P9-DGQ-201

INTERNATIONAL ENCYCLOPEDIA OF DANCE

INTERNATIONAL ENCYCLOPEDIA OF

DANCE

A project of Dance Perspectives Foundation, Inc.

FOUNDING EDITOR

Selma Jeanne Cohen

AREA EDITORS

George Dorris Nancy Goldner Beate Gordon
Nancy Reynolds David Vaughan
Suzanne Youngerman

CONSULTANTS

Thomas F. Kelly Horst Koegler Richard Ralph
Elizabeth Souritz

VOLUME 4

OXFORD UNIVERSITY PRESS
New York 1998 Oxford

OXFORD UNIVERSITY PRESS

Oxford New York
Athens Auckland Bangkok Bogotá Bombay
Buenos Aires Calcutta Cape Town Dar es Salaam
Delhi Florence Hong Kong Istanbul Karachi
Kuala Lumpur Madras Madrid Melbourne
Mexico City Nairobi Paris Singapore
Taipei Tokyo Toronto Warsaw
and associated companies in
Berlin Ibadan

Published by Oxford University Press, Inc.,
198 Madison Avenue, New York, New York 10016

This work was initiated with funds granted by the National Endowment for the Humanities, a federal agency

Library of Congress Cataloging-in-Publication Data
International encyclopedia of dance : a project of Dance Perspectives Foundation, Inc. / founding editor, Selma Jeanne Cohen; area editors, George Dorris et al.; consultants, Thomas F. Kelly et al.
p. cm.
Includes bibliographical references and index.
1. Dance—Encyclopedias. 2. Ballet—Encyclopedias. I. Cohen, Selma Jeanne, 1920-. II. Dance Perspectives Foundation.
GV1585.I586 1998 97-36562 792.6′2′03—dc21 CIP
ISBN 0-19-509462-X (set)
ISBN 0-19-512308-5 (vol. 4)

Printing (last digit): 9 8 7 6 5 4 3 2

Printed in the United States of America
on acid-free paper

K

CONTINUED

KEIL, BIRGIT (born 22 September 1944 in Kowarschen, Sudetenland), German ballet dancer. Birgit Keil grew up in Bad Kissingen, in Bavaria, where as a young girl she received her first, private ballet lessons. After her family moved to Stuttgart in 1954, she continued her dance training at the ballet school of the Württemberg State Theater, from which she was accepted into the corps de ballet of the Stuttgart Ballet in 1961. Her outstanding talent soon won her a scholarship to the Royal Ballet School in London, where she spent a year polishing her technique. Upon her return to the Stuttgart company in 1963, she was appointed a soloist by the company director, John Cranko, and later was named principal dancer, a position she held until her retirement from the stage in 1995.

Without question, Keil became the Stuttgart Ballet's foremost German ballerina, second only to Marcia Haydée, who is of Brazilian origin. As such, she danced leading roles in all the company's productions of the classic ballets and created numerous roles in ballets mounted for the company by contemporary choreographers, including not only Cranko but Kenneth MacMillan, Glen Tetley, William Forsythe, Jiří Kylián, Eliot Feld, John Neumeier, Heinz Spoerli, and Hans van Manen. As a guest ballerina in great demand, she also danced—often with her husband Vladimír Klos as her partner—with companies outside Germany, including the Vienna State Opera Ballet, the Basel Ballet, La Scala Ballet, American Ballet Theatre, the Royal Ballet (London), the Paris Opera Ballet, and the Zurich Ballet.

Among the roles Keil created in the Cranko repertory are the Queen of Hearts in *Jeu de Cartes* (1965), Eurydice in *Orpheus* (1970), B. (for Birgit) in *Initialen R.B.M.E.* (1972), and leading parts in *Scènes de Ballet* (1962), *Opus 1* (1965), *Holberg Suite* (1967), *Kyrie Eleison* (1968), *Brouillards* (1970), *The Seasons* (1971), and *Green* (1973). Other important creations were principal roles in Kenneth MacMillan's ballets *Das Lied von der Erde* (1965), *Miss Julie* (1970), *Requiem* (1976), and *My Brother, My Sisters* (1978), as well as in his television productions of *A Lot of Happiness* (1983) and *The Seven Deadly Sins* (1984). For Glen Tetley, Keil created roles in *Voluntaries* (1973) and *Daphnis and Chloe* and *Greening* (both 1975), and for Jiří Kylián she appeared in the original casts of *Return to the Strange Land,* first version (1974), *Nuages* (1976), and *Forgotten Land* (1981).

In the works of Swiss choreographer Heinz Spoerli, Keil also found many parts well suited to her talents and artistic temperament. She danced in numerous Spoerli ballets both in Germany and in Switzerland, creating roles in *Träume* (1979), *Der Rote Mantel* (1980), *Childe Harolde* (1981), *Fantasien* (1983), and *Abschied* (1985). The part of Mathilde Wesendonk in Spoerli's *Träume,* set to Richard Wagner's "Wesendonk Lieder," provided her with one of the richest performing opportunities of her entire career. Another was the title role in the Stuttgart production of *Giselle und die Wilis,* mounted especially for her by Marcia Haydée in 1989.

KEIL. John Cranko restaged his production of *Swan Lake* in 1972 expressly to showcase the classical technique, purity of line, and exceptional musicality of Birgit Keil. As Odette, she was at once radiantly feminine and vulnerably avian. (Photograph © 1972 by Leslie E. Spatt; used by permission.)

A ballerina of ladylike distinction and great elegance, Keil impressed audiences through the neatness of her technique and her genuine musicality. A certain aloofness characterized her interpretations of the great classics, among which her performances as Odette-Odile in various productions of *Swan Lake* and as the Sylph in Peter Schaufuss's production of *La Sylphide* won special acclaim. That she also possessed a lighter, even humorous talent showed when she danced the role of Katherine in Cranko's *The Taming of the Shrew;* the title role in *Die Listige Witwe* (The Merry Widow), made especially for her by Daniela Kurz in 1988; or the role of Vera Baronova in the Stuttgart Ballet's production of the Broadway musical *On Your Toes* in 1990.

Long before she retired from the stage, Keil had become a teacher of high repute, being especially well known for her pas de deux classes at the annual International Summer Academy of Dance in Cologne. At the end of her active career as a ballerina in 1995, she established the Tanzstiftung (Dance Foundation) Birgit Keil to further the careers of promising young dancers and choreographers. Among her honors and awards are the German Order of Merit, First Class (1982), a German Critics' Award (1982), an Emmy award for *A Lot of Happiness* (1984), and the John Cranko Medal (1985).

BIBLIOGRAPHY

Birgit Keil: Portrait einer Ballerina. Rev. ed. Pfullingen, Germany, 1991.

Koegler, Horst. *Stuttgart Ballet.* London, 1978.

Koegler, Horst. "Etwas in Bewegung setzen." *Ballett International* (October 1994): 22–25.

Regitz, Hartmut. "Birgit Keil: Portrait einer Ballerina." *Das Tanzarchiv* (October 1980).

HORST KOEGLER

KELLY, GENE (Eugene Curran Kelly; born 23 August 1912 in Pittsburgh, Pennsylvania, died 2 February 1996 in Beverly Hills, California), American dancer, actor, choreographer, and film director. One of the major figures of the Hollywood musical, Kelly, originally a dancer and actor, became a choreographer and director during the 1940s and early 1950s, the most prolific period of film musical production at the studios of Metro-Goldwyn-Mayer (MGM). Later, as the musical declined in popularity, Kelly became less involved in dance and concentrated on film direction. He nevertheless remained significant as the star and choreographer of some of the most revered musicals in film history.

Kelly had dance training as he was growing up, but he did not take it seriously until his teens. He soon established a reputation, however, and began staging shows, performing in clubs (often with his brother Fred), and, most important, operating a dance school, all while pursuing his academic education. He graduated from the University of Pittsburgh in 1933 with a degree in economics. Kelly continued to seek out dance teachers, to learn new material, and to improve his ballet technique. In 1938, Kelly went to New York to try to break into the theater, and within three years he had established himself as a promising choreographer and star.

Although he had minor roles in his first two Broadway shows, *Leave It to Me* (1938) and *One for the Money* (1939), his third show, *The Time of Your Life* (1939), really started his career. Kelly had had some opportunity to continue creating dances, but his first principal choreography in New York was for *Billy Rose's Diamond Horseshoe Revue* in 1940. His next two assignments, the leading role in *Pal Joey* in 1940 and dance director for *Best Foot Forward* in 1941, climaxed his stay in New York, for *Pal Joey* brought him to the attention of Hollywood.

It was as a dancer-actor that Kelly established his reputation and for which his fame endures. Nevertheless, his major contribution to dance may well be the conscious, intellectual approach to filming choreography that began even with his first film role, in *For Me and My Gal* (1942), and continued throughout his career as a dancer-actor and choreographer-director. Always open to new ideas, Kelly experimented with different forms of dance, new ways of filming dance, and combining animation and other special effects with dance. What distinguished Gene Kelly from Fred Astaire and other contributors to dance in musical films was Kelly's total involvement with the filmmaking process. Never content to be just a star or a choreographer, Kelly became familiar with all aspects of film production. Significantly, with the decline of the Hollywood studio system and of musicals as a major genre, Kelly gave up performing and choreographing. Although he continued to direct, his contribution as a choreographer seems to have been linked indelibly with his career as a dancer.

Kelly's initial Hollywood contract was with David O. Selznick, but he did *For Me and My Gal* on loan to MGM. Subsequently, MGM bought up his contract, and, with the exception of *Cover Girl* (done on loan to Columbia in 1944), all his film work as a dancer and choreographer was done for MGM. In doing *For Me and My Gal* Kelly was especially struck by the differences between film and live dance performance. As a result, he became involved as early as his second film, *Dubarry Was a Lady* (1943), with the preparation of the camera for the dance. With *Cover Girl,* his sixth film, he fully choreographed and shot those numbers in which he danced, including the experimental "Alter Ego" number where, through double exposure, he danced with himself. Kelly's success with that project made him able to continue preparing and shooting dances at MGM, and with *Anchors Aweigh* (1945), *The Pirate* (1948), and *Take Me Out to the Ball Game* (1949), he developed a choreographic style, an approach to filming

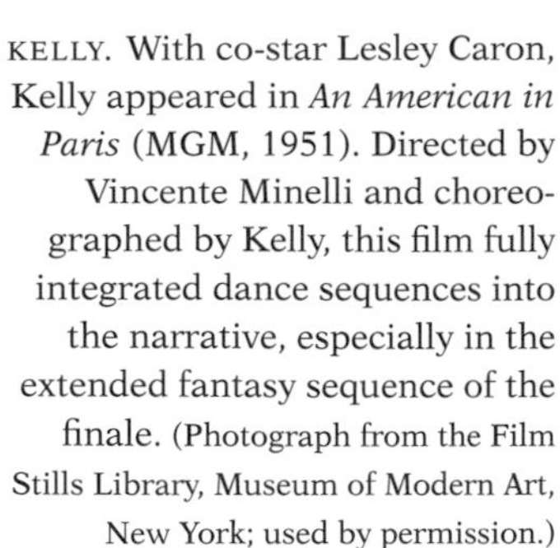

KELLY. With co-star Lesley Caron, Kelly appeared in *An American in Paris* (MGM, 1951). Directed by Vincente Minelli and choreographed by Kelly, this film fully integrated dance sequences into the narrative, especially in the extended fantasy sequence of the finale. (Photograph from the Film Stills Library, Museum of Modern Art, New York; used by permission.)

dance, and a musical star persona that would bring him acclaim over the next several years.

In conjunction with Stanley Donen, a frequent collaborator on the earlier films, Kelly had his first opportunity to direct, as well as choreograph, with *On the Town* (1949). Donen and Kelly also worked together on *Singin' in the Rain* (1952) and *It's Always Fair Weather* (1955). These three films, all starring Kelly, constitute a major trilogy of the Hollywood musical and embody most aspects of Kelly's conscious desire to integrate dance and film, to combine different types of dance, and to explore the relationship between dance and popular culture. Kelly continued to work with other directors as well, always providing his own choreography, however, and his most frequent collaborator, other than Donen, was director Vincente Minnelli, with whom he made three films, including *An American in Paris* (1951).

In all his films Kelly tried to find new ways to present dance in the musical. *On the Town, Singin' in the Rain,* and *An American in Paris* contain extended dance sequences that fully develop Kelly's integration of dance forms and experiments with filming dance. Those sequences also prefigure his all-dance film *Invitation to the Dance,* shot during 1952 but not released until 1957. Perhaps Kelly's most ambitious project, *Invitation to the Dance* attempted to combine all his ideas of the dance-film relationship. Eschewing all dialogue, Kelly tried to move beyond the apparent limits of the popular musical. He choreographed for ballet stars (Igor Youskevitch, Tamara Toumanova, Claire Sombert, and others); used symphonic music (original scores by Jacques Ibert and André Previn and an adaptation of *Schéhérazade*); and continued his experiments with animation by preparing a fairy tale with live-action dancing in a cartoon setting.

Kelly's last musical for MGM was *Les Girls* in 1957. By that time, though, his position at the studio had fallen from its high point of a few years earlier; as a result, Jack Cole was assigned to choreograph and George Cukor to direct. The studio system itself was also changing, and Kelly would continue his career mainly as an actor in dramatic roles and as a director. He directed only one other musical, *Hello, Dolly!* (1969), for which Michael Kidd choreographed the dances. Nevertheless, Kelly's continuing interest in innovative approaches to dance led also to significant work on television. In *Dancing: A Man's Game* in 1958, he investigated the relationship between dance and athletic movement, always one of his primary concerns; and in *Jack and the Beanstalk* in 1967, he pursued the combination of live action and animation earlier explored in *Anchors Aweigh* and *Invitation to the Dance.* He also did some stage work, particularly the direction for Rodgers and Hammerstein's *Flower Drum Song* in 1958 and the choreography for *Pas des Dieux* for the Paris Opera Ballet in 1960.

Kelly's eclectic dance style drew upon tap, soft-shoe, ballet, modern, jazz, folk, and ethnic dance. Moreover, an athletic-gymnastic quality was often at the foundation of his movement as a choreographer and dancer. He moved

KELLY. Swinging on a lampost in *Singin' in the Rain* (MGM, 1952), Kelly exudes a delightful, carefree charm. In this number, one of the most famous dance sequences on film, Kelly worked hard to create the well-crafted, seemingly effortless, combination of character, story, and movement. (Photograph from the Film Stills Library, Museum of Modern Art, New York; used by permission.)

easily among dance forms throughout his career, yet there was a definite progression in his work, beginning with a dominant tap and musical comedy style to greater complexity involving ballet and modern dance forms. "I don't have a name for my style of dancing," Kelly once said; "it's certainly hybrid. . . . I've borrowed from the modern dance, from the classical, and certainly from the American folk dance—tap-dancing, jitterbugging. . . . But I have tried to develop a style which is indigenous to the environment and locale in which I was reared" (quoted in Delamater, 1981, p. 156). Perhaps Kelly's most significant use of various forms was their conventional appropriateness within the context of a given film, for his characters worked through situations by means of those conventional associations. Exuberance and joy tended to be expressed through tap or other popular dance idioms, as in the title song from *Singin' in the Rain* or "I Got Rhythm" from *An American in Paris.* Pensive or romantic moments were more frequently expressed through ballet or modern dance, as in "Heather on the Hill" from *Brigadoon* or "Our Love Is Here to Stay" from *An American in Paris.* Kelly never felt confined by those conventions, however, and he often worked toward establishing new meanings and new contexts for dance forms. Kelly always operated from a tap base, but it was only one aspect of his style; he combined it with ballet turns and lifts, for example, and his natural athleticism gave his more ambitious movements a distinctive, broad, muscular quality. The title dance from *An American in Paris* displays the variety and virtuosity that epitomized Kelly's performing and choreography.

Other contemporaries of Kelly (notably Jack Cole and Eugene Loring) also were conscious of the need to prepare dances for the camera, but Kelly's work seems to represent the fulfillment of dance-film integration in the 1940s and 1950s. The full-figured photographing of dance that characterized Fred Astaire's work in the 1930s gave way to a diverse system in which material was choreographed for the camera and the camera positioned for the material. Kelly's numbers exploited the space of the film in an almost limitless fashion. Camera movement, changes in camera angle, and editing combined with dance movement to reveal new space for the dancer; areas of offscreen space became onscreen, dance space, as in "Prehistoric Man" from *On the Town* or "The Hat My Dear Old Father Wore" from *Take Me Out to the Ball Game.* Kelly felt that the kinetic force of live dance was often missing in film, and he strove to overcome that, partially by involving the camera in the movement and giving the dancer multiple directions in which to move. The dancer could move toward the camera and the camera toward the dancer—even into close-up—and those movements created for Kelly a cinematic dance force. Kelly exploited varieties of dance forms within a film context, and as a performer, choreographer, and director who was concerned especially with photographing dance, he was a culminating force in the film musical.

[*See also* Film Musicals, *article on* Hollywood Film Musicals; Tap Dance.]

BIBLIOGRAPHY

Delamater, Jerome. *Dance in the Hollywood Musical.* Ann Arbor, Mich., 1981.

Fordin, Hugh. *The World of Entertainment!* New York, 1974.

Frank, Rusty E. *Tap! The Greatest Tap Dance Stars and Their Stories, 1900–1955.* Rev. ed. New York, 1994.

Hirschhorn, Clive. *Gene Kelly: A Biography.* New York, 1984.

Wollen, Peter. *Singin' in the Rain.* London, 1992.

JEROME DELAMATER

KENT, ALLEGRA (Iris Margo Cohen; born 11 August 1937 in Santa Monica, California), American ballet dancer and author. Kent began her dance education at age nine with folk dance classes at the boarding school she attended. She came under the tutelage of Irina and Bronislava Nijinska, Carmelita Maracci, and Maria Bekefi before moving to New York and beginning to study at the School of American Ballet in September 1951. After an apprenticeship she joined the New York City Ballet as a member of the corps in 1953.

Kent danced her first featured role, in the Viola pas de deux in Jerome Robbins's *Fanfare,* in January 1954; her first created role, in "The Unanswered Question" section of George Balanchine's *Ivesiana,* was performed later that year. In 1956, the year she became a soloist, she created one of the five ballerina roles in Balanchine's *Divertimento No. 15.* In 1957 she became a principal dancer and also danced in the Broadway musical *Shinbone Alley.*

Other roles that Kent created in Balanchine ballets included one of the ensemble women in *Agon* (1957), the baton-twirling leader of the first regiment ("Corcoran Cadets") in *Stars and Stripes* (1958), the dancing Anna in the revival of *The Seven Deadly Sins* (1958), the Concerto (op. 24) in *Episodes* (1959), the principal woman in *Bugaku* (1963), and the Andante of *Brahms-Schoenberg Quartet* (1966). She is associated especially with the title role in *La Sonnambula,* which she first danced in the ballet's 1960 revival. She was in the first cast of Robbins's *Dances at a Gathering* (1969), and other roles for which she is noted include the Girl in *Afternoon of a Faun,* Odette in Balanchine's one-act version of *Swan Lake,* the Sugarplum Fairy in *The Nutcracker,* the pas de deux in *Agon,* the Second Movement of *Symphony in C,* and the fantasizing "ballerina" in *The Concert.* Her last appearances were in 1981 in John Taras's Variation VI from Trio in A Minor, a section of his *Tempo di Valse.*

Kent pursued her entire career with the New York City Ballet, performing with it—except for five leaves of absence—over a period of almost thirty years. She was a compelling performer who danced a large number of roles. During the first part of her career many of her roles utilized the remarkable elevation she had at the time, while her extraordinary flexibility and affinity for legato movement prompted Balanchine in some of his choreography for her—in *Ivesiana, Episodes,* and *Bugaku,* for example—to extend the range of partnering.

Kent married photographer Bert Stern and is the mother of three children. She is the author of an autobiography (1997) and of *Allegra Kent's Water Beauty Book* (1976), which details an exercise program she developed that uses water as the source of resistance.

BIBLIOGRAPHY

Kent, Allegra. *Once a Dancer: An Autobiography.* New York, 1997.

Mazo, Joseph H. *Dance Is a Contact Sport.* New York, 1974.

Newman, Barbara. "Speaking of Dance: Allegra Kent." *The Dancing Times* (May 1988): 742–744.

Reynolds, Nancy. *Repertory in Review: Forty Years of the New York City Ballet.* New York, 1977.

Tracy, Robert, and Sharon DeLano. *Balanchine's Ballerinas: Conversations with the Muses.* New York, 1983.

WILLIAM JAMES LAWSON

KENYA. *See* Central and East Africa. *See also* Digo Dance; Giriama Dance; Pokot Dance; *and* Samburu Dance.

KERMANI, SHEEMA (born 1950 in Rawalpindi), Pakistani dancer and choreographer. Kermani is one of a handful of professional Pakistani dancers who come from an educated, liberal, middle-class family. Studying music and dance was a tradition in her family, although no one before her pursued them professionally. The daughter of an army officer, she lived in several parts of Pakistan before settling in Karachi, where she began studying dance at the Ghanshyam Academy at the age of fifteen; however, it was not until the age of thirty that she decided to pursue dance professionally.

At the Ghanshyam Academy Kermani trained for about fifteen years in *kathak, bharata nāṭyam,* and Oḍissi, taking a year off to study fine arts at the Croydon School of Art in London. She taught art at a grammar school, held exhibitions of her paintings, and resumed her dance training. In 1971 she was employed in both the performing troupe and the teaching staff at the academy. Shortly afterward she decided to pursue dance professionally and was encouraged by the Ghanshyams to travel to India to study *bharata nāṭyam* and Oḍissi in Delhi. She has returned every year for three or four months to continue her training with Leela Samson of the Kalakshetra, Guru Mayadhar Raut of Bharatiya Kalakendra, and Aloka Pannikar of Art Kendra.

Kermani has choreographed powerful and revolutionary dances, often set to Urdu poetry, with themes addressing contemporary issues such as political violence, women's rights, and the acceptance of dance. A recent dance drama performed by Kermani and her students, *The Song of Mohenjodaro,* was based on her research on the ancient Indus civilization; she sought to show that in the ancient world classical dance was a part of the land that is now Pakistan, and thus it should not be rejected as "Indian" and as undermining Pakistani national identity.

Since Pakistani nationalism has become increasingly associated with Islam, Kermani has had to face greater opposition than *kathak* dancers, the only other classical dancers in Pakistan, because *bharata nāṭyam* and Oḍissi developed mostly under Hindu patronage and have come to be associated more closely with Hinduism than has *kathak,* which flourished under the Muslims. She was forced to cancel an anniversary concert due to bomb threats.

Nevertheless, Kermani has managed to stage numerous performances in Pakistan and abroad and has a substantial number of students in her dance classes. She has performed in Germany as a state guest and spent a year in

Delhi studying under Aloka Pannikar, on scholarship from the Indian Council of Cultural Relations. She was the first Pakistani to participate in the International Choreographer's Workshop at the American Dance Festival at Duke University. Kermani is now interested in creating her own dance style combining Pakistan's varied folk styles, *bharata nāṭyam,* Oḍissi, *kathak,* and *chhau,* a martial-arts dance; in *The Song of Mohenjodaro* she forged this fusion successfully.

An intellectual with a strong desire for social justice and change, Kermani has not only filled a void in the field of dance in Karachi, but she has also displayed courage as a women's-rights activist and tremendous talent as an actor in plays with socially relevant themes. Her long-term goal is to establish her own academy where drama, music, dance, and related arts would be taught.

INTERVIEW. Sheema Kermani, by Shayma Saiyid (Karachi, January 1995).

SHAYMA SAIYID

KERMESSE IN BRUGES. A studio portrait, taken in 1905, of Ellen Price de Plane as Eleonore and Gustav Uhlendorff as Carelis, holding the magical viola da gamba that impels everyone to dance. Both dancers made their debuts in these roles with the Royal Danish Ballet in September 1900. (Photograph 1905 by Peter Elfelt; from the Royal Library, Copenhagen.)

KERMESSE IN BRUGES. Danish title: *Kermessen i Brügge, eller De Tre Gaver.* Ballet in three acts. Choreography and libretto: August Bournonville. Music: Holger Simon Paulli. Costumes: Edvard Lehmann. First performance: 4 April 1851, Royal Theater, Copenhagen. Principals: Juliette Price (Eleonore), Andreas Füssel (Mirewelt), Georg Broderson (Adrian), Ferdinand Hoppensach (Geert), Ferdinand Hoppe (Carelis).

Inspired by Dutch genre painting with its rich tapestry of characters and dramatic chiaroscuro effects, August Bournonville devised *Kermesse in Bruges;* set in the Flemish town of Bruges in the seventeenth century. In the marketplace, the townspeople celebrate the Kermesse, a religious festival in honor of their patron saint, with dancing and merriment. This story of multiple romantic intrigues has several levels of meaning; its themes include true love and the temptations placed in the way of its fulfillment, and the forces of prejudice and ignorance opposed to science and progress.

The story tells of the amorous exploits of three brothers, Adrian, Geert, and the young hero, Carelis. As a reward for rescuing the alchemist Mirewelt and his daughter Eleonore from the hands of would-be abductors, the brothers each receive a magical gift—a sword that always brings victory, a ring that makes its wearer loved by all, and an enchanted viola da gamba whose music makes everyone dance. The last gift saves the brothers from the stake in the ballet's hilarious finale.

The critic Erik Aschengreen (1980) called the expressive pas de deux from act 1 "a romantic encounter from a vanished time" and "one of the purest Bournonville compositions." Like the pas de deux from Bournonville's *Flower Festival at Genzano,* it has gained international popularity in recent years. Major productions of *Kermesse* have been mounted by Harald Lander and Valborg Borchsenius (1942–1943), by Hans Brenaa (1957, 1979), and by Brenaa and Flemming Flindt (1966).

[*See also* Royal Danish Ballet *and the entry on Bournonville.*]

BIBLIOGRAPHY

Aschengreen, Erik, et al., eds. *Perspektiv på Bournonville.* Copenhagen, 1980.

Bournonville, August. "The Ballet Poems of August Bournonville: The Complete Scenarios." Translated by Patricia McAndrew. *Dance Chronicle* 4.2 (1981).

Bournonville, August. *My Theatre Life* (1848–1878). Translated by Patricia McAndrew (Middletown, Conn., 1979).

Hallar, Marianne, and Alette Scavenius, eds. *Bournonvilleana.* Translated by Gaye Kynoch. Copenhagen, 1992.

PATRICIA MCANDREW

KHACHATURIAN, ARAM (Aram Il'ich Khachaturian; born 6 June 1903 in Tbilisi, Armenia, died 1 May 1978 in Moscow), Soviet composer. Fairly early in his career,

Khachaturian wrote three ballets—*A Song of Happiness* (1939), *Gayané* (1942), and *Spartacus* (1956), the last being his best-known work. A fourth Khachaturian ballet score, *The Masquerade* (1944), was assembled from some of Khachaturian's incidental music by Armenian composer E. S. Ognessian. Though Khachaturian wrote nothing specifically for ballet after the mid-1950s, at least five other ballets were set to his music.

Khachaturian's father, a not very prosperous bookbinder, indulged his son by buying a piano, and the eight-year-old boy soon learned to play popular tunes by ear. At age ten he enrolled in the Commercial School of Tbilisi, where he played in the school's brass band. In 1921 he left the school without graduating. That fall he acted on a suggestion by his brother, a producer at the Second Moscow Art Theater, to pursue his studies in Moscow.

Khachaturian spent two years at Moscow University studying biology and mathematics before going to the Gnesin Musical Technical School to ask Mikhail Gnesin, an eminent pupil of Nikolai Rimsky-Korsakov, to permit him to matriculate there. Gnesin consented, and Khachaturian remained there—studying and continuing to compose—until 1929, when he enrolled in the Moscow Conservatory. He graduated with honors in 1934.

Khachaturian had written a quantity of engaging music by the time he attracted national attention in 1937 with *Song of Stalin*, a symphonic poem for chorus and orchestra. He was awarded the 1940 Stalin Prize for his Violin Concerto; in 1942 he was given a second Stalin Prize, of one-hundred thousand rubles, for *Gayané*, whose brassy "Saber Dance" was a worldwide popular hit, establishing him as one of the Soviet Union's leading composers. (In *Gayané*, Khachaturian used large portions of his earlier ballet, *A Song of Happiness*, which then disappeared as a separate entity. In 1957 *Gayané* was extensively revised, in a more symphonic style, to fit another story.)

Spartacus was the last of the great socialist spectacle ballets. Of it, Khachaturian wrote, "I thought of *Spartacus* as a monumental fresco describing the mighty avalanche of the antique rebellion of slaves on behalf of human rights." In either Leonid Yakobson's original 1956 version or Yuri Grigorovich's 1968 choreography, the ballet was incorporated into the repertories of the leading dance companies of eastern Europe.

During his career, Khachaturian garnered official honors and prestigious appointments at home as well as invitations to conduct in the West, including the United States in 1968. He fell from grace only once, in 1948, when together with Sergei Prokofiev and Dmitri Shostakovich he was accused by the Communist party's central committee of writing works that "smell strongly of the spirit of modern bourgeois culture." Khachaturian confessed his musical "guilt" in appearing to emulate Western composers, particularly Maurice Ravel, and he never strayed again. His credo was epitomized in a long article for the Soviet journal *Culture and Life*, in which he wrote of the composer's

> spiritual affinity with the people, with their vital interests, joys and sorrows, [which] actually makes him a contemporary of his epoch and determines his position as an artist and a citizen of his country. Contrary to those false theories of the so-called "pure art" created in ivory towers, a truly modern artist creates for the people, the masses, and not for a handful of select connoisseurs. (Kachaturian, 1971)

Indeed, Khachaturian was a Soviet cultural hero whose sparkling folkloristic music made few demands on the listener. He combined traditional Armenian melodies with modern orchestral techniques and, at his most brilliant, lifted folk tunes to the level of art music. At the same time, Khachaturian was capable of writing abstract music of high quality.

Orientalism is dominant in his work; some passages have a barbaric sound yet are always colorful and strongly rhythmic. He combined the rhapsodic style of the minstrels who wandered his native Caucasus with the sanctioned traditions of Soviet symphonic music. This synthesis—expressing cheerfulness, optimism, and a happy bravura—informs most of his works, which range from ballets to symphonies, concertos, chamber music, film scores, marches, and choral works. His concertos for violin and piano are part of the contemporary repertory.

[*See also* Gayané *and* Spartacus.]

BIBLIOGRAPHY

Bakst, James. *A History of Russian-Soviet Music*. New York, 1966.

Biesold, Maria. *Aram Chatschaturjan*. Wittmund, Germany, 1989.

Dorris, George. "Music for Spectacle." *Ballet Review* 6.1 (1977): 45–55.

Harris, Dale. "Khachaturian." In *The Encyclopedia of Dance and Ballet*. New York, 1977.

Khachaturian, Aram. "Music and the People." *Culture and Life* (October 1971).

"Khachaturian" (obituary). *New York Times* (3 May 1978).

Martynov, Ivan. *Aram Khachaturian*. Moscow, 1947.

Montagu-Nathan, Montagu. "Aram Ilich Khachaturian." In *The Music Masters*, vol. 4, *The Twentieth Century*, by W. R. Anderson et al. Harmondsworth, 1957.

Rybakova, Sofia. *Aram Ilich Khachaturian*. Moscow, 1975.

Schwarz, Boris. "Khachaturian, Aram." In *The New Grove Dictionary of Music and Musicians*. London, 1980.

Swift, Mary Grace. *The Art of the Dance in the U.S.S.R.* Notre Dame, Ind., 1968.

Tigranov, Georgii. *Balety A. Khachaturiana*. 2d ed. Moscow, 1974.

Tigranov, Georgii. *Aram Ilich Khachaturian*. Moscow, 1978.

Yuzefovich, Viktor. *Aram Khachaturyan*. Translated by Nicholas Kournokoff and Vladimir Bobrov. New York, 1985.

JOSEPH GALE

KHANUM, TAMARA (Tamara Khanum; born 20 March [11 April] 1906 in Margelan, Uzbekistan, died 30 June 1991 in Tashkent, Uzbekistan), folk singer, dancer, choreographer, and teacher. Tamara Khanum's birth name was Tamara Artemovna Petrosyan, but she took the sobriquet "khanum," meaning "woman." She danced and sang from an early age and made her first public appearance at the age of twelve. Among those who discovered her talent was the distinguished Uzbek writer and composer Khamza Khakimzadeh Niyazi. She made her professional debut at age fifteen in the corps de ballet of the Russian Opera House in Tashkent. Her mentors included the popular Uzbek singers and dancers Yusup Kizik Shakarjanov, Ata Hoja Saidazimov, and Usta Alim Kamilov. From 1921 to 1923 she attended E. Karganova's private ballet school in Tashkent, and in 1923 she became a pupil of Vera Maya at the Lunacharsky Theater Technicum in Moscow.

The initial period of Tamara Khanum's career came at a time when an acute social struggle was taking place in Uzbekistan. Before the October Revolution of 1917 the women in that part of Central Asia had worn cloaks that covered them from head to foot and a black horsehair veil over their face; they did not have the right to appear in the company of men. Tamara Khanum's performances carried a social message: she appeared on the stage without the traditional veil, and she called on Uzbek women to rise up against their oppressed status. Her boldness earned her the hatred of reactionary fanatics, who made several attempts on her life, but she continued to help the new system break the hold of centuries-old customs.

Tamara Khanum performed at the First World Exhibition of Folk Decorative Art in Paris in 1925 and at the First International Folk Dance Festival in London in 1935, where she and her teacher and accompanist Usta Alim Kamilov were awarded a medal. Her innovative style of performing Uzbek folk dances won recognition abroad. She and Kamilov created numbers that combined traditional Uzbek folk and professional dancing with elements of classical choreography and ballet technique (chiefly spins and movements in a circle). Some of the innovations were later incorporated into the new, diversified Uzbek choreography. This enriched dance form, with its accentuated expressive devices, helped Tamara Khanum to evolve an image of the new, emancipated Soviet woman.

Seeking a format in which she could depict the life and work of people in many different parts of the Soviet Union, Tamara Khanum gradually developed a unique type of solo song-and-dance sketch, performed in the various languages and styles of the peoples of the Soviet Union and other countries. The sketches were permeated with a modern spirit.

In 1940 Tamara Khanum helped to produce one of the earliest Uzbek ballets, *Gulandom.* The rise of Uzbek Soviet ballet was inseparably associated with Tamara Khanum's tireless work as dancer, choreographer, and teacher. In 1941 she was awarded a State Prize of the USSR, and in 1956 the title People's Artist of the USSR was conferred on her.

BIBLIOGRAPHY

Avdeeva, Lubov. *Tamara Khanum.* Tashkent, 1959.

Cohen, Selma Jeanne. "East Meets West in Central Asia." *Dance Magazine* (July 1990): 45–48.

Gray, Laurel Victoria. "Tamara Khanum: Uzbekistan's Heroine of Dance." *Arabesque* (January–February 1985): 14–15.

Gray, Laurel Victoria. "In Search of Ethnic Dance in the USSR." *Viltis* 44 (May 1985): 10–11.

Makarov, Vassili. "Tamara Khanum." In *The Soviet Ballet,* by Yuri Slonimsky et al. New York, 1947.

Obituary. *Dance Magazine* (November 1991): 34.

Shirokaia, O.I. *Tamara Khonim: Fotoalbom.* Tashkent, 1972.

LUBOV AVDEEVA
Translated from Russian

KHŌN. The Thai masked dance drama known as *khōn* developed in the Ayudhayā period (c.1600–1700) from Hindu military rituals and Thai martial arts. The term *khōn* may have been derived from Khmer *lakhol* or *lakhọn khol,* meaning "dance drama" and "royal dance drama," respectively.

The prototype of *khōn* was the martial ritual *chak nāk dükdamban* ("pulling the serpent") performed at the Indraphisēk ceremony, the coronation of a new king of Siam (now Thailand) by the earliest chief Hindu god Indra. In this ritual, military officers and civil officials, dressed and masked as demons, monkeys, and gods from Hindu mythology, pulled on opposite ends of a rope in a tug-of-war. This recreated the myth of the great serpent king, Ananta Nākharāt, who obtained ambrosia from Mount Sumen to grant eternal life for the heavenly beings. This ritual may have originated in India to be transmitted to the Thais through the Khmers. The twelfth-century sculptural reliefs depicting this myth at the original capitals of the Khmer Empire, Angkor Wat and Angkor Thom, are evidence of this ancient rite.

An art related to *khōn* is *nang* (shadow-puppet dance drama), which is known to have been performed in the early kingdom of Siam, in the fourteenth century. The two kinds of drama were usually performed together, with *nang* preceding *khōn.* Some scholars have concluded that *khōn,* because it is performed by dancers and has more elaborate dance patterns, evolved from *nang;* others contend that the two developed independently. Performers of each genre adopted aesthetic qualities from the other to perfect their art. For example, *khōn* dancers imitate the fighting poses of the exquisitely carved shadow puppets, while *nang* puppeteers manipulate their puppets to use leg and body movements of *khōn.*

There are five major types of *khōn. Khōn klāng plāeng* is performed outdoors in a big field; *khōn rōng nǭk* or *khōn nang rāo* is performed on an open stage, with a long bamboo rod serving as a bench; and *khōn nā čhǭ* is performed in front of a screen with *nang. Khōn rōng nai* is performed in the style of *lakhǭn nai,* a genre of maskless-dance drama. *Khōn chāk* is presented in a theater with painted backdrops, a modernized production style of the nineteenth century that has continued to the present.

Stories performed in *khōn* are taken from the *Rāmakian* epic. Each episode has a theme of good defeating evil. The favorite climactic scenes are battle scenes between Phra Rām (Sanskrit, Rāma), the righteous king of Ayudhayā, and Thosakan (Ravana), the immoral ruler of Longkā, a menace to the universe. It is customary that the performance end with the defeat of Thosakan and his allies, who promise revenge, fulfilled in the next day's performance. Although Thosakan is finally killed in the epic, his death is not presented onstage, because it is believed that this would cause misfortune and fatal accidents for the dance company.

The traditional *khōn* performance begins with a prelude, *Čhap Ling Hua Kham* (Catching the Monkeys in the Early Evening), a short episode about a hermit and his two monkey disciples, one white and one black, representing good and evil. After this, the main play starts with the theme of evil caused by the demon king Thosakan, who is exterminated by Phra Ram or his associates. Throughout the play comparisons are made between the two opposing rulers, their politics, social and domestic affairs, systems of government, and personalities. These comparisons were originally intended to give lessons to the audience. Much comic relief is provided by the demons *(yak),* monkeys *(ling),* soldier comedians, and court jesters, who exchange witty improvised dialogue.

The chorus and narrators *(khōn phāk)* recite the narrative and dialogue for other characters in poetic rhyme with musical accompaniment. The orchestra *(pīphāt)* consists of one or two *ranād* (wooden xylophones), *pī* (oboe), *khǭng wong* (circular gongs), a pair of *ching* (small cymbals), and two *klōng* (tympani). There are several dance tunes that represent specific actions *(nā phāt),* such as marching, fighting, flying, walking, sleeping, and manifesting supernatural powers.

Khōn masks are worshiped by dancers and artists as sacred objects, possessing a supernatural power that can bring either fortune or misfortune to the owners or wearers. In the annual Phithī Wai Khrū invocation and Phithī Khrǭp initiation ceremony, new dancers are initiated by the master teacher, who puts on the mask of Phra Phrot Rüsī (great master of dance), the mask of Phra Phirāp (god of dance, one form of the Hindu god Śiva [Shiva], and the headdress called *sōēt.* The various masks are placed on altars during the ceremony. Only initiated dancers can perform *khōn.*

Dancers of *khōn* are trained from childhood, usually starting at the ages of eight to ten. They are first assigned by the teachers to one of four categories of characters from the *Rāmakian.* The characters are Phra, a refined male human or divine being, such as Phra Ram; Nāng, a refined female human with divine attributes, such as Sīdā; Yak, a robust, vigorous demon, such as Thosakan; and Ling, a monkey, particularly Hanumān. The physical appearance and special talent suitable for each role are the major criteria in the assigning of characters. Each dancer normally undergoes rigorous training for nine to ten years in the same character, daily practicing the patterns of dance for the type and the basic movements called *māē thā* (mother movements). Dancers also learn acrobatic martial arts for fighting scenes, but present-day *khōn* has lost many of its original martial characteristics.

Until the 1930s, all *khōn* dancers were male. After Siam's revolution in 1932, female Thai dancers were permitted to play female roles, and the *khōn* dance style merged with that of *lakhǭn*. A major contributor to new features in *khōn* was Prince Narisaranuwadhiwong (1863–1947), who composed romantic songs and music for his modern production of the *Rāmakian* in the new style of *lakhǭn dükdamban.* This music is now used in modern *khōn* productions.

Khōn assumed a new political role in Thai society when King Vajiravudh (1880–1925) introduced modern politics into his royal *khōn* productions. He trained his courtiers and close associates in the art as a revival of the ancient military tradition and also as a tool to propagate his policies in support of absolute monarchy. A special school was set up under his patronage for sons of officials and middle-class families to receive free formal education as well as *khōn* training. The themes of his *khōn* productions were loyalty to the throne and patriotic sacrifice for the nation.

After the absolute monarchy was replaced by a constitutional monarchy in 1932, the Royal Khōn Troupe was transferred to the Department of Fine Arts under the administration of the Ministry of Education. Its current focus is more educational than artistic or political. Episodes chosen for productions are geared toward schoolchildren. The scripts and dances are now shortened and simplified, with added comic relief to increase *khōn's* popularity among the younger generation. Modern techniques in set and lighting design attract a new mass audience with spectacular effects and glittering costumes.

Despite the pressure of Western popular culture, *khōn* gradually regained its significance in modern Thai culture in the 1970s, through the creative effort of Mom Rātchawong Kukrit Prāmoj, a former prime minister and avid *khōn* dancer. He formed the Thammasat University Khōn Troupe, whose purpose is to train young intellectuals to be cultivated leaders of the country. Kukrit's witty dialogue and new political and social interpretations of the stories are major reasons for the success of the Thammasat Khōn. Former members of the troupe now hold many important positions in the government and private sector. They form the firm group of supporters necessary for the continuation of this ancient art.

To celebrate the golden jubilee of King Phumiphol in 1966, Professor Mattani Rutnin produced and directed a modern version of the *Rāmakien,* called *Rama-Sida.* The performance utilized *khōn* martial arts movements danced to contemporary music, spoken dialogue in poetic prose, and narratives sung in traditional *khōn* style. This new development of classical *khōn* has stimulated new interest among the modern generation.

Khōn training is now popular in Thailand's schools, colleges, and universities. The grand national performance festival in 1982—in which two thousand dancers from various schools and the National Academy of Dance participated—celebrated the bicentennial anniversary of Bangkok. Nearly one thousand dancers from all regions of Thailand took part in grand spectacles of *khōn* for two important national events in 1995 and 1996: the queen mother's royal funeral and the king's golden jubilee. This cultural heritage, taught through the generations for more than four hundred years, is still a living art in Thailand.

[*See also* Thailand. *For discussion of other Thai dance dramas, see* Lakhǭn *and* Manōhrā.]

BIBLIOGRAPHY

Aphǭn Montrīsāt, Chaturong Montrīsāt, and Montrī Trāmōte. *Wichā nātasin.* Bangkok, 1974.

Damrong Rājānubhāp, H. R. H. Prince. *Tamnān lakhǭn inao.* Bangkok, 1964.

Dhaninivat, H. R. H. Prince. "The Shadow-Play as a Possible Origin of the Masked-Play." *Journal of the Siam Society* 37.5 (1948): 26–32.

Kukrit Pramōj, Mom Rātchawong. "Nātasin." Unpublished ms., n.d.

Kukrit Pramōj, Mom Rātchawong. "Khāng Sangwian." *Sayam rāt* (27–30 October 1978): 7.

Maha Vajiravudh. "Notes on the Siamese Theatre." *Journal of the Siam Society* 55.1 (1967): 1–30.

Miettinen, Jukka O. *Classical Dance and Theatre in South-East Asia.* New York, 1992.

Rutnin, Mattani Mojdara. ed. *The Siamese Theatre.* Bangkok, 1975.

Rutnin, Mattani Mojdara. *Dance, Drama, and Theatre in Thailand.* Tokyo, 1993.

Rutnin, Mattani Mojdara. "Phatthanākār khǭng lakhǭn thai smai mai. In *Arayatham thai.* Bangkok, 1997.

Yupho, Dhanit. *The Khon and Lakon.* Bangkok, 1963.

Yupho, Dhanit. *Khōn.* Bangkok, 1968.

Yupho, Dhanit. *Silapa lakhǭn ram rüe khūmü nātasin thai.* Bangkok, 1973.

Mattani Mojdara Rutnin

KIDD, MICHAEL (Milton Gruenwald; born 12 August 1917 in Brooklyn, New York), American dancer, stage and film choreographer. Kidd began his career as a ballet dancer but turned to stage and film choreography after his initial success at creating a ballet. Although he essentially gave up performing early in his career, Kidd nevertheless made a significant contribution to the Broadway and Hollywood musical with his robust, athletic choreographic style.

After high school Kidd studied chemical engineering at City College of New York. Starting his dance training at eighteen, he attended the School of American Ballet on scholarship. He made his stage debut in 1937 in a Max Reinhardt production, *The Eternal Road.* Between 1937 and 1940 he toured with Lincoln Kirstein's Ballet Caravan, for which he worked backstage and danced, among other roles, the title character in Eugene Loring's *Billy the Kid.* Kidd served as soloist and assistant director with Loring's Dance Players in 1941–1942 and subsequently in 1942 joined Ballet Theatre as a soloist. He performed with Ballet Theatre for five years, dancing important roles in *Fancy Free, Three Virgins and a Devil,* and *Interplay,* among others. In 1945, on conductor Antal Dorati's recommendation, Kidd was given his first chance to choreograph. The result was *On Stage!,* a narrative about a backstage handyman (danced by Kidd) who helps a novice ballerina (Janet Reed) to overcome her fear of an audition. With music by Norman Dello Joio, the ballet included rehearsal scenes and was a lighthearted comment on the world of dance. Its reception suggested the direction Kidd would ultimately take: Edwin Denby's original review in the *New York Herald-Tribune* condescendingly referred to it as a "Broadway pastime"; John Martin's in the *New York Times,* more complimentary, found it "a funny, gauche, human little comedy."

Kidd never created another ballet. Instead, in 1947 he left his dancing career to choreograph the production numbers for the musical *Finian's Rainbow* and with that began a long association with Broadway and Hollywood. The first person to win four Tony awards, he also choreographed *Hold It* (1948), *Arms and the Girl* (1950), *Guys and Dolls* (1950), *Can-Can* (1953), *L'il Abner* (1956), *Destry Rides Again* (1959), *Wildcat* (1960), *Subways Are for Sleeping* (1967), and *The Rothschilds* (1970). Years later, commenting on his redirected career, Kidd said, "Maybe it was my late start in dancing, my scientific background—I don't know. At any rate I wanted a more rounded, more outgoing career than I could have with the Ballet" (quoted in Jamison, 1954).

His film choreography included *Where's Charley?* (1952), *The Band Wagon* (1953), *Seven Brides for Seven Brothers* (1954), *Guys and Dolls* (1955), *Merry Andrew* (which he also directed, 1958), *Star!* (1968), *Hello, Dolly!* (1969), and *Movie Movie* (1978). Kidd also appeared in *It's*

Always Fair Weather (1955), *Smile* (1975), and *Movie Movie.*

Beginning with *On Stage!*, Kidd frequently expressed his desire to create dances that would appeal to all audiences: "Dancing should be completely understandable—every move, every turn should mean something, should be crystal-clear to the audience" (quoted in Jamison, 1954). The broad appeal of Kidd's work was evident in the eclectic style and in the variety of dances in his shows and films. One of Kidd's particular characteristics was to blur the lines between dance and gymnastics, as evident in the barn-raising competition from *Seven Brides for Seven Brothers,* "Salud" in *Merry Andrew,* and "Dancing" from *Hello, Dolly!* In addition, he often captured the essence of certain dramatic situations through stylization of movement. "The Girl Hunt Ballet" from *The Band Wagon,* for example, parodies gangster fiction by abstracting the elements of the genre and then emphasizing them through the dance. Kidd's choreography, notable for combining ballet and other forms of dance with nondance movement, was essential to the development of the musical.

[*See,* Film Musicals *article on* Hollywood Film Musicals; *and* United States of America, *article on* Musical Theater.]

BIBLIOGRAPHY

Coleman, Emily. "The Dance Man Leaps to the Top." *New York Times Magazine* (19 April 1959).

de Mille, Agnes. *America Dances.* New York, 1980.

Denby, Edwin. *Dance Writings.* Edited by Robert Cornfield and William MacKay. New York, 1986.

Jamison, Barbara. "Kidd from Brooklyn." *New York Times Magazine* (13 June 1954).

JEROME DELAMATER

KIDD. The barn-raising scene from *Seven Brides for Seven Brothers* (1954), with Tommy Rall as an airborne brother. One of Kidd's best-loved numbers, this dance combined ballet, show dancing, and acrobatics in characteristic form. In 1997, Kidd received an Oscar for lifetime achievement as a choreographer and a performer in films. (Photograph from the Film Stills Library, Museum of Modern Art, New York; used by permission.)

KIM CH'UN-HEUNG (born 1909 in Seoul), Korean dancer, teacher, and choreographer. Kim Ch'un-heung began his study of Korean court dance and music at the age of thirteen when he entered the Yi Dynasty Royal Music Conservatory in 1922. The following year he danced at the royal court before Emperor Soonjong at a banquet commemorating the monarch's fiftieth birthday. After graduating from the Conservatory, Kim became a member of the royal court orchestra and dance troupe. In 1940 and 1941 he studied folk dance with the great master Han Song-jun. During the Korean War (1950–1953) he taught dance at an institute in Pusan. Kim returned to Seoul in 1954 to open his own institute; he also became one of the founding members of the National Classical Music Institute of Korea, the successor of the Yi Dynasty Royal Music Conservatory.

In 1956 Kim gave his first public performance with his students, and in 1960 he received the Seoul City Cultural Award. In 1963 he performed folk and masked dance drama with his students in Seoul. As a leading member of the Sahm-Ch'un-Li Dancers and Musicians of Korea, he made his American debut in 1964, appearing at twenty-seven universities and culminating in two performances at Lincoln Center's Philharmonic Hall in New York. In 1968 he was cited by the Ministry of Culture and Information for his efforts in preserving traditional dance and music; during the same year, he was designated a Human Cultural Treasure as both a dancer and musician of the Royal Ancestral Shrine Music and Dance.

In 1969 Kim presented his first choreographic work, *The Flute That Calmed Ten Thousand Waves.* In 1971 he was once again designated a Human Cultural Treasure for his performance of *ch'oyong-mu,* a royal court masked dance. In 1972 he gave a special performance of *ch'unaeng-mu* ("nightingale dance"), a court dance on which he is regarded as the leading authority, commemorating his fiftieth year in the field of traditional dance. Repeat performances of this dance were given in 1982 and 1992, commemorating his sixtieth and seventieth years in dance. In 1976 Kim again toured the United States as part of the bicentennial celebrations. In 1995, at the age of eighty-six, he taught Korean court dance and music as a visiting lecturer at the University of Hawaii.

As the only living dancer in Korea who has ever performed at court before a king, Kim has painstakingly revived a large number of old court dances that would have otherwise fallen into oblivion.

BIBLIOGRAPHY

Cho Dong-wha. "Dance." In *Korea: Its Land, People, and Culture of All Ages.* 2d ed. Seoul, 1963.

Chung Byong-ho. *Korean Traditional Dance.* Seoul, 1985.

Heyman, Alan C. "Dances of the Three-Thousand-League Land." *Dance Perspectives,* no. 19 (March 1964).

Ku Hui-suh. *Ch'um Kwa Ku Saram.* Vol. 1. Translated by Lee Kyong-hee. Seoul, 1994.

Song Kyong-rin. "Korean Court Dance." In *Korean Dance, Theater, and Cinema,* edited by the Korean National Commission for UNESCO. Seoul, 1983.

ALAN C. HEYMAN

KIM PAIK-BONG (born 1927 in Seoul), Korean dancer, choreographer, teacher, and writer. Kim Paik-bong began her study of traditional dance as a student of Ch'oi Seung-hee from 1939 to 1943 in Seoul; she later studied creative dance at Ch'oi's academy in Pyongyang. She made her debut in Tokyo in 1941 in the *Dance of the Court Lady* and, in 1943, became a member of Ch'oi Seung-hee's dance troupe, performing in Manchuria, Japan, China, and Southeast Asia. In 1947 she embarked on the modernization of Korean dance at Pyongyang's Citizen's Theater in the First Creative Dance Festival, with a series of dance poems, dance dramas, dance operas, and mass games. In 1953 she opened a private dance institute in Seoul and has since taught at such institutions of higher learning as Sudo Women's College (today King Sejong University), Sorabol Arts College, Hanyang University, and Kyunghee University, where she presently holds the title of professor emerita of dance. She is also a board member of Korea's National Academy of Arts, the Korea branch of the International Theater Institute (ITI), the Advisory Committee on the Arts to Korea's Ministry of Culture and Sports, and the National Theater. She is a member of the judging committee of the Culture and Arts Award and the Korea Dance Festival.

In 1958, as a member of a Korean friendship troupe, Kim performed in Vietnam, Thailand, the Philippines, and Hong Kong. In 1962, as a member of the Korean Folk Arts Troupe, she performed in France, Italy, Greece, and Turkey as part of an international folk arts festival. She performed again with the same troupe in Tokyo (1964) and Mexico (1968), and in the United States as part of the bicentennial celebration of American independence (1976). In 1979 she toured Europe with the National Dance Company, which performed *Moonlight Water Sprite, Flower Crown Dance, Filial Piety, Dance of Improvisation, Dance of Liberation, Fragrance of Spring, Heart of Innocence, Young Lad with a Straw Hat, In Praise of the Fatherland, Fan Dance, A Story of Our Village, The Portrait, Hometown, Drum Dance, Enchanted Land, A Maiden's Dream, Buddhist Invocation, Glory, The Emperor, My Mind, Sunset, In Memoriam, The Physician of Souls, Narcissus,* and *Beautiful Woman,* along with some of her own works. Her *Fan Dance* was subsequently (1992) designated a Dance Masterpiece by the Korean Dance Association.

Kim is the author of such publications as *Pongsan Mask Dance-Drama Dance Notation* (1977), published by the Korean Culture and Arts Foundation, and several other works on dance and dance education, published by the Ministry of Education. In addition, she is a recipient of such prizes as the Seoul City Cultural Award (1963) and the Academy of Arts Award (1975).

Kim Paik-bong is most noted as a superb dancer and dance teacher who succeeded in creating a new style of dance based on traditional forms.

[*See also* Korea, *article on* Modern Dance.]

BIBLIOGRAPHY

Cho Dong-wha. "Dance." In *Korea: Its Land, People, and Culture of All Ages*. 2d ed. Seoul, 1963.

Chung Byong-ho. *Korean Folk Dance*. Seoul, 1992.

Heyman, Alan C. "Dances of the Three-Thousand-League Land." *Dance Perspectives*, no. 19 (March 1964).

Pak Yong-ku. "Young Dancers Seek to Create Fresh Stage Idioms." In *Korean Art Guide*. 2d rev. ed. Seoul, 1986.

ALAN C. HEYMAN

KINESIOLOGY. [*To discuss a scientific and technical approach to the understanding of movement, this entry comprises two articles. The first article presents an overview of the history of the study of human movement; the second article focuses on the importance of kinesiology in prevention and treatment of dance-related injuries. For related discussion, see* Body Therapies; Dance Medicine; Photography; *and* Physics of Dance.]

An Overview

Kinesiology is the study of human movement, concentrating on the interactions between anatomy and the environment. The term *biomechanics* is frequently used interchangeably with *kinesiology.* The differences between the two terms are based on research focus rather than on precedent or technical division of the subject. Kinesiology relies on the basic sciences of anatomy, physics, physiology, and, increasingly, on biochemistry to state the laws of nature that govern organic movement.

The kinesiologist reasons deductively in the description of movement principles rather than inductively in the statement of laws. For example, based on observations of many individuals' performances of movement tasks, the kinesiologist might deduce that a particular number of describable patterns are typical in human activity. Consequently, he or she might offer the thesis that any individual's motor development or skill acquisition can be evaluated against general human movement pattern norms. As a rule, the kinesiologist does not frame biological laws that both explain and predict movement patterns for all humans.

The Elements of Kinesiology. The two major areas of study basic to kinesiology are mechanics and anatomy. Mechanics is the branch of physics that analyzes the effects of forces on matter and on material systems. Mathematics provides the tools for analysis. Anatomical studies include not only gross anatomy of the musculoskeletal and articulatory systems of the body but also neuromuscular and cardiovascular physiology.

Mechanics. The Cartesian three-dimensional coordinate system is applied to the human body as a basis for determining its center of gravity, its motional planes, and its configuration from movement to movement. Detailed analysis can be made upon this essentially geometric foundation. For example, the interrelative accelerations of the body's segments can be plotted, and centers of moments and the displacement of the center of gravity can be determined.

Three of Newton's classic laws of mechanics are systematically applied in describing the forces that cause or affect motion. Vector analysis and algebraic expressions of linear and rotational mechanics describe resultant forces, torques, moment arms (lever systems), and trajectories.

Anatomy. Muscle tissue and the mechanism for muscle contraction must be understood to analyze the function of muscles as prime movers, antagonists, accessories, and synergists in creating movements.

Anatomy of the articulatory system (the body's joints) gives information on the organic capacities for and limits on motion, on lever systems, and on the three-dimensional configuration of the whole body in motion.

Neuromuscular and cardiovascular physiology may be studied to describe more completely skill development (motor learning), physical conditioning, the sources of energy to effect and sustain muscle contraction, and the effects of energy depletion. Biochemistry is basic to the study of physiology.

The Development of Kinesiology. The development of kinesiology is rooted in the history of natural philosophy. Aristotle (384–322 BCE) is considered the father of kinesiology. He was the first philosopher to observe and record animal movement systematically. His logico-verbal method, the forerunner to the scientific method, produced three treatises, *De partibus animalium* (On the Parts of Animals), *De incessu animalium* (On the Movement of Animals), and *De generatione animalium* (On the Generation of Animals), in which he considered the relationships of anatomy and behavior to habitats.

The mathematician Archimedes (c.287–212 BCE) determined the significance of densities of masses. He is credited with being the first experimenter to demonstrate the existence of a center of mass of any given body. Galen (129–c.199 CE) advanced the practice of medicine on the thoroughness of his anatomical and physiological observations. He recommended procedures for conditioning athletes and gladiators and he noted, from direct observation, the roles of prime mover and antagonist muscles.

During the Renaissance in Italy, artist and scientist Leonardo da Vinci (1452–1519) elevated anatomical and mechanical illustration to a fine art. At his hand anatomical features were rendered with clarity and precision. Andreas Vesalius (1514–1564) of Brussels formulated the modern concept of anatomy. For Italian artists, Vesalius prepared the first comprehensive atlas of human anatomy. His *De humani corporis fabrica* (On the Makeup of the Human Body) is the classic model for anatomical illustration; in other works he attempted to depict actual movement in process and to identify its anatomical sources. In the field of mechanics, Galileo Galilei (1564–1642) demonstrated the universal principles of motion with respect to gravitation. Subsequently, Isaac Newton (1642–1727) formally expressed the laws of mechanics that laid the foundations of modern physics.

The first researcher to bring the separately emerging findings in anatomy and mechanics together into a kinesiological inquiry was Giovanni Alfonso Borelli (1608–1679), a student of Galileo. In *De mota animalium* (Animal Movement) he demonstrated that bones and joints make up lever systems and that they are articulated by muscles according to physical laws. He further calculated that external forces such as air, water, and the ground influence animal movement. Iatrophysics, the application of principles of physics in the practice of medicine, is also dated from Borelli's work. Orthopedics and physical therapy are two of the modern disciplines that have developed out of iatrophysics.

During the eighteenth and nineteenth centuries, rapid advances in technology and engineering, together with the development of neuromuscular physiology, were particularly significant for the eventual identification of kinesiology as a discipline in its own right.

In the seventeenth century Francis Glisson (1597–1677) demonstrated that muscles contract rather than expand (as his contemporary, Borelli, had thought). Later, Luigi Galvani (1737–1798), an anatomist, discovered the irritability of muscle in contact with electrical current. The

KINESIOLOGY. Advancements in photography in the late nineteenth century allowed for a dramatically improved understanding of the physical mechanics of movement. This sequence of photographic stills, from Eadweard Muybridge's *Animal Locomotion,* published in 1887, shows a man doing a handstand from two different angles. (Metropolitan Museum of Art, New York; Gift of the Philadelphia Commercial Museum, 1964 [64.661.6.30]; used by permission.)

difference between irritability and excitability was noted by Albrecht von Haller (1708–1777), who was then able to conceive the idea that contractility is an innate property of muscle. Kinesiologists' later understanding of the motor unit (the anatomical-functional relationship of the neuron to the muscle fiber), of excitatory and inhibitory responses to stimuli, and of the mechanism for muscle contraction all depended on this idea. Similarly, the "all-or-none" principle, first propounded by Henry Bowditch (1814–1911), clarified how a muscle contracts with increasing force by cumulative activation of its many motor units.

Karl Culmann (1821–1881), an engineer, made a principle of geometry, the trajectory theory, an architectural principle. The principle identifies any curve that cuts a family of curves or surfaces all at the same angle. The biologist Jules Wolff (1836–1902) observed this principle in the longitudinal section of bone, in which minimal tissue provides greatest strength in its "architectural" arrangement. Consequently, Wolff stated a fundamental law for organic growth: in their internal and external architecture, bones conform to the stresses to which they are habitually subjected.

Wolff's contemporary Adolf E. Fick (1829–1902) studied in detail the structure and mechanics of joints. He also developed the method of exercise against increasing resistance for gain in muscle strength, and he identified isometric (in the same length) and isotonic (with the same tension) contraction in the conditioning of muscle.

Using frozen cadavers, Christian Braune (1831–1892) and Otto Fisher (1861–1917) located the center of gravity of the human body. They were further able to demonstrate the significance of that center for posture and locomotion of the living body. They located the center of gravity for each segment of the body and, by use of photographs in series, known as chronophotography, analyzed the human gait mathematically.

Eadweard Muybridge (1831–1904), photographer, published his eleven-volume *Animal Locomotion* in 1887. This monumental work further demonstrated the technique of chronophotography and its usefulness in analyzing movements over uninterrupted periods of execution from two or three views simultaneously. Étienne-Jules Marey (1830–1904), physiologist, recognized the significance of photography for inspecting all biological functions and did the earliest experiments observing motion at the physiological level in the 1880s.

Guillaume Benjamin Amand Duchenne (Duchenne de Boulogne) and Jules Amar, independently, summarized the advances in the sciences of the preceding two centuries as they influenced the study of human movement. In 1867 Duchenne published the landmark volume *Physiologie des mouvements* (Physiology of Motion), in which he systematically demonstrated the dynamics of intact skeletal muscles by use of electricity. Thus the technique of electromyography was born. Amar brought together all known principles of physiology and kinesiology in *Le moteur et les bases scientifiques du travail professionel* (The Human Motor). This significant publication—translated into English in 1920—introduced a major theme for twentieth-century kinesiology: efficiency of movement in industry and sport activities.

Rudolf Laban (1879–1958), the Hungarian-born movement theorist who greatly influenced the European dance artists Mary Wigman and Kurt Jooss during the early decades of the twentieth century, was himself influenced by Amar's practical and utilitarian view. Laban's system for organizing human movement potentials and enriching personal movement experience while at the same time seeking movement efficiency was perhaps the first attempt in Western culture to blend aesthetic and practical objectives in the same principles. During World War II he was employed by the British government to speed war industry mobilization through organization of human movement in support of mass production.

In the area of neurophysiology, in 1906 Charles Sherrington published *The Integrative Action of the Nervous System*. A comprehensive accounting for all neural activity on the basis of primary reflexes, the book inspects the full range of vertebrate motion. The discussions of reciprocal enervation, bodily reinforcement of emotion, and reflex and volitional action exemplify the scope of this classic work. By the second publication of this volume in 1947, a generation of international physiologists had propelled knowledge of the field into microanatomy and biochemistry. As a result, much of the late twentieth-century research in biomechanics and kinesiology has focused on the metabolism of energy sources and on the intrinsic sense modalities for muscle action.

Among the numerous researchers whose work influenced this shift in focus are John Varoujan Basmajian and Hugh Esmor Huxley. Basmajian's *Muscles Alive* appeared in four editions between 1962 and 1978. In it the technique of electromyography was fully expanded and employed, and the interrelative degree of muscle contraction during motion was recorded for qualitative as well as quantitative analysis. Huxley was able to construct a model of the ultrastructure of muscle tissue. The electron microscope and tissue sectioning and staining techniques were then available to reveal the shadows of overlapping protein filaments, and the mechanism for muscle contraction could at last be described.

In other developments, film techniques replaced the cumbersome chronophotography, and high-speed cinematography, electronic stroboscopy, and X-ray motion pictures made three-dimensional and physiological movement visible for detailed inspection. The force platform was in use by the 1970s, making possible direct vectoral measurements of dancers' and athletes' action against the ground. Coupled with film recording, these measurements provide kinesiologists with comprehensive data for diagnosis of individual performances.

Kinesiology in Academe. The development of kinesiology in its many applications and theoretical branches can be traced to its institutionalization as an academic discipline.

In 1913 William Skarstrom, a doctor and professor of physical education at Wellesley College in Massachusetts, published his textbook, *Gymnastic Kinesiology.* The book typified the early academic approach to the subject with its assessment of human postures, analysis of the body's lever systems, and prescription of remedial and developmental calisthenic exercises.

KINESIOLOGY. Each primary body plane divides the body equally by weight: the frontal plane divides anterior from posterior; the sagittal plane, right from left; and the transverse plane, superior from inferior. The intersection of these planes creates the primary axes, coordinates X, Y, and Z. The primary axes coincide at one point, the center of gravity. (Drawing courtesy of John M. Wilson.)

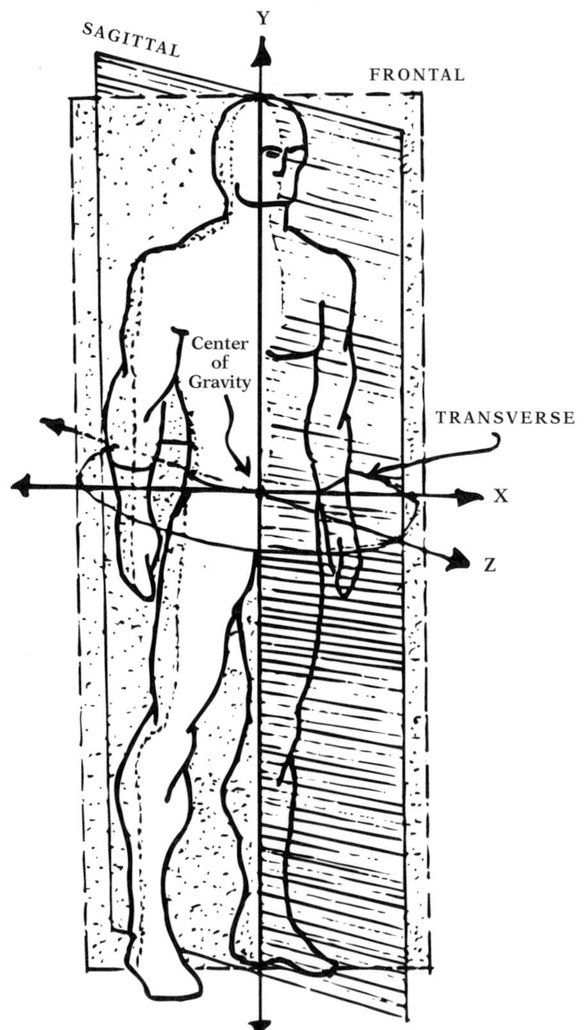

Other texts published between 1912 and 1935 considerably expanded the scope of the subject. The emphasis on scientifically based information and on experimentation, rather than on anecdotal information and pedagogical principles, put academic kinesiology in the sphere of quantitative analysis.

Wilbur Bowen and Robert Tait McKenzie's 1917 publication, *Applied Anatomy and Kinesiology: The Mechanism of Human Movement,* laid a comprehensive foundation for what was to become the traditional approach to the discipline. Special branches of study were soon to appear.

Wilhelmine Wright focused on functional anatomy for physical education and physical therapy students in her 1928 publication, *Muscle Function.* Children's developmental physical education and sport skill development were addressed by Ruth Glassow in her 1930 *Fundamentals of Physical Education.*

Arthur Steindler, a doctor and professor of orthopaedic surgery at the University of Iowa, viewed human movement analysis in terms of medical conditions. His 1935 *Mechanics of Normal and Pathological Locomotion in Man* linked orthopaedics with physical education for the first time.

Dance Kinesiology. Dance did not enjoy a particularly comfortable or productive relationship to academic kinesiology from 1910 to about 1970. Few kinesiology texts referred to dance; those that did tended to focus on moments of greatest acceleration of a limb, greatest displacement of the center of gravity, or optimal alignment to achieve balanced stance during execution of movement patterns. This quantitative approach seems too reductionist to most dancers and dance educators. It is the experience of movement—the dynamics, the rhythm, the phrasing, the gestural intent, and the motivation—that is of primary interest.

The foundations of qualitative analysis of dance and human movement began to develop in the 1930s and 1940s. The European development is clearly traceable to Laban's theories and teachings. The emphasis of his work was on movement efficiency and expression through the analysis of the mover's use of and attitude toward weight, time, space, and energy flow in relation to the environment. Following World War II, Laban's disciple, Irmgard Bartenieff, brought his theory and foundational applications with her to the United States, where she continued to explore and articulate principles that reintegrate natural neurological growth and responses with efficient movement development.

The American approach to human movement analysis originated in the work of Mabel Elsworth Todd, however, at Columbia University Teachers College in the 1930s. Todd's point of view was holistic. Her 1937 summary volume, *The Thinking Body,* was based on the best scientific information available at the time but emphasized the integrative activity of the body's many physiological systems rather than patterned activity acquisition.

Further, dance kinesiology has developed with a practical focus—to improve the performance of dance and to prevent and treat injuries. A particularly influential concept developed by Lulu Sweigard (1895–1974), a student of Todd's, incorporates techniques of imaging movement as an essential part of moving fully and efficiently. The technique, known as ideokinesis, has been further explored and developed by Irene Dowd, a neuromuscular training specialist.

Other body reeducation techniques based on kinesiological study have been incorporated into dance curricula. Those of Frederick Alexander and Moshe Feldenkrais have been particularly influential. Together with the Laban-Bartenieff Movement Fundamentals, with ideokinetic facilitation, and other systems, these approaches to human movement analysis and experience came to be known in the 1960s and 1970s as body therapies. They provide a form of clinical laboratory for kinesiological study.

Equally significant has been the influence of physical therapy and sports medicine. Celia Sparger's *Anatomy and Ballet* and Raoul Gelabert's *Anatomy for the Dancer* provided ballet dancers and their teachers "with exercises to improve technique and prevent injuries."

In the 1970s Ernest L. Washington, director of the International Center for Dance Orthopaedics and Dance Therapy in Los Angeles, rallied athletic trainers and physicians to professional dancers' medical needs. His survey, "Musculoskeletal Injuries in Theatrical Dancers" (*The American Journal of Sports Medicine,* 1978), his international clinics, and his *Dance Medicine–Health Newsletter* led the medical profession's rapidly developing interest in dancers as athletes. In 1978 Daniel Arnheim published *Dance Injuries: Their Prevention and Care,* a practical book that was not limited to the specifics of ballet technique.

By 1983 *Clinics in Sports Medicine* published an issue on dance injuries, and in 1984, as a part of the Olympic Scientific Congress, the first International Symposium on the Scientific Aspects of Dance was held at the University of Oregon.

In the 1970s and 1980s the quantitative foundations for analysis of dance were advancing and bringing dance into the traditional track of kinesiology. *The Physics of Dance* (1984) by Kenneth Laws and *Kinesiology for Dance* (1986) by Sally Fitt exemplify the full text approach to the subject. An increasing number of masters' theses, using experimental methods, were contributing data to the quantitative foundations of dance kinesiology.

Influential quantitative studies such as those conducted by Rhonda S. Ryman and Donald A. Ranney included the analysis of dance movements from the perspective of physics, using technological recording and measuring tools. Grounded in biomechanical principles, the work of diverse researchers and practitioners has expanded the field of dance kinesiology. Exploration of the connection between reflexive action and personal behavior, health, and healing is exemplified in the work of Valerie Hunt and her students at the University of California—Los Angeles. The development of generic dance techniques has been led by Joan Skinner (Skinner Releasing Technique), Bonnie Bainbridge Cohen (Mind/Body Centering), and John M. Wilson (Arthrocentric Exploration).

Beginning with the newsletter *Kinesiology for Dance* (1977–1979), edited by Martin Tracy at UCLA, research and communication in the field rapidly expanded. By 1990 several journals and anthologies devoted to the subject were being published and widely used including *The Journal of Sports Medicine and Kinesiology for Dance, Impulse,* and *Science of Dance Training,* edited by Priscilla M. Clarkson and Margaret Skrinar.

The technological developments in movement research, including computer and video analysis, began to have a major influence on dance kinesiology in both theoretical research and practical application. By the early 1990s several computer programs offered three-dimensional videographic representation of the human body in motion. But a continuing interest in personal, practical learning, hands-on and in the studio, is exemplified in the increasing use of Pilates training by both college and professional dancers, attention to nutrition and conditioning, the inclusion of yoga and meditation in their personal lives, the development of personal and generic techniques, and courses in experiential anatomy such as those developed by Andrea Olsen and Caryn McHose.

At the close of the twentieth century, dance kinesiology has not achieved a unitary disciplinary approach. Quantitative analysis of biomechanics and exercise physiology continue to follow the experimental model developed in the health-related professions and physical education since the 1920s. The body therapies, subsumed into the emerging field of somatics, predominate in dance education and, increasingly, replace traditional courses in kinesiology. It is clear that whatever the field of dance kinesiology will develop into, it will seek to build a paradigm that will include qualitative as well as quantitative analysis and that its principal learning modality will be experiential.

BIBLIOGRAPHY

Atwater, Anne E. "Kinesiology/Biomechanics Trends." *Research Quarterly for Exercise and Sport* 51.1 (1980).

Bartenieff, Irmgard, with Dori Lewis. *Body Movement: Coping with the Environment.* New York, 1980.

Braun, G. L. "Kinesiology: From Aristotle to the Twentieth Century." *Research Quarterly for Exercise and Sport* 12 (1941).

Clarkson, Priscilla M., and Margaret Skrinar, eds. *Science of Dance Training.* Champaign, Ill., 1988.

Fitt, Sally S. *Dance Kinesiology.* New York, 1988.

Glassow, Ruth B. "Modern Dance and Kinesiology." *Journal of the American Association for Health, Physical Education, Recreation* (January 1966).

Kapandji, I. *The Physiology of the Joints.* New York, 1980.

Kinesiology for Dance. Los Angeles, 1977–.

Laws, Kenneth. *The Physics of Dance.* New York, 1984.

Myers, Martha, and Margaret Pierpont. "Body Therapies and the Modern Dancer." *Dance Magazine* 57 (August 1983).

Olsen, Andrea, and Caryn McHose. *Bodystories: A Guide to Experiential Anatomy.* Barrytown, N.Y., 1991.

Seireg, Ali. "Leonardo da Vinci: The Biomechanician." In *Biomechanics,* edited by David Bootzin and Harry C. Muffley. New York, 1969.

Solomon, Ruth, Sandra C. Minton, and John Solomon, eds. *Preventing Dance Injuries: An Interdisciplinary Perspective.* Reston, Va., 1990.

Wickstrom, Roger. "Developmental Kinesiology: Maturation of Basic Motor Patterns." *Exercise and Sport Sciences Reviews* 3 (1975).

JOHN M. WILSON

Therapeutic Practices

Dance kinesiology, often referred to as dance science, is the study of human bodies in the positions and movements of dance. It concentrates on the scientific and medical aspects of dance, in contrast to the choreographic, psychological, ethnological, or sociological dimensions. Drawing from the general discipline of kinesiology (kinesis: movement), dance movement is examined from anatomical, biomechanical, physiological, neuromuscular, motor behavioral, developmental, and morphological perspectives.

Dance kinesiology is an interdisciplinary course of study bridging the fields of art and science. Science strives to objectify knowledge through methods of observation, analysis, standardized terminology, and quantifiable measurement. Dance is an expressive art form eliciting subjective responses for the purpose of communicating feelings, artistic intent, and aesthetics. A dance kinesiologist is most effective when educated in both the art of dance and in scientific methods.

Dance kinesiologists operate in a variety of capacities: medicine, education, and research. In a medical context, dance kinesiologists often work with other health professionals to assess injuries, recommend treatment, and teach preventive and rehabilitative techniques. Additional training may be required in physical therapy, athletic training, or sports medicine because of the applied clinical focus of medicine.

In education, most college and university dance curricula require courses in anatomy and kinesiology related to dance. The development of dance kinesiology pedagogy has gradually altered dance training principles to prevent injuries and enhance performance. The content of these courses has included both quantitative and qualitative theories of movement analysis.

In research, scientific investigations are conducted to study the manner in which dance movements affect the physical body. Researching dance movement involves quantitative and qualitative investigations. Quantitative studies gather statistics on types, frequencies, and numbers of dance injuries. Biomechanical analysis of specific dance movements, such as a *plié* or *grand jeté,* are studied through electromyography (EMG) and high-speed film techniques. Nutritional studies, physiological considerations of strength and endurance, and motor learning outcomes are all approached from scientific analysis using deductive and inductive research methods.

Qualitative studies are drawn from various somatic disciplines (e.g., Alexander Technique, Bartenieff Fundamentals, Feldenkrais, Ideokinesis, etc.) and Laban Movement Analysis (LMA). Qualitative research studies movement through natural observation and self-reporting techniques. Qualitative systems such as LMA and Somatics recognize the relationship between physical expression and anatomical function. Research of this nature studies the dynamic interactive process between movement and behavior. Value is given to the participants' perspectives on their experiences to understand better the synthesis of emotional and physical factors that influence expressive movement, creativity, and artistic intent.

Somatic disciplines, sometimes referred to as "body therapies," are applied kinesthetic modalities that enhance the relationship between the mental, emotional, and physical expression of movement. Somatic studies are educational techniques used to facilitate neuromuscular repatterning and increase awareness of subtle responses to fine and gross motor capacities. The process of kinesthetic reeducation occurs through physical participation, concentrating on heightened sensory awareness, refined coordination, breathing patterns, joint articulations, and efficient muscular usage. Participants of somatic disciplines are encouraged to be aware of subtle movement feelings. The inherent self-reflective process of somatic education develops integration of movement behavior. Comprehending the functional and expressive relationship of movement allows a dance kinesiologist to work with concerns of dance artistry as well as physical well-being.

Expressive qualities in dance can be defined through the LMA system. LMA offers a descriptive language and model for qualitative movement study that includes anatomy, spatial use, and dynamic range (use of force, time, flow, focus). LMA is a recordable method of movement observation that is capable of analyzing and communicating stylistic dance patterns. The application of LMA reveals predispositions to particular expressive qualities and movement patterns that could lead to injury. For example, when a dancer opens his or her arms slowly and gently in a forward upward direction, there is an expressed quality to the movement. In addition, how the arms are moved at the shoulder joint and in unison with the spine indicates if the dancer is moving efficiently. Inefficient technique patterns leave joints susceptible to injuries.

In each subspecialty of dance kinesiology, medicine, education, and research, movement analysis illuminates the specific demands of dance compared to other athletic disciplines. Dancing involves learning and proficiently performing a large number of varied spatial and rhythmic patterns. These patterns can change frequently depending on the style of dance and the choreographic project. Many dance forms involve above-normal flexibility and considerable strength and power to run, jump, and fall. These physical demands make dancers unique artistic athletes. The interplay of tremendous athletic and expressive skills results in distinct causes and types of dance injuries.

Causes of Dance Injuries. Multiple factors cause dance injuries. Rarely is one factor responsible; it is usually an accumulation of several conditions such as faulty technique; insufficient conditioning in flexibility, muscle strength, power, and endurance; improper warm-up; anatomical limitations; abrupt overload; emotional stress; improper technique level; stylistic demands; environmental conditions; nutritional deficiencies; and trauma.

• *Faulty technique* is the execution of poor movement mechanics. Improper mechanics cause muscle imbalances, uneven friction at joint sites, and stress and strain on tissue structures. This is one of the leading causes of dance injuries, which occur through repeated misuse over a sustained period.

• *Insufficient conditioning* has several categories. If a dancer lacks flexibility conditioning, the result will be tight muscles, which limit joint range of motion. If groups of muscles are not prepared to do, for example, a high leg kick, the body tissue will tear. In opposition, if a dancer has very "loose joints," what is called ligament laxity, this hypermobility will cause joint instability. An unstable joint is equally as prone to injury. Stretching can be used to condition tight muscles, and strengthening techniques must be used through joint range to improve conditions of hypermobility from ligament laxity.

• *Insufficient muscle strength, power, and endurance* result in weak muscles that fatigue easily. When a muscle is tired and does not have the capacity to perform, faulty mechanics occur and the dancer has poor movement control. Insufficient muscle strength causes compression forces to impact joint structures, which can lead to numerous soft-tissue injuries.

• *Lack of adequate warm-up* fails to prepare the circulatory and neuromuscular systems properly. A warm-up primes the cardiopulmonary systems. Increases in heart rate and blood flow through the body serve to elevate body temperature, which affects the pliability of muscle and soft tissue. A warm-up also prepares the neuromuscular system for optimal force and speed of a muscle contraction.

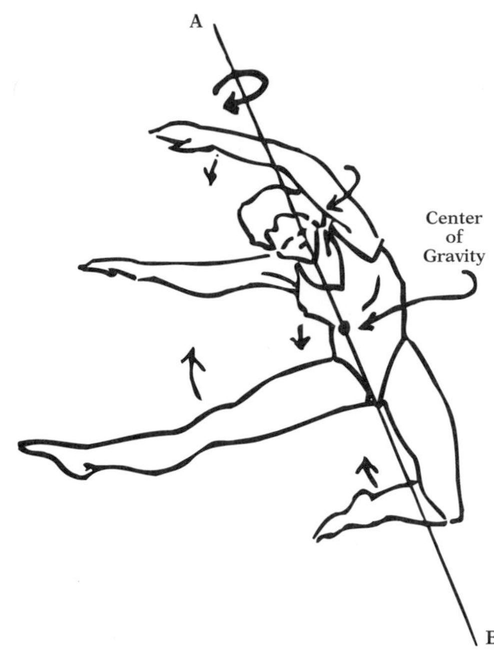

KINESIOLOGY. The dancer rotates around her axis of momentum (AB) in the air during a jump. This is the sum effect of segment torques. The center of gravity is displaced upward and laterally. (Drawing courtesy of John. M. Wilson.)

• *Anatomical predispositions* are structural abnormalities in bones and tissues that offset movement mechanics. Any abnormal bony shape, such as an altered angle in the hip joint (a greater increase or decrease in the angle between the neck and shaft of the femur) will alter efficient alignment and lead to muscle compensations and imbalances.

• *Abrupt overload* is any change in the intensity of dance training or performance. Increasing physical activity places undue stress on the body. To build physical stamina, body tissues need time to adjust to unfamiliar demands through the process of adaptation. Many overuse injuries occur in bones, muscles, ligaments, tendons, and fascia because these tissues did not have adequate adaptation time.

• *Emotional stress* is a factor that can disturb the body's equilibrium and jeopardize the cycle of general adaptation leading to physical exhaustion, illness, or injury. The hormonal and physiological changes from emotional stress result in the same nonspecific responses as physical stress.

• *Improper technique level* is the outcome of training that is too advanced for the student.

• *Stylistic demands* result from particular choreographic movements that can stress the physical structure beyond an individual's anatomical or training limits.
• *Environmental conditions* are the training and performance areas for a dancer. The most crucial environmental factor is the floor. The floor surface creates proper or improper friction levels between the dancer's feet and the floor. Floors should have shock absorption properties to absorb compressive forces so they do not transfer to joints and body tissues. The temperature of a dancing environment influences hydration and physiological functions.
• *Nutrition deficiencies* are the outcome of an improper diet. Lack of adequate nutrients, vitamins, and minerals can impair cell growth and repair, especially to bone matter, and jeopardize energy requirements along with fluid balance.
• *Trauma* is any sudden impact causing injury, such as a fall.

Types of Injuries. The multiple causes for dance injuries result in problems that affect bones, muscles, tendons, ligaments, cartilage, and fascia. All these musculoskeletal structures can be overly stretched or compressed, resulting in different types of injuries.

A fracture is a bone injury. Bone fractures vary in severity, from a "hairline" crack to complete fragmentation of bone tissue.

When a muscle is "pulled" or torn it is called a strain. Strains result from overstretching and tearing fibers. Strains range from a mild tearing stretch to a complete rupture (tearing the tendon away from the bony attachment site).

When small microtrauma tears occur in tendons, inflammation develops and the condition is called tendonitis. When fibers of a ligament tear it is called a sprain. Sprains produce stretching or tearing of ligaments and the various connective tissues structures around a joint, such as the capsule and synovial membrane. There are first-, second-, and third-degree sprains. Third-degree sprains can lead to a dislocation.

A dislocation is a separation of one bone from another. Cartilage can be torn at particular joint sites, such as the meniscus pads in the knee. Injuries to fascia are referred to as fascitis.

All musculoskeletal injuries require medical evaluation before a diagnosis or explanation of the injury can be given. Treatment for dance injuries varies depending on the choice of therapeutic approaches.

Dance Science Practitioners. A medical doctor who performs surgery, such as when a bone is broken, is called an orthopedic surgeon. Orthopedists who specialize in dance injuries have a sports medicine emphasis in their training. Other methods of health care include the following: an osteopathic physician, or D.O., is a licensed doctor with education and training similar to an M.D. Osteopathic physicians have extensive training in nonsurgical methods of musculoskeletal care, including soft-tissue manipulation. Osteopaths use medications and surgery when appropriate.

A chiropractor is a health practitioner who does not use surgery or drugs. A chiropractor will treat dancers with a combination of joint manipulation, soft-tissue stretching, physiotherapy, and exercise. Tests will be given for flexibility and range of motion at joints as well as for muscle strength and balance. Treatment may include customized exercises and taping or adjustments to the dancer's joints and soft tissues.

A physical therapist is a rehabilitation specialist who works with methods of massage, ultrasound, and prescriptive exercises. A dance physical therapist knows the biomechanics of specific dance moves and can evaluate movement dysfunction contributing to a given injury.

A massage or soft-tissue therapist does not diagnose an injury but will work with the muscles and soft tissue of the body. Scar tissue from injury or emotional trauma deforms soft tissue, often requiring hands-on pressure to release tension-holding patterns that may contribute to structural imbalances. A massage therapist should be licensed. A soft-tissue therapist will have extensive training and certification in such methods as Rolfing.

In conjunction with medical and health practitioners, movement specialists contribute to the prevention and treatment of dance injuries. Movement specialists are often dance kinesiologists or somatic educators (body therapists). Movement specialists do not diagnose or treat acute injuries but look at patterns of movement that contribute to the cause of an acute or chronic injury. Once a health practitioner has given a diagnosis, a movement specialist will evaluate the dancer's body mechanics. In addition to receiving an evaluation, the dancer will learn how to improve body awareness and enhance dance technique and conditioning.

Movement specialists have training in various methods, such as Bartenieff Fundamentals, Alexander Technique, Feldenkrais, Ideokinesis, Body-Mind Centering systems (Bonnie Cohen's work), or the Pilates Method. All movement specialists help the dancer to increase sensory and motor function, which improves coordination. As coordination improves, small errors in technique are corrected. Changing dance mechanics not only improves technique and range of motion but allows for greater qualitative movement expression.

The expanded range of therapeutic practices contributes to better care of dancers as a special population. Improved treatment of dance injuries parallels expanded educational knowledge in how to reduce injury risks. Better prevention and treatment of a dancer's physical problems increases career longevity and enhances the art form of dance.

[*See also* Dance Medicine; *for related discussion, see* Body Therapies.]

BIBLIOGRAPHY

Arnheim, D. D. *Dance Injuries: Their Prevention and Care.* 3d ed. Princeton, 1991.

Bartenieff, Irmgard, with Dori Lewis. *Body Movement: Coping with the Environment.* New York, 1980.

Berardi, Gigi. *Finding Balance.* Princeton, 1991.

Chmelar, Robin D., and Sally S. Fitt. *Diet for Dancers: A Complete Guide to Nutrition and Weight Control.* Pennington, N.J., 1990.

Clarkson, Priscilla M., and Margaret Skrinar, eds. *Science of Dance Training.* Champaign, Ill., 1988.

Clinics in Sports Medicine 2 (November 1983). Publication of a symposium on injuries to dancers, edited by James Sammarco.

Dowd, Irene. *Taking Root to Fly: Seven Articles on Functional Anatomy.* New York, 1981.

Feldenkrais, Moshe. *Awareness through Movement.* New York, 1972.

Fitt, Sally S. *Dance Kinesiology.* New York, 1988.

Howse, Justin, and Shirley Hancock. *Dance Technique and Injury Prevention.* Rev. ed. London, 1992.

Laws, Kenneth. *The Physics of Dance.* New York, 1984.

Marshall, Catherine, and Gretchen B. Rossman. *Designing Qualitative Research.* 2d ed. Newbury Park, Calif., 1994.

Micheli, Lyle J. "Back Injuries in Dance." *Clinics in Sports Medicine* 2 (November 1983): 473–484.

O'Brien Stillwell, Janet. "The Alexander Technique: An Innovation for Dancers." *Somatics* 4.2 (1983): 15–18.

Quirk, Ronald. "Ballet Injuries: The Australian Experience." *Clinics in Sports Medicine* 2 (November 1983): 504–514.

Ryan, Allan J., and Robert E. Stephens. *The Dancer's Complete Guide to Healthcare and a Long Career.* Chicago, 1988.

Ryan, Allan J., and Robert E. Stephens, eds. *Dance Medicine: A Comprehensive Guide.* Chicago, 1987.

Ryan, Allan J., and Robert E. Stephens, eds. *The Healthy Dancer.* Abr. ed. Princeton, 1989.

Shell, Caroline G., ed. *The Dancer as Athlete.* Olympic Scientific Congress Proceedings, vol. 8. Champaign, Ill., 1986.

Smyth, Mary M., and Alan M. Wing, eds. *The Psychology of Human Movement.* Orlando, Fla., 1984.

Solomon, Ruth, and Lyle J. Micheli. "Technique as a Consideration in Modern Dance Injuries." *Physician and Sports Medicine* 14 (August 1986): 83–92.

Sweigard, Lulu E. *Human Movement Potential: Its Ideokinetic Facilitation.* New York, 1974.

Todd, Mabel Elsworth. *The Thinking Body.* New York, 1937.

Zebas, Carole, and Michael Chapman. *Prevention of Sports Injuries: A Biomechanical Approach.* Dubuque, Iowa, 1990.

JUDY GANTZ

KING, KENNETH (born 25 August 1948 in Freeport, New York), choreographer, dancer, and writer. King presented his first major work in New York City while still a philosophy student at Antioch College. Originally trained as an actor, he combines dancing with various theatrical elements, including films, written and spoken texts, atmospheric lighting, costumes, and characters, to create a chain of signals and symbols that are metaphors for information and power systems or for the workings of the mind itself.

King's early pieces of the mid-1960s were influenced by the alogical structures of happenings, the subject matter of pop art, and the underground film scene of which he was also a part. His preferred choreographic techniques have long included repetition and static forms. In *cup/saucer/two dancers/radio* (1964), all the elements in the title were considered equally important in the dance, reducing the dancers to automatonlike objects. *Print-Out* (1967–1968) was King's most radical dance. In it he presented language rather than movement as the dominant force in a dance. But in many of his works since then, wordplay after the manner of James Joyce coexists with high-energy dancing. King's writing (whether in performance texts, manifestos, or other essays) shows a futurist's fascination with the technological jargon of the cybernetic age as well as a sharp political critique and whimsical humor.

The fragmentation of thought and perception has informed King's work since he began choreographing. He has dramatized this fragmentation through the use of disguises and alter egos, a conscious theatrical expression of the philosophical notion of the double, the shadow (Nietzsche), and the other (Sartre). His movement style incorporates spinning, classically extended limbs, and minute articulations of body parts, gestures, and motions. King has written of his choreographic method,

> As a dancemaker I program structural and organizational options, rather than just set specifically repeatable phrases, so the generation of (im)pulses, and the tracing and tracking of 'circuits' in space, activates the firing and fielding of signs and signals which synchronistically become part of the formal performance process. . . . It's a kind of *digital*-kinetic semiotics.
> (Quoted in Kreemer, 1987, p. 151)

King's works in the 1970s included *High Noon* ("A Portrait-Play of Friedrich Nietzsche," 1974), *Battery, Parts I, II, and III* (a celebration of the philosopher Susanne K. Langer, 1975–1976), and *RAdeoA.C.Tiv(ID)ty* (for Pierre and Marie Curie, 1976–1977). His works of the 1980s included the multimedia *Phi Project* (1981), which involved computer programmed special effects; *Space City,* a dance–film collaboration with Robyn Brentano and Andrew Horn (1981); and *Critical Path* (for R. Buckminster Fuller, 1985); *If Iphigenia* (1988; to music by Constance Demby), an exploration of Greek mythology using split and doubled characters; and *Correlations* (1989; to music by Michael Stearns), which mixed serious speculation about words and movement with verbal wit and physical antics.

In 1990 King created *Dancing Wor(l)ds,* seven solos involving dancing, talking, tongue twisters, and comic characters. The solos included a tribute to Maria-Theresa

KING. The fleet-footed King as Patrick Duncan (Isadora's brother) in *Dancing Wor(l)ds* (1990), his evening-length suite of seven solos. This costume was designed by Heather Samuels. (Photograph © 1990 by Johan Elbers; used by permission.)

Duncan, one of Isadora Duncan's adopted daughters; *Ask Mr. Snail,* in which King impersonated a lazy mollusk; and *The Tallulah Deconstruction,* in which, disguised as the actress Tallulah Bankhead in the process of becoming a painter, he explored art, film, and stardom. In 1992 he added another, serious solo to the program, *Patrick's Fourth Dansing Dance (Orestes' Spell)* (to music by Dvořák), in which he seemed to be pursued by the Furies.

All of King's dances since 1993 have featured his familiar giddy high-tech wordplay live and/or on tape, including his three solos, *Dancing and Writing (On Hermaphrodites), Through Me Many Voices* (both 1994), and *Upper Atmospheric Disturbances* (1995). King has also made two duets, to which his partners contributed text and movement: *Secret Detour* (1993/94) with Gina Bonati, and *www//alenikoffking.com* (1997) with Frances Alenikoff.

BIBLIOGRAPHY

Anderson, Jack. "Kenneth King Is a Thinking Man's Choreographer." *New York Times* (10 May 1981).

Banes, Sally. *Terpsichore in Sneakers: Post-Modern Dance.* 2d ed. Middletown, Conn., 1987. Includes a bibliography.

King, Kenneth. "On the Move: A Polemic on Dancing." *Dance Magazine* (June 1967): 56–58.

King, Kenneth. "SuperLecture." In *Young American Writers,* edited by Richard Kostelanetz. New York, 1967.

King, Kenneth. "Space, Dance, and the Galactic Matrix." In *Merce Cunningham: Dancing in Space and Time,* edited by Richard Kostelanetz. Pennington, N.J., 1992.

King, Kenneth. "SCAN." *Performing Arts Journal,* no. 50/51 (May 1995): 100–106.

Kreemer, Connie, ed. *Further Steps: Fifteen Choreographers on Modern Dance.* New York, 1987.

FILMS. *Making Dances* (Blackwood Productions, 1979). *Space City* (directed by Robyn Brentano and Andrew Horn, 1981).

SALLY BANES

KIRALFY FAMILY, Hungarian family of dancers, choreographers, and theatrical producers. Notable members were the brothers **Imre Kiralfy** (born 1845 in Pest, died 27 April 1919 in Brighton, England) and **Bolossy Kiralfy** (born 1848 in Pest, died 6 March 1932 in London) and a sister **Haniola Kiralfy** (born 1851 in Pest, died 1889?). The Kiralfy brothers, dancers and producers of theater spectacles, were the children of Anna and Jacob Königsbaum, a Hungarian nationalist who lost his fortune during the unsuccessful Revolutions of 1848. At the ages of five and three the brothers made their debut at the National Circus in Budapest, performing traditional folk dances, and for the next eight years they supported their family by performing throughout the Austro-Hungarian Empire. In 1859, Imre, Bolossy, and their younger sister Haniola moved to Berlin to study with Paul Taglioni at the Berlin Court Opera Ballet School. A year later they went to Paris to continue their training at the Paris Opera while performing in the evenings at the Boulevard theaters.

The Parisian theaters, particularly the Théâtre de la Porte-Saint-Martin, the Théâtre du Chatelet, and the Paris Opera, with their enormous spectacles, sophisticated backstage equipment, and efficient management, made a deep impression on the brothers, both of whom wanted to be producers. Their first opportunity came in 1865 when, performing in England with Haniola, they were asked to direct *The Pearl of Tokay* at the Alhambra Theatre in London. In 1868 they were given an even larger assignment by the Belgian government, a five-day public fete in Brussels that included operas, ballets, pantomimes, sports, and a pageant of four thousand soldiers.

In 1869 the Kiralfy troupe of Hungarian dancers, consisting of Haniola, Imre, and Bolossy as soloists, younger sisters Katie and Emilie as secundas, and six other dancers recruited in London, made their New York debut performing a "Magyar Czardas" in George L. Fox's *Hiccory Diccory Dock* at the Olympic Theatre. Hailed by critics for their exuberance and dazzling technical feats, the Kiralfy troupe was soon the most popular company of dancers in New York. Imre and Bolossy, however, continued to pursue their dreams of producing. They believed that America was an ideal environment for European-style extravaganzas.

With no capital, but possessing a vision, enormous energy, and a sure business sense, the brothers forced their way to the top. By October 1870 their eleven-member troupe had grown to sixty. By 1871 the brothers were demonstrating a flair for novelty and skill in maneuvering an even larger company of dancers in kaleidoscopic patterns. In an 1871 revival of Fox's greatest spectacle *Humpty Dumpty,* for example, they devised a "Dance for the Amazon Warriors" in which the male warriors locked their shields above their heads while Amazons climbed up the stairs formed by the shields.

In 1873 Imre and Bolossy purchased exclusive production rights to *The Black Crook,* the most popular spectacle of the time. They added new musical numbers and gathered the entire family for a final appearance in the "Grand Ballet of All Nations" at its opening at Niblo's Garden Theatre in New York on 18 August 1873. Shortly thereafter they retired from performing to devote themselves to their growing theatrical empire. Haniola took charge of the dancers and married Albert Parkes, drama critic for the *New York Mercury.* Katie married Edmond Gerson, Bolossy's business partner, and Emilie married Gabriel Brenauer, a diamond merchant, leaving only the youngest Kiralfy brother, Arnold, pursuing a career as a leading dancer in his brothers' productions.

In 1875 Imre and Bolossy produced Jules Verne's *Around the World in Eighty Days* at Niblo's. It featured the largest dance company New York had ever seen, with realistic stage effects that included the sinking of a steamer at sea, a balloon ascension, a railway engine pulling cars across the stage, and a live elephant. This production exemplified the Kiralfy's approach: entertainment of epic proportions, using large contingents of dancers and elaborate special effects. Although some of these productions originated with and were choreographed by the Kiralfys, most—including dancers, designs, choreography, and the translated script—were imported from European theaters. Ballet masters taught the American marching choruses the prescribed formations around visiting ballerinas, and Bolossy and Imre coordinated the whole. Importing productions gave them flexibility; often they had two spectacles running simultaneously. In 1876 they branched into real estate, building the Alhambra Palace in Philadelphia to capitalize on the U.S. centennial celebration.

In 1886, after a disagreement over business matters, Imre and Bolossy severed their partnership and began to compete fiercely. Their individual productions grew until they outgrew the interiors of even the biggest theaters and were forced to move outside. In an amphitheater on Staten Island, New York, Imre produced *The Fall of Babylon* and *Nero, or The Fall of Rome,* with casts numbering up to fifteen hundred. Bolossy built the Palisades Amusement Park on the bank of the Hudson River in New Jersey, where he produced *King Solomon: The Fall of Jerusalem.* Unlike the earlier imported spectacles, these outdoor extravaganzas were written, directed, designed, and, in most cases, choreographed by the brothers. Stage movement was worked out on giant sheets of graph paper with rubber stamps indicating groups of dancers. Intricate footwork for the ensemble was abandoned in favor of simple steps to connect the formations. Although Europeans still filled the majority of the featured dance roles, the necessity for star performers was diminished by the immense size of the cast.

KIRALFY FAMILY. In the back row of this 1869 photograph are (left to right) an unidentified woman, Katie Kiralfy, Bolossy Kiralfry, Emilie Kiralfy, Imre Kiralfy, Haniola Kiralfy, and two unidentified women. In the front row (center) is Marie Kiralfy, flanked by two unidentified women. (Photograph courtesy of Barbara Barker.)

Worsening economic conditions and financial panics in the United States in the early 1890s made the Kiralfy entertainments impractical. Moving to London, Imre mounted several spectacles at the Olympia Theatre, became the lessee and director-general of the exhibitions at Earl's Court, and built White City, a 140-acre amusement center specially equipped to house his spectacles and exhibitions. When Imre left the Olympia, Bolossy moved in, staging *Constantinople, or the Revels of the East.* The brothers continued as producers into the second decade of the twentieth century, Imre doing most of his work in London, and Bolossy dividing his time among New York, London, and elsewhere in Europe. Both produced pageants for Barnum and Bailey's Circus as well as for world's fairs and expositions.

The work of the Kiralfy brothers inspired the next generation of showmen. Their dissolving and reforming masses of dancers, transforming scenery, and lighting effects pointed the way for the early filmmakers. Epic themes narrated through movement lived on in the repertories of the early modern concert dancers, Ruth St. Denis and her students, the precision ensembles of the Tiller Girls and the Rockettes, and the circus pageants of Barnum and Bailey.

Two of Bolossy Kiralfy's children, Calvin and Verona, carried on the family tradition of traveling entertainers, becoming vaudeville performers on the Orpheum children's circuit, billed as the "Kiralfy Kiddies." The youngest Kiralfy brother, Arnold, taught and choreographed in New York and Pittsburgh.

BIBLIOGRAPHY

Barker, Barbara. "Imre Kiralfy's Patriotic Spectacles." *Dance Chronicle* 17.2 (1994): 149–178.

Guest, Ivor. *Ballet in Leicester Square.* London, 1992.

Kiralfy, Bolossy. *Bolossy Kiralfy, Creator of Great Musical Spectacles: An Autobiography.* Edited by Barbara Barker. Ann Arbor, Mich., 1988.

Kiralfy, Imre. *America: Grand Historical Spectacle, in Four Acts.* Cincinnati, 1893.

Kiralfy, Imre. "My Reminiscences." *Strand Magazine* 37 (July 1909): 646.

Marks, Edward B. *They All Had Glamour: From the Swedish Nightingale to the Naked Lady.* New York, 1944.

Odell, George C. D. *Annals of the New York Stage.* Vols. 8–12. New York, 1936–1938.

Senelick, Laurence. "Spectacle and the Kiralfys." *Dance Chronicle* 12.1 (1989): 149–154.

BARBARA BARKER

KIRGHIZIA. *See* Kyrgyzstan.

KIRKLAND, GELSEY (born 29 December 1952 in Bethlehem, Pennsylvania), American dancer and teacher. Daughter of the playwright Jack Kirkland and actress Nancy Hoadley, in 1960 Kirkland entered the School of American Ballet in New York, where her sister, Johnna, was already enrolled. Kirkland joined the New York City Ballet in the spring of 1968. She was promoted to soloist in 1969 and made a principal dancer in 1972. During her adolescent years, Kirkland made frequent guest appearances with the Eglevsky Ballet.

In 1970 George Balanchine picked Kirkland to dance the title role in his new production of *The Firebird.* In 1971 he cast her in *Suite No. 3 (Theme and Variations),* in which, dancing with the utmost precision and grace, she was an outstanding success. Kirkland also created roles in Jerome Robbins's *The Goldberg Variations* (1971), *Scherzo Fantastique* (1972), and *An Evening's Waltzes* (1973). John Clifford, John Taras, and Richard Tanner also created ballets for her.

Kirkland's repertory with New York City Ballet included *The Nutcracker, Dances at a Gathering, Harlequinade, Momentum Pro Gesualdo, Movements for Piano and Orchestra, The Cage, Concerto Barocco,* and *Symphony in C.* Wishing to expand her repertory into the classics and to dance with Mikhail Baryshnikov, Kirkland left the New York City Ballet and in the autumn of 1974 joined American Ballet Theatre. The Kirkland-Baryshnikov partnership in the succeeding years won rave reviews and new audiences to ballet.

With American Ballet Theatre Kirkland excelled in the Romantic ballets *Giselle* and *La Sylphide,* but she also achieved great success in Baryshnikov's stagings of *The Nutcracker* and *Don Quixote.* Antony Tudor recognized her gifts by using her in *Shadowplay* and *Jardin aux Lilas.* He also created leading roles for her in *The Leaves are Fading* (1975) and *Tiller in the Fields* (1978). In both of these, her youthfully rhapsodic dancing made an unforgettable impression. Her repertory with American Ballet Theatre also included *Raymonda, Three Preludes, Other Dances, La Sonnambula,* Kingdom of the Shades from *La Bayadère, Theme and Variations,* and *Les Rendezvous.*

Kirkland made frequent guest appearances with regional companies across the United States and Canada. In 1980 she triumphed with the Royal Ballet, dancing in *Giselle* and Kenneth MacMillan's *Romeo and Juliet,* partnered by Anthony Dowell. Continuing to appear sporadically with American Ballet Theatre through the early 1980s, she proved erratic and uncommitted, and in 1984 she was dismissed.

Kirkland's slight frame and flowing, airy grace disguised a formidable technique, but it was her wayward artistry and shining individuality that distinguished her. A perfectionist who from the beginning drove herself to reach for the utmost, Kirkland suffered periodic bouts of ill health, brought on by her emotional frailty, the exceptional demands she placed upon herself, and an ultimately conquered dependence on drugs.

KIRKLAND. With American Ballet Theatre, Kirkland shone in many leading roles. Here she is seen as Nikia in *La Bayadère* with Iván Nagy as Solor. Their costumes were designed by Marcos Paredes. (Photograph © 1980 by Max Waldman; used by permission.)

Following her marriage to Greg Lawrence, she and her husband co-authored two autobiographies, *Dancing on My Grave* in 1986 and, in 1990, *The Shape of Love.* Since 1986, Kirkland has taught and coached dancers in Europe and America, notably for the Royal Ballet and English National Ballet. She also appeared as a guest artist with the Royal Ballet in *The Sleeping Beauty.* In 1991 Jane Hermann, artistic director of American Ballet Theatre, invited Kirkland to join the staff of the company as a coach. Since that time Kirkland teaches and coaches but is no longer officially connected to American Ballet Theatre.

BIBLIOGRAPHY

Croce, Arlene. *Going to the Dance.* New York, 1982.
Current Biography. New York, 1975.
Dunning, Jennifer. "Gelsey Kirkland: Happy Right Where She Is." *New York Times* (31 May 1978).
Finkel, Anita. "Beyond Love and Madness." *New Dance Review* 3 (October–December 1990): 12–18.
Goodman, Saul. "Gelsey Kirkland: Brief Biography." *Dance Magazine* (December 1971): 80–81.
Gruen, John. "A New Swan Prepares for Flight." *New York Times* (5 June 1977).
Horn, Laurie. "On the Comeback Trail." *Ballet News* 4 (August 1982): 24–26.
Kirkland, Gelsey, with Greg Lawrence. *Dancing on My Grave.* Garden City, N.Y., 1986.
Kirkland, Gelsey, and Greg Lawrence. *The Shape of Love.* New York, 1990.
Perlez, Jane. "Gelsey Kirkland: The Ultimate Giselle." *New York Post* (20 December 1975).
Rockwell, John. "Gelsey Kirkland at American Ballet Theatre: Ease Does It." *New York Times* (21 December 1975).
Sandler, Ken. "Her Own Best Friend: Gelsey Kirkland Speaks about Her Career." *Ballet News* 3 (August 1981): 32–33.
"Three Views of Kirkland's Grave." *Ballet Review* 14 (Winter 1987): 77–86.
"U.S. Ballet Soars." *Time* (1 May 1978).

PATRICIA BARNES

KIROV BALLET. *See* Maryinsky Ballet.

KIRSOVA, HÉLÈNE (Ellen Wittrup Hansen; born c.1911 in Denmark, died 22 February 1962 in London), ballet dancer, teacher, choreographer, and company director. Kirsova began her dance studies with Léo Staats at the Paris Opera, having reputedly run away from her native Denmark to learn to dance in Paris. She was quickly taken into Le Ballet Franco Russe and traveled with the company to South America. Returning to Paris, she joined Ida Rubinstein's company and worked with Bronislava Nijinska before becoming a founding member of Colonel Wassily de Basil's Ballets Russes de Monte Carlo in 1932.

With Valentina Blinova she was the leading female dancer with de Basil's second company, the Monte Carlo Russian Ballet, which Leon Woizikowski led on a nine-month tour to Australia for the 1936/37 season. In Australia her dancing was received with much acclaim. Critics praised her for her dazzling technique and her imaginative powers. She scored particular success in *Le Carnaval,* in which she had a memorable partnership with Igor Youskevitch, and in *Petrouchka.*

Kirsova returned to England with the Monte Carlo Russian Ballet in 1937 but came back to Australia early in 1938 to marry Dr. Erik Fischer, Danish vice-consul in Sydney. In 1940 she established a dance school in Sydney, and in 1941 she set up a company which, from its second Sydney season onward, was called the Kirsova Ballet. The company was directed by Kirsova and led by some former members of the Covent Garden Russian Ballet who had decided not to return to Europe in 1939, at the end of the second Ballets Russes tour to Australia. They were joined by some Australian principals and a corps de ballet of dancers studying at Kirsova's school. From the very beginning Kirsova's dancers were paid award rates for their performances. The Kirsova Ballet was Australia's first professional ballet company.

Kirsova choreographed most of the works for her company, although she also mounted some of the classics, including *Les Sylphides* and *Swan Lake,* act 2. Her own works included a full-length *Faust,* based on a theme by nineteenth-century German poet Heinrich Heine, with Tamara Tchinarova in the lead role as Satana. Kirsova also encouraged Australian visual artists and composers to create for her company. She commissioned a number of designs, including those for *Faust,* from Loudon Sainthill, then at the beginning of his career as a theatrical designer. She also worked closely with the composer Henry Krips.

The Kirsova Ballet gave its last performance in 1944. Many of Kirsova's dancers then joined the Borovansky Ballet, often considered a rival company in the race to establish ballet in Australia. The reasons for the demise of the Kirsova Ballet are complicated, but they are related, in part at least, to the strength of Kirsova's personality and her unwillingness to compromise in the 1940s Australian male-dominated world of theatrical management. Kirsova ran her school in Sydney for a few more years and then retired in 1947, when she moved to Paris with her second husband, Peter Bellew. After visiting the Soviet Union in 1956, Kirsova, writing as Hélène Bellew, published *Ballet in Moscow Today* (c.1958) and was a major contributor to *Dictionnaire du ballet moderne.*

[*See also* Australia, *article on* Ballet.]

BIBLIOGRAPHY

Bellew, Hélène. *Ballet in Moscow Today.* London and Greenwich, Conn., n.d. (c.1958).

Bellew, Peter, ed. *Pioneering Ballet in Australia.* Sydney, 1945.

García-Márquez, Vicente. *The Ballets Russes: Colonel de Basil's Ballets Russes de Monte Carlo, 1932–1952.* New York, 1990.

Montague, John, and Peggie Cochrane, eds. *Dictionnaire du ballet moderne.* Paris, n.d. Translated as *Dictionary of Modern Ballet,* edited by Francis Gadan and Robert Maillard (New York, 1959).

Potter, Michelle. "A Strong Personality and a Gift for Leadership: Hélène Kirsova in Australia." *Dance Research* 8.2 (Autumn 1995): 62–76.

MICHELLE POTTER

KIRSTEIN, LINCOLN (Lincoln Edward Kirstein; born 4 May 1907 in Rochester, New York, died 5 January 1996 in New York City), American impresario, arts patron, historian, critic, theorist, editor, and ballet director. The three most important nonperformers in twentieth-century American dance might well be John Martin, Louis Horst, and Lincoln Kirstein. Kirstein's principal contribution was to bring Russian-born choreographer George Balanchine to the United States and to create a mechanism that allowed Balanchine's artistic vision to evolve in freedom for almost fifty years. He did this by providing Balanchine with his own performing laboratory, the New York City Ballet, for which Kirstein served as general director from its inception in 1948 until he retired with the title of general director emeritus in 1989, and with a continuing source of fresh material, the School of American Ballet. Kirstein—scholar and philanthropist, proselytizer and visionary—was also a catalytic influence in many other areas of the artistic life of the United States. As a young man he wrote, "the one thing I wanted was to affect people and get things done." His achievement of this goal—in art, music (briefly), publishing, and, above all, in dance—mark him as the twentieth century's truest successor to Serge Diaghilev. Kirstein was active in virgin America, not the cultured Europe that Diaghilev conquered, and he had financial resources that Diaghilev lacked. Through Balanchine, Kirstein eventually attained the continuity and stability that had eluded Diaghilev to the end.

Evocations of Kirstein's privileged youth are to be found in his thinly disguised early autobiographical novel, *Flesh Is Heir* (1932), as well as in his monograph *Entries from an Early Diary* (1973) and in *The New York City Ballet* (1974). Each portrays a febrile, questing, and brilliant but sometimes intolerant man, full of ideas, talented—but not too talented—in various arts, impassioned, restless, and inclined to bully his friends. From the beginning he associated equally with intellectuals and artists and with stylish, monied patrons. Always well connected, Kirstein's friends from youth included James Agee, Walker Evans, Philip Johnson, James Thrall Soby, Henry-Russell Hitchcock, Muriel Draper, Carl van Vechten, W. H. Auden, Hart Crane, Ben Shahn, and Archibald MacLeish. At thirteen, already enthralled by the theater (having caught Jean Cocteau's "red and gold disease"), he saw Anna Pavlova after missing his sole chance to see Vaslav Nijinsky in 1916; at fifteen, in London, he fell in love with Diaghilev's Ballets Russes, which he continued to haunt during yearly summers in Europe; in 1926, watching the Ballets Russes perform *The Firebird,* he saw George Balanchine dance Kastchei. *Flesh Is Heir* presents a description of Balanchine's *The Prodigal Son* and the funeral of Diaghilev, which the young protagonist stumbles onto by accident. Kirstein wrote, "A dynasty had ended, the king was interred on the Island of Saint Michael among the marble headstones and cypresses. . . . It was the end indeed, . . . the end of power and endeavor." Diaghilev—and Abraham Lincoln—were to remain heroes.

In 1927, while still an undergraduate at Harvard, Kirstein, with Varian Fry, founded a "magazine of arts and letters," *The Hound & Horn;* during its seven-year existence, it published writings of Ezra Pound, T. S. Eliot, Edmund Wilson, and Irving Babbitt, among many others. (One of its original editors was A. Hyatt Mayor, later curator of prints at the Metropolitan Museum of Art.) Its penultimate issue was a highly praised monograph on Henry James. Kirstein as contributor (mostly of reviews of poetry) wrote only three articles on dance, one of which, however, was a major essay called "The Diaghilev

Period." It contained a prophetic description of "the classical dance . . . [with] its cold multiplication of a thousand embroideries . . . divested of the personal." Without having met him, Kirstein thus revealed an intuitive affinity with the work of Balanchine.

In 1928, with classmates John Walker III (later director of the National Gallery in Washington, D.C.) and Edward M. M. Warburg, Kirstein founded the Harvard Society for Contemporary Art to enable works of such artists as Isamu Noguchi, Buckminster Fuller, and Alexander Calder to be publicly exhibited for the first time. In 1929, the group's faculty adviser, Alfred Barr, went to New York as the first director of the Museum of Modern Art. At the museum, through the 1940s, Kirstein would be curator, consultant, and cataloger for several exhibitions. (In later life, he emphatically rejected modern art—and what he considered the entire modernist aesthetic—championing instead the work of those classically oriented visual artists who dealt primarily with the human figure, such as Gaston Lachaise, Elie Nadelman, and Paul Cadmus.)

After graduation in 1930, Kirstein studied ballet for the first time, choosing Michel Fokine as his teacher; this resulted in a laudatory monograph on the great choreographer's work. Drawn from lengthy interviews with Fokine, Kirstein came to the unexpected conclusion that none of Fokine's ballets would survive. (With the very brief exception of *Chopiniana* in 1972, none was ever presented by a Balanchine-Kirstein company.) In the foreword to the book *Fokine,* published in 1934, Arnold Haskell, the editor, could write already of the still-youthful author:

> Kirstein is not merely an enthusiast. He is a practical man who is attempting a gigantic task, that of harnessing the immense dancing talent of America into a representative national ballet with the aid of Russian teachers and choreographers. He will probably succeed.

A few years earlier Kirstein had begun to work with Romola Nijinsky on a biography of her husband. This plunged Kirstein into research on Diaghilev and introduced him to expatriate Russians as well as to the monied society on which Diaghilev depended (and which, in lesser force, took some responsibility for Nijinsky after his illness). Perhaps here was the beginning of Kirstein's fascination with the revolutionary aspects of Nijinsky's choreography, which he explored more fully in his books *Movement and Metaphor* (1970) and *Nijinsky Dancing* (1975). A trenchant critic from the beginning, in 1934 he wrote, "Before anyone, there is Nijinsky, whose researches into the springs of action have extended, by implication at least, the limits of the human body to infinity. He presented ballet digested, reversed, renewed" (*The Nation,* 11 April). After an overwrought collaboration, Romola's biography was eventually completed by Haskell, published in 1933, and has had many subsequent reprintings.

In 1935, Kirstein's *Dance: A Short History of Classical Theatrical Dancing,* the first treatment of the subject in English, was published. It was a densely written tour de force, a survey of dance from ancient ritual to the present day (not all of it "theatrical"). Much of the material, such as dance in the United States during the nineteenth century, had scarcely been previously researched. Illustrations showed an equal grasp of diverse materials. The precocious author was then twenty-eight.

By 1933, two years before the publication of *Dance,* when Kirstein had again summered in Europe, he had become acquainted with members of the Bloomsbury circle: E. E. Cummings, G. I. Gurdjieff, Christian Bérard, Jean Genêt, Katherine Anne Porter, and, most important for his future, the composer Virgil Thomson and the artist Pavel Tchelitchev. While Tchelitchev was designing Balanchine's *Errante* for Les Ballets 1933, Thomson told Kirstein that the "progressive line from Diaghilev is with Balanchine rather than Massine." (Léonide Massine was infinitely more famous at the time.)

Through Romola, in 1933 Kirstein met Balanchine in London and invited him to the United States to found a school and a ballet company—to create an "American ballet." By mutual agreement there were to be no *Swan Lake*s, no *Giselle*s, and no guest stars. Academic classicism, representing as it did to Kirstein a reflection of the moral order of the universe, would be the starting point for a new repertory. He wrote, "What I love about the ballet is not that it looks pretty. It's the method in it. Ballet is about how to behave" (quoted in Russell, 1982). On 16 July 1933, he had written to a friend, A. Everett ("Chick") Austin, Jr., director of the Wadsworth Atheneum in Hartford, Connecticut, "we have the future in our hands." In a subsequent telegram he said that bringing Balanchine to America was "the most important thing all of us will ever do." Austin, Warburg, Johnson, and others contributed; on 17 October 1933, Balanchine arrived in New York.

With the new year, the School of American Ballet opened. Warburg was its first president (a title Kirstein assumed in 1940 when the school was incorporated as a nonprofit educational institution); Kirstein was its first director. In June 1934, students performed *Serenade,* the first ballet Balanchine choreographed in America; in December, as the Producing Company of the School of American Ballet, the group premiered *Transcendence* (among other works), a ballet about virtuosity that had the first of a number of libretti by Kirstein. In March 1935, the American Ballet, with Balanchine as ballet master, made its professional debut in New York. In a little more than a year, Balanchine had created a company and a repertory. [*See* American Ballet.]

Life for the American Ballet was over almost before it began, however; the company collapsed after one week of a projected transcontinental tour and was saved only by an invitation to become the resident ballet troupe at the Metropolitan Opera from 1935 to 1938. Meanwhile, in 1936, Kirstein created a well-intentioned but self-conscious enterprise called the Ballet Caravan, a chamber company devoted to producing new works with commissioned music and decor, using American artists and subject matter. The chief choreographers were William Dollar, Lew Christensen, and, the most original talent, Eugene Loring. Kirstein wrote libretti for ballets with such titles as *Filling Station, Yankee Clipper, Pocahontas,* and *City Portrait;* his most famous was *Billy the Kid,* presented in 1938 to music by Aaron Copland with choreography by Loring. In its four years of existence, the modest company managed to travel throughout the United States and to Havana. [*See* Ballet Caravan.] In disbanding the group, Kirstein admitted that, despite its earnest aims, Ballet Caravan lacked both the glamour and the professionalism of the Russian troupes that were then touring America and against which he railed in print for their reliance on worn-out formulas and escapist aesthetics. His invective on the subject appeared in its purest form in his *Blast at Ballet: A Corrective for the American Audience* (1938), in which he attacked not only the "so-called Russian ballet" but also managers, patrons, critics, and the public.

In 1936, Kirstein and Warburg commissioned Igor Stravinsky's score for *Jeu de Cartes* for an American Ballet Stravinsky Festival to be mounted at the Metropolitan Opera the following year (with *Apollo* and *Le Baiser de la Fée,* all choreographed by Balanchine). Thus began the composer's active involvement with a series of Balanchine-Kirstein companies. Of the masterpieces resulting from the collaboration of Balanchine and Stravinsky, possibly the greatest, as well as the most important for the establishment and, later, reputation of the New York City Ballet, were *Orpheus* (1948) and *Agon* (1957). The composer's published correspondence provides a rare glimpse of Kirstein's role behind the scenes, documenting, among other things, his contribution to the evolution of *Agon* over a period of almost ten years.

In 1941, Balanchine and Kirstein merged the American Ballet and Ballet Caravan to form the American Ballet Caravan, which lasted for just five months, touring South America with a repertory that included two major new Balanchine works, *Concerto Barocco* and *Ballet Imperial.* Kirstein was also acting as a consultant to the Museum of Modern Art on the art of Latin America. In the same year he married Fidelma Cadmus, sister of the painter Paul Cadmus.

With some five thousand of his own objects, books, photographs, sketches, and other documents as a centerpiece, in 1940 Kirstein had established the Dance Archives at the Museum of Modern Art under the curatorship of Paul Magriel; it was the first such resource in the United States. Although the archives were suspended in 1947, in 1964, in conjunction with the opening of the New York State Theater at Lincoln Center, Kirstein deposited this material (considerably augmented) in the Dance Collection of the New York Public Library for the Performing Arts. He established a conservation laboratory in this facility in 1970.

In 1942, using the vast materials of the Dance Archives—much of it unpublished—as a nucleus for research, Kirstein, Magriel, and Baird Hastings founded the magazine *Dance Index,* an unprecedented venture in the then barely defined world of dance scholarship. In existence until 1949, the periodical provided a forum for the investigations of George Chaffee (on Romantic ballet iconography), Marian Hannah Winter (on pre-Romantic ballet), Lillian Moore (on various subjects, many of them American), and Yuri Slonimsky (on Marius Petipa and Jules Perrot), among others. Monographs were published on Isadora Duncan, Martha Graham, Balanchine, Nijinsky, and several visual artists, photographers, and critics, in addition to an acclaimed issue on "Stravinsky in the Theater" (1945), in which Balanchine's famous formulation of his philosophy appeared for the first time:

> *Apollon* I look back on as the turning point in my life. [The score] seemed to tell me that I could dare not to use everything. . . . I could clarify . . . by reducing what seemed to be multiple possibilities to that one that is inevitable.

Kirstein's contribution was "Elie Nadelman: Sculptor of the Dance" (1948), a subject more fully treated in his definitive, profusely illustrated book on the artist published in 1973.

During World War II, Kirstein served in the U.S. Army in Europe and was active in recovering stolen art works. He then rejoined Balanchine and, engaging Leon Barzin as musical director, developed his most elaborate master plan for the production of dance (and the lyric theater): Ballet Society. At its center was a performing ballet company, conceived along Diaghilevian lines: "Each [new work] will have the planned collaboration of independent easel painters and progressive choreographers and musicians, employing the full use of avant-garde ideas, methods and materials," Kirstein wrote (anonymously) in the prospectus. Unlike Diaghilev, however, who rarely had more than one choreographer active at a time, Kirstein, while giving Balanchine free rein, was prepared to sponsor the efforts of several others.

In its two-year existence, Ballet Society produced sixteen new ballets, including Balanchine's seminal *The Four Temperaments, Symphony in C,* and *Orpheus.* Plans were also laid for an elaborate, two-act Balanchine work—unrealized—on the theme of Beauty and the Beast, set to music by Aleksei Haieff with scenery and costumes by Esteban Francés. Contemporary operas by Gian-Carlo

Menotti and dance other than ballet were also performed. The press was generally excellent.

But Kirstein wanted more. He envisioned a club of cognoscenti, a chosen audience that, in addition to "participating" in the creation of new works, would receive books (in the first year, monographs on Nijinsky, Pavlova, and Duncan), silk-screen prints of stage designs executed by the Pippin Press, and invitations to films (Cocteau's *Beauty and the Beast*), poetry readings (the Sitwells), exhibitions, and dance demonstrations by Balanchine. In short, Kirstein offered a complete environment for experiencing dance in all its intellectual as well as its aesthetic and sensual aspects. But financial support was inadequate. The company was able to perform only four programs yearly on unsuitable stages, and it seemed that another Kirstein-Balanchine enterprise would fail.

On the strength of *Orpheus*, however—Ballet Society's most prestigious production—Morton Baum, chairman of the Executive Committee of New York's City Center of Music and Drama, invited the company to become a resident constituent, and thus was born the New York City Ballet, which gave its first performance on 11 October 1948. It had taken fourteen years for Balanchine and Kirstein to achieve the necessary conditions for American ballet not only to exist but to grow. Along the way, Kirstein the visionary had been Kirstein the pragmatist as well, having made overtures concerning joint ventures to Massine, Sol Hurok, Ballet Theatre, and the Marquis de Cuevas, among several other unlikely partners.

In the early years of the New York City Ballet, although Balanchine was always the principal creative force, other distinguished choreographers—notably Frederick Ashton and Antony Tudor—were invited to contribute new ballets to the repertory, and several pieces were elaborately designed. But as time went on, "outsiders" became fewer; Balanchine totally dominated the repertory (with outstanding contributions by Jerome Robbins), and decor was either nonexistent or provided by house designers. Balanchine always used distinguished musical support, but long before Stravinsky's death, there ceased to be commissioned scores. There had virtually never been any libretti. In putting himself so completely at the service of Balanchine, it seems clear that Kirstein—who had once advocated a return to choreodrama, insisting that *Uncle Tom's Cabin* would make a splendid Balanchine ballet, but who later wrote of "applause machines" and necessary "novelties" in the repertory—had sublimated his own vision of the dance, as it had crystallized in the high-minded ideals of Ballet Society.

Under Kirstein's direction, the New York City Ballet expanded from an "improvised" activity to a company of 103 artists in the 1984/85 season, with a budget of $18 million and an international reputation. From 1948 until his death in 1983, Balanchine provided more than 120 new works. Of this achievement, Kirstein the critic wrote in *Dancing Times* (October 1983):

> What he recognized as especially characteristic was the force of the rhythm of New York, symbolized by the athleticism, speed, extrovert energy, the reckless dynamism in its syncopation and asymmetry, and as well a kind of impersonal mastery, an abstraction of life symbolized by the grid plan and numerical nomination of its streets and avenues. His dancers were required to move faster, with more steps in tighter sequences than previous corps. . . . The policy of his company was involved primarily with the stuff of dance rather than the presentation of personalism. . . . Only a dancer dancing can say for him, what he says to them.

The first of many New York City Ballet trips abroad was in 1950 (to England; Kirstein was an Anglophile); the first evening-long ballet, *The Nutcracker*, was mounted in 1954; Robert Irving was engaged as musical director in 1958; the company became resident at the New York State Theater in 1964 (built "for Lincoln and George," in the words of its architect, Kirstein's longtime friend Philip Johnson); in 1972 the company's Stravinsky Festival crowned one of the most fertile artistic collaborations of the twentieth century. In addition to furthering all this activity, Kirstein presided over the establishment of the New York City Ballet—an organism that had outgrown the resources of one man, even if that man was Kirstein himself—as an independent corporation with a board of directors. With the death of Balanchine, the artistic directorship passed to Peter Martins and Jerome Robbins, demonstrating that Kirstein had created an institution—for then it could be so called—that could survive the personal magnetism of its great co-founder. Permanence seemed assured. From 1934 until his retirement in 1989, Kirstein simultaneously guided the School of American Ballet from a shoestring operation to an approximation of the state-supported dance academies of Russia and France.

As a writer, the resonance of Kirstein's thought is best demonstrated in his book *Movement and Metaphor* (1970), in which he examined fifty seminal ballets through the ages in their cultural and political contexts as well as in their technical evolution. He wrote:

> The classical dance is a language, and ballets are its constructs, comparable to others formed in other idioms. The battle picture, still life, landscape; the comedy of manners, heroic tragedy; the novel of society or psychological observation create worlds based on tradition, observation, and craft. The universe projected by ballet in its brief temporal duration draws on analogous sources and is capable of maintaining similar metaphors.

More than any writer in the field, Kirstein combined erudition with an instinct for the grand gesture in print.

In his art writings, Kirstein had resurrected or enhanced a number of reputations, including those of Nadelman, Lachaise, Tchelitchev, and William Rimmer; he had, as well, mounted one of the earliest cases for photography as an art form. Two books of poetry had been inspired by his service in the army. Officially, he had held positions with the City Center of Music and Drama, Lincoln Center, the Works Progress Administration (WPA) Federal Dance Theater, American National Theater and Academy (ANTA), the American Shakespeare Festival Theater Academy, the Museum of Modern Art, and Pro Musica Antiqua. Acting privately, he had sponsored artists, courses, and performances as well as the important support activities of archiving and conservation. At the Metropolitan Museum of Art in New York, the departments of American art, twentieth-century (European) art, prints, Far Eastern art, and costume benefited from his extensive and widely varied donations, many in formerly neglected areas such as Japanese prints of the Meiji Restoration period (1868–1912).

Among the few tokens of recognition Kirstein accepted were the Royal Society of Arts Benjamin Franklin Award from Great Britain (1981), the Presidential Medal of Freedom (1984), the Municipal Arts Society award of New York City (1985), and the Brandeis University Notable Achievement Award (1986). True to his quixotic nature, he refused the offer of several other honors as irrelevant.

[*See also* New York City Ballet *and the entry on Balanchine. For discussion of Kirstein's writings, see* United States of America, *article on* Dance Research and Writing.]

BIBLIOGRAPHY

Chapman, John V. "The Aesthetic Interpretation of Dance History." *Dance Chronicle* 3.3 (1979–1980): 254–274.

Chujoy, Anatole. *The New York City Ballet.* New York, 1953.

Goldner, Nancy. *The Stravinsky Festival of the New York City Ballet.* New York, 1974.

Hamovitch, Mitzi Berger, ed. *The Hound & Horn Letters.* Athens, Ga., 1982.

Kirstein, Lincoln. *Ballet, Bias, and Belief: Three Pamphlets Collected and Other Dance Writings.* New York, 1983.

Kirstein, Lincoln. "A Ballet Master's Belief." In Kirstein's *Portrait of Mr. B: Photographs of George Balanchine.* New York, 1984.

Kirstein, Lincoln. *Mosaic: Memoirs.* New York, 1994.

Lowry, McNeil. "Conversations with Kirstein." *The New Yorker* (15–22 December 1986).

Reynolds, Nancy. *Repertory in Review: Forty Years of the New York City Ballet.* New York, 1977.

Reynolds, Nancy. "In His Image: Diaghilev and Lincoln Kirstein." In *The Ballets Russes and Its World,* edited by Nancy Baer and Lynn Garafola. New Haven, 1997.

Russell, John. "Lincoln Kirstein: A Life in Art." *New York Times Magazine* (20 June 1982).

Schwartz, Sanford. "An Aristocrat of Life and Culture." In Schwartz's *The Art Presence.* New York, 1982.

Simmonds, Harvey. *Lincoln Kirstein: The Published Writings, 1922–1977.* New York, 1978. Covers more than four hundred writings on all subjects.

Stravinsky, Igor. *Selected Correspondence.* Vol. 1. Translated and edited by Robert Craft. New York, 1982.

Taper, Bernard. *Balanchine: A Biography.* New rev. ed. Berkeley, 1996.

ARCHIVE. The Dance Collection of the New York Public Library for the Performing Arts contains extensive manuscript and other materials on all the Kirstein-Balanchine companies, as well as Kirstein's personal scrapbooks and diaries.

NANCY REYNOLDS

KITA SCHOOL, one of Japan's five schools of *nō* dance drama.

An Overview. Although counted today as one of *nō*'s five schools, the Kita school is unlike the others in not claiming direct descent from Japan's medieval troupes. It was established in the seventeenth century by Kita Shichidayū (1586–1623), who studied under a Konparu-school actor and became skilled at *nō*. While still young, Shichidayū was supported by the shogun Toyotomi Hideyoshi (1536–1598), an avid *nō* fan, and even served briefly as headmaster of the closely related Kongō school. Although he owed much to the Konparu lineage, Shichidayū borrowed freely from all the schools of *nō* in creating his own distinctive styles of dancing and performing, which are flashier and more acrobatic than those of the other four schools.

During the Edo period (1603–1868), the Kita school was supported by the Tokugawa shogunate, and a number of feudal lords *(daimyō)* studied Kita-school chanting and dancing. With the Meiji Restoration of 1868 and the return of the emperor, the fortunes of the Kita school declined, but the great artistry and great efforts of Kita Roppeita XIV (1874–1971), the fourteenth headmaster, helped restore the school to popularity. So well appreciated was Roppeita XIV that in 1955 he was declared a National Living Treasure by the Japanese government. So devoted was he to his art that—according to what may be an apocryphal tale—as an old man who could barely walk and had to be helped to the curtain, Roppeita performed flawlessly and beautifully while on stage, only to collapse again as the curtain closed. His dancing was of a level far above that of most of his contemporaries.

Kita Roppeita XV. (original name Nagayo; born 6 December 1924 in Tokyo), sixteenth headmaster of the school and the grandson of Roppeita XIV, made his debut on the *nō* stage at the age of three. Extremely active and energetic, Roppeita XV and his father, Kita Minoru (1900–1986), became well known for their performances of newly written *nō* plays, including *Tatsunokuchi* (about the persecution of Nichiren) and *Fukkatsu* (about the resurrection of Jesus). Open to experimental performances, Roppeita XV in 1968 danced on a temporary stage before an audience of more than twenty thousand, inside the building housing the swimming pool that had been used for the 1964 Olympic Games in Tokyo—thus familiarizing an enormous new public with the art of *nō*. Roppeita XV has made numerous trips abroad, especially to the United States. Many American students eagerly look forward to these visits so that they may study with him.

Among the many awards won by Roppeita XV are the Tokyo Performing Arts Festival Prix d'Honneur (1977) and Japan's Order of the Purple Ribbon (1991).

[*See also* Asian Martial Arts *and* Nō. *For discussion of other schools of* nō, *see* Hōshō School; Kanze School; Kongō School; *and* Konparu School.]

KITA SCHOOL. Kita Roppeita XV as a monstrous spider breaking out of his lair and preparing to battle Minamoto no Raikō's men in the *nō* drama *Tsuchigumo*. (Photograph by Morita Toshirō; used by permission; courtesty of Stephen Comee.)

BIBLIOGRAPHY

Keene, Donald. *Nō: The Classical Theatre of Japan*. New York, 1966.

Kodansha Encyclopedia of Japan. Tokyo, 1983. See the entries "Kita School" and "Nō."

Komparu Kunio. *The Noh Theater: Principles and Perspectives*. Translated by Jane Corddry and Stephen Comee. New York, 1983.

Nishino Haruo and Hata Hisashi, eds. *Nō, kyōgen jiten* (Dictionary of Noh and Kyogen). 2d ed. Tokyo, 1988.

STEPHEN COMEE

KNIGHT, LAKSHMI (born 30 October 1943 in Madras), Indian dancer, musician, and teacher. Knight was trained in *bharata nāṭyam* and Karnatic music by her mother, T. Balasaraswati. She began assisting her mother in teaching, both at the Music Academy in Madras and outside of India, in 1962; she also accompanied her mother in concert as a vocalist during the 1970s. Knight gave her first public concert of *bharata nāṭyam* in 1972 in Madras.

Knight has performed since then throughout India and in North America, where she has performed in most major concert venues, appearing in more than two hundred concerts over a twenty-year period. She has received several Performance and Choreography Fellowships from the U.S. National Endowment for the Arts, as well as recognition and support from the Asian Cultural Council and the Indo-U.S. Subcommission. She has performed at most major venues in India, and in 1992 she was honored with the title Nritya Choodamini by the Krishna Gana Sabha, Madras.

Knight has taught at more than a dozen dance residencies throughout the United States, including the American Dance Festival, California Institute of the Arts, Wesleyan University, the University of California, Los Angeles, and the American Society for Eastern Arts. She is artistic director of the Balasaraswati School of Indian Music and Dance, with branches in the United States and India. She has presented lectures on the subject of Indian dance throughout North America, including a series for the Jungian Foundation in New York, Congress on Research in Dance, and the Society for Ethnomusicology. She is currently writing a book, on *bharata nāṭyam* for the non-Indian audience, supported by a grant from the National Endowment for the Arts.

Her husband, Douglas Knight, is an ethnomusicologist with a specialty in South Indian drumming. He has accompanied several of India's leading artists, and he regularly accompanies Lakshmi in dance concerts. Their son, Aniruddha, studies dance with his mother and music with his uncle, T. Viswanathan.

BIBLIOGRAPHY

Arudra. "The Third Eye." *Sruti* (Madras), no. 21 (February 1986): 28–29.

Pearcey, Eilean. "Indian Dance Recitals." *Dance and Dancers* (June 1974): 44–45.
Viswanathan [Knight], Lakshmi. *Bharatanatyam: The Tamil Heritage.* Madras, 1984.

DONALD KNIGHT

KNUST, ALBRECHT (born 5 October 1896 in Hamburg, died 19 March 1978 in Essen-Werden, Germany), German ballet master and first professional notator in the Laban system. Knust was to a great extent responsible for the development of Rudolf Laban's dance notation (called Kinetography Laban or Labanotation) into a viable and comprehensive system. As a result of Knust's teaching activities, Labanotation was introduced to many European countries and to the United States.

At the beginning of his career, Knust was a participant in, and later a leader of, folk dance groups in Hamburg from 1912 to 1921. He then studied with Laban from 1921 to 1923, becoming a member of his dance theater, the Tanzbühne, in 1922. He was a teacher and later director at the Laban School in Hamburg from 1923 to 1934. In addition, he was ballet master at the Friedrichstheater Dessau from 1926 to 1927, and co-founder of the Laban Central School in Berlin from 1928 to 1929. With Azra Laban (Laban's daughter) Knust founded the first dance notation center, the Hamburger Tanzschreibstube, in 1930; from 1935, the center was based in Berlin. From 1930 to 1932, he wrote a treatise on methods of notating group movements.

Knust was the first professional notator in the Laban system. Starting in 1930, he was involved in notating Laban's movement choirs (group works for lay dancers) and his major choreographic works, and in restaging them entirely from the notated scores. He headed the dance department at the Folkwang Schule in Essen from 1934 to 1935. In 1935 and 1936, he worked with Irmgard Bartenieff to transcribe eighteenth-century court dances from the Feuillet notation system into Labanotation.

In 1937, Knust completed the first version of his *Abriss der Kinetographie Laban* (Handbook of Kinetography Laban). However, Laban's work had been banned by Germany's Nazi government, and Knust was able to circulate only a few typewritten copies. He worked in secrecy during the war years (1939–1945) in a tiny room in the Munich Opera House, and there he completed his second version of the handbook. In 1942, he again could distribute only a few copies of a typescript. The book was finally published in 1956; the English version followed in 1958. Throughout World War II, Knust also notated all the current repertory of the Munich State Opera Ballet, which was under the direction of the ballet masters Pino and Pia Mlakar.

After the war, Knust worked for five years on his eight-volume *Encyclopedia of Kinetography.* In this work he collected twenty thousand notated examples of different kinds of movement and dance styles. The encyclopedia was never published, but a few copies and microfilms of the manuscript are extant.

In 1951 Knust returned to the Folkwang Schule (later Hochschule) in Essen and became director of the Kinetographisches Institut, remaining in that position after his retirement from teaching in 1962. He was elevated to professor in 1974. In addition to extensive teaching, he also continued to notate, including many scores of the Kurt Jooss repertory.

Knust was chairman of the International Council of Kinetography Laban from 1961 and president from 1969, spearheading the effort of creating a unified system. His final work, *A Dictionary of Kinetography Laban,* was published posthumously in 1979. Some of his archives are housed at the Centre for Dance Studies in the Channel Islands, Great Britain, under the supervision of his student and colleague Roderyk Lange.

BIBLIOGRAPHY

Knust, Albrecht. *Abriss der Kinetographie Laban.* Hamburg, 1956. Translated as *Handbook of Kinetography Laban,* 2 vols. (Hamburg, 1958).
Knust, Albrecht. *A Dictionary of Kinetography Laban.* 2 vols. Estover, England, 1979.
Lange, Roderyk. "Albrecht Knust: An Appreciation." *Dance Studies* 1 (1976): 1–4.

RODERYK LANGE

KOCHNO, BORIS (born 3 [16] January 1904 in Moscow, died 9 December 1990 in Paris), Russian-French ballet scenarist, artistic collaborator, artistic director, and writer. Kochno was neither dancer, choreographer, composer, nor designer. Although known as a scenarist—his name (or his *nom de plume,* Sobeka) appears on ballet libretti dating from the early 1920s to the period of regeneration in Paris after World War II—it is clear that he had an even greater talent for work behind the scenes. Despite having only intermittent official positions after the dissolution of Serge Diaghilev's Ballets Russes following the impresario's death in 1929, Kochno continued to be a presence in the French dance world for more than half a century, during which he made a place for himself in other people's memoirs and histories as a kind of *éminence grise.*

The very young and well-educated Kochno, who was an aspiring poet with a knowledge of Russian constructivist painting and a love of cubism, arrived in Paris, via Constantinople, impoverished, in 1920. The painter Serge Soudeikine arranged for him to meet the émigré Russian ballet impresario Serge Diaghilev; within a day or two of the first interview on 27 February 1921, Kochno—eager, erudite, handsome—was engaged as secretary, a potential new favorite for Diaghilev. (Léonide Massine had departed on 19 January.) Kochno proved to be something more: in subsequent years Diaghilev acquired and lost several companions, yet Kochno (although unpaid) remained.

Along with general troubleshooting (fights and intercessions with Pablo Picasso, Bronislava Nijinska, Pavel Tchelitchev, and Georges Rouault are among the many recorded), certain specific responsibilities (he was put in charge of illustrated programs in 1925), and his duties as personal factotum to Diaghilev, Kochno was entrusted with the libretti of several major ballets (which usually meant coordinating the efforts of the volatile artistic collaborators). These included *Les Fâcheux* (1924), adapted from Molière, with choreography by Nijinska to music of Georges Auric and with scenery and costumes by Georges Braque; *Les Matelots* and *Zéphire et Flore* (both, 1925), choreographed by Massine; the extraordinarily complex "mixed media" work *Ode* (1928), choreographed by Massine to music by Nicolas Nabokov and with scenery and costumes by Tchelitchev; and several ballets by George Balanchine: *La Pastoral* (1926); *The Triumph of Neptune* (1926); *La Chatte* (1927), called Balanchine's "first modern ballet"; *The Gods Go a-Begging* (1928); *Le Bal* (1929); and *Le Fils Prodigue* (The Prodigal Son; 1929). Serge Grigoriev, Diaghilev's *régisseur,* wrote in his memoirs (1953) that as Diaghilev grew progressively less interested in the company, he left more and more artistic responsibility to Kochno. [*See* Ballets Russes de Serge Diaghilev.]

At Diaghilev's death in 1929, it was thought by some that Kochno would take over, but instead the entire enterprise collapsed, perhaps because of quarrels with Serge Lifar, who also considered himself an heir. (According to Richard Buckle [1983], however, the dancers were polled and refused Lifar's leadership.) Kochno's next work was in London, assisting in the staging of two episodes on *Cochran's Revue* of 1930: "Luna Park," choreographed by Balanchine, and "Night," choreographed by Lifar. Christian Bérard, with whom Kochno would be associated until the latter's death in 1949, designed some of the costumes.

Kochno and Balanchine were then invited by René Blum to be part of a new company, the Ballets de Monte Carlo. All three were soon to feel themselves compromised by Colonel Wassily de Basil, who acted as the company's impresario and who changed its name to the Ballets Russes de Monte Carlo. Before leaving the company in 1932, Balanchine and Kochno collaborated on *Les Bourgeois Gentilhomme,* set to music of Richard Strauss with scenery and costumes by Alexandre Benois, and the haunting *Cotillon,* to music of Emmanuel Chabrier, with scenery and costumes by Bérard. Both were created around the talents of Tamara Toumanova. Kochno also worked with Massine (and Toumanova) on *Jeux d'Enfants* (1932), set to music of Georges Bizet and with scenery and costumes by Joan Mirò.

Balanchine and Kochno next produced a season for their own company, Les Ballets 1933 (financed by the English art collector Edward James), and for the first time Kochno's name appeared as artistic director. Again in the Diaghilev manner (particularly that of the late years), the repertory was smartly dressed, with new music. In at least two of the six works presented, classical dance counted for little, and there was critical comment that "shock" and "chic" were featured. The company dissolved after less than a month in public performance. [*See* Ballets 1933.] Balanchine then went to New York, and Kochno remained in Europe, reassociating himself with the Ballets Russes de Monte Carlo as artistic adviser until 1938. While there he again worked with Nijinska, collaborating with the composer Baron d'Erlanger on the libretto for *Les Cents Baisers* (1935), a ballet stunningly dressed by Jean Hugo, and for two works choreographed by David Lichine, *Le Pavillon* (1936) and *Le Lion Amoureux* (1937). [*See* Ballets Russes de Monte Carlo.]

In 1945, Kochno surfaced again as artistic director with the acclaimed Ballets des Champs-Élysées, which he founded in Paris on a shoestring with the choreographer Roland Petit and the writer and critic Irène Lidova. Of the troupe's first success, Buckle wrote:

> There is a moment in Petit's *Les Forains* when, to a cue in [Henri] Sauguet's score, the ragged curtain of the booth erected by strolling players was suddenly lit up and flamed scarlet against the black night: it was like the waving of a banner, an assertion by Kochno and Bérard and Petit of the theatre's power to transform. (Buckle, 1983)

The Ballets des Champs-Élysées, the first important independent company in postwar France, was less interested in technical virtuosity than in the creation of atmosphere and the translation of emotion into theater.

Again, as with Diaghilev, Kochno commissioned new music and modern decors from distinguished artists—mostly French—and he brought a new generation of dancers to prominence. Important ballets created during the brief life of the company were Petit's *Le Jeune Homme et la Mort* (1946) and David Lichine's *Le Rencontre* (1948). *Le Jeune Homme et la Mort,* an expression of postwar nihilism, was set to music of J. S. Bach, with a libretto and costumes by Jean Cocteau and scenery by Georges Wakhevitch, and was danced by Jean Babilée and Nathalie Philippart. *Le Recontre,* set to music by Sauguet, with a libretto by Kochno and costumes and scenery by Bérard, featured the young Leslie Caron. Also in the repertory, in line with Kochno's intellectual bent, was the first modern mounting of August Bournonville's *La Sylphide,* reconstructed in 1947 by Victor Gsovsky, with the exquisite Nina Vyroubova in the title role. After a history of sporadic performance, the group was disbanded in 1951. [*See* Ballets des Champs-Élysées.]

In 1954, Kochno's book *Le ballet en France* was published, as handsomely produced as any of his dance works, with a cover by Henri Matisse and a lithograph by Picasso inside; his *Diaghilev et les Ballets Russes* was published in both French and English in 1970. Kochno assisted Richard Buckle in the important exhibition of Diaghilev costumes held in Edinburgh and London in 1954, to which he also lent artworks from his personal collection: drawings and watercolors by Léon Bakst, Georges Braque, Natalie Goncharova, Mikhail Larionov, Henri Matisse, Pablo Picasso, and Nikolai Roerich. In 1975, Kochno sold most of his papers to the French government, including the (unpublished) manuscript of Diaghilev's memoirs that Kochno had translated from Russian into French.

[*See also* France, *article on* Ballet since 1914.]

BIBLIOGRAPHY

Buckle, Richard. *Diaghilev.* New York, 1979.

Buckle, Richard. *In the Wake of Diaghilev.* New York, 1983.

Garafola, Lynn. *Diaghilev's Ballets Russes.* New York, 1989.

García-Márquez, Vicente. *The Ballets Russes: Colonel de Basil's Ballets Russes de Monte Carlo, 1932–1952.* New York, 1990.

Grigoriev, Serge. *The Diaghilev Ballet, 1909–1929.* Translated and edited by Vera Bowen. London, 1953.

Kochno, Boris. *Le ballet en France.* Paris, 1954.

Kochno, Boris. *Diaghilev and the Ballets Russes.* Translated by Adrienne Foulke. New York, 1970.

Kochno, Boris. *Christian Bérard.* Translated by Philip Core. New York, 1988.

Spencer, Charles. *The World of Serge Diaghilev.* Chicago, 1974.

INTERVIEW. Boris Kochno, by Nancy Reynolds (1976), Oral History Archive, New York Public Library.

ARCHIVE. Boris Kochno Collection, Bibliothèque Nationale, Paris.

NANCY REYNOLDS

KOHOMBA KANKARIYA. The elaborate ritual known as the Kohomba Kankariya is one of the most ancient folk ceremonies in Sri Lanka. This ceremony is unique to Sri Lanka and embodies a rich tradition of prehistoric and pre-Buddhist lore. Legend says that King Panduvasdeva (fifth century BCE) was afflicted by an incurable disease caused by a curse. The remedy was known only to a king in India, born not of a woman but of a flower, whom the god Sakra lured to Sri Lanka. The deity Rahu assumed the form of a boar and laid waste the garden of the King of the Flower, who chased the boar as far as Sri Lanka and struck it with his golden sword, whereupon the boar turned into a stone. After the king of Sri Lanka, who ruled in the ancient capital Anuradhapura, was cured by the King of the Flower, he decreed that this story be reenacted periodically to ensure prosperity to the land and freedom from disease.

This purification ritual, embodying elements from fertility and animistic cults, cults of deified chieftains, the ceremonial purification of neophytes, and other early forms of worship of the aboriginal Veddha people is said originally to have lasted three months and three weeks. Today, in its abridged version, it lasts two days at the most. It is deeply embedded in the cosmology and fertility rituals of a predominantly agricultural society.

The preparations and ceremonies for this ritual, also known as Kohomba Yak Kankariya or Kohomba Yak Mangallaya, extend over several weeks. The ritual is intended to appease the Kohomba god, whose abode is the *kohomba* tree *(Melia azadirachta),* the leaves and bark of which are used for purification.

The area where the Kankariya is to be held is marked off and consecrated three months in advance with the planting of a sacred post, a young sapling called the *kapa.* At an auspicious time, this mystic tree of life is set up and smeared with sandalwood, and a votive gold coin is tied to it to the accompaniment of ceremonial drums. The dance arena *(yakge)* is built to conform to the specifications of the original dance arena of the Kankariya in Anuradhapura. Another room is built to serve as a storehouse for the coconut flowers used in a special dance, the consecrated vines, and other ritual materials.

The *ves* dancers are the servants of the gods, and they alone make the preparations. The chief of the dancers, the *mulyakdessa* (a high priest), is assisted by twelve *yakdessa*s. They prepare the altars *(yahana),* collect and store oil, make cloth torches *(pandam),* and bring in vegetables, rice, yams, plantains, and other foods. They set about their tasks dressed in white and wearing mouth-covers *(mukkha vadam)* while preparing the foods. The altars are conventionally decorated with bark, banana plants in fruit, bamboo, and tender coconut leaves. The dancers wear new white cloths given by the suppliant.

The day's proceedings commence before noon with a ceremonial offering of rice at the decorated high altar. The weapons and insignia of the gods are carried by *naiyandi* dancers in a ceremonial procession from the village *devale* (temple) to the dance arena. The regalia of the principal *ves* dancer and the principal drummer are also taken there. Throughout the afternoon, offerings of food and flowers are prepared with ceremony. By evening the altars are illuminated and perfumed with incense.

The dancers, who have bathed and ritually purified themselves and dressed in their red-and-white costumes and silver ornaments, don the *ves* headgear. Flanked by their drummers, they invoke the blessings of the gods on the owner of the premises and on any sick person within. The conch shell is blown, and ceremonial drums begin. They next invoke the blessing of the supreme gods and the gods of the Kankariya, a twelvefold pantheon. This is followed by a series of dance sequences accompanied by purification chants and prayers; the devotional dance rhythms consecrate fire, incense, the turmeric water vessel, the shawl, coconut, betelnut, and food. Throughout the night the dancers continue singing verses honoring the gods, enacting sequences in pantomime narrating the epics of Sita, Vijaya, Panduwasdeva, and others. Short tales about the Kohomba god Kuveni and other figures are also dramatized. Frenzied dances depict the chase of the boar by the King of the Flower.

The closing ceremony, toward morning, is the shooting of the banana flower with the ceremonial bow and arrow. At the conclusion, the storehouse is pulled down and set on fire to dispel all evil influences.

Of the various propitiatory dance rituals of Sinhala rural folk, the Kohomba Kankariya is the most elaborate and costly. For this reason, its performance is a rare event today.

[*For articles on other dance traditions in Sri Lanka, see* Kandyan Dance; Kandy Perahera; Tovil; *and* Ves Dance. *See also,* Costume in Asian Traditions *and* Mask and Makeup, *article on* Asian Traditions.]

BIBLIOGRAPHY

Amunugana, Sarath. *Samskrtiya, Samajaya, ha Parisaraya.* Colombo, 1977.

Amunugana, Sarath. *Notes on Sinhala Culture.* Colombo, 1980.

Bowers, Faubion. *Theatre in the East: A Survey of Asian Dance and Drama.* New York, 1956.

de Zoete, Beryl. *Dance and Magic Drama in Ceylon.* London, 1957.

Disanayaka, Mudiyanse. *Udarata santikarma saha gami natya sampradaya.* Colombo, 1990.

Gunasinghe, Siri. *Masks of Ceylon.* Colombo, 1962.

Gunawardhana, Theja. *Kohomba Kankariya.* Colombo, 1979.

Kotelawala, Sicille P. C. *The Classical Dance in Sri Lanka.* New York, 1974.

Makulloluwa, W. B. *Dances of Sri Lanka.* Colombo, 1976.

Molamure, Arthur. "Aspects of the Kohomba Kankāriya: The Ceremony of a Dancer's Initiation." *Ceylon Journal of Historical and Social Studies* 1 (January–June 1958): 63–72.

Nevill, Hugh. "Sinhalese Folklore." *Journal of the Royal Asiatic Society, Ceylon Branch* 14 (1971): 58–90.

Pertold, Otaker. *Ceremonial Dances of the Sinhalese* (1930). Colombo, 1973.

Raghavan, M. D. *Dances of the Sinhalese.* Colombo, 1968.

Reed, Susan A. "The Transformation of Ritual and Dance in Sri Lanka: Kohomba Kankariya and the Kandyan Dance." Ph.D. diss., Brown University, 1991.

Sarachchandra, Ediriweera R. *The Folk Drama of Ceylon.* 2d ed. Colombo, 1966.

Sedaraman, J. I. *Nrtya ratnakaraya.* Colombo, 1992.

Sedaraman, J. I., et al. *Udarata natum kalava.* Colombo, 1992.

Seneviratna, Anuradha. *Traditional Dance of Sri Lanka.* Colombo, 1984.

SICILLE P. C. KOTELAWALA

KŌKEN. *See* Kabuki Theater.

KOLOSOVA, EVGENIA (Evgeniia Ivanovna Neyelova Kolosova; born 15 [26] September 1780 in Saint Petersburg, Russia; died 30 March [11 April] 1869 in Saint Petersburg), dancer and teacher. One of the brilliant Russian ballerinas of the first quarter of the nineteenth century, Kolosova made her mark early in her career, leaping into fame almost overnight. She graduated from the Imperial Theater School in Saint Petersburg in 1799, where she had been taught by Ivan Valberkh. In addition to grooming her into a first-class actress, he instilled in her a creative attitude toward her own career on the stage and a deep respect for the art of ballet. Kolosova's performing career began with appearances in children's roles in dramas, comic operas, and ballets. While still a student she danced in the comedy *The Trojan Wedding* and took the role of Podzora in the ballet *Oracolo,* staged by Charles Le Picq.

At the Imperial Theater School, Kolosova was trained according to the principles of pantomime and dance of the eighteenth century. Her own style was noted for majesty, strict poses with a clear line, measured movements, and a certain statuesque rigidity, but with the temperament of a tragic actress and a highly expressive gift for mime, she was able to breathe life into her roles. Her frequent appearances and extensive repertory helped her to develop her talent and polish the more difficult of her tragic roles to perfection. Kolosova appeared in ballets staged by her teacher Valberkh as well as in those of Le Picq, Chevalier Peicam de Bressoles (called Chevalier), and Charles-Louis Didelot. In Didelot's ballets especially she was able to extend her range. He knew many foreign ballerinas but considered Kolosova superior to all of them and described her talent as incomparable.

Kolosova's career spanned thirty years. Her significant roles were Ysaure in *Raoul Barbe-Bleue,* Adelaide in *Raoul de Créquis,* Medea in *Médée et Jason,* Juliet in *Romeo and Juliet,* Phaedra in *Phèdre et Hippolite,* the Girl in *The New Werther,* and Vasilisa in *Russians in Germany, or The Effects of Love for the Motherland.* Her art was a blend of classical and character dance. A recognized tragic actress in the ballet repertory, she was equally at home in social-dance plays, *divertissements,* operas, and comedies. According to her contemporaries she conferred a charming poetic quality on Russian folk dances; not only did she establish them in professional ballet, but she also arranged them for the stage. The great Russian poet Aleksandr Pushkin recorded his admiration for her performance of Russian dances.

Kolosova was the first woman to teach dance in Russia. Didelot placed her in charge of the school when he was away from Russia between 1811 and 1816, and returned to find that her talent, stage experience, and industry had enabled her to do much to improve dance teaching methods. Her art influenced the work of Maria Danilova, Anastasia Likhutina, and Avdotia Istomina. Poets dedicated verses to her, and her name has gone down in the annals and memoirs of Russian theater.

BIBLIOGRAPHY

Bakhrushin, Yuri. *Istoriia russkogo baleta.* 3d ed. Moscow, 1977.

Krasovskaya, Vera. *Russkii baletnyi teatr: Ot vozniknoveniia do serediny XIX veka.* Leningrad, 1958.

Swift, Mary Grace. *A Loftier Flight: The Life and Accomplishments of Charles Louis Didelot.* Middletown, Conn., 1974.

Wiley, Roland John, trans. and ed. *A Century of Russian Ballet: Documents and Accounts, 1810–1910.* Oxford, 1990.

NIKOLAI I. ELYASH
Translated from Russian

KOLPAKOVA, IRINA (Irina Aleksandrovna Kolpakova; born 22 May 1933 in Leningrad), dancer, teacher, and coach. Kolpakova trained at the Leningrad Ballet School under Agrippina Vaganova, graduating in 1951. Her art combined the finest features of the Saint Petersburg style—a noble manner, integrity of form, and lofty inspiration, all of which manifest Vaganova's system in its purest form. Kolpakova's gentle, refined stage presence and technically impeccable and confident dancing made her perfect for lyrical roles in the classical repertory: a sylph in Michel Fokine's *Chopiniana;* Masha in Vasily Vainonen's *The Nutcracker;* Maria in Rostislav Zakharov's *The Fountain of Bakhchisarai;* and the title role in Konstantin Sergeyev's *Cinderella.* She attained a pinnacle of artistry as Aurora, Raymonda, Giselle, and August Bournonville's Sylphide.

Kolpakova's talent, closely associated with the classical tradition, was revealed in a new light in modern choreography. She created the roles of Katerina in Yuri Grigorovich's *The Stone Flower* in 1957, His Beloved in Igor Belsky's *The Coast of Hope* in 1959, Desdemona in Vakhtang Chabukiani's *Othello* and Nina in Boris Fenster's *Masquerade* in 1960, Shirin in Grigorovich's *Legend of Love* in 1961, Ala in Georgi Aleksidze's *Scythian Suite* and the Girl in Oleg Vinogradov's *Two* (created for a program in her honor) in 1969, Eve in Natalia Kasatkina and Vladimir Vasiliov's *The Creation of the World* in 1971, the Dream Bird in Belsky's *Icarus* in 1974, Nelly in Valentin Elizariev's *Till Eulenspiegel* in 1977, and Natalia Nikolaevna in both Elizariev's *Pushkin* in 1977 and its restaging by Kasatkina and Vasiliov in 1980, among others.

Kolpakova danced in Leonid Yakobson's *The Snow Maiden* and *Dream* in 1957, Dmitri Briantsev's *Dedication* in 1977, and Leonid Lebedev's *Infanta* in 1979. Also in her repertory were the Polish Lady in Fenster's *Taras Bulba,*

KOLPAKOVA. Gaiety, elegance, and a light, high jump were characteristic of Kolpakova's dancing. She executed this perfect *grand jeté* c.1951. (Photograph from the Dance Collection, New York Public Library for the Performing Arts.)

Juliet in Leonid Lavrovsky's and in Igor Chernyshev's *Romeo and Juliet,* Kitri in Aleksandr Gorsky's *Don Quixote,* the Beautiful Maiden in Yakobson's *The Land of Miracles* and Syuimbike, the Bird Maiden in his *Shurale,* and many other roles.

Kolpakova was featured in a documentary film, *Irina Kolpakova,* and starred in the television films *Magic, The Lady and the Hooligans, Masters of the Leningrad Ballet, Irina Kolpakova Dancing, The Queen of My Heart, La Sylphide,* and others. When the Kirov Ballet first visited New York in 1961, Kolpakova was a warmly received leading ballerina. John Martin, writing in the *New York Times,* had special praise for her Giselle, the first act filled with youthful joy but tinged with foreboding. Still dancing in 1986, Kolpakova remained a gracious, lyrical sylph. The following year she left the stage and was engaged as a guest teacher and coach by American Ballet Theatre, which appointed her ballet mistress in 1990.

Kolpakova's honors and awards include the Grand Prix at the ballet competition in Vienna (1959), the Gold Star at the International Dance Festival in Paris (1965), the State

Prize of the USSR (1980), and the Anna Pavlova Prize (1982). She was named People's Artist of the USSR in 1965.

BIBLIOGRAPHY

Finch, Tamara. "Vaganova's Pupil: Irina Kolpakova." *The Dancing Times* (October 1988): 34–35.

Ilicheva, Marina. *Irina Kolpakova.* Leningrad, 1979.

Smakov, Gennady. *The Great Russian Dancers.* New York, 1984.

MARINA A. ILICHEVA
Translated from Russian

KOMAR, CHRIS (Christopher Komar; born 30 October 1947 in Milwaukee, Wisconsin, died 17 July 1996 in New York City), American dancer. Nearly all of Komar's professional career was with the Merce Cunningham Dance Company, which he joined in 1972. He graduated from the University of Wisconsin at Milwaukee with a bachelor of fine arts in dance in 1970 and was a member of its dance faculty until 1971. From 1969 to 1971 he also danced with the Milwaukee Ballet. After seeing the Cunningham company on tour, Komar went to New York to study with Merce Cunningham and soon afterward was asked to join his company. From 1973 onward he was on the faculty of the Merce Cunningham Studio in New York and in 1982 was appointed assistant to Cunningham, in which capacity he was responsible for the revival of Cunningham's dances by such companies as the Paris Opera Ballet, American Ballet Theatre, and the Rambert Dance Company, as well as for the maintenance of the repertory of Cunningham's own company.

Komar was in the original casts of most of the dances choreographed by Cunningham from 1972 on, notably *Landrover* (1972), *Sounddance* (1975), *Torse* (1976), *Travelogue* (1977), *Exchange* (1978), *Duets* (1980), *Channels/Inserts* (film, 1981), *Roaratorio* (1983), *Pictures* and *Doubles* (both 1984), *Native Green* (1985), *Points in Space* (video 1986; stage version 1987), *Fabrications* (1987), *Carousal* (1987), *Five Stone Wind* (1988), *Cargo X, August Pace,* and *Inventions* (all 1989), *Trackers* and *Loosestrife* (both 1991), *Change of Address* and *Enter* (both 1992), and *CRWDSPCR* (1993). Komar had the lightness, swiftness, and *ballon* of a classical dancer; Cunningham caught his personal quality perfectly in the grave, mysterious solo he choreographed for Komar in *Changing Steps* (1973). As Cunningham began to relinquish his own roles, Komar succeeded to some of them, notably in *Summerspace, Rune,* and *Scramble.* He also appeared in Karole Armitage's *Drastic Classicism* (1981) in New York. In 1992 he was appointed Assistant Artistic Director of the Merce Cunningham Dance Company, a position he held until his death. Komar retired from the stage in 1993 but continued to be active as a teacher and rehearsal director. In 1994 he and Meg Harper, another former Cunningham dancer, revived *Sounddance,* which had not been performed since 1980.

BIBLIOGRAPHY

Aloff, Mindy. "The Course of Events." *Dance Ink* (Fall 1993): 34–37.

Ballet Review 15 (Fall 1987): 19–40. Section entitled "Cunningham and His Dancers."

Parks, Gary. "Chris Komar Expands His Work as a Cunningham Dancer." *Dance Magazine* (March 1989): 12.

DAVID VAUGHAN

KOMLEVA, GABRIELLA (Gabriella Trofimovna Komleva; born 27 December 1938 in Leningrad), dancer and teacher. Komleva graduated from the Leningrad ballet school in 1957, after training with Vera Kostrovitskaya. In 1984 she graduated from the choreographic department of the Leningrad Conservatory. Since 1957 she has been with the Kirov (now Maryinsky) Opera and Ballet Theater, from 1980 onward as a teacher as well as a dancer.

Komleva was a ballerina of artistic range, encompassing all facets of classical dance. A reviewer noted that in her the entire history of the Kirov style was focused. Her secure technique, gift for characterization, and musicality made her famous in roles of the traditional repertory—Aurora, Kitri, Nikia, Paquita, Raymonda, Odette-Odile, Giselle, Sylphide, Esmeralda, the sylph in *Chopiniana*—and long attracted the interest of contemporary choreographers. She created the roles of the Girl who has lost her beloved in *The Coast of Hope* (1959) by Igor Belsky, the Girl in his *Leningrad Symphony* (1961), the Planet in *The Distant Planet* (1963) by Konstantin Sergeyev, Asiyat in *The Mountain Girl* (1968) by Oleg Vinogradov, Ariadne in Belsky's *Icarus* (1974), and the Maiden Beauty in Boris Eifman's version of *The Firebird* (1975). She also appeared in many miniatures staged by Leonid Yakobson, Georgi Aleksidze, Mai-Ester Murdmaa, Dmitri Briantzev, and others. Drawing imagery from music and dance, Komleva became a noted interpreter of the complex genre of dance symphony, exemplified by *Leningrad Symphony* and George Balanchine's *Le Palais de Cristal.* She performed works by foreign choreographers such as Louis Aubert's romantic *Pas de Deux,* Anton Dolin's *Pas de Quatre,* Roland Petit's *Choros,* Fanny Elssler's *Cachucha,* and José Limón's *The Moor's Pavane.* Komleva starred in a number of motion pictures and television films: *Gabriella Komleva Dances* (1981), *Leningrad Symphony* (1982), and *The Moor's Pavane* (1985). The 1979 film of *La Bayadère,* in which she participated, was honored by the British Broadcasting Corporation as the finest musical film of the year. From 1985 to 1989 she produced a television series, *The Wisdom of Terpsichore.*

Komleva was named People's Artist of the USSR in 1983 and was awarded the State Prize of the Russian Federation in 1970 for her performance as Asiyat. She was a silver medalist at the Varna International Ballet Competition in 1966, and Laureate of a USSR competition for new choreography in 1967. She continues her work in Russia, where in 1994 she revived August Bournonville's *La Sylphide* for the Bolshoi Ballet.

BIBLIOGRAPHY

Alovert, Nina, and Robert Greskovic. "A Reply to Komleva." *Dance Magazine* (October 1994): 41–45.

Belsky, Igor. "Gabriella Komleva." *Sovetskii balet,* no. 3 (1983).

Komleva, Gabriella. "Why Petipa Is Losing at Competitions." *Dance Magazine* (March 1994): 56.

Krasovskaya, Vera. "Gabriella Komleva." In *Leningradskii balet segodnia,* vol. 2, edited by V. V. Chistiakova. Leningrad, 1968.

ARKADY A. SOKOLOV-KAMINSKY
Translated from Russian

KONDRATIEVA, MARINA (Marina Viktorovna Kondrat'eva; born 1 February 1934 in Leningrad), dancer. Kondratieva studied at the Moscow Ballet School under Serafima Kholfina and Galina Petrova. In 1951, while still a student, she appeared in her first major role, at the Bolshoi Filial Theater, as Masha in Vasily Vainonen's version of *The Nutcracker.* Even at that early stage Kondratieva displayed a highly idiosyncratic lyrical gift. Upon graduation in 1952 she was accepted into the Bolshoi Ballet company. The following year she made a successful debut in the title role of Rostislav Zakharov's *Cinderella.* In 1954 she appeared as Maria in Zakharov's *The Fountain of Bakhchisarai* and as Aurora in *The Sleeping Beauty* a year later. The ballet critic Moissey Iofiev, in a 1965 analysis of Kondratieva's first roles, wrote:

> Kondratieva's art is notable for its sincerity and restrained lyricism. Her heroines are characterized by introspection and a contemplative outlook. . . . Dedication to lofty ideals, a quiet solitude in the face of fateful adversities—such is the psychological leitmotif and dominant theme of the ballerina.

In 1960 Leonid Lavrovsky produced the ballet *Paganini,* creating the role of the Muse especially for Kondratieva. She emerged as the light-winged Muse to the brilliant and elemental violin virtuoso, inspiring him to bursts of creativity and comforting him in times of trouble. Kondratieva convincingly projected herself as Paganini's good genius. One of her best creations was Giselle, in which role she appeared in 1961. She was coached for it under the expert guidance of Marina Semenova, who helped her to create many of her best roles. Kondratieva's novel Giselle seemed to radiate the soft aura of poetry. This interpretation added an interesting emotional coloring to the academically clean, transparent lines of Giselle's plastique, lending it a tender, tremulous lyricism. Also in 1961 Kondratieva created the role of Katerina in Yuri Grigorovich's *The Stone Flower,* premiered at the Bolshoi Theater. Grigorovich was impressed with her performance and cast her in leading roles in other of his ballets, such as *The Legend of Love* (1965) and *Spartacus* (1968). Her interpretations were noted for emotional depth, subtle, intelligent treatment, and a thorough understanding of Grigorovich's concept and style of plastique. In 1965 Kondratieva appeared as a romantic and enchanting Odette-Odile in *Swan Lake.* She revealed other facets of her talent in leading roles in ballets of other choreographers, including Syuimbike in Leonid Yakobson's *Shurale* (1955), the title role in Vasily Vainonen's *Gayané* (1957), Juliet in Leonid Lavrovsky's *Romeo and Juliet* (1957), the title role in Maya Plisetskaya, Natalia Ryzhenko, and Viktor Smirnov-Golovanov's *Anna Karenina* (1972), Eola in Vladimir Vasiliev's *Icarus* (1976), and Magnolia in Henrik Mayorov's *Cipollino* (1977).

Kondratieva frequently toured abroad, appearing in Great Britain, France, the United States, Canada, Japan, and Norway. In 1976 she was honored with the title People's Artist of the USSR. She retired from the stage in 1980 and has since been a ballet teacher and *répétiteur* with the Bolshoi Ballet in Moscow.

BIBLIOGRAPHY

Hering, Doris. "And Still, the Chasm." *Dance Magazine* (November 1962): 30–34.

Iofiev, Moissey. "Baletnije silueti." In *Profily iskusstva.* Moscow, 1965.

Kondratieva, Marina. "Kak vyrastayut krylya." *Teatralnaya zhizn,* no. 22 (1964).

Senior, Evan. "Is This the Second Ulanova?" *Dance and Dancers* (August 1954): 21–22.

GALINA V. INOZEMTSEVA
Translated from Russian

KONER, PAULINE (born 26 June 1912 in New York City), dancer and choreographer. Koner's style of modern dance has been based on her own eclectic dance background. She studied ballet with Michel Fokine (from 1926) and modern and ethnic dance with Michio Ito and Angel Cansino (in 1928). Koner danced with Fokine's company in 1928, with Ito in the 1928/29 season, and with Yeichi Nimura in 1930. Her New York solo debut of her own work was on 7 December 1930, at the Guild Theatre, for which John Martin proclaimed in the *New York Times* her "unquestionable right to stand alone."

In 1931, Koner starred in *Le Pas d'Acier* (choreographed by Edwin Strawbridge) at the Metropolitan Opera Ballet. She toured the Middle East in 1932 and danced in the Soviet Union during 1935 and 1936, developing a solo repertory flavored with Spanish, Oriental, and dramatic works which she performed on tour through the mid-1940s. In 1945, with Kitty Doner, she created *Choreotones* for CBS

Television a pioneering example of modern dance for television.

In her noted association with the José Limón Dance Company (1946–1960), she created roles in Limón's *The Visitation, La Malinche, The Moor's Pavane, There Is a Time,* and Humphrey's *Ruins and Visions.* She created many of her own solo parts in the Limón dances, bringing to these works a vivacity and speed indigenous to her unique style, a strong affinity for dramatic gesture, quick rhythmic changes, and sharp attack. She had an instinctive timing for demanding lifts, which are not seen in revivals. [*See the entry on Limón.*]

After founding her own company in 1949, with Doris Humphrey as artistic adviser, Koner toured extensively until 1963. [*See the entry on Humphrey.*] From 1975 to 1982, she toured with her Dance Consort, creating solo and group works for both ensembles, such as the solo *Cassandra* (1953), *The Shining Dark* (1956, based on Helen Keller), *Solitary Songs* (1963) and *Cantigas* (1978, set in part to music by George Crumb). Her long solo (about thirty minutes) *The Farewell* (1962) is considered one of her best, an elegiac tribute to Humphrey; it was set to the last section of Austrian symphonist Gustav Mahler's *Das Lied von der Erde* (Song of the Earth). Her husband Fritz Mahler (a second cousin of the composer) conducted at her official premiere on 28 February 1962, on the concert series of the Hartford Symphony (a preview performance had been sponsored by the Virginia Dance Society on 9 February 1962).

Koner's works have been performed by the Limón, Alvin Ailey, and Batsheva companies, among others. As an educator, Koner has introduced her "Elements of Performing" at many colleges, stressing motivation, dynamics, focus, and movement texture (such as point-of-pulse and suspension and rebound). Highlights of her pedagogical career include teaching at the American Dance Festival (1949–1960, and frequently through the 1970s); as an artist in residence at the North Carolina School of the Arts (1965–1976); as an adjunct professor at Brooklyn College (1975–1979); through the Fulbright Commission on a tour of Japan in 1965; and as a guest lecturer at universities throughout the United States and worldwide. Since 1986 Koner has taught at the Juilliard School, and has continued to restage her most important works for several soloists and ensembles. She received an honorary doctorate in fine arts from Rhode Island College in 1985. The 1963 *Dance Magazine* Award cited Koner's "unique sense of perfection [which brings] inspiring dimension to the medium of solo dance."

One of very few modern dancers to have made her name on her own prior to working with a major choreographer, Koner remains best known as a choreographer and dancer of solo works.

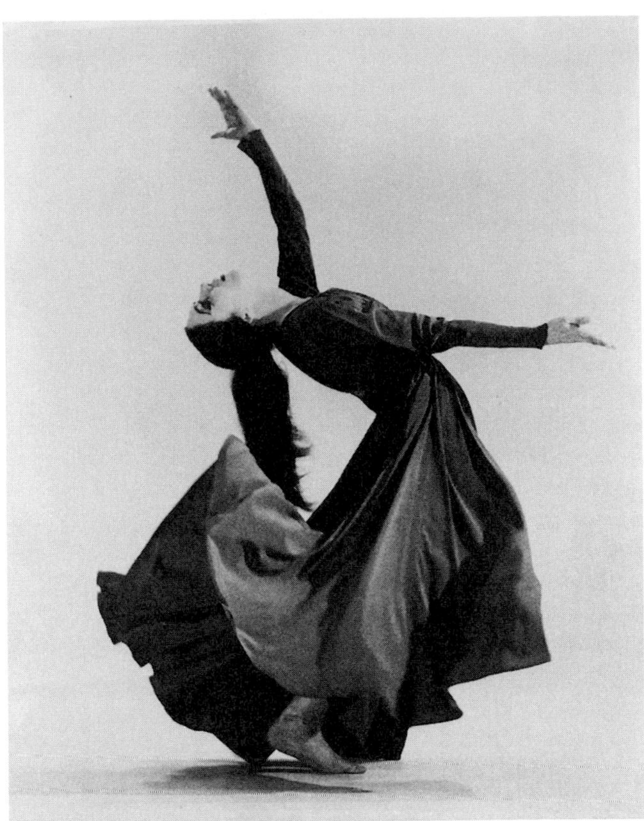

KONER. In *Solitary Songs* (1963), Koner explored the idea of total aloneness. This dance was later performed in a suite with another solo, based on a happier facet of the same theme, called *Wondrous Moment.* (Photograph by Peter Basch; used by permission.)

BIBLIOGRAPHY

Kisselgoff, Anna. "Pauline Koner's Golden Anniversary." *New York Times* (2 July 1978).

Koner, Pauline. "Intrinsic Dance." In *The Modern Dance: Seven Statements of Belief,* edited by Selma Jeanne Cohen. Middletown, Conn., 1966.

Koner, Pauline. *Solitary Song.* Durham, N.C., 1989.

Koner, Pauline. *Elements of Performance.* Chur, Switzerland, 1993.

Marks, Marcia. "Pauline Koner Speaking" (parts 1–3). *Dance Magazine* (September–November 1961).

Maynard, Olga. "Pauline Koner: A Cyclic Force." *Dance Magazine* (April 1973): 56–69.

McDonagh, Don, ed. *The Complete Guide to Modern Dance.* New York, 1976.

Pikula, Joan. "Communication and Compassion: Pauline Koner." *Dance Magazine* (March 1978): 64–69.

DAVID SEARS

KONGŌ SCHOOL, one of Japan's five schools of *nō* dance drama.

Overview. The Kongō school claims to descend directly from the Sakato-za, a troupe of medieval Yamato *sarugaku,* all four troupes of which were affiliated with

Hōryūji Temple, in the Nara area. In fact, the son of Kongō Ujikatsu (mentioned in Hōryūji records), Ujiaki (1324–1399), was the sixth headmaster of the Kongō school, and it is thought that a reference to Kongō Gon-no-kami in the *Sarugaku Dangi* (An Account of Zeami's Reflections on Art) refers to him: "Kongō was an actor [whose art had] great weight and breadth. . . . [He] played any and all types of roles . . . [and] danced in an ample and nimble style, with great concentration of strength." According to one Kongō school genealogy, the Sakato troupe disappeared with Shirō Katsuyasu (1437–1485); he was succeeded by Saburō Masaaki (1449–1526), whose childhood name, Kongōmaru, gave the troupe its new name. The Sakato Kongō line died out, however, with Ukyō Ujiyasu (1872–1936). Kongō Iwao I, the head of the Kyoto branch of the family, then succeeded as headmaster of the school. While the Kongō school style of dancing and acting is more sedate than the Kanze style, many feel it is more elegant than the severely simple Hōshō style.

KONGŌ SCHOOL. Kongō Iwao II as the young Heike nobleman Taira no Tsunemasa dancing out his death in the battle of Ichinatani in the *nō* drama *Tsunemasa.* (Photograph by Morita Toshirō; used by permission; courtesy of Stephen Comee.)

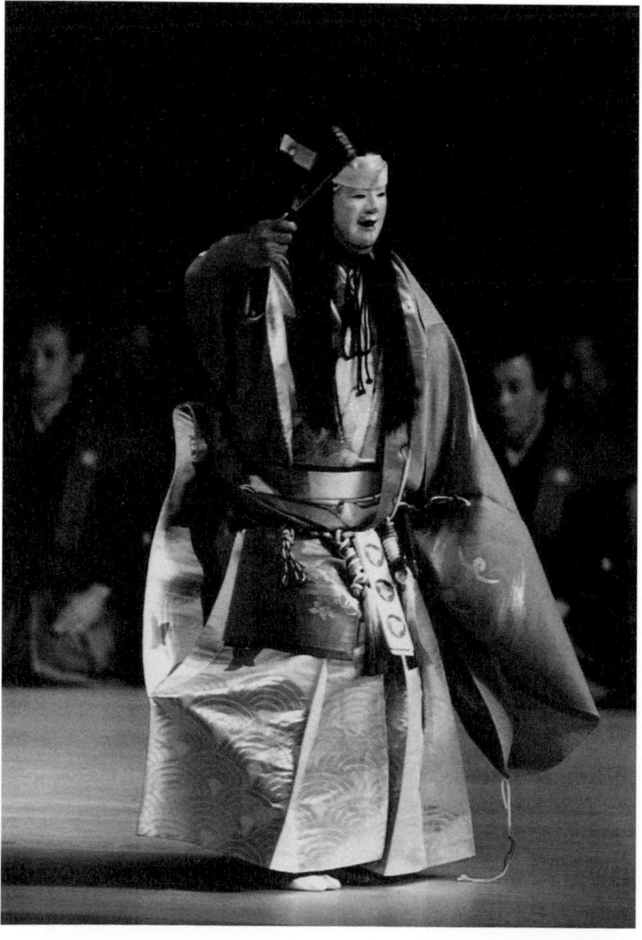

Kongō Iwao I (born 25 March 1886 in Kyoto, died 21 March 1951 in Kyoto), the twenty-fourth headmaster, made his first appearance on the *nō* stage at about the age of four and later attended the Japan School of Music in Tokyo. His efforts are largely responsible for saving the Kongō school from dying out. Well loved for the superb figure he cut on stage, he was renowned for the mysterious beauty of his dancing when portraying women.

Kongō Iwao II (born 23 December 1924 in Kyoto), the son of Iwao I, made his first appearance on the *nō* stage at the age of six and graduated from Tatsunoya University in 1945. He was one of the first *nō* actors to attend university; until his time, such education was thought unnecessary and a waste of time, because it severely cuts into the time required for a young *nō* actor to polish and perfect his dancing and acting techniques.

Iwao II has been active both in and out of Japan and in 1984 performed the play *Hagoromo* (The Feather Robe) before Pope John Paul II in the Vatican. Interested in bringing many plays that had been lost back into the *nō* repertory, he revised the play *Uzume,* about the goddess Ame-no-Uzume, and performs it at the annual festival of her shrine near Nagoya.

Iwao II has received countless awards, including the Japan Art Academy Prize (1995), and was designated the Bearer of an Important Intangible Cultural Asset (1965) and elected to the Order of the Purple Ribbon (1991) by the Japanese government.

[*See also* Nō. *For discussion of the other schools of* nō, *see* Hōshō School; Kanze School; Kita School; *and* Konparu School.]

BIBLIOGRAPHY

Keene, Donald. *Nō: The Classical Theatre of Japan.* New York, 1966.

Kodansha Encyclopedia of Japan. Tokyo, 1983. See the entries "Kongō School" and "Nō."

Komparu Kunio. *The Noh Theater: Principles and Perspectives.* Translated by Jane Corddry and Stephen Comee. New York, 1983.

Nishino Haruo and Hata Hisashi, eds. *Nō, kyōgen jiten* (Dictionary of Noh and Kyogen). 2d ed. Tokyo, 1988.

Zeami. *On the Art of the Nō Drama: The Major Treatises of Zeami.* Translated by J. Thomas Rimer and Yamazaki Masakazu. Princeton, 1984.

STEPHEN COMEE

KONI, FEDOR (Fedor Alekseevich Koni; born 1809 in Moscow, died 1879 in Saint Petersburg), Russian journalist, critic, and historian of ballet and theater. An astute observer of the Romantic era in Russia, Koni wrote during the period 1830 to 1850 for a variety of publications, including *Molva, Panteon, Literaturnaia gazeta,* and *Panteon i repertuar russkogo teatr.* His extensive reviews of the current season in Saint Petersburg included evaluations of performances by Elena Andreanova and Tatiana Glushkovska as well as by touring European dancers, including Marie Taglioni and Fanny Elssler. He also wrote historical accounts of the development of ballet in Russia.

Koni was a firm supporter of drama in ballet, writing in 1843, for example, that "ballet should be a phantasmagoria wherein objects from the real world take on an illusory, dreamlike appearance and cross the boundary of the plausible. The audience's imagination is carried along, and the further it disappears into the realm of fantasy, the more delightful." He wrote extensively about Charles-Louis Didelot's supremacy in this regard and cited such requisite qualifications for a choreographer as the ability to create poetry and to inspire mime. Koni likewise advanced the view that ballet's librettists should be selected from the ranks of the great writers.

Koni's descriptions of Taglioni were no less fervent than were those of his contemporaries. In 1847, for example, he wrote, "Marie Taglioni's talent breathed life into the moonlit fantastic characters of her father's ballets. As soon as she was gone, the spectators realized the depressing stupidity of the ballet." In his 1848 article about Andreanova's benefit performance in *Satanilla* Koni furthered his ideas about the juxtaposition of dance and drama, even advocating the predominance of drama over ballet. Koni went so far as to call ballet "an attractive addendum, drama's elegant splendor." In this regard he described Andreanova's performance as "surpassing the superlative," and he praised her natural vivacity, the speed and agility of her movements, and the expressiveness of her face.

In 1850 Koni published a comprehensive survey of ballet life in Saint Petersburg, including commentary on its development. The survey was a culmination of his personal views and a definitive statement of his aesthetics. In it Koni traced the history of dance from ancient Roman times to the Romantic era in Russia, discussing the heights it reached under Didelot and Taglioni. In addition Koni discussed the resurgent interest in ballet occasioned by the 1847–1848 tours of Andreanova in Italy and Germany and Elssler's performances in Russia. Koni also treated ballet's ability and, in his view, necessity to generalize. This characteristic precludes the portrayal of historical figures on the ballet stage, he explained, for "it is hard to convince oneself that events of world importance are unraveling from the pointed toe of a graceful ballerina."

[*For similar discussion, see the entries on Levinson, Svetlov, Volynsky, and Zotov.*]

BIBLIOGRAPHY

Koni, Fedor. "Teatral'nyi Benefis g-zha Glushkovskoi." *Molva,* no. 20 (1831).

Koni, Fedor, ed. *Panteon russkago i vsiekh evropeiskikh teatrov.* Saint Petersburg, 1840–.

Koni, Fedor. "Teatral'naia letopis'—Bol'shoi teatr—Satanilla, ili Liubov' i ad." *Panteon,* no. 3 (1848).

Koni, Fedor. "Balet v Peterburge." *Panteon i Repertuar Russkogo Teatra* 2.3 (1850).

Wiley, Roland John, trans. and ed. *A Century of Russian Ballet: Documents and Accounts, 1810–1910.* Oxford, 1990.

SUSAN COOK SUMMER

KONPARU SCHOOL, one of Japan's five schools of *nō* dance drama.

Overview. The Konparu school claims direct descent from the Enman'i-za, the oldest of the four Yamato *sarugaku* troupes, which had been under the patronage of Kōfuku Temple and Kasuga Shrine in Nara since the Kamakura period (1185–1333). The school's own tradition states that it has been involved in performing miracle plays at temples and shrines since the time of its lineal ancestor, the Chinese entertainer Hata no Kōkatsu (fl. early seventh century), and his direct descendant, Hata no Ujiyasu, an actor who performed at the court of Emperor Murakami (ruled 946–967). The earliest known head of the school is Konparu Gon-no-kami (Mitsutarō; fl. fourteenth century), who was said to have been the son of a semilegendary actor known as Bishaō Gon-no-kami). After Gon-no-kami, the school produced many noted figures, including Konparu Zenchiku, the actor, aesthetician, and playwright who revived the school and who was Zeami's son-in-law and spiritual heir, and Konparu Zenpō (1454–1532), Zenchiku's grandson (and Zeami's great-grandson), who left behind many well-loved plays, such as *Arashiyama* (Mount Storm) and perhaps even the perennial favorite *Hagoromo* (The Feather Robe).

The Konparu school was loved by, and flourished under, Toyotomi Hideyoshi (1536–1598), but declined during the Edo period (1603–1868). Konparu-school actor Sakurama Banba (1835–1917), along with Hōshō Kurō (1837–1917) and Umewaka Minoru (1828–1909), worked ceaselessly to ensure that *nō* would not die away after the Meiji Restoration (1868). His descendant Sakurama Michio (1897–1983) was such an excellent dancer he was designated the Bearer of an Important Intangible Cultural Asset.

The Konparu school, which still maintains close ties with Nara, the birthplace of all *nō,* is the most traditional of the five schools. Its chanting, dancing, and acting are rather staid and elegant, without the starkness of the Hōshō school or the brilliance of the Kanze school.

Konparu Nobutaka (born 12 April 1910 in Tokyo) is the school's seventy-ninth headmaster. He studied *nō* only briefly under his father, Konparu Mitsutarō Hachijō (1886–1922), the seventy-eighth head of the school. Nobutaka made his stage debut at the age of seven, a little late for a *nō* actor. After graduating from Kansai University with a bachelor's degree in Japanese literature, he devoted much time and effort to organizing the repertory by revising the Konparu texts of the Shōwa era (1926–1989) and reinstating lost plays such as *Ohara Gokō* (The Imperial Visit to Ohara) and *Obasute* (An Old Woman Abandoned) back into the active repertory.

In 1971, Nobutaka participated in a cultural mission sent to perform *nō* in the United States and Canada. He has served two terms as the director of the Japan Nō Association. Perhaps the most prestigious of the many awards he has received is the Fourth Order of the Sacred Treasure, which was bestowed on him by the Japanese government in 1990.

[*See also* Nō. *For discussion of other schools of* nō, *see* Hōshō School; Kanze School; Kita School; *and* Kongō School.]

BIBLIOGRAPHY

Keene, Donald. *Nō: The Classical Theatre of Japan.* New York, 1966.

Kodansha Encyclopedia of Japan. Tokyo, 1983. See the entries "Komparu School," "Komparu Zenchiku," and "Nō."

Komparu Kunio. *The Noh Theater: Principles and Perspectives.* Translated by Jane Corddry and Stephen Comee. New York, 1983.

Komparu Nobutaka. *Takigi Noh.* Tokyo, 1987.

Nishino Haruo and Hata Hisashi, eds. *Nō, kyōgen jiten* (Dictionary of Noh and Kyogen). 2d ed. Tokyo, 1988.

STEPHEN COMEE

KONPARU ZENCHIKU (original name Ujinobu; posthumously given the Buddhist name Ken'ō Zenchiku; born 1405 in Yamato, present-day Nara Prefecture, Japan, died c.1470 near Kyoto), *nō* actor, aesthetician, and playwright. Zenchiku is traditionally said to have served as the thirtieth headmaster of the Konparu school, which was active mainly in the Nara area.

Zenchiku was the son of Konparu Yasaburō (twenty-ninth headmaster), grandson of Konparu Gon-no-kami, and great-grandson of Bishaō Gon-no-kami (twenty-sixth headmaster). As Yasaburō is mentioned by neither Zeami nor Zenchiku, it is assumed he died at a young age. The role played by Zenchiku in the history of *nō* is closely tied to the life and career of the great *nō* theorist and playwright Zeami. As a youth, Zenchiku studied with Zeami, and he married Zeami's daughter (c.1427). Although Zeami named him his artistic successor, the headmastership of the Kanze school was given to Zeami's adopted son Motoshige (On'ami)—whom Zeami had already disowned—by the shogun Yoshinori, who greatly favored the young actor. Thus, Zenchiku shared in Zeami's disfavor and downfall. While Zeami was in exile on the island of Sado, Zenchiku cared for Zeami's wife, his mother-in-law.

Zeami wrote two treatises especially for Zenchiku: *Rikugi* (Six Principles) and *Shūgyoku Tokka* (Finding Gems and Gaining the Flower). Zeami's natural sons Motomasa and Motoyoshi also entrusted to Zenchiku copies of Zeami's *Kakyō* (The Mirror of the Flower) and *Sandō* (Three Elements [in Writing Nō Plays]). Zeami and his children all looked on Zenchiku not only as a great actor and superb dancer but also as the only hope for the continuance of their art. In the *Kyakuraika* (The Return of the Flower), written about a year after Motomasa's untimely death in 1422, Zeami wrote of Zenchiku, "He will become an uncommonly skilled actor with a distinctive style. . . . Motomasa permitted [Zenchiku] to view one of our most secret treatises, no doubt thinking that other than he there was no one who could preserve our school's name for future generations."

Although Zenchiku actually did become quite a popular actor, On'ami remained more popular. Zenchiku was able, however, to restore the Konparu (Enman'i) troupe to a more stable position. He left a number of excellent plays, including *Bashō* (The Plantain), *Kamo* (The God of Kamo Shrine), and *Teika* (Teika and the Vines of Love). The *shite* (main characters) in his plays tend to be intricate gestalts formed of natural forces and poetic image—in stark contrast to Zeami's more vivid characters and greater variety of dramatic form. Zenchiku uses the art of poetry itself as a major theme, reflecting his concept of poetry as "the essence of *nō*."

In 1468, to avoid the troubles caused by the Ōnin Wars (1467–1477), he retired to a retreat near that of his friend the Zen priest and poet Ikkyū (1394–1481), the forty-seventh head of Kyoto's Daitoku Temple and son of Emperor Go-Komatsu (ruled 1392–1412). Zenchiku's relationship with Ikkyū is thought to have lent a Zen coloring to his later writings. As Ikkyū was an acquaintance of the great *renga* ("linked verse") poet Sōgi (1421–1502), Zenchiku was exposed not only to Zen thought but also to court poetry. Konparu-school legends state that Zenchiku performed *nō* for Ikkyū and Sōgi, but this cannot be corroborated.

Zenchiku left behind a number of aesthetic treatises, the most important of which are *Rokurin ichiro* (Six Circles, One Dewdrop, 1455) and *Kabu zuinō ki* (The Essence of Song and Dance, 1456).

[*See also* Nō *and the entry on* Zeami.]

BIBLIOGRAPHY

Keene, Donald. *Nō: The Classical Theatre of Japan.* New York, 1966.

Kodansha Encyclopedia of Japan. Tokyo, 1983. See the entries "Komparu School," "Komparu Zenchiku," and "Nō."

Komparu Kunio. *The Noh Theater: Principles and Perspectives.* Translated by Jane Corddry and Stephen Comee. New York, 1983.

Nishino Haruo and Hata Hisashi, eds. *Nō, kyōgen jiten* (Dictionary of Noh and Kyogen). 2d ed. Tokyo. See entries "Konparu School" and "Konparu Zenchiku."

Thornhill, Arthur H., III. *Six Circles, One Dewdrop: The Religio-Aesthetic World of Komparu Zenchiku.* Princeton, 1993.

STEPHEN COMEE

KONSERVATORIET. Full Danish title: *Konservatoriet, eller Et Avisfrieri.* Ballet in two acts. Choreography and libretto: August Bournonville. Music: Holger Simon Paulli. First performance: 6 May 1849, Royal Theater, Copenhagen. Principals: Juliette Price (Eliza), Pauline Funck (Victorine), Ferdinand Hoppe (Alexis, Dancer, and Teacher), Wilhelm Erik Funck (Erneste, Violinist).

One of August Bournonville's most popular works, *Konservatoriet* was originally a two-act vaudeville ballet based on the choreographer's memories of dancing and amorous escapades during his student days in Paris of the 1820s. A poignant secondary plot concerns an itinerant musician's desire to have his daughter trained in a proper ballet school; it was inspired by a similar request addressed to Bournonville himself by a family of English pantomimists, the Prices.

Act 1 is set in the dancing school of the Paris Conservatory, where the inspector, Dufour, outrages his housekeeper and one-time fiancée by seeking a wife through a matrimonial advertisement. The dancers sympathize with the fiancée and, after their ballet class, decide to teach Dufour a lesson and reunite him with the offended spinster. This they do in hilarious fashion in act 2, set at a restaurant in the Paris suburb of Saint-Germain-en-Laye.

The ballet was performed in its entirety until 1934, though the dancing school portion of act 1 had already been presented alone as a *divertissement* ten years earlier; the latter was given its definitive form by Harald Lander and Valborg Borchsenius in 1941. *Konservatoriet* as we know it today is a graceful, elegant dancing lesson. Under the watchful eye of the ballet master, the corps performs *pas d'école* with variations, starting with an exacting adagio sequence; the students—adults and, at one point, children—then dance their way through the vocabulary of French classical steps. A pas de trois by the ballet master and the soloists Eliza and Victorine is followed by an increasingly complex series of *enchaînements* (some of these can be found in the Friday lesson of the manual on Bournonville training), which culminates in dazzling *brisés* for a male soloist and a finale performed by the entire company.

Konservatoriet has been called the purest choreographic expression of the school of Auguste Vestris, with whom Bournonville studied. Since the 1960s it has entered the repertories of companies throughout the world.

[*See also* Royal Danish Ballet *and the entry on Bournonville.*]

BIBLIOGRAPHY

Aschengreen, Erik, et al., eds. *Perspektiv på Bournonville.* Copenhagen, 1980.

Bournonville, August. "The Ballet Poems of August Bournonville: The Complete Scenarios." Translated by Patricia McAndrew. *Dance Chronicle* 4.1 (1981).

Bournonville, August. *My Theatre Life* (1848–1878). Translated by Patricia McAndrew (Middletown, Conn., 1979).

Hallar, Marianne, and Alette Scavenius, eds. *Bournonvilleana.* Translated by Gaye Kynoch. Copenhagen, 1992.

PATRICIA MCANDREW

KONSERVATORIET. The 1933 Royal Danish Ballet production of *Konservatoriet* starred Margot Lander as Victorine, Else Højgaard as Eliza, and Børge Ralov as Alexis, dancers at the Paris Opera. Here, in act 1, scene 4, after the ballet class is over, Victorine scans a newspaper while Erneste, the violinist (Leif Ørnberg), Eliza, and Alexis look on. Erneste has just called his friends' attention to an amusing matrimonial advertisement, which leads them to decide to play a prank. (Photograph by Holger Damgaard; from the Royal Library, Copenhagen.)

KORDAX. Literary descriptions of the *kordax,* a wild and lascivious dance of Mediterranean antiquity, mention kicking the buttocks, rotating the hips, slapping the thighs, and leaping as its characteristic movements. In Greece, Italy, and Asia Minor through nine centuries, it was performed by men or by women, in groups or solo. It is impossible to tell to what extent the dance changed over time, although it seems certain that its lewd qualities and its principal movements remained constant.

The earliest record of performance of the *kordax* dates from the fifth century BCE, when it figured among the dances of actors and the chorus in Greek comedy. Although the comic playwright Aristophanes denied using the *kordax* in his *Clouds,* most scholars assume that his claim is ironic and that his characters and choruses probably danced the *kordax,* if not in the *Clouds,* then elsewhere. In Aristophanes' *Wasps,* for example, Philocleon's description of his own dance and the chorus's comment on it suggest movements associated with the *kordax.*

Numerous philosophers and orators condemned the *kordax* and associated it with drunken and degenerate conduct. Plato, among the earliest writers to judge the dances of comedy morally corrupt, was the precursor of later moralistic assessments of the *kordax.* In the third century BCE the orator Demosthenes denounced the shameless performances of the *kordax* in the court of Philip of Macedon. As late as the fourth century CE the *kordax* retained its stigma as a vulgar dance (as in Athenaeus's *Deipnosophists*).

Although many Roman antiquarians and lexicographers associated the *kordax* solely with the dance of Greek comedy, some reported the dance in other contexts. In the first century CE, maidens, perhaps trained temple dancers, performed a dance called the *kordax* at shrines for Artemis. How closely these ritual dances resembled the *kordax* of the fifth-century BCE comic chorus is unclear. The associations of the rites with fertility may account for the attested hip and belly rotations of the dances. Other fiction and satires written during the Roman Empire mention that the *kordax* was performed at banquets and revels.

[*See also* Greece, *article on* Dance in Ancient Greece.]

BIBLIOGRAPHY

Aristophanes. *Clouds* 540–544; *Wasps* 1484–1537.
Athenaeus. *Deipnosophists* 14.630–631.
Demosthenes. *Olynthiac* 2.
Lawler, Lillian B. *The Dance of the Ancient Greek Theatre.* Iowa City, 1964.
Pausanius 6.22.1.
Plato. *Laws* 816.
Smigel, Elizabeth [Libby]. "Redefinitions of the Fifth-century Greek Chorus Using a Methodology Applied to Aristophanes' *Thesmophoriazusae.*" Master's thesis, York University, 1982.

LIBBY SMIGEL

KOREA. [*To survey the dance traditions of Korea, this entry comprises four articles:*

The first article presents a historical overview of Korean dance; the second explores the Yangju *and* Pongsan *masked dance dramas; the third discusses the importance of Western-derived contemporary dance; the fourth provides a brief history of scholarship and writing.*]

An Overview

Some forty million Korean speakers occupy a peninsula of East Asia some six hundred miles (970 kilometers) long, separating the Yellow Sea to the west from the Sea of Japan to the east. The People's Republic of China lies to the north and west and Russia to the northeast. The Korean people are northern Asians who moved south into the peninsula in prehistoric times. Korea was traditionally founded in 2333 BCE; recorded history begins with the Three Kingdoms. Their rivalry resulted in the kingdom of Silla emerging strongly by the third century CE, later forging an alliance with the Tang dynasty of China and unifying the peoples of the peninsula by the seventh century. The Koryŏ dynasty began its rule in 935, was disrupted by Mongol invasions from China, and was dominated in a thirteenth-century Mongol-controlled alliance. The Yi dynasty (1392–1910) established Confucianism as the state religion and built a capital at Hanyang (now Seoul). Contact with the West began during the Yi dynasty, at the end of the nineteenth century. With internal unrest as the pretext, both China and Japan sent troops to Korea in 1894; Japan proved dominant and kept Korea under colonial rule, annexing it in 1910 and occupying it until the end of World War II.

The Allies had promised Korea an independent nation but divided it into two zones of occupation, with Soviet troops in the northern zone and American in the southern. In 1948 two separate Korean regimes were established—the Republic of Korea in the south and the Democratic People's Republic (under Communism) in the north. In 1950, North Korea attempted to unite the country, sending troops into South Korea; until 1953 United Nations forces fought to keep them separate. Since then, both nations remain with a border at the 38th parallel, and economic talks have ensued but none on unification; both countries are highly industrialized, and Confucianism, Buddhism, and Christianity are the dominant religious traditions.

The ancient Chinese chronicle *Writings of the Later Han and Wei Dynasties*, compiled sometime during the sixth to seventh centuries CE, states that during the thirteenth century BCE many tribes were roaming the northern and central parts of the Korean peninsula, and that during the tenth or eleventh month of the year they held sacred ceremonial festivals that they celebrated with songs and invocatory group dances.

In the Three Han Kingdoms in the south, thanksgiving festivals were held twice annually, after rice transplanting and after the harvest. The *Munhon Tonggo,* an ancient Korean literary work, describes these dances:

> [They were] performed by a dozen or so dancers who lined up in a single file and followed the leader, raising their hands up and down and stamping on the ground to the accompaniment of music. . . . The ceremonies were presided over by a leader who might well have been a *mudang,* a folk ritual practitioner, who was, at the same time, lyricist, composer-musician, and dancer.

The earliest-known Chinese reference to these various types of ritual festivities is found in the *Sanguozhi* (History of the Three Kingdoms), compiled in 297 CE, in the section dealing with the "eastern people" (the inhabitants of Korea). It tells of the rituals practiced by various tribes until the third century CE: "In the fifth month, they sacrifice to spirits; all day and night, without rest, they sing, dance and drink wine."

In these ancient rituals dedicated to deities, held before the outset of farm work and after the agricultural cycle was completed, labor and the arts rose from a common source and existed in harmony. Continuously handed down through succeeding generations, the traditions came to form the basic character of Korean culture; thus the Korean dances of folk rites, folk games, farmers' festivals, and masked dance dramas are not considered separate entities but rather as part of an integrated whole along with the ritual, music, and drama.

During the emergence of the Three Kingdoms—the period of Silla, Paekje, and Koguryŏ (c.18 BCE–918 CE)—the indigenous folk religion was augmented with Buddhist and Confucian thought from China, resulting in many modifications in dance. Korea's kings and courtiers of this period were deeply involved with the dance of continental Asia; however, they did not merely enjoy it but also added a decorative and artistic element that was highly individualistic. Affecting not only the silken finery worn in royal court dances, but even the rough-hewn dances of the common folk, the influence of Asian continental civilization changed Korean culture. Nonetheless, even when Koreans adopted and assimilated types of movement, techniques, ornamentation, and costumes from other cultures, they always added their own special characteristics. From this admixture, over time they created new forms and refined them into a subtle and delicate art.

In their dance Koreans emphasized not only outer form but also innate character, "a spiritual inner beauty aside from outwardly aesthetic features" (Heyman, 1964). They valued freedom of expression and movement, particularly in folk dances, and their strong national individuality.

KOREA: An Overview. Sung Hae-oh performing a traditional-style Korean fan dance. Her posture shows the opposing principles of weight (her bent knees suggest the pull of gravity) and weightlessness (her extended arms and open fans suggest wings and the flight of birds). (Photograph © 1967 by John van Lund; used by permission.)

It was through their many ancient rituals, however, that the Koreans attested to a strong attachment to the land; this source provided the spiritual foundation from which traditional dance emerged and evolved. The underlying aesthetic of Korean dance begins with the moment the elegant foot, encased within the sesame seed–like *poson* (the traditional-style Korean bootee), takes its first step. The dancer's step expresses the character of a bird's flight, a crane or a heron; the dancer's foot (where female), hidden beneath the folds of a long, wide, flowing skirt (the *ch'ima),* is like a bird in hiding, assimilating both freedom and adherence to the earth and consolidating them. Korean dance appears only lightly dependent on the ground; it overflows with airy beauty yet retains gravity.

Koreans seek the infinite and eternal in the flow of life, the continual flux of *yin* to *yang* (the opposing principles of the universe: male–female, darkness–light, goodness–evil, truth–treachery, beauty–desolation, and so on). In Korean dance the interrelatedness of the whole—arms with chest, chest with breathing, breathing with lifting away from and giving in to gravity, all reflected in hand movements—makes the dance seem to revolve like the eternally changing *yin* and *yang,* between heaviness and lightness.

This feeling of heaviness, termed *mugopta,* is an important aspect of Korean dance, especially in the classical style. Although in neighboring Japan dance also emphasizes heaviness, for the Japanese this is a downward force that represents *ochitsuita* (a sense of immovability or stability). Roske-Cho (1980) sees this downward force as characteristic of the Japanese aesthetics of *mujo-kan,* the feeling of transitoriness that is a manifestation of attachment to earthly life. In Korean dance, however, this heaviness is felt as a rejuvenating force, which the dancer uses to rise again (Loken-Kim, 1982).

From the prehistoric to the Tribal States period, and until the beginning of the Three Kingdoms era, life in Korea was based largely on expediency. Therefore, the dances of that early period were largely dedicated to various gods in an attempt to ward off adversity. In this society, no distinction was made between aristocrat and commoner. Later, however, with the establishment of a class structure, the upper classes became actively involved in the creation of music and dance, and a new and different art accordingly developed. A good example of this is the *hwarang,* an organization of young noblemen who delighted in the performance of an art that was elegant, erudite, and aesthetically pleasing. As time passed, they acquired great discipline and technique in the execution of ritual dance. At the height of the Buddhist period, during the Koryŏ dynasty (918–1392 CE), the high priests, who had acquired knowledge of Buddhist ritual music and dance from China, brought it to a high degree of excellence.

Thus dance, first a part of the work and everyday life of the common people, later became an elite means of training body and spirit as well as of religious and ideological expression. Still later, during the Yi dynasty (1392–1910), under the code of Confucian ethics, the performance of music and dance was relegated to a professional entertainer class (and designated as a lower caste). The aristocracy and literati were restricted from taking part in music or dance performance, and thereby the distinction between performer and spectator had become clearly defined.

After the fall of the Yi dynasty and the advent of the modern period, Korea acquired theater in the Western sense—an indoor theater with a stage, proscenium, lighting, and scenery—which had been virtually nonexistent until that time. All arts, especially dance, underwent dramatic changes and were soon far beyond the common people. The resulting gap, not one of class distinction, was rather due to the aspirations of the performers themselves, who continuously innovated and refined their art until it appealed only to an elite, ever-diminishing audience of connoisseurs and lost popular support. Folk dance was not entirely forgotten, but performance in which the audience played an active role was badly neglected.

The continuity of Korea's traditional culture was interrupted, first by the Japanese colonial annexation in 1910 that brought an end to the Yi dynasty, and later by the devastating Korean War (1950–1953). The war brought an onslaught of Western culture that drove the traditional arts, already weakened by Japanese oppression, into near extinction. Many dance forms without traditional roots emerged after this time.

Contemporary Korean dance theater has turned in search of its lost roots. This quest is not merely for the sake of modernization or superficially approaching both the modern and the traditional of East and West; instead, Korean artists are looking in new directions, with a strong consciousness about the nation's cultural heritage in creating new works.

Folk Dance. Many forms of folk dance exist in Korea, including both those performed by professional folk dancers in theaters and on television and those performed by the common people at seasonal festivities and folk rituals. The two most distinctive types are farmers' festival music and dance, often referred to as *nongak* (agricultural music), and *t'al'ch'um,* the masked dance dramas.

Of all traditional dances in Korea, those performed by the farmers are the most spirited and exciting, filled with verve and rhythmic invention. The farmers' festival music and dance, *nongak,* is the descendant of rituals during the prehistoric and Tribal States periods, making it one of the oldest forms of dance extant in Korea today. During the Three Kingdoms period, in addition to its ritual function, it was also utilized for military drill purposes by the rulers of the time, who formed the farmers into a peasant militia against frequent invasions. The costume worn by the dancers retains military vestiges to this day, and, particularly in North Kyŏngsang Province, the dancers still simulate such military maneuvers as assembly, recruitment, parade, retreat, charge, and the triumphal return of the peasant soldiery. They form into parallel lines, advance and retreat in accordance with flag signals, and march toward each other as if in combat.

As time passed, though the farmers' dance retained ties to folk religion, it gradually came to be used more for entertainment. For example, a farmers' dance is occasionally accompanied by a procession of masked dancers or miming skits known as *chapsaek* (variegated colors). The main characters are an aristocrat, who carries a long bamboo pipe and a folding fan; a hunter, who carries a rifle and from whose belt a pheasant dangles; a Buddhist monk; a procuress; and a small child who dances on the shoulders of an adult male as he parades around the performance area.

The musical instruments employed are almost all percussive and are played by the farmers themselves as they dance. They include a small gong, played by the leader of the group; a large gong, which marks out the fundamental beat; an hourglass-shaped drum, which is played on both sides and is secured to the performer's waist and shoulders; a round, barrel-shaped drum, again used largely for sounding the fundamental beat; and a small, round-handled drum, which is struck on both sides as the player dances and twirls a long paper streamer attached to a swivel on his hat. The only melodic instruments are a conical oboe with a wooden bore and flared bell at the end and, occasionally, a long clarion.

Nongak was not only for ritual and entertainment but also to enhance work in the fields. In addition to being performed by the farmers themselves, it was on occasion played by professional or semiprofessional groups of roving musicians and dancers who assisted in village shrine rituals and exorcistic rites. They sometimes performed masked dances and puppet dramas as well.

The masked dance dramas, *t'al'ch'um,* which are believed to be of Central Asian origin, were introduced into Korea from China during the Three Kingdoms period and then transmitted from Korea to Japan. At that time they were Buddhist morality plays (somewhat akin to the mystery cycles—enactments of the life of Jesus—in medieval Europe). Later, during the Yi dynasty, they were transformed into comic plays that satirized the corrupt Buddhist clergy of the time, the decadent aristocracy, and the triangular relationship of husband, wife, and concubine. Masked dance dramas were also performed at folk rituals, mainly to exorcise evil but also for entertainment.

The themes in this genre are basically the same throughout Korea, but regional differences exist in the masks and dance movements. Those of the northwest are large, gruff, and grotesque, whereas the movements of the central and southern regions are smaller and gentler, and the masks are more humanlike. The materials used in making the masks also differ according to region. Those of Hwanghae and South Kyŏngsang provinces are made basically of *papier mâché,* those of Kyŏnggi Province of gourd, and those of North Kyŏngsang and Kangwŏn provinces of wood.

The colors of the masks symbolize five points of the compass: blue is east, red south, white west, black north, and yellow the center. Thus, at seasonal festivals, when the old monk, who wears a black mask, is defeated by the prodigal, who wears a red mask, it is symbolic of the "Battle of Summer and Winter" (since south is associated with summer and north with winter).

The dialogue, which is often racy and vulgar, is limited to certain characters. In some dramas such as the Lion Dance performed in South Hamgyŏng Province during lunar New Year festivities, it is almost absent.

KOREA: An Overview. In this scene from a Pongsan *t'al'ch'um* drama, an old monk (left) woos a young courtesan. (Photograph from the archives of The Asia Society, New York.)

Salp'uri. The genre known as *salp'uri* ("to exorcise evil") is derived from a folk ritual of southwestern Korea. It is a gay, beautiful, bewitching solo dance usually but not necessarily performed by women. The *salp'uri* is a joyful improvisatory dance that tells no story, yet has the power to move the spirit deeply. Nowhere are the uniquely distinctive Korean characteristics of *mot* and *hung* more apparent than in the *salp'uri.* The dancer's movements are infused with irrepressible joy, almost with giddiness. The dance illustrates one of the main principles of authentic Korean art, that of deriving the maximum effect from the minimum material. The costume is free of heavy adornment, employing only the plain white native costume, a white silken scarf, and occasionally a small round-handled drum of the type used in *nongak* for the fast portion of the dance.

It is believed in Korea that an evil force *(sal)* has taken possession of a person suffering great difficulties, but that one can survive if the evil is exorcised. *Salp'uri* enables one to face and overcome evil by understanding the essence of evil itself. This is impossible without a clear appreciation of the real world and the struggle of life, itself a process of *salp'uri.* Such conflict is also the structural principle of the masked dance drama. *Salp'uri* unites one with divine power; at this point the artistic impulse is brought to a climax and bursts forth in song and dance; this ultimate experience in *salp'uri* is called *shinmyong.*

Salp'uri is performed to the accompaniment of a wind and percussion ensemble (strings are sometimes added), which starts off in a slow, rippling tempo in 12/8 meter and is very gradually accelerated to a fast-moving 6/8. The musical texture is uniquely heterophonic, little resembling other existing Asian musical forms. Invariably a singer joins the ensemble, but the song consists only of meaningless syllables sung in time with the music.

Ritual Dance. Confucian ritual dance is performed twice a year at the Confucian Shrine and once at the Royal Ancestor Shrine by girls from the Traditional Music High School in Seoul. At one time, these dances were performed only by men, because women were customarily barred from all Confucian ceremonies.

The ritual dances, called *il-mu* (line formation dance), are of two types: the civil dance symbolizes peace and prosperity, and the military dance represents glorious military achievements. *Il-mu* consists of a series of simple ritual movements—stately arm motions, bowing, turning, and posturing, with little foot motion. It is performed solely for the purpose of the ceremony. Like the music that accompanies it, this dance was probably introduced into Korea from Song-dynasty China in 1116 CE. It is part of a ceremony said to be one of the oldest and most authentic still being performed in the East Asian cultural tradition. The *il-mu,* employing sixty-four dancers (eight lines of eight dancers), is also performed at the Royal Ancestor Shrine Ceremony, but with some modifications. It was re-created from a dance performed at the Confucian Shrine around the middle of the fifteenth century.

Korea today is the only nation in Asia where Buddhist ritual dance may still be seen. The dances, which are believed to have undergone alteration in Korea from their original (Indian) prototypes, during the late Koryŏ or early Yi-dynasty period, are performed at temples by monks or nuns during large-scale memorial services for the dead. They are of three basic types: the Butterfly Dance, so called because of the extremely broad sleeves of the dancer's costume, which hang from the shoulder to the floor along the entire length of the arm; the Cymbal Dance, in which the performers hold large cymbals that they twirl over and around their heads as they dance; and the Drum Dance, in which the performer dances before a large round drum struck at certain intervals during the dance.

Perhaps the most notable characteristic of Buddhist ritual dance is the position of the feet—perpendicular to each other, with the heel of the left foot raised slightly and touching the right between the instep and ankle joint. At the same time, the knees are bent as in a *plié.* This posture occurs in no other type of Korean traditional dance. It is assumed at the start of the dance, after each series of movements, and at the end of the dance.

Korean folk ritual dance, often generically referred to as "shaman dance," differs in each region of the country and contains many similarities to that region's nonritual folk dance. Generally, however, the folk ritual dances of the North are dynamic, at times attaining very rapid tempos in which the dancer engages in frenetic jumping movements; those of the South are usually calm and passive, performed to a slow, rippling tempo in 12/8 or 6/8 meter.

KOREA: An Overview. Kim Keum-ha, a trained shaman *(sei supmu),* demonstrates the "Ritual of Good Fortune," a shaman dance typical of North Korean folk ritual. (Photograph from the archives of The Asia Society, New York.)

Court Dance. Royal court dance, or *chongjae* ("offering one's talent"), emerged during the Koryŏ period in two forms—the *tangak chongjae,* court banquet dances of Chinese origin, and *hyangak chongjae,* those of Korean origin. These dances, which reached their zenith in the Yi dynasty, at one time comprised a very large repertory, but only about fifteen are actively performed today. Today, there is, however, an effort to restore many of the dances that were allowed to fall into oblivion.

The court dance represents the epitome of elegance, taste, refinement, restraint, and resplendent beauty; it is seen by audiences as the very essence of Korean culture. It features a subtle and restrained exposition of innermost feelings; for this reason, the dancer's overt physical features are hidden to the greatest extent possible. Such restraint is a byproduct of the influence of Confucianism, which was the state religion during the Yi dynasty. It contrasts with folk dance, which manifests somewhat more overt freedom in movement and expression.

A Korean word that adequately describes many of the dance movements is *chong'joong'dong,* denoting quiescence; it may be translated as "motion within stillness" or, conversely, "stillness within motion." The characteristic calm and quietness of Korean court dance are achieved through carefully controlled movements executed with tremendous energy.

Korean dance has an essentially flowing kinetic quality, rather than being punctuated by static sculptural positions. The dancer is never still; something is always moving, and this quality alone makes the dance appear flowing, graceful, and gentle. The limited differentiation of body parts, the delicacy of their movement, and the generally slow rhythms (especially in the court dances) give the dances a low movement density. The audience is not watching for technical virtuosity but rather for the spirit of the dance, the joy and ecstasy (*mot* and *hung*).

Graceful shoulder movements are of particular importance, and the slow rising and sinking movement of the knees inside the long, full skirt is considered to be integral with the breathing of the dancers. They step elegantly from the heel, but the soles of their feet are not revealed to the audience. Neither are their hands, which are completely covered by long, wide rainbow-colored sleeves. (Such movements as hopping and hip-swaying are considered highly improper.)

Court dance today is performed mostly by female dancers of the National Classical Music Institute of Korea (now the Korean Traditional Performing Arts Center), the successor of the Yi dynasty's Royal Conservatory of Music and Dance.

[*For further general discussion, see* Asian Dance Traditions *and* Costume in Asian Traditions. *See also the entries on Han Young-Sook, Kim Ch'un-heung, and Lee Maebang.*]

KOREA: An Overview. In this Korean court dance, the performer stays in a small space, delineated by a straw mat. The striped sleeve extensions serve to hide her hands and elongate her movements. As she executes the graceful rising and sinking movements of the dance, her facial expression remains impassive. (Photograph from the archives of The Asia Society, New York.)

BIBLIOGRAPHY

Ch'ae Hui-wan. "*Shinmyong* as an Artistic Experience in Group Performance." Translated by Alan C. Heyman. *Korea Journal* 21 (October 1981).

Chang Sa-hun. "Farmer's Band Music." Translated by Hahn Manyong in *Traditional Performing Arts of Korea.* Seoul, 1975.

Cho Dong-wha. "Dance." In *Korea: Its Land, People, and Culture of All Ages.* 2d ed. Seoul, 1963.

Chung Byong-ho et al. "Korean Dance Movement Patterns." *Korean Culture and Arts Foundation* (January 1980).

Han Ok-hi. "Folk Dance." Translated by Alan C. Heyman in *Survey of Korean Arts,* vol. 2, *Folk Arts.* Seoul, 1974.

Heyman, Alan C. "Dances of the Three-Thousand-League Land." *Dance Perspectives,* no. 19 (March 1964).

Heyman, Alan C. "*P'ansori:* The Dramatic-Epic-Narrative Song of Korea." In *Essays on Asian Music and Theater,* by Alan C. Heyman and William P. Malm. New York, 1972.

Heyman, Alan C. "*Chak-Bop:* The Buddhist Ceremonial Dance of Korea." *Journal of Korean Dance* 1 (May 1982).

Howard, Keith. "*Nongak,* the *Changgu,* and Kim Pyong-sop's *Kaein Changgu Nori*" (parts 1–2). *Korea Journal* 23 (May–June 1983).

Kim Ch'un-heung. "A Notated Score of Korean Dance Movements." In *Cultural Properties Bureau, Ministry of Culture and Information, Republic of China* (September 1969).

Kim Ch'un-heung. "Korean Traditional Folk and Mask Dance." *Survey of Korean Arts*, vol. 2, *Folk Arts*. Seoul, 1974.

Kim On-kyong. "A Comparative Study of the Dance Movements of the Aristocrat and the Servant in the Tongnae Yayu Mask Dance-Drama." *Journal of Korean Dance* 1 (May 1982).

Kim Paik-bong. "A Notated Dance Movement Score of the Pongsan Mask Dance-Drama." *Korean Culture and Arts Foundation* (December 1976).

Kim Yong-jun. "The Five Great *P'ansori*." *Cholla Province Traditional Music Institute* (January 1966).

King, Eleanor. "Reflections on Korean Dance." *Korea Journal* 17 (August 1977).

Lee Byong-won. "Korean Dance." *Korean Music and Dance* (October 1981).

Lee Du-hyon. "Korean Mask Dance-Drama." Translated by Alan C. Heyman in *Traditional Performing Arts of Korea*. Seoul, 1975.

Loken-Kim, Christine. "Moving in the Korean Way: Movement Characteristics of the Korean People as Expressed in Their Dance." Unpublished ms., April 1982.

Loken-Kim, Christine, and Juliette T. Crump. "Qualitative Change in Performances of Two Generations of Korean Dancers." *Dance Research Journal* 25 (Fall 1993).

Roske-Cho, W. S. "*Mot* and the Japanese Aesthetical Feeling of *Mujokan*." *Korea Journal* 20 (July 1980).

Song Kyong-rin. "Introduction to Korean Folk Dance." Translated by Alan C. Heyman in *Survey of Korean Arts*, vol. 2, *Folk Arts*. Seoul, 1974.

Yi Po-hyong. "*P'ansori*." *Survey of Korean Arts*, vol. 2, *Folk Arts*. Seoul, 1974.

Yi Po-hyong. "The Genetic Relationship of Farmer's Music and Dance to Village Communal Shaman Rituals in Korea." Translated by Alan C. Heyman. *Korea Journal* 21 (October 1981).

ALAN C. HEYMAN

Masked Dance Drama

The genre known in Korean as Yangju *pyŏl sandae nori* (masked dance drama) developed as a local variation of the *sandae* drama cycle performed throughout the Seoul region of Korea. The old town of Yangju was situated at a busy intersection from which roads fanned out to several towns. Yangju was also an important stopping point on the way to Seoul. Traditionally, the Yangju masked dance drama was performed on the eve of the lunar New Year, on the eighth day of the fourth lunar month (the Buddha's birthday), at the Tano festival (the fifth day of the fifth lunar month), and at Ch'usŏk, the autumn harvest festival on the fifteenth day of the eighth lunar month.

The Yangju play, like other masked dramas of Korea, is composed largely of dance with accompanying music to which song is added. It includes scenes in which speech is absent and only pantomime and gesture are employed. Scenes that include both monologue and dialogue appear largely for comedic purposes as well as for acting out the part of the drama that calls for speaking roles.

Compared with other masked dances, the Yangju dance drama is executed with more refinement and beauty of form. The different dance patterns (*sawi*) employed in the *pyŏl sandae* drama are more detailed than those used in other mask dances. They are divided into two kinds: that of the *kŏdŭrŭm* dance and those of the *kkaekki* dance. These two kinds are further subdivided into ten different dance patterns. All the basic patterns of Korean folk dance can be observed among them.

The Yangju play employs the *samhyŏn yukkak* instrumental ensemble consisting of two bamboo oboes, one bamboo transverse flute, one two-stringed fiddle, one hourglass-shaped drum, a barrel drum, and a small gong. These instruments produce the accompanying dance rhythms: *yŏmbul* (a six-beat rhythmic pattern), *t'aryŏng* (a twelve-beat pattern) with the accent on the ninth beat), and *kutkŏri* (also a twelve-beat pattern).

The order of scenes in a Yangju play is not strictly adhered to by the players. That is, the Yangju drama is not a through-composed play like traditional Western drama; it rather resembles the *commedia dell'arte* or the British-style revue. The drama is usually divided into eight episodes. The themes of the play may be broadly outlined as follows: ceremonial dances for the exorcism of evil spirits and shamanistic rituals; satire of the ideological hypocrisy of apostate monks; criticism of the privileged status of the gentry; conflict between male and female as a critique of the tyranny of the male; and the misery of the everyday life of the common people. The Yangju *pyŏl sandae nori* has been designated by the Korean government as an Important Intangible Cultural Property.

The plot of another dance drama, the Pongsan *t'al'ch'um*, is clearly of the *sandae-dogam* tradition. However, its music, dance, and dialogue carry the distinct flavor of northwestern Korean folk art. Pongsan, in the northwestern province of Hwanghae, was a thriving market town during the eighteenth and nineteenth centuries. Prosperous townspeople fostered a local tradition of masked dance drama, and players were called upon to perform at welcoming ceremonies for visiting Chinese envoys. The Pongsan *t'al'ch'um* was part of this tradition.

Originally, the play's primary function was religious; performances were held to commemorate the birthday of the Buddha, on the eve of the eighth day of the fourth lunar month. In the nineteenth century, the masked dance drama was incorporated into the magnificant folk festival held to celebrate Tano, the fifth day of the fifth lunar month. The Tano festival was held at a relatively slack point in the busy agricultural calendar, just before the arduous work of summer rice-planting begins. As part of the festival, a performance of masked dance drama would be held to expel evil and invoke blessings for a good harvest in the coming year.

The main themes of the Pongsan *t'al'ch'um* are evident in three kinds of dramatic action: satire involving degenerate monks, mockery of aristocrats, and the portrayal of the everyday life of the common people. The Pongsan

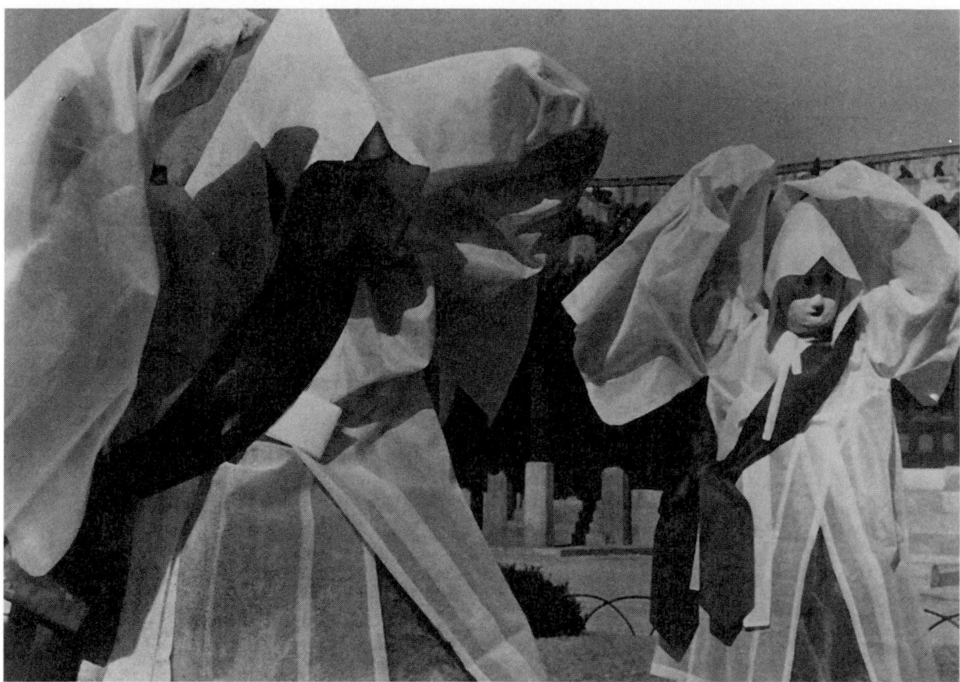

KOREA: Masked Dance Drama. Pongsan *t'al'ch'um* is a Korean masked drama satirizing corrupt monks and noblemen. The hooded robes and sashes worn by these two performers are stylized monk costumes. (Photograph from the archives of The Asia Society, New York.)

drama is divided into the following seven episodes: (1) a ceremonial opening dance by Four Young Monks; (2) the Eight Buddhist Monks; (3) dance and songs by Sadang and Kŏsa; (4) the Old Monk's Dance, comprising three scenes—the Old Monk and the Young Shaman, the Shoe Seller, and the Prodigal; (5) the Lion Dance; (6) the Noblemen and their Servant; and (7) the Old Couple.

The Pongsan *t'al'ch'um* also employs the *samhyŏn yukkak* instrumental ensemble. The dance movements *(sawi)* utilized in Pongsan drama include the *oe-sawi* (the hand circles the head once), and *kop-sawi* (the hand circles across the front of the head first and then circles behind in the opposite direction). The *kkaekki-ch'um* (the hand circles the head once, then the right hand is placed on the shoulder and the left hand waves a willow branch up and down) is characteristic of the prodigal, Ch'wibari. The servant, Malttugi, dances in the *tuŏ-ch'um* pattern, waving a riding crop around in front of him, circling it over his head in the opposite direction, holding it in front of him with both hands on the handle, and finally wielding it to drive the aristocrats into the pigsty. The old woman, Miyal, dances the *kung-dung' i-ch'um,* a swaying motion of the hips. Distinct walking patterns are also used by the various characters. Ch'wibari employs the *Kŭdŭrŭm* strutting motion, and Miyal the *kalji-ja kŏlŭm* or zig-zag motion. The Pongsan *t'al'ch'um* has also been designated an Important Intangible Cultural Property by the Korean government.

[*See also* Mask and Makeup, *article on* Asian Traditions.]

BIBLIOGRAPHY

Korean National Commission, UNESCO. *Traditional Performing Arts of Korea.* Seoul, 1975.

Lee Du-hyon. *Han'guk kamyon'gŭk.* Seoul, 1969. Includes an English summary.

LEE DU-HYON

Modern Dance

The history of modern dance in Korea began in 1922, when Ishii Baku, a pioneer of modern dance in Japan who studied with Isadora Duncan, visited Seoul and performed the *Neue Tanz* ("new dance"), as it was called in German, that he had learned in Europe. The impact was so great that some young dance students left immediately for Tokyo to study under the famous Japanese dance master. They included Cho T'aek-won and Ch'oi Seung-hee, who later made distinguished contributions to the development of modern dance in Korea. Both were devoted to creating their own dance expression by combining the modern dance techniques they had learned in Japan with the unique spiritual motifs they drew from Korean traditional dance. They composed a number of works that successfully conveyed the subtle lyricism inherent in Korean expressive arts and the atmosphere of Korean folklore with fresh stage idioms borrowed from contemporary dances of the West. In 1937, Ch'oi Seung-hee embarked on a two-year tour of the United States, Latin America, and Europe under the aegis of impresario Sol Hurok, giving more than one hundred performances that drew acclaim from the critics of *Le Figaro* and other journals.

Another major stream of modern Korean dance was led by Yuk Wan-sun, founder of the Modern Dance Association of Korea and formerly professor of modern dance at Ewha Women's University in Seoul. She introduced the techniques of Martha Graham, with whom she had studied in New York. She attained great success in Korea with her choreographic version of *Jesus Christ Superstar*, in which she also performed.

Hong Sin-cha, a leading artist of the younger generation in the world of Korean contemporary dance, studied at Columbia University under the tutelage of Alwin Nikolais and Meredith Monk. Until 1990 she was based in New York, where she organized a troupe called Laughing Stone. In performances in Seoul in 1973 and 1975 she attempted to express Korean spiritualism through contemporary dance techniques, to much acclaim. She is now teaching and performing in her own studio near Seoul.

Korea's long history and unique cultural heritage has been explored as a valuable source of inspiration by many other modern dancers, including Nam Jeong-ho, Lee Jung-hee, and Kim Hyon-ok, all of whom studied in France and the United States. Numerous small dance companies, organized in recent years in Seoul and other cities, are striving to rediscover Korea's indigenous dance culture and translate it into modern dance expression, to communicate with Korean audiences and those of the entire world. Ch'ang Mu Hoe (Creative Dance Company), led by Kim Mae-ja, is one of the most active groups in this experimental movement. The Korean Dance Festival, sponsored by the Korean Culture and Arts Foundation, has been encouraging the activities of many modern dance companies by offering them an annual forum.

KOREA: Modern Dance. Lee Kyung-ok is one of a new generation of Korean choreographers to come out of Kyung Hee University. A 1986 graduate, she made a strong impression with her debut work *Short Breath*. She is seen here in a 1989 dance called *There Is a Cliff Over There*. (Photograph by Cho Dae-hyung; courtesy of Christopher Caines.)

[*See also the entries on Ch'oi Seung-hee, Cho T'aek-won, Hong Sin-cha, Kim Paik-bong, and Lee Sun-ock.*]

BIBLIOGRAPHY

Hong Shin-cha. *Mouth to Tail: The Dance World of Hong Shin-cha*. Seoul, 1994.

Pak Yong-ku. "Young Dancers Seek to Create Fresh Stage Idioms." In *Korean Art Guide*. 2d rev. ed. Seoul, 1986.

ALAN C. HEYMAN

Dance Research and Publication

A great deal has been written about Korean dance, some of it for use by scholars, some intended solely to document events, and some as anecdotal comment by those who observed dance performances. The content ranges from brief introductions intended for the first-time visitor to Korea to detailed information forming a basis for subsequent research.

There is a continuous tradition of government involvement with dance writing dating from as long ago as the Koryŏ dynasty (918–1392). This is not surprising, because the performing arts played an important role in court entertainment. As a result, many historical accounts at least mention that dance was performed as part of a particular celebratory event.

Two early works in Korean stand out for their major contributions to information about dance in early times. The first, known as the *Koryosa akchi* (Music Chapter of the History of the Koryŏ Dynasty), sets a precedent reflected in many later writings; dance is included with discussions of music. This chapter is noteworthy for its documentation of interchanges between China and Korea that included both music and dance.

The second important early document is the *Akhak kwebom* (Treatise on Music), published in 1493. Devoted entirely to an explication of theoretical and practical matters relating to music and dance, it specifically refers to some twenty dances and provides descriptions of dance costumes and implements used by dancers.

From the end of the fifteenth century, dance was referred to occasionally in informal court histories, but it was not until the late nineteenth century that it was officially documented in a substantial way. Beginning in the late 1800s, government logs (known as *holgi* and *uigwe*) were kept to record information about court banquets, which documented not only the event but also its preparation. They included explanations of why events were held and descriptions of all the planning phases. They also provided floor plans of processionals and dances, as well as costume illustrations, song texts, and verbal descriptions of movement.

With the end of the Yi dynasty in 1910, the royal court, once the focal point for upper-class entertainment, ceased to exist. South Korean government involvement with dance writing, however, continued in the twentieth century. In 1962 the Korean government adopted a system for recognizing outstanding artistic works and the individuals who keep these works alive. Individual dances and the performers and teachers of these dances may be designated Cultural Treasures. Each time a new dance becomes a Cultural Treasure, the Ministry of Culture commissions a monograph containing historical information about the dance, verbal and sometimes pictorial descriptions of movements, information about costuming and music, and biographical sketches of the individuals officially designated to perpetuate the dance. These documents are difficult to obtain because they are reproduced in limited numbers and are kept primarily in government offices.

The South Korean government has started to make information on the Cultural Treasures more accessible through other kinds of publications. For example, in the early 1980s, the government-supported Kungnip Kugagwon (National Classical Music Institute, now the Korean Traditional Performing Arts Center) began to publish facsimiles of selected eighteenth-century court documents (for example, the facsimile of King Honjong's 1848 *chinchan ulgwe*); in 1961 Hanguk Munhwa Poho Hyophoe (the Society for the Preservation of Korean Culture) published *T'al'ch'um taesajip,* a volume that contains the Korean-language scripts of twelve masked dance dramas that are Cultural Treasures. In 1983 the Office of Cultural Properties (affiliated with the Ministry of Culture and Information, now the Ministry of Culture and Sports) published a large volume with lavish color photographs featuring seventy-nine Cultural Treasures, including dance.

South Korea has also published sections on dance in numerous large works and separate small texts on dance. Many of these are general, however, and do not add to existing knowledge because they are simply republications of information already available in print. Two government-supported organizations now publish annual compilations that include factual information on dance—*Hanguk yesulji* (Yearbook of Korean Arts), published by Taehan Minguk Yesulwon (the Korean National Academy of Arts), and *Munye yongam* (Yearbook of Literature and Arts), published by Hanguk Munwha Yesul Chinnungwon (the Korean Culture and Arts Foundation). Each volume contains statistics on arts organizations in various regions, descriptions of these organizations, and lists of awards and performing calendars from the preceding year.

The South Korean government's most significant contemporary contribution to writings on dance may be the encyclopedia of traditional Korean culture. This multivolume work, begun in 1980, is being compiled by the Hanguk Chongshin Munwha Yon'guwon (the Academy of Korean Studies), a major government-funded research institute. One section will be devoted to dance.

Because Korea had no early indigenous written form, the earliest documents were written in Chinese characters. Later documents contained a mixture of Chinese characters and those of the Korean alphabet, which was devised in the mid-fifteenth century. Contemporary efforts have been made to translate some of the earliest works from the Chinese system into Korean; the most significant translations so far for dance are *Koryosa akchi* (translated by Ch'a Chu-hwan, 1974) and *Akhak kwebom* (translated by Lee Hye-gu, book 1, 1955; book 2, 1961).

Regular periodic publications on dance began in 1961 with the introduction of the *Korea Journal,* an English-language publication of the Korean National Commission for UNESCO. From its earliest days, the journal has frequently included articles on dance that span such subjects as history, criticism of recent performances, and book reviews. Authors are of diverse background and include older Korean scholars and performers of the court dance of the Yi dynasty as well as younger non-Korean academicians. Photographs are occasionally included with articles, but reproduction quality is not always good. A selection of these articles was reprinted by the Korean National Commission in 1983 in *Korean Dance Theatre and Cinema,* but none was identified as having been published earlier in the *Korea Journal.*

Among Korean-language periodicals that occasionally feature articles on folk dancers and folk dance performances are *Kong kan* (Space), *Pouri kip'un namu* (Deep-Rooted Tree), and *Madang* (Playground). The first Korean-language periodical devoted entirely to dance is the monthly *Ch'um* (Dance), which began in 1978. Its articles emphasize the contemporary dance genres, particularly Western-style modern dance and ballet, but they occasionally focus on traditional Korean dance. Also included are critiques of performances, information on current dance events, and interviews.

Hanguk muyong yon'gu (Korean Dance Studies), published primarily in Korean with occasional articles or abstracts in English, began in 1982. It is published by Hanguk Muyong Yon'guhoe (the Society of Korean Dance Studies), an organization founded in 1981, which is concerned with the scholarly study of dance in Korea. The journal's articles cover a broad range of topics, including contemporary dance education, descriptions of traditions, and dance genres. In addition to publishing the journal, the organization holds occasional dance conferences and workshops.

Korean Culture, an English-language quarterly published since 1980 by the Korean Cultural Service of Los Angeles, California, occasionally contains dance articles that vary in scholarly level. Photographs are often included and are generally of good quality.

The most recent addition to periodicals is *Koreana,* published by Hanguk Kukche Munhwa Hyophoe (the International Cultural Society of Korea, now the Korea Foundation). The first issue of this quarterly appeared at the end of 1987 and contained a dance review and brief announcements of current dance events. The publisher's statement of intent in the first volume indicated that future issues would include major articles on dance. This has since been done in volume 3, number 2, of 1989 and in volume 7, number 4, of 1993. The journal is lavishly illustrated.

A valuable source of current information is *Newsreview,* published since 1972 weekly in Korea, in English. It contains brief summaries of contemporary events. Although its focus is primarily economic and political, almost every issue contains one or more pages on the arts, including dance. Despite the brevity of many articles—sometimes only a single paragraph—and their lay orientation, they provide useful information on the current dance scene.

The first books containing substantial broad histories of traditional Korean dance were published in 1977. *Hanguk muyongsa* (History of Korean Dance) was written by Kim Mae-ja, a dance professor who is also a performer, and *Hanguk chont'ong muyong yon'gu* (Study of Traditional Korean Dance) by a music professor, Chang Sa-hun. In addition to text, both volumes contain photographs of portions of early government manuscripts that are not otherwise readily accessible.

Many performance series have been presented in Korea in the 1970s, 1980s, and 1990s focusing on individuals considered to be highly skilled dancers, although they are not necessarily identified as Cultural Treasures. In 1985, the Korean newspaper *Hanguk ilbo* published a beautifully illustrated book presenting biographical sketches of many of these artists, *Hangukui myongmu* (Korea's Famous Dancers) by Ku Hi-so. It contains photographs by Chong Pom-t'ae.

Numerous works have attempted to describe Korean dance movements. The earliest records (for example, *Akhak kwebom* and the *holgi*) give verbal descriptions. The Cultural Treasure documents employ both verbal descriptions and stick figures. A 1971 survey, Kim Chong-yon's *Hanguk Muyong Togam* (A Survey of Korean Dance), uses line drawings and verbal descriptions, as well as Western musical notation, to characterize eleven dances and their basic arm and foot movements. Kim Paek-pong's 1976 work, *Pongsan t'al'ch'um mubo* (Pongsan T'al'ch'um Dance Notation) documents a masked dance drama form by using elaborate figure drawings aligned with musical notation. Several texts on basic dance movements contain single-frame photographs of dance performances. Examples include Chong Byong-ho, *Ch'um sawi* (Dance Movements, 1980, republished in 1985 with an expanded introduction, under the title *Hanguk ch'um,* Korean Dance); and Kim Myong-su, *Lee Tong'an T'ae p'yongmu yon'gu* (A Study of Lee Tong'an's T'aep'yongmu, 1983). *Dances of Korea,* published in English in 1962, is the only work that has recorded Korean dance using a formalized, universally applicable system of movement notation. It was written by a Korean, Cho Won-kyung, with an American, Carl Wolz, using the Labanotation of Rudolf Laban.

An important resource for researchers is Song Bang'-song's *An Annotated Bibliography of Korean Music,* published in 1971. Although the author is an ethnomusicologist rather than a dance researcher, the book contains substantial entries on dance. Its index, organized by author and subject, makes items on dance easy to find. Seven supplements to its bibliography, including dance items, have been published in the periodicals *Korea Journal* (1974 and 1975) and *Asian Music* (1978).

Except for articles in English-language periodicals and occasionally in other sources, most works on Korean dance are published in the Korean language. A significant exception is the English-language writing of an American, Alan Heyman. A long-time resident of Korea, Heyman has studied both music and dance and has written the only major overview of Korean dance in English, *Dances of the Three-Thousand-League Land.* Originally published in the United States in 1964, more than ten years before the publication of the first histories written by Koreans, it was reprinted in 1970 and again, in Korea, in 1981. Heyman is the most prolific non-Korean author in this field.

Because of the diverse contexts in which dance occurs, authors often combine dance research with other disciplines. Among the most prolific early Korean writers are Chang Sa-hun, a musicologist; Lee Du-hyon, a folklorist who has published extensively on masked-dance drama (for example, *Hanguk kamyonguk,* Korean Masked Dance Drama, 1969); and Song Kyong-rin, a former court musician and author of *Hanguk chont'ong muyong* (Traditional Korean Dance, 1979).

Trained dancers are now becoming more involved in writing. There have been recent publications by such authors as Kim Mae-ja, Moon Il-chi (for example, *Nabi ch'um ch'um sawuiae kwanhan yon'gu,* A Study of the Dance Movements of the Butterfly Dance, 1969), and Kim On-kyong (*Hanguk minsok muyong yon'gu,* A Study of Korean Folk Dance, 1982).

Both traditional and contemporary dance forms are being extensively documented on videotape by the National Theater and the Korean Culture and Arts Foundation. The foundation also maintains a library of both pictorial and written materials. These resources, accessible to the public, should prove valuable for research in the years ahead.

Noteworthy is the 1985 establishment of the Culture and Art Promotion Support Council. It was initiated by private businesspeople to assist the arts by fostering cooperation among businesses, artists, and cultural organizations. It is not yet clear whether its efforts will focus on performance, research, or publication.

Grants for dance research are provided by the International Cultural Society of Korea (now the Korea Foundation), the Korean Culture and Arts Foundation, and the Academy of Korean Studies, all government-supported.

A few Korean universities offer a degree with a major in dance; some focus on Western theatrical dance forms (ballet and modern dance), and others on traditional Korean forms. Some graduate students write their theses on traditional dance genres. These are published, usually in limited quantities, and may be distributed by the authors to interested individuals. Although students of the dance departments of Ewha Women's University and Sejong University are responsible for the majority of dance theses, students of Seoul National University and other colleges have also contributed to dance literature. No rigorous training programs in dance research methodologies have yet been established. With only a few exceptions—for example, Lee Sun-ock, who studied at New York University—the language barrier has prevented Korean students from studying in research-oriented dance programs in other parts of the world. This same barrier has prevented the study of Korean dance by many non-Koreans.

ALAN C. HEYMAN and LEE DU-HYON

KOREN, SERGEI (Sergei Gavrilovich Koren; born 6 September 1907 in Saint Petersburg, died 6 September 1969 in Moscow), Russian choreographer, coach, and art director. Koren graduated from the Leningrad Choreographic Institute in 1927, where he trained under the master teacher Vladimir Ponomarev. From 1927 to 1930 he was a soloist with the Leningrad Maly Theater, and then with the State Academic Theater for Opera and Ballet from 1930 to 1942. When he transferred to Moscow's Bolshoi Ballet in 1942 he remained a solo dancer until 1960 and thereafter until his death was a choreographer and coach. In the 1940s and 1950s he was also the director and choreographer for a number of folk dance companies. He prepared concert programs and staged dances in operas as well as a version of *Swan Lake* in Kishinev in 1968. He danced in the ballet films *Romeo and Juliet* as Mercutio, *Taras Bulba* as Ostap, and *Sombrero,* and starred in the first Soviet television ballet, *Count Nulin,* with choreography by Vladimir Varkovitsky.

Koren was an outstanding character dancer whose art embodied every aspect of the form: staged folk dances such as the Panaderos in *Raymonda* and concert programs of Spanish and other national dances; studies of characteristic national dances in roles such as Espada the matador in the Petipa-Gorsky *Don Quixote,* Nurali in Rostislav Zakharov's *The Fountain of Bakhchisarai,* and Zaal in Vakhtang Chabukiani's *Heart of the Hills;* and roles requiring characterization, such as Mercutio in Leonid Lavrovsky's *Romeo and Juliet* and Li Shan-fu in his *The Red Flower,* and Cavalier Ripafratta in Vasily Vainonen's *Mirandolina.*

Boris Lvov-Anokhin (1982) summarized Koren's contribution to character dance:

> All of Koren's work on the ballet stage was marked by a struggle against the 'passive role' of character dance and for its active place in ballet as an element of rich imaginativeness. . . . Koren recognized the dramatic significance of character dance, but he raised it to the summits of musical abstraction that, as it had seemed before him, were accessible only to classical dance.

A natural classical dancer with solid training and elongated, well-proportioned body lines (he often served as a model for well-known sculptors and artists), Koren chose character dance as the genre best suited to his artistic temperament, aggressive dancing style, and gift for acting. He had enormous stage presence; each of his numbers, even if it was as brief as a panaderos, elicited a storm of applause. Lvov-Anokhin quotes Irakly Andronikov, a notable Soviet author and art critic, as having said,

> Koren is inimitable! There will never be another dancer like him. His dance was expressive and meaningful to the limit. That sparkling series of consummate movements and poses lasted less than a minute, yet each of them could be regarded as the ultimate because it was invariably refined, unexpected, and determined.

Koren was honored with a number of awards: Merited Artist of the Russian Federation (1939); State Prize of the USSR (1950); People's Artist of the Kabardino-Balkarian ASSR (1957); and Merited Art Worker of the North Ossetian ASSR (1960).

BIBLIOGRAPHY

Bellew, Hélène. *Ballet in Moscow Today.* London, 1956.

Lvov-Anokhin, Boris. "Ego rysokoye iskusstvo tantsa v kharaktere." *Sovetskii balet* 5 (1982).

Lvov-Anokhin, Boris. *Sergei Koren* (in Russian). Moscow, 1988.

GALINA V. BELYAYEVA-CHELOMBITKO
Translated from Russian

KOROVIN, KONSTANTIN (Konstantin Alexeevich Korovin; born 23 December 1861 in Moscow, died 11 September 1939 in Paris), Russian-French scenery designer. In 1874 Korovin entered the Moscow Institute of Painting, Sculpture, and Architecture, where he studied principally as a landscapist. In 1885 he made the acquaintance of the art patron Savva Mamontov and became an important member of the Abramtsevo neonationalist colony. At this time Korovin began to work as a stage designer, contributing to Mamontov's productions of *The Snow Maiden (Snegurochka), Sadko, Khovanshchina, Prince Igor,* and other pieces. It was also in this period he became friends with Feodor Chaliapin.

In the late 1880s and early 1890s Korovin traveled throughout Europe and was greatly influenced by impressionism. He was also close to the *Mir iskusstva* (World of Art) group.

In 1900 Korovin was appointed resident designer for the Bolshoi Theater, where he worked on a number of productions, including Cesar Pugni's ballet *The Little Humpbacked Horse* (1901). From the early years of the century onward he was active in many opera, drama, and ballet productions. In 1923 Korovin emigrated to Paris, where, for the rest of the decade, he worked for a number of émigré troupes, though with little success.

Although not avant-garde in the sense that Natalia Goncharova and Mikhail Larionov were, Korovin is one of the most famous of Russia's stage designers. He belonged to the new generation of stylists at the end of the nineteenth century and was much indebted to neonationalism, impressionism, and Art Nouveau. During his lifetime he decorated eighty operas, thirty-seven ballets, and seventeen dramas. He brought to the Russian stage a vitality that was lacking in the conventional Imperial theaters, and, as Alexandre Benois recalled of the 1898 production of *Sadko,* "Korovin's decors amazed us by their daring approach" (Benois, *Reminiscences,* p. 197). Even so, Serge Diaghilev asked Korovin to design only one ballet for him, *Les Orientales* (Paris, 1910, assisted by Léon Bakst), perhaps because Korovin was too picturesque and paid little attention to scenic space and volume in his set design.

BIBLIOGRAPHY

Benois, Alexandre. *Reminiscences of the Russian Ballet.* Translated by Mary Britnieva. London, 1941.

Gusarova, Alla. *Konstantin Korovin* (in Russian). Moscow, 1990. Includes an English summary.

Kamensky, Alexander. *Konstantin Korovin.* Translated by Inna Sorokina. Leningrad, 1988.

Kogan, Dora. *Konstantin Korovin* (in Russian). Moscow, 1964.

Turchin, Valerii. *Konstantin Korovin* (in Russian). Moscow, 1991.

ARCHIVES. Bakhrushin Museum, Moscow. Tretiakov Gallery, Moscow.

JOHN E. BOWLT

KOSLOV, THEODORE (Fedor Mikhailovich Kozlov; born 4 [16] February 1882 in Moscow, died 21 November 1956 in Hollywood, California), Russian dancer, choreographer, and teacher. In films, in vaudeville, and at his schools, Theodore Koslov popularized and disseminated the imperial Russian dance tradition in the United States. He introduced American audiences to Serge Diaghilev's repertory in his unauthorized versions of Michel Fokine's ballets and pioneered the performance of Russian ballet in vaudeville. He also trained some of the first American classical dancers of the twentieth century.

Koslov graduated from the Moscow Theater School and entered the Bolshoi Ballet in 1900. He went to Saint Petersburg to attend Nikolai Legat's "class of perfection" and joined the Maryinsky Theater as a demi-soloist. In 1904 he returned to the Bolshoi for six years. His repertory encompassed both classical and character roles: Rothbart, the pas de trois, and the Spanish dances in *Swan Lake;* the Prince in *The Magic Mirror;* and Mato in *Salammbô.* He was remembered as a virtuoso who could perform a pirouette of eighteen revolutions.

Koslov, his brother Alexis, and his wife Alexandra Baldina danced in Diaghilev's first seasons, and also with Tamara Karsavina at the London Coliseum. In 1910 the Koslovs were the first Russian ballet dancers in United States vaudeville. Koslov also staged pirated versions of Fokine's *Schéhérazade, Cléopâtre,* and *Les Sylphides* for Gertrude Hoffman.

Koslov taught in New York and worked in London music halls until 1915, when he staged the Broadway shows *Maid in America, The Passing Show of 1915,* and *A World of Pleasure.* In 1916 he appeared in cabaret and on the Keith vaudeville circuit. In Los Angeles, Cecil B. De Mille signed him for a series of films. He opened a school there, appeared in more than twenty films, and staged ballets for operas and movie prologues. For Hollywood Bowl seasons from 1926 to 1939 he choreographed *Shingandi* and adapted Fokine's *Schéhérazade, Chopin Memories* (as he renamed *Les Sylphides*), *Petrouchka,* and *Le Spectre de la Rose.* At the invitation of and with support from the cultural elite of Dallas, Texas, Koslov formed the Koslov Ballet in 1929. Astutely gauging the expectation of his audiences, he again offered popularizations of the Russian ballet repertory, along with his own *Dionysia, The Romance of the Infanta,* and *Shingandi.* The company lasted until 1934.

Koslov's teaching was his lasting contribution. His school, with branches in Texas and Chicago, was modeled on the Imperial Theater School. He trained Agnes de Mille, Nana Gollner, and Dimitri Romanoff.

BIBLIOGRAPHY

Garafola, Lynn. *Diaghilev's Ballets Russes.* New York, 1989.

Krasovskaya, Vera. *Russkii baletnyi teatr nachala dvadtsatogo veka,* vol. 2, *Tantsovshchiki.* Leningrad, 1972.

Legat, Nikolai. "'The Class of Perfection' of the Imperial Ballet School." *The Dancing Times* (July 1931): 324–327.

Prevots, Naima. *Dancing in the Sun: Hollywood Choreographers, 1915–1937.* Ann Arbor, Mich., 1987.

SUZANNE CARBONNEAU

KRAKOWIAK. A gay Polish dance derived from folk dances in the region around Kraków, the *krakowiak,* or *cracovienne,* features a 2/4 meter, syncopated rhythm, and a quick tempo. Its characteristic rhythm of two eighth notes followed by a quarter note appeared in musical compositions as early as the sixteenth century. Since the eighteenth century, it has become common in music by Polish composers.

Sometimes danced by a couple but was usually performed by a larger number of dancers, the *krakowiak* features percusive sounds of stamping feet and the clicking of heels. Karol Czerniawski, a nineteenth-century scholar of Polish national dances, described it as follows:

> The [male] dancer grasps the waist of his partner, usually with his right arm but sometimes with his left, holds his free arm high in the air, and sets off on his round at an amble . . . vigorous and strong, stamping in time or striking the brass ringlets hung at his waist with his free hand to make a rattling sound. (Czerniawski, 1858, p. 73)

The boldest and strongest dancer led the others. He began the dance by singing in front of the musicians, an action later repeated by other dancers. Next he chased his partner, who then reversed roles and chased him. He punctuated the dance with stamping and heel-clicking in the air.

Like the *mazur,* or mazurka, the *krakowiak* was incorporated into a number of ballets. From the eighteenth century onward, stage presentations of the *krakowiak* set patriotic texts to its swaggering, rhythmic accompaniment, and operas and ballets popularized both the dance and the national sentiment. When Fanny Elssler danced a *cracovienne* as a solo in Joseph Mazilier's ballet *La Gipsy* at the Paris Opera in 1839, Théophile Gautier wrote in *La presse:*

> It is a combination of rhythmical precision, charming abandon, and an energetic and bouncy speed that surpasses the imagination, and the metallic chatter of her spurs, like castanets worn on the heels, adds a marked accent to the steps and gives the dance a character of joyful vivacity that is quite irresistible.

In Saint Petersburg, the Polish dancer Feliks Krzesiński (known as Kshessinsky in Russia) became a favorite of Tsar Nicholas I as a performer of Polish national dances on the stage of the Maryinsky Theater. Along with the *mazur* (mazurka) and *polonez* (polonaise), the *krakowiak* was among his specialities. He often performed these dancers with one of his daughters, Julia or Matilda, both of whom were members of the Imperial Ballet.

BIBLIOGRAPHY

Czerniawski, Karol. *O tańcach narodowych.* Warsaw, 1858.

Gautier, Théophile. *Gautier on Dance.* Translated and edited by Ivor Guest. London, 1986.

Glapa, Adam, and Alfonx Kowalski. *Tańce i zabawy wielkopolskie.* Wrocław, 1961.

Gloger, Zygmunt. *Encyklopeida staropolska.* 4 vols. Warsaw, 1900–1903. Reprint, Warsaw, 1972.

Grażyna Dąbrowska

KRAKOWIAK: A double-ring figure performed by the ensemble of Mazowsze, the Polish State Dance Company, a folkloric troupe founded in 1948 by Tadeusz Sygietyński and Mira Zimińska. (Photograph by D. Gładysz.)

KRASOVSKAYA, VERA (Vera Mikhailovna Krasovskaia; born 19 August [1 September] 1915 in Petrograd), Russian ballet critic and historian. Krasovskaya graduated from the Leningrad ballet school, where she studied under Agrippina Vaganova. In 1933 she joined the Kirov Ballet, dancing there until 1941. Her first press articles appeared in 1941. In 1946 she began studies at the Leningrad Ostrovsky Institute of the Theater (since 1961 it has formed part of the State Institute of Music, Theater, and Cinematography) and in 1951 joined its staff. Holder of a doctorate in art criticism since 1955, she gained a professorship in 1975.

A veteran ballet critic and historian, Krasovskaya has written over two hundred articles for various Russian and foreign ballet periodicals. For the most part these are profiles of Russian dancers and choreographers, analyses of their work, and surveys of Leningrad ballet seasons. In the latter half of the 1950s, which were marked by reaction against undue emphasis on ballet's dramatic element and by an appreciation of the need to restore dance to its preeminent position, Krasovskaya was in the forefront of those who strongly advocated new ideas and fresh approaches. In her many articles, such as "Lyricism and Drama in Ballet Theater," published in *Teatr i zhizn* (The Theater and Life) in 1957, Krasovskaya surveyed and conceptualized the modern ballet scene, identified laws governing the evolution of ballet and its trends, and made shrewd predictions, soon to come true. In her articles devoted to the state of the art in the USSR Krasovskaya analyzed various ballets and the work of individual dancers in light of the new elements they contributed to the heritage of Soviet art.

Parallel to her work as a critic, Krasovskaya has maintained a busy schedule of research in the field of ballet history. She first stepped into the realm of ballet scholarship at a time when Soviet ballet historians of the older generation, above all her teacher Yuri Slonimsky, were beginning a systematic study of the history of Russian ballet. They developed a series of books dealing with individual phenomena, periods, and leading personalities on the Russian ballet scene. Over the years she gathered enough material for a book summarizing these data and tracing the evolution of ballet, *Ballet Theater in Russia* (four volumes, 1958–1972), which contains important assessments of the aesthetic principles and philosophies of Marius Petipa, Michel Fokine, and other outstanding Russian choreographers. It provided the basis for a textbook on the history of Russian ballet, which appeared in 1978. Individual themes are elaborated by Krasovskaya in her *Anna Pavlova* (1964), *Nijinsky* (1974; an English translation appeared in 1979), and other books.

Krasovskaya next undertook a major project, her *magnum opus, Zapadno-evropeisky baletny teatr* (Western European Ballet Theater), the first comprehensive history of ballet outside Russia to appear in Russian since 1917. By 1996 four volumes had appeared, bringing the history through the Romantic period. In the meantime two more important biographies had been published: *Nikita Dolgushin* (1985) and *Agrippina Iakovlevna Vaganova* (1989). In addition to her many books Krasovskaya has contributed to a number of major reference works on ballet, including the *Soviet Encyclopedia of Ballet* (1981).

BIBLIOGRAPHY

Krasovskaya, Vera. *Russkii baletnyi teatr: Ot vozniknoveniia do serediny XIX veka.* Leningrad, 1958.

Krasovskaya, Vera. *Russkii baletnyi teatr vtoroi poloviny deviatnadtsatogo veka.* Leningrad, 1963.

Krasovskaya, Vera. *Russkii baletnyi teatr nachala dvadtatogo veka.* 2 vols. Leningrad, 1971–1972.

Krasovskaya, Vera. *Istoriia russkogo baleta.* Leningrad, 1978.

Krasovskaya, Vera. *Agrippina Iakovlevna Vaganova.* Leningrad, 1989.

Trabskii, A. I. *Bibliograficheskii ukazatel trudov Very Mikhailovny Krasovskoi.* Leningrad, 1980.

ELIZABETH SOURITZ
Translated from Russian

KRAUS, GERTRUD (born 6 May 1903 in Vienna, died 23 November 1977 in Tel Aviv), dancer, choreographer, and teacher. Kraus began her artistic career as a piano student at the Vienna State Academy. Through accompanying modern dance classes at the academy, she became interested in dance. After graduation she became a student of Gertrud Bodenwieser and for a short time danced in her company. In 1926 Kraus founded her own dance studio and gave her first solo recital. Among her students were Mia Slavenska, Fred Berk (Fritz Berger), and Manon Ehrfur (Chaufour).

Her dances, created in the expressionist style of the period, often dealt with social and Jewish topics. Kraus toured Europe alone and with her group. In 1930 she participated with the group in the International Dancers' Congress held in Munich, performing her dance cycle *Songs of the Ghetto* to music by Joseph Achron. In 1931, Kraus was invited to perform in Palestine and Egypt. She continued to dance and teach in Vienna until 1935; then she immigrated to Palestine. Settling in Tel Aviv, she founded the Gertrud Kraus Dance Group, which toured the country, often performing with the Palestine Orchestra (later the Israel Philharmonic) and within the framework of the Popular Opera.

Kraus's studio became the focal point of modern dance in Israel. In 1950 she helped to found and became the artistic director of the short-lived Israel Ballet (1950–1952). She gave her last solo performance in 1954. After that time she concentrated on teaching, choreographing pageants for several kibbutzim, and sculpting and painting at her home in the Ein-Hod artists' village near Haifa.

Most of Israel's dancers and choreographers regard her as the main influence in shaping their art. After a dance department was founded at the Rubin Academy of Music and Dance in Jerusalem, she became one of the chief teachers. She was appointed professor of dance when the department received academic accreditation. In 1963, Kraus was awarded the prestigious Israel Prize for her lifetime achievements. During her last years, she served as artistic adviser to the Batsheva Dance Company and the Kibbutz Dance Company.

Kraus's best-known dances were the 1926 *Strange Guest,* to music by Pablo Sarasate; the 1927 *Tired Death,* to music by Franz Salmhofer; the 1933 *A City Waits,* to music by Marcel Rubin; the 1937 *Spanish Dance,* about the Spanish Civil War, to folk tunes; the 1946 *A City Symphony,* to music by George Gershwin; and several solo and group works to music by Israeli composers, Marc Lavri and Yehoyachim Stutschewsky, among others.

In her last years Kraus was mainly active as a painter and sculptor. In 1988, three of Kraus's works—*The Poet's Dream, Allegro Barbaro,* and *Carousel*—were reconstructed by Kraus former dancer Naomi Aleskovsky and were performed in Israel and abroad, as well as videotaped.

[*See also* Israel, *overview article.*]

BIBLIOGRAPHY

Amort, Andrea. "Ausdruckstanz in Österreich bis 1938." In *Ausdruckstanz.* Wilhelmshaven, 1992.

Eshel, Ruth. *Dancing with the Dream.* Tel Aviv, 1991.

Hoffmann, Christine. "Deutschsprachige Ausdruckstänzerinnen und ihre Emigration." *Tanzforschung Jahrbuch* 4 (1993): 43–59.

Ingber, Judith Brin. "Conversations with Gertrud Kraus." *Dance Magazine* (March 1976).

Kraus, Hans Felix. *Die Tänzerin Gertrud Kraus.* Vienna, 1938. Includes fifteen lithographs.

Manor, Giora. *The Life and Dance of Gertrud Kraus.* Tel Aviv, 1977.

Manor, Giora. "Influenced and Influencing—Dancing in Foreign Lands." In *Ausdruckstanz.* Wilhelmshaven, 1992.

Manor, Giora, ed. *Gertrud Kraus* (Album). Tel Aviv, 1988.

GIORA MANOR

KRESNIK, JOHANN (born 12 December 1939 in Sankt Margarethen, Carinthia), Austrian dancer, choreographer, and company director, active in Germany. Growing up in rural Austria, Johann Kresnik was only three years old when his father was shot in his presence by Slovenian partisans during World War II, a traumatic experience that would haunt him for years to come and that would be reflected in many of his choreographic works. He had his first stage experiences at the Graz Theater, where as a teenager he appeared as a supernumerary in parts that required certain athletic abilities. From such small parts he progressed to dancing roles while he was still a student in the ballet school of the theater. He became a professional dancer upon joining the corps de ballet at the Graz Theater in 1959, thereafter following ballet master Jean Deroc to Bremen in 1960 and to Cologne in 1962.

In Cologne, Kresnik profited greatly from his training with Leon Woizikowski and from the opportunity to try his hand at choreography. His early pieces, created for local workshop performances, were marked by strong social criticism. Influenced by the snowballing social protests of the so-called student movement of the 1960s, his ballets, which he preferred to call "choreographic theater," showed an increasing political awareness. His treatments of topical subjects were heavily biased by his explicitly left-wing sympathies and were done somewhat in the style and manner of the early Soviet agitprop theater. His works were filled with aggression, hatred, brutality, vulgarity, and even obscenity. The expressive powers of the *danse d'école* rated very low.

In 1968, Kresnik became ballet master and choreographer at the Bremen Theater, where he worked in close collaboration with the drama department and where, during the next ten years, he fully developed his blockbuster, hard-edged, poster-style type of political revue. Working in Heidelberg from 1980 to 1989, he continued his crusade against what he considered the fascist, war-mongering tendencies of Western society, combining a deep-rooted hatred for Germany's Nazi past with contempt for America's capitalism and for what he viewed as American imperialism. He returned to Bremen in 1989 and stayed there until 1994, when he moved his dancers to Berlin. There his company forms an independent group within the playhouse setup of the Volksbühne (Folk Theater) and continues to present works with strong political content. Kresnik's advanced years have in no way mellowed his radical, left-wing bias.

Kresnik has also worked as a drama director and as a guest producer and/or choreographer in Vienna, Munich, Mannheim, Stuttgart, Salzburg, Moscow, Hamburg, and, at the invitation of the Goethe Institute, Brazil. While he has attracted an ever-growing following—mostly young people with antiestablishment leanings—he has not been without detractors. He has been accused of using coarse and blatant methods of attracting attention, including unconcealed communist propaganda, and of exhibiting obvious deficiencies in craftmanship. Nevertheless, there can be no doubt about the elementary force with which he overwhelms his audiences. His regular collaborators include the composers Walter Haupt, Peter Raben, and Kurt Schwertsik and the designers V. A. Wöfl, Anne Steiner, and Gottfried Helnwein.

Even a selected list of Kresnik's works must include the following important creations: *O Sela Pei* (1967), *Paradise?* (1968), *Susi Creemcheese* (1969), *PIGasUS* (1970), *Swan Lake & Co.* (1973), *The Nibelungs* (1974), *Jesus Ltd.*

(1977), *Mars* (1983), *Sale* (1984), *Sylvia Plath* (1985), *Pasolini* (1985), *Murderer Woyzeck* (1987), *Macbeth* (1988), *Oedipus* (1989), *King Lear* (1991), *Rosa Luxemburg* (1993), *Francis Bacon* (1993), *Frida Kahlo* (1994), *Othello* (1995), and *Hansel and Gretel* (1995).

BIBLIOGRAPHY

Kraus, Hildegard. *Johann Kresnik* (in German). Frankfurt am Main, 1990.

Schilcher, Susanne. *Tanztheater: Tradition und Freiheiten*. Hamburg, 1987.

Schmidt, Jochen. *Tanztheater in Deutschland*. Frankfurt am Main, 1982.

Schulz, Winfried. *Johann Kresnik: Choreographisches Theater*. Heidelberg, 1985.

HORST KOEGLER

KREUTZBERG, HARALD (born 11 December 1902 in Liberec [Reichenberg], Czechoslovakia, died 25 April 1968 in Muri, Switzerland), German dancer, choreographer, and teacher. Kreutzberg was one of the most important and impressive personalities of interpretive (or expressionist) dance, distinguished particularly by his theatricality and dramatic humor. He made his debut at the age of five in Wrocław (Breslau), in the operetta *Der Fidele Bauer*. At the age of eight he began studying with Erna Grondona in Leipzig. After further study at a school of the arts in Dresden, he began working as a dress designer. He entered classes for amateurs at Mary Wigman's Dresden school, but he was quickly promoted by Wigman to the training class, where he executed his first choreography, *Trommelspuk* (Drum Spook), to rhythmic accompaniment by bass drum and gong.

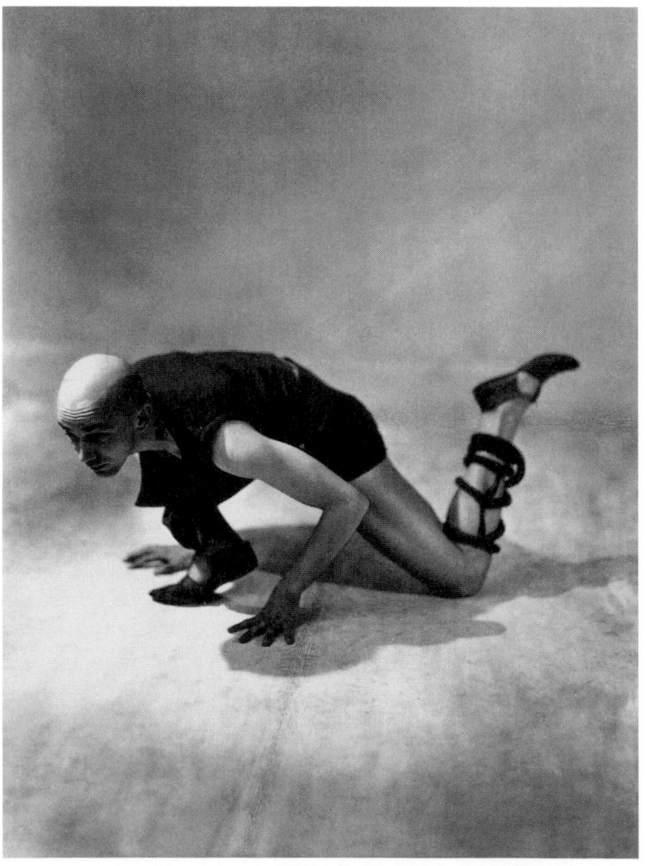

KREUTZBERG. A leading figure of *Ausdruckstanz*, the characteristically bald-headed Kreutzberg is seen here, c.1933, in a strikingly modern pose. (Photograph by Soichi Sunami.)

In 1922 Max Terpis, a Wigman student who had just been called to Hanover as a ballet master, hired Kreutzberg for his company. While at Hanover, Kreutzberg undertook his first guest performances, with the soloist Frieda Holst. In 1924 he followed Terpis to a position as solo dancer at the Berlin State Opera, where he was extremely successful in the role of Anxiety in Terpis's initial piece, *Die Nächtlichen* (Nocturnal), an expressive dance drama about human passions. In 1926 Kreutzberg took the role of the court jester in Terpis's ballet-pantomime *Don Morte*, based on a story by Edgar Allen Poe, at the Berlin Krolloper. For this role he had his head completely shaved, and thereafter he retained this feature permanently as his trademark. Friedrich Wilckens, who composed the music for *Don Morte* and became acquainted with Kreutzberg through this work, was Kreutzberg's closest collaborator for the rest of his life, writing the music for most of his ballets and acting as his manager.

In 1926 Kreutzberg and Elisabeth Grube, soloist of the Berlin State Opera, performed a solo and duet guest program. The role of the master of ceremonies in Gozzi's *Turandot*, presented at the Salzburg Festival, brought him international recognition. The following year Reinhardt gave him the speaking part of Puck in his production of *A Midsummer Night's Dream*, again for the Salzburg Festival. His acting experience led Kreutzberg to integrate speech into his dances, although dance remained the dominant medium of expression. A concert appearance with Reinhardt in New York followed; this introduced Kreutzberg to American audiences and brought him recognition as a representative of modern dance.

In 1927 Kreutzberg returned to Hanover as a soloist in Yvonne Georgi's company. With Georgi, in 1928 he gave a concert in New York. In 1929 he undertook with her the first of several American tours, chiefly of solo works. A Boston critic H. T. Parker wrote in 1929:

> [Mary] Wigman . . . sought a freedom, suppleness, variety and mastery of motion of which the classicists never dreamed, that the reformers saw only in distant vision. Mr. Kreutzberg—with Miss Georgi not too far behind—is full-furnished exemplar of this new liberty and abundance. His body is the ready, manifold servant of imagination and will. It takes, on the instant, any contour that he desires, be it curve or angle, perpendicular

> or diagonal; weaves itself into intricate patterns; vibrates to rhythm and counter-rhythm; defines the long line; snaps out the short phrase; runs a gamut of intensities and shadings.
>
> (Taylor, 1982, p. 202)

Kreutzberg's joint dance evenings with Georgi ended at the Berlin State Opera in 1931 with *Die Planeten* (The Planets) and *Le Train Bleu* (The Blue Train). Ruth Page was his partner in subsequent U.S. tours. Extended tours in Europe made Kreutzberg one of the best-known dancers of his time. At the Olympic Games festival in Berlin in 1936, Kreutzberg executed the group production *Waffentanz* (Weapons Dance); however, solos and duets continued to be the core of his choreographic work. He again made international tours after World War II, the last in 1959. After this he made individual appearances as an actor and worked on opera productions, but he devoted most of his time to teaching in the school he founded in 1955 in Bern.

As a dancer, Kreutzberg did not form a school in the way that Kurt Jooss did, but he was nevertheless one of the most important personalities in interpretive dance. His expressive style, reinforced by costumes and masks of his own creation, was revealed chiefly through dramatic power and comic movement. Oriented toward expressionistic gesticulation, with a stylization reduced to its essence, Kreutzberg remained true to the basic feeling of interpretive dance.

BIBLIOGRAPHY

Forster, Marianne. "Reconstructing European Modern Dance: Bodenwieser, Chladek, Leeder, Kreutzberg, Hoyer." In *Dance Reconstructed*, edited by Barbara Palfy. New Brunswick, N.J., 1993.

Kreutzberg, Harald. *Über sich selbst.* Detmold, 1938.

Parker, Henry Taylor. *Motion Arrested: Dance Reviews of H. T. Parker.* Edited by Olive Holmes. Middletown, Conn., 1982.

Pirchan, Emil. *Harald Kreutzberg.* Vienna, 1941.

Turbyfill, Mark. *Ruth Page—Kreutzberg.* Chicago, 1935.

Wille, Hansjürgen. *Harald Kreutzberg—Yvonne Georgi.* Leipzig, 1930.

FILM. Barzel Collection, Newberry Library, Chicago.

HEDWIG MÜLLER
Translated from German

KREUTZER, RODOLPHE (born 16 November 1766 in Versailles, died 6 January 1831 in Geneva), French violinist, composer, and teacher. Kreutzer received his first musical education from his father, a German immigrant musician. From 1778, Anton Stamitz taught him violin and composition. Sometime between 1782 and 1784 Kreutzer met Giovanni Battista Viotti and was much influenced by his style of playing and composing. He performed his own first violin concerto at the Concert Spirituel in 1784. Kreutzer came under the protection of Queen Marie Antoinette and was accepted as a member of the King's Chapel in 1783. From 1789 he was a leading virtuoso and helped to form the French violin school. Kreutzer began composing operas in 1790; in 1791 he had successes with *Paul et Virginie* and *Lodoïska,* both performed at the Opéra-Comique.

The Revolutionary period produced great activity in the musical world, and Kreutzer was very much in the center. He became professor of violin at the Conservatoire in 1795, a position he held until 1826. He toured in Italy in 1796, and in 1798, with Count Bernadotte in Vienna, he met Beethoven. In 1801 he was given the position of solo violinist at the Paris Opera, where he had considerable success with the opera *Astyanax.* In the following years he composed many operas. He had an important position in Napoleon's chapel, and after 1815 he became master of the King's Chapel. His career as a violinist ended in 1810, but he retained his official positions until 1826. At this time Kreutzer's style was out of fashion, and his last opera, *Mathilde,* was refused by the Opera in 1826.

Kreutzer is today mainly remembered as a representative of the French violin school. He composed a great many works for his instrument and was an important teacher. Beethoven dedicated a sonata to him in 1803.

Kreutzer's first ballet score, *Paul et Virginie* (1806), was a successful arrangement of melodies from his own *opéra comique,* and was performed at the Opera for at least fifteen years. His ballet scores of the Restoration were often created in collaboration with other musicians: Henri-Montan Berton and Louis-Luc de Persuis took part in *L'Heureux Retour* (1815), and Persuis in *Le Carnaval de Venise* (1816). For the wedding of the duc de Berry, Kreutzer participated in the creation of the *opéra-ballet Les Dieux Rivaux* (1816), together with Gaspare Spontini, Persuis, and Berton. Kreutzer's last two ballet scores, *La Servante Justifiée* (1818) and *Clari* (1820), were composed by him alone.

Kreutzer's music is simple and elegant, with a sense of local color. Too often his musical thinking does not progress beyond simple melody and accompaniment. The score of *Le Carnaval de Venise* typifies the pre-Romantic period in both structure and character. The overture is in two tempi, using melodies from the ballet and quoting a coda from Mozart's opera *Don Giovanni.* The score is full of Italian folk tunes, *barcarolas* and *tarantellas*, and as a leading motif Kreutzer used the famous Italian song "O Mamma, Mamma Cara."

BIBLIOGRAPHY

Beaumont, Cyril W. *Complete Book of Ballets.* London, 1937.

Constant, Pierre. *La Conservatoire Nationale de Musique et de déclamation.* Paris, 1900.

Fétis, François-Joseph. Obituary. *La revue musicale* (15 January 1831).

Guest, Ivor. *The Romantic Ballet in Paris.* 2d rev. ed. London, 1980.

Hardy, Joseph. *Rodolphe Kreutzer, sa jeuness à Versailles.* Paris, 1910.

Kling, Henri. *Rodolphe Kreutzer.* Brussels, 1898.

OLE NØRLYNG

KRIGER, VIKTORINA (Viktorina Vladimirovna Krieger; born 28 March [9 April] 1893 in Saint Petersburg, died 23 December 1978 in Moscow), dancer, ballet critic, founder and director of Moscow Art Ballet. Kriger was a leading ballerina of the Bolshoi Ballet from 1910 to 1948, and the founder in 1929 and director until 1938 of the Moscow Art Ballet. As a ballet critic and public figure she showed a striking individuality. After her graduation in 1910 from the Moscow theatrical school, where she was trained in Vasily Tikhomirov's class, Kriger achieved mastery of classical dance technique. A gifted actress, she had played minor dramatic roles at the Maly Theater in her childhood. Every role in ballet she created was primarily a human character, a brilliant alloy of virtuosic dance and human spirit.

Kriger's first leading roles were in productions by Aleksandr Gorsky. The Tsar Maiden in *The Little Humpbacked Horse* in 1915, Kitri in *Don Quixote* in 1916, and Swanilda in *Coppélia* in 1917 brought her public recognition as an actress-dancer. The demoniac Odile in Gorsky's version of *Swan Lake,* Zarema, consumed with passion, in Rostislav Zakharov's *The Fountain of Bakhchisarai,* the selfless Tao-Hoa in Lev Laschilin and Tikhomirov's *The Red Poppy,* the vicious fairy Carabosse in Asaf Messerer's version of *The Sleeping Beauty,* the cruel Stepmother in Zakharov's *Cinderella*—such was the wide range of characters created by Kriger, invariably vivid, active, and colored with her own individuality.

Kriger was one of the first dancers to appreciate the significance of Konstantin Stanislavsky's and Vladimir Nemirovich-Danchenko's innovative quests for the musical theater. As Nemirovich-Danchenko sought to educate and raise a "singing actor," Kriger saw her task in training a "dancing actor." The activities of the Moscow Art Ballet headed by Kriger attracted the attention of Nemirovich-Danchenko, who reputedly remarked, "This is a troupe that lives by our principles." The ballet troupe was later integrated into the company of Nemirovich-Danchenko's musical theater.

Kriger was among the first ballerinas to make Soviet ballet internationally famous. She successfully toured the United States and Europe from 1920 to 1923. Her activities as a critic and author are also worthy of note. She wrote the book *Moi zapiski* (My Notes) and many articles, essays, and reviews in Moscow newspapers, in which she upheld whatever was new, progressive, and talented in Soviet and world ballet. From 1955 to 1963 she was director of the Bolshoi Theater Museum. Kriger was awarded the State Prize of the USSR in 1946.

BIBLIOGRAPHY

Borel, Ludmila. "Viktorina Kriger." *Sovetskii Balet,* no. 2 (1983).
Chudnovskii, Mikhail. *Viktorina Kriger* (in Russian). Moscow, 1964.
Iving, Viktor. *Viktorina Kriger* (in Russian). Moscow, 1928.
Kriger, Viktorina. *Moizapiski.* Moscow, 1930.
Raffé, W. G. "What the Russians Are Trying to Do in Ballet." *Dance Magazine* (March 1948): 32–39.
Swift, Mary Grace. *The Art of the Dance in the U.S.S.R.* Notre Dame, 1968.

LUDMILA I. BOREL
Translated from Russian

KRISHNAMURTHI, YAMINI (born 1933 in Karnataka), Indian dancer and choreographer. Yamini Krishnamurthi was trained in *bharata nāṭyam* under the guidance of Rukmini Devi for five years and participated in various dance dramas at Kalakshetra. She was further trained by Conjeevaram Elappa Pillai and Tanjore Kitappa Pillai, and she studied Kuchipudi with Venugopalakrishna Sharma of Kuchipudi and Oḍissi with Pankajcharan Das of Puri in Orissa.

Krishnamurthi gave her first public performance, known as *Arengetram,* in Madras in 1957. She moved to Delhi in 1958 with her family. Her younger sister, Jyotishmati, led the musicians for Yamini's recitals for many

KRISHNAMURTHI. Seen here in a pose from Kuchipudi, Krishnamurthi is also a skilled performer of *bharata nāṭyam.* (Photograph from the archives of The Asia Society, New York.)

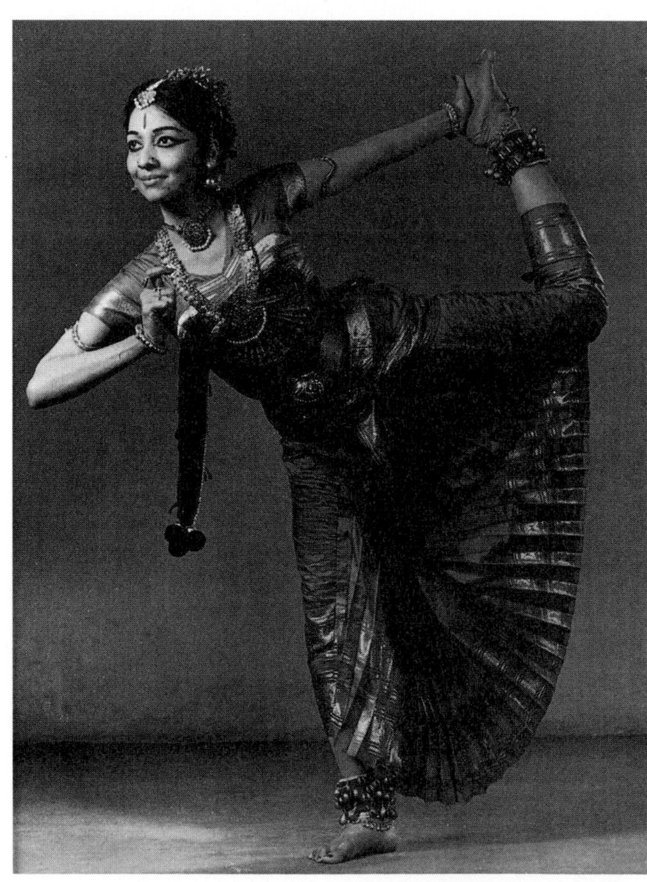

years. When in Delhi Yamini taught dance for some time at Sangeet Bharati. Recently she has choreographed a Vedic dance drama taking hymns from the *Ṛgveda*, the ancient scriptures, and using Vedic chants.

Krishnamurthi was influenced by the *pandanallur* style of *bharata nāṭyam*. Her *nṛtta* (pure, rhythmic dance that is free from depicting a story or mood) is chiseled and dynamic. Her lines are arresting and her movements powerful and energetic. She has set standards that have influenced younger dancers. Her *abhinaya* (expressive dance) is provocative; she is uninhibited in displaying passion within the traditional framework. She has tremendous assurance and a theatrical stage presence.

Krishnamurthi lives in Delhi and runs a school called Nritya Kaustubha on land given to her by the government of India. She has been honored by the Central Sangeet Natak Akademi and the government of India. A twenty-minute color documentary, produced by the Films Division of the government of India and directed by Balawant Gargi, records Krishnamurthi's *bharata nāṭyam* dances and an Oḍissi dance. She has written *Natya* (1983), a monograph on Indian classical dance, and an autobiography, *A Passion for Dance* (1995) with Renuker Khandekar. In 1990 she began work on a television series on classical dance and its relation to architecture, temples, and Sanskrit literature.

BIBLIOGRAPHY

Kothari, Sunil, ed. *Bharata Natyam: Indian Classical Dance Art*. Bombay, 1979.

Krishnamurthi, Yamini. *Satya Bhama: The Aesthetic Ideal of Womanhood*. Bombay, 1973.

Krishnamurthi, Yamini. *Natya*. Madras, 1983.

SUNIL KOTHARI

KRIZA, JOHN (born 15 January 1919 in Berwyn, Illinois, died 18 August 1975 in Naples, Florida), American dancer and teacher. An especially versatile and popular leading dancer with Ballet Theatre for twenty-five years, John Kriza, the son of Czech immigrants, began studying dance in Chicago at an early age. His earliest teachers were Mildred Prchal, Bentley Stone, and Walter Camryn; he later studied with Anton Dolin, Pierre Vladimiroff and, Valentina Pereyaslavec.

Kriza received his professional start from Ruth Page, who hired him in 1938 for the government-sponsored WPA Ballet. In 1939 he toured South America with Page's Chicago Civic Opera Ballet. Arriving in New York, he joined Ballet Theatre in 1940. The first role created on him was in Dolin's *Romantic Age* (1942); he subsequently originated roles in Antony Tudor's *Dim Lustre* (1943), Jerome Robbins's *Fancy Free* (1944), George Balanchine's *Waltz Academy* (1944), Bronislava Nijinska's *Harvest Time* (1945), Simon Semenoff's *Gift of the Magi* (1945), Michael Kidd's *On Stage!* (1945), Robbins's *Interplay* (1945) and *Facsimile* (1946), Agnes de Mille's *Fall River Legend* (1948), Herbert Ross's *Caprichos* (1950), Kenneth MacMillan's *Winter's Eve* (1957), Ross's *Concerto* (1958) and Bentley Stone's *L'Inconnue* (1965).

Kriza accumulated a vast and diverse repertory, with the title role of Eugene Loring's *Billy the Kid* being his most celebrated part. He danced lead roles in de Mille's *Rodeo, Tally Ho,* and *Rib of Eve;* Michel Fokine's *Les Sylphides, Petrouchka, Bluebeard,* and *Helen of Troy;* Tudor's *Romeo and Juliet, Jardin aux Lilas, Dark Elegies,* and *Offenbach in the Underworld;* Massine's *Aleko;* Frederick Ashton's *Les Patineurs;* and David Lichine's *Graduation Ball.* His more classical roles included the male leads in *Giselle, Swan Lake,* and *Aurora's Wedding.*

Particularly noted for his dramatic abilities, Kriza also embodied a distinctly American style. Although not a classical virtuoso, he was praised for his lyrical and poetic qualities. He remained with Ballet Theatre until his 1966 retirement from the stage but always pursued outside ventures during layoff periods. He toured South America with the Kirstein-Balanchine American Ballet Caravan in 1941, creating roles in several ballets, including Tudor's *Time Table,* and he guested occasionally with the Chicago Opera Ballet and the New York City Ballet. He performed in nightclubs; on Broadway in *Folies Bergère* (1940), *Panama Hattie* (1941), and *Concert Varieties* (1944); and in summer stock in *Kiss Me, Kate* and *Brigadoon.*

Following his retirement, Kriza served for several years as assistant to American Ballet Theatre's directors. He continued to coach various companies and teach; during the 1970s he was on the dance faculty of University of Indiana at Bloomington. He made his last stage appearance at American Ballet Theatre's thirty-fifth anniversary gala in January 1975.

BIBLIOGRAPHY

Lansdale, Nelson. "Versatile John Kriza." *Dance Magazine* (July 1954): 33–34.

Payne, Charles. *American Ballet Theatre.* New York, 1978.

Terry, Walter. Obituary. *New York Times* (20 August 1975).

SUSAN REITER

KRÖLLER, HEINRICH (born 25 July 1880 in Munich, died 25 July 1930 in Würzburg), German dancer, choreographer, ballet master, and opera producer. At a time when ballet had uncertain prospects, Kröller gave new life and radiance to theatrical dance in Germany and neighboring countries by adapting classical ballet to the expressionist theater. He may be viewed, with Michel Fokine and Rudolf Laban, as an early twentieth-century innovator. These three men, so close in age, represent profoundly different visions of dance.

Born into a middle-class family, at the age of nine Kröller became a student of Flora Jungmann in Munich's Court Theater Ballet School. By the age of twenty he was an official student soloist; in 1903 he was named solo dancer, and in 1906 first solo dancer. Wanting more recognition, however, he left Germany and found it at the Paris Opera, performing with Carlotta Zambelli and Léo Staats. In the fall of 1907 Augustin Berger lured him to the Dresden Opera with a seven-year contract. In 1912 Kröller married Julia Bergmann, an esteemed Munich solo dancer; the couple had two sons.

The German tour of the Ballets Russes awakened Kröller's choreographic fantasies, which were reinforced by the new impulses of the Dalcroze school in Hellerau. When choreographic research for his Dresden partner, prima ballerina Clara Gabler, led him in 1915 to the post of ballet master in Frankfurt, Kröller's previously constricted energies exploded in opera dances and ballet pieces that brought him widespread attention. After his years of apprenticeship, Kröller returned to his native Munich in 1917, as ballet master, and began what has been referred to as the Heinrich Kröller era.

In the fall of 1919 Kröller assumed the additional post of ballet director at the Berlin State Opera, which he held until the fall of 1922. It was in this stronghold of modern theater that he proved himself. There, the success of his version of *Die Josephslegende* in February 1921 won him a permanent place in the German theater world. His own dancing, as well as his choreography and direction, contributed greatly to his reputation.

In an effort to lure Kröller to Vienna, the composer Richard Strauss wrote to him, "I can offer you only one sphere of activity, the like of which, I believe, cannot be found in Europe." The prospect of having a great composer near him led Kröller to sign a five-year contract with the Vienna State Opera and to cancel his Berlin contract while maintaining his Munich post. He was a tireless creator, and the works choreographed in 1922 for these three leading theaters included *Der Grüne Heinrich* (Greenhorn Henry), *Carnaval, Neue Silhouetten, Sylvia, Die Josephslegende,* and *Schéhérazade.*

In Munich, Kröller worked out plans that were marked by an emphasis on the contemporary. In 1924 he began linking his choreographic works to the music of new tonal composers such as Béla Bártok, Igor Stravinsky, Ernst Krenek, and Arthur Honegger. His modern ballet evenings were to be an evolutionary counterweight to the revolutionary modern dance movement, which was then dominant. The idea that ballet should be dismantled and that genuine dance could be shaped only outside the theater was foreign to Kröller's convictions. For him, a work had to contain at least a dramatic core and usually had to tell a story. His dramatic sensitivity required credibility and clarity of subject, from which sprang the components that shaped the dance. He felt that new forms and solutions could be found by transformation, without rejecting the tradition of theatrical dance. On this point Fokine and Kröller agreed.

Kröller stopped dancing in 1925, but he continued as ballet master and remained much sought after as an opera director. His production for the first performance of *Die Vögel* (The Birds; 1920), to music by Walter Braunfels, was regarded as a landmark because of its choreographic fantasy. It persuasively resolved arguments about the search for contemporary operatic forms. Other works—*Mikado* (1926), *Das Geheime Königreich* (The Secret Kingdom; 1928), *Orfeo* (1929), *Schwanda der Dudelsackpfeifer* (Schwanda the Bagpiper; 1929), and *Zigeunerbaron* (The Gypsy Baron; 1930)—excelled through their sensitivity of style and wealth of imagination.

By December 1927 Kröller's only commitment was to Munich, where he had been working for years with Leo Pasetti, a stage and costume designer who shared his production values. Together they produced forty successful works. The principal performers of his modern ballet repertory in Munich were Johanna Tolzer, Anny Gerzer, Walther Matthes, and Otto Ornelli; the theatrical importance of Kröller's works can be read in the names of their conductors—Bruno Walter, Karl Böhm, Robert Heger, and Richard Strauss among them.

"There is only one dance; we speak a language that has various dialects," was Kröller's maxim, delivered at the artistic exchange of ideas at the Third Convention in 1930. That same year, an illness, diagnosed too late, led to his death on his fiftieth birthday.

BIBLIOGRAPHY

Mlakar, Pia, and Pino Mlakar. "Eine Gedenkstunde für Heinrich Kröller." *Das Tanzarchiv* 28 (July 1980): 382–394.

Mlakar, Pia, and Pino Mlakar. *Unsterblicher Theatertanz: 300 Jahre Ballettgeschichte der Oper in München.* Wilhelmshaven, 1992.

See, Max. "Tänzer, Choreograph und Regisseur in der Zeitenwende." *Neu Zeitschrift für Musik* 9 (1970).

PIA MLAKAR and PINO MLAKAR

KRONSTAM, HENNING (born 29 June 1934 in Copenhagen, died 28 May 1995 in Copenhagen), Danish dancer, director, producer, and teacher. Perhaps the most influential person in the Royal Danish Ballet in the second half of the twentieth century, Kronstam was trained by Harald Lander and Vera Volkova. He entered the ballet school of the Royal Theater in Copenhagen in 1943. He made his official debut with the Royal Danish Ballet as the Drummer in *Graduation Ball* in 1952, the same year he became a member of the company. He was appointed *solodanser* (principal dancer) in 1956 and *førstesolodanser* in 1966, the same year he became head of the ballet school.

Kronstam's great breakthrough as a romantic dancer came in 1955, when, within a few months of his twentieth birthday, he danced the role of the Poet in the first Danish production of George Balanchine's *Night Shadow* and that of Romeo in *Romeo and Juliet,* which was created by Frederick Ashton for the Royal Danish Ballet. Mona Vangsaae was his Juliet.

Tall, dark, and handsome, and possessing a superb technique, Kronstam was a classical dancer first and foremost. When the Russian classics *Swan Lake, The Sleeping Beauty,* and *The Nutcracker* came to Denmark for the first time in full-length productions, he danced the role of the prince in each of them. He also danced the entire Bournonville repertory: his portrayal of James in *La Sylphide* beautifully expressed his understanding of the feelings and anxieties of this romantic youth. Although he was trained classically, Kronstam developed a deep sensitivity to new choreographic tendencies and other dance styles. When international choreographers came to Copenhagen in the 1950s and 1960s, they all wanted Kronstam to dance their works. He was Balanchine's Apollo on *Apollon Musagète,* and, later, as the producer of that work in Copenhagen, he showed great understanding of Balanchine's neoclassical style. He danced the works of Glen Tetley, Murray Louis, and Paul Taylor, but his most impressive triumph in the modern dance repertory was as Iago in José Limón's *The Moor's Pavane* on 1971.

By then it was clear that the *danseur noble* had developed into an impressive and strong character dancer. Kronstam was brutal as Jean in Birgit Cullberg's *Miss Julie* and absolutely mad as the Teacher in Flemming Flindt's *The Lesson,* but he was most moving as the title figure in Roland Petit's *Cyrano de Bergerac,* where his artistic temper ably combined the comic and the tragic. His artistic temperament was also evident in John Cranko's *The Lady and the Fool,* where, as in many other ballets, he danced with Kirsten Simone. The leading couple of the period, they also toured abroad as guest artists with, among other companies, the Chicago Ballet. Kronstam danced about 130 different roles; no other Danish dancer had so broad an artistic range.

While his rivals Erik Bruhn and Flemming Flindt made their careers abroad, Kronstam stayed home, and Danish audiences loved him for it. He was honored with a knighthood in 1964.

Kronstam served as artistic director of the Royal Danish Ballet from 1978 to 1985. During his tenure he stressed the classical line, and his greatest success was the first Bournonville Festival, held in 1979. After he resigned as director of the company, he continued on as a producer and coach until 1993. Kronstam was an extremely important influence on several generations of Danish dancers. No one had his keen understanding of the repertory and his appreciation for the style of the company.

[*See also* Royal Danish Ballet.]

BIBLIOGRAPHY

Aschengreen, Erik. "Henning Kronstam." *Saisons de la danse,* no. 91 (February 1977): 20–24.

Aschengreen, Erik. "Kronstam, Henning." In *Dansk biografisk leksikon.* 3d ed. Copenhagen, 1979–.

Aschengreen, Erik. "The Royal Danish Ballet Season of 1954–1955." *Dance Chronicle* 18.3 (1995): 419–426.

Jackson, George. "Falling in Love Again." *Dance View* 9 (June 1992): 31–37.

Kragh-Jacobsen, Svend. *Twenty Solodancers of the Royal Danish Ballet.* Copenhagen, 1965.

Tomalonis, Alexandra. "Bournonville's Gifts." *Dance View* 9 (June 1992): 42–54.

Tomalonis, Alexandra. "Dancing for Ashton and Balanchine: Talking with Henning Kronstam." *Dance View* 11 (Summer 1994): 24–55.

ERIK ASCHENGREEN

KṚṢṆĀṬṬAM. A genre of Indian dance drama, *kṛṣṇāṭṭam* depicts the life of the Hindu god Kṛṣṇa. It is performed exclusively by an all-male troupe at Guruvayur Temple in Kerala from November through May.

Facts on the origin and development of *kṛṣṇāṭṭam* are few. Records indicate that its Sanskrit text, the *Kṛṣṇagīti* (songs about Kṛṣṇa), was composed in 1652 by Manaveda of the royal family of Calicut. No records have been found of the first performance of the theatrical version. According to oral tradition, *kṛṣṇāṭṭam* continued as a court art until 1958, when the troupe moved to Guruvayur.

Changes have occurred in *kṛṣṇāṭṭam* since its departure from court, such as the increased use of codified hand language and a modified style of singing, both showing the influence of *kathakaḷi,* a later genre of dance drama. *kṛṣṇāṭṭam's* choreography still adheres to traditions at least 125 years old, taught at Guruvayur to students who learn through performing minor roles and observing the performances of master artists.

The seclusion of *kṛṣṇāṭṭam* in the court and temple, and its similarity to *kathakaḷi* in costume and makeup—which *kathakaḷi* borrowed from *kṛṣṇāṭṭam*—have obscured public awareness of *kṛṣṇāṭṭam's* unique features. Conspicuous among them are its choreography, masks, and two rarely portrayed scenes of Kṛṣṇa's life. Examples of exceptional choreography are the pure dances accompanying the prayer songs that conclude each episode and the dances performed in battle and journey scenes. Both body movements and dance patterns are largely circular. The dancing is accompanied by two vocalists singing the text and by musicians playing a gong, cymbals, and three drums—*suddha maddaḷam, topi maddaḷam,* and *iṭekkya*—or to

KṚṢṆĀṬṬAM. A dance drama depicting scenes from the life of Kṛṣṇa, *kṛṣṇāṭṭam* is performed exclusively by an all-male troupe at Guravayur Temple in Kerala. In this scene, a bird character, at left, appears with Kṛṣṇa. (Photograph © 1985 by Jack Vartoogian; used by permission.)

percussion alone. The wooden masks, two to three feet high, are strikingly designed; some have several heads and others have grotesque features. The two scenes rare in traditional Indian theater are in the first episode, the baby Kṛṣṇa learning to walk, and in the final episode, his death.

[*For related discussion, see* Kathakaḷi.]

BIBLIOGRAPHY

Ashton-Sikora, Martha Bush, and Robert P. Sikora. *Krishnattam.* Oxford, 1993.

Ragini Devi. *Dance Dialects of India.* 2d rev. ed. Delhi, 1990.

Sarabhai, Mrinalini. "Krishnattam." *Marg* 19 (March 1966): 43–45.

MARTHA BUSH ASHTON-SIKORA

KSHESSINSKY FAMILY, Polish-Russian family of dancers. Notable members were the father, Feliks, and three children, Julia, Iosif, and Matilda.

Feliks Kshessinsky (Pol., Feliks Adam Walerian Krzesiński; Russ., Feliks Ivanovich Kshesinskii; born 5 [17] February 1821 in Warsaw, died 3 [16] June 1905 at his estate at Siverskaya, Russia), character dancer, choreographer, and teacher. As a boy, Kshessinsky studied at the Warsaw Ballet School under Maurice Pion and Roman Turczynowicz. By the time he was fourteen, in 1835, he had begun to make professional appearances, and in 1838 he was engaged by the Warsaw Ballet. Promoted to principal dancer in 1843, he danced in the Polish capital until 1852, appearing at first in classical roles but later devoting himself entirely to character dances and mimed roles. He was generally acclaimed as the "best of the best" dancers of the *mazur*, the *krakowiak*, and the *polonez*, and he counted among his fans no less a personage than Tsar Nicholas I of Russia, an avid balletomane.

At the invitation of the tsar, Kshessinsky made his Russian debut as The Best Man in the ballet *Kraków Wedding (Les Noces Paysannes)* at the Aleksandrinsky Theater in Saint Petersburg on 30 January 1853. His performance was such a success that he was invited to join the ballet of the Maryinsky Theater, where he soon gained great popularity through his performances of Polish, Hungarian, and Gypsy dances. Because of his talent for acting, he was also frequently cast in important mime roles: the King of Nubia in *La Fille du Pharaon*, the Khan in *The Little Humpbacked Horse*, Claude Frollo in *Esmeralda*, the High Brahmin in *La Bayadère*, Inigo in *Paquita*, and others. For the Maryinsky, he staged productions of several ballets, including *Robert and Bertram, or Two Thieves* (1858), and *divertissements*, including a suite of *Lezghian Dances* (1864) set to music by the Polish composer Jan Stefani.

In addition to his theatrical work, Kshessinsky gave private lessons in character dancing. As in Poland, he was famous especially for his execution of the mazurka, both on the stage and in the ballroom, and he is credited with making this dance one of the most popular in Russia. In her memoirs, his younger daughter Matilda quotes a review of her father's performance of a mazurka:

> It is difficult to imagine a prouder, livelier or more fiery performance of this national dance. Kschessinsky gave it a stamp of grandeur and nobility. It was due to him, or as it has been said,

to his lightness of leg, that the mazurka first received the overwhelming popularity which it was to enjoy in our capital's high society. (Kshessinska, trans. Haskell, 1960, p. 15)

In 1898 Feliks Kshessinsky was awarded the title of Honorary Artist of the Imperial Theaters.

Julia Kshessinska (Iulia [Genrietta] Feliksovna Kshesinska; born 22 April [3 May] 1865 in Saint Petersburg, died January 1969 in Paris), character dancer. The elder daughter of the renowned character dancer Feliks Kshessinsky, Julia Kshessinska studied ballet as a nonresident student at the Imperial Theater School. Upon her graduation in 1883, she joined the ballet company of the Maryinsky Theater as a *coryphée,* and in 1894 she was promoted to the rank of second dancer. Like her father, she gained fame as a character dancer and was considered to be an excellent mime. She was adept at the mazurka, the Kshessinsky family specialty, which she often performed on the Maryinsky stage with her father.

Described by contemporaries as a very beautiful woman, Julia Kshessinska was apparently lacking in neither vanity nor daring, for her personnel file in the Maryinsky archives reflects a certain number of fines, for unauthorized alterations of costumes and for wearing an excessive amount of jewelry on stage. Among her more important roles were Damaianti in Marius Petipa's *The Talisman* and La Nuit de Nil in his *Cinderella.* She retired from the Maryinsky in December 1902 and a few months later married Baron Aleksandr Logguinovich Zeddeler, who thereupon left the Preobrazhensky Regiment to enter the Ministry of Communiciations. Widowed in 1921, Julia Kshessinska settled with her younger sister Matilda in Paris, where she died in 1969 at the advanced age of 103.

Iosif Kshessinsky (Iosif Feliksovich Kshesinskii; born 5 [17] February 1868 in Saint Petersburg, died 18 August 1942 in Leningrad), ballet dancer and teacher. Following in the footsteps of his elder sister, Iosif Kshessinsky studied ballet at the Imperial Theater School in Saint Petersburg and, upon his graduation in 1886, joined the ballet company at the Maryinsky Theater. Like his sister and his father, he became known as a character dancer and as a master of pantomime.

During his career at the Maryinsky, Kshessinsky danced in *divertissements* in numerous operas as well as in ballets by Marius Petipa and Michel Fokine. His main parts included Inigo in *Paquita,* Florestan in *The Sleeping Beauty,* the Pharaoh and the King of Nubia in *La Fille du Pharaon,* the Rajah in *La Bayadère,* the Colonel in *Halte de Cavalerie,* Claude Frollo and Phoebus in *Esmeralda,* Marcus Antonius in *Les Nuits Egyptiennes,* Conrad in *Le Corsaire,* and Viscount René in *Le Pavillon d'Armide,* among others. During the Soviet era, he created the parts of Pantalone and the Favorite in productions of, respectively, *Pulcinella* (1926) and *A Serf Ballerina* (1927).

From 1896 to 1905 Kshessinsky was a teacher at the Imperial Theater School, where Anna Pavlova and Lydia Kyasht were among his pupils. In 1905 he was expelled from the Maryinsky for his active part in the dancers' strike, but he rejoined the company in 1914 and remained a member until 1928. After the Russian Revolution, Kshessinsky was again engaged to teach at the ballet school, from 1918 to 1927, under Soviet auspices. In 1929 *The Red Poppy* was staged under his direction at the Vybork House of Culture in Leningrad, and Kshessinsky himself performed the role of the Soviet ship captain. During the years 1928–1930 he organized and led a touring youth company in which some leading Soviet dancers, including Konstantin Sergeyev, began their careers in ballet. He died in 1942, during the Nazi siege of Leningrad.

Matilda Kshessinska (Matil'da-Mariia Feliksovna Kshesinskaia; born 19 [31] August 1872 at Ligovo, near Saint Petersburg, died 6 December 1971 in Paris), ballet

KSHESSINSKY FAMILY. Matilda Kshessinska and Feliks Kshessinsky pose in Polish costume, c.1904, prior to dancing the mazurka, the family specialty. Renowned as a character dancer, Feliks Kshessinsky was eighty-three years old when this photograph was taken. (Photograph from the Dance Collection, New York Public Library for the Performing Arts.)

dancer and teacher. Like her siblings, Julia and Iosif, Matilda Kshessinska was trained at the Imperial Theater School in Saint Petersburg and, upon her graduation in 1890, was invited to join the ballet company at the Maryinsky Theater. After her debut, at the age of eighteen, she rapidly rose through the ranks. She was appointed *ballerina* in 1892, *prima ballerina* in 1893, and *prima ballerina assoluta*, an honor rarely accorded, in 1895. She performed as leading dancer of the Imperial Ballet until 1904 and continued to appear as a guest artist thereafter, until the Revolution in 1917. She is generally recognized as the last great Russian ballerina of the imperial age.

As a student at the Imperial Theater School, Matilda Kshessinska (also known as Mathilde and as Kschessinska II) had been impeccably trained by such master teachers as Lev Ivanov, Christian Johansson, and Enrico Cecchetti. Thoroughly schooled in the academic classical technique, she soon found favor with Marius Petipa and quickly distinguished herself as an interpreter of his works, notably as Marietta in *Kalkabrino,* as the Shadow of Mlada in *Mlada,* as the Wheat Ear (or Corn) in *Les Saisons,* and as Odette-Odile in *Swan Lake.* (She was the first Russian ballerina to master the thirty-two *fouettés* that are now regularly performed in the Black Swan pas de deux.) Her greatest roles, however, were Aurora in *The Sleeping Beauty,* the title role in *Esmeralda,* Thérèse in *Halte de Cavalerie,* Lise in *La Fille Mal Gardée,* Nikia in *La Bayadère,* and Aspicia in *La Fille du Pharaon.* She appeared as a guest artist in Vienna (1903), Paris (1908–1909), and Warsaw (1909), and she danced as guest ballerina with Serge Diaghilev's company in the 1911/12 season, appearing in London, Monte Carlo, Vienna, and Budapest. Notably, Kshessinska also danced in several of Fokine's works—*Eunice* in 1907, *Les Sylphides* in 1911, and *Eros* in 1915—but found herself not well suited to his choreographic style.

KSHESSINSKY FAMILY. A studio portrait of Matilda Kshessinska in costume as Galatea, from Lev Ivanov's *Acis and Galatea* (1896). (Photograph from the State Museum of Theatrical and Musical Arts, Saint Petersburg.)

She was, first and foremost, a Petipa ballerina, and she gloried in the *demi-caractère* roles that allowed her to display her bravura, cheerfulness, and refined classical form. Although Bronislava Nijinska later dismissed Kshessinska's virtuoso dancing as vulgar acrobatics, Tamara Karsavina claimed that she was not only a spectacular technician but a supreme actress as well. Whatever the truth about her dancing, Kshessinska was undoubtedly a great star of the imperial Russian ballet stage.

She was also a dominant force in backstage politics and a figure of some importance in Russian social history. As the youthful mistress of the tsarevich, who later became Tsar Nicholas II, and subsequently as the morganatic wife of the Grand Duke Andrei, Kshessinska enjoyed the wealth, prestige, and power of an aristocrat. In one famous incident, in 1901, a small fine was levied against her by Prince Sergei Volkonsky, director of the Imperial Theaters, for altering her costume in *La Camargo.* She immediately appealed to the tsar, who ordered the fine rescinded, whereupon Volkonsky resigned his post and Kshessinska's preeminent position in the Imperial Theaters, and in imperial favor, was reaffirmed. For a number of years, her palace on the Kronversky Prospect was a center of social life in Saint Petersburg, and it eventually proved a fitting site for Lenin's address to the citizens of Petrograd after his return from exile in 1917.

In 1920 Kshessinska settled in France and in 1921 married the Grand Duke Andrei, thereafter styling herself as H.S.H. The Princess Marie Romanovsky-Krassinsky. In 1929 she opened a ballet studio in Paris, where she lived and taught for many years. Among her pupils were Tatiana Riabouchinska, Boris Kniaseff, André Eglevsky, and such famous ballerinas as Yvette Chauviré and Margot Fonteyn. Her teaching was acclaimed for its lyric quality and its emphasis on especially beautiful *port de bras.*

KSHESSINSKY FAMILY. Matilda Kshessinska with her pet goat, which appeared with her in Perrot's *Esmeralda,* revived especially for her in 1899. Known as a virtuoso, Kshessinska was acclaimed in this ballet for her "eloquent and expressive acting." After her triumph in the part, no other Maryinsky ballerina danced it until she left the stage in 1917. (Photograph reprinted from Kshessinska, 1960.)

Kshessinska made her final appearance on stage at a gala event at Covent Garden, London, in 1936. At the age of almost sixty-four, she performed a traditional Russian dance, for which an appreciative audience rewarded her with numerous curtain calls and baskets of flowers.

BIBLIOGRAPHY

Bakhrushin, Yuri. *Istoriia russkogo baleta.* 3d ed. Moscow, 1977.

Breazeale, Helene. "In Search of Mathilde Kschessinska." *Dance Magazine* (March 1995): 72–73.

Dąbrowski, Stanislaw, and Zbigniew Raszewski, eds. *Słownik biograficzny Teatru Polskiego, 1765–1965.* 2 vols. Warsaw, 1973, 1994.

Gregory, John. *The Legat Saga.* 2d ed. London, 1993.

Karsavina, Tamara. *Theatre Street.* Rev. and enl. ed. London, 1948.

Kouznetsova, Tatiana. "L'impériatrice Mathilde." *Danser* (September 1993): 42–45.

Krasovskaya, Vera. *Russkii baletnyi teatr nachala dvadtatogo veka,* vol. 2, *Tantsovshchiki.* Leningrad, 1972.

Kshessinska, Matilda (Marie Romanovsky-Krassinsky). *Souvenirs de la Kschessinska.* Paris, 1960. Translated by Arnold L. Haskell as *Dancing in Petersburg: The Memoirs of Kschessinska* (London, 1960).

Macdonald, Nesta. "Kschessinska with Diaghilev in 1911." *The Dancing Times* (November 1971): 73–76.

Maynard, Olga. "Kschessinska at Ninety-nine." *Dance Magazine* (November 1971): 22–24.

Pudełek, Janina. *Warszawski balet romantyczny, 1802–1866.* Warsaw, 1968.

Teliakovsky, Vladimir. "Memoirs: St. Petersburg Ballet." Translated by Nina Dimitrievich. *Dance Research* 9 (Spring 1991): 26–39.

Teliakovsky, Vladimir. "Memoirs: The Balletomanes." Translated by Nina Dimitrievich. *Dance Research* 12 (Spring 1994): 41–47.

Wiley, Roland John, ed. and trans. *A Century of Russian Ballet: Documents and Eyewitness Accounts, 1810–1910.* Oxford, 1990. See especially "Recollections of T. A. Stukolkin, Artist of the Imperial Theatres," pp. 108–134.

ARCHIVES. The manuscript of Iosif Kshessinsky's memoirs is preserved in the Library of the A. A. Bakhrushin State Theatrical Museum in Moscow. Letters belonging to Matilda Kshessinska can be found in the Saint Petersburg Theatrical Library. The archives of the Maryinsky Theater, in Saint Petersburg and Moscow, include the personal files of all four members of the Kshessinsky family.

CLAUDE CONYERS
Based on materials submitted by Janina Pudełek, Victor V. Vanslov, and Irina Klyagin

KUCHIPUDI. The traditional Indian dance drama Kuchipudi is performed by male dancers belonging to the brahman caste, highest in the hierarchy of the Hindu caste system and usually indicative of the occupation of scholar, teacher, or priest. The word *Kuchipudi* is derived from the name of a village situated in the estuary of the Krishna River in Andhra Pradesh, a state in the center of the southeastern coast of India. Kuchipudi is an abbreviated form of the original name of the village, Kuchelapuram or Kushilavapuram ("city of actors"); it has been the nurturing ground of this form of dance drama for about four hundred years.

The period between the sixth and tenth centuries saw the emergence of a new form of Indian religion, the cult of *madhura bhakti* (sweet devotion). Its devotees believed that God could be approached best not through austere rituals and stern puritanism but through the ecstatic outpouring of song, dance, and drama, in which God was visualized as the Cosmic Beloved, the Supreme Soul and Spirit *(paramātman).* The singer–dancer–actor personifies the lover, the human soul *(jīvātman)* longing for union with the Beloved.

The sixteenth-century Siddhendra Yogi belonged to such an order of mystics. From boyhood he was a devotee of the god Kṛṣṇa (Krishna). Married in childhood to a beautiful girl but kept apart from her until she attained maturity, he devoted his time to intense study of the scriptures and became a noted scholar. On the night that he was to consummate the marriage, he was unable to find a ferryman who would take him across to his bride's village and decided to swim. There was a torrential downpour and Siddhendra Yogi, facing a watery death, cried out to Kṛṣṇa to come to his aid. The Divine Voice came, assuring him of protection but extracting the promise that he would renounce his marriage vows and devote his life solely to singing and dancing to the deity's glory. The Kuchipudi dance drama was revealed to him in that moment of enlightenment.

KUCHIPUDI. Mallika Sarabhai in a pose from Kuchipudi, a traditional dance drama from the village of the same name. Created by the sixteenth-century composer Siddhenda Yogi as a form of devotion to Kṛṣṇa, Kuchipudi is traditionally performed only by members of the brahman caste. (Photography © 1994 by Jack Vartoogian; used by permission.)

Siddhendra Yogi's devotion found expression in a beautiful lyric opera, *Bhāmākalāpam,* which has as its central character Satyabhāmā, the proud and passionate wife of Kṛṣṇa. Also called *Srī Kṛṣṇaparijātam* or *Parijātāpahāranam,* it recounts the story of how Satyabhāmā compelled Kṛṣṇa to plant the *parijāta* (a celestial tree) in her garden, having been told by the mischievous sage Nārada that Kṛṣṇa had given a flower from that tree to his other wife, Rukminī. The role of Satyabhāmā is a complex and demanding one, portraying a wide range of emotions. It is the most coveted role in the Kuchipudi repertory, and it is mandatory for every Kuchipudi dancer to perform it at least once during his lifetime.

Siddhendra Yogi trained a group of young brahman boys to enact the Kuchipudi roles and traveled with his company throughout Andhra. Their performance so enthralled the presiding governor, Nawab Abdul Hasan Tanisha, that he gave them Kuchipudi village. Since that time the village has belonged to ten traditional brahman families, and every male child born into one of these families must take a vow that, to his dying day, he will sing and dance in honor of Kṛṣṇa. Thus the art has been maintained as a sacred obligation. Even though the village's traditional troupe is exclusively male, in recent times women have been allowed to learn the female roles in these dance dramas.

The technique employed in Kuchipudi is harmoniously balanced between the three aspects of Indian dance, *nṛtta, nṛtya,* and *nāṭya,* as expounded in the ancient texts. *Nṛtta,* or abstract dance that stresses rhythmic movement involving the entire body, usually precedes, concludes, or punctuates a story. *Nṛtya* conveys the subject matter with coordinated hand gestures, footwork, and body movement. *Nāṭya* involves dramatic acting prominently; one of its features is *vācika abhinaya,* or acting with the spoken word and accompanying gestures. Solo numbers within the main story are either entirely rhythmic—for example, *jātīśvaram* and *tillānā,* which display the dancer's technical virtuosity—or combine rhythmic and expressive dance—for example, the many *śabdams*, in which phrases of acting alternate with phrases of dance. Some of the well-known *śabdams* are *Kṛṣṇa Śabdam* (the milkmaid invites Kṛṣṇa), *Daśāvatāra* (the ten incarnations of the god Viṣṇu), *Maṇḍuka Śabdam* (Viṣṇu's rescue of the elephant king from the crocodile), and *Rāmapattābhiśeka Śabdam* (the story of the epic *Rāmāyaṇa* up to Rāma's coronation). Such solo dances usually serve as interludes within the main story.

Another popular number from the Kuchipudi repertory, *Bālagopāla Tharaṅgam,* describes the childhood pranks and exploits of Kṛṣṇa, interspersed with rhythmic sequences and concluding with a dance on a metal plate *(thālī)*—a remarkable balancing feat. Sometimes the dancer places a pot of water on his head while dancing on the plate. The *taraṅgam* is an extract from *Kṛṣṇa-Līlā-Taraṅgiṇī,* an opera in Sanskrit composed by Tirtha Narayana, a disciple of Siddhendra Yogi.

In addition to classical Sanskrit texts, Kuchipudi employs Telugu, the spoken language of Andhra. It is a mellifluous tongue that lends itself admirably to the immense range of dramatic portrayal that is the essence of this style.

Kuchipudi costume is usually a more ornamental version of the *dhoti,* the lower garment worn by men in India. One end of it covers the chest, overlapping the blouse if the performer is enacting a female role. A much-ornamented false braid is worn by male dancers performing female roles, especially that of Satyabhāmā, who was proud of her long hair. The male roles are costumed according to the character, divine, heroic, demonic, comic, or saintly. The music is also adapted to the theme and uses arrangements and instrumentation similar to those of *bharata nāṭyam*, but featuring more lilt and charm.

[*See* Asian Dance Traditions, *overview article. For general discussion, see* India, *article on* History of Indian Dance. *See also the entries on Reddy, Vedantam Satyam, and Vempati Chinna Satyam.*]

BIBLIOGRAPHY

Acharya, C. R., and Mallika Sarabhai. *Understanding Kuchipudi.* New Delhi, 1992.

Khokar, Mohan. *Bharata Natyam and Kuchipudi.* New York, 1976.

Kothari, Sunil. "The Tradition of Kuchipudi Dance-Dramas." *Quarterly Journal of the National Centre for the Performing Arts* 14 (June 1985): 1–10.

Massey, Reginald, and Jamila Massey. *The Dances of India: A General Survey and Dancer's Guide.* London, 1989.

Ragini Devi. *Dance Dialects of India.* 2d rev. ed. Delhi, 1990.

Raman, Pattabhi. "Interview: Swapnasundari, a Thoughtful Terpsichorean." *Sruti* (Madras), no. 13 (November 1984): 21–31.

Uma Rama Rao, K. *Kuchipudi Bharatam, or, Kuchipudi Dance.* Delhi, 1992.

RITHA DEVI

KUDELKA, JAMES (born 10 September 1955 in Newmarket, Ontario), Canadian dancer, choreographer, and company director. Born on a farm on the outskirts of Toronto, Kudelka was one of six children in a family that encouraged interest in the arts. He began dance lessons when he was four, and in 1965, when he was ten, he entered the National Ballet School in Toronto, where he proved to be a precocious student. When he was eleven he mounted George Balanchine's *Concerto Barocco* on his classmates and created his own dance steps for the parts he could not remember. At fourteen, he caught the eye of ballerina Veronica Tennant with a pas de deux, *Encounter*, choreographed to excerpts from Bach's *Goldberg Variations.* Tennant was to become a mentor to Kudelka when he joined the National Ballet of Canada in 1972 at sixteen.

Kudelka's premature entrance into the company before completing his training was the result of an unusual maturity coupled with a rebelliousness that the school had found difficult to control. That Kudelka was a misfit during his formative years and was physically distanced from his family had important repercussions on his choreography; he has produced a significant body of work dealing either overtly or obliquely with themes of angst, rejection, repression, loneliness, and humiliation. Indeed, many of his ballets carry a menacing undercurrent and explore the dark side of human nature.

Within a year of joining the National Ballet of Canada in 1972, Kudelka created for the company choreographic workshop a pas de deux for Tennant and Winthrop Corey entitled *Sonata*, to music by César Franck. Two other workshop ballets, *A Party* and *Washington Square*, joined the company's repertory in 1977 and 1979, respectively. The former, set to music by Benjamin Britten, follows the

KUDELKA. Jacques Drapeau and members of Les Grands Ballets Canadiens in a 1986 performance of Kudelka's *In Paradisum*, created in 1983 to music by Michael J. Baker. The unisex costumes were designed by Denis Joffre; lighting was by Nicholas Cernovitch. (Photograph by Dominique Durocher; used by permission.)

KUDELKA. Martine Lamy and Robert Conn in *Pastorale,* mounted for the National Ballet of Canada in 1990. Kudelka is noted for his unusually inventive pas de deux, which frequently demonstrate the beauty of linear tension between the partners, as seen here. (Photograph by Lydia Pawelak; used by permission.)

romantic entanglements at a chic get-together. The latter, set to an original score by Michael Conway Baker and inspired by the famous Henry James novella, depicts the psychological interplay between the spinster Catherine Sloper (a tour de force for Tennant), her tyrannical father, and her feckless suitor. The work was revived in 1996.

As a dancer, Kudelka's clean technique, speed, musicality, and dramatic flair led to his promotion to soloist in 1976. He excelled in strong character portrayals in story ballets as well as abstract roles in neoclassical works, and he was also considered a very sensitive partner. Unfortunately, Kudelka's years with the National Ballet were not entirely happy ones. Even though he was appointed resident choreographer in 1980, he chafed under the leadership of artistic director Alexander Grant, whom he felt did not give high priority to the creation of original work.

In 1979 Kudelka spent seven months in Europe, where he was particularly affected by such dance works as Kenneth MacMillan's antiwar ballet *Gloria.* In 1980 he was invited to participate in a choreographic seminar held at the Banff Centre for the Arts in Alberta during which each choreographer was matched with a different composer each afternoon for the creation of a new work. Thrust into this world of modern dance, with its use of parallel placement, grounded center, and equality between the sexes, Kudelka experienced an epiphany about the possibilities of choreographic vocabulary.

The Rape of Lucrece (inspired by Shakespeare's poem) and *Playhouse,* both created in 1980, constituted Kudelka's first public foray into parallel placement rather than turnout. *Playhouse,* set to a driving score by Dmitri Shostakovitch, epitomized Kudelka's disenchantment with the company. A Master (played alternately by a female and male dancer) attempts to rouse her/his charges into some kind of action while they affect indifference or incomprehension. (The dancers not only hated the physical challenges of the work, they rebelled against its implied attack against them.) Continued discontent with the company led Kudelka to accept an invitation in 1981 to join the Montreal-based Les Grands Ballets Canadiens as a principal dancer.

Kudelka was given *carte blanche* to create original work, and in 1984 he was appointed resident choreographer, having produced his first acknowledged masterpiece the previous year. Set to an original score by Michael J. Baker, *In Paradisum* is a moving portrayal of grief and reconciliation with death. In 1986 a chronic back problem forced Kudelka to give up dancing.

The flowering of Kudelka's choreographic craft in the encouraging climate of Les Grands Ballets Canadiens—despite eventual differences over repertory and casting with artistic director Lawrence Rhodes—cannot be underestimated. Key works during this period, such as *Alliances* (1984), set to Brahms's Piano Concerto no. 1 for Les Grands; *The Heart of the Matter* (1986), set to Sergei Prokofiev's Piano Concerto no. 2 for the Joffrey Ballet (Kudelka's first piece for a high-profile American company); and *Dreams of Harmony* (1987), set to Schumann's Second Symphony for the San Francisco Ballet, sealed his reputation as a world-class choreographer. These works also marked a shift away from narrative pieces into explorations of abstract dance set to large-scale instrumental music. Critics have praised Kudelka's deep understanding of the emotional landscape of his scores.

Kudelka has no one characteristic style *per se,* but his works do share a similar choreographic language. They are distinguished by complex partnering with difficult hand manipulations and innovative lifts, dense footwork, a vocabulary that combines classical ballet and modern dance, fast changes in weight and direction, unpredictable and unexpected movement patterns, off-balance and shared weight, and structures based on tension and struggle. Kudelka, who has called himself a "conscientious observer," once stated that all of his works deal with love, sex, and death. He described his choreography to one critic as "nonlinear, dramatic, abstract narratives," and even his pure dance pieces are infused with an ambiguity of implied relationships.

Excellent examples of Kudelka's versatility in both classic and contemporary dance are found in two pieces from 1991: *Fifteen Heterosexual Duets,* set to Beethoven's "Kreutzer Sonata" for Toronto Dance Theatre, and for Les Grands Ballets Canadiens, *Désir,* which uses Prokofiev's waltzes from the opera *War and Peace* and the ballet *Cinderella.* Each work contains only duets, but of totally different types. Whereas *Désir* is a lush, romantic, and passionate on-pointe ballet, the more seasoned couples in the witty *Fifteen Heterosexual Duets* are anchored in real life. In both pieces, however, Kudelka delineates character, as each duet within each piece is its own sharply etched cameo of a relationship. The Toronto theater community honored *Fifteen Heterosexual Duets* with the 1991 Dora Mavor Moore Award for Choreography.

Kudelka reentered Toronto's ballet world in stages. In 1988 he was invited to create a piece for the opening of the Betty Oliphant Theatre at the National Ballet School; *Signatures,* a humorous history of ballet, used dancers from the National Ballet of Canada, including prima ballerina Karen Kain, another Kudelka muse. His sumptuous epic *Pastorale,* set to Beethoven's Sixth Symphony and presented in 1990 by the National Ballet of Canada, contrasts the behavior of urban sophisticates and country dwellers. *New York Times* critic Anna Kisselgoff wrote that *Pastorale* confirmed Kudelka as "the most imaginative choreographic voice to come out of ballet in the last decade." His *Musings,* a showcase for Kain created for Toronto's Glory of Mozart Festival in 1991, also entered the National Ballet of Canada's repertory.

Following the success of *Pastorale,* Reid Anderson, then artistic director of the National Ballet of Canada, invited Kudelka to rejoin the company. Kudelka, who had become a freelance choreographer in 1990, accepted the position, which he assumed in 1992. Kudelka elected to call the National Ballet of Canada position artist in residence rather than resident choreographer so that he could coach, teach, be an artistic consultant, and appear on stage as well as create new works. Since returning to the company, Kudelka has performed to great acclaim such character roles as Doctor Coppélius in Bruhn's *Coppélia* and Friar Laurence and the Duke of Verona in Cranko's *Romeo and Juliet.*

Again able to mount full-scale productions rather than ballets with minimal sets and costumes, Kudelka returned choreographically to the complex and often controversial narrative subjects that had dominated his early work. His 1993 version of *The Miraculous Mandarin,* set to Béla Bartók's famous score, dealt with child abuse and had an openly homosexual theme. His 1994 presentation of *Spring Awakening,* inspired by the Frank Wedekind play and using original music by Michael J. Baker, focused on the psychological damage of repressed sexual feelings and also touched on homosexuality. *The Actress,* set in 1994 to Frédéric Chopin preludes and including clever pastiches of the standard repertory, depicted a backstage look at the tangled relationships of a prima ballerina. A watershed in Kudelka's career occurred in 1995 with the lavish National Ballet of Canada production of *The Nutcracker,* his first full-length ballet.

Kudelka has also continued to create highly acclaimed abstract allegorical ballets set to great pieces of music. With the San Francisco Ballet he has presented, among other works, *The Comfort Zone* (1989), set to Beethoven's Triple Concerto, and *The End* (1992), set to Brahms's Fourth Symphony. Switching to the avant-garde, in 1995 he set *Terra Firma* to a score by Michael Torke. *Cruel World* (1994), set to Petr Tchaikovsky's *Souvenir de Florence,* and *States of Grace* (1995), set to Paul Hindemith's *Mathis de Maler Symphony,* are among the many works he has contributed to American Ballet Theatre. Kudelka works are also in the repertory of the Royal Winnipeg Ballet, Ballet British Columbia, the Boston Ballet, the Houston Ballet, the BalletMet (Columbus, Ohio), and the Compañía Nacional de Danza (Mexico City). He has made solos for contemporary dancers Nancy Colohan (New York) and Toronto's Peggy Baker and Patricia Fraser, as well as contemporary dance companies, including Chicago's Hubbard Street Dance Company, Montreal's Danse Cité, and Les Ballets Jazz de Montréal. A Kudelka *Romeo and Juliet* duet is featured in Rhombus Media's 1990 television video *Prokofiev by Two.* A behind-the-scenes look at the creation of *The Actress* is the subject of Anthony Azzopardi's documentary film *Making Ballet,* which first aired on CBC on 15 February 1995. In 1993 Kudelka was honored with Canada's most prestigious dance prize, the Jean A. Chalmers Choreographic Award.

KUDELKA. Karen Kain and Rex Harrington in *The Actress,* created especially for Kain by Kudelka in 1995. (Photograph by Lydia Pawelak; used by permission.)

Kudelka's first work set on a European company was *Le Baiser de la Fée,* to Stravinsky's score, for Birmingham Royal Ballet in the summer of 1996. Kudelka was appointed artistic director of the National Ballet of Canada, 1 June 1996.

BIBLIOGRAPHY

Ayre, John. "Four Hard Lives in the Dance Business." *Saturday Night* (October 1976): 40–46.

Citron, Paula. "James Kudelka: Profile of an Enigma." *Dance in Canada* (Spring 1985): 10–18.

Citron, Paula. "James Kudelka: Out of the Depths." *Dance Magazine* (February 1994): 94–97.

Citron, Paula. "Holiday Treat." *O'Keefe Centre's Performance Magazine* (December 1995–February 1996): 49–56.

Doob, Penelope Reed. "James Kudelka, Then and Now." *National Ballet of Canada's Performance Magazine* (December 1995–February 1996): 11–18.

Kain, Karen, with Stephen Godfrey and Penelope Reed Doob. *Movement Never Lies: An Autobiography.* Toronto, 1994.

Kareda, Urjo. "The Turning Point." *Saturday Night* (March 1985): 55–58.

Officer, Jill, ed. *The Encyclopedia of Theatre Dance in Canada* (electronic). Toronto, 1989.

Rafelman, Rachel. "Snowflakes, Fairies, and a Really Big Tree." *Toronto Life* (December 1995): 50–55.

Tobias, Tobi. "Found Objects." *New York Magazine* (30 May 1994).

Windreich, Leland. "Full Circle." *Dance International* (Fall 1993): 10–15.

Young, Pamela. "The Master." *Maclean's* (21 February 1994).

PAULA CITRON

KUN, ZSUZSA (Zsuzsa Kunwasa; born 9 December 1934 in Budapest), Hungarian dancer. A pupil of Ferenc Nádasi from 1943 to 1949 at the ballet school of the Budapest Opera, Kun continued her studies in the 1950s at the Bolshoi Ballet and at the Choreographic Institute, both in Moscow. Her tutors in Russia included Marina Semenova, Elisaveta Gerdt, Aleksandr Lapauri, and Olga Lepeshinskaya.

Engaged by the Budapest Opera in 1949, Kun became a soloist in 1953. Beginning with an impressive Zarema in Rostislav Zakharov's *The Fountain of Bakhchisarai* in 1952, she danced all principal parts in the repertory, soon becoming the leading ballerina of the company and keeping that position until the early 1970s. In addition to her unforgettable title roles in Leonid Lavrovsky's *Giselle* and *Romeo and Juliet,* she covered the entire stylistic range of the Budapest Ballet, dancing the Gypsy Sári in Gyula Harangozó's *The Kerchief* (1953) and the title role in his *Schéhérazade* (1959); Odette-Odile in both versions of Messerer's *Swan Lake* (1960 and 1969); the principal parts in Imre Eck's *Le Sacre du Printemps* (1963) and in Petr Gusev's *Sleeping Beauty* (1967); Flavia in László Seregi's *Spartacus* (1968); Lise in Frederick Ashton's *La Fille Mal Gardée* (1971); and the title role in Seregi's *Sylvia* (1972). Even after a knee injury she could still re-create some of her roles, but she retired from the stage in 1977.

In addition to her participation in almost all guest performances of the Budapest Ballet abroad, Kun danced as a guest artist in the Soviet Union, Switzerland, East Germany, London, and Sydney between 1956 and 1972. She appeared with the Saratov Ballet in *The Kerchief* (1956), in concert programs in 1958, and danced Zarema (1960), Giselle (1962 and 1968), and Juliet (1969) at the Bolshoi. Her Giselle was a great success in Tbilisi (1960), in Novosibirsk, Ufa, and Perm (1962), in Odessa and Tallinn (1968), and at the Kirov (Maryinsky) Theater (1968). Her Odette-Odile was seen in Yerevan and Baku (1965), Zurich (1966), Basel (1968), Berlin and Prague (1972), and she danced Aurora in Yugoslavia twice (1968 and 1972).

Kun toured the Soviet Union and visited Munich with a concert program in 1966; she danced three times in East Germany in 1960, appeared in Vichy in 1961, and was guest ballerina with London's Festival Ballet four times between 1960 and 1965, in *The Nutcracker* and *Swan Lake.* She danced the principal parts in these ballets in Sydney in 1972. A biographical film on her was produced in 1967. She directed and narrated the Hungarian television film *Ballet Shoe.*

Her renderings were highly sensitive, intellectually and emotionally fervent, with a poetic style and technique of great clarity, particularly individual as Giselle and as Juliet. At home and abroad she was looked on as a *prima ballerina* of the classical-dramatic school but owing to her portrayals of the more intellectual heroines of *Le Sacre du Printemps, The Miraculous Mandarin,* and *Spartacus,* she was also acknowledged as a worthy exponent of modern works. She was a ballerina of most convincing expressive power in both lyrical and dramatic roles.

Kun's honors included second prize at the World Youth Festival, Bucharest (1953); first prize at the World Youth Festival, Warsaw (1955); the Liszt Prize (1960); and the Kossuth Prize (1962).

BIBLIOGRAPHY

Herf, Estelle. "Zsuzsa Kun, Ballerina from Budapest." *Ballet Today* (March 1964): 33–35.

Körtvélyes, Géza, and György Lőrinc. *The Budapest Ballet: The Ballet Ensemble of the Hungarian State Opera House.* Vol. 1. Translated by Gedeon P. Dienes and Éva Rácz. Budapest, 1971.

Kun, Zsuzsa. "A Subjective Comment after a Budapest Ballet Night." *Hungarian Music News,* no. 1 (1978): 4–5.

GÉZA KÖRTVÉLYES

!KUNG SAN DANCE. The !Kung San, a hunting and gathering people, live in the northwestern section of the Kalahari desert in Botswana. Their nightlong healing dance is the most important of their dances. It is the cen-

!KUNG SAN DANCE. Ceremonial dancers circle around the */gao* (bending, at center), a shaman who has begun to go into a trance. Another shaman holds his arm. (Photograph reprinted from Marshall, 1969.)

tral event in the !Kung healing tradition, which is more than a medical system that treats disease; it is also essential to the community's enhancement and maintenance.

The dance involves the entire community and is a major social as well as ritual event. It is an opportunity for self-expression and reestablishing the individual's sense of group identity. Although the dances are done for enjoyment, the healing of sickness, both manifest and latent, remains critical.

The dance is performed at night, usually about four times a month. Women sit around a fire, singing and rhythmically clapping; men dance around the singing women, who sometimes join the men. As the singing and dancing intensifies, *n/um* (spiritual or healing energy) is activated in the healers, most of whom are among the dancing men. As their *n/um* "heats up," the healers experience *!kia* (an enhancement of consciousness). At this time, the healer comes into contact with the spiritual world, which makes healing possible. All who are at the dance are healed. Before the sun rises fully the next morning, the dance usually ends. Those at the dance find it exciting, joyful, and powerful. "Being at a dance makes our hearts happy," the !Kung say.

The music of the dance comes basically from part singing and the women's complex clapping. Several healing songs are used, named for "strong" things that are considered to possess *n/um,* such as honey, the elephant, and the mamba snake. The structure of the healing dance music is intricate and varies endlessly, with disciplined improvisation inside the bounds of repeated musical phrases. The eerie sound of the dancers' leg rattles adds another dimension to the songs and sharply clapped cadences. The music is a vehicle of transcendence for the healers and others participating in the dance.

Mood changes many times during the dance; several periods of intense healing may be interspersed with periods when no one is in the *!kia* state. The healers' passage into *!kia* is terrifying and dangerous, requiring that the healers enter the "death of *!kia.*" Healing is accomplished through a laying on of hands; the sickness is taken into the healers and then expelled from them. Healing is difficult, painful work, as expressed in the healers' *kowhedeli,* their intense moans and shrieks, as they expel the sickness. These moans and shrieks themselves become part of the healing dance sound.

The healing dance is open and public. Becoming a healer is not an unusual event. By the time they reach adulthood, approximately 50 percent of the men and more than 10 percent of the women have become healers.

In the traditional healing dance, men and women make different but equally valued contributions, which reflects the egalitarian nature of !Kung life. The healers readily acknowledge their reliance on the singers. The women sing and clap to provide not only impetus for *!kia* but also protection for the healers as their spirits travel outside their bodies. The healing dance is thus not only an art but also a concerted effort of the entire community to resolve social conflict, banish misfortune, and reaffirm its spiritual life.

[*See also* Southern Africa.]

BIBLIOGRAPHY

England, Nicholas M. *Music among the Zu/wasi and Related Peoples of Namibia, Botswana, and Angola.* New York, 1995.

Katz, Richard. *Boiling Energy: Community Healing among the Kalahari !Kung.* Cambridge, Mass., 1982.

Lee, Richard B. *The !Kung San.* Cambridge, 1979.

Marshall, Lorna. "The Medicine Dance of the !Kung Bushmen." *Africa* 39.4 (1969): 347–381.

Schadeberg, Jürgen. *The Kalahari Bushmen Dance.* London, 1982.

Sugawara, Kazuyoshi. "Interactional Aspects of the Body in Co-Presence: Observations on the Central Kalahari San." In *Culture Embodied,* edited by Michael Moerman and Masaichi Nomura, Senri Ethnological Studies, no. 27. Osaka, 1990.

FILM. J. Marshall, *N/um Tchai: The Ceremonial Dance of the !Kung Bushmen* (Watertown, Mass.: Documentary Educational Resources, 1965).

RECORDING. *Healing Music of the Kalahari San* (New York: Folkways Records, 1982), with notes by Richard Katz, Megan Biesele, and M. Shostak.

RICHARD KATZ and MEGAN BIESELE

KUNQU is an ancient and sophisticated Chinese performing art that integrates vocal and instrumental music, drama, and dance. *Kunqu* originated in Kunshan county in Zhejiang Province and is sometimes called "Kunshan Opera." It became popular in the fourteenth century in this region, during the Yuan dynasty (1271–1368) and the succeeding early Ming dynasty (1368–1644).

The origins of *kunqu* can be traced as far back as the Tang dynasty (618–906), and in the Song dynasty (906–1271) the melodies arose that would ultimately be transformed into *kunqu* tunes. These matured during the Song and the succeeding Yuan dynasty. By the Qing dynasty (1644–1911), *nanxi* (southern theater) and *zaju* (vaudeville) further evolved into Kunshan, Yiyang, and other regional musical theaters. The main difference between the two is that *nanxi* employed *nanqu* (southern melodies) while *zaju* used *beiqu* (northern melodies).

During the Ming dynasty, regional operas continued to develop and became popular in many areas, and tune patterns based on the ballads of the various areas emerged and were incorporated. By the end of the Ming dynasty and the beginning of the Qing, *kunqu* had gained the leading position among regional operas.

Wei Liangfu, a prominent musician of the Jaijing (1522–1566) and Longqing (1567–1572) periods of the Ming dynasty and a native of Kunshan in the south, made outstanding contributions to the development of opera. By uniting the traditions of southern and northern popular music, using southern melodies as the main musical form and assimilating various artistic features from the Haiyan and Yiyang operas, as well as popular tunes from the lower Yangzi River, he created a delicate, gentle melodic pattern known as *shuimo qiang* (water-grounded tune), which enriched both vocal and instrumental music. *Di,* a horizontal bamboo recorder, *guan,* a bamboo wind instrument, *sheng,* a reed-pipe wind instrument, and *xiao,* a vertical bamboo flute, provided musical accompaniment, along with stringed instruments. The first *kunqu* opera ever performed was *The Romance of the Yarn-Washing Girl,* written by the short-story writer Liang Bolong, also a Kunshan native. The music became known for its sweet, exquisite artistic appeal.

Kunqu libretti are generally grand in scale, rich in language, complex in plot, and skillful in characterization. The plots often feature talented scholars, beautiful damsels, emperors, princes, and noble ladies. The action determines the choice of tunes and physical movement.

The instrumental melodies and songs are marked by rhythmic cadence and rhyme. The musical structure of *kunqu* is based on *qupai* (tune patterns). Compared with *zaju* of the Yuan dynasty and *nanxi* in its earlier stage, *kunqu* possesses a richer store of tunes and is more flexible in their application, perhaps because it combines the best traits of both southern and northern melodies. *Kunqu* uses the *gong* key, a note in the ancient Chinese five-note scale that corresponds to one in numbered musical notation. Some one thousand tune patterns have been used in *kunqu.*

In contrast to the conspicuous rhythmic cadence of the tune patterns, its acting and dance stress poetic and pictorial effects. Movements are generally slow and meticulous, drawn to a great extent from the traditions of ancient folk dance, court dance, and Tang and Song dance. Performance is marked by a lyrical quality, and the style is considered much gentler than that of the Beijing Opera.

Characterization is based on an elaborate set of stylized roles involving such types as the leading man *(sheng);* leading lady *(dan);* painted face *(jing);* middle-aged man *(mo);* clown *(chou);* middle-aged woman, *(tie);* and old man *(wai).* Each type of role further includes minor characters; for example, there are a minor *sheng* and minor *dan,* as well as lesser roles such as *lao dan,* the old woman, or *fu jing,* the middle painted face. Sophisticated costuming and makeup play an integral part in creating these characterizations.

The extant *kunqu* repertory includes such works as *Picking up a Picture, Invoking the Lady in the Picture, Love Song, Stealing a Poem, A Stroll in the Garden and Starting up from the Dream, The Gossipy Fat Girl, Marrying Off His Sister, Water Fight,* and *Borrowing a Fan.* Large-scale operas include *The Peony Pavilion* and *The Peach Blossom Fan.*

[*See also* Asian Dance Traditions, *overview article; and* China, *article on* Dance in Opera.]

BIBLIOGRAPHY

Mackerras, Colin. *The Chinese Theatre in Modern Times: From 1849 to the Present Day.* Amherst, Mass., 1975.

Mackerras, Colin, ed. *Chinese Theater from Its Origins to the Present Day.* Honolulu, 1983.

Scott, A. C. *The Classical Theatre of China.* London, 1957.

Wang Kefen et al., eds. *A Dictionary of Chinese Dance* (in Chinese). Beijing, 1994.

Yung, Bell. *Cantonese Opera: Performance as Creative Process.* Cambridge, 1989.

Zung, Cecelia. *Secrets of the Chinese Drama* (1937). New York, 1964.

YE SHAOLAN

KŮRA, MIROSLAV (born 26 May 1929 in Brno, Czechoslovakia), Czech dancer and choreographer. After being introduced to ballet by his older brother Gustav, Kůra obtained his dance basics in Brno (1939–1941) at the school of Ivo Váňa Psota, who also became his first ballet director. Kůra was also engaged at Katowice (1941–1943) and Nuremberg (1943–1944). After World War II he performed in Brno (1945–1946), in Bratislava (1946–1948), and again in Brno (1948–1949); Saša Machov then lured him to the National Theater in Prague (1949–1951). After Machov's death, Kůra worked in Košice (1951–1953), Bratislava (1953–1954), and again in Prague (1954–1964). He concluded his career as an active dancer in Brno, where he worked also as ballet director (1964–1966) and as choreographer (1967–1973). In 1966–1967, the only gap in his final tenure at Brno, he directed the ballet in Skopje, Yugoslavia. In 1973 Kůra was offered the post of ballet director at the National Theater in Prague, where after 1978 and until his retirement in 1991, he worked as choreographer.

It has been said of Kůra that he was the greatest male ballet dancer in the history of Czechoslovak ballet. His failure to gain international recognition must be accounted for by the isolation of Czechoslovak dance art during his peak years. Two Czech choreographers, Psota and Machov, distinctly influenced Kůra's artistic profile. Whereas Psota insisted on a virtuoso and stylistically pure execution of any given role, Machov emphasized the dramatic side of the interpretation—emotional depth, psychological truth, and dramatically worked-through roles. Their student succeeded in connecting masterful technical brilliance with spirited expression, but integral to this fusion were personal qualities that Kůra brought to bear on Psota and Machov's pedagogical influences: strong talent and a captivating stage presence that radiated from each step and gesture.

As a dancer Kůra was unusual in that he was not limited to a specific style; he excelled in the roles of the *danseur noble*—Siegfried, Désiré, and Albrecht—as well as in demi-classical, *demi-caractère,* character, and even burlesque roles—Spartacus, Iago in *Othello,* Petrouchka. All of his roles—he created more than forty—shared a rare tenderness and conviction, a truly human as well as theatrical dimension. Kůra also had impeccable feeling for proportion in stylization and exaggeration and for exact, expressive, creatively effective planting of movement onto the stage space. In addition he had an attractive appearance, a wonderful physical disposition, and a particularly elastic softness of movement, manly lyricism, and dramatic strength. On stage he always executed even the most difficult *tours de force* as a matter of course, with complete confidence and lightness. The audience never got the impression that he was acting; he became his characters.

Also important was Kůra's choreographic output. He choreographed more than thirty stage productions as well as many others for television, the latter primarily in collaboration with director Petr Weigl. Kůra's best works were sensitive, stylistically pure musical versions of classical opuses, for example, *Swan Lake,* staged in Brno in 1966; *Giselle,* also in Brno, in 1968; and the *chef d'oeuvre* among his productions, Sergei Prokofiev's *Romeo and Juliet,* performed at the Prague National Theater in 1971 (the film version was awarded the Grand Prix d'Italia). Among the important choreographies of his later period were *Passion* (1976, to music by Georges Bizet and others); *Complaint about the Destruction of the Town of Ur* (1976, to music by Luboš Fišer); *Špalíček* to music by Bohuslav Martinů and performed in Brno in 1973 and Bratislava in 1984. Kůra's choreographies comprised few original elements; they mostly sprang from a firm base of classical vocabulary that Kůra personally modified and colored—for example, with unusual arm gestures or head and torso curvatures. Kůra's achievements have been recognized with many awards and titles.

BIBLIOGRAPHY

Pilka, Jiří. *Miroslav Kůra.* Prague, 1979.

Rey, Jan. "Change and Growth in Czechoslovakia." *Dance and Dancers* (October 1960): 14–17.

Schmidová, Lidka. *Československý balet.* Prague, 1962.

Windreich, Leland. "Prague." *Ballet Review* 23 (Fall 1995): 9–13.

VLADIMÍR VAŠUT
Translated from Czech

KURATH, GERTRUDE PROKOSCH (born 19 August 1903 in Chicago, Illinois, died 1 August 1992 in Ann Arbor, Michigan), dancer, scholar, and author, known as the "mother of dance ethnology." Kurath was born into a family that cherished intellectual and artistic pursuits: her mother was a pianist, and her father, a linguist, was Sterling Professor at Yale University. Kurath received two degrees from Bryn Mawr, a bachelor of arts in 1922 and a master of arts in 1928 in art history, which later led her to reconstruct Renaissance and Baroque dances. In 1930 she married the renowned linguist Hans Kurath. They had two children, Ellen and Edward.

Kurath's continuing studies of performance arts included theater at the Yale School of Drama, and music—harmony and Gregorian chant, as well as piano, viola, violin, guitar, and organ. Her dance and movement studies encompassed the techniques of Dalcroze, Chalif, H'Doubler, Mensendieck, and Duncan, as well as improvisation, ballet, tap, jazz, gymnastics, English folk dancing, and Spanish and Mexican dance. Among her many teachers were Riva Hoffman, Doris Humphrey, and Ruth Page.

For several years Kurath had her own dance company in Rhode Island. During her career she performed, choreographed, taught, coached, and lectured throughout the United States. She sometimes used the stage name Tula. Her fieldwork in dance ethnology began in the 1940s with the *moriscas* of Mexico and, in collaboration with the anthropologist William Fenton, among the Iroquois. Her later fieldwork focused on the Aztec, Otomi, Zapotec, Tarascan, and Yaqui peoples of Mexico, the Pueblo Tewa peoples and Penitentes of New Mexico, Native Americans of the Great Lakes area, and African-American dancers in Michigan.

Although best known for her studies of Native American dance, Kurath also made pioneering theoretical and methodological contributions to dance ethnology generally. She developed a glyph shorthand to record dances, adapting concepts from Rudolf Laban's movement notation (Labanotation). Convenient in the field and easy for nondancers to read, it is used extensively in her writings. From 1931 through 1983, Kurath published eleven books, 132 articles, 128 reviews, and hundreds of entries for eight encyclopedias and dictionaries; she also performed editorial duties for numerous journals.

BIBLIOGRAPHY

Kealiinohomoku, Joann W., and Frank J. Gillis. "Special Bibliography: Gertrude Prokosch Kurath." *Ethnomusicology* 14 (January 1970): 114–128.

Kealiinohomoku, Joann W. "The Conviction of Gertrude Prokosch Kurath about the Interconnections of Dance and Music." *UCLA Journal of Dance Ethnology* 19 (1995): 1–5.

Kealiinohomoku, Joann W. "A Tribute to Gertrude Prokosch Kurath." *UCLA Journal of Dance Ethnologists* 10 (1986): 3–6.

Kealiinohomoku, Joann W. "In Memorium: Gertrude Prokosch Kurath: August 19, 1903–August 1, 1992." *Dance Research Journal* 24.2 (1992): 70.

Kurath, Gertrude Prokosch. *Dance Memoirs.* Cambridge, Mass., 1983.

Malm, Joyce R. "Gertrude Kurath Collection, University of Michigan, Ann Arbor." *Dance Research Journal* 23 (Spring 1991): 61.

JOANN W. KEALIINOHOMOKU

KURBET, VLADIMIR (Vladimir Kuzmich Kurbet; born 5 December 1930 in Susleny, Moldavian Soviet Socialist Republic), director of Zhok, the Moldovan folk dance company. Kurbet began his career as a choreographer in his native village, where he led a group of amateur folk dancers. In 1954 he established another amateur company in the village of Karagash in the Slobodzei district. Three years later he led this group to one of the top prizes at the World Festival of Youth and Students in Moscow. Thereafter, Kurbet was invited to become choreographer of Zhok, and he has been its artistic director since 1958. At the same time he was studying music at the Nyagi music school in Kishinev, from which he graduated in 1966.

The genuine folkloric foundation and original character style of Kurbet's first productions infused fresh blood into the repertory of the company and won broad popularity throughout Moldova. Works like *Zhok Ferarilor* to folk tunes arranged by Georgi Tyrtseu, *Betuta* to folk tunes arranged by Aleksandr Kamenetsky, and *Khory Fetelor* to music by David Fedov revealed Kurbet's artistic individuality and his command of sophisticated syncopated rhythms. This style was used in innovative ways in dance suites to folk music arranged by Vladimir Rotaru: *Gaiduki* and *Vioara* (1964) and *Stremoshaske* and *Tserenyaske* (1967). In the latter the measured and somewhat heavy, swaying movements of the body combine with rhythmically complex movements of the legs and with light leaps.

Vivid theatrical effects and distinctive stylization mark Kurbet's choreography. *Meruntsika* (1960) to music by Kamenetsky was remarkable for its intricate rhythmic patterns of leg movements. In contrast, the lyrical *Kreitsele* (1967) to Rotaru's music was based on quite simple movements. In 1984 there was the poetic *Dragaika* to music by Todor Kiriyak, which praised peasant work and was reminiscent of rites dedicated to wheat harvesting. Among Kurbet's dance suites are *The Carpathians* and a Gypsy scene, both to music by Rotaru, and *Mertsyshor,* based on a folk legend set to music by Vasily Goya.

Zhok is one of the most popular dance companies in Russia and has toured to many countries. Kurbet is the author of three books: *Moldavian Folk Dances,* with M. M. Marder (1969), *Pa vatra khorepor* (At the Cradle of Round Dance; 1973), and *Promotor ai aratei populari* (Representatives of Folk Art; 1979). He was named People's Artist of the USSR in 1981.

BIBLIOGRAPHY

Chokanu, Ion. *Pashilui, Vladimir Kurbet.* Kishinev, 1982.

Koroleva, Elfrida A. *Khoreografischeskoe iskusstvo Moldavii.* Kishinev, 1970.

Koroleva, Elfrida A., ed. *Moldavskii baletyni teatr.* Kishinev, 1990.

Kurbet, Vladimir. *Pa vatra khorepor.* Kishinev, 1973.

ELFRIDA A. KOROLEVA
Translated from Russian

KURDISH DANCE. The Kurds are a nomadic people whose homeland (Kurdistan) and population (of some 10 million) are now divided among mountainous rural regions of Syria, Turkey, Iran, Iraq, and Armenia; small numbers live in Israel and the Republic of Georgia, (and a separatist movement is headquartered in Paris, France). They speak an Iranian (a Persian) language, and some believe them to be the descendants of the ancient Medes. Without a state of their own, the Kurds place great importance on such cultural forms and identity markers as dancing.

Kurds perform four types of dances: group dances; solo improvisational dances; processionals; and ritual and religious dances. The first two are the most popular and widespread types. Social dancing does not attract opprobrium among the Kurds, probably because the professional solo dancing that has been associated with moral laxity has never been practiced in their area.

On social occasions, such as weddings, dancing is a key form of entertainment; it may last many hours. Dancers are connected to one another by a variety of hand, shoulder, and belt holds during group dances. The dances, similar to the Arabic *dabkah,* have short repetitive choreographic phrases, punctuated by dips, rhythmic movements of the arms, stamping, and clapping. The lines and circles sometimes have up to one hundred dancers.

Music is usually provided by the *sorna* (a kind of shawm, an early form of the double-reed oboe) and the *dohol,* a double-headed drum that is beaten with sticks and played from the Balkan Peninsula east into China. The dancers often sing. More than forty dances are named in the musical literature (Dzalil, 1973). The group dances are part of a wide repertory of dances, step patterns, music, and movements that are also in the dance repertories of Turkey, Armenia, Greece, Azerbaijan, and the Pontic (Black Sea area), as well as among Iraqi Arabs and the Aramaic-speaking Christian Assyrians.

Solo dancing is also performed in festive contexts, often in the center of a circle of people who either clap or sing and watch. One or more dancers may improvise freely within the regional style. Kurdish solo dancing is not as elaborate as many of the improvisational styles found farther east. Processional dances have been reported, but no details are known of their choreographic form.

The majority of Kurds practice Sunni Islam and respect the prohibition of dance and music for religious ceremonies. However, as in many parts of the Islamic world, certain non-Sunni sects and groups do utilize movement within their rituals. For example, the Sufi sect among the Kurds use movement to achieve an ecstatic state; similarly, the Yazīdī, a group of Kurds living mostly in Iraq, utilize and revere ceremonial music and dance.

[*See also* Iran]

BIBLIOGRAPHY

Christensen, Dieter. "Tanzlieder der Hakkari-Kurden: Eine materialkritische studie." *Jahrbuch für Musikalischevolks und Völkerkunde* 1 (1963):11–47.

Christensen, Dieter. "Ein Tanzlied der Hakkari-Kurden und seine Variantez." *Baessler-Archiv* 23 (1975):195–215.

Dzhalil, Dzhalile, comp. *Kurdskie narodnye pesni i instrumentalnye melodii.* Moscow, 1973.

Hansen, Henny Harald. *The Kurdish Woman's Life.* Copenhagen, 1961.

Kendal, Nezan. "Kurdish Music and Dance." *World of Music* 21.1 (1979):19–28.

Shiloah, Amnon. "Kurdish Music." In *The New Grove Dictionary of Music and Musicians.* London, 1980.

Anthony V. Shay

KŪṬIYĀṬṬAM. India's *kūṭiyāṭṭam* is a genre of drama, not of dance; however, some of its major elements are similar to those of the important dance traditions of India, such as *kathakaḷi* and *bharata nāṭyam. Kūṭiyāṭṭam* is practiced exclusively in the central and south central area of the state of Kerala on the southwestern coast of India.

Kūṭiyāṭṭam is preserved by a small community of temple servants, perhaps no more than two dozen in all, who have maintained the practice of performing Sanskrit plays. Historical evidence suggests that reforms were made in *kūṭiyāṭṭam* in the tenth century CE but that the form was created perhaps as early as the second century CE, making it the oldest extant tradition of theater on the Indian subcontinent, and perhaps in the world.

In its traditional setting, portions of Sanskrit plays are performed over a period of days, or sometimes weeks, in permanent, specially designed temple theaters. Although audiences may sit on three sides of the acting area, the shows are intended to be seen from the front of the stage, with the spectators sitting below the actors and looking up at them. Because most Kerala temples are off-limits to non-Hindus, it is impossible for interested outsiders to see *kūṭiyāṭṭam* in its proper setting. On rare occasions cultural societies sponsor performances in halls or proscenium theaters outside the temple compounds, but the setting of these performances bears little resemblance to the temple theaters.

Although dance plays very little part in *kūṭiyāṭṭam,* this drama, like Indian classical dance, employs elaborate system of gesture language and facial expression to convey meaning and emotion, with complementary rhythmic accompaniments. The actors often recite a Sanskrit or Prakrit verse from a play in one of many patterns of vocal expression called *rāga*s, executing the appropriate hand gestures for each word; they then repeat the same gesture sequence to the accompaniment of drums, often in a much slower tempo and to various rhythmic patterns, exaggerating the facial expressions and focusing on the sentiment *(rasa)* of the content. [*See* Rāga.] Then they progress to the next verse or segment of dialogue. In former times the actors repeated the same material a third time, chanting the verse and executing the gestures without the drum accompaniment. Naturally, this repetition prolongs the performance so that one act of a play, normally the largest single unit enacted in *kūṭiyāṭṭam,* may take six to nine hours to complete, even though it might be performed in a naturalistic manner in about half an hour. With the ritual preliminaries, introduction of characters, expansion of the story line, and performance of the complete act, a full-scale *kūṭiyāṭṭam* event may last from five to thirty-five days.

The "dance of hands and face" is not the only dance element present in *kūṭiyāṭṭam.* Special movement sequences are used during the entrance of characters *(purappadu);*

these movements are known as *krīyas*, and each sequence has a name. The *krīyas* are short and are normally performed one after another. The actor holds a conventional gesture associated with the character he is portraying, to the accompaniment of special drum patterns which punctuate the striking of the actor's feet against the floor. A few other conventional movements are used to suggest a long journey, taking a walk to a garden or in the forest, preparing for battle, imitating the movements of various birds and animals, and so on. Rather than calling these dance movements, it is more appropriate to describe them as conventional patterns of movement to the accompaniment of drums; they do not resemble the elaborate patterns of movement in space and time in Indian classical dance.

Today *kūṭiyāṭṭam* is taught by the oldest members of the acting families. Instruction of the young is carried out in the private gymnasiums (*kalari*s) of families and in public educational institutions such as the Kerala Kalamandalam. The knowledge of *kūṭiyāṭṭam* is preserved by the family elders and passed down from generation to generation. Acting manuals called *kramadīpikā*s and *attaprakāra*s in the possession of the actor families guide the teachers in the correct techniques for executing selected acts of a limited number of Sanskrit plays. The *kramadīpikā*s contain instructions regarding songs, dances, *rāga*s, and numerous stage directions. The *attaprakāra*s contain instructions for performing the introductory verses of specific acts, as well as a variety of commentaries on costuming, makeup, and other theatrical subjects. Sometimes the instructions for a given play contain contradictory details, and only a skilled teacher can understand and interpret them.

Kūṭiyāṭṭam actors use a wide range of gestures with specific and implied meanings, with a vocabulary of slightly more than six hundred hand gestures. The text from which most of the gestures are derived is the *Hastalakṣanadīpikā*, a Sanskrit work in Malayalam script.

KŪṬIYĀṬṬAM. Only a small community of temple servants continue to practice *kūṭiyāṭṭam*, a dance drama from the central region of Kerala that is one of the world's oldest living theater traditions. (Photograph from the archives of The Asia Society, New York.)

BIBLIOGRAPHY

Bharatha Iyer, K. *Kutiyattam: The Sanskrit Drama of Kerala.* Bombay, 1962.

Enros, Pragna Thakkar. "Producing Sanskrit Plays in the Tradition of Kutiyattam." In *Sanskrit Drama in Performance,* edited by Rachel Van M. Baumer and James R. Brandon. Honolulu, 1981.

Kunjunni Raja, K. *Kutiyattam: An Introduction.* New Delhi, 1964.

Kunjunni Raja, K. "Kootiyattam: A General Survey." *Quarterly Journal of the National Centre for the Performing Arts* 3 (June 1974): 1–12.

Vatsyayan, Kapila. *Traditional Indian Theatre: Multiple Streams.* New Delhi, 1980.

FARLEY RICHMOND

KYLIÁN, JIŘÍ (born 21 March 1947 in Prague), Czech dancer, choreographer, and ballet director. In 1962, at the age of fifteen, Jiří Kylián began his dance studies at the Prague Conservatory, where he was a pupil of Zora Semberova in the National Ballet School. In 1967, having been awarded a grant from the British Council, he continued his studies at the Royal Ballet School in London. Thoroughly trained in classical ballet, he also studied modern dance techniques, particularly that of Martha Graham, as well as music theory and practice. As a student, he also developed a particular interest in folk music and dance.

In 1968, Kylián made his debut as a dancer with the Stuttgart Ballet, directed by John Cranko. Although he was soon promoted to soloist, it was not long before it became apparent that Kylián's principal talent was for choreography, for which he displayed a natural bent. In 1970 he choreographed his first ballet, *Paradox,* set to his own music, for a Noverre Society gala performance in Stuttgart and soon followed it with *Kommen und Gehen* (1970), set to the music of Béla Bartók, for the Stuttgart Ballet. Other early works included *Viewers,* set to the music of Frank Martin for the Netherlands Dance Theater in 1973, and *Rückkehr ins Fremde Land* (Return to the Strange Land), set to the music of Leoš Janáček, which he choreographed for the Stuttgart Ballet, first as a pas de trois in 1974 and then in a fuller version in 1975.

The success of Kylián's early works led to his appointment as co–artistic director, with Hans Knill, of the Netherlands Dance Theater, located in the Hague, in 1975. Success followed success, with *Verklärte Nacht* (Transfigured Night), set to the music of Arnold Schoenberg in 1975; *Symfonie in D,* set to music by Franz Joseph Haydn, in 1976; and *November Steps,* set to the score by Tōru Takemitsu in 1977. With *Sinfonietta,* choreographed to music by Janáček and performed at the Spoleto Festival in Charleston, South Carolina, in 1978, Kylián was thrust into international prominence. That same year he became sole artistic director of the Netherlands Dance Theater, where over the next two decades he would establish himself as one of the foremost choreographers in Europe.

Influenced mainly by John Cranko, Glen Tetley, and, since the 1980s, by William Forsythe, Kylián's dance works represent a new form of ballet expressionism in which emotional eloquence and polished elegance are well balanced. His dynamic choreographies are often impressive for their speed and vitality, thanks to many swirling and whirling movements, in a fluent idiom that combines the vocabularies of classical ballet and Graham technique. The content of his dances is often emotionally colored by relational patterns; a recurrent theme concerns the need to belong and to be comforted, specifically the need of women who seek protection by men.

Kylián's themes are often inspired by folklore. The jubilation of *Sinfonietta* (1978), for example, is a pure expression of his love of his Czech homeland and his joy and happiness in his memories of it. Other ballets showing his interest in Slavonic folk dance are *Dream Dances* (1979), set to music by Luciano Berio, and *Svadebka* (Les Noces, or The Wedding; 1982), to the score by Igor Stravinsky. A trip to Australia in 1981 inspired Kylián to choreograph several works incorporating concepts and images from the cultures of Australian Aborigines: *Nomaden* (1981), to music by Stravinsky; *Stamping Ground* (1983), to music by Carlos Chávez; and *Dreamtime* (1983), to music by Takemitsu.

Religious sentiments have periodically surfaced in Kylián's ballets ever since such early works as *Symphony of Psalms* (1978), to Stravinsky's score, and *Glagolitic Mass* (1979), to Janáček's music. Humor is also prominent is such works as *Symfonie in D,* a parody of ballet that he reworked three times (1976, 1977, 1981); *L'Enfant et les Sortilèges* (1984), to the score by Maurice Ravel; and *Six Dances* (1986), set to music by W. A. Mozart. Since the late 1980s, Kylián has also experimented with a more abstract approach, emphasizing dance as pure movement construction, starting with *No More Play* (1988), set to music by Anton Webern.

Other works created by Kylián for the Netherlands Dance Theater include *Soldier's Mass* (1980), also called *Field Mass,* set to music by Bohuslav Martinů; *L'Histoire du Soldat* (1986), set to the Stravinsky score; a third version of *Heart's Labyrinth* (1987), set to music by Schoenberg; *Falling Angels* (1989), set to music by Steve Reich; and *Sarabande* (1990), set to music by J. S. Bach. His productivity has continued unabated through the 1990s, and his musical tastes have continued to range widely, from Bach and Mozart to John Cage and Kan Ishii. Recent works include *Petite Mort* (1991), *Tiger Lily* (1994), *Arcimbolo* (1995), *La Bella Figura* (1995), and *Anna and Ostriches* (1996).

Kylián has been the recipient of many prizes and honors given by various organizations in Sweden, Great

KYLIÁN. David MacGillivray, Charie Evans, and Bernard Sauvé of Ballet British Columbia in a 1988 performance of Kylián's *Return to the Strange Land,* created in 1975. Along with the glorious *Sinfonietta,* this spare, clean work is among Kylián's most popular ballets. Both are set to the music of his Czech compatriot Leoš Janáček. (Photograph © by David Cooper; used by permission.)

Britain, Denmark, and France as well as in the Netherlands. He is married to the Dutch dancer Sabine Kupferberg, who led the original cast of *Sinfonietta,* his first major international success.

[*See also* Netherlands Dance Theater.]

BIBLIOGRAPHY

Garske, Rolf. "In Love with Music and Movement." *Ballett International* 10 (March 1987): 6–13.

Hense, Peter, and Luuk Utrecht. *Het Nederlands Dans Theater en de balletten van Jiří Kylián.* Amsterdam, 1981.

Klooss, Helma. "Jiří Kylián: Three's Company." *Dance Magazine* (June 1991): 56–60.

Kylián, Jiří. "New and Free Artistic Thought and Feeling." *Tanz International* 2 (January 1991): 82–87.

Lanz, Isabelle. *A Garden of Dance.* Amsterdam, 1995.

Mannoni, Gérard. *Kylián* (in French). Arles, 1989.

Merrett, Sue. "Spotlight on Jiří Kylián." *The Dancing Times* (May 1991): 763.

Schaik, Eva van. "Master of Ceremonies, Seeker of Truths." *Ballett International/Tanz Aktuell* (June 1995): 36–39.

Scheier, Helmut. "Choreographing in Symbols." *Ballett International/Tanz Aktuell* (October 1994): 14–21.

Versteeg, Coos. *Nederlands Dans Theater: Een revolutionaire geschiedenis.* Amsterdam, 1987.

LUUK UTRECHT

KYŌGEN. [*To explore the general characteristics and importance of dance in* kyōgen *plays, this entry comprises two articles. The first article presents a history of the genre, its development and general characteristics. The second focuses on the two extant schools of* kyōgen, *the Izumi school and the Ōkura school. For related discussions, see* Japan, *article on* Dance Traditions; *and* Mask and Makeup, *article on* Asian Traditions.]

An Overview

Developed in Japan in the fourteenth century during the Kamakura and Muromachi periods, *kyōgen* plays are stylized comedies that have been transmitted through strict imitation of masters and that are still performed today. The Chinese characters for *kyōgen* mean "outrageous speech," referring to situational skits incorporating farce, satire, comedy of manners, parody, and fantasy. In a typical program, *kyōgen* plays alternate with their opposites—the masked, austere, religious plays of *nō*. Though strictly codified, *kyōgen* retains a colloquial earthy humor and a spontaneous exuberance that have allowed it to adapt to modern performance circumstances.

Kyōgen and *nō* developed as two branches of a form that synthesized elements from religious, agricultural, and popular urban forms in the fourteenth century. Earlier, in the seventh century, *sangaku* (scattered music) had been imported from China and Korea into Japan, where it contrasted with the more formal court music and dance. *Sangaku* included songs, skits, and simple dances as well as juggling, acrobatics, and magic tricks. Strolling *sangaku* players traveled throughout Japan, borrowing from local folk entertainments. Some troupes became affiliated with shrines and temples, offering their arts as sideshow attractions to lure worshipers. These entertainments soon incorporated Japanese elements, and the Chinese ideograms for the word *sangaku* were changed to read *sarugaku,* meaning "monkey music."

Various syncretic forms emerged in the Muromachi period (1392–1573) to compete for popularity. These arts evolved through competition for audiences, fluid borrowing between the imperial court and commoners, and movement between rural and urban areas. *Kyōgen* borrowed music from *imayo* (present-day songs), *enkyoku* (party music), and *ennen* (Buddhist long-life prayers). Its dance forms derived from rustic dances called *dengaku* (rice field music) and *shirabyōshi* ("white rhythm" dance). Narration style derived from *hojushi* (explanatory skits concerning esoteric Buddhism), folk tales, and *renga,* or linked comic verse. *Sarugaku,* then, was an inclusive form, comprising a variety of entertainments adapted to specific audiences that split into the serious and comic theatrical forms of *nō* and *kyōgen.*

Zeami, the great choreographer and theoretician of the *nō* theater, accorded *kyōgen* a permanent place on the *sarugaku* stage, alternating with *nō* plays. A typical program consisted of four to five *nō* plays interspersed with three or four *kyōgen* plays. An interval actor, known as an *ai-kyōgen,* would also appear between sections of a *nō* play as a servant, priest, or low official who would relate the history of the setting in colloquial language.

Though *kyōgen* plays originated as satires of actual persons, censorship coupled with creative stylization over many centuries produced a collection of fixed character-types immediately recognizable by their costumes and bearing. Lords and masters trail long pantaloons, which they flick imperiously behind them when they turn. Servants wear broad checks and stripes, hold their hands at their sides, and bow low. Gods, wearing fierce, often grotesque masks, stand with feet at a wide angle, arms away from their bodies, chests out. Women, always played by men, cross their feet narrowly in front of each other and wear turbans with dangling strips that are tucked into their belts. Old men and women use sticks for support, bend low, and shuffle forward. Masks are employed in only a few plays—to portray gods, nonhuman characters (mosquito, monkey, fox), and ugly women. Plots also follow strict formulas: bridegrooms make terrible first impressions on their fathers-in-law; proud and silly masters are outwitted by their servants; shrewish

KYŌGEN. Stylized comedies, *kyōgen* plays are performed as interludes in *nō* dramas. In this episode, Shigeyama Sengorō (now called Sensaku IV) rows a priest, portrayed by Kaoru Matsumoto, across a river in the drama *Satsumanokami.* (Photograph by Osamu Muranaka; used by permission; courtesy of Jonah Salz.)

wives chastize henpecked husbands; arrogant mountain priests prove to be charlatans; gods are healed by mortals, and city slickers bested by country bumpkins. Inversion, gentle mocking satire, and escalating fantasy are *kyōgen*'s elemental comic weapons.

There is also a darker, more grotesque genre of *kyōgen* plays, in which blind men are beaten, lame men are mocked, and servants are ordered to kill their bosom buddies. These bittersweet dramas of deformity and death, temptation and punishment, share themes with European morality plays and the modern tragicomedies of Samuel Beckett and have influenced some contemporary Japanese experimental theater, including works by Abe Kōbō, Terayama Shuji, and Betsuyaku Minoru.

Kyōgen are transmitted orally and by example of masters taught from birth in a strict headmaster-and-disciple system *(iemoto)*. The *kyōgen* actor learns *kata* (fixed forms) for walking, dancing, and vocalizing, which he then uses in increasingly complex patterns and variations. Only when he has mastered the *kata* is the actor expected to infuse them with his own personality. *Kyōgen*'s fascination lies in this underlying tension between precisely controlled action and spontaneous feeling.

Kata are considered "paths" perfected over hundreds of years of trial and error. Yet far from being inflexible rules, *kata* vary with an actor's age, experience, and ability as well as with audience size, configuration, and sophistication. The *kyōgen* actor learns to adapt to particular performance conditions and to the changing tastes of the times. His career is said "to start as a monkey and end as a fox," denoting the important initiation and graduation roles—that of the monkey in *Utsubo Zaru* (The Monkey-Skin Quiver), played by the child actor at as young an age as three years, and that of the fox in *Tsuri Gitsune* (Fox Trapping), played in young manhood as a graduation from formal lessons at around the age of twenty.

Although generally considered a dialogue drama (unique in all of classical Asian drama, over half of all *kyōgen* plays contain some song and dance. Basic dance *kata* such as *hiraki* (opening), *komawari* (small turns), and *sayu* (right–left), abstract movements are performed in various combinations, often accompanied by stylized gestures: lifting a sake cup, riding a bamboo horse, portraying a rabbit's ears and hopping. *Kyōgen* dance incorporates folk, popular, and religious forms and is generally more mimetic than *nō*. The drunken, stumbling, yet ecstatically graceful dance is one of *kyōgen*'s signature pieces, and the auspicious, ancient *sambaso* features bell-ringing and stamping in an energetic prayer for fertility.

The *kyōgen* vocal technique is a wavelike pattern that infuses all dialogue, song, and accompanying movement. The voice is loud and resonant, developed for projecting on outdoor stages, at temples, and at festivals. Sometimes compared to the sensation of slicing through green bamboo, the *kyōgen* actor's voice must reach the last row of the audience. The energy generated by this compressed, singsong rhythm brings the audience into the same breathing pattern as that of the actors, who, once in control, can then move the audience to surprise and laughter.

Kyōgen dialogue is full of overlapping banter, repeated catchphrases ("This is a problem. What shall I do?"), puns, parodies of Chinese poetry and *nō* plays, and exclamations. Street vendors' cries, popular drinking songs and romantic ballads, and children's songs appear frequently. The aural pattern extends to mime, which is never silent. "Zukazukazukari" accompanies motions denoting the sawing of wood; "sarasarasara" is used when sliding a door open. To create these actions, the *kyōgen* master employs his chief tool and property: the fan. Closed, the fan is a sword, a pipe, a drumstick; open, it is a sake ladle and cup, a branch, a wing. Stage space is similarly manipulated through simple, clear actions: a long journey is compressed into a triangular walk; a character kneels and "disappears."

Kabuki actors took their acting lessons from *kyōgen* actors, whose abilities range from formal, deadpan delivery to realistic pathos. Many modern Japanese theater groups have also studied *kyōgen* acting technique and dramaturgy. Popular *kyōgen* actors have adapted Aristophanes, French medieval farce, Shakespeare, and science fiction to *kyōgen* and have appeared in modern dance, opera, and experimental theater. *Kyōgen* is the consummate actor's art, requiring strict adherence to prescribed rules, one of which is to adapt to the shifting times, audience expectations, and performance space. After six hundred years of continuous transformation, *kyōgen* remains a supple and classic stage art.

[*For related discussion, see* Nō.]

BIBLIOGRAPHY

Fujii, Takeo. "Humor and Satire in Early English Comedy and Japanese Kyogen." In *Drama: A Cross-Cultural Study in Dramatic Arts.* Hirakata, Japan, 1983.

Gondo Yoshikazu. *Kyōgen nyūmon.* Kyoto, 1996.

Hisashi Hata et al. *Kyōgen.* Tokyo, 1982.

Kenny, Don. *The Kyogen Book: An Anthology of Japanese Classical Comedies.* Tokyo, 1989.

Kitagawa Tadahiko. *Hyogen hyakuban* (A Hundred Kyogen Plays). Kyoto, 1964.

Kobayashi Seki. *Kyōgen o tanoshimu* (Enjoying Kyogen). Tokyo, 1972.

Kobayashi Seki. *Kyōgen Handbook.* Tokyo, 1995.

Makoto Ueda. *Literary and Art Theories of Japan.* Tokyo, 1967.

McKinnon, Richard. *Selected Plays of Kyogen.* Tokyo, 1968.

Morley, Carol. *Transformation, Miracles, and Mischief: the Mountain Priest Plays of Kyogen.* Ithaca, New York, 1994.

Motohiko Izumi. *Kyōgen e no shoukai* (An Invitation to Kyogen). Tokyo, 1991.

O'Neill, P. G. "Kyogen." In *Kodansha Encyclopedia of Japan.* Tokyo, 1983.

Shio Sakanishi. *Japanese Folk Plays.* Tokyo, 1960.

Teele, Rebecca, comp. *No/Kyogen Masks and Performance.* Claremont, Calif., 1984.

VIDEO. "This Is Kyogen" and "Busu (Poison Sugar)" (Akira Shigeyama International Projects, 1995).

JONAH SALZ

Kyōgen Schools

Performers of *kyōgen* belong to two extant schools, or lines—the Izumi school and the Ōkura school—both of which appear to have originated in Japan in the early fifteenth century.

Izumi School. The Izumi school was founded by the Sasaki and Yamawaki families in the city of Sakamoto in the Land of Omi (present-day Shiga prefecture) during the early part of the Muromachi period (1394–1466). By the time of the third-generation headmaster, however, the school had moved to the then-capital, Kyoto, and its members bore the family name Torikai.

The seventh-generation headmaster, Izumi Motonobu, officially organized the Izumi school of *kyōgen* in the middle of the seventeenth century, during the Edo period (1603–1868), a time when the third Tokugawa shogun, Iemitsu, was encouraging the fixation of the feudal system through all levels of society—including the entrenchment of the headmaster/school system in all the traditional and contemporary arts and crafts. Because Izumi Motonobu's family was not large enough to form a strong school, he took the Miyake and Nomura families under the Izumi-school umbrella, and this reinforced organization served both the Tokugawa clan of Owari and the imperial court in Kyoto. The tenth headmaster, Izumi Motokazu, however, moved with his immediate family to Nagoya, while parts of the Miyake family moved to Osaka and Kanazawa and the Nomura family moved to Kumamoto.

Up to the Meiji Restoration (1868), the Izumi school as a whole remained in service to the imperial court in Kyoto, while the Okura school and the now-defunct Sagi school served the shogunate. By the turn of the twentieth century, the headquarters and most of the families of the Izumi school had moved to Tokyo, where the school is centered to this day (with parts of the Nomura family remaining in Nagoya and Kanazawa).

Kyōgen differs from the other traditional arts of Japan in that the position of headmaster has never been very strong in *kyōgen.* In 1907, for example, the sixteenth Izumi headmaster, Motokiyo, expelled three actors from the school for performing an important play without his permission. But the rest of the *kyōgen* and *nō* world sympathized with the wayward actors, and most of the other actors in the Izumi school joined with them to form a new faction. Motokiyo fell into disfavor and found it very difficult to get work during the remaining five years of his life. His successor, Mototeru, the seventeenth headmaster,

KYŌGEN. The Noho Theater Group of Kyoto has presented *kyōgen*-style interpretations of the plays of Samuel Beckett. In this 1981 performance, Akira Shigeyama (right) and Yasushi Maruishi portray, respectively, Blind Man and Lama Man in Beckett's *Rough for Theatre I.* (Photograph by Yoshihiro Hosomi; courtesy of Jonah Salz.)

died at a very early age in 1916, leaving the position empty. In 1940, Yamawaki Motoyasu became the eighteenth headmaster, but was considered such a troublemaker that he was forced to retire three years later. Finally, in 1943, the nineteenth headmaster, Izumi Motohide, was installed in the post. He was just six years old at the time, and his power was always tenuous at best. He earned a great deal of disapprobation by permitting his two young daughters to become *kyōgen* actors—the first female actors in *kyōgen* history—and by pushing his young son, then in his mid-teens, into roles that traditionally have not been attempted by actors until their mid-twenties or early thirties. Then his sudden death at the end of 1995 left the school without a recognized headmaster, since none of the other actors in the school will accept his son (in his early twenties) as headmaster and have joined together to nullify his claims to that position.

Today there are thirty accredited actors in the Izumi school. Most live in Tokyo, but several reside in Nagoya and Kanazawa. Nomura is the predominant family name, but the headmaster uses the family name Izumi, and his younger brother and one of his daughters use the family name Miyake.

Ōkura School. Laying claim to illustrious origins, the Ōkura school traces itself back to Konparu Zenchiku (1405–1470), the son-in-law and successor of the great theoretician of *nō* drama, Zeami. The earliest historical records, however, seem to indicate that, like the Izumi school, the Ōkura school originated in the city of Sakamoto near the beginning of the fifteenth century, moving to the Land of Tanba (present-day Hyōgo prefecture) during the time of the seventh headmaster, Hiyoshi Yaemon, toward the end of the Muromachi period (1394–1466). [*See the entires on Komparu Zenchiku and Zeami.*]

Confirmable historical records of the school begin in the Edo period (1603–1867), with the tenth headmaster, Ōkura Yaemon (1610–1672). Through the Edo period, the Ōkura school was primarily in the service of the shogunate. After the Meiji restoration of 1868, few actors were left in the Ōkura school; the twenty-second headmaster moved to Nara, where he died in 1881, leaving the post empty. The school was kept alive, however, by a number of regional branches, including the Yamamoto family in Tokyo and the Shigeyama, Ōkura, and Zenchiku families in the Kamigata area (Osaka and Kyoto).

In 1941, Ōkura Yataro married the adopted daughter of Ōkura Torakazu (who was twenty-third headmaster in name only) and became the twenty-fourth headmaster of the school. In 1946, Yataro moved to Tokyo, where he has lived ever since, and formed a company centered around himself, his younger brother Zenchiku Keigorō, and their sons and grandsons.

Today there are eighty officially accredited actors in the Ōkura school. The Ōkura and Yamamoto families live in Tokyo; the Shigeyama family in Kyoto; and the Zenchiku family in Osaka. In both the Ōkura and Izumi schools there are also quite a number of minor actors who have other family names and who are scattered around Japan.

Repertories and Styles. The plays of *kyōgen* evolved through actors' use of a repertory of stock characters and comic situations. There is little documentary evidence concerning the plays' development until the scripts were finally written down—in something very close to their present form—around the beginning of the Edo period, in the seventeenth century. Writing in 1721, a *kyōgen* actor of the Ōkura school attributed authorship of fifty-nine plays to a Kamakura-period Buddhist priest named Genne (1269–1350). This actor, however, listed only the titles of the plays, and no other source credits Genne as having any relationship to *kyōgen,* so this claim appears suspect. In their present official repertories, the Izumi school lists 254 plays and the Ōkura school 180; because so many plays are shared by both schools, the combined total comes to only 257.

The styles of the two schools produce the same general atmosphere and effect, but it is possible to draw subtle distinctions between their techniques. Izumi-school acting is typified by a tight, precise style that creates a vortex of energy, which draws the audience in and holds its attention. By contrast, Ōkura-school acting is typified by a casual, earthy style that elicits laughter through direct appeal to the audience.

[*For further discussion of a branch of the Ōkura school, see the entry on the Shigeyama family. For biographies of dancer-actors of the Izumi school, see the entries on Nomura Manzo VI and Nomura Mansaku II.*]

BIBLIOGRAPHY

Furukawa Hisashi et al. *The Kyogen Encyclopedia.* Vol. 2 (Kyōgen Jiten Jikohen). Tokyo, 1976.

Kenny, Don. *The Kyogen Book: An Anthology of Japanese Classical Comedies.* Tokyo, 1989.

Don Kenny

KYRGYZSTAN. Separated from Russia by Kazakhstan on the north, Kyrgyzstan is in central Asia, bounded by China on the east, Tajikistan on the south, and Uzbekistan on the west. The Kyrgyz (who were formerly called Kara-Kyrgyz) are a Muslim Turko-Mongolian people; they occupied the area from the thirteenth century onward under khanate rule. Annexed by Russia by 1876, after the Revolution of 1917, it became an autonomous area, was reorganized in 1926, and was made a constituent republic of the USSR in 1936. Kyrgyzstan became an independent state in 1991 after the dissolution of the USSR; it is among the poorest of the new republics.

Folk Dance. Records of Kyrgyz folk dance have not survived, although some information on the character of dance lore can be found in the epic *Manas,* an encyclopedic collection of folk myths, fairy tales, and legends, and in the testimony of explorers who described the musical culture of the Kyrgyz. The art of folk musicians, known as *komuz* players, the mimicry, gestures, and imitative movements of the folk jesters *(al-kuuduldars),* and some original folk games and rites also contain some dance elements. During the Soviet era, an interest in reclaiming traditional dances emerged. In the 1930s amateur groups proliferated, and numerous contests and festivals of folk art were held to demonstrate the achievements of talented dancers. Many folk games, such as *selkinchek* ("swings"), became sources of inspiration for the creation of new dances.

Theatrical Dance. In 1926 a music and drama studio was established in Frunze, now Bishkek, the Kyrgyz capital. Its students performed folk and ballet dances at youth festivals. In 1936 the studio became a musical drama theater with a ballet company under the direction of Nikolai Kholfin, who sought to introduce progressive methods into choreography. Based on a thorough study of the folk games, rituals, tasks, costumes, and music of the Kyrgyz, Kholfin revived folk dances in the first national opera, *Aichurek* (Moon Beauty; 1939), composed by Vladimir Vlasov, Abdfyias Maldybayev, and Vladimir Fere, and in the musical dramas *Altyn Kyz* (Golden Girl; 1937) and *Adjal Arduna* (Not Death but Life; 1938). Very popular with audiences were the numerous dances and games in these productions—the group dance *djash kerbez,* the maidens' round dance *jomok biy,* the warlike horse-riders' dance *adaman,* and the women's dances *kviz elecheki* and *kyzdaryn kyyaly.* Dance folklore also provided basic material for Kholfin's first Kyrgyz ballet, *Anar* (1940), to music by Vlasov and Fere. The ballet tells of the love of the maiden Anar and the youth Kadyr who rebel against patriarchal customs and despotic feudal rule. The ballet depicted picturesque scenes of folk life.

The theater became an opera and ballet theater in 1942, presenting classics as well as original ballets. One of the most important productions was the ballet *Cholpon* (Morning Star), choreographed by Lev Kramarevsky to music by Mikhail Rauchwerger in 1944 (new version by Nurdin Tugelov, 1953 and 1958). The ballet tells the story of a young girl, Cholpon, whose faithful love helps her to overcome prejudice and also the evil charms of the sorceress Aidai. The national repertory was expanded with the first comic ballet, *Kuiruchuk* (1960), choreographed by Tugelov to music by Kalyi Moldobasanov and Herman Okunev. It recounts the life of the popular folk clown Khudaibergen Omurzakov. The productions of classics from the standard repertory not only acquainted Kyrgyz audiences with the most important Russian, Soviet, and foreign ballets but also expanded the horizons for national choreography and set the stage for the quest for modern themes among dancers and choreographers.

Starting in the late 1970s the company actively worked on heroic themes, including productions of Aram Khachaturian's *Spartacus* in 1969 and Emin Aristakesian's *Prometheus* in 1971. The ballet *Immortality* (1972), choreographed by Uran Sarbagishev to music by Chary Nurymov, praised the staunchness of the Soviet people in the struggle against fascism. Also in the repertory were ballets based on themes from world as well as native literature, for example, the works of the Kyrgyz author Chingiz Aitmatov; notable among these was the ballet oratorio *Mother's Field* (1975), in which Sarbagishev closely followed the author's narrative. Talgonai has lost three sons and her husband at the front. As if conversing with the earth, her nurturer and witness to all her life, she recalls her youth, happy times, and losses. The images arising in her memory are portrayed by choreographed scenes in which classical dance is blended with motifs from national folk dances.

Sarbagishev remains chief choreographer of the company, with principal dancers Aisulu Tokombayeva, Cholponbek Bazarbayev, Arstanbek Irsaliev, Svetlana Tukbulatova, Rosa Tairova, Anvarbek Ryskulov, Kemel Suleimanov, and Bolot Kuttubayev. A ballet school was founded in 1980; its director is Aidai Shukurbekova. The national theatrical folk dance company has been working on a permanent basis since 1966 under the direction of Melisbek Asylbashev.

[*See also the entry on* Makhmud Esambayev.]

Robert K. Urasguildiyev
Translated from Russian

L

LABAN, RUDOLF (Rudolf Jean Baptiste Attila Laban de Varalja; born 15 December 1879 in Poszony [Bratislava], Hungary, died 1 July 1958 in Addlestone, England), innovative, multifaceted dance theorist, choreographer, and educator. Laban's father, a military governor, was away a great deal in Rudolf's youth. The boy and his three younger sisters were raised by an architect uncle, Antoine Sendlein, his wife, and by grandparents. Laban attended grammar school in Poszony and boarding school in Vienna. His main interests were painting, puppet theater, *tableaux vivants* performances, opera, backstage life in the Poszony and Vienna theaters, scene painting, riding, fencing, and adventurous travel in the Balkans while his father was stationed in Bosnia and Herzegovina. His experience of Sufi Islam and Mevlevi dervish rituals profoundly affected him. In 1899, as a cadet at the Militär Akademie in Wiener Neustadt, he admired military life and was interested in massed parades and maneuvers, but his artistic leaning proved stronger.

In 1900, after briefly working with Hermann Obrist in Munich, Laban enrolled at the Écoles des Beaux-Arts in Paris to study architecture and philosophy, but his attendance was erratic. He had a studio in Montparnasse and a small house for his wife Martha Fricke, a painter, in Saint-Maurice near the Bois de Vincennes. He lived the bohemian life of an artist, drew caricatures and posters in the Art Nouveau style, studied the Delsarte method, and began watching and writing down movement and behavior, occasionally working in cabaret and boulevard theaters. Through the Écoles he learned the principles of Rosicrucianism, an approach to life as a spiritual quest, which informed his entire career. In 1907 his wife died. Stunned, Laban sent his two children to her parents near Hanover and left Paris incapacitated by the first of many bouts of profound depression and self-doubt. He returned to Vienna, where his own father had retired.

Laban married Maja Lederer, a singer, in 1910. They moved to Munich, and in 1912 he began a struggling school on Theresienstrasse in the artists' quarter, experimenting with *Tanz-Ton-Wort* (Dance-Sound-Word) ideas. Although still earning as a painter (he successfully published caricatures in the satirical magazine *Jugend*), he was moving more and more toward the performing arts.

It was in Munich that Laban began his great struggle to establish dance as an autonomous art form. He did it by rejecting the dominance of music, still exhibited in the work of Isadora Duncan, Ruth St. Denis, and especially of Émile Jaques-Dalcroze and in ballet. For dance to stand on its own, it needed an approach to its material relevant to industrial society. Discarding the fashionable return to ancient Greece and looking at how to develop beyond ballet's steps and mime, Laban decided to research the medium of movement itself and define its principles of organization—a monumental task.

Although there is no direct evidence that Wassily Kandinsky and Laban met, they undertook similar work in the same street in Munich—Schwabing. Hans Brandenburg, a writer and critic, was a mutual friend and Obrist was a mutual teacher. Kandinsky's efforts to free painting from representation led him and his Blaue Reiter group to face the structures of his medium, just as his friend Arnold Schoenberg did with music. Each of the three men searched for the spiritual basis of his art form; each established a new way of motivating and organizing his material. In particular, similarities can be seen between Kandinsky's *innere Notwendigkeit* (inner necessity) and Laban's concept of inner effort, and between Schoenberg's emerging *Harmonielehre* (theory of harmony) for atonality and Laban's *Harmonielehre* for the dancer's space.

In summer 1912 Laban was invited with his dancers to Monte Verità, Ascona, on Lake Maggiore in Switzerland. He taught *Tonkunst, Wortkunst, Bewegungskunst,* and *Plastikkunst* in this arcadian center, which he called his dance farm. These experiments in rural living (gardening, weaving, cooking, building), in free thinking, and in the arts were the foundation of his later *Bewegungschöre* (movement choirs) and successful community dance work. It is probable that it was on Monte Verità that his conviction grew that people need to be in harmony with nature and the cosmos to be wholly human.

The similarity between his thinking and that of the mystic G. I. Gurdjieff cannot be ignored. He saw movement as the common denominator of all things: rhythm, oscillation, pulsation, tension and relaxation, attraction and repulsion, stability and mobility, circling, swinging—the fundamentals shared by humans and their environment. Position and stillness were for him illusory, for all is in flux and change. He feared the industrial age of the ma-

LABAN. Six identically clad masked dancers form an asymmetrical grouping in Laban's 1920s satirical work, *Die Grünen Clowns* (The Green Clowns). A characteristic sense of weight is clearly conveyed, especially by the dancer at right. (Photograph by Wide World Photos; reprinted from Elizabeth Seldon, *The Dancer's Quest,* 1935.)

chine, as did many others, as destructive of human culture, reducing humanity to the level of the automaton. In Ascona he experimented with the means to combat this tendency. His time there was not either idealistic or escapist, but essentially practical: it was a daily search for an essential alternative to the dehumanizing processes of the twentieth century.

In 1912 Laban was joined by Suzanne Perrottet, who left her teaching post with Dalcroze, to live and work with Laban. In 1913 Marie Wiegmann (later Mary Wigman, also from Dalcroze) joined him. In 1914 they prepared a large work for the Deutsche Werkbunde Exhibition in Cologne of Brandenburg's *Der Sieg des Opfers* (The Triumph of the Victor), but the declaration of war prevented the performances.

The Munich school, now in Schwanthalerstrasse, was abandoned. Laban reopened in Zurich, Switzerland, in Seegartenstrasse, with Wigman and Perrottet as helpers. Perrottet's musical background and talent for children's work left Laban free to work with Wigman on the theory and practice of movement syntax and, thus, on how it could be written down in a notation system. He finalized his concept of the spatial and dynamic content of movement (choreutics and eukinetics) from which his later choreology and kinetography (Labanotation) were developed. He prepared the first edition of *Die Welt des Tänzers* (The Dancer's World), published 1920, in which he expressed his basic credo of the coexistence of the two worlds "of silence" and "of adventure"—of the spiritual world and of the material world—and that the world of the dance could be a means of synthesis. He gave several lecture series on dance ethnology and with Wigman as his soloist gave performances on expressionist theater with his adult pupils.

The Dada movement in Zurich attracted Laban's dancers, who in turn attracted the Dadaists. Käthe Wulff and Sophie Täuber were prominent Laban Dadaists. Laban himself remained aloof from the nihilistic performances and manifestos of the Cabaret Voltaire.

In 1916 Dussia Bereska, a Russian dancer, joined him, and in 1917 his astounding *Sang an der Sonne* (Song to the Sun) was produced, a three-part event danced on the hillside as part of a Masonic festival. Part 1 was at sunset, part 2 at midnight, and part 3 at dawn, with the sun and bonfires as part of the set, along with movement, voices, processions, and audience participation.

Laban's reputation became established as an innovator and dance philosopher and also as a charismatic figure and womanizer. With no money, a growing family (Maja bore five children and Susanne one), hounded by the Hungarian army to enlist and by the Swiss immigration authorities to prove financial independence, again dogged by ill health and self-doubt, the war years were traumatic.

Laban finally abandoned domesticity in 1919, leaving a school in Zurich, run by Perrottet and Wulff. He gained entry to Germany and began his major dance career as the central protagonist of the Absolute Dance. This he did through an astonishingly energetic and committed lifestyle composed of several concurrent strands: dance theater, dance as education, community dance, dance literacy, dance politics, dance theory, and the beginnings of dance therapy.

Laban started his Tanzbühne Laban (1921) with Bereska, in Stuttgart, and was guest choreographer at the Mannheim National Theater. He created his first theater piece, *Die Geblendeten* (The Deluded), and his first rendering of the *Tannhäuser* Bacchanale, using his own experimental dance group, which included Kurt Jooss, Edgar Frank, Herta Feist, Albrecht Knust, and Jens Keith, along with twenty dancers from the theater. After a long summer school at Gleschendorf in 1922, he found a sponsor in Hamburg for his dancers. The works he created there include *Der Schwingende Tempel* (The Swinging Temple; 1922), the first full-length abstract "dance symphony"; *Fausts Erlösung* (1922), Goethe's *Faust* spoken by a speech choir and enacted by a dance choir; *Prometheus* (1923), Aeschylus's *Prometheus,* also with a speech choir; *Gaukelei* (Jugglery; 1923), a dance drama commenting on tyranny, which was danced in silence; *Komödie,* or *Casanova* (1923), a comedy about the idiocies of love; *Terpsichore* (1925) to music by Handel, with a singer; *Narrenspiegel* (Fool's Mirror; 1925), a dance ballad commenting on the duality of life; *Don Juan* (1926), a dance drama to the Gluck score; *Ritterballett* (Ballet of the Knights), a commissioned work to a Beethoven score; *Nacht* (Night; 1927), a satirical *dynamische Materialisation* using mundane movement, jazz, silence, and words.

Besides this work, from 1922 to 1928 Laban and Bereska ran his Kammertanzbühne Laban, a smaller company. They created and toured some thirty-five dances, ranging from solos and duos such as *Orchidée, Marotte, Mondäne,* and *Dithyramb;* quartets such as *Marsch* and *Ballade;* comedies such as *Oben und Unten;* decorative works such as *Zaubergarten* and *Drachentöterei;* and the satire *Die Grünen Clowns.*

His stated aim was to offer diversity and to have meaning and substance behind even the merest piece. His methods were absolutely innovative: they used improvisation; very little or no music; communal decision making; a new, free approach to the body in both movement and costume; interchangeable roles; nonmetric rhythms; and wholehearted, full-bodied movement contrasted with delicate hand and arm studies. The same dance might be performed in different costumes or with different sound or by a different sex and number of dancers. The motivation ranged from "a delight in line" to a comment on "inner stirrings," decorative, rhythmic, grotesque, and ecstatic themes, as well as pictorial imagery.

In 1926 he toured with Gert Ruth Loeszer, using Wagnerian themes without music, which caused the kind of furor to which he and his circle were accustomed. Loeszer, who became ballet mistress at Düsseldorf, was an accomplished dancer and one of the few Laban dancers keen on nudity.

In 1930 Laban was appointed director of movement and dance at the Prussian Theaters in Berlin. He was ballet master at the State Opera (Unter den Linden), where he choreographed many opera dances, including *Prince Igor, Rienzi, Geisha, Salome,* and *Margarete* and gave dance performances at the Kroll Theater. His works were notorious for their freedom from the usual restrictions of the ballet tradition and for his opposition to the star system. In 1930 and 1931 he choreographed the *Tannhäuser* bacchanale at the Bayreuth Wagner Festival, assisted by Kurt Jooss, for which there were both ecstatic and critical notices. With the beginning of the Third Reich in 1933 and the termination of his contract at the Opera in 1934, he was appointed director of the Deutsche Tanzbühne, a newly created organization to promote German dance, a post directly under the Nazi Ministry of Propaganda.

Alongside his theater work, Laban developed the movement-choir concept, a mode of dancing for large groups of amateurs. His aim was to make celebratory works primarily for the enjoyment of the performers and thereby to reestablish dance as a central feature of community life—a phenomenon largely destroyed by the industrial revolution. The Hamburger Bewegungschöre Laban was the first to be established, in 1922; by 1924 there were six others, in Frankfurt, Stuttgart, Munster, Gera, Bern, and Budapest. The number continued to grow rapidly.

The first major movement-choir work Laban choreographed was *Lichtwende* (Dawning Light; 1923), followed by *Agamemnons Tod* (Death of Agamemnon; 1924), *Dämmernden Rhythmen* (Rhythms of Twilight; 1925), *Titan* (1927), and *Alltag und Fest* (Everyday Life and Festival; 1929). [*See* Movement Choir.]

In June 1929, Laban was appointed to direct the Viennese Festzug des Handwerkes und der Gewerbe (Pageant of Crafts and Guilds), a massive procession around the

Ringstrasse, last held fifty years before. Laban managed to engage the cooperation of the guilds. Up to ten thousand participants—from umbrella makers to plasterers, clockmakers, bakers, and metalworkers—danced the actions of their crafts with specially written music by Max Brand and Egon Wellesz. It was a phenomenal piece of imaginative organization, which nearly came to grief because of the weather and the vagaries of the first mobile loudspeakers for phonograph recordings of the music.

After he had established his main school in Hamburg, on Tiergartenstrasse (1922), and later on Schwanenwik, Laban schools opened all over Germany and also in Italy, France, Hungary, Yugoslavia, Holland, and Czechoslavakia. By 1926 there were twenty-one quoted in the magazine *Schönheit*.

Laban's central school was eventually housed at the Folkwang Schule in Essen in 1929, with Jooss as its director. Laban lived a peripatetic existence, visiting his various schools "once a month," an essential charismatic and inspiring figure.

The aims of Laban's schools were to provide professional dance training, supply dancers for his companies, and train leaders of amateur dance-and-movement choirs. Unlike his acolytes, and especially Wigman, Laban was not anti-ballet but instead saw his work as a development of the ballet tradition, more suitable to the machine age of the twentieth century. His work centered on developing the body, through a system of movement exercises. The exercises were based on spatial scales and on dynamic/rhythmic studies, both in given movement and in improvisation and creativity. The relatedness of the dancer to his or her environment and to other dancers was central through expressive movement, group form, and group improvisation. Artistry and creativity were emphasized, which distinguished Laban's work from physical-culture systems (Bode, Günther, Mensendieck, Loheland, Medau). His students were required to pass in notation and in theory and practice of dance and be reexamined each year to gain the Laban Diploma.

Laban published two books on dance teaching: *Gymnastik und Tanz* (1926) and *Des Kindes Gymnastik und Tanz* (1929). They contain photographs, many of which are of nude or seminude dancers. This is misleading, for although nudity was popular, and Jenny Gertz, a Laban-trained teacher, taught children's classes nude, Laban never did. However he was persuaded to use nudity for publicity for his work, to the amusement of his close colleagues and to the annoyance of the more staid majority.

After his concentrated work with Wigman in Ascona and Zurich during the war years (1914–1918), Laban worked ceaselessly to find the right solution for developing a notation system for movement as well as for dance. Building on what was already there, namely, Raoul-Auger Feuillet's and Pierre Beauchamp's systems, he devised several symbol systems to express his developing choreological analysis. Eventually, in 1927, during the summer school following the First Dancers' Congress at Magdeburg, while working with Jooss, Sigurd Leeder, and Bereska, the final formulation was reached. *Kinetographie Laban* was published in 1928 by Universal Edition in Vienna. It was further developed in the 1930s, primarily by Knust and Leeder.

Much of choreology was still called choregraphy at that time—that is, dance writing, using the Feuillet meaning of the word. In 1926 Laban published *Choreographie*, in which he explains his thinking and gives several solutions to notation problems, all later subsumed or abandoned. In autumn 1926 his Choreographisches Institut was set up in Theaterstrasse Würzburg, for purposes of research and collecting choreographic knowledge—in other words, for developing dance as a discipline with a choreological body of knowledge. It was staffed by Loeszer, Bereska, Robert Robst, and Gertrud Snell. It moved to Gillstrasse in Berlin in 1927, attracting many students who later went on to prominent professions in dance (Aurelio Milloss, Pino and Pia Mlakar, Ilse Loesch), and to the Folkwang Schule in Essen in 1929, where it was subsumed in the Zentrale Schule Laban.

In 1928 the journal *Schrifttanz* was published, initiated by Laban and edited by Alfred Schlee of Universal Edition. It was the first serious dance magazine, aiming to provide a forum for discussing and promoting all forms of dance writing, including questions of notation and of dance theory, dance history, and dance aesthetics. It included writers from many dance fields, but it was dominated by the Laban circle. In 1932 it was subsumed into the magazine *Der Tanz*, which in 1933 was manipulated into an organ for Nazi culture.

Laban realized that in order to reestablish dance as a serious art form, capable of standing as an equal to its sister arts, he must overcome its image as an effeminate, thoughtless, slightly pornographic profession. He therefore set about establishing dance for men by introducing the kind of movement that was attractive to the young German male—virile looking, impactive, strongly rhythmic, and good for the development of an athletic body. Hamburg's men's movement choir is an example of his success in the amateur dance field. Laban's theater works include major roles for men such as the Fool in *Narrenspiegel*, the title role in *Don Juan*, the Tyrant in *Gaukelei*, and the Servant in *Komödie*. His companies included strong male dancers such as Frank, Robst, and Jooss, at a time when female solo dancers were plentiful.

Laban's loathing for privilege led him to use a democratic structure for his companies. His dismissal of the soloists of the Berlin Opera Ballet in 1932 is an example of his credo in action. His movement choirs also exhibited his belief in each person's autonomy, value, and need for social interaction. He was advocating not crowd behavior but group interdependence and intradependence.

Laban had set about improving the lot of the professional dancer by helping to establish the Deutscher Tänzerbund (1927) and by promoting improvements in security, social benefits, and applications of the law for dancers. He had been on the organizing committee for, and undoubtedly dominated, the First Dancers' Congress (1927) in Magdeburg, the Second in Essen (1928), and the Third in Munich (1930).

Laban was socially conscious all of his life, but he was politically naive. In 1934 he was at the pinnacle of his career, completely absorbed in his work and believing he could overcome the Nazi problem just as he had overcome all the immense problems in establishing dance. While his Jewish friends and colleagues left Germany (Jooss, Martin Gleisner, Sylvia Bodmer), the dance community as a whole hung on. His autobiography *Ein Leben für den Tanz* (A Life for Dance), published in 1935, makes no mention of political problems. Yet, in the same year, he, Wigman, Gret Palucca, and Harald Kreutzberg, among others, were used to promote the National Socialist doctrine for dance in an official pamphlet. It was the Berlin Olympics of 1936 that triggered his downfall. His massive movement choir *Vom Tauwind und der Neuen Freude* (Of Warm Breeze and New Joy), prepared for the Dietrich-Eckhart open-air theater for the cultural celebrations surrounding "Hitler's Olympics," was disallowed. Its personal censorship by Dr. Josef Goebbels was followed by Laban's dismissal. He took refuge in Schloss Banz, Staffelberg. His schools, movement choirs, notation system, and books were all declared anti-German, and his colleagues were harassed. His name, so prominent in the publications of 1935 and 1936, was absent thereafter.

The Nazis achieved a chillingly efficient annihilation of Laban's work. It was as if he had never been. Only in isolated instances was his work ever referred to again publicly, and it was not until the 1980s that Germany looked again at his astounding achievement for dance in their country.

In 1937 Laban, by then penniless, managed to obtain a visa to France with the help of Rolf de Maré and in November arrived in Paris. Ill both physically and mentally, and in deep shock, he was found in a destitute state by Lisa Ullmann, a Jooss-Leeder teacher, who had gained her Laban Diploma in Berlin under Lotte Wedekind. Jooss brought him to Dartington Hall in Devon, England, where Jooss, Les Ballets Jooss, and the Jooss-Leeder school (late of the Folkwang Schule in Essen) were guests of Dorothy and Leonard Elmhirst.

Laban spent two years at Dartington, at first almost as a recluse, being nursed back to health by Ullmann. Having lost all his papers in Germany, he attempted to recall some of the essentials of his theories in a document that

LABAN. A scene from *Agamemnons Tod* (Death of Agamemnon; 1924), with the Hamburger Bewegungschöre Laban. (Photograph reprinted from Elizabeth Seldon, *The Dancer's Quest*, 1935.)

became the first half of his book *Choreutics,* published posthumously in 1966.

Gradually, Laban began a new career, branching out along several concurrent lines—in industry, education, recreation, therapy, and drama. While at Dartington Hall, Laban was introduced to F. C. Lawrence, a management consultant interested in motion study. Lawrence needed a movement expert to help him train women for men's manual work in wartime and to place people in the right management jobs. Together they developed the Laban/Lawrence system of movement observation. Laban worked in a variety of manufacturing situations to assist the war effort. The use of the word *effort,* the English translation of the German *Antrieb,* comes from this period. With Lawrence he published *Effort* in 1947.

In 1940 all aliens were required to leave Dartington, and Laban, with Ullmann, found a place to live in rural Wales, at Rock House, in Newtown. They had very little income apart from the continuing generosity of the Elmhirsts. Ullmann attempted to earn by teaching movement classes, through the Keep Fit Association and Local Education Authority. Educational thinking in Britain, much influenced by the American John Dewey's child-centered methods, creative learning, and discovery methods, provided an ideal ambience for Laban's ideas. Several educators who had studied with Wigman in the 1930s welcomed Laban and Ullmann, and so began the period of creative dance in British schools, based on training given at The Modern Dance Holiday Courses by Ullmann, Joan Goodrich, and Diana Jordan.

In 1942 Laban and Ullmann moved to Manchester—Laban to work with Lawrence and both to teach teachers. The Laban Guild, primarily for teachers, was started, and in 1946 Ullmann opened the Art of Movement Studio in Manchester, where Sylvia Bodmer taught and Laban acted as a mentor. For two short years the Art of Movement Studio offered courses for dancers. Laban still believed theater work might be possible. In 1948, however, the Ministry of Education approved one-year courses for teachers. Laban's work, under Ullmann, became entirely education oriented and child centered and rapidly developed an influence in schools. Laban published *Modern Educational Dance* in 1948.

Laban, needing relief from the child-oriented emphasis around him (in which he was frankly not interested), taught at the Bradford Civic Theatre with Esmé Church, producing and writing several movement plays, eventually assisted by Geraldine Stephenson. He also was associated closely with Theatre Workshop—with Joan Littlewood, Jean Newlove, and Ewan McColl—the left-wing theater group working in Manchester.

The British Drama League took up his work; indeed, it had begun to do so already in 1934, under Annie Boalth's influence, and he taught many courses for them. He published *Mastery of Movement on the Stage* in 1950. Through Dartington Hall, Laban worked at Withymead, a center for Jungian arts therapy, developing a method of using creative dance and movement for therapeutic purposes.

In 1953 the Art of Movement Studio moved to Addlestone, Surrey, with Marion North, Valerie Preston, and Geraldine Stephenson as faculty. By 1954 the Laban Centre, continuing the role of his Berlin Choreographisches Institut, functioned as Laban's laboratory. He became increasingly isolated, partly as a result of Ullmann's protectiveness, and partly because he was working on an intellectual and intuitive plane few people could share. He took little joy in the company of the teachers who came to the Art of Movement Studio to study the particular brand of his work developed for British schools. He was deeply engrossed in the spiritual truths for which movement provided a clue. His mature research into movement and personality crystalized in his last years, stimulated by a Jungian colleague, Bill Carpenter. The book they were writing has never been published.

Laban died in 1958, but his work did not die with him. The overall influence of the man on dance in the Weimar Republic is reflected in the contemporary writings of Wigman, Brandenburg, Böhme, Schikowski, Schlee, and Joseph Lewitan. He was a giant in his time, not always understood but recognized as the source of a new dance era.

Laban was not a choreographer of outstanding works, but one who consistently experimented with new aspects of his medium. He was interested in confronting the problems of space, sources of motion, casting, tradition, expression, gesture, abstraction, sound, and audience reaction; as soon as he had solved the problem at hand, he lost interest and moved on to the next. Hence, he left the completion of works, both dances and books, to others, having been himself the essential catalyst to get them underway. He was not a good dancer, technically, but had a presence in which his larger-than-life personality filled the stage. Personal appearances were in demand, but an accident in 1926 during a performance of *Don Juan* put an end not only to his own dancing but also to his permanent company's prospects. In assessing his contribution to dance theater, it is his innovative and continually developing processes of choreography that are extraordinary. The products themselves were uneven and some, such as *Nacht,* so avant-garde as to attract considerable abuse and egg throwing. Some of the choreographic devices of the 1930s, regarded as new, were in fact practiced by Laban in the 1920s. His influence on his students' lives is consistently enormous. Many who came for a week found they had begun a life's work.

Laban changed the face of community dance. With the decline of folk dance, he offered a way of participating in an art form that, although severely ravaged by the Third Reich, reappeared in other guises in Britain almost immediately and is again reemerging in Europe and in America.

Ullmann's influence is important. Without her, it is possible that Laban might never have recovered from the shock and deprivation of 1936. Without her, the British schools' creative-dance explosion of the 1950s and early 1960s might never have happened. However, she, like everyone else, was not capable of dealing with the breadth of his genius alone. Under her leadership, her version of Laban's work for schools grew and is still discernible, although partially engulfed by contemporary dance technique and choreography from the United States and shifts in education policy. She initiated the International Council of Kinetography Laban in 1959 and retired in 1972.

Laban's work began to spread to the United States in the 1930s, primarily through the work of his students and of disciples of Wigman and Jooss. Hanya Holm opened her Wigman school in New York in 1931. Her influence was later developed by her student Alwin Nikolais. The Dance Notation Bureau was founded in 1940 and developed under the guidance of students of Laban or Leeder—Ann Hutchinson, Helen Priest Rogers, and Irmgard Bartenieff. In the United States, the term *Labanotation* replaced *Kinetography*. Labanalysis, or Laban Movement Analysis, became the American adaptation of choreology.

After Laban's death it was inevitable that none of his pupils could encompass his work. The unity he professed and practiced of art, education, recreation, and work became specialized. His theater work was virtually unknown, and the application of his theories developed along separate lines.

In the late 1970s the Laban/Bartenieff Institute of Movement Studies was established in New York City as a center for the study of Laban's movement principles, as understood by Bartenieff in discussion with Warren Lamb. Also in New York City, the Dance Notation Bureau specializes in his notation, with a branch at Ohio State University in Columbus. In London the Laban Centre for Movement and Dance developed rapidly under Marion North, with Bonnie Bird's cooperation. It pioneered the first British bachelor's, master's, and Ph.D. degrees in dance. It offers the range of dance experience Laban pioneered in the Weimar Republic: community dance, dance theater, dance documentation, dance therapy, and performance with the sociology and practice of dance. All students learn Laban's choreological concepts, which are applied to contemporary needs. The Laban Centre houses the Laban Collection, a working archive of documents, films, photographs, and audio- and videotapes of Laban-centered materials, specializing in the period from 1900 to 1942. Ullmann's collection of papers and drawings are housed in the National Resource Centre for Dance at Surrey University.

As with any genius, the period following Laban's death was uneasy. However, gradually, despite misinterpretation and diminished representations of his work, the key essentials of this many-faceted man are being discovered. His notation, by which he is best known, is overstated as his main contribution. He was above all else an artist/researcher who is emerging more clearly as the father of modern dance in Europe and the leading dance theorist of the twentieth century.

[*See also* Labanotation *and* Laban Principles of Movement.]

BIBLIOGRAPHY

Brandenburg, Hans. *Der moderne Tanz.* 3d ed. Munich, 1921.

Brandenburg, Hans. *Das Theater und das neue Deutschland.* Jena, 1919.

Gleisner, Martin. *Tanz für Alle.* Leipzig, 1928.

Green, Martin. *Mountain of Truth.* Hanover, N.H., 1986.

Hodgson, John, and Valerie Preston-Dunlop. *Rudolf Laban: An Introduction to His Work and Influence.* Plymouth, 1990.

Koegler, Horst. "In the Shadow of the Swastika: Dance in Germany, 1929–1936." *Dance Perspectives,* no. 57 (Spring 1974).

Laban Art of Movement Guild Magazine, no. 15 (1954); no. 63 (1979); no. 65 (1980).

Laban, Rudolf. *Principles of Dance and Movement Notation.* London, 1956.

Laban, Rudolf. *A Life for Dance.* Translated and annotated by Lisa Ullmann. London, 1975.

Lewitan, Joseph. "Laban der Tanz-Tribun." *Der Tanz* 2 (1929): 2–7.

Maletic, Vera. *Body—Space—Expression: The Development of Rudolf Laban's Movement and Dance Concepts.* Berlin, 1987.

Preston-Dunlop, Valerie. "Laban and the Nazis: Toward an Understanding of Rudolf Laban and the Third Reich." *Update Dance/USA* 7 (August–September 1989): 12–13, 19–22.

Preston-Dunlop, Valerie. "Rudolf Laban: The Making of Modern Dance." *Dance Theatre Journal* 7 (Winter 1989): 11–16; 7 (February 1990): 10–13.

Preston-Dunlop, Valerie. "Rudolf Laban and Kurt Jooss in Exile." In *Theatre and Film in Exile: German Artists in Great Britain, 1933–1945,* edited by Günter Berghaus. Oxford, 1989.

Preston-Dunlop, Valerie. "Laban, Schoenberg, and Kandinsky, 1899–1938." In *La danse tracée.* Paris, 1990. Exhibition catalog, Centre Georges Pompidou.

Preston-Dunlop, Valerie, and Susanne Lahusen, eds. *Schrifttanz: A View of German Dance in the Weimar Republic.* London, 1990.

Die Schönheit 1–2 (1926).

Schrifttanz Eine Vierteljahresschrift . . . Vienna 1928–31. Reprinted with an introduction. Hildesheim, 1991.

Singchor und Tanz (December 1929).

Die Tat (June 1920); (June 1922); (November 1927).

Terpis, Max. *Tanz und Tänzer.* Zurich, 1946.

Wigman, Mary. "Rudolf von Labans Lehre vom Tanz." *Die Neue Schaubühne* 5 (September 1921).

Wigman, Mary. *The Mary Wigman Book.* Translated and edited by Walter Sorell. Middletown, Conn., 1975.

ARCHIVES. Dartington Hall Records, Dartington Hall, Devon, England. Laban Collection, Laban Centre for Movement and Dance, London. National Resource Centre for Dance, University of Surrey, Guildford. Tanzarchiv, Cologne. Tanzarchiv, Leipzig.

VALERIE PRESTON-DUNLOP

LABANOTATION. Also known as Kinetography Laban, Labanotation is a movement notation system originated by Rudolf Laban (1879–1958) in Germany and subsequently further developed by his followers in Europe and the United States. Laban first evolved a shorthand for his theories about lines of movement in space (which he called space harmony). Realizing that a universally applicable system was needed, he explored the idea of placing movement indications on a cross representing the body. A sequence of movements was written on a series of crosses, reading from left to right.

Laban credits choreographer Kurt Jooss with the idea of modifying the cross into a vertical staff representing the vertically standing body. Reading the movement indications from the bottom of the page upward provided an unbroken representation of fluent, continuous movement. Dussia Bereska, one of Laban's principal dancers, suggested that the length of a movement sign should indicate the duration of the action—long signs for sustained movement, short signs for sudden actions.

By establishing a constant basic unit for the regular beat, or time pulse, the writer could indicate exact rhythms through the lengths of the symbols. This third development led to the publication of Laban's *Schrifttanz* (Written Dance, 1928). In 1930 an English-French edition was issued, together with a collection of dances and studies, *Kleine Tänze mit Vorübungen.* Laban also launched the periodical *Schrifttanz* in 1928. He emphasized that it was not *Tanzschrift* (dance script) but "written dance"; his concern was with dance in written form rather than with a notation system; the difference is subtle but significant.

Laban's daughter Azra was an early contributor to the development of the system, but the first person to become completely involved in it and to make it his life's work was Albrecht Knust, who established the first notation center, created reading materials, and published handbooks on the system in 1897. His work with large-movement choirs led to his unique contribution on group notation. Knust became resident notator for Pia and Pino Mlakar at the opera house in Munich. When cut off from other activities during World War II, he worked on his eight-volume encyclopedia of the system, which then was circulated in a very limited edition in typescript form. [*See the entry on Knust.*]

The system also fascinated a colleague of Jooss's, Sigurd Leeder, who used it regularly in his school and contributed many lively and imaginative ideas to it that grew out of his rich understanding of movement subtleties. A student of Leeder's at the Jooss-Leeder Dance School in England, Ann Hutchinson, was asked to notate four of Jooss's ballets in 1938–1939. Returning to her native New York, armed with this practical experience, she met with three young women who had learned the system from other sources. Helen Priest had been a student of Knust in Germany, while Henrietta Greenhood and Janey Price had been students of Irma Betz at the Hanya Holm Studio in New York City.

Betz, who died shortly before Hutchinson's arrival, had met Laban during his 1926 visit to the United States and had studied the system subsequently through correspondence. Differences in usage soon became apparent and, as a result, in 1940, the Dance Notation Bureau was formed. The bureau's stated aim was to further the art of dance through the use of a system of notation. Its first task was to act as a center of information and a clearinghouse. In sorting out the differences, it soon became apparent that aspects rooted in Laban's movement theories would have to be modified if the system were to function universally for all forms of movement.

Hutchinson, like Knust, also made notation her life's work, pioneering the spread of the system in the United States and becoming the director and the leading force at the bureau.

The particular contribution Hutchinson and her colleagues made at the bureau, notably Nadia Chilkovsky Nahumck, Lucy Venable, and (later) Muriel Topaz, was the practical application of the system and its gradual refinement through daily use as well as theoretical discussions. Teaching materials, textbooks, a magazine *(The Dance Notation Record),* and a trade pamphlet *(The Labanotator)* kept practitioners in touch. Use of the system to record George Balanchine's ballets as well as many modern-dance choreographies, notably those by Doris Humphrey, spread interest in the system.

Early on, Laban gave Hutchinson carte blanche to develop the system, declaring that he no longer wanted to be concerned with details. Before his death in 1958, he officially handed the mantle of responsibility to Hutchinson, Knust, Leeder, and Lisa Ullmann. In 1959, Ullmann called together specialists from different countries to form the International Council of Kinetography Laban (ICKL), the first of many biennial conferences. In addition to the four core members selected by Laban, founding members included such leading practitioners as Valerie Preston (United Kingdom), Mária Szentpál (Hungary), Vera Maletić (the former Yugoslavia), Jacqueline Challet (France), Irmgard Bartenieff (United States), and Roderyk Lange (Poland). The ICKL's prime purpose was to unify the system by sharing and combining ideas and usages developed independently in different countries as a result of war-produced isolation.

In the United States, Nahumck was the first to establish Labanotation as part of the dance curriculum at every level at the Philadelphia Dance Academy. She was also the first to publish books combining the notation with dance education. Many college dance departments incorporated use of the notation, notably the Juilliard School in New York City. In the United Kingdom, Valerie Preston-Dunlop saw the value of motif writing in connection with Laban's modern education dance and produced a series of books in which she organized the motif ideas and expanded their use. This broad description of movement concepts and motifs had already proved valuable in teaching children as well as in choreographic exploration.

In establishing the Language of Dance Centre in London in 1967, Hutchinson changed the focus in the use of Labanotation from study of the system itself to its functional use as an integral part of dance and movement education. Her book *Your Move* (1983) was the first of its kind to present this new approach.

Laban's wartime work in industry led to the development of "Effort," the qualitative aspects of movement. His first work-study investigations of the functional placement of tools and fatigue-reducing exercises led to an awareness of each person's innate movement preferences in the use of time, space, energy, and flow. Effort notation evolved to record observations on these inborn patterns; it provided "profiles" that aided the placement of individuals in jobs that required their natural skills. Personnel assessment was expanded by Warren Lamb, who further defined "shape" aspects and who, with Pamela Ramsden, evolved action profiling, a technique that assists businesses in their top-team planning. This work, which originated in the United Kingdom, has spread to other countries.

Application of Effort-Shape analysis has enriched dance studies as well as physio- and psychotherapy. Bartenieff, who studied with both Laban and Lamb, applied with remarkable results the knowledge gained from her hospital work with polio victims. Graduates of the Laban/Bartenieff Institute of Movement Studies, which she founded in 1978, spread the work to many different fields. Effort-shape notation was at one time considered to be separate from Labanotation, but experiments have shown that a very complete description of a movement can be obtained by combining the two.

Thus, the Labanotation system encompasses three areas of specialization: motif description (the movement idea), structured description (in which specific information is given regarding use of the body, type of movement, and timing), and effort-shape description (use of energy flow, inner states and drives, and the shaping of movement).

The structured form of Labanotation is an alphabet system in which movement patterns are spelled out according to the components contained in any given movement. It answers the questions what? (the body), where? (space), when? (time), and how? (manner of performance).

The body is represented by a vertical three-line staff with columns for supports and for the main parts of the body. The center line of this staff divides the body symmetrically into right and left sides. Direction is indicated pictorially by the shape of the symbol; the missing third dimension, the vertical line, or the level is shown by the shading of the direction symbol. Placement of the symbol on the staff indicates which part of the body is moving into the stated direction. Timing, or duration, is shown by the visual device of the length of the symbol. The center line of the staff also represents time passing by and, for structured time, is marked off into regular beats and measures (bars), thus allowing the precise indication of rhythms. One symbol contains four pieces of information: the timing by its length, the direction by its shape, the level by its shading, and the part of the body involved by its placement on the staff.

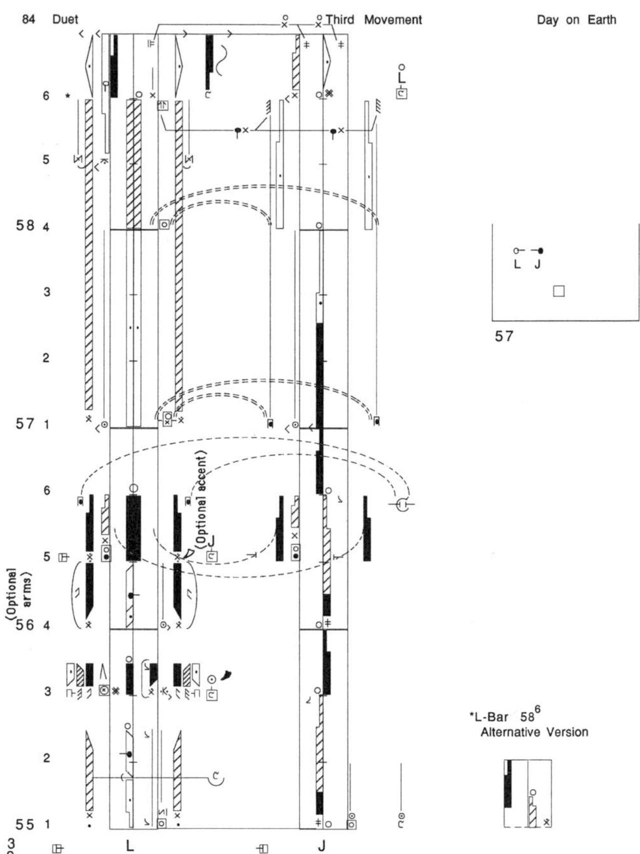

LABANOTATION. This example of Labanotation shows bars 55 through 58 of a duet from Doris Humphrey's *Day on Earth* (1947) as notated by Muriel Topaz. The two dancers are identified by the letters L and J, and the staff is read from bottom to top. The meter (identified on the lower left-hand side) is 3/2. The four bars of notation are grouped into two bars of six counts each. (Courtesy of the Dance Notation Bureau, New York.)

Movement analysis includes all forms of flexion, extension, rotation, contact, relationship, and location—indeed, all the facts and ideas about movement that have been encountered through application of the system to many different fields, movement disciplines, and choreographic ideas. Labanotation emphasizes the process of movement rather than positions.

Each Labanotation specialist has contributed knowledge and experience to its further development. Although a shorthand for the system was never developed, professional notators working at speed have evolved quick devices, particularly for known movement patterns. In finished scores these are carefully spelled out, often in a glossary, thus providing access to the full information. Like a language, the system can be used at a highly sophisticated level or in a simple, more rudimentary form, when only general statements are needed.

Because it incorporates a universal movement analysis, Labanotation serves as an enriching education tool. Textbooks on Labanotation (Kinetography Laban) have been published in many languages. Books of dances and scores of ballets have been published, and many scores can be rented for classroom study. An increasing number of books on movement techniques now also include the information in notated form. Learned articles and theses include notated examples.

Centers specializing in teaching and publishing Labanotation exist in several countries. The Dance Notation Bureau in New York City specializes in training notators and reconstructors to work with ballet and contemporary dance companies. The system's greatest strength is the democratic cooperation of the many people who have contributed to its present high state of development and widespread use through notating, in addition to dance, everyday interactions, animal movement, and athletic activities.

[*See also* Notation. *Many of the figures mentioned herein are the subjects of independent entries; see especially the entry on Laban.*]

BIBLIOGRAPHY

Guest, Ann Hutchinson. *Labanotation.* 3d rev. ed. New York, 1977.

Guest, Ann Hutchinson. *Your Move: A New Approach to the Study of Movement and Dance.* 2 vols. New York, 1983, 1995.

Guest, Ann Hutchinson. *Choreo-Graphics: A Comparison of Dance Notation Systems from the Fifteenth Century to the Present.* New York, 1989.

Guest, Ann Hutchinson. *Advanced Labanotation.* New York, 1991.

Knust, Albrecht. *A Dictionary of Kinetography Laban.* 2 vols. 2d ed. Estover, England, 1979.

Laban, Rudolf. *Principles of Dance and Movement Notation.* London, 1956.

Nahumck, Nadia Chilkovsky. *Introduction to Dance Literacy.* Roodepoort, S.A., 1978.

Preston-Dunlop, Valerie. *Readers in Kinetography Laban.* 3 vols. London, 1966–1967.

Preston-Dunlop, Valerie. *Practical Kinetography Laban.* Brooklyn, 1969.

Venable, Lucy. "Archives of the Dance: LabanWriter—There Had to Be a Better Way." *Dance Research* 9 (Autumn 1991): 76–88.

Warner, MaryJane. *Laban Notation Scores: An International Bibliography.* New York, 1984–.

ANN HUTCHINSON GUEST

LABAN PRINCIPLES OF MOVEMENT ANALYSIS. Rudolf Laban undertook an in-depth investigation of movement in life and art. In contrast to traditional approaches to movement studies, which examined phenomena in isolation, Laban's approach was based on his belief in a contextual understanding of movement principles. He drew from his multiple experiences as artist-designer, dancer, choreographer, director, teacher, and time-and-motion analyst to establish a theoretical framework for analyzing and notating movement. His view of dance as human expression connected to universal forms of movement directed him to seek common denominators among all types of movement.

Three major systems of movement classification constitute Laban's theoretical framework: general movement analysis and description, which also underlie his system of notation, called *Kinetography Laban* or *Labanotation;* a theory investigating the spatial structure of movement and dance, referred to as *Space Harmony* or *Choreutics;* and a theory dealing with the dynamic rhythm of movement and dance, first known as *Eukinetics* and subsequently as *Effort.*

Two contemporary developments of Laban's concepts and principles of movement analysis may be added to these. One is Effort-Shape, drawn from Laban's concept of affinities between the movement's energy, or effort, and its spatial unfolding, as developed by his student Warren Lamb. The other is Laban Movement Analysis, in which his principles are coupled with Bartenieff Fundamentals, a system that combines the Laban frame-work with insights from physical therapy and the body sciences, as developed by Laban's student Irmgard Bartenieff.

Laban began his investigation of movement in the 1910s and refined and expanded his theories and their applications until his death; his students and colleagues continue to develop his work. Thus ideas, terminology, and interpretations have varied over the years. Some aspects are conceived differently by different people; others are controversial. This article emphasizes Laban's formulation of underlying principles.

In general, Laban's principles are marked by the following conceptions. The view of movement as a dynamic process and not as static states underlies all of his writings. All movement components, such as aspects of space, weight, time, flow, and body sequencing, are considered interdependent. The system encompasses the analysis of both quantitative features of movement (that is, what body part moves in which direction and with what timing) and qualitative features (that is, with what dynamics). All movement analysis is approached from the point of view of the link between the mental and the physical. In *Choreutics* (1939), Laban outlined a contemporary choreology, or science of movement, as "a kind of grammar and syntax of the language of movement, dealing not only with the outer form of movement but also with its mental and emotional content." His system is based on the discipline of movement and dance itself; it defines common denominators of all types of movement and provides a means of differentiating them through description, classification, and notation. The vocabulary describes movement and dance in their own terms.

Laban's theoretical framework aims at delineating principles of human movement as a means of understanding this phenomenon, while also providing a practical tool for anyone interested in movement. Thus Laban principles have been applied not only to dance and choreography but also to theater, sports, dance therapy, and other forms of body therapies and the psychotherapies; to research in nonverbal communication and other topics in the behavioral and social sciences; and to management consulting, injury prevention and treatment, and other educational, research, and creative endeavors.

In presenting Laban's principles, however, translation and interpretation are essential. Laban's early German texts, at times written in a rhapsodic style, are not amenable to literal translation; many of his English texts present no lesser challenges because of their Central European structure and style. Even concepts formed in England and terminology selected from the English language require interpretation.

General Movement and Dance Analysis. Laban's first books, written in German in the 1920s—*Die Welt des Tänzers* (The Dancer's World), *Gymnastik und Tanz* (Gymnastics and Dance), and *Des Kindes Gymnastik und Tanz* (Gymnastics and Dance for the Child)—deal with movement and dance both generally and contextually. In *Choreographie,* however, he approached a dynamic description of dance elements and an outline of a system of dance notation. The 1928 publication of "Grundprinzipien der Bewegungsschrift" (Fundamental Principles of Movement Notation) and *Schrifttanz: Methodik, Orthographie, Erläuterungen* (Methodics, Orthography, Explanations) marks the birth of Laban's system of notation, to which he dedicated his last book, *Principles of Dance and Movement Notation.*

The analysis of bodily actions is presented in *The Mastery of Movement on the Stage* and in its revised version, *The Mastery of Movement.* Actions of the whole body and its parts are examined for the purpose of training the body as an instrument of expression. The initial analysis of actions—determining which body parts move, their direction(s) in space, the duration of the movement, and the degree of muscular energy used—is also considered more globally within three aspects of rhythm that "are always united, though one can occupy the foreground of an action." *Space rhythm* consists of the alternative use of various directions that results in shapes, such as combinations of straight, curved, and twisted. *Shaping* can occur sequentially or simultaneously, not unlike melody and harmony in music. *Time rhythm* evolves from a sequence of movements of equal or different lengths; this temporal division can be related to metrical or free rhythms. *Weight rhythm* results from muscular energy or force in terms of degrees of muscular tension and accents. In associating weight and time, Laban draws an analogy between movement and Greek poetic metrics, identifying such sequences as trochee, iamb, dactyl, or anapest. Also related to rhythm is phrasing, which can be distinguished through various emphases of the space, time, and weight components.

The second edition of *The Mastery of Movement* revised by Lisa Ullmann in 1960, elaborates on the observation and analysis of movement styles. Because style is seen as "a special selection of movement originated from racial, social period and other characteristics," detailed guidelines are provided for observing bodily actions from the perspective of the subdivision of body, time, space, and energy, as well as relationships. These observation points have served as a foundation for the development of several research tools in comparative analysis of style, such as the "choreometric coding book" designed by Irmgard Bartenieff and Forrestine Paulay with Alan Lomax (1968); its purpose is to describe dance style profiles for eight world culture regions. Analyses of choreographic style, such as Elizabeth Kagan's comparison of works by Paul Taylor and Doris Humphrey (1978) or Vera Maletić's comparison of pieces by Twyla Tharp and Dan Wagoner, have also integrated the observation of bodily components into the research design.

Space Harmony and Choreutics. In his formulation of organizing principles of movement in space, Laban drew from many sources. The theory and notation of social dances that laid the foundation for ballet (published by Feuillet in 1700) was a point of departure for his directional orientation. He observed that the structuring of forms in nature, including crystals, plants, and animals, is subject to spatial laws not unlike those that underlie the harmonious movement of the human body. Laban's view of human movement as a continuous creation of fragments of crystalline forms was also supported by the ancient knowledge of dynamic crystallization, which brought Plato to classify the five regular solids (cube, octahedron, tetrahedron, icosahedron, and dodecahedron). Laban believed that movement in various spatial directions contains a form-building force, similar to the building of crystalline forms. He thus found basic ordering principles in movement sequences, including particular sets of directions and counterdirections within crystalline structures such as octahedron, cube, and icosahedron. Laban referred to the theory and practice of ordering movement in space as *Space Harmony;* he also coined the term *Choreutics* (from Greek *choros,* circle-dance, and *eu,* good or harmonious).

Laban's principles of Space Harmony are drawn from several works. His 1926 book *Choreographie* presented the first outline of his theory of movement in space. The manuscript for his major book on Space Harmony was written

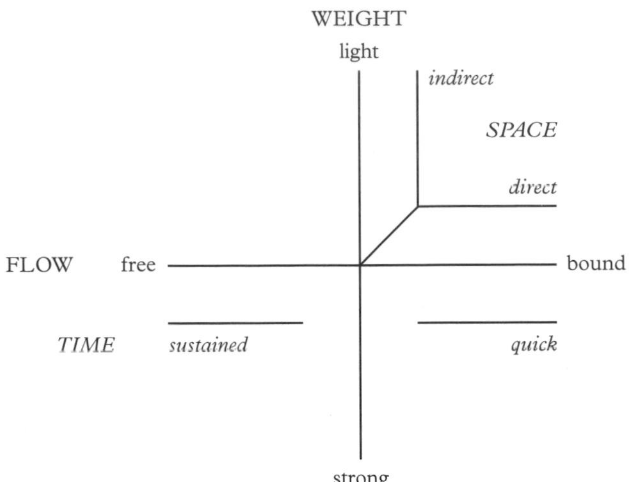

LABAN PRINCIPLES OF MOVEMENT ANALYSIS. The Effort graph is composed of four axes that show the effort factors of weight, space, time, and flow. A short diagonal line serves as a positional reference. Weight is indicated by the vertical axis, with the opposing elements of lightness and strength indicated, respectively, at top and at bottom. The horizontal axis indicates flow, with free flow at left and bound flow at right. The time factor, whose extremes are sustained (left) and quick (right), is indicated by the broken horizontal axis. The two opposing attitudes toward space—direct and indirect—are indicated by the inner horizontal and vertical lines at upper right.

in England in 1939 and published posthumously as *Choreutics* in 1966, annotated and edited by Ullmann. A succinct survey of Laban's theory of movement in space can also be found in "The Conception of the Sphere of the Movement," in his *Modern Educational Dance* (1948).

Kinesphere and Directional Orientation. Laban distinguished general space from the "reach space" immediately around the body, which he called the *kinesphere* (from Greek *kinesis,* movement, and *sphaira,* ball or sphere). The kinesphere is mapped by means of directions that radiate from the center of the upright body. Directions are associated with two states of equilibrium, the stable and the mobile or labile. Dimensional directions are predominantly stable owing to the balancing of the body mass around the center of weight and its perpendicular relationship to the support. Diagonal directions move the body center out of the vertical alignment over the support and thus promote lability or mobility. (Laban used the term *lability* in his German writings and *mobility* in the English books.)

Spatial Scales and Rings. By linking directions according to various harmonic principles, such as opposition, parallelism, and equilibrium, Laban identified spatial forms of greater or lesser complexity, referred to as "scales" and "rings." Not unlike musical intervals and scales, these forms are sequences of balancing tensions embodying various spatial relations. The latter result from three ways of connecting points of the kinesphere: (1) centrally, moving from the center of the body outward, or the reverse, with the possibility of continuing the movement through the center to the opposite side of the kinesphere, thus engaging contraction and extension of the joints; (2) peripherally, moving around the center allowing the joints to use various degrees of extension; and (3) transversally, starting the movement on the periphery of the body, approaching by bypassing the center, and continuing toward the opposite end point of the periphery (in this kind of transition finer shadings of contraction between two extensions are performed).

The crystalline form of the dimensional scale is the octahedron incorporating the three dimensions: the height of the body with the arms stretched upward and legs placed downward; the width, when unfolding limbs to right and left; and the depth, with the swinging of the extremities forward and backward in locomotion. The order of the scale is designed according to principles of countertension (or opposition) and of equilibrium. Each movement into one pole of the dimensions is followed by a movement into its opposite pole. Thus high is followed by low, sideways across by sideways open, and backward by forward. This sequence can also be performed emphasizing the spatial "intents" of the movements—that is, on rising-sinking, crossing-opening, and retreating-advancing actions. The vertical and horizontal structure of the scale also promotes the principle of stability. For example, much of the classical ballet vocabulary, such as the basic arm positions, fits within an octahedral form.

The crystalline structure for the diagonal scale is the cube that incorporates the four space diagonals and their eight directions. The order of the scale is also arranged according to the principles of countermovement and equilibrium. The spatial intent of diagonal directions is more complex because each direction includes three-dimensional intents, such as rising, opening, advancing-sinking, crossing, and retreating. In contrast to the predominant stability of the dimensional scale, the diagonal scale is the prototype for mobility; thus its movements lead to locomotion, elevation, and falling. Many of the flying leaps of ballet align the body in a diagonal direction.

The crystalline form of the icosahedron provides for a greater number of scales and rings. In its inner structure, the dimensional planes—vertical ("door"), horizontal ("table"), and sagittal ("wheel")—correspond to the forward-backward, up-down, and right-left body symmetries.

The twelve points of the planes are linked peripherally and/or transversally in the following scales and rings. The prototypes for peripheral circuits are the four peripheral standard scales around the four diagonals that link all twelve directions within one interval distance (that is, to the next closest point). They are also referred to as "primary scales," being among the first scales Laban designed.

Prototypes for the transversal scales that link all twelve directions are four transversal standard scales—two A-scales (according to the right-left symmetry) and two B-scales (formed through the forward-backward symmetry in relation to the A-scales). Each of the four scales consists of twelve transversals (movements that bypass the body center while linking two points of the kinesphere) inclined toward three different diagonals, the fourth one becoming the structural axis of the scale. The twelve transversals, or inclinations, alternate in the order of flat (inclined toward the side-to-side horizontal), steep inclination (gravitating toward the vertical), and flowing inclination (moving toward the forward-backward horizontal); this spatial rhythm is repeated four times in accomplishing the circuit of the scale. The inner harmonic structure of the scale is further manifest in terms of *volutes,* coiling movements formed by the obtuse angle of juncture of two inclinations, and *steeples,* angular movements formed by two inclinations linked under a sharp angle. In addition to icosahedral scales, there are spatial forms called *rings* that are structured peripherally, transversally, and by mixing both links. Many modern dance forms are icosahedral, emphasizing spiraling and twisting of the torso and limbs in three dimensions.

These spatial structures offer numerous suggestions for dance technique and composition. Because some areas of space are more easily reached than others, the potential of moving in twenty-six directions is challenging. Furthermore, the mastery of a greater range of diagonal, off-balance directions and of various dimensional, balancing situations can provide for both skillful performance and an extended movement vocabulary. The choreographer can select from the directions, organize their order, and design the bodily performance in sequential or simultaneous phrases. While the spatial order of icosahedral rings and scales is kept constant, various compositional manipulations can be applied, such as variations with regard to bodily actions, size, and rhythmic-dynamic qualities.

The identification of various spatial structures is also a significant component of movement assessment and dance-style analysis. For instance, discernible choreutic fragments and units as embodied in choreography are the basis of Valerie Preston-Dunlop's analysis of style in the works of Martha Graham, Doris Humphrey, Bronislava Nijinska, and others (1979, 1981).

Theory of Eukinetics and Effort. Laban's first investigations into the dynamic structure of movement focused on expressive qualities in dance. Complementary to Choreutics, he referred to this area as *Eukinetics* (*eu,* "good" or "harmonious," and *kinesis,* "movement") and defined it as exploring good movement in terms of harmonic principles in dance. In the 1920s and 1930s Eukinetics, along with Choreutics, was seen as an integral part of choreology. While Choreutics considers laws of structuring movement within the rhythm of forms, Eukinetics deals with temporal and dynamic occurrences within the rendering of expression; it is the fusion of three factors of movement—the sequentiality of time, strength of force, and extension of space—which gives movement the intended expression.

As an expansion of Eukinetics, in the 1940s Laban developed Effort Theory, which considers the various qualities of mind-body movement involved in human exertion in general. The concept of effort and its theory are developed in several of Laban's books. The first one, *Effort,* was an outcome of his collaboration with F. C. Lawrence, an

LABAN PRINCIPLES OF MOVEMENT ANALYSIS. The eight basic effort actions consist of all possible combinations of the weight, space, and time factors. For instance, slashing (indicated at upper left), utilizes indirectness (space), quickness (time), and strength (weight). The opposite action, gliding, uses directness (space), sustainment (time), and lightness (weight). Similarly, pressing (direct, slow, strong) and flicking (indirect, quick, light) are effort opposites—as are wringing (indirect, sustained, strong) and dabbing (direct, quick, light), and punching (direct, quick, strong) and floating (indirect, sustained, light).

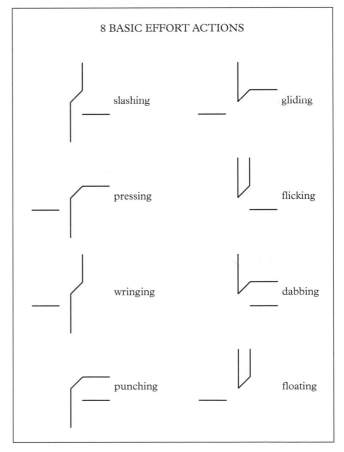

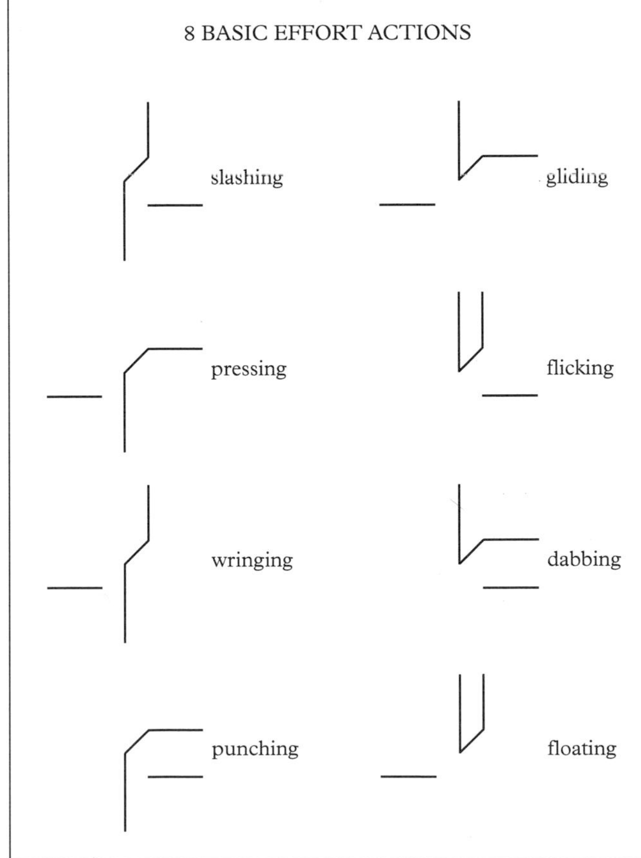

industrial management consultant who had invited Laban to record industrial processes and to assist with time-and-motion studies. While this first book focused on effort in work and industry, *Modern Educational Dance* proposed a new kind of dance education or "free dance technique" based on the practice of effort sequences. *The Mastery of Movement on the Stage* (1950) and the subsequent *The Mastery of Movement* (revised by Ullmann) elaborate on effort expression in mime, acting, and dance.

Laban's use of the term *effort* differs from its common usage denoting activity that requires substantial expenditure of energy. Laban sees effort as the inner impulse—a movement sensation, thought, feeling, or emotion—from which movement originates; it constitutes the link between mental and physical components of movement. The manifestations of this inner impulse or movement motivation can be described in terms of movement factors. There is no movement that does not evolve in space as well as in time, bringing the weight of the body into the flow of change. Hence every human movement engages the four motion factors—space, time, weight, and flow—in a more or less active or clear fashion. The particular emphases on, or selections from, these factors make up what Laban calls the characteristic effort patterns of a person. More specifically, the effort patterns result from mental or inner attitudes of resisting or accepting the physical conditions influencing movement: the mover's attitudes of fighting against or of contending with the four motion factors result in polarities of opposing effort elements of space, direct and flexible/indirect; weight, strong/firm and light/fine touch; time, sudden and sustained; and flow, bound and free. To notate effort elements and their combinations, Laban designed the Effort graph, which reflects the concept of polarities.

Laban correlates attitudes toward the motion factors to various levels of consciousness. Attitudes toward space are associated with attention and the human's powers of thinking; attitudes toward weight with intention and with sensing; attitudes toward time with decision making and intuition; and attitudes toward flow with progression and feeling. A link is apparent between Laban's concept of effort and C. G. Jung's division of consciousness.

Combinations of two effort elements denoting inner attitudes or states are observable in transitions between actions and are frequently elaborated in dance. For example, while the combination of weight and time elements creates a rhythmical, earthy, intimate mood, its opposite association of space with flow elements gives a more abstract, remote mood. Associations of space and time elements create an alert attitude; opposite combinations of weight and flow are more dreamlike and unaware. The combination of flow and time can create a mobile, adaptable attitude; by contrast, associations of space and weight are likely to produce a stable, steadfast attitude. Each of the six combinations has four potential variations; thus the combinations of weight and time may include light and free, strong and bound, strong and free, and light and bound variations. There are twenty-four distinct qualities within this range, which Laban calls *incomplete efforts* or *inner attitudes.*

Combinations of three effort elements produce more intense and pronounced movement expressions, which are referred to as *movement drives.* The action drive combines space, weight, and time elements, while flow remains latent. The eight possible combinations of the above elements are also described as "basic effort actions" of thrusting or punching–floating, pressing–flicking, gliding–slashing, and dabbing–wringing. Several terms in the ballet vocabulary derive from the description of the quality of performance; for example, *battement* ("beating") is a direct, strong, and sudden gesture, while *glissade* ("glide") has a direct, light, and sustained quality.

When the flow factor replaces qualities of space, the action may transform into a more emotionally stressed drive, also referred to as a *passion drive.* It includes the eight possible combinations of weight, time, and flow that override the clarity of spatial placement and shaping. When the flow factor is substituted for the weight factor, the movement may change into a more weightless, vision-like drive; its eight possible combinations of space, time, and flow override the bodily import.

When the flow factor replaces time qualities, the movement transforms into a timeless, spell-like drive; its eight possible combinations of space, weight, and flow override the sense for timing. As shown above, each of the four drives has eight potential variations, and they provide thirty-two more qualities.

Maximum intensity is achieved in exceptional performances when all four effort elements are clearly present in a so-called *complete effort action.* The combination of space, time, and flow allows for sixteen more distinct variations. The descriptive names Laban gave to these inner attitudes or states and movement drives are intended as metaphors of the experience rather than technical terms.

Effort observation and training can be an important component in achieving efficiency in any skill, including dance performance. Identifying the effort patterns and expanding the potential range can lead both to more balanced actions and to a performance richer in dynamic variation.

Not unlike Space Harmony, effort analysis is a significant tool in movement assessment, mime and dance characterization, and style description. For instance, particular combinations of effort elements are a significant component in Marion North's (1972) personality assessment of children. In describing the dynamic image of Martha Graham's choreography and performance, Billie

Lepczyk pointed to bound flow as a salient quality of aesthetic value. In her analysis of *The Shakers,* Suzanne Youngerman (1978) observed that Doris Humphrey's juxtaposition of contrasting effort states and drives contributed significantly to the choreographic rendering of inner conflicts.

Effort–Space Affinities. The interrelationship of Eukinetics and Choreutics, or of Effort and Space Harmony, is manifest in Laban's view of harmonic relationships between the dynamics of bodily actions and their spatial patterns. Laban found close correlations between effort elements and dimensional directions. These were based on his observation that a light movement has a tendency upward, and a strong movement aims downward; a straight, direct movement is correlative with movement across the body, and a roundabout, flexible movement is correlative with an opening outward; a quick, sudden movement tends backward, and a slow, sustained one reaches forward. Elaborating compounds of these, Laban arrived at the "eight basic effort actions," which correspond with the eight diagonal directions. Accordingly, a light-flexible-sustained movement is associated with the high-open-forward diagonal, or a strong-direct-sudden one with the down-across-back diagonal.

Laban's observation of dynamic characteristics of deep, medium, and high movers was related to the area of affinities; these considerations may also be seen as analogous to the predominant pitch and quality of a singer's voice. Laban saw the difference among the three types of movers as influenced by bodily structure, as well as by mental and emotional qualities. The high dancer shows some degree of tension in order to act against gravity and produce an erect carriage, light gestures, and leaps; clarity of design is also among his or her attributes. The deep dancer, who feels more comfortable nearer to the ground, displays strength and rhythmicality, favoring stamping and crouching actions. The medium dancer prefers freely flowing, swinging, and turning actions in the horizontal level in space. This characterization of the three types of movers and dancers arises from Laban's involvement with "movement choirs" in the early 1920s. An awareness of one's own tendencies may facilitate efficient work toward expanding the natural range.

Laban's concept of affinities between effort elements and dimensional directions was the point of departure for Warren Lamb's elaborations of effort and shape relationships. Initially Laban's student and assistant in developing the Laban-Lawrence Effort Assessment test, Lamb evolved his own methodology in the 1950s; it is now applied in the action profiling of management teams. It emphasizes degrees of affinity between shape and effort variations, including Lamb's elaboration of "flow of shape" in addition to the flow of effort; the observation of posture (action involving whole-body adjustment) in relation to gesture (confined to isolated body parts) is also a significant variable.

Students and Collaborators. When designing his principles of analysis and notation, Laban frequently established creative collaborations with his disciples, who also taught with him or directed Laban schools. Between 1913 and 1920 dancer-choreographer Mary Wigman was the first person to perform and test Laban's "movement harmony" sequences based on spatial forms. Wigman and Suzanne Perrottet (both former students of Émile Jaques-Dalcroze) were also teaching assistants in the Schools for the Art of Movement in Munich and Zurich. In the 1920s Laban's concert partner, Ruth Loeser, taught Space Harmony at the Choreographic Institute Laban, and Laban's assistant, Gertrud Snell, compiled a survey of Choreutics. (This survey and Laban's 1939 manuscript, annotated and edited by Lisa Ullmann, form the text of *Choreutics,* 1966.)

During the 1920s dancer-choreographer Kurt Jooss assisted Laban with the formulation of Eukinetics; Jooss continued teaching it (along with Choreutics) in the Folkwang Schule in Essen (associated with the Central School Laban and the Choreographic Institute Laban). In the 1930s Eukinetics and Choreutics were also taught in the Jooss-Leeder School of Dance at Dartington Hall in England. Jooss and Dussia Bereska—the artistic director of the Laban Chamber Dance Theatre—were instrumental in elaborating Laban's system of notation.

There were many German collaborators and disciples of Laban's sociopedagogical ideas in the 1920s and early 1930s; particularly instrumental in formulating methodologies for movement choirs and conducting them were Albrecht Knust and Martin Gleisner. Gleisner also published *Tanz für Alle* (Dance for All, 1928), which gives a theoretical foundation for this recreational activity. During the 1930s and 1940s, because of the rise and spread of Nazism, several Laban associates and students—including Jooss—transferred their activity to England and the United States. While Jooss and Ullmann found a supportive environment in the English arts center and progressive school Dartington Hall, Irmgard Bartenieff and Irma Otte-Betz introduced Laban's principles and notation to American audiences. Sylvia Bodmer transferred her pedagogical and choreographic activities to England in the 1940s and became the co-founder and artistic director of the Manchester Dance Circle. Laban's chief collaborator in England and the annotator of his manuscripts, Lisa Ullmann, founded the Art of Movement Studio in 1946; in the 1970s the Studio merged with the University of London's Goldsmith's College. Here, other Laban student-collaborators were trained, such as Warren Lamb, Valerie Preston (later Preston-Dunlop), Geraldine Stephenson, Marion North, and Joan Russell. Ullmann, Preston, North, and Russell applied and elaborated Laban's ideas and movement classification in recreational and educational frameworks; Stephenson continued Laban's link between movement and drama, working in the theater and for the British Broadcasting Corporation (BBC). Lamb and North expanded Laban's effort theory through personal investigation in behavioral sciences—Lamb in management consultancy, developing the assessment system Action Profiling, and North in personality assessment through movement for children and babies. Preston-Dunlop developed motif writing for purposes of describing movement ideas and has conducted research in choreographic style based on choreutic analysis.

In the United Kingdom, Laban's work is continued chiefly at the Laban Centre for Movement and Dance, at the University of London, and through the Laban International courses, established in 1979 as a continuation of modern dance holiday courses founded in 1942.

In the United States, the Laban/Bartenieff Institute of Movement Studies is a center for training in and development of Laban-based movement analysis. The Dance Notation Bureau in New York, and its extension branch at Ohio State University, specialize in Labanotation. Laban's work has had a worldwide impact, primarily through the spread of principles of modern educational dance in the British Commonwealth countries and through the adoption of his notation system for the documentation of theatrical, folk, and traditional dance.

Laban's concepts and classification of movement are increasingly applied as research instruments in several other disciplines, such as anthropology, choreology, psychology, and nonverbal communication. Bartenieff's individual and collaborative activities created several interdisciplinary cross-fertilizations between movement–dance and physical therapy, psychotherapy, and anthropology; the study of movement and dance styles undertaken with her assistant Forrestine Paulay resulted in "choreometric profiles." Bartenieff Fundamentals, which incorporates Laban principles, is often used in conditioning the body for dance and injury prevention and treatment.

The 1976 Labananalysis Research Workshop at Ohio State University's department of dance, under the direction of Lucy Venable, designed a coding sheet for the distinction of ethnic, historical, and choreographic styles. Movement classification had been compiled from two complementary systems—Labanotation and Effort/Shape—with some parameters from North and from the Bartenieff-Paulay choreometric project. Several subsequent choreological projects used Labananalysis (Labanotation and Effort/Shape), among them the work of Elizabeth Kagan (1978), Suzanne Youngerman (1978), and Jill Gellerman (1978).

Martha Davis, initially Bartenieff's student and assistant, through her dual training in movement and psychology has integrated movement and nonverbal communication theories. Psychoanalyst Judith Kestenberg has designed ways of observing by using and expanding some Effort/Shape parameters in the context of Freudian developmental phases.

The breadth of Laban's original conception enabled his movement classification to provide a sufficiently broad base for further development of his germinal idea as well as further application in other theoretical frameworks. Thus one can agree with Selma Jeanne Cohen (1983) that because of its systematic classification, Laban's theory is "one of the most important for modern dance thought."

[*See also* Labanotation *and the entry on Laban.*]

BIBLIOGRAPHY

Bartenieff, Irmgard, Martha Davis, and Forrestine Paulay. *Four Adaptations of Effort Theory in Research and Teaching.* New York, 1970. See Bartenieff, "The Roots of Laban Theory: Aesthetics and Beyond."

Bartenieff, Irmgard, with Dori Lewis. *Body Movement: Coping with the Environment.* New York, 1980.

Bodmer, Sylvia. *Studies Based on Crystalloid Dance Forms.* 1979.

Cohen, Selma Jeanne. "Dance as an Art of Imitation." In *What Is Dance?*, edited by Roger Copeland and Marshall Cohen. New York, 1983.

Curl, Gordon. "Philosophic Foundations." *Laban Art of Movement Guild Magazine* (1966–1969).

Davis, Martha. *Towards Understanding the Intrinsic in Human Movement.* New York, 1973.

Davis, Martha. "Laban Analysis of Nonverbal Communication." In *Nonverbal Communication,* edited by Shirley Weitz. 2d ed. New York, 1979.

Dell, Cecily. *A Primer for Movement Description: Using Effort-Shape and Supplementary Concepts.* Rev. ed. New York, 1977.

Foster, John. *The Influences of Rudolph Laban.* London, 1977.

Gellerman, Jill. "The Mayim Pattern as an Indicator of Cultural Attitudes in Three American Hasidic Communities: A Comparative Approach Based on Labananalysis." *CORD Dance Research Annual* 9 (1978): 111–144.

Gleisner, Martin. *Tanz für Alle.* Leipzig, 1928.

Hodgson, John, and Valerie Preston-Dunlop. *Rudolf Laban: An Introduction to His Work and Influence.* Plymouth, 1990.

Kagan, Elizabeth. "Towards the Analysis of a Score: A Comparative Study of 'Three Epitaphs' by Paul Taylor and 'Water Study' by Doris Humphrey." *CORD Dance Research Annual* 9 (1978): 75–92.

Kestenberg, Judith S. *The Role of Movement Patterns in Development.* Vol. 1. New York, 1967.

Kestenberg, Judith S., and J. Mark Sossin. *The Role of Movement Patterns in Development,* vol. 2, *Epilogue and Glossary.* New York, 1979.

Laban, Rudolf. *Die Welt des Tänzers.* Stuttgart, 1920.

Laban, Rudolf. *Choreographie.* Vol. 1. Jena, 1926a.

Laban, Rudolf. *Gymnastik und Tanz.* 2d ed. Oldenburg, 1926b.

Laban, Rudolf. *Des Kindes Gymnastik und Tanz.* 2d ed. Oldenburg, 1926c.

Laban, Rudolf. "Die Entwicklung der Bewegungsschrift." *Der Schrifttanz* 1.2 (October 1928a).

Laban, Rudolf. "Grundprinzipien der Bewegungsschrift." *Der Schrifttanz* 1.1 (July 1928b).

Laban, Rudolf. *Schrifttanz: Methodik, Orthographie, Erläuterungen.* Vienna, 1928c.

Laban, Rudolf. *Choreutics* (1939). Edited by Lisa Ullmann. London, 1966.

Laban, Rudolf, and F. C. Lawrence. *Effort.* London, 1947.

Laban, Rudolf. *Modern Educational Dance.* London, 1948.
Laban, Rudolf. *The Mastery of Movement* (1950). Edited by Lisa Ullmann. 2d rev. ed. London, 1980.
Laban, Rudolf. *Principles of Dance and Movement Notation.* London, 1956.
Laban, Rudolf. *A Vision of Dynamic Space.* Edited by Lisa Ullmann. London, 1984.
Lamb, Warren. *Posture and Gesture.* London, 1965.
Lamb, Warren, and David Turner. *Management Behaviour.* London, 1969.
Lamb, Warren, and Elizabeth Watson. *Body Code.* London, 1979.
Lomax, Alan, ed. *Folk Song Style and Culture.* Washington, D.C., 1968.
Main Currents in Modern Thought 31 (1974).
Maletić, Vera. *Body-Space-Expression: The Development of Rudolf Laban's Movement and Dance Concepts.* Berlin, 1987.
Moore, Carol-Lynne. *Executives in Action.* Plymouth, 1982.
North, Marion. *Personality Assessment through Movement.* Boston, 1972.
North, Marion. *Movement and Dance Education: A Guide for the Primary and Middle School Teacher.* London, 1973a.
Pforsich, Janis L. "Labananalysis and Dance Style Research." *CORD Dance Research Annual* 9 (1978): 59–74.
Preston-Dunlop, Valerie. *Readers in Kinetography Laban, Series B: Motif Writing for Dance.* London, 1967.
Preston-Dunlop, Valerie. *Practical Kinetography Laban.* Brooklyn, 1969.
Preston-Dunlop, Valerie. "Choreutics: The Study of Logical Spatial Forms in Dance." In *Dancing and Dance Theory,* edited by Valerie Preston-Dunlop. London, 1979.
Preston-Dunlop, Valerie. *A Handbook for Dance in Education.* 2d ed. London, 1987.
Preston-Dunlop, Valerie. "Laban and the Nazis: Toward an Understanding of Rudolf Laban and the Third Reich." *Updata Dance/USA* 7 (August–September 1989): 12–13, 19–22.
Preston-Dunlop, Valerie, and Charlotte Purkis. "Rudolf Laban: The Making of Modern Dance." *Dance Theatre Journal* 7 (Winter 1989): 11–16; 7 (February 1990): 10–13.
Preston-Dunlop, Valerie, and Susanne Lahusen, eds. *Schrifttanz: A View of German Dance in the Weimar Republic.* London, 1990.
Ramsden, Pamela. *Top Team Planning: A Study of the Power of the Individual Motivation in Management.* London, 1973.
Russell, Joan. *Creative Dance in the Secondary School.* London, 1969.
Russell, Joan. *Creative Dance in the Primary School.* 3d ed. Plymouth, 1987.
Snell, Gertrud. "Grundlagen einer Allgemeiner Tanzlehre." *Der Schrifttanz* 2.1 (January 1929); 2.2 (May 1929); 3.2 (May 1930).
Ullmann, Lisa. "Space Harmony" (parts 1–4). *Laban Art of Movement Guild Magazine* (1952–1956).
Youngerman, Suzanne. "The Translation of a Culture into Choreography: A Study of Doris Humphrey's 'The Shakers' Based on Laban-analysis." *CORD Dance Research Annual* 9 (1978): 93–110.

ARCHIVES. Laban Archive, National Resource Centre for Dance, University of Surrey. Laban Collection, Laban Centre for Movement and Dance, London.

VERA MALETIĆ

L'ABBÉ, ANTHONY (Antoine [?] de l'Abbé; born in France, died after 1738), dancer, dancing master, choreographer. L'Abbé was already renowned as a theatrical dancer in Paris when Thomas Betterton brought him to Lincoln's Inn Fields theater in London in 1698. His early appearance before the king, with his compatriot Claude Ballon, signaled his immediate success in the English court. Betterton allegedly became jealous of L'Abbé's popularity: an anonymous satirist wrote in 1702, "Yet nothing will our modern plays enhance, but Dame Ragou, L'Abbé or Ladder Dance."

By 1707 L'Abbé became dancing master at the Queen's Theatre. In addition to composing dances and dancing himself, he taught theatrical dancing and formed many successful careers. His later fame as a genteel master should not overshadow his important contribution to English stage dancing: by 1715 he was the most successful dancer based in London. John Essex wrote in *The Dancing-Master: or, The Art of Dancing Explained* (1728) that "His talent chiefly lay in the grave Movement, and he excelled all that ever appeared on the *English* Stage in that Character."

John Weaver in *Orchesography* (1706) also refers to L'Abbé's "admirable Compositions . . . in Ballet." L'Abbé's early theatrical dances appeared in *The French Dancing-Master* (c.1700), now lost. His ball and stage dances were notated and collected by Le Roussau, who published them as *A New Collection of Dances* (c.1725). This work, one of the most important surviving collections of eighteenth-century dances, includes works performed by leading dancers at Lincoln's Inn Fields and at Drury Lane.

After L'Abbé's retirement, his pupil, De La Garde, continued his theatrical work and, with Edmund Pemberton, was responsible for notating his later dances. Weaver stated in *Anatomical and Mechanical Lectures upon Dancing* (1721) that De La Garde's own excellence as a teacher derived from the "just Notions, and first Instructions, [that he received] from that great Master in every Branch of this Art, Monsieur L'Abbé."

Shortly after the death of Queen Anne in 1714, L'Abbé became court dancing master to the granddaughters of George I. In addition to teaching members of the royal family, L'Abbé composed and published an annual royal ball dance during much of George I's reign.

L'Abbé's annual dances include "The Princess Royal" (1715), "The Princess Anna" (1716), and "The Royal George" (1717); valuable collections exist in the Bodleian Library at Oxford (Don.d.45) and in the British Library (h.801, h.801.a–c). Kellom Tomlinson mentions several of L'Abbé's dances in *The Art of Dancing* (1735), and Pemberton published L'Abbé's "A Passacaille" in *An Essay for the Further Improvement of Dancing* (1711). Francis Peacock claimed that, like Mister Isaac, L'Abbé made a fortune from the sale of his notated dances (*Sketches,* 1805).

L'Abbé retained his post under George II and continued to teach his daughters. Essex felt that the princesses' "noble Presence, easy Deportment, and graceful Carriage" reflected his fine teaching.

After Mister Isaac's retirement, L'Abbé became the leader of the dancing profession in London and remained a figure of unrivaled influence and prestige until the mid-1730s. He led English masters in a rapprochement with their French colleagues. Under Mister Isaac, Thomas Caverley, and John Weaver, there had been something of a distancing process as an English style and an English profession established themselves and as theatrical dancing masters, under the influence of Weaver and Christopher Rich, experimented with dramatic dance. Among the subscribers to L'Abbé's *New Collection* were many of the greatest French masters, whom L'Abbé had doubtless known in Paris: Guillaume-Louis Pecour, Claude Ballon (whom Weaver had attacked in print), François Marcel (Jean-Georges Noverre's and Gioranni Gallini's teacher), Michel Blondy, Dumoulin, and André Deshayes, among many others. In 1731, L'Abbé added his approbation to that of Pecour for the second English edition of Pierre Rameau's *Le maître à danser (The Dancing Master)*, thus further embracing the French profession. L'Abbé remained in London until 1738, when he retired to Paris.

BIBLIOGRAPHY

Goff, Moira, and Jennifer Thorp. "Dance Notations Published in England, c.1700–1740." *Dance Research* 9 (Autumn 1991): 32–50.

Goff, Moira. "Dancing-Masters in Early Eighteenth-Century London." *Historical Dance* 3.3 (1994): 17–23.

Highfill, Philip H., Jr., et al., eds. *A Biographical Dictionary of Actors, Actresses, Musicians, Dancers, Managers, and Other Stage Personnel in London, 1660–1800.* Carbondale, Ill., 1973–.

L'Abbé, Anthony. *A New Collection of Dances* (1725). Edited by Carol G. Marsh. London, 1991.

Marsh, Carol. "French Court Dance in England, 1706–1740: A Study of the Sources." Ph.D. diss., City University of New York, 1985.

Rader, Patricia Weeks. "Harlequin and Hussar: Hester Santlow's Dancing Career in London, 1706–1733." Master's thesis, City University of New York, 1992.

Thorp, Jennifer, and Ken Pierce. "Taste and Ingenuity." *Historical Dance* 3.3 (1994): 3–16.

RICHARD RALPH

LABYRINTH DANCES. Little is known with certainty about the origin of the labyrinth and labyrinth dances, but ancient tradition ascribes it to Crete between the second and third milennia BCE. The typical labyrinth design (the so-called universal maze)—either circular or rectangular, with only one path doubling and redoubling its way into a center and back to the entry—is found in prehistoric European stone carvings, but its original significance and its possible status as rudimentary choreographic notation remain unknown despite abundant speculation. The earliest textual reference to a possible labyrinth dance is in *The Iliad* (eighth century BCE); it describes a ritual dance (sometimes linked with the *geranos*, or "crane dance") of youths and maidens in a dancing place like that built for Ariadne by Daedalus, mythical creator of the Cretan labyrinth. The earliest visual evidence may be the Tragliatella Wine Pitcher (seventh–sixth centuries BCE), showing two mounted men and a line of nine warriors emerging from a labyrinth labeled *truia*. Scholars have speculated that *truia* may mean "dancing place," or may refer to Troy.

Unambiguous mention of rituals involving a labyrinth pattern are found in Virgil's *Aeneid*, which describes the Troy game—part tournament, part equestrian ballet—performed by young men on horseback at Anchises' funeral games. This ritual existed in imperial Rome, as Suetonius and Pliny note, and is the earliest certain example of a labyrinthine dance. Plutarch (c.46–120) reports that Theseus celebrated his victory over the Minotaur and his escape from the Cretan labyrinth by a serpentine group dance, called "The Crane," that imitated the winding of the labyrinth and was still performed in Plutarch's time. Among the early Christians, Gregory of Nazianzus (330–390) follows Homer in associating the "harmonious dance of Knossos, Daedalian work" with the labyrinth, while Marius Victorinus (fourth century CE) links Theseus's labyrinth dance on Delos with a mimesis of the movements of the heavens. None of these early sources, however, tells us much about actual as opposed to mythical labyrinth dances.

Only in the late Middle Ages can the existence of labyrinth dances performed on foot be confirmed. While labyrinth dances may have existed in any of the numerous French and Italian cathedrals containing large labyrinth mosaics in their naves, and while some evidence suggests the practice of labyrinth dances at Sens and Chartres, only at Auxerre are there extensive records (1396 and later) of an Easter labyrinth dance. At sunset, the dean and canons gathered in the nave labyrinth, where a new canon presented the dean with a *pelota* ("ball"). While singing Wipo's Easter sequence, *Victimae paschale laudes*, the dean performed a *tripudium* within the labyrinth as the canons danced a *chorea* ("carol") around, or perhaps through, the labyrinth in a "garland-like" fashion. [*See* Tripudium.] All the while, the *pelota* was thrown back and forth. Afterward the group repaired to a communal meal. The significance of the Auxerre ritual is clear in the context of medieval labyrinth lore, whereby the labyrinth sometimes symbolized hell and Theseus, who slew the Minotaur with the aid of a ball of pitch (rammed in the beast's mouth before the fatal blow) and a ball of thread (to guide Theseus's returning steps), sometimes symbolized Christ. The Auxerre dance, then, imitates Christ's descent into the labyrinth of Hell and his rescue of the just souls therein (the Harrowing of Hell and Resurrection). The first fully described labyrinth dance, was thus a Christian ritual, an excellent example of the many kinds of dancing permitted and indeed encouraged by the medieval Christian church.

Labyrinth dances may have also been associated with turf mazes cut into English fields and with stone labyrinths in Scandinavia, many of which bear names such as Maiden's Dance or Stone Dance. However, in the absence of firm dating and reliable records, interpretation remains uncertain. Indeed, many studies of both labyrinths and dance through the Middle Ages rely more on conjecture than on fact and must be viewed with skepticism. There is, for instance, no evidence at all for the accepted belief that medieval labyrinth rituals were related to pilgrimage.

Labyrinthine dances also figure in Renaissance masques (such as Jonson's *Pleasure Reconciled to Virtue*) and in theatrical dances from the Baroque era to the present. (Examples include François Dolivet's ballets for Lully's *Thesée* (1675), Gasparo Angiolini's *Teseo in Creta* (1782), Léonide Massine's *Labyrinth* (1941), John Taras's *The Minotaur* and Martha Graham's *Errand into the Maze* (1947), Merce Cunningham's *Labyrinthian Dances* and Birgit Åkesson's *The Minotaur* (1958), José Udaeta's *El Laberinto* (1963), Kuert Stuyf's *Labyrinth* (1966), John Butler's *Labyrinth* (1968) and *The Minotaur* (1970), Glen Tetley's *Laborintus* (1972), and Susana Audeoud's *Labyrinth* (1984).

In recent and ancient works alike, the image of the labyrinth is most often used metaphorically. It attracts and incorporates a wide range of associations—complex artistry, difficulty, inextricability, impenetrability, magnificent design, utter chaos, transcendence, confusion—many of which are peculiar to a given period and culture. It is impossible to interpret the meaning of labyrinthine imagery in any particular dance without an understanding of the appropriate historical context.

[*For related discussion, see* Crete, *article on* Dance in Ancient Crete.]

BIBLIOGRAPHY

Backman, Eugène Louis. *Religious Dances in the Christian Church and in Popular Medicine.* Translated by E. Classen. London, 1952.

Batschelet-Massini, W. "Labyrinthzeichnungen in Handschriften." *Codices Manuscripti* 2 (1978).

Doob, Penelope Reed. "The Labyrinth in Medieval Culture." *Revue de l'Université d'Ottawa* 52 (1982).

Doob, Penelope Reed. "The Auxerre Labyrinth Ritual." In *The Myriad Faces of Dance: Proceedings of the Eighth Annual Conference, Society of Dance History Scholars, University of New Mexico, 15–17 February 1985,* compiled by Christena L. Schlundt. Riverside, Calif., 1985.

Doob, Penelope Reed. *The Idea of the Labyrinth from Classical Antiquity through the Middle Ages.* Ithaca, N.Y., 1990.

Homer. *Iliad* 18.590–606.

Kern, Hermann. *Labyrinthe.* Munich, 1982.

Krönig, Wolfgang. "Osterfreude und liturgisches Spiel." *Quatember: Vierteljahreshefte für Erneuerung und Einheit der Kirche* 43 (1979).

Lawler, Lillian B. *The Dance in Ancient Greece.* Middletown, Conn., 1964.

Matthews, W. H. *Mazes and Labyrinths.* London, 1922.

Plutarch. *Theseus* 21.

Schnapper, Edith B. "Labyrinths and Labyrinth Dances in Christian Churches." In *Festschrift Otto Erich Deutsch,* edited by Jan LaRue and Wolfgang Rehm. Kassel, 1963.

Virgil. *Aeneid* 5.553–603.

PENELOPE REED DOOB

LAC DES CYGNES, LE. *See* Swan Lake.

LACOTTE, PIERRE (born 4 April 1932 in Châtou, near Paris), French ballet dancer, choreographer, teacher, and company director. Pierre Lacotte studied at the Paris Opera Ballet School with Carlotta Zambelli, Gustave Ricaux, and Serge Lifar. He also studied privately with Lubov Egorova, Madame Rousanne (Rousanne Sarkissian), and Nicholas Zverev. After joining the Paris Opera Ballet in 1946, Lacotte rose through the ranks and became a *premier danseur* in 1952, but he did not remain long with the company. Wishing to pursue opportunities for choreography, he left the Paris Opera in 1955 to form his own company, Les Ballets de la Tour Eiffel. For this troupe, featuring dancer Josette Clavier, he created his first important works, including *La Nuit Est une Sorcière,* to music by Sidney Bechet; *Gosse de Paris,* to music by Charles Aznavour; and *Concertino,* to music by Antonio Vivaldi.

In 1956 Lacotte went to New York as principal male dancer with the Metropolitan Opera Ballet, remaining until the end of the 1956/57 season. He returned to Europe and resumed his dancing career as a guest artist with various troupes, but after seriously injuring his knee in 1959, he reestablished his own company. He choreographed *Such Sweet Thunder,* to music by Duke Ellington, for an appearance by Les Ballets de la Tour Eiffel at the Berlin Festival in 1959.

In 1962 Lacotte became the director of the newly founded Ballet National Jeunesses Musicales de France, where he danced as well as choreographed. Many of his works were made for the ballerina of the company, Ghislaine Thesmar, a dancer of exceptional delicacy and charm. Among his works in the company repertory were *Simple Symphony* (1962), to music by Benjamin Britten; *Bifurcation* (1963), to music by Francesco Geminiani; *Hamlet* (1964), to music by William Walton; *Hippolyte et Aricie* (1965), to music by Jean-Philippe Rameau; *Combat de Tancredi* (1966), to music by Rafaello de Banfield; and *La Proie* (1967), to music by Arnold Schoenberg. Several of these works were televised. In 1966, Lacotte set two works for Ballet Rambert in London: *Intermède,* to music by Vivaldi, and *Numeros,* to modern jazz. In 1968 he and Thesmar were married.

Despite his interest in contemporary music and ballet, Lacotte had an abiding interest in works of the Romantic era and the Second Empire in France. His first attempt at restoration based on historical records was a pas de deux from Gaetano Donizetti's opera *La Favorite,* which had had its premiere at the Paris Opera in December 1840. This pas de deux was seen in a 1970 production of the opera at the Teatro La Fenice in Venice. Lacotte's next success, and one of his greatest triumphs, was a 1971 production for French television, a reconstruction of *La Sylphide* as it had been given at the Paris Opera in 1832, with choreography by Filippo Taglioni to the score by Jean Schneitzhoeffer. Starring Thesmar in the title role, this production, based on painstaking research, reopened the doors of the Opera to Lacotte, who was invited to mount it there in 1972. Having been a teacher of adagio classes at the Conservatoire Nationale Supérieur de Musique et de Danse since 1970, he was also invited to teach adagio classes at the Paris Opera Ballet School in 1972. In 1975 he revived the three-act version of *Coppélia,* following the original choreography of Arthur Saint-Léon, which had not been seen at the Opera since 1870, and in 1976 he revived Marie Taglioni's only ballet, *Le Papillon,* which she had created for Emma Livry to music by Jacques Offenbach in 1860. Lacotte made his last appearances on the stage in these two works.

From the mid-1970s onward, Lacotte established himself as France's leading authority on nineteenth-century ballet. He recreated Saint-Léon's famous pas de six from *La Vivandière* (1844), to the music of Cesare Pugni, for the Opéra-Comique in 1976, and he mounted a production of Filippo Taglioni's ballet *La Fille de Danube* (1836), to music of Adolphe Adam, for the Teatro Colón in Buenos Aires. Also in 1978 he mounted *Giselle* for the Ballet du Rhin in Strasbourg, using the best of the original 1841 version by Jules Perrot and Jean Coralli at the Paris Opera and the 1884 production by Marius Petipa at the Bolshoi Theater in Saint Petersburg.

In 1979, as a guest artist in Russia, Lacotte mounted *La Sylphide* for the Novosibirsk Ballet and *Le Papillon,* the pas de six from *La Vivandière,* and "La Cachucha," Fanny Elssler's famous dance from *Le Diable Boiteau* (1836), for the Kirov Ballet in Leningrad. In 1980 he revived Filippo Taglioni's two-act *Nathalie, ou La Laitière Suisse* (The Swiss Milkmaid; 1821), to music by Adalbert Gyrowetz, for the Young Classical Ballet in Leningrad. In 1981, he reconstructed Joseph Mazilier's three-act *Marco Spada, ou La Fille du Bandit* (1857), to music by Daniel Auber, for the Rome Opera Ballet. In 1984, for French television, he reconstructed "La Cracovienne," Elssler's solo from Mazilier's ballet *La Gipsy* (1839), and in 1987, for Italian television, he revived Taglioni's "Ballet of the Nuns" from Giacomo Meyerbeer's opera *Robert le Diable* (1831).

Despite his success, and worldwide demand for his productions of historic ballets, the validity of Lacotte's reconstructions was often questioned, because he had not revealed the precise sources of his information. In two essays published in the early 1980s, he has set forth his ideas on reconstruction and revival (see Lacotte, 1981, 1982), and in a book published in 1987, Jean-Pierre Pastori has attempted to summarize Lacotte's views and thoughts on issues involved in historic reconstruction.

After Thesmar retired from the stage in 1983, she and Lacotte were invited by the royal family of Monaco to revive the Ballets de Monte-Carlo, of which they served as joint directors from 1985 to 1988 and for which Lacotte mounted some of his works. Thereafter, Lacotte served as artistic director of the opera ballet in Verona, Italy, but he returned to France in 1991 to assume the post vacated by Patrick Dupond as artistic director of the Ballet National de Nancy et de Lorraine.

BIBLIOGRAPHY

Babsky, Monique, and Olivier Mauvaisin. "Pierre Lacotte." *Saisons de la danse,* no. 166 (Summer 1984).

Cournand, Gilberte. "Sompteuse résurrection." *Saisons de la danse,* no. 248 (July–August 1993):17–18.

Lacotte, Pierre. "La conservation du ballet." In *Le ballet,* edited by André Vladimir Hofmann. Paris, 1981.

Lacotte, Pierre. "Looking for *La Sylphide.*" *Dance and Dancers* (October 1982):14–16.

Pastori, Jean-Pierre. *Pierre Lacotte: Tradition* (in French). Lausanne, 1987.

Salas, Roger. "L'ombra, ritrovata del balletto romantico." *Balletto oggi* (July–August 1993):12–16.

Stuart, Otis. "'A Really Good School Is International.'" *Ballett International* 7 (October 1984):16–21. Interview with Lacotte.

MONIQUE BABSKY
Translated from French

LA FONTAINE, MADEMOISELLE DE (*fl.* 1681–1693), French dancer. Mademoiselle de La Fontaine is known to us only through ballet and early opera programs. In 1696, Jean Nicolas Du Tralage wrote that "she had been one of the best dancers at the Opera," had retired in 1692, and was living at a convent of the Religieuses de l'Assomption in Paris, "not as a nun, but as a resident who can go about as she pleases." A small poem praising her decision to leave the Paris Opera, a "school of vice," ended Du Tralage's remembrance of one of the earliest known professional female dancers of the French stage.

Mademoiselle de La Fontaine debuted in court ballets when the genre was almost extinct, as well as in Jean-Baptiste Lully's operas during their formative years. Dance historians usually associate her name with the ballet *Le Triomphe de l'Amour* (1681). Although the production's libretto and account book mention only thirteen male professional dancers and the most distinguished members of the court, the Parfaict brothers list La Fontaine, along with Mesdemoiselles Carré and Pesan, among the dancers. *Le Triomphe de l'Amour* was given twice in 1681 and only once more the following year; André Campra revived it in 1705. La Fontaine therefore must have been part of the second or third performance at the Paris Opera, in May 1681 or January 1682, or both.

Mademoiselle de La Fontaine's name appeared in the programs for the following ballets and operas: *Proserpine* (1681); *Atys* and *Persée*, with Guillaume-Louis Pecour as a partner (1682); *Phaëton* (1683); *Amadis de Gaule*, with Mesdemoiselles Carré and Pesan, Pierre Beauchamps, Michel Blondy, and Claude Ballon (January 1684); *Roland* (1685); *Le Temple de la Païx*, a court ballet produced for Louis XIV in October 1685, with Mademoiselle Desmatin, Pierre Beauchamps, Guillaume-Louis Pecour, Anne-Louis Lestang, Romain Dumirail, Claude Marc Magny, and Jean Favier; *Ballet de la Jeunesse*, *Armide et Renaud*, and *Acis et Galathée* (1686); *Achille et Polyxène* (1687); *Zéphire et Flore* (1688); *Le Palais de Flore* performed at Trianon for Louis XIV in January 1689, with Mesdemoiselles Lesueur and Durieux and Marie-Thérèse Subligny; *Thétis et Pélée* and a revival of *Atys*, with Subligny, Pecour, and Magny (1689); *Orphée* and *Cadmus et Hermione*, with Subligny, Pecour, Lestang, Blondy, and Ballon (1690); and *Le Bourgeois Gentilhomme* at Versailles in 1691.

In 1692, La Fontaine retired to a convent but reemerged the following year to perform in *Didon*, with Subligny, Lestang, and Blondy. This was her last recorded appearance. She died in 1738 in another convent, near La Croix-Rouge in Paris.

BIBLIOGRAPHY

Du Tralage, Jean Nicolas. *Notes et documents sur l'histoire des théâtres de Paris aux XVIIe siècle.* Paris, 1880.

Lajarte, Théodore de. *Bibliothèque musicale du Théâtre de l'Opéra* (1878). 2 vols. Geneva, 1969.

Migel, Parmenia. *The Ballerinas: From the Court of Louis XIV to Pavlova.* New York, 1972.

Parfaict, François, and Claude Parfaict. *Histoire générale du théâtre françois.* Paris, 1734–.

RÉGINE ASTIER

LAING, HUGH (Hugh Skinner; born 6 June 1911 in Barbados, British West Indies, died 10 May 1988 in New York), English dancer. Talented in art as a youth, Laing went to London in 1930 to study at the Grosvenor School of Modern Art under Iain Macnab. Although his interest in the visual arts remained with him, Laing found himself strongly drawn to dance. In 1932 he began classes with Marie Rambert and later studied with the Cecchetti teacher Margaret Craske. At the Rambert studio, Laing's qualities caught the eye of Antony Tudor, one of Rambert's stable of young choreographers, and there began a lifelong creative association and friendship.

LAING. The Young Man from the House Opposite, in Antony Tudor's *Pillar of Fire* (1942), was perhaps Laing's most memorable role. Pictured here with Nora Kaye as Hagar, Laing was the incarnation of sexual desire. He brought intelligence and understanding to the role as well as his astonishing good looks. (Photograph from the Dance Collection, New York Public Library for the Performing Arts.)

Laing created roles in many of Tudor's early ballets: *Atalanta of the East* (1933), *The Planets* (1934), *The Descent of Hebe* (1935), *Jardin aux Lilas* (1936), and *Dark Elegies* (1937). His first significant non-Tudor role was in 1932 as Florestan in Michel Fokine's *Le Carnaval.* Other roles included Frederick Ashton's *Mephisto Valse* (1934) and *Valentine's Eve* (1935) and in 1936 Vaslav Nijinsky's *L'Après-midi d'un Faune.* When Tudor formed his London Ballet company in 1938, Laing went with him and created further roles in Tudor's *The Judgment of Paris*, *Gala Performance*, and *Soirée Musicale* (all 1938).

The following year, at the invitation of the co-founder of Ballet Theatre, Richard Pleasant, Laing went with Tudor to the United States and in 1940 joined the company. Laing's charismatic good looks and remarkable interpretive gifts made an immediate impression, and he quickly became one of the company's most significant dancers, winning particular acclaim in Tudor's great dramatic ballets, which included not only the early Rambert works *Jardin aux Lilas* and *Dark Elegies* but also those mounted for Ballet Theatre: *Pillar of Fire* (1942), *Dim Lustre* and *Romeo and Juliet* (both 1943), and *Undertow* (1945).

Laing joined the New York City Ballet from 1950 to 1952 and created the role of Armand in Tudor's *The Lady of the Camellias* (1951). He had great success in George Balanchine's revivals of *The Prodigal Son* and *Tyl Ulenspiegel* and in Ashton's *Illuminations.* Returning to Ballet Theatre in 1954, Laing remained with them until 1956, creating roles in Léonide Massine's *Aleko* (1942) and Agnes de Mille's *Tally-Ho* (1944). His repertory also included Jerome Robbins's *Facsimile* (1946), Fokine's *Petrouchka,* and the classic *Giselle,* in which he partnered both Alicia Alonso and Tamara Toumanova.

Perhaps the most theatrical dancer of our time, indeed a legendary performer, Laing worked with this century's greatest choreographers—Tudor, Ashton, Fokine, Massine, de Mille, Robbins, and Balanchine—during the course of his career. Married to Diana Adams for seven years, he became a commercial photographer after his retirement from the stage and assisted Tudor in restagings of his ballets until contracting cancer.

BIBLIOGRAPHY

Cohen, Selma Jeanne. "Antony Tudor: The Years in America and After." *Dance Perspectives,* no. 18 (1963).

Current Biography 7 (November 1946).

Percival, John. "Antony Tudor: The Years in England." *Dance Perspectives,* no. 17 (1963).

Perlmutter, Donna. *Shadowplay: The Life of Antony Tudor.* New York, 1991.

Szmyd, Linda. "Antony Tudor: Ballet Theatre Years." *Choreography and Dance* 1.2 (1989): 3–26.

PATRICIA BARNES

LAITIÈRE SUISSE, LA. *See* Swiss Milkmaid, The.

LAKE, MOLLY (born 3 June 1900 in Cornwall, England, died 2 October 1986 in London), British dancer, director, and choreographer. A devoted pupil of Enrico Cecchetti in London, Lake was one of the finest expositors of his system of teaching and a founding member of the Cecchetti Society, established in London in 1922. Trained as well by Serafina Astafieva and in Paris by Lubov Egorova and Vera Trefilova, she danced with Anna Pavlova's company, with the Markova-Dolin Ballet, with which she appeared in 1936 in the first cast of Keith Lester's noted restaging of Jules Perrot's *Pas de Quatre,* and then with Lester's short-lived Arts Theatre Ballet. She was one of the original members and leading dancers of the Ballet Guild, founded in 1941 to encourage young dancers and choreographers. This small company gave its first performance in Bath, toured throughout Great Britain, and during the war gave camp shows for ENSA (Entertainments National Service Association) in England, France, Belgium, and Germany.

In 1945, Lake and Travis Kemp, her husband, preempted most of the repertory and personnel of the Ballet Guild to form another small company, originally called the Embassy Ballet and later known as the Continental Ballet. The new choreography she provided for this group consisted of short nineteenth-century period pieces, stylistically similar to those in Pavlova's repertory, with titles like *La Petite Fadette, Victorian Bouquet,* and *Valse Viennoise.* Their titles alone survive.

In 1954, Lake and Kemp became the joint directors of the ballet school at the Ankara State University of Music in Turkey, a school the Turkish government had established only six years earlier according to guidelines suggested by Ninette de Valois. Lake remained there for twenty years. She returned to England with Kemp in 1974 and resumed teaching, at the London School of Contemporary Dance from 1975 to 1979, and then at her own Lake School of Dancing.

BIBLIOGRAPHY

Benari, Naomi. *Vagabonds and Strolling Dancers: The Lives and Times of Molly Lake and Travis Kemp.* London, 1990.

Noble, Peter, ed. *British Ballet.* London, 1949.

BARBARA NEWMAN

LAKHIA, KUMUDINI (born 17 May 1929 in Allahabad), Indian dancer and choreographer. Kumudini Lakhia was trained in *kathak* dance from childhood by Ashique Hussain Khan and began her professional career in 1944 at the age of fifteen, performing at the Allahabad Music Conference. Later, after joining Ram Gopal's company in Bangalore, she trained in the Jaipur *gharānā,* that is, the Jaipur school of *kathak,* under Radhelal Misra. She traveled extensively in Europe and the United States as one of Ram Gopal's leading partners, winning acclaim for her dancing in both *kathak* and *bharata nāṭyam.* With Ram Gopal's company, she danced the role of Queen Mumtaz Mahal in *The Legend of the Taj Mahal* at the Edinburgh Festival.

While working in Ram Gopal's troupe, she married Rajani Lakhia, and she then returned to India for further training in *kathak* under the masters Shambhu Maharaj of the Lucknow *gharānā* and Sundarprasad of the Jaipur *gharānā.* She appeared in the dance dramas of Sri Ram Bharatiya Kala Kendra in Delhi, and with Krishna Kumar and Birju Maharaj in *Malati Madhava* and *Kumar Shambhava* in the 1950s and 1960s.

In 1961 Lakhia settled in Ahmedabad, where she established Kadamb, an academy of classical *kathak* dance and music, in 1963. She trained a number of female dancers and a few males. She began choreographing group dances in an innovative, experimental style, seen by critics as a meaningful departure from the traditional *kathak* format. Works such as *Dhabkar, Drishtikon, Duvidha, Yugal, Venunada, Premchakshu, Okha Haran, Dashavatara, Atah Kim, The Peg, Tarana, Shravan,* and *Samasamvedan* changed the nature of *kathak,* introducing contemporary sensibilities and modern theatrical presentation. Lakhia explored the *kathak* genre, looking at its possibilities and using space and group composition imaginatively.

Lakhia possesses a sense of programming, color, and design that enables her to create patterns of unusual beauty, retaining the essential quality of *kathak* movement but giving it a new look. Her works benefit from the wide experience of her years with Ram Gopal as well as from her own creativity. She has received excellent support from Atul Desai, the composer for all her choreography.

Lakhia lives in Ahmedabad, where she trains students in *kathak;* her notable pupils include Daksha Sheth, Aditi Mangaldas, Maulik Shah, Ishira Parikh, and Shubha Desai and Darshini Desai. She has a son, Sri Raj, and a daughter, Maitreyi. She continues to choreograph and to take part in national and international dance festivals. Her contributions have been honored by the Padamshri award of the government of India and by the Central Sangeet Natak Akademi award. She has held several prestigious positions, serving as vice president of UNESCO's International Dance Council and as chairman of the Gujarat State Sangeet Nritya Natak Akademi.

BIBLIOGRAPHY

Dove, Simon. "'Navanritya': New Dance." *Ballett International* 13 (November 1990): 24–27.

Kothari, Sunil. *Kathak: Indian Classical Dance Art.* New Delhi, 1989.

Misra, Susheela. *Some Dancers of India.* New Delhi, 1992.

Percival, John. "Dancing Differently." *Dance and Dancers* (August–October 1993): 8–9.

Rubidge, Sarah. "Modern Movement and Traditional Tales." *Dance Theatre Journal* 10 (Spring–Summer 1993): 32–37.

SUNIL KOTHARI

LAKHỌN. The term *lakhọn* (also spelled *lakon*) for "Thai dance drama" is probably derived from the Javanese word *lagon,* which means "dance drama." Some Thai scholars, however, associate the term with Nakọn Sīthammarāt, a city in southern Thailand where older forms of dance drama, *lakhọn norā* and *lakhọn chātrī,* are well established.

There are three major subgenres of *lakhọn. Lakhọn ram* is dance drama with poetic narratives sung by a chorus and solo singers, and poetic prose dialogue is spoken by dancer-actors. *Lakhọn rōng* is operetta with narratives sung by a chorus and dialogue sung and spoken by actor-singers. *Lakhọn phūt* is spoken drama in poetry or prose.

Until the nineteenth century, *lakhọn* denoted classical and folk dance drama in various styles. Both *lakhọn rōng* and *lakhọn phūt* are modern dramatic forms with Western influences, which were introduced during the reign of King Chulalongkorn (1868–1910).

The stories performed in traditional *lakhọn ram* are taken from India's *jātaka* tales ("birth stories"), usually the adventures and romances of kings and princes who were *phōthisat* (future Buddhas, avatars in Buddha's previous lives). One of the oldest forms of *lakhọn* is the *nōrā chātrī* of southern Thailand, which tells the romantic tale of Phra Suthon and Manōhrā and other *jātaka* stories. This southern folk drama developed into *lakhọn chātrī* in the eighteenth century. It incorporated many features of the central Thai folk dance drama, *lakhọn nọk,* but preserved most of its indigenous southern characteristics—for example, the swift hand and foot movements, the music, the long, curved bronze fingernails, and the headdress.

Lakhọn nọk, an old form of *lakhọn ram* performed in the central part of Thailand, was probably developed in the Ayudhayā period, in the seventeenth century or even earlier. *Lakhọn nai* is the shortened name of *lakhọn nāng nai* (dance drama of the ladies of the inner court), a later development in the Ayudhayā period of the eighteenth century.

There are many differences between *lakhọn nọk* and *lakhọn nai* in stories, style of dancing, musical accompaniment, characterization, interpretation and expression, costumes, and dramatic purposes. The stories of *lakhọn nọk* are *Jātaka* tales from the Mahayana Buddhist collection *Panyāsa-Chādok* (Fifty Lives of Phōthisat), with emphasis on comic and melodramatic scenes. The style of dancing is simple, fast, and action-oriented. It is a folk dance drama for popular audiences.

Lakhọn nai, by contrast, is a court entertainment focusing on elaborate, refined movements presented with grace and charm, purely for their romantic and aesthetic qualities. Stories in *lakhọn nai* are from the epics *Rāmakian, Romance of Inao,* and *Unarut,* with emphasis on love scenes and domestic affairs among members of the aristocracy and the royal family. The expression of emotion is therefore very subtle, in the sophisticated manner of the courtiers. While characters in *lakhọn nọk* are usually two-dimensional, those in *lakhọn nai* show psychological complexity and depth.

The costumes of both dance-drama genres are similar, but in the past *lakhọn nai,* as an entertainment for the elite and members of the royal family, displayed the richness, luxury, and high fashion of the royal court and used exquisite costumes and ornaments to imitate royal attire. King Mongkut, Rama IV (1851–1868) prohibited other *lakhọn* troupes from imitating royal costumes or using gold ornaments, which were prerogatives of the royal family.

Lakhon nǫk and *lakhǫn nai* use different styles of music. The orchestra for both consists of a *ranād* (bamboo xylophone), *pī* (oboe), *taphōn* (two-faced drum), *khǫng wong* (a circle of gongs), *klǫng* (tympani), and *ching* (small cymbals). The tunes for specific actions *(nā phāt)* in *lakhǫn nǫk* are shorter, faster, and simpler than those in *lakhǫn nai*, which accompany elaborate and beautiful dances.

Training for *lakhǫn ram*, both folk and classical, usually starts in childhood. Pupils proceed through the basic patterns of dance handed down from older generations, with some modernized choreography added by outstanding artists of past royal courts or of the National Theater and National Academy of Dance. Actors of *lakhǫn phūt*, by contrast, are mostly self-taught.

In the reign of King Somdet Phra Phuttha Lōet Lā, Rama II (1809–1824), dance movements and music for both dance dramas were perfected. The king and his court poets composed many episodes from the *Rāmakian* and *Inao* as well as plays for the *lakhǫn nǫk* to be performed by the royal dance troupe. The dance styles of both theater forms merged, and *lakhǫn nǫk* developed more refined qualities in its dramatic texts, dance patterns, characterization, and even comic relief.

Other dance troupes later imitated the classical style of royal *lakhǫn nai* and *lakhǫn nǫk*, using King Rama II's compositions and choreography. *Lakhǫn* and *khōn* productions of the National Theater today continue to depend on his dramatic texts, but they use modern condensed versions and concentrate on rapid storytelling, comic dialogues, dance numbers with modern choreography, spectacular set designs, and colorful costumes rather than the traditional complex and refined dance movements.

Melodies and songs composed by Prince Narisarānuwadhiwong (1863–1947) were later additions to the traditional *lakhǫn nōk, lakhǫn nai*, and *khōn* repertory, intended to attract the interest of modern audiences. The three types of dance drama are now regularly performed and taught by the National Theater and National Academy of Dance. Occasionally, private organizations and educational institutions present amateur productions.

As a result of modernization under Western influence during the long reign of King Chulalongkorn, Rama V (1868–1910), three new forms of *lakhǫn* developed from traditional forms. *Lakhǫn phanthāng* emerged from *lakhǫn nōk*, based on stories taken from historical legends and chronicles and using modernized versions of period costumes. *Lakhǫn dukdamban*, created by Prince Narisaranuwadhiwong and Chao Phrayā Thēwētwongwiwat, was an offshoot of the royal *lakhǫn nai* and *lakhǫn nǫk* with new features in music, songs sung by dancers, rapid action, contemporary dialogue, and modern theater techniques. The third form, *lakhǫn rōng*, was a Thai attempt at imitating Western operetta, with Thai music and stories adapted from Western plays set in the contemporary period and fashion.

A new dramatic genre drawn from Western tradition, the spoken play or *lakhǫn phūt*, also evolved during this period. Schooled in England, King Vajiravudh, Rama VI (ruled 1910–1925), was an avid amateur actor and playwright. His translations—adaptations of French and English plays, including Shakespeare—as well as his own plays earned him the title "Father of Thai *lakhǫn phūt*." The king also introduced new styles of acting, directing, makeup, and stage production.

The king's political themes emphasized support of an absolute monarchy and served as an instrument to stir public interest and patriotic support for his concerns about Western colonialism, Russian socialism, the Chinese monopoly of commerce and trade, and various economic and social problems. In his reign, *lakhǫn phūt* became an effective means of propagating loyalty to the throne as well as of educating the public. Later playwrights who followed in his footsteps included Luang Wichitwathakān, who wrote patriotic and nationalistic musical plays during the 1940s and 1950s, and Somphop Čhantharaprahpā, author of royalist dance dramas in the 1970s.

Lakhǫn phūt became more popular during World War II and the postwar period, when the importation of foreign films was not permitted. Many companies offered high salaries to popular actors and invested in music, dance, costumes, and sets. Costumes and makeup in *lakhǫn phūt* still preserve many of the traditional theatrical qualities of *lakhǫn ram*.

During the 1950s and 1960s, with the influx of Western films, both *lakhǫn ram* and *lakhǫn phūt* lost most of their audience. Recently, however, both have been revived on television. Tales from traditional *lakhǫn nǫk, lakhǫn nai*, and *khōn* are regularly presented in modern costume. All television channels have their own *lakhōn thōrathat* (television dramas), most of which present domestic stories with social themes or satires. Thus the tradition of *lakhǫn* is still very influential in the Thai entertainment world.

During the 1970s and 1980s, training in modern *lakhǫn phūt* developed in leading Thai universities, using Western methods, particularly those of Konstantin Stanislavsky, thus generating an emphasis on realistic acting in Thai classical and modern dance. During the 1990s, artists have been giving new interpretations to classical dance dramas and integrating contemporary and classical dances, spoken modern prose, and sung narratives into the traditional styles. Successful experimental productions from 1994 to 1996 include Mattani Rutnin's *Busaba-Unakan* (1994) and *Rama-Sida* (1996); Parichat Jungwiwathanaporn's *Phimphilalai* (1995); and *Savitri* (1996) produced by a freelance dance-drama group directed by Nuchawadee Bamrungtrakul and Ornchuma Yuthawong. These creative experiments have succeeded in relating classical *lakhọ̄n* traditions to a new generation.

[*See also* Thailand. *For discussion of other Thai dance dramas, see* Khōn *and* Manōhrā.]

BIBLIOGRAPHY

Aphọ̄n Montrīsāt, Chaturong Montrīsāt, and Montrī Trāmōte. *Wichā nātasin.* Bangkok, 1974.

Damrong Rājānubhāp, H. R. H. Prince. *Tamnān lakhọ̄n inao.* Bangkok, 1964.

Kukrit Pramōj, Mom Rātchawong. "Nātasin." Unpublished ms., n.d.

Maha Vajiravudh. "Notes on the Siamese Theatre." *Journal of the Siam Society* 55.1 (1967): 1–30.

Miettinen, Jukka O. *Classical Dance and Theatre in South-East Asia.* New York, 1992.

Mojdara Rutnin, Mattani, ed. *The Siamese Theatre.* Bangkok, 1975.

Mojdara Rutnin, Mattani. "Phathanākān khọ̄ng nātasin lae kān lakhọ̄n thai smai mai." Unpublished ms., 1983–1984.

Mojdara Rutnin, Mattani. *Dance, Drama, and Theatre in Thailand.* Tokyo, 1993.

Yupho, Dhanit. *The Khon and Lakon.* Bangkok, 1963.

Yupho, Dhanit. *Silapa lakhọ̄n ram rüe khūmü nātasin thai.* Bangkok, 1973.

MATTANI MOJDARA RUTNIN

LAKSHMI. *See* Knight, Lakshmi.

LAMBERT, CONSTANT (Leonard Constant Lambert; born 23 August 1905 in London, died 21 August 1951 in London), English composer, conductor, and pianist. Lambert showed early aptitude for music and in 1922 won a scholarship to the Royal College of Music in London, where one of his teachers was Ralph Vaughan Williams. Lambert's interest in dance was first aroused at this time, and in 1924, while a student, he composed two ballet scores on his own initiative: *Prize-Fight,* for small orchestra, and *Mr. Bear Squash-you-all-flat,* for wind quintet, percussion, and piano. Both are unpublished and have no record of performance.

During this time he became associated with the Sitwells, an English literary family, and their friend, the composer William Walton, who dedicated *Façade* to Lambert in its original form, music with recitation. Lambert was the co-reciter with Edith Sitwell at an early public performance in 1926, and he himself composed the first eleven bars of one item, "Four in the Morning." A "suite dansée," *Adam and Eve,* was composed by Lambert in 1925; after he and a friend played it in two-piano form for Serge Diaghilev, who was then interested in British composers, Lambert was invited to compose a work for Diaghilev's Ballets Russes.

Romeo and Juliet was Diaghilev's choice, and the ballet was produced at Monte Carlo in 1926 with choreography by Bronislava Nijinska, to whom Lambert dedicated the music. This made use of the *Adam and Eve* score, but with cuts, changes, and some newly composed sections, lasting about thirty minutes in two tableaux. At Diaghilev's behest, Christopher Wood, the commissioned designer, was replaced at a late stage by the surrealists Max Ernst and Joan Miró, and the setting was changed to a theatrical rehearsal situation.

Lambert was dismayed at these changes and attempted to have the work withdrawn, as he described in a letter to his mother (Shead, 1973). The ballet, first danced by Tamara Karsavina and Serge Lifar, was moderately well received at Monte Carlo, but its decor provoked a riot of opposing factions in Paris. It was well received in London, although frequent published comments on the unusually ill-judged relationship (for a Diaghilev production) between the decor and music suggest that the composer made his displeasure known.

The *Romeo and Juliet* music comprises a suite of classical dance and other forms. It is scored for small orchestra, and its character owes much to the example of Igor Stravinsky and the influence of the then fashionable neoclassical French school. The diatonic harmony incorporates structural dissonance and clear-cut rhythms with few or no emotional associations, in a manner Lambert was later to deride in others.

Lambert continued the idiom in his next ballet, *Pomona,* composed on an invitation from Nijinska, who first choreographed it at the Teatro Colón in Buenos Aires in 1927. Most of this music originated as a divertimento in seven movements for concert performance, written shortly before, to which were added a passacaglia from the 1925 *Adam and Eve* and an introduction derived from an independent *Pastorale* for piano.

The subject concerns the pursuit of Pomona, goddess of fruits in Roman mythology, by Vertumnus, a god of seasons, a theme retained by Frederick Ashton when he created his *Pomona* ballet for the debut program of the Camargo Society in London on 19 October 1930. This ballet was the major success on that occasion, and Ashton later reworked it at Sadler's Wells Theatre in 1933 and for Margot Fonteyn and Robert Helpmann in 1937.

Meanwhile, Lambert broadened his musical interests to include a fondness for American jazz, primarily as represented by Duke Ellington, in whose support Lambert wrote knowledgeably and sympathetically in the 1930s. He composed a short *Elegiac Blues* (1927) in memory of the black singer Florence Mills and the same year completed his best-known concert work, *The Rio Grande.* A setting for solo piano, chorus, and orchestra of a poem by Sacheverell Sitwell, its fantasy and form were reconciled by an original musical texture woven from Ellingtonian jazz, Latin American rhythms, and the shifting harmonies of Frederick Delius. Ashton made use of it in 1931 for the Camargo Society ballet called *A Day in a Southern Port,* but he reverted to Lambert's title at Sadler's Wells in 1935, when Fonteyn danced her first principal role as the Creole Girl.

After arranging a reduced orchestration of Wolfgang Amadeus Mozart's *Les Petits Riens* for Ninette de Valois in 1931, Lambert was engaged as the first conductor and music director of the fledgling Vic-Wells (later Sadler's Wells) Ballet, to which he devoted most of his next sixteen years. De Valois wrote:

> He was at his best when seated with us at the piano working out cuts, sequences and the general development of a score he was arranging. . . . He had a carefully acquired knowledge of different types of dancers . . . and sympathetic understanding shown where licence could be permitted that was not to the detriment of the musical or choreographic flow. Yet he was a great disciplinarian. . . . His word was law, and a law respected by all the artists. (De Valois, 1977)

Lambert's performance contribution was threefold. He musically supervised and conducted the classics of the Maryinsky heritage as transplanted to Britain—*Coppélia, Swan Lake, Giselle,* and *The Sleeping Beauty*—setting uncompromising musical standards given the resources available. He took comparable care with new works such as *Job,* set to music by Williams that Lambert arranged for reduced orchestra, and *Checkmate,* to music by Arthur Bliss. He also arranged skillfully crafted anthologies of existing music tailored to the choreographic needs of specific ballets.

These furnished the music for *Les Rendezvous* (1932), to music by Daniel Auber; *Apparitions* (1933), to Franz Liszt; *Les Patineurs* (1937), to Giacomo Meyerbeer; *Harlequin in the Street* (1938), to François Couperin; *Dante Sonata* (1940), to Liszt; *The Prospect before Us* (1940), to William Boyce; *Comus* (1942), to Henry Purcell; and *Ballabile* (1950), to Emmanuel Chabrier. The last three were for de Valois, Helpmann, and Roland Petit, respectively; the rest were for Ashton, whose *Les Rendezvous* and *Les Patineurs* have had continued longevity in the repertories of the Royal Ballet and other companies.

During the 1930s Lambert augmented his income by writing music criticism of a Shavian wit and polemic, briefly for *The Nation and Athenaeum* until it was merged into *The New Statesman and Nation,* then for the now-defunct *Sunday Referee.* His fluent writing found more extended expression in the equally polemical book, *Music Ho! A Study of Music in Decline* (1934). Besides expressing his views on music of that time, the book attacked aspects of Diaghilev's artistic methods and principles based on his own unfortunate experience.

In 1931 Lambert composed a concerto for piano and nine instruments, an abrasive, pungently scored work with melodic and rhythmic elements of jazz, and nine movements of incidental music for a production of Oscar Wilde's *Salomé,* including a "Dance of the Seven Veils," choreographed by de Valois, that he had scored for clarinet, trumpet, cello, and percussion. The opening theme of this dance recurred in Lambert's largest-scale work, *Summer's Last Will and Testament,* a choral and orchestral "masque," as he called it, with words by the sixteenth-century writer Thomas Nashe. This work occupied him intermittently for some three years before it was first performed in 1935.

His next major work was the ballet *Horoscope,* the most successful of his dance scores, premiered at Sadler's Wells on 27 January 1938. Ashton's choreography had an astrological theme devised by Lambert, whose music was dedicated to Fonteyn. The score, for symphonic orchestra, comprises a short "Prelude" in palindromic form, "Dance for the Followers of Leo," "Saraband for the Followers of Virgo," "Variations for Young Man and Young Woman," "Bacchanale," "Waltz for the Gemini," "Pas de Deux," "Invocation to the Moon," and "Finale."

While relying to some extent on the repetition of certain rhythmic and harmonic traits, the music for *Horoscope* has engaging melodic appeal and was as well liked as the ballet. Its success was cut short two years later when the sets and costumes, together with the full score and parts, were left behind in Holland when the Sadler's Wells Ballet, which was on tour, escaped the invading German army by a matter of hours. The work was never revived, but a concert suite of five movements became popular in the postwar years. A 1967 record reissue preserves Lambert's 1940s recording of the "Saraband" and "Bacchanale," as well as *The Rio Grande,* together with the "Gemini Waltz" conducted by Robert Irving.

Lame since childhood, Lambert was unfit for military service and spent the war years playing piano for the depleted ballet company when there was no orchestra available for the company's tours. As one of the company's two pianists, he sometimes gave up to six evening and three matinee performances in one week. He made all the necessary musical arrangements, conducted whenever there was an orchestra, and recited the Gertrude Stein text for Ashton's *A Wedding Bouquet* as a substitute for the chorus, a practice continued ever since.

Lambert conducted *The Sleeping Beauty* for the postwar reopening of Covent Garden, and he made and conducted his own edition of Purcell's *The Fairy Queen* as the first opera there after the war. He had conducted Purcell's *Dido and Aeneas* at Sadler's Wells in 1931 and Giacomo Puccini's *Manon Lescaut* and *Turandot* at Covent Garden, the former in 1937 and the latter in 1939 and 1947. With the inauguration of the British Broadcasting Corporation's "Third Program" in 1946, Lambert made numerous broadcasts, often with little-known music by Liszt, Chabrier, Erik Satie, and other composers he admired.

Worsening alcoholism led to Lambert's resignation from a salaried post with the Sadler's Wells Ballet in 1947, but he was made one of the artistic directors on an advisory basis and continued as a guest conductor, in which capacity he conducted the company's 1949 debut performance at the Metropolitan Opera House in New York. His last composition was for another Ashton ballet, *Tiresias*, which Lambert had first proposed twenty years earlier to the Camargo Society. It came to fruition at Covent Garden on 9 July 1951, only to be found disappointing in performance.

Among the reasons suggested for the ballet's failure was the undue length of Lambert's score, which had stretched from an intended thirty minutes to more than an hour. Lambert's declining health, affected by previously undiagnosed diabetes, compelled much of the orchestration to be undertaken by others, among them Irving, Humphrey Searle, and Alan Rawsthorne. The score, for symphonic orchestra with no violins or violas, is divided into three scenes and is characterized by dissonant polytonality, with the interval of the tritone related to the bisexuality of the protagonist.

Further exhausted by the demands of the new ballet, Lambert died six weeks after the premiere. A shortened version with music edited by Elisabeth Lutyens continued in repertory until 1954, but the score was unpublished. Lambert was nevertheless a prime architect of the British ballet tradition and is so remembered on the title page of each Royal Ballet program.

BIBLIOGRAPHY

de Valois, Ninette. "Constant Lambert." In de Valois's *Step by Step*. London, 1977.

Irving Robert. "Constant Lambert." In *The Decca Book of Ballet*, edited by David Drew. London, 1958.

Lambert, Constant. *Music Ho! A Study of Music in Decline*. London, 1934.

Motion, Andrew. *The Lamberts: George, Constant, and Kit*. London, 1986.

Shead, Richard. *Constant Lambert*. London, 1973.

Sorley Walker, Kathrine. *Ninette de Valois: Idealist without Illusions*. London, 1987.

Vaughan, David. *Frederick Ashton and His Ballets*. London, 1977.

NOËL GOODWIN

LAMHUT, PHYLLIS (born 14 November 1933 in Brooklyn, New York), American dancer, choreographer, and teacher. Lamhut trained in modern dance primarily with Alwin Nikolais at the Henry Street Playhouse, beginning in 1948 at the age of fifteen; she also studied modern dance with Merce Cunningham (1961–1971), ballet and body placement with Zena Rommett, ballet with Peter Saul (both in the 1960s), and circus arts with Hovey Burgess (1969–1970).

Lamhut was a featured dancer with the Nikolais Company from its inception in 1948 until 1969, creating roles in more than twenty-five works, including *Imago, Kaleidoscope, Sanctum, Tower, Tent, Prism,* and *Vaudeville of the Elements*. Concurrently, she was the leading female dancer with the Murray Louis Company from 1963 to 1969, appearing most prominently in *Junk Dances, A Gothic Tale, Proximities, Interims, Go 6, Landscapes,* and *Suite for Diverse Performers*.

Lamhut began choreographing in 1949 and founded the Phyllis Lamhut Dance Company in 1970. She has choreographed more than one hundred works, from solos to full-evening group pieces, in a wide range of styles, working since 1980 with commissioned scores, often with composers Robert Moran, Andy Teirstein, and Ben Hazard. Lamhut is known for her comedic sense as a performer, but much of her choreography is dramatic. She has said, "I consider myself an individual artist. I listen to my inner voice, and I structure my imagination. I am committed to the art of motion and its expressiveness and to the process of choreography." Her dances have been shown in a variety of spaces from theaters to gymnasiums and city plazas. Among her eclectic works are *House* (1971), *Hearts of Palm* (1975), *Brain Waves* (1976), *Dyad* (1977), *Mirage Blanc, Disclinations,* and *Essence* (all 1978), *Musical Suite* (1979), *Passing* (1980), *Stones, Bones and Skin* (1982), *For Spirits and Kings* (1983), *Collapsing Spaces and Tilting Times* (1984), *Klein Kunst* (Small Art) (1985), *Die Bewegung* (The Movement) (1986), *Utopia* (1988), *Man* (a response to the AIDS crisis; 1989), *Dislocations* (1993), *Deadly Sins* (1995), and *Adjustments* (1996). Lamhut has also made three pieces for the Limón Dance Company: *Cleave* (1990), *Fantômes* (1994), and *Sacred Conversations* (1993), a solo for Carla Maxwell.

Lamhut has received fellowships from the Guggenheim and CAPS foundations, and from the New York Foundation for the Arts, as well as several grants from the New York State Council on the Arts and from Meet the Composer. She was the first woman in modern dance to receive a three-year choreographer's fellowship from the National Endowment for the Arts. She has taught at the Henry Street Playhouse, the Nikolais-Louis Laboratory, and Dance Theater Workshop in New York City. She has been on the faculty of the Tisch School of the Arts at New York University since 1986 and has taught in universities throughout the United States and around the world. She has also directed several national and international seminars, including the National Association of Regional Ballet Craft of Choreography Conference (1984), the Canadian National Choreographic Seminar (1985), the Carlisle Project's "New Impulses" choreography workshop (1995), and a workshop on dance and music at Hebrew University in Jerusalem (1996), funded by the Israeli government. Lamhut's publications include several articles on Alwin Nikolais.

BIBLIOGRAPHY

Anderson, Jack. "Phyllis Lamhut." *Dance Magazine* (February 1975): 62–65.

Lamhut, Phyllis. "A Response to the National Endowment for the Arts' Essay." In *A Debate on Government Funding for the Arts, Kansas Journal of Law and Public Policy,* vol 2, no. 1 (Spring 1992). Lawrence, Kans., 1992.
Lamhut, Phyllis. "Views on the Arts." *Poor Dancer's Almanac.* New York, 1991.
McDonagh, Don, ed. *The Complete Guide to Modern Dance.* New York, 1976.
Vaughan, David. "Phyllis Lamhut Dance Company." *Dance Magazine* (June 1985): 24–25.
Zupp, Nancy T. "An Analysis and Comparison of the Choreographic Process of Alwin Nikolais, Murray Louis, and Phyllis Lamhut." Ph.D. diss.,University of North Carolina, Greensboro, 1978.

AMANDA SMITH

LAMI, EUGÈNE LOUIS (born 12 January 1800 in Paris, France, died 19 December 1890 in Paris), French costume designer. Paradoxically, Lami owes the main part of his fame in the dance world to a costume he probably did not design: the long white "Romantic tutu" worn by Marie Taglioni in the title role of *La Sylphide* (1832). No sketch of the costume was ever found among his designs for this ballet, and he apparently never claimed credit for it (Fischer, 1931). Although most dance historians today agree that the Romantic tutu was not Lami's invention (cf. Guest, 1981), his name remains inextricably linked with it because of the mystery attached to the "missing" sketch. [*See* Tutu.]

LAMI. For the 1832 premiere of *La Sylphide* at the Paris Opera, Lami designed this Scottish costume, complete with dirk, sword, and shield, for Joseph Mazilier, who danced the role of James. (Photographic reproduction from Bibliothèque de l'Opéra, Paris; courtesy of the Dance Collection, New York Public Library for the Performing Arts.)

Lami specialized in military uniforms, which he meticulously reproduced both in lithographs and in costume designs for the Paris Opera, for which he worked as an independent designer between 1830 and 1835. He designed the uniforms for Jean-Louis Aumer's ballet *Manon Lescaut* (1830), collaborating with Hippolyte Lecomte, the costume designer for the production. Lami was also renowned for his regional costumes, such as the Scottish costumes he designed for Filippo Taglioni's ballet *La Sylphide.* In 1832 he designed one of the ten sets for the *opéra-ballet La Tentation,* astonishing audiences with his vision of a demon's chamber in a subterranean hall dominated by an enormous blazing stairway. He also designed costumes for the ballets *L'Orgie* (1831) and *L'Île des Pirates* (1835).

Lami was not, however, primarily a theatrical designer. A student of Horace Vernet and Antoine Gros, he exhibited historical and battle paintings at the prestigious Paris Salons between 1824 and 1878. His smaller-scale watercolors and lithographs chronicled aristocratic Parisian society. Many of these works depict fashionable Parisians at fêtes, balls, or the theater. His well-known watercolor of the Foyer de la Danse at the Paris Opera (1841) portrays Fanny Elssler, Jean Coralli, Louis Véron, and other notable personages of the day.

BIBLIOGRAPHY

Fischer, Carlos. *Les costumes de l'Opéra.* Paris, 1931.
Guest, Ivor. *The Romantic Ballet in Paris.* 2d rev. ed. London, 1980.
Guest, Ivor. "Costume and the Nineteenth Century Dancer." In *Designing for the Dancer,* by Roy Strong et al. London, 1981.
Lemoisne, Paul-André. *L'oeuvre d'Eugène Lami, 1800–1890.* Paris, 1914.
Wild, Nicole. *Décors et costumes du XIXe siècle,* vol. 1, *Opéra de Paris.* Paris, 1987.

SUSAN AU

LANCHBERY, JOHN (John Arthur Lanchbery; born 15 May 1923 in London), English conductor and composer. Lanchbery began violin lessons when eight years old and started composing at much the same time; he later continued his studies at the Royal Academy of Music, London, to which he returned after war service. While working part time in music publishing, he obtained the conductor's post with Metropolitan Ballet, a London-based touring company, with which he worked from early 1948 until the company folded from lack of funds at the end of 1949.

During this time he learned his craft, conducting performances throughout Great Britain and working with such dancers as Sonia Arova, Svetlana Beriosova, Celia Franca, Erik Bruhn, and Poul Gnatt. His first music arrangement was the orchestration for piano and strings of the second movement from Petr Ilich Tchaikovsky's Piano Trio in A Minor (op. 50) for John Taras's *Designs with Strings* (1948), and he composed original music for *Pleasuredrome* and *The Eve of Saint Agnes,* the latter for Franca as choreographer-dancer in one of the first commissioned ballets shown on British Broadcasting Corporation (BBC) television.

After composing several motion picture scores, Lanchbery became conductor in 1951 with what was then the Sadler's Wells Theatre Ballet, where he remained until 1959, when he moved to the Royal Ballet at Covent Garden, briefly under Hugo Rignold, then as principal conductor from 1960 to 1972. His subsequent conducting appointments were as music director for the Australian Ballet from 1972 to 1978, and for American Ballet Theatre from 1978 to 1980. Since then he has continued freelance conducting and recording in the United States, Great Britain, and elsewhere.

While with the Sadler's Wells company, Lanchbery made a symphony-orchestra arrangement of three jazz pieces by Stan Kenton and did the arrangements for Kenneth MacMillan's first professional ballet, *Somnambulism* (1953), as well as arranging works by the Catalan composer Federico Mompou for MacMillan's *House of Birds* (1955). He then made a major transcription and revision of the 1828 Ferdinand Hérold music for *La Fille Mal Gardée* to suit the needs of Frederick Ashton's new version for the Royal Ballet (1960).

Lanchbery further collaborated with Ashton successfully in adapting Felix Mendelssohn for *The Dream* (1964), orchestrating Erik Satie's *Trois Gnossiennes* for *Monotones* (1966), making some minor revisions in 1970 to Ludwig van Beethoven's 1801 ballet *The Creatures of Prometheus,* and adapting some Frédéric Chopin works for *A Month in the Country* (1976). He was asked to rewrite the 1869 Léon Minkus score for Rudolf Nureyev's version of *Don Quixote* (1966). He again made revisions to Minkus for Natalia Makarova's production of *La Bayadère* for American Ballet Theatre in 1980.

Lanchbery suggested adapting Franz Liszt's works for MacMillan's *Mayerling* (1978). His three-act score draws on more than thirty works, from *A Faust Symphony* to the *Mephisto Polka* and the *Transcendental Studies,* as well as on Liszt's transcriptions of Franz Schubert in the *Soirées de Vienne* for the formal dances at the wedding ball. Lanchbery pointed out that Liszt's keyboard music has a number of instrumental allusions, suggesting that Liszt "thought orchestrally as well as pianistically." Liszt's orchestration in other works was kept intact.

Lanchbery also became adept at transforming operas and operettas into nonvocal ballet music, beginning with Jacques Offenbach's *The Tales of Hoffmann* for Peter Darrell and the Scottish Ballet in 1972. This was followed by Franz Lehár's *The Merry Widow* for Ronald Hynd and the Australian Ballet in 1975, and three years later by Johann Strauss's *Die Fledermaus,* which became Hynd's *Rosalinda* for PACT (Performing Arts Council of the Transvaal) Ballet in Johannesburg, South Africa, and then for London's Festival Ballet.

Lanchbery has said that the musical character of particular composers affects his approach to orchestration in his adaptations. In the case of operatic music, he notes,

> what you cannot do is to take the original orchestration, put the voice part on a trumpet or an oboe and hope it will sound right. It doesn't. You have to take it apart and re-weave it, as it were. (Lanchbery, 1978)

His aim is always to balance the interests of composer and choreographer, and in conducting he combines a craftsman's ability to reconcile the sometimes conflicting demands of music and the dancers' capabilities with an artist's understanding of the music's nature and purpose.

His major film scores include *The Tales of Beatrix Potter* (1971), for which he drew on themes from nineteenth century salon music for Ashton's choreography of the Victorian children's stories, and *The Turning Point* (1977), which featured Leslie Browne, Mikhail Baryshnikov, and American Ballet Theatre, and is mostly an adaptation of existing ballet scores although it includes a Duke Ellington number and two original contributions by Lanchbery.

Kenneth LaFave has quoted Lanchbery in defining his aims as a ballet conductor:

> The important element is that of the orchestra contributing to a dramatic work, being part of it instead of just churning out the music from the pit. . . . Unfortunately some companies treat the music as rather unimportant, almost like a necessary evil. That is an attitude I want to stamp out. I'd like to feel that, wherever I go, I'm fighting a crusade for ballet music. Music has been the Cinderella of ballet for too long. (La Fave, 1981)

In 1989, Lanchbery received the Queen Elizabeth II Coronation Award from the Royal Academy of Dancing, Great Britain's highest accolade in dance.

BIBLIOGRAPHY

LaFave, Kenneth. "Music Man." *Ballet News* 3 (December 1981): 30–31.

Lanchbery, John. "The Conductor Who Arranges Things." *Dance and Dancers* (March 1978): 24–27.

Nice, David. "Arranged Marriages." *Opera House,* no. 6 (September 1995): 34–38.

NOËL GOODWIN

LANDER, HARALD (Alfred Bernhardt Stevnsborg; born 25 February 1905 in Copenhagen, died 14 September 1971 in Copenhagen), Danish dancer, ballet master, and teacher. Lander was a ballet pupil at the Royal Danish Ballet School (1913), a dancer (1923), soloist (1929), and ballet master (1932–1951) at the Royal Danish Theater, and a leader of the Paris Opera's ballet school (1956–1963). Even though Lander's small stature precluded his becoming a leading classical dancer, he possessed a strong turning and jumping technique, which enabled him to execute three *tours en l'air.* Lander belonged to the generation profoundly influenced by Michel Fokine, with whom he studied in the United States in 1927 and 1928. Lander also studied Russian and especially Spanish national dances.

During his nineteen years as artistic leader of the Royal Danish Ballet, Lander created thirty ballets, brought new life into the Danish repertory, staged works by Petipa and Fokine, and made *divertissements* for operas and plays. At the same time he gave daily classes to the company, alternating Bournonville with Russian technique day by day.

Lander changed the company's artistic composition in six years. In 1938 he found the dancers were capable of performing Russian classical ballet and staged *Swan Lake.* During the German occupation of World War II, from 1940 to 1945, Lander made the Royal Ballet a bastion of Danish culture, creating a positive public attitude which still exists.

Lander's first works had continued Bournonville's approach to dramaturgy. The action took place in exotic locales—*Gaucho* (1931) in Latin America, *Tata* (1932) in Hungary, and *Zaporogerne* (1934) in Russia, with designs after Ilya Yefimovich Repin's paintings. The last in this series was *Boléro* (1934), with a Spanish milieu.

A turning point came on 12 November 1936, when Lander staged Bertholt Brecht and Kurt Weill's *The Seven Deadly Sins.* Lander showed that he was able to handle a burning issue and political satire. The ballet was performed only twice because the German ambassador made an unofficial protest to the Danish foreign ministry.

An important series of collaborations began between Lander and a number of the best Danish artists—all dedicated antifascists. Among them were the composer Knudåge Riisager, the dramatist and scenic designer Kjeld Abell, and the scenic designers Svend Johansen and Erik Nordgren. The first product had a typical Abell libretto: a modern emancipated young woman is locked up in the museum of the classical sculptor Bertel Thorvaldsen in Copenhagen. This ballet, *Thorvaldsen,* with music by Johan Hye-Knudsen (premiered 21 November 1938), was a capricious but deeply humanistic call for an alliance between Danish youth and the classical democratic ideals of Greece and Rome.

Denmark was occupied by Germany on 9 April 1940, and half a year later Harald Lander presented his first example of official ballet art, *Troldmandens Lærling* (The Sorcerer's Apprentice), on 17 October 1940. The symbolism was clear to the Danes. Hitler, another unlucky witch-pupil, had started something he never could master. The idea was emphasized by the designer's use of "decadent" American cartoon styling. During 1942, the year of the greatest Nazi victories, Lander created an entire series of political ballets: *Slaraffenland* (The Land of Milk and Honey); *Qarrtsiluni,* after an Eskimo legend about a drummer who dances to the moment of the sun's return; *Fest-Polonaise,* expressing belief in the natural goodness of human beings quite the opposite of the *Führer Kult* in Germany and Italy; and the moving *Våren* (The Spring), to Edvard Grieg's music, a homage to the fighting spirit of Norway.

During the occupation, Lander also restaged five Bournonville ballets, showing that even they expressed an ideal far from that of the fascists. The old repertory had lost popularity before the war owing to the successes of modern ballets by Lander and Ralov, but its future was saved by Lander during these dark, cruel years.

After the liberation, most of Lander's political ballets fell from popularity. Their symbolism became dated, while their weaker elements (except for *Qarrtsiluni*) became obvious. Together with Riisager, the composer of the brilliant scores for both *Qarrtsiluni* and *Slaraffenland,* Lander tried to create a new political, ethical ballet. In 1946, *Fugl Fønix* (The Phoenix) was a brilliant symbol of newborn liberty. The opening scene with its image of fire and the rebirth of the phoenix showed a choreographer in development.

The collaboration with Riisager made the aesthetic of symphonic ballet actual for Lander, but he was unsuccessful when he attempted to deal with literary symbolism. The peak of Lander's approach to the symphonic ballet was *Études* (1948).

Harald Lander organized the first two Danish ballet festivals in 1950 and 1951, drawing international notice. Leading ballet critics from the United States, Great Britain, and France felt that the old French-Danish Romantic ballet was still alive in Copenhagen, side by side with Lander's and Ralov's interesting modern ballets in a national vein.

Lander's first wife, Margot Lander (Margot Florentz-Gerhardt), scored a deserved success as first soloist in the first ballet festival but retired the following season. His second wife, Toni Lander (Toni Pihl Petersen), was a central performer in the 1951 festival. Lander's personal affairs shocked Denmark in August 1951, when seventeen members of the Royal Danish Ballet accused him of immoral behavior and cruel artistic leadership. Lander was acquitted, however, and the conflict resulted in a more aware generation of dancers who did not accept the old dictatorship of ballet masters.

In the fall of 1951, Lander accepted an offer from the Paris Opera, and in 1952 successfully staged the third *entrée, Les Fleurs,* in the spectacular *opéra-ballet Les Indes Galantes.* He also staged Vincenzo Galeotti's *The Whims of Cupid and the Ballet Master* (1786) and his own *Études.* Lander directed the ballet school attached to the Paris Opera from 1956 to 1963. After his departure from Denmark, he also worked with several other companies, including Festival Ballet in London, Le Grand Ballet du Marquis de Cueves in Milan, Ballet Theatre in New York, and German and Scandinavian companies. As a choreographer, however, he never regained his earlier inventive and professional qualities.

Historically, Harald Lander opened the Royal Ballet in Copenhagen to new artistic trends and techniques without sacrificing its Danish character. His own choreography was built on and born from his company; that became both Lander's strength and weakness as a creative artist.

BIBLIOGRAPHY

Anderson, Jack, and George Dorris. "A Conversation with Svend Kragh-Jacobsen." *Ballet Review* 5.4 (1975–1976): 1–20.

Fridericia, Allan. *Harald Lander og hans balletter.* Copenhagen, 1951.

Jackson, George. "Falling in Love Again." *Dance View* 9 (June 1992): 31–37.

Lander, Harald. *Thi kendes for ret? Erindringer.* Copenhagen, 1951.

Lander, Harald. *Ballet er en krævende kunst.* Edited by Lise Lander and Erik Aschengreen. Copenhagen, 1972.

Lander, Harald. "Avant-première." *Saisons de la Danse,* no. 82 (March 1976): 18–19.

Schønberg, Bent. *Harald Lander i Paris.* Copenhagen, 1952.

Tomalonis, Alexandra. "Bournonville's Gifts." *Dance View* 9 (June 1992): 42–54.

ALLAN FRIDERICIA

LANDER, MARGOT (Margot Florentz-Gerhardt; born 23 August 1910 in Copenhagen, died 18 July 1961 in Copenhagen), Danish dancer. Lander entered the Royal Theater ballet school in Copenhagen in 1917. She joined the Royal Danish Ballet in 1928, became a principal dancer in 1933 and premiere principal dancer in 1942, and was named *ingenio et arti* in 1938. Though she was brought up in the period when Bournonville was the only training method, she was nonetheless open to the new currents that came to Copenhagen with Michel Fokine and George Balanchine, who were guest choreographers at the Danish ballet in 1925 and 1930/31. When the Royal Danish Ballet flourished in the 1930s and 1940s under the artistic direction of Harald Lander, the repertory was centered around Margot Lander. She held the same position in Denmark as Margot Fonteyn occupied in Great Britain and as Galina Ulanova held in the Soviet Union. [*See* Royal Danish Ballet.]

Margot Lander was an excellent Bournonville dancer: full of life as Teresina in *Napoli,* temperamental as the troll Birthe in *A Folk Tale,* and thoroughly Spanish in *La Ventana* and *Far from Denmark.* But her great successes were in roles from outside the Bournonville canon, in international ballets that Harald Lander brought to Denmark. She was the first Swan Princess—she danced it deeply and with soul—in a one-act version of the Petr Ilich Tchaikovsky classic *Swan Lake* in 1938. She was sparkling as Swanilda in *Coppélia,* a part she danced more than one hundred times between 1934 and her farewell performance in 1950. But she surprised no one more than Lander, who had bound her talent to the *demi-caractère* repertory, when in 1946 she showed herself to be a great dramatic dancer-actor in *Giselle.*

The new repertory that Harald Lander created over his twenty years with the company was built largely to showcase Lander, whom he married in 1932. She was Anna in his *The Seven Deadly Sins* in 1936, danced the lead in his *Våren* (The Spring) in 1946, and she and her partner, Børge Ralov, danced in red and white as the leading couple in *Fest-Polonaise* (1942), one of the ballets that Harald Lander used to issue a moral statement against the German occupation of Denmark. Harald Lander's greatest work, *Études,* was created for Margot Lander in 1948, but it was his later wife, Toni Lander, who brought it out into the world.

Margot Lander's career climaxed in the 1940s, when because of World War II there was no possibility for international recognition, but her position in Denmark was unchallenged. She had a stronger technique than had ever been seen before in Denmark, and as a ballerina with great stage presence she displayed a deep artistic understanding and had the talent to convey an impressive range of feeling to her audiences.

BIBLIOGRAPHY

Anderson, Jack, and George Dorris. "A Conversation with Svend Kragh-Jacobsen." *Ballet Review* 5.4 (1975–1976): 1–20.

Aschengreen, Erik. "Lander, Margot." In *Dansk biografisk leksikon.* 3d ed. Copenhagen, 1979–.

Kragh-Jacobsen, Svend. *Margot Lander.* Copenhagen, 1948.

"The Other Margot." *Dance and Dancers* (November 1983): 13.

Poulsen, Ulla. "Margot Lander's Farewell." *The Dancing Times* (April 1950): 414–416.

ERIK ASCHENGREEN

LANDER, TONI (Toni Pihl Peterson; born 19 June 1931 in Gentofte, Denmark, died 19 May 1985 in Salt Lake City), Danish dancer and teacher. Lander was the strongest technician among female Danish dancers since World War II. She was schooled at the Royal Danish Ballet by Harald Lander (her husband from 1950 to 1964), who made her a soloist in 1950, one year after her breakthrough as the ballerina in his *Études*. She accompanied her husband when he left Copenhagen in 1951 and danced with the Original Ballet Russe in London, the Paris Opera Ballet, London Festival Ballet, American Ballet Theatre, and—again—with the Royal Danish Ballet from 1971 to 1976. There she danced Desdemona in José Limón's *The Moor's Pavane* and worked as a teacher.

She was in charge of the school at Ballet West in Salt Lake City, Utah, where she worked with her second husband, Bruce Marks, whom she married in 1966. From *Études* (which Lander directed in Budapest, Paris, New York, and Toronto) to *The Moor's Pavane,* she developed steadily from a cool and brilliant dancer to a powerful dramatic interpreter. Her versatility included quick, light footwork; dazzling transitions and changes of direction; fullness of movement; high elevation; excellent balance; and strong pantomimic ability. Her most important roles were the title characters in Birgit Cullberg's *Miss Julie* and *The Moon Reindeer;* Caroline in Antony Tudor's *Jardin aux Lilas;* the lead in *La Sylphide;* and Myrtha in *Giselle* (she also danced the last named on television with American Ballet Theatre).

TONI LANDER. With Bruce Marks in Harald Lander's *Études,* staged for American Ballet Theatre in 1961. The three principal parts were danced by Lander, Marks, and Royes Fernandez. Lander displayed both delicacy and daring in executing numerous bravura passages in the ballerina's role. (Photograph © by Fred Fehl; used by permission.)

BIBLIOGRAPHY

Anderson, Jack, and George Dorris. "A Conversation with Svend Kragh-Jacobsen." *Ballet Review* 5.4 (1975–1976): 1–20.

Kragh-Jacobsen, Svend. *Twenty Solodancers of the Royal Danish Ballet.* Copenhagen, 1965.

Lander, Toni. "Fair New World." *Dance Scope* 5 (Spring 1971): 40–42.

Newman, Barbara. *Striking a Balance: Dancers Talk about Dancing.* Rev. ed. New York, 1992.

Vaughan, David. "Toni Lander." *Ballet Review* 14 (Spring 1986): 53–56.

HENRIK LUNDGREN

LANG, PEARL (born 29 May 1922 in Chicago), American dancer, choreographer, and teacher. At about the age of six Lang was taken to see the Irma Duncan Dancers. At the age of twelve she began to study with Francis Allis, from whom she gained a strong basic technique. From 1938 to 1941 she was a student in a special program for the creatively gifted at the University of Chicago. While in Chicago she also worked with Nicholas Tsoukalas and in the Federal Dance Project under the direction of Ruth Page. Her work with Martha Graham began with a June course in New York, and was followed by a season's scholarship. Additional dance training included instruction with Louis Horst, Muriel Stuart, and Nennette Charisse, among others. After a brief time as an understudy with the Graham company, as Pearl Lack she made her debut in 1941 in *Punch and the Judy.* Lang was a soloist with the Graham company from 1942 to 1952; she was the first performer selected to dance Graham roles as the Three Marys in *El Penitente* in 1947 at the Ziegfeld Theater in New York. In 1954 she toured Europe with the company as a guest artist. She performed in musicals, too, including *One Touch of Venus* (1943), *Carousel* (1945), *Finian's Rainbow* (1947), and *Allegro* (1947).

In 1952 Lang formed her own company. Among her many choreographed works, two solos for herself, *Moonsong* and *Windsong* (both 1952), are especially remembered. *Rites* (1953), a group work, and *Shirah* (1960), created from the theme of a mystical Hasidic tale, are considered to among her signature pieces. Writing in the *Village Voice*, Deborah Jowitt noted that Lang made

> the ideas in the play bloom vividly. . . . She is adroit in her use of stiffly exuberant Hasidic dance steps; and the way the men clutch themselves, hunch forward, and twist their torsos from side to side in short jerks eloquently expresses their doggedness. . . . Lang's own rippling, sweetly sinuous style makes a poignant contrast.

Formerly director of modern dance at Jacob's Pillow, appointed by founder Ted Shawn, she has taught, performed, and choreographed at the American Dance Festi-

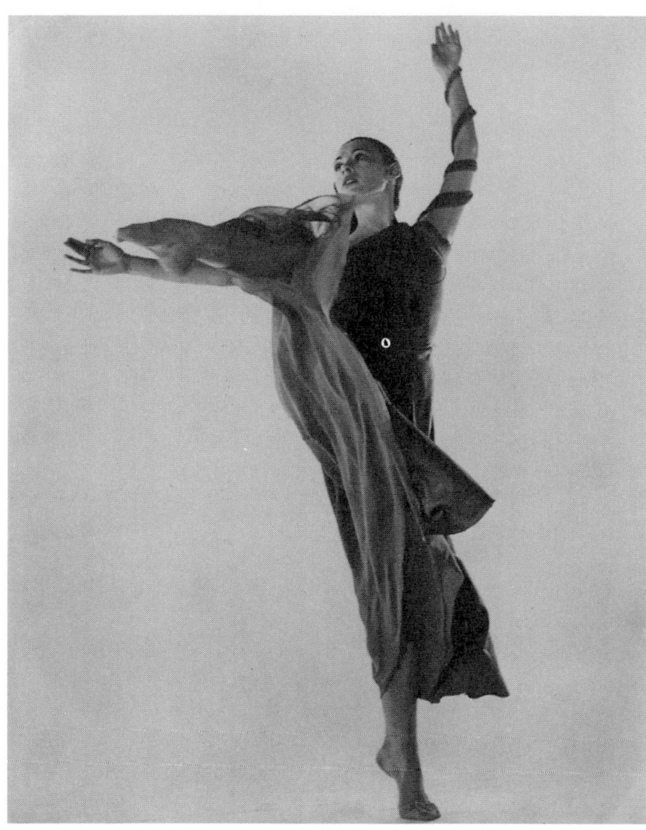

LANG. In her *Song of Deborah,* Lang exhibited the technical artistry that won her admiration as a leading Graham dancer and as a soloist in her own company. (Photograph, c.1949, from the archives at Jacob's Pillow, Becket, Massachusetts.)

val; has been a guest teacher throughout the United States and in Germany, Switzerland, and Sweden; and has taught at the Yale University School of Drama, Juilliard School, and the Neighborhood Playhouse. She was a Guggenheim fellow in 1960 and 1969. In 1975 she performed again with the Graham company in *Adorations*. In 1975 she choreographed *The Possessed,* a work based on Ansky's *The Dybbuk,* a Yiddish play.

Lang is known for her performance lyricism, strength, integrity, and radiance, and for making a positive and continuing contribution to the world of modern dance.

BIBLIOGRAPHY

Cohen-Stratyner, Barbara Naomi. "Lang, Pearl." In *Biographical Dictionary of Dance.* New York, 1982.

Lang, Pearl. "Correspondence: A Refutation." *Dance Observer* (January 1959):6–7.

Tobias, Tobi. "Lang." *Dance Magazine* (September 1974):47–54.

SARAH ALBERTI CHAPMAN

LANNER, KATTI (Katharina Josefa Lanner; born 14 September 1829 in Vienna, died 15 November 1908 in London), Austrian dancer, choreographer, and ballet mistress. Daughter of the famed Viennese waltz composer Joseph Lanner, Katti Lanner began her dance training at the age of fourteen under Pietro Campilli and André Isidore Carey at the Vienna Court Opera school. In 1845, she made her debut at the Kärntnertor Theater and until 1856 performed in Vienna, appearing in ballets with Fanny Elssler, Marie Taglioni, and Paul Taglioni.

In 1856 Lanner left Vienna, and the following year she became choreographer and ballet mistress at the Hamburg Opera House. Her first work was titled *Uriella, Demon of the Night* (1857). She organized a children's ballet, took the Hamburg Ballet on tour to Berlin, and made guest appearances elsewhere. At the same time she organized the Viennese Ballet and Pantomime Troupe as a touring company, to which she increasingly devoted her attention.

At the Teatro São Carlos in Lisbon during the 1870–1871 season, Lanner and her troupe appeared in repertory from the Romantic ballet, including *Giselle.* A critic there considered her "the best ballerina known." In 1871 Lanner made her New York debut as the star of the troupe's *Giselle,* a success repeated in London later the same year.

Lanner and her troupe returned to New York in 1872 for the opening of Niblo's Garden, performing the extravaganza *Leo and Lotus* and the pantomime *Azarel.* According to *The Spirit of the Times,* the performance of *Azarel* "passed under the forming hands of Madame Katti Lanner and comes forth well proportioned, harmonious, exact in time, graceful in its evolutions and beautiful in its groupings. Madame Lanner is a true artist, a very light dancer but in nothing is her talent better shown than in the molding of the corps de ballet." The following year Lanner choreographed a ballet for fifty children as part of Augustin Daly's revival of *A Midsummer Night's Dream.*

On returning to Europe in 1876 Lanner took on the direction of the first National Training School for Dancing, founded by James Mapleson of Her Majesty's Theatre, London. She was thus instrumental in establishing an institutional basis for English ballet. In 1887 she became ballet mistress at the Empire Theatre. During her twenty years there she produced thirty-four ballets, many in collaboration with the composers Leopold Wenzel and Hervé (pen name of Florimond Ronger) and the designer C. Wilhelm (William John Charles Pitcher). Notable productions included *The Sports of England* (1887), *The Paris Exhibition* (1889), *Round the Town* (1892–1895), *Faust* (1895), and *The Dancing Doll* (1904–1905). Although Lanner had to make concessions to music hall audiences, she kept classical ballet alive in England during its so-called twilight years.

BIBLIOGRAPHY

Beaumont, Cyril W. "Our First National School of Dancing." *The Dancing Times* (August 1967):588–589.

Guest, Ivor. *The Empire Ballet.* London, 1962.
Guest, Ivor. *Ballet in Leicester Square.* London, 1992.
Lange, Fritz. *Josef Lanner und Johann Strauss: Ihre Zeit, ihr Leben und ihre Werke.* Vienna, 1904.
Sasportes, José. *História da dança em Portugal.* Lisbon, 1970.
Wenzel, Joachim E. *Geschichte der Hamburger Oper, 1678–1978.* Hamburg, 1978.

BETTY JUNE MYERS

LANY FAMILY, French brother and sister active during the mid-eighteenth century.

Jean-Barthélemy Lany (born 24 March 1718 in Paris, died 20 March 1786 in Paris), dancer and choreographer. The son of a ballet master, Jean Lany, Jean-Barthélemy joined the Paris Opera as solo dancer in 1740. He appeared in the works of composers André-Cardinal Destouches (*Issé,* 1741), Jean-Joseph Mouret (*Les Amours de Ragonde,* 1742), Jean-Phillippe Rameau (*Hippolyte et Aricie,* 1742; *Les Indes Galantes,* 1743), Joseph Bodin de Boismortier (*Don Quichotte chez la Duchesse,* 1743), and André Campra (*Hésione,* 1743). In 1743 he became ballet master to Emperor Frederick the Great in Berlin. His troupe included his two sisters, Louise-Madeleine (who was just starting her brilliant career) and Charlotte (an artist of lesser importance), as well as the great choreographer Jean-Georges Noverre. After creating numerous works in Berlin, Lany returned to the Paris Opera in 1747 as dancer and ballet master.

The comic spirit he displayed in his brilliant variations brought him public attention. He worked on numerous ballets by Rameau, both new and revivals, including *Les Fêtes d'Hébé* (1747); *Les Fêtes de l'Hymen et de l'Amour* (1748); *Platée, Naïs,* and *Zoroastre* (1749); *La Guirlande, ou Les Fleurs Enchantées, Acante et Céphise,* and *Pygmalion* (1751); *Les Fêtes de Polymnie* (1753); *Les Surprises de l'Amour* (1757); and *Les Paladins* (1760). Other works he produced included *Le Carnaval du Parnasse* (1749); *Titon et l'Aurore* and *Les Fêtes de Paphos* (1753) by Jean-Joseph Mondonville; *Les Amours de Tempé* (1752), *Enée et Lavinie* (1758), *Canente* (1761), and *Polixène* (1763) by Antoine Dauvergne, *Ismène* (1747); *Le Prince de Noisy* (1760) by Jean-Féry Rebel and François Francoeur; Campra's *Tancrède* (1750); Mouret's *Les Cinq Sens, Omphale* by Destouches (1751); Boismortier's *Daphnis et Chloé* (1752); and Jean-Jacques Rousseau's *Le Devin du Village,* danced for the first time at Fontainebleau on 18 October 1752.

Lany appeared with the Paris Opera for the last time in 1769. He danced again at Versailles in 1770 for the wedding of the Dauphin, in ballets composed by Michel-Jean Bandieri de Laval, including Rameau's *Castor et Pollux, La Tour Enchantée,* by Rebel and Francoeur; Pierre-Alexandre Monsigny's *Aline, Reine de Golconde;* and Mondonville's *Les Projets de l'Amour.*

Lany worked in Turin in 1773 and in London in 1775, returning as a choreographer to the Paris Opera, where Gaëtan Vestris, his assistant since 1761, had succeeded him as ballet master in 1770. Because of Vestris's intrigues and interference (Vestris had even challenged him to a duel in 1754 during a rehearsal), Lany now turned to teaching. His pupils included Maximilien Gardel and Jean Dauberval.

In his *Lettres sur la danse,* Noverre provides clear and detailed judgments of his contemporaries, including Lany. "Arched" dancers like Lany are strong and sinewy, he remarks, but not all of them are able to turn these characteristics to good advantage, as Lany did. Noverre described Lany as tense and extroverted, vigorous but adroit; precision was the soul of his performance, and the formation of his steps was unique in its clarity, variety, and brilliance. "He is the most skillful dancer I know," Noverre added. This striking precision, allied with a keen musical sensitivity, gave "remarkable spirit, vivacity, and gaiety" to his dancing. Aware that he lacked mobility and dignity, he preferred comic dancing. In addition, he created a new genre, the *pâtres,* a comic pastoral, to be distinguished from the gallant *demi-charactère bergerie,* "in which he obtained the most striking success." As a choreographer, Lany seemed to lack imagination when composing new works, but he was able to exploit his superior qualities as a performer.

Louise-Madeleine Lany (born 1733 in Paris, died 1777 in Paris), dancer. Louise-Madeleine Lany was a pupil of her brother, whose severity as a teacher created in her, according to Noverre, a timidity that restricted her self-expression. It also left her with perfect technique. She made her debut at the Opéra-Comique in 1743, dancing with Noverre in Charles-Simon Favart's parody of *Les Indes Galantes* called *L'Ambigu de la Folie.*

She accompanied her brother to Berlin. Upon her return to France, she triumphed at the Paris Opera on 25 July 1747 in Rameau's *Les Fêtes d'Hébé,* which she danced with her brother. Other vehicles for their talents were *Platée, Naïs, Zoroastre, Le Carnaval du Parnasse,* Collin de Blamont's *Les Caractères de l'Amour* (1749), *Tancrède,* and Brassac's *Léandre et Héro* (1750).

In 1750 she danced in Lyon with Marie Camargo and Noverre, and then in Turin. Back again at the Paris Opera, she shone in such works as *Les Cinq Sens, La Guirlande, Les Surprises de l'Amour, Les Paladins, Daphnis et Chloé, Les Amours de Tempé, Enée et Lavinie, Canente, Titon et l'Aurore, Les Fêtes de Paphos;* and *Le Prince de Noisy.* She retired in 1767.

Noverre admired her proud and elegant bearing and her dancing "written with perfection." If her *entrechat six* was not the best on the stage of the Paris Opera, as has been claimed, it certainly had a special grace. Engravings show her in a hoop skirt that displays her ankles to maximum advantage for this step. A worthy successor of Camargo, she was lively and had excellent elevation, along with the art of concealing effort behind a charming ease. "Every woman would like to dance like her," Noverre remarked. He summed up her glory in the following judgment: "Mademoiselle Lany has outshone all those whose qualities consisted of beauty, precision, and daring performance; she is the leading dancer in the world."

BIBLIOGRAPHY

Campardon, Émile. *L'Académie Royale de Musique au XVIIIe siècle.* 2 vols. Paris, 1884.

Kapp, Julius. *200 Jahre Staatsoper im Bild: Aus Anlass des 100jährigen Jubiläums der Berliner Staatsoper im Auftrage der Generalintendenz der Preussischen Staatstheater.* Berlin, 1942.

MacCormack, Gilson B. "The French Ballet at the Court of Frederick the Great." *The Dancing Times* (December 1932): 252–255.

Noverre, Jean-Georges. *Lettres sur les arts imitateurs en général et sur la danse en particulier.* 2 vols. Paris, 1807. Edited by Fernand Divoire as *Lettres sur la danse et les arts imitateurs* (Paris, 1952).

JEANNINE DORVANE
Translated from French

LAOS. The Lao People's Democratic Republic is a communist state in Southeast Asia, with a 4.1 million population in about 92,000 square miles (240,000 square kilometers). China is to the north, Vietnam to the east, Cambodia to the south, and Thailand and Myanmar (formerly Burma) to the west. The Lao people are believed to be descended from the Thai. In the mid-fourteenth century, the Lan Xang kingdom was founded and Buddhism was introduced from India. By the seventeenth century, the kingdom extended throughout the Indochinese peninsula and war was constant with Siam and the other neighboring empires. Indochina was colonized by France in the nineteenth century and Laos was given semi-autonomy in 1949 within the French Union. After 1950, however, Laos was disrupted by the bitter struggle between the communist-backed Pathet Lao and the Western-backed royalists. In 1975, the Pathet Lao gained control; with communist victories that year in Vietnam and Cambodia as well, many Laotians fled to Thailand, Europe, and the Americas.

Highland Dance Forms. More than half the population of Laos consists of tribal and non-Lao highland groups whose dance traditions bear little similarity to lowland Lao dance forms. Although tribal theater seems unknown among them, groups such as the Hmong (in Chinese, Miao), Mien (Yao), and Kmhmu celebrate the New Year with dance and music, both as participants and as entertainers. These celebrations are also important occasions for courtship. The Hmong are noted for dancing acrobatically while simultaneously playing the mouth organ. Highland people who have settled in the West as refugees continue the same traditions but often modify them to suit a more modern environment; they even include rock bands and the latest Western and Southeast Asian social dance styles, which are mixed with the traditional forms or juxtaposed against them.

Lowland Dance Forms. Of the lowland ethnic Lao dance forms, the most predominant village entertainment is provided by one or more *mohlams* (experts in singing), whose extemporized and/or memorized verses may be enhanced by elaborate hand, arm, and body gestures. When the entertainer is not seated, the musical interludes between verses may be entirely danced; the hands rotate in opposition, with the thumb and forefinger touching, the remaining fingers outstretched, and the performer wheeling slowly around in tiny, circling steps. The customary musical accompaniment is the *khen* (a mouth organ), whose player may join in the slow, rotating movements of the dancer.

Dance movements similar to those of the *mohlam* are found in the popular social dance called *lamvong* ("song circle"), in which individuals or couples form a large ring, circling constantly, their steps varying according to the type of song being sung. A similar dance is found in Cambodia, where it is called *ramvong.* When dance band or rock music is played, some of these traditional movements are combined with modern steps.

Classical Dance. The origins of Lao classical dance can be traced to the kingdom of Lang Xan, founded by Prince Fa Nguan at Luang Prabang. In 1353, Fa Nguan introduced Khmer dance and music from Cambodia to his court; it was adapted to Lao tastes, modified by Thai influences, and was maintained until the government was overthrown by the Pathet Lao in 1975. Because the Lao court was never as large as those of Cambodia or Thailand, performances featured smaller ensembles and offered only excerpts from the *Rāmāyana* rather than the entire dance drama.

Lao Dance Today. In 1959, the Natasin School of Music and Drama was established in Vientiane; both classical and folkloric training in dance are provided, and a professional troupe is retained. Their repertory is more inventive and Thai-influenced than that of the more conservative palace troupe in Luang Prabang, which sought to preserve the traditional Lao classical style of dance.

After the Pathet Lao regime began in 1975, some representatives of both the Luang Prabang Palace ensemble and the Lao Natasin school escaped from Laos and tried to continue performing abroad, particularly in the United States and France. The Luang Prabang dancers have resettled in Nashville, Tennessee, and the Natasin group has founded a community of artists in Des Moines, Iowa. Both groups are contending with the difficulties faced by all large performing companies in the Americas.

BIBLIOGRAPHY

Brandon, James R. *Theatre in Southeast Asia.* Cambridge, Mass., 1967.

Compton, Carol J. *Courting Poetry in Laos: A Textual and Linguistic Analysis.* Northern Illinois University, Center for Southeast Asian Studies. Dekalb, Ill., 1979.
Mahony, Therese Mary. "The White Parasol and the Red Star: The Lao Classical Music Culture in a Climate of Change." Ph.D. diss., University of California, Los Angeles, 1995.
Rattanovong, Houmphanh. "The Lam Lüang: A Popular Entertainment," in *Selected Reports in Ethnomusicology,* vol. 9, edited by A. Catlin. Ethnomusicology Department, University of California, Los Angeles, 1992.
Sahai, Sachchidanand. *The Rāmāyāna in Laos.* Delhi, 1976.

AMY CATLIN

LARIONOV, MIKHAIL (Mikhail Fedorovich Larionov; born 22 May 1881 in Tiraspol, Bessarabia, died 10 May 1964 in Fontenay-aux-Roses, France), Russian-French scenery and costume designer. In 1898 Larionov entered the Moscow Institute of Painting, Sculpture, and Architecture, where in 1900 he met the artists Natalia Goncharova, who was to become his lifelong companion. In 1906, the pair were represented in Serge Diaghilev's Salon d'Automne, the occasion for their first trip to Paris. Originally somewhat impressionist in style, both moved steadily toward brighter, bolder colors and were active in a number of experimental arts groups in Russia, including the Jack of Diamonds, Donkey's Tail, and the Target. Around 1912, Larionov formulated a semi-abstract style that he called rayonism and described as "spatial forms arising from the intersection of reflected rays of various objects, forms chosen by the will of the artist."

In 1914 Larionov joined Diaghilev in Paris; following army duty in World War I (in which he was wounded), he rejoined Diaghilev in Lausanne, Switzerland, and began working closely with Léonide Massine on the preparations for *Soleil de Nuit* and *Contes Russes*. *Le Chout* (1921) and *Le Renard* (1922) followed. The arrival of Larionov and Goncharova marked the definitive end of the first period of the Ballets Russes, in which the Russian vision of Léon Bakst, Alexandre Benois, and Nikolai Roerich had predominated.

Inspired by indigenous Russian art forms such as the *lubok* (hand-colored print), the painted tin tray, the signboard, and the icon, Larionov brought to avant-garde Russian art a vigor and spontaneity that contrasted sharply with the conventions of realism and academic art. As he and Goncharova declared in one of their manifestos of 1913, "Simple, uncorrupted folk are closer to us than the artistic husk that clings to modern art, like flies to honey."

Rejecting the measured elegance of *Mir iskusstva* (World of Art) artists such as Benois and Mstislav Dobujinsky, Larionov and Goncharova transformed Russian theatrical design, injecting it with a new and rude force—something that only the ancient mummers and fair-

LARIONOV. For Bronislava Nijinska's *Le Renard* (1922), set to Stravinsky's score, Larionov designed this costume for the role of Renard (the fox) disguised as a nun. (Photograph from the Dance Collection, New York Public Library for the Performing Arts.)

ground theaters had previously possessed and restoring the element of farce to the professional stage, including the ballet. His designs for *Soleil de Nuit* (1915), *Histoires Naturelles* (1915), *Le Chout* (1921) and *Le Renard* (1922, 1929) rely for their effect on a tension between narrative sequence and unexpected jokes, grotesquerie, and vulgarity. *Le Renard* particularly relied on the "barbarism" of Larionov's designs, and, despite of Igor Stravinsky's discordant music and Bronislava Nijinska's complex choreography, the ballet scored a remarkable success in both 1922 and 1929.

Perhaps Larionov's most radical ballet design was for *Le Chout*. In it, he combined his interest in primitive art with his rayonist ideas to produce sets and costumes that were at once vulgar and sophisticated. From a practical standpoint, however, Larionov's costumes were unwieldly, and Diaghilev was forced to threaten the dancers with penalties to make them dance in clothes that interfered with their movements. Even though Diaghilev spoke of *Le Chout* in laudatory terms, its courageous modernism had a cool reception in both Paris and London. The London *Times* (10 June 1921) even remarked that "one hardly finds in it a touch of that art which has made the Diaghilev ballet famous throughout Europe and beyond it."

Nevertheless, Larionov always thought seriously about the onstage interaction of his costumes and sets, emphasizing the direct links between the costume and the movement. Not even in his fantastic, futurist costumes for the unrealized *Histoires Naturelles* (much influenced by the contemporary work of Fortunato Depero) did Larionov lose sight of the relation of his designs to the moving body, which was one reason that many dancers and choreographers—including Massine and Serge Lifar—consistently admired him.

After 1930, except for occasional activities, Larionov and Goncharova lived unrecognized and impoverished, but in 1954 their names were resurrected at Richard Buckle's "The Diaghilev Exhibition" in Edinburgh and London.

[*For related discussion, see* Scenic Design. *See also the entries on the principal figures mentioned herein.*]

BIBLIOGRAPHY

Baer, Nancy Van Norman. *The Art of Enchantment: Diaghilev's Ballets Russes, 1909–1929.* San Francisco, 1988.

Bowlt, John E., ed. and trans. *Russian Art of the Avant-Garde.* Rev. and enl. ed. New York, 1988. Contains manifestos by Larionov in English translation.

Garafola, Lynn. *Diaghilev's Ballets Russes.* New York, 1989.

Garafola, Lynn. "The Making of Ballet Modernism." *Dance Research Journal* 20 (Winter 1989): 23–32.

George, Waldemar. *Larionov.* Paris, 1966.

Larionov, Mikhail. *Une avant-garde explosive.* Lausanne, 1978.

Nathalie Gontcharova/Michel Larionov. Paris, 1995. Exhibition catalogue, Centre Georges Pompidou.

Parton, Anthony. *Mikhail Larionov and the Russian Avant-Garde.* London, 1993.

ARCHIVE. Victoria and Albert Museum, London.

JOHN E. BOWLT

LARSEN, NEILS BJØRN (born 5 October 1913 in Copenhagen), Danish dancer, choreographer, and director. Larsen attended the Royal Ballet School in Copenhagen from the age of seven and had his entire education there until he graduated in 1921. He was appointed a principal dancer of the Royal Danish Ballet in 1942. He developed his talent for character dancing early in his career and became the company's most outstanding mime, not only in the Bournonville repertory but also in many other ballets. His special gift and originality as an actor-dancer served as inspiration for several generations of Danish dancers. He also enjoyed international fame as a guest artist with such companies as the National Ballet of Canada, the Berlin Opera Ballet, and the London Festival Ballet. With the last, he danced his most famous Bournonville character, the witch Madge, in Peter Schaufuss's celebrated 1979 version of *La Sylphide.*

Larsen's talent for mime and character dancing was stimulated during a stay with Trudi Schoop, whose touring group he joined for several seasons between 1935 and 1939. He created the role of Angakok the Sorcerer in the 1942 Greenlandic ballet *Qaartsiluni,* choreographed by Harald Lander to music by Knudåge Riisager, and he performed as the Charlatan in *Petrouchka* in 1943. He danced his first Doctor Coppélius in 1945 with the Royal Danish Ballet, recreating the role in 1957 and 1959 at the Greek Theater, Los Angeles. When Léonide Massine produced *Symphonie Fantastique,* to music by Hector Berlioz, for the Royal Danish Ballet in 1948, Larsen had the leading role. In Frederick Ashton's *Romeo and Juliet* (1955),

LARSEN. At age seventy-two, Larsen's farewell performance with the Royal Danish Ballet was as Madge the witch in *La Sylphide.* He later appeared as guest performer in this role with several foreign companies. (Photograph from the Dance Collection, New York Public Library for the Performing Arts.)

Larsen alternated in the roles of Tybalt and Mercutio; he was Lord Capulet in the revival for the London Festival Ballet in 1985. In 1963, he danced Mother Simone in Ashton's version of *La Fille Mal Gardée.* Larsen also performed numerous characters in the Bournonville repertory. He gave his farewell performance as Madge in *La Sylphide* in April 1986.

During World War II, Larsen had his own company, Neils Bjørn Balletten. He choreographed thirteen works for the group, mostly lighthearted fare. After the war, he was the first in Denmark to choreograph American musicals, including *Oklahoma!, Annie Get Your Gun,* and *Show Boat.*

Besides dancing with the company, Larsen was director of the Royal Danish Ballet from 1951 to 1956 and again from 1958 to 1965. He brought to Denmark the period's most important choreographers—Ashton, Kenneth MacMillan, George Balanchine, Jerome Robbins, Roland Petit, and Birgit Cullberg. His first choreography for the Royal Danish Ballet was *Den Detroniserede Dyretæmmer* (The Dethroned Animal Tamer) in 1944. He made *Sylvia,* to music by Léo Delibes, in 1948; *Drift* (Urge), to music by George Gershwin in 1951; and *Peter and the Wolf,* to the score by Sergei Prokofiev in 1960. In addition, from 1956 to 1980, Larsen was responsible for the Pantomime Theater in Copenhagen's Tivoli Gardens, for which he choreographed fifteen ballets.

BIBLIOGRAPHY

Aschengreen, Erik. "The Royal Danish Ballet Season of 1954–1955." *Dance Chronicle* 18.3 (1995):419–426.

Cunningham, Kitty. "Niels Bjørn Larsen: A Life in Mime." *Ballet Review* 10 (Summer 1982):88–94.

Mørk, Ebbe. *Bag mange masker.* Copenhagen, 1974.

Newman, Barbara. *Striking a Balance: Dancers Talk about Dancing.* Rev. ed. New York, 1992.

EBBE MØRK

LASSEN, ELNA (born 27 August 1901 in Lyngby, Denmark, died 19 September 1930 in Copenhagen), Danish dancer. Among female Danish dancers in the first half of the twentieth century, Lassen was undoubtedly the strongest technician. However, she had only a short time to prove her extraordinary gifts and skill. She was a pupil at the Royal Theater from 1909 to 1918. Her educator was the dancer Valborg Borchsenius, who taught her the true Bournonville style—later Lassen would excel in parts like Celeste in *Toreadoren* and Teresina in *Napoli* by the Danish choreographer. She was a dancer at the Royal Theater from 1918 to 1921 but, finding the challenges too small, left for the United States (1921–1924), where she studied with Michel Fokine.

Upon her return to Denmark, Lassen had a breakthrough as Swanilda in *Coppélia,* and when Fokine directed three ballets in Copenhagen in 1925 he chose her for the Ballerina in *Petrouchka* and as one of the soloists in *Les Sylphides.* She was the first Danish Firebird in 1928, showing an impeccable technique. When Max Reinhardt came to Denmark in 1930, he immediately recognized her possibilities: he had a waltz created especially for her during the production of *Die Fledermaus.* She was invited to Berlin to show this dance at Reinhardt's twenty-fifth anniversary, in front of an international public, on 30 May 1930. Three months later she committed suicide. Reinhardt commemorated her in a Danish newspaper: "She was a unique artist by her combination of Bournonville's school and Fokine's lines. She had a sparkling temperament and a soft, graceful charm. . . . In my opinion she was the greatest next to [Anna] Pavlova."

BIBLIOGRAPHY

Anderson, Jack, and George Dorris. "A Conversation with Svend Kragh-Jacobsen." *Ballet Review* 5.4 (1975–1976): 1–20.

Kragh-Jacobsen, Svend. *Ballettens blomstring ude og hjemme.* Copenhagen, 1945.

HENRIK LUNDGREN

LATVIA. One of the three Baltic states, with Estonia to the north, Lithuania to the south, and the Baltic Sea to the west, Latvia was invaded by Crusaders in the thirteenth century and for seven centuries thereafter was under German, Polish, Swedish, and Russian domination. Latvia became an independent state only after World War I, passing back and forth between Germany and Russia from 1914 to 1918, until it achieved self-rule in the Baltic Wars of Liberation. It remained an independent republic until the Soviet-German agreement of 1939 ceded it to the USSR, into which it was officially adopted in 1940. During World War II it was occupied by Germany but retaken by the USSR in 1945. After an abortive coup the Soviet Union, just prior to its dissolution in 1991, recognized Latvia's independence but did not withdraw troops until 1994. Today's population is Latvian, Russian, Ukrainian, and Belarusian.

Folk Dance. The buffoons, mimes, jesters, and clowns that were common in many parts of Europe were absent from early Latvia. Latvian folk dance reflected both the quiet tenor of village life and the local mythology. The principal expressive outlet was in the numerous folk songs, called *dainas,* after the Latvian national legend that voiced a protest against oppression. The tempo and structure of the *dainas* made them suitable for dancing, and these dances formed the basis for the resurgence of folk dance interest in the 1930s, when the collection of dance folklore and the establishment of folk dance circles began. This work enabled reproduction of the best-known dances, collected in fragments from various districts of Latvia. The popularity of folk dance grew considerably after World War II. The government of Soviet Latvia included folk dance in the programs of traditional song festivals. After 1948 the song and dance festivals were held every five years, with as many as thirty thousand participants. These festivals were followed by school children's song and dance festivals and Baltic students' festivals. Folk dance also became part of theatrical performance, and although in some forms it is highly artistic it has never abandoned its folk roots. The nationwide work of collecting and studying dance folklore also led to an assimilation of classical ballet forms into folk dance. Latvian choreographers eliminated accidental and foreign elements from dance and reinforced its most characteristic features.

Traditional dances are typically couple dances and group dances. Many are native to specific regions, but the following may be considered common to all Latvia. In the *gatbec-deya,* couples stroll between a line of boys and a line of girls. Latvian folk decorative motifs, such as the sun, the fir tree, and the star, are visible in the figures. The *sudmalinyas,* danced to a song about the work of millers, dramatizes the work of grinding grain. The *achups* is a dance for four to eight couples that is based on square and cross forms. In the *adjinish,* young men follow girls and sing, "Dance, dance, girl. If you dance beautifully and lightly, you will be my bride." The *belka,* performed by girls, imitates the actions of squirrels; it is light and free in mood.

Contemporary folk dances have been constructed to preserve the traits of the Baltic people. The dancers, wearing national costume, perform in a reserved manner. The complex floor patterns of the dances make them especially suited to performances by large groups in stadiums and on large, open stages.

Theatrical Dance. The first full-length ballet in Latvia was performed at the National Opera House on 1 December 1921. It was *La Fille Mal Gardée,* staged by Nicholas Sergeyev from the Maryinsky Theater in Russia. The foundation of Latvian ballet was laid by Aleksandra Fedorova, a former soloist of the Maryinsky. During her work in the capital, Riga, as a ballerina and choreographer (1925–1932) as well as a coach (1925–1937), she produced eighteen ballets from the Russian classical repertory. She was followed by other ballet masters: Anatole Vilzak (1932–1933), Mečislav Pianovsky (1933–1934), Michel Fokine (1929), Leonid Zhukov (1931), and Vasily Tikhomirov (1933).

From 1934 to 1944 Latvian ballet developed through the efforts of Osvald Lemanis, the first talented choreographer wholly educated in Latvia. His *The Triumph of Love* (1935) to music by M. Janis Medinj was the first classical ballet with a Latvian theme and character; it incorporated typically Latvian dances. Lemanis also created other ballets: *Ilga* (1937) to music by Janis Vitolinjs, *Autumn,* and *The Nightingale and a Rose* (1939) by Janis Kalninjs, many dances and ballet miniatures, and his own interpretations of works from the classical repertory.

Ballet of the post–World War II period was closely associated with the work of Elena Tangiyeva-Birzniece. She began as a ballerina and teacher and in 1956 became chief choreographer. Her productions followed the principles of academic ballet. She created the first Latvian Soviet ballet, *Laima* (1947) to music by Anatole Lepin, as well as *Rigonda* (1959) to music by Romuald Grinblat, *The Precious Stones* (1961) to music by Jarol Vitols, and other nationalistic ballets. Between 1950 and 1961 Evgeny Changa, the first Latvian choreographer with an academic ballet education and a pupil of Rostislav Zakharov, worked side by side with Tangiyeva-Birzniece. His finest productions were the national ballet *Freedom Sanctuary* to music by Adolf Skulte (1951 and 1955), *Staburadze* by Alfreds Kalninjs (1957), and innovative interpretations of *Romeo and Juliet* in 1953 and *Spartacus* in 1960.

These choreographers initiated two different trends in ballet: Tangiyeva-Birzniece, an advocate of academic dance, sought to achieve an absolute harmony of movements and to fuse music and dance; Changa favored dramatic ballet. The ballets of Tangiyeva-Birzniece appealed to the audience through their harmonious and musically precise dance scenes. Changa impressed the audience with his dramatic passion and fantasy.

In today's Latvian ballet, similar examples can be found in the art of choreographers Irene Strode and Alexander Lembergs of the Academic Opera and Ballet Theater of Latvia. Strode gravitated to the trend upheld by her teacher Tangiyeva-Birzniece and achieved her best results in ballets such as *The Garland of Flowers* (1965) to music by Peteris Barison and *The Rose of Turaids* (1966) by Janis Kepitis. Lembergs, who choreographed dramatic ballets, served as chief choreographer longer than any of his predecessors. In addition to producing revivals of the classic ballets, he created the first original Latvian ballets for children: *Spiriditis* (1965) and *The Magic Bird of Lolita* (1979), both to music by Arvid Jilinski, and in collaboration with Tamara Vityn *The Gold of the Incas* (1969) to music by Oleg Barskov. His most successful productions included his own interpretations of psychological themes, such as *Scaramouche* and *Carmen,* both in 1971; *Notre-Dame de Paris* in 1970; and *Romeo and Juliet* in 1982.

The integrity of style in Latvian ballet owes much to the activities of the ballet school founded in Riga in 1932. Today all members of the company are graduates of this school.

The ballet stars in the 1930s were Tangiyeva-Birzniece, Edith Pfeiffer, Mirdza Grike, Osvald Lemanis, and Karij Plucos. They danced in the first foreign tours of the Latvian ballet. Anna Priede adorned the Latvian stage from

1937 to 1962, dancing a wide range of roles: Odette and Odile, Giselle, Laurencia, Juliet, Kitri, and Aurora. Velta Vilcinja (born 1938) was a dramatic ballerina; Juliet, Zarema, the Baroness in *Freedom Sanctuary,* and the Dying Swan were her major roles. Zita Errs (born 1950) was known for her tragic Esmeralda, her childlike Juliet, and her radiant Aurora. Inessa Dumpe (born 1959) danced the roles of the Swan, Kitri, Juliet, and Eve in *The Creation of the World.* Among the *premiers danseurs,* Plucis and Lemanis were followed by Alexander Lembergs, the first virtuoso dancer of the new, athletic stamp. Harald Rittenberg (born 1932) was an admired Romeo for a whole generation of spectators. Gennady Gorbanev (born 1950) was a *premier danseur* of the 1970s and 1980s.

There have been two other Latvian ballet companies. From the early 1920s until 1950 there was one at the Liepaja Opera House. The first ballet was staged there by Anna Stedelaube in 1926. From 1934 onward the company was directed by Albert Kozlovsky.

The other company, directed by Janita Janina Pankrat, is that of the Riga Operetta Theater. Rather than dance secondary scenes in operas, the company often plays the most important part of the cast. Pankrat's choreographic fantasy thrives in original dance *divertissements.* She also pioneered the genre of modern variety dance. Today many professional variety dance companies perform, one of which is directed by Pankrat.

Among the first professional folk-based choreographers were Tangiyeva-Birzniece, Strode, and other masters of ballet. Folk dance companies enriched their repertories with some difficult, innovative, and meaningful works, and the number of companies steadily grew, as did their artistic skill and knowledge. In the 1960s, when the total number of amateur and professional dancers had reached about ten thousand (Latvia's population was then about two million), folk dance companies were founded nationwide. Their members were amateurs, but they had long-standing traditions and a distinctive style of dance; they also had their own choreographers, orchestras, and vocal groups, their own sets of costumes, regular schedules of concerts, and a vast repertory. The university's Dancis company, the Liesma company of the Central Printers' Club, the Kalve company of the Agricultural Academy, the Rotalja company of the cultural center of the VEF radio factory—over fifty folk dance companies in all—became an appreciable factor in Latvian culture, and their directors, such as Milda Lasmane, called "Mother of Latvian Dance," Harijs-Suna, Alfred Spura, and Aja Baumann, won renown. New dances appeared in folk choreography in addition to the three main genres; ritual dances, family dances, and dances associated with seasons of the year were joined by dances of city life, dances on themes of work, space exploration, and modern professions, and children's dances.

In April 1968 a professional Latvian folk dance company, Daile, was formed under the direction of Uldis Jagata. The most distinctive items in its repertory are traditional folk dances interpreted by modern choreographers, dances incorporating other elements of folklore, and modern rhythmic dances.

Many folk dance companies have their own studios that hold classes for children. The Daile dance company opened its own dance school, and university-level institutions also have folk dance studios. In 1978 the Latvian Conservatory of Music opened a department to train folk dance experts, including professional choreographers.

BIBLIOGRAPHY

"The Baltic Republics." *Ballett International* 13 (June–July 1990): 54–56.

Behrman, Renate. "The Latvian Ballet." *The Dancing Times* (October 1937): 11–13.

Brants, Georgs. *The Latvian Ballet.* Riga, 1937.

Karasyova, Nina. "Choreographer from Latvia: Elena Tangieva-Birzniek." *Ballet Today* (March 1963): 26.

Keiss, Vera. "The Latvian Ballet." *Ballet Today* (October 1963): 20–22.

Krolls, Otto. *Karalis Gaida.* Cikaga, 1962.

Liepa, Maris. *Vchera i segodnia v balete.* 2d ed. Moscow, 1986.

Roslavleva, Natalia. "Latvian Ballet Has Fine Past and a Promising Future." *Dance News* (October 1966): 9.

Swift, Mary Grace. *The Art of the Dance in the U.S.S.R.* Notre Dame, 1968.

Stals, Georgs. "The Latvian Ballet." *The Dancing Times* (June 1934): 246–249.

Stals, Georgs. "The First Latvian Original Ballet." *The Dancing Times* (August 1935): 486–487.

Stals, Georgs. "New Ballet in Riga." *The Dancing Times* (February 1937): 620–621.

Stals, Georgs. *Latviesu balets.* Riga, 1972.

Stein, Bonnie Sue. "Dance Struggles in the Baltics." *Dance Magazine* (September 1990): 20.

Tihonovs, Jakovs. *Rigas balets.* Riga, 1979.

Voskresenska, Jelena. *Latviesu padomju balets.* Riga, 1978. Includes an English summary.

ERIK U. V. TIVUM
Translated from Latvian

LAUCHERY, ÉTIENNE (also Stephan Lauchery; born September 1732 in Lyon, died 5 January 1820 in Berlin), French dancer, choreographer, and ballet director. Nothing is known of Étienne Lauchery's early dance training; there is no basis for Anton Pichler's assumption that Lauchery studied at the Opera in Paris and was trained by Jean-Georges Noverre. In 1746 he was engaged as a dancer in Mannheim, where his father, Laurentius, was ballet master, and he had probably been trained by his father. In 1756 he became principal dance master there at an annual salary of four hundred guilders. In 1774 he was promoted to first ballet master in Mannheim; but from 1764 to 1772 he had served simultaneously as ballet master in Kassel. In 1778 Lauchery went with the court to Munich; nevertheless ballet in Mannheim and Kassel continued, and it competed successfully with the ballet in Stuttgart.

Lauchery promoted every form of ballet known in his day but was particularly effective as a dramatic choreographer and practitioner of the *ballet d'action.* He divided his productions into twelve to fifteen scenes that usually required two or three different stage sets. The story lines were carried by the actors; the corps de ballet had a figurative role, serving to establish atmosphere or historical setting. Lauchery classified his works as tragic, tragic-pantomime, heroic, heroic-tragic-pantomime, pastoral-heroic, historical, comic, and allegorical. All his complete works probably functioned as interludes between the acts of operas, without any connection to the subject of the opera. Lauchery was certainly familiar with Noverre's letters on the ballet, but he did not follow Noverre's call for thematic unity of opera and ballet.

From 1780 to 1786 Lauchery was once again in Kassel. It is not known for certain where he was engaged in 1787; some speculate he was in Lyon. From 1788 to 1813 he was ballet master in Berlin, where his work enjoyed much recognition, and he was often awarded special prizes by the king. Little is known about Lauchery's choreographic works in Berlin because of war damage to the State Opera Archives and the German National Library there. He produced four to six ballets a year as entr'actes for operas and dramas; he also collaborated as choreographer in the staging of ballet entr'actes for operas and dramas, including in 1803 *Iphigénie en Tauride* (the 1778 opera by Christoph Willibald Gluck).

Lauchery's son Albert was a solo dancer and later director of the ballet school in Berlin.

BIBLIOGRAPHY

Derra de Moroda, Friderica. "Die Ballettmeister, vor, zur Zeit und nach J. G. Noverre." *Das Tanzarchiv* 24 (August 1976): 281–289.

Kloiber, Rudolf. "Die dramatischen Ballette von Christian Cannabich." Ph.D. diss., University of Munich, 1928.

Pichler, Anton. *Chronik des grossherzoglichen Hof- und National-Theaters in Mannheim.* Mannheim, 1879.

Stahl, Ernst L. *Die klassische Zeit des Mannheimer Theaters,* vol. 1, *Das europäische Mannheim.* Mannheim, 1940.

Walter, Friedrich. *Geschichte des Theaters und der Musik am kurpfälzischen Hofe.* Leipzig, 1898.

KURT PETERMANN

LAURENCIA. Ballet in three acts. Choreography: Vakhtang Chabukiani. Music: Aleksandr Krein. Libretto: Evgeny Mandelberg. Scenery: Simon Virsaladze. First performance: 22 March 1939, Maryinsky Theater, Saint Petersburg. Principals: Natalia Dudinskaya (Laurencia), Vakhtang Chabukiani (Frondoso), Boris Shavrov (Gomez).

Laurencia played a significant part in the history of Soviet choreography as a ballet on a heroic theme. It was in the repertory for more than thirty-five years. Using folklore and virtuosic classical dance, Chabukiani staged a picturesque and innovative ballet based largely on corps de ballet dances. The work was produced at a time of intense public interest in Spain, where the Civil War was in progress, and the authors borrowed the principal elements of the plot from Lope de Vega's *Fuente Ovejuna.*

LAURENCIA. A scene from act 1 of a 1956 Bolshoi Ballet production, with Maya Plisetskaya, seated on the burro, as Laurencia. (Photograph from the Bolshoi Theater Museum, Moscow.)

The scene is the village of Fuente Ovejuna of Castille in fifteenth-century Spain. The village alderman's daughter falls in love with the peasant Frondoso. However, the local knight commander, a cruel and willful man, opposes their happy union. Frondoso is jailed. Laurencia stirs the peasants to rebellion. They defeat the tyrant and celebrate victory. Chabukiani lent Spanish color to numerous scenes of the ballet, and made the characters lifelike rather than archetypal. The peasants, the alderman Esteban, and Laurencia's and Frondoso's friends Mengo, Pascuala, and Jasinta oppose the knight commander Gomez, his soldiers, and his servants.

The star of the original production was Natalia Dudinskaya as Laurencia; Chabukiani as Frondoso charmed the audience with his soaring dance. The role of Laurencia was danced by Maya Plisetskaya at the Bolshoi Theater in Moscow in 1956 and by Nina Timofeyeva at the Kremlin Palace of Congresses in Moscow in 1963. The ballet was performed in many Russian cities and in other eastern European countries.

BIBLIOGRAPHY

Beaumont, Cyril W. *Supplement to Complete Book of Ballets.* London, 1942.

Krasovskaya, Vera. *Vakhtang Chabukiani.* 2d ed. Leningrad, 1960.

Krasovskaya, Vera, ed. *Sovetskii baletnyi teatr, 1917–1967.* Moscow, 1976.

Lawson, Joan. "Another New Soviet Ballet: *Laurencia.*" *Dancing Times* (October 1940): 11–13.

Lawson, Joan. "A Short History of the Soviet Ballet, 1917–1943." *Dance Index* 2 (June–July 1943): 77–96.

Macaulay, Alastair. "Back to the Sixties: Laurentia and, Above All, Fille." *Dancing Times* (March 1990): 568–573.

Roslavleva, Natalia. *Era of the Russian Ballet* (1966). New York, 1979.

Swift, Mary Grace. *The Art of the Dance in the U.S.S.R.* Notre Dame, 1968.

ELFRIDA A. KOROLEVA
Translated from Russian

LAUTERER, ARCH (born 1904, died 1957 in Oakland, California), scenery and lighting designer. Lauterer taught at Western Reserve University, Cleveland College, the Traphagan School, Mills College, and most significantly, Bennington College in Vermont (1933–1943), where his collaboration with major choreographers in the field of modern dance created a new "world for dance to live in" (Lloyd, 7 August 1943).

Based on the idea that scenic aspects of modern dance are more closely related to its origin in the studio than to its roots in traditional theater, Lauterer transformed Bennington's inadequate Vermont State Armory stage into a spacious multilevel arena with side "fins" through which large groups of dancers could enter and exit. When he redesigned the Bennington College Theater in 1940 he was able to introduce more sophisticated devices, some new to the theater. His classes in stagecraft, design, and production encompassed the whole process of creating dance as communication, and his teaching has been hailed as a major influence by many students who later achieved distinction as teachers, choreographers, and performers.

Stemming from the ideas of Adolphe-François Appia, Lauterer's theories dealt with space and light as fluid, living choreographic elements with which he created an environment for dance that matched its form and function in every respect. His designs, usually unadorned by painted decor, functioned as a realm of fantasy in which dancers moved amid sculptural forms, platforms, ramps, and the like, creating what he termed "resistance—the dynamic expression of forms, [which] sharpens the meaning, both kinesthetically and emotionally, of the dance movement" (Lloyd, 7 August 1943). These functional settings replaced the ubiquitous velvet-curtained proscenium stage, and the stark look of his architectural designs provided a model to which modern dance has adhered for the most part.

Lauterer's first collaboration with Martha Graham at Bennington was her *Panorama* (1935), followed by *American Document, El Penitente, Letter to the World, Punch and the Judy,* and *Deaths and Entrances.* For Doris Humphrey, he designed *Passacaglia in C Minor* (1938) and *Decade;* for Hanya Holm, *Trend* (1937), *Dances of Work and Play,* and *Dance Sonata.* He worked, as well, with Eleanor King, Louise Kloepper, Marian Van Tuyl, and Charles Weidman. His collaboration with Holm continued at Perry-Mansfield Camp in Steamboat Springs, Colorado, with *The Golden Fleece* and *Tragic Exodus.* There he also designed *Four Walls* (1944) with choreographer Merce Cunningham.

[*See also* American Document; Deaths and Entrances; Letter to the World; Trend; *and* Scenic Design.]

BIBLIOGRAPHY

"Collaboration Is Multiplication." *Christian Science Monitor,* 7 August 1943. Interview with Margaret Lloyd.

Kriegsman, Sali Ann. *Modern Dance in America: The Bennington Years.* Boston, 1981.

Lauterer, Arch. "Notes on Production of Dance-Drama," "Lecture-Demonstration," "Stage Design in Our Time," and "The Image of Man's Spirit." *Impulse* (1959). Included in a special issue devoted to Lauterer.

MALCOLM MCCORMICK

LAVAL, ANTOINE BANDIERI DE (born 1698 in Paris, died 20 October 1767 in Paris), French dancer, teacher, choreographer, and director of the Académie Royale de Danse. His father, also named Antoine Bandieri de Laval, was a native of Lucca in Italy, and one of Louis XIV's vaulting and riding masters. His mother was Catherine Dufort, sister of the famous ballerina Elisabeth Dufort, and his uncle was none other than Claude Ballon, dancing master to Louis XV—and one of the most celebrated dancers of his time. With such an auspicious background, the young Laval was enabled to bring his own talent to the fore. He made an early and brillant debut at the Paris Opera at the age of eighteen. Rapidly rising to the rank of *premier danseur,* he became the leading ballerinas' favorite partner. When Marie Sallé added to her repertory Françoise Prévost's famous *Les Caractères de la Danse,* she rechoreographed the piece as a duet for herself and Laval. "They danced *Les Caractères* at the end of *Alceste,* in their street clothes and without masks, to the great delight of a packed audience," wrote the *Mercure* on 17 February 1729. From 1726 to 1729 Laval made several ballets at the Jesuit Collège Louis-le-Grand, in collaboration with the dancer Malter.

While still in his early thirties, Laval began to fill the various positions at court caused by the progressive retirement of his uncle, Claude Ballon. In 1731 his first appointment was Dancing Master to the Children of France (Mâitre-à-danser des Enfants de France). In 1739, he received the position of court ballets choreographer, and at the death of his uncle in 1744, replaced him as head of the Académie Royale de Danse.

Laval had married Anne-Benigne Nicolet, a jeweler's daughter, on 17 February 1722. Claude Ballon and his two sons had been witnesses. Five sons and six daughters were born to the couple. The eldest son joined the navy and died a royal councilor, a superintendant, and a comptroller in the Gaudaloupe Islands. The second son, Michel-Jean, followed in his father's footsteps, inheriting all his court positions.

When Laval died in Paris, on 20 October 1767, his obituary recalled the magnificent ballets that he had choreographed for the marriage of the dauphin (France's crown prince) and those he had devised for the Fontainebleau fêtes of 1753 and 1754:

> One still remembers the gracious and regal style in which they were composed . . . and to these talents, Antoine de Laval added the qualities of rare integrity and openness, which made him respected in his own family and esteemed by all those who knew him. (*Le nécrologe des hommes,* 1769)

[*See also* Académie Royale de Danse *and* Ballet de Collège.]

BIBLIOGRAPHY

Despréaux,Jean-Étienne. *Mes passe-temps: Chansons suivies de l'art de la danse.* Vol. 2. Paris, 1806.

Mercure de France (17, 28, 29 February 1929).

Poinsinet de Sivry, J., et al. *Le nécrologe des hommes célèbres de France, par une société de gens de lettres.* Paris, 1767–.

Ranum, Patricia. "Les 'Caractères' des danses françaises." *Recherches sur la musique française classique* 23 (1985): 45–70.

Rice, Paul F. *The Performing Arts at Fontainebleau from Louis XIV to Louis XVI.* Ann Arbor, 1989.

ARCHIVES: Archives Nationales, Paris: Serie 01 75. Bibliothèque Nationale, Paris: Fichier Laborde, VI, no. 2079.

RÉGINE ASTIER

LAVROVSKY, LEONID (Leonid Mikhailovich Lavrovskii; born 5 [18] June 1905 in Saint Petersburg, died 26 November 1967 in Paris), Russian dancer, choreographer, and teacher. Upon graduation from the Petrograd Ballet School in 1922, where he studied under Vladimir Ponomarev, Lavrovsky joined the Petrograd State Academic Theater for Opera and Ballet as a solo dancer. Until 1935 he danced leading roles in both classical and modern ballets, among which were Jean de Brienne in Marius Petipa's *Raymonda,* Prince Siegfried in Petipa and Lev Ivanov's *Swan Lake,* the male principal in Michel Fokine's *Chopiniana* and Amoun in his *Une Nuit d'Égypte,* an Actor in Vasily Vainonen's *The Flames of Paris,* and a Young Coolie in the Leningrad version of *The Red Poppy* choreographed by Fedor Lopukhov, Ponomarev, and Leonid Leontiev. Lavrovsky's style was marked by a dignified virility, expressive plastique, and a musical sensibility that soon became a fundamental principle in his choreography.

Throughout his dancing career, Lavrovsky tried his hand at choreography. In 1927 he produced *Valse Triste,* a concert piece set to the music of Jean Sibelius. The following year he choreographed the ballet *The Seasons,* set to the score by Tchaikovsky, and used music by Robert Schumann for *Études Symphoniques* at the Leningrad Choreographic Institute. In 1934 he produced the ballet *Fadetta,* based on George Sand's novel *La Petite Fadette* and set to the music of Léo Delibes's *Sylvia. Fadetta* was created amid an ongoing controversy in ballet circles that focused on the function of dancing; on whether narrative content could be the backbone of any performance, ballet included; on the emotional impact of a ballet performance as a whole; and on ballet imagery. *Fadetta* not only met all criteria but also became a landmark in the development of Soviet choreography.

In 1935 Lavrovsky ended his career as a dancer to turn his full attention to choreography. From 1935 to 1938 he was director of the ballet company of Leningrad's Maly Opera Theater, whence he moved to the Kirov Opera and Ballet Theater in Leningrad, serving as artistic director of ballet until 1942. After fulfilling a one-year directorship with the Spendiarov Opera and Ballet Theater in Erevan, Armenia, in 1944 Lavrovsky joined the Bolshoi Ballet in Moscow, serving as chief choreographer, with a hiatus between 1956 and 1960, until 1964. As a choreographer he sought to derive deeper meaning from and broaden the range of themes used for ballet and to devise new forms of dance vocabulary. He nevertheless toed the Party line in his early work by asserting the supremacy of realism in Soviet ballet, which owes its international recognition to him.

After *Fadetta,* Lavrovsky produced *Katerina,* set to the music of Anton Rubinstein and Adolphe Adam. The ballet was first staged by the Leningrad Choreographic Institute in 1935 and performed a year later by the parent Kirov Ballet. In *Katerina* Lavrovsky succeeded in expressing the narrative through movement and mime. Three years later he interpreted Aleksandr Pushkin's romantic poem *The Prisoner of the Caucasus,* choreographed to music by Boris Asafiev. First presented at the Maly Opera Theater, the ballet was an instant success. The critic Igor Solmertinsky summed up its impact: "In this production the choreographer promotes and carries farther an artistic principle justly viewed as the treasured asset of Soviet choreography—the ability to reveal human personality and human character using the expressive idiom of dance."

Lavrovsky's productions of the 1930s and 1940s were noted for their use of serious literature. His interpretation of Shakespeare's *Romeo and Juliet,* which had its premiere in 1940 at the Kirov, was the pioneering effort by a Soviet choreographer to adapt Shakespeare to ballet. The fact that it was the first staged interpretation of Sergei Prokofiev's score in the Soviet Union lent added significance. Its sophisticated rhythms, lyricism, dramatic suspense, and philosophical message required unconventional structure and choreography. Lavrovsky's solution was to weld together various forms of dance, imaginatively arrange the action scenes, alternate tense crowd scenes with romantic pas de deux, and drive the narrative with expressive mime. He probed and realistically captured the protagonists' emotions and agonies. The aesthetic, dramatic, and choreographic impact of that production, regarded in the annals of Soviet ballet as the most accomplished interpretation of Shakespeare, was tremendous; it heralded a new era in Soviet ballet. In 1946 it was recreated at the Bolshoi Theater; it was also added to the repertory of other Soviet ballet companies and was staged by companies outside the Soviet Union. *Romeo and Juliet* gave several generations of dancers a creative outlet. In 1955 Lavrovsky collaborated with the filmmaker L. Arnshtam to produce a screen version of the ballet that featured the Bolshoi Ballet stars Galina Ulanova as Juliet, Yuri Zhdanov as Romeo, Sergei Koren as Mercutio, and Aleksei Yermolayev as Tybalt. In 1973 the British Broadcasting Corporation filmed the ballet for television.

Another milestone in Lavrovsky's career was his turn toward creating ballets to scores originally composed for concert performance. In 1960 he produced *Paganini,* a one-act ballet to the music by Sergei Rachmaninov. The critic Boris Anokhin wrote: "The expressiveness of Rachmaninov's music prompted the ballet master to arrive at an unusual choreographic solution. *Paganini* is the embodiment of demonic creative force and drive, is overwhelmed by storms of delight and despair, of exultation and fury. The role of Paganini is made up of extremely difficult movements calling for breakneck speed, which accounts for the highly dynamic quality of the dance." In *Paganini* there were no sets, mime, or realism; everything was stylized. Paganini did not carry an actual violin; the impression of virtuosic playing was created by his fluttering fingers and impulsive hand movements. After *Paganini* Lavrovsky staged Prokofiev's *Classical Symphony* in 1966 for the Moscow School of Choreography. These two works revealed Lavrovsky's quest for a new style and method of composition. The multilayered ensemble dances he created in these ballets put him on a par with the foremost Soviet choreographers.

At the peak of his career, in the 1960s, Lavrovsky devoted himself to treading the uncharted waters of symbolism, while retaining his basic artistic principles. Contemporary themes dominated his thinking, ambitions, and endeavors, but did not achieve fruition. He was well aware of the importance of creating a modern ballet that would depict contemporary protagonists, but he could not find a suitable scenario. One such, *Rus, Wave Thy Wings,* dedicated to the poet Sergei Esenin, was never staged. In his memoirs Lavrovsky set out to explore the pitfalls confronting ballet when it tries to absorb new material furnished by life. In his view the problems arose from the difficulty in identifying and generalizing images of life coupled with the imperfection of expressive means. Pursuing a perfect synthesis Lavrovsky attempted a string of scenarios, some fairly complete, which were never realized.

Lavrovsky was well grounded in the masterpieces of classical ballet. His version of *Giselle* was first performed by the Bolshoi Ballet in 1944 and remains in its repertory; it was also staged by theater companies in Budapest, Helsinki, and Belgrade in 1958. In 1945 Lavrovsky mounted his own version of *Raymonda,* to Reinhold Glière's score, at the Bolshoi Theater. Among his original ballets, all presented at the Bolshoi Theater, were *The Red Poppy* (1949) to Glière, *The Tale of the Stone Flower* (1954; Helsinki, 1961) to Prokofiev, and *Night City* (1961) to Béla Bartók, and for the Moscow School of Choreography *Pages from a Life* (1967) to music by Andrei Balanchivadze. Lavrovsky either devised or was co-author of the libretti of all his ballets. He pioneered many trends in Soviet choreography. During his tenure, 1959–1964, as ballet master of the Moscow Ice Revue, he created shows such as *Winter Fantasy, Snow Fantasy,* and *Cinderella,* which are staples of the company's repertory. From 1962 to 1967 Lavrovsky taught in the Choreography Department of the Lunacharsky Theater Technicum in Moscow. In his lifetime he attracted many disciples, among whom were Soviet choreographers such as Evgeny Changa, Aleksei Chichinadze, and M. Mnatsakanian. Lavrovsky became artistic director of the Moscow School of Choreography in 1964. In 1965 he was named People's Artist of the Soviet Union. He won the State Prize of the USSR in 1946, 1947, and 1950.

BIBLIOGRAPHY

Cox, A. J. "Leonid Lavrovsky." *Ballet Today* (December 1956):6.

Demidov, Alexander P. *The Russian Ballet: Past and Present.* Translated by Guy Daniels. Garden City, N.Y., 1977.

Roslavleva, Natalia. *Era of the Russian Ballet* (1966). New York, 1979.

Swift, Mary Grace. *The Art of the Dance in the U.S.S.R.* Notre Dame, 1968.

MUSA S. KLEIMENOVA
Translated from Russian

LAVROVSKY, MIKHAIL (Mikhail Leonidovich Lavrovskii; born 29 October 1941 in Tbilisi, Georgian Soviet Socialist Republic), dancer and choreographer. The son of the choreographer Leonid Lavrovsky, Mikhail graduated from the Moscow Ballet School, where he studied under Olga Khodot, Nikolai Tarasov, and Gleb Evdokimov. Upon graduation in 1961 Lavrovsky joined the Bolshoi Ballet, where he was a soloist until 1988. He was a dancer-actor of a distinctly heroic and romantic stamp who interpreted his characters as manly, noble, dynamic, and honest. Lavrovsky's professionalism and technical brilliance made him a dancer with an exceptionally broad range and enabled him to tackle any choreographic experiment. His consummate technique, polished by his coach Aleksei Yermolayev and by his father, put Lavrovsky in the forefront of the Bolshoi's male dancers early in his career. During this period he danced a series of memorable roles, including Georgi's Son in his father's *Pages from a Life,* Philippe in Vasily Vainonen's *The Flames of Paris,* Prince Charming in Rostislav Zakharov's *Cinderella* and Vatslav in his *The Fountain of Bakhchisarai,* Frondoso in Vakhtang Chabukiani's *Laurencia,* and Medzhnun in Kasyan Goleizovsky's *Leili and Medzhnun.* Under Yuri Grigorovich's direction, Lavrovsky was given leading roles in the Bolshoi's principal repertory after 1965, appearing as Siegfried in *Swan Lake;* the Nutcracker, Paganini, Spartacus, and Ivan the Terrible in the ballets of the same name; and Basil in *Don Quixote,* Solor in *La Bayadère,* Viktor in *The Angara,* Romeo in *Romeo and Juliet,* Ferkhad in *Legend of Love,* and Artinov in Vladimir Vasiliev's *Aniuta.*

Of Lavrovsky's repertory roles, his lyrical-romantic interpretation of Albrecht in *Giselle* was one of the best portrayals of his career. Another lyrical protagonist he danced brilliantly was Romeo. First created by him in the 1967 ballet film *Romeo and Juliet,* choreographed by Natalia Ryzhenko and Viktor Smirnov-Golovanov to Tchaikovsky's score, the role took on a heroic quality a year later in the *Romeo and Juliet* Lavrovsky produced to Prokofiev's score. Lavrovsky deepened the tragic dimension of the character over the years, revealing it with added force in his father's version of the ballet, which Mikhail revived for Tbilisi's Opera and Ballet Theater (this production was brought to the Kirov Ballet in 1991). Lavrovsky also portrayed a lively Basil in Aleksandr Gorsky's version of Marius Petipa's *Don Quixote.* His participation in Grigorovich's productions represented a special chapter in his career. Above all, he created a memorable interpretation of Spartacus, which earned him the Lenin Prize in 1970.

Lavrovsky also appeared in a number of films. In addition to Romeo, he starred as Hippolytus in *Phaedra,* the Dreamer in *White Nights,* Albrecht in *Giselle,* the title role in *Mziri,* Herman in *The Three Cards,* and the title role in *Prometheus.* He also directed two ballet films: *Mziri* (1977), a television film, was awarded first place at the 1978 Seventh Dance Films and Videotape Festival held in the United States; *Prometheus* was produced in 1984.

In 1979 Lavrovsky graduated from the Choreography Department of the Lunacharsky Theater Technicum in Moscow, where he studied under Rostislav Zakharov. Thereafter, Lavrovsky combined his work as a premier danseur with the Bolshoi Ballet and his duties as artistic director of the ballet company of the Paliashvili Opera and Ballet Theater in Tbilisi, where he staged his father's one-act version of *Romeo and Juliet* in 1982, and two original ballets to the music of George Gershwin: *Porgy and Bess* in 1984 and *The Dreamer* in 1989. In *Porgy and Bess* Lavrovsky attempted to blend classical and jazz dance styles for the role of Bess, which was interpreted by two ballerinas, one dancing the real and the other the idealized Bess. The poetic pas de deux and pas de trois are among the highlights of the work, along with convincing portrayals of the other characters. Another Gershwin ballet, *Jazz Café* (1992), Lavrovsky mounted for the Moscow Operetta Theater. After his retirement as a dancer

MIKHAIL LAVROVSKY. In his first year at the Bolshoi Ballet, Lavrovsky won acclaim for his performances as the slave in *Spartacus.* (Photograph reprinted from a Boshoi Ballet souvenir program, 1962.)

Lavrovsky began to travel outside the Soviet Union and became one of the first Soviet choreographers to collaborate with companies in the West, notably Ballet Arizona for which he created *Bach Suite No. 2 for Flute* (1987), and for Atlanta Ballet *Fantasy on the Theme of Casanova* (1989) as well as several one-act ballets. He also worked in California and Australia.

Mikhail Lavrovsky was named People's Artist of the USSR in 1976 and received the State Prize of the USSR in 1977. He took first place at the 1965 International Ballet Competition in Varna, and he won the Nijinsky Prize in Paris in 1972.

BIBLIOGRAPHY

Avaliani, Noi, and Leonid Zhdanov, comps. *Bolshoi's Young Dancers.* Translated by Natalie Ward. Moscow, 1975.

Helpern, Alice. "Informal Meeting with Mikhail Lavrovsky, Visiting Soviet Choreographer." In *Proceedings of the Tenth Annual Conference, Society of Dance History Scholars, University of California, Irvine, 13–15 February 1987,* compiled by Christena L. Schlundt. Riverside, Calif., 1987.

Lavrovsky, Leonid. *Dokumenty, stati, vospominaniia.* Moscow, 1983.

Lvov-Anokhin, Boris. *Mastera bolshogo baleta.* Moscow, 1976.

Swift, Mary Grace. *The Art of the Dance in the U.S.S.R.* Notre Dame, 1968.

Tyurin, Yuri P. "Mikhail Lavrovsky." *Trud aktera* 21 (1976).

VALERIA I. URALSKAYA
Translated from Russian

LAZZINI, JOSEPH (born 1927 in Marseille), French dancer and choreographer. Lazzini studied dance in Nice and made his debut in the corps de ballet of the Marseille Opera in 1945. He became *premier danseur* at the Nice Opera in 1946 and then a *première danseur étoile* with the San Carlo Opera in Naples. His primary interest, however, was creating new dances.

From 1954 to 1957 he was a dancer and choreographer with the Liège Opera, where he presented *L'Ode des Ruines* (music by Tchaikovsky) in 1955 and *Orpheus* (music by Igor Stravinsky) in 1956. He spent one year at the Capitole in Toulouse, where he created an obsessive vision in *Valse* (music by Ravel) in 1959. He demonstrated the full range of his abilities at the Marseille Opera from 1959 to 1968, where he revived traditional ballets, including *La Fille Mal Gardée, Giselle, Les Sylphides,* and *Coppélia.* He imparted a decisive impetus to the company, for which he created original and powerful works that were sometimes controversial, including *Hommage à Jérôme Bosch* (music by Jan Meyerowitz); *Les Illuminations* (music by Emmanuel Bondeville); *The Miraculous Mandarin* (music by Béla Bartók); *E = MC²* (music by Aleksandr Mosolov), a powerful evocation of matter in fusion, forged by human beings; *Lascaux* (music by John Antill), a depiction of primitive eroticism; *The Prodigal Son* (music by Sergei Prokofiev); and *Ecce Homo* (music by Berghmans), a study of crucified man as victim of the human condition. He gave *Salomé* (music by Jean-Baptiste Miroglio) at the Ballet-Théâtre Contemporain of Amiens in 1968.

The Ministry of Cultural Affairs appointed him to direct the Théâtre Français de la Danse. Here he revived his best ballets and created *Les Métaboles* (music by Henri Dutilleux), *Une Saison en Enfer* (music by Prodomidès) and *Pour Deux Orchestres à Cordes et Deux Danseurs* (music by Kazimierz Serocki). At the Paris Opera in 1972 he put on *Cantadagio,* a work inspired by the music of Gustav Mahler; in 1973 he presented *Adagietto* at the Théâtre de l'Quest-Parisien. This was followed in 1974 by *Patchwork* at the Théâtre des Champs-Élysées and a restaging of *The Nutcracker* at Toulouse in 1978.

A film buff and a man of the theater as well as a choreographer, Lazzini merges body rhythm, decorative elements, lighting, and even the stage itself in total movement. Nourished by the anguish of the human condition, his work presents a phantasmagorical world that reflects ever-present anxiety.

At the 1963 Festival de Paris, Lazzini was awarded the prize for best choreographer. He was awarded the prize of the Université de la Danse in 1965.

After several reconstructions of *La Fille Mal Gardée,* Lazzini presented a new version at the Capitole in Toulouse in November 1985. Based on the score by Ferdinand Hérold and Peter Hertel, enriched by contributions from numerous composers—among them Riccardo Drigo, Léon Minkus, Gioachino Rossini, and Léo Delibes—and orchestrated by Jean-Michel Damase, this total revision of the ballet originally choreographed by Jean Dauberval was first performed at the Paris Opera on 28 April 1987.

At a music festival in Bordeaux in May 1990, in homage to Henri Sauguet, Lazzini produced three ballets with scores composed by Sauget just before his death: *Four Images of the Seasons,* to an excerpt from the *Symphonie Allégorique,* whose original choreography was by Léonide Massine; *Ballet of a Grand Love* (with Elisabeth Maurin and Wilfried Romoli), inspired by *The Lady of the Camellias,* realized in 1957 by Tatjana Gsovsky; and a modern recreation of *La Chatte* (with Françoise Legrée and Yassen Valchanov), originally presented by George Balanchine in 1927 with Diaghilev's Ballets Russes.

BIBLIOGRAPHY

André, Bernd. "Ballettklassiker im neuem Glanz." *Ballett-Journal/Das Tanzarchiv* 43 (February 1995): 30–31.

Bourcier, Paul. "Danser aujourd'hui." In Bourcier's *Histoire de la danse en Occident.* Paris, 1978.

Chabrier, Victor [Camarat, Victor]. *Lazzini et le ballet.* Manosque, 1967.

Christout, Marie-Françoise. "Away and Home." *Dance and Dancers* (June 1968): 19–21.

"Dossier spécial Marseille." *Pour la Danse* (April 1979): 16–32.

Marmin, Olivier. "*Les Salomé* de Lazzini." *Saisons de la danse,* no. 272 (September 1995): 52–53.

Percival, John. "France Dances." *Dance and Dancers* (October 1987): 20–26.
Planells, Martine. "Joseph Lazzini prestissimo." *Danser* (July–August 1990): 30–31.
Rossel, Lucile. "Lazzini." *Saisons de la danse* (April 1969).

JEANNINE DORVANE
Translated from French

LEAPS. *For discussion of jumps and leaps in ballet, see* Ballet Technique, *article on* Jumping Movements.

LEBANON. In many respects, Lebanon is unique among the Arab states of the Middle East, and this uniqueness is reflected in its dance traditions, particularly in the number of professional performances given. Lebanon is a country more urban than rural, although most residents of Beirut, its capital, have some village relations or associations. Because the nation is small, no village is more than a few miles from Beirut or from such other urban centers as Sidon or Tripoli. Lebanon's population is highly educated, and nomads (bedouins) account for only a miniscule percentage. The country's many religious groups and sects—mainly Christian and Islamic—seem to have had little effect on the dance traditions that are common to all Lebanese.

There are three basic dance forms in Lebanon and throughout the rest of the Levant (the eastern Mediterranean region of Syria, Jordon, Israel, Palestine, and northern Egypt): solo improvisational dancing, group dances, and combat dances.

Solo Improvisational Dancing. In the Levant, nearly everyone performs solo improvisational dances, which range from unimposing displays at informal domestic gatherings to highly professional performances, principally in the Egyptian style (*danse du ventre,* the belly dance), as was offered in the many nightclubs and cabarets of pre-civil war (pre-1975) Beirut and in other urban centers and resorts. Both men and women perform solo at informal festivities, sometimes in a very versatile and skilled fashion. The men often inject comically erotic or satiric movements in their dancing or display agility in balancing jugs or other objects on their heads, while isolating and shaking their shoulders, hips, or other parts of the body. Whether men and women dance in each other's presence depends on their or their family's religious convictions and/or their social conservatism, as well as the relationships and the number of participants in the dance.

Virtually all people in the Levant recognize the *danse du ventre* as non-Levantine. They call it *raqṣ al-sharq* ("Oriental dance") or *raqṣ al-miṣrī* ("Egyptian dance"), indicating its foreign origins.

Virtually all professional performers of the *danse du ventre* are women, often famous in the Arab world, and non-Lebanese. Their performances, depending on their skill and the milieu, are virtually the same in all particulars as those seen in Cairo or in Middle Eastern nightclubs and cabarets in large Western cities.

Group Dances. The most popular group dance is the *dabkah,* a line dance known to all Lebanese, of whatever

LEBANON. *Dabkah* is a popular line dance, often performed at weddings and other gatherings. The leader of the group waves a handkerchief to rouse and direct the dancers. There are different methods of linking, including clasping hands, resting an arm on the shoulder of the adjacent dancer, or gripping his belt. Here, a line of men and women (mostly out of view) dances to the accompaniment of a musican playing a *zurna* (also called *zamr* and *ghayṭah*). (Photograph from the collection of Metin And.)

background. It has many steps and patterns, several of which are usually known in each village; they offer the leader, who also sets the patterns for the entire line, a scope for improvisation. The line is usually joined by arms on shoulders (less often by holding hands), and the leader signals changes of dance patterns and the tempo for the musicians by means of a handkerchief or scarf. *Dabkah*s may be sexually segregated, or mixed, depending on the (religious and/or geographic) setting.

So beloved and indigenous are *dabkah* dances that urban professional performers (especially the Lebanese) invent increasingly intricate steps, patterns, and movements—not disdaining the incorporation of such foreign elements as Russian-style squats and kicks. The costumes and the music, too, are constantly changed and updated. The performers of the traditional *dabkah* refer to these glossy stage performances as the "new" folk dances. As modern and slick as these stage performances can be, they are still an extension of traditional dance expression. No stage presentation, musical concert of a major Lebanese singing star, Lebanese film, festival, or social gathering—such as a *hafla* or wedding—would be considered complete without a group performance of the *dabkah*.

Combat Dance. Represented by sword and shield dancing *(ṣeif wa ters),* the combat dance is today performed less and less often. It probably originated as a pyrrhic dance and is related to the sword and shield dances of Bursa, Turkey. The performers hold real swords and dance with only one partner, most often a brother, cousin, or lifelong friend. The dance is accompanied by instrumental music (unlike the Bursa version, which is unaccompanied), with the musicians following the performers' movements. The first part of the dance is a slow, formal salute and circling, followed by combat gestures, often improvised. Minor wounds may be inflicted, but because the performers are so close to each other, they can usually anticipate each other's movements. If one partner leaves the village or dies, the remaining partner generally no longer performs.

As a result of the political situation in the Middle East, the Levant's major folkloric festival, an annual event at Baalbek in northeastern Lebanon was held from 1955 to 1975. It has been replaced by an annual festival in Jarash, Jordan, which began in 1982. The Jarash festival features artists from the Arab world and international groups. The Beit al-Din festival began in the 1980s and features Lebanese folklore as well as Western performing arts. Other regional festivals also showcase local dancing.

[*See also* Bedouin Dance. *For general discussion, see* Middle East.]

BIBLIOGRAPHY

Shay, Anthony V. "Traditional Music and Dances of Lebanon." *Viltis* 35 (December 1976): 6–10.

ANTHONY V. SHAY

LECLAIR, ANDRÉ (born 29 January 1930 in Brussels), Belgian ballet dancer, choreographer, and teacher. Leclair studied classical ballet with Monique Querida in Brussels and with Victor Gsovsky in Paris. In 1947 he danced with Roland Petit's Ballets des Champs-Élysées. In 1949 he joined the dance company of the Koninklijke Muntschouwburg in Brussels, where he was a principal dancer, together with Jean de Cock and Jacques Sausin.

Leclair interrupted his career in Belgium by joining Les Ballets Jean Babilée (1953) and the Norwegian National Ballet (1954). He returned to the Muntschouwburg to debut as a choreographer in the 1955/56 season with *Francesca da Rimini.* He later was associated with Maurice Béjart's Ballet du XXe Siècle, for which he created *Accroche-coeur* (1961), *L'Enigme* (1964), *Ode* (1964), *Masques Ostendais* (1965), and *Symphonie No. 9* (1966).

In 1966 Leclair went to Antwerp to work as ballet teacher for the Royal Flemish Opera, and in 1968 he became director of its ballet company. In 1970 he was appointed choreographer with the Royal Ballet of Flanders, for which he created various works.

In 1979 Leclair received the award of the Belgian Union of the Friends of Terpsichore for his thirty years of dance experience and his fifty choreographed works. His work is characterized by the use of virtuosic elements of classical technique and is almost always set in Baroque decor. His *Offenbach Follies* (1974) received the Television Award in Knokke, Belgium. One of his masterworks is *Ritus Paganus* (1972), set to the music of François Glorieux.

BIBLIOGRAPHY

Barbier, Rina. *Van operaballet naar Ballet van Vlaanderen.* Antwerp, 1973.

Peters, Kurt. "Koninklijk Ballet van Vlaanderen immer jubiläumsreif." *Das Tanzarchiv* 28 (July 1980): 409–412.

Van de stomme van portici tot de lentewijding. Brussels, 1980.

LUC VERVAEKE

LE CLERCQ, TANAQUIL (born 2 October 1929 in Paris), American ballet dancer, teacher, and author. The daughter of a French father and an American mother, Le Clercq was brought from Paris to New York at the age of three and a half. Reared in a cosmopolitan, urban environment, she received her education at the French Lycée in Manhattan and the King-Coit School. At age seven, she began ballet classes with Mikhail Mordkin. Four years later she won a scholarship competition at the School of American Ballet and began studying there in October 1941. In 1945, while still a student, she created the role of the second ballerina in George Balanchine's *Symphonie Concertante.* At the first performance of Ballet Society in 1946, she created Choleric in Balanchine's *The Four Temperaments* and the Princess in his *Spellbound Child;* the

LE CLERCQ. A studio portrait in costume for Balanchine's *Bourrée Fantasque* (1949), in which she created a leading role. In the second section, set to Chabrier's *Bourrée Fantasque* (1891), Le Clercq and Jerome Robbins were ideally matched in a satirical choreographic commentary on dance. (Photograph from the Dance Collection, New York Public Library for the Performing Arts.)

same year she received the Ballet Society Fellowship Award. When Ballet Society became New York City Ballet in 1948, Le Clercq, a charter member, was its first principal dancer to have trained from childhood at its affiliated school, the School of American Ballet.

Among the more than twenty-five roles that Le Clercq created in Balanchine ballets were the Leader of the Bacchantes in *Orpheus* (1948), the first section of *Bourrée Fantasque* (1949), the Eighth Waltz and La Valse in *La Valse* (1951), the leading role in *Metamorphoses* (1952), Dewdrop in *The Nutcracker* (1954), the Rondo in *Western Symphony* (1954), and one of the five ballerinas in *Divertimento No. 15* (1956). Her other Balanchine roles included the second movement of *Symphony in C* and Polyhymnia in *Apollo*. She also created Sacred Love in Frederick Ashton's *Illuminations* (1950), the Girl in Jerome Robbins's *Afternoon of a Faun* (1953), and one of the featured roles in his *The Concert* (1956). A comic ballet, *The Concert* originally contained a serious, introspective solo for Le Clercq that was dropped after she no longer danced.

Le Clercq's dancing career ended in 1956 when she contracted paralytic polio. In a professional career that was barely ten years long, Le Clercq established herself as a great dancer. Possessing a radiant theatrical presence—and illuminating her roles with elegance, grace, and wit—she was the epitome of Balanchine's ballerina ideal.

From 1952 to 1969, Le Clercq was married to Balanchine. She is the author of two books, *Mourka: The Autobiography of a Cat* (1964) and *The Ballet Cookbook* (1966), and from 1974 to 1982 she taught at the school of the Dance Theatre of Harlem.

BIBLIOGRAPHY

Denby, Edwin. *Dance Writings*. Edited by Robert Cornfield and William MacKay. New York, 1986.

Garis, Robert. "The Balanchine Enterprise." *Ballet Review* 21 (Spring 1993): 24–44.

Lobenthal, Joel. "Tanaquil Le Clercq." *Ballet Review* 12 (Fall 1984): 74–86.

Montague, Sarah. *The Ballerina*. New York, 1980.

Newman, Barbara. *Striking a Balance: Dancers Talk about Dancing*. Rev. ed. New York, 1992.

Palatsky, Eugene. "Tanaquil Le Clercq." *Dance Magazine* (October 1957).

Reynolds, Nancy. *Repertory in Review: Forty Years of the New York City Ballet*. New York, 1977.

Taper, Bernard. *Balanchine: A Biography*. New rev. ed. New York, 1984.

WILLIAM JAMES LAWSON

LECOMTE, EUGÉNIE (born c.1811, probably in France, died after 1843), dancer. Lecomte was a competent dancer who excelled in roles such as Helena in Giacomo Meyerbeer's opera *Robert le Diable*. Her husband, John R. Lecomte, was a tenor and theatrical manager in Lyon and elsewhere. Her brother was the dancer Jules Martin.

Since numerous members of the Lecomte and Martin families appear in the performance listings of theaters in Bordeaux, Lille, Rouen, and Lyon as well as in Paris, it is difficult to distinguish or identify them definitively. In 1829 a Madame Lecomte danced at Lyon and in 1830 in Brussels. The year 1832 found the Lecomte couple performing at the Berlin Royal Theater. In the spring of 1832, Madame Lecomte danced at the King's Theatre in London in the ballets *La Somnambule* and *L'Anneau Magique*. From 1833 to 1836, the couple appeared in Lyon and Rouen. From December 1836 to July 1837 an "Anna" Lecomte was under contract to the Imperial Theater in Saint Petersburg; probably it was the same person.

Madame Lecomte debuted in the United States on 23 November 1837 at the Park Theatre, dancing Helena in *Robert le Diable*. She soon added *La Bayadère* and *Masaniello* to her repertory, with her husband singing in the latter. Following an engagement in Philadelphia in early 1838, she returned to the Park Theatre to dance in *The Dew Drop* and *The Mountain Sylph*. A failure of the stage machinery resulted in a disabling injury that cut short her Park engagement. Lecomte then traveled the Mississippi route south, danced in various theaters along the way, and finally arrived for her performances in New Orleans in December 1838. After engagements in Mobile, Alabama, and Havana, Cuba, she returned to New York in April 1839. There, in addition to her former offerings, she performed *La Fille Mal Gardée.*

Lecomte's performances received mixed reviews. The reviewer of *The Albion* noted:

> It is impossible, in speaking of this danseuse, to dispute that she is the most highly finished proficient in her art, that this country has ever witnessed; she has perfect mastery over her muscles, limbs, and positions; grace and elegance are in all her motions, difficulties she sets at defiance. . . . Shall we confess after this, that although she draws down wonder and surprise, she fails to fascinate and fix admiration. It is all professional, and none of it is feminine.

Several observers agreed with the evaluation of actor-manager Francis Courtney Wemyss (1797–1859): "Although an excellent dancer, her figure was too large to render her efforts agreeable to the eye."

During the summer of 1839, Lecomte returned to Europe, where she gathered together a corps of dancers who returned with her to the United States in mid-October. Among the group were Jean Petipa and his son Marius, with whom she had collaborated in Europe. Lecomte's company opened at the National Theatre on 29 October in *La Tarentule.* Later the company also gave *Jocko, the Brazilian Ape.* At the Bowery Theatre they performed *Marco Bombo, or The Bragging Sergeant.* Marius Petipa relates in his memoirs that because payment of their salaries was continually delayed, he and his father soon returned to Europe. Lecomte and the rest of her company continued to tour, playing New York again in January and November of 1841; they also performed in Charleston, South Carolina, and Petersburg, Virginia, and in Philadelphia during that season.

By this time, Fanny Elssler had arrived in the United States, eclipsing lesser dancers such as Lecomte. In addition, various notices indicate that Lecomte had gained a bit more weight than even the standards of that age allowed. In 1843 she appeared at Covent Garden, London, in *The Maid of Cashmere,* a performance described in the London *Times* as "a dismal failure." Her career appears to fade away after this point in the provincial theaters of France.

Lecomte's brother, Jules Martin, remained in the United States with his wife, Egerie, and became a respected dancing master in Philadelphia.

BIBLIOGRAPHY

Moore, Lillian. "The Petipa Family in Europe and America." *Dance Index* 1 (May 1942): 72–84.

Swift, Mary Grace. *Belles and Beaux on Their Toes: Dancing Stars in Young America.* Washington, D.C., 1980.

Wemyss, Francis Courtney. *Twenty-Six Years of the Life of an Actor and Manager.* 2 vols. New York, 1847.

ARCHIVE. Dance Collection, New York Public Library for the Performing Arts.

MARY GRACE SWIFT

LECOMTE, HIPPOLYTE (born 28 December 1781 in Puiseaux, France, died 25 July 1857 in Paris), French costume designer, painter, and lithographer. Although Lecomte, costume designer at the Paris Opera between 1825 and 1831, is not known for any major innovations, his work anticipates some aspects of costume design that developed further during the Romantic period. His interest in detailed and accurate historical and regional costumes prefigured the Romantic ballet's vogue for ballets of local color. The simple white dress he designed for Pauline Montessu's sleepwalking scene in *La Somnambule* (1827) was a progenitor of one of the most famous ballet costumes of all time, the Romantic tutu worn by Marie Taglioni in the title role of *La Sylphide* (1832). [*See* Tutu.]

Lecomte was a painter and lithographer as well as a designer; he specialized in history, battle, and landscape paintings, many of which he exhibited at the Parisian Salons between 1804 and 1847. He published several series of plates of regional, military, and theatrical costumes, some of which were copied and sold in statuettes of Rockingham porcelain. His book illustrations included the fables of La Fontaine and the *contes* of Perrault; appropriately enough, he designed the costumes for Jean-Louis Aumer's *La Belle au Bois Dormant* (1829) at the Paris Opera. Lecomte's interest in history served him well as a costume designer. He researched the costumes of Neapolitans in the 1650s for Daniel Auber's opera *La Muette de Portici* (1828). His designs for Aumer's ballet *Manon Lescaut* (1830), based on the 1731 novel by Antoine-François Prévost, recalled the costumes designed by Boquet, Gillot, and Bérain; however, many of his other costume designs betray, in their high-waisted silhouettes, the influence of the Parisian fashions of his era.

During the Bourbon restoration, Lecomte was the official costume designer for court fêtes and ceremonies. He also worked for the Théâtre Italien and the Opéra-Comique. His costume designs for ballets at the Paris Opera also include *Mars et Vénus* (1826), *Astolphe et Joconde* (1827), and *Le Sicilien* (1827).

BIBLIOGRAPHY

Fischer, Carlos. *Les costumes de l'Opéra.* Paris, 1931.

Wild, Nicole. *Décors et costumes du XIXe siècle,* vol. 1, *Opéra de Paris.* Paris, 1987.

SUSAN AU

LEE, MARY ANN (born c.1823 in Philadelphia, died 25 January 1899), American dancer. Lee was America's first native-born ballerina. She was the daughter of an actor, Charles Lee, whose early death imposed upon her the burden of supporting herself and her widowed mother. Necessity encouraged her versatility, and her career was characterized by acting ability as well as dancing. She first appeared on stage at the age of eleven and acted a variety of roles. She received dance training under Paul H. Hazard, who had once been a member of the corps de ballet of the Paris Opera.

On 30 December 1837 Lee made her debut as a dancer at the Chestnut Street Theater in Philadelphia, performing the role of Fatima in *The Maid of Cashmere,* an English-language version of *Le Dieu et la Bayadère* (later known as *La Bayadère*), an *opéra-ballet* with music by Daniel Auber. Also making her debut at that time was Augusta Maywood, Lee's rival; both dancers were well received. According to newspaper accounts, Maywood was the superior dancer, but Lee had a winsome quality that endeared her to audiences throughout her performing career.

For several years Lee continued to dance at the Chestnut Street Theater. Then, because of her rivalry with Maywood, she moved to the Walnut Street Theater, where she had the staunch support of the manager, Francis Courtney Wemyss, who produced a ballet especially for her. She appeared as Queen Lily of the Silver Stream in *The Lily Queen,* and, although the ballet was short-lived, she continued to perform in the theater's supportive environment. On 27 April 1839 she played the leading role of Zoloë in *La Bayadère,* which ultimately led to her New York debut in the same role later that year.

While again in New York in 1840, Lee took advantage of the fact that the great Austrian ballerina Fanny Elssler was also appearing there. Under the tutelage of James Sylvain, Elssler's partner, she learned some of the ballerina's famous dances, such as "La Cachucha," "La Smolenska," and "La Cracovienne." Soon afterward she toured extensively in the United States, performing many of these dances and becoming a popular favorite. Upon returning from her tour of 1842, she danced with Eugénie Lecomte in the ballet from Giacomo Meyerbeer's opera *Robert le Diable.*

By this time Lee had achieved a measure of success; had she remained in the United States, she might have continued to perform as an average dancer whose personality ensured her popularity with audiences. In 1844, however, her career took a turn that secured her place in history. In November she sailed to France, where she studied at the Paris Opera with the choreographer Jean Coralli. After a year, not only had she improved her technique, but she had also acquired a knowledge of some of the great Romantic ballets—*Giselle, La Fille du Danube,* and *La Jolie Fille de Gand*—which she brought back to the United States. Shortly after her return she began to prepare productions of these ballets.

On 24 November 1845, *La Jolie Fille de Gand* made its American premiere at the Arch Street Theater in Philadelphia. Reports state that it was staged in its original grandeur, not a surprising fact since Philadelphia was the cultural center of the United States at the time, boasting some of the finest theaters outside Europe. Lee danced the role of Beatrix and displayed her improved technique; appearing with her was George Washington Smith.

The success of *La Jolie Fille de Gand* was followed in the same year by the American premiere of *La Fille du Danube.* Lee danced the leading role of Fleur des Champs, which later became the title of the ballet; she was again partnered by Smith.

Lee then left for Boston, where on 1 January 1846 she presented the first American performance of *Giselle.* She danced the title role, with Smith as Albrecht. Following

LEE. This illustration appeared on the cover of sheet music for "La Smolenska," an 1842 *divertissement* originally danced by Fanny Elssler but staged for Lee by James Sylvain. (Dance Collection, New York Public Library for the Performing Arts.)

this historic performance, Lee began an extended tour of the United States in 1846. Although she had reached a pinnacle of success during this period, she also began to experience poor health.

In the spring of 1847 Lee gave her farewell performances, though she danced occasionally thereafter. Her contributions to her profession were noteworthy. Though she does not appear to have been an exceptional technician, she possessed certain qualities that endeared her to audiences: physical beauty, genuineness, and stage presence. Without the flamboyance of many of her contemporaries, she was nonetheless a pioneer in bringing new ballets to the United States from Europe.

BIBLIOGRAPHY

Barker, Barbara. *Ballet or Ballyhoo: The American Careers of Maria Bonfanti, Rita Sangalli, and Giuseppina Morlacchi.* New York, 1984.

Farrell, Rita Katz. "Star-Spangled Giselles." *Ballet News* 6 (September 1984): 15–20.

Maynard, Olga. "Barbara Weisberger and the Pennsylvania Ballet." *Dance Magazine* (March 1975): 45–60.

Ludlow, Noah M. "Miss Lee, Danseuse." In Ludlow's *Dramatic Life as I Found It.* St. Louis, 1880.

Moore, Lillian. "Mary Ann Lee: First American Giselle." *Dance Index* 1 (May 1943): 60–71.

Swift, Mary Grace. *Belles and Beaux on Their Toes: Dancing Stars in Young America.* Washington, D.C., 1980.

ARCHIVE. Dance Collection, New York Public Library for the Performing Arts.

BARBARA FERRERI MALINSKY

LEEDER, SIGURD (born 14 August 1902 in Hamburg, died 20 June 1981 in Herisau, Switzerland), German dancer, choreographer, and teacher. Leeder was the outstanding dance teacher of his generation in his ability to stimulate movement exploration and evoke movement concepts through creative imagery. He related aspects of movement to everyday life and to art, drawing and painting in particular.

Leeder discovered expressive movement as a child in communicating with a deaf-mute playmate through dancing and acting. At the Hamburger Kunstgewerbe Schule he became acquainted with Sarah Norden, an early student of Rudolf Laban, who confirmed and stimulated Leeder's gift for dance. His career as a dancer and actor, begun at the Hamburger Kammerspiele in 1920, led to recitals of his own solos and choreography for his group.

Leeder's meeting with Kurt Jooss in 1924 resulted in a twenty-three-year collaboration, first as performers in their programs called *Zwei Tänzer,* then as directors of the dance department at the School for Music, Speech and Movement at Münster. As co-director with Jooss, Leeder built up the dance department of the Folkwang Schule in Essen and established his method of teaching modern dance. From Jooss he had learned Laban's Space Harmony (Choreutics), and from Laban himself the concepts of dynamics (Eukinetics), both of which Leeder used creatively throughout his teaching career; his classroom approach was to build up dancelike Studies from initial movement exploration. Leeder's Studies are not movement sequences but complex dance compositions with special themes. He recorded them all in kinetography, to which he made an important contribution, both through translating movement ideas into symbols and through practical application of the system in teaching and choreographing.

After a period as teacher for Ida Rubinstein and her company in Paris, Leeder moved from Essen to England with Jooss and headed the Jooss-Leeder School of Dance, Dartington Hall, Devon, until the outbreak of World War II. Performing again during the war, he toured the United States and Europe with Les Ballets Jooss as dancer, teacher, and choreographer. In 1947 he established his own school in London, attracting students worldwide.

The best of Leeder's students became members of the Studio Group, for which he choreographed many works. In 1959 he was called to Santiago to organize and head the dance department at the University of Chile. He returned to Europe in 1964 and moved his London school to Herisau, Switzerland, to which students from around the world traveled to experience his enlightening and charismatic teaching. Since his death in 1981 the school has continued under the direction of Grete Müller, his former co-director, using the deep-rooted principles that he established.

BIBLIOGRAPHY

Forster, Marianne. "Sigurd Leeder." *Ballett-Journal/Das Tanzarchiv* 29 (January 1981): 60–61.

Forster, Marianne. "Reconstructing European Modern Dance: Bodenwieser, Chladek, Leeder, Kreutzberg, Hoyer." In *Dance Reconstructed,* edited by Barbara Palfy. New Brunswick, N.J., 1993.

Guest, Ann Hutchinson. "Images for the Dance: The Teaching Method of Sigurd Leeder." *Ballett International* 8 (October 1985): 14–21.

Müller, Margaret. "The Impassioned Teacher of Dance: Sigurd Leeder." *Ballett International* 8 (June–July 1985): 28–30.

GRETE MÜLLER

LEE MAE-BANG (born 5 May 1927 in Makpo), Korean dancer, teacher, and choreographer. Lee Mae-bang began to study Korean traditional dance at the age of six under the tutelage of his grandfather, and at the age of seven under a renowned *kisaeng* (female entertainer, the Korean counterpart of the Japanese *geisha*). Both taught him the *sungmu* (a Buddhist monk's dance) and the art of drumming that goes with it. At fifteen he had already mastered the *sungmu* to the extent that he was invited to tour the countryside with a folk music and dance troupe. During the same year, 1942, he studied the *kommu* (sword dance).

In 1950 Lee established his first dance institute in Kunsan; he performed with his students for the first time in Kwangju in 1953. He soon moved his institute to Seoul, and in 1956 he made his debut in Pusan. In 1962 he gave his first overseas performances in Japan, the United States, South America, Europe, and Tunisia. He toured the Korean countryside with his students in 1976, performing his first dance creation, *Sword of the Spirit.* In 1978 he performed with a folk music and dance troupe at the International Folk Arts Festival in Rennes, France, and the following year gave a presentation at a dance festival commemorating the tenth anniversary of the establishment of Korean Airlines.

Lee won acclaim for his 1981 performance of the *sungmu* at the Kennedy Center in Washington, D.C. In 1982 he performed the *salp'uri* (dance of exorcism) at the Festival of Great Korean Dancers in Seoul. He took part in the Performing Arts Festival of the 1986 Asian Games in Seoul. The following year, he was designated a Human Cultural Treasure by the Korean government for his superb rendition of the *sungmu.* He participated in the Performing Arts Festival of the 1988 Olympic Games in Seoul. He was again designated a Human Cultural Treasure in 1990 for his interpretation of the *salp'uri.* In 1991 he was a leading member of a large music and dance company that performed in Los Angeles and at Carnegie Hall in New York to commemorate Korea's entry into the United Nations.

Lee Mae-bang is the leading living exponent of the *sungmu* and the *salp'uri.* The fact that many of his students have become accomplished dancers may in itself serve as a testimonial to his mastery of Korean traditional folk dance technique and artistry.

BIBLIOGRAPHY

Cho Dong-wha. "Dance." In *Korea: Its Land, People, and Culture of All Ages.* 2d ed. Seoul, 1963.

Chung Byong-ho. *Korean Folk Dance.* Seoul, 1992.

Ku Hui-suh. *Ch'um Kwa Ku Saram.* Vol. 3. Translated by Lee Kyong-hee. Seoul, 1994.

Song Kyong-rin. "Introduction to Korean Folk Dance." Translated by Alan C. Heyman in *Survey of Korean Arts,* vol. 2, *Folk Arts.* Seoul, 1974.

ALAN C. HEYMAN

LEE SUN-OCK (born 14 January 1943 in Kaesong), Korean dancer, choreographer, teacher, and author. As a Korean traditional and modern dancer and choreographer, Lee Sun-ock began her training in traditional dance when she was nine. She studied with such dancers as Han Young-sook and Lee Mae-bang, both of whom have been designated Human Cultural Treasures by the Korean government. Moving to the United States in 1969, she made her New York debut in 1972 at Carnegie Recital Hall and later performed at the Asia Society, La Mama, and at Lincoln Center's Alice Tully Hall and Avery Fisher Hall (now Philharmonic Hall), as well as at numerous other theaters throughout the United States and abroad. In 1973 she collaborated on Nam June Paik's worldwide video art production *Global Groove,* and she has been a resident artist of the Asia Society Performing Arts Program since 1974. In 1975 she taught at New York City's High School of Performing Arts. At that time she became interested in Zen dance and formed the Lee Sun-ock Zen Dance Company, with which she later toured in Europe and Asia.

In 1976 Lee became a founding member of the Asian New Dance Coalition. She performed Zen dance in Stockholm at the International Theater Institute Conference in 1977. In 1978 she participated in the Festival of Traditional Arts in Rennes, France, and in the First Asian Dance Conference in Hawaii. In the same year she began to teach at New York University's Dance Education Program, where she earned a doctor of arts degree in dance in 1984 with a dissertation entitled "The Evolvement of Yimoko III: Zen Dance Choreography." In 1980 the National Endowment for the Arts gave her the Choreographic Award for her Zen dance creations. She published her first book, volume 1 of *Zen Dance: Meditation in Movement,* in 1985, followed by volume 2 in 1988. In 1984 she performed Zen dance in several Asian countries and conducted a research project collecting and documenting videotapes of Korean traditional dance for the Korean and Asian Performing Arts Center, of which she is presently artistic director. During the same year, she performed in *Mystics and Masters: The Meeting Ground of Thomas Merton* at Saint Bartholomew's Church in New York.

Lee coordinated the 1985 Asian Traditional and Contemporary Dance and Music Festival, of which she is currently artistic director, at La Mama, where she also coordinated a Mini Asian Music and Dance Festival for the Third World Institute of Theater Arts Studies. She participated in the 1985 mixed-media performance, *Zen Dance / Zen Painting,* at the Korean Cultural Service Gallery in New York, and also in the first Asian Alliance Arts Festival at the Henry Street Settlement in New York. In 1986 she performed *Zen Dance / Zen Painting* at the Asia Society for its Meditation and the Arts series of events; participated in and performed at the thirtieth anniversary of the American Dance Guild's Arts and Collaboration Conference in North Carolina; and performed her composition *Lotus II* at the Maison des Cultures du Monde in Paris. She taught at the University of Hawaii in 1987 and performed *Lotus II* for the World Peacemaking Conference.

In 1988 she gave workshops on Zen dance for A.E.G.I.S. in Lebanon, Massachusetts; participated in the Open Gate's conference Through the Arts to the Sacred in England; lectured on Zen dance in China at the Dance Academy of Beijing; participated and performed at the Third Asian Dance Conference sponsored by the Academy of performing Arts in Hong Kong; and performed at the Han River International Jazz Festival in Seoul as part of the Olympic Arts Festival. In 1991 she performed her compositions *Lotus I, Lotus II,* and *Lotus III* and gave the New York premiere of *Lotus IV* at the Korean Zen Festival sponsored by the Asia Society, a performance that the *New York Times* dance critic Anna Kisselgoff called "completely original" and "totally creative." In 1993 she performed her *Lotus VI: Simudo* (Taming the Bull) at the First Asian Contemporary Dance Festival at La Mama. Lee again collaborated with Nam June Paik in 1994 in the world premiere of *The School of Korean Zen Dance,* presented at the Court House in New York and later at Le Rond Point in Paris.

Lee presently teaches Zen Dance: Meditation in Movement at the New York Open Center. She is also director of the Zen Temple of Crosskill in New Jersey, where she has recorded a set of three videotapes entitled *Zen Meditation Exercise: Toning Body and Mind.* She is best known for her creation of Zen dance, which spans the cultures and dance styles of East and West. Her work has been recognized and acclaimed internationally for its beauty, its power to evoke deep inner feelings, and its innovative approach to cross-cultural arts.

[*See also* Korea, *article on* Modern Dance.]

BIBLIOGRAPHY

Lee Sun-ock and John Chang McCurdy. *Zen Dance: Meditation in Movement.* 2 vols. Seoul, 1985–1988.

ALAN C. HEYMAN

LEGET FAMILY. Nikolai Legat was Anna Pavlova's partner on her 1909 tour of western Europe. Here they are seen as Colin and Lise in *La Fille Mal Gardée,* staged by Petipa and Ivanov after Dauberval. (Photograph by Schneider, Berlin; from the Dance Collection, New York Public Library for the Performing Arts.)

LEGAT FAMILY, Russian ballet dancers of Swedish descent. The father, Gustav, and his two sons, Nikolai and Sergei, were notable performers on the stages of imperial Russia.

Gustav Legat (Gustav Ivanovich Legat; born 20 January [1 February] 1837, died 20 July [1 August] 1895 in Saint Petersburg). Having studied ballet under Marius Petipa at the Imperial Theater School in Saint Petersburg, Gustav Legat worked at the Maryinsky Theater between 1857 and 1869. In 1865 and again in 1868 he danced at Moscow's Bolshoi Theater, where, in 1865, he produced Jules Perrot's *Le Délire d'un Peintre.* From 1869 to 1875 he danced at the Bolshoi Theater, during which time, from 1872 to 1874, he also taught at its school. Retiring in 1875, he returned to the Bolshoi in 1882. During the 1885/86 season, he rejoined the Maryinsky company.

Gustav Legat was a classical dancer with an impressive technique. Some of the best-known and most important roles he created include Alvares in *Le Délire d'un Peintre,* Sandro in Julius Reisinger's *Stella* (1875), and the Miller in Fortunato Bernadelli's *Le Ballet des Meuniers.*

Nikolai Legat (Nikolai Gustavovich Legat; born 15 [27] December 1869, died 24 January 1937 in London), dancer, teacher, and choreographer. He studied at the Imperial Theater School in Saint Petersburg under his father and later under Nikolai Volkov, Pavel Gerdt, and Christian Johansson. Upon his graduation in 1888, he became a leading classical dancer with the Maryinsky Theater company. He possessed a polished technique, a commanding stage presence, and considerable acting skill.

Nikolai Legat partnered some of the foremost ballerinas of the day, including Anna Pavlova, Matilda Kshessinska, Tamara Karsavina, and Olga Preobrajenska. Among his principal roles were Siegfried in *Swan Lake,* Prince Désiré in *The Sleeping Beauty,* Albrecht in *Giselle,* Jean de Brienne in *Raymonda,* Basil in *Don Quixote,* Harlequin in *Les Millions d'Arlequin,* Franz in *Coppélia,* and Gringoire in *Esmeralda.* Beginning in 1907 he made guest appearances in Paris, Berlin, Leipzig, Prague, Vienna, and Warsaw. In 1902 he was made assistant ballet master of the Maryinsky Theater and in 1905 its joint ballet master with his brother Sergei. He became chief choreographer and ballet master in 1910, succeeding Marius Petipa.

Nikolai Legat carefully preserved Petipa's legacy and traditions. Not always responsive to new ideas and change, he stoutly resisted any attempt to erode the school of classical dance. He produced a series of admirable ballets at the Maryinsky Theater, including Josef Bayer's *The Fairy Doll* (1903), choreographed in collaboration with his brother Sergei; Aleksandr Mikhailov's *Puss in Boots* (1906); and Thomas Hartman's *The Blood-Red Flower* (1907). He also revived some of Petipa's ballets, including *Les Saisons* in 1907, *Le Talisman* in 1909, and *Barbe-Bleue* in 1910.

Between 1896 and 1914, Nikolai Legat also taught at the Imperial Theater School in Saint Petersburg, succeeding Johansson as director of the class of perfection in 1905. A highly successful teacher, Legat had a genius for combining instruction in the fundamentals of classical dance with an individualized approach to each of his pupils. Among the galaxy of dancers he trained were Anna Pavlova, Michel Fokine, Tamara Karsavina, Lydia Kyasht, Vaslav Nijinsky, Bronislava Nijinska, Agrippina Vaganova, and Fedor Lopukhov.

In 1914 Legat left the Maryinsky Theater when the management, displeased by his conservative outlook, which they saw as an obstacle to efforts to modernize the repertory, failed to renew his contract. Following his forced resignation, he staged two ballets at the Popular Cultural Center in Saint Petersburg in 1915: *The White Lily,* to music by Boris Asafiev, and *The Rose of Margitta,* to music by Johann Armsheimer. Legat also taught at Akim Volynsky's School of Russian Ballet in Petrograd, gave private lessons, and in 1914–1915 went on tour in France and England, where he appeared in music halls in Paris and London with his wife, Nadine Nikolaeva.

Because of the outbreak of World War I in Europe, Legat was unable to return to Russia until after the Revolution of 1917. When he did return, after several years' absence, he was unsuccessful in finding a place for himself in the emerging world of Soviet ballet. Thus, in 1922 he left his homeland and immigrated to western Europe. There, he taught ballet classes in London and Paris, served for a short time as ballet master for Serge Diaghilev's Ballets Russes, and in 1926 settled in London and opened a school in Colet Gardens. Among his pupils were Alexandra Danilova, Lydia Lopokova, Ninette de Valois, Alicia Markova, Anton Dolin, Serge Lifar, and Margot Fonteyn. After his death in 1937, the school continued to operate under the direction of his widow, Nadine Nikolaeva-Legat.

Known primarily as a dancer and teacher of extraordinary talent, Legat was also a skilled caricaturist and a competent writer. While still in Saint Petersburg, he published in 1903 an album entitled *Russky balet v karikaturakh* (Russian Ballet in Caricature), produced in collaboration with his brother. His book on the development of Russian ballet technique was translated as *The Story of the Russian School* and published in London in 1932.

Sergei Legat (Sergei Gustavovich Legat; born 15 [27] September 1875 in Moscow, died 19 October [1 November] 1905 in Saint Petersburg), dancer and teacher. Sergei

LEGAT FAMILY. Sergei Legat in a studio portrait, late 1890s, possibly in costume as Jean de Brienne in *Raymonda.* (Photograph from the State Museum of Theatrical and Musical Arts, Saint Petersburg.)

Legat attended the Imperial Theater School in Saint Petersburg, where he studied under Pavel Gerdt, Christian Johansson, and Lev Ivanov. From 1894 onward he worked at the Maryinsky Theater. An extremely handsome man, he was also a talented actor who specialized in roles of the classical repertory. He was especially admired for his performances as Ta-Hor in *La Fille du Pharaon,* Lucien in *Paquita,* Jean de Brienne in *Raymonda,* Pierre in *Halte de Cavalerie,* Arthur in *Barbe-Bleue,* and Vestris in *Camargo*—all ballets choreographed by Marius Petipa—as well as Acis in Lev Ivanov's *Acis and Galatea* and Colin in the Petipa-Ivanov version of *La Fille Mal Gardée.* In most of these roles he danced as partner of the leading ballerinas at the Maryinsky, including Tamara Karsavina.

Together with his wife, the ballerina Marie Petipa (Maria Mariusovna Petipa, 1857–1930), a much admired character dancer, Legat went on tour in 1902–1903 to Vienna, Paris, Monte Carlo, and Budapest. Upon his return, in 1903, he and his brother Nikolai were co-producers of the ballet *The Fairy Doll,* to Josef Bayer's score and with sets and costumes by Léon Bakst, at the Maryinsky Theater. From 1896 onward he taught mime and partnering at the Imperial Theater School in Saint Petersburg, and from 1898 he served as teacher and *répétiteur* for the ballet company of the Maryinsky Theater. Under intense pressure during the dancers' strike of 1905, he committed suicide at the age of twenty-nine.

BIBLIOGRAPHY

Gregory, John. "Legendary Dancers: Nikolai Legat." *The Dancing Times* (October 1987).

Gregory, John, ed., with André Eglevsky. *Heritage of a Ballet Master: Nicholas Legat.* London, 1978.

Karsavina, Tamara. "Nikolai Legat." *The Dancing Times* (August 1964).

Krasovskaya, Vera. *Russkii baletnyi teatr vtoroi poloviny XIX veka.* Leningrad, 1963.

Krasovskaya, Vera. *Russkii baletnyi teatr nachala XX veka.* Leningrad, 1972.

Legat, Nicholas. *The Story of the Russian School.* Translated by Sir Paul Dukes. London, 1939.

Legat, Nicholas. *Ballet Russe: Memoirs of Nicholas Legat.* Translated by Sir Paul Dukes. London, 1939.

Nikolaeva-Legat, Nadine. *Ballet Education.* London, 1947. Includes excerpts from the diaries and notebooks of Nikolai Legat.

VICTOR V. VANSLOV
Translated from Russian

LEGEND OF JOSEPH. *See* Josephslegende, Die.

LEGEND OF LOVE. Russian title: *Legenda o Lyubvi.* Ballet in three acts. Choreography: Yuri Grigorovich. Music: Arif Melikov. Libretto: Nazım Hikmet and Yuri Grigorovich. Scenery and costumes: Simon Virsaladze. First performance: 23 March 1961, Kirov Theater, Leningrad. Principals: Olga Moiseyeva (Mekhmene Banu), Irina Kolpakova (Shirien), Aleksandr Gribov (Ferkhad), Anatoly Gridin (Vizier).

Based on a well-known play by the Turkish poet and revolutionary journalist Nazım Hikmet, *Legend of Love* is a complex choreographic drama of passion and sacrifice, rich in imagery and symbolism. In order to cure her sister Shirien, Queen Mekhmene Banu is compelled to part with her beauty. Thereafter, upon learning of the flight of Shirien and her beloved, the young artist Ferkhad, the enraged queen, who also loves Ferkhad, orders her servants to catch the fugitives. She commands Ferkhad to build a canal across the mountains to bring water to the people of her parched land; only then will she allow him to marry Shirien. Shirien is in despair. Ferkhad abandons his beloved to bring happiness to the people.

The ballet is remarkable for its ideological and moral message, psychologically complex images, and tense action. The basis for the choreography is classical dance in its well-developed ensemble and symphonic forms. Grigorovich relied on individual elements of oriental patterns and modern dance, which are organically integrated into the classical foundation. Each of the protagonists is surrounded by a corps de ballet that provides an accompaniment for his or her experiences and intensifies the psychological expression. This effect is especially strong in the scene depicting Mekhmene Banu's agonizing sadness. Her "monologue" is accompanied by the performance of a corps de ballet seconding her thoughts and emotions.

Grigorovich lent an active character to mass scenes, basing them on polyphonic principles as complex, multilayered, and meaningful choreographic structures. For example, in the scene of the pursuit of the fugitives, the Vizier, who leads the chase, and Makhmene Banu, who soars over the scene, are united in a common dance. In the key interactions among the three protagonists—meeting, conflict, parting, and so forth—the action stops, the stage grows dark, the orchestra falls silent except for the strings, and the trio of Ferkhad, Shirien, and Mekhmene Banu retreats to the back of the stage. This method reminds one of arrested action in operatic ensembles or a close-up in films.

Duets are of great significance in the work. For example, the five contrasting duets of Ferkhad and Shirien reveal the full story of their relationship. The action develops against the background of stage scenery that resembles an open book of oriental illustrations or a painted screen used in folk theater. Every scene is like an illustration on a page of this book. Oriental fixtures produce fantastic stage lighting that emphasizes the legendary character of the events.

The ballet has been produced in many cities in the former Soviet Union and in eastern Europe. It was mounted for the Bolshoi Ballet in Moscow in 1965 with a cast including Maya Plisetskaya (Mekhmene Banu), Natalia Bessmertnova (Shirien), and Maris Liepa (Ferkhad).

BIBLIOGRAPHY

Balanchine, George, with Francis Mason. *Balanchine's Complete Stories of the Great Ballets*. Rev. and enl. ed. Garden City, N.Y., 1977.

Beaumont, Cyril W. *Complete Book of Ballets*. Rev. ed. London, 1951.

Haskell, Arnold L. "Russian Logbook" (parts 1–3). *The Dancing Times* (June–September 1962).

Karp, Poel M. "Legenda o Lyubvi." *Teatr*, no. 9 (1961).

Lvov-Anokhin, Boris. "Legenda o Lyubvi v Bolshom." *Teatr*, no. 9 (1965).

MacMahon, Deirdre. "'Corridor to the Muses.'" *Ballet Review* 12 (Spring 1984): 57–65.

Vanslov, Victor V. *Balety Grigorovicha i problemy khoreografii*. 2d ed. Moscow, 1971.

VICTOR V. VANSLOV
Translated from Russian

LEGNANI, PIERINA (born 30 September 1868 in Milan, died 15 November 1930 in Milan), Italian dancer. Legnani studied under Caterina Beretta in Milan and was an exponent of nineteenth-century Italian virtuoso ballet of the school of Carlo Blasis. In 1890 she appeared as *prima ballerina* at the Alhambra Theatre in London in the ballet *Salandra* by Eugenio Casati. In 1892 she was appointed *prima ballerina* at the Teatro alla Scala in Milan. Petite and of no great beauty, she must have been endowed with considerable talent, for the following year the Maryinsky Theater in Saint Petersburg engaged her as *prima ballerina assoluta*. During her stay there she had the opportunity to study at the school of Nikolai Legat.

Legnani first displayed her technical prowess in the title role of *Cinderella* (1893; choreography by Enrico Cecchetti, Lev Ivanov, and Marius Petipa). She first won acclaim as a major artist, however, on the evening of 15 January 1895, when she performed in the uncut version of *Swan Lake* by Petipa and Ivanov. The audience was particularly impressed by the famous thirty-two *ronds de jambe fouettés* that she introduced in the Odile variation during the third act. Reports of the time mention not only this technical accomplishment but also Legnani's special interpretation of Odette-Odile. The young pupils of the Imperial School at that time, among them Anna Pavlova and Tamara Karsavina, were struck by the celebrated ballerina's breathtaking virtuosity. Karsavina wrote in her memoirs, "Legnani had infinite charm and grace, and her qualities, combined with an extraordinarily brilliant execution, left the detractors of the Italian school totally speechless."

The enthusiasm of balletomanes and dancers was shared by the critics. In *History of Dance*, the scholar Sergei Khudekov wrote:

> Legnani was the highest ideal of plastic movement. She had none of those jerky movements that are so often found in Italian ballerinas. Her movements were graceful, plastic, feminine, but lacked sensuousness or expressiveness, and this explains why she never appeared at the Paris Opera. . . . Therefore Legnani has assimilated, albeit unwittingly, the stylistic refinement and the elegant manner of Russian dancers. . . . In *Swan Lake* she evoked the fascinating image of a dancing swan. Legnani truly seemed to be living those heady moments of poetic melancholy. Every one of her movements was cloaked in ineffable languor. In this role she reached the peak of her art.

LEGNANI. Creator of the dual role of Odette-Odile in the 1895 production of *Swan Lake* in Saint Petersburg, Legnani is remembered today chiefly for having introduced the famous sequence of thirty-two *fouettés* into the Black Swan pas de deux. Pictured here in her costume for Odette, the White Swan, she was designated *prima ballerina assoluta* of the Maryinsky Theater, an honor subsequently accorded to only one other dancer, Matilda Kshessinska, a favorite of Tsar Nicholas II. (Photograph from the Dance Collection, New York Public Library for the Performing Arts.)

Among Legnani's best interpretations were all the leading roles in the ballets of Petipa, who adapted for her a new version of *Coppélia*, created in collaboration with Cecchetti in 1894, and also *The Talisman* (1895), *Le Halte de Cavalerie* (1896), *La Perle* (1896), *Barbe-Bleue* (1896), *Raymonda* (1898), *L'Épreuve de Damis* (1900), *Les Élvèves de Dupré* (1900), and *Les Ruses d'Amour* (1900).

Legnani last appeared in public for a farewell performance in Saint Petersburg on 28 January 1901, in *La Camargo* by Léon Minkus and Petipa. On that occasion she was presented with a silver slipper, which is now kept at the Theater Museum of La Scala. She retired to Lake Como, but she continued to officiate on the examining board of La Scala Ballet School until July 1930, four months before her death.

BIBLIOGRAPHY

Gregory, John. "Legendary Dancers: Pierina Legnani." *The Dancing Times* (December 1987): 237.

Gregory, John. *The Legat Saga.* 2d ed. London, 1993.

Guest, Ivor. *Ballet in Leicester Square.* London, 1992.

Karsavina, Tamara. *Theatre Street.* Rev. and enl. ed. London, 1948.

Khudekov, Sergei. *Istoriia tantsev.* 4 vols. St. Petersburg, 1914–1918.

Lifar, Serge. *A History of Russian Ballet* (1950). Translated by Arnold L. Haskell. New York, 1954.

Migel, Parmenia. *The Ballerinas: From the Court of Louis XIV to Pavlova.* New York, 1972.

Rossi, Luigi. "Legnani, Pierina." In *Dizionario del balletto.* Vercelli, 1977.

ALBERTO TESTA
Translated from Italian

LÉGONG. A characteristic element of the *légong* performance is a unison duet performed by two dancers (also called *légong*), which occurs as part of the pure dance section preceding the development of the narrative. These two *légong* appear in perfect synchronization. (Photograph from the archives of The Asia Society, New York.)

LÉGONG. Bali's most stylistically formalized female dance form, *légong* was traditionally performed by a group of three preadolescent girls, although this age distinction has most often been disregarded recently in the contexts of institutionalized education and the tourist trade. Traditionally, *légong* was of special interest to local princes, who might choose their *légong* dancers from among the village youngsters, taking them into the court to be trained under their supervision. *Légong* is thus considered a court genre, sometimes referred to as *légong keraton,* or palace *légong.* This reflects its links to *gambuh,* the formal dance drama influenced by fifteenth-century Javanese courts. This aspect of the *légong* tradition has continued to the present day in villages such as Saba and Peliatan. The classic *légong* music ensemble is *gamelan pelégongan* or *semar pegulingan;* sweet and delicate-sounding, they were traditionally placed just outside the king's bedchamber.

Légong must have evolved when the indigenous gestural language, exemplified by the ritual *sang hyang dedari,* took on an entirely new dramatic character under the influence of such forms as *gambuh.* Whereas *sang hyang* is considered as performance in company with gods, *légong* is a dance done for human audiences. Many of *sang hyang*'s spontaneous gestures, based on motions observed in nature, were incorporated into the fixed choreographic style of *gambuh.* The word *légong* derives from *leg* ("gentle, swaying movement") and *gong,* referring to the accompanying instrumental ensemble. Costume elements such as the *gelungan* headdress were also taken from *gambuh.*

One chronicle, the *Babad Dalem* of Sukawati village, attributes the creation of *légong* to a dream that came to I Déwa Agung Madé Karna, a king of Sukawati reigning around 1775 to 1825. During meditation, he saw celestial maidens dancing in heaven, clad in beautiful costumes and golden headdresses. He then had nine masks carved and used *sang hyang* dancers, one pair at a time, to recreate the choreography he saw in his dream. This *sang hyang légong* is still performed with the original masks, taking place in the innermost temple courtyard during a ceremony held every six months in Ketéwel.

Some time later a new form of *légong* called *nandir* was created. It is performed by two boys without masks. Also around the turn of the nineteenth century, a *nandir* for two girls was choreographed. The *kebiar* style of the 1920s infused a more energetic element into the dance as well as a more direct relationship between dancer and gamelan. It was during this period that the *condong* character was brought in. Functioning within the dance drama as female attendant, bird of ill omen, or any of a number of other characters, the *condong* also provides the lengthy first segment of *légong.* It is particularly in this opening, prestory segment that the unique characteristics of *légong* are displayed, as a dynamic crosscurrent of intense, percussive energy and delicate, tranquil lines together create a rhapsodic quality of movement that exists in its own realm, outside any specific narrative context. The structure of the dance reflects compositional aspects of *gambuh,* including, within the first section, a *pengawit* ("head"), *pengawak* ("body"), and *pengécét* ("tail") sequence.

This pure dance, or *igel ngugal,* precedes the narrative, as the condong establishes the mood and language of movement in a solo segment. Then the other two dancers, referred to as *légong,* perform a sequence in unison and often in symmetrical patterns, closely coordinated with the cymbals and drums, while the gamelan plays somewhat more slowly. For the following *pengecet* segment, the *gamelan* doubles its tempo while the dancers mirror each other's darting movements.

The second section of the dance brings in the story line as the tempo slows to accommodate a different melody. The third section enacts a departure *(pangkat)* usually involving a fight *(pesiat).* The last section of the dance is a nonnarrative epilogue *(pekaad).*

The most prevalent theme is *Lasem,* drawn from Java's Malat literature. The king of Lasem finds a beautiful woman, Langkesari, lost in the forest. He brings her home and locks her in a stone house. Langkesari's brother, the king of Daha, discovers where she is being held, but the king of Lasem will not give her up. Lasem takes leave of his distraught wife and daughter and goes out to battle. As he leaves his palace, a great crow attacks him, and although he beats it away, it is nonetheless a bad omen. The king reflects that although he will die, he will surely ascend to heaven, since he is to die on the field of battle. As he climbs onto his chariot, he draws blood again by scraping his foot, yet another ill omen. He goes to battle and is killed. The actual *légong* version depicts only the parting scenes between the king, Queen Prameswari, and Langkesari, followed by his fight with the bird of ill omen, or *gúwak.*

Other dramatic narratives are *Legodbawa, Kutir,* and rarely *Calonarang. Semaradana* is performed with the addition of *panasar* and *kartala* narrators, a *baris* dancer, and others. Three versions of *légong* without a particular plot are *Kupu-kupu Tarum, Kuntul,* and *Jobog,* in which the dancers represent butterflies, herons, and monkeys.

The narrative versions of *légong* traditionally employ a vocalist *(juru tandak)* who sits among the gamelan musicians, providing voices for characters as well as sung poetry *(tandak)* to clarify the story and its changing moods. The traditional *gamelan pelégongan* has all but given way to the dominant *gamelan gong kebiar,* and the thirty- or forty-five-minute *légong* is often shortened to fifteen minutes, adapting to the requirements of tourist entertainment.

[*See also* Indonesia, *articles on Balinese dance traditions.*]

BIBLIOGRAPHY

Bandem, I Madé. *Perkembangan Legong Keraton Sebagai Seni Pertunjukan.* Denpasar, 1974.

Bandem, I Madé, and Fredrik Eugene DeBoer. *Balinese Dance in Transition: Kaja and Kelod.* 2d ed. New York, 1995.

Covarrubias, Miguel. *Island of Bali.* New York, 1937.

de Zoete, Beryl, and Walter Spies. *Dance and Drama in Bali* (1938). New ed. New York, 1973.

Dibia, I Wayan. "Arja: A Sung Dance-Drama of Bali; A Study of Change and Transformation." Ph.D. diss., University of California, Los Angeles, 1992.

Herbst, Edward. *Voices in Bali: Energy and Perceptions in Vocal Music and Dance Theater.* Hanover and London, 1997.

Hitchcock, Michael, and Lucy Norris. *Bali, the Imaginary Museum: The Photographs of Walter Spies and Beryl de Zoete.* New York, 1995.

Holt, Claire. *Art in Indonesia: Continuities and Change.* Ithaca, N.Y., 1967.

McPhee, Colin. "Children and Music in Bali." In *Childhood in Contemporary Cultures,* edited by Margaret Mead and Martha Wolfenstein. Chicago, 1955.

Siegel, Marcia B. "Liminality in Balinese Dance." *Drama Review* 35 (Winter 1991): 84–91.

EDWARD HERBST

LENINGRAD SYMPHONY. Russian title: *Sedmaya Simfoniya.* Ballet in one act and three scenes. Choreography: Igor Belsky. Music: Dmitri Shostakovich. Libretto: Igor Belsky. Scenery: Mikhail Gordon. First performance: 14 April 1961, Kirov Opera and Ballet Theater, Leningrad. Principals: Gabriella Komleva (The Girl), Yuri Soloviev (The Young Man).

The ballet's three scenes are "Peaceful Life," "Invasion," and "Requiem." As the curtain opens, a beam of light cuts through the darkness and illuminates on the backdrop a bar—the composer's autograph—from Dmitri Shostakovich's Seventh Symphony ("Leningrad"). Then the whole backdrop is lighted more and more to show a silhouette of the Neva embankment. The majestic sounds of the symphony are heard. Young men, the protagonist among them, leap into the air in a forceful dance as though testing their strength and then march in step as if at a sports parade. Young couples stroll in the dimness of twilight. The Young Man and the Girl also appear. Pensive and dreamy intonations of present and future happiness prevail.

Suddenly the peace is broken by a dry drumbeat. This alien theme—representing war—grows and breaks the tranquility. A giant bloodstained hand creeps toward the city and covers the whole sky; war destroys hope and subordinates all to its inexorable demands. The youths march off to battle, during which they are overcome, imprisoned, and executed. Only one attempts to save himself by turning traitor, but he is confronted by the Girl, who symbolizes the people's vengeance. The invaders take over. Their orgy of atrocities reaches its culmination and they prepare to celebrate victory.

At this critical moment the native land brings back to life its loyal sons and defenders. The Young Man is among them. They go into battle again, but they are heavily outnumbered. Soviet soldiers die while wiping out enemy hordes. One surviving invader circles over the dead like a vulture. He swoops down upon the dying Young Man. The latter gathers his last strength and kills the hateful enemy, the last member of the enemy force. The Young Man staggers forward toward the future and then stands still like a monument in bronze. A mournful composition of women's figures is a symbol of tragic war experiences: the women enter the scene as a reminder of the war and its irretrievable losses. The Girl's arms stretching toward the audience seem to appeal to today's generation: "It should never happen again!"

The *Leningrad Symphony*'s theme of the Soviet people's war against the Nazi invaders suggested to Igor Belsky the idea to stage a ballet devoted to people's responsibility for the destiny of the world. Symphonic music required generalization of choreographic images, which Belsky achieved by the method of symphonic dance—an opposition and development of choreographic themes. Therein Belsky found an accurate criterion for the stage action, which remained closely linked with the development of the music.

BIBLIOGRAPHY

Krasovskaya, Vera. "Balet-simfoniia." *Sovetskaia Kul'tura* (5 August 1961).

Vanslov, Victor V. "Balet-simfoniia." *Sovetskaia Muzyka*, no. 2 (1962).

ARKADY A. SOKOLOV-KAMINSKY
Translated from Russian

LEPESHINSKAYA. The virtuosity, beauty, and comic talent required by the role of Kitri in *Don Quixote* made Lepeshinskaya an ideal interpreter. She is seen here with Asaf Messerer as Basilio, c.1940. Some Russian balletomanes claim that no other dancer has ever matched the joyfulness and excitement of her performances as Kitri. (Photograph from the Dance Collection, New York Public Library for the Performing Arts.)

LEPESHINSKAYA, OLGA (Ol'ga Vasilevna Lepeshinskaia; born 15 [28] September 1916), dancer and teacher. In 1933 Lepeshinskaya graduated from the Moscow Ballet School, where she had studied under Olga Charpentier, Elena Adamovich, Viktor Semenov, and Aleksandr Chekrygin. She then joined the Bolshoi Ballet, where she remained until her retirement as a dancer in 1963. Her successful debut as the peasant girl Lise in Aleksandr Gorsky's version of *La Fille Mal Gardée* was followed by appearances as Suok in Igor Moiseyev's *Three Fat Men*, Aurora in Asaf Messerer's version of *The Sleeping Beauty*, Kitri in Gorsky's *Don Quixote*, and Oksana in Rostislav Zakharov's *Taras Bulba*. These performances set Lepeshinskaya in the first rank of Soviet ballerinas. Although not an exemplar of pure academic style, her virtuosic technique, coupled with a gift for characterization, enabled her to live her roles. Lepeshinskaya was a highly popular ballerina because she broadened the expressive language of classical dance to make it readily understandable to a wide audience. Her art sprang from a balanced combination of the Moscow school style and an imaginative search for effective artistic imagery in the contemporary repertory.

Lepeshinskaya was able to take a wide range of roles—from farce to high drama, romance to tragedy—but her strength lay in comedy and in the heroics of Soviet ballet. Some of her best portrayals included the title role in *Svetlana* (1939), choreographed by Nikolai Popko, Lev Pospekhin, and Aleksandr Radunsky; Jeanne in Vasily Vainonen's *The Flames of Paris* in 1947; Tao-Hoa in Leonid Lavrovsky's *The Red Poppy* and Parasha in Zakharov's *The*

Bronze Horseman in 1949; and Sari in Konstantin Sergeyev's *The Path of Thunder* in 1959. Those that brought her greatest fame were the title role in Zakharov's *Cinderella* (1945); Swanilda in *Coppélia,* choreographed by Evgenia Dolinskaya and Radunsky after Gorsky; the title role in Vainonen's *Mirandolina* (1949); and Asol in *Crimson Sails,* choreographed by Radunsky, Popko, and Pospekhin in 1943. Her concert appearances constituted a special chapter in Lepeshinskaya's career. During World War II she performed for troops at the front in a series of miniatures specially staged for her by Leonid Yakobson, such as *Blind Girl* and *The Hunter and the Bird.* Lepeshinskaya also appeared in a series of ballet films, including *Count Nulin* and *Prince Igor;* in the latter she danced Chaga in the *Polovtsian Dances.*

In 1963 Lepeshinskaya retired from the stage and became a ballet teacher. She was invited on several occasions to serve as guest teacher and *répétiteur* in Italy, Hungary, East and West Germany, Japan, Sweden, and Austria. In the 1970s and 1980s she wrote newspaper reviews of ballet and hosted a special ballet program on Central Television, Moscow. A People's Artist of the USSR and winner of successive State Prizes (1941, 1946, 1947, and 1950), Lepeshinskaya was repeatedly elected a deputy of the Moscow City Council.

BIBLIOGRAPHY

Dolgopolov, Mikhail. "Olga Lepeshinskaya." In *The Soviet Ballet,* by Yuri Slonimsky et al. New York, 1947.

"Four Russian Dancers of Today." *The Dancing Times* (October 1941):12–14.

Iakovlev, M. A., ed. *Mastera bolshogo teatra.* Moscow, 1976.

Lepeshinskaya, Olga. "Life of a Soviet Ballerina." *Dance News* (January 1946):6–7.

Martin, John. "Reports from Russia." *Dance Magazine* (September 1956):14–21, 58–64.

Roslavleva, Natalia. *Era of the Russian Ballet* (1966). New York, 1979.

Solodovnikov, Aleksandr. *Olga Lepeshinskaiia.* Moscow, 1983.

Swift, Mary Grace. *The Art of the Dance in the U.S.S.R.* Notre Dame, 1968.

MUSA S. KLEIMENOVA
Translated from Russian

LE PICQ, CHARLES (also known as Lepic, Pick, or Lepij; born 1744 in Naples, died 1806 in Saint Petersburg), dancer, choreographer, and director. Le Picq began his career in 1761 as a dancer in the corps de ballet of the Stuttgart Theater. A student of Jean-Georges Noverre, who had been invited by the duke of Württemberg to direct the ballet, Le Picq was named *danseur sérieux* in 1763. In February 1763 he collaborated in the creation of Noverre's *Médée et Jason* and appeared in his *La Mort d'Hercule.* In 1764 he set out with his wife, Anna Binetti, on the first of many tours of Europe, including visits to Venice, Vienna, and Warsaw.

From December 1765 to March 1767 Le Picq was principal dancer of an Italian troupe in Warsaw. From 1769 to 1772 he was a choreographer and dancer at the Teatro San Benedetto in Venice, where he created *Orphée et Euridice, Les Triomphes et les Victoires d'Hercule,* and *Le Sacrifice d'Iphigenie,* and mounted Noverre's *Médée et Jason.* He also presented Noverre's *Hymenée et Cryseus* in Milan. Between 1773 and 1776, in Naples, he presented his own ballets *Aminta et Clori* and *La Partie de Chasse d'Henri IV* and staged *Armide, Orphée et Euridice, Adèle de Ponthieu,* and *Les Horaces et les Curiaces,* by Noverre.

In 1776 Le Picq followed Noverre to the Paris Opera, where his *entrées* in *Alceste,* set to music by Christoph Willibald Gluck, and *L'Union de l'Amour et des Arts,* to music by Etienne-Joseph Floquet, were highly successful. He collaborated in the performance of Noverre's *Les Caprices de Galathée* before the court at Fontainebleau on 30 September 1776. It was repeated on 17 November in Paris, where Le Picq and Marie-Madeleine Guimard aroused the enthusiasm of the audience. After a new engagement at the Teatro San Benedetto, where he mounted *Télémaque dans l'Île de Calypso* and *Les Trois Horaces et les Trois Curiaces* (1777), he returned to the Paris Opera to dance Noverre's *Apelles et Campaspe* with Guimard and Gaëtan Vestris. The intrigues by the jealous Vestris and Maximilien Gardel caused him to leave Paris, and in 1781 he returned to Naples. In 1782 he joined Noverre at the King's Theatre in London, where he danced brilliantly in *Apollon et les Muses, Apelles et Campaspe,* and *Le Déserteur,* to music by Pierre-Alexandre Monsigny and choreography by Jean Dauberval. Between 1782 and 1785 Le Picq presented his own ballets, including *L'Enlèvement des Sabines, Le Tuteur Trompé*—in which he danced seguidillas with Spanish expertise—*Les Épouses Persanes, Les Amours d'Alexandre et Roxane, Sémiramis, Le Jugement de Pâris, Le Convive de Pierre* (music by Gluck), and *Macbeth.*

In 1786 Le Picq and his second wife, Gertrude Rossi, were engaged at the court of Catherine the Great in Saint Petersburg, where Gertrude was named *prima ballerina.* Together with Giuseppe Canziani, Le Picq designed the dances for Molière's *Le Bourgeois Gentilhomme* (1789) and for *Le Commandant d'Oleq,* a major historical spectacle conceived by the empress and performed at the Hermitage Theater on 15 October 1790. He was also responsible for the ballets *Bergère* (1790), *Didon Abandonnée* (1795), *La Belle Arsène* (1795), *Les Amours de Bayard* (1798), and *Tancrède* (1798). He staged *Le Déserteur,* Maximilien Gardel's *L'Oracle,* and Noverre's *Mort d'Hercule, Psyché et l'Amour, Médée et Jason, Adèle de Ponthieu,* and *Annette et Lubin.*

Still Noverre's faithful disciple, Le Picq succeeded in getting his mentor's *Lettres sur la danse* published by Emperor Alexander I in 1803. Noverre was delighted at the recognition given to Le Picq in Saint Petersburg and considered him, along with Vestris, the model of the ideal dancer, writing:

> The beautiful proportions of his figure, the nobility of his face, the enchanting harmony of his movements, and the delicate polish of his execution were made all the more amazing by their apparent case and the fact that any physical exertion was always gracefully concealed. The combination of these attributes won him success both at court and with the general public.

In his choreography, Noverre said Le Picq shared with Jean Dauberval, Sébastien Gallet, and Gardel the gift of "combining taste, imagination, and genius with the deep knowledge of their art." Perhaps the master was being indulgent; Le Picq's entire career was linked with that of the famous choreographer, whose principles he assimilated, whose works he carefully staged wherever he was engaged, and whose innovative ideas he applied. A defender of the *ballet d'action,* Le Picq was also one of the first Frenchmen before Charles-Louis Didelot to give classical dance lasting impetus in Russia.

BIBLIOGRAPHY

Guest, Ivor. *The Romantic Ballet in England.* London, 1972.

Lifar, Serge. *A History of Russian Ballet* (1950). Translated by Arnold L. Haskell. New York, 1954.

Lynham, Deryck. *The Chevalier Noverre: Father of Modern Ballet.* London, 1950.

Massaro, Maria Nevilla. "Balli e ballerini fra Padova e Venezia." *La Danza Italiana* 5–6 (Autumn 1987):77–88.

Noverre, Jean-Georges. *Lettres sur les arts imitateurs en général et sur la danse en particulier.* 2 vols. Paris, 1807. Edited by Fernand Divoire as *Lettres sur la danse et les arts imitateurs* (Paris, 1952).

Swift, Mary Grace. *A Loftier Flight: The Life and Accomplishments of Charles Louis Didelot.* Middletown, Conn., 1974.

Winter, Marian Hannah. *The Pre-Romantic Ballet.* London, 1974.

JEANNINE DORVANE
Translated from French

LEPRI, GIOVANNI (*fl.* 1847–1881, died probably in Mexico c.1892), Italian ballet dancer, choreographer, and teacher. Nothing is known of Lepri's early life. At some time in his youth, probably in the early 1840s, he became a pupil of Carlo Blasis, who directed a ballet school in Milan. Contemporary records show that he began his performing career in 1847. Thereafter, he distinguished himself as a *primo ballerino di rango francese* (i.e., *premier danseur*) as well as in mime roles, dancing in ballets by the leading choreographers of the day and partnering some of the most famous female dancers of his age.

During 1847 and 1848, Lepri is known to have danced in Piacenza, Cremona, and Florence. His name subsequently appears in records of productions in several other cities in Italy. In Turin, he danced at the Teatro Carignano in 1851, and he appeared at the Teatro Regio in Antonio Cortesi's *La Gerusalemme Liberata* during the 1852/53 season. In Florence, he danced in Blasis's *Le Galanterie Parigine* in 1853, and in Rome, during the 1853/54 season, he appeared at the Teatro di Apollo in Emmanuele Viotti's *Margherita di Scozia,* partnering Amalia Ferraris.

In 1857, Lepri was engaged at the Teatro alla Scala in Milan, where he appeared several times until 1862. During his first year in Milan he danced in *Il Conte di Montecristi* by Giuseppe Rota, produced by Efisio Catte, and in Pasquale Borri's *La Giocoliera* (The Woman Juggler). He subsequently partnered Caterina Beretta in Borri's *Rodolfo* and *Fiammella* and in Raffaele Rossi's *Jenny.* In 1862, he partnered Amina Boschetti in *I Viaggiatori dell'Isola dell'Amore* (Travelers on the Island of Love) by Antonio Monticini, produced by Gaspare Pratesi. By this time, Lepri had begun to choreograph: two pas de deux by him are documented in Francesco Magri's *Elisa di Senneville,* produced at the Teatro Carignano, Turin, in 1860.

About 1863, Lepri moved to Florence, where he had earned the favor of the public dancing in the 1860 and 1861 seasons in Rota's *Bianchi e Negri* (Whites and Blacks), with Olimpia Corilla, and *Il Giuocatore* (The Gambler). In 1864 he was appointed director of the newly established ballet school and teacher of the finishing class at the Teatro La Pergola, where he continued also to dance until 1867. In 1865 at Lugo, he performed in *Le Quattro Stagioni* (The Four Seasons), the *divertissement* from Giuseppe Verdi's opera *I Vespri Siciliani,* choreographed by Cesare Cecchetti, father of the dancer Enrico, who was at that time Lepri's pupil.

Under Lepri's direction, the school at La Pergola flourished in the years from 1866 to 1870, when Florence was the capital of the Kingdom of Italy, but it was closed in 1872. At this school, which was only for girls, Lepri's pupils included Virginia Zucchi and Giuseppina de Maria, later to become the wife of Enrico Cecchetti. Cecchetti himself studied privately with Lepri, by virtue of a clause in the school regulations allowing teachers to keep private students. Indeed, Lepri is remembered today chiefly as Cecchetti's teacher.

Details of Lepri's later years are as obscure as those of his early life. It is known that he left Italy and went abroad, probably in the late 1870s, to work as ballet master for *Castles in Spain,* an extravaganza in which his daughter, Amalia Lepri, headed the cast. After tours through Spain, Cuba, and Mexico, this production was presented at the Metropolitan Alcazar Theater in New York City in 1881.

BIBLIOGRAPHY

Blasis, Carlo. *Delle composizioni coreografiche e delle opere letterarie di Carlo Blasis.* Milan, 1854.

"The Cecchetti Society." *The Dancing Times* (June 1959): 1–16.

Poesio, Giannandrea. "Maestro's Early Years." *The Dancing Times* (September 1992): 1125–1127.

Poesio, Giannandrea. "Il maestro Giovanni Lepri e la sua scuola fiorentina." *Chorégraphie* 1 (Spring 1993): 68–75.

Poesio, Giannandrea. "Cecchetti: The Influence of Tradition." In *Dance History*, edited by Janet Adshead Lansdale and June Layson, 2d ed., pp. 117–131. London, 1994.

ARCHIVES. Lillian Moore's unpublished research notes, headed "Giovanni and Amalia Lepri," are held in the Dance Collection, New York Public Library for the Performing Arts.

CLAUDIA CELI
Translated from Italian

LERMAN, LIZ (born 25 December 1947 in Los Angeles), American dancer, choreographer, and author. The foremost exponent and practitioner of community-based dance in the United States, Lerman established Dance Exchange in Washington, D.C., in 1976. Comprising a company of elderly dancers, a school, and a touring company, Dance Exchange was streamlined in 1993 into one cross-generational company, Liz Lerman Dance Exchange. The current company, whose members range in age from twenty-four to seventy-two, operates on three fronts: touring and performance; community projects; and professional training for artists interested in community work.

Lerman's philosophy is that dance belongs to everyone. Since creating *Woman of the Clear Vision* in 1975, a dance in which she honored her recently deceased mother and worked with elderly adults from a Washington senior center, Lerman has presented a full spectrum of people and experiences on the dance stage. At the same time she strives to bring dance to the broadest possible community. Examples of this include the 1980s *Fanfare for the Common Man* (also called *May Dance on the Mall*), in which Lerman had eight hundred people dancing on the steps of the Lincoln Memorial. Another example is *Still Crossing* (1986), a dance commissioned to celebrate the centennial of the Statue of Liberty and that Lerman designed to incorporate local community members wherever her company is on tour.

Lerman's interest in content-driven dance links her to a long line of modern-dance humanists, including Doris Humphrey and Helen Tamiris. While many of her contemporaries pursued abstract and formalist issues in dance, Lerman took a more personal route. Beginning with her earliest solo, *New York City Winter* (1974), she talked and danced. Since then, the text has ranged from the autobiographical to the political and historical (Lerman was a history major at Brandeis University in Waltham, Massachusetts). She incorporates storytelling and narrative from all her company members into her choreography, and her performances typically invite audience feedback.

In 1994 Lerman wrote in her article published in *Movement Research*, "I think that people are mostly so removed from physical learning that dance concerts are too distant a form in which to feel the connection that those of us

LERMAN. Members of the intergenerational, interracial Liz Lerman Dance Exchange in a weight-sharing pose from *Flying into the Middle.* The dancers are (left to right) Lerman, Jeffrey Gunshol, Thomas Dwyer, and Kimberli Boyd. Lerman's work is deeply personal, often derived from stories of her dancers, yet it retains a strong political element. She has made a reputation teaching dance to people from all walks of life, including the elderly and "disadvantaged" populations. (Photograph © 1995 by Beatriz Schiller; used by permission.)

making dance seem to expect. Thus, the emphasis in my own work is on community and participation—and yes, the use of language as a way into the physical memory, kinship, and feeling, and the ultimately nonverbal, non-translatable experience that dance can sometimes bring about."

Lerman has been developing a "Critical Response Process" by which creative artists can solicit and receive structured, positive feedback on works in progress from their peers. She offers training workshops in this method as part of the residency activities of the Liz Lerman Dance Exchange.

BIBLIOGRAPHY

Harding, Cathryn. "Liz Lerman: Seeking a Wider Spectrum." *Dance Magazine* (January 1996): 78–82.

Kriegsman, Alan M. "Liz Lerman, Democrat of Dance." *Washington Post* (26 April 1987).

Lerman, Liz. *Teaching Dance to Senior Adults.* Springfield, Ill., 1984.

Lerman, Liz. "Toward a Process for Critical Response." *High Performance,* no. 64 (Winter 1993): 46–49.

Lerman, Liz. "By All Possible Means." *Movement Research* (Fall–Winter 1994–1995).

CATHRYN HARDING

LESTANG, ANNE-LOUIS (died 3 January 1737), French dancer, teacher, choreographer, and dance academician. Lestang was often referred to as "Lestang *cadet,*" which distinguished him from his older but equally famous brother. With Guillaume-Louis Pecour, he was considered the ornament of the Paris Opera at the turn of the eighteenth century. Both dancers were often compared, and they engaged in a friendly rivalry. Both were sought after in the best social circles, for "it was a pleasure to be in their company" (Rameau, 1725).

Lestang made his debut at the Paris Opera in *Atys* in 1676. Described by the Parfaict brothers in their *Histoire manuscrite de l'Académie Royale de Musique,* "he was tall, with beautiful arms and a well-turned leg [and] he danced until 1702." He was always celebrated for "this certain air special to men of quality but rarely seen in a dancer" (Le Cerf, 1705, p. 12). Lestang was also noted for the precision of his steps and somewhat criticized for the coldness of his dance and the poor invention of his choreography. At Pierre Beauchamps's retirement from the Académie Royale de Musique in 1687, the composition of ballets was entrusted to Lestang and Pecour, who collaborated on such productions as *Achille et Polyxène* in 1687 and *Thétis et Pélée* in 1689. Lestang, "little satisfied" with his works turned over the whole production of ballets to Pecour, keeping for himself, as was the custom, only the composition of his own solos.

Lestang retired from the Paris Opera with a pension of eight hundred livres and was listed among the members of the Académie Royale de Danse in 1730. He married at least twice, the second time to Catherine Buret, a widow, on 15 June 1736. Lestang died on 3 January 1737, at his home on the rue d'Orléans in Paris. An inventory of his estate was made on 17 January of the same year; this sixty-page document itemized what seems to have been an extremely luxurious and wealthy household.

BIBLIOGRAPHY

Almanach des spectacles de Paris, ou Calendrier historique et chronologique des théâtres. Paris, 1773.

Le Cerf de la Viéville, Jean-Laurent, seigneur de Freneuse. *Comparaison de la musique italienne et de la musique françoise.* 3 vols. Paris, 1704–1706 and Brussels, 1705.

Parfaict, François, and Claude Parfaict, *Histoire manuscrite de l'Académie Royale de Musique.* Paris, n.d. Manuscript located in Bibliothèque Nationale, Paris, fr.12355.

Rameau, Pierre. *Le maître à danser.* Paris, 1725. Translated by Cyril W. Beaumont as *The Dancing Master (*London, 1931).

ARCHIVES. Archives Nationales, Paris: Y.342, f.159. Archives Opéra, Paris: Finances, Arch. 18.

RÉGINE ASTIER

LESTER, KEITH (born 9 April 1904 in Guildford, Surrey, died 8 June 1993 in London), British ballet dancer, choreographer, and teacher. After becoming a double scholar at Saint Paul's School in London, Keith Lester determined to pursue a career as an archaeologist. He changed his mind in 1921 after seeing a performance of *The Sleeping Princess* by the Ballets Russes de Serge Diaghilev, then appearing in an extended run at the Alhambra Theatre. This spectacular production inspired Lester to begin training as a dancer. His first instructor in ballet was a youngster exactly his own age: Anton Dolin, who taught a class at Serafina Astafieva's studio in Chelsea and who had appeared in the corps de ballet of *The Sleeping Princess.* Lester later studied with Astafieva herself and with Nicholas Legat. Despite his limited training, he made his stage debut in 1923, in dances arranged by Michel Fokine for *Hassan,* a play by James Elroy Flecker, at His Majesty's Theatre.

Within a few years, Lester became a striking dancer and strong partner, and he was chosen by Lydia Kyasht as partner for her tours (1925–1927). At age twenty-four, he was invited to become Tamara Karsavina's partner; he joined her in Riga, and they subsequently toured Europe from 1928 to 1930. In 1931, he was engaged by the Teatro Colón, Buenos Aires, to partner Olga Spessivtseva in the classics and other works that Fokine was reviving there at that time.

Back in London in 1932, Lester appeared in Max Reinhardt's production of *The Miracle,* in dances choreographed by Léonide Massine. Joining the Ida Rubinstein Ballet for its Paris Opera season in 1934, he created roles in Fokine's *Sémirimis* and in Kurt Jooss's *Persephone*. After touring the United States in a revue, he returned to England and joined the newly formed Markova–Dolin Ballet in 1935 as dancer and choreographer. His wide experience, plus his historical knowledge, inspired his distinguished choreographic career. For the Markova–Dolin company, his first creation was *David* (1935), a dramatic ballet on a biblical theme set to a score by Maurice Jacobson. This was followed in 1936 by a careful reconstruction of Jules Perrot's 1845 *Pas de Quatre*, a Romantic *divertissement* set to music by Cesare Pugni. These were the most notable of his several creations before he left in 1937 to dance and choreograph Shakespearean productions for Robert Atkins in the Regents Park open-air theater.

Two serious operations in 1939 curtailed Lester's dancing career, but later that year he choreographed *Pas des Déesses*, again using music by Pugni, for the London Ballet. In 1940 with Harold Turner, he formed Arts Theatre Ballet, for which he created several works, including *De Profundis*, with music by Chopin, and *The Glen*, with music by Mendelssohn. The company merged with Ballet Rambert and Lester left to tour in musicals. From 1945 until 1964, he directed dance and created some 150 ballets at London's Windmill Theatre.

Having taught pas de deux and choreography at the Royal Academy of Dancing since 1960, Lester became a permanent member of the staff in 1964. He was appointed co-principal of the academy's Teacher Training College in 1968 and principal in 1970. Upon his retirement in 1975, he was named a fellow of the Royal Academy of Dancing.

BIBLIOGRAPHY

Benari, Naomi. *Vagabonds and Strolling Dancers: The Lives and Times of Molly Lake and Travis Kemp*. London, 1990.

Karsavina, Tamara. "An English Partner: Keith Lester." *The Dancing Times* (December 1967): 143–148.

Lester, Keith. "Choreographers at Work: A Method in Their Madness." *The Dancing Times* (February 1941): 264.

Lester, Keith. "Dancers at the Windmill." *The Dancing Times* (November 1964): 91.

Lester, Keith. "Rubinstein Revisited." *Dance Research* 1 (Autumn 1983): 21–31.

Noble, Peter, ed. *British Ballet*. London, 1949.

PETER WILLIAMS

LETTER TO THE WORLD. Choreography: Martha Graham. Music: Hunter Johnson. Scenery: Arch Lauterer. Costumes: Edythe Gilfond. First performance: 11 August 1940, Bennington College Theater, Bennington, Vermont, Martha Graham and Dance Group. Principals: Martha Graham (The One in Red), Margaret Meredith (The One in White), Jane Dudley (The Ancestress), Erick Hawkins (The Lover), Merce Cunningham (March).

In *Letter to the World*, Martha Graham associated herself with the reclusive New England poetess Emily Dickinson, capturing the wildness and freshness of a spirit who defied, through her art, the nineteenth-century Puritan traditions that circumscribed her life. Not only can the sedate Emily who speaks the poems and the high-spirited Emily who dances be thought of as alter egos, but many of the other characters, who appear and disappear with the ease of fantasies, can also be considered aspects of the heroine. Children play, young men and women dance as if at a party, a buoyant young man bounds toward Emily as she sits on her bench ("Dear March, come in . . ."), a lover—severe and strong and, in the end, unattainable—dances with the heroine. The most potent figure is the Ancestress, a remorseless and giant figure in black, who can be seen as death and also as smothering tradition. It is she who causes Emily to envision her own funeral, she who cleaves the lovers apart. Like many of Graham's dances, *Letter to the World* ends with the heroine's achieving self-knowledge: the woman will retreat into a life of solitude in order that the mind and heart of the artist may range free.

The dance was not a success when first presented at the Bennington Festival, but Graham edited and reworked it. Jean Erdman took over the role of The One in Red (now identified as One Who Speaks), and the character was more fully integrated into the choreography. After its New York premiere in January 1940, *Letter to the World* was acclaimed a masterpiece.

BIBLIOGRAPHY

Sears, David. "Graham Masterworks in Revival." *Ballet Review* 10.2 (1982): 25–34.

Siegel, Marcia B. *The Shapes of Change: Images of American Dance*. New York, 1979.

DEBORAH JOWITT

LEVENTHAL, VALERY (Valerii Iakovlevich Leventhal; born 17 August 1938 in Moscow), Russian scenery designer and librettist. Leventhal was trained in the Art Department of the Institute of Cinematography in Moscow. From his earliest stage designs of 1963–1964, he proved equally adept at designing for ballet, drama, and opera. His first works in ballet—*Cinderella* in 1964 and *Romeo and Juliet* in 1965—were produced in collaboration with the choreographer Oleg Vinogradov at the Novosibirsk Opera and Ballet Theater. For *Cinderella*, Leventhal invented a fairy-tale world of naiveté, frailty, and transparency: luminescent and glimmering, silvery trees with long branches extending upward formed an alley that plunged deeply upstage. For *Romeo and Juliet* he built a three-tiered arcade based on architectural motifs of the early Renaissance and the Shakespearean stage: around the arcade was a painted scene of a white town with pointed houses whose outlines, which he had dis-

LEVANTHAL. A model of Leventhal's set design for the Bolshoi Ballet's production of *The Seagull* (1980), with scenario based on Anton Chekov's 1895 play. (Photograph by Viktor Berezkin; courtesy of Elizabeth Souritz.)

cerned in the rhythms of Prokofiev's music, conveyed anxiety.

In 1965 Leventhal began designing for the Bolshoi Ballet. He designed Maya Plisetskaya's productions of *Anna Karenina* (1972) and *The Seagull* (1980), in the latter creating an environment of light and air in an impressionist mood. He also worked with Vladimir Vasiliev on the restaging of *Icarus* in 1976 and *Macbeth* (1980), in which Leventhal showed the romantic and tragic colors of his palette. Among Leventhal's other works in ballet are *Till Eulenspiegel,* choreographed by Otar Dadishkiliani in Minsk in 1974; *Cippolino* (1977) and *The Little Prince* (1983), choreographed by Henrik Mayorov for the Bolshoi; productions of *Swan Lake* in Novy Sad in 1982 and Vilnius in 1983; and Plisetskaya's open-air production of *Raymonda* at the Baths of Caracalla in Rome in 1984. He also designed television ballets, including *Romeo and Juliet, Trapeze, Transfigured Night,* and *Phaedra.* He became a People's Artist of the Russian Federation in 1981.

BIBLIOGRAPHY

Berezkin, Viktor. "Khudozhnik v teatralnom spektakle: Tvorchestvo Valeriia Leventalia." *Iskusstvo,* no. 4 (1974).

Demidov, Alexander P. *The Russian Ballet: Past and Present.* Translated by Guy Daniels. Garden City, N.Y., 1977.

Kapterova, Galina, ed. *Maya Plisetskaya.* Translated by Kathleen Cook. Moscow, 1976.

Lutskaia, Elena. "Valerii Levental." *Teatr,* no. 2 (1980).

Lutskaia, Elena. *Valerii Levental* (in Russian). Moscow, 1989.

VIKTOR I. BEREZKIN
Translated from Russian

LEVINSON, ANDRÉ (Andrei Iakovlevich Levinson; born 1 January 1887 in Saint Petersburg, died 3 December 1933 in Paris), Russian ballet and literary critic. A critic of international standing, Levinson is best known for his landmark critiques of the Serge Diaghilev enterprise and for his vigorous support of the classical tradition. In both literature and the arts he reached a foremost position as a perspicacious and highly erudite writer. His breadth and sophistication established a new basis and standard for dance criticism throughout Europe and the United States.

Levinson graduated from the Imperial University of Saint Petersburg and joined its faculty as a professor of French literature. His critical work was well established by 1911, when his reviews of Diaghilev's Ballets Russes appeared in such leading newspapers and journals as *Rech', Apollon,* and *Zhizn' iskusstva.* In his distinctively forceful, often ironic style, Levinson proclaimed his disapproval of Diaghilev's subordination of dance to costumes, decor, and music, and he voiced his fear that ballet's classical tradition was being eroded for the sake of evanescent novelty. Without denying the pictorial splendor of the so-called new ballet, or Michel Fokine's genius for innovation, Levinson wrote that the company was leading ballet along the path of "suicide on the public stage" (1982, p. 48), a path restrained only by classical pedagogy.

Levinson left Russia during the Revolution and in 1921 settled in Paris, where he taught at the Sorbonne and became one of the most influential critics of the French capital. His reviews, which appeared in *Candide, Zhar-Ptitsa, Theatre Arts Monthly, La revue musicale,* and *Sovremennye zapiski,* were not confined to the realm of ballet; they included articles on Loie Fuller, Spanish dancers, Negro ensembles, Oriental performers, and music-hall shows. Levinson also conducted annual seminars at the Comédie des Champs-Élysées.

Although he was rooted in the classical tradition, Levinson hailed the choreographic reforms of Isadora Duncan and likened her aesthetic foundation to pre-Raphaelitism and Quattrocento painting. He felt it was Duncan who, through her cult of athleticism, brought the art of the dance to an ever greater audience.

Complementing his prolific career as a critic, Levinson also wrote numerous full-length works on dance and aesthetics. These included *Mastera baleta* (1914), *Staryi i novyi balet* (1918), a biography of Léon Bakst (1922), *La danse au théâtre* (1924), *La Argentina* (1928), a biography of Marie Taglioni (1929), and *La danse d'aujourd'hui* (1929).

Levinson was elected to the Légion d'Honneur in 1927, and in 1932 be became a naturalized French citizen. Following his death one month before his forty-seventh birthday, two books of his appeared, *Les visages de la danse* (1933) and *Serge Lifar: Destin d'un danseur* (1934).

[*For similar discussion, see the entries on Koni, Svetlov, Volynsky, and Zotov.*]

BIBLIOGRAPHY

Garafola, Lynn. "Politics in Paradise: André Levinson's Classicism." *New Dance Review* 6 (Spring 1994): 12–18.

Jowitt, Deborah. "Levinson from Paris." *Ballet Review* 21 (Summer 1993): 6–9.

Levinson, André. *Bakst: The Story of the Artist's Life.* New York, 1922.

Levinson, André. *Marie Taglioni* (1929). Translated by Cyril W. Beaumont. London, 1977.

Levinson, André. *Ballet Old and New.* Translated by Susan Cook Summer. New York, 1982.

Levinson, André. *André Levinson on Dance: Writings from Paris in the Twenties.* Edited by Joan Acocella and Lynn Garafola. Middletown, Conn., 1991.

Scholl, Tim. "From Apollon to Apollo." *Ballet Review* 21 (Winter 1993): 82–96.

Taplin, Diana Theodores. "On Critics and Criticism of Dance." In *New Directions in Dance,* edited by Diana Theodores Taplin. Toronto, 1979.

SUSAN COOK SUMMER

LEVI-TANAI, SARA (born 1911 in Jerusalem), Israeli choreographer and company director. Levi-Tanai was born of Yemenite Jewish parents but raised in an orphanage. She was trained to be a kindergarten teacher at the Levinsky Teachers' Seminary in Tel Aviv, where she also studied music with Yoel Engel, discovering her talents as a musician and songwriter.

During World War II, Levi-Tanai lived at Kibbutz Ramat Hakovesh, an episode she later considered a turning point in her life. That community was seeking a deeply rooted culture, looking for special, authentic ways to express Jewish forms in the arts, and for six years she organized holiday pageants there. In 1944 with a group from her kibbutz she attended the Dalia Festival, the first Israeli folk dance gathering; it influenced all those that followed. Her dances in *El Ginat Egoz,* set to her own music were hits of the festivals and became instant classics of the new Israeli folklore movement. In 1948/49 she taught at the Tel Aviv Seminary for Music Teachers, where she met Ovadia Tuvia, an Israeli composer, and a group of Yemenite youth who sang in his chorales. With Tuvia she created *From the Sources of Yemen,* a program using those performers. The group became the nucleus of the Sara Levi-Tanai Company in 1949; in 1951 it became known as the Inbal Dance Theatre. [*See* Inbal Dance Theatre.]

Levi-Tanai's first dances, she noted later, were connected to the earth, to her ancestral landscape, and especially to the desert. The cultural foundation for her work, she claimed, was embedded in Jewish literature. Yet, she was also keenly aware that she was working in the modern era, a different framework. In her 1980 article, "The Source of the Movement Language of Inbal," she explained that she wanted "to bring out the spiritual beauty contained in the traditional cultural values" of the Yemenite Jews, to express them "in terms of a national and universal contemporary stage language."

True to her heritage, Levi-Tanai's dances do not cover wide spaces because Yemenite dances took place at indoor family gatherings rather than outdoors. The movement is predominately vertical, with syncopated stepping patterns; the arms are held close to the body, with fluttering and decorous hand movements. Using these basic techniques, in 1953 after researching traditional marriage customs she produced her signature work, *Yemenite Wedding.* Other important works created for Inbal were inspired by Israel's landscape and peoples, by the Bible, and by Jewish liturgy.

Levi-Tanai was awarded the Prize of the Theater of Nations in 1962 and the Israel Prize in 1973. When traveling with her company within Israel or on extensive tours abroad, Levi-Tanai would often give charismatic curtain speeches about her work. Despite the managerial turnover of her company, Inbal receives municipal and state-financed support as well as support from the artistic world. In 1989 Levi-Tanai realized one of her dreams—permanent quarters for the company on the site, ironically, of her own elementary school in a picturesque Yemenite neighborhood of Old Tel Aviv. In 1990 she premiered *Your Legs, Musiah* at the Carmiel Festival in Israel. Commissioned by the Organization of Jewish Survivors of Vilna (now Vilnius, Lithuania), this work went beyond the Yemenite themes for which she is known, dealing with the Holocaust and a dancer crippled in the Nazi concentration camp of Auschwitz. In her eighties, in 1991 Levi-Tanai became director emeritus of the company, now part of a larger dance center with a greater overall ethnic dance emphasis.

BIBLIOGRAPHY

Ingber, Judith Brin. "Shorashim: The Roots of Israeli Folk Dance." *Dance Perspectives* 59 (Autumn 1974).

Ingber, Judith Brin. "The Priestesses." *Dance Chronicle* 18.3 (1995): 453–465.

Levi-Tanai, Sara. "The Source of the Movement Language of Inbal." *Israel Dance* (1980): 10–14.

Manor, Giora. *Inbal, Quest for a Movement Language.* Tel Aviv, 1975.

JUDITH BRIN INGBER

LEWITZKY, BELLA (born 13 January 1916 in Los Angeles), American dancer, choreographer, and teacher. One of the great dancers of her time, Lewitzky was also a highly articulate advocate for dance and a gifted teacher and choreographer. She studied modern dance with Lester Horton, who became her mentor and most influential teacher. In a remarkable fifteen-year association, Lewitzky became Horton's leading dancer, his choreographic collaborator, and a master teacher of his technique. In 1948 she, Horton, William Bowne, and her husband Newell Reynolds cofounded the Dance Theater, for which she created roles in *The Beloved* (1948), a revision of *Salomé* (1948), and *Warsaw Ghetto* (1949). Under the direction of Horton and Lewitzky, the Dance Theater produced many outstanding artists, including Alvin Ailey and Carmen de Lavallade. In 1950 Lewitzky left Horton to pursue her artistic development independently, and in 1951 she opened a school, Dance Associates. She was the principal teacher-choreographer at Idyllwild School of Music and the Arts from 1954 to 1972, and she became chair of the dance program there in 1958.

In 1966, at age fifty, she founded the Bella Lewitzky Dance Company and continued actively as a performer. Unlike the dramatic and socially conscious work she had done with Horton, her choreography in this period emerged with decided leanings toward pure movement. Her dancers became noted for their purity of line, strength, agility, and elevation. The company's important early works were the lyrical *Trio for Saki* (1966), Lewitzky's brilliant solo *On the Brink of Time* (1969), and the group pieces *Kinaesonata* (1970) and *Pietas* (1971). Successful appearances at the Connecticut College American Dance Festival and at the Brooklyn Academy of Music in 1971 led to extended tours throughout the United States and Europe. Writing about Lewitzky's New York debut at the Brooklyn Academy of Music at age fifty-four, Clive Barnes, then of the *New York Times,* described her as "one of America's great modern dancers."

Beginning in the late 1960s, Lewitzky was in great demand as a speaker and as a master teacher. Her incisive lecture-demonstrations with the company were a model of their kind. In 1969 the company was chosen to participate in the Artist-in-Schools IMPACT program and won high praise for that work. Her teaching was centered at the University of Southern California for a number of years. She later became founding dean of the School of Dance at the California Institute of the Arts. She resigned from that position in 1972 to meet an increasing number of requests for performances by the company.

Four collaborators in particular made important contributions to Lewitzky's later work: architect Newell Reynolds designed the set for *Spaces Between* (1974); the innovative fashion designer Rudi Gernreich contributed

LEWITSKY. Sean Greene and Kurt Fleisheimer float Nora Reynolds in Bella Lewitsky's *Greening* (1976), set to music by Aaron Copland. (Photograph from the Dance Collection, New York Public Library for the Performing Arts.)

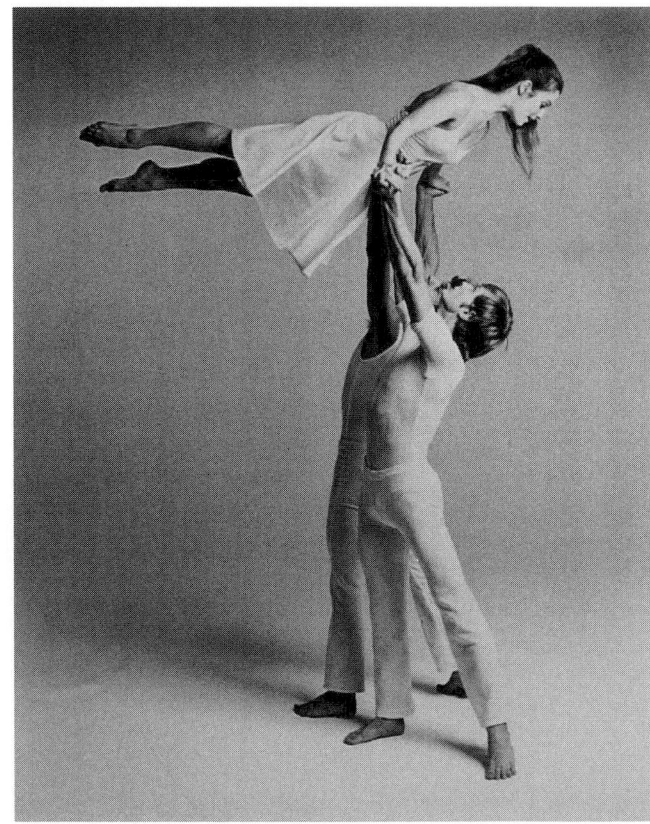

extraordinary costume designs and sets for the 1976 work *Inscape* and other productions; Larry Attaway, musical director of the company, composed many scores in the repertory; and Lewitzky's manager for more than twenty years, Darlene Neel, designed lighting and costumes for many works.

Lewitzky served on various important arts boards in California as well as nationwide. She was vice-chair of the Dance Panel of the National Endowment for the Arts for three years, and from 1983 to 1986, at the appointment of Governor Jerry Brown, she served on the California Arts Council. In 1984 she was producer of the Dance Component of the highly successful ten-week Olympic Arts Festival in Los Angeles. Lewitzky also was the recipient of numerous awards recognizing her outstanding achievements in the field of dance. These included the *Dance Magazine* Award (1978), a Guggenheim fellowship, several honorary doctorates, numerous mayoral and state proclamations in her honor, the first Governor's Award (State of California) for lifetime achievement in the performing arts (1989), the first award for dance from the Los Angeles Arts Council (1989), and the Tiffany Award (1990).

In 1995, marking another turning point in her eventful career, Lewitzky announced her "intention to pursue new projects," which would preclude her continuing her company's extensive touring and performing schedule. The company was slated to conclude operation at the end of the 1996/97 farewell season. This is an unfinished story, and only time will tell what directions this brilliant artist pursued after her retirement from the concert field. She has every intention of continuing her work in dance.

[*See also the entry on Horton.*]

BIBLIOGRAPHY

Alenikoff, Frances. "Lewitzky Looks Back and Ahead." *Dance News* (June 1978): 3.

Brown, Jean Morrison, ed. *The Vision of Modern Dance*. Rev. ed. Princeton, 1984.

Moore, Elvi. "Bella Lewitzky: A Legend Turned Real." *Dance Chronicle* 2.1 (1978): 1–78.

Rosen, Lillie. "A Conversation with Bella Lewitzky." *Ballet Review* 10 (Fall 1982): 81–94.

Warren, Larry. *Lester Horton, Modern Dance Pioneer*. New York, 1977.

LARRY WARREN

LIBRARIES AND MUSEUMS. The recorded history of dance is found in libraries, museums, and archives throughout the world. Libraries in the traditional sense are known for their printed resources and ability to lend, whereas museums are known for their image-based objects, artifacts, and depictions as well as the ability to exhibit. Archives are generally thought of as repositories of manuscripts and other print-based primary resources in which circulation and browsing in stack areas is prohibited. Increasingly, however, distinctions among the three types of institutions have lessened, as libraries exhibit holdings with greater frequency, museums incorporate in-house libraries of print materials, and archives are actively sought for deposit in both. Individual institutions determine appropriate formats based on budgets, collecting mission, and physical environment.

Dance collections are housed in a variety of public and private contexts, on college campuses, and in large metropolitan areas. They vary in size, scope, and subject specificity. Many libraries and museums consider dance a priority area for collecting and thus vigorously acquire, catalog, and preserve both print and nonprint items about dance and dancers. These unique repositories often reflect the history of dance in a specific geographic region or focus on a specific dance form, such as folk dance or ballet. Many dance archives are established through the donation of personal papers and memorabilia representing the lifetime accumulation of a dance specialist, writer, collector, or enthusiast; others, as extensions of music, theater, or performing arts collections that serve to facilitate research and study. Librarians, curators, company directors, and dancers alike are chiefly responsible for overseeing the development and preservation of collections. Items are often systematically acquired to ensure complete coverage of a particular historical period, dance style, or artist's work. Some dance companies form partnerships with libraries for the collection and preservation of company records, whereas others create them in-house.

It is difficult to pinpoint when dance materials first began to be accumulated, organized, and exhibited by institutions. Most museums possess random artifacts depicting dancers or dance rituals from ancient periods, but the oldest established collections were founded in the mid-nineteenth century. The roots of many European libraries lie in opera houses and theaters, such as those of the Paris Opera, established in 1882, and London's Palace Theatre. Still others developed out of personal collections of the aristocracy originating in the sixteenth and seventeenth centuries, such as that of the Royal Library, now a part of the Swedish National Library in Stockholm. Earliest materials included texts, sketches, paintings, costumes, and sculpture; twentieth-century collections tend to be more varied.

The elusive nature of the moving image makes dance difficult to capture and describe, and thus the field has been poorly documented throughout its history. Because there is no single, standard, universal form for representing dance movement, as in the field of music, dances have been recorded in various ways. The diversity of materials and formats revealing the richness of dance heritage is often astonishing. Books, periodicals and newspapers, costumes, photographs, drawings, paintings, sculpture, lithographs, props, scrapbooks, diaries, posters, and programs all are important pieces of the dance record. In recent decades, films, videotapes, CD-ROM technology, and other electronic resources have emerged as equally vital. Scholars piece together the past by finding clues from these various records. The wide variety of formats, however, poses problems for libraries and museums, which continually wrestle with space considerations, access to collections, and the prevention of the deterioration of materials.

Significant growth of all types of dance materials, particularly in video and film, occurred during the latter half of the twentieth century. Many libraries and museums created distinct moving-image archives that are climate controlled and house master copies of tapes. Reconstructing dances from the past necessitates the unearthing of original choreographies and creates an urgent need for accurate documentation and adequate preservation of original records. Initially it was thought that films and videos would be the salvation of the dance record, but in fact, these nonarchival mediums will deteriorate in approximately ten years without proper care.

In 1991, two separate but related groups, the Dance Heritage Coalition and the Dance Librarians Discussion Group, the latter affiliated with the American Library Association, were established in order to address a number of issues related to dance materials. Both continue to develop projects and direct their energies toward improving dance documentation, access to dance materials, preserving dance materials, and fostering education and training for individuals involved in dance research and collections.

In the past gaining access to dance materials was difficult, often necessitating a trip to the institution where they were housed. It is still not uncommon to find primary resources uncataloged and unprocessed in storage areas. In most repositories, however, items are cataloged and listed in traditional card catalogs and in archival or museum registers. Access has been dramatically improved as card catalogs are computerized and information is transmitted beyond the confines of the facility where the materials are housed.

Libraries and museums in countries that have undergone widespread economic growth and expansion generally use electronic catalogs instead of traditional card catalogs. Through digitization, that is, the transfer of data to machine-readable format, even the smallest library-archive has the potential to become a global resource. Digitizing not only serves to document the information in word and/or picture, it also preserves the data for the future and makes it accessible to other computer users. Thus within a matter of seconds a dance researcher in Indiana can learn about the collections held at the National Resource Centre for Dance in Great Britain via the World Wide Web. Full-motion video clips of dance performances can be inserted into textual documents, Labanotation scores can be created using LabanWriter software, and collections of dance photographs can be viewed via video disc technology. Future technological developments will undoubtedly enhance accessibility to a greater extent.

The following international libraries, museums, and archives hold noteworthy collections of dance and dance-related materials. All allow varying degrees of access, though in many cases appointments must be made in advance. Each is significant in terms of size, breadth and depth, and/or ownership of rare, unique items. Coverage and descriptions are sparse for countries where political conditions have restricted public dissemination of information.

Africa. Although dance is an integral part of cultures on the African continent, dance research is still an emerging field. Many libraries and museums house scattered dance resources, but no single institution has yet to target dance as a priority collection area. Some universities are, however, developing programs of dance study that include repositories for dance materials.

Egypt. Established in 1958, the library at the Cairo Institute of Ballet is an important resource, containing more than thirty-five hundred books and periodicals. The institute houses departments of classical ballet, choreography, and graduate studies. The Ministry of Culture and Information oversees its administration as well as that of another repository of dance-related materials, the Higher Institute for Theatrical Arts, also in Cairo.

Ghana. Dance and related materials are held in the Dance Library of the Institute of African Studies and School of Performing Arts at the University of Ghana in Accra.

Kenya. Research in dance is conducted at the Institute of African Studies, which is a part of the University of Nairobi, founded in 1965.

Nigeria. Programs of dance study and theater arts are gradually being implemented at the Universities of Ibadan and Port Harcourt, both of which are growing resource centers. In addition, a dance library is at the University of Calabar.

Sudan. Ballet materials are kept at the Institute of Music, Drama, and Folklore in Khartoum.

Asia

Bali. Many traditional books and materials on dance and the performing arts are housed at the Gedong Kirtya Library located in Singaraja in northern Bali. The National Dance College of Bali, located to the south in Denpasar, also has a library.

China. The Central Ballet of China at the Beijing School of Dancing has a collection of dance books. Two other Beijing institutions have significant dance resources as well, the libraries of the Chinese Theater Institute (classic opera) and the Central Theater Institute, which specializes in modern Western theater. The Center for Literary Research, Theater Division, has strong theater collections. Dance materials are also located at the Dance Research Institute and at the China National Arts Academy.

India. The records of India's rich dance traditions are located in an array of dance repositories, many in private libraries. Among the most important are the palace collections of the Maharajah Serfoji Sarasvathi in Madras, established in 1919, consisting of manuscripts, masks, costumes, props, musical instruments, and cassettes. Similar collections are found in the libraries of the Maharajah in Seraikella and Bihar and at the Temple of Chitrakoot in Uttar Pradesh.

Dance resources in the city of Madras are the Kalakshetra College of Fine Arts library and the Adyar Library at the Theosophical Society.

Several schools are home to other dance collections. Chief among them are the National School of Dramatic Art in New Delhi and the Darpena Academy of Performing Arts in Usmanpura, Ahmadabad. The latter, founded in 1948, is recognized as a center for the study and performance of the classic dance of Ahmadabad. Its library contains many books, programs, posters, set designs, and costumes. Other libraries connected to schools are those at the Academy of Dance, Drama, and Music and the National School of Dramatic Art, both in New Delhi. The library affiliated with the dance department at Rabindra Bharata University in Calcutta is yet another resource.

New Delhi is also the location of the Society for the Promotion, Analysis and Research of Traditional Arts, established in 1985. Diverse materials and subject coverage distinguish its holdings, which include masks, costumes, photographs, and objets d'art. The library located at the Indira Gandhi National Centre for Arts additionally holds many dance items.

In Purulia, West Bengal, the Sparta Purulia Chhau Dance Museum, established in 1988, houses a small book collection, periodicals, films, and photographs of dance in opera, musical theater, and festivals. It contains a unique collection of costumes and masks. Another West Bengal source for dance items is the Shantiniketan Library.

Indonesia. Dance materials can be found in the library at the Jakarta Institute of the Arts (IKJ).

Japan. The Eiryo Ashihara Collection at the National Diet Library in Tokyo consists of several thousand volumes on dance, written in English as well as Japanese. Ashihara was a dance critic who introduced many Western dance forms to Japan in the 1940s and 1950s. A published catalog of all items in the collection is available.

The Shochiku-Otani Library in Tokyo, a private facility, collects materials on all traditional Japanese theater forms, including dance; *kabuki* and *bunraku* are particular subject strengths.

The Tsubouchi Memorial Theatre Museum at Waseda University has a wide variety of dance collections. Many dance forms are covered: *kabuki,* primitive and folk dancing, *nō* and *kyōgen* dance drama, *shinpa,* and *shingaku,* among others. The museum houses programs, books, and posters and occasionally hosts exhibitions.

Other resources of dance-research materials include the National Theater Museum, the Hijikata Tatsumi Archives (Hijikata was the creator of *butō*), the Dance Collection at Ochanomizu University, Bunkyu-ku, which opened in the 1980s, and the Japan Foundation, which owns many films of *kabuki, nō,* and *jiuta-mai.*

The National Theater Documentation Service in Tokyo is linked to the National Theater and covers all traditional Japanese performing arts.

The Misono Theater Library, in Nagoya, has resources on all performing arts.

Java. A major source for materials on all arts and culture is the library at the Royal Magukunagaran Court, located in Solo.

Korea. Dance collections are found in the libraries at Sung Kyun Kwan University and Sookmyung Women's University in Seoul.

Philippines. The National Library of the Philippines in Manila contains materials about many performing arts. Other resources are the Folk Arts Center, which has regional dance materials, the library at the University of the Philippines, and the library at the Cultural Center of the Philippines in Manila.

Taiwan. Three Taipei institutions are excellent resources for dance researchers: the National Taiwan Art Education Institute, the National Taiwan Academy of Arts, and the National Institute of the Arts.

Thailand. The National Museum in Bangkok contains many performing arts items, such as theatrical masks, marionettes, and shadow-play figures.

Vietnam. The Institute of Research in Musicology and Choreography in Hanoi, which was established in 1976, supports an active dance education program as well as a library.

Australia/New Zealand. A number of repositories for dance were established in Australia during the latter half of the twentieth century.

The National Library in Sydney holds comprehensive dance collections in print and supports an active oral history program. In addition, Sydney is the site of the State Film Library, which includes materials on dance.

The prodigious Dennis Wolanski Library and Archives of the Performing Arts is housed in the Sydney Opera House. More than three hundred thousand programs are on file, as are special collections on British actor Fred Leslie; Anna Pavlova; the First Australian Ballet; the "first

Australian-born disciple of the New Dance," Irene Vera Young; and many other Australian dancers. It also contains an extensive collection of posters, prints, and slides on the history of dance.

The Gertrud Bodenwieser Archives are in the private home of Mary Cuckson in Sydney.

Additional dance resources are found at the New South Wales Conservatorium of Music, the Library of New South Wales, the Australia Council in North Sydney, and the Australian Elizabethan Theatre Trust in Chippendale, New South Wales.

The Australian Archives of the Dance, founded in 1972 in Flemington, Victoria, includes the Dr. Ringland Anderson Collection of films and the Nanette Kuehn Collection of photographs; both focus on the De Basil Ballets Russes.

Other repositories include the Australian Institute of Aboriginal Studies in Canberra and the Perth Theatre Trust as well as the Queensland Performing Arts Trust in South Brisbane, which owns the Marjorie Hollinshed Collection of ballet materials.

The Performing Arts Collection of South Australia, founded in 1979 at the Adelaide Festival Centre, retains a variety of dance items, such as costumes, slides, films, posters, and prints. The Performing Arts Museum at the Victorian Arts Centre was founded in 1982.

The Australian Association for Dance Education Resource Centre in Flemington holds more than one thousand books and five hundred journals as well as clippings, programs, posters, and an extensive oral history collection.

Europe. Some of the oldest dance archives are located in European countries with long-standing ballet and folk dance traditions. Because ballet is a codified form of dance, it appears to have left more records than other dance forms, and folk dances are often retained through the musical scores.

Austria. The foremost collection is the Derra de Moroda Archives at the Institute of Musicology, Salzburg University. Friderica Derra de Moroda was a dancer, choreographer, and dance researcher who at her death in 1978, willed her personal library to the institute. It is a rich resource of more than twenty-five hundred titles, covering ballet, folk dance, notation systems, and the Free Dance movement.

Dance materials at the Austrian National Library are in the Music Collection, the Theater Collection, and the Riki-Raab Archiv.

Dance items reside in the Library of the Institute of Theater Studies at the University of Vienna as well as in the Library of the Academy of Music and Arts. The latter, founded in 1909, offers books, periodicals, and audiovisual programs on all performing arts.

Belgium. Contredanse, a documentation and information center for dance located in Brussels, collects press clippings related to contradance as well as books, texts, programs, and periodicals. Located at Performance House "La Bellone," the center, established in 1980, houses many additional performing arts materials, including photographs and a videotape library. Much of the collection is computerized. Another Brussels organization, Folkraft-Europe, houses a collection of dance scores in Labanotation. The Dance Information Center (Dans-Informatiecentrum), an additional resource, is located in Ghent.

Czech Republic. The library at the Theater Institute in Prague includes dance materials. The Information and Advisory Center for Local Culture also houses a library. Established in 1991, it holds many dance, theater, and music collections.

Denmark. Dance research in Denmark is a dynamic, growing endeavor. The Danish Dance History Archive at Copenhagen University's Institute of Musicology, founded in 1979, holds materials covering all forms of dance in Denmark. It also has an active documentation center that videotapes performances of all types. In addition it publishes a yearbook, *Information from the Danish Dance History Archive,* hosts conferences, and reconstructs historic dances.

Dance documentation and collection is conducted also at the Danish Folklore Archives in Copenhagen, which has many video and audio recordings of field research in local and regional dance traditions.

The Theater Museum (Teatermuseet) is another rich resource in Copenhagen. Manuscripts, photographs, and costumes are found in the museum's various collections, which were begun in 1912. Subjects covered in the dance items are primarily Danish ballet and mime theaters.

The Archives and Library of the Royal Theater, begun in 1748, contain the recorded history of ballet, opera, and theater presentations at the Royal Theater. All sorts of materials are collected: costumes, programs, press clippings, photographs, designs, and more.

The Royal Library, founded by King Frederick III in 1673, contains August Bournonville's diaries and many letters, musical scores, and photographs of his ballets.

The Nordic Society for Folk Dance Research, which was established in 1977 in Copenhagen, supports studies of Nordic dance and collects dance materials.

Estonia. The library at the State Theater of Opera and Ballet of Estonia, begun in 1906, is located in Tallin.

Finland. Important holdings in dance are in the Helsinki Theater Museum, which mounts exhibitions of materials depicting Finnish dance performances. The Central Library for Performing Arts and Dance is located there as well.

France. In France, under the auspices of the National Library, the Museum and Library of the Paris Opera was established in 1882. It contains large collections of dance items, including more than fifty thousand books, thirty thousand libretti, fifty thousand photographs, drawings, scenery models, jewelry, original letters, musical scores, and some fifteen thousand costume and scenery drawings. Special archives include the International Archive of the Dance, donated by Rolf de Maré in 1952, as well as the papers of French choreographers, dancers, and impresarios, such as Jean-Louis Aumer, Emilie Collomb, Boris Kochno, Serge Lifar, Max de Rieux, and Marie Taglioni.

Other repositories of dance information in Paris include: the Library of the Arsenal, which includes theater arts and holds books, programs, and posters; the National Library, Toulouse-Philidor Collection, as well as the Department of Performing Arts; the Cinémathèque de la Danse, National Film Library; the Public Library for Information (Bibliothèque Publique d'Information) at the Georges Pompidou Centre; the library at the National Conservatory of Music and Dance of Paris (Conservatoire National Supérieur de Musique et de Danse de Paris).

The Education Institute of Music and Dance (Institut Pédagogique Musical et Choréographique) in Paris is an outstanding documentation center for dance, having amassed collections of dance books, periodicals, theses, videotapes, and photographs.

The Jean Vilar House, located in Avignon and affiliated with the National Library Performing Arts Division, is a research and documentation facility containing books, periodicals, and slides. Established in 1979, it houses a large videotape library and regularly exhibits items from the collections. The original archive, dating back to 1895, belonged to collector August Rondel, who carefully compiled a diverse array of historic records. Dance materials include documents on both French and international dancers, public balls, and technical works.

The Musée National des Arts et Traditions Populaires has dance materials relating to French rural society, mid-eighteenth through twentieth centuries.

Germany. Germany is home to several interesting dance repositories. The German Dance Archive in Cologne was founded in 1985 but actually began in 1945 as the private collection of Kurt Peters. It holds more than seven thousand volumes covering German stage dance, *Ausdruckstanz,* and other modern dance forms in Germany. The main special collections include materials on the *Triadic Ballet* of Oskar Schlemmer, ballet photos by Dietmar Dunhoft, and the letters of German dancing master Friedrich Albert Zorn. The archive holds costumes, works of art, more than five hundred thousand newspaper clippings, a postage stamp collection, dance masks from Mary Wigman's *Totentanz* and Harald Kreutzberg's *Eternal Circle,* and a historic collection of dance cards. The archive also publishes a journal, *Ballet-Journal/Das Tanzarchiv,* which is issued five times a year.

The Dance Archive of the Academy of Arts in Leipzig is just as prominent. Founded by Kurt Petermann in 1957 at the Institute of Folk Art Studies, it covers a broad array of topics in its thousands of programs, musical scores, photos, and books as well as its large film collection of ballets and regional performances. In addition the archive houses items on German folk dance, children's dance, pantomime, and prominent German dancers, much of it computerized.

The Tanzmedia München/Information Center for Contemporary Dance and Video Archive was established in 1989 in Munich.

The Württemberg State Library (Württembergische Landesbibliothek) in Stuttgart contains the Doris Niles and Serge Leslie Dance Collection, which is especially strong in eighteenth- and nineteenth-century materials. A published list of its more than two thousand items, collected by former dancers and teachers, is *A Bibliography of the Dance Collection of Doris Niles and Serge Leslie* (London, 1966; repr. 1981). Resources extend beyond books into photographs, audiovisual materials, ballet programs, and set and costume designs.

The Library at the Academy of Arts and Music, established in Berlin in 1975, has a large collection of musical scores. It also contains the Karl Heinz Taubert Collection of historical dance materials as well as manuscripts and photographs of Mary Wigman.

Other resources include: the Bundesarchiv Koblenz, the German Theater Museum in Munich, the Düsseldorf Theater Museum, and the Theater Museum of the University of Cologne, which has stage and costume designs of Les Ballets Jooss.

Greece. The Dora Stratou Society Library and Archives in Athens is a vital resource for dance photographs and films, and it supports an active education and research program on national and regional dances. The archive, established in 1953 by the late Dora Stratou, is a component of the Dora Stratou Greek Dances Theatre. It houses more than twenty-five hundred village-made costumes worn during performances.

Hungary. Sources for dance information are the Budapest Dance Archives, founded by Edith Kaposi in 1969, the Institute for Musicology at the Hungarian Academy of Sciences, the Library and Archives of the Association of Hungarian Dance Artists, and the National Folk Dance Archives.

The Hungarian State Opera Archives and Museum, also located in Budapest, houses a small collection of ballet scripts, posters, and press clippings. The Hungarian Theater Institute holds more than forty-five hundred books, vast photograph collections, manuscripts, slides, and films as well as cassettes on ballet and other dance forms.

Italy. The Dance Documentation Center in Genzano (Centro Documentazione Danza di Genzano), founded in 1985, has many videotapes and books.

Perhaps the foremost library and museum in the country is that of the Teatro alla Scala in Milan. The library, which opened in 1913, features thousands of ballet libretti, drawings, playbills, and the correspondence of prominent dancers. Volumes of Alessandro Sanquirico costume designs are at the National Library of Braidense, also in Milan. In addition, the Milan-based National Academy of Dance (Accademia Nazionale di Danza) supports a library.

The Center for Documentation and Research in Dance (Centro di Documentazione e di Ricerca della Danza), which began in 1987, is located in Turin. Alberto Testa made the original contribution of materials to this archive, which includes some rare items. Materials consist of books, periodicals, scripts, films, disks, and cassettes. Turin also is the site of the Andrea della Corte Public Library of Music, which contains performing arts documents and audiovisual materials, many on dance.

The Rolandi Collection at the Institute for Literature, Theatre, and Melodrama of the Giorgio Cini Foundation in Venice consists of more than thirty-six thousand ballet and opera libretti. Dance researchers may also be interested in the large performing arts collections at the Venice Biennale Archive of the History of the Contemporary Arts. Its numerous collections include press clippings, posters, photographs, videotapes, recordings, and disks.

In Reggio Emelia, the municipal library "A Panizzi," founded in 1796, holds many dance materials among its four hundred thousand-plus volumes and ten thousand manuscripts.

The Bucardo Theater Library in Rome has records of Italian drama, lyric theater, ballet, and set design.

The Netherlands. The most comprehensive dance collection in the Netherlands belonged to the library in the Centraal Dansberaad (CDB) in The Hague from 1956 to 1985 and was then moved to the Netherlands Dance Institute in Amsterdam to become the Netherlands Documentation Center for the Dance. In 1993 its administration was taken over by the Theater Instituut Nederland. This Dance Collection has significant holdings in both Dutch and international dance performances, and it abounds in video as well as printed materials. Master videos are stored in the archives, with copies made for viewing purposes. The book collection covers dance technique, therapy, ballroom, and dance-related topics. Special archives include materials on Anna Pavlova, *Ausdruckstanz*, Netherlands Ballet, National Ballet, Ballet van de Lage Landen, Ballet van de Nederlands Opera, Gertrude Laistikow, Corrie Hartong, and Hans Snoek. The center also supports an oral history project and holds large collections of photographs, press clippings, costumes, and programs that date from 1910. Catalogs of the holdings are available.

The Music Library, Haags Gemeentemuseum, founded in 1935, contains a dance collection, and The Hague Municipal Library has early dance books dating to before 1850.

The Opernbare Bibliotheek Theater and Film Collection in Groningen has a large collection of performing arts materials in many languages, including some ballet and other dance items. Another repository is located at the Brabant Dance Academy in Tilburg.

Poland. Owing to widespread destruction during World War II, Poland has few comprehensive libraries and museums. However, the Polish Theater Museum holds many items related to dance. Established in Warsaw in 1957, it owns original set designs for ballets and hosts exhibitions. In addition, the Institute of Fine Arts in Warsaw has a small library that includes materials on dance, as does the Wielki Theater.

Portugal. A small book and periodical collection is found at the National Theater Museum, established in 1985 in Lisbon. In addition to posters, prints, and programs, the museum features more than ten thousand reels of microfilm, a large clippings file, photographs, and a costume collection.

Romania. A significant collection of dance and theater materials is located in the library at the Art History Institute in Bucharest.

Spain. Spain's wealth of dance resources generally are found in large metropolitan areas. In Madrid, the Music Department of the National Library of Spain holds scores and programs. Dance manuscripts and pre-nineteenth-century and other old books are found in the Barbieri Collection. Other dance materials are held by the private Juan March Foundation, which was created in 1977.

The most prodigious dance collection is found in the Documentation Center (Palau Guell) of the Theater Institute in Barcelona. The center has scores of scene designs and costumes, posters, programs, and prints related to dance performance as well as one hundred twenty-five thousand-plus volumes dating back to 1913. Special collections include the Alphonso Puig Legacy of books and pictures, the Tortola Valencia Collection of programs and photographs, the Dalcroze Legacy, consisting of letters, programs, books, pictures and press clippings, and the T. Aites Archive. Another resource in Barcelona is the Center for Musical Documentation.

The Centre de Documentacio de la Generalitat de Cataluña in Barcelona contains archives of many Spanish dancers, including Llonguere's papers and the José Subira legacy. Another prominent institution, the Centre de Promocio de la Cultura Popular i Tradicional Catalana holds many dance items and features a unique database of more than twenty-two hundred dances from Catalonia.

South of Madrid, in Seville, the Andalusian Center for Theater Documentation was created in 1991 to collect, preserve, analyze, and distribute information about Andalusian performing arts. The collections contain more than twelve thousand five hundred monographs in addition to videotapes, compact discs, periodicals, programs, brochures, libretti, and more. Data in this public facility can be accessed by a variety of databases. The Andalusian Center for Flamenco is located in Jerez de la Frontera, near Cádiz. The library, housed in an eighteenth-century palace, stores books and videotapes and the archival "manuscripts and letters of famous flamenco artists. An excellent source of dance music scores is located in Granada, at the Andalusian Documentation Center for Music.

Sweden. The Dance Museum (Dansmuseet) in Stockholm, founded in 1950 by Rolf de Maré and Bengt Häger, contains primary resource materials about de Maré and Les Ballets Suédois. The UNESCO Dance and Video Collection also is housed here, in climate-controlled vaults. Adjacent to the museum is the prodigious Carina-Ari Dance Library for dance literature, established in 1969. More than fifteen thousand books, periodicals, and manuscripts are held by the museum, which has strong collections in Asian and African dance, the history of classical ballet, the development of modern dance in Europe, and European folk dance. Some records have been computerized.

The Drottningholm Court Theater archive in Stockholm was established in 1777, the same year the theater opened. The archive has significant holdings in dance, including drawings, set designs, paintings, and engravings. Registers from the Royal Theater as early as 1773 are preserved here as well, along with posters and programs. The Drottningholm library also serves as the official repository for archival materials from the Royal Swedish Opera. More recent materials at the Royal Swedish Opera's in-house Archives and Collections consist of masks, portraits, costume designs, and videotapes, among other items.

One of the oldest European arts collections is the Royal Library, a division of the Swedish National Library in Stockholm. Performing arts materials are located in the Manuscript Department, the Maps and Prints Department, and the general library. Of particular interest for dance researchers are the Jean-Georges Noverre manuscripts and the more than fifteen hundred ballet posters.

Other resources include the Music Museum, which houses a myriad of dance records, and the Stockholm University Department of Theater and Cinema Arts Library, which has a large performing arts collection. The Museum of Theatre History in Göteborg covers all aspects of opera, musicals, and dance theater.

Switzerland. The Serge Lifar Archives are located at the Archives de la Ville in Lausanne. Lifar donated them at his death in 1986. Correspondence of Émile Jaques-Dalcroze is contained in the Swiss Theater Collection, established in 1927 in Bern.

United Kingdom. Many dance collections, some long-established and others newly emerging, are located in the United Kingdom. Most reside within the London metropolitan area; however, several interesting archives are found in other regions.

The National Resource Centre for Dance at the University of Surrey in Guildford, established in 1982, offers many services as well as collections. As one of the leading dance information centers, its holdings include records from various dance companies, a Laban archive, the Claire H. de Robilant Collection (Bournonville, Noverre, and Latin American Dance), the Warren Lamb Archive, the Lisa Ullmann Archive, and records of dance associations and societies. The center also publishes a quarterly journal, *Dance: Current Awareness Bulletin,* which indexes articles from dance periodicals.

The Pavlova Museum at Ivy House in London opened in February 1974.

The Vaughan Williams Memorial Library, administered by the English Folk Dance and Song Society at Cecil Sharp House, published a catalog of its holdings in 1973. The library's special holdings include the Cecil Sharp Collection of manuscripts and books on folk dance, the Butterworth Collection on folk dance and song, and the Melusine Wood Collection of historical dance books.

Thousands of dance films are held by the National Film Archive at the British Film Institute. These include documentaries, short films, and Hollywood musicals as well as films on English dance, newsreels, films by Marie Rambert, and copies of BBC-televised dance programs.

The vast Victoria and Albert Museum, parent body of the outstanding Theatre Museum, founded in 1974, is the most extensive repository of theatrical dance history in England. Rich collections of costumes, set models, props, books, and prints are housed here, as are many special dance collections, among them, the London Archives of the Dance, Serge Diaghilev costumes, the Beard Collection of seventeenth-century illustrations, author Cyril W. Beaumont's personal papers, and the Enthoven Collection of more than one million playbills, manuscripts, and lithographs from London stage productions dating back as early as 1718. The museum mounts at least two exhibitions annually. The Department of Prints and Drawings, located in the Henry Cole Wing, holds numerous posters, paintings, and objets d'art on dance.

The Royal Opera House Library and Museum, Covent Garden, has collections of dance books, some manuscripts, drawings, and a large photograph collection. Most items document the Royal Ballet and its predecessor, the Sadler's Wells Ballet.

Company archives are plentiful in London. The Rambert Dance Company Archive, established in 1982, holds materials pertaining to the original company, Ballet Rambert, founded in 1934, as well as to personalities involved with it. Original sets are housed here, as are photographs, lighting plots, notated scores, films, programs, and items about the Rambert School. The Marie Rambert–Ashley Dukes Collection of Romantic Ballet Prints is outstanding. Records of the English National Ballet (formerly the London Festival Ballet) are deposited in the archive at Markova House in London.

Two special collections at the Library of the Laban Centre for Movement and Dance are the Peter Williams Collection (photographs, programs, and ephemera) and the Laban Collection (materials on the life and work of choreographer, teacher, and notator Rudolf Laban). The library also contains many books, periodicals, and an extensive photographic collection focused largely on contemporary dance. Conference proceedings and reports, dissertations and theses from students at the center, and videos also are available in the library, which opened at the end of 1989. Computerized data files are used to access many of these resources.

The library at the Benesh Institute of Choreology contains more than five hundred dance scores recorded in Benesh Movement Notation as well as a diverse collection of books on choreography, anthropological research, dance technique, and related topics. Established in 1962, the library has recorded its holdings in *An International Listing of Benesh Movement Notation: Scores of Professional Dance Works Recorded 1955–1985*, by Irmgard E. Berry.

Important dance materials are also found at the library and archives at the Royal Academy of Dancing, London. Among these resources is a collection of rare dance books from the sixteenth century, part of the P. J. S. Richardson bequest; a vast photographic archive belonging to G. B. L. Wilson; and the personal library of books, scores, and early dance manuals of the late Sir Frederick Ashton.

The library at the Imperial Society of Teachers of Dancing (ISTD), a relatively new establishment, has a strong, general collection that supports the curriculum of the ISTD certificate program.

The Raymond Mander and Joe Mitchenson Theatre Collection in Beckenham, Kent, is considered one of the finest in the world. Once a private archive, in 1977 it became a charitable trust, and visitors may now use the collection by appointment. It is richly endowed with ballet designs, scene and costume sketches, costumes, and ephemera.

The library of the Roehampton Institute of Higher Education in southwest London has more than four thousand books about dance in addition to clippings, films, periodicals, and videotapes. Items are accessible by computer.

The Brighton Public Library has the Angiolini-Clericetti Collection of rare books on dance.

The Knust Collection at the Centre for Dance Studies, located on Jersey in the Channel Islands, is an interesting private collection of unique items. It consists of the late Albrecht Knust's personal archives and copyrighted notation scores.

In Aberdeen, Scotland, the Central Library contains the A. Cosmo Mitchell Bequest of materials on the history and technique of ballroom dancing, focusing especially on the period between 1910 and 1930. Mitchell, who was a dance teacher, established the bequest in 1932. The book collection is comparatively small, but the collection's numerous pamphlets, periodicals, and reports provide varied information on Scottish, ballroom, and classical dance. The John Glen Collection at the National Library of Scotland in Edinburgh consists primarily of books on English country dances but also includes some manuscripts of Scottish dance music.

The Royal Scottish Academy of Music and Dance in Glasgow contains a library of books, cassettes, and compact discs. Seventeenth- and eighteenth-century Scottish folk and dance music is found in the Athol Collection at the Perth and Kinross District Libraries in Perth.

Former Yugoslavia. Dance and other performing arts materials are housed at the Slovenian Theater and Film Museum in Ljubljana and at the Museum of Literature and Theater Art of Bosnia and Herzegovina in Sarajevo. Both have varied collections of posters, programs, photographs, and videos of regional dances as well as ballet performances. The Museum of the Performing Arts of Serbia in Belgrade, founded in 1950, includes a library of seventy-five hundred volumes.

The National Theater of Croatia and the Theater Institute, both in Zagreb, have collections of dance books, periodicals, scene designs, prints and programs, and costume sketches.

Middle East. The most significant repository in the Middle East, the Dance Library of Israel, is located in Tel Aviv. Founded in 1975 by Anne Wilson Wangh, the library owns more than three thousand books, eight hundred hours of videotape and film, slides, research papers, photographs, posters, and letters. Its special collections consist of the archives of Fred Berk, Bronislav Hubermann, Joachim Stotchewsky, and Menasha Ravinia. All forms of dance are represented.

Russia and Former Soviet Republics. Archives and museums in Russia underwent massive reorganization after 1991, with significant changes made with regard to public access to the institutions as well as to their materials. Information about repositories of all types, once impossible to retrieve, has gradually become available in the form of descriptive directories, however brief. The nature of individual collections within the repositories, however, cannot yet be ascertained short of visiting in person.

The State Institute of Theater, Music and Cinematography, located in Saint Petersburg, is repository of the Gevergeev Collection of dance materials on Russian ballet as well as materials about Michel Fokine and Lev Ivanov. The Central Music Library and the Kirov Theater Museum of the Kirov State Academic Theater for Opera and Ballet also are in Saint Petersburg. The former owns a vast collection of original Russian musical scores for ballet and opera and numerous personal letters together with other papers of Russian composers and musicians. All records of dance performances held at the Kirov are collected in the library there. The State Central Archive of Literature and Art of Saint Petersburg holds materials concerned with theater, film, music, and other arts in the Leningrad/Saint Petersburg region. Another major repository is the Saint Petersburg State Museum of Theater and Music, which has divisions of photographs and reproductions, posters and playbills, drawings, prints and engravings, and manuscripts and documents.

The A. V. Lunacharsky Museum, established in 1918 in Saint Petersburg, is one of the largest holdings of theater and music materials in Russia. Among its riches are the collections of the Aleksandrinsky, Maryinsky, and Makhailovsky theaters, including personal papers, set drawings, engravings, and numerous photographs. Other archives include personal papers belonging to Bronislava Nijinska, Olga Preobrajenska, Elena Andreyanova, Serge Diaghilev, Antoinetta Dell'Era, Fanny Elssler, Michel Fokine, Ekaterina Geltser, Adam Glushkovsky, Tamara Karsavina, Konstantin Korovin, Matilda Kshessinska, Pierina Legnani, Marie Taglioni, Virginia Zucchi, and Carlotta Zambelli. Original designs of Léon Bakst, Alexandre Benois, Louis Boquet, and Ivan Vsevolozhsky also are kept here.

Another Saint Petersburg resource is the Konstantin Sergeyev Ballet Foundation, an independent organization that preserves and promotes the legacy of its namesake. The Foundation engages in research activities related to Sergeyev's life and collects and disseminates materials about him.

The State Central Archives of Literature and Arts located in Moscow, founded in 1941, holds considerable ballet material in its Arts Division. The Russian State Library of Art retains rare books on dance history as well as engravings, photographs, and picture postcards. Additional items are found at the Archives of the Office of the Imperial Theaters and at the Bolshoi Theater Museum. More than seventy-five thousand items are in the Bolshoi's holdings, including personal letters and three notebooks in which Vaslav Nijinsky described his choreographic system.

The A. A. Bakhrushin State Central Theatrical Museum, established in Moscow in 1894, is the oldest Russian theatrical museum and holds many interesting dance and dance-related archival collections. Many of them are found in the Archive-Manuscript Division, which includes the papers of more than four hundred theatrical figures in Russian history. Separate divisions house photographs and negatives, posters and programs, scene design, books, and audiovisual materials. Archives of Marius Petipa and Aleksandr Gorsky also are here, as is the Razsokhinskaya Collection of more than three thousand volumes on the history of Russian ballet.

Moscow also is home to the M. I. Glinka State Central Museum of Musical Culture, which stores dance materials in several different departments. Thirty-five-thousand-plus opera, ballet, and concert programs and posters from various performances during the period 1883–1988 are kept here, as are scene and costume sketches of musicals and ballet theater productions.

Ukraine. Dance and folklore items are held in the Ukrainian State Museum in Kiev.

A huge library of more than three hundred thousand volumes is affiliated with the Chelyabinsk State Institute of Art and Culture, where courses in ballet, choreography, and theater are taught.

Uzbekistan. The Museum of Uzbek History, Culture, and Art, established in 1874 and located in Sovetskaya, contains many dance materials. Three other resources are located in Tashkent: the Tamara Khanum Museum, a private collection of folk and theatrical costumes as well as archival materials documenting the life of the museum's namesake; the Mukarram Turgunbayeva Museum, named for the artistic director of Bakhor, Uzbekistan's premier dance ensemble; and the Khamza Institute, located on Independence Square, which houses an archive holding dance-related materials.

North America

Canada. Canadian dance archives, libraries, and museums grew significantly in the late twentieth century. Most repositories are located in urban areas in the eastern region, but some are in universities.

The University of Quebec in Montreal (Université du Québec à Montréal), Arts Library (Bibliothèque des Arts), founded in 1944, contains paintings, sculpture, and many other visual art forms, including dance. The Dance Library (Bibliothèque de la Danse), also in Montreal, is an engaging component of Les Grands Ballets Canadiens. As the official archive for the company, the library contains more than thirty-five hundred volumes concerning a variety of dance-related topics. An extensive periodical collection, piano scores, posters, photographs, and newspaper clippings have been organized and maintained by the curator, former company dancer Vincent Warren.

Other eastern-region resources are the Centre for Newfoundland Studies in Saint John's, the Archives of the

Stratford Shakespearean Festival in Ontario, and several divisions of the National Archives in Ottawa.

The Dana Porter Library at the University of Waterloo in London, Ontario, houses the Henry Crapo Collection, which includes rare manuals by Fabritio Caroso and Jean-Georges Noverre as well as other historic treatises. The Crapo Collection, stored in the Doris Lewis Rare Book Room, consists of three thousand-plus titles, most of which were identified and published in a 1983 catalog.

The city of Toronto is the home of several major, diverse dance collections. The Metropolitan Toronto Reference Library Arts Department holds an extraordinary number of books in its regular circulating collections as well as archives of posters, programs, photographs, and slides emphasizing Canadian theater ballet that are housed in the Special Collections Room. More than five thousand items, consisting of original sketches, photographs, designs, slides, notebooks, letters, and interviews, are in the Mary Kerr collection of set and costume designs. Kerr designed sets and costumes for such groups as the Stratford (Ontario) Festival, the National Ballet of Canada, and the Danny Grossman Dance Theater. Other archival collections include the papers of teacher/director Boris Volkoff, dance critic Ralph Hicklin, Ballet Academy founder Bettina Byers, Mary Wigman, and journalist/dance critic John Fraser.

Dance Collection Danse Archives in Toronto is a unique repository established in 1984 to preserve and share Canadian theatrical dance materials in electronic format. Some printed materials are published as well. Codirectors Lawrence and Miriam Adams have produced on computer the *Encyclopedia of Theatre Dance in Canada,* which contains nearly six thousand entries. Another unique Toronto archive is that of the National Ballet of Canada. Appointments are required to view the materials in this private collection, which was established in 1975. Among the items are a large collection of personal papers from founding artistic director Celia Franca and the Erik Bruhn Library of some three hundred books.

Scott Library at York University in Toronto houses research-level dance materials, which support active scholarship in the university's large, graduate dance program. The Sound and Moving Image Library on campus is a repository of dance videos. Descriptions of holdings are readily accessible through Yorkline, the campus-wide network, and further assistance is provided by the thirty-five-page publication *Dance: A Guide to Reference Sources in York Libraries.* The Sound and Moving Image Library also holds copies of tapes submitted for the Jean A. Chalmers Choreographic Award.

In the province of Saskatchewan, the organization Dance Saskatchewan maintains a strong collection of dance materials at its headquarters in Saskatoon. The University of British Columbia Fine Arts Library in Vancouver has significant holdings on the history of costume and dance. The Provincial Archives in Manitoba hold dance records from the Royal Winnipeg Ballet as well as the personal papers of Kathleen M. Richardson, a former Royal Winnipeg Ballet board member and president.

Other western Canadian sites include the library at the University of Calgary in Alberta and McPherson Library at the University of Victoria, British Columbia.

One of the largest dance collections in Canada is held by the Vancouver Public Library in its Fine Arts and Music Division. The regular monograph collection is comprehensive, whereas the program file dates back to 1905. Other files contain newspaper clippings, press releases, and posters.

The Vancouver Ballet Society, founded in 1946, has an established archive that includes newspaper clippings, photographs, and ongoing records of the group's activities. It is largely supported by donations from individuals and dance companies.

Mexico and Central America. CENIDI-Danza, "José Limón," the National Center for Research, Documentation and Information of the Dance (Centro Nacional de Investigación, Documentación e Información de la Danza) is the predominant repository in Mexico. Begun in 1983, it formerly was the Mexican Archives of the Dance. Housed at the National Center for the Arts in Mexico City, CENIDI-Danza actively documents programs in addition to acquiring both print and nonprint materials. The collections focuses on dance in Mexico, with special archives that include papers of choreographers Anna Sokolow and José Limón, dance educator and choreographer Waldeen, and sisters Nellie and Gloria Campobello, who figured in the development of dance in Mexico.

Another Mexico City resource is the Art Library at the National Free University of Mexico (Universidad Nacional Autónoma de Mexico), Institute of Aesthetics Research. It contains materials on dance and all other performing and fine arts.

General collections of performing arts books and periodicals are held at the University of Costa Rica Library in San José.

United States. Dance archives/libraries/museums are located throughout the United States. Notable repositories are found in university libraries that support graduate dance programs, a handful of research libraries and museums, and some private collections.

New York City, the acknowledged capital of dance, is blessed with an abundance of library and museum dance collections. The Dance Collection of the New York Public Library for the Performing Arts at Lincoln Center is unquestionably the world's foremost repository of dance documentation. Founded in 1944 by Genevieve Oswald, the collection comprises more than forty thousand books, four hundred thousand clippings and reviews, seven thousand videos, one hundred fifty thousand photographic negatives, and more. It covers all forms and styles of dance, from folk and modern to ballet, social, and ethnic. Numerous special collections are included; the Jerome Robbins Archive of the Recorded Moving Image is only one of several used by visiting scholars. The Asian Dance Archive includes Indonesian materials and *bugaku* manuscripts from the imperial household of Japan. Collections on American dance pioneers abound; Isadora Duncan, Ruth St. Denis and Ted Shawn, Hanya Holm, José and Pauline Limón, Louis Horst, and Agnes de Mille are extensively represented. Scenery and costume designs constitute the Rouben Ter-Arutunian Collection, and rare ballet manuals are found in the Cia Fornaroli–Walter Toscanini Collection. Lincoln Kirstein's and Lillian Moore's papers also are there, among many others. Ephemeral items include woodcuts, engravings, and oral history tapes. All holdings of the Dance Collection are documented in the multivolume *Dictionary Catalog of the New York Public Library Dance Collection* (1975) and its annual supplements. The catalog is also issued in CD-ROM format as *Dance on Disc.* Articles published since 1990 in the Dance Collection's more than fifty periodical subscriptions are listed in *Index to Dance Periodicals* (G. K. Hall). In addition to the noncirculating Dance Collection, another library of circulating dance materials is housed at the same Lincoln Center location.

The Dance Notation Bureau (DNB) library is an international repository for dance notation scores and related materials. The DNB library includes a research collection of master tapes (video, audio, and film), scores, programs, lighting plots, and other primary resources. Books and periodicals, photocopied scores, and other materials also are available for circulation, and collections are accessible electronically.

The Dance Theatre of Harlem Library/Archives consists of videotapes, programs, and books documenting the history of the company. Many additional items, such as photos and posters, also are found there. Other New York dance companies with established archives are those of Merce Cunningham and José Limón.

New York City is also home to three private archives of resources on black dance: the Ernie Smith Collection, the Joe Nash Black Dance Collection, and the Hatch-Billops Collection of performing arts materials. The formidable Schomburg Center for Research in Black Culture owns much material on Alvin Ailey and other dancers and performing artists.

The Ninety-second Street YM-YWHA, the oldest Jewish community center in the United States, established in 1874, has a library filled with dance resources. Materials chiefly document the numerous dance performances that have taken place at the 92nd Street Y since the 1930s as well as its dance education program.

Libraries affiliated with several educational institutions in New York City have cultivated collections of dance materials. The Juilliard School, Lila Acheson Wallace Library, holds many notated dance scores as well as books on technique and history. The Oral History Research Office at Columbia University owns fifty-six hundred pages of transcribed taped interviews with dancers who were in residence at the Bennington College Summer School of Dance from 1934 through 1939 and the college's Summer School of the Arts from 1940 through 1942. The Laban-Bartenieff Institute of Movement Studies Library on East Fourth Street has a small collection of titles on the subject of human movement.

Archives at the Shubert Theater are another excellent New York City resource. The archive, housed in the Lyceum Theater, contains many dance and dance-related materials.

The Dance Films Association, while not a lending library, holds hundreds of films and videos for purchase and in 1991 published the *Dance Film and Video Guide,* a catalog of the association's holdings.

Farther upstate in Saratoga Springs is the National Museum of Dance. The museum, which opened its doors in 1986, is building collections related to dance companies, personalities, and history. It supports an active exhibition program and eventually will house a resource center.

The University of the Arts in Philadelphia owns a strong, comprehensive collection in dance, including the Lattimore-Nahumck Dance Archive of books and papers. The private Charlotte Cushman Club, established in 1907, holds many dance books, programs, and newspaper clippings. Visual materials documenting the performances of the Littlefield Ballet Company can be found at the Free Library of Philadelphia.

The Carnegie Library Music and Arts Department in Pittsburgh has more than 1,750 dance books on its shelves, and the Special Collections Department at Hillman Library, University of Pittsburgh, holds unique archival materials. The Anna Pavlova–Karl G. Heinrich Collection comprises scrapbooks, original sketches, clippings, posters, and programs that document early twentieth-century dance in Pittsburgh as well as the Pittsburgh Civic Ballet. The department also houses the Curtis Theater Collection, which contains many programs from dance performances in the region.

Firestone Library at Princeton University in New Jersey houses the vast William Seymour Theater Collection, within which is the Richard Pleasant Dance Collection. Pleasant cofounded Ballet Theatre and the McCarter Theater in Princeton and was involved in numerous public relations activities throughout his life.

The Wadsworth Athenaeum in Hartford, Connecticut, holds many items related to dancer Serge Lifar. The repository also houses original set and costume designs from the Ballet Russe de Monte Carlo. The archives at nearby Connecticut College retain dance documents from the historic School of Dance and American Dance Festival for the period 1948–1968. Many photos, newspaper clippings, and publicity files also are held here.

Farther north lies the "cradle" of modern dance, Bennington College in Bennington, Vermont. Archival papers collected in the library include Bennington Summer School of Dance records from the 1930s.

The oldest established repository of dance materials in the United States is the Harvard Theater Collection, founded in 1901 by George Pierce Baker and located in the Harvard College Library. Shaped by early curator (1940–1969) William Bird van Lennep and writer-historian Lillian Moore, these dance holdings include numerous rare and important primary research collections. Prominent among them are the George Chaffee Collection of prints and drawings on the history of ballet; the William Como–*Dance Magazine* Collection on contemporary dance during the mid-twentieth century; and the Sergeyev Collection of primary Russian ballet materials from the late imperial period, including original choreographic notations and orchestral parts. Photographic collections include the Lindquist archive from four decades of dance activities at Jacob's Pillow and the Angus McBean images of British ballet in the 1930s. A vast array of other items include libretti, photographs, slides, lithographs and etchings, countless playbills, prints, and much more.

The Aphin Music Library at the Boston Conservatory of Music is home to the Jan Veen–Katrine Amory Hooper Memorial Dance Collection, a general collection of some one thousand titles. The Special Collections Department at Mugar Memorial Library, Boston University, holds the personal papers of Nora Kaye and Herbert Ross as well as other materials related to Murray Louis, Fred and Adele Astaire, Hanya Holm, Tamara Geva, and Gene Kelly. The collection of Mary Rice Morgan, consisting of rare ballet works, is at the Berkshire Athenaeum in Pittsfield, Massachusetts.

The Werner-Josten Library of the Performing Arts at Smith College in Northampton, Massachusetts, has a strong general collection of dance items, and the archives at nearby Jacob's Pillow Dance Festival in Becket, Massachusetts, is rich in the history of dance and especially in materials related to founder Ted Shawn, Ruth St. Denis, and the Denishawn Dance Company.

Archives of the Country Dance and Song Society and of the Ralph Page Collection are housed at Dimond Library, University of New Hampshire in Durham. The Page collection contains materials primarily on contradance and square dance and includes manuscripts, as well as Page's diaries and letters.

The American Dance Festival Archives located in Durham, North Carolina, holds extensive documentation of the history of the festival in the form of administrative files, press materials, slides, correspondence, artwork, more than one thousand videotapes, and much more.

The Special Collections Department at Jackson Library, University of North Carolina in Greensboro, has a unique collection of rare dance volumes from the sixteenth through eighteenth centuries. It also has manuscripts and papers of dance educators Joyce Boorman, Gladys Andrews Fleming, Ruth L. Murray, and Virginia Tanner as well as historical, modern dance, and dance notation books.

Several divisions of the Library of Congress in Washington, D.C., own a wide variety of dance materials. The Performing Arts Library at the John F. Kennedy Center for the Performing Arts primarily houses book collections, whereas the Music Division, located in the James Madison Memorial Building, contains the majority of dance holdings. Several special collections in the Music Division are noteworthy: memorabilia from dancer-actress Gwen Verdon and dancer-choreographer Bob Fosse and Russian impresario Serge Diaghilev's personal music library, including his notebooks; the papers of principal Ballets Russes dancer Serge Lifar are among them. Other special collections are rare manuals once belonging to English dancing masters, the personal papers of choreographer-teacher Franziska Boas, and the Martha Graham Videotape Collection. Additional Graham materials, specifically on *Appalachian Spring,* are in the Coolidge Collection. A unique collection of dance photographs by Arnold Genthe is located in the Prints and Photographs Division, and thousands of films and videos can be found in the Motion Picture, Broadcasting, and Recorded Sound Division.

Rogers Library, on the campus of Goucher College in Towson, Maryland, has dance and dance therapy materials.

The Belknap Collection for the Performing Arts at the University of Florida, Gainesville, houses boxes of Ruth St. Denis–Ted Shawn materials as well as documents about La Meri, many souvenir programs, and photographs.

A number of unique dance resources are located in the midregion of the United States. The Chicago Dance Archive at the distinguished Newberry Library, created by former curator Carolyn Sheehy, contains a myriad of company records and personal papers of area dancers and choreographers. Among them are the Hubbard Street Dance Company archives, records of the Chicago City Ballet and the Stone-Camryn Ballet, and critic Ann Barzel's collection of books, magazines, posters, and programs. Barzel's dance films, made as early as 1937, along with extensive video collections of other dancers and dance performances, are housed at the Chicago Dance Collection, which is a part of the Arts Department, Harold Washington Library Center. The center also has a Folk Dance Collection consisting of more than fifty loose-leaf notebooks. An index leads users to the descriptions of the folk dances from all nations. In addition, the Eliza Stigler Collection of dance books on ballet and dance history holds many titles on Spanish dance. There is also a small collection of memorabilia on Ruth Page.

The Applied Life Studies Library at the University of Illinois, Champaign-Urbana, has acquired a broad array of materials in the areas of sports, recreation, biomechanics, and rehabilitation as well as comprehensive coverage of all forms and styles of dance. It also houses a collection of twentieth-century dance programs. A large collection of personal papers belonging to dancer-choreographer-anthropologist Katherine Dunham is in the Special Collections Department at Morris Library, Southern Illinois University in Carbondale. The Dunham Museum in East Saint Louis, Illinois, also is a rich resource of dance images, instruments, and other elements of dance performance.

The E. Azalia Hackley Memorial Collection of Negro Music, Dance, and Drama, founded in 1921, housed in the Music and Performing Arts Department of the Detroit Public Library, has extensive dance holdings. Across the state, a comprehensive collection emphasizing dance history is held by the Harper C. Maybee Music and Dance Library at Western Michigan University in Kalamazoo.

Three noteworthy repositories reside on the Ohio State University campus in Columbus: the Music/Dance Library, which covers dance in a broad sense; the Dance Notation Bureau Library Extension, which is housed in the Dance Department; and the Twyla Tharp Archives at the Jerome Lawrence and Robert E. Lee Theater Research Institute Library. Tharp's collections are prodigious, and many items, such as costumes, are stored in other buildings. Records include administrative files for her company, costume sketches, programs and photographs, and videotape.

A small archive of rare dance books, primarily on ballet, is located in the Anatole Chujoy Memorial Dance Collection at the College Conservatory of Music in Cincinnati, Ohio.

The Performing Arts Archives at the University of Minnesota Libraries in Saint Paul holds records of the Minnesota Dance Theatre and the Pacific Northwest Ballet. Dance educator Gertrude Lippincott donated her personal library of books to the Saint Paul Public Library, and others have since added items to create significant holdings in dance, most of which circulate to the public.

The Public Library of Nashville and Davidson County, located in Nashville, Tennessee, owns the Jeter-Smith Dance Collection. Nashville is also home to Vanderbilt University, and the Special Collections Department of its Heard Library holds the Francis Robinson Collection of Theatre, Music, and Dance. Acquired in 1980, the collection consists of more than four thousand volumes as well as one hundred cubic feet of manuscripts, which have been identified and published in *The Francis Robinson Collection of Theatre, Music, and Dance: A Manuscripts Catalog* (1986). Signed photographs of dancers and choreographers as well as personal correspondence and playbills abound in this collection.

The Wichita Public Library in Wichita, Kansas, holds a unique collection of dance materials in its Art and Music Division. From 1968 to 1972 the American Dance Symposia were held in Wichita, and records of the lectures and performances are available here. Many prominent dance personalities appeared at the symposia, and the library has more than three hundred hours of audiotape as well as hundreds of photographs featuring, among others, Juana de Laban, Léonide Massine, Alphonse Cimber, Willam Christensen, Martha Hill, and Eleo Pomare.

The state of Texas is home to several dance repositories. The vast Theatre Arts Collection at the Harry Ransom Humanities Research Center, University of Texas, Austin, is a major resource. The Fred Fehl Collection of Theatre and Dance Photographs comprises more than two hundred thousand photographs, two hundred and fifty thousand negatives, and programs. Many Ballets Russes materials are found here, as are the Marquis de Cuevas Collection, the Bob Goldy archive of theatrical photographs, and many set designs by León Bakst, Alexandre Benois, Cecil Beaton, and Jo Mielziner. Papers of Vernon Castle, Augustin Daly, and George M. Cohan also are here, as are collections of ephemera relating to Ruth St. Denis, Katherine Litz, Igor Youskevitch, James Clouser, and the companies of the marquis de Cuevas. The Fine Arts Library on the same campus also houses a significant collection of dance and dance history materials.

The Marion Koogler McNay Art Museum, in San Antonio, holds the Tobin Collection, which is concerned primarily with set and costume designs. Most noteworthy are those of Bakst, Benois, Natalia Goncharova, Pavel Tchelitchev, and Mikhail Larionov.

The Blagg-Huey Library at Texas Woman's University in Denton contains personal papers of many early modern dancers, notably Ted Shawn, José Limón, Hanya Holm, and Charles Weidman. The archives also holds numerous oral history interviews of dancers as well as several manuscript collections.

The Dallas Public Library's Theatre, Film, and Dance Archives houses the Juana de Laban Dance Collection, which, until it was processed, consisted of sixty-three boxes and thousands of books and periodicals. Rare letters from many well-known dancers and writers are contained in the collection. Another grouping, the Mary Bywaters Collection, documents dance activities and personalities from the Dallas region. The Hamon Arts Library at Meadows School of the Arts, Southern Methodist University, holds a wealth of performing arts materials.

In Honolulu, the Hawaii Archives of Ethnic Music at the University of Hawaii concentrates its collecting efforts on dance in Asia and the Pacific. It contains many videos of dance performances as well as photographs.

The San Francisco Performing Arts Library and Museum, located in the heart of downtown, was established in 1947 by theatrical designer Russell Hartley with the goal of collecting and preserving the history of all types of dance in San Francisco. Numerous special collections of manuscripts and photographs are housed here, among them the Lew Christensen Collection, the Isadora Duncan Collection, the Job Collection of modern dance materials, and the San Francisco Ballet Collection.

The Lawton Harris Folk Dance Collection, held at the University of the Pacific Library in Stockton, California, is international in scope and features more than seventeen thousand musical scores, one thousand videos, and 13,500 descriptions of folk, square, and round dances. The Jane Bourne Parton Collection of Books on the Dance at Mills College Library in Oakland is small but holds many rare treatises on the Ballets Russes.

The Southern California region is an especially fertile area for primary research in dance. The Special Collections Department, University of California at Irvine, holds the Eugene Loring Collection, donated in 1974. San Francisco dancer and teacher Ruth Clark Lert also donated her entire library of modern dance materials, just as author and teacher Olga Maynard did with her personal papers.

The Department of Special Collections at the University of California, Los Angeles, includes the Arthur Todd Collection, donated in 1968, and a host of other manuscript collections. Many Ruth St. Denis materials are here, including a copy of her personal diary. Other dance archives include the papers of Gordon Craig, Mary Desti, Ernest Belcher, Gower Champion, Daniel Nagrin, and Maud Allan. The Henry E. Huntington Library in San Marino also has Ruth St. Denis materials.

Dancer, teacher, press agent, and critic Dorathi Bock Pierre donated her personal library of more than eleven thousand photographs, programs, posters, letters, and other dance items to the Beverly Hills Public Library with the stipulation that much of it be made available for circulation. Special items kept in a reading room reflect Pierre's extensive dance- and theater-related travels and other endeavors throughout the twentieth century.

The Goldwyn Hollywood Regional Library, a branch of the Los Angeles Public Library system, contains dance materials in its Special Collections Department. More than four hundred dance programs, most from New York and Los Angeles productions dating from 1930 to the present, are kept in files. Dance programs of Gladys Littell and Ruth St. Denis from 1947 to 1957 also are housed here, as are photographs, fliers, programs, and brochures.

Cross-Cultural Dance Resources, located in Flagstaff, Arizona, supports a library focusing on the anthropology of dance. Visiting scholars and members of the organization may use the facility, which includes books, clippings, videos, and films. Interesting collections of costumes and musical instruments are found there as well.

The Special Collections Department at the University of Arizona in Tucson holds dance programs from 1890 through 1941, including performances by Anna Pavlova, Ruth St. Denis, Les Ballets Jooss, and the Ballets Russes.

The Lloyd Shaw Dance Archives in Albuquerque, New Mexico, has been designated the National Square Dance Repository. Founded in 1977, it houses a variety of archival collections: the Dance Away Library of more than five thousand items, the C. Thomas Collection of two thousand-plus square dance items, the Bob Osgood Collection of square dance recordings, and Square Dance Hall of Fame portraits. Additional items include clothing, film and videotapes, records, sheet music, and letters.

The Lyric Theatre and Dance Collection at Golden Library, Eastern New Mexico University in Portales, consists mainly of boxes of listed items, phonograph records, periodical volumes, and a small book collection.

The Carson-Brierly Dance Library on the northeast campus of the University of Denver in Colorado is named after teacher Martha Faure Carson and dance enthusiast Justin Brierly. Among its special collections are the International Folk Dance Library, the Ballet Division, and the Oral History Collection of interviews with famous dancers and choreographers.

The Utah Ballet Archives, housed in the Special Collections Department, University of Utah Libraries, holds papers related to Ballet West as well as to the company's first director, William Christensen.

The Dance Collection located in the Art, Music, and Media Department at the Seattle Public Library contains a strong, comprehensive array of dance materials. The collection's unique features include seventy-five vertical files on local dancers and companies. Scrapbooks of Robert Joffrey, Eleanor King, Bill Evans, Pacific Northwest Ballet, and the First Chamber Dance Company are available. The collection's dance card file, which contains some twelve thousand five hundred entries, provides information on techniques, steps, costumes, and other subjects covered in selected books and periodicals.

The Cornish College Library, also in Seattle, has dance and performing arts holdings.

South America

Chile. The Municipal Ballet Archive "Elena Poliakova" is located at the Santiago Municipal Theater. Founded in 1965 by Claire de Robilant, it contains books, photographs, signed ballet slippers, and newspaper clippings.

The University of Chile Arts School supports the Library of Music and Dance (Biblioteca de Música y Danza), which was founded in 1935. It includes varied holdings in ballet and other dance forms. Additional items can be viewed at the National Museum of Fine Arts.

Uruguay. The Florencio Sanchez Theatre Library in Montevideo has a variety of materials on ballet, dance in general, and mime.

Venezuela. Caracas is home to the developing dance documentation center Trayectodanza. Its primary objective is to collect materials on dance in Venezuela, but items on all aspects of dance have been acquired as well. Since February 1993 the center has accumulated a video library and various print materials, such as posters, newspaper clippings, slides, photographs, programs, and brochures. Numerous personal scrapbooks and other donated items document the activities of Venezuelan teachers and performers, such as Henry Danton, Conchita Crededdio, and Vincente Abad. Another source of dance information is the library at the Center for Fine Arts in Maracaibo. Founded in 1954, the center supports a school of ballet and modern dance.

BIBLIOGRAPHY

Ash, Lee, and William G. Miller. *Subject Collections.* 7th ed. Detroit, 1993.

Bassett, Peter. "Archives of the Dance (15): The Library of the Laban Centre for Movement and Dance." *Dance Research* 12 (Spring 1994): 48–59.

Bopp [Strow], Mary S. *Research in Dance: A Guide to Resources.* New York, 1993.

Brinson, Peter. *Background to European Ballet.* New York, 1966.

"Centro Andaluz de Flamenco" (Jerez, Spain). Dance Collection, New York Public Library for the Performing Arts.

Cohen-Stratyner, Barbara Naomi, and Brigitte Kueppers, eds. *Preserving America's Performing Arts: Papers from the Conference on Preservation Management for Performing Arts Collection, April 28–May 1, 1982, Washington, D.C.* New York, 1985.

Collier, Clifford, and Pierre Guilmette. *Dance Resources in Canadian Libraries/Resources sur la danse des bibliothèques canadiennes.* Ottawa, 1982.

"Contredanse" (Brussels). Dance Collection, New York Public Library for the Performing Arts.

Dahms, Sibylle. "The Derra de Moroda Dance Archives at the University of Salzburg." *Dance Research* 1 (Autumn 1983): 69–79.

"Dance Archives." *Ballett International/Tanz Actuell* (June 1994): 6.

"The Dance Museum Stockholm." *Dance Research* 4.2 (1986): 78–80.

Dictionary Catalog of the New York Public Library Dance Collection. New York, 1975.

Fowler, James. "Early Dance Holdings of the Theatre Museum, London." *Dance Research* 7 (Autumn 1989): 81–88.

Franchi, Francesca. "Dance Material in the Archives of the Royal Opera House, Covent Garden." *Dance Research* 6 (Autumn 1988): 78–82.

Freese, Joan. "Dance Preservation: A Report from the Field." *Dance View* 12 (Winter 1994–1995): 9–14.

Gallico, Alison, ed. *Directory of Special Collections in Western Europe.* London, 1993.

Grimsted, Patricia Kennedy, ed. *Archives in Russia 1993: A Brief Directory.* Washington, D.C., 1993.

Guest, Ivor. "The Library and Archives of the Paris Opera Preserved." *Dance Research* 2 (Summer 1984): 68–76.

Henry, Tricia. "The Joy of Modem: Computer Access to Resources in Dance." *Dance Research Journal* 26 (Spring 1994): 56–58.

"Instituto del Teatro" (Barcelona). Dance Collection, New York Public Library for the Performing Arts.

Kahane, Martine. "The Library and Archives of the Paris Opera: Part 2." *Dance Research* 3 (Autumn 1984): 67–71.

"Konstantin Sergeev Ballet Foundation" (St. Petersburg). Dance Collection, New York Public Library for the Performing Arts.

Kopp, Leslie Hansen. "Preserve: Assuring Dance a Life Beyond Performance." *Performing Arts Resources* 15 (1990): 7–18.

Lewanski, Rudolf J. *Guide to Italian Libraries and Archives.* New York, 1979.

Library of Congress Music, Theater, Dance: An Illustrated Guide. Washington, D.C., 1993.

Morris, Geraldine. "Ashton's London Library." *The Dancing Times* (November 1994): 131.

Nugent, Ann. "For Freddy, Yes for Freddy . . ." *Dance Now* 3 (Autumn 1994): 26–33.

Penman, Robert. "Making History: The BBC Television, Film, and Videotape Library." *Dance Research* 5 (Autumn 1987): 61–68.

Pritchard, Jane. "The Rambert Dance Company Archive." *Dance Research* 6 (Spring 1988): 59–69.

Rachow, Louis A. "Theatre and Performing Arts Collections." *Special Collections* 1 (Fall 1981): 3–11.

Stark, Alan. "Research in Dance Worldwide: Mexico." *Dance Research Journal* 26 (Fall 1994): 73–78.

Steinberg, Stephen. "Dance Holdings of the San Francisco Performing Arts Library and Museum." *Dance Research* 8 (Autumn 1990): 69–79.

Troester, Maura. "Barzel Collections Are a Bonanza for Dance Scholars." *Dance Magazine* (January 1994): 44.

Ugolo, C. E. "Research in Dance Worldwide: Nigeria." *Dance Research Journal* 26 (Fall 1994): 71–72.

Vaughan, David. "Building an Archive: Merce Cunningham Dance Company." *Dance Research* 2 (Spring 1984): 61–67.

Veinstein, André, ed. *Performing Arts Libraries and Museums of the World/Bibliothèques et musées des arts du spectacles dans le monde.* 4th ed. Paris, 1992.

Willimas, Moelwyn I., ed. *A Directory of Rare Book and Special Collections in the UK and Republic of Ireland.* London, 1985.

Windreich, Leland. "Collector and Archivist Vincent Warren." *Dance International* 22 (Winter 1994–1995): 26.

Woodcock, Sarah C. "Later Dance Holdings of the Theatre Museum, London." *Dance Research* 8 (Spring 1990): 62–77.

World Guide to Libraries. 9th ed. New York, 1991.

Zidouemba, Dominique. *Directory of Documentation, Libraries, and Archives Services in Africa.* Paris, 1977.

MARY R. STROW

LIBRETTI FOR DANCE. [*To explore the use of printed scenarios for an audience attending theatrical dance performances, this entry comprises three articles. The first article surveys practices in sixteenth- and seventeenth-century France; the companion articles focus on the evolution of libretti into twentieth-century program notes.*]

Sixteenth- and Seventeenth-Century Libretti

Throughout the sixteenth and seventeenth centuries in France, the libretto was the scenario (outline or synopsis) of a court entertainment, in which spoken and sung acts alternated with interludes of dance. The libretto tells us both more and less than we might expect. It provides direct insight into the themes, characters, and structure of performance but only indirect glimpses of the dance and movement aspects of performance. Thus libretti are documents that record the textual aspects of ballet but only, incidentally, the performance aspects. Libretti are, however, important sources of information about dance in court spectacle. For example, libretti help the researcher when known dances are named; these may then be researched in contemporaneous dance manuals. Libretti also provide the social historian with information on those among the nobility who danced and which roles they performed. Occasional appended introductions provide interpretive material for the critical theorist. In the field of historical dance, where sources are limited, the libretto is a central if somewhat problematic reference.

The publishing of a libretto extended the fame of the person commissioning a court ballet performance while prolonging the luster of that unique occasion—often an event with political and social overtones. Such a motivation led to the most elaborate productions, as, for example, Baltazar de Beaujoyeulx's *Le Balet Comique de la Royne* (1581). In these cases, the libretto is essentially a festival book. Libretti published in small format were distributed to the audience before the performance. Such libretti—the vast majority—contained few if any illustrations; their purpose was to help viewers identify characters and understand the visual allegories of the performance.

Libretti have been useful in establishing the evolution of French court ballet from the late sixteenth century to the 1670s. They have indicated shifts in the relationship of the spoken or sung texts to the interlude during which, traditionally, the dancing occurred. They have indicated the shifts in literary style, from Jean Antoine de Baïf's *vers mesuré* of the 1570s, to the burlesque verse of the 1620s, to the alexandrines of Isaac de Benserade in the 1650s. They have also indicated the changes in scenographic (set) conventions, from the *scène dispersée* of composite spectacle, to the *pièce à machine* developments of melodramatic works, to the emphasis on masquerade traditions in burlesque ballet, and to combinations of these various traditions in comic ballet. Above all, libretti reveal that for about a century court ballet in France evolved significantly in style and content before the reign of Louis XIV (1643–1715) and the development of court performance as an instrument of politics and diplomacy. Scholarly focus has been all too frequently on Louis XIV's court performance and insufficient attention has been given to the traditions being rehabilitated, suppressed, or recombined from the recent historical past.

The libretto began within the larger genre of festival books. It functioned as publicity for an event and, when distributed to the audience, as part of the process of interpreting the abstruse meanings within the performance. In the absence of formal dance notation or extensive descriptions of the performance aspects of French court entertainment, libretti continue to be a major source for the study of court ballet history and theory.

BIBLIOGRAPHY

Canova-Green, Marie-Claude. "Mises en texte du spectacle du pouvoir." In Canova-Green's *La politique-spectacle au grand siècle: Les rapports franco-anglais.* Paris, 1993.

Fournel, Victor. *Les contemporains de Molière, recueil de comédies, rares ou peu connues, jouées de 1650 à 1680, avec l'histoire de chaque théâtre,* vol. 2, Hôtel de Bourgogne (suite), Théâtre de la cour (ballets et mascarades) (1965). Geneva, 1967.

Franko, Mark. *Dance as Text: Ideologies of the Baroque body.* Cambridge, 1993.

Lacroix, Paul, ed. *Ballet set mascarades de cour de Henri III à Louis XIV* (1868–1870). 6 vols. Geneva, 1968.

McGowan, Margaret M. *L'art du ballet de cour en France, 1581–1643.* Paris, 1963.

Watanabe-O'Kelly, Helen. "Festival books in Europe from Renaissance to Rococco." *The Seventeenth Century* 3 (Autumn 1988): 181–201.

Yates, Frances A. *The French Academies of the Sixteenth Century.* London, 1947.

MARK FRANKO

Eighteenth-Century Libretti

Commonly termed *le livret* in France and the program (or programme) in England, libretti are printed scenarios that list the choreographer, composers, publishers, date and theater of presentation, cast of characters and dancers, censor's stamp, summary of the story to be danced or mimed and, once in a while, the set and costume designer. They were sold at theaters to help the audience to understand the action and to establish a kind of early copyright for the choreographer. Occasionally, they mention specific gestures and dramatic movement action. For the dance historian, they are an invaluable, durable witness that often contains rare sources of information about the ballet and its artists.

Libretti are also important indications of the taste of the times and contemporary preferences for certain literary themes or expressions of a particular writing style. In the early eighteenth century, mythological and pastoral stories predominated. According to Guillaume-Louis Pecour in *Règles pour faire des ballets,* a manuscript found in the Bibliothèque de l'Opéra in Paris, "the ancient myth and fable are essential sources for a ballet. The choreographer may create a new fable but it should be based upon an ancient story." The airy, luxuriant realms of Mount Olympus provided the setting for antique gods and goddesses. Entertaining Baroque *divertissements* with fine footwork and fancy designs kept the audience's attention. Scenes were only loosely connected to the story, while magical transformations on stage were achieved with marvels of engineering. The dancing filled the eye, if not the heart. Also prevalent at the time were ballets taken from theatrical or operatic plots; they might describe an exotic tale, a historical event, or a comic story, with the heroine in danger of being kidnapped by the evil villian; in catering to popular taste, however, happy endings prevailed in practically all eighteenth-century ballets.

In Italy in the early eighteenth century, libretti provided little information about the ballets or dancers. Performances of dances, often interchangeable in the ballet repertory, were listed in the libretto as *ballo primo* or *ballo secundo,* to be performed during intermissions of the operas. A set number of ballet entries was assigned according to an artist's rank in the theater's hierarchy. A typical ballet company in a major opera house in about 1715 consisted of ten male and ten female dancers, a choreographer, a scene designer, and a costume designer. From two sheets, slightly larger than present-day playbills, the libretto grew to forty pages. The purpose was no longer simply to give credit to the ballet's creators, but to explicate the plot of the drama being danced on stage. The libretti of the middle and latter years of the century not only told the story in complete detail, but described the scenery, the use of "machinery," and, to some extent, the movements performed.

Although the premiere of these ballets might occur at court in private theaters, most were also presented at the large opera houses. The libretti show the rising importance of the ballet as, beginning in 1747, the dancers' names are listed (Hansell, 1980, p. 642). By midcentury, a company of thirty dancers was not uncommon in the most important opera houses in Italy—in Bologna, Milan, Naples, Padua, Parma, Rome, Turin, and Venice. Each of these had a resident ballet company and a ballet master who went from one theater to another, to show his brilliance and increase his reputation. Paris and London, Vienna and Moscow were not too far for these well-traveled choreographers.

All of Europe, including Russia, looked to Paris for decisions about aristocratic taste, fashion, and literary inspiration. In London, theater managers seduced Parisian dancers with the promise of more money and fame. Ballet libretti or programmes mimicked those at the Paris Opera and exploited fads and popular themes of the moment. Occasionally they reverted to English stories that told of heroic gestures from Brittanic legend.

In early eighteenth-century France, with somewhat more description of the ballets (because they were literary in inspiration), the development of the use of the *livret* is linked to the increasing importance of ballet as an independent art form. Gradually, the choreographer began to write his *livrets* to serve his own purposes—with a prologue and a dedication that clarified his personal view of the work or the problems of production. Aesthetic values were debated or apologies offered when not enough time or money was available. The choreographer/librettist was generally a highly skilled dancer, sometimes the musical composer, and often quite educated.

In making a ballet separate from an opera, and thus creating a twenty- or thirty-minute piece complete unto itself, the choreographer produced a more cohesive, coherent, and structured work. The antique unities of time, place, and action, so common to seventeenth-century neoclassic theater, were disputed but often used because they emphasized structure. All action that was too complex or that needed explanation (previously conveyed through song or dialogue) was to be avoided. The *livret* served as a means to concretize the simplified action of the ballets. In the early eighteenth century, Italian *commedia dell'arte* artists who visited England and France also influenced ballet. There was a tendency to integrate pantomime into the Baroque dance forms characteristic of ballet, which needed connection and dramatic material. In France, attention was given to this gestural technique of dance expression in *Les Horaces,* presented in 1714 at the Château de Sceaux. Act 4, scene 5, of Pierre Corneille's tragedy was transposed into a formal dumb show measured by music (Winter, 1974, p. 48). It was mimed in an improvisational way by Claude Ballon and Françoise Prévost, two performers from the Paris Opera. This radical approach to a dramatic scene initiated a more naturalistic style in which gesture depended on psychological observation and justified the complaints of eighteenth-century writers about empty virtuosic ballet steps. English artists also sought ideas from pantomimes of the time. John Weaver created the *Loves of Mars and Venus* in 1717 in London. His libretto describes a collection of dances in which the "passions" were interpreted in a clear language of gesture: "To strike the hand open, rais'd above our Head; is an exalting expression of Triumph. . . . Grief is express'd by hanging down the Head; wringing the Hands and striking the Breast."

Early on, France became the focal point of revolutionary thinking about ballet. In the mid-eighteenth century, Denis Diderot, Jean d'Alembert, Jean-Jacques Rousseau and many others collected scientific articles for what became the *Encyclopédie.* These extraordinary volumes contained articles on dance, and on ballet in particular. Louis de Cahusac, who wrote the *Traité historique de la danse* in 1754, was primarily a librettist for the opera. He wrote the article on ballet for the *Encyclopédie* in 1752, emphasizing the importance of "unity of design" and a tight and moving plot—just as the scenes and plot of a play are written, so, too, the scenes of a dance should be carefully structured in the written *livret.* The scenario would move the audience intensely by a touching story, a kind of ballet that was to be called the *ballet d'action.* Indeed, several choreographers had already been working rather skillfully with this idea. As early as 1740, Franz Hilverding produced dance dramas for the Viennese court: Jean Racine's *Britannicus,* Crébillon's *Idoméneo,* and Voltaire's *Alzira,* tragedies when happy endings in ballet were *de rigueur.* Hilverding was to have an important effect on Italian dancing masters such as Gaspero Angiolini; the connection between Hilverding and Italian dancers was intimate, and most historians believe that pantomimic dancing was well established in Italy by 1740.

Perhaps the most important figure in this discussion of *livrets* is the extraordinary ballet master Jean-Georges Noverre. He published his *Lettres sur la danse et les arts imitateurs* in 1760, urging that the choreographer write his *livrets* with form and skill. He advocated the use of a variety of subjects, emphasizing that the composer must look to life for his stories, not just to mythology and pastoral sources: peasants as well as kings have a place in ballet. If the subject is guided by suspense, new events must be used to further the mystery. Noverre worked to facilitate transitions and to ensure their logic and motives. He chose scenarios from the greatest playwrights, knowing that their work brought to the stage the truth of human emotion and "une peinture vivante des passions"—a living picture of passions. The libretto suggests and sentimentalizes experiences, and Noverre admitted that the language of dance is more allusive than directly expressive. With this in mind, he wrote sadly that without the *livret,* the audience was in the dark.

> In all honesty, I will confess that the *livrets* are the interpreters of the pantomime, which is still a baby: I shall admit that the *livret* tells the historical or mythological story and states clearly what the dance can only vaguely hint, because our dancers are not Greeks and Romans. (Winter, 1974, p. 121)

The appetite for scenarios that moved the audience to pity and tears, but that did not need the assistance of a printed pamphlet, became a cause célèbre of Angiolini, Hilverding's pupil. Angiolini sought diverse themes as the subjects of his ballets. *La Scoporta dell America du Cristoforo Columbo* (Turin, 1757), one of Angiolini's earliest ballet-pantomimes, capitalizes on the eighteenth-century fascination with exotic settings. He created ballets based on Roman history (e.g., *La Morte di Cleopatra,* Milan, 1780) and many melodramatic romances in which the heroine is abducted and only reunited with her true love in the last scene (*Le Roi et le Fermier,* Vienna, 1774).

After 1750, most ballet stories tell tales that startle and touch the viewer. Spectacle, with huge storms and dramatic scene designs, heightens the sense of wonder and suspense. Music also reflects the changing taste in expressivity. The reforms of the opera libretto initiated by Raniero di Calzabigi (1719–1795), who collaborated with Christoph Willibald Gluck (1714–1787), as did Angiolini, had their effect on ballet. More and more, instead of Psyche or Mélide, favorite mythological characters, it was Sara or Dorotea whose lives and loves were threatened by an evil lord or mayor. However, whether the subject was history, mythology, or temporarily star-crossed lovers, the tone became dramatic. The reformers had been heard, and the choreographers created ballets with a single plot, even if the libretti never adhered to the classical unities. Dramatic sensibility conquered the eighteenth century and all the elements of theatrical presentation contributed to this tight totality.

Angiolini responded heatedly to Noverre's *Lettres sur la danse* in the *aviso,* or preface, to his ballet *Le Festin de Pierre, ou Don Juan* (October 1761). Thus, in a new development, the *aviso* became the forum for an artistic discussion as well as a personal statement. Angiolini seconds many of Noverre's ideas: the use of pantomime to touch and move the audience by achieving truth, the use of good dancers, the freedom to move the body without heavy costumes, the elimination of the *divertissement.* Unlike Noverre, however, he does not believe that a ballet can be developed like a play. In the theater, a play takes three hours, a ballet only an hour and a half. In 1773, Angiolini published a pamphlet in which he particularly criticizes Noverre's fondness for an overly long and detailed libretto. In the *aviso* to the ballet *Thésée en Crète* (Vienna, 1774), the Italian choreographer argues that "the programs are . . . an abuse." If the ballet pantomimes were unintelligible without the crutch of the printed scenario, the movements of the ballet should clarify the plot. However, though the debate continued, in a sense it was Noverre who won: many-paged, minutely detailed libretti remained the norm to the end of the century.

In France, one of the more interesting developments in scenarios was the desire to interpret reality on the ballet stage. Certainly the French Revolution participated in this clarity of thinking. Jean Dauberval, a pupil of Noverre, created what became a very significant ballet, *La Fille Mal Gardée* (1 July 1789). Many aspects of its detailed *livret* reflect the romantic view of rural life and of the peasant, with background workers as important scenic accompaniments. Dauberval's success as a choreographer in Bordeaux depended upon this important change in ballet stories that sought inspiration from the middle and lower classes. Maximilien Gardel created several works that took their plot from popular stories of the "boulevard theatres:" *Ninette à la Cour* (1778), *Mirza et Lindor* (1779), and *Le Déserteur* (1784) spoke of money and love, the real interests of the middle class, as Diderot understood when he wrote his treatises on middle-class drama. Diderot consciously tried to proclaim the theater an agency of social reform and to entrust to it the gospel of philanthropy. The impact of his plays was intended to spring from their truth to nature, a truth tied to a new perception of what "natural man" and his mortality exemplified.

Even for creative artists, old ideas perish with difficulty. Pierre Gardel's best-known and most enduring ballets were based upon mythological subjects: *Psyché* (1790) claimed to have had 564 presentations, second only to *Coppélia*. In the tradition of Noverre, Gardel wrote meticulously detailed *livrets,* with prefaces that really gave insight into his personality and concerns. *Psyché* was most appreciated by the audiences of the Revolution, perhaps because it harkened back to a time of seeming plenty and harmony. Charles-Louis Didelot also wrote long, rather poetic and detailed *livrets,* but he tended to much more invention with the mythological plots.

In more southern climes, Salvatore Viganò, also a pupil of Dauberval and Noverre, fulfilled their prophecies with his archaeological correctness in costume and decoration and performances by actor-dancers, rather than dancer-acrobats. Viganò's first choreodrama, or ballet, was called *Raoul, Signor de Crechi, ossia La Tirannida Represa* (Venice, 1791). His countryman Vincenzo Galeotti was also strongly influenced by the *ballet d'action* of Noverre and Angiolini and was the first to utilize romantic themes in Scandinavia.

Thus, at the turn of the century, the ballet is marked by a strong central plot, an interest in heroes and heroines who touch the audience, large-scale spectacle with a new emphasis on music that foretells the action, and a developing freedom of technique applied to the whole corps of dancers. It was ballet that, in the early decades of the nineteenth century, helped to create the emerging current of romanticism. Without the detailed *livrets* of these descendants of the *ballet d'action,* it would have been very difficult indeed to know what those ballets were about.

BIBLIOGRAPHY

Angiolini, Gaspero. *Dissertation sur les ballets pantomimes des anciens, pour servir de programme au ballet pantomime tragique de Semiramis.* Vienna, 1765.

Angiolini, Gaspero. *Riflessioni sopra l'uso dei programmi ne'balli pantomimi.* Milan, 1775.

Barnett, Dene, with Jeanette Massy-Westropp. *The Art of Gesture: The Practices and Principles of Eighteenth-Century Acting.* Heidelberg, 1987.

Boulenger de Rivery, C. F. F. *Recherches historiques et critiques sur quelques anciens spectacles et particulièrement sur les mimes et sur les pantomimes.* Paris, 1751.

Brainard, Ingrid. "The Speaking Body: Gaspero Angiolini's *Rhétorique Muette* and the Ballet d'Action in the Eighteenth Century." In *Critica Musica: Essays in Honor of Paul Brainard.* London, 1995.

"Cahusac, Diderot, and Noverre: Three Revolutionary French Writers on the Eighteenth-Century Dance." *Theatre Journal* 35 (May 1983): 168–178.

Carones, Laura. "Noverre and Angiolini: Polemical Letters." *Dance Research* 5 (Spring 1987): 42–54.

Chazin-Bennahum, Judith. *Dance in the Shadow of the Guillotine.* Carbondale, Ill., 1988.

Cohen, Selma Jeanne. *"Freme di Gelosia!* Italian Ballet Librettos, 1766–1865." *Bulletin of the New York Public Library* 67 (November 1963): 555–564.

Cohen, Selma Jeanne, ed. *Dance as a Theatre Art.* New York, 1974.

Christout, Marie-Françoise. *Le merveilleux et le théâtre du silence.* Paris, 1965.

Chronology of Magri's Career. Compiled for Gennaro Magri session, Society of Dance History Scholars Conference, Minneapolis, Minnisota, June 1996. (To be included in the *Proceedings.*)

Franko, Mark. *Dance as Text: Ideologies of the Baroque Body.* New York, 1993.

Gallini, Giovanni. *A Treatise on the Art of Dancing.* London, 1762.

Hansell, Kathleen Kuzmick. "Opera and Ballet at the Regio Ducal Teatro of Milan, 1771–1776: A Musical and Social History." Ph.D. diss., University of California, Berkeley, 1980.

Harris-Warrick, Rebecca, and Marsh, Carol. *Musical Theatre at the Court of Louis XIV: Le Mariage de la Grosse Cathos.* Cambridge, England, 1994.

Hilton, Wendy. *Dance of Court and Theatre: The French Noble Style, 1690–1725.* Princeton, 1981.

Kirstein, Lincoln. *Movement and Metaphor: Four Centuries of Ballet.* New York, 1970.

Magri, Gennaro. *Trattato teorico-prattico di ballo.* Naples, 1779. Translated by Mary Skeaping as *Theoretical and Practical Treatise on Dancing.* London, 1988.

Noverre, Jean-Georges. *Lettres sur la danse et sur les ballets.* Stuttgart and Lyon, 1760. Translated by Cyril W. Beamont as *Letters on Dancing and Ballets.* London, 1930.

Oliver, Alfred Richard. *The Encyclopedists as Critics of Music.* New York, 1947.

Price, Curtis A., et al. *Italian Opera in Late Eighteenth-Century London,* vol. 1, *The King's Theatre, Haymarket, 1778–1791.* London, 1995.

Ralph, Richard. *The Life and Works of John Weaver: An Account of His Life, Writings, and Theatrical Productions.* London, 1985.

Schwartz, Judith L., and Christena L. Schlundt. *French Court Dance and Dance Music: A Guide to Primary Source Writings, 1643–1789.* Stuyvesant, N.Y., 1987.

Tani, Gino. "Angiolini, Gasparo." In *Enciclopedio dello spettacolo.* Rome, 1954–.

Tozzi, Lorenzo. *Il balletto pantomimo del settecento: Gaspare Angiolini.* L'Aquila, Italy, 1972.

Winter, Marian Hannah. *The Pre-Romantic Ballet.* London, 1974.

JUDITH CHAZIN-BENNAHUM

Nineteenth- and Twentieth-Century Libretti

The history of the libretto is to some extent the history of society's ideas about the communicative powers or purposes of dance. Nineteenth-century ballets often told elaborate stories crammed with incident and complicated by characters who were not always what they appeared to be. To tell these stories, choreographers accepted the aid of conventional mime and the written word. Ballet libretti were often many pages long. In the twentieth century, reformers such as Michel Fokine rejected conventional mime and insisted that narrative ballets be legible in terms of movement alone; Fokine scorned verbal aids. Under his influence, the complex personal relationships and ingenious twists of plot beloved in the nineteenth century went out of favor.

The pioneers of modern dance also helped to hasten the demise of the nineteenth-century story ballet. Isadora Duncan, Martha Graham, and others focused on basic and universal human emotions, which needed no verbal translation since they were shared by everyone. Both ballet and modern dance choreographers began to eliminate stories to concentrate on aesthetic qualities such as flow of movement, design in space, and musical relationships, qualities that are better experienced than described. Once it was no longer necessary to explain a complicated sequence of events to the audience, libretti dwindled into the more concise texts called program notes.

Nineteenth Century. Libretti were published in pamphlet form throughout most of the nineteenth century. They were distributed or sold to the audience and occasionally reprinted in periodicals as parts of reviews. Some were bilingual, often with parallel columns of text in the two languages. Because of their multitude of detail, these libretti are a delight to the historian. They provide data on the locations and dates of premieres, the collaborators, and the *dramatis personae.* Dances were often listed separately, a practice that has carried over to the programs of twentieth-century musical comedies, which often provide a separate list of the "musical numbers." The choreographer sometimes made a verbal statement about his aims in a preface or foreword. For example, August Bournonville wrote in the libretto of *Psyché* (1850): "Psyché performs no *pas d'école;* she executes neither pirouettes nor tours de force. The performance becomes no dazzling fireworks display but, if possible, a stroll through a museum where lifelike statues, groupings, cameos, and bas-reliefs alternate with one another" (Bournonville, 1981).

The libretto often prepared the audience by explaining events that had occurred prior to those depicted onstage. This enabled the choreographer to extract his plots from long stories or histories, such as the *Odyssey* or the conquest of Peru. In *Helena und Paris* (1807), Jean Coralli could thus plunge directly into the climactic confrontation between Paris and Menelaus without feeling obliged to choreograph the whole of the Trojan War.

The libretto provided an act-by-act, sometimes scene-by-scene, account of the action onstage. Descriptions of the setting often preceded each section; these could be as pithy and concise as "The temple of Diana. Evening," or they could build up a graphic image of the stage picture, even suggesting its atmosphere. Théophile Gautier's libretto for Coralli's *La Péri* describes the second act thus:

> Le théâtre représente la terrasse du palais d'Achmet. . . . Au delà, vue de Caire à vol d'oiseau: multitude de plates-formes coupées de ruelles étroites. . . . Ça et là, quelques touffes de caroubiers, de palmiers.—Dômes, tours, coupoles, minarets.—Dans le lointain, tout au fond, l'on aperçoit vaguement les trois grandes pyramides de Giseh et les sables du désert. A l'une des fenêtres du palais scintille un reflet de lumière; il fait un clair de lune splendide. (The scene shows the terrace of Achmet's palace. . . . Beyond, as the crow flies, a view of Cairo: a multitude of platforms crossed with narrow alleys. . . . Here and there some clumps of carob and palms.—Domes, towers, cupolas, minarets.—In the far distance one can vaguely see the three great pyramids of Giza and the desert sand. At one of the palace windows a light reflection twinkles; there is splendid moonlight.)

Many libretti included brief exchanges of dialogue. These were probably a literary convention rather than actual stage practice, although the gist of their meanings may have been conveyed through mime.

Since the plots of many nineteenth-century ballets centered on disguise, role-playing, mistaken identity, transvestism, magical transformations, and the like (a few examples are *Giselle, Le Diable Boiteux, Ondine, La Gipsy, Coppélia, Napoli,* and *Swan Lake*), libretti helped the audience keep track of characters and permitted them to enjoy an insider's knowledge of true identities and relationships. Even if the viewer missed the clues planted by the action, he or she could still learn from the libretto that the doll that came to life was really Swanilda in a borrowed dress, or that the glamorous gatecrasher at Siegfried's ball was not Odette but the treacherous Odile.

The nineteenth-century libretto also elaborated on states of mind that the dancers might have had trouble communicating in conventional mime. In the libretto for Filippo Taglioni's *La Fille du Danube* (1836), we see Rudolf's madness not only in the concrete terms of his "yeux hagards" (wild eyes) and "cheveux hérissés" (hair on end), but we are also given an insight into his disordered mind: "Le désespoir des autres, les honneurs qui l'attendent, s'il oublie ce fatal amour, tout l'a trouvé insensible; la gloire n'est plus rien pour lui." (Other people's desperation, the honors that await him, if he can forget this fatal love, to all this he is insensible; glory no longer means anything to him.)

More elaborate forms of the libretto, illustrated with woodcuts and engravings and enriched with critical analyses, were published in serial form in Paris in the 1830s and 1840s; these could be purchased at the theater or by subscription, like a periodical. One such series was the *Album des théâtres* (1836/37), which covered the most popular plays, operas, and ballets of its day. Another was *Les beautés de l'Opéra* (1844/45), collected and published as a single volume in 1845; an English version appeared under the title *Beauties of the Opera and Ballet* (1845). Each installment of the series, published as a pamphlet, was devoted to a single work.

Nineteenth-century audiences also received house programs, similar to those of the twentieth century. In 1847, patrons of Her Majesty's Theatre in London received a program, the first page of which resembled a playbill. Within it were synopses of only two of the evening's many offerings—one chosen from among the operas, the other from among the ballets. This meant that some fairly complex works (for example, Jules Perrot's *Alma* of 1842) went undescribed on certain evenings, the management giving priority to the newer repertory.

Toward the end of the nineteenth century, the pamphlet type of libretto became rare. A late example is the libretto for Imre Kiralfy's *America* (1893), which was copiously illustrated with chromolithographs. The closest twentieth-century equivalent to the nineteenth-century libretto is the souvenir program devoted to a single ballet, although this usually emphasizes illustrations rather than text.

Twentieth Century. Program notes have replaced the libretto, although they are occasionally omitted in favor of no explanation at all. The British critic Arnold L. Haskell has called program notes "a branch of public relations," pointing out that, unlike the libretto, they are not intended to explain the dance work to the audience; to do so would be to usurp the function of the dance. Instead, program notes should "provide a clue to the atmosphere much in the way that a drop curtain sometimes does" (Haskell, 1961).

The length of the program notes depends on the amount of information the choreographer wishes to impart verbally to the audience. Narrative works are frequently, though not inevitably, accompanied by plot synopses; sometimes viewers are left to puzzle out the action for themselves. Program notes may also consist of epigraphs, extracts of poetry or prose, or musical or historical analyses. The choreographer, composer, or another person may comment on the work. Doris Humphrey's *The Race of Life* (1938) was accompanied by the observations of *New Yorker* wit and author Dorothy Parker: "This sequence represents the life story of a man and his wife; or several days, a month or year in their life and in that of their child. Anything may be read into it or left out of it without making a great deal of difference."

Program notes may be altered from time to time, sometimes in response to the needs of the audience. In 1938, the year of its premiere, Humphrey's *Passacaglia in C Minor* was accompanied by notes that read, in part, "The music has been used as a departure point for the creation of an abstract composition with dramatic overtones." New notes published in 1940 imply a desire to rectify a misunderstanding:

> This dance is known technically as an abstraction, which is highly misleading as a title. Actually, each movement and each phrase is dramatic in origin. The dancers are expressing moods here—at one time it is heroic courage in the face of adversity, at another it is light-heartedness. . . . The mistake is to look for a dramatic story any more than one would look for it in a symphony.

The loss of a linear sequence of events in some twentieth-century choreography has required that program notes also depart from traditional narrative techniques. Events in a dance work may not move from one point in time to another; instead, they may occur simultaneously or in flashbacks. Aspects of a single character may be divided among two or more performers, and symbolism and allegory may bestow multiple meanings upon characters, events, and objects. The program notes for Martha Graham's *Deaths and Entrances* (1958) show how this type of work may be verbally presented to the audience:

> *Deaths and Entrances* is essentially a drama of poetic experience rather than a story of incident. The action takes place in . . . an ancient house on a stormy evening. The central characters are three sisters, like the Brontë sisters, and the action is concerned with their relationships with each other and with the men they have known. During the course of this violent night they relive their childhood and youth. It is a night when time is suspended, when the sight and touch of simple objects like a shell or a goblet or a vase serve to revivify memory, to bring about deaths and entrances of old hopes, and fears, hatreds, madness, dreams of romance and finally, at a peak of violence, to bring understanding.

That the twentieth-century audience still likes to have verbal explanations of the dances it sees is demonstrated by the number and popularity of books that describe the plots or intentions of the current repertory. George Balanchine himself, so often considered an antiverbalist, lent his name to the many editions of *Balanchine's Stories of the Great Ballets,* first published in 1954, which were substantially written by Francis Mason. Similar collections of stories have been made by Cyril W. Beaumont (whose 1937 work *Complete Book of Ballets* was extended by several supplements), Peter Brinson, Mary Clarke, Clement Crisp, John Gruen, Rosalyn Krokover, Grace Robert, Walter Terry, and many others. New books of this type appear as the repertory changes.

BIBLIOGRAPHY

Bournonville, August. "The Ballet Poems of August Bournonville: The Complete Scenarios, Part Five." Translated by Patricia McAndrew. *Dance Chronicle* 4.2 (1981): 155–193.

Cohen, Selma Jeanne. "*Freme di Gelosia!* Italian Ballet Librettos, 1766–1865." *Bulletin of the New York Public Library* 67 (November 1963): 555–564.

Haskell, Arnold L. "The Writing of Programme Notes." *The Dancing Times* 51 (March 1961): 348–349.

SUSAN AU

LIBYA. *See* North Africa.

LICHINE, DAVID (David Liechtenstein; born 25 October 1910 in Rostov-on-Don, died 26 June 1972 in Los Angeles), Russian-American dancer, ballet master, and choreographer. Lichine studied with Lubov Egorova, Pierre Vladimiroff, and Bronislava Nijinska in Paris. He made his debut with the Ida Rubinstein Ballet in 1928 and danced with the Pavlova company in 1930. A charter member of Colonel W. de Basil's Ballets Russes, 1932–1941, he created roles in George Balanchine's *Cotillon* and *Le Bourgeois Gentilhomme* (1932); in Léonide Massine's *Beach, Présages, Choreartium, Le Beau Danube* (1933), and *Union Pacific* (1934); and in Nijinska's *Les Cent Baisers* (1935). He is remembered for a brilliant rendition of the Bluebird in *Aurora's Wedding* and for a sensual portrayal of the title role in Vaslav Nijinsky's *L'Après-midi d'un Faune.*

LICHINE. The ingenuous charm of *Graduation Ball,* created in 1940 for the Original Ballet Russe, has made it one of Lichine's most durable works. Here he is seen in the leading male role as the First Junior Cadet. (Photograph © by Maurice Seymour; used by permission.)

Lichine made a modest debut as choreographer with *Nocturne* (1933) and followed with *Les Imaginaires* (1934) and *Le Pavillon* (1936). More successful were *Francesca da Rimini* (1937) and two new versions of ballets originally created by Balanchine for Diaghilev's Ballets Russes: *Les Dieux Mendiants* (1937) and *The Prodigal Son* (1938). The latter was considered by many to be Lichine's masterpiece for its innovative style and its remarkable fusion of drama, humor, and tenderness. In it and in *Protée* (1938) and *Graduation Ball* (1940), Lichine created the principal male roles himself; an injury prevented him from dancing the Prodigal at the premiere, which fell to Anton Dolin. In 1946, Lichine staged *Cain and Abel* for the company for its last American tour, joining them with his wife, Tatiana Riabouchinska, for guest appearances at Covent Garden and in Spain for the 1947–1948 tour.

Kathrine Sorley Walker (1983) has assessed Lichine's contribution to the de Basil company in her history of the organization, noting that Lichine fared best in those works created under the guidance of his mentor, Henry Clifford (notably *Francesca da Rimini* and *Protée*), but she laments his inability to arrive at a characteristic style. His failure to attain the status of a Michel Fokine or a Massine was due largely to his haphazard education and membership in a ballet organization with no home base. "He was, successfully or otherwise," she notes, "constantly devising new movement that looked even farther forward than the symphonic ballets—too far ahead, often, to be acceptable at the time."

For Ballet Theatre, Lichine restaged Fokine's abandoned *Helen of Troy* (1942), created *Fair at Sorochinsk* (1943), and a new version of *Graduation Ball* (1944), with decor by Mstislav Doboujinsky. With Riabouchinska he was a frequent guest star with that company between 1944 and 1955, dancing in his own ballets and in various Ballets Russes revivals. In 1955 he returned to set *The Sphinx* with Nora Kaye and Igor Youskevitch.

After World War II Lichine settled in Los Angeles and divided his time between ballet and the commercial dance theater. In 1947 he restaged *The Prodigal Son* and created *Evolución del Movimiento* for the ballet at the Teatro Colón in Buenos Aires. In 1948 he choreographed new works for the Ballets des Champs-Élysées in Paris: *La Rencontre* (an earlier version of *The Sphinx*) and *La Création,* one of the earliest ballets danced in silence. For London Festival Ballet Lichine created a new version of Riccardo Drigo's *Harlequinade* (1950); *Symphonic Impressions* (1951), set to Georges Bizet's Symphony in C; *Concerto Grosso en Ballet* (1952); *Concerti* and a full-length version of *The Nutcracker* in collaboration with Alexander Benois (1957); and *Vision of Chopin* (1959). He traveled extensively, setting ballets for the Borovansky Ballet, the Berlin Opera Ballet, and Le Grand Ballet du Marquis de Cuevas, serving also as ballet master and choreographer at the Teatro alla Scala in Milan and the Royal Opera House in Amsterdam. During this productive decade, Arthur Franks (1954) regarded Lichine as "one of the most important figures in post-1945 choreography," suggesting that stability of background would have allowed him to emerge as one of the major choreographers of his time.

Lichine's elaborate ballets for the musical *Rhapsody* (1944) were highly praised, and his work in Hollywood musicals brought him success, both as performer and choreographer. His most memorable works for films were "Two Silhouettes" with Riabouchinska in the Walt Disney production *Make Mine Music* (1946) and the ballet sequences for Cyd Charisse in MGM's *The Unfinished Dance* (1947). Lichine spent his last years in Los Angeles co-directing, with his wife, the Los Angeles Ballet Theatre and its school.

BIBLIOGRAPHY

Anthony, Gordon. "A Hero of the 1930's: David Lichine." *The Dancing Times* (November 1972): 82.

Beaumont, Cyril W. *Ballets Past and Present*. London, 1955.

Deveson, Rosemary. *Dancing for de Basil: Letters to Her Parents from Rosemary Deveson, 1938–1940*. Toronto, 1996.

Franks, A. H. *Twentieth-Century Ballet*. New York, 1954.

García-Márquez, Vicente. *The Ballets Russes: Colonel de Basil's Ballets Russes de Monte Carlo, 1932–1952*. New York, 1990.

Lichine, David. "Thoughts of a Choreographer." *Ballet* 4 (September 1947): 13–15.

Osato, Sono. *Distant Dances*. New York, 1980.

Reynolds, Nancy, and Susan Reimer-Torn. "Graduation Ball." In *Dance Classics*. Pennington, N.J., 1991.

Sorley Walker, Kathrine. *De Basil's Ballets Russes*. New York, 1983.

LELAND WINDREICH

LIEBESLIEDER WALZER. The original cast of dancers (clockwise, from the right): Diana Adams and Bill Carter, Melissa Hayden and Jonathan Watts, Violette Verdy and Nicholas Magallanes, Jillana and Conrad Ludlow. (Photograph from the Dance Collection, New York Public Library for the Performing Arts. Choreography by George Balanchine © The George Balanchine Trust.)

LIEBESLIEDER WALZER. Ballet in two parts. Choreography: George Balanchine. Music: Johannes Brahms; *Liebeslieder* (op. 52) and *Neue Liebeslieder* (op. 65), waltzes for piano duet and vocal quartet, set to poems by Friedrich Daumer and Johann Wolfgang von Goethe. Scenery: David Hays. Costumes: Barbara Karinska. First performance: 22 November 1960, City Center of Music and Drama, New York, New York City Ballet. Pianists: Louise Sherman, Robert Irving. Singers: Angeline Rasmussen, Mitzi Wilson, Frank Poretta, Herbert Beattie. Dancers: Diana Adams, William (Bill) Carter; Melissa Hayden, Jonathan Watts; Jillana, Conrad Ludlow; Violette Verdy, Nicholas Magallanes.

Balanchine's *Liebeslieder Walzer*, an hour-long marathon of pas de deux, is the choreographer's most extended, intricate, and intimate confessional about love. The ballet, entirely in 3/4 time, paradoxically combines austerity with sensuality in an intoxicating atmosphere that expresses the limitless intensity of human passion while only intimating at narrative drama. Like the similarly stirring and inscrutable *Serenade*, created by Balanchine in 1934, *Liebeslieder Walzer* springs from a deep, unfathomable well of the choreographer's imagination, out of which pours endless dance invention. Unlike the earlier work, however, *Liebeslieder's* characters are real people, not dancers, adhering to clearly defined social protocol. Thus, their emotions are conveyed ambiguously through partial, suggestive nuances.

Liebeslieder alludes to the custom of *Hausmusik*, home entertainment among nineteenth-century music lovers, for which the Brahms waltzes were composed. Part 1, consisting of eighteen waltzes, takes place in a setting suggestive of a salon in the home of a wealthy German family. Four couples clad in formal evening dress exhibit impeccable manners as they listen and waltz to the music performed by onstage singers and pianists. The dancers then retreat into a garden, and the curtain is briefly lowered. As part 2 unfolds, we see that the women have exchanged their ball gowns and slippers for ballet dresses and pointe shoes and that the salon atmosphere has given way to an unspecified celestial setting. Under a starry sky, the four couples dance a sequence of fourteen waltzes in which balletic invention expresses heightened romantic fantasy. Yet the real and idealistic aspects of love bridge the two sections: the couples in the ballroom aspire toward a passion of fantastic proportions; their ethereal counterparts remain aware of the emotional bonds they formed in the ballroom. At the end, the performers return to the salon, once more in evening dress. In the mellow glow of candlelight, they listen—enraptured and, perhaps, transfigured—to the final waltz, the only one set to a poem by Goethe.

Balanchine's ravishing movement invention to the lengthy, nonballetic score was considered daring and bold by reviewers. It was immediately hailed as a rich exploration of the waltz form and of relationships between men and women, and it has subsequently influenced the works of innumerable choreographers, among them Jerome Robbins and Eliot Feld.

After 1964, when the New York City Ballet left City Center and began to dance on the more spacious stage of the New York State Theater at Lincoln Center, *Liebeslieder Walzer* was rarely performed and was eventually dropped from the repertory, partly because the intimate setting was unsuitable, partly because hiring accomplished singers had become very expensive, and partly because an ideal cast was unavailable. The ballet was revived in 1984 in a production staged by Karin von Aroldingen as a tribute to Balanchine and Karinska. Karinska's original costumes were recreated, and a sumptuous new setting was designed by David Mitchell, based on a rococo salon in the Amalienberg pavilion in Munich. On 10 May 1984, an enthusiastic audience gave its complete approval to the assembled cast, which consisted of Suzanne Farrell (in the Adams role) and Sean Lavery, Patricia McBride (in the Hayden role) and Bart Cook, Stephanie Saland (in the Jillana role) and Ib Andersen, and Kyra Nichols (in the central role created by Verdy) and Joseph Duell.

BIBLIOGRAPHY

Balanchine, George, with Francis Mason. *Balanchine's Complete Stories of the Great Ballets.* Rev. and enl. ed. Garden City, N.Y., 1977.

Choreography by George Balanchine: A Catalogue of Works. New York, 1984.

Cohen, Selma Jeanne. "Balanchine's Waltzes." New York City Ballet program (February 1965).

Croce, Arlene. "Love-Song Waltzes." *The New Yorker* (June 1984).

Greskovic, Robert. "Making a Place for *Liebeslieder Walzer*." Playbill (24 May 1984).

Jowitt, Deborah. "The Waltz: Encyclopedia of Passion." *The Village Voice* (29 May 1984).

Kirstein, Lincoln. *Thirty Years: The New York City Ballet.* New York, 1978.

Martin, John. "Ballet: Brahms' Waltzes." *New York Times* (23 November 1960).

Moore, Lillian. "The Recent Ballets of George Balanchine." *Ballet Annual* 16 (1962): 109–114.

Reynolds, Nancy. *Repertory in Review: Forty Years of the New York City Ballet.* New York, 1977.

Tobias, Tobi. "Balanchine's Love Songs: Remembering *Liebeslieder Walzer*." *Dance Magazine* (May 1984): 38–41.

FILM. *Liebeslieder Walzer* (1961), available in the Dance Collection, New York Public Library for the Performing Arts.

REBA ANN ADLER

LIEPA, ANDRIS (Andris Marisovich Liepa; born 6 January 1962 in Moscow), Russian dancer. Son of the dancer Maris Liepa and Moscow repertory actress Margarita Zhigunova, Andris Liepa graduated from the Moscow Choreographic School in 1981. His first professional appearance took place a year before he graduated, when he danced the role of Franz in the Bolshoi School production of *Coppélia* in 1980. Upon graduation he was accepted into the Bolshoi Ballet; in 1983 was promoted to the rank of soloist.

In his first years with the company Liepa seemed to be the clear favorite of Yuri Grigorovich. He performed al-

ANDRIS LIEPA. Romeo is one of Liepa's most successful roles. With Nina Ananiashvili as Juliet, he appeared at New York's Metropolitan Opera House, 25 June 1992. (Photograph © 1992 by Jack Vartoogian; used by permission.)

most all the leading roles in Grigorovich's versions of the standard classical repertory—the Prince in *The Nutcracker,* Albrecht in *Giselle,* Jean de Brienne in *Raymonda,* Prince Désiré in *The Sleeping Beauty,* and Romeo in *Romeo and Juliet.* In 1988 Liepa was invited by Peter Martins to appear, together with his partner Nina Ananiashvili, with the New York City Ballet as guest artists. This was the first officially permitted guest engagement of Bolshoi dancers in the United States in more than fifty years. Later the same year Liepa was given permission to sign a year-long contract with American Ballet Theatre and was assured that his position at the Bolshoi would be held for him; after his return home in 1989, however, Liepa had to look for a job elsewhere. In 1990 he appeared as a guest artist with the Kirov Ballet and had several other invitations.

In 1991 an injury prevented Liepa from fulfilling his engagements. This interruption of his performing career gave him an opportunity to work on another project, reviving Michel Fokine's ballets for the Russian stage. In 1990, at a Nijinsky gala in Saint Petersburg, he performed *Le Spectre de la Rose* with great success. In 1993, together with Isabelle Fokine and his sister Ilsa Liepa, he reconstructed *The Firebird, Schéhérazade,* and *Petrouchka.* The premiere of the program took place on 5 January at the Maryinsky Theater and on 20 January at the Bolshoi Theater.

Liepa is recognized as a typical Bolshoi dancer, physically and dramatically powerful, athletic and yet lyrical. His early performances manifested some Bolshoi mannerisms that he later managed to overcome. He has sharp, light, high jumps and expressive Russian arms. As always characteristic of the Moscow school, Liepa is a noble partner who nevertheless preserves his own stage presence. He has been one of the very few Russian dancers of his generation to have opportunities to try different dance vocabularies and styles. The transition from the grand poses and aplomb of the Bolshoi style to the speed and intricate footwork of the New York City Ballet, which he had to make in just a few weeks, required hard work, flexibility, and sensitivity to stylistic diversity.

BIBLIOGRAPHY

Alovert, Nina. "Andris Liepa: Romeo . . ." *Dance Magazine* (June 1992): 32–36.

Alovert, Nina. "The Return of the Firebird." *Dance Magazine* (June 1993): 70–71.

Flatow, Sheryl. "Ananiashvili and Liepa at the New York City Ballet: Glasnost in Action." *Dance Magazine* (June 1988): 48–51.

Kokich, Kim Alexandra. "A Conversation with the Liepas." *Ballet Review* 15 (Summer 1987): 39–42.

Pierpont, Claudia Roth. "Clio's Revenge." *Ballet Review* 16 (Spring 1988): 29–43.

Verdy, Violette. "Violette Verdy on the Bolshoi." *Ballet Review* 15 (Summer 1987): 15–38.

IRINA KLYAGIN

LIEPA, MARIS (Maris Rudol'f Eduardovich Liepa; born 17 July 1936 in Riga, Latvian Soviet Socialist Republic, died 26 March 1989 in Moscow), dancer, teacher, and choreographer. Liepa studied at the Riga ballet school under Valentin Blinov and graduated in 1955 from the Moscow ballet school, where he studied in Nikolai Tarasov's class. From 1956 to 1960 he danced solo roles at the Stanislavsky and Nemirovich-Danchenko Musical Theater in Moscow. He was a leading soloist for the Bolshoi Ballet from 1960 to 1983.

Liepa's dance was remarkable for its manliness, virtuosity, broad and strong movements, and sculptural effects. The vividness of his performance stemmed from the harmony between his dance and his acting. His main classical roles at the Bolshoi were Albrecht in *Giselle,* Desiré in *The Sleeping Beauty,* and Siegfried in *Swan Lake.* Liepa excelled in roles of the modern repertory: the Devil in *L'Histoire du Soldat,* choreographed in 1964 by Eduard Suve; Ferkhad in the 1965 premiere of Yuri Grigorovich's *Leg-*

MARIS LIEPA. One of the great dancer-actors of the twentieth century, Maris Liepa was known for academically perfect technique. He is seen here as Crassus, the debauched Roman general who defeats Spartacus, a performance that won him the 1970 Lenin Prize. (Photograph from the Dance Collection, New York Public Library for the Performing Arts.)

end of Love; Vronsky and later Karenin in the 1972 *Anna Karenina,* by Maya Plisetskaya, Natalia Ryzhenko, and Viktor Smirnov-Golovanov; and Prince Lemon in Henrik Mayorov's 1977 ballet *Cippolino.* Liepa's signature role was Crassus in *Spartacus,* created for him by Grigorovich in 1968, in which Liepa portrayed an archetypal image of lust for power, violence, and evil, evoking associations with fascism.

Liepa revived Michel Fokine's *Le Spectre de la Rose* for the Bolshoi in 1967, Aleksandr Gorsky's *Don Quixote* at the Dnepropetrovsk Opera House in 1979, and *The Sleeping Beauty* at the Sofia Opera House in 1983. He directed the screen version of *Music for a Birthday* (1980), and also starred in several motion picture ballets—*Hamlet* by Viktor Kamkov, *Spartacus,* and *Galatea* by Dmitri Briantsev—as well as in dramatic and dancing roles in feature films. He also staged dances in dramas. Liepa published articles on ballet and the autobiography *Vchera i segodnia v balete* (Yesterday and Today in Ballet), in which he conveys his joy at meeting with the great choreographers of our time.

From 1963 to 1980 Liepa taught at the Moscow ballet school. In 1983 he became choreographer at the Sofia Opera House in Bulgaria. He was named People's Artist of the USSR in 1966 and received the Lenin Prize in 1970, the Vaslav Nijinsky Prize in 1971, and the Marius Petipa Prize in 1977.

BIBLIOGRAPHY

Barnes, Patricia. *Maris Liepa.* Brooklyn, 1975.

Demidov, Alexander P. *The Russian Ballet: Past and Present.* Translated by Guy Daniels. Garden City, N.Y., 1977.

Kokich, Kim Alexandra. "A Conversation with the Liepas." *Ballet Review* 15 (Summer 1987): 39–42.

Liepa, Maris. *Vchera i segodnia v balete.* 2d ed. Moscow, 1986.

Lvov-Anokhin, Boris. *Mastera Bolshogo Baleta.* Moscow, 1976.

Roslavleva, Natalia. *Maris Liepa.* Moscow, 1978.

Tarasov, Nikolai. *Ballet Technique for the Male Dancer.* Translated by Elizabeth Kraft. Garden City, N.Y., 1985. Includes Liepa's "A Word about the Teacher."

VICTOR V. VANSLOV
Translated from Russian

LIFAR, SERGE (Sergei Mikhailovich Serdkin; born 2 April 1905 in Kiev, died 15 December 1986 in Lausanne), Russian dancer, choreographer, and teacher. As a very young man Serge Lifar became an international ballet star. Gifted with intelligence and charisma, he had a profound influence on the rebirth and expansion of ballet in France, first with the Ballets Russes of Serge Diaghilev and then at the Paris Opera. His daring innovations aroused a wide variety of reactions, from glowing enthusiasm to hostility.

The son of a civil servant working for the Russian Forestry Commission, Lifar studied piano at the Kiev Conservatory of Music, where one of his fellow students was Vladimir Horowitz. The Russian Revolution of 1917 put an end to his musical studies. Despite a physique ideal for dance (the sculptor Aristide Maillol would use him as a model), he discovered dance only in 1921, when he accompanied a friend to the Kiev studio of Bronislava Nijinska; she refused to accept him as a private pupil, however, so he registered for a time in her classes at the state-run Central Studio of the Kiev Opera Ballet. He also studied expressive execution and makeup with the comedian known as Davydoff.

When Nijinska rejoined Diaghilev in 1921, she sent for five of her Kiev students to work with her, and Lifar replaced one student who dropped out. On 3 December 1922, he left Russia for France and the Ballets Russes. Lifar made his debut in Monte Carlo on 17 April 1923 in *Le Mariage d'Aurore* and participated in the creation of *Les Noces.* Alexandre Benois brought him to public attention in the role of the Boy with the Accordion in *Petrouchka,* but Diaghilev, thinking the young man undisciplined, reprimanded him for giving too much importance to a dying slave in *Schéhérazade.*

Subsequently, however, Diaghilev assigned Lifar roles as the Officer in *Les Fâcheaux* and a Gigolo in *Le Train Bleu.* He also encouraged Lifar to supplement his education in Spain and Italy and to improve his imperfect technique with Enrico Cecchetti in Turin. Lifar made such rapid progress that after an examination conducted by Diaghilev and his staff, he was made a soloist in *Cimarosiana* and *La Boutique Fantasque.* His creation of Boreas in *Zéphire et Flore* (1925) won him the position of first dancer, as the successor to Anatole Vilzak. He continued to improve, studying with Vera Trefilova, Lubov Egorova, and Nikolai Legat, but he owed his triumph as the French Sailor in *Les Matelots* to his youthful spontaneity, and his success as the Officer in *Barabau* to his charisma. After Anton Dolin's departure from the company, Lifar became its chief male star.

Lifar brought a great range of talents to Diaghilev's ballets. His performances with Vera Nemchinova in the company's one-act version of *Swan Lake* (revived in 1924) served as his initiation into the classical repertory as a soloist. In a company otherwise noted for the domination of its male stars, Lifar's partnering showcased the feminine lyricism of Tamara Karsavina in *Romeo and Juliet* and of Olga Spessivtseva in *The Firebird.* He performed in the brutal *Pas d'Acier* and the intellectual *Ode.* George Balanchine called attention to his athletic harmony in *La Chatte* and cast him in the idealized title role of *Apollon Musagète* (dedicated to Lifar by the composer Igor Stravinsky), which glorified Lifar's radiant elevation.

At Diaghilev's urging, Lifar finally made his debut as a choreographer with the acrobatic *Le Renard,* to music by Stravinsky. The year 1929 held other milestones for him—his performance in the title role of Balanchine's new work

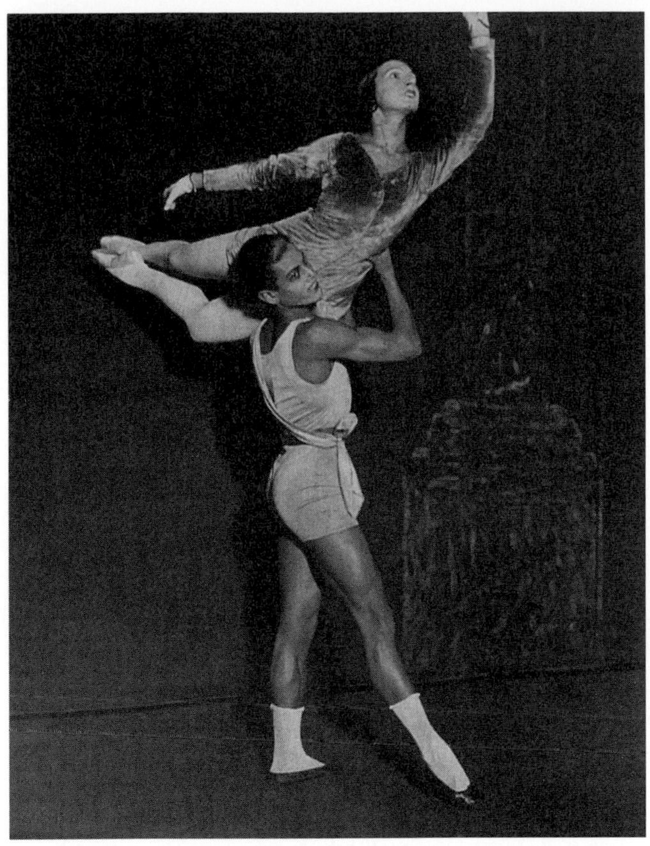

LIFAR. As the leading Athlete in Bronislava Nijinksa's *Les Biches* (1924), Lifar carries Vera Nemchinova as La Garçonne. (Photograph © by *The* (London) *Times;* from the Dance Collection, New York Public Library for the Performing Arts.)

The Prodigal Son, in which Lifar gave free rein to his dramatic passion, and the death of Diaghilev, his spiritual father, resulting in the dispersal of the Ballets Russes.

Lifar's long association with the Paris Opera began in 1929 through a commission by the Opera's director, Jacques Rouché, to choreograph a new version of *The Creatures of Prometheus,* set to the original score by Beethoven. (Lifar was originally engaged to dance Prometheus, but his role expanded when Balanchine, the commissioned choreographer, fell ill.) Charmed by the hero, Lifar restructured the story to strengthen his part, to the outrage of the librettists. He also introduced technical innovations into the role, including falls and double *tours en l'air* with folded and crossed legs. The figure of Prometheus would be prophetic: like the firegiver of myth, Lifar would bring new fire and life to French ballet.

In 1930 Lifar traveled to London to perform with Cochran's Revue, dancing in several pieces by Balanchine and choreographing *La Nuit* (music by Henri Sauguet, design by Christian Bérard). On Lifar's return to the Paris Opera in 1931, Rouché made him both ballet master and first dancer. That year Lifar staged various lesser works; he then surprised the critics and subscription audiences with his daring inventions in *Bacchus et Ariadne,* set to music by Albert Roussel and designed by Giorgio de'Chirico, particularly in the pas de deux, which he danced with Spessivtseva in the center of a labyrinth created by the legs of sixteen female dancers lying on the floor. Lifar's audacities as a novice choreographer could be clumsy, but his early audiences were induced to accept them by his exceptional performing qualities.

At the Paris Opera Lifar encouraged the rehabilitation of male dancing. At first he tended to use the corps de ballet as a backdrop to the soloists, but as the corps improved, he showcased their developing capabilities in more striking choreography. Thanks to Rouché's constant and enlightened support, Lifar was gradually able to impose indispensable reforms on the Opera; he had the house chandeliers extinguished during performances, and he made the male dancers shave off their mustaches and the ballerinas cease wearing personal jewelry onstage. He

LIFAR. George Balanchine's *The Prodigal Son* (1929), the last production of Diaghilev's Ballets Russes, provided Lifar with one of his most famous roles. In this scene, Lifar (The Prodigal Son) is restrained by Anton Dolin and Léon Woizikowski (Servants to the Prodigal Son). (Photograph from the Dance Collection, New York Public Library for the Performing Arts. Choreography by George Balanchine © The George Balanchine Trust.)

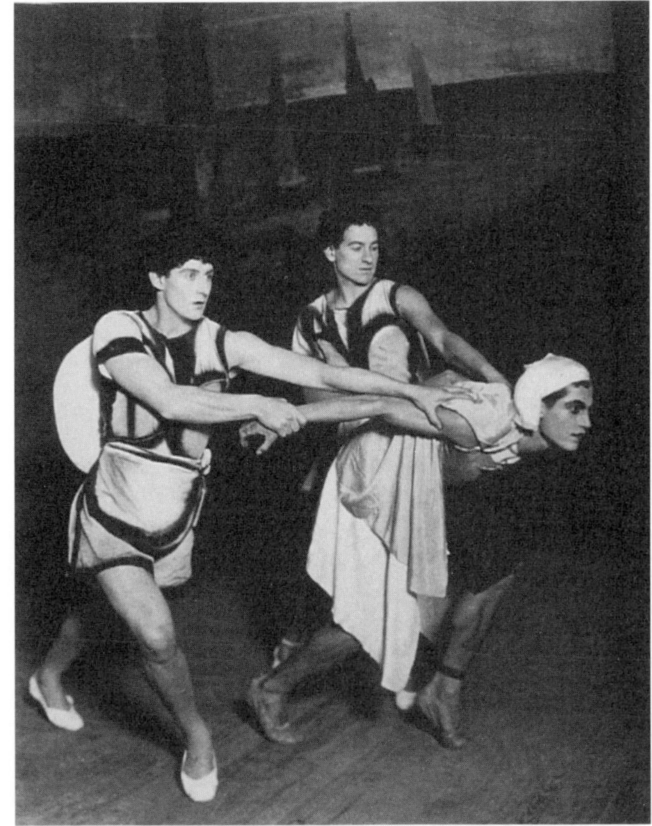

closed the Foyer de la Danse (rehearsal hall) to the public; it had been infamous as a meeting ground for ballet girls and their predatory admirers. The dominance of opera was weakened by the inauguration of a full evening of ballet every Wednesday, along with special ballet months. The critic Anna Kisselgoff wrote, "He made the ballerinas dance on pointe when they often preferred demi-pointe." Kisselgoff also noted that Lifar "asked his ballerinas to knuckle over on toe, to achieve an off-center look that rendered the old ballet silhouettes more dynamic." He added two new positions to ballet's basic five—sixth, with feet together and parallel, and seventh, with feet parallel in a slight stride.

After 1932 Lifar endeavored to gain the goodwill of classicism's defenders, including the critic André Levinson, who had demanded, "Banish this barbarian from our national academy!" Levinson nonetheless applauded Lifar's restagings of *Le Spectre de la Rose,* excerpts from *The Sleeping Beauty* (under the title *Divertissement de Petipa*), and the mazurka from *Les Sylphides,* which Lifar introduced into his *Suite de Danses.*

With his favorite partner, Spessivtseva, he restaged *Giselle;* in it, guided by Pierre Vladimiroff, he would for twenty-five years be the most affecting of Albrechts, bringing the character from insouciant spontaneity to overwhelming passion. Especially notable was his second-act *entrée* with lilies and a long, trailing cloak. He also focused on other performers. Anxious to revive the French classical school, he started an adagio class at the Paris Opera, turning it into a laboratory in which he developed his neoclassical style and forged a new generation of dancers. Kisselgoff wrote that Lifar sent many of his dancers to study with the Russian emigré teachers of Paris "to soften the Milanese influences in the Paris Opéra School."

Extroverted in temperament, Lifar always tried to make dance an expression of action or feelings, in the manner of the eighteenth-century choreographer Jean-Georges Noverre. There were two principal emphases in his work, heroic ballets and ballet comedies. He exploited both genres in alternation, almost abandoning abstraction but never ceasing to integrate dramatic expression with formal concerns. In *La Vie de Polichinelle* (1934), to music by Nicolas Nabokov, he demonstrated a new flexibility, arranging the dancers on several superimposed stage levels while the mischievous Polichinelle bounded from one level—and situation—to another.

The year 1935 was another milestone. The verve of *Polichinelle* was repeated by Suzanne Lorcia and Serge Peretti in Lifar's well-received *Salade,* and he achieved a new sensual expressiveness as a solo performer with *Prélude à L'Après-midi d'un Faune.* In his 1935 book *Manifeste du chorégraphe,* he defended the primacy of the choreographic element in ballet over decor and music; he illustrated his theory onstage in his ballet *Icare,* performed to a stark percussion score (by Arthur Honegger and Georges Szyfer) of rhythmic counts based on the bodily rhythms that inspired the dance. *Icare* was one of Lifar's masterpieces, immediately bringing him public acclaim.

The heroic cycle Lifar began with *Icare* continued with *David Triomphant* (1937), to music by Vittorio Rieti, design by Fernand Léger, *Alexandre le Grand* (1937), to music by Philippe Gaubert, and *Aenéas* (1938), set to music by Roussel. These ballets spotlighted his partners—Yvette Chauviré, Solange Schwarz, and Suzanne Lorcia—in a wide variety of adagios and gave the corps de ballet an increasingly dramatic presence. Gradually developing the importance of female dance in his work, Lifar gave Lycette Darsonval the title role in *Oriane et le Prince d'Amour* (1938), to music by Florent Schmitt; he transformed Schwarz into a Degas dancer, with himself as Apollo, in *Entre Deux Rondes* (1940), set to music by Marcel Samuel-Rousseau.

During the German occupation of France, Lifar emphasized the autonomy of French ballet with a restaging of *Sylvia* (1941) and with intense activity that produced several masterpieces. *Le Chevalier et la Damoiselle* (1941), to music by Gaubert, evoked the legend of a fawn princess, danced by Schwarz, rescued by Lifar as a knight-errant. Exceptionally original, this ballet featured medieval animal stylization, a triple duel, and adagios. Also during 1941, Lifar dedicated to Chauviré his perilous and symbolic variation, *Istar,* to music by Vincent d'Indy, and he portrayed bullfighting in *Boléro,* set to the music of Maurice Ravel.

The next year, in the Burgundian drama *Joan de Zarissa* (1942), to music by Werner Egk, the entire company was galvanized around a triumphant Lifar as a seducer-revolutionary. "Lifar's demoniac Don Juan drags love to death as an appointed victim," wrote Jean Cocteau, "but a victim that finds the forces of revolt within itself right to the end." His *Les Animaux Modèles* (1942), libretto from Jean de La Fontaine, set to music by Francis Poulenc, represented France in its golden age, while *L'Amour Sorcier* (1943), to music by Manuel de Falla, evoked a Spain embodied by Teresina, and served as the debut of Roland Petit.

Eager to discover and encourage new talents, Lifar created *Romeo and Juliet* (1942) with Ludmilla Tcherina; and for his students Janine Charrat, Petit, Zizi Jeanmaire, and Colette Marchand, he staged variations and adagios, sometimes set to poems. For the Paris Opera, he designed the uncharacteristically abstract *Suite en Blanc* (1943), to music by Édouard Lalo, based on *Namouna;* its exemplary variations often appeared as excerpts in ballet competitions. In *Guignol et Pandore* (1944), to music by André Jolivet, the story of two Lyon marionettes, Lifar revived his comedic strain. The metaphysical *Mirages* (1944), to music by Sauguet, a project for Chauviré and Michel Renault, was probably Lifar's most perfect ballet.

After the liberation, Lifar was accused of having collaborated with the Nazis (it remains unclear whether he actually was guilty) and was dismissed from the Paris Opera, along with Rouché. Nevertheless, Lifar's energy continued unabated. He left Paris in 1945 to found and direct the Nouveau Ballet de Monte Carlo, where he was joined by his faithful disciples Chauviré, Charrat, Jeanmaire, Olga Adabache, Alexandre Kalioujny, and Vladimir Skouratoff. In 1946 for that company he choreographed five ballets: *Aubade,* to music by Poulenc, *Dramma per Musica,* to music by Bach, *Chota Roustaveli,* to music by Honegger and others, *La Péri,* to music by Paul Dukas, and *Night on the Bare Mountain,* set to music by Modest Mussorgsky. *Nautéos* (1947), to music by Jeanne Leleu, was subsequently restaged at the Paris Opera. The brilliance of Lifar's Monaco seasons, his tours, and persistent demand among both the general public and ballet circles brought his recall to the Paris Opera in 1947, first as ballet master and then, in 1949, as a performer. During this second period, however, his autonomy was reduced by the presence of other administrators, official regulations, and prescribed casting, with a resulting unevenness in his abundant output.

Lifar's *Septuor* (1950), to music by Letèce, was dedicated to the hopes of the ballet. During this period he also produced the oratorio *Jeanne au Bûcher* (1950), to music by Egk, *Le Chevalier Errant* (1950), to music by Jacques Ibert, and, most notably, *Phèdre* (1950), to music by Georges Auric, design by Jean Cocteau, a stylization of the Greek tragedy, to which its performers, including Tamara Toumanova and Nina Vyroubova, did ample justice. The three-act *Snow White* (1951), to music by Maurice Yvain, represented an attempt to return to the genre of the fairy-tale ballet; *Fourberies* (1952), to music by Rossini, harked back to the spirit of Molière.

While still performing himself, Lifar also did justice to his dancers Chauviré and Vyroubova, particularly in *Variations* and *Grand Pas* (1953). This period was dominated by his *Les Noces Fantastiques* (1954) set to music by Marcel Delannoy; its inventive richness and exceptional performances eclipsed even his *Firebird* (1954), to music by Stravinsky. Lifar's last noteworthy creation for the Opera was the allegorical *Chemin de Lumière* (1957), to music by Auric. In 1957 he left the company again, this time over a disagreement with the director. From that time he traveled widely, setting new work for companies in Europe and South America. For Le Grand Ballet du Marquis de Cuevas, for instance, he choreographed *L'Amour et Son Destin* (1957), to music by Tchaikovsky.

Over the three decades between his second departure from the Opera and his death, Lifar returned to the company only three times, but it continued to be his preferred setting, despite his differences with its administrators. Here he staged *Le Grand Cirque* (1969), in which Michaël Denard came to public attention. In 1977 Lifar featured

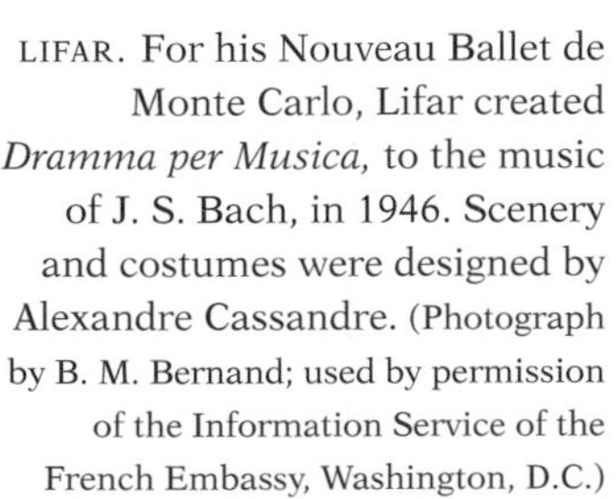

LIFAR. For his Nouveau Ballet de Monte Carlo, Lifar created *Dramma per Musica,* to the music of J. S. Bach, in 1946. Scenery and costumes were designed by Alexandre Cassandre. (Photograph by B. M. Bernand; used by permission of the Information Service of the French Embassy, Washington, D.C.)

the troupe in the kind of spectacle demanded by the public but too seldom offered by the Paris Opera.

Despite his longstanding desire for notational and film records (in 1943 he had proposed a film library of dance), Lifar's works go unrecorded. Modeled from life, they have been passed on by oral tradition alone, and like his style they appear vulnerable to erosion over time. Nevertheless, they are milestones in the development of European ballet.

To train his performers and to keep the public informed, Lifar brought dance into the Sorbonne, Paris's great university. In 1947 he founded the Institut Chorégraphique, now the Université de la Danse, which awards prizes and organizes conferences, demonstrations, and retrospectives. In 1953 he revived the Académie de Danse, founded in 1661, and invited Balanchine, Léonide Massine, Frederick Ashton, and other leading figures to it. He designed, published articles, and wrote twenty-nine historical studies, including *Giselle* (1942), *A History of Russian Ballet* (1939; English edition, 1950), and various autobiographical, polemical, and theoretical works, such as the *Traité de chorégraphie* (1952). He participated in several films, from *La Mort du Cygne* (1937) to *Spectre de la Danse* (1960). He was also a prodigious collector of art and artifacts associated with dancing. (After an unsuccessful New York tour in 1933, he sold a portion of his collection to the Wadsworth Atheneum in Hartford, Connecticut.)

"The soul of dance dwells in him," the poet Paul Valéry wrote. "He is too great an artist, and too sure and conscious a creator, not to have an extremely clear and broad idea of the essence of his art." Lifar was a member of the Institut de France (Académie des Beaux-Arts, 1968), a Commandeur des Arts et Lettres, and a Chevalier de la Légion d'Honneur.

[See also Icare *and* Paris Opera.]

BIBLIOGRAPHY

Garafola, Lynn. *Diaghilev's Ballets Russes.* New York, 1989.

García-Márquez, Vicente. *The Ballets Russes: Colonel de Basil's Ballets Russes de Monte Carlo, 1932–1952.* New York, 1990.

Gruen, John. *The Private World of Ballet.* New York, 1975.

Hersin, André-Philippe. "Hommage à Serge Lifar." *Saisons de la Danse,* no. 218 (November 1990): 19–21.

Laurent, Jean, and Julie Sazonova. *Serge Lifar, rénovateur du ballet français.* Paris, 1960.

Levinson, André. *Serge Lifar, destin d'un danseur.* Paris, 1934.

Lidova, Irène. "The Marquis and His Ballet." *Dance and Dancers* (July 1993): 18–20.

Lifar, Serge. *La danse.* Paris, 1938.

Lifar, Serge. *Traité de danse académique.* Paris, 1949.

Lifar, Serge. *Traité de chorégraphie.* Paris, 1952.

Lifar, Serge. *Au service de la danse.* Paris, 1958.

Lifar, Serge. *Ma Vie: From Kiev to Kiev.* Translated by John H. Mason. New York, 1970.

Lifar, Serge. *Les mémoires d'Icare.* Monaco, 1993.

Mail, Léone. "Le style 'néo-classique' de Serge Lifar." In *Hommage à Serge Lifar.* Paris, 1988.

Moore, Lillian. "Serge Lifar." In Moore's *Artists of the Dance.* New York, 1938.

Newman, Barbara. *Striking a Balance: Dancers Talk about Dancing.* Rev. ed. New York, 1992.

Shaïkevitch, André. *Serge Lifar et le ballet contemporain.* Paris, 1950.

Shaïkevitch, André. *Serge Lifar et le destin de ballet de l'Opéra.* Paris, 1971.

Valéry, Paul, and Jean Cocteau. *Serge Lifar à l'Opéra.* Paris, 1943.

MARIE-FRANÇOISE CHRISTOUT
Translated from French

LIGHTING FOR DANCE. [*This entry comprises two articles on the use of illumination in the performance of dance. The first article presents the history and development of theatrical lighting techniques; the second discusses practical techniques that can enhance choreography.*]

Historical Overview

The history of theatrical lighting can be traced to the late fifteenth century, when princely Renaissance entertainments began the slow transition from outdoor pageantry to indoor spectacle. This transformation took nearly a century to complete, during which time the basic components of designed lighting—placement, angle, control, color, and movement—were identified. Inextricably linked to theater architecture (the shape of the performance space and its relationship to the viewer) and to scenic design, lighting is a practical art: problems are solved as they arise, solutions are refined, and the subsequent stage of development is usually triggered by architectural or technological advances.

The need for illumination did not exist on classical and medieval stages because performances took place outside during daylight hours. Yet theatrical lighting has antecedents in the ancient torchlight processions, in the sailors' rigging that raised and lowered the *aulium* (canvas awning) for shading Roman spectators from the sun, and in the writings of Vitruvius (first century BCE), whose ten-volume *De architectura* was discovered in 1414 at Sankt Gallen and eventually published in an Italian translation in 1521. There were aesthetic connections, too, with the flashes and smoky effects of Hell's Mouth, where devils cavorted for audiences in the Middle Ages.

During the late sixteenth century in England, the popular unroofed Elizabethan playhouses fashioned an outdoor lighting device to brighten the playing area on gloomy winter afternoons when twilight came early. These crude implements, called cressets, were made from large ropes twisted into coils, covered in pitch, placed in small iron cages, and set aflame. Unresolved until the late nineteenth century, the major lighting hazard—fire—was a serious problem well before the Renaissance. At the in-

LIGHTING FOR DANCE: Historical Overview. This engraving, by Le Pautre after Jean Berain, shows a court ballet danced before Louis XIV and the Princesse de Conti in 1683. The lighting, provided by candelabra overhead and sconces on the walls, unites, rather than separates, audience and performers. (Reprinted from Cyril Beaumont, *Ballet Design: Past and Present*, London, 1946.)

famous Bal des Ardents of 1393, five noblemen were accidentally torched as they performed *The Masque of Wild Men* at the Hall of Saint Pol in Paris.

The logistical difficulties of arranging feudal entertainments in the banquet hall were first surmounted by Italians, whose multiple skills as builders, painters, machinists, and engineers gave a true Renaissance cast to their role as court architect. There was not enough room indoors to accommodate the row of separate mansions common to the medieval multiple-stage organization. Conventions were borrowed from the visual arts, especially the newly rediscovered painted perspective that gave the illusion of more space. Torches, sconces, standing candelabra, and chandeliers were used to achieve simple visibility and were not placed, in the beginning, to distinguish the performance area from any other part of the hall. The advantage of indoor productions was singular: the architect gained more control over the proceedings.

The pattern of importing Italian ingenuity to enhance French diversions began early in the sixteenth century when Francis I started modeling himself on princes of the great houses of Urbino, Este, and Medici. Leonardo da Vinci settled at Amboise in 1516. Sebastiano Serlio (1475–1554), the most influential theorist of the period, was brought to Fontainebleau in 1540. Five years later his seminal *De architectura* (with its notable passages on perspective) was published simultaneously in French and Italian. Serlio became the authority on the arrangement of scenes in the banquet hall, and he advocated setting the emotional tone for an entertainment through its visual accoutrements. Other significant innovators were Bernardo Buontalenti (1536–1608), machinist and designer to the Medici, and Di Somi, whose *Dialogues on Stage Affairs* is the advice of a man practicing his craft in the 1560s. He recommends concealing the sources of light for the performance area, increasing illumination by employing reflectors (a polished barber's basin could be quite effective as a moon), texturing the design with shadow, and keying the overall effect to feelings expressed: happy *divertissements* should be bright; melancholy intervals, dim.

The production of *Le Balet Comique de la Royne* at the Louvre's Salle de Bourbon in 1581 was the culmination of these practices as well as the end of an era. A combination of multiple settings and rolling vehicles with a scene fixed behind an arcaded frame, this Valois fête glowed with colored light. Mullioned windows in Circe's palace were fitted with stained glass, a technique known since the eleventh century; the placement of torches behind the windows caused brightly hued shafts to fall on the garden below. The same effect could also be achieved by setting a large bottle of colored water in front of a powerful flame—a candle, torch, or wick-burning oil lamp (known since prehistoric times) of the type associated with Aladdin. It is important to note that the lighting for *Balet Comique* was designed to enhance the spectacle, not to increase visibility. [*See* Balet Comique de la Royne, Le.]

Influenced to a degree by the new absolutism, the next phase of scenic design attempted to organize the entire stage picture within a frame. The Teatro Olimpico, with its triple arcade, opened in Vicenza in 1585. In France the ballet *Alcine* (1610) was the first to compress all the scenery behind a single, decorative opening. The seven-

LIGHTING FOR DANCE: Historical Overview. The Blue Grotto on the Isle of Capri, from act 2 of August Bournonville's *Napoli.* The introduction of electrical stage lighting enabled nineteenth-century designers to create highly illusionistic environments, as described in this ballet's libretto: "One sees the empty grotto. Its dark pillars form the foreground; the water, with its magical play of color, fills up the interior of the cave, and in the far background, sunlight pours in through the low and narrow entrance." Set design by Thorolf Pedersen (1903), after the original design by C. F. Christensen (1842); lighting designer unknown. (Photograph c.1903; from the collection of the Royal Theater, Copenhagen.)

teenth-century Teatro Farnese at Parma was equipped with a complete set of wings. A new generation of theorists refined theatrical possibilities. Although his recommendation was not heeded at the time, Angelo Ingegneri (c.1550–c.1613) urged that the area designated for spectator seating be darkened. Josef Furtenbach (1591–1667) included valuable drawings in a treatise that spread Mediterranean conventions to northern Europe, and Inigo Jones (1573–1652) carried Italianate skills to England.

As the shape of architectural space changed, the possibilities for placing sources of light increased. In *Architectura civilis* (1628), Furtenbach refers to a trough filled with lamps at the upstage reaches of the playing space, thus providing back light. Glass globes, especially blown for theatrical purposes, were made with a handle that could fit into ring holders or into holes drilled into a board. These *bozze* were set into vertical poles in the wings. When the poles were turned manually, marvelous flickers and flashes could be effected, and simulated shadows might suggest the offstage progress of carriages, processions, or military drills.

Nicola Sabbattini (1574–1654) stressed the importance of sidelighting in *Practica di fabricar scene e machine ne' teatri* (1638) and demonstrated a method for suspending tin cylinders over each lamp to dim the light. He also indicated the placement of lamps at the downstage edge in the footlights area, but these lamps were not used in dance entertainments until the practice of descending from the stage to perform at audience level was abandoned.

Traps, complex rigging systems, and a batten for lamps just behind the proscenium in what in the twentieth century became known as the "first electric" position made it possible to produce elaborate special effects. The brilliant scene painter Giacomo Torelli (nicknamed "il gran stregoni") was invited to Paris by Cardinal Mazarin in 1645. Torelli's disciple Gaspare Vigarani (1586–1663) later constructed the Salle des Machines in the Tuileries. The fabulous collaborations at the court of Louis XIV by Molière, Pierre Beauchamps, and Jean-Baptiste Lully were mounted indoors or outdoors at Versailles with the most advanced technology. There are both written descriptions and drawn illustrations of these achievements.

The eighteenth century, for the most part, witnessed an elaboration of previously developed techniques. After 1765 all light sources except the footlights (alternately abolished and restored for four hundred years) were hidden behind the proscenium arch. Overhead chandeliers and wall sconces provided general illumination in the house and on stage. Lamps with individual reflectors were concealed overhead as well as on wing ladders. These lamps can still be seen today at Sweden's Drottningholm Theatre, built in 1766 as part of the palace of Queen Louisa Ulrika. Often naked flames unprotected by any sort of cage or encasement, they caused many theater fires.

Lighting reforms were carried out at Drury Lane (London) by David Garrick, who sponsored the English tour of his friend Jean-Georges Noverre's *Les Fêtes Chinoises.* The period's emphasis was on directional light from the sides and experiments with traps of floating light. Troughs were filled with oil-burning lamps or with fish oil on which wicks stuck through pieces of cork bobbed and floated; rigged with a counterweight system, they could be raised or lowered through traps in the floor. Garrick's designer Philip James de Loutherbourg (1740–1812) became adept at creating special effects with fog and flames. In his *Treatise on Theatres* (1790), George Saunders suggested placing sconces with reflectors on the front of boxes closest to the stage to provide front lighting, but pictorial evidence indicates that this practice was not adopted until much later.

British engineer William Murdock lit his Cornish home with coal gas in 1792. The greatest changes in lighting since the Renaissance followed. Gaslight offered a more powerful source of illumination that could be controlled precisely by the opening and shutting of valves. First used in England to light the exterior of Covent Garden in 1815, the new system was soon installed in the auditorium and then backstage. During the decade from 1817 to 1827 most public buildings in western Europe and the United States were equipped with gas facilities. The number of theater fires doubled. The Paris Opera was fitted with twenty-eight miles of gas piping and nine hundred and sixty gas jets controlled by eighty-eight stopcocks. Handles for the valves were manipulated (usually by the prompter) at a brass-plated table calibrated with settings at low, medium, and high. Colored glass media in red, blue, and green (the primary hues for mixing light) were employed along with blinds of colored cloth. Flexible gas hoses in the wings provided the source for special effects, and the eerie grottoes of the Romantic ballet were quickly perfected.

There also were experiments with dioramas, semicircular expanses of painted fabric (forerunners of the contemporary cyclorama) that wrapped the stage in panoramic vistas, eliminating the wings altogether. For the 1856 production of Joseph Mazilier's *Le Corsaire* at the Paris Opera, the storm and the wrecking of the corsair's ship were produced in this manner. It was rumored that two hundred of the tsar's militia marched underneath a painted canvas to simulate tossing waves during a similar scene when the opera was produced in Russia.

The intense blue glow of gaslight cast fanciful shadows that were integral to effecting a supernatural atmosphere. The requisite gas jets were sometimes sheathed with glass chimneys, but usually the flame was totally exposed. When Emma Livry ignited herself by brushing against one of these gas jets at a rehearsal for *La Muette de Portici* in 1862, the accident marked the close of the French Romantic epoch as well as the beginning of a new phase of technology.

Limelight, the brilliance from heated lime (calcium oxide), discovered by Thomas Drummond in 1816, next gained ascendancy as the principal method for spotlighting performers. Electricity powered by carbon arcs also served this purpose and was so successful in creating an effect of the rising sun at the Paris Opera in 1846 that it soon was incorporated for floodlighting productions of both opera and ballet. Enclosed in a metal hood, the arc light—with its lens and parabolic mirror reflector—was the prototype of the modern spotlight. By 1879 a reliable incandescent bulb was perfected simultaneously in England by Sir Joseph William Swan and in the United States by Thomas Alva Edison. Edison's carbon filament encased in an evacuated glass bulb, paired with his first public generating station, allowed eighty-five customers in New York City to light the interiors of their homes with electricity.

The Paris Hippodrome was lit totally by Jablochkoff candles, a refined version of carbon arc light, in 1878. A year later the California Theatre in San Francisco installed electricity. Other institutions quickly followed suit. Richard D'Oyly Carte's Savoy Theatre pioneered the practice in London in 1881. The Bürn Theatre in Austria and the Paris Opera were completely fitted with incandescent lamps in 1882 and 1886, respectively. This is chronicled in detail in Lefèvre's *L'électricité au théâtre* (1895).

The pace of developments quickened with new concepts. The most significant theory was articulated by the Swiss innovator Adolphe Appia (1862–1928), whose *Die Musik und die Inszenierung* (1899) distilled his experience producing Wagnerian opera. Appia saw that light could provide comprehensive artistic unity to the entire *mise-en-scène,* evoking mood as well as a three-dimensional environment for the performer. Sculpting theatrical space with the *chiaroscuro* potential of designed lighting, he brought out the expressive qualities of mass and form while heightening the spectator's sensual and emotional responses. His ideas were borrowed and elaborated on by Gordon Craig in *The Art of the Theatre* (1905), *On the Art of the Theatre* (1911), and *The Theatre Advancing* (1921). [*See the entry on Appia.*]

Louis Tiffany's beautiful glass *objets d'art* opened up a rainbow of possibilities for advanced media. The archetypal American art dancer Loie Fuller invented a phosphorescent medium and perfected a system of placing painted glass slides in front of her lighting instruments to project colorful patterns onto the swirling lengths of silk surrounding her figure. By merging science with art she epitomized Art Nouveau and captured an image that summarized the late nineteenth century. Mariano Fortuny (1871–1949) built a sky dome that allowed reflected light to be thrown onto bands of colored silk, producing an exquisite though impractical stage ambience.

The British actress Ellen Terry declared that electricity caused the stage to be "revealed in all its naked trashiness," but this very effect augmented naturalistic productions. Known for his realistic spectacles and fascination with sunrises, American director David Belasco (1859–1931) established a laboratory for lighting research in New York City. His electrician, Louis Hartman, was one of the first theatrical technicians to work exclusively on the problems of light. The artist who specializes solely in lighting design did not emerge until the second half of the twentieth century. Other theater directors who conducted notable experiments with light were Henry Irving (1838–1905), Max Reinhardt (1873–1943), Harley Granville-Barker (1877–1946), Jacques Copeau (1878–1949), Eugene Vakhtangov (1883–1922), and Alexander Tairov (1885–1950).

The early twentieth century saw rapid technological progress. A few inventions that expanded the parameters of lighting design were the Schwabe-Haseit system, the Linnebach projector, the GKP projecting process, Wilfred's color organ, and Munroe R. Pevear's pure-color media. By 1922, scientifically designed reflectors were available and improved methods for positioning the lamp, reflector, and lens within a metal encasement had been determined. The stepped lens, devised for lighthouse beams by Augustin Jean Fresnel (1788–1827), was adapted for the theater in a miniature version, called a Fresnel lens, capable of diffusing light evenly over a specific area. The tungsten filaments and gas-filled incandescent bulbs of the 1930s increased brilliance. Improved switchboards offered greater control, particularly George Izenour's electric console (1947).

Since World War II equipment has been developed to refine and accelerate the process of raising and dimming light. The old resistance dimmer was supplanted by an autotransformer and the silicon-controlled rectifier (SCR). The capacity for multiscene presets was added, and Izenour's punchcard system was one of several methods for simplifying execution while stepping up the potential complexity of lighting cues. Computer boards followed in quick succession. A 1985 version incorporated a digitally controlled dimmer that received information

LIGHTING FOR DANCE: Historical Overview. Twyla Tharp's *Fait Accompli*, at the Brooklyn Academy of Music, 1984. For this work, with movement derived from boxing, Jennifer Tipton created a lighting design featuring 144 unmasked backlights. The exposed lamps, the stage fog that reveals the beams of downlight, and the blazingly bright stage floor poetically evoked a sports arena. Tipton's work exploits the creative possibilities inherent in the precise focus of contemporary lighting instruments and the exact timing of computer-controlled dimmer systems. (Photograph © 1984 by Beatriz Schiller; used by permission.)

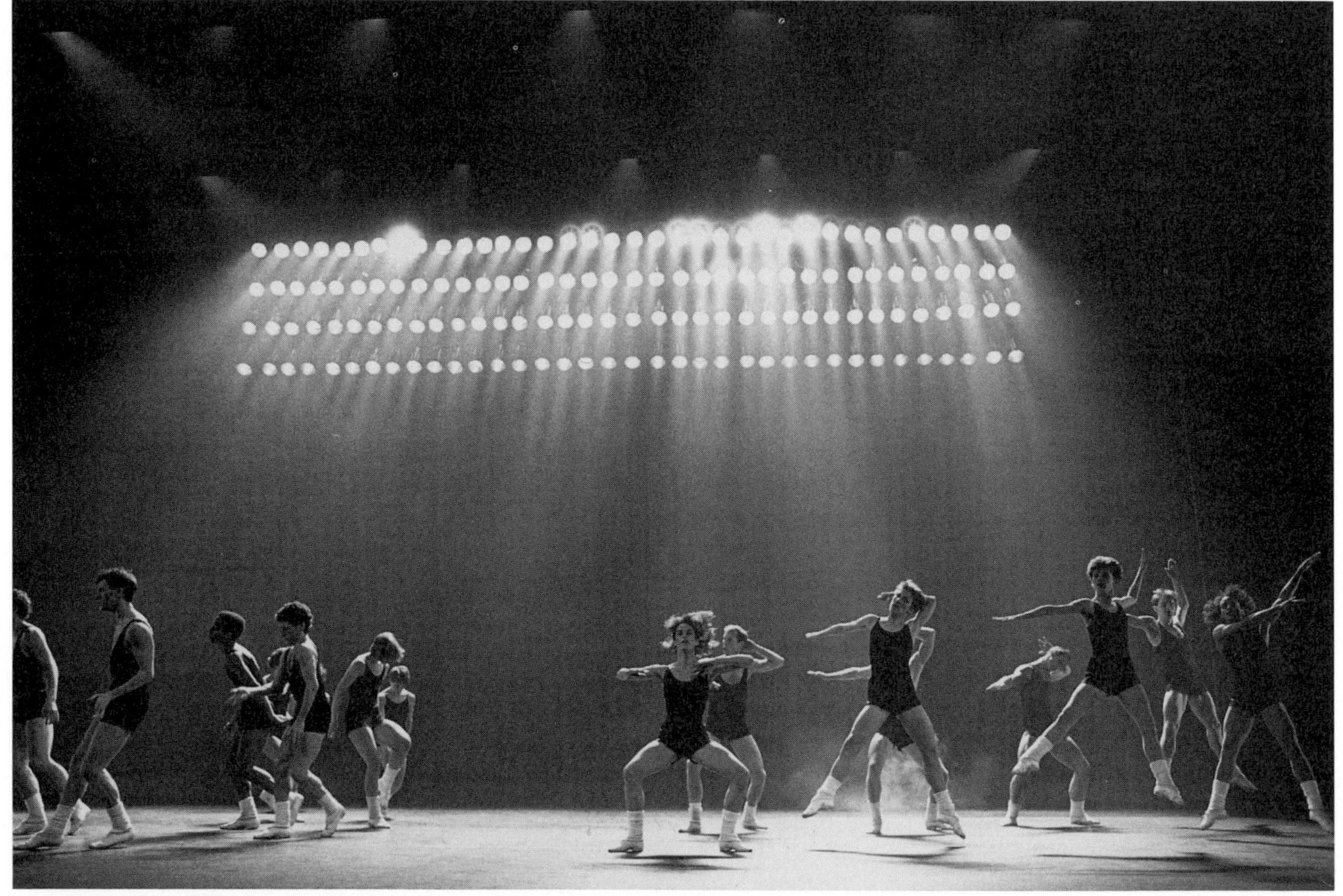

from the computer by means of a coaxial cable in a transmission process similar to that of cable television.

Contemporary architecture—pragmatically built theater plants with the capacity for state-of-the-art technology—has made it possible to increase the number of positions for lighting instruments in the auditorium (for front light) so that they can function efficiently and still be unobtrusive.

The greatest achievement of the twentieth century was the recognition of lighting design as an art. A handful of individuals brought that about, including the few who were able to meet the very specific demands of lighting dance. Aesthetically, a precedent was set by Robert Edmond Jones (1887–1954), who was the first American to design for a world-class dance ensemble. Jones worked with Vaslav Nijinsky on *Tyl Eulenspiegel* in 1916 during the second season of Ballets Russes de Serge Diaghilev in the United States. Although the idea incubated over a decade, Jones realized that designing a dance production was not at all the same as collaborating on a play.

The next major landmark was the system devised by Stanley McCandless (1897–1967), a Harvard-trained architect who taught lighting at the Yale School of Drama. Although it was developed for actors, McCandless's approach was the keystone for subsequent accomplishments in theatrical lighting. Basically, he divided the stage into six general areas. Each side of all six rectangles was then hung with two instruments (one gelled warm, one cool) focused at a 45-degree angle to emphasize the actor's eyes and to approximate the direction of natural light from the sun. There was considerably more theory behind McCandless's work, but this technique provided the framework for each production's made-to-measure design. His books, *A Syllabus of Stage Lighting* and *A Method of Lighting the Stage*, are probably the most influential publications ever written on the topic. He also trained the first generation of American specialists in lighting.

As a teenager, Jean Rosenthal (1912–1969) studied at the Neighborhood Playhouse School of the Theatre with Martha Graham and Louis Horst from 1928 until 1930. One of the few purely native art forms, modern dance was producing its first crop of major choreographers. It was an exciting time. Rosenthal was enchanted. A year later she matriculated at Yale to study lighting with McCandless. Among her earliest professional assignments were her positions as lighting designer and production supervisor for the Martha Graham Dance Company (1938–1966) and with Ballet Society and its renamed successor, the New York City Ballet (1947–1957). For Balanchine's magnificent *Nutcracker*, she designed both the lighting and the magical Christmas tree. Rosenthal's credits range from Broadway across the continent in dance, theater, and opera. In 1942 she lit the President's Inaugural Ball and in 1959 worked to create lighting effects for Judy Garland's appearance at the Metropolitan Opera House. As an artist, she went beyond McCandless's concept to evolve a three-dimensional light-around-the-body style in which the entire anatomy is as important to the dancer as the face and eyes are to the actor. Rosenthal used carefully controlled illumination from all directions, varying intensity and color to give the impression of light and shade on a stage that, in fact, had no shadows. [*See the entry on Rosenthal.*]

As dance became a more fully integrated component of musical comedy, Broadway complemented the concert circuit as a venue for dance-lighting development. Abe Feder and Peggy Clark made significant contributions, as did Jo Mielziner, but it was two of Rosenthal's protégés, Tharon Musser and Thomas R. Skelton, who took the field even further. Musser, who also studied at Yale, graduated to become lighting designer and stage manager for the Limón Dance Company and for the American Dance Festival, among many other affiliations. Musser earned the distinction of being the first designer to use a computer board on Broadway: for Michael Bennett's production of *A Chorus Line*. During the 1940s, Skelton, who at the time was studying to be a theater director at Middlebury College in Vermont, saw Graham perform in New York. That concert—designed by Rosenthal—convinced Skelton to pursue lighting design for dance, and he later became the world's leading authority on the subject. Above all, he perceived that the angle of light must follow the axis of movement. As articulated in his "Handbook of Dance Stagecraft" (published in *Dance Magazine*), Skelton's method provides a base for lighting a dance with fifteen instruments or five thousand. His system accomplished for the dancer and choreographer what McCandless had achieved for the actor and director.

Designing and consulting internationally led Skelton to study anthropology and become an expert on presenting ethnic dance in a format that does not compromise its authenticity. In addition to working on Broadway and teaching lighting at Yale and the American Dance Festival, he has maintained long-term relationships with the Paul Taylor Dance Company, the Joffrey Ballet, the New York City Ballet, Feld Ballets/NY (now Ballet Tech), and the Ohio Ballet. Two of Skelton's former apprentices, Jennifer Tipton and Beverly Emmons, have joined him and Rosenthal and Musser as leaders in the field.

United Scenic Artists (USA), the union for designers of sets, costumes, and lights, was founded in 1918. Admission to a limited membership was based on the ability to pass rigorous tests on all three aspects. Having won acceptance, initiates were deemed competent to work in all areas, a concept inherited from the Renaissance. However, the rapid proliferation of information in the late twentieth century led to greater specialization, and in 1963 USA changed its policies to reflect that reality. Those admitted to the union before that date are classified as "all class" designers. Since 1963, members must be informed on all three facets of production but may choose a single area of concentration; each is recognized as a separate, though related, discipline. The twentieth-century technological explosion provided the lighting designer in particular with the tools for turning this craft into an art.

For both designer and choreographer a human form is ultimately at the center of any vision. A beautiful dance may be performed without sets, costumes, or even music. But without light, the dance is imperceptible.

[*See also* Designing for Dance.]

BIBLIOGRAPHY

Appia, Adolphe-François. *The Work of Living Art: A Theory of the Theatre* (18–). Translated by H. D. Albright. Coral Gables, Fla., 1960.

Harris, Margaret Haile. *Loïe Fuller: Magician of Light.* Richmond, Va., 1979.

Jackson, Barry. "Diaghilev: Lighting Designer." *Dance Chronicle* 14.1 (1991): 1–35.

Marigny, Chris de. "Light, Real Time, and Jennifer Tipton." *Dance Theatre Journal* 11 (Winter 1993–1994): 12–15.

McCandless, Stanley R. *A Method of Lighting for the Stage.* 4th ed. New York, 1958.

Parker, W. Oren, and Harvey K. Smith. *Scene Design and Stage Lighting.* 2d ed. New York, 1968.

Rees, Timothy. *Theatre Lighting in the Age of Gas.* London, 1978.

Rosenthal, Jean, and Lael Wertenbaker. *The Magic of Light.* Boston, 1972.

Skelton, Thomas R. "Handbook of Dance Stagecraft" (parts 1–3). *Dance Magazine* (October 1955–October 1957).

CAMILLE HARDY

Theory and Practice

Lighting dance is an art integral to dance itself. We see the shape, feel the rhythm, sense the passion—perceive dance on its many levels and in its many forms—by the light that reveals it.

Masking. No discussion of lighting in dance is complete without a discussion of masking. Black legs (high, narrow cloth panels hung on either side of the stage) and borders (short, wide panels hung above the stage)—and a black backdrop when appropriate—are used to mask or hide the backstage areas and the lighting instruments from the view of the audience. This black cloth should if at all possible be velour, because its deep pile absorbs light and softens shadows more than any other material. This drapery is used to frame the stage picture; beyond that, it must virtually disappear. It should be as neat as possible, with no pleats, drapes, or folds to catch the light. The borders should make a straight line at the bottom, especially when the audience sees the upstage border against a sky or light-colored drop. The line of the leg at the edge of the stage should be straight and vertical, not swagged. There should be no lint, white or dirty spots, or places that will command the attention of the audience and thus defeat the purpose of masking. Backdrops should have no wrinkles. Any spot or wrinkle will call attention to the material and destroy the illusion. All the beautiful light in the world is worth nothing if the dancers' surroundings are sloppy, tacky, or untended.

The masking, should be arranged to give the dance as much space as possible. The wing openings need to be at least six feet (two meters) wide to allow room for dancers and light booms (vertical pipes in the wings to which side lights are attached). The booms themselves should be at least six to eight feet (two to two-and-a-half meters) offstage of the leg line (the imaginary line made by the inner, onstage edge of the legs) to allow the light to cover the

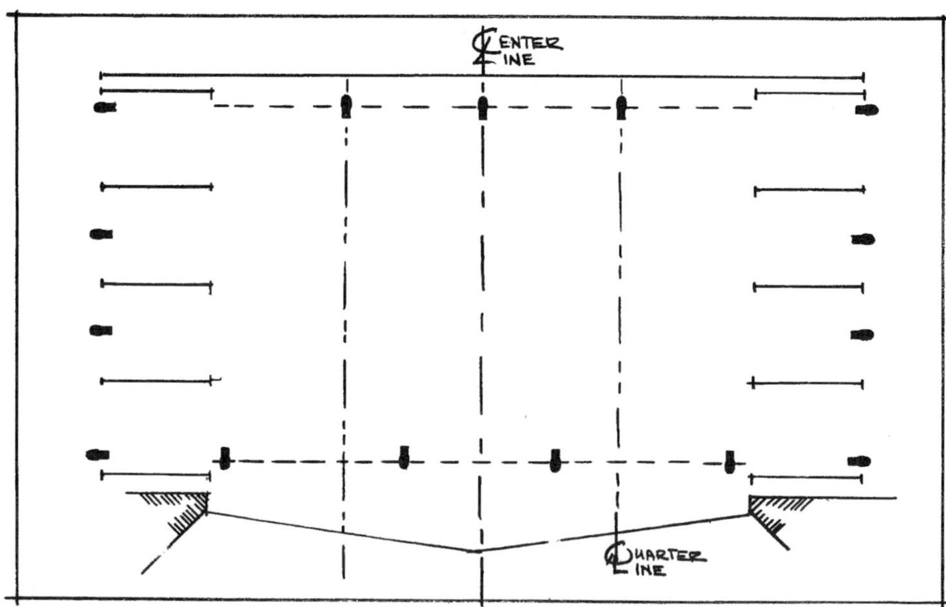

LIGHTING FOR DANCE: Theory and Practice. Figure 1. Ground plan of a proscenium stage, indicating the dimensions of the stage, the location of the legs, and the fundamental positions of side-, front-, and backlights. (Drawing by Jennifer Tipton.)

stage, to be out of sight of the audience, and to allow fast-moving dancers to enter and exit freely. Backdrops should be as far upstage as possible. Ideally if there should be enough depth to allow space between a backdrop and the dancing space so that light spill on the backdrop from the front- and sidelights can be minimized.

Placement of Lights. To allow dance to be seen, light must carve the body out of space. Exact and carefully planned placement of the lights on the stage allows this to happen. The boundaries of the dancing space are marked by light (see figure 1). Sidelight, the chief workhorse of dance lighting, is placed in the first and fourth wings as far downstage and upstage, respectively, as possible, to delineate the upstage and downstage limits of the dancing space, and in the center of the midstage wings to allow maximum coverage at the near side. Low lights, fondly called "kickers" or "shinbusters," are placed as low as possible in order to "cut" the space away from the floor. Backlights are placed as far upstage as possible to push the bodies away from the background. Frontlights are placed to the side, just inside the leg line, so that light can hit the dancers without hitting the legs, (that is, the masking for the wings) thus separating the dancers from their surroundings. If any of these lighting positions is compromised, then the dance space itself is compromised. A large stage can be reduced considerably in size if the light does not delineate its full space, if it does not cover the full space from any and all of the above-mentioned angles.

Angle. In theater one must see actors' faces to hear the words they speak; frontlight is therefore essential. In dance it is more important to see movement, to see three-dimensional bodies in space, to be able to perceive the exact positions of an arm, a leg, a tangle of bodies. It is sidelight that reveals three-dimensional space most effectively and efficiently. The entire width of the stage can be lit with one light hung at head height on a boom at the side offstage, in the wings; therefore, the side is a very economical position for lighting, and provides the precise angles that reveal the body better than any others. Low lights not only separate the space from the floor but are the only lights able to reach under tutus; therefore, they are able to soften shadows on the dancers' legs and make leg movements more clearly visible. Downlights are often used in dance to isolate a particular area; however, they are not at a good angle to reveal movement or the body without distorting the viewers' perception of it. When low sidelight (having been "cut" carefully off the floor), is added, downlights can be effectively used to define a small area around the dancer. The body well lit by sidelight seems isolated in the small space.

A good balance of light from all angles—side, front, and back—best reveals bodies in space. Sidelight from many positions—low, mid (waist high) head high, high-boom (from lights hung above head-high lights on the booms in the wings), and pipe-end (from lights hung at the offstage ends of the pipes above the stage)—is helpful in achieving this balance.

Color. The choice of color is always a reflection of the taste of the designer, but there are general principles to consider. Color in sidelights hung at an accessible place on the booms can be changed from dance to dance—even during a dance—and, therefore, will make the most noticeable difference from piece to piece in an evening's program. Front- and backlight are less accessible during a performance, so a flexible variety of color washes from these angles is desirable. The ability to light the full stage space in each color from any chosen angle, to avoid limiting the dancers' space, is important.

Saturated color is often used in dance. Although it is useful for creating atmosphere and a sense of "place" when appropriately handled, all too often color is used gratuitously, for no real reason except that dance, unlike theater, is thought to provide an occasion for using deep colors. Dancers with green faces are just as bizarre as actors with green faces. A dance is as badly served as a play if it is lit with oversaturated and inappropriate color. One strategy is to use color from the upstage diagonal back position—to light the air, light the space, light the floor with deep color, without changing the color of skin or costumes.

Control. In dance, as in theater, the ideal is to have each light controlled on a separate dimmer, but economic limitations make this a dream rarely realized. It is difficult to choose which lights should work together. The simplest division of control is front, back, side from stage left, and side from stage right. Here again the personal taste of the designer will determine how the control of the light is further divided. The particular dances, or the sequences of the dances, in a company's repertory, are critical factors in making these choices.

Dynamics. Perhaps the most personal considerations for lighting dance have to do with the choice of when the light will move and at what speed the change will occur—the dynamics of the light. The dynamics of the dance itself will be deeply affected by the dynamics of the light; therefore, the designer must be sensitive to the dance. Too many dances are distorted because the light moves in the wrong places or moves too quickly or slowly. The choice of whether the movement of light will parallel the dance or run counter to it is extremely important and will indeed determine how the audience perceives the piece.

The main factor in determining what the dynamics of the light should be in a dance is likely to be the music or sound score. Music establishes a basic rhythm that is interrupted only by choice of the choreographer. The movement of the light should respond to the music in the same way, interrupting the rhythm only by choice of the designer.

Style. The style of lighting will vary according to the type of dance being lit. Angle does not vary much from style to style, yet color will be vastly different. Classical ballet is choreographed to show purity of line and fluidity of movement; color in the light should allow the audience to perceive body line without distortion. More saturated color may be used to emphasize the drama of a dance. Choice of color is personal to the designer, but it must be universal to the extent that most of the audience responds to the color in the same way that the designer does. The dynamics or movement of light will also reflect what kind of dance is being performed. Light cues in classical ballet may be designed to be almost imperceptible, whereas a jazz piece may have cues that shift color and focus quite abruptly. Contrast of light and shadow—chiaroscuro—is helpful in creating atmosphere. For a dramatic dance this contrast may be quite extreme. For a jazz dance the shadows may be softened by contrasting colors in the light.

Lighting a Sky. One of the most difficult chores in dance lighting is to make an expanse of material approximately sixty feet wide by thirty feet high (fifty-five by twenty-seven meters) give the illusion of being a sky. One of the problems is to light the center of the drop as well as the top. In addition to the striplights (long units comprising a row of several lamps, each in a separate cell) that light the cyclorama from overhead, another set can be placed far enough downstage to direct the light toward the center of the drop. The main reason for the difficulty in creating the illusion of sky is that the sky has a translucent quality that is difficult to simulate with frontlight on a piece of material. There are two ways to counteract this problem. The first is to hang a transparent drop—of sharkstooth or even bobbinette scrim (a light, sheer, loosely woven material)—downstage of the drop. The fact that there are two surfaces confuses the eye and gives the illusion that there is no surface. The second way, the best and easiest, but also the most expensive is to use a seamless translucent drop with a ground row of lights (that is, lights placed on the floor) directed toward a bounce drop (made from a material specifically designed to reflect, or "bounce," light back toward the audience) behind it. The ideal distance between the two drops is three feet (one meter). The ground row should be focused on the bounce drop; in fact, no light from it should hit the translucent drop, because this light will make a line that is visible to the audience. Striplights overhead between the drops are useful as well. Unless the light is very bright (and blue light, often needed for sky effects, is never very bright), light from the floor and from overhead will leave a dark area in the center of the drop. This area can be filled in with light from the front, from those striplights that are hung far enough downstage to light the center of the drop. This arrangement makes it possible to achieve a great deal of variety in the background by using different colors from the three different positions (see figure 2).

Repertory. All lighting for dance is repertory lighting, that is, lighting not restricted to any one piece and flexible enough to accommodate the changing pieces of repertory. Flexibility in color and control are paramount. The basic lighting setup for a company should make variety and

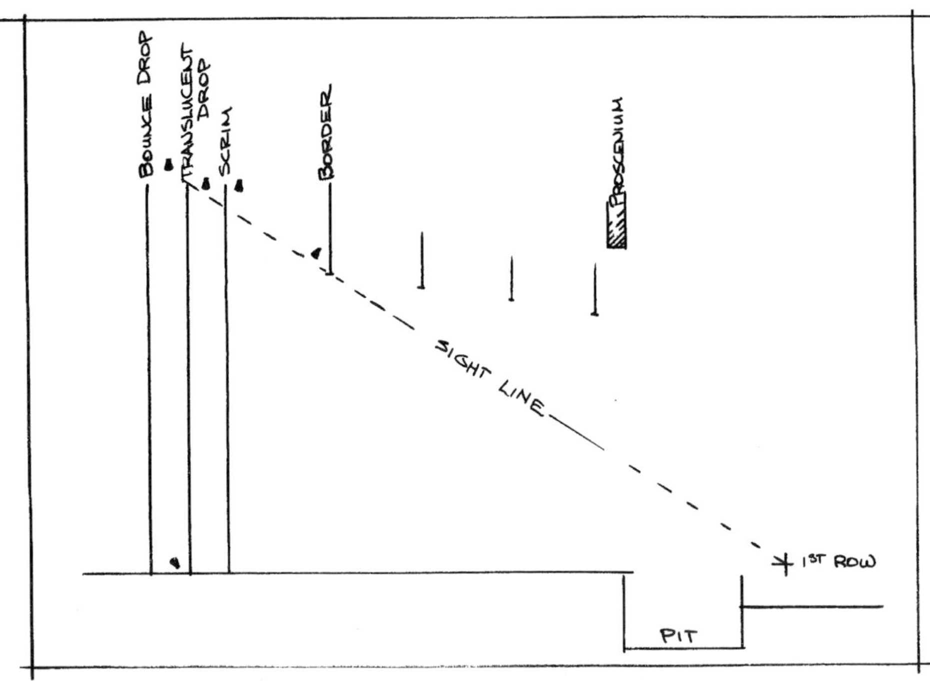

LIGHTING FOR DANCE: Theory and Practice. Figure 2. Sectional view of the stage, showing the five angles from which the cyclorama may be lit (the small black symbols indicate lighting unit postions). The diagram also shows how the upstage border is hung to hide all the overstage cyc units from the view of the audience. (Drawing by Jennifer Tipton.)

separation possible without the addition of many new lights for each new dance. Here are some suggested light plots, beginning with the most minimal and developing it into a larger plot appropriate for a ballet company. The addition of systems and choice of colors should respond to the needs of each new piece added to the repertory; there is no prescribed order to the addition of systems.

Four lights on stands about seven feet (2.1 meters) high on each side of a space forty feet wide by thirty feet deep (twelve by nine meters) are the minimum number necessary to make a dance visible. They can define a dance space within a larger space, such as a gymnasium, but they provide only visibility—with no possibility for variety, color, atmosphere, or movement of light.

A small modern dance company can achieve variety and good visibility with approximately forty lights and a set of striplights controlled by twenty-four dimmers (see figure 3). A small ballet company can add more variety to the plot with the addition of backlight washes in two colors, low sidelights, and sidelight washes in two colors (the added height on the boom makes two lights necessary to cover the width of the stage, one focused near and one far; see figure 4). These lights can be controlled with a reasonable degree of flexibility by approximately forty dimmers.

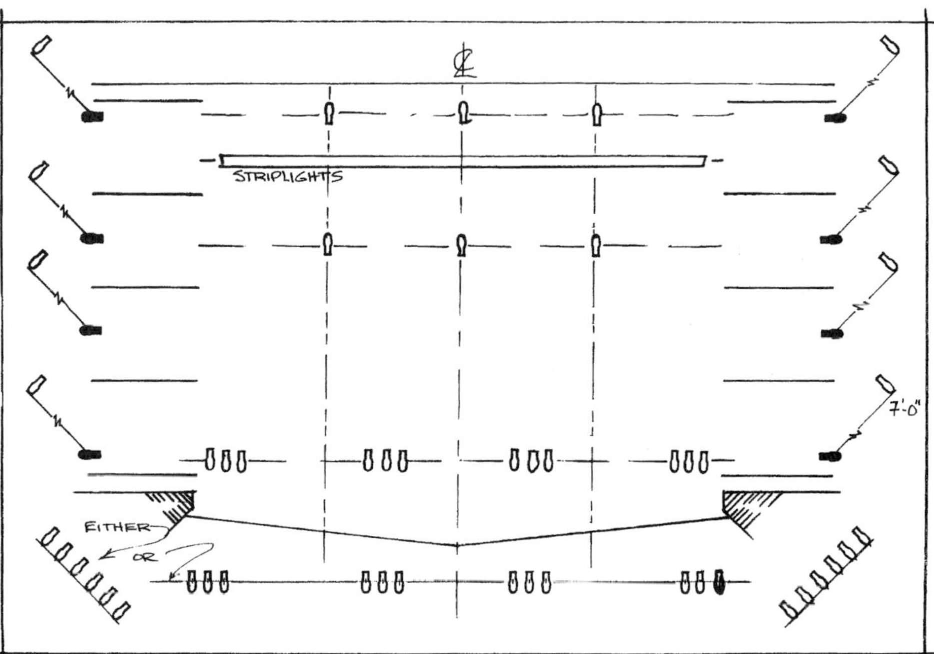

LIGHTING FOR DANCE: Theory and Practice. Figure 3. Repertory lighting plot for a small modern dance company. This plot includes head-high sidelights, one system of backlight, three colors of frontlight, striplights for the cyc, and twelve units focused on the front diagonals from the "box boom" or "slot" positions in the house. (Drawing by Jennifer Tipton.)

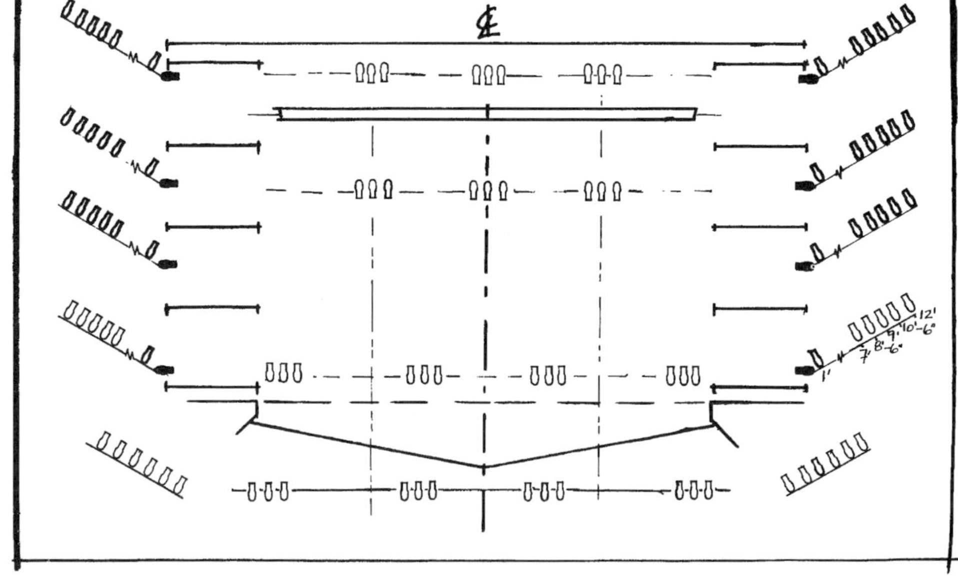

LIGHTING FOR DANCE: Theory and Practice. Figure 4. Repertory plot for a small ballet company. This plot adds floor lights, sidelight washes in two colors, and three colors of backlight to the basic plot represented by Figure 3. (Drawing by Jennifer Tipton.)

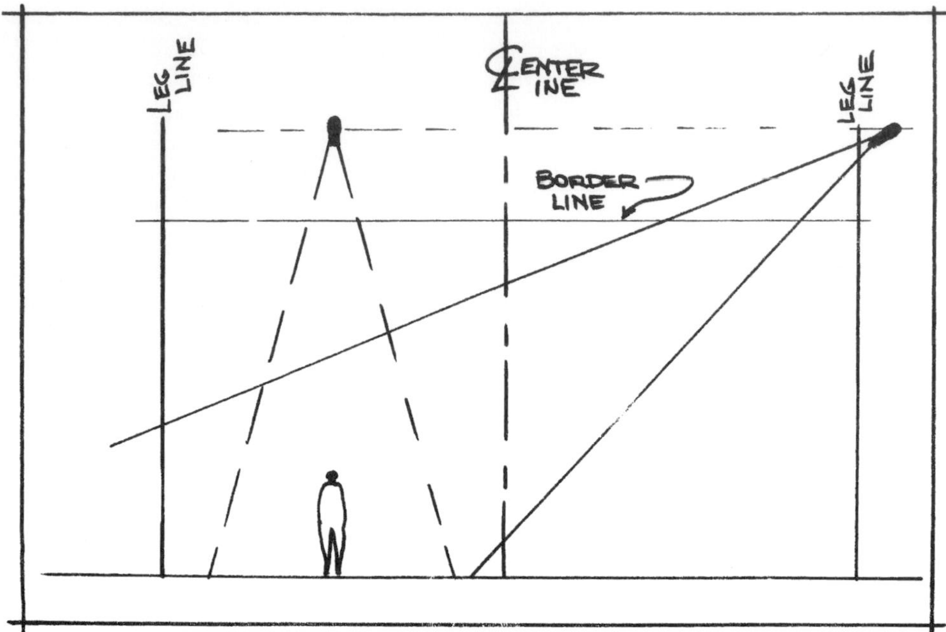

LIGHTING FOR DANCE: Theory and Practice. Figure 5. The proscenium stage drawn in front elevation. The diagram shows the difference between downlight and high-side crosslight as means of providing isolation on the quarterline. The crosslight must be focused high enough to illuminate dancers in jumps and lifts close to the leg line. (Drawing by Jennifer Tipton.)

Further flexibility can be gained by adding nine downlights, individually placed downstage, midstage, and upstage at the centerline and two quarterlines, all separately controlled. Downlights do not provide good visibility, however, so an alternative is to mount lights on the ends of each overhead pipe and focus them to the far quarterline. These lights cover about the same area on the floor as downlights because most of the light is lost in the wing, but as high sidelight they provide much more visibility (see figure 5). Still, they provide an alternative for the quarterline but not the centerline downlights, because crosslight into the center lights the entire floor and defeats the purpose of isolation.

Touring. Dance companies tour extensively, making it difficult to maintain the technical standards they set for their productions. Most ballet companies are able to travel with their own equipment and masking, whether rented or owned. Modern dance companies, on the other hand, are dependent on their local sponsors to provide the lights and drapery. This may mean that the company must perform with minimum resources; it certainly means that a great deal of flexibility is required in the lighting. A company may be forced to perform on a stage with beige masking hung in fullness three inches above a shiny gymnasium-type floor to facilitate mopping. In such a circumstance all the lighting equipment in the world will not help. What will help is a black scrim hung as a background even over the existing drop, helping to erase the lines made by the pleats in the beige drop or to cover up the dirt and the holes in the rag called a sky drop and softening the light that spills on it. It will give an illusion of space, allowing the audience to focus on the dancers and not on the surroundings. Bodies may even sometimes be better seen if side masking is pulled out, leaving the light booms to mark the dance space. Whatever lights are used the space needs to be open, lit evenly from all angles in all chosen colors, and separated from what surrounds it. Compromise can be made in the light on tour if it is done wisely, but the stage itself should always be neat.

For a company traveling with its own equipment, the problem is to maintain the same volume of space so that the light will be the same, so that adjustment of cues will be minimal, and so that the focus will vary little from place to place. As time grows more expensive, less of it is reserved for rehearsal and lighting. A performance will always happen, but as the economic squeeze increases, it becomes more difficult to maintain the quality of that performance.

Other Considerations. Light can provide scenery for dances to create variety in an evening's program. Lighting backgrounds with different colors is the easiest way to create a different place for each dance. Slides and gobos or templates (perforated metal or etched glass discs inserted in a lighting unit between the lamp and the lens), which create patterns when projected on a sky drop or scrim, also make scenic backgrounds. Smoke or haze in the air will reveal beams of light and make a composition in the space above the dancers. A designer must be sensitive to this spatial architecture; the needs of the visual composition may be more important than the light on the dancers. Light shapes space and creates a place for the dance to happen.

There are in addition many kinds of special lighting effects that are useful in particular circumstances, such as strobes, colorwheels and color scrollers, mirrorballs, lasers, and computer-controlled moving lights.

Alternative Spaces. The discussion of dance lighting so far has referred to proscenium stages. Most companies prefer this kind of performance space because it controls the angle from which the audience sees the line of the body and the shape of the dance. Most lighting designers also prefer to use light from a specific audience point of view. There are, however, some contemporary choreographers who choose to work in "found" spaces with the audience on three or four sides or even intermingled with the dancers. Here the guidelines for lighting are determined by the spaces themselves.

In all circumstances the types of lights used need not be limited to those designed specifically for stage use. The possibilities for lighting are as many and as varied as the designer can imagine. There are no rules.

BIBLIOGRAPHY

Armstrong, Leslie, and Roger Morgan. *Space for Dance*. New York, 1984.

Corbett, Tom, and Trisha Gorman. "Inseparable Techniques: Lighting for Dance; Makeup for Dance." *Dance Teacher Now* 3.3 (1981): 18–28.

Gillette, J. Michael. *Theatrical Design and Production*. 2d ed. Mountain View, Calif., 1992.

Harris, Margaret Haile. *Loie Fuller: Magician of Light*. Richmond, Va., 1979.

Izenour, George C. *Theater Technology*. New York, 1988.

Lippincott, Gertrude. *Dance Production*. Washington, D.C., 1956.

Louis, Murray, and Ruth E. Grauert. "Alwin Nikolais's Total Theater." *Dance Magazine* (December 1979): 56–69.

Pilbrow, Richard. *Stage Lighting*. Rev. ed. New York, 1979.

"The Performance: Costumes, Lights, Planning, Sets, Money, Music." *Dance Teacher Now* 2.1 (1980): 3–36.

Rosenthal, Jean, and Lael Wertenbaker. *The Magic of Light*. New York, 1972.

Schlaich, Joan, and Betty DuPont, eds. *Dance: The Art of Production*. Princeton, 1988.

Shyer, Laurence. *Robert Wilson and His Collaborators*. New York, 1989.

JENNIFER TIPTON

LILAC GARDEN.

See Jardin aux Lilas.

LIMÓN, JOSÉ (José Arcadia Limón; born 12 January 1908 in Culiacán, Sinaloa, Mexico, died 2 December 1972 in Flemington, New Jersey), dancer and choreographer. Remembered as one of modern dance's greatest male dancers and choreographers, Limón was the oldest of eleven children born to Florencio Limón, a musician of French and Spanish descent, and Francisca Traslaviña Limón, of Mexican lineage with a trace of Yaqui Indian blood in her ancestry. Limón's memories of his early childhood in Mexico—the vibrancy of Spanish and Mexican dancing and music, the ritual of the bullfight, the violence of the Mexican Revolution—provided artistic inspiration and choreographic material throughout his life. In 1915, the Limón family immigrated to the United States. Florencio Limón's search for work as a musical arranger forced the family to travel for several years before they settled permanently in Los Angeles. Poverty, sickness and constant traveling contributed to the deaths of several of the younger children and, later, to Francisca's death during childbirth.

Limón studied painting and music, exhibiting talent in both. While at the University of California, Los Angeles, he chose to become a painter and in 1928 left school to pursue his career in New York. Once in New York, however, his inability to produce a masterpiece frustrated him. He laid down his brushes along with his artistic ambitions. Friends persuaded him to attend a dance concert given by the German dancers Harald Kreutzberg and Yvonne Georgi. Kreutzberg's dancing so enthralled and moved Limón that, at the age of twenty, he decided to become a dancer.

He enrolled in modern dance classes at the Humphrey-Weidman Studio, where Doris Humphrey and Charles Weidman were teaching. They and their accompanist, Pauline Lawrence, had recently left the Denishawn company. Limón's large, powerful build (he was over six feet tall) required him to find a way to control his limbs and his weight within a technique that was designed for smaller, more supple bodies. He devised a series of exercises that isolated the different body parts and developed control of the weight within each. Later, his own teaching of this more complex distribution of weight added another technical dimension to the Humphrey-Weidman style.

Limón soon became a member of the Humphrey-Weidman company, performing and teaching on tour and at the company's summer residencies at the Bennington College Dance Festival. He came to be known for the natural, animal-like grace of his dancing and for the dignity and elegance of his bearing.

Doris Humphrey encouraged his choreographic ventures. Shown at the Humphrey-Weidman Studio, his early solos, duets, and trios were concerned primarily with exploration of pure movement. They showed some promise for, in 1937, the Bennington Dance Festival awarded Limón one of its first choreographic fellowships.

In 1940, after a decade with the company, Limón left for California, where he joined former Martha Graham dancer and choreographer, May O'Donnell. Together they created several dances with which they toured the West Coast. After a year, Pauline Lawrence joined Limón in San Francisco, where they were married on 3 October 1941.

Some months later, the couple returned to New York where Limón rejoined the Humphrey-Weidman company as a principal dancer. In 1942 he premiered *Chaconne*, a solo about the majesty of the human spirit. As the first dance in which he set his choreography within a strong emotional and thematic context, *Chaconne* marked the beginning of his maturation as a choreographer.

Shortly thereafter Limón was drafted and was assigned to Special Services at Fort Lee, Virginia, where he choreographed camp shows for the servicemen. On leaves he returned to New York to choreograph for the Humphrey-Weidman company. He created *Western Folk Suite* in 1943 and *Concerto Grosso* in 1945.

When the severe arthritis in her hip forced Doris Humphrey to stop dancing in 1944, she turned exclusively to choreography and to the furthering of Limón's career. The Limón Company was formed in 1946 with soloist Pauline Koner and three Humphrey-Weidman dancers (all of whom left within two years): Letitia Ide, Miriam Pandor, and Beatrice Seckler. Later, Jooss dancer Lucas Hoving, Betty Jones, and Ruth Currier joined the company. Between 1946 and her death in 1958, Humphrey served as artistic director for the Limón Company and created for it some of her greatest work: *Lament for Ignacio Sánchez Mejías, Day on Earth,* and *Ruins and Visions.* In addition, under her expert guidance, Limón developed and refined his own creative talent.

LIMÓN. The choreographer in his celebrated solo *Chaconne* (1942), danced to the music of J. S. Bach. (Photograph © by Barbara Morgan; used by permission.)

La Malinche, a trio based on a Mexican legend of love, politics, and betrayal, was the first piece Limón choreographed and performed with his new company. Though primarily a story dance, the exploration of the characters' emotional motivations in *La Malinche* presaged the kind of character development that emerged with greater depth in Limón's later work.

In 1949, at the American Dance Festival at Connecticut College, Limón premiered his masterpiece and signature work, *The Moor's Pavane.* Based on the story of Shakespeare's *Othello,* the piece represented a distillation of Limón's use of drama and character. The covert alliances, the characters' jealousy, love, and rage erupted in dramatic episodes framed by the stately pavane. Limón received the *Dance Magazine* Award for this work in 1950. [*See* Moor's Pavane, The.]

The Instituto Nacional de Bellas Artes of Mexico invited Limón to come to Mexico City to choreograph and perform in 1951. Mexican themes and rhythms predominated in the works he created during the residency. For the first time Limón experimented with large groups, incorporating both Mexican dancers and his company members into the thirty-dancer cast of *Los Cuatros Soles* and into the twenty-six-dancer cast of *Redes.*

The next seven years were greatly productive for Limón. Plot and character development figured prominently in his work of this period. Aided by Humphrey's invaluable advice, he created *The Exiles* (1950), *The Visitation* (1952), *The Traitor* (1954), *There Is a Time* and *The Emperor Jones,* both in 1956.

During this time, the Limón Company taught classes in New York, at the American Dance Festival during the summers, and on tour. It was in these classes that some of the major components of the Limón technique—the isolation of weight in different body parts; successional lifts in the spine and limbs; and fall, rebound, and suspension—were beginning to be identified and taught.

Limón was asked to join the faculty of the Juilliard School's new dance department in 1951. Here he had the opportunity to refine the teaching of Limón technique, and was able once again to work with large groups of dancers. With access to more male dancers, he also began to choreograph for all-male casts. Two men's works, *The Traitor* (1954) and *Scherzo* (1955), premiered at the American Dance Festival; a third, *The Emperor Jones,* was commissioned in 1956 by the Empire State Music Festival.

The Limón Company gained international recognition when it was chosen to tour South America in 1954 as the first modern dance company to participate in the U.S. State Department's Cultural Exchange Program. Subsequently, the company was sent to Europe in 1957, to South and Central America in 1960, and to Asia and Australia in 1963. The year after Limón's death, in 1973, another State Department tour took them to the Soviet Union.

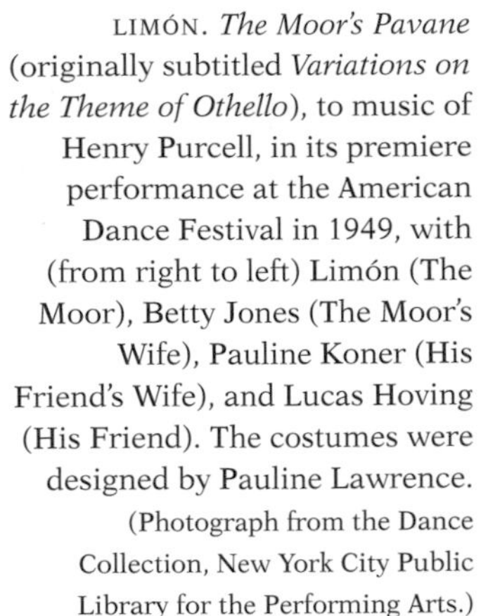

LIMÓN. *The Moor's Pavane* (originally subtitled *Variations on the Theme of Othello*), to music of Henry Purcell, in its premiere performance at the American Dance Festival in 1949, with (from right to left) Limón (The Moor), Betty Jones (The Moor's Wife), Pauline Koner (His Friend's Wife), and Lucas Hoving (His Friend). The costumes were designed by Pauline Lawrence. (Photograph from the Dance Collection, New York City Public Library for the Performing Arts.)

During the 1957 European tour, the company performed in cities still devastated by World War II. The Polish people, struggling to rebuild their lives, inspired Limón to choreograph another of his major works, *Missa Brevis.* Composed to Zoltan Kodály's music, *Missa Brevis in Tempore Belli,* this large group work was created as a testimony to the tenacity and power of the human spirit.

The year 1958 included both the premiere of *Missa Brevis,* to great acclaim, and the death of Humphrey. Though Limón continued to choreograph, the absence of his mentor affected his work for several years.

The Juilliard School became a training ground for new company members. In 1963, for the Asian tour, Limón added a group of younger dancers from Juilliard to the company. After the tour, the original company members left to pursue independent careers while some of the newer members, including Sarah Stackhouse, Louis Falco, Jennifer Muller, and Daniel Lewis, remained.

Limón's tribute to Doris Humphrey, *A Choreographic Offering* (1964), commissioned by the American Dance Festival, marked the beginning of a resurgence in his creativity. After this, Limón began to use more abstract themes and to focus on manipulating large groups of dancers. *The Winged* (1966), an ensemble work for sixteen, was simply about flight and mythical winged creatures. He also began to experiment with different types of sound and musical accompaniment. For *The Winged* he created a sound collage of electronic sounds, birds chirping, the sound of the wind, and a jazz score. The collage served as "incidental music" and showed a departure from Limón's usual adherence to the structures and rhythms of accompanying music. Later he incorporated spoken text, voice scores, and taped speeches into his sound collages.

In the fall of 1967, Limón entered the hospital for the first of several operations for cancer of the prostate. Later that year, however, he was working again and performing limited roles. Within two years he stopped dancing completely and concentrated on his choreography and on his company.

Experimentation with sound and form continued. In *The Unsung* (1970) a group of eight men danced in silence, to no accompaniment except the sound of their own feet—brushing, running, leaping, and stamping. A tribute to the Native American people and essentially plotless, the dance took its shape from a series of eight solos, each named for a Native American leader.

During the next two years, Limón's dances continued to mine the ideas and structures he had begun to explore in *The Unsung.* His *Dances for Isadora* was another series of solos, each of which portrayed a different aspect of the legendary Isadora Duncan. His last work, *Carlota,* the story of Carlota and Maximilian, emperor of Mexico (1864–1867), was created in 1972. It showed a return to his early use of plot; this time, though, the work was danced in silence. On 2 December 1972 José Limón died in a hospital not far from his New Jersey farm.

Dancers who have worked with Limón invariably say that he made his dancers feel special and helped them to discover and manifest their own strengths. He was most concerned with the truth in his work and in the performance of it. To this end he trained dancers to use each part of their bodies as an expressive tool. Men, in particular, responded to Limón's dancing and choreography because they saw in it a male passion and strength.

During his lifetime, Limón choreographed seventy-four works, of which twenty exist in the repertories of modern dance companies, such as Alvin Ailey American Dance Theater, Netherlands Dance Theater, Daniel Lewis Dance, Utah Repertory Dance Theater, and the Limón Dance Company, and in such ballet companies as American Ballet Theatre, Compañía Nacional de Danza (Mexico City), Dresden Ballet, Hamburg Ballet, Joffrey Ballet, Maggio Danza (Florence, Italy), Miami City Ballet, Oakland Ballet, Pacific Northwest Ballet, Paris Opera Ballet, Pennsylvania Ballet, Royal Danish Ballet, Royal Swedish Ballet, and the National Ballet of Canada. In 1950, his exceptional choreographic ability was honored by a *Dance Magazine* Award for *The Moor's Pavane.* Limón also received the Capezio Dance Award in 1950 and a second *Dance Magazine* Award in 1957. He was awarded honorary doctorates of Fine Arts by Wesleyan University in 1960, by Colby College in 1967, by the University of North Carolina in 1968, and by Oberlin College in 1971. The New York State Council on the Arts named him artistic director of the short-lived American Dance Theatre in 1964. The Limón Company still performs and teaches all over the world.

In his own words, José Limón tried to

> compose works that are involved with man's basic tragedy and the grandeur of his spirit . . . to dig beneath empty formalisms, displays of technical virtuosity, and the slick surface; to probe the human entity for the powerful, often crude, beauty of the gesture that speaks of man's humanity.
>
> (Limón, 1966)

[*See also the entries on Humphrey and Koner.*]

BIBLIOGRAPHY

Becker, Svea. "From Humphrey to Limón: A Modern Dance Tradition." *Dance Notation Journal* 2 (Spring 1984): 37–52.

Cohen, Selma Jeanne, ed. *The Modern Dance: Seven Statements of Belief.* Middletown, Conn., 1966.

Hill, Martha. "José Limón and His Biblical Works." *Choreography and Dance* 2.3 (1992): 57–61.

Humphrey, Doris. *Doris Humphrey, an Artist First: An Autobiography.* Edited by Selma Jeanne Cohen. Middletown, Conn., 1977.

Lewis, Daniel, with Lesley Farlow. *The Illustrated Dance Technique of José Limón.* New York, 1984.

Limón, José. "The Modern Dance as an Unpopular Art." *Juilliard Review Annual* (1964–1965): 31.

Limón, José. "An American Accent." In *The Modern Dance: Seven Statements of Belief,* edited by Selma Jeanne Cohen. Middletown, Conn., 1966.

Martin, John. "The Dancer as an Artist." *New York Times Magazine* (12 April 1958).

McDonagh, Don. *The Rise and Fall and Rise of Modern Dance.* Rev. ed. Pennington, N.J., 1990.

Owen, Norton, ed. *Limón: A Catalogue of Dances.* New York, 1994.

Pollack, Barbara, and Charles Woodford. *Dance Is a Moment: A Portrait of José Limón in Words and Pictures.* Pennington, N.J., 1993.

Van Gelder, Lawrence. Obituary. *New York Times* (4 December 1972).

Waung, Juliette, and Sheldon Schwartz, comps. "The Choreographic Works of José Limón." Unpublished chronology, Juilliard School of Music and Dance, New York. Originally compiled by Waung in 1957, supplemented by Schwartz in 1973.

NOTATED SCORES. The Dance Notation Bureau, New York, contains Labanotation scores of many of Limón's works.

ARCHIVE. Limón's unpublished writings and letters are in the files of the Juilliard School of Music and Dance, New York. The José Limón and Pauline Lawrence Limón Collection is held in the Dance Collection, New York Public Library for the Performing Arts.

DANIEL LEWIS and LESLEY FARLOW

LINDEN, ANYA (Anya Eltenton; born 3 January 1933 in Manchester, England), British dancer. Having received her early training from Theodore Koslov in California, Linden entered the Sadler's Wells Ballet School in 1947. She first performed with the company as a student, in 1949; she entered the corps in 1951 and was promoted to soloist in 1954 and to principal in 1958 when the English writer Cyril Swinson called her "the first dancer of ballerina status to emerge from the School since the war."

A calm, lyrical dancer, dynamically serene, Linden quietly mastered all the challenges of the classical repertory in logical sequence. Starting with the peasant pas de deux in *Giselle,* the Bluebird pas de deux, and the Mazurka in *Les Sylphides,* she moved with assurance into Swanilda, Cinderella, and the Lilac Fairy, then on to Aurora and eventually into the more dramatic classical roles of Odette-Odile, Myrtha, and Giselle. Her range was equally broad in modern works, extending from pure dance roles in *Ballet Imperial, Homage to the Queen,* and *Birthday Offering* to highly dramatic ones: Ophelia, the Wife in *The Invitation,* and the Red Queen in *Checkmate.* Responding to her cool, piquant qualities, Kenneth MacMillan created four roles for her—in *Noctambules* (1956), *Solitaire* (1957), and *Agon* (1957) and as the dancing Anna in his first treatment of *The Seven Deadly Sins,* at the Edinburgh Festival in 1961.

Linden married John Sainsbury in 1963 and retired in 1965. As Lady Sainsbury, she became a member of the advisory panel of the Royal Ballet Choreographic Group, the board of directors of Ballet Rambert, and the board of governors of the Royal Ballet School.

BIBLIOGRAPHY

Bland, Alexander. *The Royal Ballet: The First Fifty Years.* London, 1981.

Clarke, Mary. "The Royal Ballet at Home." *The Dancing Times* (April 1958): 325–327.

Swinson, Cyril. *The Royal Ballet Today.* London, 1958.

BARBARA NEWMAN

LINDY HOP. Also known as the jitterbug or swing dancing, this exuberant, sometimes wild, social dance is done to swing music. Originating in Harlem in the late 1920s, the Lindy Hop developed out of four previously popular social dances, the Charleston, the Collegiate, the Breakaway, and, according to dance historian Marshall Stearns, the Texas Tommy. Certain elements of the Lindy can be traced back to African and early African-American dance forms. The post–Civil War migration of free blacks from the South to cities in the North and the later celebratory atmosphere of the jazz age also influenced the flowering of jazz dance and music.

Done in couples with the man traditionally leading, the Lindy incorporates a common vocabulary of steps danced in an unset order as well as improvisational dancing. One basic step is the Lindy circle. Done in a modified ballroom position, partners dance in a circular path around a shared central axis, exploiting centrifugal force and momentum. In the characteristic swingout, the woman is guided out on an oblong path, almost rebounding back as she returns to her partner. Improvisational sections, called a break or breakaway, may be inserted into the dance during musical breaks. The break may incorporate specific Lindy variations, jazz steps, and/or individual movements unique to the dancers. During the break, sometimes referred to as the dancer's chance to "shine," a couple may or may not choose to separate. Staying connected by only one hand, or breaking the connection completely, allows for more creative freedom. The rhythm, originally an eight-count structure with six-count variations, is given vitality through intricate footwork and syncopated movements. As the Lindy became popular in the late 1930s, dance schools created a simplified six-count basic Lindy in order to market the dance to the public. As a performance art, the Lindy may involve ensemble dancing, choreographed routines, and acrobatic airsteps.

Most sources agree that the name *Lindy Hop* became attached to the dance shortly after Charles Lindbergh completed the first solo transatlantic flight on 20 May 1927. Shorty Snowden, a much-admired dancer at the time, is credited with naming the Lindy Hop when, shortly after the momentous event, he was asked by reporters at a Manhattan Casino dance marathon what dance he was doing. Perhaps Snowden was influenced by such headlines as "Lindy Hops the Atlantic," but in actuality, he probably renamed the currently popular Breakaway, which he likely was doing that evening.

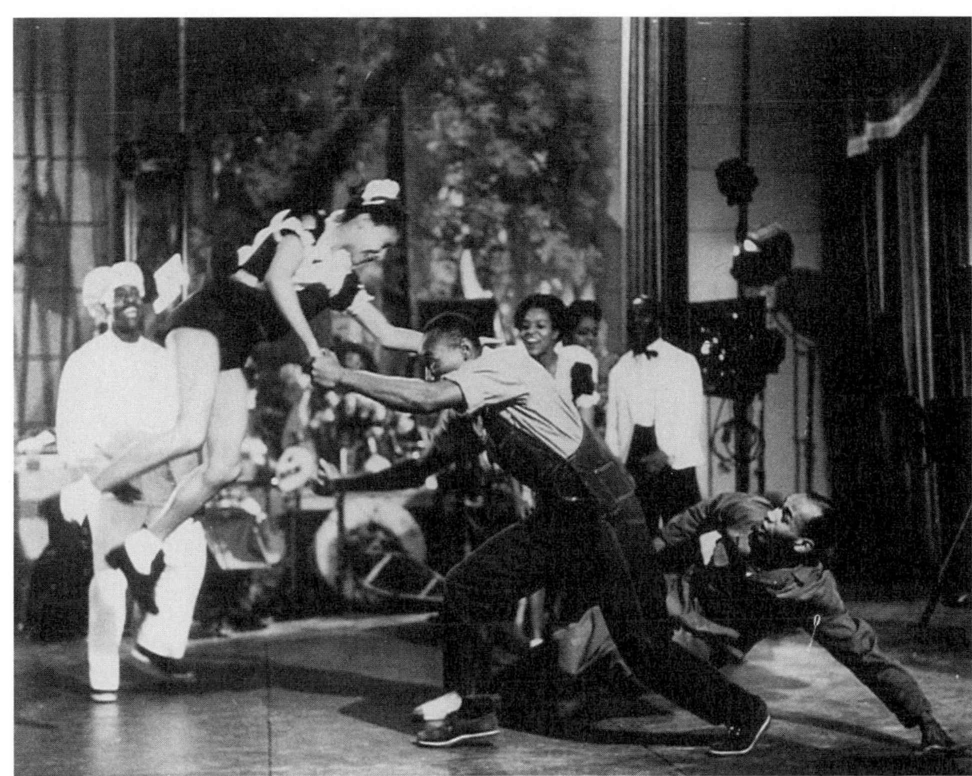

LINDY HOP. Whitey's Lindy Hoppers on the set of the film *Hellzapoppin'* (1941). At center, Ann Johnson and Frankie Manning perform an airstep called the Snatch, while (left to right) Billie Ricker, Willmae Ricker, Al Minns, and William Downs look on. Manning, a major figure in the development of the Lindy Hop, is credited with having created the first Lindy airstep, c.1935. In the 1980s and 1990s, he has helped lead a revival in swing dancing. (Photograph from the collection of Cynthia Millman and Frankie Manning.)

LINDY HOP. The Lindy Hop is one of many dances with African-American origins to became hugely popular in white mainstream culture. This photograph, taken in 1935, at the height of the swing era, shows a white couple in a characteristically lively Lindy step. (Photograph used by permission of AP/Wide World Photos.)

Snowden's upright style of dancing, which emphasized complex footwork, was soon overshadowed by a newer, more acrobatic style of Lindy originated by Frankie Manning, a younger dancer who idolized Snowden. Circa late 1935, Manning created the first Lindy airstep and synchronized ensemble Lindy routines. Earlier he had developed the style of dancing more horizontally to the floor in order to create a wilder, abandoned effect. According to jazz historian Ernie Smith the more swinging jazz of the big band era (1935–1945) influenced Lindy Hoppers toward a smoother, more elongated style of dance than the original more upright, bouncier style that was inspired by early jazz. [*See the entry on Manning.*]

The famed Savoy Ballroom in Harlem was the center of the universe for Lindy Hoppers. Encouraged by Herbert "Whitey" White, a Savoy bouncer, Manning and a new generation of enthusiastic young dancers continued to expand the vocabulary of floor steps as well as airsteps. This feverishly creative period was often stoked by a friendly competitiveness among the dancers for prizes awarded at weekly dance contests held at the Savoy, at the Apollo Theatre, and at the annual Harvest Moon Ball competition in Madison Square Garden that began in 1935. Impromptu performances for appreciative, often tipping, Savoy patrons also inspired the dancers.

In the mid-1930s, as the swing music of Count Basie, Benny Goodman, Duke Ellington, Jimmie Lunceford, and others was embraced by the nation, the Lindy Hop became the rage among the younger set. From the latter half of this decade onward, the Lindy Hop was commonly known as the jitterbug. This enormously popular social dance, as practiced by the masses, might have lacked the acrobatic airsteps of performance Lindy but not its enthusiasm or energy.

Attesting to its immense popularity, in 1943 *Life* featured a cover story on the Lindy Hop, proclaiming it "America's national dance" and "this country's only native and original dance form" along with tap dance. Hundreds of other newspaper and magazine articles on the Lindy corroborated its cultural importance.

The combination of swing music's popularity, Manning's audience-pleasing innovations, and the irrepressible talent of the Savoy elite helped catapult the Lindy from the ballroom to stage and screen. Foreseeing the Lindy's rising star, Whitey began organizing professional (meaning a signed contract was involved) dance troupes in 1936. He often booked several performing groups at a time. Appearing under various names, but most often as Whitey's Lindy Hoppers, his groups toured the globe until World War II; they performed in nightclubs, theaters, revues, on Broadway (*Hot Mikado,* 1939; *Swingin' the Dream,* 1939), at the 1939 World's Fair Hall of Music, in a soundie (a brief film shown within jukeboxes to accompany the record) with the Duke Ellington Orchestra (*Hot Chocolates,* 1941), and in several films, including *A Day at the Races* (1937) and *Hellzapoppin'* (1941).

These exceptionally talented dancers were known for their frenetic ensemble routines, uniquely expressive solos, and breathtakingly daring airsteps. Manning, recruited by Whitey as a dancer, soon became his chief choreographer as the young man's choreographic and leadership talents became apparent. Among the many notable dancers in the troupe were Norma Miller, Willamae Ricker, Leon James, and Al Minns.

The term *swing dance* became associated with the Lindy as swing music came into vogue. After the war, swing dancing slowly declined in popularity as other social dances, particularly nontouch dance types, came into favor and big bands became too expensive to run and hire. The Lindy lifted its head briefly in the 1950s, to the early rock-and-roll music of such groups as Bill Haley and the Comets, with the dance sometimes taking its name from the music.

Swing dance has since become an umbrella term for all of the permutations and regional variations in this family of social dances, including rock-and-roll (1950s' style), jive (England), boogie-woogie (Germany), Carolina Shag, Saint Louis Shag, and West Coast Swing styles, such as the Dallas Push and Houston Whip. West Coast Swing, which originated in California during World War II, is danced in a slotted spatial pattern to rhythm-and-blues (R&B) music, tends to be more upright, and has developed its own vocabulary of steps, mostly to a six-count rhythm.

A revival of swing dance took place in the mid-1980s as touch dancing came back into style, and the revival has continued. In the 1990s, Manning was increasingly in demand as a teacher, choreographer, performer, and lecturer, and Norma Miller also was much sought after to share her knowlege of swing dancing. More than three hundred and fifty ongoing organizations were formed in the United States and Europe to preserve and promote swing dancing. These societies and clubs sponsor dances, classes, workshops, weekends, festivals, camps, conventions, competitions, products, and newsletters. Run by amateurs and/or professionals, the swing dance world is diverse in terms of age, race, nationality, and occupation—but not enthusiasm.

[*See also* Social Dance, *article on* Twentieth-Century Social Dance to 1960. *For related discussion, see* United States of America, *article on* African-American Social Dance.]

BIBLIOGRAPHY

Crease, Robert P. "Swing Story." *Atlantic Monthly* (February 1986).

Crease, Robert P. "Divine Frivolity: Hollywood Representations of the Lindy Hop, 1937–1942." In *Representing Jazz,* edited by Krin Gabbard. Durham, N.C., 1995.

Engelbrecht, Barbara. "Swinging at the Savoy." *Dance Research Journal* 15 (Spring 1983): 3–10.

"The Lindy Hop: A True National Folk Dance Has Been Born in the U.S.A." *Life* (23 August 1943).

Malcolm X. *The Autobiography of Malcolm X.* New York, 1964. Includes a vivid description of the experience of Lindy hopping in the chapter "Laura."

Miller, Norma, with Everette Jensen. *Swingin' at the Savoy: The Memoir of a Jazz Dancer.* Philadelphia, 1996. Features memoirs of original Savoy Lindy Hopper Norma Miller; "Portrait of the Swing Era" by Ernie Smith; and "The Future of the Lindy and the New York Swing Society" by Robert P. Crease.

Monaghan, Terry. "A Lindy Double" (parts 1–2). *Dancing Times* (May–June 1995).

Smith, Ernie. "Films." In *The New Grove Dictionary of Jazz.* London, 1988.

Stearns, Marshall, and Jean Stearns. *Jazz Dance.* New York, 1968.

Van Vechten, Carl. *Parties* (1930). New York, 1977. Includes a vivid description of Lindy Hop (pp. 157–159).

FILMS. *Hellzapoppin'* (1941), starring Olsen and Johnson, with the best Lindy Hop scene ever captured on film, choreographed by Frankie Manning for Whitey's Lindy Hoppers. Mura Dehn, *The Spirit Moves: Jazz Dance from the Turn of the Century 'till 1950* and *The Spirit Moves: Savoy Ballroom of Harlem* (both New York, c.1950), Dance Collection, New York Public Library for the Performing Arts.

VIDEOTAPES. *Eye on Dance* (WNYC-TV, New York, 1989), an interview with Frankie Manning and dance writer Robert P. Crease, including some rare film footage. "Jitterbug," *National Geographic Explorer* (PBS, 1991), documentary on the history and current revival of swing dancing.

ARCHIVES. Ernie Smith Jazz and Film Dance Collection (social dance reel) in the Moving Image and Recorded Sound Collection, Schomburg Center for Research in Black Culture, New York Public Library. New York Swing Dance Society Archives, Dance Collection, New York Public Library for the Performing Arts.

CYNTHIA R. MILLMAN

LINGUISTICS AND DANCE. *See* Methodologies in the Study of Dance, *article on* Linguistics.

LINKE, SUSANNE (born 19 June 1944 in Lüneberg, Germany), dancer, teacher, and choreographer. Susanne Linke studied dance in Berlin at the Mary Wigman Studio from 1964 to 1967, then in Essen at the Folkwang Schule from 1967 to 1970. She was a member of the Folkwang Tanzstudio from 1970 to 1973, where her colleagues included Pina Bausch, Reinhild Hoffmann, and Jean Cébron. From 1975 to 1985 she was artistic director of the Folkwang Tanzstudio, for which she choreographed numerous small-scale works, showing herself strongly influenced by Wigman, Dore Hoyer, and other pioneers of the early German modern dance movement. She has a broad sense of humor, which occasionally shows in her titles, such as *Bathtubbing* (1980) or *We Can't All Be Swans* (1982). She works mostly to musical collages. Her other important pieces are *L'Histoire Obscure* (1977), *The Next One, Please* (1978), *Frauenballett* (1981), and *Am Reigenplatz* (after Euripides' *Bacchae;* 1983).

Linke was director of the Folkwang Tanzstudio from 1975 to 1985, the first two years in collaboration with Reinhild Hoffmann. In 1983, she performed and taught in Buenos Aires. In 1984 she danced with the José Limón Dance Company at Saratoga Springs, New York, performing her own solos, which included the American premiere of *Flood,* danced with a long roll of blue fabric. Jennifer Dunning, writing in the *New York Times,* found her a "powerful physical presence." Two years later Linke returned to the United States to choreograph *Also Egmont, Bitte* for the Limón company, using a recording of a rehearsal of the Beethoven overture to accompany scenes about the staging of a ballet.

Back in Germany, Linke re-created two dances by Dore Hoyer—*Hommage à Dore Hoyer (Affectos Humanos)* (1985), to music by Dimitrij Wiatowitsch, and *Hommage à Dore Hoyer (Affekte)* (1988). Other recent works include *JardinCour* (1988), *Effekte* (1990), to music by Pierre Henry, *Ruhr-Ort* (1991), to music by Ludger Brümmer, and *?Tristan und Isolde?* (1992), to music by Brümmer, which she created for the Netherlands Dance Theater. Since 1994 she has co-directed (with Urs Dietrich) the Bremer Tanztheater, for which she has choreographed *Märkische Landschaft* (1994), to music by Peter Hollinger, and *Hamletszenen* (1996), to music by Ronald Steckel.

BIBLIOGRAPHY

"An Interview with Susanne Linke." *Choreography and Dance* 2.1 (1992): 133–135.

Kirchner, Birgit. "Dancing Really Does Make Sense." *Ballett International* 6 (December 1983): 22–28.

Schlicher, Susanne. "Tradition und Freiheit alm Biographie." In Schlicher's *Tanztheater.* Reinbeck, 1987.

Schmidt, Jochen. "Susanne Linke: Die Einzelgängerin." In *Tanztheater in Deutschland,* pp. 144–157. Berlin, 1992.

HORST KOEGLER

LITHUANIA. [*To survey traditional and theatrical dance in the republic of Lithuania, this entry comprises two articles. The first article discusses the history of traditional dance; the second explores the development of ballet.*]

Traditional Dance

Bordering on the Baltic Sea in the west, Lithuania is bounded by Latvia to the north, Belarus to the east, Poland to the south, and Kaliningrad (a territory of Russia) to the southwest. A flatland drained by the Nemen River, Lithuania is an agricultural and dairying country. Its people are mainly Lithuanian Balts, speaking a Baltic language, and descended from those who settled along the Nemen River about 1500 BCE.

In the thirteenth century, Lithuania formed a strong unified state for protection from the Livonian and Teutonic knights; by absorbing nearby Russian principalities, Lithuania became one of the largest states in medieval Europe. Lithuania gradually merged with Poland, between 1386 and 1569, thus coming under Russian control in 1795 when Poland was partitioned by Russia, Prussia, and Austria.

Lithuanian folk dances were recorded by travelers beginning in the ninth century; the English traveler Wulfstan, in describing the customs of the Balts (887–901), mentioned funeral games. Sources from the thirteenth to eighteenth centuries also have descriptions from travelers about Lithuania and its customs. Most sixteenth to eighteenth century examples are from so-called Minor (or Prussian) Lithuania, the Balts' lands conquered by thirteenth-century Crusaders on both sides of the rivers Nemen and Poregolia (now in the Russian territory of Kaliningrad). Minor Lithuania was formed in the sixteenth century in the northeast of Prussia, where Lithuanians lived compactly from the sixteenth to nineteenth centuries. Their calendar, funerals, weddings, and fishermen dances were described by several chroniclers. From 1698 to 1707 Michael Praetorius made engravings of some Lithuanian folk dances: the wedding dance of women, *žalia rūtelė* ("green rue"), and a dance of men, *heiduka.*

Since the nineteenth century, most information about folk dance comes from Major Lithuania (and to it belongs the state of Lithuania). Here, not only foreigners but also Lithuanians described the folk dances. The first Lithuanian dance melodies were published in the nineteenth century; unfortunately, there were no descriptions of the movements. The first collections of folk dances and games were published in 1911.

Very little scholarly attention was paid to the folk tradition in Lithuania for a long time. Lithuanian folklore collectors first began by recording the songs—huge collections of songs were published just before the twentieth century—but not the dances. Mainstream scholarly opinion has been that the folk songs are the most significant and interesting part of Lithuanian musical folklore. Lithuanian dances and games of ancient origin were usually accompanied with a song rather than with an instrument. According to old sources and the descriptions of traditional dances and games, it is possible to say that the women and girls were the main dancers and singers.

The character of the dances was stately—slow and quiet—and the steps were not complicated but based on walking. The typical choreographical drawings show a circle, some lines, a snake, a spiral, a "bridge" and so on. The group dances were performed with men, but led by women, and they have the same patterns. The men's dances were very few, but these few had higher jumps and stronger movements. In general, the origin of Lithuanian folk dance lies in a female culture. It is based on small, low steps, with symmetry of movement; the music is based on two-beat meter with a quadratic structure (2/4 time). For the most part, Lithuanian folk dance is group dance. Solo dances do not exist except for some brief examples in ritual and some moments found in improvisational games and dances.

Lithuanian couple dances were mentioned for the first time in eighteenth-century sources. Since the nineteenth century, couple dances from other countries came to Lithuania, such as the polka, waltz, quadrille, and krakowiak; these have complicated steps and a fast tempo. The accompaniment of instrumental music also became more popular. The dances of the Slavs had their influence in the southeast part of Lithuania, whereas

LITHUANIA: Traditional Dance. Two Lithuanian women in traditional "good" clothes perform a couple dance, c.1930. Note the stylish high-heeled pumps worn by the younger woman on the left. (Photograph courtesy of Lietuvos Vaizdo Ir Garso Archyvas, Vilnius.)

dances from western Europe and especially from Germany had their influence in the northwestern part of Lithuania. The role of the man as the leader became stronger in couple dances but women continued to lead the group dances with singing, even when they performed with the men. This wave of couple and quadrille-style dances stimulated new Lithuanian versions. Various forms are fixtures all over Lithuania. They were especially popular at the end of the nineteenth century and at the beginning of the twentieth century; some few survive even today.

Until the nineteenth century, ritual choreography is mentioned most often in the old sources. All Lithuanian ritual dance and games were related through the ancient pre-Christian religion and worldview of the Balts. The fourteenth and fifteenth centuries were the closing epoch of Lithuania's prosperity as one of the largest states in Europe—with territory extending from the Baltic to the Black Sea. Although Lithuania adopted Christianity in 1387 (the last state to do so in Europe), the ancient religion of the Balts lasted officially until the beginning of the fifteenth century. The ancient religion and culture endured in rural areas until the seventeenth century, but traces could still be found in the nineteenth century and even later. Information about Lithuanian ritual choreography was recorded only in the time when the rituals were fast disappearing. Ritual dances and games continued until World War I but soon after vanished and were described only as memories. The ritual calendrical celebrations and wedding dances are the main descriptions. These include the games of Advent to Christmas, the dances of masks for Carnival, circle dances devoted to a cult of the sun and those to protect the harvest in summer, special wedding dances that mark the changing of the bride's status, and those that bring together the two families. Some few even testify that ritual choreography still existed for birthday celebrations and funerals at the turn of the twentieth century. Only a few descriptions of very doubtful origin exist for Lithuanian war and hunting dances.

Folk Choreography. Folk choreography in Lithuania is classified into four groups: danced *sutartinės,* dances, roundelays, and games.

Danced sutartinės. These are the most original and most ancient group of the Lithuanian ethnochoreography—performed mainly by women. *Sutartinės* were danced and sung by couples. The song was executed as imitational polyphony (a canon) or as contrasting polyphony. In polyphony, voices with the same melody sound together but constantly form dissonances. The singers must be very attentive, listening to each other, because they must blend in a strict rhythmic and melodic way.

The word *sutartinė* means "to agree" in English. The connection between the music and the dance movements is great, since all are based on the same principles of execution. For example, in performing those dances with imitational polyphony, not only are the melody and words repeated in a canon but also the movements—the steps, rotations, clapping, turnings arm-in-arm, illustrative movements, and so forth. *Sutartinės* of the canon type are mostly danced in a circle, in a square, and, less often in a line by couples.

With contrasting polyphony, the dance was performed differently. Usually two couples dance standing either in a cross or with one couple in front of another. While one couple is singing and dancing (moving forward and back, turning arm-in-arm, etc.), the other couple stands in silence; later, the couples change roles. *Sutartinės* with contrasting polyphony are danced less often in a circle. Some *sutartinės* are played on instruments, but their music, like those sung, provide no information about the dance movements. *Sutartinės* were originally danced at various ceremonies. They have disappeared from the countryside and are only executed as reconstructions by the amateur and professional folk ensembles.

Dances. Social, couple, and quadrille dances with instrumental accompaniment are in this group. Their organized steps are subordinated to the musical rhythm, and various figures form their choreography. Most of Lithuanian couple dances are not complicated; the same movements are repeated many times. Usually they are based on two or three steps and their combinations, with figures such as rotations, walking to the side and back, clapping, and such. Quadrilles became popular in Lithuania in the nineteenth century. In some places the quadrille remained the main dance at a party until the 1950s and later. Sometimes a quadrille was danced for hours without any break. Lithuanian quadrilles are based on a walking step, and have many stanzas (5–12), each with different combinations of the figures. A very typical way of dancing is for each couple to repeat the same figure. Usually the rotation figure is also repeated in every stanza as a refrain.

Roundelays. These group dances, performed while singing, are called roundelays (choreographers have given wide meaning to this term, but the village people use the term only for dances round in form). Usually roundelays consist of two parts: in the first part the dancers sing rhythmically while walking or standing; in the second part they turn, weave, creep, or illustrate the words of the song. Roundelays are divided into groups based on form—circles, lines, chain (snake), bridge, gates. Roundelays were usually danced between the other dances, the girls and women leading them; some were danced by children. Nowadays the roundelays danced are of later origin—those that came into Lithuania at the turn of the twentieth century. The most popular way of dancing them is for the dancers to choose their own partners. Some roundelays still danced are of ancient origin—coming from ancient rituals.

Games. Another division of the ethnochoreography is called "games." Here the free and natural movements of the participants only partly depend on a song's rhythm or do not depend on it at all. Some are only spoken, without singing. In many cases the games do not have a clear structure, because they are very static, very free, or may be improvised by one or a few players. Some games are similar to the roundelays, having a clear structure, usually of two parts. The most popular types of Lithuanian games include: catching, hiding, blindfolded, a figure of gates, taking players from one group to another, matchmaking, and so on. Lithuanian games originally were related to a season—one in step with the ceremonial year—thus most are known from the games of Advent to Christmas. Later, some of them were forgotten and others were changed into leisure activities and children's games. They also lost their musical accompaniment (the singing).

This classification of Lithuanian ethnochoreography is not strict, as it is difficult to distinguish a dance from a roundelay and a roundelay from a game. A strict classification does not exist in the countryside either; for example, a roundelay (so named by a choreographer) might be called either a game or dance in the countryside. Some mixed forms are characteristic too, when a game is changed into a dance. Often many figures from the roundelays or the game motifs are plaited into a dance of differing origin (as a polka or a quadrille).

Traditional dancing no longer exists in Lithuania, but folk dances are usually performed by various ensembles on special occasions (at concerts, after work in the fields). Contemporary Lithuanian folk dancers may be divided into four groups:

1. Those who learned in traditional village surroundings are people born in the 1920s and 1930s. Some have formed dance ensembles. They mostly perform the later couple dances, the quadrilles and roundelays, and some games. The young people of the countryside usually do not continue in the folk dance tradition.

2. The second group includes dancers of all ages—children, youth, adults, and elderly—who live in the towns. They form folk ensembles and learn to dance from the first group. They also learn the dances from old descriptions and are reconstructing some forms that no longer exist, like the *sutartinės*.

These two groups are as close to authentic as they can be in their manner of folk dancing. However, two other groups emerged during the Soviet period, when song-and-dance ensembles were founded based on Russian examples. These ensembles execute a stylized and otherwise quite changed set of "folk" dances. Choreographers especially create very complicated, mass choreographies, composers write the music, and poets write the words to the songs. The dancers' training is similar to that of classical ballet.

3. The dancers who form this group are dancing composed, stylized staged dances as described above. Often they give dance and choreography lessons to train children in the secondary schools.

4. Some dancers of the third group perform real folk

dances, but these are in a balletic style and so they are not authentic.

Lithuanian folk dances are nowadays, in most cases, performed by folk ensembles in concert, at festivals, for evening parties, and during the festivities of families and other groups. Folk ensembles promote folk dances at various regional centers of ethnic activity. The Lithuanian Folkculture Centre coordinates all such activities. Usually there are six to ten seminars and camps (in summer) each year. The Section of Choreographical Folklore was established at the Lithuanian Folkculture Centre in 1986; it organizes and promotes folk dances, is publishing collections of dances, and has also created the central archives of Lithuanian folk dance. The staff members are collecting folk dances both from fieldwork and from other archives. Most of the material consists of cards with descriptions (11,000 items). The descriptions include illustrations. Another part of the archives consists of videotapes (300–400 hours). Searches for specific dances may be made by the name of the dance and its region.

Few research works on folk dance are published in Lithuania. Choreographers who created the stylized stage dances published the first books about Lithuanian folk dance (J. Lingys, E. Morkūniene, and K. Poškaitis). E. Venskauskaitė in the Section of Choreographical Folklore and Dalia Urbanavičienė in the Department of Ethnomusicology at the Lithuanian Academy of Music are continuing further research.

BIBLIOGRAPHY

Beliajus, Vytautas. *The Dance of Lietuva.* Chicago, 1951.

Beliajus, Vytautas. "The Lithuanian Tour Experience" (parts 1–4). *Viltis* (December 1985–May 1986).

Breichmanas, Genovaite. "Lithuanian Folk Dance." *Viltis* 55 (March–April 1995): 6.

"Dance Selection." *Viltis* 54 (May–June 1994): 20.

Davidson, Mary E. "Lithuania and Her Dances." *The Dancing Times* (June 1939): 285–286.

Lingys, Juozas. "Lithuanian Folk Dances." *Rosin the Bow* 5.7 (1954): 5–12.

Lingys, Juozas. *Lietuvisku sokiu pyne.* 4 vols. Vilnius, 1978–1985.

Sagys, Alexandra. "The Thirteenth National Song Fest in Vilnius." *Viltis* 49 (December 1990): 13–15.

Tkachenko, Tamara. *Narodnyi tanets.* 2d ed. Moscow, 1967.

Dalia Urbanavičienė

Theatrical Dance

Although historically there were traditional participatory dances in Lithuania, it was not until the sixteenth and seventeenth centuries that dances were included in theatrical presentations at schools. From about that time ballet

LITHUANIA: Theatrical Dance. Marius Petipa's *Raymonda* was staged for the National Ballet of Lithuania by Nicholas Zvereff in 1933. With sets and costumes designed by Mstislav Dobuzhinsky, Zvereff's production starred Vera Nemchinova as Raymonda and Anatole Oubоukoff as Jean de Brienne. (Photograph from the archives of the Theater Museum, Vilnius.)

troupes danced at the courts of the grand dukes and some magnates of Lithuania.

Ballet. After independence in 1920, an opera house was opened in Kaunas, then the capital and the largest city on the Nemen River. Olga Dubeneckienė staged the dances for their first productions, and in 1921 she opened Lithuania's first ballet studio there. The Russian choreographer Paul Petroff worked in Kaunas from 1925 to 1930. He staged the first professional ballet, *Coppélia,* and Olga Malėjinaitė, Jadvyga Jovaišaitė, and Bronius Kelbauskas danced in it. In the company from 1931 to 1935 were the famous Russian dancers Vera Nemchinova and Anatole Oboukhoff and the choreographer Nicholas Zvereff. They revived classical ballets and one-act ballets from the repertory of Serge Diaghilev (for example, *Aubade* by George Balanchine and *Boléro* by Bronislava Nijinska) and created three one-act ballets by Lithuanian composers: *Jūratė ir Kastytis, Piršlybos,* and *Šokių Sukūry* (In the Whirlwind). In 1935 the company toured Monte Carlo and London. The first Lithuanian choreographer, Bronius Kelbauskas, created many ballets. In *Sužadėtinė* (The Bride), he blended classical dance with elements drawn from national folklore.

LITHUANIA: Theatrical Dance. Eglė Špokaitė and Edvardas Smalakys in Jurijus Smoriginas's *Carmen,* set to music by Rodion Shchedrin. (Photograph by Mikhail Rashkovsky; used by permission.)

With the occupation of Lithuania by the Soviet Union in 1940, Germany from 1941 to 1944, and reversion to the Soviet Union in 1945, most ballet artists emigrated. In 1948 the ballet theater was transferred to Lithuania's traditional and restored capital, Vilnius. Its leading dancers were Marija Juozapaitytė, Genovaitė Sabaliauskaitė, Tamara Sventickaitė, Henrikas Banys, and Henrikas Kunavičius. From 1952 to 1976, the chief choreographer was Vytautas Grivickas; he staged the Lithuanian ballets *On the Seashore, Audronė,* and *Eglė, Queen of Grass Snakes.* They were notable for their well-developed action and the stylization of Lithuanian folklore. His leading artists were Leokadija Aškelovičiūtė, Raimundas Minderis, Vytautas Kudžma, Svetlana Masaniova, and Nina Antonova. From 1974 to 1977, chief choreographer Elegijus Bukaitis produced the ballet *Aistros* (Passions) with a new style of choreography, one without a story. From 1978 to 1990, the company was led by Vytautas Brazdylis. His *Baltaragio Malūnas* (The Baltaragis Mill), in which he used modern dance steps, was very popular. The principals of the company were then Jonas Katakinas, Petras Skirmantas, Loreta Bartusevičiūtė, Nelli Beredina, and Aleksandr Molodov. Jolanta Valeikaitė, winner of the Moscow, Varna, and Paris ballet competitions, has danced in Essen, Germany, since 1994.

In 1992, Tatjana Sedunova became the artistic director of the company, which consists of seventy-five dancers. Most have graduated from the Vilnius Ballet School (opened in 1952) but also from the Moscow and Saint Petersburg ballet schools. Since 1989 the leading dancers of the company have been Eglė Špokaitė (winner of competitions in Perm, Saint Petersburg, and Helinski), Živilė Baikštytė (third prize in a New York competition), Rūta Jezerskytė (first prize in Lausanne), Edvardas Smalakys, and Mindaugas Baužys. The company and its soloists have toured in Europe and the Americas. The company's repertory has always consisted mostly of nineteenth-century classical ballets—those composed by Fedor Lopukhov, Maya Plisetskaya, Nikolai Boyarchikov, Oleg Vinogradov, Vladimir Vasiliev, Antol Fodor, and Mai-Ester Murdmaa. Jurijus Smoriginas, the contemporary Lithuanian choreographer, created the ballets *House of Alba, Fedra,* and *Macbeth.* Egidijus Domeika has staged the ballets *Caligula* and *Eglė, Queen of Grass Snakes.* Ballet companies also reside in Kaunas and at the Klaipėda Musical Theater.

Modern Dance. In 1939 Danutė Nasvytytė, the pioneer of Lithuanian modern dance, finished her studies at the school of Jutta Klamt in Berlin. From 1939 to 1943 she danced and had her studio in Kaunas. Her pupil, Kira Daujotytė, taught modern dance for forty years. Since 1980, Birutė Letukaitė has been the artistic director of the

Aura company, for which the guest choreographers Royston Maldoom, Tamar Rogoff, and Yane-Claude Roulin worked. Aura has participated in festivals in Germany and England. In 1994, French contemporary dance companies started traveling to Lithuania, and in 1995, the Lithuanian Dance Information Center began organizing modern and contemporary dance workshops.

BIBLIOGRAPHY

"The Baltic Republics." *Ballett International* 13 (June–July 1990): 54–56.

Ruzgaitė, Aliodija, and K. Landsbergas. *Teatr opery i baleta Litovskoi SSR: Vilnius Balet.* Vilnius, 1976.

Stein, Bonnie Sue. "Dance Struggles in the Baltics." *Dance Magazine* (September 1990): 20.

Swift, Mary Grace. *The Art of the Dance in the U.S.S.R.* Notre Dame, 1968.

Teatr opery i baleta Litovskoi SSR: Gosudarstvennyi akademicheskii teatr opery i baleta Litovskoi SSR, 1920–1925. Vilnius, 1955.

Aliodija Ruzgaitė

LITTLEFIELD, CATHERINE (born 16 September 1905 in Philadelphia, died 19 November 1951 in Chicago), American dancer and choreographer. Littlefield, founder of the Philadelphia Ballet, was the eldest of four children born to James and Caroline Littlefield; her mother, her sister Dorothie, and her brother Carl were also active in dance. The impetus for her achievement was provided by her early exposure to dance and theater through her mother. Raised in an atmosphere of strong discipline, Caroline Littlefield became enamored of the theater when she first saw a performance of the Philadelphia Opera Company. She subsequently answered calls for extras from among the subscribers and was soon walking on. Her classical ballet training under the tutelage of Romulus Carpenter started too late for her to achieve virtuoso status, but she attained the rank of soloist.

In addition to performing, in 1908 Caroline Littlefield founded the Littlefield School, an influential force in the development of American ballet. Affectionately referred to as "Mommie," she was the director and driving force behind the school, which provided rigorous training for such American dancers as Lucille Bremer, Karen Conrad, Douglas Coudy, Jane Deering, William Dollar, Norma Gentner, Miriam Golden, Joan McCracken, and Jack Potteiger. The school continued through the 1940s, providing instruction of high quality for a generation of American dancers.

In 1934, when George Balanchine founded the School of American Ballet in New York City, he selected from the Littlefield School dancers who became the nucleus of his company; he also recruited Dorothie Littlefield to teach the junior division at the School of American Ballet. When Balanchine's Ballet Theatre was organized in 1939, it too drew dancers from the Littlefield School. In this environment of high standards Catherine and her siblings had been trained.

Catherine was seen by Florenz Ziegfeld in a Philadelphia Junior League presentation, *Why Not,* and he hired her to appear in *Sally* in 1921. This was followed by other performances in musical theater, such as the *Ziegfeld Follies* (1922), *Kid Boots* (1923), *Annie Dear* (1924), *Louis XIV* (1925), and *La Valse* (1932). Although she attained a measure of success in musical theater, Catherine was not satisfied to remain at this level of performance. She continued to grow artistically, augmenting her training at home and abroad, studying with Luigi Albertieri in New York and with Leo Staats and Lubov Egorova in Paris. At their mother's initiative, Catherine and Dorothie with as many as twenty students from the Littlefield School made an annual summer trip to France. From the mid-1920s to the late 1930s, these trips provided the students opportunities for additional study and exposure to the cultural life of Paris. It was on one of these excursions that Catherine met George Balanchine.

In learning the techniques of both Italian and French opera ballet, Catherine prepared for the next step in her career, that of performer-choreographer with three companies: the Philadelphia Civic Ballet, of which her mother had become director; the Philadelphia La Scala, an Italian opera company; and the Philadelphia Opera Company. In addition to her activities in opera ballet, she often composed and produced dances for live performances given as prologues to movies, which were popular in the 1920s at Philadelphia area theaters.

The Littlefields were affected by the onset of the Depression, when the activities of the Philadelphia Opera Company ceased. Catherine, however, pursued other dance interests. She participated in a movement to create a "new dance" that would communicate human problems to the American people, using accessible themes. Some choreographers developed new dance styles by codifying systems of movement; others, including Catherine Littlefield, characterized this new dance through incorporating American historical and ethnic material and themes of social concern. Moreover, for the first time in United States history, there was government subsidy for the arts. The Federal Theater Project was formed in 1935 and provided jobs for dancers, helping to legitimize the art form.

In 1935 Catherine Littlefield founded the Littlefield Ballet, later renamed the Philadelphia Ballet, with her mother as company director. True to the spirit of the times, the company announced its goals: it would strive to present the best in classical and modern classical dance; new ballets would be produced occasionally, with music specially written for dance; and the company would present what it believed to be a true American ballet. It further stated that it would give performances not only in large but also in small auditoriums, at popular prices, in order to develop a ballet-conscious public in all sections of the city and region. On 25 October 1935 the Littlefield Ballet took its first steps in a modest suburban setting. From its inception to its disbanding in 1941, it provided a forum for American musicians, composers, scenic and costume designers, choreographers, and dancers.

Dorothie Littlefield, who had been performing with the Ballet Russe in Europe, returned to America to become first soloist with the Littlefield Ballet. With training received both at the Littlefield School and abroad, she was an excellent technician and performer whose choreographic memory was a valuable asset in rehearsing the company in the early years. Carl Littlefield, also trained in the Littlefield School, had developed a pure classical style and was an excellent partner to Catherine. He often performed under the pseudonym of Carl Cleighton to establish his own identity.

Having succeeded in establishing a permanent repertory ballet company—the first to be exclusively composed of and directed by Americans—Catherine Littlefield produced many ballets in that first season of 1935/36, including *The Minstrel, The Snow Queen, The Fairy Doll,* and the American premier of *Daphnis and Chloë,* in which she starred with Thomas Cannon. Performed at the Academy of Music with the Philadelphia Orchestra, it was the work she considered her best. In addition, the Philadelphia Ballet's repertory included works choreographed by other members of the company, such as *Aubade* and *Prince Igor* by Alexis Dolinoff and *Fête Champêtre* by Edward Caton. This prodigious first season was well received; the second one, also at the Academy of Music, presented a complete three-act version of Littlefield's version of *The Sleeping Beauty* with approximately one hundred dancers and eighty-five musicians.

Having provided her company with a core of classical works, Catherine Littlefield turned to American themes. In 1937 she choreographed two ballets, *Barn Dance* and *Terminal,* which were unique for the time in their use of American music and the American folk idiom. When the company toured Europe in 1937—the first American ballet company to do so—*Barn Dance* and *Terminal* captivated Europeans in Paris, London, and Brussels. On that tour Littlefield received the Médaille de la Renaissance Française at the Archives of Dance in Paris. Later that year other examples of Americana were presented, including *Parable in Blue,* a symphonic-jazz ballet; *The Rising Sun,* a ballet history of old Philadelphia; and *Let the Righteous be Glad.*

The year 1938 was one of recognition for Catherine Littlefield. On 13 January 1938 there was a command performance for President Franklin D. Roosevelt. She was awarded the Gold Medal of the Pennsylvania Arts and Sciences Society for her distinguished service in the arts and sciences and in recognition of her creativity in the development of an American ballet.

Littlefield ventured beyond Philadelphia to choreograph for the Chicago Civic Opera for two seasons, 1938/39 and 1939/40. She produced several opera ballets as well as other pieces of Americana, such as *Café Society,* a commentary on night life, and *Ladies' Better Dresses,* a satire on the fashion industry. In 1939, the Littlefield Ballet (as it was once again called) became the official resident company of the Chicago Civic Opera, thus achieving national rather than regional status. By 1941 it had replaced Ballet Theatre as the official ballet of the Chicago Opera. The growth and success of the company prompted the arrangement of another European tour in 1942; however, in 1941, most of the male dancers resigned from the company to enlist in the service during World War II.

Although her company had disbanded, the following decade provided Catherine Littlefield with the opportunity to explore other vehicles for her choreography, such as musical theater and ice shows. She choreographed *American Jubilee* for the New York World's Fair in 1940, producing for this extravaganza an extraordinary dance for ninety bicycles, "Won't You Be My Bicycle Girl," which was the *pièce de résistance* of the show. In 1944 *Barn Dance* was revived by Ballet Theatre, with Dorothie Littlefield and Thomas Cannon appearing in their original roles.

Catherine Littlefield made no attempt to reassemble the ballet company. Throughout the 1940s she choreographed Broadway musicals, including *Hold on to Your Hats, Crazy with the Heat, A Kiss for Cinderella, Follow the Girls, The Firebrand of Florence,* and *Sweethearts.* In the same decade she pioneered in choreographing ice shows, contributing an artistic dimension to ice-skating. Some of the ice revues that bore the stamp of her ingenuity were *It Happens on Ice, Stars on Ice, Hats Off to Ice, Icetime,* and *Howdy, Mr. Ice.* As an outgrowth of these experiences, Littlefield worked with Sonja Henie on programs for her ice performances, which included *The Hollywood Ice Revue.* Early television provided still other opportunities for her, and between 1949 and 1951 she was the choreographer for *The Jimmy Durante Show.*

BIBLIOGRAPHY

Barzel, Ann. "The Littlefields." *Dance Magazine* (May 1945): 10–11; (June 1945): 8–9.

Hering, Doris. "The Littlefield Legacy." *Dance Magazine* (September 1993): 48–51.

Kirstein, Lincoln. *Ballet, Bias, and Belief: Three Pamphlets Collected and Other Dance Writings.* New York, 1983.

Schmitz, Nancy Brooks. "The Contribution of the Littlefields to Concert Dance in Philadelphia." In *Proceedings of the Ninth Annual Conference, Society of Dance History Scholars, City College, City University of New York, 14–17 February 1986,* compiled by Christena L. Schlundt. Riverside, Calif., 1986.

Schmitz, Nancy Brooks. *A Profile of Catherine Littlefield.* Philadelphia, 1986.

Schmitz, Nancy Brooks. "Catherine Littlefield and Anna Sokolow: Artists Reflecting Society in the 1930s." In *Dance: Current Selected Research,* vol. 1, edited by Lynnette Y. Overby and James H. Humphrey. New York, 1989.

ARCHIVE. Music Department, Free Library of Philadelphia.

BARBARA FERRERI MALINSKY

LITTLE HUMPBACKED HORSE, THE. Russian title: *Konek-gorbunok.* Also known as *The Tsar-Maiden.* Ballet in four acts and nine scenes. Choreography: Arthur Saint-Léon. Music: Cesare Pugni. Libretto: Arthur Saint-Léon. Scenery: A. Roller, G. Wagner, M. Shisko, A. Bredov. Costumes: A. Charlemagne. First performance: 3 [15] December 1864, Maryinsky Theater, Saint Petersburg, Russia. Principals: Marfa Muravieva (Tsar-Maiden), Feliks Kshessinsky (Khan), Nikolai Troitsky (Ivanushka).

The story of *The Little Humpbacked Horse* is based on the fairy tale of the same name written by Petr Yershov. Ivanushka, the Fool, helped by the Little Humpbacked Horse with its magical powers, performs a series of miraculous exploits: he brings to the Khan a foreign beauty, the Tsar-Maiden, recovers the ring lost by her from the bottom of the sea, and emerges unscathed from a cauldron of fiercely boiling water in which the Khan perishes. Ivanushka marries the Tsar-Maiden to the tumultuous approval and rejoicing of the people, whereupon the Little Humpbacked Horse bids them farewell and vanishes.

The ballet was replete with striking scenic effects, such as transformations and rapid scene shifts. It was, in fact, a colorful mosaic of fairground popular entertainment scenes with mass and solo Russian dances followed by stylized oriental dances in the Khan's chambers. The oriental scene preceded the classical dance of frescoes come to life, a grand classical ensemble of nereids and the Tsar-Maiden on the Isle of Nereids, and a series of dances in the underwater kingdom that involved various denizens of the deep: oysters, lobsters, and even a whale. The ballet ended with a spectacular *divertissement* parade of national dances.

Unlike Yershov's fairy tale the central character of the ballet is the Tsar-Maiden, rather than Ivanushka the Fool. To differentiate the negative (Khan's wife) and comic (Ivanushka) characters Saint-Léon made extensive use of character dance. Despite the rather poorly developed role of Ivanushka, its first interpreters lent it the attractive quality of a naive and unpretentious Russian folk tale. The role of the Tsar-Maiden was largely based on pure classical dance, only partly embellished with characteristic features of traditional Russian folk plastique. As interpreted by Marfa Muravieva, the image of the Tsar-Maiden took on a poetic and unmistakably Russian character, albeit stylized.

THE LITTLE HUMPBACKED HORSE. Because the essential Russian nature of this fairy tale was not fully understood by its French creator, Arthur Saint-Léon, generations of Russian choreographers have reworked the ballet. In Aleksandr Radunsky's 1963 version, set to music by Rodion Shchedrin, the Tsar was played by Radunsky, Ivanushka by Vladimir Vasiliev. (Photograph reprinted from Victor Komissarzhevsky, *Maya Plisetskaya,* Moscow, 1965.)

The democratic wing of contemporary critics at the time attacked the ballet's pseudofolk style and distortions of Yershov's original fairy tale, the subtle poetry of which was replaced by Saint-Léon's lavish extravaganza. Nonetheless, *The Little Humpbacked Horse* survived the barrage of criticism and had a long and successful run; for a long time it was the only ballet on a Russian theme playing in Russian theaters.

Many ballet masters and choreographers reworked Saint-Léon's first version. In 1895 *The Little Humpbacked Horse* was substantially revised by Marius Petipa for the Maryinsky Theater. Petipa produced anew most of the folk dances in the ballet to give the action easily recognizable national characteristics. In 1900 the *divertissement* of the final act was complemented with Liszt's Second Rhapsody, set by Lev Ivanov. The result was a symphonically developed Hungarian dance that conveyed the impetuous and spontaneous temperament of the Hungarian people.

In 1901 Aleksandr Gorsky produced a revised version of the ballet for Moscow's Bolshoi Theater. He saturated the ballet with a plethora of dances that engaged almost the whole of the Bolshoi Ballet's female section. Gorsky introduced into the musical score dance fragments from Tchaikovsky, Glazunov, Anton Simon, and other composers and added a few dances of his own, including a Slav dance to music by Antonín Dvořák and the pas de deux of the Pearl and Water Sprite to music by Andrei Arends. In the 1912 revival of the ballet at the Maryinsky Theater, Gorsky staged the pas de deux to music by Boris Asafiev. In the 1914 Bolshoi revival, the *divertissement* of the final act was complemented with a Gypsy dance, while the pas de deux was replaced by a pas de trois of the Ocean and Two Pearls marked by interesting choreographic innovations. Many of the dances composed by Gorsky eventually became popular concert numbers. Gorsky's version of *The Little Humpbacked Horse* was revived by many theaters throughout the Soviet Union.

After 1960 Cesare Pugni's score was absent from the ballet repertory of Soviet theaters, having been replaced by a new ballet of the same name choreographed by Aleksandr Radunsky to music by Rodion Shchedrin. This version was filmed in 1961, starring Maya Plisetskaya and Vladimir Vasiliev. In 1963 Igor Belsky produced the ballet for the Maly Theater in Leningrad. For a full list of productions of *The Little Humpbacked Horse* in the Soviet Union to 1980, see the *Encyclopedia of Ballet,* published in Moscow in 1981.

BIBLIOGRAPHY

Krasovskaya, Vera. *Russkii baletnyi teatr vtoroi poloviny deviatnadtsatogo veka.* Leningrad, 1963. See pages 74–83.

Krasovskaya, Vera. *Russkii baletnyi teatr nachala dvadtsatogo veka,* vol. 1, *Khoreografy.* Leningrad, 1971. See pages 129–131, 276–277.

Slonimsky, Yuri. *Mastera baleta.* Leningrad, 1937. See pages 156–162.

Wiley, Roland John. *A Century of Russian Ballet. Oxford,* 1990.

ELENA G. FEDORENKO
Translated from Russian

LITURGICAL DANCE. The terms *sacred dance, liturgical dance,* and *religious dance* are often used interchangeably. However, *liturgical dance* suggests that which is performed only as part of the liturgy or worship service, whereas *sacred* or *religious dance* suggests a broader category of dance. The styles of sacred dance are diverse; modern dance is probably most common today, but folk, ballet, and jazz are also popular. Like dance in general, sacred dance is exploring the blending of art forms. Mime and drama are some of the increasingly common combinations. What sets liturgical or sacred dance apart is its intention to inspire a religious experience in the congregation or audience and the dancer. The creative source of the dance is considered to be God.

Liturgical or sacred dance, though not a modern phenomenon, is experiencing a renewal in the worship practices of many faiths. This renewal is particularly dramatic for the Christian church because dance in worship drastically declined during the Protestant Reformation of the sixteenth century and all but disappeared with the Puritans in the seventeenth century. Although historical documents reveal that dance has never been totally absent from the church, most Christians are not aware of their religious dance tradition and falsely believe that liturgical dance is a new development.

Early in the twentieth century, artists such as Ted Shawn and Ruth St. Denis, who explored religious themes and evoked a strong spiritual depth in their dances, helped to generate a movement that revived liturgical dance that continues to flourish. Initially dances with religious themes were performed on stage by professionals but gradually began to appear in worship services as churches became receptive to them. Ted Shawn first performed in Christian worship in 1917 in the Interdenominational Church in San Francisco. He had been training for the Methodist ministry, but when he discovered dance as an expression of faith and worship, he redirected his life. He began to tour and generally was well received.

In the 1930s Erika Thimey moved to the United States from Germany and began to dance in Unitarian churches in Chicago, New York, and Boston. In the 1940s Margaret Fisk Taylor was dancing and leading a dance choir in New Hampshire. She led innumerable workshops and wrote many books on the practical as well as the philosophical and historical issues of liturgical dance.

Many more leaders gradually emerged in those early years: Evelyn Broadbent, Barbara Mettler, Mary Jane Wolbers, Robert Storer, Louise Matlage, Virginia Lucke, Pat Sonen, Mary Anthony, Forrest Coggan, Nels Anderson, Toni Intravaia, and Constance Fisher. All of them emphasized both the sacred and the dance aspects of their art. Sometimes one quality is accentuated at the expense of the other; the need to maintain a balance between the two has challenged sacred dancers through the years.

By the late 1940s and early 1950s there was a clearly recognized movement of liturgical dance, which in 1956 grew into the Eastern Regional Sacred Dance Association. In 1958 it became the more geographically inclusive Sacred Dance Guild. An interfaith organization, its original purpose as stated in its bylaws was "to stimulate interest in dance as a religious art form, and to provide a means of communication and training for dance choirs." New members have commonly reported that until their discovery of the guild they thought they were the only ones practicing sacred dance.

Over the years the many activities in sacred dance have evolved into several clearly defined but diverse categories. The first is the sacred dance choir, for which the guild was originally formed. A dancing choir is an integral part of the life of a church and functions similarly to a singing choir; that is, it artistically enhances the worship service. Dance expertise and style cover a broad spectrum from simple gestures to more demanding forms. A sacred dance choir often performs during the special seasons of the church year, such as Christmas, Easter, Pentecost, and Thanksgiving, although it is not limited to those times. All age groups can participate.

The second category of sacred dance is that performed by the professional dancer or dance company. These dancers have a much wider scope of ministry than the local congregation, traveling throughout the United States and other countries. They perform religious dances in concert and in worship services.

The third category is congregational dance. In simple movements usually led by someone, the whole congregation moves joyfully, playfully, or reverently, often while simultaneously singing a simple song or refrain. Congregational dance is most easily introduced to a church in an informal setting such as a religious retreat.

The fourth category is personal dance prayer. Spontaneously inspired, many dancers, whether novice or professional, report experiencing spiritual communion with God when freely and privately worshipping in movement. It is a form of prayer that may express joy, pain, humility, confession, obedience, cleansing, ecstasy, or love.

The fifth category is healing dance, used therapeutically for emotional or physical well-being. For example, in a nursing or convalescent home simple, joyful movements often give patients more flexibility both in body and in spirit. Recognizing that everyone has unmet emotional needs, many workshop leaders provide dance experiences that help grief, anger, depression, poor self-esteem, and so on.

Other liturgical dance important for religious expression includes Hasidic and other Jewish genres; Sufi dances; ecstatic dance, as in some Pentecostal, black, and charismatic churches; and dance in religious education, through which Bible stories or spiritual themes are enacted with gestures and dance.

Fully recognizing that these different forms of sacred dance emerged from the religious community at large, the Sacred Dance Guild has been extremely instrumental in their development, particularly in the United States, Canada, Europe, and Australia. Every year, in addition to many local and regional workshops, the Sacred Dance Guild hosts a major festival in which a wide variety of topics are explored: for example, working with children, the sacred aspects of sacred dance, creative process, use of music and architectural space in churches, improvisation, suitable Bible passages, historic worship, mask making, dancing Christmas carols and spirituals, sign language, mime, non-Western dance forms, and holistic awareness. Technique classes are always available, as are special concerts and worship services.

Some of the most influential leaders in the realm of contemporary sacred dance are Carla De Sola, director of the Omega Liturgical Dance Company at the Church of Saint John the Divine in New York City, who has encouraged the deep spiritual quality of liturgical dance; Carolyn Deitering, director of Romans XII dance group, Tucson, Arizona, who has taught extensively about dance in the liturgy; Doug Adams, professor of the arts in religion at the Pacific School of Religion, Berkeley, California, who has pioneered the area of congregational dance; and Judith Rock, associate director of Body and Soul Dance Company, Berkeley, California, who is clarifying the theological base and expression of liturgical and sacred dance.

[*See also* Bible, Dance in the; Christianity and Dance; Islam and Dance; Jewish Dance Traditions; *and* Shaker Dance.]

BIBLIOGRAPHY

Adams, Doug. *Congregational Dancing in Christian Worship.* Rev. ed. Austin, 1980.

Backman, Eugène Louis. *Religious Dances in the Christian Church and in Popular Medicine.* Translated by E. Classen. London, 1952.

Deitering, Carolyn. *Actions, Gestures, and Bodily Attitudes.* Saratoga, Calif., 1980.

De Sola, Carla. *The Spirit Moves.* Washington, D.C., 1977.

Reed, Carlynn. *And We Have Danced.* Austin, 1978.

Rock, Judith. *Theology in the Shape of Dance.* N.p., 1978.

Taylor, Margaret Fisk. *A Time to Dance.* Aurora, Ill., 1976.

CARLYNN REED

LITZ, KATHERINE (born 1918 in Denver, Colorado, died 1978 in New York), American dancer and choreographer. Litz was one of the most curious, compelling, and magically comical performer-choreographers of her generation and an important solo figure in modern dance, essentially unconnected to any artistic school. She began to study the Humphrey-Weidman technique of dance in her native Denver. She came to New York in the mid-1930s to study with Charles Weidman, who soon took her into the Humphrey-Weidman company. She remained for five years, creating roles in some of Doris Humphrey's most important works and coming under the influence of fellow company member Sybil Shearer. Shearer had assisted Agnes de Mille and introduced Litz to her.

In the early 1940s, Litz joined de Mille's small touring company, then danced de Mille's choreography in the national company of *Oklahoma!* in Chicago for two years, where she also taught in Shearer's new dance program at Roosevelt College. In 1945 Litz was back in New York, dancing for de Mille in the Broadway show *Carousel* and studying with Shearer's teacher Yuri Bilstin. When *Carousel* went on tour in 1947, Litz stayed home to marry the American painter Charles Oscar and begin her choreographic career.

In 1948, Litz presented two solos in a New York concert at the Ninety-second Street YM-YWHA. She also choreographed and performed a leading role (the biblical Susanna) in the American National Theatre and Acadamy's (ANTA) production of *Ballet Ballads.* Two years later Litz gave her first full-length concert of solo and group works. In the 1950s she was assumed to be part of the dance avant-garde led by Merce Cunningham, because she used controversial music—a score by Morton Feldman for *Thoughts out of Season* (1951, 1954) and music by Arnold Schoenberg for *The Lure* (1954). But her heart did not belong to abstract dance alone; she also explored her dancers' dramatic gifts—especially those of Ray Harrison, with whom she had choreographed several duets. The eventual result was her finest ensemble work, *Dracula* (1959), with a cast of outstanding soloists including Harrison, Charles Weidman, Gemze de Lappe, Buzz Miller, and Aileen Passloff.

Although Litz never kept a permanent company, she always found dancers to work with, especially since she continually taught and performed in colleges and dance festivals throughout the United States and gave concerts in New York of both new work and revivals. Starting in the late 1950s, she also acquired a reputation in theater circles. She had broadened her training to include ballet, voice, speech, and acting, and she began to perform in off-Broadway productions such as the 1960 *Ubu Roi,* and many plays thereafter at the Judson Poets' Theater.

Litz's finest achievement, however, was her collection of solos for herself, which she mostly kept alive in her repertory. These semi-precise, semi-illusory sketches of motion aligned with costume, character, and gesture were like nothing else in modern dance. Even their titles are remarkable: *Daughter of Virtue* (1949), *Fire in the Snow* (1949), *Blood of the Lamb* (1950), *The Long Night* (1950), *The Glyph* (1951), *And No Birds Sang* (1952), *Super Duper Jet Girl* (1953), *Vaudeville: Madame Belinda Bender's Dancing School* (1953), *The Story of Love from Fear to Flight* (1953), and *Homage to Lillian Gish* (1978). Some of the solos were serious, some were funny, but all were odd. Using repeated, incantatory movement, small shifts of attitude, and subtle musical counterpoint, Litz conveyed the essences of the extraordinary girls, women, and creatures of her imagination. She was the only cartoonist-visionary in dance.

BIBLIOGRAPHY

Kendall, Elizabeth B. "Katherine Litz: Daughter of Virtue." *Ballet Review* 7.2–3 (1978–1979): 1–9.

Maynard, Olga. "Katherine Litz Talks to Olga Maynard." *Dance Magazine* (January 1967): 52–59; (February 1967): 56–64.

Siegel, Marcia B., ed. "Dancers' Notes." *Dance Perspectives,* no. 38 (1969).

ELIZABETH B. KENDALL

LIVRY, EMMA (Emma-Marie Emarot; born 24 December 1842 in Paris, died 26 July 1863 in Neuilly), French ballet dancer. The daughter of a Paris Opera dancer and Baron Charles de Chassiron, Livry studied ballet at the studio of Madame Dominique (Caroline Lassiat), a former Opera dancer who also trained Giuseppina Bozzacchi and Léontine Beaugrand. In 1858, at age fifteen, Livry made a brilliant debut at the Opera in the title role of Filippo Taglioni's ballet *La Sylphide,* originally created for his daughter Marie in 1832. The noted critic Paul de Saint-Victor, writing in *La presse* (25 October 1858), described Livry thus: "Tall, supple, and slim, she has the slenderness of extreme youth, arms that float like shawls, and a very innocent and sweet face." The poet Théodore de Banville was so moved by her performance that he wrote a poem about her.

Hearing of Livry's success in her own most famous role, Marie Taglioni came to Paris expressly to see her. Enchanted by the young woman's artistry, she wrote, "I should dance as she does." Taglioni accepted a position at the Opera as a teacher of the *classe de perfectionnement* so

LIVRY. In Félicien David's opera *Herculaneum* (1859), Livry appeared as Erigone in a *divertissement* choreographed by Joseph Mazilier. This lithograph by Adolphe Menut depicts her in costume for the role, one of the highlights of her short career. It was printed in *Les danseuses del'Opéra* (Paris, c.1860). (Courtesy of Madison U. Sowell and Debra H. Sowell, Brigham Young University, Provo, Utah.)

that she could supervise Livry's progress. Livry thus became her protégée. In 1859 Livry danced in the *divertissement* of Félicien David's opera *Herculanum* and was so successful that she was given a three-year contract as *première danseuse.*

On 26 November 1860, Livry appeared at the Opera in the leading role of Marie Taglioni's *Le Papillon,* set to music by Jacques Offenbach and a libretto by Jules-Henri Vernoy de Saint-Georges. In the only ballet choreographed by Taglioni, she danced the only role she ever created. The ballet was so successful that Napoleon III went to see it twice. Saint-Victor, too, was once again greatly impressed by the qualities of Livry's dancing. In *La presse* (2 December 1860), he exclaimed, "What modest grace! What airy lightness! She has an elevation that soars and a bound that carries one away. Her success was immense." In the same day's issue of *Le moniteur universel,* Pier-Angelo Fiorentino was the first to describe the dancer's technical movements, mentioning a "variation that was such a surprise for the audience . . . in which she danced downstage with *temps piqués sur la pointe,* and *jetés en tournant* that she executed with unusual daring." Taglioni was so pleased with Livry's dancing that she gave her a photograph inscribed "Faites-moi oublier. Ne m'oubliez pas" (Make me forget. Don't forget me), and Livry's performance so impressed the sculptor Jean-Auguste Barre that he created a statue of her in her costume.

While the Opera made plans for another ballet for Livry, also to be directed by Marie Taglioni, Livry agreed to dance the role of Fenella in Daniel Auber's opera *La Muette de Portici.* During the general rehearsal on 15 November 1862, Livry ventured too close to the gaslights on the stage and her tarlatan petticoats caught fire. Severely burned, she died after eight months of intense suffering. Théophile Gautier was among those who followed the hearse bearing her corpse to the Cimetière du Montmartre. He wrote her eulogy several days later.

BIBLIOGRAPHY

Beaumont, Cyril W. *Three French Dancers of the Nineteenth Century: Duvernay—Livry—Beaugrand.* London, 1935.

Beaumont, Cyril W. *Complete Book of Ballets.* London, 1937.

Gautier, Théophile. *Gautier on Dance.* Translated and edited by Ivor Guest. London, 1986.

Guest, Ivor. "Centenary: Emma Livry, 1842–63." *Ballet Annual* 18 (1964): 54–60.

Guest, Ivor. *The Ballet of the Second Empire.* London, 1974.

Guest, Ivor. Program notes, *La Sylphide,* Paris Opera Ballet, 24 December 1976.

Moore, Lillian. "Emma Livry." In Moore's *Artists of the Dance.* New York, 1932.

Moore, Lillian. "The Tragedy of Emma Livry." *Dance Magazine* (June 1952): 38–39.

Woodcock, Sarah C. "Margaret Rolfe's Memoirs of Marie Taglioni, Part 1." *Dance Research* 7 (Spring 1989): 3–19.

MONIQUE BABSKY
Translated from French

LLOYD, MAUDE (born 16 August 1908 in Cape Town), South African–born British dancer and writer. From an early age, Maude Lloyd studied dance with Helen Webb in Cape Town, where her first stage appearances were in pupils' recitals at the local town hall. She was awarded a scholarship to study the Cecchetti technique in London, with the idea that she should become a teacher. Arriving in London, at age sixteen-and-a-half, she went to study with Marie Rambert and danced in the performances then being given by first-generation Rambert students. One of these performances was of dances arranged by Frederick Ashton and Rambert for Henry Purcell's *The Fairy Queen,* given by the Purcell Opera Society in 1927. Lloyd went back to South Africa in 1928, but she returned to England permanently in 1930 and became a leading dancer in the regular Sunday performances of Rambert's Ballet Club. At the same time she danced in the classic revivals and new ballets given by the Camargo Society (1930–1933).

Lloyd's aristocratic beauty and great artistry were an inspiration to the young, developing choreographers of that time, especially Frederick Ashton and Antony Tudor. She inherited many roles originally choreographed for Alicia Markova. Among the many roles she created, the most notable were the Reflection in Ashton's *The Lady of Shalott* and Olivia in Tudor's *Cross-Garter'd* (both 1931); Venus in Tudor's *The Planets* (1934); Solange in Ashton's *Valentine's Eve* and Night in Tudor's *Descent of Hebe* (both 1935); Caroline in Tudor's *Jardin aux Lilas* (1936); and the pas de deux in his *Dark Elegies* (1937). During these years, she also danced for a season with the Markova-Dolin Ballet, as well as in many early British Broadcasting Corporation (BBC-TV) ballet transmissions, mainly from the Rambert repertory, including Tudor's experimental *Fugue for Four Cameras* (1937).

In 1938 Lloyd joined Tudor's newly formed London Ballet and created roles in two of his works—Tirolese in *Soirée Musicale* and La Déese de la Danse, the ballerina from Milan, in *Gala Performance* (1938). In late 1939, after Tudor's departure, she and Peggy van Praagh took over the direction of the company, for which Andrée Howard choreographed *La Fête Étrange* (1940), with Lloyd as the Young Châtelaine, her last created role. She stopped dancing in 1941, but from 1951 on she collaborated with her husband, Nigel Gosling, writing, under the *nom de plume* of Alexander Bland, many important dance books until Gosling's death in 1982.

BIBLIOGRAPHY

Bland, Alexander. *Observer of the Dance, 1958–1982.* London, 1985.

Crisp, Clement, et al., eds. *Ballet Rambert: Fifty Years and On.* Rev. and enl. ed. Ilkley, England, 1981.

Hunt, Marilyn. "A Conversation with Maude Lloyd." *Ballet Review* 11 (Fall 1983): 5–26.

Lloyd, Maude. "Some Recollections of the English Ballet." *Dance Research* 3 (Autumn 1984): 39–52.

PETER WILLIAMS

LONDON CONTEMPORARY DANCE THEATRE. Founded in 1976 by Robin Howard, the London Contemporary Dance Theatre was Howard's attempt to establish a foothold for modern dance in Britain. The Martha Graham Dance Company's visit to the United Kingdom in 1954 was the first appearance of any American modern dance company there and was generally very poorly received. Visits by American modern dance companies increased during the 1960s. The Limón Dance Company visited in 1957, and Howard sponsored a highly successful second visit by Graham in 1963, to London and the Edinburgh Festival, followed in 1964 with seasons by the Alvin Ailey, Merce Cunningham, and Paul Taylor companies. Apart from the Ballet Rambert's shift toward modern dance in 1966, modern and experimental activity by British groups was only minor.

Howard decided that introducing Graham's classwork and method was the ideal way to establish a modern-dance tradition in England. In 1963 a group of British dancers was sent on scholarship to train for a year at the Martha Graham School in New York. Graham company dancers Ethel Winter, Mary Hinkson, and Bertram Ross were invited to England to teach and to give lectures in 1965, which included a week with the educational Ballet for All. In 1966 a regular school was established, the London School of Contemporary Dance, later named the London Contemporary Dance School.

The 1967 performances of the London Contemporary Dance Group, now the London Contemporary Dance Theatre, directed by Robert Cohan, then co-director of the Martha Graham Dance Company, were given at the Adeline Genée Theatre in East Grinstead, Surrey, supported by an Arts Council grant. Cohan led the performers with two other American guest artists, Robert Powell and Noemi Lapzeson, who appeared with the London Contemporary Dance Theatre into the early 1970s (as did William Louther, who joined in 1969).

Under the auspices of the Contemporary Dance Trust, the company and school moved to The Place Theatre in 1969. Cohan then became permanent artistic director of the company (a position he occupied until 1989) and regular seasons began, at first in The Place Theatre, the earliest important small-scale dance venue in London. Beginning in 1970, the dancers were offered a full year of

LONDON CONTEMPORARY DANCE THEATER. Members of the company in Robert North's *Dressed to Kill* (1974), with scenery and costumes by Peter Farmer. (Photograph by Anthony Crickmay; used by permission of the Board of Trustees of the Theatre Museum, London.)

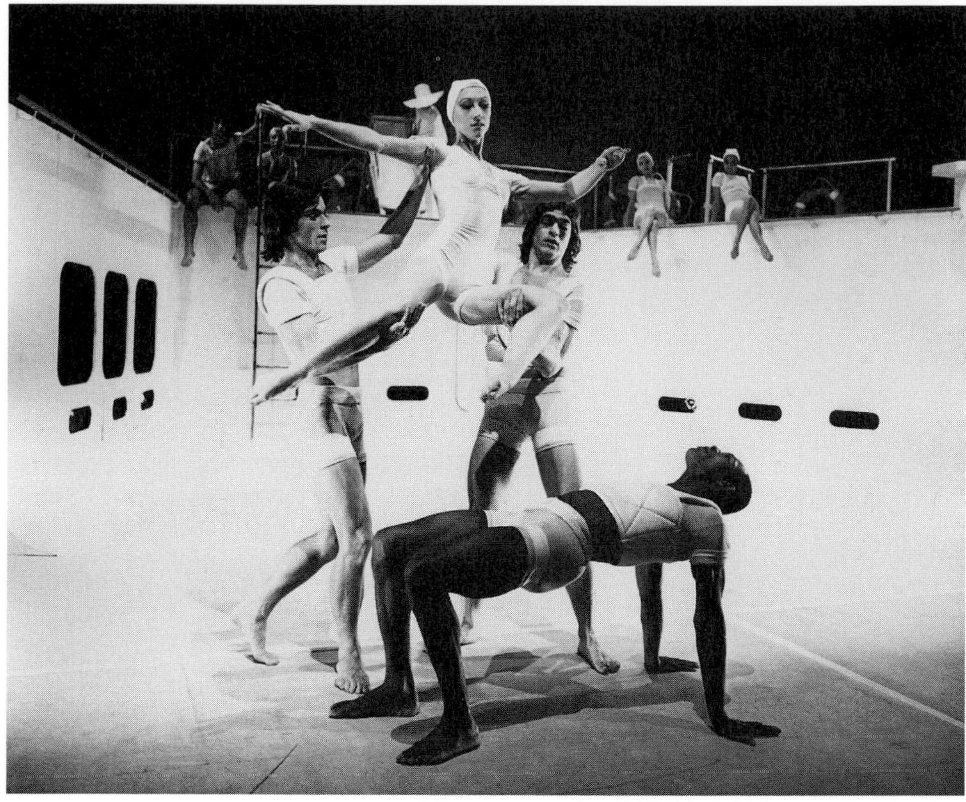

LONDON CONTEMPORARY DANCE THEATRE. Robert Cohan's popular 1974 comic work *Waterless Method of Swimming Instruction,* with design by Ian Murray Clark. (Photograph by Anthony Crickmay; used by permission of the Board of Trustees of the Theatre Museum, London.)

employment with the aid of major grants from the Gulbenkian Foundation and the Arts Council.

From 1973 the company performed regularly at the Sadler's Wells Theatre. It built itself an international reputation, touring extensively in the United Kingdom and abroad; it made its United States debut at the American Dance Festival in New London, Connecticut, in 1977 and first performed in New York in 1983. In 1984 and 1988, it was chosen as the sole dance company to represent Britain at the Olympic Arts Festivals in Los Angeles and Seoul, Korea. In 1990, London Contemporary Dance Theatre became the first major contemporary dance company to perform in Moscow.

The company varied in size from twelve to twenty dancers and developed without soloists, drawing dancers directly from its school. Because many of the dancers remained in the company for many years, the London Contemporary Dance Theatre appeared as an exceptionally coherent working community. Dancers who attracted critical attention over the years include Linda Gibbs, Siobhan Davies, Kate Harrison, Patrick Harding-Irmer, Micha Bergese, Robert North, and Tom Jobe.

The London Contemporary Dance Theatre repertory included over 165 works in 1983, with forty-five by Cohan alone. Much of his work has psychological content or contains complex, sometimes confusing literary references, and clearly stems from Graham's vocabulary. Though some of Cohan's works have been produced simply, such as *Chamber Dances* (1982) and the popular *Class* (1975), and are a celebration of his dancers' technique, Cohan is essentially a man of the theater. Pieces with visual effects achieved through costume, decor, and lighting have particularly excited audiences: *Cell* (1969), which suggested mental persecution and confinement within a box set, and *Waterless Method of Swimming Instruction* (1974), a lighthearted work depicting a swimming pool and assorted bathers. The production element is similarly strong in the company's only full-length works, also by Cohan: *Stages* (1971), a multimedia event relating the myth of the hero to contemporary culture that was successfully sent to some of the largest theaters in Britain; *Dances of Love and Death* (1982), which introduces a series of figures from popular mythology; and *The Phantasmagoria* (1987), a collaboration with Jobe and with Darshan Singh Bhuller.

Cohan's work more than any other molded company style, and Cohan instilled his own theatrical interest in choreographers within the company. Designers Peter Farmer and Norberto Chiesa made frequent contributions, and Jenny Henry worked with costuming. From 1969 into the mid-1980s, John B. Read acted as chief lighting designer, introducing side-lighting techniques known in the United States but relatively new to the

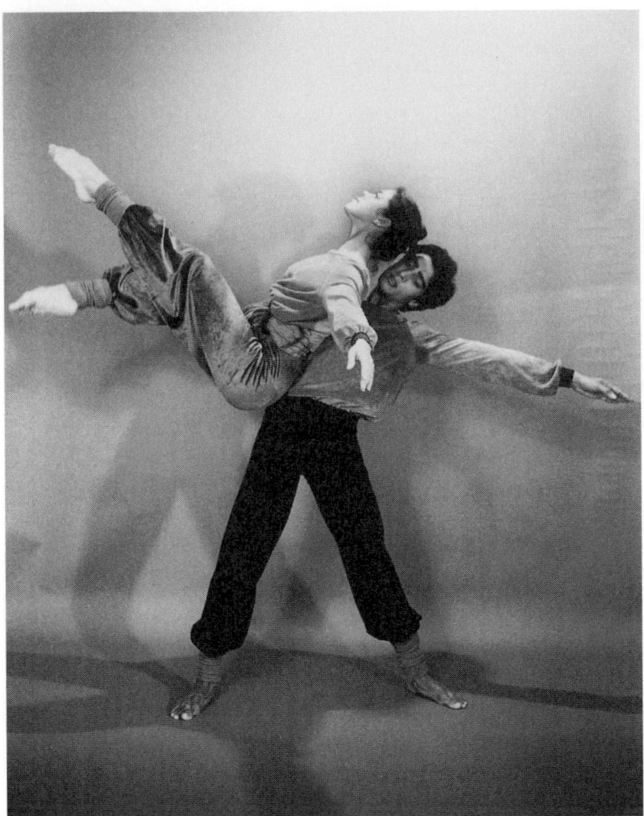

LONDON CONTEMPORARY DANCE THEATRE. Darshan Singh Bhuller and Lauren Potter in Richard Alston's duet-based *Doublework* (1978), an austere piece for three couples danced in silence, with costumes by Jenny Henry. (Photograph © by David Buckland; used by permission.)

United Kingdom then—techniques that enhanced the sleek, dramatic company image and emphasized body contours.

In the early years, Cohan added many works by guest choreographers to the repertory, including revivals of Graham's *El Penitente* in 1969 and *Diversion of Angels* in 1974; Paul Taylor's *Three Epitaphs* and *Duet* in 1970; Alvin Ailey's *Hermit Songs* in 1969; and Talley Beatty's *The Road of the Phoebe Snow* in 1971, and new works by, for instance, Anna Sokolow, Remy Charlip, Dan Wagoner, and the Dutch choreographer Pauline de Groot. During this period, the repertory acquired works by choreographers from within the school or company: Richard Alston, Barry Moreland, Robert North (associate choreographer, 1974–1981), Siobhan Davies (associate choreographer, 1974–1989; resident choreographer, 1983–1987), and Micha Bergese (associate choreographer, 1977–1979).

Moreland, an Australian with extensive ballet training, created six works for the company between 1969 and 1972. Most of these were cast in the Graham mold: studies in psychological symbolism reflecting an interest in ritual and stage effects. *Kontakion*, the last, was a thirty-minute dance version of the New Testament.

North, an American who had studied at the Royal Ballet School and in New York, appeared with the London Contemporary Dance Theatre in 1967 and then performed with the Graham company before rejoining the company in 1969. Before becoming artistic director of the Ballet Rambert in 1981, North created seventeen works for the London Contemporary Dance Theatre. Vigorous yet lyrical, and sometimes exhibiting jazz elements, these works are wide ranging, extroverted, and theatrical. His most popular work, the all-male *Troy Game* (1974), a tongue-in-cheek athletic display, was revised for the Dance Theatre of Harlem (1979) and the Royal Ballet (1980). His *Dreams with Silences* (1978) was inspired by the music of Johannes Brahms, *Scriabin Preludes and Studies* (1978) by the music of Aleksandr Scriabin, and *Songs and Dances* (1981) by the music of Franz Schubert.

Siobhan Davies, one of the first students in the school, was the most interesting choreographer to emerge from the ranks of the company. Her earliest work, *Relay* (1972), was based on sports movement and *Pilot* (1974) on images of travelers with suitcases; *Sphinx* (1977) was framed by enigmatic solos for the choreographer herself. A few pieces, such as *Something to Tell* (1980), contained a more clearly defined dramatic content. Davies's work for the company tended toward abstraction, and the literary content implied by the titles of many works she created has been combined with and even subsumed by movement vocabulary, structure, and spatial patterning that became increasingly intricate over the years.

Davies's style is characterized by its gentleness and understatement. She introduced a more intimate quality, of cushioned movement, than is found in any other company work, which she contrasts with broad, ecstatic statements that emphasize the risk of fall and the recovery of weight. Davies collaborated on several occasions with the designer David Buckland. [*See the entry on Davies.*]

Bergese, a German musician who joined the company in 1970, created ten works before leaving in 1979. Under the strong artistic influence of Cohan, his early works *Hinterland* (1975), *Da Capo al Fine* (1975), and *Nema* (1976), were based on a narrative, often incorporating autobiographic and spectacular production elements. Later works, including *Solo Ride* (1978), were more simply produced and demonstrated a more highly structured movement content.

From the mid-1970s to the late 1980s, the choreographic emphasis of the London Contemporary Dance Theatre has been largely on work produced from within the company. This policy has encouraged creative activity from within the ranks and helped to solve the problem of ever-tightening budgetary controls. It also, however, prompted criticism that the company had become too inbred and too unaware of new developments in dance and that the dancers lacked choreographic talent. However, there were exceptions: Taylor's *Cloven Kingdom* and *Esplanade* were added to the repertory in 1979 and 1982, respectively; Jerome Robbins's *Moves* was added in 1986; and Rosalind Newman's *John Somebody* was created for the company in 1987, the first evidence of postmodernism.

The London Contemporary Dance Theatre proved instrumental in stimulating a new range of music for dance in the United Kingdom, commissioning scores from experimental composers and composers of electronic music, among them Bob Downes, Michael Finnissy, Geoffrey Burgon, and Barrington Pheloung, who became the company's first full-time musical adviser in 1979, a position he held until 1986. In 1970 Peter Maxwell Davies composed a score for Moreland's *Nocturnal Dances;* Davies's more important *Vesalii Icones,* conceived for solo dancer and chamber ensemble, was first performed at the Queen Elizabeth Hall in London in 1969 and entered the repertory in 1970.

The company was the first to establish strong links among the professional dance world, the community, and colleagues in education; it built from a tradition of lecture-demonstrations and small-scale performances speeding radical changes in dance education in the United Kingdom. Many of the dancers in the company were experienced teachers as well as performers. In 1976 the company took part in a nine-week residency in colleges and universities in Yorkshire and Liverpool, the first of its kind in the United Kingdom. The lecture-demonstrations, classes, and public rehearsals (Cohan created *Khamsin*

LONDON CONTEMPORARY DANCE THEATRE. *Red Steps,* by choreographer Siobhan Davies, with design by Hugh O'Donnell, shows the influence of Merce Cunningham and his collaborators on contemporary English dance. (Photograph © by David Buckland; used by permission.)

during the residency) met with outstanding success, stimulating interest in modern dance well beyond the confines of the host institutions. The residency is an idea that many other British groups have since taken up vigorously.

In the 1970s, methods of training dancers changed. While the root was Graham technique, this term was replaced in 1976 (though direct links with the Graham company continued until 1980) by *contemporary dance technique*. Cohan and his fellow teachers at the school responded to the British style, which they considered naturally more elastic and less emotionally charged and athletic than the Graham style.

The company school, which offers full-time vocational training in modern dance, has won an international reputation and attracts many students from abroad. In 1967 Patricia Huchinson was appointed its first principal; in 1970 former Graham dancer Jane Dudley arrived from the United States to head Graham studies (ballet was introduced from the start and body conditioning was added later). Another former Graham dancer, Nina Fonaroff, came in 1972 to head the choreographic department; her inclusion of composition classes was unprecedented in the curricula of British dance schools. Under Dr. Richard Ralph, the principal until 1996, the school began to offer from 1980 a bachelor of arts degree with honors in dance validated by the University of Kent, to which were added the degrees of master of art from 1991 and doctor of philosophy from 1994.

Visiting artists and teachers with a range of styles and choreographic principles have always played an important part in school life. In addition to full-time training, the school offers classes for children and has a flourishing evening department and a program of vacation and weekend courses. In 1989 the American choreographer Dan Wagoner became artistic director but relinquished the position in 1991; he was succeeded by another American, Nancy Duncan.

During the 1980s the company had developed a number of exciting, mature, and strongly dramatic dancers who were ideally suited to Cohan's expressive style and theatrical repertory. The 1990s saw many changes to the repertory as well as to company training and personnel; and, though looking both to the future as well as to its tradition, the company seemed more and more unsure of its direction. Company training and style became increasingly eclectic and encompassed a wide range of choreographers' new works. Christopher Bruce's *Rooster*, restaged in 1992 to songs by the Rolling Stones, exploited the energetic enthusiasm of the new, almost exclusively young company of dancers, while Richard Alston's *Perilous Night* (1993), to John Cage's composition of the same name for prepared piano, was a virtuosic solo made for Darshan Singh Bhuller, the longest-serving member of the company. Singh Bhuller, who joined the company as dancer in 1980 and as choreographer the following year, created *Fall Like Rain* (1993), which looked back on the company's history. Following in the footsteps of Graham and Cohan, Singh Bhuller returned to myth, in this case Yadahpati, an Asian mythological deity, bringer of rain, who can see, ironically in the circumstances, into the past and the future. Singh Bhuller's acrobatic choreography and theatrical effects were elements also in keeping with company tradition. Another former company member, Jonathan Lunn, created new works during this period, including *Hang Up*, an intense duet that used text by the playwright Anthony Minghella.

The repertory also included works by relatively little-known choreographers in Britain: for example, the German-based Amanda Miller (*My Father's Vertigo*, 1992; *The Previous Night*, 1993); the avant-garde Israeli choreographers Liat Dror and Nir Ben-Gal (*Rikud*, 1991); the French choreographer Angelin Preljocaj (*Sand Skin*, 1993). Since Cohan's retirement, the company had been dogged by funding and management problems, together with the succession of short-term artistic directorships, and these ambitious projects, though worthy of Howard's and Cohan's original vision, received muted audience response.

In 1994, in acknowledgment of the rapidly changing face of dance in Britain and the need for greater company flexibility, a decision was made to restructure the activities of the Contemporary Dance Trust and to disband the company. Richard Alston, one of London Contemporary Dance School's first graduates, was appointed artist in residence in 1993, with responsibility for coordinating and expanding The Place as a choreographic center. Since October 1994 he has presided as artistic director over the new organization, which brings together all the various activities of the dance trust including The Place Theatre, the school, The Video Place, The Data Place, and education and community programs. He also heads a new smaller choreographer-led group, the Richard Alston Dance Company, which had its inaugural season at The Place Theatre in autumn 1994.

London Contemporary Dance Theatre was awarded the 1994 Laurence Olivier Award for outstanding achievement in dance in recognition of its 1993 London season, an award it had won previously in 1990. In 1988, Robert Cohan was named a Commander of the British Empire in recognition of his outstanding contribution to dance in the United Kingdom.

The importance of the London Contemporary Dance Theatre and its school to British dance cannot be overestimated. Together they have given rise to a considerable body of small-group and experimental dance activity in Britain, training its choreographers and its dancers. Many of these moved beyond Graham's principles while continuing to value the alternative to ballet that the London

Contemporary Dance Theatre and the London Contemporary Dance School afforded. That the school and company have been a major influence in the history of modern dance in the United Kingdom is testimony to Robin Howard's foresight and to Robert Cohan's gifts as leader, teacher, and director.

[*For related discussion, see* Great Britain, *article on* Modern Dance.]

BIBLIOGRAPHY

Clarke, Mary, and Clement Crisp. *London Contemporary Dance Theatre: The First Twenty-One Years.* London, 1989.

"The Contemporary Ballet Trust: Background to a New Venture." *The Dancing Times* (September 1969).

Elgin, Kathy, ed. *London Contemporary Dance Theatre.* London, 1982.

"Getting to Know You: Robert Cohan Talks to D&D about London Contemporary Dance Theatre's Residencies in the Regional Centres." *Dance and Dancers* (April 1976).

Mackrell, Judith. *Out of Line: The Story of British New Dance.* London, 1992.

Percival, John. "London's Own Contemporary Dance Theatre." *Dance Magazine* (November 1975).

FILM. *This Is The Place* (1972).

STEPHANIE JORDAN and BONNIE ROWELL

LONDON FESTIVAL BALLET. *See* English National Ballet.

LONGWAYS. One of several types of formation or figure dances, the longways has existed at least since the fifteenth century but was prevalent, especially in English country dances, from the seventeenth century on. It was adapted to French ballroom dance under the name of *contredanse* in the seventeenth century, performed in Germany, where it was called the anglaise, during the eighteenth century, and lives on in the contra dances of New England and the South of the United States. [*See* Anglaise.]

Longways can be danced by three or four couples (longways for six, longways for eight) or any number of couples, positioned one behind the other, with the men at the left hand of the women and all initially facing the "presence" (the king, queen, or other ranking personage) or "top of the hall." In the first edition of John Playford's *English Dancing Master* (1651), longways for six and eight together were the most numerous; gradually, however, the smaller longways were almost completely replaced by the larger ones "for as many as will." [*See* Country Dance.]

All longways begin at the top of the formation. The first couple initiates the action, which soon involves the second couple as well. The two couples together dance the figures specific to the choreography and end having changed places with one another: couple 1 is now in second place and couple 2 has moved up into first place, at the top. The lead couple then dances the figures with couple 3; the place change happens as before; couple 1 is now in third place. In a "longways for as many as will," as the first couple begins dancing with couple 4, the couple at the top of the formation (the original couple 2) also begins to dance with the adjacent couple (the original couple 3). The lead couple continues down the set, with the other couples following in turn after having previously reached top place. The dance goes on until the lead couple, having danced all the way down to the bottom of the set, has again returned to first place.

Because the gradual progression of the first couple (usually the highest-ranking one, the one to be honored, or the hosts of the event) takes time enough to allow the rest of the participants to observe the pattern before the figures actually reach them, longways of this type were well suited to novices. Young beginners traditionally were placed at the bottom of the set and were expected to execute the figures without error when their turn came. The principle of progression also prevails in the longways for three or four couples.

Longways progressions can take place with each person remaining on his or her side of the set or crossing over to the other side. In the latter case, either the crossing is followed by a two-hand turn that takes both dancers back to their "normal" positions but one place further down the set (as in "La Gasconne" in Raoul-Auger Feuillet's *Recüeil de contredances* [1706], and also in Feuillet and Essex's *For the Further Improvement of Dancing* [1710]), or the figure in its entirety is repeated, bringing the couple back to original positions. Feuillet also describes and notates a progression in which the first gentleman, having changed places with his lady during the first figure, moves down the set on the women's side and does not return to his own side until he has arrived at the bottom of the formation. The lady makes the same progression on the men's side.

The variety of progression patterns in country dances and contredanses is nearly as great as that of the figures themselves. One variation resulted from an effort to involve more couples sooner in the configuration of the longways: Thomas Wilson (c.1820) divided the "long set" into smaller, "minor sets"; the first couples of all minor sets begin the figures simultaneously and progressions take place within the minor set. Because most figures involve two or three couples, minor sets are usually for four couples.

This principle was adopted, with further modifications, by country-dance revivalist Cecil Sharp in the early twentieth century. It is favored today in recreations of seventeenth- and eighteenth-century longways performed by the English Country Dance Society and its American counterpart.

BIBLIOGRAPHY

Guilcher, Jean-Michel. *La contredanse et les renouvellements de la danse française.* Paris, 1969.

Sharp, Cecil J., et al. *The Country Dance Book.* 6 vols. London, 1909–1927.

Sharp, Cecil J. *An Introduction to the English Country Dance.* London, 1919.

Taubert, Karl Heinz. *Die Anglaise . . . mit dem Portefeuille Englischer Tänze von Joseph Lanz.* Zurich, 1983.

Wittman, Carl. "An Analysis of John Playford's 'English Dancing Master' (1651)." Master's thesis, Goddard College, 1981.

INGRID BRAINARD

LÓPEZ, PILAR (Pilar López Julvez; born 4 June 1906 in San Sebastian, Spain), Spanish dancer and teacher. Together with her sister La Argentinita, Pilar López is generally acknowledged as the dancer most responsible for shaping a line of major Spanish male dancers active from the 1950s through the present. Her thorough knowledge of the Spanish dance tradition, her pure style and elegant line, and her meticulous approach to production details have all left their mark on dancers who have long since formed their own companies, including José Greco, Manolo Vargas, Roberto Ximénez, and Antonio Gades.

LÓPEZ. Roberto Sega and López in *Café de Chinitas.* (Photograph by Annemarie Heinrich; used by permission.)

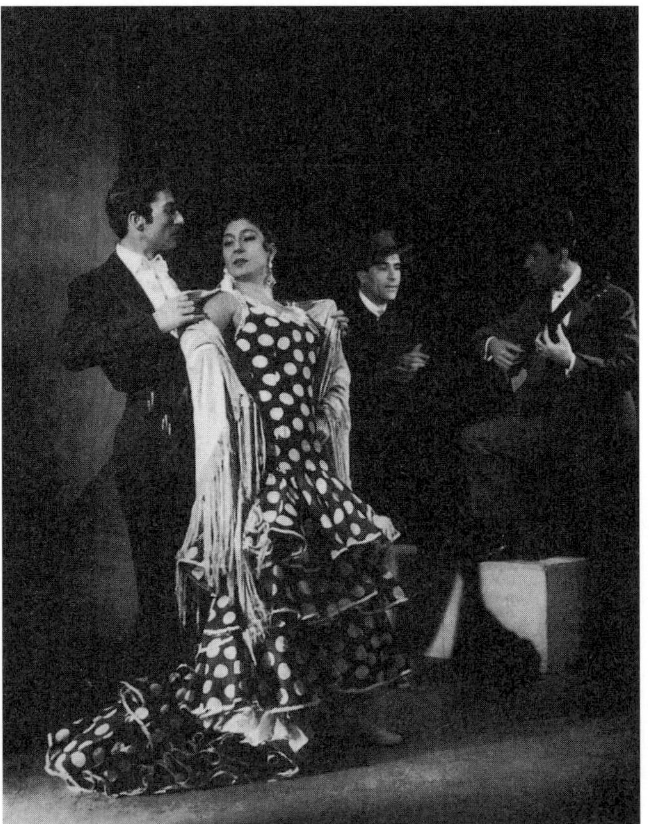

Pilar López began dancing with her older sister—already a well-known performer under her professional name—when López was seven years old. Most of López's dance training came from her sister Encarnación, known as Argentinita. She made her official debut in 1929 in Madrid and then toured with the Velasco Company.

In 1933 López joined the Madrid Ballet, the company of legendary Gypsy performers assembled by Argentinita and Federico García Lorca. Except for a concert tour with Rafael Ortega in 1934, López remained in her sister's company, leaving Spain with her at the outbreak of the Spanish Civil War. They toured Europe, Latin America, and the United States, where the sisters settled in 1939.

After Argentinita's death in 1945, López returned to Spain with a repertory that was the closest thing to a national ballet that Spain possessed. Those remaining from La Argentinita's prewar circle of friends urged Pilar to carry on her sister's work, and in 1946 she founded her own Ballet Español with José Greco, Manolo Vargas, Nila Amparo, Elvira Real, and guitarist Luis Maravilla. Pastora Imperio and Rafael Ortega were guest artists that first season.

Over the next fifteen years her company fostered many well-known dancers: in addition to those already named, they included Alberto Lorca, Alejandro Vega, Eduardo Serrano, Alberto Portillo, and Dorita Ruiz, as well as Lola de Ronda and Nana Lorca, both of whom later danced with José Greco. During that time López expanded not only the company but also the repertory her sister had left, choreographing such works as *La Zapatera y el Emborazo* (1949), which included Argentinita's *El Zorongo Gitano.* The Ballet Español performed works jointly choreographed by López and Argentinita, such as *Boléro* and *Pictures of Goya;* and López also revived many of her sister's most beloved dances, including *El Huayno, Café de Chinitas, L'Espagnolade* and the turn-of-the-century *zarzuela* solo that became a signature piece for López, *La Boda de Luis Alonso.*

The Ballet Español was especially well received in England, where it performed many times. Ivor Guest (1951) called López "a queen among dancers," and Peter Williams, drawing an analogy between her work and the academic ballet tradition, praised her ability to bring the operetta style to life: "In much the same way that Markova can evoke the style of Romantic ballet, so can López evoke the almost lost schools of Spanish dance. . . . It is my belief that Pilar López is the one person in Spain who can preserve the truth in its dance" (Williams, 1959).

Pilar López retired to Spain in the early 1960s, but her company continued to perform there occasionally throughout the decade. In the 1980s she lived outside Madrid with her husband, Tomas Rios, a noted conductor and composer who managed her company for many years.

[*See also the entry on Argentinita.*]

BIBLIOGRAPHY

Brunelleschi, Elsa. "The Spanish Ballet of Pilar López." *Ballet* 11 (November 1951): 32–39.

Guest, Ivor. "The Ballet Espagnol of Pilar Lopez." *Ballet Today* (November 1951): 8–10.

Murías Vila, Carlos. "Souvenirs: Doña Pilar López." *Danser* (April 1994): 50–52.

Pedroso y Sturdza, Dolores de. "Contemporary Theatrical Dancing in Spain." *Foyer* (Winter 1951–1952): 43–46.

"Personality of the Month: Pilar Lopez." *Dance and Dancers* (October 1957): 5.

Pohren, D. E. *Lives and Legends of Flamenco.* Madrid, 1964.

Williams, Peter. "Ballet Español." *Dance and Dancers* (February 1956): 31.

Williams, Peter. "The First Lady of Spanish Dance." *Dance and Dancers* (July 1959): 20–23.

Williams, Peter. "Manzanares to Merseyside." *Dance and Dancers* (November 1960): 17–20.

JUDY FARRAR BURNS

LOPOKOVA, LYDIA (Lidiia Vasil'evna Lopukhova; born 9 [21] October 1891 in Saint Petersburg, died 8 June 1981 in Seaford, England), Russian-English ballet dancer and actress. The Lupukhov family included four siblings—Fedor, Evgenia, Lydia, and Andrei—who began their professional lives as ballet dancers. Like her brothers and sister, Lydia was trained at the Imperial Theater School in Saint Petersburg, where she studied with Michel Fokine. Upon her graduation in 1909, she joined the corps de ballet of the Maryinsky Theater and a year later was promoted to *coryphée.* At Fokine's suggestion, she participated in Serge Diaghilev's 1910 Saison Russe in Paris, achieving great personal success in the Bluebird pas de deux and as Tamara Karsavina's replacement in *Le Carnaval* and *The Firebird.* With her brother Fedor, sister Evgenia, and Alexandre Volinine, Lopokova then left Europe for a tour of the United States, where she remained until 1916, performing in Gertrude Hoffman's Saisons Russes (1911) and Mikhail Mordkin's All-Star Imperial Russian Ballet (1911), and in revues, musicals, and dramatic plays.

In early 1916, Lopokova rejoined Diaghilev's Ballets Russes in New York and quickly became its leading star, adding *Le Spectre de la Rose, Petrouchka,* and *Les Papillons* to her repertory during the company's two nationwide tours. Between 1917 and 1922 (except for a hiatus in 1919–1921, when she returned to the United States and appeared on Broadway in *The Rose Girl*), Lopokova established herself as a favorite with the British public and a brilliant interpreter of Léonide Massine's ballets, which exploited her genius for comedy. As Mariuccia in *Les Femmes de Bonne Humeur* (1917), wrote Cyril W. Beaumont, "She was so full of vitality, so exhilarating, . . . so spontaneous in all her actions . . . that she radiated happiness whenever she appeared." Her Can-Can Dancer in *La Boutique Fantasque* (1919) was another triumph. Although her performance in *Les Sylphides* was often praised, she was not strictly a classical dancer, and the role of Aurora, which she danced in the production of *The Sleeping Princess* (1921/22) at London's Alhambra Theatre, lay outside the range of her *demi-caractère* style. She garnered praise, however, for her performance as the Lilac Fairy. After 1922, Lopokova made only guest appearances with the Ballets Russes. She frequently appeared with a small company at the London Coliseum, however, and in 1924 she created the role of the Street Dancer in Massine's *Le Beau Danube,* presented by Comte Étienne de Beaumont's Soirées de Paris.

LOPOKOVA. A studio portrait of Lopokova in costume as the Girl in *Le Spectre de la Rose,* taken shortly after she rejoined the Diaghilev company in New York in 1916. (Photograph by Ira L. Hill; from the Dance Collection, New York Public Library for the Performing Arts.)

Lopokova's marriage in 1925 to the renowned economist John Maynard Keynes brought her into the Bloomsbury circle of intellectuals and did great service to British ballet through Keynes's chairmanship of the body that became the British Arts Council. For the Camargo Society, of which Keynes was treasurer, Lopokova created roles in "Jodelling Song" and "Tango Pasodoble" in Frederick Ashton's *Façade* (1931) and danced the title role in *Coppélia* (1933), which she had learned from Nikolai Legat. She also appeared in a number of dramatic roles, including Olivia in *Twelfth Night* (1933), Nora in *A Doll's House* (1934), and Célimène in *The Misanthrope* (1937), although praise for her acting ability was tempered by criticism of her accent. An artist of great independence who was not afraid to stand up to "Big Serge," as she called Diaghilev, Lopokova was one of the era's best-loved ballerinas, remembered by colleagues for her unfailing wit, gaiety, and kindness.

BIBLIOGRAPHY

Beaumont, Cyril W. *The Art of Lydia Lopokova.* London, 1920.

Garafola, Lynn. *Diaghilev's Ballets Russes.* New York and Oxford, 1989.

Hill, Polly, and Richard Keynes, eds. *Lydia and Maynard: The Letters of Lydia Lopokova and John Maynard Keynes.* London, 1989.

Keynes, Milo, ed. *Lydia Lopokova.* London, 1983. A collection of essays by various contributors, including Fedor Lupukhov, Anton Dolin, Ninette de Valois, Frederick Ashton, and Cecil Beaton; several pieces of writing by Lopokova are appended.

Lopokova, Lydia. "Serge Diaghileff." Obituary. *The Nation and Athenaeum* (31 August 1929). Reprinted in Keynes (1983).

Montagu-Nathan, Montagu. "Keynes and the Ballet." *Ballet* 11 (April 1951): 12–18.

Pritchard, Jane. "London's Favourite Ballerina." *The Dancing Times* (December 1989).

ARCHIVE. John Maynard Keynes Papers, King's College Library, University of Cambridge.

LYNN GARAFOLA

LOPUKHOV, FEDOR (Fedor Vasil'evich Lopukhov; born 8 [20] October 1886 in Saint Petersburg, Russia; died 28 January 1973 in Leningrad), dancer, choreographer, teacher, and theorist. Graduating in 1905 from the Saint Petersburg Maryinsky Theater school, where he studied under Nikolai Legat, Lopukhov appeared as Acis in the graduation performance of *Acis and Galatea* by Michel Fokine. Between 1905 and 1909 and again between 1911 and 1922, Lopukhov was a soloist with the Maryinsky Ballet company. In 1909–1910 he was a soloist at Moscow's Bolshoi Theater and in 1910–1911 he toured the United States with Anna Pavlova. In 1922, when the USSR was undergoing a period of economic privations, Lopukhov headed the ballet troupe of the Petrograd Opera and Ballet Theater (as the Maryinsky was then called). He was its artistic director until 1930, returning from 1944 to 1946 and 1951 to 1956. Lopukhov founded the ballet troupe of Leningrad's Maly (now Modest Mussorgsky) Opera House and headed it from 1931 to 1935. He was director of the choreography department at the Leningrad Choreographic Institute between 1936 and 1941. He produced ballets for Moscow's Bolshoi Theater and the Stanislavsky and Nemirovich-Danchenko Theater, and had a hand in launching ballet companies in various constituent republics of the Soviet Union, including Belarus, Lithuania, Turkmenistan, and Uzbekistan. He also produced ballets for all the theaters in which he served as artistic director.

Lopukhov established centers for the training of professional choreographers and ballet masters, the first of their kind in the history of Soviet ballet. In 1937 such a center was set up in the Leningrad Choreographic Institute, and Lopukhov supervised the training until 1941. In 1962 Lopukhov was appointed head of the choreography department at the Leningrad Conservatory, heading it until his death in 1973; he held a professorship from 1965 onward. Among his many pupils who later achieved prominence in the ballet world were Vladimir Varkovitsky, Boris Fenster, Aleksandr Obrant, Konstantin Boyarsky, Georgi Aleksidze, and Nikolai Boyarchikov.

In the 1920s Lopukhov was one of the first Soviet choreographers to revive for the sake of posterity classical ballets that included *The Sleeping Beauty, Raymonda, Swan Lake,* and *Don Quixote.* While retaining the basic choreography and style of these ballets, he choreographed new episodes for those that had been either lost or omitted from the original scores. He took more liberties with the *mise en scène* of old ballets in order to suit them to the times. Lopukhov made his debut as choreographer by staging the ballet *Dream,* to the music of Nikolai Shcherbachev, and *The Mexican Tavern,* to music by Leonid Goncharov. Both were given at the Theater of Musical Drama by dancers of the Maryinsky Theater in 1916. In 1921 Lopukhov presented a new version of Igor Stravinsky's *Firebird* and the dance symphony *The Magnificence of the Universe* to Beethoven's Fourth Symphony (1923). In the latter, following Fokine's lead in the area of plotless ballets as exemplified by his *Chopiniana* and *Les Préludes,* Lopukhov turned his attention to symphonic music and the idea of using some of its basic principles in ballet. *The Magnificence of the Universe* was in six parts: Introduction, "The Birth of Light, the Genesis of the Sun"; Part One, "Life in Death and Death in Life"; Part Two, "Thermal Energy," Part Three, "The Joy of Existence"; Part Four, "Perpetual Motion," and Finale, "The Grandeur of Creation." Each part dealt with a particular aspect of the creation of the world and nature. Lopukhov's dance symphony opened a new chapter in the annals of ballet theater. Significantly, the innovative works of George Balanchine, who danced in the premiere, and of Léonide Massine began with *The Magnificence of the Universe.* However, for all its original treatment, the first performance of Lopukhov's dance symphony was its last.

Lopukhov realized his concept of the choreographed symphony in a series of productions and substantiated it in his theoretical works. In *Puti baletmeistera (The Path of the Choreographer)*, published in 1925, Lopukhov claimed that a new type of ballet was in the making, a ballet employing strictly musical and choreographic means of expression to convey its message, without any identifiable plot, reliance on period scenery and costume, or mimed episodes. This type of ballet would exist alongside its traditional cousin, which was based on a concrete plot complete with all the familiar ballet paraphernalia, and would be able to express ideas that until then had been inaccessible to the ballet theater. The problem of dance symphonism, which dominated the work of choreographers from 1925 to 1975, was at the center of discussion in the ballet world of the 1920s. Lopukhov declared that a new stage had been reached in the relationship between ballet and music, and that the choreographer was now expected to express in the language of dance not only tempo and rhythm, but also a wide range of subjects, harmonic structures, sound dynamics, intonational patterns, and instrumentation. He subsequently spelled out his ideas on the substantive content of choreography in two major theoretical works: *Shestdesiat let v balete* (My Sixty Years in Ballet, 1966) and *Khoreograficheskie otkrovennosti* (Choreographic Confessions, 1972).

Throughout the 1920s, Lopukhov was looking for a model of integrated ballet production as he introduced into his works elements such as the spoken word, singing, buffoonery, and eccentric tricks, selected circus acts, and elements of puppetry. He brought forth these ideas particularly in *Night on the Bare Mountain* (1924), to the music of Modest Mussorgsky, *Pulcinella* (1926), by Igor Stravinsky, and *Le Renard* (1927), by Stravinsky. Carrying on the traditions of theater long established in Russia, Lopukhov's productions had a tremendous theatrical appeal and were remarkable for their well-rounded dramaturgy and thrilling intrigues. Lopukhov also made the first attempt to create convincing ballet on a contemporary revolutionary subject using the conventions and expressive means of ballet. Called *The Red Whirlwind* (1924), the ballet was set to music by Vladimir Deshevov and consisted of two parts, dubbed "processes": the first used abstract imagery to describe the growth and spread of revolutionary ideas; the second portrayed through dance archetypal characters of the day. *The Red Whirlwind* influenced the content and structure of Sergei Prokofiev's score *Le Pas d'Acier* (1925), choreographed by Léonide Massine in 1927. Lopukhov pressed his search for a convincing ballet treatment of contemporary subjects with Reinhold Glière's *The Red Poppy*, staged in 1929 in collaboration with Vladimir Ponomarev and Leonid Leontiev, in which Lopukhov choreographed the first act and supervised the entire production, and *The Bolt* (1931), to Dmitri Shostakovich's score, an example of satirical ballet. Lopukhov's production of *The Serf Ballerina* (1927), to the music of Klimenty Korchmarev, was the first of a long series of drama ballets that would dominate the Soviet ballet scene in the 1930s and 1940s.

In a sense, Lopukhov's work brought together in convincing combination the principles of Marius Petipa and Fokine, which until then had been generally regarded as incompatible. An organic blend of canonical forms and the abstract imagery of classical dance compositions are readily traceable to the work of Petipa, while the methods of conveying the ballet's plot, dramatic action, and characters in the language of dance were typical of Fokine's ballet theater. A major landmark in the evolution of Soviet ballet was reached when Lopukhov staged *The Ice Maiden* (1927), to music by Edvard Grieg. Lopukhov displayed his flair for fresh approaches and expressive means in his ingenious handling of the canons and forms of Romantic ballet. He enhanced classical dance by weaving acrobatic sequences into the fabric of the ballet, a device that became established in ballet technique. Lopukhov reinterpreted Romantic images and made the fantastic heroine, the Ice Maiden whose enchanting beauty was cruel, symbolize the inclement forces of nature and the harsh realities of man's own world. The Ice Maiden beckoned the hero with a promise of love, but, being the obedient tool of more powerful forces, she gave him death instead. In the acts set in the countryside, Lopukhov drew heavily on Norwegian folk dance.

A new version of *The Nutcracker*, staged by Lopukhov in 1929, was his contribution to the process of its reinterpretation, initiated by Aleksandr Gorsky. Seeking to bring Tchaikovsky's evocative music closer to the spirit of E. T. A. Hoffmann's fairy tale, Lopukhov introduced a number of episodes that were absent from the original libretto: A prehistory, a scene involving the heroine playing with her dolls, called "Dolls Are People, Too," and a scene describing adult diversions called "People Are Like Dolls, Really." An intermingling of real life, fantasy, and fairy tale, coupled with a juxtaposition of humdrum reality and the exciting world of a child's imagination, gave greater philosophical depth and sophistication to the ballet. Lopukhov also turned his attention to various topical subjects as he looked for effective expressive means to portray his contemporaries in the language of modern plastique. He evolved various choreographic methods to reflect the inner space of their minds. In his programmatic ballets, Lopukhov exposed the essential instability, brittleness, fleeting nature, and fickleness of humans and their natural environment. He tried to show the destinies of people—strong and weak alike, purposeful or irresolute, with exalted ideals or base instincts—as unpredictable if not inscrutable. Lopukhov's thinking in the 1920s was well ahead of its time and did not take root in the practice of Soviet ballet for many years. This could not but affect his career, forcing him to change jobs frequently and sometimes putting him out on a limb without the support and encouragement of people who would share his philosophy.

In 1930 Lopukhov formed a ballet troupe at Leningrad's Maly Opera House, to be used as a kind of laboratory-workshop for experiments in comic ballet. In particular, he choreographed new versions with new librettos of Riccardo Drigo's *Harlequinade* in 1933 and Léo Delibes's *Coppélia* in 1934. Lopukhov set the action of both ballets in a specific historical period, with the result that events that were shrouded in mystery in the old versions were given quite real, down-to-earth explanations by Lopukhov. Dmitri Shostakovich's *Bright Stream,* staged by Lopukhov at the Maly Opera House in 1935 and at Moscow's Bolshoi Theater in 1936, was an interesting ballet-vaudeville on a topical Soviet subject—the lofty meaning of work and the enthusiasm of the Soviet people for building a new society. Such flaws as there were in the libretto were more than compensated for by Shostakovich's delightful music and Lopukhov's generous dance palette. Using classical dance in the ballet, Lopukhov proved that it could be a convincing medium for conveying modern ideas and concepts, if appropriately handled. As he said in a booklet about his work on the ballet, published in Leningrad in 1935, "No one should find it odd to see a Soviet Komsomol boy or girl, or a young collective farmer, or even an engineer or university professor speak the language of classical dance."

In the years before, during, and after World War II Lopukhov helped his fellow choreographers in a number of constituent republics of the USSR create their first ballets dealing with local national themes. In particular, he assisted Aleksei Yermolayev in the creation of *The Nightingale* (1939), to the music of Mikhail Kroshner, first performed at the Minsk Opera and Ballet Theater; collaborated with Mukarram Turgunbaeva and Usta Alim Kamilov on *Akbilyak* (1943), to music by Sergei Vasilenko, staged at the Navoi Theater in Tashkent; with Vladimir Burmeister on *Christmas Eve* (1938), to music by Boris Asafiev, performed at Moscow's Stanislavsky and Nemirovich-Danchenko Theater; and for the Kirov Ballet *Taras Bulba* (1940), to the music of Vasily Soloviev-Sedoi and *Spring Tale* (1947), to music by Boris Asafiev based on Tchaikovsky. In the last two ballets of his long career—*Love Ballad* (1959), to a musical score composed of excerpts from Tchaikovsky's *The Seasons,* first performed at Leningrad's Maly Opera House, and *Pictures at an Exhibition* (1963), to Modest Mussorgsky's score, premiered at Moscow's Stanislavsky and Nemirovich-Danchenko Theater—Lopukhov responded to the renewed interest of the Soviet ballet community in one-act ballets and ballet miniatures and offered his own choreographic treatment of minor forms in ballet as a thematic suite. Each of the ballets created by Lopukhov, especially those of the 1920s, was a trailblazing effort that eventually prompted the emergence of new trends in ballet in the Soviet Union and in the rest of the world. He was named People's Artist of the Russian Federation in 1956.

BIBLIOGRAPHY

Alovert, Nina. "Lopukhov's Legacy." *Dance Magazine* (March 1989): 42–46.

Devereux, Tony. "Legend of a Lost Choreographer" (parts 1–2). *The Dancing Times* (January–February 1988).

Dobrovolskaya, Galina N. *Fyodor Lopukhov* (in Russian). Leningrad, 1976.

Joffe, Lydia. "The Lopukov Dynasty." *Dance Magazine* (January 1967): 35.

Lopukhov, Fedor. *Shestdesiat let v balete.* Moscow, 1966.

Lopukhov, Fedor. *Khoreograficheskie otkrovennosti.* Moscow, 1972.

Souritz, Elizabeth. *Soviet Choreographers in the 1920s.* Translated by Lynn Visson. Durham, N.C., 1990.

Swift, Mary Grace. *The Art of the Dance in the U.S.S.R.* Notre Dame, 1968.

GALINA N. DOBROVOLSKAYA
Translated from Russian

LOQUASTO, SANTO (born c.1944 in Wilkes-Barre, Pennsylvania), American costume and stage designer. Santo Loquasto was already a dynamic force in theatrical stage design when he began his collaboration with Twyla Tharp on *Sue's Leg* in 1975. Responding to the choreographer's devices, Loquasto's costumes raised the vernacular to the theatrical: dancers' practice clothes—the usual layered jumble of sweatpants, pullovers, and leg warmers—were rendered in rich satins and wools in tones of beige, brown, and gold. While allowing for freedom of movement without distraction, the costumes reflected Tharp's style of apparent looseness refined to a classical edge, her desultory elegance. Tharp has said of Loquasto, "He's so good because he has an eye that can read, describe and exaggerate in the right ways" (*Newsweek,* 21 March 1977).

Loquasto graduated from the Yale School of Drama in 1969 and designed for regional theater before going to New York in 1971, where he was an immediate success. In 1977 his hyperrealistic junkshop for *American Buffalo* and his spectral, almost evanescent interior for *The Cherry Orchard* were revealed in premieres in a single week, demonstrating his range and adaptability.

Loquasto shared in the success of Tharp's *Push Comes to Shove* for American Ballet Theatre in 1976 and continued to design a range of works for her, including the full-length Broadway productions of *When We Were Very Young* (1980) and *The Catherine Wheel* (1981). At the same time he took on more traditional ballet assignments, in which his work has treated balletic conventions with irony. His designs for Jerome Robbins's *The Four Seasons* (1979) were, like the choreography, a conscious pastiche of opera-house traditions and excesses; his sets and costumes for American Ballet Theatre's *Cinderella* (1983) were criticized for the effects he deliberately evoked in order to avoid stereotypes, trying to reveal, in his words, "the cold and sophisticated world in which this innocent flourished and triumphed."

[*See also* Scenic Design.]

BIBLIOGRAPHY

Berkvist, Robert. "A Designing Man in the Theater." *New York Times* (16 September 1977).

Current Biography (June 1981). Includes a full biography and list of productions.

Kissel, Howard. "Arts and People." *Women's Wear Daily* (20 April 1984).

Kroll, Jack. "Setting the Stage." *Newsweek* (21 March 1977).

Loquasto, Santo. Interview. *Theatre Crafts* (October 1973).

Rowes, Barbara. "Ballet, Broadway, or Films: Santo Loquasto Is the Designer in Demand for Sets and Costumes." *People* (17 November 1980).

CLAUDIA ROTH PIERPONT

LORING. A scene from the Ballet Caravan production of *Yankee Clipper* (1937), with Fred Danieli, Loring, and Michael Kidd. Set to music by Paul Bowles and a libretto by Lincoln Kirstein, Loring's ballet depicted the cycle of a New England sailor's life in the mid-nineteenth century. (Photograph from the Dance Collection, New York Public Library for the Performing Arts.)

LORING, EUGENE (LeRoy Kerpestein, born c.1911 in Milwaukee, Wisconsin, died 30 August 1982 in Kingston, New York), American dancer, choreographer, and teacher. Having studied music and acrobatics, Kerpestein began to perform with the Wisconsin Players, a small dramatic troupe in Milwaukee, sometime in the early 1930s. Influenced by the director of the company, Boris Glagolin, who encouraged his actor-dancers to combine expressive gesture with the spoken text in a meaningful, dramatic interpretation, Kerpestein expanded his studies to include ballet and tap dancing. As he gained confidence, he determined to embark upon a theatrical career, whereupon he adopted the professional name of Eugene Loring.

Loring's first choreographies were dances for Glagolin's theatrical spectacles. Friends of Lincoln Kirstein saw these efforts and persuaded Loring to go to New York to study with George Balanchine at his new School of American Ballet. There Loring continued his training not only with Balanchine but with such outstanding teachers as Anatole Vilzak, Muriel Stuart, and Pierre Vladimiroff. He made his professional debut in 1934, dancing in a company led by Michel Fokine, who impressed upon him the importance of a true synthesis of the arts in ballet and the expressive potential of the academic vocabulary.

Loring was a true *demi-caractère* dancer. Kirstein would later recall that Loring reminded him of the film actor James Cagney: "both were alike in their stubby strength, concentration, and physicality" (Kirstein, 1973, p. 52). Dancing with the American Ballet and with its successor, Ballet Caravan, Loring appeared in the first professional productions of three important Balanchine ballets, *Alma Mater* (1935), *Reminiscence* (1935), and *The Card Party* (1937). He also created several notable roles in his own works for Ballet Caravan and Ballet Theatre (later called American Ballet Theatre) as well as in Lew Christensen's *Filling Station* (1938), Adolph Bolm's *Peter and the Wolf* (1940), and Agnes de Mille's *Three Virgins and a Devil* (1941).

Loring's theatrical talents found their greatest outlet, however, not in performance but in choreography. For Ballet Caravan he produced four works, all based on American themes. The first of these, *Harlequin for President* (1936), a satire on the presidential electoral process, was a mélange of good-natured jokes and buffoonery, very much in the tradition of the Italian *commedia dell'arte.* Loring's later works would be more distinctively American in character, and more soundly crafted. *Yankee Clipper* (1937), recounting the adventures of a farm boy who sails around the world, showed Loring's knowledge and mastery of the classical ballet vocabulary for men. *Billy the Kid* (1938) retold the legend of America's favorite cowboy and presented romantic images of the great American West, in sharp contrast to the grim scenario of *City Portrait* (1939), which focused on the conflict and hopelessness of an urban family. Loring himself created the central characters in *Harlequin for President, Yankee Clipper,* and *Billy the Kid,* which was almost immediately recognized as a classic work of Americana and which firmly established his reputation as an important American choreographer. [*See* Billy the Kid.]

In 1940, Loring collaborated with the author William Saroyan in the creation of *The Great American Goof,* a ballet-play with words, for the newly organized Ballet Theatre. Loring went on to star in Saroyan's play *The Beautiful People* (1941), illustrating to audiences and critics that an effective dramatic interpretation could result from the fusion of acting and dance. Encouraged by his success and wishing to create a new form of lyric ballet theater, Loring founded a company of his own, Dance Players, in the fall of 1941. Although the company folded the following year, Loring did manage to create a few ballets for the group that attracted favorable attention. Walter Terry, a leading critic, commended *Prairie* (1942) for finding its dramatic power "not in a human character but in the character of the land itself. . . . The movements of *Prairie* suggested the very sweep of a new land and the robust qualities of the people who cherished it" (*New York Herald Tribune,* 25 April 1942).

Thereafter, Loring did some of his best work for the popular stage and screen, beginning with *Carmen Jones* (1943). In the dances he devised for this Broadway adaptation of Georges Bizet's opera *Carmen,* Loring was especially commended for his integrity and honesty of movement in the "Toreador Song," conceived not as a bullfight but as a boxing match. In subsequent Broadway shows—*Three Wishes for Jamie* (1952) and *Silk Stockings* (1955)—and in numerous Hollywood films—among them *Yolanda and the Thief* (1945), *Ziegfeld Follies* (1946), *Mexican Hayride* (1948), *The Toast of New Orleans* (1950), *Deep in My Heart* (1954), *Meet Me in Las Vegas* (1955), *Funny Face* (1956), and *Silk Stockings* (1957)—Loring successfully fused ballet, modern, and jazz styles in his production numbers. He also devised challenging choreography for his male dancers. In all his later films and in works created for television—such as *Capital of the World* (1953)—he experimented with visual effects and camera angles, conscious that he was choreographing for the camera rather than for a theatrical audience.

In the late 1940s Loring began to codify his theatrical dance concepts into a comprehensive curriculum for the education of dancers. The course of instruction at the American School of Dance, which he founded in Hollywood in 1948, and at the University of California at Irvine, where he founded a dance department in 1965, prepares dancers for professional rather than academic careers. It includes training in ballet, jazz, modern, ethnic, and "freestyle" dance as well as courses in dance history, choreography, acting for dancers, and Kinesiography, Loring's own system of dance notation. Freestyle dance, incorporating elements of ballet, modern dance, and jazz dance, evolved from Loring's desire to free dance from stylistic restriction, increasing expressive possibilities for both the choreographer and the performer. Loring sold his school in 1974 in order to concentrate on his duties at the University of California.

[*See also* Notation.]

BIBLIOGRAPHY

Canna, D. J., and Eugene Loring. *Kineseography: The Loring System of Dance Notation.* Hollywood, 1955.

Delamater, Jerome. *Dance in the Hollywood Musical.* Ann Arbor, Mich., 1981. Includes an interview with Loring.

Guest, Ann Hutchinson. "Selma Jeanne Cohen and Eugene Loring's *Kinesiography*." *Dance Chronicle* 18.2 (1995): 195–206.

Kirstein, Lincoln. *The New York City Ballet.* With photographs by Martha Swope and George Platt Lynes. New York, 1973.

Lloyd, Margaret, and Selma Jeanne Cohen. "Eugene Loring's Very American School of Dance." *Dance Magazine* 30 (August 1956): 30–33.

Martin, John. "Summing Up." *New York Times* (3 May 1942).

Maynard, Olga. *The American Ballet.* Philadelphia, 1959.

Maynard, Olga. "Eugene Loring Talks to Olga Maynard" (parts 1–2). *Dance Magazine* (July–August 1966).

Moulton, Robert D. "Choreography in Musical Comedy and Revue on the New York Stage from 1925 through 1950." Master's thesis, University of Minnesota, 1957.

Obituary. *Variety* (15 September 1982).

Reynolds, Nancy. *Repertory in Review: Forty Years of the New York City Ballet.* New York, 1977.

INTERVIEW. Eugene Loring, by Marian Horosko (1966), Dance Collection, New York Public Library for the Performing Arts.

VIDEOTAPE. Eugene Loring, "Capital of the World," *Omnibus* (WCBS-TV, New York, 1953).

Reba Ann Adler

LOSCH, TILLY (Ottilie Ethel Leopoldine Losch; born 15 November 1903 in Vienna, died 24 December 1975 in New York City), dancer, actress, choreographer, and painter. Trained at the ballet school of the Vienna Opera, as a student Losch appeared with the Vienna Opera Ballet, making her debut in 1913 in Louis Frappart's *Wiener Walzer.* She became a member of the corps de ballet on 1 March 1918, a *coryphée* on 1 February 1921 and, on the recommendation of the ballet master Heinrich Kröller and opera co-director Richard Strauss, a soloist on 1 January 1924.

Losch was neither a classicist like Gusti Pichler nor an academic technician like Adele Krausenecker, but a new type that had evolved toward modern dance from the balletic *caractère* and *demi-caractère* categories. A bit gamin, charming despite astringency, she appeared in traditional Viennese ballets (the Chinese Lady Doll in Josef Hassreiter's *Die Puppenfee* was her first solo) and in works by the Russian Georgi Kyaksht and the Italian Nicola Guerra, but she came to prominence in ballets by the German Heinrich Kröller (creating in 1924 the role of Princess Tea Blossom in *Schlagobers* and in 1927 the title role in *Das Lockende Phantom*). According to Kröller, "What and how Losch dances (in *Phantom*) has nothing to do with tradition, though the steps are balletic . . . the body is free and plastic." She had studied modern dance, performing with Grete Wiesenthal in 1919 and taking classes with Mary Wigman in 1924.

Losch danced and acted at the Vienna Burgtheater and Akademietheater and, from 1925 through 1926, at the Salzburg Festival. In 1924, she choreographed and danced in Max Reinhardt's Berlin production of Shakespeare's *A Midsummer Night's Dream,* resigning from the Vienna Opera Ballet on 31 August 1927 to continue to work with Reinhardt in Salzburg.

Later that year, she made her New York debut with the Reinhardt company and her London debut in Noël Coward's *This Year of Grace,* the first of a series of musicals produced by Charles B. Cochran, for which she danced and provided choreography. Her "hand dance" (cochoreographed with Hedy Pfundmayr) fascinated viewers in London and New York, as it had in Austria. In 1931 she choreographed *The Gang's All Here* and appeared with Fred and Adele Astaire in *The Band Wagon* (dancing on pointe, partnered by Fred Astaire in ballroom shoes). In 1932 she performed the part of the Nun in Reinhardt's production of Karl Volmoeller's *The Miracle.* These years set a pattern of transatlantic commuting.

Losch also gave dance recitals. Arnold Haskell called her one of the few "continental" dancers who does not disappoint by just posing. To him, she seemed well trained in ballet though not a virtuoso. Her real interest, however, lay in exotic dances.

Edward James, a wealthy Londoner whom Losch married in 1931, founded Les Ballets 1933. The company appeared only that year in Paris and London. George Balanchine, whom Losch befriended in 1924 in Berlin and who subsequently helped her to choreograph some of her dances, headed the troupe. Losch danced leading roles in three of the six items of the all-Balanchine repertory: *Les Sept Péchés Capitaux, Errante,* and *Les Valses de Beethoven.* In 1934 James won a divorce from Losch, claiming that she had committed adultery with Prince Serge Obolensky. She then resumed her London theater career in A. P. Herbert's *Streamline.*

In Hollywood films, Losch was cast in exotic acting-dancing roles, in *The Garden of Allah* (1936) and in *The Good Earth* (1937). She married Lord Carnarvon in 1939. The following year, she performed as a guest artist with Ballet Theatre at City College's Lewisohn Stadium in New York, on 1–2 August, in Antony Tudor's *Goya Pastorale.* She divorced Carnarvon in 1948. After appearing in still another exotic acting-dancing role in the 1947 film *Duel in the Sun* and choreographing the Salzburg Festival production of a Ferdinand Raimund play in 1950, Losch concentrated on painting, which she had begun in 1938. Her art works are held by major collections, including the Barnes Foundation.

BIBLIOGRAPHY

Amort, Andrea. "Die Geschichte des Balletts der Wiener Staatsoper, 1918–1942." Ph.D. diss., University of Vienna, 1981.

Cullum, Winifred. "Dancer to Star: Tilly Losch." *American Dance* (September 1940): 9.

Haskell, Arnold L. "Tilly Losch." In Haskell's *Penelope Spencer and Other Studies.* 2d ed. London, 1931.

Koller, Ann Marie. "Tilly Losch." In *Österreichisches Biographisches Lexicon.* Graz, 1957–.

Losch, Tilly. "The Dance of the Flame." *New York Times* (31 January 1937).

Newnham, John K. "Tilly Losch in Hollywood's Most Costly Film." *The Dancing Times* (December 1946): 134–135.

ARCHIVE. Dance Collection, New York Public Library for the Performing Arts.

GEORGE JACKSON

LOUIS XIV (born 5 September 1638 in Saint-Germain-en-Laye, died 1 September 1715 in Versailles), king of France and patron of dance. Like his father Louis XIII, Louis XIV showed a talent for dance at an early age; as a young child, he is said to have enjoyed the burlesque masquerades of *La Finta Pazza* (1645). At the age of eight he appeared at the end of *Orfeo* (1647) at the theater in the royal palace. Cardinal Mazarin, the first minister, was accused of stressing dance instead of grammar in Louis's education, but his grace and elegance on the stage eventually helped him win the hearts of his rebellious subjects. He made his official debut in the roles of a knight and a "tricotet poitevin" in the ballet *Cassandre* (1651). In the sumptuous ballet *Les Fêtes de Bacchus* he danced a Drunken Thief, a Bacchant, a Frozen Man, a Titan, and a Muse.

After the insurrection of the Fronde, Louis XIV used the court ballet as a tool for displaying to Europe his prestige as a heroic prince. In *Le Ballet de la Nuit* (1653), he first played the role of Apollo, who was to become his emblem as the Sun King. Alone or with partners from among the professional dancers or the nobility, he performed a variety of comic, poetic, and mythological roles, in which he demonstrated harmony of gesture and an easy bearing, sense of rhythm, and *leggedria* ("lightness") that surprised the Italian ambassadors. He generally appeared several times a week in ballets, until his sudden decision to retire because of the burdens of his office. His last appearance was in 1670, in *Les Amants Magnifiques.*

A student and patron of dancing master Pierre Beauchamps, Louis founded the Académie Royale de Danse in 1661, with thirteen accomplished dancing masters, for the purpose of defining the principles of academic dance and training dancers for his ballets. He kept a watchful eye on the purity of the French school through his Règlement de l'Opéra (Opera Regulations) of 1713.

[*See also* Académie Royale de Danse; Ballet de Cour; Ballet Technique, History of, *article on* French Court Dance.]

BIBLIOGRAPHY

Christout, Marie-Françoise. *Le ballet de cour de Louis XIV, 1643–1672.* Paris, 1967.

Coeyman, Barbara. "Theatres for Opera and Ballet during the Reigns of Louis XIV and Louis XV." *Early Music* 18 (February 1990): 22–37.

Erlanger, Philippea. *Louis XIV.* Paris, 1965.

Franko, Mark. "Double Bodies: Androgyny and Power in the Performance of Louis XIV." *Drama Review* 38 (Winter 1994): 71–82.

Gaigneron, Axelle de. "Louis XIV, roi de l'Amérique." *Connaissance des Arts* (March 1984): 48–55.

Guilmard-Geddes, Laurence. "De l'iconographie de quelques figures de ballet sous le règne de Louis XIV." *Recherche en Dance* 2 (1983): 39–44.

Harris-Warrick, Rebecca. "Ballroom Dancing at the Court of Louis XIV." *Early Music* 14.1 (1986): 41–49.

Harris-Warrick, Rebecca, and Carol G. Marsh. *Musical Theatre at the Court of Louis XIV: Le Mariage de la Grosse Cathos.* Cambridge, 1994.

Purkis, Helen. "Le Ballet Royale de la Nuit (1653) et l'influence italienne." *Studi Francesi* 13 (1969): 77–83.

Rice, Paul F. *The Performing Arts at Fontainebleau from Louis XIV to Louis XVI.* Ann Arbor, 1989.

Saint-Maurice, Thomas François Chabod, marquis de. *Lettres sur la cour de Louis XIV.* 2 vols. Edited by Jean Lemoine. Paris, 1911–1912.

MARIE-FRANÇOISE CHRISTOUT
Translated from French

LOUIS, MURRAY (Murray Louis Fuchs; born 4 November 1926 in Brooklyn), American dancer, choreographer, and teacher. Louis received a B.A. in dramatic arts from New York University in 1951. He also studied with Anna Halprin at San Francisco State College. Louis began what was to be an important association with Alwin Nikolais in 1949 at the Henry Street Playhouse in New York City. Louis was lead soloist in the Nikolais Dance Theatre until 1969 and was associate director of the playhouse, where, as a teacher, he was instrumental in the formation of the Nikolais-Louis dance technique. Louis is a remarkable dancer whose control and articulation of the body have been consistently praised. His choreography is often noted for its humor and kinetic wit.

Louis developed his company primarily with Nikolais dancers (Phyllis Lamhut, Gladys Bailin, Mimi Garrard, Bill Frank, Michael Ballard, and others) during the period from 1953 to 1969. In 1969 he formed his own permanent company, which toured nationally and internationally. In 1989 the Louis Company incorporated with Nikolais to become a group of ten members called Nikolais and Murray Louis Dance Company. The company has performed work of both choreographers, usually on the same program.

Louis's major solo works are *Chimera* (1966) and *Déjà Vu* (1977). Group works include *Junk Dances* (1964), *Hoopla* (1971), *Porcelain Dialogues* (1974), *Schubert* (1977), *Afternoon* (1980), and *Four Brubeck Pieces* (1984). Louis has used music ranging from electronic scores by Nikolais to jazz compositions by Dave Brubeck and classical music of Brahms and Tchaikovsky. Before his death, Nikolais created most of the lighting and stage effects for Louis's choreography. Louis has choreographed works for the Hamburg Ballet, the Royal Danish Ballet, the Scottish Ballet, and the Batsheva Dance Company of Israel. In 1975 and 1978 he worked with Rudolf Nureyev choreographing both group and solo works.

A highly concerned and outspoken advocate for dance, Louis has been a pioneer teacher of master classes and workshops throughout the United States. His book *Inside Dance* (1981), which stemmed from articles written for *Dance Magazine,* forms an intimate view of a dancer's life and concerns. In 1972 he filmed *Dance as an Art Form,* a series of five films based on the principles of the Nikolais/Louis technique ("Space," "Shape," "Time," "Motion," and "The Body as an Instrument"). Louis's solo works have been filmed as *Murray Louis in Concert;* the documentary *Nik and Murray* was made in 1987 as part of the

LOUIS. The choreographer in *Déjà Vu* (1977), one of his major solo works. (Photograph © 1978 by Jack Vartoogian; used by permission.)

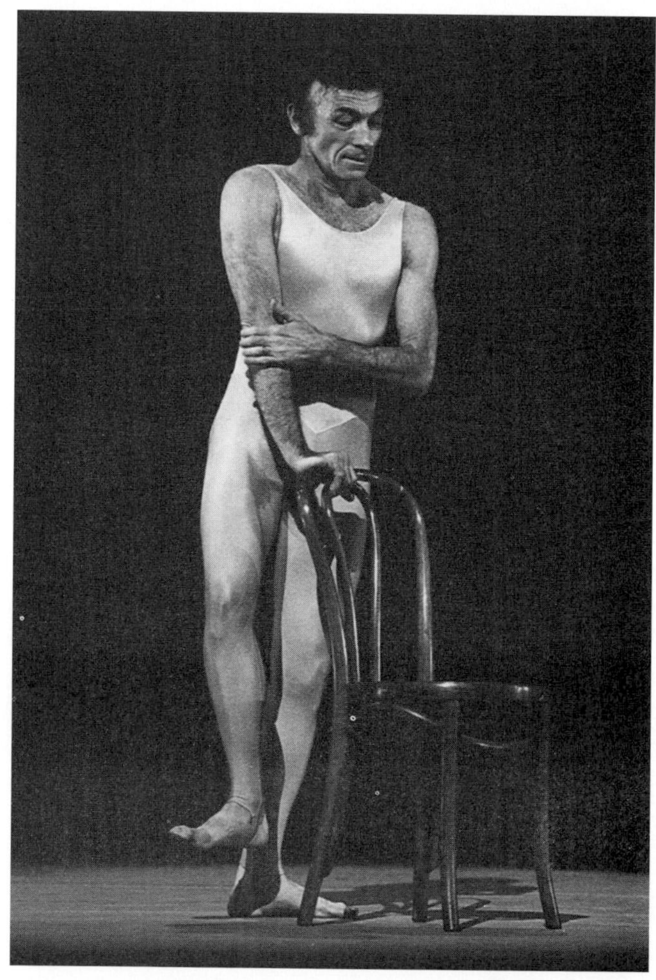

Public Broadcasting Service *American Masters* series. Louis has served as a member of the dance panel of the National Endowment for the Arts, and he received the *Dance Magazine* Award in 1977.

BIBLIOGRAPHY

Cunningham, Kitty. *Conversations with a Dancer.* New York, 1980.

Louis, Murray. *Inside Dance.* New York, 1980.

Louis, Murray. *Murray Louis on Dance.* Chicago, 1992.

Zupp, Nancy T. "An Analysis and Comparison of the Choreographic Process of Alwin Nikolais, Murray Louis, and Phyllis Lamhut." Ph.D. diss., University of North Carolina, Greensboro, 1978.

KITTY CUNNINGHAM

LOURE. A French Baroque court and theater dance, *loure* also refers to an optional movement of the instrumental suites. The word *loure,* which is probably derived from the Latin *lura,* a "bag" or "purse," in Normandy referred to a bagpipe. The bags of the pipes were made from animals' stomachs, and the peasants of lower Normandy called the stomach *la loure.* It has therefore been surmised that the music for the *loure* (also called *gigue lente*) was associated with the Normandy bagpipe; however, any original relationship between the *gigue* and *gigue lente* remains obscure.

At Louis XIV's court (ruled 1643–1715), the *gigue* was used in the early *ballets de cour* ("court ballets") of Jean-Baptiste Lully (1632–1687), while a piece titled "Loure" did not appear until his *Les Fêtes de l'Amour et de Bacchus* (1672). The first published *loure* is by Raoul-Auger Feuillet, disguised under the title "Sarabande Espagnole," in his 1700 collection of his own dances. The music is from *Le Bourgeois Gentilhomme: Ballet des Nations* (1670). In French dance music, both the *gigue* and *loure* usually have a 6/4 time signature, and the predominant rhythm within the measure is ♩. ♪ ♩ ♩. ♪ ♩. Their musical tempi, however, are markedly different, because twice as many steps are danced in one measure of a *loure.* The *gigue,* which contains many springing steps, is the liveliest of the Baroque dances, while the *loure* (the *gigue lente* [slow *gigue*]), with about one-third springing steps, is described as being one of the slowest and most majestic.

Some twenty-five examples of the *loure* are extant in eighteenth-century dance notation. With one or two exceptions, notably Guillaume-Louis Pecour's ballroom dance "Aimable Vainqueur" [*see* below], they are virtuosic theater dances for men and women. Two *loures* by Pecour (1653–1729) are solos for a woman: his "Entrée pour une Femme," danced by Mademoiselle Marie-Catherine Guyot in Theobaldo di Gatti's *Scylla,* and the "Entrée Espagnolle," published in 1704 and danced by Mademoiselle Marie-Thérèse Perdou de Subligny in André Campra's *L'Europe Galante.* The choreography of the former has the circle for its choreographic theme. It begins with turning paths in space; then the dancer balances while executing *tours (ronds) de jambe en l'air,* the climax occurring when these are combined with whole *pirouettes en dehors* and *en dedans.* The choreography of the latter contrasts slow balances with quick springs. The *loure* was also referred to as a Spanish *gigue* and was frequently used for Spanish *entrées,* with the characteristic rhythm:

A beautiful *loure* of moderate technical difficulty is Pecour's *gigue lente,* danced by Monsieur Dumerail and Mademoiselle Victoire to the "Air des Graces" in Campra's *Hésione.* The remaining *loures* are almost all virtuosic solos and duets for male dancers.

According to eighteenth-century dance theorists, the *loure* is a dance in quadruple meter, or time, that is, the dance has two *pas composés,* or *temps* (step-units), instead of the usual one, danced in a measure. The dancer is moving in triple meter, but making a strong duple beat with the rhythmic stress that occurs at the beginning of each step-unit:

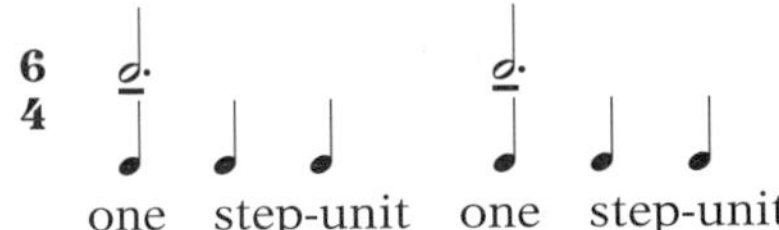

A *loure* will sometimes be written in 3/[4] time to clarify the triple-meter performance of the units as though to two measures of triple time.

The step-units are most frequently combined so that there is less activity on the quarter-note beats 2 or 5, or on both. This results in a long, rhythmic pull on beats 1 and 4, a quality also produced when two springs are made over three quarter notes. A step-unit of two springs is seldom repeated in a measure, and the following unit often has a step on each quarter note, the two combined giving a rhythm usually found in the melodic line; for example, in the least active measures, *élevés,* preceded by *pliés,* mark the duple beat:

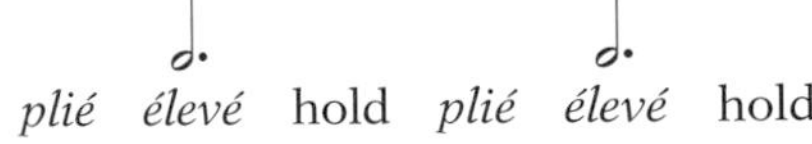

At the other end of the scale of activity, eighth-note rhythms are introduced into the step-units, often coinciding with a less active musical measure. For example, in the *loure* from *Scylla:*

Music

Dance

With two step-units in a measure, the cadential step occurs not on the downbeat but on the second half-note beat—the steps in the first half of the measure being quite active.

Musically, the *loure* is most frequently bipartite, with strains of diverse and often unequal lengths. The *gigue lente* from *Hésione* has a strain of ten measures followed by one of sixteen, while the two strains of a *loure* from Lully's *Acis et Galatée* (1686) have nine and thirteen measures. The *loure* from *Scylla*, with strains of four and eight measures, is exceptionally short. The musical repeats are usually A-A-B-B and, as in the majority of Baroque dances, a new figure is choreographed for each.

The two step-units in a measure make for extended dance figures with long inner phrases that, with their intricate step-sequences, make considerable demands on the dancers' powers of rhythmic phrasing and musicality. The long, slow swing of the duple beat and the smooth majesty of the dance must be maintained, even while the quickest step-patterns are being clearly articulated.

The most beloved ballroom *danse à deux* (couple dance) was Pecour's triple-meter *loure* "Aimable Vainqueur," composed to the air of that name from Campra's *Hésione*. Published in 1701, Pecour's new dance was composed at the royal retreat at Marly and first performed for the king by the comte de Brionne and Mademoiselle Bournonville. The king expressed great satisfaction, and the dance immediately became popular owing to the beauty of its air and choreography, which combine nobility and tenderness to evoke a refined and delicate atmosphere of love.

This *loure* is in triple meter, with one step-unit per measure, and the choreography flows in complete accord with the music. After the first four measures have fulfilled the required advance toward the Presence (the person or persons of highest social rank), the dancers focus almost entirely on each other, until the final steps and the Honours, after dancing, acknowledge the Presence once more.

The *loure* continued to appear in the operas of Jean-Philippe Rameau (1683–1764). In instrumental music, the two most famous *loures* are in J. S. Bach's Violin Partita in E Minor and his French Suite in G Major.

[*See also* Ballet Technique, History of, *article on* French Court Dance.]

BIBLIOGRAPHY

Boyden, David D. "Loure." In *New Grove Dictionary of Music and Musicians*. London, 1980.

Feuillet, Raoul-Auger. "Traité de la cadence." In Feuillet's *Recüeil de dances contenant un très grand nombres des meillieures entrées de ballet de M. Pécour.* Paris, 1704. Translated by John Weaver as *A Small Treatise of Time and Cadence in Dancing*. London, 1706.

Hilton, Wendy. *Dance of Court and Theater: The French Noble Style 1690–1725*. Princeton, 1981.

WENDY HILTON

LOWSKI, WOYTEK (Wojciech Wiesiołłowski; born 11 October 1939 in Brest Litovsk), Polish dancer and teacher. Woytek Lowski studied at the Warsaw Ballet School of the Wielki Theater with Leon Wójcikowski (also known as Woizikowski). He joined the Warsaw Opera Ballet in 1956 and was promoted to soloist in 1958. From 1961 to 1963 he studied at the Leningrad Choreographic School with Olga Jordan and Aleksandr Pushkin, also dancing with the Kirov Ballet. He was a soloist with the Warsaw Ballet (1963–1966), Maurice Béjart's Ballet du XXe Siècle (1966–1971), Cologne's TanzForum (1971), and the Ballet de Marseille (1972–1973). Relocating to the United States, he became a principal dancer with the Boston Ballet (1973–1979). In Pushkin's opinion he had "a high jump and a very good extension, beautiful *tours par terre* and *en l'air*, forceful expression; he danced emotionally with an inner temperament." He was also an excellent partner. As a soloist he debuted in Woizikowski's *L'Après-midi d'un Faune* (1958; after Vaslav Nijinsky).

Appearing with so broad a range of companies, Lowski naturally danced a wide variety of roles. In addition to the classics, he appeared in works by Béjart, George Balanchine, Agnes de Mille, Norman Walker, Roland Petit, and Birgit Cullberg. At the end of his career, Lowski toured extensively as a partner to Eleanor D'Antuono.

Lowski received his teacher's diploma in Leningrad in 1963 and sporadically led classes throughout his career. Since 1979 he has devoted himself to pedagogy. He has taught at Rosella Hightower's center in Cannes and at ballet and opera theaters in Boston, Nancy, Paris, Rome, Basel, Hamburg, Berlin, and Rio de Janeiro. Beginning in 1982 he taught at American Ballet Theatre in New York. He won second prize at the first International Ballet Competition in Varna, Bulgaria, in 1964.

BIBLIOGRAPHY

Horosko, Marian. "Woytek Lowski: ABT's Aristocrat of the Classroom." *Dance Magazine* (April 1983): 82–86.

Stoop, Norma McLain. "Woytek Lowski: An Exchange of Emotion." *Dance Magazine* (June 1976): 58–61.

PAWEŁ CHYNOWSKI

LUIGI. *See* Jazz Dance.

LUISILLO (Luis Pérez Davila; born 1928 in Mexico City), dancer. Luisillo began his international career in the Spanish dance company of Carmen Amaya and in 1950 formed a partnership with Teresa Amaya. From these associations he gained a professionalism that stood him in good stead when he formed his own company, Luisillo and His Spanish Dance Theater, in 1956. Based in Spain, this company was one of the first to employ for-

LUISILLO. With a member of his company, Luisillo performed a lively Spanish folk dance, late 1950s. (Photograph reprinted from Horst Koegler, *Ballett International*, Berlin, 1960, fig. 170.)

eigners; South African, Australian, and British dancers were glad of the opportunity to join a Spanish dance troupe.

The company that Luisillo formed with his partner Teresa Amaya in 1950 led to extensive international touring, and his strong sense of theater produced a theatrical presentation with wide appeal. Luisillo created ballets such as *Gitanos de la Alpujarra, Sinfonía Sevillana,* and *Nocturno Flamenco;* these and similar ballets made use of all the different forms of Spanish dance. He filled the stage with colorful regional dances and was able to express all the emotions of love and pain in solos and duets. He particularly excelled in *escuela bolera.*

After disbanding his company, Luisillo opened a *tablao* (theater), Los Cabales, in the center of Madrid, which is frequented by both tourists and local dance aficionados. In the 1980s, he reformed his Spanish Dance Theater, which toured throughout Spain. Luisillo has also served as president of the Spanish Dance Society of South Africa.

BIBLIOGRAPHY

Airoldi, Elsa. "Luisillo." *Danza & Danza,* no. 36 (September 1989): 4.

Brunelleschi, Elsa. "Spanish Dancing Old and New." *Ballet* 11 (January–February 1951): 7–17.

Brunelleschi, Elsa. "Three Spanish Dancers." *Ballet Annual* 12 (1958): 109–112.

Segura, Felipe. "Luisillo (Luis Pérez Dávila)." *Cuadernos del CID-DANZA,* no. 16 (1987): 19–20.

Williams, Peter. "Luisillo on a Fresh Path for Spanish Dance." *Dance and Dancers* (May 1961): 15–17.

PHILIPPA HEALE

LUKOM, ELENA (Elena Mikhailovna Liukom; born 23 April [5 May] 1891 in Saint Petersburg, died 27 February 1968 in Leningrad), dancer, teacher, and author. Lukom graduated from the Saint Petersburg Theater School in 1909, where she studied under Michel Fokine, and joined the ballet company of the Maryinsky Theater. For the 1910 Saison Russe in Paris she danced in Diaghilev's Ballets Russes. Returning to Russia, from 1912 onward she danced solo roles, steadily advancing to the leading position in the company. Lukom was the most famous and active ballerina of Leningrad after the Revolution of 1917, contributing to the revision of the classical tradition and its democratization. Her talent and aesthetic views helped her to make the refinements of ballet comprehensible to the new popular audiences, who rewarded her with affection. Even in the early part of her career she had been called a performer in the new style for her expressive, soaring technique and sensitivity to the nuances in the music, so that her dancing looked like inspired improvisation. A faithful pupil of Fokine, she proved to be a good actress in both lyrical and comic roles.

In her thirty-year career Lukom rapidly mastered a large and varied repertory of more than thirty-five roles. She was the charming and simple Lise in *La Fille Mal Gardée,* the coquettish Colombine in Fokine's *Le Carnaval,* the gentle and cunning Medora in *Le Corsaire,* the delicate Nikia in *La Bayadère,* and the temperamental Kitri in *Don Quixote* as well as an incomparable Giselle and Esmeralda. She moved away from idealizing Romantic heroines, discovering instead the poetry in their natural charm and human emotions. Her flair for invention found expression in various ways: experiments on the concert stage, where she danced with her regular partner Boris Shavrov in duets based on acrobatic lifts, and collaboration with the innovative choreographer Fedor Lopukhov. The peak of Lukom's achievement was the contemporary heroine of Lopukhov's *The Red Poppy* (1929).

One of the founders of the Soviet school of dance, Lukom greatly influenced many of the finest Leningrad dancers of the 1930s and 1940s. In 1925 she was one of the first ballet dancers to be awarded the title of Merited Artist of the Republic, and in 1960 she received the title of Merited Art Worker of the Russian Federation. Her memoir on her career was published in 1940.

BIBLIOGRAPHY

Krasovskaya, Vera. *Russkii baletnyi teatr nachala dvadtsatogo veka,* vol. 2, *Tantsovshchiki.* Leningrad, 1972.

Lukom, Elena. *Moya rabota v balete.* Moscow, 1940.

Obituary. *Dance and Dancers* (August 1970): 3.

Rozanova, Olga. *Elena Liukom* (in Russian). Leningrad, 1983.

OLGA ROZANOVA
Translated from Russian

LULLY, JEAN-BAPTISTE (Giovanni Battista Lulli; born 29 November 1632 in Florence, Italy, died 22 March 1687 in Paris), French composer, violinist, choreographer, and director of theatrical spectacles. The son of a Florentine miller, Giovanni Battista Lulli was only thirteen when he arrived in France, and he never returned to his native land. He entered the employ of Mademoiselle de Montpensier, a cousin of Louis XIV who wanted to perfect her Italian. Thanks to his contact with the musicians employed by the princess, and the organists Nicolas Métru, Nicolas Gigault, and François Roberday, he developed exceptional gifts for composition and for the violin, which he played perfectly. However, it was his abilities as a dancer that were most admired at the time and that brought him to the attention of the king. On 23 February 1653, three months after he left the service of Mademoiselle de Montpensier, he danced no fewer than five roles at the court in *Le Ballet de la Nuit.* His success was so great that several weeks later, on 16 March, Louis XIV appointed him *compositeur de la musique instrumentale* ("composer of instrumental music"). Between 1653 and 1655 he attracted attention through his choreographic prowess and his humor in works in which he most frequently danced next to the young sovereign, with whom he enjoyed a kind of a camaraderie that he put to good use. After 1655 his role in the composition of the ballets, which he shared with other musicians, became preponderant, and his name gradually eclipsed those of his collaborators. The ballets *Alcidiane* (14 February 1658) and *La Raillerie* (19 February 1659) made particular contributions to his fame.

In 1660 Lully created ballet *entrées* for celebrations of the Peace of the Pyrénées and the marriage of the king. They were introduced into Francesco Cavalli's opera *Serse,* performed on 22 November. In May of the following year he was named *surintendant et compositeur de la musique de la chambre* ("superintendant and composer of chamber music") by Louis XIV, who had just taken control of the affairs of the kingdom following the death of Cardinal Mazarin. This situation instigated Lully to request naturalization papers in December. He further strengthened his ties with France by his marriage on 24 July 1662 to Madeleine Lambert, the only daughter of Michel Lambert, the king's musician. That same year he again collaborated with Cavalli, composing twenty-six *entrées* for the opera *Ercole Amante.* Lully continued to supply *ballets de cour,* including *entrées* for *Les Amours Déguisés* (1664) and *La Naissance de Vénus* (1665), and *Flore* (1669).

After 1664, he turned toward another theatrical genre, the *comédie-ballet,* which had been inaugurated in 1661 by Molière with *Les Fâcheux.* Molière collaborated with Lully in writing several of these theater pieces, which included episodes of singing and dancing. The collaboration of the two "grands Baptistes" ("great Baptists"; Molière's real name was Jean-Baptiste Poquelin) lasted almost eight years and produced a series of masterpieces: *Le Mariage Forcé* (1664) and the sumptuous *La Princesse d'Élide,* given as part of the fête, *Les Plaisirs de l'Île Enchantée,* at Versailles in 1664; *L'Amour Médecin* (1665); *Le Sicilien ou L'Amour Peintre;* (1667); *George Dandin* (1668); *Monsieur de Pourceaugnac* (1669); *Les Amants Magnifiques* (1670); and *Le Bourgeois Gentilhomme* (1670). *Psyché,* a *tragédie-ballet* staged on 17 January 1671, marked another important stage in the composer's career. In this elaborately mounted work, Lully set to music verses by Molière, Pierre Corneille, and Philippe Quinault, the last of whom was henceforth to be his principal collaborator.

The following year Lully quarreled with Molière; Lully had purchased the license for productions at the Paris Opera, which he enforced with draconian severity, notably by forbidding Molière's troupe to use a great orchestra and to include choruses in their performances. His attitude was justified only by his fear of having to compete with another Paris theater. Lully's own theater, the Académie Royale de Musique in Paris, did in fact initially have difficulties that were not finally resolved until after Molière's death in 1673. The following year Lully's *Alceste* caused a scandal when performed for the public, but his later operas were generally received with increasing praise. [*See the entry on Molière*]

The *ballet de cour,* the Italian opera, and the *comédie-ballet* had prepared Lully to work in the lyric theater. All that was needed to make *Psyché* a genuine opera was the recitatives, which he added later when he performed the work in his theater in 1678. His first spectacle for the Parisians was *Les Fêtes de l'Amour et de Bacchus* (1672), which consisted of *divertissements* previously done for the court. Pressed for time, Lully assembled the best passages from *La Princesse d'Élide, George Dandin, Les Amants Magnifiques,* and *Le Bourgeois Gentilhomme.* The following year he put on *Cadmus et Hermione,* an original work. This opera, which was the fruit of the collaboration between Lully and Quinault, also inaugurated a new genre, the *tragédie en musique* ("tragedy in music"), known after the end of the eighteenth century as *tragédie lyrique* ("lyric tragedy"). In this theatrical form, which emphasized a dramatic action expressed by both singer and orchestra, dance also occupied an important place through a *diver-*

tissement in each act, which helped to vary and embellish the spectacle. Other *tragédies lyriques* by the composer, generally one a year, followed *Cadmus et Hermione: Alceste; Le Triomphe d'Alcide* (1674), *Thésée* (1675), *Atys* (1676), *Isis* (1677), *Psyché* (1678), *Bellérophon* (1679), *Proserpine* (1680), *Persée* (1682), *Phaëton* (1683), *Amadis* (1684), *Roland* (1685), and *Armide* (1686). Lully also experimented with other genres, including a pastorale, *Acis et Galatée* (1686), and two "ballets," *Le Triomphe de l'Amour* (1681) and *Le Temple de la Paix* (1685), which can really be considered operas, because of the role played by vocal music in these works. *Le Triomphe de l'Amour* is still reminiscent of the *ballets de cour* because of its series of *entrées,* while *Le Temple de la Paix* bears a greater resemblance to lyric works because of its more consistent and logical plot. *Le Triomphe de l'Amour* also provided an opportunity for the director of the Paris Opera to introduce professional female dancers for the first time on the Parisian lyric stage, led by Mademoiselle de La Fontaine.

Lully had the assistance of Louis XIV in his administrative tasks. The king witnessed at his various residences the creation of several operas by the artist before they were performed in Paris, ensuring a certain amount of publicity, while the sets and machinery used in the royal theaters were sometimes offered for use in the Paris performances. However, the composer apparently suffered some kind of disgrace at court in 1686, one year before his death. His work was nevertheless admired and even enjoyed exceptional dissemination both in France and in the rest of Europe, where for more than a century it represented French lyric art. Lully's *tragédies lyriques* were performed during his lifetime in England, Germany, and the Netherlands, and composers as famous as Henry Purcell and Johann Sebastian Bach were influenced by his music, particularly his dance suites.

Ballet music occupies an important place in Lully's work. In the *ballets de cour,* the *comédie-ballets,* and the operas, conventional dances frequently appear: *bourrées, menuets, gavottes, sarabandes, canaries, courantes, galliardes, loures, rigaudons,* and *passepieds. Chaconnes* and *passacailles* also play an important role, contributing a majestic brilliance to the spectacle and giving the composer an opportunity to create pieces with a complex instrumental texture. The dances in *Amadis* and *Armide,* particularly noteworthy in this regard, are among the most successful orchestral pieces left by the artist. However, he wrote many *menuets,* which together with his *gigues* attracted increasing interest. As fashions changed, some dances, for example the *galliardes,* were even dropped from the operas in favor of new types, such as the *rigaudons.*

Following the *ballet de cour*'s traditions, Lully introduced into his lyric works free dances that revealed the nature of a character or dramatic action. The Abbé Dubos called these works *airs charactérisez,* which, corresponding to an (albeit vague) idea, enabled the spectator to follow the dramatic action more easily, thus rendering it more plausible. This conformity of the music to the dramatic content of the scene is one of the most characteristic features of French opera of the seventeenth and eighteenth centuries. The fury of the demons, the shivering of the people in the frozen north, or the terror aroused by fatal dreams or premonitions could thus be described. Pierre Beauchamps and Hilaire d'Olivet often staged the choreographies that conveyed these meanings, but sometimes the composer himself demonstrated to the dancers steps that he invented, corresponding to his intentions in the score. Lully created dances that could extend drama and comment on an entire dramatic action. For the third act of *Alceste* he invented a kind of pantomime designed to described the sorrow of the weeping women and grieving men mourning the death of the Princess Alceste: "A paroxysm of grief overcomes the two bereaved groups; some of them rend their garments, some tear their hair, and at the foot of the statue of Alceste everyone breaks the adornments carried in his hand."

A composer, choreographer, and director of theatrical spectacles, Lully also trained performers—including singers such as Louis Gaulard Dumesny and Marie le Rochois, but certainly dancers as well. Louis Lestang and Guillaume-Louis Pecour both made their debuts under his direction. After the composer's death, Pecour made ballets for the Opera, and early in the eighteenth century he published choreographies, some of which were designed for lyric works by Lully: *Cadmus et Hermione, Thésée, Atys, Persée,* and *Phaëton.*

Lully also taught musical composition. One of his pupils was Pascal Colasse, who, after Lully's death in 1687, completed the composer's unfinished lyric tragedy *Achille et Polyxène.* For almost a century Lully's successors at the Opera were to adopt his musical ideas, thereby making it possible for the French lyric art to enjoy an exceptional flowering.

[*See also* Ballet de Cour, *article on* Ballet de Cour, 1643–1685; *and* Opéra-Ballet and Tragédie Lyrique.]

BIBLIOGRAPHY

Anthony, James R. "Towards a Principal Source for Lully's Court Ballets: Foucault vs. Philidor." *Recherches sur la musique française classique* 25 (1987): 79–103.

Beaussant, Philippe. *Lully, ou Le musicien du soleil.* Paris, 1992.

Bernardi, Paola, et al. *Modo di diffusione al di fuori del contesto teatrale delle opere e dei balletti di Giovanni Battista Lulli.* Rome, 1989.

Cassaro, James P. "A Critical Edition of Jean-Baptiste Lully's *Ballet des Saisons.*" Master's thesis, Cornell University, 1993.

Christoub, Marie-Françoise. *Le ballet de cour de Louis XIV.* Paris, 1967.

Couvreur, Manuel. *Jean-Baptiste Lully: Musique et dramaturgie au service du prince.* Brussels, 1992.

Daniels, Margaret. "Passacaille d'Armide." In *Proceedings of the Sixth Annual Conference, Society of Dance History Scholars, the Ohio State University, 11–13 February 1983,* compiled by Christena L. Schlundt. Milwaukee, 1983.

Heyer, John, ed. *Jean-Baptiste Lully and the Music of the French Baroque.* New York, 1989.

Hilton, Wendy. "Dance to Music by Jean-Baptiste Lully." *Early Music* 14 (February 1986): 51–63.

La Gorce, Jérôme de, and Herbert Schneider, eds. *Jean-Baptiste Lully: Actes du colloque, Saint-Germain-en-Laye, Heidelberg, 1987.* Laaber, 1990.

La Gorce, Jérôme de. *Lully, un âje d'or de l'opéra français.* Paris, 1991.

La Laurencie, Lionel de. *Lully.* 2d ed. Paris, 1919.

Little, Meredith Ellis. "The Dances of J. B. Lully." Ph.D.diss., Stanford University, 1967.

Little, Meredith Ellis, and Suzanne G. Cusick. "Inventory of the Dances of Jean-Baptiste Lully." *Recherches sur la musique française classique* 9 (1969): 21–55.

Newman, Joyce. *Jean-Baptiste Lully and His Tragédies Lyriques.* Ann Arbor, Mich., 1979.

Prunières, Henry. *Lully.* 2d ed. Paris, 1927.

Russell, Craig H. "Lully and French Dance in Imperial Spain." In *Proceedings of the Fourteenth Annual Conference, Society of Dance History Scholars, New World School of the Arts, Miami, Florida, 8–10 February 1991,* compiled by Christena L. Schlundt. Riverside, Calif., 1991.

Schneider, Herbert. *Die Rezeption der Opern Lullys im Frankreich des ancien régime.* Tutzing, 1982.

JÉRÔME DE LA GORCE
Translated from French

LYONNOIS, MARIE-FRANÇOISE (Marie-Françoise Rampon; born 18 November 1728 in Strasbourg, died after 1790), French dancer. Lyonnois made her debut at the Paris Opera on 16 June 1744 in *L'École des Amants,* at an annual salary of six hundred livres. She danced regularly in theatrical performances, creating roles in *Les Fêtes de Polymnie* and Jean-Philippe Rameau's *Le Temple de la Gloire,* which she danced before Louis XV in Versailles in 1745; she already had a solo *entrée,* an indication of her rapid progress. The salary increases and bonuses paid to her both at the Paris Opera and at the court bear witness to her talent and growing favor. She danced in Rameau's *Platée* and *Naïs* and triumphed critically as Hatred in his *Zoroastre.* During a revival of *Les Indes Galantes* in 1751, she danced a polonaise and the *entrée Les Sauvages* with precision, power, and lightness. She was applauded in a *pas chinois* she performed with Jean-Barthélemy Lany in *Issé* (1756). A *demi-caractère* dancer, she was often his partner in the popular pas de deux of the shepherds in *Les Fêtes Grecques et Romaines,* as well as in the pantomime-ballet *Les Noces de Village* (1763). Greatly admired at the court, she created the leading role in Rameau's *Les Fêtes d'Hébé, ou Les Talents Lyriques.*

Age and a fondness for alcohol, together with the fame of her young rival Marie Allard, led to Lyonnois's withdrawal from the stage in 1767. She was awarded a pension of one thousand livres from the Paris Opera and six hundred from the court. Nothing is known of her after 1790. Famed for her beauty, she combined mastery with communicative gaiety and sprightly vivacity, excelling in the roles of shepherdess and seductive demon. She may have been the first dancer to perform the *gargouillade.*

Lyonnois had a brother, born in 1730, whose name is not recorded. He joined the Paris Opera in 1746. A *danseur noble,* valued for his lightness and harmonious style, he was eclipsed by the personalities of Louis Dupré and Gaëtan Vestris and retired from the stage in 1767. He was awarded membership in the Acádemie Royale de Danse in 1757.

BIBLIOGRAPHY

Amelot. *Mémoires pour servir à l'histoire de l'Académie Royale de Musique depuis 1663 jusqu'à 1778.* N.p.,n.d. Paris Opéra, Library.

Bachaumont, Louis Petit de. *Mémoires secrets.* 36 vols. Paris, 1777–1789.

Campardon, Émile. *L'Académie Royale de Musique au XVIIIe siècle.* 2 vols. Paris, 1884.

MARIE-FRANÇOISE CHRISTOUT
Translated from French

M

MACDONALD, BRIAN (born 14 May 1928 in Montreal), Canadian choreographer and company director. One of Canada's most prolific and widely known choreographers, Macdonald began training in Montreal with Gerald Crevier and Elizabeth Leese. Following graduation from McGill University, where he studied history, philosophy, and English, Macdonald supported his dance studies with work as a music critic for the *Montreal Herald* from 1949 to 1951. He joined the newly formed National Ballet of Canada in 1951, but his dancing career was cut short two years later by a severe injury.

Macdonald's loyalty to his Canadian roots was early manifested in his founding of the short-lived Montreal Theatre Ballet (1956), which was dedicated to using choreography, music, and stage design by Canadian artists. In 1957, Macdonald's diverse theatrical talents became widely known through the long-running Canadian satirical review *My Fur Lady,* which he directed and choreographed and in which he performed. With *The Darkling* (1958), Macdonald began a long association with the Royal Winnipeg Ballet, for which, by 1970, he had choreographed twelve ballets, notably *Rose Latulippe* (1966)—Canada's first evening-length narrative ballet—and *The Shining People of Leonard Cohen* (1970).

During the late 1960s and early 1970s Macdonald worked mostly abroad as a director and choreographer, creating new ballets and restaging earlier works for various companies: *Time Out of Mind* (Joffrey Ballet, 1963), *Hymn* (Norwegian National Ballet, 1963), *While the Spider Slept* (Royal Swedish Ballet, 1965), *Martha's Vineyard* (Batsheva Dance Company, 1971), *The Lottery* (Harkness Ballet, 1974), and *Prologue to a Tragedy* and *Remembranzes* (Ballet Nacional de Cuba, 1978). Outside Canada, Macdonald's works have also appeared in the repertories of the Paris Opera Ballet, the German Opera Ballet, the Royal Danish Ballet, the London Festival Ballet, Alvin Ailey American Dance Theatre, and several smaller companies. Macdonald was artistic director of the Royal Swedish Ballet (1964–1966), of the Harkness Ballet (1967–1968), and of the Batsheva Dance Company (1971–1972).

MACDONALD. *Rose Latulippe* was choreographed by Macdonald for the Royal Winnipeg Ballet in 1966 as part of Canada's centennial celebration. Based on a French-Canadian legend with some similarities to the plot of *Giselle,* it is acknowledged as the first full-length ballet on a Canadian theme. (Photograph by Douglas Spillane; courtesy of the Royal Winnipeg Ballet.)

MACDONALD. *Theft* (1995), set to music by R. Murray Schafer, featured Tara Birtwhistle, Paul De Strouper, Brandon Downs, and David Lucas. (Photograph by Bruce Monk; used by permission; courtesy of the Royal Winnipeg Ballet.)

With his Swedish-born wife, the ballerina Annette av Paul, Macdonald then resettled in Canada and in 1973 tried to establish a new Festival Ballet Company at the National Arts Centre in Ottawa. He created his own full-length version of the Romeo and Juliet story, *Star Cross'd,* using music by Canadian composer Harry Freedman and including excerpts from Shakespeare's play. This later reappeared as *Romeo and Juliet* in the repertory of the Montreal-based Les Grands Ballets Canadiens, of which Macdonald became artistic director in 1974. He relinquished this post three years later but retained the title of resident choreographer.

In Montreal, Macdonald once again chose to emphasize Canadian creative talent by utilizing local composers and designers for his ballets. His many works for Les Grands Ballets Canadiens have met with varying degrees of success. Popular ballets such as *Tam Ti Delam* (1974) and *Fête Carignan* (1978) draw on the folk heritage of French Canada. *Newcomers* (1980), for the National Ballet of Canada, celebrated Canada's pioneers. Others, such as *Étapes* (1982) and *Findings* (1983) reflect—according to some critics, ambiguously—Macdonald's critical view of contemporary society and its mores.

Although some of Macdonald's best choreography has been created in a neoclassical style and nonnarrative context, all his work is marked by a strong theatrical flair. Since the 1950s he has choreographed and directed for television; in the 1980s his longstanding interest in opera and musical theater came to occupy a substantial part of his time. He has directed operas in Canada, France, and the United States. His innovative productions of Gilbert and Sullivan operettas for the Stratford Festival in Ontario—*The Mikado* (1982), *The Gondoliers* (1983), and *Iolanthe* (1984)—were widely acclaimed. Appointed an associate director of the Stratford Festival in 1983, he has continued to direct operettas and productions of classic Broadway musicals. Since 1982 he has also been head of the summer dance program at the Banff Centre for Continuing Education in Alberta. Working with young professional dancers, he has staged annual festival performances that include restaged or newly created works of his own, new works commissioned from emerging choreographers, and works by such twentieth-century masters as George Balanchine.

[*See also* Grands Ballets Canadiens, Les, *and* Royal Winnipeg Ballet.]

BIBLIOGRAPHY

Crabb, Michael. "Les Grands Ballets Canadiens." *The Dancing Times* (July 1982): 744–745.

Kaiser, Pat. "Macdonald Speaks." *Canadian Dance News* 2 (June 1981): 6.

Macdonald, Brian. "*Rose Latulippe:* A Canadian Legend and Ballet." *Dance News* (December 1966): 58.

Macdonald, Brian. "The Chance to Dream." In *Visions: Ballet and Its Future,* edited by Michael Crabb. Toronto, 1978.

Stoop, Norma McLain. "The Canadian Cosmopolitan." *Dance Magazine* (April 1984): 62–65.

Wyman, Max. *Dance Canada: An Illustrated History.* Vancouver, 1989.

MICHAEL CRABB

MACEDONIA. *See* Yugoslavia.

MACHOV, SAŠA (František Mařha; born 16 July 1903 in Zhoř u Pacova, Bohemia, died 23 June 1951 in Prague), Czech dancer, choreographer, and director. While he was a student at the Industrial Academy in Prague, Machov began to study ballet with Jelizaveta Nikolská. He became close to the young, theater avant-garde, and from 1927 to 1929, at the Liberated Theater, he danced, acted in small roles, and choreographed productions.

Machov's relationship with the most significant creative personalities of the modern Czech stage formed his artistic and worldly opinions. Perhaps the greatest of these influences was Emil František Burian, whose ballet *The Bassoon and the Flute* Machov guest choreographed at the National Theater in Prague in 1929. From 1929 to 1934 Machov served as ballet director in Ostrava, where he acquired experience and routines. Decisive also in forming his personality was his engagement at the progressive, leftist-oriented Prague Theater D35-D36, founded and directed by Burian. Machov not only danced and choreographed, he also acted and became assistant director of the theater. "D," which stood for the "dance" element, was completely integrated into the overall shape of the dramatic productions and thus created the theater's distinctive profile. The dance element functioned also by itself, for example, in Machov's ballet to the music of Leoš Janáček's *Lachian Dances* (1936).

During this time Machov's choreographic style began to crystalize, and contemporary critics pointed out his "Czechness." From 1936 to 1938 Machov worked as choreographer and dancer at another progressive Prague theater, led by the actor-clowns Jiří Voskovec and Jan Werich. Their Liberated Theater, of the revue-musical type, used humor to fight the growing threat of fascism. The theater was very popular as well as successful until the fall of 1938, when the deteriorating political situation forced it to liquidate.

After the Nazis occupied Czechoslovakia, Machov managed to escape to Greece, where he worked as *chef de ballet* of the Royal Theater in Athens from 1939 to 1941, when Greece was invaded by Italy. Machov then volunteered for the African corps of the Czechoslovak army and took part in the fighting in the desert before being transferred from Tobruk to London in 1943. At the request of the Sadler's Wells opera, Machov was released from the army to collaborate as a dancer and choreographer on Bedřich Smetana's *Bartered Bride* in 1943; he then began to direct operas for Sadler's Wells, among them *Così Fan Tutte* and *Madama Butterfly*.

After the war and his return to Czechoslovakia, Machov directed operas in Brno (1945–1946) and soon thereafter was called to the Prague National Theater to become the *chef de ballet*. Within five years Machov had worked miracles: from a company diverse in age and technique he created a homogeneous, enthusiastic group that experienced one success after another. Inspired by the example of the English ballet, Machov aspired to formulate a specifically Czech national ballet. The backbone of this repertory, therefore, was ballets by national composers. Some such new works were *Weddings* by Václav Nelhýbel in 1947 and *The Philosophy Lesson* in 1949 and *Viktorka* in 1950, both by Zbyněk Vostřák. The true *chef-d'oeuvre* for Machov's choreography was the premiere of Sergei Prokofiev's *Romeo and Juliet* in 1950.

Machov was both a sensitive choreographer and an outstanding director. His productions were exemplary for their broad-minded, tight, and well-thought-out constructions; they never appeared contrived or dry but rather were filled with emotion and dramatic excitement. Machov had exceptional feeling for detail, dramatic abbreviation, and poetic movement metaphor. His style could be compared to that of Frederick Ashton: his choreographies were inventive, musical, sensitive to the musical style of the work, and always replete with content. Machov's premature death, by suicide as a tragic consequence of political persecution under the communist regime, did not allow him to attain even greater mastery of the genre; even so, he remains the greatest founding personage of modern Czech ballet.

BIBLIOGRAPHY

Holzknecht, Václav. *Jaroslav Ježek a Osvobozené divadlo*. Prague, 1957.

Jenčík, Josef. *Skoky do prázdna*. Prague, 1947.

Rey, Jan. "70 let baletu Národního divadla." *Divadlo* 4 (1953).

Rey, Jan. "Change and Growth in Czechoslovakia." *Dance and Dancers* (October 1960): 14–17.

Schmidová, Lidka. *Československý balet*. Prague, 1962.

Vašut, Vladimír. "Saša Machov a E. F. Burian." *Taneční Listy* 5 (1976).

Vašut, Vladimír. *Státní divadlo v Ostravae-60 let*. Ostrave, 1979.

Vašut, Vladimír. *Saša Machov*. Prague, 1986.

VLADIMÍR VAŠUT
Translated from Czech

MACMILLAN, KENNETH (born 11 December 1929 in Dunfermline, Scotland, died 29 October 1992 in London), dancer and choreographer. Kenneth MacMillan was often called a "product of the Royal Ballet," which indeed he was, but his early background was an unlikely one for an innovative choreographer working within the classical idiom. As a small boy he was taken to see, and was fascinated by, Hollywood musicals, especially those featuring Fred Astaire and Ginger Rogers, and he attempted to emulate their elegant tap routines. He won local talent contests in Great Yarmouth, Norfolk, where his family had moved. In his early teens, MacMillan took part in amateur theatricals and, with his limited pocket money, paid for tap-dancing lessons; later, during World War II, he joined a revue that toured U.S. bomber bases in Norfolk. Through reading *The Dancing Times* in the local library, he learned of the existence of ballet and decided on a career as a classical dancer.

Without telling his family, MacMillan approached Phyllis Adams, the principal of a local ballet school, who was so intrigued that an adolescent boy should seek, of his own volition, to be a ballet dancer that she taught him free of charge. MacMillan was ambitious, and after only eighteen months of study, he forged his father's signature on a letter applying for an audition for the Sadler's Wells Ballet School in London. When his request was granted, he acquitted himself well. Ninette de Valois was so impressed by his talent that she accepted him immediately for the spring term of 1945.

After the war, with the reopening of London's Royal Opera House, Covent Garden, as a permanent home for the Sadler's Wells (later Royal) Ballet in 1946, de Valois developed another, smaller company—the Sadler's Wells Theatre Ballet, based at Sadler's Wells but also undertaking long regional tours. At the end of the summer term of 1946, MacMillan joined the new company. It was a company crammed with young talent, but MacMillan soon established himself as a fine classical artist with a strong stage presence that made him useful in character roles. In autumn 1948, MacMillan was transferred to the company

MACMILLAN. The Royal Ballet gave the first performance of MacMillan's *Le Baiser de la Fée* on 12 April 1960. In this scene the Fairy (Svetlana Beriosova) and her attendants take the Young Man (Donald MacLeary) to the Land beyond Time and Place. Scenery and costumes were designed by Kenneth Rowell. (Photograph © by Zoë Dominic; used by permission.)

at the Royal Opera House, where he continued to make his mark as a classical dancer. He was with the company when it made its debut in New York City in 1949. That initial visit gave him a continuing love of, and fascination with, the United States.

At the end of 1951, MacMillan became afflicted with a growing neurosis that affected his performances: stage fright. In despair, he went to de Valois, who advised him to take a rest for three months. During this period of inactivity, MacMillan's friend and colleague, John Cranko, planned a season in England of his own works, at a tiny theater at Henley-on-Thames; he suggested that MacMillan join his *ad hoc* company of dancers. MacMillan did so and found the experience enjoyable, thanks to the relaxed atmosphere that contrasted with the high-pressure discipline of the company at the Royal Opera House. In the autumn, at de Valois's suggestion, MacMillan rejoined the Sadler's Wells Theatre Ballet, with its convivial family atmosphere, and was rewarded with a number of major roles, several created for him.

About this time MacMillan joined a group of company dancers intent on giving regular choreographic workshops. When one of the choreographers dropped out at the last minute, MacMillan was persuaded to produce something quickly to fill the gap. To a jazz score by Stan Kenton, he created *Somnambulism,* first performed in 1953, the theme of which was the effect of dreams on human behavior. To his surprise, it was the hit of the evening—MacMillan had discovered his real talent. He continued dancing but managed to find time to produce *Laiderette,* to music by Frank Martin, first performed in 1954. This was another immediate success, with its theme of rejection and its leading character something of a social outcast, a combination that would frequently recur throughout MacMillan's career. De Valois wanted to take the ballet into the company's repertory, but the use of a harpsichord in the score proved a difficulty. Instead, she commissioned him to create a new ballet for the Sadler's Wells Theatre Ballet. (*Laiderette,* however, was taken into the repertory of Ballet Rambert in 1955.)

While in New York in 1949, MacMillan had bought a recording of two Igor Stravinsky scores; he decided to use one of them, *Danses Concertantes,* for his first commissioned work. The ballet, first performed in 1955, was full of choreographic invention and was an instant success for both MacMillan and its young designer, Nicholas Georgiadis, thus initiating a collaboration that lasted throughout their careers.

With the success of this ballet, MacMillan gave up dancing and was appointed resident choreographer to the Sadler's Wells Theatre Ballet. During the next two years he produced three more works, two for the company—*House of Birds* (1955), to music by F. Mompou, and *Solitaire* (1956), to music by Malcolm Arnold—and his first for the main company at Covent Garden, *Noctambules* (1956), to a commissioned score by Humphrey Searle. All of these were favorably received. In 1957, Lucia Chase commissioned MacMillan's first work for American Ballet Theatre, *Winter's Eve* (to music by Benjamin Britten), in which Nora Kaye appeared as a blind woman. This was given a mixed reception by New York critics; it was followed by *Journey,* to music by Béla Bartók, first given at an American Ballet Theatre choreographic workshop in 1957; this work, also made for Nora Kaye, was better received and was taken into the repertory.

Until this time, MacMillan's ballets had been somewhat influenced by the French postwar school of existentialist fantasy. But now, impressed by the work of new young British playwrights, such as John Osborne and Harold Pinter, he turned to some realistic themes. His next work, *The Burrow* (1957), was about a group of characters hiding from the state police of a totalitarian regime. This theme prompted the supposition that it was based on *The Diary of Anne Frank,* which had recently been dramatized, but MacMillan said that his source was a short story by Franz Kafka. In *The Burrow,* he first used the talents of a young dancer, Lynn Seymour, who was to become something of a muse for MacMillan; he created a number of memorable roles for her over the ensuing twenty years.

Both of MacMillan's next two ballets were to Stravinsky scores, and both were for the Royal Ballet. His version of *Agon* (1958) was only a partial success, and his *Le Baiser de la Fée* (1960), though full of beautiful choreography, did not last long in the repertory. (It was, however, revived in a new production in 1986.) There followed *The Invitation,* for the second company (now called the touring section of the Royal Ballet), first performed on 10 November 1960. A powerful study of the emotional and physical awakening of two adolescents, this ballet established Seymour as the company's leading dramatic dancer and advanced MacMillan's reputation as a choreographer prepared to tackle subjects previously considered unsuitable for ballet.

In 1961, Western Theatre Ballet, a small regional company, commissioned MacMillan to choreograph the Brecht-Weill allegory *The Seven Deadly Sins* (later revised for the Royal Ballet in 1973). *Diversions* (1961), to a score by Arthur Bliss, was a plotless work of great technical complexity for the Royal Ballet; it was followed by his version of *The Rite of Spring* (1962), a large-scale interpretation of Stravinsky's famous score, which introduced Mon-

MACMILLAN. At the premiere of MacMillan's *Romeo and Juliet* in February 1965, Margot Fonteyn and Rudolf Nureyev danced the title roles. In later performances, Lynn Seymour and Christopher Gable, seen here at far left, portrayed the famous "star-crossed" lovers. Scenery and costumes were designed by Nicholas Georgiadis. (Photograph from the Dance Collection, New York Public Library for the Performing Arts.)

ica Mason as the Chosen Maiden, a role she danced with great intensity and power for the next twenty years. *Symphony* (1963) was another abstract work, to the first symphony of Dmitri Shostakovitch, and with a leading role for Seymour.

John Cranko, having created an adventurous young company in Stuttgart, Germany, commissioned MacMillan to produce a work for it. He devised *Las Hermanas* (1963), a study of repressed spinsterhood, based on Federico García Lorca's play *The House of Bernarda Alba,* to a score by Frank Martin. First performed at Stuttgart, it was later taken into the repertories of Western Theatre Ballet and American Ballet Theatre. It was also taken into the Royal Ballet touring section, and for this company, he produced a version of Darius Milhaud's *Création du Monde* (1964). When the main company presented a special program to honor the quatercentenary of Shakespeare's birth, on 2 April 1964, it included MacMillan's *Images of Love,* based on Shakespeare's sonnets; this was considered at best an interesting failure.

MACMILLAN. *Das Lied von der Erde* was created for the Stuttgart Ballet in the autumn of 1965. Mounted for the Royal Ballet as *The Song of the Earth* the following year, it featured Monica Mason and Anthony Dowell, seen here. (Photograph from the Dance Collection, New York Public Library for the Performing Arts.)

MacMillan's first full-length work was a version of Sergei Prokofiev's *Romeo and Juliet,* commissioned by Frederick Ashton when he became director of the Royal Ballet. First performed in 1965, the ballet was a major triumph and became a mainstay of the Royal Ballet repertory. It was taken into the repertory of the Royal Swedish Ballet in 1969 and into that of American Ballet Theatre in 1985. Again the leading female role was created for Seymour, with Christopher Gable as her Romeo, though the first performance was danced by Margot Fonteyn and Rudolf Nureyev.

Nine months later, Cranko commissioned another work from MacMillan. MacMillan had long wanted to create a ballet to Gustav Mahler's symphonic song cycle *Song of the Earth,* but the board of directors of the Royal Opera House considered the score to be sacrosanct. Cranko, however, was receptive to the idea, and when MacMillan's ballet was given its first performance in Stuttgart in 1965, it was generally considered a masterpiece. It entered the repertory of the Royal Ballet six months later and has been revived by the Paris Opera Ballet.

In 1966, MacMillan was invited to become director of the Berlin Opera Ballet. Encouraged by Ashton, he accepted; he took with him Seymour, as his ballerina, among others. On the opening night of his first season in Berlin, David Webster, general administrator of the Royal Opera House, London, offered MacMillan the directorship of the Royal Ballet on Ashton's retirement three years hence. MacMillan's directorship of the Berlin company was highly successful. He created a prestigious classical company, for which he produced a spectacular version of *The Sleeping Beauty* (1967), with designs by Barry Kay, and an intensely dramatic version of *Swan Lake* (1969), with designs by Georgiadis. His own works for the company included the plotless *Concerto* (1966), to music by Shostakovitch, which also entered the repertories of both Royal Ballet companies as well as those of the Stuttgart Ballet and American Ballet Theatre, and a one-act expressionist ballet, *Anastasia* (1967), to music by Bohuslav Martinů, based on Polish amnesia victim Anna Andersen's claim to be the sole survivor of the tsar's family, executed during the Russian Revolution. Seymour danced the leading roles in all these productions. During this period MacMillan created two more works for the Stuttgart company, *Sphinx* (1968) and *Miss Julie* (1970), to music by Andrej Panufnik.

MacMillan took up his appointment as director of the Royal Ballet in autumn 1970. He inherited various plans from the board of directors, including the combining of the resources of both Royal Ballet companies, of which the smaller would become an experimental group of soloists (known for a time as the New Group). This resulted in the dismissal of a number of dancers, for which MacMillan received much criticism, though he was in no way responsible for the decision. The plan did not work well, so the company reverted to its previous form, under the direction of Peter Wright, and was renamed Sadler's Wells Royal Ballet (subsequently Birmingham Royal Ballet).

An anti-MacMillan faction continued to attack MacMillan's artistic and administrative decisions, bringing him to a state of deep depression. In 1972 he met and subsequently married Deborah Williams, an Australian artist. A daughter, Charlotte, was born in 1973, and this happy marriage gave MacMillan the stability and equanimity essential to continue as a creative artist.

During his seven years as director of the Royal Ballet, MacMillan produced five new one-act works: *Triad* (1972), to music by Prokofiev, also taken into American Ballet Theatre's repertory; a reworking of *The Seven Deadly Sins* (1973); *Elite Syncopations* (1974), to ragtime music by Scott Joplin and others, in both Royal repertories and that of the National Ballet of Canada; *The Four Seasons* (1975), to music by Verdi, which was revived by the ballet of the Paris Opera; and *Rituals* (1975), on Japanese themes. He also created two full-length works: an expanded version of *Anastasia* (1971), with the first two acts danced to music of Tchaikovsky, again with Seymour in the title role; and *Manon* (1972), to music by Massenet, arranged by Leighton Lucas. *Manon*'s first performance, with Antoinette Sibley in the title role, received a somewhat cool critical reception, but the ballet went on to become a great popular success, rivaling that of *Romeo and Juliet. Manon* also went into the repertories of the Royal Swedish Ballet, the Paris Opera Ballet, and American Ballet Theatre.

MacMillan's production of *The Sleeping Beauty* (1973) was not a success in London and was soon replaced by a new one by de Valois. Three of his one-act works for the Sadler's Wells Royal Ballet, *Checkpoint* (1970), *Ballade* (1972), and *The Poltroon* (1972), did not remain long in the repertory. As director of the Royal Ballet, MacMillan brought into the repertory five works by Jerome Robbins, three by George Balanchine, three by Glen Tetley, two by Cranko, two by Hans van Manen, and one by John Neumeier. In the same period, he also produced the beautiful *Requiem* (1976), to the Gabriel Fauré score, for the Stuttgart Ballet as a personal tribute to the memory of Cranko. Although this music had been considered unsuitable for ballet by the board of directors at Covent Garden, they relented and the ballet was taken into the repertory.

In 1977, MacMillan decided to resign as director of the Royal Ballet to concentrate on choreography. The immediate result was the three-act *Mayerling* (1978), an anti-Romantic study of the double suicide of Crown Prince Rudolf of Austria-Hungary and his young mistress Mary Vetsera, danced to music by Franz Liszt, arranged by John Lanchbery. Once again, Seymour brought her extraordinary intensity to the role of the willful young woman,

MACMILLAN. *Anastasia*, a three-act ballet focusing on the youngest daughter of Tsar Nicholas II, was created in 1967 as a vehicle for the dramatic dancing of Lynn Seymour. She is seen here in act 2, set to Tchaikovsky's Third Symphony, at a ball in the Winter Palace in Saint Petersburg. (Photograph from the Dance Collection, New York Public Library for the Performing Arts.)

and David Wall scored a personal triumph as the doomed princeling. A television program, produced by London Weekend Television in the same year, documented the creation of the ballet and its first performance.

A few months later, for the Stuttgart Ballet, MacMillan produced another dark piece, *My Brother, My Sisters* (1978), to music by Arnold Schoenberg and by Anton von Webern; this, too, went into the Royal Ballet repertory. Toward the end of the year, he choreographed *Metaboles* (1978) for the Paris Opera Ballet.

Returning to the Royal Ballet, he created *La Fin du Jour* (1979), to Maurice Ravel's G Major Piano Concerto. This ballet, inspired by the atmosphere and extravagant fashions of the 1930s, was a great success, as was *Playground* (1979), a study in madness for the Sadler's Wells Royal Ballet. A more somber look at the past was *Gloria* (1980), to the Francis Poulenc score, a tribute to the lost generation of World War I; this was considered by many to be one of MacMillan's finest ballets. *Isadora* (1981), a full-length work based on the life of Isadora Duncan, to a

MACMILLAN. Set to music of Massenet, MacMillan's *Manon* was first presented in March 1974 with Antoinette Sibley in the title role and Anthony Dowell as her lover. The ballet roughly follows the plot of the Abbé Prévost's *Histoire du chevalier des Grieux et de Manon Lescaut* (1731). (Photograph © by Leslie E. Spatt; used by permission.)

commissioned score by Richard Rodney Bennett, attempted to extend the scope of the large-scale narrative work by introducing a text written by the novelist Gillian Freeman and spoken by an actress. The title role was danced not by Seymour (who had impersonated Duncan in Ashton's *Five Brahms Waltzes in the Manner of Isadora Duncan*) but by Merle Park. By some, this piece was criticized for not taking the art of Duncan seriously enough, to say nothing of that of Loie Fuller, who was parodied in one scene.

MacMillan renewed his association with American Ballet Theatre with *Wild Boy* (1981), conceived as a vehicle for Mikhail Baryshnikov soon after he became director of the company. *Verdi Variations* (1982), devised as a gala showpiece for Elisabetta Terabust and Peter Schaufuss, was later expanded into a one-act ballet, *Quartet* (1982), for the Sadler's Wells Royal Ballet. In November 1982 the Royal Ballet presented an all-Stravinsky program, for which MacMillan choreographed a version of *Orpheus,* with Schaufuss as guest artist in the title role.

Valley of Shadows (1983), for the Royal Ballet, was based on a novel by Giorgio Bassani, *The Garden of the Finzi-Contini.* With its study of the Fascist persecution of the Jews in Italy during World War II and its depiction of a Nazi concentration camp, this ballet went to the limit of MacMillan's belief that classical ballet can deal with even the harshest themes of modern life. Here, he used for the first time the histrionic talents of the young dancer Alessandra Ferri. Still in an expressionist vein, his *Different Drummer* (1984) was a ballet version of Georg Büchner's seminal play *Wozzeck* (the basis of Alban Berg's opera *Wozzeck*), although MacMillan used as his score Schoenberg's expressionist string sextet, *Verklärte Nacht* (Transfigured Night).

In 1984, Baryshnikov suggested to MacMillan that he should become associate artistic director of American Ballet Theatre, and he accepted the offer. An immediate result of this appointment was the company's acquisition of MacMillan's *Romeo and Juliet.* Ferri also went to American Ballet Theatre and danced the role of Juliet. MacMillan's first new work for the company was another *Requiem* (1986), this time to the score by Andrew Lloyd Webber; it won a mixed reception from American critics.

In 1989, a projected full-length production of *The Prince of the Pagodas* (originally created in 1957 by MacMillan's contemporary and colleague John Cranko) was postponed when MacMillan suffered a heart attack while in Australia. The fairy-tale ballet, which received its premiere in

MACMILLAN. The plot of *Mayerling* centers on Crown Prince Rudolf of Austria-Hungary, tracing his gradual moral and physical decline from the time of his marriage to his death by suicide, with his teenage mistress Mary Vetsera, at the hunting lodge of Mayerling. At the premiere in February 1978, the role of Rudolf was created by David Wall, seen here with Genesia Rosato as an exuberant Princess Louise, dancing at their wedding celebration. (Photograph from the Dance Collection, New York Public Library for the Performing Arts.)

MACMILLAN. A memorial tribute to youths who perished in the trenches of World War I, *Gloria* (1980) was set to music by Francis Poulenc. Scenery and costumes were designed by Andy Klunder. Julian Hosking, Jennifer Penney, and Wayne Eagling were in the original cast. (Photograph from the Dance Collection, New York Public Library for the Performing Arts.)

March 1990, was revived mainly because of Benjamin Britten's only ballet score. It marked MacMillan's return to the pure classical style, but while full of beautifully inventive sequences, the work was seriously flawed by its clotted scenario, containing elements of *King Lear, Beauty and the Beast,* and *The Sleeping Beauty.*

In February 1991, MacMillan created *Winter Dreams,* to music by Tchaikovsky, a one-act work based on the 1901 play by Anton Chekhov, *Three Sisters,* with leading roles for the choreographer's latest muse, Darcey Bussell, and the former Bolshoi Ballet star Irek Mukhamedov, who became a permanent member of the Royal Ballet. A ballet in MacMillan's most romantic and lyrical vein, it was a resounding success and was adapted for television in 1992.

Much more controversial was *The Judas Tree* (1992), to music by Brian Elias. A study in betrayal, the ballet, with a cast of fourteen men and one woman, contains scenes of gang-rape, murder, and suicide—with biblical overtones. Savage and powerful, the work revealed MacMillan at his most disturbingly inventive. *The Judas Tree* proved to be MacMillan's last work; on 29 October 1992, he suffered sudden heart failure while backstage at the Royal Opera, during the last act of his *Mayerling,* in which Mukhamedov was making his debut as the dissolute Austrian Crown Prince Rudolf (who with his mistress committed suicide at the royal lodge called Mayerling in 1889).

MacMillan's premature death was a terrible loss to British ballet in general and the Royal Ballet in particular, but he left an extensive repertory that will challenge dancers for generations to come. MacMillan's work has established ballet as one of the most expressive forms of theatre.

[*See also* Royal Ballet.]

BIBLIOGRAPHY

Bintley, David. "Sir Kenneth MacMillan, 1929–1992." *Dance Now* 1 (Winter 1992–1993): 42–45.

Bland, Alexander. *The Royal Ballet: The First Fifty Years.* London, 1981.

Crisp, Clement. "Anastasia: Kenneth MacMillan Talks to Clement Crisp." *About the House* 3 (Summer 1971): 11–13.

Hunt, Marilyn. "The Malcontent Is Mellowing." *Dance Magazine* (September 1991): 50–54.

Kane, Angela. "Kenneth MacMillan: Rebel with a Cause." *The Dancing Times* 80 (November 1989): 1–8.

Thorpe, Edward. *Kenneth MacMillan: The Man and His Ballets.* London, 1985.

Thorpe, Edward. "Kenneth MacMillan: Legend and Legacy." *Opera House* (December 1993–March 1994): 62–67.

EDWARD THORPE

MADSEN, EGON (born 24 August 1942 in Ringe, on the island of Fyn), Danish ballet dancer and company director. Madsen began his dance training at the age of nine in classes taught by Thea Jolles in Århus, a seaport city on the eastern shore of Jutland. Refused admission to the Royal Danish Ballet School (because of his frail physique), he continued his studies with Jolles until he was fifteen, dancing as a member of her company, the Danish Children's Ballet. In 1957, he went to Copenhagen, where he joined the company of the famed Pantomime Theater at the Tivoli Gardens and continued his ballet training in private classes with Birger Bartholin and Edite Frandsen. In 1959 he joined Elsa-Marianne von Rosen's Scandinavian Ballet as a soloist, touring Sweden and Denmark for the next three years. In 1961, he went to Germany to audition for John Cranko, the newly appointed artistic director of the Stuttgart Ballet. Engaged as a soloist and soon named a principal dancer, he would remain with the Stuttgart Ballet for the next two decades, creating many important roles in works by Cranko, Kenneth MacMillan, Glen Tetley, and John Neumeier.

Madsen charmed his audiences with his mercurial temperament and high spirits, as he was a "born bouncer" and an irrepressible comedian. The Joker in Cranko's *Jeu de Cartes* (1965), set to Stravinsky's rollicking score, was perhaps his most winning creation. However, he also had an introspective side, which inspired him to such fine creations as Lensky in Cranko's *Onegin* (1965) and leading roles in ballets such as *Brouillards* (1970), a haunting work set to piano preludes by Debussy, and *Initialen R.B.M.E.* (1972), in which he danced the principal part in the fourth movement (identified as "E." for Egon) of Brahms's Second Piano Concerto in B-flat. His dramatic abilities were demonstrated in roles such as the Messenger of Death in MacMillan's *Das Lied von der Erde* (Song of the Earth; 1965) and Armand Duval in Neumeier's *Die Kameliendamen* (The Lady of the Camellias; 1978), and his classical technique was frequently on view in the princely roles in *Swan Lake* and *The Nutcracker.*

At the end of the 1980/81 season, having been awarded the John Cranko Medal for his services in preserving the Cranko heritage, Madsen left the Stuttgart Ballet to take up an appointment as director of the ballet company attached to the Frankfurt Opera House. As head of the Frankfurt Ballet, he attempted to consolidate the company's reputation by building a mixed repertory of nineteenth-century classics such as *Giselle,* neoclassical works by George Balanchine, story ballets by Cranko, and contemporary ballets by choreographers such as Jiří Kylián and William Forsythe. His efforts were not successful, and he left Frankfurt in 1984. Subsequent posts as artistic director of the Royal Swedish Ballet (1984–1986) and of the ballet company at the Teatro Comunale in Florence (1986–1988) also proved unsatisfactory.

Returning to Germany, Madsen rejoined the Stuttgart Ballet as a ballet master in 1990 and was appointed assistant artistic director in 1991. He remained in this post until the end of the 1995/96 season, when he once again left the company. A splendid dancer and a fine teacher, he has been unable to achieve lasting success at the level of company management.

BIBLIOGRAPHY

"Egon Madsen" (in English). *Stuttgarter Ballett Annual* 3 (1980).

Geitel, Klaus. "Egon Madsen, oder die Metamorphosen dees Harlekin." In *Ballett 1977: Chronik und Bilanz des Ballettjahres,* edited by Horst Koegler et al. Hanover, 1977.

Goodman, Saul. "Egon Madsen and Susanne Hanke." *Dance Magazine* (October 1969): 66–69.

Regitz, Hartmut. "Die Heimkehr des verlorenon Sohnes." *Ballett-Journal/Das Tanzarchiv* 38 (June 1990): 50–52.

Stuart, Otis. "Form and Meaning: An Interview with Egon Madsen." *Ballett International* 7 (May 1984): 6–9.

Horst Koegler

MAGALLANES, NICHOLAS (born 27 November 1922 in Camargo, Mexico, died 1 May 1977 in New York), Mexican-American dancer. Magallanes was brought to the United States from Mexico at age five and grew up in and around New York City. Fascinated after seeing his first ballet performance, the teenage Magallanes auditioned for George Balanchine, who accepted him for the fledgling School of American Ballet. Thus began Magallanes's lifelong association with the dance enterprises of Balanchine and Lincoln Kirstein. He first appeared professionally in Ballet Caravan's *A Thousand Times Neigh!* at the 1939 New York World's Fair. He danced briefly with Catherine Littlefield's Littlefield Ballet, toured South America with American Ballet Caravan (1941), and appeared on Broadway in *The Merry Widow* (1943), Balanchine's *Song of Norway* (1944), and Ruth Page's *Music in My Heart* (1947). He danced with Ballet Russe de Monte Carlo (1943–1946), Ballet Society (1946–1948), and, from 1948 until shortly before his death, as a principal with the New York City Ballet.

Magallanes created some two dozen Balanchine roles, notably in *Night Shadow (La Sonnambula), Orpheus* (title role), *La Valse, The Nutcracker* (Cavalier), *Western Symphony* (second movement), *Allegro Brillante, Square Dance, Episodes II, Liebeslieder Walzer,* and *A Midsummer Night's Dream* (Lysander). He was also closely identified with Balanchine's *Serenade, Le Baiser de la Fée, Concerto Barocco, Symphony in C,* and *The Four Temperaments.* Among his other major creations were the Poet in Frederick Ashton's *Illuminations* and An Intruder in Jerome Robbins's *The Cage.*

Never a virtuoso, Magallanes made his mark as an exemplary partner for nearly all the New York City Ballet's ballerinas through the 1960s and as a dancer-actor of unique lyric gifts. A handsome, slender man, he could embody to perfection the Balanchine archetype of the yearning lover-poet, bringing a special romantic grace and fervor to Orpheus, the Poet in *La Sonnambula,* and the melancholy heroes of *La Valse* and *Serenade.*

BIBLIOGRAPHY

Croce, Arlene. *Going to the Dance.* New York, 1982.

Current Biography. New York, 1955.

Reynolds, Nancy. *Repertory in Review: Forty Years of the New York City Ballet.* New York, 1977.

Anne Murphy

MAHAPATRA, KELUCHARAN (known as Guru Kelucharan Mahapatra; born 1 August 1926 in Raghurajpur, Orissa), Indian dancer, choreographer, and teacher. Born into a family of traditional painters, Kelucharan Mahapatra studied dance under Mohan Goswami. He began performing in a theatrical company as a *gōtipūa,* a boy who dances in female costume in a devotional context. He also mastered the *pakhavaj* or double-barreled drum used in temple dances. Although he was forced to support himself with manual labor even as a child, he persisted in his studies. He also took lessons from guru Pankajcharan Das, an Oḍissi male dancer of the *māhārī* community. The *māhārīs* were female dancers dedicated to the temple who danced for the gods.

Mahapatra performed with various theatrical companies and then joined Kala Vikash Kendra, a school in Cuttack which taught Oḍissi, music, and folk dance. When Oḍissi began to attract the attention of connoisseurs of classical Indian dance, Mahapatra led in the development of the genre. He drew inspiration from the relief sculptures in Orissa's temples and from traditional painting to choreograph solo and group dances which remain in the present repertory of Oḍissi. Working with the violinist Bhubaneswara Misra, he also composed the music for his dances. One of the gifted architects of neo-Oḍissi dance—along with guru Pankajcharan Das, guru Deba Prasad Das, and Mayadhar Raut—he ensured it a permanent place in the world of Indian classical dance. A host of his disciples have become well-known soloists, including Sanjukta Panigrahi, Kum Kum Mohanty (nee Das), Sonal Mansingh, Madhavi Mughal, and Mahapatra's own son Ratikant Mahapatra.

Mahapatra choreographed a number of dance dramas, including some based on the mystical erotic poem *Gīta Govinda* and works especially created for the Konaraka Dance Festival; these are preserved in the repertory of the Odissi Research Centre. A precious record of his performances and choreography survives in *Bhavantarana,* a film about him by Kumar Shahani, and in several other documentaries.

Mahapatra has received several awards, including the Central Sangeet Natak Akademi award, the Kalidasa Sanman, the Padamshri, and the Padma Bhushan award from the government of India, as well as honors from several Orissan art institutions. He conducts dance workshops, dividing his time among Bhubaneswar and other parts of India and training many students. He has had a lasting influence on the Oḍissi dance genre.

BIBLIOGRAPHY

Kothari, Sunil, and Avinash Pasricha. *Odissi: Indian Classical Dance Art.* Bombay, 1990.

Schechner, Richard. "Collaborating on Odissi." *Drama Review* 32 (Spring 1988): 128–138.

SUNIL KOTHARI

MAHARAJ, BIRJU (born 4 February 1938 in Lucknow), Indian dancer and choreographer. Maharaj represents the seventh generation of the family that originated and developed the *kathak* dance style of Lucknow, a North Indian city. He is the son and disciple of Acchan Maharaj, who was a court dancer in the former state of Rampur (now Uttar Pradesh) and was considered one of the great *kathak* dancers of his generation. He died when Birju was only eight years old; after that the youth was guided by his uncles.

The youngest artist to receive the award for dance from the government of India's Academy for Dance, Drama and Music, Maharaj directs the Baharatiya Kala Kendra in New Delhi, an institution devoted to the propagation of the classical arts. He has performed extensively in India, Europe, the Middle East, Southeast Asia, the Soviet Union, and the United States.

A high degree of technical skill is necessary in *kathak* dance, but Maharaj goes beyond virtuoso technique. He is noted for his beautiful hand gestures, mobile face, and large, expressive eyes. He is so skilled in the manipulation of the ankle bells that accent his movement that he can make any number sound at a time—even a single bell.

Maharaj is also an expert drummer and singer in the northern Indian style. Known for his imaginative choreography, he has created many dance dramas, including one about the great Indian patron of dance, music, and poetry, Nawab Wajid Ali Shah.

Maharaj's subtlety of interpretation, elegance of expression, and depth of dramatic sense have made him one of the greatest *kathak* dancers. In recent years, he and his company have represented India at almost all the major Festivals of India in countries outside India, including the United States, Germany, and Russia. He has been awarded the title of Padmabhushan, a great honor. His students are now spread all over the world, particularly in Western countries.

BIBLIOGRAPHY

Brooks, Valerie. "Heart of the Matter." *Ballet News* 7 (September 1985): 11–16.

Hall, Fernau. "Maharaj and Indian Classics." *Daily Telegraph* (22 September 1981).

Khokar, Mohan. "Lucknow Gharana." *Marg* 12.4 (1959).

Misra, Susheela. *Some Dancers of India.* New Delhi, 1992.

Najan, Nala. "Procession of Indian Dance" (parts 1–2). *Arabesque* 12.2–3 (1986).

Schmidt, Jochen. "Divine Law versus the Body: The Laborious Rebirth of Indian Dance." *Ballett International/Tanz Aktuell* (August–September 1994): 70–75.

Schmidt, Jochen. "A Living Legend." *Ballett International/Tanz Aktuell* (May 1995): 52–53.

RITHA DEVI

MAKAROVA, NATALIA (Natalia Romanovna Makarova; born 21 November 1940 in Leningrad), Russian-American ballet dancer, actress, and producer. At the age of thirteen, Makarova entered the Vaganova Ballet School in Leningrad. Her teachers included Mikhail Mikhailovsky (who had made his stage debut in Marius Petipa's time), Nikolai Ivanovsky, and Elena Shiripina. On graduation in 1959, Makarova entered the Kirov Ballet company. Her talent and skill had been evident at her graduation performance of the adagio from *Giselle,* act 2, when her affinity for the Romantic style was at once recognized.

She danced her first Giselle (with Nikita Dolgushin as Albrecht) on 27 December 1959 in her initial season at the Kirov. Many more major roles followed, for which she was variously coached by Natalia Dudinskaya, Tatiana Vecheslova, and Alla Shelest, all leading exponents of the classical repertory and pupils of Agrippina Vaganova. Makarova danced the roles of Odette-Odile in *Swan Lake,* Aurora and Princess Florine in *The Sleeping Beauty,* Nikia and Gamsatti in *La Bayadère,* Masha in *The Nutcracker,* Maria in *The Fountain of Bakhchisarai,* and the Tsar Maiden in *The Little Humpbacked Horse.* She danced leading roles in *Raymonda, Romeo and Juliet* (choreographed by Leonid Lavrovsky), *Chopiniana, Le Corsaire, Leningrad Symphony* (choreographed by Igor Belsky), *Goryanka* (choreographed by Oleg Vinogradov), *Cinderella,* and *Distant Planet* (choreographed by Konstantin Sergeyev). She also appeared in ballets by Leonid Yakobson, with whom she had a special sympathy, including *Country of Wonder, The Bedbug,* and certain of his choreographic miniatures.

MAKAROVA. Using four marzurkas and a waltz by Chopin, Jerome Robbins created *Other Dances* for Makarova and Mikhail Baryshnikov to perform at a gala benefit for the New York Public Library for the Performing Arts, given at the Metropolitan Opera House on 9 May 1976. Makarova's lovely dress was designed by Santo Loquasto. (Photograph © 1976 by Max Waldman; used by permission.)

Makarova emerged during the 1960s as a ballerina whose ideal physique was matched by exceptional emotional power. As first-place winner of the 1965 International Ballet Competition and a Merited Artist of the RSFSR (Russian Soviet Federated Socialist Republic), she was chosen to appear as Giselle in Sergeyev's farewell performance in that ballet. Makarova was first seen in the West in 1961, when the Kirov Ballet made its initial appearance in London at the Royal Opera House, Covent Garden. Nearly ten years later, at the end of the Kirov Ballet's season at the Royal Festival Hall, on 3 September 1970, Makarova opted to remain in the West. In *A Dance Autobiography,* a commentary on the art of the ballerina written at the height of her career and published in 1979, Makarova details her reasons for taking this step toward artistic freedom.

Makarova went to New York City in 1971, where she joined American Ballet Theatre; this company remained a base for much of her work and provided her with an extensive classical and modern repertory. She also established strong links with the Royal Ballet as a regular and much-loved guest artist. Her partnership with Anthony Dowell was exceptionally fruitful in the classical repertory as well as in the ballets of Kenneth MacMillan and Frederick Ashton. In MacMillan's *Romeo and Juliet* and *Manon,* she gave interpretations combining beauty of style with exultant emotion, and she has been a notable Woman in his *Song of the Earth.* For Ashton she was both a beguiling Cinderella and a superbly impulsive Natalia Petrovna in *A Month in the Country.* Very potent, too, were her appearances in such varied roles as Jerome Robbins's *Dances at a Gathering* (in which she danced the scherzo), Ninette de Valois's *Checkmate* (Black Queen), Glen Tetley's *Voluntaries,* and Nijinska's *Les Biches* (La Garçonne). As a guest dancer with many companies, she was hailed in both the classical and contemporary repertories: the Royal Danish Ballet; the Paris Opera Ballet; the National Ballet of Canada; the Marseille Opera Ballet; the Scottish Ballet; companies in Hamburg, Stuttgart, and Munich; and in Brazil, Australia, South Africa, and Italy.

In traditional works she established standards of lyric intensity and poetic eloquence; in such lighter works as American Ballet Theatre's stagings of *Don Quixote, La Fille Mal Gardée,* and *Coppélia,* she was a joyous and high-spirited comedienne. Her intense psychic involvement with a role and her ability to pierce to the heart of a character's emotions made her unforgettable in John Cranko's *Onegin* as Tatiana, as Roland Petit's Carmen, and as Esmeralda in his *Notre-Dame de Paris.* In 1980, Makarova produced for American Ballet Theatre the first full-length staging in the West of Petipa's *La Bayadère* (she had, six years previously, staged its Kingdom of the Shades scene for the company). This was an intelligent and honorable revision of a great classic, restoring a version of act 5 that had been abandoned in Leningrad in 1919 in which the drama is properly resolved, as Petipa had intended. With superb designs by PierLuigi Samaritani, this *La Bayadère* remains an impressive and important production; it was subsequently produced for the Royal Ballet and for the Royal Swedish Ballet.

In November 1980 Makarova appeared in a season at the Uris Theater, New York, with a group of guest stars and a corps de ballet. She presented her staging of the *Paquita grand pas de deux* and appeared in ballets by Maurice Béjart, George Balanchine, Barry Moreland, and Lorca Massine. An injury at this time curtailed her performances, but her return to dancing showed her power undiminished in her traditional repertory and in such varied new roles as the Nightingale in the Ashton production of Igor Stravinsky's *Le Rossignol* at the Metropolitan Opera House, New York, in December 1981 and a triumphant Broadway debut in the New York revival of the musical *On Your Toes* in March 1983, which won her an Antoinette Perry ("Tony") Award.

In the summer of 1988 the Kirov Ballet was again performing in London and, thanks to *glasnost,* Makarova was reunited with her parent company when she danced the second-act adagio from *Swan Lake,* partnered by Konstantin Zaklinsky, with the Kirov corps de ballet of swans surrounding her. In January of the following year Makarova returned to Leningrad to dance at the Kirov Theater—a visit recorded in a BBC-TV documentary. This sensational performance, in which Makarova danced two pas de deux from Cranko's *Onegin* with Alexander Sombart, was hailed by the Leningrad audience and by Makarova's Kirov colleagues. It marked the end of her career as a classical ballerina. Since 1988 she has concentrated on her work as an actress.

The unifying elements in the multiplicity of Makarova's balletic roles, as in all her work, has been her concern for vivid truth in performance and the classic underpinning of the dance itself. The inspired and intuitive quality of her interpretations comes from her quest to make each role anew in every performance. This outpouring of seemingly spontaneous feeling is matched and controlled by a dance style that retains all the distinction and classic rigor of her Kirov training.

BIBLIOGRAPHY

Austin, Richard. *Natalya Makarova.* London, 1978.

Makarova, Natalia. *A Dance Autobiography.* New York, 1979.

"Makarova Today." *Ballet News* 1 (March 1980).

CLEMENT CRISP

MALAWI. *See* Central and East Africa.

MALAYSIA. The Southeast Asian country of Malaysia has territory on both the southern Malay Peninsula and on the northern part of the island of Borneo. Before independence, all of Malaysia had been governed by Britain. Although parts were colonized by the Portuguese and Dutch in the late 1700s and early 1800s, Britain dominated the area by the mid-1800s for tin production and rubber plantations and formed the Federated Malay States in 1896. Independence came in 1957, but in 1963 Malaya joined with Sarawak and Sabah (both on Borneo) and Singapore to create the federation of Malaysia (Singapore withdrew in 1965). The country is pluralistc, and every ethnic group has minority status within the federation. Among the people of East Malaysia (the northern shores of the former Borneo) and the jungles of West Malaysia (peninsular Southeast Asia) are found many traditional dances as well as dance dramas. Chinese opera and Indian *bangsawan* theater and dance are also parts of Malaysia's culture. This article, however, deals only with traditional *(desa)* arts as defined by the Malaysian government.

Trance Dances. Indonesian trance dance forms are found in the *kuda kepang* hobby-horse dances of Johore and East Malaysia as well as in the *barong* mythical animal dances. Both dances may develop plots in which Islamic and Javanese legends are mixed.

The *dabus* dance is performed by groups of male dancers carrying iron rods and wearing warriors' costumes similar to those of analogous Javanese dancers. The *dabus* shares with other warrior dances an emphasis on strong leg movements. The musical accompaniment consists of drums, songs, and *serunai* (reed aerophones).

The northern states of Malaysia have a strong tradition of shamanism, both male and female, reflected in the *putri* (or *puteri*) dances, which involve tossing the head to induce trance. [*See* Shamanism.] The accompaniment consists of *rebab* (spiked fiddle), two-headed *gendang* drums, gongs, and an upturned brass bowl called a *bantil.* The dances resemble those of *mayong,* a form of dance drama, except that the *putri* dancer both moves and sings alone; they may also include sudden leg movements drawn from Thai tradition. Once trance is induced, the dancing usually stops and communication begins between the *putri* (who now is possessed) and the *rebab* player, who interviews the spirit.

Islamic and Festival Dance. Arabic texts are often taught through *zikir* songs led by a tambourine or frame-drum performer and repeated by lines of young men, who may begin performing hand gestures while seated and then continue with standing dance steps. These *rodat* and *hadrah* dances are also done by troupes featuring lines of men, some dressed as women. A more secular Arab dance is the *zapin*. Weddings, circumcisions, and holidays frequently include Islamic dances, but Southeast Asian *bersilat* fight dances accompanied by *serunai*, drums, and gongs are also common, as are candle dances *(tari inari* or *tari lilin)*.

Folk and Social Dance. There are many regional fishing and rice-cultivating folk dances in Malaysia, and *ronggeng* and modern *joget* social dances are widespread. *Ronggeng* grew out of exposure to sixteenth-century Portuguese dances, but indigenous elements prevail. Couples or lines of dancers perform hand gestures and steps while facing but not touching their partners. The music may be provided by a Western violin, Southeast Asian gongs, an Arab frame drum, or a dance band. Modern *joget* dances are similar, and new genres continue to appear, reflecting Malaysia's creativity in dance.

Court Dances. Remnants of the dances of the sultans' courts survive in Malaysia through performance by private troupes or by support of national programs. Two major forms are the *joget* of Trengganu and the *ashek* (or *asyek*) of Kelantan.

Joget is an example of marginal survival, in that it maintains dances imported long ago from Indonesia, where they are now extinct. Javanese and Islamic stories are accompanied by one of Malaysia's few gamelan metallophone ensembles. The costumes reflect earlier Javanese styles, and the choreography contains backbends, hand gestures, and flicks of waist scarves that imply the same origin as do the symmetrical groupings in straight and circular floor patterns.

The court of Patani (now part of Thailand) was the source of many court traditions, including *ashek*, which survived in Kelantan. Originally a group female dance accompanied by a special drum, a *rebab*, and a xylophone, today it is a solo dance accompanied by a *serunai* (oboe) and by percussion. It exploits thc three basic positions of Malaysian professional dance—sitting, kneeling, and standing. Hand gestures are particularly refined in *ashek*,

MALAYSIA. In 1991, Manuel Alum presented an arranged program of traditional and modern dances, entitled *Made in Malaysia: A Shamanistic Journey*, at The Asia Society, New York. *(above)* Omar Ismail as the Shaman with Idris Mamat, playing the *rebab*. *(left)* Several *mayong* dancers, with eyes downcast, in the midst of creating fluid gestures with their hands. (Photographs © 1991 by Jack Vartoogian; used by permission.)

reflecting the Malaysian word for dance, *tari,* which refers to such movements.

Theatrical Dance. *Mayong,* a village survival of early court drama, and *mek mulung,* a folk-generated variant of it, are valuable examples of the provincial remnants of Indonesian, continental Southeast Asian, and Islamic traditions as subjected to indigenous Malaysian creativity. The resulting mixture is unique, particularly in its heterophonic chorus style. The dramas are also important as sources of information about Malaysian legends. The opening dance of each performance follows the *ashek* choreographic sequence and uses some of its hand movements. The many other dances that appear throughout a play are circular and simple in gesture. All performers except the clowns and musicians are female, and no distinction is evident between male and female role dances except in walking and fighting scenes.

The *tari ragam* dance in *mayong* is derived from the *manōhrā* genre performed by Thai communities living in Malaysia. These dance dramas are performed only by men, some in female attire. The major role is the Manōhrā, a mythical bird; the standard dance interludes involve a series of figure-eight patterns in which dancers try to touch the bird's tail (a transvestite's buttocks). Like *mayong, manōhrā* develops its plot slowly with many comic and dance interruptions. The stories are based on regional oral narrative traditions.

[*See also* Mayong. *For related discussion, see* Manōhrā.]

BIBLIOGRAPHY

Harun Mat Piah, ed. *Gamelan Malaysia.* Kuala Lumpur, 1983.

Jennings, Sue. "Temiar Dance and the Maintenance of Order." In *Society and the Dance,* edited by Paul Spencer. Cambridge, 1985.

Malm, William P., and Amin Sweeney. *Studies in Malaysian Oral and Musical Traditions: Music in Kelantan, Malaysia, and Some of Its Cultural Implications.* Michigan Papers on South and Southeast Asia, no. 8. Ann Arbor, 1974.

Miettinen, Jukka O. *Classical Dance and Theatre in South-East Asia.* New York, 1992.

Mohd Anis Md Nor. *Zapin: Folk Dance of the Malay World.* New York, 1993.

Sheppard, Mubin. *Tama Indera, a Royal Pleasure Ground: Malay Decorative Arts and Pastimes.* London, 1972.

Sheppard, Mubin. *Taman Saujana: Dance, Drama, Music, and Magic in Malaya Long and Not-So-Long Ago.* Petaling Jaya, 1983.

Sooi, Beng Tan. "The Performing Arts in Malaysia: State and Society." *Asian Music* 21.1 (1989–1990): 137–171.

WILLIAM P. MALM

MALI. *See* Sub-Saharan Africa. *See also* Bamana Dance *and* Dogan Dance.

MANEN, HANS VAN (born 11 July 1932 in Amstelveen), Dutch dancer and choreographer. Trained by Sonia Gaskell, Darja Collin, Françoise Adret, and Nora Kiss, Hans van Manen joined Ballet Recital in 1951 and the Ballet of the Amsterdam Opera in 1952; there he was demi-soloist in 1953 and soloist in 1955. His first choreography for this company was *Feestgericht* (music by L. Ponse, 1957), which was soon followed by *Intermezzo* (music by Arthur Honegger, 1958) and *Mouvements Symphoniques* (music by Haydn, 1958). After a season with Wim Sonneveld's cabaret revue *Rim Ram,* he joined the Ballets de Paris of Roland Petit in 1959.

A year later van Manen became a member of the newly founded Netherlands Dance Theater, as dancer, choreographer, and joint artistic director with Benjamin Harkarvy. For this company he produced thirty ballets. Among them are *Klaar af* (music by Duke Ellington, 1960), *Voet bij stuk* (music by Dave Brubeck, 1962), *Symphony in Three Movements* (music by Igor Stravinsky, 1963), *Opus Twelve* (music by Béla Bartók, 1964), *Essay in Silence* (music by Oliver Messiaen, 1965), *Metaforen* (music by D. Lesur, 1965), *Point of No Return* (music by W. Pijper, 1966), *Five Sketches* (music by Paul Hindemith, 1966), *Three Pieces* (music by G. Bacewicz, 1968), *Solo for Voice 1* (music by John Cage, 1968), *Squares* (music by Erik Satie, 1969), *Situation* (music collage, 1970), *Mutations* (with Glen Tetley, music by Karlheinz Stockhausen, 1970), *Grosse Fuge* (music by Beethoven, 1971), *Opus Lemaître* (music by Bach, 1972), *Septet Extra* (music by Camille Saint-Saëns, 1973), *Noble et Sentimentale* (music by Maurice Ravel, 1975), *Lieder ohne Worte* (music by Felix Mendelssohn, 1977), *Memories of the Body* (music collage, 1979), and *Concert voor Piano and Blazers* (music by Stravinsky, 1979). Meanwhile, he also produced forty ballets for television and stage shows.

In 1970 van Manen left Netherlands Dance Theater, and after three seasons working as a free-lance choreographer with several European and American companies, he joined the Dutch National Ballet in 1973 as choreographer and ballet master. From 1973 to 1984 he made nineteen ballets for this company. Among them are *Twilight* (music by Cage, 1972), *Daphnis and Chloë* (music by Ravel, 1972), *Adagio Hammerklavier* (music by Beethoven, 1973), *Le Sacre du Printemps* (music by Stravinsky, 1974), *Kwintet* (music by Mozart, 1974), *Ebony Concerto and a Tango* (music by Stravinsky, 1976), *Octet Opus 20* (music by Mendelssohn, 1977), *Five Tangos* (music by Piazzola, 1977), *Dumbarton Oaks* (music by Stravinsky, 1978), *Live* (music by Liszt, 1979), *Enlage* (music by Johann Strauss the younger, 1980), *Pianovariaties I* (music by Bach and Luigi Dallapiccola, 1980), *Pianovariaties II* (music by Sergei Prokofiev, 1981), *Five Short Stories* (music collage, 1982), *Pianovariaties III* (music by Satie, 1982), *Pianovariaties IV* (music by Claude Debussy, 1982), *In and Out* (music by Anderson and N. Hagen, 1983), and *Pianovariaties V* (music by Debussy, 1984). Many of these ballets are now included in the repertories of companies in Germany, England, Denmark, Austria, Switzerland, and the United States.

Van Manen also created *Snippers* (music by Terry Riley, 1970), *Ajaka-Boembi* (music by Scraggs and Chopin, 1971), and *Assortimento* (music by Debussy, 1973) for the Dutch Scapino Ballet (now known as Scapino Rotterdam); *Keep Going* (music by Berio, 1971) for the Düsseldorf Ballet; *Four Schumann Pieces* (music by Schumann, 1975) for London's Royal Ballet; *Premier Grand Trio* (music by Schubert, 1978) for the Vienna State Opera; and *Portrait* (music by Satie, 1983) for Dansproduktie Rotterdam.

Van Manen was named an Officer of the Orde van Oranje-Nassau (1970) and received the Prize of Dutch Theater Critics (1974), the H. J. Reyninck Medal (1976), and the Sonia Gaskell Prize in Choreography (1991).

A fervent admirer of George Balanchine's choreographic concepts and influenced directly by Jerome Robbins, Glen Tetley, and John Butler, van Manen is strongly inspired by conceptual art. Averse to any symbolism, he wants to visualize the musical score, experimenting with all the possibilities within motion. His creations often result in sudden and surprising effects that clash with traditional expectations. Expanding the academic idiom with movements from daily life, he often takes a simple question as his source of inspiration. For example, what happens when the same series of movements is repeated within changing contexts? What is the effect of replacing ballet slippers with pumps? How can one make a classical pas de deux for two men? In the solution of these choreographic challenges he often deals with themes of aggression, sexuality, the control and outbursts of erotic relationships, and relations between individuals and groups.

MANEN. Andrea Boardman and Jay Booker of Les Grands Ballets Canadiens in van Manen's *Black Cake*, originally set on Netherlands Dance Theater in 1989. (Photograph © 1994 by David Cooper; used by permission.)

MANEN. Nathalie Caris and Wim Broeckx of the Dutch National Ballet in van Manen's *Twilight* (1972), set to music by John Cage. (Photograph © 1992 by Deen van Meer; used by permission.)

Not believing in purely abstract ballets, van Manen creates dance dramas without telling a story or referring to literal backgrounds. His use of everyday movements often throws into relief the suspense in the human relationships among the dancers and creates humorous effects. Important in all his ballets is the climactic end: van Manen always displays an unpessimistic attitude, and he never presents his dancers as definite losers or winners. Coincidence or chance seems to be banished; everything on stage fulfills a function. Van Manen has stated that all his dances are about dance, and that the movements result from clearly articulated principles that are integrated into one dramatic concept.

In an early stage of his choreographic career van Manen was already interested in the possibilities of video and film. He showed this very strikingly not only in his television ballets but also in his co-production with Glen Tetley of *Mutations* (1970). In 1979 his interest in video resulted in the ballet *Live,* created around the possibilities of the Carré Theater of Amsterdam and introducing a cameraman for the live recording of the dancer as she performs a solo.

Conforming to van Manen's clearly structured choreographies, the stage designs are mostly sober, stylish, and abstract. Many of his ballets have had decor and costumes designed by the painter Jean-Paul Vroom. In his choice of music van Manen was often experimented with various genres—eighteenth-century chamber music, Romantic orchestral pieces, *Lieder,* jazz, and contemporary music. In the late 1970s he showed a strong preference for piano music, concluding with a series of five variations on the piano music of Bach, Dallapiccola, Prokofiev, Satie, and Debussy.

[*See also* Dutch National Ballet *and* Netherlands Dance Theater.]

BIBLIOGRAPHY

Dekker, Keso. *Hans van Manen + Modern Ballet in Nederland.* Amsterdam, 1981.

Fenger, Ulrike J. "Betrachtungen zur Tanzsprache Hans van Manens." *Tanzforschung Jahrbuch* 4 (1993): 95–127.

Jonkers, Marc, ed. *Hans van Manen: Photographs, Facts, Opinions.* Amsterdam, 1992.

Koegler, Horst, et al., eds. *Ballett 1972: Chronik und Bilanz des Ballettjahres.* Velber bei Hannover, 1972.

Loney, Glenn. "Hans van Manen." *Dance Magazine* (February 1974): 70–77.

Manen, Hans van, et al. *Grand pas classique: Curiosities Kept Alive, or The Perfect Ballet.* Edited by Annemarie de Wildt. Amsterdam, 1989.

Schaik, Eva van. *Op gespannen voet: Geschiedenis van de Nederlandse theaterdans vanaf 1900.* Haarlem, 1981.

Schaik, Eva van. "Movement and Form: Interview with hans van Manen." *Ballett International* 7 (January 1984): 20–23.

Schaik, Eva van. "The Amused Muse." *Ballett International/Tanz Aktuell* (November 1995): 36–45.

Schmidt, Jochen. *Das Ballet und die andere Künst.* Cologne, 1980.

Schmidt, Jochen. *Der Zeitgenosse als Klassiker über den Hollandischen choreographen Hans van Manen.* Cologne, 1987.

Weigelt, Gert. "Dance Has Many Faces." *Ballett International* 9 (July–August 1986): 20–27.

EVA VAN SCHAIK

MANIPUR. The state of Manipur is in the far northeastern corner of India. The predominant ethnic group is the Meitei, a distinct cultural group of Mongoloid stock, closely related to northern Burmese and Thai peoples and speaking a Tibeto-Burman language. There are many other ethnic groups in Manipur state, including branches of the Naga people.

The indigenous religious beliefs of the Meiteis were animistic; the presence of Hinduism is believed to have begun as early as the sixth century CE, with later, sporadic migrations of brahman Hindu families. Much of this migration was from Bengal, as evidenced by the fact that the script in use in Manipur is derived from Bengali. In the sixteenth to eighteenth centuries, Vaiṣṇava Hinduism and the cult of Rādhā-Kṛṣṇa were introduced. This sect of Hinduism, centered about the deity Viṣṇu (Vishnu) and particularly the worship of Kṛṣṇa (Krishna), an *avatāra* or incarnation of Viṣṇu, had an important effect on the dance tradition of Manipur.

The deeper levels of the pre-Hindu Meitei dance tradition are rich and complex. This tradition includes fairly simple community or folk dances, usually performed in connection with a festival. It also includes martial dances performed by men with spears, shields, and swords, with a distinct element of acrobatics. The Meitei dance tradition is best seen, however, in the month-long spring ceremonies of the Lai Haraoba, performed before the shrines of the ancient deities of Umenglai and Lairembi. The Lai Haraoba symbolizes the creation of the world; ritual and dance are blended, as are solo dances by hereditary priests and priestesses with group dances by the people of the community. A stringed instrument called the *pena* provides the accompaniment.

The pattern of blending solo with group dances is seen also in performances of dance within the Vaiṣṇava tradition. These are principally the dances seen in the *rās līlā,* relating stories of Kṛṣṇa as a child and young man, growing up among cowherds; Kṛṣṇa's beloved Rādhā, his brother Balarām, and the *gopīs* (cowherdesses) also figure in these stories. [*See* Rās Līlā.]

It is the dances in the tradition of the *rās līlā* that have come to be known most widely in other parts of India and elsewhere as Manipuri dance. The spread of this genre owes its impetus to the Indian poet Rabindranath Tagore. He felt the need for developing a fuller curriculum in the arts at Vishvabharati University at Shantiniketan, and like other national figures, he also felt that the people were being dispossessed of important aspects of their cultural heritage. He had seen Manipuri dance and was impressed by its graceful movement and somewhat restrained quality. Respectable middle-class Indian society had rejected dance as a fitting subject in education on the basis of the stigma associating it with professionals and prostitutes of low social and ritual status. Manipuri dance, however, came from outside the cultural context of Bengal and urban North India and had no connections with the class of professional courtesans, so it was ideal for Tagore's purpose.

Tagore's first major step was to establish dance as a regular part of education at Vishvabharati University in 1926, when he brought the celebrated teacher Nabakumar Sinha to teach Manipuri dance. Later Nabakumar Sinha, who was originally from Tripura, left to teach in Ahmedabad and Bombay, and the popularity of Manipuri dance among girls from respectable families became established in urban society. Still later, new teachers from Manipur came to Bengal and moved on to teach in the larger cities of North India. This was a critical turning point in the history of dance in India: the reintroduction of dance as a "respectable" art had begun. Thus Tagore, along with other intellectuals who saw the decline of much of India's cultural heritage in the first quarter of the twentieth century, contributed greatly to the renaissance of traditional dance and its reestablishment in the evolving society.

Aside from the dance forms mentioned here, there are many other occasions for dance in Manipur, and many other themes, such as the story of the ill-fated lovers Khamba and Thoibi. There are dances with drums and with large cymbals. There is a Vaiṣṇava devotional celebration called the *saṅkīrtan* in which dance and music play an important part.

Manipuri dance, both the older pre-Hindu tradition and the dances associated with the Vaiṣṇava religion, is extremely plastic, with a strong visual continuity of pattern: circular and parabolic, like a continuous thread of arabesques and curves. One of the appealing features of Manipuri dance is that it is graceful and appears to be unlabored and easy to learn. This is extremely deceptive; it may be easily imitated, but to perform it well is difficult. In the quality of its movement, it reveals its close ties with dance traditions farther east. The technique and conception of movement are demonstrably related to the movement concepts of the nearby peoples of Myanmar and the southern, Indianized portion of Central Asia. Much has been written on the extent of Sanskritization of Manipuri dance. Although a degree of Sanskritization has taken place, the Manipuri tradition stands on its own, a distinct entity apart from the mainstream of choreographic styles of North and South India.

[*See also* Asian Dance Traditions, *overview article;* Costume in Asian Traditions; *and the entries on the Jhaveri sisters and Bipin Singh.*]

BIBLIOGRAPHY

Anand, Mulk Raj, ed. *Classical and Folk Dances of India.* Bombay, 1963.

Datta, Birendranath, ed. *Traditional Performing Arts of North-East India.* Guwahati, Assam, 1990–.

Doshi, Saryu, ed. *Dances of Manipur: The Classical Tradition.* Bombay, 1989.

Lightfoot, Louise. *Dance-Rituals of Manipur, India.* Hong Kong, 1958.

Ragini Devi. *Dance Dialects of India.* 2d rev. ed. Delhi, 1990.

Samson, Leela. *Rhythm in Joy: Classical Indian Dance Traditions.* New Delhi, 1987.

Vatsyayan, Kapila. *Traditions of Indian Folk Dance.* 2d ed. New Delhi, 1987.

CLIFFORD REIS JONES

MANNING, FRANKIE (born 26 May 1914 in Jacksonville, Florida), American dancer and choreographer. Manning played a major and continuing role in the development of the Lindy Hop. During its heyday, in the 1920s, 1930s, and 1940s, he was responsible for a number of steps and important stylistic and choreographic innovations. Decades later, in the 1980s and 1990s he contributed significantly to the swing dance revival.

While growing up in New York's Harlem, Manning listened to early jazz and watched his mother and her friends do social dances of the era, including the Black Bottom, Charleston, Mess Around, Blues, Collegiate, and Breakaway. At age fourteen he started playing hookey from Sunday afternoon church activities in order to attend teenage dances at Harlem's Alhambra Ballroom, where he became enthralled with the newly popular Lindy Hop. Excelling in the dance, he "graduated" to the Renaissance Ballroom around 1930. He finally ventured to the legendary Savoy Ballroom, in late 1933, quickly becoming a regular.

In 1934 Manning was invited to join Whitey's Lindy Hoppers by manager Herbert ("Whitey") White. This troupe of elite dancers evolved from talented enthusiasts to sought-after professionals in the ensuing years. Manning soon displayed choreographic abilities as well as enormous talent as a performer. Whitey encouraged him as a dancer and gave him responsibilities that included choreographing (although this term was not used at the time) routines and managing the group on tours. Manning invented numerous steps, including variations on the Charleston and the movement, called the Slide-Through, in which a man slides a woman through his legs from front to back. Inspired by his desire to attain the leading edge in a dance contest, Manning is best known for creating, circa late 1935, the first aerial, or airstep, called Over-the-Back. In aerials, the woman is forcefully guided through the air by her partner in a choreographed sequence in time to the accompanying swing music. Usually named according to the woman's trajectory, the aerial caught on, and many more were created by Manning and others.

Around the same time, Manning contributed to Lindy group choreography by creating the first synchronized, ensemble Lindy routine. He also introduced slow-motion segments as a contrast to the frenetic pace of Lindy Hopping and action freezes for rhythmic punctuation. A year earlier he had begun dancing with his body positioned more horizontally to the floor in order to create a more exciting line. Manning had a knack for taking movement ideas from various sources, including circuses, gymnasiums, and other dancers, a step further, thus creating new movements. His innovations, most of which continue to be done, greatly contributed to the theatrical appeal of the Lindy and, hence, its international popularity.

As one of Whitey's Lindy Hoppers, Manning toured the United States as well as Europe, South America, and Australia until the start of World War II. He performed in the swankiest nightspots with all of the swing era greats, including Count Basie, Duke Ellington, Billie Holiday, and Ella Fitzgerald. He danced in and choreographed several films, for which he received no credit, including in 1941 *Hellzapoppin'* and with Duke Ellington *Hot Chocolates* (a soundie, officially called a Panoram, a brief film projected within jukeboxes for the duration of the song; produced by Mills Music from 1940 to 1944, they usually featured the recording artists but sometimes showed dancers or other performers). Manning danced on Broadway and at the 1939 New York World's Fair. He was featured in numerous newspaper and magazine articles, including one in *Life* magazine (1941).

After World War II, Manning started his own troupe, the Congaroo Dancers. In 1954, with gigs having become scarce, Manning took a job at the U.S. Post Office, where he worked for thirty years.

In 1986 two young dance teachers from California, Erin Stevens and Steven Mitchell, tracked Manning down and begged him to pass on his Lindy expertise to them. Manning soon began teaching regularly at a dance studio in New York City and attending swing dances sponsored by the newly established New York Swing Dance Society. To his surprise he found that more and more younger dancers were eager to study with him. As an octogenarian in great demand, he teaches, choreographs, and performs throughout the United States and in Europe. Manning's later professional work includes choreography for the Alvin Ailey American Dance Theater in 1989. He was dance consultant-performer for director Spike Lee's film *Malcolm X* and director-choreographer for Debbie Allen's movie for television *Stompin' at the Savoy,* both in 1992. Manning's numerous honors include a 1989 Tony award for his choreography in Broadway's *Black and Blue* and a National Endowment for the Arts Choreographer's Fellowship Grant in 1994.

Manning has contributed to the late twentieth-century swing dance revival by sharing his memories of the swing era, by passing on the original Savoy Lindy steps, and by inspiring others with his love of dance.

[*See also* Lindy Hop. *For related discussion, see* United States of America, *article on* African-American Social Dance.]

BIBLIOGRAPHY

Amelar, Sarah. "The Shim-Sham Man: For Dancer Frankie Manning, It Don't Mean a Thing If It Ain't Got That Swing—Even at 80." *New York Newsday* (6 June 1994).

Crease, Robert P. "Last of the Lindy Hoppers." *Village Voice* (25 August 1987).

"81-Year-Old Dancer Thrills Crowd at Library of Congress." *Jet* (19 June 1995).

Monaghan, Terry. "A Lindy Double: Frank Manning and the JLH Celebrate Anniversaries." *Dancing Times* (May 1995): 787–789.

Smith, Ernie. "FRANKIE-ISMS: The Defining of a Lindy Legend." *Hoppin'* 1 (Spring 1994): 4–5.

FILM AND VIDEOTAPE. *Hellzapoppin'* (1941), starring Olsen and Johnson, with the best Lindy Hop scene ever captured on film, choreographed by Frankie Manning for Whitey's Lindy Hoppers. "Back into Swing," a segment on the ABC television network news magazine *20/20* (1989), focusing on Frankie Manning's early years as a Lindy Hop innovator and his emergence from retirement to help lead the swing dance revival.

CYNTHIA R. MILLMAN

MANŌHRĀ. The Thai dance drama *Manōhrā,* also rendered *Manōrā* or *Nōrā,* takes its name from a heavenly bird-maiden and princess who is the heroine of the Buddhist myth "Suthon Chādok." The tale recounts the romance of Suthon, a handsome human prince, and Manōhrā, a beautiful *kinnarī* (half bird, half woman). Belonging to different species and worlds, the two lovers are destined to undergo trials and suffering to prove their true love and virtues, a Buddhist theme prevalent in *jātaka* tales ("birth stories"). Because of its combination of romance, myth, and adventure, *Manōhrā* has always enjoyed popularity as a dance drama.

In southern Thai dialect, *Manōhrā* is shortened to *Nōrā. Nōrā* also refers to the dance and dance drama genres and to the dancers themselves. It is used as a title before the dancer's name (e.g., Nōrā Am, Nōrā Tōēm).

One of the oldest genres of dance dramas in Asia, the *nōrā chātrī* of southern Thailand features this tale in a sensual and ritualistic dance style with rhythmic, rapid musical accompaniment. The dance movements imitate those of birds and animals.

Nōrā chātrī includes dance dramas based on other *jātaka* stories, later plays with contemporary themes, and the latest political or social gossip. Modern jazz instruments have been added to the orchestra, and modern folk songs are sung by dancers to attract young audiences. *Nōrā chātrī* developed into *lakhọ̄n chātrī* in eighteenth-century central Siam (now Thailand) and in the city of Bangkok, incorporating features from the central Thai folk dance drama, *lakhọ̄n nōk.*

Traditionally, *nōrā* dancers were all male, playing both male and female roles; nowadays, some female dancers are allowed to perform. Traditional *nōrā* costumes consist of golden headdresses *(sōēt),* wings, tails, long trousers covered with embroidered material, long golden fingernails, and ornaments worn on the bare chest. In the 1940s the government compelled the dancers to wear shirts and socks; this practice continues today.

There are twelve basic patterns of dance movements in *nōrā,* called *mǣ thā* ("mother movements") or *thā sipọ̄ng* ("twelve movements"). These are followed by more elaborate dance sequences, most of which imitate natural movements of birds and animals; some are very acrobatic and demanding.

An invocation and initiation ceremony usually precedes a *nōrā* performance. In this ceremony the master *nōrā* dancer and his disciples worship gods and the spirits of teachers, parents, and rulers to receive their blessings.

Then they start dancing for the gods to show their special talents and to please the supernatural beings. Master *nōrā* dancers are believed by villagers to possess healing powers, and they often perform shamanistic rites in the villages.

In 1955, Thailand's Department of Fine Arts produced a modernized version of *Manōhrā* in the form of *lakhǫn chātrī*, a dance drama in classical style combined with the original southern dance style of *nōrā chātrī*. The sensual sacrificial dance of *Manōhrā*—the *Manōhrā Būchayan*, as choreographed by Khunying Phaeo Snidwongsēnī and exquisitely danced by Bunnāk Swētanai—enraptured modern Thai audiences. It has since been regarded as a gem of Thai classical dance and a role much sought by young aspiring dancers.

Various choreographers have experimented in ballet and modern dance using *Manōhrā* as the theme. One noted example is a Thai-French classical ballet choreographed in 1962 by Geneviève Lespagnol Damond (from L'Opéra Monte Carlo and the Marquis de Cuevas Ballet) now a resident of Bangkok, to music by the present king of Thailand, Bhūmibol Adulyadēj. Another is a spectacular Chinese-Russian ballet by the National Troupe of the People's Republic of China, presented in Asia and Thailand in the late 1970s; it combines the dance style of a Thai tribe living in southern China with Russian ballet leaps and vigorous movements. During the 1990s, a female Japanese dancer and former student at the Withayalai Natasin (National Dance College of Thailand) started a Thai school of dance in Japan where *Manōhrā* is taught. She had previously danced the leading role in a production of *Manōhrā* with Bangkok's Thai National Troupe. This cross-cultural *Manōhrā* is significant to the expansion of *Manōhrā* dance beyond the borders of Thailand. *Manōhrā* thus remains a living tradition in Asian culture and extends its art and influence into the Western world.

[*See also* Thailand. *For discussion of other Thai dance dramas, see* Khōn *and* Lakhǫn.]

BIBLIOGRAPHY

Bot Lakhǫn Khrang Krung Kao: Ruang Nāng Manōhrā Lae Sangthǫng. Bangkok, 1965.

Damrong Rājānubhāp, H. R. H. Prince. *Tamnān Lakhǫn Inao*. Bangkok, 1964.

Ginsburg, Henry D. "The Manora Dance-Drama." *Journal of the Siam Society* 60 (1972): 169–181.

Jaini, Padmanabh. "The Story of Sudhana and Manohra: An Analysis of the Texts and Borobudur Reliefs." *Bulletin of the School of Oriental and African Studies* 29.3 (1966).

Miettinen, Jukka O. *Classical Dance and Theatre in South-East Asia*. New York, 1992.

Nicolas, René. "Le lakhon Nora, ou Lakhon chatri et les origines du théâtre classique siamois." *Journal of the Siam Society* 18 (1924): 84–110.

Rutnin, Mattani Mojdara, ed. *The Siamese Theatre*. Bangkok, 1975.

Rutnin, Mattani Mojdara. *Dance, Drama, and Theatre in Thailand*. Tokyo, 1993.

Rutnin, Mattani Mojdara. "Phatthanākān Khǫng Lakhǫn Thai Smai Mai." In *Arayatham Thai*. Bangkok, 1997.

Phinyo Chittham. *Nōrā*. Songkhlā, 1965.

Suthiwong Phongphaibun, ed. *Manōhrā Nibāt Chabap Wat Matchimawāt*. Songkhlā, 1970.

MATTANI MOJDARA RUTNIN

MANON. Dramatic ballet in three acts. Choreography: Kenneth MacMillan. Music: Jules Massenet, orchestrated and arranged by Leighton Lucas. Libretto: Kenneth MacMillan, based on *L'histoire du chevalier des Grieux et de Manon Lescaut* (1731) by Antoine-François Prévost d'Exiles. Scenery and costumes: Nicholas Georgiadis. First performance: 7 March 1974, Royal Opera House, London, Royal Ballet. Principals: Antoinette Sibley (Manon), Anthony Dowell (Des Grieux), David Wall (Lescaut), Derek Rencher (Monsieur G.M.).

Based directly on Abbé Prévost's novel, rather than on any of its operatic renderings, *Manon* portrays the story of corrupted innocence, sensual love, and rapacious greed in the extravagantly passionate dance language that has become MacMillan's trademark. Although he avoided Massenet's opera music for the work, commissioning a score comprised of selections from twenty-four Massenet sources, MacMillan gave the narrative a decidedly operatic structure, alternating intimate pas de deux of extraordinary invention and striking beauty with elaborate crowd scenes.

Framed by undistinguished dances for beggars, courtesans, guards, and noblemen, the heart of the story and the best of the choreography lie in the pas de deux. The major set pieces depict three stages in the doomed affair between the captivating, amoral Manon and the besotted Des Grieux: the innocent joy of their first meeting, the erotic and emotional profundity of their love, and the anguish of separation at Manon's death.

Having given herself eagerly to Des Grieux, Manon is introduced to Parisian society by her dissolute brother, Lescaut. Seduced by Monsieur G.M.'s wealth, for which she is even greedier than for love, she quickly enters a loveless liaison with him. Her spurning of Des Grieux goads him into cheating at cards to win enough money to regain her affection. When she is denounced as a prostitute and deported to Louisiana, he follows her faithfully, eventually killing the jailer who has raped her. Left with nothing but each other, they flee to the desert, where she dies, haunted by specters of her short-lived freedom from squalor.

MacMillan evoked Manon's capriciousness, Des Grieux's devotion, and Lescaut's decadence and charm with brilliant choreographic fluency, eliciting memorable characterizations from the original cast and offering unlimited challenges to subsequent interpreters. These have

MANON. Antoinette Sibley in the title role and Anthony Dowell as Des Grieux, photographed during the premiere performance. (Photograph © by Lesley E. Spatt; used by permission.)

included, in the title role, Natalia Makarova, Jennifer Penney, Lynn Seymour, Lesley Collier, Altynai Asylmuratova, Sylvie Guillem, and Viviana Durante. Anthony Dowell and David Wall later exchanged roles with some success, and Rudolf Nureyev danced Des Grieux. A performance with Penney, Dowell (Des Grieux), and Wall (Lescaut) was televised from Covent Garden in 1982 and is available on videocassette.

BIBLIOGRAPHY

Balanchine, George, with Francis Mason. *Balanchine's Complete Stories of the Great Ballets*. Rev. and enl. ed. Garden City, N.Y., 1977.

Laughlin, Patricia. "The Making of *Manon*." *Dance Australia* (February–March 1994): 18–21.

Maynard, Olga. "A Brief for *Manon*." *Dance Magazine* (August 1974): 46–52.

Newman, Barbara. *Antoinette Sibley: Reflections of a Ballerina*. London, 1986.

Reiter, Susan. "Making Do." *Dance View* 11 (Winter 1993–1994): 24–28.

Sulcas, Roslyn. "*Manon* Revisited." *Dance and Dancers* (February–March 1991): 18–20.

Thorpe, Edward. *Kenneth MacMillan: The Man and the Ballets*. London, 1985.

BARBARA NEWMAN

MANSINGH, SONAL (born 30 April 1944 in Bombay), Indian dancer and choreographer. The outstanding contemporary dancer Sonal Mansingh received her training in classical *bharata nāṭyam* from U. S. Krishna Rao and his wife U. K. Chandrabhaga Devi, acquiring a sound foundation in the Pandanallur school. She studied *abhinaya* (histrionics) with the legendary Mylapore Gauri Amma. Later she acquired proficiency in Oḍissi dance under Guru Kelucharan Mahapatra; she was praised for her mastery of the two dance forms.

Possessed of an inquiring mind, Mansingh extended the horizons of Oḍissi by choreographing new dance numbers in her repertory. Despite their imaginative nature, these works are firmly rooted in the neoclassical tradition of the genre and adhere to the aesthetic principles of Indian classical dance.

In recent years Mansingh has explored further, creating works such as *Draupadi* which incorporate the spoken word, singing, *abhinaya*, drama, and the use of properties and modern technology. Her *Panchakaya*, based on the stories of the five virgins of Indian mythology, combines *bharata nāṭyam* and Oḍissi techniques harmoniously. With her arresting stage presence, tasteful costumes, and fine technique, Mansingh articulates her ideas through both her dancing and her introductions, which make her complex creations accessible to the audience. She is also a gifted writer, and her choreographer's notes are informative to connoisseur and lay audience alike.

Mansingh heads the Centre for Indian Classical Dance in Delhi, where she offers training in classical *bharata nāṭyam* and Oḍissi as well as Sanskrit and music, and choreographs new works. Her honors include the Padmabhushan and Central Sangeet Natak Akademi awards.

In addition to her many responsibilities in Delhi, she performs regularly in festivals at home and abroad.

BIBLIOGRAPHY

Kothari, Sunil. *Bharata Natyam: Indian Classical Dance.* Bombay, 1979.

Kothari, Sunil, and Avinash Pasricha. *Odissi: Indian Classical Dance Art.* Bombay, 1990.

Pearcey, Eilean. "Sonal Mansingh." *Dance and Dancers* (August 1979): 35–36.

"Sonal Mansingh Dance Group." In *Eighth Festival of Asian Arts.* Hong Kong, 1983.

SUNIL KOTHARI

MANUALS. *See* Technical Manuals.

MANZOTTI, LUIGI (born 2 February 1835 in Milan, died 15 March 1905 in Milan), Italian dancer and choreographer. Of humble origin, Manzotti was attracted to the art of mime in adolescence. He was a devoted follower of dramatic actors, so he enrolled in the school of mime associated with the Teatro alla Scala's ballet school in Milan. He learned the rudiments from Giuseppe Bocci, advanced rapidly, and in just a few months was able to appear on stage at the Canobbiana in Milan in *L'Incoronazione di Corinna in Roma* by Pasquale Borri. He was an unqualified success and went on to perform at the Teatro La Pergola in Florence and the Teatro Alibert in Rome.

Manzotti was advised to devote his talents to choreography, and in 1858 he created his successful first ballet, *La Morte di Masaniello.* Manzotti's first major work was *Pietro Micca* (1872), in which he also performed; it was a patriotic ballet that aroused emotion and excitement in an audience caught up in the recent events of the Italian Risorgimento. Giovanni Chiti wrote the music, and Manzotti's contribution of the mime was decisive in terms of expression, especially in an emotional scene in which Pietro Micca, before sacrificing himself for love of country, bids farewell to his wife.

In the same year Manzotti was called by the choreographer Ferdinando Pratesi to be the leading mime in the ballet *Bianca di Nevers,* performed at Teatro alla Scala in 1875. In 1876 he put on a successful version of the ballet *Rolla,* which he restaged the same year at the Teatro Regio in Turin. The theater manager, Giuseppe Depanis, asked him to compose a major dance work especially for that theater. The result was *Sieba* (1878), with music by Romualdo Marenco, who was to become Manzotti's loyal collaborator, and scenes and costumes by Alfredo Edel, another valuable associate. This ballet clearly displayed the trend toward colossal productions that was to become a dominant characteristic of Manzotti, with large crowd scenes and endless scenic effects. The setting of *Sieba* is phantasmagoric, using amazing scenic machinery (including ships on stage) to evoke an archaic and fanciful Nordic era.

At this point, the choreographer was called on to explore the leading issues of an era in the full flush of Positivism—progress, civilization, discovery, and industrialization—while catering to the rather decadent taste for post-Romantic ballet. Manzotti launched his spectacular productions, presaging a vulgarization of theatrical dance. After tours in Italy and France, Manzotti settled in Milan where, on 11 January 1881 he gave the first performance of *Excelsior* at La Scala, a choreographic event replete with historical, allegorical, and fantastic allusions, in six parts and eleven scenes. It depicts a titanic struggle between progress and regression, from the age of the Spanish Inquisition to the cutting of the tunnel through Mont Cenis, showing the prodigious discoveries and technological advances of the imminent twentieth century. It was a veritable convoy of sets, not only displaying a sumptuous panorama of history and society but also serving as a vehicle of ideology. More than five hundred people took part in the first acts, led by Rosina Viale, Bice Vergani, Carlo Montanara, Carlo Coppi, and Cesare Coppini.

The triumph at La Scala (from January to October there were around one hundred performances) were followed by successes in Europe and America. In Paris *Excelsior* was staged by a new theater, the Eden, which was built specially for the occasion. In 1885 it was performed at Her Majesty's Theater, London, with Enrico Cecchetti and Giovannina Limido as the principal performers. After the turn of the century it was presented in various versions: one in 1914 filmed in part by Luca Comerio; one in Milan in 1916 by Renato Simoni; one in 1931 at the Teatro San Carlo in Naples, staged by Pratesi; and eventually in adaptations for marionette theater by the Piccoli di Podrecca and the Colla Brothers Marionettes. Other important revivals have included Florence in 1967; Milan in 1976; Rome in 1976; and the Teatro San Carlo in Naples in 1996.

Manzotti wanted to stage more colossal productions, and in 1886 he presented *Amor,* another collaboration with Marenco and Edel. *Amor* (an anagram for *Roma*) was an exaltation of love and brotherhood between peoples in the form of an epic poem that outdid even *Excelsior* in requiring an enormous deployment of crowds and animals. Manzotti then proceeded to conquer the field of athletics with his ballet *Sport* (1897) and, finally, at the turn of the century, embarked on a minor operetta, *Rosa d'Amore,* with music by Josef Bayer (1899).

Manzotti's productions would not be considered ballets in today's sense; rather, they were series of tales told through mime and choreography, interspersed with performances by a large corps of dancers performing in orderly rows. In the midst of these arrangements, Manzotti was able to give both solo dancers and duos an opportunity to display brilliant virtuosity in the academic tradition.

Many of Manzotti's choreographic innovations were later adopted and developed by twentieth-century musical theater. The rows of chorus girls in big revues and American musicals have their roots in the grand productions of Manzotti. The athletic and acrobatic devices used by choreographers such as Kasyan Goleizovsky, Bronislava Nijinska, Serge Lifar, Léonide Massine, and George Balanchine during the final phase of the Ballets Russes can also be found in Manzotti's *Sport*.

MANZOTTI. Spectacular ballets were staged in Milan in the late nineteenth century. Here, from *L'illustrazione italiane,* is the Orgy Scene from *Amor* (1886), choreographed and staged by Manzotti at the Teatro alla Scala. The enormous cast is arranged before the peristyle of the Temple of Venus in ancient Rome. (Dance Collection, New York Public Library for the Performing Arts.)

BIBLIOGRAPHY

Beaumont, Cyril W. *Complete Book of Ballets.* London, 1937.

Calo, Maria Amata. "L'Excelsior in pellicola." *Chorégraphie* 3 (Spring 1995): 46–78.

Cavazza, Serafino. *Romualdo Marenco e la vita novese dell'800.* Novi, 1957.

Grillo, Elena. "L'Italietta del Ballo Excelsior." *Chorégraphie* 3 (Spring 1995): 79–82.

Guest, Ivor. *The Divine Virginia: A Biography of Virginia Zucchi.* New York, 1977.

Lo Iacono, Concetta. "Manzotti e Marenco." *Nuova rivista musicale italiana* (July–September 1987): 421–446.

Lynham, Deryck. *Ballet Then and Now.* London, 1947.

Monaldi, Gino. *Le regine della danza nel secolo XIX.* Turin, 1910.

"Sala del Maggio musicale fiorentino." Program, Teatro Comunale, Florence, 1967.

Sasportes, José. "Virtuosismo e spettacolarità: La risposte italiane alla decadenza del balletto romantico." In *Tornando a Stiffelio: Atti del convegno internazionale di studi,* edited by Giovanni Morelli. Florence, 1987.

Testa, Alberto. "I Maestri danzanti." In *Il dramma* 11 (November 1994).

ARCHIVE. Teatro alla Scala, Milan.

ALBERTO TESTA
Translated from Italian

MAORI DANCE. The initial settlement of Aotearoa (the islands of New Zealand) may have been made by seafarers before 1000 CE. These were Polynesian voyagers, probably using outrigger canoes, from the Cook, Society, and Marquesas island chains. They found the islands' climates and natural resources markedly different from those of East Polynesia. Later waves of Polynesian migrants undoubtedly had to compete for land and defend it. Warfare, conquests, migrations, and interbreeding occurred, and Maori tribal identities developed. A tribe (or a federation of tribes) called itself a *waka* ("canoe" in their Malayo-Polynesian language), a reference to the common vehicle of migration to New Zealand.

Tribal art forms, especially the carving of wood, bone, or stone, developed a range of stylizations of the human body, head, and face. A protruding tongue is a frequent motif, suggesting an emphasis on the primary importance of speech, of oratory and song-text. The men's *haka taparahi* (ceremonial war dance) and *peruperu* (war dance) share the aesthetic principles of these carved images. Evidence of tribal differences can still be found today in the dance terms for hip, foot, and leg movements, as well as in the style of *ringa* (hand actions). The ownership of specific compositions is also determined by tribal affiliation.

Neither contact with the colonial European culture since the early nineteenth century nor increased contact among tribes has eliminated Maori tribal rivalries, which form the basis of regional and national dance competitions. New Zealand was visited by the Dutch explorer Abel Tasman in 1642, by British explorer Captain James Cook four times between 1769 and 1777, and by whalers, traders, and missionaries before becoming a British colony (with a settlement at Wellington) in 1840. Wars over settlers moving onto Maori lands continued until 1870.

Haka is the generic term as both noun and verb for a traditional dance and its accompanying song chant; the dancers are their own musicians. No extra singers or accompanying instruments are used. Maori dance uses dynamic emphases for rhythmic accents; early nineteenth-century European observers described the result as "posture dances." Those early accounts frequently translated *haka* as "war dance," although more perceptive writers recognized the highly demonstrative dance style as the favored Maori form of welcome, which issued challenge and greeting in tandem.

MAORI DANCE. Modern-day Maori, in various types of Western garb, still assemble for sessions of traditional dance. *(left)* Contemporary men are untattooed but dance in a menacing fashion with carved wooden spears and war clubs. *(above)* Backing the men's dance, Maori women sing and use hand gestures to elucidate the ceremonial poetry. (Photographs by Ken George; courtesy of Jennifer Shennan.)

The genuine war dance *(peruperu)* excelled as an expression of bellicose, massed defiance. It was performed with weapons when warriors faced their enemies in battle. According to the renowned *haka* exponent Arapeta Awatere (1975), the psychological aims of the *peruperu* were to demoralize the enemy "by gestures, by posture, by controlled chanting, by conditioning to look ugly, furious, to roll the fiery eye, to glare the light of battle. '*Peruperu*' is the intensive form of *peru*, anger [and also means 'eyebrow']."

The *tū ngārahu* was the traditional performance of the *haka* to divine the outcome of a pending expedition by a *taua* ("war party"). Any mistake or timing error was taken to be a bad omen; even today, a *haka* performance on a *marae* (ceremonial gathering place) retains this potential.

The *haka taparahi* is a male ceremonial dance used for many auspicious occasions. Although performed without weapons, it is threatening, aggressive, and sexually evocative. Even though tribal differences may influence the extent of their role, several women may serve as *manungangāhu* ("sentries" or "leaders") from the sidelines, exhorting the dancers through gesticulation and *pūkana* (exaggerated face and eye expressions). These *haka* are chanted, shouted, declaimed, and screamed; in fact, every physical action of the dance is intended to heighten the oral delivery.

The *wero* ("challenge") is a part of the rituals of welcome onto the *marae*. Performed by a single warrior (or sometimes by three in succession), the dance demands rigorous knowledge of the extensive vocabulary of stylized body movement, weapons manipulation, and control of balance. As a solo performance, the *wero* is not conceptualized as a dance genre, but outsiders to the tradition are likely to regard it in that light.

The *haka pōwhiri* is the traditional welcome performed whenever *manuhiri* ("visitors") are called onto the *marae*. In this chant dance, the senior women of the *tangata whenua* ("home people") wave branches of greenery from the front line of the assembled group to call the *manuhiri* forward.

Other chants—*ngeri, pōkeka,* and *pātere*—also incorporate stylized gestures, postures, and facial expressions. The timing in these performances, however, is spontaneous and by individual inspiration, as opposed to the uniformity and precision demanded in the various types of *haka*.

Poi dances, which are perhaps the most widely known Maori dances, are nowadays performed throughout New Zealand. Before European colonization, however, they were not known in every tribal area but were most developed in the Taranaki region. The *poi* is a ball made of *raupo* ("bulrush reed"), which is tied to a long or short cord and used singly or in pairs. The *poi* is swung and tossed at a range of speeds from very slow to very fast; percussive effects are obtained by slapping the ball with the hand or on other parts of the body.

Throughout Maori history, young people in particular favored dances for entertainment and courtship. These dances were described in many legends as well as in early European accounts.

The Maori also had the custom of adapting existing song texts to particular occasions or audiences by substituting suitable place or personal names. For example, the *waiata kori* or *waiata-a-ringa* (action song) is a twentieth-century dance genre that developed out of a borrowed European melody, a new text in Maori, and stylized gestures borrowed and modified from several traditional genres. Some of the original *waiata kori* are now associated with the circumstances of their composition. Today's genre has become quite sophisticated, with new *ringa* used to portray images in new song texts. The *waiata kori* are the main message-bearing vehicles of contemporary Maori composers. They are performed on many public occasions, including informal school or community gatherings and massed multitribal welcomes to visiting dignitaries.

According to Maori legend, dance originated in the quivering, shimmering heat waves that rise from the ground in the height of summer. The sun, Rā, has two wives—Hine Takurua in the winter, and Hine Raumati in the summer. It is Rā's offspring by Hine Raumati that can be seen dancing during the summer. This quivering motion is *wiri*, the energy or life force that permeates expressive movement and brings it to life as dance. Numerous Maori terms distinguish subtleties in the quivering motion that permeates all dance and chant forms—for example, the *wero*, and even *whaikōrero* (traditional oratory), with its fantastic rapid rotational vibration of the forearm through the wrist and hand. Without *wiri*, a dance performance would be considered invalid or dead.

Maori dances tend to be group rather than solo forms, a practice emphasizing their importance to family, community, and tribe. The overriding impact of all Maori dance performance comes from the performing group's solidarity. In the strongly rectangular formation of rank and file, the performers neither separate from one another nor move about during the dance; the starting position is close to, if not the same as, the ending position. Such a form epitomizes the expression "standing dance."

Maori society places a high value on dancing. In general, older performers are aesthetically preferred. Sexual imagery in the *haka*, for example, is impressively portrayed by mature, well-built men who are able to bend deeply or lunge with their entire body weight forward. Women of generous proportions may move with a graceful balance that is deceptively simple. Maori dance, then, is the group expression in song, poetry, and movement of mature and experienced adults, rather than a virtuosic display of youthful technique and skill.

[*For more general discussion, see* New Zealand; *for discussion on similar traditions, see* Polynesia.]

BIBLIOGRAPHY

Armstrong, Alan. *Maori Games and Hakas.* Wellington, N.Z., 1964.

Armstrong, Alan, and Reupena Ngata. *Maori Action Songs.* Wellington, N.Z., 1960.

Awatere, Arapeta. "Review of Mitcalfe 1974." *Polynesian Society Journal* 84.4 (1975).

Best, Elsdon. *Games and Pastimes of the Maori.* Wellington, N.Z., 1925.

Karetu, T. S.. *Nga waiata a Taua.* Wellington, N.Z., 1977.

Karetu, Timoti. *Haka! The Dance of a Noble People.* Wellington, N.Z., 1993.

McLean, Mervyn. *An Annotated Bibliography of Oceanic Music and Dance* and *Supplement.* Auckland, 1977–1981.

Shennan, Jennifer. "Approaches to the Study of Dance in Oceania: Is the Dancer Carrying an Umbrella or Not?" *Journal of the Polynesian Society* 90.2 (1981).

Shennan, Jennifer. *The Maori Action Song.* 2 vols. Wellington, N.Z., 1984–1985.

Shennan, Jennifer. "Maori Dance Terminology." *Dance Studies* 15 (1991).

Youngerman, Suzanne. "Maori Dancing since the Eighteenth Century." *Ethnomusicology* 18 (January 1974): 75–100.

JENNIFER SHENNAN

MARACCI, CARMELITA (born 1911 in Goldfield, Nevada, died 26 July 1987 in Hollywood, California), American concert dancer and teacher. Raised in California, Carmelita Maracci (also known as Carma Lita or Carmalita), already had a reputation as a dancer on the West Coast, when John Martin, dance critic of the *New York Times,* wrote in 1937, "It is rarely that a dancer so succeeds in combining exquisiteness with passion in making every movement possess not only surface finish but inner importance." Thereafter, for the next fifteen or so years, critics could not find enough superlatives. She was called a "tornado," one of the most electrifying performers of her generation. Sol Hurok described her as Isadora Duncan, Anna Pavlova, and Vicente Escudero in one. In *Dance to the Piper* (1952), Agnes de Mille left a vivid, poignant description of Maracci's theatrical power.

Although impeccably schooled in Cecchetti ballet technique, Maracci was most inspired by the Latin experience. Among her noted dances were *Live for the One Who Bore You* (later called *Viva Tu Madre,* to music of Nino Albanese, who often accompanied her in concert), in which the dancer became "the abstract of Spain," performing the entire dance while seated on a stool; *Another Goyescas,* a comic solo in which Maracci, an outstanding mime, took the roles of a man and a woman (in this, dance critic Walter Terry called her at once "malicious, humorous, and beautiful"); and a parody of historical ballet styles, *Carlotta Grisi: In Retrospect.* By turns, Maracci performed in toe shoes, in bare feet, in high heels—often using castanets—in a personal fusion of classical, modern, and Spanish dance. Her musical accompaniment ranged from Beethoven to Spanish folk. In everything, she was described as a "creator literally possessed by her creations."

Known for expressing her temperament both on and off the stage, Maracci referred to herself as a "political" performer. Clearly, she was an uncompromising individualist, touring the United States with a tiny concert group, performing one-night stands, never appearing on major stages, even in her rare New York appearances, despite overwhelming critical response. A dispute with Hurok, the most powerful impresario in America, was disastrous for her later career. Although she had been approached by Ballet Theatre when it was still in the process of formation, nothing came of it, and her sole affiliation with a major company was her mounting of a suite of her concert pieces, called *Circo de España,* for Ballet Theatre in 1951 (in which her own performance was termed "triumphant").

Around the mid-1950s Maracci ceased to appear onstage. Attaining near-legendary status as a teacher as well as a performer, she attracted such pupils to her Los Angeles studios as Cynthia Gregory, Allegra Kent, Donald Saddler, Christine Sarry, and Bill Carter.

BIBLIOGRAPHY

Armitage, Merle. *Dance Memoranda.* Edited by Edwin Corle. 2d ed. New York, 1946.

de Mille, Agnes. *Dance to the Piper.* Boston, 1952.

de Mille, Agnes. *Portrait Gallery.* Boston, 1990.

Knowles, Jocelyn W. "Lessons with Carmelita Maracci." *Dance Magazine* (May 1964): 38–41.

Maracci, Carmelita. "Close-Up of Modern Dance Today: Symposium." *Dance Magazine* (March 1958): 38–41.

Maracci, Carmelita. "The Symbolic and Psychological Aspects of the Dance." In *The Dance Has Many Faces,* 2d ed., edited by Walter Sorell. New York, 1966.

Page, Ruth. "Classwork: Carmelita Maracci." In Page's *Class: Notes on Dance Classes around the World, 1915–1980.* Princeton, N.J., 1984.

Perlmutter, Donna. "Carmelita Maracci." *Dance Magazine* (November 1987): 32–33.

FILM. The Dance Collection of the New York Public Library for the Performing Arts houses an 8½ minute black-and-white silent performance film shot at Jacob's Pillow (1954), containing fragments of *Carlotta Grisi: In Retrospect.*

NANCY REYNOLDS

MARCEL, FRANÇOIS (François Robert Marcel; died 1759 in Paris), French dancer, teacher, choreographer, and dean of the Académie Royale de Danse. Marcel's father, Jacques, and his brother, Jacques-Antoine, were also dancing masters.

In 1708 the two brothers' names began to appear on the programs of the Académie Royale de Musique. In June 1710, François Marcel became an overnight success at the premiere of *Les Fêtes Vénitiennes.* An unusual part in the fourth act of this ballet, that of a dancing master who performs and sings at the same time, had defeated the *premier danseurs*. The role fell to the relatively unknown Marcel, "who had somewhat of a voice and much inclination for singing" (Rameau, 1725).

From that time on, Marcel's career took off, and the public raved about his talents. In 1714 J. C. Nemeitz listed Marcel among the best dancers at the Paris Opera; the Parfaict brothers, in their history of the Académie Royale de Musique, described him as "the most beautiful figure in the world for the noble dancers." "His pas-de-deux with Blondy . . . forced the admiration," wrote Rameau (1725).

Perhaps the fullest account of Marcel's character, idiosyncrasies, and working habits is to be found in choreographer Jean-Georges Noverre's *Lettres sur la danse* (1803–1804). With his usual biting tongue, Noverre claims that the dancer's good looks were his greatest asset and the cause of his great popularity with the fair sex, who found him "charming, delightful, and divine." Noverre adds that "he sang agreeably, and he danced the minuet with an elegance, a self-assurance, and a self-satisfaction common to the demi-talents."

History has forever linked the name of Marcel with the dance that brought him fame: the minuet. He not only "danced it to its utmost perfection" (Gallini, 1762) but also refined it to such a degree that, by the end of the eighteenth century, the dance had become the measure by which all fine dancing was to be judged. "The old minuet was always danced on the tip of the toes," wrote Guillemin (1784). "Marcel gave the idea of lowering the heel while bending and gliding the step softly while rising."

"So many things in a minuet," Marcel is said to have mumbled while watching a student's performance (Despréaux, 1806). And indeed, with its precise footwork and pattern, its reverences, taking and leaving of hands, and handling of hats, gloves, fan, and train, the grand ballroom minuet of the eighteenth century contained in a capsule form the complete teaching of the dancing master and the complete training of the courtier. "When a man dances the minuet well," said Marcel, "he has graces in all his actions" (Despréaux, 1806).

Most European educators endorsed the statement, and Marcel's internationally famous studio became a hothouse where the graces of the century were nurtured. "Apply yourself diligently to Marcel's lectures," Lord Chesterfield repeatedly urged his son in 1751, for "if Marcel never produced a student for the stage" (Despréaux, 1806), he imparted to his pupils "a superior air of genteelness that distinguished them from the other masters' pupils" (Gallini, 1772). Noverre (1803–1804) reported in his *Lettres* that all the well-to-do foreigners, the women of the court, and the rich bankers' wives aspired to be taught by Marcel, and that the "reunion of the two sexes brought him a considerable income."

Elected in 1719 to membership in the Académie Royale de Danse, as a replacement for Jean Favier, Marcel rose to the rank of dean about 1752. On 25 November 1722 he married Jeanne La Comme. At his death in 1759, his only heir was his brother Jacques-Antoine, who gave up Marcel's inheritance for being "too onerous" (Archives de la Seine, 1760).

[*See also* Académie Royale de Danse.]

BIBLIOGRAPHY

Astier, Régine. "François Marcel and the Art of Teaching Dance in the Eighteenth Century." *Dance Research* 2 (Summer 1984): 11–23.

Chesterfield, Philip Dormer Stanhope, 4th Earl of. *Letters Written by the Late Right Honourable Philip Dormer Stanhope, Earl of Chesterfield, to His Son, Philip Stanhope, Esq.* 12th ed., enl. London, 1806.

"La danza." In *Libro di modo*. Madrid, 1796.

Despréaux, Jean-Étienne. *Mes passe-temps: Chansons suivies de l'art de la danse*. Vol. 2. Paris, 1806.

Gallini, Giovanni. *A Treatise on the Art of Dancing*. London, 1762. See in particular, "The Character of M. Marcel, a Celebrated Poem by M. Durat."

Guillemin. *Chorégraphie, ou L'art de décrire la danse*. Paris, 1784.

Mereau. *Réflexions sur le maintien et sur le moyen d'en corriger les défauts*. Gotha, 1760.

Nemeitz, J. C. *Séjour de Paris*. Paris, 1727.

Noverre, Jean-Georges. *Lettres sur la danse, sur les ballets et les arts*. 4 vols. St. Petersburg, 1803–1804.

Parfaict, François, and Claude Parfaict, *Histoire manuscrite de l'Académie Royale de Musique*. Paris, n.d. Manuscript located in Paris, Bibliothèque Nationale, fr. 12355.

Rameau, Pierre. *Le maître à danser*. Paris, 1725. Translated by Cyril W. Beaumont as *The Dancing Master* (London, 1931).

RÉGINE ASTIER

MARENCO, ROMUALDO (born 1 March 1841 in Novi Ligure, Italy, died 9 October 1907 in Milan), Italian composer and conductor. Marenco made an early debut as a composer with *Lo Sbarco di Garibaldi a Marsala* (Garibaldi's Arrival in Marsala) at the Teatro Doria in Genoa; he also played the violin and the bassoon during the performance. Afterward Marenco resumed his studies and toured as a violinist. In 1873 he became first violinist and director of ballet music at La Scala Ballet in Milan, serving in that capacity for seven seasons. He composed three operas and two operettas, but his name is most closely linked with the composition of ballets, particularly in collaboration with choreographers Luigi Manzotti, Antonio Pallerini, and Ferdinando and Giovanni Pratesi, on large historical or allegorical themes, providing many opportunities for lavish displays involving large numbers of dancers.

Marenco was closely involved in the great successes of Manzotti, including *Sieba* (Turin, 1878); the spectacular *Excelsior* (Milan, 1881), detailing the triumph of progress and light in the modern world; *Amor* (Milan, 1886); and

Sport (Milan, 1897). Although the music is often decried by modern critics, the sheer energy of Marenco's score for *Excelsior* has been an important element in the ballet's success (it was performed 103 times in its first year; in 1883 it opened the Eden-Théâtre in Paris, where it ran for nine months; and since 1967 it has been revived successfully in Florence and Milan).

The success of Marenco's music was based primarily on his rhythmic vitality, catchy tunes, and vivid orchestration, but his works were carefully molded to support the choreographic spectacle. Popular dance rhythms, such as the waltz, the polka, and the galop, added vivacity, making the scores readily acceptable to large audiences. In this Marenco was typical of the craftspersons, many of them Italian, who provided music for choreographical spectacle before Léo Delibes and Petr Ilich Tchaikovsky began to change the way composers regarded ballet music.

Some of the other more notable of Marenco's more than twenty ballets were Pratesi's *Armida* (Milan, 1868); Pallerini's *Amore ed Arte* (1870) and *I Setti Peccati Capitali* (1873), both of which premiered in Milan; Pratesi's *Tentazione* (Milan, 1874) and *Day-Sin* (Venice, 1880); Marzagora's *Dai Natha* (Milan, 1882); Pratesi's *L'Astro degli Afgan* (Milan, 1883); Raffaele Grassi's *Teodora* (Milan, 1889); and Pratesi's *Bacco e Gambrinus* (Milan, 1904) and *Luce* (Milan, 1905).

BIBLIOGRAPHY

Lo Iacono, Concetta. "Manzotti e Marenco." *Nuova Rivista Musicale Italiana* (July-September 1987): 421–446.

"Marenco, Romualdo." In *Enciclopedia dello spettacolo.* Rome, 1954–.

ARCHIVE. Walter Toscanini Collection of Research Materials in Dance, New York Public Library for the Performing Arts.

GEORGE DORRIS and ALBERTO TESTA

MARIANAS ISLANDS. *See* Melanesia.

MARIO, I KETUT (born c.1897 in Bali, died 22 March 1968), Indonesian dancer, choreographer, and teacher. The most celebrated innovator of twentieth-century Balinese dance, I Ketut Mario was regarded as the first exponent of the *kebiar* ("lightning") dance genre. Mario, as he was known to international audiences through the writings of Beryl de Zoete, Miguel Covarrubias, and John Coast, was born in Belaluan, Denpasar, and was raised by Anak Agung Ngurah Madé Kaleran. He was dancing as a Sisya (one of the female students of the sorceress) in a performance of the magic drama *Calonarang* in 1906 (just as the *rājā* of Tabanan and his followers committed suicide in a *puputan* ["the end"] while facing the overwhelming Dutch army). From an early age Mario cultivated his dancing, studying the *baris, Calonarang,* and *jauk* genres with I Salit and Pan Candri, both from Mengwi Gedé, Denpasar. Mario later moved to Banjar Lebah, Tabanan, which remained his home for the rest of his life.

Mario first heard a *kebiar* orchestra around 1919, when a gamelan group from the village of Bantiran, North Bali, performed at a cremation ceremony in Tabanan. The realization of his creation, *Kebiar Duduk,* derived strong motivation from the rich rhythms of these *kebiar* compositions. Jagaraga and Bungkulan are the North Balinese villages where this explosive musical style came into being; around 1914 performers in Jagaraga created a pure dance which intimately followed and reflected every nuance of the musical phrases, without any narrative element. Bungkulan had created a musical innovation by using the neglected *trompong*—a melodic gong-chime—as a featured melodic instrument.

By 1925 Mario had created the revolutionary *Kebiar Duduk,* a virtuosic dance in which a solo male dancer simultaneously played the *trompong.* His sinuous twirling of the instrument's mallets, used like batons, was a fanciful choreographic extension of his musicality. The squatting or sitting *(duduk)* position characterizing the dance was necessitated by the position used for playing the *trompong.* Whereas all previous Balinese dance had maintained an upright standing position, the *Kebiar Duduk* dancer circles the floor in a half-squatting position. Emphasis is on the torso, the body bends and circles as the arms and hands bend and circle in their own orbits around the head, and the face changes expression dramatically. The dancer holds a fan, which exaggerates the bending motions and gives the impression of a windmill turning.

Innovative as it was, *Kebiar Duduk* was not cut off from its sources. The dance reflected and fused movements from the *baris* and *légong keraton* traditional genres. Balinese artists say the dance is a *tari banci* (hermaphrodite role) because the quality of movement mixes *keras* ("strong") and *alus* ("refined") qualities.

Kebiar Duduk interpreted in dance a new musical form like a roller coaster of melody and rhythm. In earlier male dances, such as *baris* and *jauk,* the gamelan followed and reflected the movements of the dancer; Mario, however, helped create a new equilibrium, with each dance gesture dependent on the music. Mario's slender figure was considered perfect for interpreting every nuance of the gamelan's dynamics in an elegant combined-gender style. With Mario performing the dance himself, the form grew over time as his own choreographic and musical ideas informed each other. Although some Balinese classicists did not appreciate his departure from classical form, the work has endured and spawned generations of choreographic heirs.

Mario worked closely with the famed Gong Pangkung gamelan orchestra of Tabanan and later became associ-

MARIO. Dancers Ni Gusti Ayu Raka (left) and I Sampih (right) were the original performers in Mario's *Tumulilingan Mengisep Sari* (The Bumblebee Sips Honey), created for a 1952/53 tour of the United States and Europe. While perfecting this *kebiar*-style dance, Mario reduced it from its initial length of thirty minutes to fifteen minutes. It remains a popular work, although later generations of dancers have added their own variations and innovations. (Photograph from the Dance Collection, New York Public Library for the Performing Arts.)

ated with another ensemble, Gong Belaluan of Denpasar. An illness around 1931 forced him to stop dancing, but he continued to teach. By the early 1950s he was inactive artistically, living in Tabanan with his wife and working in a government office. The coaxing of John Coast and Anak Agung Gedé Mandra of Peliatan brought him back into choreographing and teaching. Twenty-five years after the creation of *Kebiar Duduk,* they asked Mario to create a dance based on the theme of a cockfight. This grew into a collaborative process of composition with the younger dancer I Sampih. The dance, *Sabungan Ayam,* is still performed in Peliatan's repertory.

In preparation for a 1952–1953 tour of the United States and Europe, Coast and Gedé Mandra asked Mario to create a dance on the theme of bumblebees in a garden. A young girl, Ni Gusti Ayu Raka Rasmin, and a young man, I Sampih, were chosen to perform it. The original *kebiar* music for this fifteen-minute work, *Tumulilingan,* was composed by Mario's colleague from Tabanan, Pan Sukra, for a different dance, but had apparently not been used. Once the gamelan of Peliatan had learned Pan Sukra's composition, Peliatan's musicians Gedé Mandra, Madé Lebah, and Gusti Kompiang rearranged and refined the composition further in rehearsal with Mario and the dancers. The complete name of the dance is *Tumulilingan Mengisep Sari* (The Bumblebee Sips Honey). It remains popular, although several innovations and variations have been created by succeeding generations of dancers. Mario accompanied the dance tour of Peliatan in 1952 and again visited the United States with the Gong Pangkung ensemble from Tabanan.

Two other dances created by Mario are *Kakelik* and *Ngejuk Capung,* both performed around 1967 by the Gong Pangkung of Tabanan. At that time I Gusti Ngurah Raka also performed a dance similar to *Tumulilingan,* and Mario offered a rare performance of *Kebiar Duduk.*

Throughout his life Mario was a government office worker at the Tabanan judicial court and in the landscape department. His artistic honors include the Dharma Kusuma from the governor of Bali, and the Wijaya Kusuma. I Mario's main artistic descendants were I Wayan Rindi of Lebah, Denpasar, and I Gusti Ngurah Raka from Tabanan, both of whom widely disseminated the *kebiar* dance aesthetic.

BIBLIOGRAPHY

Bandem, I Madé. "Kehidupan Mario Dalam Seni." Paper presented at Baliologi Conference, Denpasar, 1984.

Bandem, I Madé, and Frederik de Boer. *Balinese Dance in Transition: Kaja and Kelod.* 2d ed. New York, 1995.

Bandem, N.L.N. Swasthi Wijaya. "Dramatari Calonarang Di Singapadu." Master's thesis, Akademi Seni Tari Indonesia, 1982.

Baum, Vicki. *A Tale of Bali.* New York, 1938.

Covarrubias, Miguel. *Island of Bali* (1937). New York, 1956.

Coast, John. *Dancing Out of Bali.* London, 1954.

de Zoete, Beryl, and Walter Spies. *Dance and Drama in Bali* (1938). New ed. New York, 1973.

Dibia, I Wayan. "Arja: A Sung Dance-Drama of Bali; A Study of Change and Transformation." Ph.D. diss., University of California, Los Angeles, 1992.

Herbst, Edward. *Voices in Bali: Energies and Perceptions in Vocal Music and Dance Theater.* Hanover and London, 1997.
Holt, Claire. *Art in Indonesia, Continuities and Change.* Ithaca, 1967.
Lendra, I Wayan. "Bali and Grotowski; Some Parallels in the Training Process." *Drama Review* 35 (Winter 1991): 113–128.
McPhee, Colin. *A House in Bali.* New York, 1946.
McPhee, Colin. *A Club of Small Men.* New York, 1948.
McPhee, Colin. "Children and Music in Bali." In *Childhood in Contemporary Cultures,* edited by Margaret Mead and Martha Wolfenstein. Chicago, 1955.
McPhee, Colin. *Music in Bali.* New Haven, 1966.
McPhee, Colin. "Dance in Bali." In *Traditional Balinese Culture,* edited by Jane Belo. New York, 1970: 290–321.
Ornstein, Ruby. "Gamelan Gong Kebyar: The Development of a Balinese Musical Tradition." Ph.D. diss., University of California, Los Angeles.
Tenzer, Michael. *Balinese Music.* Singapore, 1992.
Vickers, Adrian. *Bali: A Paradise Created.* Singapore, 1989.

EDWARD HERBST

MARKÓ, IVÁN (born 29 March 1947 in Balassagyarmat, Hungary), Hungarian dancer, choreographer, and ballet director. Markó graduated from the State Ballet Institute at Budapest in 1967. He joined the Budapest Opera Ballet Company and danced such roles as Vatslav in *The Fountain of Bakhchisarai,* the Student in *The Miraculous Mandarin,* Albrecht in *Giselle,* and the title role in *The Wooden Prince.* He joined Maurice Béjart's Ballet du XXe Siècle in 1972 and for seven years danced principal roles in *The Firebird; Opus 5; Ninth Symphony; Nijinsky, Clown de Dieu,* and other ballets. In 1974, Hungarian television produced a film on his life and work.

In 1979, at the zenith of his career as a solo dancer, Markó went home to head a small group selected from the graduates of the State Ballet Institute, for whom he choreographed his first work, *Those Loved by the Sun,* to ten movements of Carl Orff's *Carmina Burana,* to be performed at their graduation. This piece opened the premiere of the new Győr Ballet, with two other works by Markó—*Dream Night,* five poetic scenes to Richard Wagner's "Wesendonk Lieder," and the polyphonic *Stations of the Cross* to music by Richard Strauss, a passionate survey of the world, including friends and lovers, art and science, birth and death. Another ballet, *Samurai,* consisted of three scenes of self-discipline that seemed to have been carved in ivory by the powerful talent of dancer Viktor Fülöp.

MARKÓ. With the Ballet du XXe Siècle, Markó appeared in the title role of Béjart's third version (1970) of *The Firebird.* (Photograph from the Dance Collection, New York Public Library for the Performing Arts.)

In subsequent years Markó evolved his own "total theater" in both form and content. *Ancestors and Descendants* (to Leonard Bernstein's Third Symphony) shows man roaming the globe eternally, questioning the power of God. In *The Moment of Truth,* subtitled *Ceremony and Ritual for F. G. Lorca,* Markó penetrates the universe of Federico García Lorca in a set of scenes that reflect the great Spanish poet's life and death. Markó's wanderings through the personal yet universal struggles of his heroes led him to three contradictory figures: Don Juan in *Don Juan's Shadow upon Us* (1982, music by Strauss), Faust, and Franz Kafka's Joseph K, who is called Mr. K/M in the ballet. In a set of impressive and spectacular scenes, Markó convincingly identifies himself with his heroes in their desire for pleasure, purity, and knowledge.

Markó has also produced two powerful cycles of dramatic visions of prehistory, myth, and religion in his *Taboos and Fetishes* (1982) and *Totem* (1984), both to musical collage and sound effects. The latter premiered together with a restaging of the former, serving as twin statements of how Markó, the artist, sees the ethical and social evolution of mankind. His vision of the universe came to full realization in *Glowing Planets,* produced in the Budapest Sports Palace in the summer of 1983 against a set of "space architecture" designed by his constant collaborator Judit Gombár.

The Miraculous Mandarin (1981, music by Béla Bartók) and *Seasons* (premiered in 1982 in the Theater an der Wien, Vienna, under the title *Haydn Getanzt*) are unlike most of his other works, for which the sound accompaniment is usually selected, arranged, and tailored to his message; these two display Markó's individual approach to preexisting music. His *Mandarin* is a revolt against the original text (but not against the score): here the Mandarin's appearance for his last struggle is replaced by his birth, and his murder by departure into life; the Girl is not a streetwalker but a mother protecting her son. In *Seasons,* by contrast, Markó faithfully interprets Franz Joseph Haydn's intentions and moods in the neoclassical idiom, interspersed with elements of character dances, setting the year's rhythms in a series of scenes going from and back to the calm whiteness of winter.

Markó uses a vast variety of props, including paraphernalia of daily life such as chairs, tables, beds, sticks, or a house with windows flung open. More symbolic props include huge crosses, undulating veils, shrouds, turning disks, and complicated scaffoldings as well as thrones and burning candles. These sets are born out of his and Gombár's rich imaginations and realized in János Hani's elaborate lighting, which may attempt to replicate stars, suns, and other celestial phenomena.

The young dancers under Markó master a high standard of classical technique and also seem to be capable of assimilating elements of modern styles. As a dancer, Markó is in perfect control of his body and can meet his own high technical choreographic requirements. Markó's second six years as head of the Győr Ballet brought about twenty productions, including three full-evening works: a dance drama, *Jesus, the Son of Man* (1986, music by Franz Liszt, Iannis Xenakis, and Dmitri Shostakovich); a set of historical pictures, *Bulgakov and the Others* (1987, music by Aleksandr Borodin, Igor Stravinsky, Sergei Prokofiev, and Shostakovich); and the dance play *On the Periphery of Life* (1990, music by Bartók and Zoltán Kodály). In addition, there was the pas de deux *Prospero* (1987, music by Franz Schubert).

Jesus, the Son of Man portrays a modern family gathering to celebrate the christening of a newborn and being slain by machine-gun fire. After some episodes from the Gospels, in a picturesque and spectacular rendering, Jesus (Markó) carries the cross, accompanied by children. In *Bulgakov,* a shabby and intimidated little Author (Markó) wishing to write the true history of Russia appears in a series of sarcastic vignettes inspired by Nikolai Gogol, Fedor Dostoyevsky, and Anton Chekhov, showing rulers from Ivan the Terrible to Stalin. In *On the Periphery of Life,* an Organ-Grinder (Markó) and an Angel are involved in twentieth-century dramatic scenes in suburban tenement houses, symbolizing a universal struggle for a better world.

Markó left the Győr Ballet in 1991 and went to Jerusalem, where his dance drama *The Wall* premiered with great success in 1992. Returning to Hungary in 1995 he staged a triple bill, "Dance for Life," for the Hungarian Festival Ballet (consisting of five solo dancers of the Opera Ballet and the corps de ballet of the Madách Theater) on the stage of the Congress Palace, Budapest. The first ballet, *Traveler of the Desert,* tells about love, the root of the three great religions; the last, *Dance for Life,* is a biographical confession about the eternal conflicts of master and disciples.

[*See also* Győr Ballet.]

BIBLIOGRAPHY

Fuchs, Lívia. "The Győr Ballet Abroad." *Hungarian Dance News,* no. 1 (1987): 20–21.

Hegyi, Gábor, and Iván Markó. *Szentföldi látomások: Keresztény-Zsidó párbeszéd.* Budapest, n.d.

Mészáros, Tamás. *Markó táncszinháza.* Budapest, c.1985.

Mészáros, Tamás. *The Lord of Dreams: The Dance Theatre of Iván Markó.* Translated by Myrtill Nádasi. Budapest, 1989.

Pór, Anna. "Önéletleirás táncban elbeszélve" (Life Story Told in Dance). *Táncművészet* 1 (1996): 18–19.

Stoop, Norma McClain. "'Budapest Knows Iván Markó.'" *Dance Magazine* (January 1973): 36–38.

Whittock, Patricia. "Iván Markó and Others." *The Dancing Times* (May 1989): 755–757.

GEDEON P. DIENES

MARKOVA, ALICIA (Lillian Alicia Marks; born 1 December 1910 in London), dancer. As a child Alicia Marks studied dancing at the Thorne Academy at the suggestion of her family doctor as an exercise to strengthen her legs and feet. Her precocious ability won her a first engagement in the pantomime *Dick Whittington* at the age of ten. Her acceptance as a pupil in the studio of Serafina Astafieva, a product of the Saint Petersburg Imperial Ballet School who had danced in the ballet at the Maryinsky Theater and in the early seasons of Serge Diaghilev's Ballets Russes, would prove to be important. Astafieva opened her London school in 1916; among her other pupils was Anton Dolin. Marks's exceptional gifts—ease of execution and a rare delicacy and grace—were so shaped by Astafieva that Diaghilev decided to engage the child for his company, and in January 1925 Alicia Marks, just fourteen years and one month old, became Alicia Markova and a member of the Ballets Russes.

Over the next few years, Markova's teachers included Enrico Cecchetti, Lubov Tchernicheva, and Nicholas Legat. Her early roles included Odette in a special performance of the act 2 adagio from *Swan Lake* (for which she was coached by Matilda Kshessinska and George Balanchine) and the Nightingale in the premiere of George Balanchine's *Le Chant du Rossignol* (1925). There followed a thorough grounding in the repertory as a member of the corps de ballet and as soloist, and the emergence of the "little English girl" as an artist capable of sustaining such principal roles as the heroine of *La Chatte,* Florine in the Bluebird pas de deux, and the pas de deux in *Cimarosiana.* Diaghilev had planned to feature her in *Giselle* as second cast to Olga Spessivtseva, but his death in August 1929 forced the Ballets Russes to close.

Markova thus found herself, at the age of eighteen, bereft of artistic home and artistic prospects. However, she was soon involved in the early activities of the emergent British ballet. At the Ballet Club, leading roles were created for her in Frederick Ashton's *La Péri* (1931), *Foyer de Danse* (1932), *Les Masques* (1933), and *Mephisto Waltz* (1934), in Antony Tudor's *Lysistrata* (1932), and in Ninette de Valois's *Bar aux Folies-Bergère* (1934). Markova was

MARKOVA. The title role of *Giselle* was unquestionably Markova's most famous portrayal. Here she is pictured in the Ballet Theatre production, c.1942, at a moment early in act 1. Poised *sur la pointe en attitude,* she is listening to discover the hiding place of her sweetheart, who has just knocked on the door of her cottage. Anton Dolin, as Albrecht, can be seen in the background, standing at the corner of the cottage and blowing kisses in her direction. Edwin Denby, dean of American dance critics, said that Markova's Giselle was the "greatest glory" of Ballet Theatre. (Photograph by Walter E. Owen; from the Dance Collection, New York Public Library for the Performing Arts.)

also an important figure in the Camargo Society, creating roles in de Valois's *Cephalus and Procris* (1931) and in Ashton's *Façade* (1931) and *High Yellow* (1932) and sharing performances of *Swan Lake,* act 2, with Spessivtseva. In *Façade* she danced the Polka—her final double *tour en l'air* has, it seems, never been duplicated—and took over the role of the Debutante from Lydia Lopokova.

By January 1932, Markova had also made guest appearances with the Vic-Wells Ballet in its initial season; she helped de Valois mount *Les Sylphides* and danced with Anton Dolin in *Swan Lake* act 2 before joining the company as its first permanent ballerina for the next season, 1932 to 1933. Ashton made *Les Rendezvous* (1933) for Markova and Stanislas Idzikowski, and de Valois created the roles of Alicia in *The Haunted Ballroom* (1934) and the Betrayed Girl in *The Rake's Progress* (1935) for her. Markova was also the inspiration for three major classic stagings mounted by Nicholas Sergeyev for the Vic-Wells company: *Giselle* (1 January 1934), *The Nutcracker* (30 January 1934), and four acts of *Swan Lake* (30 November 1934). In her portrayal of Giselle, Markova assumed a role that she made gloriously her own for the next three decades; in it audiences were to delight in her brilliant technique, that simplicity of means that was ever an ideal of her art, a prodigious lightness, and a rare sensitivity of musical understanding and phrasing. Markova's Giselle was unrivaled in delicacy and clarity of image, the tender, sensitive girl of the first act touching in her subsequent madness; the impalpable wili appearing in the night air like mist. In *The Nutcracker* Markova produced dancing as light as spun sugar. With the 1934 *Swan Lake* a notable Odette-Odile was born, with a purity of expression and classical restraint for the swan queen, and a penetrating, flashing malice for the enchantress.

In these classic roles Markova remained throughout her career a repository of correct steps and pure style: her exceptional memory retains the texts of ballets far more authentically in both step and manner than later generations of producers and dancers care to admit.

Markova had been intermittently partnered throughout this period by Anton Dolin, and their friendship, which dated from Astafieva's studio, and their complementary stage personalities, brought about the creation in the autumn of 1935 of a ballet company—the Markova-Dolin Ballet—which was formed to show ballet to the public throughout Britain on lengthy tours and in London seasons. The repertory included the classics already closely associated with Markova and Dolin, and also new works by Keith Lester, whose *Pas de Quatre* was the first to reveal Markova's uncanny physical and temperamental sympathy with Marie Taglioni, and by Wendy Toye (whose *Aucassin and Nicolette* was created for Markova and Dolin). In 1937, Bronislava Nijinska joined the company as choreographer and ballet mistress, staging *Les Biches (The House Party),* with Markova as La Garçonne, and *La Bien Aimée (The Beloved),* also for Markova.

After two successful years the company disbanded, and Markova accepted an invitation from Léonide Massine to join the Ballet Russe de Monte Carlo, of which he had become artistic director. Markova made her American debut with that company in 1938, in *Giselle,* with Serge Lifar as her partner. (Lifar also partnered Markova in this ballet during the 1938 London season; the various incidents of these performances are vividly told in Markova's *Giselle and I.*) Markova created roles in two of Massine's symphonic ballets: the Spirit of Air in *Seventh Symphony* and the Woman in *Rouge et Noir,* in both of which her partner was Igor Youskevich, and the Princess Turandot in his *Vienna—1814.* Her repertory with this company also included Michel Fokine's *Les Elfes, L'Epreuve d'Amour,* and *Petrouchka,* Balanchine's *Card Game, Swan Lake,* act 2, and *Coppélia.*

In the summer of 1941, Markova and Dolin ran a summer school at Jacob's Pillow, and this presaged the renewal of their partnership when, in the autumn of 1941, Markova joined Ballet Theatre (later called American Ballet Theatre), of which Dolin was a principal dancer. Markova was now able to work with Michel Fokine, who had restaged *Les Sylphides* for the company and worked extensively with Markova on its three ballerina roles. He also coached her in *The Dying Swan* and created the role of Floretta for her in *Bluebeard* (Mexico City, 1941), his last completed ballet. In 1942 Markova was also reunited with Massine, who staged his *Aleko* for Ballet Theatre, with Markova as Zemphira and George Skibine as her partner, and *Don Domingo,* in which Dolin was her partner. Dolin's version of *Pas de Quatre* and his *Romantic Age* were also created as vehicles for Markova. For Antony Tudor she danced Caroline in *Jardin aux Lilas* and in 1943 an unforgettable Juliet in his *Romeo and Juliet,* which was hailed as a portrait of extraordinary emotional intensity and sustained imaginative power. Markova's artistry at this time reached its maturity; Edwin Denby and John Martin, among many other critics, offer potent testimony to her greatness.

In 1944 Markova and Dolin were engaged by Billy Rose to join his revue *The Seven Lively Arts,* which also involved the diverse talents of Beatrice Lillie, Bert Lahr, and Benny Goodman. A special ballet score was needed, and at Markova's suggestion Igor Stravinsky was invited to compose *Scènes de Ballet,* which Dolin choreographed. In the mid-1940s Markova and Dolin were also seen in concert performances in such vast auditoriums as Lewisohn Stadium in New York and the Hollywood Bowl, and a newly formed Markova-Dolin Ballet made tours, with Markova seen in dances made for her by Nijinska, such as *Autumn Song* and *Mephisto Waltz.* Markova returned to Ballet Theatre, where she was seen as the Firebird in Adolph Bolm's staging (with designs by Marc Chagall, 1945), but when in 1946 Ballet Theatre made its first visit to Covent Garden, London, Markova and Dolin were contracted by Sol Hurok to bolster the New York season of the sadly declining de Basil Ballets Russes. John Taras, the company ballet master, made a *Camille* as a showcase for Markova and Dolin, with designs by Cecil Beaton. In the following year, Dolin made *The Lady of the Camellias* for Markova with their own troupe, and Jerome Robbins confected a hilarious *Pas de Trois* to music from Hector Berlioz's *Damnation de Faust* for Markova, Dolin, and André Eglevsky (Markova missed the first performances because of illness and was replaced by Rosella Hightower, though she later danced the role with mocking wit).

In 1948 Markova and Dolin were invited to appear with the Sadler's Wells Ballet at Covent Garden. After an initial gala performance of the *Don Quixote* pas de deux (danced two days after landing from a transatlantic crossing) the London audience was ecstatically reunited after five years with Markova and Dolin in *Giselle, Swan Lake,* and *Les Sylphides,* with the added excitement of seeing them for the first time in a full-length *Sleeping Beauty,* a performance memorable for Markova's jewel-like clarity and the grandeur of her manner and for Dolin's elegance and no-

MARKOVA. A studio portrait in costume as Marie Taglioni in *Pas de Quatre,* Jules Perrot's famous "dance for four" reconstructed by Keith Lester in 1936. In Anton Dolin's production, Markova danced this role with several companies. (Photograph by Cecil Beaton; used by permission of Sotheby's of Bond Street, London.)

bility. Markova and Dolin now embarked on extensive tours to Central America, the Philippines, Honolulu, Mexico, and major American cities, which confirmed their immense public following. They returned to London to give a series of dance recitals that were seen by eight thousand people each night in the Harringay Arena. There followed a tour of Britain, with supporting corps de ballet and soloists, in 1949. This ensemble was further to be expanded to form a permanent company, whose title, Festival Ballet, was chosen by Markova as a tribute to the forthcoming Festival of Britain. During the next two years Markova was seen in her major classical roles and in the Fokine repertory—both vital elements in winning the company its great popularity. David Lichine created *Symphonic Impressions* for Markova and Dolin in 1951. In the following year an injury obliged Markova to withdraw from the company, though she later returned to make guest appearances.

She spent the rest of the 1950s as a guest star, appearing with the Royal Ballet, American Ballet Theatre, and Le Grand Ballet du Marquis de Cuevas (with whom she danced August Bournonville's *La Sylphide* for the first time), and she made concert appearances with Milorad Miskovich as her partner. She also danced at the Teatro Colón (Buenos Aires), in Cuba, in Milan, at the Nervi Festival, at Jacob's Pillow, and with the Royal Winnipeg Ballet, everywhere revealing that refinement and lyrical clarity of style so sweetly and naturally allied to profound musical understanding. *Giselle* and *Les Sylphides,* ballets she had danced many hundreds of times, were still lit by new insights in performance, and new partnerships included the celebrated Giselles she danced with Erik Bruhn and Vladimir Skouratoff. She was seen in *Orfeo* (music by Christoph Willibald Gluck) at the Metropolitan Opera House, New York, in the Christmas entertainment *Where the Rainbow Ends* in London, and in *The Merry Widow* with Ruth Page's Chicago Ballet on Broadway. She made many television appearances in London and New York and was the first dancer to work with John Logie Baird in his experimental programs in London in the early 1930s. She danced to the *William Tell* ballet music (with Borge Ralov) in an Italian opera season in London, and joined Ram Gopal for a London season (1960) in which she appeared in a Rādhā-Kṛṣṇa duet.

MARKOVA. A studio portrait of Hugh Laing and Markova in Léonide Massine's *Aleko* (1942). (Photograph by Carl Van Vechten; used by permission of the Estate of Carl Van Vechten.)

In January 1963 Markova announced her retirement from the stage, and in that year her services to ballet—already noted in the award of the Commander of the Order of the British Empire—were further recognized with the Dame of the Order of the British Empire. At this time she accepted the position of director of ballet at the Metropolitan Opera House, New York, which she retained until 1969. Two years later she became professor of ballet and the performing arts at the University of Cincinnati. She returned to London in 1974. After her retirement from dancing Markova made many stagings of ballets: she produced the dances in operas at the Metropolitan Opera House and recreated ballets in which she had starred, among them *Les Sylphides* (for London Festival Ballet; Northern Ballet Theatre; the Australian Ballet; the Royal Ballet School; and the Royal Winnipeg Ballet) and *Le Carnaval* (for Niagara Frontier Ballet). She is a governor of the Royal Ballet and a regular guest teacher at the Royal Ballet School and at the annual Yorkshire Ballet Seminars held at Ilkley. Of her many television appearances, the latest was a series of master classes for the British Broadcasting Corporation (BBC-TV) on certain of her greatest roles. Her seventieth birthday in 1980 was marked by a celebratory documentary shown by BBC-TV.

BIBLIOGRAPHY

"The Alicia Markova Story" (parts 1–4). *Ballet Today* (August–November 1955).

Anthony, Gordon. *Markova.* London, 1935.

Beaumont, Cyril W. *Markova.* London, 1935.

Dance and Dancers (January 1955).

Dolin, Anton. *Markova: Her Life and Art.* London, 1953.

Fay, Anthony. "Alicia Markova: Her Appearances in America." *Dance Magazine* (June 1977): 47–55.
Fisher, Hugh. *Markova.* London, 1954.
Lidova, Irène. "Alicia Markova." *Les Saisons de la Danse,* no. 73 (April 1975).
Markova, Alicia. *Giselle and I.* London, 1960.
Markova, Alicia. *Markova Remembers.* Boston, 1986.
Nemenschousky, Léon. *A Day with Alicia Markova.* Translated by Margaret McGregor. London, 1960.
Vaughan, David. "Conversations with Markova." *Dance Magazine* (June 1977): 56–62.

CLEMENT CRISP

MARKS, BRUCE (born 31 January 1937 in Brooklyn, New York), American dancer, choreographer, and administrator. Although most of his early training and performing were in modern dance, Marks achieved success as a ballet *danseur noble* of particularly expressive power. As an administrator he has been committed to preserving classical traditions as well as encouraging innovation.

An early talent for gymnastics led Marks to study dance and attend the High School of Performing Arts in New York City, where he concentrated on modern technique. He began his professional career while still in school, creating the role of the Son in Pearl Lang's *Ironic Rite.* He continued to perform with Lang, later becoming her partner and creating leading roles in her works.

After a year at Brandeis University, he began studies at the Juilliard School (New York) with Margaret Craske and Antony Tudor. The following year he continued his studies with them at the Metropolitan Opera Ballet school. His friendship with Tudor would be long-standing, and he later danced in many Tudor works, including *Pillar of Fire* and *Lilac Garden.* In 1956 he joined the Metropolitan Opera Ballet as a member of the corps and in 1958 was promoted to the rank of soloist.

In 1961 Marks joined American Ballet Theatre as a lead dancer, performing in George Balanchine's *Theme and Variations* and in the company premiere of Harald Lander's *Études.* He performed with the company until 1971, dancing a wide repertory that included both classical and modern works. He danced the roles of the Moor in José Limón's *The Moor's Pavane* and Jean in Birgit Cullberg's *Miss Julie* and created the leading role in Eliot Feld's *At Midnight.* He won particular acclaim for his performance as Siegfried in *Swan Lake.*

While with American Ballet Theatre he performed as a guest artist with the Royal Swedish Ballet (1963–1964), the London Festival Ballet (1965), and Eliot Feld's American Ballet Company (1969). In 1966 he began appearing as a guest artist with the Royal Danish Ballet and in 1971 joined that company as a principal dancer, the first American to do so.

In 1976 Marks became artistic co-director with his wife, Toni Lander, of Ballet West in Salt Lake City, Utah, and was promoted to director in 1978. He was responsible for the growth of the company and its repertory, including the 1985 revival of *Abdallah,* a long-missing work of August Bournonville.

In June 1985 Marks was appointed artistic director of the Boston Ballet, where he sponsored the Discovery Festival to introduce modern dance works to the repertory; a choreographer's competition to encourage new ballet choreography; and in 1990 a staging of *Swan Lake* by Konstantin Sergeyev that represented the first full-scale collaboration between Soviet and American ballet artists. He also led a six-year campaign to build a state-of-the-art studio, performance space, school, and headquarters for the Boston Ballet.

Marks began his choreographic career in 1970 with the creation of *Clockwise,* for Eliot Feld's company. He has created more than thirty works, some of which have been set by more than one company, and has served in a number of national and international administrative positions. He created the National Choreographic Project for the National Endowment for the Arts and served on its Dance Panel from 1979 to 1981 (as chairman in 1981). He has also served as chairman of the International Performing Arts Touring Committee (1979) and was a member of the USA-USSR Joint Committee on Theatre and Dance Studies and chairman of Dance/USA and of the Jackson International Ballet Competition.

BIBLIOGRAPHY

Goodman, Saul. "Brief Biography: Bruce Marks." *Dance Magazine* (December 1961): 64–65.
Marks, Bruce. "The Male Image." *Dance Perspectives,* no. 40 (Winter 1969).
Mason, Francis. "A Conversation with Bruce Marks." *Ballet Review* 22 (Winter 1994): 41–59.
Newman, Barbara. *Striking a Balance: Dancers Talk about Dancing.* Rev. ed. New York, 1992.

KATY MATHESON

MARO AKAJI (born 23 February 1943 in Kanazawa, Ishikawa Prefecture, Japan), *butō* performer and choreographer. Maro became an actor of the Jokyo ("situation") Theater under artistic director Karajuro, in 1967. In 1972, Maro established Dai Rakudakan (Great Camel Battleship), intending to create new theatrical art in which drama and *butō* would form a harmonious whole. The company presented its inaugural dance, *Dance Anzu Machine* that same year. Besides Maro, the original members included Amagatsu Ushio (later with Sankai Juku), Osuga Isamu (later of Byakkosha, which dissolved in 1994), Tanigawa Toshiyuki, Bishop Yamada (of the Hokuho *butō* school), Murobushi Ko (who later moved to Germany with his Butō-ha Sebi company), and the late Tanimura Tatsuro (of Dance Love Machine). Dai Rakudakan performed *Phallic Mythology* in 1973 and *The Goldfish of Divine Play* in 1975; the company's dances featured fierce, large-scale props and emphasized the wild beauty of male bodies. The company was invited to perform at the American Dance Festival and at the Festival d'Avignon in France in 1982 and toured in the United States in 1987; in 1991 it performed in Melbourne, Australia.

Dai Rakudakan's dance was strongly influenced by Hijikata Tatsumi. Its pieces are always group dances of five or more *butō* performers. Maro's subject matter is often evil spirits, and he emphasizes the fictionality of staged dance. For example, *The Tale of the Supernatural Sea-Dappled Horse* (1982) deals with a man (Maro) who wanders from place to place in search of a legendary horse in order to inscribe "a mark of the sea" on it; on his way he encounters an evil spirit and a desolate landscape. Other dancers play the roles of spirits and mourners. When it was performed at the outdoor theater in Avignon in 1982, a storm caused seventy panels suspended on a high wall to sway, effectively creating an atmosphere of a world of death—in which dancers danced transcendentally. In 1992, in commemoration of the company's twentieth anniversary, it performed *Ugetsu—Hell Rising to Heaven*. The dance, in which hell ascends to heaven, strongly reflects Maro's philosophy of embracing every kind of evil.

BIBLIOGRAPHY

Anderson, Jack. "New York Newsletter." *The Dancing Times* (June 1987): 778–779.

Horton, Charles. "Reports: Durham." *Ballet News* 4 (November 1982): 37.

"Japan's 'Dairakudakan.'" *Attitude* 1.4 (1982): 3–5.

Trucco, Terry. "When West Meets East." *Ballet News* 4 (July 1982): 10–15.

ARCHIVES. Dance Collection, New York Public Library for the Performing Arts.

HASEGAWA ROKU
Translated from Japanese

MARSHALL ISLANDS. *See* Micronesia.

MARSICANO, MERLE (Merle Petersen; born c.1920 in Philadelphia, died 1983 in New York), American dancer and choreographer. Marsicano studied tap dancing with Edna Wroe, ballet with Ethel Phillips and Mikhail Mordkin, Spanish dance with Angel Cansino, and modern dance with Ruth St. Denis and Martha Graham. Her style, however, was uniquely her own, and she remained steadfast in her belief that each dancer-choreographer must discover her own way of moving.

Marsicano made no use of floor movements; she neither jumped nor turned. Instead, she made time stand still as she wove patterns with her feet, a subtly flexible torso, and eloquent arms. She seemed to will the air to become heavy or weightless as she passed through it. Her early solos, beginning in the 1950s and including *Figure of Memory, Fragment of a Greek Tragedy,* and *Time Out of Season,* were to scores by contemporary American composers; she also used jazz (for example, *Gone!* to music by Miles Davis) to extraordinary effect.

In later years Marsicano trained a small group of women for whom she created *Disquieting Muses, They Who Are Not Named, The Garden,* and other works. Arlene Croce (1977) wrote of her performances, "It may be the most economical yet the most luxurious dance theater we have." She left no school, nor would she have wished to.

BIBLIOGRAPHY

Como, William. "Peril and Delight." *Dance Magazine* (May 1965): 25–27.

Croce, Arlene. "The Theatre of Merle Marsicano." In Croce's *Afterimages.* New York, 1977.

Marsicano, Merle. "The Dance . . . Further Thoughts." *Dance Observer* (April 1958): 53.

Marsicano, Merle. "Thoughts on Dance." In *The Dance Has Many Faces,* edited by Walter Sorell. 2d ed. New York, 1966.

P. W. MANCHESTER

MARTIAL ARTS. *For discussion of martial arts in Asia, see* Asian Martial Arts. *See also* China, *overview article;* Chhau; India, *article on* History of Indian Dance; Kathakaḷi; *and for parallel traditions in Thailand, see* Khōn. *For stylized self-defense as dance in Indonesia, see* Indonesia, *article on* Javanese Dance Traditions *and* Pencak.

MARTIN, JOHN (born 2 June 1893 in Louisville, Kentucky, died 19 May 1985 in Saratoga Springs, New York), American dance critic and theorist. After a brief career in acting and service in the U.S. Army, Martin worked as director and press agent for various theater enterprises, becoming especially interested in the work of the Russian actor, director, and drama teacher Konstantin Stanislavsky (1863–1938), a concern that was to have a considerable influence on his attitude toward dance. In 1927 Martin was asked to write dance reviews for the *New York Times* by the paper's music critic, Olin Downes, who wanted him to help out for six months. Martin retired from the *Times* in 1962; by then he had witnessed not only the birth of a new American dance form but had been instrumental in winning a devoted public for it.

The first full-time dance critic on a major American newspaper, Martin was more than a reviewer; he was a crusader. Most important among his causes was the new modern dance. Sensing the expressive principles of

Stanislavsky in the work of such young choreographers as Martha Graham and Doris Humphrey, he determined to convince a largely indifferent audience of their importance. Both choreographers said later that they could not have succeeded to the extent they did without Martin's support.

Martin described what he called "expressive dance" as starting from life instead of from fixed convention; it was subjectively created movement. The kinds of movement could be vastly different. To Martin, modern dance was not a technique; it was a point of view. The choreographer arouses emotions in the audience to change their feeling about something, to extend the range of their personal experience. Martin had a mission: to "open the eyes" of the audience, to get them to see the significance of this new dance that was often not pretty and that often told them truths they did not especially want to hear. He won.

Another situation that he started to fight when he first went to the *Times* was the state law that prohibited Sunday concerts. The law was repealed in 1932.

While he promoted his ideas in writing, from 1931 to 1934 Martin also presented an important series of lecture-demonstrations at the New School for Social Research; from 1934 to 1939 he also taught at the Bennington School of the Dance in Vermont.

In addition to his reviews and the important "think" pieces that he wrote for the Sunday paper, Martin was also the author of several books: *The Modern Dance* (1933), *Introduction to the Dance* (1939), *The Dance* (1945), and *World Book of Modern Ballet* (1952). He received the Capezio Award in 1969.

In later years Martin was accused by some of betraying the cause of modern dance, for he began to praise the work of George Balanchine and the New York City Ballet as he became more critical of some expressionist choreographers. But the scene had changed. The ideas of modern dance had become accepted; his cajoling was no longer so necessary. Further, many of the younger choreographers had become more concretely dramatic, whereas Martin had insisted that modern dance should present not a literal rendition of an experience but its essence.

Martin's philosophy of criticism remained the same. Criticism, he asserted, was not a science; a critic simply reacted to what was presented. Martin went to the theater, he said, "like a sponge—I just sit there and let it go through me." He wanted to be "alert, but open, with no preconceptions and no expectations in particular." Of his reviews, Doris Hering wrote in *Dance Magazine* that they were "literate without being highbrow, capable of enthusiasm without oozing nectar, sensible without being matter-of-fact."

BIBLIOGRAPHY

Martin, John. *World Book of Modern Ballet.* Cleveland and New York, 1952.

"Walter Terry Interviews John Martin." *Dance Magazine* (January 1956): 36–39.

ARCHIVES. Back issues of the *New York Times,* 1927–1962, contain reviews and essays by Martin.

SELMA JEANNE COHEN

MARTINS, PETER (born 27 October 1946 in Copenhagen), Danish-American ballet dancer, choreographer, teacher, and company director. When Peter Martins was accepted, at the age of eight, into the Royal Danish Ballet School, he had already been studying social dancing for three years. Photographs show him as a boy of angelic good looks, erect carriage, and modest deportment. In his third year as a student at the Royal Ballet School, he began the course of technical study laid down in the nineteenth century by August Bournonville, which forms the core of the school's curriculum, and by the time he was twelve he had begun to study with Stanley Williams, whom Martins considers to have been a formative influence as well as a continuing support throughout his career. [*See the entry on Williams.*]

In 1964, at age eighteen, Martins made an unofficial debut with the Royal Danish Ballet while he was still an apprentice, dancing alongside Erik Bruhn as one of the two male leads in *Garden Party,* a ballet by Frank Schaufuss. Two weeks later, he made his scheduled debut in *Moods,* a new work choreographed by Hans Brenaa. In 1967, he was named a *solodanser* (soloist, or principal dancer), one of the youngest in the company's history. In the spring of that year he danced the title role in George Balanchine's *Apollo* for the first time, having been coached by Henning Kronstram, and during the following summer he danced the role several times with the New York City Ballet, which was performing at the Edinburgh Festival. As a last-minute replacement for an injured Jacques d'Amboise, he danced opposite Suzanne Farrell and received coaching from Balanchine himself. Both Farrell and Balanchine were to play important parts in his future. For the next three years, Martins performed as a principal dancer of the Royal Danish Ballet and as a guest artist with New York City Ballet. In mid-1970, he joined New York City Ballet as a permanent member.

Because of Martins's tall stature and elegant bearing, Balanchine saw him as a *danseur noble,* and as an ideal partner for Suzanne Farrell. He cast the handsome blond Dane as a courtly cavalier in numerous works: *The Nutcracker, Symphony in C* (first and second movements), the *Diamonds* section of *Jewels, Swan Lake, Ballet Imperial,* and *Liebeslieder Walzer.* Jerome Robbins used him as the Boy in Green for his *Dances at a Gathering* during its premiere year, 1969, and then created parts especially for him in *In the Night* (1970) and *The Goldberg Variations* (1971).

MARTINS. As Franz in Balanchine's production of *Coppélia,* Martins had an unusual opportunity to display his sly wit and boyish charm as well as the elegant line and soaring jump depicted here. (Photograph © 1976 by Linda Vartoogian; used by permission. Choreography by George Balanchine © The George Balanchine Trust.)

The 1972 Stravinsky Festival at New York City Ballet marked the beginning of a new phase in Martins's work with Balanchine. The ballet master cast him in two new ballets, *Violin Concerto* and *Duo Concertant.* As roles in other Balanchine works followed, Balanchine's casting of Martins became more diversified. In 1974 Martins began to perform a sly, foxy Franz in *Coppélia.* In 1976 Balanchine showed Martins's various facets in a single ballet: in the first part of *Union Jack,* Martins was the straight-spined leader of the Menzies clan of high-stepping Scotsmen; in the last part, he was a devilish, cigarette-chewing jack-tar doing a rubber-legged hornpipe.

In 1977 Martins choreographed his first ballet, *Calcium Light Night,* a pas de deux for Heather Watts and Daniel Duell set to music by Charles Ives. After its successful premiere with Martins's own group, Balanchine saw it and encouraged Martins to do more choreography for the New York City Ballet and for its affiliate, the School of American Ballet. (*Calcium Light Night* not only went into the company repertory as an independent work but also appeared as a section of Balanchine's *Ivesiana* for a time in 1978.) Other early works by Martins were *Rossini Pas de Deux* (1978), *Sonate di Scarlatti* (1979), *Eight Easy Pieces* (1980), and *The Magic Flute* (1981). For the New York City Ballet Tchaikovsky Festival in 1981, he made *Symphony No. 1,* and for the Stravinsky Centennial Celebration in 1982 he made *Piano-Rag-Music* and *Concerto for Two Solo Pianos.* During these years, he also created dances for other ballet companies, for opera companies, for ice skaters, and for musical comedies. His *Tango-Tango* (1978), set to two tangos, one by Joseph Gade and one by Igor Stravinsky, and danced by ice skaters JoJo Starbuck and John Curry, was a memorable number on the program of Curry's *Ice Dancing* tour in the late 1970s.

In addition to performing and choreographing, Martins had begun teaching a company class for New York City Ballet in 1976. In the autumn of 1981 he was appointed to the roster of the company's ballet masters, joining Balanchine, Robbins, and John Taras. In mid-March 1983, when Balanchine was seriously ill, Martins was appointed ballet master in chief, alongside Robbins. After Balanchine's death in April 1983, Robbins limited his responsibilities to choreography, and the overall direction of the company fell to Martins, as did the chairmanship of the faculty at the School of American Ballet. In June 1983, Martins announced that he would retire from performing at the end of the year with a performance of the cavalier to the Sugarplum Fairy in *The Nutcracker.* The following December, he and Suzanne Farrell made their last official appearance together in the one-thousandth performance of Balanchine's famous production of this Yuletide favorite. [*See the entry on Farrell.*]

When Martins first appeared as a guest artist with the New York City Ballet, the elegance, precision, and control of his dancing made him an immediate standout. The longer he worked with the company, the more the coolness and correctness of his manner mellowed. The classical vocabulary with which his body communicated became richer, more inflected. He became more a part of Balanchine's aesthetic even though he continued to remain somewhat apart from Balanchine's dancers. Through his work with New York City Ballet—especially in roles in such later Balanchine works as *Tzigane* (1975), *Chaconne* (1976), *Vienna Waltzes* (1977), and *Robert Schumann's "Davidsbündlertänze"* (1980)—Martins's dancing and partnering set standards for a whole generation of classical dancers. The purity and energy that Martins names as paramount concerns in classical dancing readily describe his own work.

As a choreographer, Martins continued on the course set for him by Balanchine. In an interview with Jonathan Cott, Balanchine spoke of ballet mastering as follows: "To be a choreographer, you must be a great dancer—maybe not *great,* but better than the dancers who come to you. . . . You have to invent and teach these people something they don't know" (*Rolling Stone,* 12 May 1983). When he chose to groom Martins as ballet master for New York City Ballet, Balanchine acted on these beliefs, and Martins has tried earnestly to live up to them. Notable among his numerous works are *A Schubertiad* (1984), *Songs of Auvergne* (1986), *Les Gentilhommes* (1987), and *Barber Violin Concerto* (1988). Perhaps most successful are his works using music by contemporary composers, including *Ecstatic Orange* (1987), set to music by Michael Torke, and *The Chairman Dances* (1988) and *Fearful Symmetries* (1990), both set to music by John Adams.

Martins became sole head of the New York City Ballet in 1990. In addition to creating new ballets regularly, he has coordinated special concentrations of new works, such as the American Music Festival (1988) and the Diamond Project (1992 and 1994). In 1990 he produced a festival of Robbins's ballets, and in 1993 he oversaw an eight-week Balanchine Celebration, which presented seventy-three of Balanchine's ballets in repertory, generally presented in chronological order. He has also exhibited a flair for restaging classics of the nineteenth-century repertory. He staged Bournonville's *La Sylphide* for the Pennsylvania Ballet in 1985 and for the San Francisco Ballet in 1986. In 1991, for the New York City Ballet, he directed a staging "after Marius Petipa" of *The Sleeping Beauty,* which reduced, by way of internal cuts, the three-act-plus-prologue scheme to a two-act production. For the fall of 1996 he staged a complete production of *Swan Lake* for the Royal Danish Ballet.

[*See also* New York City Ballet.]

BIBLIOGRAPHY

Caras, Steven. *Peter Martins: Prince of the Dance.* New York, 1986.

Gradinger, Malve. "Faith in the Power of Classical Ballet." *Ballett International/Tanz Aktuell* (December 1995): 32–35.

Greskovic, Robert. "New York City Ballet: A Year and Its Dancers." *Ballet Review* 7.4 (1978–1979): 1–107.

Gruen, John. "Martins Talks Back: Peter's Perspectives." *Dance Magazine* (November 1987): 38–42.

Gruen, John. *People Who Dance: Twenty-two Dancers Tell Their Own Stories.* Princeton, N.J., 1988.

Martins, Peter, with Robert Cornfield. *Far from Denmark.* Boston, 1982.

Newman, Barbara. *Striking a Balance: Dancers Talk about Dancing.* Rev. ed. New York, 1992.

Paltrow, Scot J. "Peter Martins: Off-Balance." *Los Angeles Times Magazine* (6 December 1992).

Trustman, Deborah. "Peter Martins, Prince of the Dance." *New York Times Magazine* (9 November 1980).

ROBERT GRESKOVIC

MARTYN, LAUREL (Laurel Gill; born 23 July 1916 in Toowoomba, Queensland), Australian dancer, teacher, choreographer, and director. Martyn first studied dance in Brisbane, Queensland, then in London, where she won the prestigious Adeline Genée competition. Her choreographic career also began in London. She won second prize in the Pavlova-Casket choreographic competition with her ballet *Sigrid,* which she later remounted in Australia. A member of Sadler's Wells Ballet from 1935 through 1938, under Ninette de Valois, she returned to Australia in 1938 and joined Edouard Borovansky's infant company as ballerina in 1940, dancing the title role in his ballet *Vltava.* Martyn continued with his company until 1945, when she left with some other dancers to form the Victorian Ballet Guild, presenting ballets in Melbourne, interstate, and New Zealand for thirty years.

Beginning largely with intimate works presented for the Melbourne Ballet Club, the company moved to larger works, including the first Australian production of *Sylvia,* choreographed by Martyn. When the company began to receive official grants, it changed its name to Ballet Victoria and became more ambitious. Jonathan Taylor was invited from the Ballet Rambert to produce ballets, including *Star's End,* which he created for the company in 1975.

The company scored a coup when it signed Mikhail Baryshnikov and Natalia Makarova to visit Australia; their style and technique drew enthusiastic audiences both in Melbourne and on tour. Attempting to repeat this triumph with Valery and Galina Panov, the company lost heavily in New Zealand, went into receivership, and was disbanded in 1976. Garth Welch, who had been appointed deputy to Martyn, continued to direct the Ballet Victoria school until the end of the year.

As a local company, the Ballet Guild had been a valuable and progressive organization, producing more than ninety ballets, most of them new. More than thirty of them were the work of Martyn herself, including her early works *Sigrid* and the significant *En Saga,* set to the Sibelius tone poem, which she had begun in London and introduced into the repertory of the Borovansky Ballet in 1941.

The company attracted artists and musicians as well as developing a steady following. Several dancers who made their names with the Australian Ballet or elsewhere received their training with the Guild. Martyn herself was a dancer of distinction and finesse, both in strictly classical roles and in *demi-caractère.* After the demise of Ballet Victoria, Martyn pursued a career as a teacher and writer. She developed a training course for teachers of classical dance, and in 1985 she wrote *Let Them Dance,* a book on the subject of teaching children under the age of ten. She restaged *Le Carnaval* for the Australian Ballet and has been a frequent guest artist with that company.

BIBLIOGRAPHY

Denton, Meg Abbie. "Reviving Lost Works." *Brolga* no. 2 (June 1995): 57–67.

Grove, Robin. "Silent Stories." *Brolga* no. 1 (December 1994): 9–16.

In Honor of Laurel Martyn, OBE. Special issue of *Brolga* no. 4 (June 1996).

Martyn, Laurel. *Let Them Dance: A Preparation for Dance and Life.* London, 1985.

Pask, Edward H. *Ballet in Australia: The Second Act, 1940–1980.* Melbourne, 1982.

MICHELLE POTTER
Based on material submitted by
Geoffrey William Hutton

MARYINSKY BALLET. [*To survey the background, development, and style of one of the great Russian ballet companies, this entry comprises two articles. The first is an overview, tracing the history of the company from its origins to the present; the second is a brief note on the cultural and technical elements contributing to the distinctive Maryinsky style of dancing.*]

Historical Overview

The ballet company of the Maryinsky Theater in Saint Petersburg is one of the oldest in the world, having marked its two-hundredth anniversary in 1983. During the nineteenth century, the Maryinsky became one of the great Imperial Theaters of Russia, and its ballet company was rivaled only by the leading companies of western Europe. During the Soviet era of the twentieth century, after Saint Petersburg was renamed Leningrad and the Maryinsky Theater had become the Leningrad Academic Theater of Opera and Ballet named for S. M. Kirov, the company was familiarly known in the West as the Kirov Ballet. Following the dissolution of the Soviet Union in 1991, the theater once again became known as the Maryinsky.

The development of the tradition of the Maryinsky Ballet is inseparably linked with the destiny of the national culture, with historical events, and with the life of the people of Russia. This company is considered the cradle of Russian classical ballet. Its productions and interpretations defined the elements of the dramatic structure, style, and performance traditions of the Russian school of ballet.

Origins. The Saint Petersburg ballet, born in the 1730s during the reign of Empress Anna, began as one of the components of court performances, those solemn and magnificent spectacles in which singing, declamation, and musical and dancing scenes glorified the autocratic power, the deeds of the tsar, and the victories of Russian arms. For the staging of such performances foreign choreographers, musicians, and composers were invited. In 1736 the Italian virtuoso, ballet master, and teacher Antonio Rinaldi (called Fossano) began performing in Saint Petersburg. Students of the Gentry Services High School, taught by the French dancing master Jean-Baptiste Landé, appeared in Fossano's works. The origins of Russian Ballet were thus founded in Italian and French traditions.

Landé. In 1738 Jean-Baptiste Landé organized the first Russian ballet school. From among the court servants he took twelve young girls and boys who became the performers of the court spectacles and joined the Russian Opera and Ballet Troupe, formed in 1742 on the occasion of Empress Elizabeth's coronation. In 1755 still another ballet school opened in the summer palace of Peter III in Oranienbaum. A graduate, Timofei Bublikov, became the first Russian dancer to win fame abroad. Contemporaries especially delighted in his tragic roles in allegorical ballets. Russian artists proved to be not simply diligent students of foreign masters; they creatively interpreted the choreography they were taught, introducing traditional characteristics of Russian folk dance: musicality, spirituality, and expressiveness. A subtle sense of melody and rhythm, breadth and flow of gestures, deftness and daring characterized the first Russian professionals, who transformed the strict regulations of French ballet and the fiery and virtuosic dance of *commedia dell'arte* into an art form of their own. Among the best performers of that time were Aksinia Sergeeva and Andrei Nesterov.

Hilverding, Le Picq, and Canziani. The Austrian ballet master Franz Hilverding worked in Saint Petersburg from 1759 to 1765, producing *The Return of Spring* in 1760. In 1766 his Italian pupil Gaspero Angiolini went to Russia where he lived for fifteen productive years, staging the first Russian heroic patriotic ballet *Semira* (1772), based on Aleksandr Sumarokov's tragedy. French dancer and ballet master Charles Le Picq worked in Saint Petersburg from 1786 to 1798. He was a devoted pupil of Jean-Georges Noverre, in whose ideas of dramatic dance he believed, and staged many Noverre ballets, including *Médée et Jason* (1789). However, Le Picq had to respect the taste and demands of the court of Catherine II (the Great) by giving performances of special magnificence and spectacular effects. Continuing the tradition of the *ballet d'action,* ballet master Giuseppe Canziani served in Saint Petersburg from 1779 to 1782 and again from 1784 to 1792. He staged the ballets *Ariadne and Bacchus* (1789) and *Pyramus and Thisbe* (1791). Along with Le Picq he took part in a grandiose spectacle at the theater in the Hermitage, *The Early Reign of Oleg,* based on a scenario by Catherine II (1791). Canziani proved to be an excellent teacher, training among many other remarkable artists the gifted dancer and first Russian ballet master, Ivan Valberkh.

In 1783 the Bolshoi, or Kamenny ("stone"), Theater opened in Saint Petersburg opposite the site where the Maryinsky Theater stands now. It staged drama, opera, and ballet. Choreographic performances were already an independent genre but usually occurred as a component of opera or drama. The ballet at times contained singing and dramatic dialogue. In the late eighteenth century important Italian artists worked as scene designers in the Russian musical theater: Giuseppe Valeriani, Antonio and Carlo Bibiena, and others. Their architectural designs in Baroque style provided spectacular backgrounds that lacked geographical or historical authenticity. In fairy-tale ballets machines were used to raise characters into the air or lower them under the stage. Ballet costumes adhered to fashionable attire but were less weighty.

MARYINSKY BALLET. Marius Petipa was the principal choreographer of the Imperial Theaters from 1862 until 1903. Of his more than fifty works, none is more famous than *The Sleeping Beauty*, first performed at the Maryinsky Theater in January 1890 and still performed today, more than a century later. A major revision was made by Konstantin Sergeyev in 1952. This 1961 photograph shows the six fairies in a pose from the prologue, "The Christening": at center is Inna Zubkovskaya as the Lilac Fairy; she is flanked by (from left to right) Natalia Makarova as Tenderness, Galina Kekisheva as Bountiful, Ninel Kurgapkina as Courage, and Nonna Yastrebova as Joyful; kneeling in front is Ludmila Alekseeva as Carefree. (Photograph from the Dance Collection, New York Public Library for the Performing Arts.)

Nineteenth Century. In the nineteenth century, ballet in Saint Petersburg flowered as a fully professional art. All the technical aspects of production were in place to support the ever broadening repertory, and an increasing number of well-trained dancers was available from the school, which was already firmly established with a disciplined curriculum. The composition of the company became much as it is known today—an integration of soloists with a strong corps de ballet—which allowed for a diversification of thematic sources for choreography. Unchanging were the essential Russian qualities of nobility, purity, expressiveness, and musicality, and this in spite of the continuing need to bring in foreign ballet masters. The European trends these masters brought with them were adopted but transmuted in Russia.

Didelot and Valberkh. In 1801 Charles-Louis Didelot arrived in Saint Petersburg. The conditions of the stage and its staff of talented musicians, designers, and performers gave scope to his poetic fantasy. Didelot's Anacreontic ballets *Flore et Zéphire* (1808) and *Psyche et l'Amour* (1809), the mythological *Theseus and Ariadne* (1817), the fairy tale *Kenzi et Tao* (1819), and the dramatic *La Chaumière Hongroise* (1817) and *Raoul de Créquis* (1819) told of human characters, heroes and heroines who fought for love and honor, displaying a broad emotional range. One of the first attempts to stage a Russian literary classic was Didelot's ballet *The Prisoner of the Caucasus* (1823), based on the poem by Aleksandr Pushkin.

Didelot's experiments led to the development of a theatrical form in which the action proceeded by use of dramatic pantomime and expressive dance. In his ballets dance was freed from the affectations of Rococo style and the strict conventions of classicism; it discovered naturalness, feeling, and picturesqueness that allow us to speak about the emergence in his work of a new stylistic direction—romanticism. Didelot opened up to his contemporaries the vast expressive possibilities of the corps de ballet, doubling the composition of the company. He integrated the dances of soloists, *coryphées,* and corps de ballet into an artistic whole, preparing the way for the innovations in ensemble dance that would evolve in the era of Romantic ballet. The decor supported this trend. At the end of the eighteenth century the leading designer in Saint Petersburg was Peter Gonzaga, who brought to scene painting the spirit of romanticism. He significantly lightened theatrical costumes and replaced cumbersome wigs with intricate but natural hair styles. In mythological and fantastic ballets Didelot's male dancers came onstage in short chitons; women wore long transparent tunics and tights.

Working with Didelot was Ivan Valberkh, who had graduated from the theater school in 1786. Valberkh choreographed thirty-six ballets. He was interested in the serious ideological and moral problems of his time, the drama of ordinary people. In his ballet *The New Werther* (1799), broadly based on Goethe, he tried to reflect real life in contemporary Moscow. Valberkh returned repeatedly in his creative work to world literature: *The New Stern* (1801), *Romeo and Juliet* (1809), *Paul et Virginie* (1810). With *Russia's Triumph, or The Russians in Paris* (1814), he responded to the Patriotic War of 1812. The Italians Catterino Cavos, who was music director of the theater, and Ferdinand Antonolini composed music for the ballets of Didelot and Valberkh. Working in close collaboration with the choreographers, they submitted to the needs of the pantomimic action, at the same time responding sensitively to the poetic essence of the ballet.

MARYINSKY BALLET. In 1894, Petipa planned a new production of *Swan Lake* but fell ill and was unable to complete it by himself. He assigned Lev Ivanov to choreograph the two lakeside scenes, now famous for their lyrical romanticism. Since its premiere on 27 January 1895, the Petipa-Ivanov *Swan Lake* has never been absent from the Maryinsky repertory. This photograph, dating from the early 1960s, shows the classical purity of the Maryinsky's corps de ballet. (Photograph from the Dance Collection, New York Public Library for the Performing Arts.)

MARYINSKY BALLET. Petipa staged a new version of *Le Corsaire* at the Maryinsky in January 1899. Loosely based on Lord Byron's epic poem *The Corsair,* the libretto tells a complicated tale of the love of the pirate Conrad for Medora, a Greek woman captured by Turkish slave traders. The spectacular revival produced by Petr Gusev and Oleg Vinogradov in 1987 includes many virtuosic solos, pas de deux, ensemble pieces, and character dances. Here Amelina Kashirina (center) is seen in the final pose of the "Algerian Dance" in the Turkish slave market. (Photograph © 1989 by Jack Vartoogian; used by permission.)

"By the time of Pushkin, ballet had already prevailed over classical comedy and tragedy," wrote the leading critic Vissarion Belinsky about the Saint Petersburg company. The success owed to the mastery of the leading dancers. One of the brightest performers was Evgenia Kolosova. A versatile actress, she appeared successfully in operatic and dramatic roles, but above all amazed audiences with her pantomime in ballet tragedies. The expressiveness of her pantomime, her spirituality, and her plastique beauty enabled her to reveal the feelings of her heroines.

The talent of the dancer Avdotia Istomina, celebrated by Pushkin in his verse novel *Eugene Onegin,* was revealed in the ballets of Didelot. Contemporaries noted her virtuosic technique and great dramatic talent. She delighted her audience, performing in the most diverse roles: comedies (Lise in *La Fille Mal Gardée*), lyric dramas (Flora in *Flore et Zéphire*), and tragedies (the title role in *Inez de Castro*). She enhanced the protagonists in the first Pushkin ballets staged in Russia. In Didelot's *The Prisoner of the Caucasus* she performed the role of the Circassian Kaselkya, and in Adam Glushkovsky's *Ruslan and Ludmila* she was Ludmila.

A combination of expressive dance and pantomimic artistry distinguished the other leading dancer of the time, Ekaterina Teleshova, to whom another great Russian poet, Aleksandr Griboedov, dedicated inspired verses. Teleshova, like Istomina, developed as an artist in Didelot's productions. As a pupil she made her debut in his *Flore et Zéphire* in the role of Hymen. In her subsequent performances Teleshova's interpretations integrated the aesthetic of the choreographer. Her repertory was distinguished by its wide range, from the blithe young charmer in *Ruslan and Ludmila* to the tragic Phaedra in *Phaedra and Hippolytus.* In her maturity she created the remarkable image of Fenella in *La Muette de Portici.*

Among other ballerinas, many authors in their memoirs praised Anastasia Novitskaya as the one who "with inexpressible lightness and purity combined tenderness and modesty"; Marie Danilova in whose airy dance one could perceive mysteriousness; and Natalia Likhutina, fascinating in roles of "good-natured girls, innocent and risable."

For fifty years (1822-1872) Nikolai Golts appeared on the Saint Petersburg stage, a versatile and leading performer of noble, *demi-caractère,* and character roles. He began his career in the role of Rostislav, the young

MARYINSKY BALLET. Anna Pavlova as Armida and Vaslav Nijinsky as Armida's Slave in *Le Pavillon d'Armide,* choreographed by Michel Fokine and first performed at the Maryinsky in November 1907. The eighteen-year-old Nijinsky created a sensation. (Photograph by Fischer, Saint Petersburg; from the Dance Collection, New York Public Library for the Performing Arts.)

Slavonic prince, in Didelot's *The Prisoner of the Caucasus,* then performed in ballets of Filippo Taglioni, Jules Perrot, Arthur Saint-Léon, and Marius Petipa. His partners were the notable ballerinas of the time: Avdotia Istomina, Evgenia Kolosova, Ekaterina Teleshova, Marie Taglioni, Carlotta Grisi, and others.

By the 1830s the corps de ballet of the Saint Petersburg company, like the soloists, were graduates of the school, trained in one methodological system and possessed of one performing manner—all of which helped choreographers achieve unity of style and artistic integrity of production. However, Romantic ballet did not develop, because a period of reaction, which set in after the suppression of the Decembrist revolt of 1825, affected all aspects of Russian life. Subsidized by the imperial treasury the Saint Petersburg company depended fully on the taste of the tsar's court. In hiring ballet masters the officials of the imperial theaters cared most about their ability to compose magnificent and entertaining spectacles with effective theatrical machinery and hosts of dancers. Only foreign ballet masters were allowed to lead the company, and the principal roles were invariably given to guest artists.

When Didelot resigned in 1832 the officials replaced him with the French ballet masters Alexis Blache and Antoine Titus, who proved to be skillful craftsmen but not inventive creators. They conscientiously transferred the new Parisian productions to the Russian stage. For example, Titus was known in Saint Petersburg for his staging of Romantic masterpieces: for *La Sylphide* of Filippo Taglioni in 1835 and *Giselle* of Jules Perrot and Jean Coralli in 1842. In 1837 Marie Taglioni herself performed *La Sylphide* in Saint Petersburg. The art of the legendary ballerina left a notable imprint on Russian performance. Her ethereal romanticism was far from the more realistic romanticism of Didelot, which was closely linked with real life. The dramatic dance of Didelot's ballets had anticipated Romantic choreography; consequently the art of Taglioni found itself on prepared ground in Russia. The traditions of romanticism were maintained by the company even in that period when they were lost in Europe.

From 1830 to 1860 many important western Europeans appeared on the Saint Petersburg stage. In 1836 the opera and ballet troupes broke off from the dramatic company, which was transferred to the building of the Aleksandrinsky Theater. From 1834 until the end of the century the artist and decor machinist Andreas Roller designed the ballet productions. Roller closely followed all the new decorative work in Europe, but he was devoid of original visions. Such stagnation remained fixed in musical theater decor for a long time. From the repertory of Taglioni, who staged nearly all of his ballets in Saint Petersburg, only *La Sylphide* was preserved (the last revival took place in 1922). The rest of his ballets were lost by the mid-nineteenth century. However, the structural principles of his productions provided the foundation for subsequent developments in Russian ballet.

Perrot. Working from 1848 to 1859, Jules Perrot introduced a different kind of romanticism to Saint Petersburg. His arrival heralded the guest appearances of Fanny Elssler. In contrast to the airy, dreamlike Marie Taglioni, Elssler presented the earthy, passionate embodiment of the many-sided feminine spirit. Her individuality was fully disclosed in the ballets of Perrot. Also important to Russia was Perrot's talent for staging dramatic works from literature. His *La Esmeralda,* after Victor Hugo, and version of *Le Corsaire,* after Byron, are often revived.

Despite special favors to foreign artists, Saint Petersburg did not accept a universally recognized reputation on faith. Famous visiting ballerinas were criticized as well as praised; some Russian performers were found comparable to the most brilliant guests. The first Russian Giselle, Elena Andreyanova, was able to unite in her art the lyrical, unearthly dance of Taglioni and the lively, dramatic character dance of Elssler. The poetry of romanticism manifested itself most fully in her. She was a beautiful Sylphide, Peri, Florinda in *Le Diable Boiteux,* and the title role in *Paquita.* The life of the ballet *Giselle* was extended by the talented interpreters of the title role. The ballet proved to be one of the most frequently played in the repertory throughout the long history of the company. *Giselle* concentrated the company's performing traditions—the expressiveness inherent in the pure nobility of classical dance; the gift to transmit beauty along with the complexity of humankind's spiritual world.

Johansson, Petipa, and Saint-Léon. In the 1840s two foreigners entered the ballet company of the Bolshoi, finding in Russia a second homeland. In 1841 the Swede Christian Johansson arrived, and in 1847 the Frenchman Marius Petipa. Johansson acquainted Saint Petersburg with the tradition of the Danish classicist August Bournonville and as dancer and teacher exerted much influence on the formation of the company's performance style. He stressed clarity and noble manner. The significance of Petipa to the destiny of the Saint Petersburg ballet was already great, but later became all-important.

In 1859, opposite the Bolshoi Theater, the Maryinsky Theater was built to the design of the architect Alberto Cavos on the site of a circus destroyed by fire. Although it opened in 1860 ballet performances remained at the Bolshoi Theater until 1880. Public enthusiasm after the reforms of 1861, which abolished the right of a landlord to own his serfs, affected all the arts, but ballet was not touched. It became a spectacle for the privileged aristocratic audience and acquired even more the character of an entertainment. The plots in new ballets only connected separate numbers, justifying the splendid *divertissements.* Yet the tradition of Russian choreography was maintained in the professionalism of ballet training and the creative talents of the performers and ballet masters. The lyrical dancer Nadezhda Bogdanova preferred the Romantic repertory. In the roles of Giselle, Esmeralda, and Margarita in *Faust* she delighted audiences with the purity, spontaneity, and sincerity of her characters. In her poetic dance, subtleties predominated. Marius Petipa's wife, Maria Surovshchikova, conquered the audience with her grace and expressive pantomime. Her creative work was closely linked with the beginning period of Petipa's activities in Russia, when he staged a series of short, lyrical-comic ballets for his wife. Surovshchikova enjoyed special success in *travesti* roles. The Romantic dancer Marfa Muravieva possessed harmonic perfection of line and subtle musicality that gave her dance an eloquent expressiveness.

The creative work of the French ballet master Arthur Saint-Léon, who was in Saint Petersburg from 1859 to 1869, was shaped by the wish to please the taste of the directors of the Imperial Theaters and the tsar's court. Yet the inventiveness of the choreographer, who could startle audiences with an unexpected *divertissement* or effective character dances, did not compensate for the substantive poverty of his compositions. The Russian audience met coldly the Saint-Léon ballets that had received approbation in western Europe. In search of subjects that would excite the public's interest he turned to the then popular fairy tale *The Little Humpbacked Horse.* However, here he remained true to himself. Eliminating the satirical element from his composition, he used the story of Ivan the Fool only as occasion for the demonstration of a large number of classical and character dances. The ballet was clearly monarchical and so was enthusiastically accepted by official Saint Petersburg, but the democratic Russian audience was sharply critical of this new work. Inspired by the success of his creation with the court audience Saint-Léon in his next work decided to turn to Pushkin, but in his ballet *The Goldfish,* the Pushkin tale well known and loved in Russia was distorted beyond recognition. That led to his misfortune. In 1869 Saint-Léon's contract was not renewed, and the post of ballet master was taken up by Petipa.

MARYINSKY BALLET. The great ballerina Galina Ulanova created the role of Juliet in Leonid Lavrovsky's *Romeo and Juliet* on 11 January 1940 at the Maryinsky Theater. Her Romeo was danced by Konstantin Sergeyev. Both she and he returned to dance in the 1960 revival, during which this photograph was taken. (Photograph by Albert Kahn; from the Dance Collection, New York Public Library for the Performing Arts.)

Petipa and Ivanov. Petipa led the company for thirty-four years. During that time in western Europe ballet was in crisis—shedding traditions, school, and repertory—but in Russia it developed in maturity, scale, and a distinctive aesthetic. Petipa had entered a major company that possessed great potential, which he was able to realize. At the same time, like his predecessor Didelot, Petipa did not remain indifferent to the democratic tendencies that were taking place in the developing Russian culture. This powerful influence was reflected in his work through his selection of themes that had ideological and philosophical bearing. For Petipa the ballet had to embody human ideas, not just turn on the novelty of technique, as in western Europe. He was sensitive to individual performers, yet simultaneously exacting with regard to the musical and poetic imagery of the dance.

A second ballet master, Lev Ivanov, was appointed to the theater in 1882 to assist Petipa in carrying out a series of new productions and revivals. Among the many dances choreographed by Ivanov, the *Polovtsian Dances* in Aleksandr Borodin's opera *Prince Igor* (1890) were distinguished by the increasing dynamism and tension of the dancing, which produced a range of emotions and conveyed the image of nomads galloping on the steppes. Ivanov's choreography for the second act of *Swan Lake,* the "white" lake scene, first shown in 1894, influenced later creations, such as Michel Fokine's *The Dying Swan. Swan Lake* revealed Ivanov's talent as a creator of large-scale compositions that pointed the way toward plastique, symphonically structured dance. Ivanov's last masterpiece was his production of the Second Hungarian Rhapsody of Franz Liszt, which was included in the *divertissement* of *The Little Humpbacked Horse* in 1900 and which continued his experiment in symphonic character dance, begun with the *Polovtsian Dances*. Here again Ivanov aimed to re-create the image of the music.

MARYINSKY BALLET. Yuri Grigorovich staged his version of *The Stone Flower* for the Maryinsky in the spring of 1957. Pictured here, c.1961, are Igor Chernyshev as Danila, the stone cutter, and Kaleria Fedicheva as the Mistress of the Copper Mountain. (Photograph from the Dance Collection, New York Public Library for the Performing Arts.)

The ballets of Petipa and Ivanov revealed the gifts of the Russian ballerina Ekaterina Vazem, who created Nikia in *La Bayadère.* Possessed of virtuosity and perfection of line, she subsequently took up teaching. Many future ballerinas studied with her or with artists who passed through her school, notably Agrippina Vaganova. The talent of Evgenia Sokolova was different; her dancing was distinguished by a lyrical softness and an emotional quality. The role of Kitri in the Saint Petersburg premiere of *Don Quixote* Petipa entrusted to the temperamental Aleksandra Vergina.

However, at the end of the 1880s, the practice of inviting foreign guests was revived. Maria Gorshenkova, who had a rare jump, and the poetic Varvara Nikitina received leading roles only after the departure of their foreign creators. Italy had introduced animation to the strict canons of academic ballet. Thus the unusual expressiveness of Virginia Zucchi, for example, stirred the foundations of conventional pantomime. At the same time the Italian visitors perceived the special characteristics of Russian performance: spirituality, understanding, and musicality. Carlotta Brianza, the first Aurora in *The Sleeping Beauty,* combined virtuosity with grace and softness. But the best achievement was that of Pierina Legnani, who brought the thirty-two *fouettés* to Russia.

In the last half of the nineteenth century the position of premier danseur was held by Pavel Gerdt, who set the standard as a *danseur noble.* A different style of male dancing was introduced with the arrival in Saint Petersburg of the virtuoso Enrico Cecchetti in 1891. Among the best character dancers were Marie Petipa, Feliks Kshessinsky, Alfred Bekefi, and Aleksandr Shiriaev. The leading mime was Timofei Stukolkin.

Twentieth Century. In the first decade of the twentieth century six ballerinas stood out: Olga Preobrajenska, Matilda Kshessinska, Vera Trefilova, Agrippina Vaganova, Julia Sedova, and Lubov Egorova. Their partners were Nikolai and Sergei Legat, Michel Fokine, and Samuil Andreonov. Virtuosic variations were entrusted to Georgi

Kyaksht and Mikhail Obukhov. No mere museum, the company developed tradition creatively. Petipa declared (Nekhendzi, 1971), "I count the Saint Petersburg ballet first in the world, precisely because it has preserved serious art, which has been lost abroad." After the dismissal of Petipa in 1903, however, a need for aesthetic reform was felt. The supporters of change urged stylistic integrity, historical authenticity, and naturalness of movement.

Fokine. The practical embodiment of these ideas was found in the innovative productions of Michel Fokine, who favored the one-act ballet with pared-down, continuous action, and with precisely conveyed stylistic coloring. In 1907 and 1908, Fokine created his first important ballets for the Maryinsky, including *Chopiniana* and *Une Nuit d'Égypte*. For the next three years he worked with the *saisons russes* of Serge Diaghilev in Paris. Fokine extended the academic limits of ballet and developed the gifts of Anna Pavlova, Tamara Karsavina, and Vaslav Nijinsky. From 1912 to 1917 Fokine again choreographed at the Maryinsky, where he renewed the aesthetic of dances within operas, rejecting the practice of inserted numbers and drawing the dances closer in style to the epoch and spirit of the opera. To this day in Russia, Fokine's choreography for the *Polovtsian Dances* is used in Borodin's opera *Prince Igor* as well as his dances for Glinka's opera *Ruslan and Ludmila*. His *Chopiniana* and other Fokine ballets also remain current in the repertory. Developing the ideas of Ivanov, he sharpened plastique and enhanced movement with ingenious details. Among the dancers of this generation were Olga Spessivtseva, a classicist of rare purity, and Pierre Vladimiroff, who was distinguished for his heroic qualities.

The 1917 Revolution rocked ballet tradition. Experiments reflected the new reality, and contemporary innovations penetrated performing style. Bold acrobatic lifts, wild turns, and jumps were introduced. A spirit of daring and of enthusiastic competition saturated the traditional choreographies with democracy; new works reflected the dynamic events and feelings of the times. In this period the talents of leading dancers such as Elisaveta Gerdt, Elena Lukom, Boris Shavrov, and Mikhail Dudko came to light.

Lopukhov and His Successors. In 1922 Fedor Lopukhov was placed at the head of the company. Under his guidance, the theater carefully preserved the finest ballets of Petipa, Ivanov, and Fokine. Experimenting in the sphere of musically structured and expressive dance, Lopukhov staged dance symphonies such as *The Magnificence of the Universe* (1923), in which George Balanchine performed just before his immigration to the West in 1924. Two colleagues of Lopukhov who were especially interested in interpreting his ideas were the young performers Olga Mungalova and Petr Gusev. The cultivation of Lopukhov's theories and his experiments in drama and ex-

MARYINSKY BALLET. Igor Belsky mounted *Leningrad Symphony* for the Maryinsky in April 1961. Set to the first movement of Shostakovich's Seventh Symphony, the ballet is in three sections: "Serene Happiness," "Invasion," and "Requiem." In the second section, a group of Nazi soldiers goosestep into the scene, as the siege of Leningrad begins. (Photograph from a souvenir program, Leningrad-Kirov Ballet, 1961.)

pressive methods influenced the development of Soviet ballet. In 1929 Lopukhov, with Vladimir Ponomarev and Leonid Leontiev, staged *The Red Poppy*, the seminal Soviet ballet (to music by Glière), on the Leningrad stage, and in 1930 another ballet on a contemporary theme, *The Golden Age*, was created by Vasily Vainonen, Leonid Yakobson, and Vladimir Chesnakov (to music by Shostakovich). Collaborative productions such as these reflected the concurrent social condition.

Beginning with Lopukhov's directorship the repertory ceased to be based on the creations of only one ballet master; the company's doors opened to the diverse experimental trends pursued by a new generation of choreographers. The decade of the 1930s was marked by the active searches of these choreographers and dancers. A new type of work emerged: the drama ballet *(drambalet)*, which had dramatic structure and expressive means, and synthesized pantomime and dance. The creators of these productions aspired to embody clear ideological concepts and psychologically cultivated images. The choreographer worked like the director of a play, and the performance combined the qualities of dancers and actors. The ballet intensively assimilated the teaching of Konstantin Stanislavsky, aspiring to reflect his ideas of characterization. On the Leningrad stage there were new productions: Vainonen's *The Flames of Paris* (1932), Rostislav Zakharov's *The Fountain of Bakhchisarai* (1934), Vakhtang

Chabukiani's *Laurencia* (1939), and Leonid Lavrovsky's *Romeo and Juliet* (1940). These ballets were noteworthy for the creation of Galina Ulanova's Maria and Juliet, Konstantin Sergeyev's Vaslav and Romeo, Natalia Dudinskaya's Laurencia, Chabukiani's Frondoso, and Nina Anisimova's Teresa. In this period the study of acting and the use of folklore motifs enlarged the expressive possibilities of choreography. Character dance gave ballet a natural coloring, democratized the spectacle, and in several productions, such as *The Flames of Paris*, appeared as the basis of the dance score.

In the years of World War II, the main part of the company was evacuated to Perm, where they performed works from the repertory and created new ones, such as Anisimova's *Gayané* (1942). Rallied by the ballerina Olga Jordan the artists who were left in blockaded Leningrad—in spite of hunger, cold, and artillery fire—continued to give concerts. They went to the front and performed in factories and hospitals. In the 1940s young artists in the company were Igor Belsky, Boris Bregvadze, Yuri Grigorovich, Inna Zubkovskaya, Ninel Kurgapkina, Askold Makarov, Olga Moiseyeva, Ninel Petrova, Vsevolod Ukhov, Konstantin Shatilov, and Nonna Yastrebova. An immediate response to the heroic deeds of the Soviet people in the war was Vladimir Burmeister's *Tatiana* (1947), in which the heroic image of a patriot was created by Tatiana Vecheslova. In *Militsa* (1947), based on the struggle of the Yugoslav partisans against the Fascists, Vainonen continued the search for an expressive interpretation of folk dance. Boris Fenster's *Taras Bulba* (1955), based on a short story by Gogol, worked on the theme of patriotism. Ballets based on Pushkin continued with Zakharov's *The Bronze Horseman* (1949). The last two, however, showed that the choreographic embodiment of important social and political problems required a more varied means of expressiveness. Konstantin Sergeyev's *Cinderella* (1946), Lopukhov's *Spring Tale* (1947), and Yakobson's *Shurale* (1950) testified to the powerful possibilities that the rich vocabulary of classicism mixed with folk dance and character dance possessed for communication with audiences.

A great surge of creativity marked the 1950s into the 1970s. Konstantin Sergeyev, who directed the company from 1951 to 1954 and again from 1961 to 1970, played a crucial role in preserving the ballets *Raymonda, Swan Lake,* and *The Sleeping Beauty.* Leonid Yakobson protested against this conservative repertory that consisted of only classical ballets and revived drama ballets of the 1930s and 1940s. In 1956, using movement patterned on classical Greek art, he choreographed Aram Khachaturian's music to *Spartacus,* and in 1958 his *Choreographic Miniatures* united the resources of literature and real-life stories, using both classical and character dance enriched by motifs taken from sculpture, painting, and graphics. In *The Bedbug* (1962) he succeeded in depicting the poet Vladimir Mayakovsky's satiric play, in which images of the postrevolutionary bourgeoisie were formed. Yakobson's *The Twelve* (1964) was based on the revolutionary poetry of Aleksandr Blok. In 1953 Sergeyev staged *Path of Thunder,* which was devoted to the struggle against racism. Yuri Grigorovich's *The Stone Flower* (1957) and *Legend of Love* (1963) and Igor Belsky's *The Coast of Hope* (1959) and *Leningrad Symphony* (1961) revitalized the traditions of symphonic dance (structured according to musical form) that had been cultivated by Petipa and Lopukhov, and continued the princi-

MARYINSKY BALLET. In 1989, two works by George Balanchine were mounted at the Maryinsky: *Theme and Variations,* staged by Francia Russell, and *Scotch Symphony,* staged by Suzanne Farrell. Both had their official premieres on the same day, 21 February 1989. Altynai Asylmuratova and Konstantin Zaklinsky danced the principal roles in *Theme and Variations,* pictured here. (Photograph © 1989 by Jack Vartoogian; used by permission. Choreography by George Balanchine © The George Balanchine Trust.)

ples of theatrical-musical action affirmed by Fokine. The new methods brought out the gifts of emerging young artists: Aleksandr Gribov, Anatoly Gridin, Irina Kolpakova, Alla Osipenko, and later Gabriella Komleva, Alla Sizova, and Yuri Soloviev, whose work was a model of the subtle combination of classical dance and the techniques of contemporary choreographers. These qualities were revealed to the West when the company toured for the first time in 1961 to Paris, London, and New York. Other notable productions of the period were Oleg Vinogradov's *The Mountain Girl* (1968) and *The Creation of the World* (1971) by Natalia Kasatkina and Vladimir Vasiliov. These ballets were performed by both experienced and young dancers: Kaleria Fedicheva, Natalia Makarova, Valery Panov, Oleg Sokolov, Mikhail Baryshnikov, Vadim Gulyaev, Natalia Bolshakova, Galina Ragozina, Vadim Budarin, and Svetlana Efremova. Soviet choreographers were turning to the music of contemporary composers, such as Prokofiev, Shostakovich, and Khachaturian.

Vinogradov. In 1977 Oleg Vinogradov was appointed artistic director and chief choreographer of the Kirov Ballet, where he remains. While conscientiously preserving the nineteenth-century classics with revivals of *Giselle, La Bayadère, Swan Lake, The Sleeping Beauty, Raymonda, Don Quixote,* and *Le Corsaire,* Vinogradov also widened the repertory with August Bournonville's *La Sylphide* in 1981 and *Napoli* in 1982, staged by Elsa-Marianne von Rosen, as well as segments of ballets and individual works revived by Russian and foreign choreographers. In fact, Vinogradov was the first Soviet director to welcome Western choreography, staging Roland Petit's *Nôtre-Dame de Paris* in 1978, Antal Fodor's rock ballet *Proba* in 1988, and some works of Maurice Béjart. In 1989 the company performed for the first time ballets by George Balanchine, *Scotch Symphony* and *Theme and Variations,* followed in 1992 by *Apollo* and in 1996 by *Symphony in C.* The repertory of Western ballets was supplemented in 1992 by Antony Tudor's *Jardin aux Lilas* and *The Leaves Are Fading,* and Jerome Robbins's *In the Night.* In 1993 André Prokovsky choreographed *Anna Karenina* for the company.

During this time Vinogradov himself has created many ballets that differ in style and choreographic language. *The Fairy of the Rondane Mountains* (1980) is in neo-Romantic style; his 1992 *Coppélia* and 1994 *La Fille Mal Gardée* and *Cinderella* are neoclassical. In *The Inspector-General* (1980) he continued the tradition of choreographic satire, while in *The Knight in a Tiger Skin* (1985) he applied both plasticity and graphic precision. *The Battleship Potemkin* (1986) and *Petrouchka* in 1990 were his response to contemporary social problems. His ballet *The Resurrection* (1996) resulted from his philosophical reflections on life. The dancers he has fostered are Galina Mezentseva, Olga Chenchikova, Liubov Kunakova, Tatiana Terekhova, Altynai Asylmuratova, Zhanna Ayupova, Yulia Makhalina, Konstantin Zaklinsky, and Farukh Ruzimatov.

[*For related discussion see* Russia, *articles on theatrical dance. Many of the figures and works mentioned herein are the subjects of independent entries.*]

BIBLIOGRAPHY

Barnes, Clive. "The Maryinsky in New York." *Dance and Dancers* (August 1992): 26–31.

Bogdanov-Berezovskii, V. M. *Leningradskii gosudarstvennyi ordena Lenina akademicheskii teatr opery i baleta imemi S. M. Kirova.* Leningrad, 1959.

Degen, Arsen, and Igor Vasilievich Stupnikov. *Leningradskii balet, 1917–1987.* Leningrad, 1988.

Degen, Arsen. "Then and Now at the Maryinsky Theater." *Ballet Review* 20 (Summer 1992): 40–48.

Gregory, John, and Alexander Ukladnikov. *Leningrad's Ballet: Maryinsky to Kirov.* London, 1981.

Greskovic, Robert. "Kirov Today." *Dance View* 10 (Winter 1993): 2–9.

Kaplan, Larry. "The Kirov Up Close." *Ballet Review* 20 (Fall 1992): 16–24.

Karsavina, Tamara. *Theatre Street.* Rev. and enl. ed. London, 1948.

Kendall, Elizabeth B. "Reflections: The Kirov." *New Yorker* (8 June 1992).

Koni, Fedor. "Balet v Peterburge." *Panteon i Repertuar Russkogo Teatra* 2.3 (1850).

Krasovskaya, Vera. *Russkii baletnyi teatr: Ot vozniknoveniia do serediny XIX veka.* Leningrad, 1958.

Krasovskaya, Vera. *Russkii baletnyi teatr vtoroi poloviny deviatnadtsatogo veka.* Leningrad, 1963.

Krasovskaya, Vera. *Russkii baletnyi teatr nachala dvadtsatogo veka,* vol. 1, *Khoreografy;* vol. 2, *Tantsovshchiki.* Leningrad, 1971–1972.

Krasovskaya, Vera, ed. *Sovetskii baletnyi teatr, 1917–1967.* Moscow, 1976.

Lopukhov, Fedor. *Shestdesiat let v balete.* Moscow, 1966.

MacMahon, Deirdre. "'Corridor to the Muses': Myth and Realism in Leningrad's Ballet." *Ballet Review* 12 (Spring 1984): 57–65.

Nekhendzi, Anna, ed. *Marius Petipa: Materialy, vospominaniia, stati.* Leningrad, 1971.

Percival, John. "Where the Classical Ballet Grew Up." *Dance and Dancers* (July 1993): 8–11.

Slonimsky, Yuri. *Sovetskii balet.* Moscow, 1950.

Souritz, Elizabeth. *Soviet Choreographers in the 1920s.* Translated by Lynn Visson. Durham, N.C., 1990.

Svetlov, Valerian. *Terpsikhora.* Saint Petersburg, 1906.

Teliakovsky, Vladimir. "Memoirs: St. Petersburg Ballet." Translated by Nina Dimitrievich. *Dance Research* 9 (Spring 1991): 26–39.

Valberkh, Ivan. *Iz arkhiva baletmeistera.* Moscow, 1948.

Wiley, Roland John, trans. and ed. *A Century of Russian Ballet: Documents and Accounts, 1810–1910.* Oxford, 1990.

Marina A. Ilicheva
Translated from Russian

Maryinsky Style

A number of components make up the distinctive style of the Maryinsky Ballet. One is a tradition that goes back to the beginning of the nineteenth century. That tradition was built on discipline, within the school as well as the theater. Ballet master Charles-Louis Didelot was charmed by the discipline of the company and made use of it; nowhere else could he be as strict as in Saint Petersburg. This discipline has been preserved for more than a century, and Agrippina Vaganova insisted that her pupils abide by it.

A second component is the environment. There is the climate—cold and crisp in the prolonged winters, poetic in the white nights of summer. There is also the architecture: the old part of the city was constructed along horizontal lines: pure, flowing, and noble. With this comes the heritage from Marius Petipa, who appreciated the architecture and the whole image of Saint Petersburg and, above all, loved Theater Street, with its rows of strong, fine columns. His corps de ballet of wilis in his version of *Giselle* was created according to the standards of the style he found in Saint Petersburg's ballet, which he tuned to his sublime dreams and brought to perfection. The wilis of today are Saint Petersburg wilis, as is the corps de ballet of *Swan Lake*. Lev Ivanov, recalling all the nereids and shades of Petipa's ballets, created his own poetical vision of a white corps de ballet—and Ivanov's sensibilities were also conditioned by Saint Petersburg.

The word *aristocratic* might be used in reference to the Kirov style, meaning that nothing should be exaggerated or rude in performance. What is said about the corps de ballet applies also to the soloists and to the relationship between partners. Aurora in *The Sleeping Beauty* and Odette in *Swan Lake* are modest, proud, and very well-bred. Their beloved princes gallantly esteem their feelings. It can be said that the well-known symphonic (musically structured) dance of the Russian ballet was born on the Maryinsky stage, owing to the company's musicality of style.

BIBLIOGRAPHY

Krasovskaya, Vera. *Russkii baletnyi teatr: Ot vozniknoveniia do serediny XIX veka*. Leningrad, 1958.

Krasovskaya, Vera. *Russkii baletnyi teatr vtoroi poloviny deviatnadtsatogo veka*. Leningrad, 1963.

Krasovskaya, Vera. *Russkii baletnyi teatr nachala dvadtsatogo veka*, vol. 1, *Khoreografy;* vol. 2, *Tantsovshchiki*. Leningrad, 1971–1972.

Krasovskaya, Vera, ed. *Sovetskii baletnyi teatr, 1917–1967*. Moscow, 1976.

VERA M. KRASOVSKAYA
Translated from Russian

MASK AND MAKEUP. [*This entry comprises three articles focusing on the use of body adornment and facial transformation in three broad areas of world cultures: African, Asian, and European. For related discussion, see* Costume in African Traditions; Costume in Asian Traditions; *and* Costume in Western Traditions.]

African Traditions

Masking is ancient in Africa. In the Saharan rock art of Tassili n'Ajjer in Algeria, a painting is dated to about 3000 BCE, showing a masquerader with his legs spread as if on horseback, shielding another figure. Historical accounts of masquerades have come from travelers—the earliest from Shams al-Dīn al-Ṭanjī ibn Baṭṭūṭa, a Muslim who visited the Mali Empire of West Africa in the fourteenth century. He witnessed masqueraders singing the praises of the king's predecessors while dressed as birds with wooden heads, red beaks, and feathers. One of the first illustrations of an African mask to appear in European literature, published in François Froger's journal

MASK AND MAKEUP: African Traditions. A masquerade of the Sitemu subgroup of the Baga people in Guinea. The performers are completely hidden beneath raffia and cloth skirts. A female spirit (Tiyambo) is represented in the headdress in the foreground. The other two headdresses represent rabbit figures (Sibondel). (Photograph © 1987 by Frederick Lamp; used by permission.)

MASK AND MAKEUP: African Traditions. Performers of *ngongoti,* a stilt dance of the Makonde people in southeastern Tanzania. This group represented the Southern Zone at a national arts and language competition held at the Sheikh Amri Abeid Stadium in Arusha, Tanzania. (Photograph © 1992 by Kelly Askew; used by permission.)

in 1698, depicts a masquerader wearing an antelope-like face covering, believed to be associated with circumcision rituals. Apart from the wide, bent-kneed stance of the figure in the Tassili rock painting, other early sources provide few clues to masqueraders' postures, gestures, or dance.

Geographically, in sub-Saharan Africa masquerading is performed approximately from Senegal in West Africa eastward to Cameroon, southward along the Atlantic coast to Congo and Angola, then eastward to Kenya, Tanzania, and Mozambique.

Even today the literature on African masked dance is sparse. Dance descriptions tend to be embedded in writing devoted primarily to analyzing cultural institutions that support masking or to the masks as art objects. As a result, the contexts of masked dance are only indirectly and superficially indicated.

Many African societies believe that spirits coexist with people, affecting their lives and environment. Masking, which gives visible form to such spirits, is regarded with awe—as reflected in African terminologies used to describe masquerades. As Herbert Cole (1970) has pointed out:

> Few African languages have a word which accurately translates as mask: BaKwele say *buoobkuk,* "face of the forest spirit." Ibo say *isi mmuo* "spirit head." Lega say *lukuwakongo* "death gathers in." Jukun say *bakindo* to indicate a broad supernatural category including the high god, ancestors, bush and other spirits both visible and tangible as well as invisible and intangible.

Thus the English words *mask* and *masquerade* do not adequately convey the spiritual nature of the African concept.

The anthropologist Simon Ottenberg (1982) argued that in West Africa masquerades essentially "deal with commonly held repressed materials," such as taboos, Oedipal conflicts, children's associations with parental figures, and sexual matters. In creating images of spirits through masking rituals, people can express their deepest feelings publicly and attempt to manage these emotions for their own benefit as well as that of society.

In traditional Africa, the sacred and the secular are not clearly distinguishable. Masquerade performances function on both planes at once; as such they are involved in social control, initiations, rites of passage, funerals, ancestor commemorations, leadership and politics, economics and agriculture, education and socialization, as well as aesthetic experiences. Simultaneously efficacious and entertaining, they bridge the human and spirit realms in elaborate spectacles—transitory manifestations of otherworldly entities that are periodically re-created or regenerated in the phenomenal world.

Masqueraders enter the village from either a sacred grove in the bush or from a shrine. They are frequently accompanied by guides, interpreters, servants, or crowd-controllers, who mediate between these spirit beings and members of the community. There are often prohibitions against touching and seeing masqueraders. Despite these precautions for keeping the realm of the spirits separate from that of humans, considerable interaction takes place between masqueraders and spectators. Once in the vil-

MASK AND MAKEUP: African Traditions. Traditionally performed during secret-society death rites and for *dama* ceremonies, the masked dances of the Dogon people have been adapted for tourist entertainment. The *kanaga* mask seen here is perhaps the most recognizable of the Dogon masks. The wooden superstructure has been variously interpreted—some see it as symbolizing the human position between heaven and earth. (Photograph © by Michel Huet; used by permission.)

lage, the masqueraders dance in a central square, in the market, or at the crossroads, and spectators join in the performance by singing, following, or even accompanying the masqueraders in dance. Indeed, masquerades represent artistic expression by countless performers and interpreters. Their otherworldliness is conveyed in their costuming, in the music and chants that accompany them, and in their dances.

Masquerade styles in Africa have a conceptual continuum from figurative to abstract. At the figurative extreme, masqueraders usually don carved, stitched, or woven human or animal masks; the masquerader's human form is always evident, alluring the inherent humanness within the spirit realm. Figurative masquerades, which are the most common, usually feature dances that emphasize stepping and stamping. To a percussive accompaniment, masqueraders concentrate on leg and foot patterns; the rest of the body accommodates and occasionally punctuates the stamping movements.

The lavish Gelede masquerades of the western Yoruba peoples of Nigeria and the Republic of Benin occur annually when the first rains fall, at funeral services, and in times of crisis such as drought or famine. Held to honor the female forces in the universe, Gelede ceremonies are expressions of the Yoruba belief that women elders, ancestors, and deities possess extraordinary powers. The purpose of Gelede is to appease and harness these forces so that they can benefit society as a whole. The masqueraders—all male but who represent men, women, and animals—place carved wooden masks on top of their heads, giving the appearance of an extended neck. The costumes consist of a multitude of women's head ties and wrappers arranged to exaggerate male and female body contours. Males are depicted with large chests; women are shown with massive hips and buttocks and long pointed breasts, which bob up and down during the dance. The masqueraders stamp out intricate rhythmic patterns, sending the dust flying.

At the nonfigurative end of the continuum, masqueraders synthesize costume and movement for a total transformation of the human body into a kind of abstract kinetic sculpture. These masqueraders, who tend to focus on the nonhuman qualities of spirits, strive for a unified, thoroughly integrated dance image in which legs and arms are often imperceptible.

In any African culture, both figurative and nonfigurative masquerade forms may exist in a single context, as they do among the Okpela, a northern Edo people of west-central Nigeria. During the Olimi festival, held annually to honor ancestors and to purify the community, figurative masqueraders commemorate "dead mothers." Women of high economic or social standing take nonfigurative roles in the same ceremonies to represent the "dead fathers." The "dead mothers" are anthropomorphic in form and wear stitched and stuffed cloth masks with human faces and snug-fitting, appliquéd costumes, to expose the contours of the body, enhancing each step and rhythm. The "dead fathers" wear a faceless costume that is designed to inspire awe—an amorphous cloth tube is sewn at the bottom and gathered at the top around a wooden stem.

The dances reinforce the visual distinctions: the "dead mother" masquerade dances employ rapid, complex rhythmic patterns, with intricate leg and footwork; the "dead father" sweeps across the ground in a disguised run, manipulating and rolling his cloth over the ground. Underscoring its nonhuman image, local people say, the "dead father walks leaving no footprint on the ground."

Masked stilt-dancing is also widespread in sub-Saharan Africa, existing in such places as Mali among the Dogon, Liberia and Côte d'Ivoire among the Dan, southern Nigeria among the Isoko, Gabon among the BaNdzabi of the Ogooué basin, and Tanzania among the Makonde. The stilts vary in height from twelve inches to twelve feet (30 centimeters to 4 meters). Dan stilts are so tall that the dancers can sit on their rooftops. Robert Thompson (1979) described a stilt masquerader thus:

> [He] crosses his stilts before his body. He relaxes his elbows, waist, and knees and sits down on thin air, posterior brought perilously below the level of his knees. He rises and walks with giant steps. He stands, staring down, at the admiring populace ten feet below. He jumps backwards seven times. He twists his body at the waist and swings his enormous legs, literally dancing. . . . Gle gbee (long spirit, the Dan name for stilt-dance) deliberately begins to fall, to be saved by young followers who artfully prevent his body from dashing against the ground.

Within any sub-Saharan African culture, great diversity exists in forms and styles of masquerading. For example, the Baule, an agricultural people of Côte d'Ivoire who live between the Komoé and Bandama rivers, have three distinct masking traditions, called *Bonu Amuen, Gba gba,* and *Goli.* The *Bonu Amuen* are fearsome bush spirits that resemble herd animals such as antelopes and buffalo. The masqueraders wear raffia costumes and helmet masks with gaping jaws and prominent teeth. They dance to protect the community, to discipline women, and to honor deceased dancers and important men at funerals. Women of childbearing age are prohibited from seeing them.

Hans Himmelheber filmed a *Bonu Amuen* masquerader known as Do in the village of Tetekro. Accompanied by drums, gongs, and flute, Do moves with short, quick movements, sharply twisting his upper torso and head from side to side so that his raffia costume flies back and forth. Sometimes unmasked male dancers appear to taunt him by shaking bunches of smoldering fiber in his face. He charges them, and they step back, pivot, and leap into a full turn, with knees lifted and torsos leaning backward. In another scene, Do sits on a chair shaking his knees rapidly up and down in opposition to each other so that he appears agitated. As he sits, a man decapitates a chicken at his feet, passes it over Do's head three times in a counterclockwise direction, and tosses it away over the heads of the spectators. Do then stands up sharply and darts off, charging members of the audience as he goes.

A second dance masquerade, *Gba gba,* is among the oldest in Baule country. It is considered a women's dance although the men masquerade. They portray real people and both domestic and wild animals in their various relationships to humans. They dance to entertain the community on special occasions, as well as at the funerals of women and those associated with *Gba gba* performances.

The masquerade begins with the entrance of Gba gba (Bird), who wears a cloth mask with cowrie eyes and a layered raffia costume that bounces and sways in response to his movements. His dance consists primarily of short segments that emphasize rapid foot rhythms and end either in a spinning turn, a long slide on the heel of one foot, or, most often, a forward roll on the ground. After his somersault, Gba gba sometimes sits and subtly twitches his head in different directions, evoking animal-like behavior. Another masquerader, representing a ram, wears a mask to which a long woven cloth is attached, covering the body of the performer. Bending forward at a 45-degree angle, the masquerader steps around the dance space, sometimes crouching near the ground like a four-legged animal.

Gba gba also features two masqueraders portraying females, one of whom wears a woman's long wrapper and a long cloth extending down from the mask. A small girl follows about eight feet (2.8 meters) behind; both performers dance upright using small, gentle, repetitive steps. The other "female" masquerader does a dance similar to the first and is likewise accompanied by a young girl. The small, delicate steps propel the dancers' bodies across the ground, as their shoulders rock repetitively backward and forward. The masquerade ends with the appearance of

MASK AND MAKEUP: African Traditions. These men, of the Ife people of central Nigeria, are priests of Ọbatala, the Yoruba deity *(orisha)* who fashions the human body. The conical, beaded crowns, seen here, are their characteristic headgear. (Photograph © by Pierre Verger; used by permission.)

two children wearing identical costumes of fresh green fibers. They are accompanied only by the handclapping of their peers. With an elder male attendant standing by to instruct them, they perform a rapid, repetitive step-catch-step and then fall to the ground and roll.

The Baule adopted *Goli* from a small Mande-speaking people, the Wan, in the early twentieth century. *Goli* is performed on occasions similar to those for *Gba gba:* traditional days of rest, visits from dignitaries, celebrations of good harvests, and funerals. In contrast to *Gba gba,* which is often performed at women's funerals, *Goli* is performed only at men's funerals. The *Goli* masqueraders perform to calabash instruments strung with cowry shells that, when manipulated, produce a rasping rhythmic sound. The masqueraders appear in pairs, and each performer takes a turn while facing one of the musicians. They perform quick stamping patterns and a rapid scissor step and periodically whirl around. Performers carry wooden rods in their hands that are thrust between their legs and then over their heads to whack the animal hides attached to their backs, punctuating the end of a movement sequence with a loud thump.

MASK AND MAKEUP: African Traditions. Young initiates of the Alur people, of the Lake Mobutu region of Congo, dance in a tight-knit line. Their bodies and faces are decorated with white paint. (Photograph © by Michel Huet; used by permission.)

Among the most widespread masking societies are the all-male Poro and its female counterpart Sande (or Bundu). The former is found from Temne and Kono territory in central Sierra Leone southward and eastward to Bassa and Mano territory in central Liberia; the latter is found throughout Sierra Leone and northwestern Liberia. These societies dominate the social, religious, and political lives of their members and traditionally involve everyone in a community.

The distribution of masking appears to reflect social organization. Masquerades do not exist among nomadic peoples or pastoralists. Even within strong masquerading areas there are large pockets where it did not exist traditionally. For example, neither the Voltaic peoples of Ghana (that is, the Lobi, Grusi, Mooré, and Gourma) nor the Twi-speakers of Ghana, Togo, and Benin have a history of masquerades. René Bravmann (1979) attributes the absence of masking among the Twi-speaking, forest-dwelling Akan to three factors: strong political, social, and law-enforcement systems that serve the same functions as masking; a lack of the kinds of formal initiations and men's associations that support masking groups elsewhere; and the value that the Akan place on openness—the antithesis of the notion of concealment inherent in masking.

In all but one area of Africa, women are forbidden to masquerade. The one notable exception occurs in the widespread Sande (or Bundu) type of secret society found principally among Mande- and Mel-speaking peoples throughout Sierra Leone and northwestern Liberia; here, women dance in fiber costumes and wooden helmet masks. In many other areas, however, women are required to shut themselves indoors and close their windows during certain masquerades.

Although men are usually the masqueraders, women generally perform the possession or trance dances that dominate many sub-Saharan African religious rituals. The Yoruba of southwestern Nigeria and Benin explain these performance roles in terms of their concept of the nature of men and women. Men's essential power is overt; they are perceived to be "hard" or "hot." The power of women on the other hand is covert; women are thus "gentle," "cool," and receptive. In masking, men cover and conceal their exteriors. When women are possessed by a deity in a trance, the spirit of that deity enters their "inner head," that is, their interior. Even when men become possession priests among the Yoruba, they are generally referred to as the "wives" of the deity and often dress in female garb and hairstyles. They become ritually receptive, thus like women in their relationship to the deity.

Despite the spread of Islam and Christianity throughout much of sub-Saharan Africa, masquerades continue to flourish and evolve. In Malawi, the northern Maravi (Chewa) parody the Virgin Mary in an anti-Christian masquerade known as *malaya.* Masking also thrives among Islamized peoples, a fact that, according to René Bravmann (1975), "directly contradict[s] the well-established dictum that Islam has had a totally destructive effect upon the arts, especially upon masking." Bravmann theorizes that masking in sub-Saharan Africa provides solutions to local problems that Islam does not address. Among the northwestern Bono, Maude-Dioula, Ligbi, and Hwela of Ghana and Côte d'Ivoire, two masking societies, the Gbain and Do, are controlled by Muslims. Gbain masqueraders in full-length raffia costumes represent bush buffalo. They perform daring feats, such as leaping onto rooftops and sitting on glowing coals, during nighttime rituals intended to rid the community of witchcraft. Upon completion of dances that include leaping, crouching, kneeling, and rapid turning, the masqueraders go through the town in search of witches. The Do masqueraders, in contrast, wear face masks that depict humans or domesticated animals. They perform publicly, mostly in pairs, during the daylight hours at various Muslim celebrations, funerals, and marriages. Their dances are vigorous and amusing, demonstrating technical agility.

The Zara of Bobo-Dioula in southwestern Burkina Faso are unique among Islamized Africans in that they evoke ancient pan-Islamic spirits known as *djinn* through their *lo gue* ("white masks") masquerades. Always performed at night, *lo gue* centers on a white-clad masquerader known as Gyinna-Gyinna (the djinn spirit made manifest), who vaults with a bamboo pole and performs vigorous pirouettes to convey the warmth or heat of the spirit. One song asserts, "If one touches the body of Gyinna, *'anewo togo,'* it is like fire." Therefore people avoid touching or looking directly at the masquerader to prevent injury from the heat he emits. Because the djinn are perceived to be tall and lean, height and slenderness are important attributes for the dancer. Gyinna-Gyinna's mask—white cloth that fits tightly around the face—is topped by a wooden crest with long rods projecting out of the top of the head so that the Gyinna-Gyinna masquerader stands nearly eight feet (2.8 meters) tall. *Lo gue* is performed annually to confront and pacify the djinn and thereby protect the Zara community.

An example of the way cultures adapt their masked dances to new situations was analyzed by Pascal Imperato (1971) among the Dogon of Mali. Traditionally, masked dances of the Dogon were performed by a secret association of circumcised males during funeral ceremonies, to lead the deceased's soul to its final resting place and to consecrate its passage into the realm of the ancestors. Masked dances were also performed during death anniversary ceremonies called *dama.* This tradition slowly changed in the 1930s as European impact increased in Dogon country. Early in the 1930s, the anthropologist Marcel Griaule began to study and write about Dogon culture; at about the same time a group of Dogon dancers performed in Paris. As a result, tourism in Dogon country increased throughout the 1940s and 1950s, and dancers in the scenic village of Sanga performed sporadically for visiting colonial officials and tourists. By 1950 each performer was receiving a fee. In the early 1960s the Malian National Folklore Troupe was formed. The erosion of the traditional men's association that produced the masked dances, combined with a new emphasis on tourism, pro-

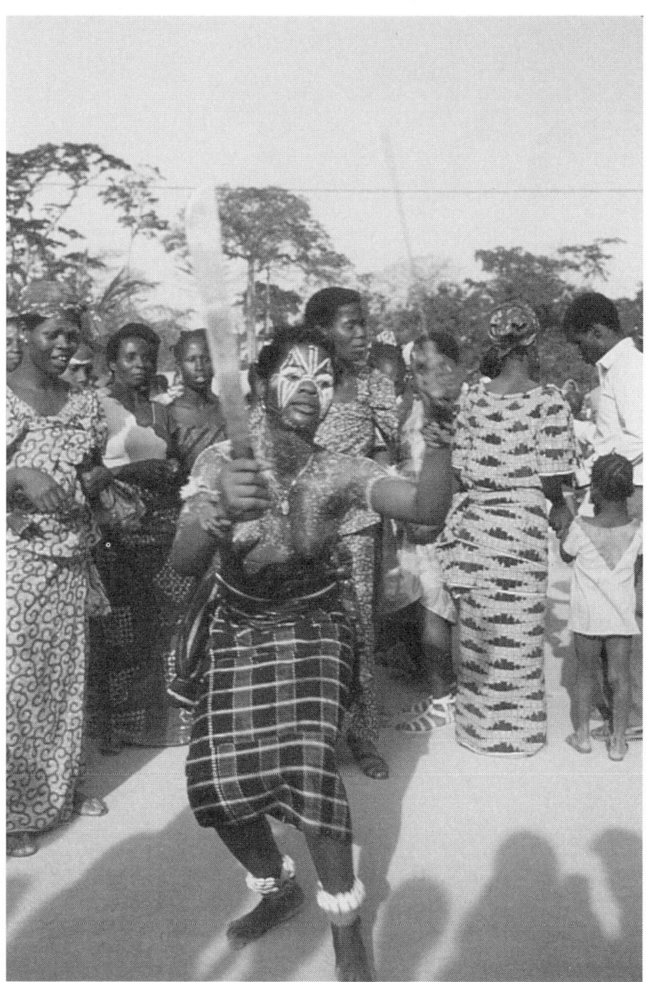

MASK AND MAKEUP: African Traditions. This knife dance is performed only at the end of a Guéré initiation rite. The Guéré are a people of southwestern Côte d'Ivoire. This dancer, Goho Norbertine, was photographed in Blolequin, Canton Néao. (Photograph © 1986 by Monni Adams; used by permission.)

MASK AND MAKEUP: African Traditions. Bamileke dancers of the central Cameroon highlands wearing characteristic long-nosed, high-hatted, beaded masks. (Private collection.)

duced a new form of masked dancing adapted from the old.

The masks have become less abstract and more naturalistic, and they are painted with commercial paint rather than vegetal dyes. Likewise, the costumes are now dyed with commercial inks and are less carefully constructed, with many of the hand accessories eliminated. Many songs, chants, and mime segments have been trimmed or eliminated, so that masquerades that once lasted two to three hours are now about fifteen minutes long. The size of the audience, too, has decreased to a handful of Europeans and local children, in contrast to the traditional audience made up of the entire village. Performances that were traditionally held in a variety of places around the village are now danced in the village square under silk-cotton trees, a more picturesque setting for photographers.

The dances have been altered or abbreviated to satisfy a foreign audience: fewer types of dances are performed, with less spectacular feats, and segments of miming are deleted. The traditional homage to the elders is no longer danced, and the masqueraders' high-pitched howling has also been deemphasized. Imperato found that little of the *bede* ("young girl") and *sirige* ("house") funeral masquerades, which consist mostly of ritual gestures rather than dance, has been transferred to the theatrical arena. Yet a traditional action in which the masquerader bends forward to touch the top of his twenty-foot (almost 7-meter) *sirige* mask to the ground to ask the deceased's pardon, has been translated into a spectacular acrobatic feat: as the masquerader bends his head forward, he jumps into the air with both legs pressed together.

With all these adaptations, the performance nevertheless maintains some spiritual integrity. Imperato noted that during a performance in 1968 two stilt dancers fell to the ground. After they were carried off, a group of masqueraders knelt down, wiping the ground with their fly whisks in ritual mourning to prevent the impending death of the fallen dancers.

Not only do existing forms change, but new ones too are continually introduced, usually from neighboring cultures. In addition, the importation of new masquerade forms and dances from distant sources—such as the introduction of the *bumba-meu-boi* masquerade from Brazil into Lagos, Nigeria, by Afro-Brazilians of Yoruba ancestry—is not uncommon. For example, masking in southern Ghana, popularly known as "Fancy Dress," was

MASK AND MAKEUP: African Traditions. A *zauli* mask of the Guro people of central Côte d'Ivoire. (Photograph © 1993 by Jenny Lynn McNutt; used by permission.)

probably introduced between 1822 and 1874 by West Indian troops brought by the colonial administration to help check Ashanti invasions. Many aspects of the Fancy Dress masquerades, as performed by members of voluntary masking associations, are identical to those of the Caribbean-style Carnival. The masks are made of molded wire screen or *papier-mâché* and are usually painted pink, beige, or another light color. The costumes consist of relatively close-fitting tunics and trousers of brightly colored cotton, cut in geometric shapes, and pieced together in patchwork fashion. Masqueraders often wear European-style tights and gloves. They perform on commission for such occasions as Easter, Christmas, New Year's Day, traditional festivals, installations of chiefs, dignitaries' visits, and funerals of deceased Fancy Dress members. Each Fancy Dress group has its own distinct garb. Most of the masquerades are generalized characters, but others are specific and include Old Man, Ship's Captain, White Man, Stilt Dancer, Ghost, Latrine-boy, Overalls, Cow, Goat, and Monkey. There has even been a twice life-sized Neville Chamberlain (British prime minister, 1937–1940), with a top hat and high collar.

A Fancy Dress performance takes the form of a procession through the streets, the masqueraders in front followed by a Carnival-style band of brasses, fifes, and snare drums playing improvised music that the participants call "blues" or "highlife." The most popular dance in sub-Saharan Africa is the highlife, which includes repeated posturing, high-stepping, strutting, and exaggerated arm swinging. Fancy Dress masqueraders in Kumasi in 1975 danced down the street in unmistakable Calypso style.

In Africa, dance masquerades have long been an aesthetic means incorporated into evaluating and managing life's situations. Current evidence suggests that they will continue in this vein, influencing and responding to ever changing conditions.

[*See also,* Costume in African Traditions. *For general discussion, see* Sub-Saharan Africa, *overview article.*]

BIBLIOGRAPHY

Adams, Marie Jeanne, ed. *Ethnologische Zeitschrift Zürich I.* Bern, 1980.

Åkesson, Birgit. *Källvattnets mask: Om dans i Afrika.* Stockholm, 1983.

Azevedo, Warren L. d'. "Mask Makers and Myth in Western Liberia." In *Primitive Art and Society,* edited by Anthony Forge. London, 1973.

Blackmun, Barbara, and J. Matthew Schoffeleers. "Masks of Malawi." *African Arts* 5 (Summer 1972).

Borgatti, Jean. "Dead Mothers of Okpella." *African Arts* 12 (August 1979a).

Borgatti, Jean. *From the Hands of Lawrence Ajanaku.* Los Angeles, 1979b.

Bravmann, René A. *Islam and Tribal Art in West Africa.* London, 1974.

Bravmann, René A. "Masking Tradition and Figurative Art among the Islamized Mande." In *African Images: Essays in African Iconology,* edited by Daniel F. McCall and Edna G. Bay. New York, 1975.

Bravmann, René A. "Gyinna-Gyinna: Making the Djinn Manifest." *African Arts* 10 (April 1977).

Bravmann, René A. "Gur and Manding Masquerades in Ghana." *African Arts* 13 (November 1979).

Brentjes, Burchard. *African Rock Art.* Translated by Anthony Dent. London, 1969.

Cole, Herbert M., et al. *African Arts of Transformation.* Santa Barbara, Calif., 1970.

Cole, Herbert M., and Doran H. Ross. *The Arts of Ghana.* Los Angeles, 1977.

Drewal, Henry John. "Efe/Gelede: The Educative Role of the Arts in Traditional Yoruba Culture." Ph.D. diss., Columbia University, 1973.

Drewal, Henry John. "African Masked Theatre." *Mime Journal,* no. 2 (1975): 36–53.

Drewal, Henry John, and Margaret Thompson-Drewal. *Gelede: Art and Female Power among the Yoruba.* Bloomington, 1983.

Fischer, Eberhard, and Hans Himmelheber. *Die Kunst der Dan.* Zurich, 1976.

Fischer, Eberhard. "Dan Forest Spirits: Masks in Dan Villages." *African Arts* 11 (January 1978).

Griaule, Marcel. *Les masques dogons* (1938). 4th ed. Paris, 1994.

Huet, Michel. *The Dance, Art, and Ritual of Africa.* New York, 1978.

Huet, Michel, and Claude Savary. *Africa Dances.* London, 1995.

Imperato, Pascal James. "The Dance of the Tyi Wara." *African Arts* 4 (Autumn 1970).

Imperato, Pascal James. "Contemporary Adapted Dances of the Dogon." *African Arts* 5 (Autumn 1971).

Imperato, Pascal James. "Bambara and Malinke Ton Masquerades." *African Arts* 13 (August 1980).

Imperato, Pascal James. "The Depiction of Beautiful Women in Malian Youth Association Masquerades." *African Arts* 27 (January 1994): 58–65.

Kedjanyi, J. "Masquerade Societies in Ghana." *Research Review* 3.2 (1967).

Kubik, Gerhard. *Maskentraditionen im bantu-sprachigen Afrika.* Munich, 1993.

Lamp, Frederick. "Frogs into Princes: The Temne Rabai Initiation." *African Arts* 11 (January 1978).

Lamp, Frederick. *African Art of the West Atlantic Coast.* New York, 1979.

Lhote, Henri. *The Search for the Tassili Frescoes.* Translated by Alan H. Brodrick. New York, 1959.

Messenger, John Cowan. "Anang Art, Drama, and Social Control." *African Studies Bulletin* 5.2 (1962).

Mubitana, Kafungulwa. "Wiko Masquerades." *African Arts* 4 (Spring 1971).

Nadel, S. F. *Nupe Religion.* London, 1954.

Obafemi, Olu. "The Kinetic Aesthetics of the Festival Masquerade Dance in Africa." In *Beyond Performance: Dance Scholarship Today,* edited by Susan Au and Frank-Manuel Peter. Berlin, 1989.

Onyeneke, Augustine O. *The Dead among the Living: Masquerades in Igbo Society.* Aachen, 1987.

Ottenberg, Simon. "Humorous Masks and Serious Politics among Afikpo Ibo." In *African Art and Leadership,* edited by Douglas Fraser and Herbert M. Cole. Madison, Wis., 1972.

Ottenberg, Simon. "Illusion, Communication, and Psychology in West African Masquerades." *Ethos* 10 (Summer 1982): 149–185.

Peek, Philip M. "Isoko Artists and Their Audiences." *African Arts* 13 (May 1980).

Phillips, Ruth B. "Masking in Mende Sande Society Initiation Rituals." *Africa* 48.3 (1978).

Sieber, Roy. "Masks as Agents of Social Control." In *The Many Faces of Primitive Art,* edited by Douglas Fraser. Englewood Cliffs., N.J., 1966.

Siroto, Leon. "*Gon:* A Mask Used in Competition for Leadership among the Bakwele." In *African Art and Leadership,* edited by Douglas Fraser and Herbert M. Cole. Madison, Wis., 1972.

Thompson, Robert Farris. *African Art in Motion: Icon and Act.* 2d ed. Los Angeles, 1979.

Thompson-Drewal, Margaret, and Glorianne Jackson, comps. *Sources on African and African-Related Dance.* New York, 1974.

Thompson-Drewal, Margaret, and Henry John Drewal. "More Powerful Than Each Other: An Egbado Classification of Egungun." *African Arts* 11 (Spring 1978).

Thompson-Drewal, Margaret. "Appendix B (Dance)." In *From the Hands of Lawrence Ajanaku,* by Jean Borgatti. Los Angeles, 1979.

Vogel, Susan M. "Baule Art as the Expression of a World View." Ph.D. diss., New York University, 1977.

Vrydagh, P. Andre. "Makisi of Zambia." *African Arts* 10 (July 1977).

Weil, Peter M. "The Masked Figure and Social Control." *Africa* 41 (October 1971).

Wembah- Rashid, J. A. R. "Isinyago and Midimu: Masked Dancers of Tanzania and Mozambique." *African Arts* 4 (Winter 1971).

Willett, Frank. *African Art.* Rev. ed. New York, 1993.

FILMS. The following films are available in the series Encyclopaedia Cinematographica (Göttingen). *Baule (Westafrika, Elfenbeinkuste)—"gbagba"—Maskentanz* (1965). *Baule (Westafrika, Elfenbeinkuste)—"goli"—Maskentanz* (1965). *Baule (Westafrika, Elfenbeinkuste)—Auftritt der "do"—Maske in Tetekro* (1970). *Baule (Westafrika, Elfenbeinkuste)—"gbagba"—Maskentanz in Asouakro. I: Eilnmarsch, Tanz des Gbagba, Schafsmaske* (1970). *Baule (Westafrika, Elfenbeinkuste)—"gbagba"—Maskentanz in Asouakro. II: Rote, schwarze und weiße Maske, Ameisenmaske, Kindermasken* (1970). *Baule (Westafrika, Elfenbeinkuste)—"goli"—Maskenfest in Agbanjansou* (1970).

MARGARET THOMPSON-DREWAL

Asian Traditions

The transformation of the face is a crucial element in many forms of Asian dance drama. Masks and makeup are not used as means of simple disguise in Asia; they are employed as sophisticated techniques for making the invisible world visible. Whereas the naked face of a performer is limited to the human expressions of an individual ego, the presence of a mask or makeup enables the dancer-actor to suggest another, often a higher, realm of meaning—dense with allusions to ancestors, gods, and archetypal human aspirations. The specific references intended by facial transformations in dance-drama performances vary from culture to culture and within cultures from one form to another. Sometimes the emphasis is on religious meaning, and sometimes it is more on secular aesthetics, but the two realms are not as easily distinguishable in Asian performance as they are in the West.

Wearing masks or codified patterns of makeup signifies that the performer is serving an art form that deemphasizes the individual in favor of larger concerns. The performance task shifts away from self-expression or display of individual talents and moves toward the depiction of god, ancestor, or archetype in physical form. The body movements become extensions of the transformed face, and the individual face beneath it (the face of the performer) is rendered inconsequential. This attitude of submitting one's physical and emotional skills to the needs of the mask is epitomized in the preperformance ritual practiced by mask performers in many cultures: meditating on the mask or making sacrificial offerings to it.

In preperformance rituals that focus on the mask or the application of makeup, as well as in the training of the dancer-actor that shapes the attitude toward the mask or makeup, the facial transformation is invested with paradox, mystery, and power. In some cases the transformation links the past to the present by giving a concrete form to historical figures and legendary ancestors, whose invocation is necessary for the spiritual health of the community. In other cases the transformation indicates a representation of divinities whose blessings are desired or possession by spirits whose exorcism is necessary. Even in the most secular of Asian dance dramas the performer is

MASK AND MAKEUP: Asian Dance Traditions. Masked performer from Bhutan. The eye holes of Bhutanese masks are often so small that performers need guides to lead them around the stage. (Photograph by Diane Glazer; used by permission of The Asia Society, New York.)

conscious of the makeup or the mask as a catalyst for converting the language and movement of the masked body into transcendant symbols of human ideals or natural forces. Unlike Western performance in which such symbolic use of masks or stylized makeup often strikes the viewer as stultified or pretentious, Asian traditions have succeeded in charging stylized facial transformations with a performance style that is simultaneously immediate and universal, specifically indicative at the same time that it is suggestively resonant. The powerful impact of masks and makeup in Asian dance drama is due partly to audience familiarity with the conventions being used and also to the great attention given to the subtle performance technique of making the mask come alive, an art almost unknown to modern Western performers and audiences. The mask or makeup is little more than an awkwardly artificial face until the performer animates it with techniques acquired through long study of muscular manipulations, breathing control, and spiritual discipline. Animated with complex performance skills in cultural contexts that value the significance of a spiritual realm in a material world, facial masks in Asia transcend the connotation of concealment, enabling performers and audiences to reach sophisticated levels of revelation. Facial transformations in Asian dance drama artfully uncover much more than they disguise.

Japan. The *nō* theater of Japan demonstrates one of the world's most refined uses of mask aesthetics. Two of the central principles of *nō* expounded by *nō* master Zeami in his fourteenth-century text *Kadensho* are *yugen* and *monomane*, and both are embodied by the suggestive use of masks. *Monomane* is an elaborate concept of performance that can be roughly translated as "imitation of things as they exist," and in one sense the features of *nō* masks imitate those of individual characters. *Yugen* is a complementary concept of performance that shifts emphasis to the intangible aspects of existence that can only be implied, and *nō* masks are also capable of evoking the mystery of unseen worlds.

Although *nō* is a secular theater form, its aesthetics cannot be separated from the combination of Shintō and Buddhist beliefs that pervaded Japanese culture when the form was evolving. The stories and action appeal to the senses in immediate ways that reflect the Shintō celebration of the sensory world and, correspondingly, the masks are realistic depictions of young women, warriors, and old men. But *nō* is also permeated with an awareness of an unseen world of spirituality and essences that reflects the influence of Buddhism, and this acknowledgment of unseen mystery is also mirrored in the use of the masks.

The subdued and hypnotic movements of the actor deemphasize active conflict and shift attention to inner actions by creating a meditative mood. The focus of the meditation in *nō* is often on the mask and the way its movements reveal inner states of thought and emotion. Many *nō* masks are relatively neutral in expression, and the actor is trained to keep his neck muscles immobile during performance except for slight movements that purposefully create the illusion that the mask's expression is changing. These illusions are created by changing shadows, created as the mask tilts in different directions. When the angle of the mask is tilted downward, the shadows that fall on the face make the character appear to be deep in thought, an effect known as clouding *(kumorashi)*. If the mask is tilted upward, a lightening of shadows gives the illusion of a happier emotional state, an effect known as brightening *(terashi)*.

As in other masked forms, the actor in *nō* is restricted in his interpretation of a character by the qualities of the mask. Several types of masks (old man, woman, warrior, demon, and others) are used repeatedly to fit these character types as they occur in the stories of the *nō* repertory. Only if a performer has access to two versions of a single character type (a youthful warrior and a more experienced warrior, for example) would it be possible to interpret a character with nuanced variations. The performer is clearly serving the mask, not forcing the mask to fit any kind of personal interpretation. Individuality in performance is discouraged to such an extent that even in the representation of unmasked characters, the actor-dancer is forced to keep the face as unchanging as if it were a mask.

Kyōgen plays, which are performed as comic interludes between the more stately *nō* dramas, also use masks but only to depict overtly nonhuman characters like demons and animals. The human characters in *kyōgen* deal with more earthly conflicts than do their counterparts in *nō*, and they perform with very simple and naturalistic makeup.

Kabuki theater is a more popular form of Japanese drama than *nō*, and much of its appeal lies in heightening emotion with bold acting techniques that are in sharp contrast to the restraints of *nō*. The muted expressions of *nō* masks give way to extravagantly colored makeup as the means for facial transformation in *kabuki*. The bold faces of white, blue, and red paint are highly stylized and conform to a code of characterization that matches specific patterns to specific character types. The code of painted faces for the male characters is called *kumadori*, and it functions primarily to exaggerate and maintain the tensions in facial muscles so that the actor appears to be in a heightened emotional state at all times. The style of makeup conforms with the style of *kabuki* performance, in providing much more opportunity for individual virtuosity in acting than is possible in the refined world of *nō* drama, but the stylized patterns of the makeup still inhibit individual interpretations of characters to a greater extent than the naturalistic makeup of the West.

MASK AND MAKEUP: Asian Dance Traditions. (*above*) The *kabuki* style of makeup called *kumadori* emphasizes, rather than covers, the lines of the face to create exaggerated facial expressions. These *kumadori* illustrations show (from left to right): the *mukimi guma* worn by the title character in *Sukeroku*; the *saruguma* (monkey *kuma*) worn by Benkei in *Gohiiki Kanjinchō*; the sujiguma (lines *kuma*) seen on Gongorō in *Shibaraku*; the *tsuchigumo no kuma* (earth spider *kuma*) worn by the Earth Spider in *Tsuchigumo*; and another version of *saruguma*, this one worn by Asahina in *Soga no Taimen*. Painted on a white background, the colors red, black, and brown are used in varying proportions in the makeup. (*left*) Ichikawa Ennosuke III, a versatile *kabuki* actor who portrays all types of characters, appears here as the Demon in *Kurozuka*. (Drawings above reprinted from Fujita Hiroshi, *Kabuki Handobukku*, Tokyo, 1994, by permission of Sanseido. Photograph at left © 1977 by Jack Vartoogian; used by permission.)

The characters of *kabuki* inhabit a larger-than-life realm of heroism and heightened action. Their exotic makeup is one of their passports to that mythic realm, but it also predetermines that their actions conform to the passions painted on their faces. It is only in contrast to the *nō* theatre that *kabuki* seems blatantly direct in its expression. The makeup still serves the function of helping the actor to reveal invisible qualities, most notably for the female impersonators (the *onnagata*), whose makeup consists of idealized feminine features delicately painted onto a white base. This facial transformation is one of the key elements in the actor's eerily sensual representation of universally female qualities, which appear more feminine than the movements of most women. The makeup helps the actor to transcend realism, where his impersonation would seem ludicrous and would reveal to his audience an otherworldly conception of the eternal feminine ideal.

China. The dominant dance-drama genre in China is Beijing Opera, which developed as a combination of a variety of folk forms. No masks are used in Beijing Opera and the major characters wear naturalistic makeup that does not transform their faces substantially. The clowns wear patches of white makeup around their eyes and nose; the category of warrior characters known as *qing* wear extravagant painted designs in which colors signify personality traits. Red indicates loyalty. White is for deceitful characters and traitors. Black denotes honesty. Blue stresses courage and ferocity. Beijing Opera relies on spectacle and athletic performance skills, so the faces of the performers are not central to the action. A legend explaining the origin of the painted faces for warrior characters suggests that a Chinese prince of the fifth century BCE found his effeminate features to be unsuitable to waging warfare, then painted fierce designs on his face before going into battle. This story connects the painted faces of the Beijing Opera to an ancient Chinese belief in the magical powers of facial transformation. In the case of the warrior prince, the painted face invests one with strength over enemies. In old rituals connected to funeral ceremonies, the Chinese often used masks to ward off demons.

Indonesia. On the island of Bali in Indonesia, the art of facial transformation thrives with vibrancy and variety. Masks and makeup are applied to the faces of dancer-actors in a wide spectrum of dance-drama forms that range from sacred possession to secular entertainment.

The most religiously potent performance is that which depicts the battle of the Barong mask against the Rangda mask. Barong is a figure in Balinese religion (a mixture of Hinduism, Buddhism, and animism) who represents the universal forces of good; Rangda is a widow-witch representing evil. Their symbolic conflict is performed to preserve the world's balance between benign and malignant forces. The mask of Rangda is imbued with such great spiritual power that it induces trance possession not only in the wearer but in the nonmasked dancers who encounter Rangda. Another form of the Rangda witch mask is known as Calonarang. Only individuals with great psychic discipline and maturity are permitted to wear the mask of Rangda, but even with this precaution there are legends of dancers who have been driven permanently mad by the experience of possession by Rangda or Calonarang.

MASK AND MAKEUP: Asian Dance Traditions. Half-masks are used to depict the comic narrator figures of Balinese *topéng* dramas. Here, I Wayan Teduh portrays Kartala, one such character, in the village of Sukawati, Bali. (Photograph © by Edward Herbst; used by permission.)

MASK AND MAKEUP: Asian Dance Traditions. Endo Suanda, a Sundanese mask-maker and performer, is seen here regarding his own work, in a characteristic wide-legged stance. (Photograph from the archives of The Asia Society, New York.)

Topéng is another form of masked drama in Bali, but the possession of the performer by the *topéng* mask is not as complete or violent as the possession that occurs with the mask of Rangda. In *topéng,* performed only by men, the masks are associated with the stories of legendary ancestors; although the masks are revered as sacred objects, the performer is conscious of performing a movement technique during the dance. At the same time, the dancer is also conscious of the spiritual and physical demands of the mask, restricting movement patterns to those in harmony with the form and archetypal character of the particular mask. The aim of a *topéng* dancer is to develop a "bond" with the mask, known as *taksu.* An actor who meditates on the mask's form and respects its spiritual origins is able to bring the mask alive in a way that transcends technical proficiency. A dancer without *taksu* is said to be like a carpenter, who merely pushes around the wooden face without making it breathe. Within the form of *topéng,* hierarchies have developed for some masks to be more potently sacred than others. The most revered mask is that of the mad god-king Siddya Karya; it can only be worn by the most experienced dancers. Half masks, which leave part of the dancer's face exposed, depict the more coarse and common characters of the clown narrators, who serve as a link between the divine world of the masked gods and the mundane world.

Arja is a more secular form of dance drama performed by women, who wear stylized makeup to help transform themselves into a state in which they can depict the legends of Balinese gods and heroes. The notion of spiritual possession is less connected to the wearing of *arja* makeup than to the donning of *topéng* masks, but the faces of the *arja* dancers are blessed with holy water and ritual chants before each performance and their link to the more sacred form of *topéng* is strengthened by the existence of hybrid performances—known as *prémbon*—in which the masked male *topéng* dancers perform in the same stories with nonmasked female *arja* dancers.

MASK AND MAKEUP. Asian Dance Traditions. A dancer portraying Hanumān, commander of the monkey army, wears a *papier mâché* mask in a Javanese *wayang wong* performance at the Dalem Pujokusuman in Jogjakarta. (Photograph © by Jukka O. Miettinen; used by permission.)

In Java, the dance dramas involving facial transformations are preserved more as cultural artifacts than as the living performance traditions that exist in Bali. In Java intriguing connections exist between dramas employing makeup known as *wayang wong,* masked dramas called *wayang topéng,* wooden rod puppets called *wayang golek,* and shadow puppets known as *wayang kulit.* The legends of Javanese gods and heroes are acted through the wooden puppets; these are one step closer to the concrete human form than are the ethereal shadow puppets who play characters that appear only in light or its absence. The masked dramas danced by actors with wooden faces bring the acting one step still closer to a secular human incarnation, and this is even more fully realized in the dances known as *wayang wong,* where the action is played out by dancers wearing only makeup. The role of facial transformation in mediating between visible and invisible worlds is seen in a variety of manifestations that range from shadows of faces, to wooden puppet representations of faces, to masks, to makeup. Each step is one phase less removed from the everyday world of the audience, but all are linked with the basic human impulse to use performance as a means of connecting the community to the realms of spirituality and mystery inaccessible to ordinary experience.

Of the other Indonesian islands, the most notable use of facial transformation is in the Feast of the Dead on the island of Borneo. During this ceremony that accompanies funerals, masks are used to represent the spirits who will carry departed souls from the realm of the living to the realm of the dead.

India. Representing characters from the great Hindu epics, the actors of *kathakaḷi* dance drama wear elaborately stylized makeup that categorizes them into distinct types. The *pacca* are the divine, heroic, and royal characters, such as Viṣṇu (Vishnu) or Rāma, with bright green faces. The *katti* are demonic characters with some noble qualities. Their faces are green as are those of the *pacca,* but they are distinguished by a red-and-white mustache design that extends from cheek to cheek and carries up across the nose and forehead, forming a knife-shaped design over each eyebrow (*katti* means "knife"). *Tati* characters are crude and bearded; some have large round false noses, which render them slightly comical (Hanuman the monkey is a variation of this type). *Kari* is the female demon type that sometimes wears false breasts and an apron. A wide variety of painted characters fall under the type termed *teppu.* The most realistic characters are called *minukku.*

Kathakaḷi makeup transforms the face and prepares the actor to enter a heroic and mythic realm of performance, but other forms of dance drama in India use makeup as a means of inducing religious possession in the performer.

MASK AND MAKEUP: Asian Dance Traditions. A *katti* character of Kathakaḷi, made up as the demon king Rāvaṇa. (Photograph by Clifford R. Jones; used by permission of The Asia Society.)

In *teyyam kettu* of the Cannanore District of Kerala, the performer believes that he is painting a deity onto his face when he puts on makeup. A variety of deities are invoked in this way, but the resulting performances do not have the technical acting skills demonstrated by the highly trained *kathakaḷi* dancers. The use of makeup to induce trance suggests a possible link between the secularized use of makeup in modern *kathakaḷi* and the more sacred forms of Hindu dance drama to which its past is linked.

Chhau dance is a form of folk drama in India that uses masks to enact minor myths. Although *chhau* performance cannot be categorized as possession, actor-dancers report feeling inspired to move in ways that are suggested by the touch of the mask. The mask thus deepens the transformation of the performer into the character. The two regions in which *chhau* is performed are Purulia, where it is passed on unchanged as a folk tradition, and Seraikella, where it is being reshaped more self-consciously by teachers and choreographers. On the continuum between spiritual possession and secular technique, the use of facial transformation in *chhau* seems to lie somewhere between the trances of *teyyam kettu* and the self-conscious artistry of *kathakaḷi*.

Korea. The continuum of masked performance that stretches from religious ritual to secular performance in Korea is present in the tradition of *pongsan* masked dances. The emphasis in most such dances is on popular entertainment, but many of the stories depict the masks of Buddhist monks driving out the masks of demonic spirits. In some regions of Korea, the masks are burned after each performance as an offering to forces that will help crops grow more bountifully and protect the district from plagues. In other regions, masks once customarily hung on gateways to repel the entrance of demons. Some versions of this dance were originally performed on the birthday of the Buddha.

Other forms of masked dramas in Korea retain varying degrees of sacred meaning. The *pyolsin* masked drama of

MASK AND MAKEUP: Asian Dance Traditions. In this scene from a Korean *pongsan t'al'ch'um* (masked dance drama), an old monk attempts to seduce a young courtesan by offering her a necklace. (Photograph from the archives of The Asia Society, New York.)

MASK AND MAKEUP: Asian Dance Traditions. *Tovil* is a Sinhala exorcism dance, traditionally performed to combat disease. Here, the performer Somapala appears in a *tovil* mask and costume for the *Naga Raksha* (Snake Demon's Dance). (Photograph from the archives of The Asia Society, New York.)

Hahoe begins with ritualistic offerings to the masks before the chest containing them is opened. Villagers believed that the failure to complete this ceremony would unleash bad spirits. In the more secularized masked dramas, such as the *pyol-sandae* masked dance drama of Yangju, the emphasis shifts to the exorcism of more human forms of evil, such as moral hypocrisy and abuse of privileges. In these masked performances, the aristocrats and literati are criticized through farcical parodies of their unethical behavior in love and worship.

The Korean lion dance of Pukchong combines the spectacle of popular entertainment and the ritual purpose of exorcising evil and bringing good fortune. Two performers manipulate the mask of the lion, often visiting each house in a village to give its residents blessings and receive gifts of money or food.

Sri Lanka. In Sri Lanka, masks are sometimes used to give visible form to the invisible world of sickness and disease. The *sanni yakuma* is a dance in which the demon of disease and his servants represent specific ills, ranging from blindness to hallucinations to flatulence. One mask portrays the chief demon and eighteen of his servants in a single headpiece. Other masks represent the sickness demons individually.

The elements of trance, possession, and magic potency present in the *sanni yakuma* masked dances are not factors in the Sri Lankan masked dance *kolam-natima.* This is now performed primarily as an entertainment that dramatizes myths of legendary heroes, gods, and demons. The religious content of the dances and the long unchanging tradition of the masked dance has led some observers to speculate that this masked drama was once charged with ritualistic significance and religious power that have been gradually forgotten as the performances became more popular, commercial, and secular.

Conclusion. In all their manifestations, Asian forms of facial transformation serve to bring performers and audiences closer to a vision of dance and drama that transcends ordinary reality. The mask or painted face serves as a mediator between visible and invisible worlds, between present and past, between humanity and the gods, and between the earthbound and the ideal. The intentions behind these facial transformations range from secular aesthetics to sacred ritual, and the effects they have on the language and movement performed by the transformed face range from a moderate increase in dramatic interest to a radical shift in perceptual perspective. In all cases, however, the use of facial transformation in Asian performance charges dramatic meaning by the added resonances that the naked face would be unable to project.

[*For general discussion on costume, see* Costume in Asian Traditions. *For specific masking traditions, see* Indonesia, *article on* Balinese Mask Dance Theater; *and* Korea, *article on* Masked Dance Drama. *For masking traditions in Thailand, see* Khōn. *For Japanese masking traditions, see* Kyōgen, Nō, *and* Kabuki Theater. *For dance types in India utilizing specialized makeup, see* Kathakaḷi *and* Chhau.]

BIBLIOGRAPHY

Bethe, Monica, and Karen Brazell. *Dance in the Nō Theater.* Ithaca, N.Y., 1982.

Gargi, Balwant. *Folk Theater of India.* Seattle, 1966.

Jones, Clifford Reis, and Betty True Jones. *Kathakali.* New York, 1970.

Keene, Donald. *Nō: The Classical Theatre of Japan.* New York, 1966.

Khaznadar, Cherif, ed. *Les masques et leurs fonctions.* Rennes, 1980.

Korean National Commission, UNESCO. *Traditional Performing Arts of Korea.* Seoul, 1975.

Lommel, Andreas. *Masks: Their Meaning and Function.* New York, 1970.

Miettinen, Jukka O. *Classical Dance and Theatre in South-East Asia.* New York, 1992.

Pertold, Otaker. *Ceremonial Dances of the Sinhalese* (1930). Colombo, Sri Lanka, 1973.

Scott, A. C. *The Kabuki Theatre of Japan.* New York, 1955.

Wu Zuguang et al. *Peking Opera and Mei Lanfang.* Beijing, 1981.

RON JENKINS

European Traditions

Masks appear to have answered a basic need in humans from very early times. They are known to have been used as early as fifteen thousand years ago, during the Old Stone Age. In the Western world they may be traced from primitive animistic rites and early religious pageantry to the orgiastic dances that honor the ancient Greek deities Dionysus and Apollo and to the theater masks of Greek tragedy and comedy. They survived in early Christian drama and iconography into the Middle Ages, when they were used along with expressionistic makeup in morality plays and other theatrical representations of biblical history. In the early Renaissance, theatrical forms incorporating dance assimilated masking as a matter of course; the use of masks was confirmed by the excavation of archaeological artifacts and the translation of classical works substantiating their significance in the theater of ancient Greece.

Before the construction of proscenium stages, masks were a means of creating aesthetic distance in *entrées* staged in crowded ballrooms. They were consistent with the formalism of courtly dancing as a means of achieving uniformity in choruses of dancing Shepherds, Sailors, Pleasures, Nymphs, Priests, and so on. They also facilitated travesty (men playing female roles). They became a convenient device for hiding nervous starts and grimaces in the execution of difficult steps. In keeping with the classical tradition of personal modesty, masks allowed European courtiers to perform alongside social inferiors or even professional dancers without embarrassment. Although masks were a universally accepted convention in royal court spectacles and theatrical dancing as late as the last quarter of the eighteenth century, they were by no means required on all occasions. Dancers performing in the noble style had the option of wearing makeup; masked and unmasked dancers performed together, and the masks were removed at the end of a performance and before general dancing began.

Renaissance masks were molded of leather and stiffened with varnish, made of *papier-mâché* on a wooden matrix, or sometimes carved of wood. If not attached to a headdress, they were held in place by means of ribbons or an inner mouthpiece. Grotesque masks for comic or fantastic characters—devils, cities, winds, Moors, savages, and so on—were often highly inventive in design and coloration. Those for noble-style dancing adhered to formal concepts of male and female beauty as seen in the idealized art of ancient Greece and Rome: symmetrical oval face with straight nose, short upper lip, and well-arched brows. They were lacquered to an enameled finish in light tones of pink and white or sometimes painted gold, silver, or black. The expressions were open, pleasant, and, although passive or neutral, not without presence. To indicate age or specific character, these masks might be given an appropriate expression or an exaggerated form.

By the mid-seventeenth century, the acceptance of women on the stage made the mask somewhat obsolete as part of female disguise (travesty). After 1661 professional dancers who were trained at the French Académie Royale de Danse gradually replaced aristocratic amateurs and introduced expressive techniques that made the immobile expression of a mask a handicap. There is no indication that the important innovators of the early decades of the eighteenth century—Françoise Prévost, Marie Sallé, and Marie Camargo—adhered strictly to their use.

That masks persisted, however, in the eighteenth-century *ballet de cour* and the opera is evident from choreographer Jean-Georges Noverre's famous diatribe against them in his *Lettres sur la danse* (1760); he not only proposed the elimination of conventionalized gesture, large headdresses, and panniers but also asked dancers to "do away with those lifeless masks, but feeble copies of nature, they hide your features, they stifle, so to speak, your emotions and thus deprive you of your most important

MASK AND MAKEUP: European Traditions. In the late seventeenth and early eighteenth centuries, the mask was considered a crucial element of the dancer's costume. This engraving, after Jean Berain, depicts a dancer at the Paris Opera, during the reign of Louis XIV. (Bibliothèque de l'Opéra, Paris.)

means of expression." His criticism suggests that masked dancers had the appearance of robotlike uniformity. When the famous dancer Maximilien Gardel discarded his mask in performances at the Paris Opera in 1773, public approval prompted other performers to follow suit, and the convention of masking in ballet fell into disuse. Within half a century, the advent of the Romantic ballet and the melodramatic pathos of the *ballet blanc* had created an environment in which masks had no place. In their stead, dancers adopted what was in effect a mobile mask—a conventionalized makeup that idealized and enlarged their features to project varieties of expression.

In the early twentieth century, under Serge Diaghilev's direction, designers for the Ballets Russes sometimes concealed dancers' faces with modernistic masks or extended elements of costume. In 1917, the artist Pablo Picasso created for Léonide Massine's ballet *Parade* oversized masks in the form of giant structures, representing parts of houses, megaphones, and models of cylinders and cubes. In Germany, during the years preceding World War I, the painter Oskar Schlemmer (later the director of the Bauhaus stage) attempted to reduce dance to its essential and fundamental aspects. With the help of his brother Carl, he produced innovative costumes and masks that transformed dancers into impersonal abstract human forms resembling modernistic sculpture. Their use of masks in the famous *Triadic Ballet,* performed in Stuttgart in 1922, has been widely misunderstood as representing a desire to mechanize or exchange the living, organic being for one that functioned as a machine. Instead, they were conceived as intensifications of expression; like other aspects of Oskar Schlemmer's work in the theater, they were intended to induce what he called "pure feeling." [*See* Bauhaus, Dance and the.]

MASK AND MAKEUP: European Traditions. Pablo Picasso created the cubist designs for Léonide Massine's *Parade,* presented in 1917 by Diaghilev's Ballets Russes at the Théâtre du Chatelet, Paris. Seen here is the costume for the Manager in Evening Dress. (Photograph reprinted from Cyril Beaumont, *Ballet Design: Past and Present,* London, 1946.)

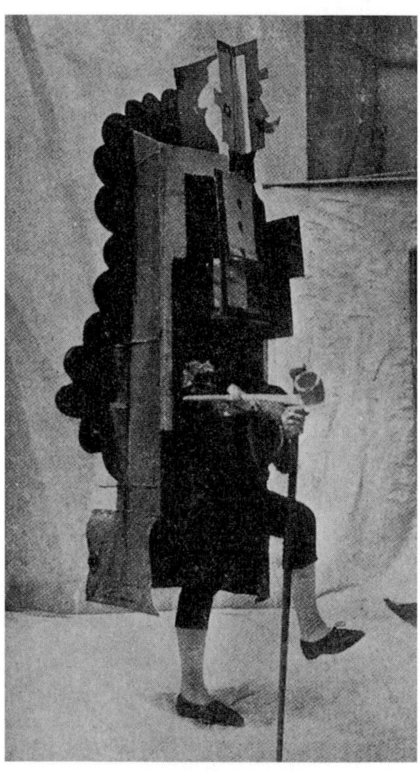

Modern dance welcomed the use of masks as a means of depersonalizing and enlarging, abstracting its themes to the most pungent essences. German expressionist dancer Mary Wigman used them to great effect in many of her powerful evocations of subjective experience. In the United States, Margaret Severn popularized the masks of illustrator W. T. Benda in theater of the 1920s. These were seen in Broadway revues and concert dance and were used as objects of art for display or interior decoration.

In Paris in 1932, Kurt Jooss produced *The Green Table,* in which dancers wore striking masks that fully covered their heads. In this way they were transformed into balding, white-haired spoilers who represented international politicians haggling over a conference table covered with green cloth. Largely due to the power of this memorable scene, his ballet has remained successful in its many revivals.

Experimental choreographer Alwin Nikolais stated that through his use of imaginative masks, props, costumes, and scenery, he attempted to re-create the dancer as an archetype, transcending personal pedestrian emotionalism. His use of dancers as the motivating force for masked costumes produced abstract effects that were evocative and potently theatrical. Like Oskar Schlemmer, however, Nikolais was accused of dehumanization.

In the postmodern era, only choreographer Erick Hawkins continued to use masks with any frequency. In keeping with the lean and clean-lined elegance of his costuming, his masks, sophisticated sculptural abstractions, were designed to lend an atmosphere of ritual.

Contemporary ballet and modern dance have largely neglected the transfiguring, symbolic potential of masking, using it only occasionally for straightforward narrative exposition. Contemporary choreography, however, which stresses abstract relationships in space, line, and mass, or the intrinsic kinetic energy underlying movement, seems best served by dancers who are willing to forgo facial expression. As a result, their faces often convey the impression of a mask substitute, presenting a neu-

MASK AND MAKEUP: European Traditions. The 1941 solo *Trickster Coyote* was Erick Hawkins's first dance to use imagery and masks inspired by the Native Americans of the southwestern United States. Throughout his career, Hawkins remained interested in the abstract design and ritual implications of masks. (Photograph © by Barbara Morgan; used by permission of the Barbara Morgan Archives, Hastings-on-Hudson, New York.)

tral and alert but passive countenance. The carriage of the head is sufficient to lend variety or focus to choreographic patterns; only the direction of the pupils of the eyes remains significant—thus eye makeup has been exaggerated. The general effect is an impersonal uniformity and classical formalism that is reminiscent of the Renaissance and Baroque stage, with life perhaps imitating the art of the mask.

As used by dancers, makeup both counteracts the unnaturalness of stage lighting and ensures that facial features and expression are legible at a distance. Although modern stage lighting closely simulates natural light, it inevitably absorbs some of the skin's natural color. It often creates a shifting kaleidoscope of several sets of shadows or, striking the face from all directions, flattens and broadens features. Makeup is thus necessary to replace color, accentuate features, and restore definition and character by artificially replacing the normal shadows that give depth and solidity of form to the face. To counteract the loss of continuity that occurs in rapid movement, dance makeup is traditionally somewhat more exaggerated than that used by other types of performers.

Medieval religious prohibitions against cosmetics gave face painting in the theater a particular significance—it usually was associated with sin and thus was used to disfigure the face, an agreed-upon sign of moral depravity. Abstractions such as pride, lust, deceit, and devilish temptation were represented by the painted face. Applying makeup on the stage was a symbolic act of conceit—a "shift of faces," connoting temptation. Red-and-white makeup constituted a "brand," a sign of sin and lust; spots were an indication of falsehood and spiritual dissolution, the suggestion of syphilitic blotches and the ugliness of sin that face paint could hide. Black was the fiend's color, associated with sexual temptation; masking blackened faces with white visors represented deceit.

The Crusaders are usually credited with introducing cosmetics of the Middle Eastern harem to European women, and the Gothic love of masquerade soon found use for it in the *moresca*, a dance duel using costume, masks, female impersonation, blackface, and other forms of face painting. [*See* Moresca.] Torches and lanterns illuminating ballrooms in the early Renaissance and the grease and wax candles used in the sixteenth and seventeenth centuries were more yellow than was natural light. They absorbed the red of the cheeks and lips and robbed the eyes of their sparkle, making them appear narrow and less expressive. To counteract this, performers used a variety of dry powders, paints, and washes that tended to be pink, relying on light for yellow tones. Products to whiten

MASK AND MAKEUP: European Traditions. Alwin Nikolais used masks, along with other design elements—including costumes, props and special lighting—to create kaleidoscopic visual effects. Here, two of his dancers, in geometrically patterned costumes, pose in *Gallery*. (Photograph © 1978 by Jack Vartoogian, used by permission.)

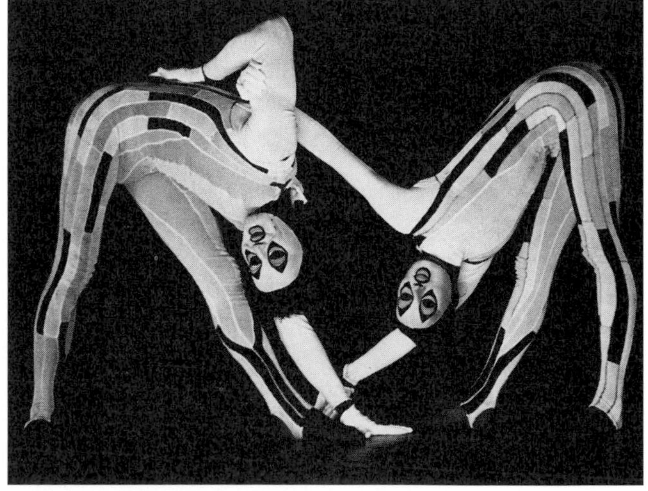

MASK AND MAKEUP: European Traditions. With her face dramatically painted, Lydia Sokolova appeared as the wicked witch Kikimora in Léonide Massine's *Contes Russes* (1917). The central scene, telling the story of Kikimora and her unfortunate cat, was first performed in 1916 in San Sebastian, Spain. (Stravinsky-Diaghilev Foundation, New York.)

the face included poisonous white lead (ceruse), powdered borax, beaten egg whites with egg shells, and lemon juice with ground hog's bones. A vermilion color was made from red ocher and mercuric oxide. Men as well as women dyed their hair to a preferred blond color, and women shaped their eyebrows and raised their hairlines by drastic plucking.

In Renaissance court spectacles, masks were a means of unifying choruses of dancers and presenting grotesque or comic characters. Makeup came into use onstage, for the first time, as a means of beautifying dancers' features and making them more legible at a distance. By Louis XIV's time (ruled 1643–1715), women placed cork or wax in their mouths to puff out their cheeks. They also wore beauty patches, of taffeta or gummed paper, to cover blemishes. These acquired elaborate symbolism: the "gallant" wore one on the cheek, the "passionate" wore one on the corner of her eye, the "coquette" one near her lip, and so on. Hair and wigs were powdered, and makeup was needed to counteract the pallid effect this had on complexions. Over a white foundation, eyebrows were emphasized with black pencil or were shaved and replaced with mouse-skin substitutes. Veins were sometimes accentuated with blue paint. Cheeks were rouged with color prepared in loose cakes and dishes or affixed to Spanish wool (fibers saturated with color) and Spanish papers, laid on with a camel-hair brush or by the moistened tip of the little finger. No attempt was made to appear natural, members of the court having adopted a deliberately artificial style of face makeup that was reminiscent of their theater masks. Only women of the demimonde then appeared with naturalistic coloring.

In Europe, construction of large theaters with proscenium stages increased the distance between audience and performer so that exaggeration was necessary; makeup for the stage appears to have been very heavy and masklike. There were complaints about its being troweled on or cracking and of performers so heavily enameled with paint that they were incapable of showing emotion.

Gas lighting, introduced in the first quarter of the nineteenth century, was very yellow and made stronger colors in stage makeup necessary. The ballet girl of the Romantic era would have supplied her dressing table with a candle, a packet of wax matches, half a dozen corks, a rabbit's foot, a box of refined rice powder, an envelope containing powdered Chinese vermilion, and a steel knitting needle. She often had to be content with lard, but if she could afford it she protected her skin with butter, first spreading it on and then removing the excess with a towel. Having boiled the vermilion in milk to make it more workable, she rubbed it dry onto her cheeks. Next she lit the candle and held the knitting needle in its flame until enough soot accumulated to darken her eyelashes. Then, after burning a cork until it was a rich black, she passed it lightly over her eyebrows to darken them. She dusted her face with a light layer of rice powder, using the rabbit's foot to spread it evenly; when this was done the gleam of butter had disappeared and the bright vermilion had softened to a rosy pink. As a final touch she worked a little vermilion with butter and created a tiny rosebud mouth. Tooth whitener and mastic, a thick white liquid "enamel" used to whiten arms and shoulders, completed the stage image. In the *ballet blanc,* the dancer's gown fused with the whiteness of her makeup to create a shimmering unearthly presence. The total effect was of alabaster perfection.

Using greasy substances in connection with theatrical makeup is at least as old as the early 1700s. By 1825, pigment was customarily applied over some kind of greasy base; grease and oil were likewise used to remove makeup in onstage transformations and at the end of a performance. Nevertheless, until the late 1800s, all makeup, whether used with grease or some liquid medium, was basically powder. Often the ingredients were toxic substances that, when rubbed into the pores of the skin, had poisonous effects and sometimes caused death.

Performers had experimented with combinations of grease and paint from 1820 to 1870, but the first to be put on the market in a convenient form (in 1873) was invented by the Wagnerian opera singer Ludwig Leichner. His sticks of makeup wrapped in foil or paper were available in many colors and facilitated precise blending and lining. Moreover, these paints were made from innocuous ingredients so that stage makeup was finally safe to wear. They had the added advantage of being impervious to perspiration and soon superseded the old-fashioned powder makeup. With the introduction of electricity, stage lighting could for the first time be effectively colored to control some of its effects on makeup. It then needed to be lighter and applied more subtly.

The dancers of Diaghilev's Ballets Russes in Paris used exotic makeup to compete for attention in productions that were supercharged with color and sound. The designers, Léon Bakst and Alexandre Benois, specified all manner of fantastic colorations and linings for the face—lavender and green eyeshadow, silver and gold dust—and soon fashionable women followed suit. The Russian dancers were expert at creating transforming makeup, and Vaslav Nijinsky in particular depended on the process of altering his appearance through makeup to realize a role; his uncanny ability to adapt his facial muscles to a painted visage was an important aspect of his genius. In 1909 Michel Fokine reintroduced the ghostlike wilis of the Romantic ballet, in his *Les Sylphides*—with the added advantage of blue and green electric lights to heighten the illusion of moonlight mistiness and transparency. Because rouge and brown shading turn to blackish violet in blue light, makeup had to be stark white, with eyes and eyebrows in black and shaded with blue or green.

During the period of the Ballets Russes (1909–1929), the image of both male and female ballet dancers as heavily made-up personalities was firmly established. Films, vaudeville, and Broadway theater exploited this stereotype, and the ballerina's masklike features and severe hairstyle became a symbolic prototype for theatrical glamour. By the 1940s, ballet dancers carried makeup to extremes, enlarging their eyes with false eyelashes, shading, and liners extended beyond a proportional relationship to the rest of the face—even in works based on rustic American themes and homely subjects. This convention persisted until the 1950s, when the popularity of George Balanchine's choreography, which tended to draw attention to itself rather than enshrining glamorous personalities, ended the myth of the ballerina as an exotic hybrid. Ballet dancers today tend to wear a more naturalistic makeup, reserving the exaggerated classical mask for revivals of ballets from the Romantic and classical eras.

In modern dance, Ruth St. Denis and Martha Graham were notable for their expert use of makeup. But many of their contemporaries rejected theatrical effects that were reminiscent of the artificiality of the ballet and preferred naturalistic makeup or none at all. This was more in keeping with their straightforward themes, plain costumes, bare feet, and simple hairstyles. In recent years, however, modern dance has adopted most of the presentational

MASK AND MAKEUP: European Traditions. Nadia Nerina, dramatically made up and wearing the traditional feathered headdress of the Firebird in the Royal Ballet production, staged by Serge Grigoriev and Lubov Tchernicheva after Fokine. Bold makeup serves to render the dancer's expression more visible to an audience in the theater. Here, dark thick strokes of eyeliner and eyebrow pencil are designed to make her eyes appear larger than life. The upward slant of the eye makeup is common Western convention in the portrayal of exotic figures. (Photograph from the Dance Collection, New York Public Library for the Performing Arts.)

techniques of the ballet and popular theater, including the standard makeup.

[*See also the entries on the principal figures mentioned herein.*]

BIBLIOGRAPHY

Angeloglou, Maggie. *A History of Make-Up.* New York, 1970.

Drew-Bear, Annette. "Face-Painting in Renaissance Tragedy." In *Essays in Dramatic Technique,* edited by Alan C. Dessen. Renaissance Drama, 12. Evanston, Ill., 1981.

Gregor, Joseph. *Masks of the World.* London, 1936.

Kirstein, Lincoln. *Dance.* New York, 1935. Republished as *The Book of the Dance* (Garden City, N.Y., 1942).

Noverre, Jean-Georges. *Lettres sur la danse et sur les ballets.* Stuttgart and Lyon, 1760. Translated by Cyril W. Beaumont as *Letters on Dancing and Ballets* (London, 1930).

Spencer, Lindley Powers. "Masks in Theatre." Master's thesis, University of Wisconsin, 1968.

Strenkovsky, Serge. *The Art of Make-Up.* New York, 1937.

MALCOLM MCCORMICK

MASLOW, SOPHIE (born 22 March 1911 in New York City), American dancer and choreographer. Maslow studied with Blanche Talmud and Martha Graham at the Neighborhood Playhouse. In 1931 she joined the Graham company, performing for twelve years in works that included *Primitive Mysteries, American Lyric, Every Soul Is a Circus, Letter to the World,* and *Deaths and Entrances.*

In the mid-1930s Maslow became involved with the New Dance League, and created her first choreography for its annual recitals. These early works, often political, included *Prelude to a May First Song* (1935), *Two Songs about Lenin* (1935), and *Women of Spain* (1937). Later, as a student and assistant to Louis Horst, she performed several solo studies in concert.

About this period in her work, Margaret Lloyd (1979) remarked that "her dances are instinct with folk feeling, modern in form. . . . Anything is legitimate, she thinks, that helps to hurdle the barrier between dancer and audience, that sends the idea or mood or emotion straight into the hearts and minds of the people."

In 1942, after sharing a concert program, Maslow, Jane Dudley, and William Bales formed The Dudley-Maslow-Bales Trio, which performed until 1954, often in an expanded version associated with the New Dance Group. All three taught at the New Dance Group Studio. Maslow's *Dust Bowl Ballads* (1941) and *Folksay* (1942), both set to songs by Woody Guthrie, were popular early works, followed by *Champion* (1948), based on a story by Ring Lardner, *The Village I Knew* (1949), from stories by Sholom Aleichem, and *Manhattan Celebration* (1954), set to Israeli folk songs. [*See* New Dance Group.]

In 1978 Anna Kisselgoff wrote about *The Village I Knew* in the *New York Times:* "Miss Maslow's fine achievement is not to trade on folklore. In the end, the humanity of the vignettes is found not in the few cheerful moments of gossip and courtship. . . . It is found in the genuine pathos of the final exodus scene. In this sadness, lies the truth of *The Village I Knew.*"

Maslow choreographed the annual Ḥannukah Festival at Madison Square Garden from 1955 to 1967 and staged operas for the New York City Opera, notably *The Dybbuk* and *The Golem.* Her Broadway credits include *Sandhog* (1954), *The Shoemaker and the Peddler* (1960), and Sholom Aleichem's *The Big Winner* (1974).

In addition, Maslow continued to choreograph for Sophie Maslow and Company, which has appeared regularly in New York City since 1956, and for the New Dance Group Studio company, The Group Dance Theater, New York City Dance Theater Company, and The Danscompany, which she founded in 1975 with Joyce Trisler. Major works have included *Raincheck* (1958); *Poem* (1963), with text by Lawrence Ferlinghetti; *From the Book of Ruth* (1964), set to music by Aram Khatchaturian; *Neither Rest Nor Harbor* (1969); *Ladino Suite* (1969), set to traditional music; *Touch the Earth* (1973), to Native American songs; *Such Sweet Thunder* (1975), set to music by Duke Ellington; *The Decathalon Etudes* (1976); and *Woody Sez* (1980).

Maslow is a recipient of grants from the National Endowment for the Arts, the New York State Council for the Arts, the New York City Cultural Foundation, and the Martha Graham Foundation. She was awarded an honorary doctorate degree in humanities from Skidmore College and the Award of Artistry from the American Dance Guild in 1991.

BIBLIOGRAPHY

Lloyd, Margaret. *The Borzoi Book of Modern Dance.* New York, 1949.

ARCHIVE. Dance Collection, New York Public Library for the Performing Arts.

ANN VACHON

MASON, MONICA (born 6 September 1941 in Johannesburg, South Africa), dancer and teacher. Mason trained with Ruth Inglestone, Reina Berman, and Frank Staff in her native South Africa and with Nesta Brooking in England before entering the Royal Ballet School at fifteen. She was the youngest dancer in the Royal Ballet when she joined it at sixteen and was still a member of the corps when Kenneth MacMillan selected her to create the Chosen Maiden in *The Rite of Spring* (1962).

The technical power and theatrical flair she first unleashed in this arduous pivotal role evolved into her stylistic trademarks. A principal by 1967, she became a uniquely modern ballerina. Over the years, she grew into a sensitive interpretive performer, tuned anew for each role. Her range encompassed the classicism of Odette-Odile, Nikia in *La Bayadère,* and the Fairy of the Woodland Glade in *The Sleeping Beauty,* as well as the sardonic humor of a deadpan Webster in *A Wedding Bouquet* and the droll Calliope Rag in *Élite Syncopations.* Alongside the austerity of purely abstract roles—in *Serenade* and particularly in *Song of the Earth*—she set intensely dramatic characterizations: Lady Elgar in *Enigma Variations,* the frustrated Wife in *The Invitation,* the ruthless Black Queen in *Checkmate.* With equal ease she could be a mythical creature, Myrtha or the Firebird; a malevolent one, such as the imperious Carabosse; or one created entirely out of its music, as in *Les Noces, Liebeslieder Walzer,* or *Dances at a Gathering.*

Her initial link with MacMillan proved an enduring one. Having appeared in nearly all his ballets in the Royal Ballet repertory, and created roles in seven of them, in 1980 she was appointed *répétiteur* (rehearsal director) for his works. She has also taught classical variations to the senior girls at the Royal Ballet School since 1980. In 1984, Mason became the company's principal *répétiteur.* She was named assistant to the director in 1988 and assistant director in 1991.

BIBLIOGRAPHY

Bland, Alexander. *The Royal Ballet: The First Fifty Years.* London, 1981.

Newman, Barbara. *Striking a Balance: Dancers Talk about Dancing.* Rev. ed. New York, 1992.

BARBARA NEWMAN

MASQUE AND ANTIMASQUE. The English court masque achieved its essential form as a literary and dramatic genre in the early decades of the seventeenth century under the supervision of innovative poets such as Ben Jonson and Thomas Campion and enterprising scene designers such as the architect Inigo Jones. Its singularity as a distinctive genre was established under the creative direction of continental dancing masters such as Master Confesse and Master Bochan who, with British counterparts such as Thomas Giles and Jerome (or Jeremy) Herne, designed dance presentations to be viewed in dramatic contexts, thus making a new and significant contribution to the theatrical arts. The genesis of the masque may be traced back several centuries to popular folk rituals, such as mummers' plays, sword dances, and Morris dances, as well as to contemporaneous continental song and dance spectacles, such as the French *ballet de cour* ("court ballet"; flourished in France, 1580–1660) and the Italian *commedia dell'arte* ("comedy of art"; developed in Italy, 1500s–1700s). As a social rite, the masque had flourished prominently at the sixteenth-century Tudor courts of Henry VIII and Elizabeth I, where it was often referred to as a "disguising"; but it attained the peak of its development as a sophisticated, scenically elaborated dance-drama form under the special fostering of the first of the Stuart monarchs, James I (died 1625) and his consort Anne of Denmark, and under Charles I (died 1649) and his consort Henrietta Maria of France.

At the height of the development of the masque, dancing constituted the chief element in its makeup. Choreographers and dancing masters, working in conjunction with composers, vocalists, and instrumentalists in its preparation and enactment, were essentially more significant than scenic designers, costumers, or even librettists. Its three kinds of dances—masque, antimasque, and social—were artistically juxtaposed on most occasions to form, despite their essential differences, a coherently integrated whole. The first group, consisting of three masque dances—the entry, the main, and the exit dances of the masquers—were specially choreographed company dances, featuring patterned movements of an abstract and sometimes geometrically esoteric sort (sometimes characterized as hieroglyphical). These were performed after several weeks of arduous rehearsal by those members of the nobility constituting the specially selected masquers for a given occasion, who were said to have brought the masque to court. In performing each of their three dances, the vizarded (visored) masquers—and these, composed of a small group usually of six, eight, or even ten or twelve—were often described as having "made a masque."

The second group of dances consisted largely of realistically devised mime movements for the antimasquers—the professional dancers who, as inhabitants of a nether world contrasting with the realm of the high-born masquers—made extensive use of bizarre, antic music and dance to enhance their often satiric pantomimic art. Their presentations often consisted of far more pantomime than of actual dance routines. Following these two groups, a third class of dance, called the revels—consisting of the various social dances of the period—were undertaken by the masquers and their partners, whom they would invite from the audience at the height of their presentation to perform in the special dancing place adjacent to an elaborately constructed stage setting. Here, those partners could be said to have been invited to share in the fictive golden world of the setting devised by the masquewright. These social dances, most of which were of continental origin, usually took up far more than an hour's activity in an evening's performance. In this revels section, the masquers and their partners began with stately measures and, in carefully ordered sequence, concluded with dances of a more informal and fanciful sort: *passamezzos* and sometimes specially choreographed measures first, and then the more sprightly dances in triple meter such as *galliardes, corantos, lavoltas, brawls* (or *branles*), and, on occasion, even country dances. Often these dance items were drawn from an established social dance sequence known as "the old measures."

Of the various groups concerned with executing these dances in the typical masque of the early 1600s sponsored by King James, by far the most important and prominent were the offerings of the aristocratic masquers. Most often clad in the composite garb of Roman soldier and medieval knight (as such they joined together the heroic figures of two great pre-Renaissance civilizations), they arrived as a representative body in formal procession before their monarch, variously to pay homage, to avow anew and reenact their fealty, to bring felicitations for his sovereign prescience, and to subject themselves (if need be) to his regenerative and curative powers as the emissary of Jove himself in this quasi-religious ritual. The individual masque performance might indeed be seen as a secular rite. Complementing the lord masquers were the lady masquers, who often appeared in impressive roles; if they were not goddesses, as in Samuel Daniel's *The Vision of the Twelve Goddesses* (1604), then they might be representatives of the constituent elements of beauty, as in Ben Jonson's *Masque of Beauty* (1608).

The form of the typical court masque was ordinarily very simple. An ideal and its opposite were prominently contrasted with one another through masque and antimasque. The masquers themselves were seen as triumphantly energized through the powerful magic of their monarch, and it was a given that the opposing antic figures were to be ultimately dismissed in scorn and ridicule. The masquers then would turn to invite guests from the courtly assemblage to join in their revels.

Although the four dozen or so court masques that survive in libretto for the period 1604 to 1640 display considerable variation in formality and informality, the fable (plot) of the typical piece was necessarily slight, and it was developed in stages that roughly approximated the following sequence:

1. The introductory song or dialogue inaugurated by a presenter announcing the subject to be explored.
2. The performance of one or two antimasques to serve as contrasts to the ideal commended in the masque.
3. The entry dance of the vizarded lord or lady masquers bringing the masque to the king and the assemblage.
4. The interpositioned songs and spoken dialogue.
5. The main dance of the masquers.
6. The Address to the State, spoken or sung, constituting not only the masquers' affirmation of fealty but also recognizing and honoring their monarch's powers of resolving all issues of significance.

MASQUE AND ANTIMASQUE. A design by Inigo Jones of a Roman setting for the 1632 masque *Albion's Triumph.* In addition to designing the Banqueting House at the royal palace of White Hall, London, where the Stuart court masques were performed, Jones controlled the visual aspects—scenery, costumes, and stage machinery—of more than fifty court entertainments. (Devonshire Collection, Chatsworth; photograph used by permission of the Chatsworth Settlement Trustees.)

7. The masquers' invitation to partners from the audience to join in social dances with them in the revels.
8. The final speeches or songs and the masquers' disvisoring.
9. The withdrawing dance of the masquers.
10. The king, as honored host, repaying in reception those bringing the masque to court, in this way displaying his benign acceptance of their greetings as well as his boundless favor.

Despite the many variables that could be identified in individual masques, the one constant group appearing in all masques consists of items 3, 5, and 9. Without the inclusion of these three specially choreographed masque dances, sometimes called (however inappropriately) terminal dances, the dramatic genre at hand can no longer be considered a masque. Also noteworthy in individual masques are the often conscious thinness of plotting; the free and easy shifting between sung and spoken segments of text; and the loosely organized episodes spoken in verse and prose, the last of which adds considerably to a sense of informality and improvisation. There is an easy give and take between audience and performers.

Although songs are frequently introduced, varying from solo aria to dialogue song to choral hymn, their texts are always limited to describing or exalting the masque dancers or addressing the monarch and do not provide (as in opera) the emotional vehicle of song for the personalized expression of a vocalist. In the masque, a soloist is most often, when not a presenter figure, an unnamed voice from a choral group. Only rarely was the text of a masque intended to be sung from beginning to end. The verses to be sung, sometimes set to preexisting tunes, were on occasion given out to be set by various composers. In Jacobean times, the chief composers of vocal music were Alfonso Ferrabosco II, Robert Johnson, John Coprario, and Nicholas Lanier; in Caroline times, William and Henry Lawes were the chief contributors. William Lawes's scores for James Shirley's *The Triumph of Peace* (1634) and William Davenant's *The Triumphs of the Prince d'Amour* (1636) and *Britannia Triumphans* (1638) consist of beautifully organized solo and choral vocal items. In most cases, however, the original Jacobean scores—never expected to be repeated and hence never preserved—were the work of several collaborating choreographers and composers. Since the masquers are the focal performers, and since they express themselves only in movement and never speak or sing, the masque may be seen as an ancestor of ballet.

Virtually all of the Jacobean and Caroline court masques were occasional in nature and hence received only a single performance. For example, the royal wedding of a princess or a prince's investiture as Prince of Wales were considered appropriate subjects for public celebration by means of a masque's formal song and dance. A few masques, however, including Jonson's *Lovers Made Men* (1617) and Shirley's *The Triumph of Peace* (1634), do manage to transcend their immediate occasions and, through editorial adaptation and reconstruction, have managed to hold the stage.

In early Stuart times, one other group besides the nobility was invited to present masques at court on various occasions; this group consisted of representatives of the legal profession as well as the students of the Inns of Court. They brought to court, in lavish outdoor processions through the streets of London, elaborately decorated pageant wagons carrying richly costumed masquers flanked by dozens of mounted attendants and illuminated by torches and flambeaux. It was deemed fitting for members of that important profession, serving as the bulwark of a royalist society, to pay due respect to their monarch and to present their felicitations on such occasions as a marriage of state or the institution of a Prince of Wales.

At a typical masque performance the king, in a lavish display of regal magnificence, was ushered into White Hall to an imposing overture played on cornets and hautboys (oboes). He took his place at a canopied seat, known as the State, centrally located at one end of the hall opposite the stage; thus seated, he was suitably surrounded by his retinue and by ambassadors from the major continental courts. Thomas Campion's *Masque in Honour of the Marriage of Lord Hayes* (1607) employed about three dozen instrumentalists and vocalists, with the musicians placed to the right and left of the stage and the vocalists in the central part of the stage facing the auditorium. The audience, seated on both sides of the dancing place of White Hall, could view all activity both on the stage and on the State as well as before them in the dancing place. When everything was in readiness, and the king gave the signal for the musicians to begin, the audience, turning their view to the stage, could clearly view the following activity:

> On the right hand whereof were consorted ten musicians, with bass and mean lutes, a bandora, a double sackbut, and an harpsichord, with two treble violins; on the other side somewhat nearer the screen were placed nine violins and three lutes; and to answer both the consorts (as it were a triangle) six cornetts, and six Chapel voices, were seated almost right against them, in a place raised higher in respect of the piercing sound of those instruments. (Campion, 1607, p. 1)

By contrast, the Caroline productions of the Inns of Court were sometimes even more elaborate in their music complements than were the Jacobean productions. The Longleat papers of Sir Bulstrode Whitelocke for James Shirley's *The Triumph of Peace* (1634) provide for no fewer than sixty-nine instrumentalists and vocalists.

The audience, composed exclusively of the aristocracy, numbered almost six hundred and could occupy the scaffolded sides of the three successively constructed royal banqueting halls (in 1581, 1607, and 1623, each known as Whitehall) in which most performances were held. The appearance of that audience was described in an eyewitness account written to the Venetian court about Jonson's *Pleasure Reconciled to Virtue* (1618): "Every box was filled notably with the most noble and richly arrayed ladies, in number some six hundred and more." Extravagantly bejeweled and beplumed, they often came wearing special low-heeled shoes suitable for dancing, escorted by noble gallants in equally fine accoutrements.

In performance, the group of masquers could be composed entirely of lords, entirely of ladies, or, on rarer occasions, by a mixed group of both. They moved in solemn silence, never speaking or singing. Their vizards effaced their individual personages to emphasize the harmonious single-mindedness of the six, eight, or ten bluebloods constituting the masquing group. As votaries, if not of the gods, then of legendary heroes such as Perseus, Daedalus, Prometheus, or Orpheus, the masquers—especially those of Jonson masques—often underwent marvelous transmutations of varying kinds. As lovers in *Lovers Made Men* (1617), they could discover that their native wit might free them from the bondage of the passions. As revelers in *Pleasure Reconciled to Virtue* (1618), they could exercise discrimination between debilitating pleasure and energizing refreshment. And as patrons of art in *The Vision of Delight* (1617) they could learn to distinguish between idle fancy and true wonder. Even more grandly, as candidates capable of perfection in *Mercury Vindicated from the Alchemists* (1616), they could rebel against the delusions of specious philosophy and learn to follow the dictates of a wise Nature. Later, after their roles in a given masque had been established through their entry and main dances, they were expected, at a climactic moment just after the revels, to remove their vizards. Here they revealed to their partners from the assemblage their individual personages as inherent possessors of the virtues and ideals that they as a group, committed to a Renaissance version of noblesse oblige, had exemplified through their specially choreographed dances.

Variously named as dancing masters in expense accounts and libretti in Jacobean times are Thomas Giles, Jerome (or Jeremy) Herne, Master Confesse, and Master Bochan. Bochan's name is a pseudonym for Jacques Cordier, noted for having taught many of the queens of Europe to dance. In this period, courtesy manuals such as Fabritio Caroso's *Il ballarino* (1581) and Baldassare Castiglione's *Il cortegiano* (translated into English from the Italian by the Elizabethan Thomas Hoby as *The Courtier* in 1561) established the basis for the advocacy of dancing not only as an emblem of social harmony befitting the new humanism but also as the ideal way, in Caroso's words, of representing "the affections of the mind as attuned to the movements of the body." In Caroline times, dancing masters such as Master DeNoe and Master Sebastian carried on the traditions of their Jacobean forbears. Like them they not only taught social dances, but in masques such as Shirley's *The Triumph of Peace* (1634), they "set the figures" for the specially choreographed dances of the masquers and the antimasquers alike. They often made good use of skillful dancers from among the nobility for the terminal dances. In Samuel Daniel's *The Vision of the Twelve Goddesses* (1604), the Lady Lucy, countess of Bedford, a famous patroness of poets, served as rector chori to lead the ladies in performing a masque dance "with great majesty and art." The libretto described it as "consisting of diverse strains, framed unto motions circular, square, triangular, with other proportions rare and full of variety." On occasion, the dancing masters, with violin in hand, provided tunes for the three masque dances as well as the antic measures, and sometimes they took nonmasquing roles in productions. In Ben Jonson's *Beauty* (1608), it was Thomas Giles as a professional who danced the role of the River Thamesis. By the 1630s, the one or two antic dances of most Jacobean masques were subdivided to include a dozen and more episodes in each production, apparently making enormous demands on the dancers' pantomimic skills.

For example, in the libretto of *Hymenaei* (1606), Jonson admiringly described its main dance as one in which the lords paired with the lady masquers in this double masque "danced forth a most neat and curious measure, full of subtlety and device: . . . The strains were all notably different, some of them formed into letters very signifying to the name of the Bridegroom, and ended in a manner of a chain, linking hands." In Jonson's *Beauty* (1608), the masquers represented a diamond, and in *Pleasure Reconciled to Virtue* (1618) they formed a pyramidical figure (which they sustained for a while in the dancing) at whose apex was Prince Charles, whose institution as Prince of Wales was celebrated in this masque. Daedalus's first song spells out the movements of the entry, urging the masquers to interweave a "curious knot" and to order the labyrinthine nature of the actions of humankind into a coherent entwining, so that the spectators might be delightfully edified by their performances.

There survives a document, British Library Additional Manuscript 10,444, that dates from the early seventeenth century and contains a remarkable collection of 138 dance tunes for Jacobean court masques. Written down by Sir Nicholas LeStrange, a Gray's Inn–trained lawyer (he had matriculated in 1618) who was also a musical amateur and an indefatigable music copyist, these dances are preserved in the skeletal form of treble and bassus parts only. Among the 138 dances transcribed by LeStrange are no fewer than fifteen sets of terminal dances for the entry, the main, and the exit dances of masquers in Jacobean masques. Most of these tunes represent the ad hoc improvisations of the dancing masters as they rehearsed, with violin in hand, their aristocratic charges. Later these tunes were in many cases turned over to composers to be set for instrumental consorts as used in actual performance. Cognate versions—many in four- or five-part consort arrangements—for some sixty of these tunes survive in various manuscript and printed sources of the period.

Essentially formal, stately, even majestic in manner, the music of each set projects a venerable dignity even while it displays considerable variation in mood from that of other sets. Each dance usually consists of two strains of duple meter, four beats in a measure, each strain four to eight measures long and on occasion irregular—and these are sometimes followed by one or even two strains of triple meter, each commonly six to sixteen measures long. The rhythm in the duple strains in a set of three masque dances is that of the almain, a vigorous four-beats-in-a-measure processional dance. Frequently the tunes of Additional Manuscript 10,444 appearing in concordances are simply titled "almain." This designation is important for indicating for terminal dances the rather heavy step and brisk pace of this company dance, which, in its final strain, sometimes possesses appropriate music for a distinguishing closing caper, or "leap." The rhythm of the triple-meter strains, however, is that of the *coranto*. The first of the terminal dances, the entry, is usually the shortest; the main dance of a set is frequently the most extended of the three. Sometimes the relationship of the music of the three in a given set is stylistically or thematically integrated. Their melodic lines are also often thematically or rhythmically allied, and their keys invariably display close major and minor key relationships.

Most Jacobean terminal sets—many of them the impromptu compositions of dancing masters—display an inherent charm and simplicity, their melodic spontaneity their most attractive feature, and the consort settings provided by composers such as Alfonso Ferrabosco II, Robert Johnson, John Coprario, and Thomas Lupo are worthy of note. Caroline terminal dances often exhibit similar combinations of successive duple- and triple-meter strains as they are introduced into the scores of individual masques. In the 1630s William and Henry Lawes, Simon Ives, John Withy, William Young, and Thomas Warlock were among the contributors to the composite music scores of most masques, and their surviving pieces, though few in number in contrast to the Jacobean settings preserved, reveal terminal dances whose essential attractiveness largely depended on a decided advance in dramatic accentuation, with a more careful articulation of melodic line and an enterprising introduction of a more sophisticated harmonic texture.

The antimasquers, unlike the masquers, were professional dancers, all male. They played several roles, all typical of the inhabitants of a fallen world. As foil figures to the focal performers, they served as "*anti*-masquers"; as grotesques often appearing before the masque proper, they could be seen as "*ante*-masquers"; as farcical wags, they clearly could be recognized as "*antic*-masquers"; and as eccentrics often trading on the quaint, inapposite, and obsolete, they could even be regarded as "*antique*-masquers." They never played all four roles at once, but several were usually combined to project a marked individuality as well as a trenchant humor. The latter, occasionally burgeoning forth into perceptive satire, contributed most effectively to the preservation of necessary tonal equilibrium in many masques.

MASQUE AND ANTIMASQUE. A typical costume by Inigo Jones, identified as a "Knight Masquer." (Devonshire Collection, Chatsworth; photograph used by permission of the Chatsworth Settlement Trustees.)

The largest collection of antic dance music, like the ritual masque dances, is preserved in British Library Additional Manuscript 10,444. As with the ritual masque dances recorded there, these are all Jacobean. They are richly varied in their marked informality. Although sometimes quite slight—particularly those composed of two duple meter strains—in items clearly intended for a single antimasquer's entry and show, the most memorable specimens are those items that are more generous in length, often composed of no fewer than five or six strains, each in a different meter. These were evidently intended for a connected series of antic *divertisssements*. In some performances, especially of Inns of Court masques, an actor serving as master of ceremonies managed the stage movement of dancers, singers, and actors. One such master of ceremonies, named Capriccio, described as "nature's noble-man," appeared in George Chapman's *Masque of the Middle Temple and Lincoln's Inn* (1613), and his surviving dance tune was probably used as the vehicle not only for his spectacular entry but also for leading into the subsequent entries of the antimasquers in his retinue.

It is not surprising that many concordances to antic dance tunes are titled "coranto," since frequently they display a strain or two in very rapid time, then often juxtapose slow and fast binary and ternary strains. Such wide variations in tempo virtually never occur in the more stable and more limitedly varied terminal dances. Antimasque dance music is dramatic, even arresting, in other ways. The frequent use of rapid running-scale passages and insistently reiterated notes, sometimes capped at the close of phrases by fermata (pauses), suggests that the professional dancers at certain moments in performance, after some striking visual movement or gesture, suddenly assumed tableau-like poses. In the words of some libretto accounts, the antics have "made a stand." One senses very clearly that the dancing master, not the composer, most frequently called the antic tune.

This antic world, on its lowest level, was an animal world sometimes real and sometimes mythic. Characteristic dances set forth the essential nature of its denizens, whether they were bears, goats, or birds. The inhabitants of the antimasque world of spirits now made visible—fairies, satyrs, devils, furies, witches—demanded dance music that clearly conveyed the flavor or appearance of the executants or the typical stances and characteristic movements that myth and legend have long ascribed to them. The satyrs in Jonson's *Oberon, the Fairy Prince* (1611), as the libretto reveals, "fell suddenly into an antic dance full of gesture and swift motion, and continued it till the crowing of the cock," while the fairies in the same masque, as they celebrated Henry as Prince of Wales, were urged to let their "nimble feet / Tread subtle circles, that may always meet / In point to him; and figures to express / The grace of him." Appropriately outlandish were the dances of the witches in Jonson's *Queens* (1609), who "with a strange and sudden music . . . fell into a magical dance, full of preposterous change and gesticulation."

In the realm of the human but in a category of the droll and the grotesque were antics whose actions were devised to contrast with the virtues and ideals displayed by the masquers, including such diverse beings as a sleepy schoolman "overcome with fantasy," errant pilgrims, mountebanks, bacchanalians, roaring boys, and the rebel followers of such political activists of the past as Jack Straw and Jack Cade, the progeny of error, ignorance, misapprehension, or (more usually) simply of misguided energy. The febrile perturbations of "The Fools' Masque," intended for Francis Beaumont's *The Masque of the Inner Temple and Gray's Inn* (1613), for example, bespeak unmitigated vacancy and stupidity, and the repetition of a convulsive-sounding motif suggests the inanity of their unrelenting opposition to their fellow antics. "The Nymphs' Dance" for the same masque provides a delicate contrast.

Sometimes pantomime artists, enacting comic roles in the midst of their dances, provided the antimasque. They appear frequently in antimasque as lovers, a plot motif recurring through several masques from as early as Campion's *The Lords' Masque* (1613), where twelve frantics "all presented in sundry habits and humours" included a lover and a self-lover as well as "a melancholic man full of fear" and "a schoolman overcome with fantasy." As counterparts to the idealized love displayed by knight masquers, such antic dancers spell out the vagaries of those who miss or misgauge the true mark of love. Their sufferings are diverse and manifold—utter dejection, lachrymose self-pity, fierce resentment, and injured pride. Such moods are defined, most whimsically, through extravagant and exaggerated sentiment in a series of dances for the doleful principals of Jonson's *Lovers Made Men* (1617), lovers who have emotionally lost their bearings and become mere ghosts of themselves through a self-inflicted demise.

This motif was even more elaborately developed in Jonson's later *Love's Triumph through Callipollis* (1631), where twelve lovers are described with their turbulent idiosyncrasies. Inigo Jones's surviving drawings for four of these very figures are not only based on the *Balli di Sfessania* of Jacques Callot (1597–1635), but carry the names of their *commedia dell'arte* prototypes, the four being equated respectively with Captain Ceremonia, Scaramouche, Pantalon, and Captain Spavento.

To counterbalance the sophistication of such continental influences as the *commedia dell'arte*, Stuart masquewrights often derived and preserved from a native mumming tradition much that was equally important. In some Jacobean masques the inclusion of a stylized sword dance, a *matachina*, to be performed by antics, was of significance in demonstrating the genre's indebtedness to a traditional kind of folk drama. In Jonson's *The Haddington Masque* (1608), the armed Cupid attended by twelve boys in antic attire were described in an eyewitness account as having danced a matachina, acting it "very antiquely."

It has been noted that Randle Cotgrave, in his Elizabethan French-English dictionary, equates *danser les buffons* with the English "to dance a Morris"; but most authorities have insisted that many significant differences exist between the ritual dances of the swordsmen and the Morris dancers, especially in the nature of the stories that they dramatize or sometimes imply. Yet both Morris men and sword dancers, with equal fervor, may be said to celebrate fertility as well as life's continuance. The blackening of the faces of both mummers and swordsmen (which made them "Moorish" and supplies the usually accepted explanation of the derivation of the term *Morris*) provides a counterpart on the folk level with the same concern for impersonality as noted in the vizarded court masquers.

The good-luck-bearing executants—the agents of fertility and continuance—demanded from their hosts as recompense for their performance only "all silver and no brass," as a phrase puts it in an Irish mummers' play quoted by Henry Glassie (1975). In like manner, the august masquers of the early Stuart court requested and received appropriate recompense from their monarch, to whom they had given, as in Jonson's *Oberon* (1611), "the honor of their being." Their reward was the assurance, as the foremost Sylvan of this masque states it,

that they may live
Sustained'd in form, fame, and felicity,
From rage of fortune, or the fear to die.

[*See also* Renaissance Fêtes and Triumphs *and the entry on Inigo Jones*.]

BIBLIOGRAPHY

Anglo, Sydney. "The Evolution of the Early Tudor Disguising, Pageant, and the Mask." *Renaissance Drama* 1 (1968).

Baskervill, Charles R. *The Elizabethan Jig and Related Song Drama.* Chicago, 1929.

Brody, Alan. *The English Mummers and Their Plays: Traces of Ancient History.* London, 1970.

Brotanek, Rudolf. *Die englischen Maskenspiele.* Vienna, 1902.

Caroso, Fabritio. *Nobiltà di dame* (1600). Translated and edited by Julia Sutton. Oxford, 1986.

Davis, Walter R., ed. *The Works of Thomas Campion.* Garden City, N.Y., 1967.

Dean-Smith, Margaret. "Folk-Play Origins of the English Masque." *Folk-Lore* 65 (1954).

Dolmetsch, Mabel. *Dances of England and France from 1450 to 1600.* London, 1949.

Glassie, Henry. *All Silver and No Brass.* Bloomington, 1975.

Herford, C. H., and Simpson, P. and E., eds. *Ben Jonson.* Vols. 7–10. Oxford, 1925–1952.

Lauze, François de. *Apologie de la danse, 1623: A Treatise of Instruction in Dancing and Deportment.* Translated by Joan Wildeblood. London, 1952.

Lefkowitz, Murray. *Trois masques à la cour de Charles Ier d'Angleterre.* Paris, 1970.

Meagher, John C. *Method and Meaning in Jonson's Masques.* Notre Dame, Ind., 1966.

Nicoll, Allardyce. *Stuart Masques and the Renaissance Stage.* New York, 1938.

Orgel, Stephen. *The Jonsonian Masque.* Cambridge, Mass., 1965.

Orgel, Stephen, and Roy Strong. *Inigo Jones: The Theatre of the Stuart Court.* 2 vols. Berkeley, 1973.

Reyher, Paul. *Les masques anglais.* Paris, 1909.

Sabol, Andrew J., ed. *A Score for* Lovers Made Men, *a Masque by Ben Jonson.* Providence, R.I., 1963.

Sabol, Andrew J., ed. *Four Hundred Songs and Dances from the Stuart Masque.* Enl. ed. Hanover, N.H., 1982.

Sabol, Andrew J., ed. *A Score for* The Lords' Masque *by Thomas Campion.* Providence, R.I., 1993.

Spencer, T. J. B., and Stanley Wells, eds. *A Book of Masques: In Honour of Allardyce Nicoll.* London, 1967.

Ward, John M. "The English Measure." *Early Music* 14 (February 1986): 15–21.

Ward, John M. "Newly Devis'd Measures for Jacobean Masques." *Acta Musicologica* 60 (1988).

ANDREW J. SABOL

MASQUERADES are fashionable assemblies at which persons wear masks and disguises and divert themselves with dancing, conversation, and other amusements. The origin of the term *masquerade* is obscure: etymologists suggest either an Arabic source—*maskharah* ("laughing-stock," "buffoon")—or a connection with the Old French *mascurer* ("to blacken the face"). The early forms *mascurado* and *mascarado* appear in English in the sixteenth century. Although the two words are sometimes used interchangeably, the masquerade should be distinguished from the masque. In contrast to the masque, a dramatic performance involving actors and spectators, the masquerade is an all-inclusive, unstructured occasion—less a theatrical event than a social gathering distinguished by costumed revelry, intrigue, and license.

The custom of masquerading originated in European Carnival tradition. Sixteenth-century travelers described *mascuradoes* in Italy and Spain at Carnival time (then from October through Lent), during which participants disguised themselves as devils and other supernatural creatures. In England, masked entertainments were held on traditional holidays such as Shrovetide and Twelfth Night at the court of Henry VIII; *Hall's Chronicle* for 1548 records a royal masked dance at Epiphany "after the maner of Italie." In the next century, elaborate masked balls were introduced during the winter season at France's court of Versailles, as the memoirs of the duc de Saint-Simon attest. Participants at these early court masquerades typically displayed themselves in a variety of extravagant allegorical and exotic disguises.

The true *grand siècle* of the masquerade, however, was the eighteenth century. The popularity of the diversion among royalty persisted: Louis XV, George II, Empress Maria Theresa, and Gustav III of Sweden were noted devotees. But the fashion for masquerades spread to other

MASQUERADES. "The World in Masquerade" is depicted in this eighteenth-century Dutch print. Several dozen revelers, in a wide array of disguise, including characters from the *commedia dell'arte,* have gathered in a large room. (Dance Collection, New York Public Library for the Performing Arts.)

ranks of society, too, thanks to the work of promoters and entrepreneurs. By midcentury the public masked ball was a well-established form of commercial entertainment in many European cities. Traditional Carnival centers—Venice, Rome, Florence, and Paris—were especially famed for their masquerades, but similar diversions are also recorded at such far-flung outposts as Saint Petersburg, where the *metamorphose* (the transvestite ball) was a popular amusement at the imperial court, and at Edinburgh, site of the first Scottish masquerade at Duff House in 1773.

In England, public masquerades took place first in London at the Haymarket in the 1710s and 1720s, under the management of the Swiss impresario and opera promoter "Count" John James Heidegger (c.1659–1749). Tickets were sold to the general public for a few shillings; as many as seven hundred persons attended each week. Heidegger's "Midnight Masquerade" quickly became notorious as a scene of excess, riot, and erotic impropriety. Public masquerades came under vociferous attack from moralists and divines in the 1720s, and a large antimasquerade literature survives from that period. Despite such criticism, however, the masquerade flourished into the 1780s. Large subscription masquerades were held at Ranelagh and Vauxhall, the Pantheon, and at Carlisle House later in the century, often with several thousand persons taking part. *Town and Country Magazine* for May 1770 reported a masquerade at the Pantheon attended by "near two thousand persons." Masked assemblies fell out of fashion only in the last decades of the century, when a new spirit of moral and social conservatism gradually took hold following the French Revolution. Despite a few nostalgic revivals during the Regency period, the public masquerade was a moribund institution in England by the turn of the century. On the Continent, in contrast, where the traditions of *travesti* and saturnalia were more deeply entrenched, large masquerades continued well into the nineteenth century. Contemporary Parisian masked balls are depicted in the novels of Honoré de Balzac and Gustave Flaubert.

In their heyday, the lavish masquerades of *ancien régime* Europe preserved—if in a somewhat secularized and stylized way—the festive ethos of Carnival. The masked ball was typically a nocturnal affair, held in sumptuously decorated and illuminated rooms. Thanks to the anonymity granted by disguise, collective behavior was unrestrained. The masquerade's contemporary reputation for licentiousness was to a large extent well deserved. Ordinary social forms were overturned, and a general spirit of libertinage prevailed. Particularly at the less reputable assemblies, sexual intrigue, prostitution, drinking, and gambling were ubiquitous activities. One contemporary called the masquerade a "Sodom for Lewdness."

Costumes were elegant and fantastic. In addition to the conventional black mask and domino (a loose, all-enfolding cloak of Venetian origin), popular masquerade costume types included foreign or exotic fancy dress, ecclesiastical parodies, transvestite costume, picturesque occupational dress, animal or supernatural disguise, *commedia dell'arte* costume, and dresses representing various theatrical, historical, and allegorical figures. "Turkish" or pseudo-Oriental costume was in particular vogue throughout the century. This fantastical multiplicity in the realm of sartorial spectacle was replicated in the diverse nature of the masquerade crowd itself, which typically drew, like Carnival, on both sexes and all ranks of society. Where else, asked a character in an English comedy of 1717, can one see "a *Nobleman* [dressed] like a *Cynder-Wench,* a *Colonel of Dragoons* like a *Country Rat-Catcher,* a *Lady of Quality* in *Dutch Trowsers,* and a *Woman of the Town* in a *Ruff* and *Farthingale?*" In both the visual and the sociological sense, the masquerade was indeed, as Joseph Addison (1672–1719) wrote in the *Spectator,* a "Promiscuous Assembly."

The masquerade has a colorful place in the history of social dance. Dancing was a staple entertainment at masquerades; especially popular were dances of a boisterous or suggestive nature. Thomas Morley had noted in his *Introduction to Practicall Musicke* of 1597 that the Italians performed galliards at their *mascuradoes;* in the next century, another writer described seeing Charles II and his court dance "with a great deal of wild frolick" at a Restoration masquerade. In Daniel Defoe's novel *Roxana* (1724), the heroine performs a *courante* and an "Antick" at a masquerade, as well as a "very fine Figure, invented by a famous Master at *Paris,* for a Lady or a Gentleman to dance single." An observer from the 1720s commented on the "scurvy Dancing" seen at Heidegger's assemblies; later in the century, Horace Walpole described masqueraders in "Old English" garb performing a maypole dance at the Jubilee Masquerade at Ranelagh in 1749.

Contemporaries took particular delight at the sight of incongruous masked couples performing together. A writer for the *Weekly Journal* in January 1724 observed a "pretty Nun" and a "Presbyterian Parson" dance a minuet together at a Haymarket masquerade, in company with "a Devil and a Quaker, a Turk and a female Rope-Dancer, a Judge and an Indian Queen." Other writers were less enchanted with such terpsichorean farce: the author of the *Short Remarks on Masquerades* (1721) blamed masquerades for encouraging "amorous and mixed Dancing" and charged that "the Devil himself, who danced in the daughter of *Herodias,* was the Original of this Lascivious Dancing."

A number of visual representations of dance at masquerades exist. Giovanni Domenico Tiepolo's remarkable painting *Carnival Scene* (1791–1793) shows masked figures dressed in *commedia* costume performing a lively contradance. Dancing figures can also be discerned in William Hogarth's satirical *Masquerade Ticket* (1727) and in his painting *The Happy Marriage: The Masked Ball at Wanstead* (c.1745). An anonymous view of the rotunda at Ranelagh from 1751 shows masqueraders performing a maypole dance in celebration of the birthday of the prince of Wales. Perhaps the most sardonic treatment of the theme is Thomas Rowlandson's *The English Dance of Death: The Masquerade* (1814–1816), in which cavorting Regency masqueraders are unpleasantly surprised by the figure of a skeleton dancing in their midst.

BIBLIOGRAPHY

Anonymous [ascribed to Charles Owen]. *The Conduct of the Stage Consider'd . . . with Short Remarks upon the Original and Pernicious Consequences of Masquerades.* London, 1721.

Castle, Terry. "Eros and Liberty at the English Masquerade, 1710–1790." *Eighteenth-Century Studies* 17 (Winter 1983–1984): 156–176.

Castle, Terry. *Masquerade and Civilization: The Carnivalesque in Eighteenth-Century English Culture and Fiction.* Stanford, Calif., 1986.

Griffin, Benjamin. *The Masquerade, or, An Evening's Intrigue.* London, 1717.

Pilon, Edmond, and Frédéric Saisset. *Les fêtes en Europe au XVIIIe siècle.* Saint-Gratien, c.1907.

Ribeiro, Aileen. "The Exotic Diversion: The Dress Worn at Masquerades in Eighteenth-Century London." *Connoisseur* 200 (January 1978): 27–31.

Ribeiro, Aileen. "The Elegant Art of Fancy Dress." In *An Elegant Art: Fashion and Fantasy in the Eighteenth Century,* edited by Edward Maeder. Los Angeles, 1983.

TERRY CASTLE

MASSINE, LÉONIDE (Leonid Fedorovich Miasin; born 3 August 1896 in Moscow, died 15 March 1979 in Borken, Germany), Russian dancer and choreographer. By breaking away from classical tradition, Massine created a new genre in ballet during the early twentieth century. Massine's choreography incorporated *demi-caractère* stylizations, ethnic influences, and an unusually powerful dramatic sense. The themes of his ballets, the symphonic music he chose, and even the movements he prescribed were all frequently focal points of artistic controversy, particularly among musicians and music lovers. He employed sharp, angular designs in movement contrasted against dynamic characterizations through gesture. These, and complex rhythmic patterns of rapid footwork, were the trademarks of Massine's style.

Massine's ballets also had a profound effect on choreographic experimentation in their strong relationship with decorative art and music. He sought a synthesis of performance and fine arts. This striving for artistic integration was a vital creative force throughout Massine's career and a legacy from his mentor, Serge Diaghilev.

Diaghilev was instrumental in discovering and nurturing Massine's creative genius. As Diaghilev's protégé, Massine was recognized both for his innovative choreography and for his brilliance as a dancer. His performances were ignited with tremendous spirit and energy. Although his choreography was controversial, his extraordinary musicality and innate sense of rhythm were indisputable. These gifts were deeply rooted in his early years.

Early Career. Leonid Fedorovich Miasin (the spelling was changed by Diaghilev) was the last of five children in a working-class family in Moscow. His father played French horn in the Bolshoi Theater orchestra, and his mother sang in its opera chorus, but the youngest Massine was the only child to pursue an artistic education. He was accepted to the Bolshoi Theater School (also known as the Imperial Theater School), and like most of its students he appeared on the Bolshoi stage in operas and ballets, as well as in plays at the Maly Theater.

MASSINE. With *La Boutique Fastasque* (1919), Massine invented a new kind of ballet based on a series of *demi-caractère divertissements* that advance the plot and lead up to a rollicking finale. As the male Can-Can Dancer, he performed a principal role. A London audience greeted the premiere with thunderous applause and shouts of enthusiastic approval. (Photograph from the Dance Collection, New York Public Library for the Performing Arts.)

As his studies progressed, Massine's interest in dance began to be overshadowed by a growing interest in acting. In December 1913, however, Massine's performance of the tarantella in *Swan Lake* with the Bolshoi caught Diaghilev's eye, and after a brief audition with Michel Fokine, he was invited to join Diaghilev's Ballets Russes.

Massine began intensive ballet training under Enrico Cecchetti, who was employed by Diaghilev to train the company's dancers. He diligently studied classical technique and often recorded the lessons, but he also realized that his own physique and style were not sympathetic with that tradition.

Nevertheless, in May 1914 Massine made his debut with the Ballets Russes in the title role of Fokine's *Die Josephslegende.* The performance was notable for Massine's mastery of the stage and commanding presence, though not for his technique.

By the time war broke out in Europe in late 1914, Massine had become Diaghilev's lover and artistic favorite, replacing Vaslav Nijinsky in both roles. The company was not performing at the time, so Diaghilev took Massine to Italy, where he was first exposed to many of the great masterpieces of Western and particularly Italian Renaissance art and architecture.

First Choreographic Work. Inspired by his new surroundings and encouraged by Diaghilev, Massine developed the idea for a new ballet, *Liturgie.* The Russian painter Natalia Goncharova met Massine and Diaghilev in Rome, where they began to discuss the Byzantine theme the new ballet was to have. It was proposed that Igor Stravinsky provide music for the piece, but he declined. The entire project was set aside when the war forced the Russian artists to leave Italy and return home.

Undaunted by the fate of *Liturgie,* Massine became enthralled with the choreographic process. His next ballet, presented in concert, was *Le Soleil de Nuit* (1915; later called *Midnight Sun*). Although the story was only loosely based on Nikolai Rimsky-Korsakov's opera *The Snow Maiden,* the ballet was set to music from that score. The Russian artist Mikhail Larionov designed the costumes and scenery in the bright colors of the Russian peasantry. As designer, Larionov assumed the task of supervising Massine's choreographic work. The movement patterns reflected the angularity and asymmetric groupings of Larionov's painting style. The first performance of *Le Soleil de Nuit* took place in 1915 at a charity performance for the Red Cross in Geneva. Massine also danced the leading role. The ballet was a resounding success and led Massine to take on the dual role of choreographer and principal dancer with the Diaghilev company.

As his technique grew more assured, Massine was given the opportunity to perform many principal roles in the company's repertory in ballets such as *Schéhérezade* and *Petrouchka.* When the Ballets Russes came to the United States in 1916, Massine was one of the dancers who replaced the absent Nijinsky.

Following Diaghilev's suggestion, he next created *Les Femmes de Bonne Humeur* (The Good-Humored Ladies) in 1917. The ballet displayed Massine's innovative style. The work's eighteenth-century setting was not so much replicated in movement as it was intimated by choreographic stylizations of the period. Departing from classical tradition, Massine gave his dancers—especially the women—angular movements of the hands and wrists.

Diaghilev and Massine then went to Rome to begin the creation of a new work, *Parade.* Jean Cocteau had already written the scenario when Diaghilev commissioned Erik Satie to compose the score and Pablo Picasso to provide the set and costume designs. *Parade* was presented on 18 May, 1917 in the Théâtre du Châtelet, Paris. On the whole, its use of modern art forms alienated the public and press, marking the beginning of the general air of controversy that would surround many of Massine's future ballets. [*See* Parade.]

In 1917, at the invitation of King Alfonso XIII, the Ballets Russes journeyed to Spain, where Massine soon became enchanted by the intricate rhythmic patterns of flamenco. Preparations for the creation of a Spanish ballet were begun, with Massine creating movement to a score contributed by Manuel de Falla. The choreographer and composer, accompanied by Diaghilev and the Spanish dancer Félix Fernández, with whom Massine was studying, toured Spain gathering folk tunes and dances. Progress was fitful; funds were frozen and political conditions hindered travel for the Russian troupe. The ballet rested in limbo for two years but was resurrected when Picasso was recruited to design the decor in 1919.

When the completed ballet, *Le Tricorne* (The Three-Cornered Hat) received its premiere later that year in London, Massine's choreography was seen in its fullest expression to date. The dances he created were in tone, interpretation, and rhythm quite Spanish, but the steps themselves were unmistakably Massine's. The work succeeded admirably in creating an ethnic atmosphere, making it a *demi-caractère* ballet. Massine danced the leading role, and his explosive solo cemented his reputation as a superior performing artist. *Le Tricorne* is still considered one of his outstanding achievements. [*See* Tricorne, Le.]

While still at work on *Le Tricorne,* Massine created *La Boutique Fantasque,* a forerunner of more lively works. Inspired by the music of Gioacchino Rossini, Massine conjured up a colorful cast of characters for his fantastic toyshop, including two Tarantella Dancers, two Can-Can Dancers, and a pack of cards represented by Queens of Diamonds and Clubs and Kings of Spades and Hearts. André Derain's costumes and scenery were bright, gay, and as fanciful as the music and choreography. *La Boutique Fantasque* premiered before *Le Tricorne* in 1919, delighting the critics and ameliorating their displeasure with *Parade.*

MASSINE. Based on Molière's 1661 *comédie-ballet* of the same name, *Les Fâcheux* (The Bores; 1927) was a revision of a failed work made by Bronislava Nijinska in 1924. Massine's version was only marginally better than the original. He is seen here with Nicolas Efimoff. (Photograph from the Dance Collection, New York Public Library for the Performing Arts.)

Massine's next creative endeavor, *Le Chant du Rossignol,* was blasted by the press, though the audiences at its premiere performances in Paris responded more positively. Stravinsky's score was originally intended as an opera, but Diaghilev decided to make it into a ballet, with Henri Matisse executing set and costume designs. Though Massine was able to work closely with Matisse, his collaboration with Stravinsky was minimal.

It was not uncommon for several projects to be pursued at one time. The ballet *Pulcinella,* for example, was conceived as *Le Chant du Rossignol* was reaching completion. While in Italy with Diaghilev in the summer of 1919, Massine had investigated *commedia dell'arte* themes and was eager to develop his interpretation of the Italian comedy.

The plot for *Pulcinella* was taken from an early eighteenth-century manuscript, *The Four Pulcinellas Who Look Alike.* Diaghilev suggested music by Giambattista Pergolesi and, together with Massine, selected the score. Diaghilev commissioned Stravinsky to provide updated orchestrations. Meanwhile, Massine was creating choreography for a large-scale ballet to what he had understood would be full orchestral accompaniment; but Stravinsky,

MASSINE. *Le Sacre du Printemps* was first mounted by Massine in 1920, when he re-created the work for Diaghilev's Ballets Russes. He staged it again ten years later for the League of Composers in the United States. Leopold Stokowski conducted the Philadelphia Orchestra; Nikolai Roerich collaborated on scenic and costume design; Martha Graham danced the role of the Chosen Virgin. The ballet was presented in April 1930, first at the Philadelphia Academy of Music and then at the Metropolitan Opera House in New York. This photograph was taken on the Metropolitan stage; Graham stands at center, with fist upraised. (Photograph from the Dance Collection, New York Public Library for the Performing Arts.)

true to his own style as well as Pergolesi's, produced a score for a small orchestra. Stravinsky's invention forced Massine to tone down and change much of his choreography in order to harmonize with the music. Picasso suggested a contemporary setting for the Neapolitan ballet, but Diaghilev insisted on a more authentic rendering of the *commedia* style. The final, vividly colored costumes were traditional, including masks. They contrasted well with the abstract scenery. *Pulcinella* proved enormously successful when first presented in May 1920.

After the success of *Pulcinella,* Diaghilev decided that Massine should re-create *Le Sacre du Printemps,* originally choreographed by Nijinsky. No one could remember the choreography accurately, so Massine had to create his own interpretation of Stravinsky's score. He spent several weeks in Switzerland with Stravinsky to study the music; their artistic communication was exemplary in this instance. The ballet was rehearsed in England prior to being presented on an all-Massine program in Paris in December 1920.

Break with Diaghilev. During the last few weeks of rehearsal in England, Massine and a young English member of the company, Vera Savina (Vera Clark), began to spend much of their free time together. After the season in Paris, the company went on to Rome. There Diaghilev grew aware of the attraction between Massine and Savina and summarily dismissed Massine from the company.

The young couple returned to London a few weeks later and were married. Before long, they were making preparations to take a group of dancers who had also left Diaghilev's company on a tour of South America. In Buenos Aires, the group danced excerpts from Massine's ballets and several pas de deux from Fokine ballets. Massine auditioned local talent, expanded the size of his little company, and extended the tour into Brazil. Directing the company, managing and arranging the tours, and dancing leading roles every night, Massine did not have time or energy to create any new ballets.

During Massine's absence, the Diaghilev company had appeared in London in a financially disastrous production of *The Sleeping Princess.* This left several dancers available for employment, so Massine recruited Lydia Lopokova, Lydia Sokolova, Ninette de Valois, and others for a limited tour of England and Scotland.

Now settled in London, the Massines endeavored to establish a dancing school. They rented a studio near Oxford Street and enrolled their first students, one of whom was Frederick Ashton. Still, Massine had little time or opportunity to create his own works. Though freed from the restraints imposed by Diaghilev, his new independent life also had its limitations. Nonetheless, Massine was soon invited by Comte Étienne de Beaumont to participate in Les Soirées de Paris, a charitable series to raise funds for widows and Russian refugees.

The first ballet Massine produced for Beaumont was *Le Beau Danube,* mounted in Paris on 17 May 1924. It was a lighthearted work suffused with its choreographer's characteristic spontaneity and audience-stimulating panache. The steps were more classically based than in some of his earlier works but remained in the *demi-caractère* idiom. Set to waltz tunes by Johann Strauss the younger, the choreography flowed freely to the music's lilting rhythms. The elegant musicality of *Le Beau Danube* contrasted sharply with the dynamic thrust of *Le Tricorne,* and this work may have been seen as a reaction to the powerful Spanish rhythms with which Massine had been so taken.

Le Beau Danube was followed in the same year by *Salade* (originally *Insalade*), based on *commedia* themes with designs by Beaumont. Also in 1924 came *Gigue* and *Mercure. Gigue* was set in a garden at Versailles, with music by Domenico Scarlatti, Johann Sebastian Bach, and George Frideric Handel and designs by André Derain.

MASSINE. Created for Colonel de Basil's Ballets Russes de Monte Carlo, *Les Présages* (1933) was Massine's first symphonic ballet. The fourth movement concerned the conflict between Man (The Hero) and Fate. Here, David Lichine as the Hero stands centerstage, framed by members of the female and male ensembles. Sets and costumes were designed by André Masson. (Photograph from the Dance Collection, New York Public Library for the Performing Arts.)

MASSINE. For René Blum's new Ballet Russe de Monte Carlo, Massine made *Gaîté Parisienne* (1938). A lively tale of love and flirtation set in a fashionable Parisian café of the Second Empire, it was danced to a selection of tunes from the works of Jacques Offenbach. Although some British balletomanes sniffily resisted its charm, Americans fell in love with it immediately. In the United States, it quickly became the new company's signature work, as much for the performances of its stars as for its choreographic merits. Here the excitable Peruvian (Massine) is lifted off his feet by the sight of the Baron (Frederic Franklin) planting a lusty kiss on the lips of the Glove Seller (Milada Miladova). (Photograph from the Dance Collection, New York Public Library for the Performing Arts.)

Mercure, the last ballet for Beaumont's Soirées, featured music by Satie and set and costume designs by Picasso. Massine danced the leads in all these ballets.

By the end of 1924, Massine and Savina had separated. She returned to Diaghilev's troupe, while Massine performed in English music hall revues until January 1925. At that time, he rejoined the Ballets Russes as guest choreographer. Diaghilev had two ballets for him to choreograph—*Zéphire et Flore* and *Les Matelots.* Massine was also asked to dance and took on the leading role in *L'Oiseau Bleu* (the Bluebird pas de deux) opposite Savina.

Reunion with Diaghilev. As productive and pleasant as the association with Beaumont had been, the creative opportunities and environment Diaghilev provided remained unparalleled in Massine's career. His reunion with his former mentor proved a fertile one. *Zéphire et Flore* was the first ballet he completed. The idea for it was suggested by Boris Kochno, who wanted to re-create the eighteenth century *ballet d'action,* but with a contemporary movement style. Massine's collaborators were the composer Vladimir Dukelsky and the painter Georges Braque, who did the scenic design. The initial performance of the work in Monte Carlo led Diaghilev to make changes in Braque's designs before the Paris opening. The choreography emphasized the best qualities of certain of the company's dancers, particularly Alice Nikitina and Anton Dolin and reaffirmed Diaghilev's confidence in Massine. (Diaghilev had seen *Le Beau Danube* and thought it in very poor taste.) Audiences, however, did not care for the ballet.

Les Matelots was much more popular. Again inspired by Kochno, this virtually plotless ballet was a frolicking suite of dances for three sailors—Spanish, French, and American—and two young girls. Georges Auric's music was as charming as the choreography, and Pedro Pruna's decor captured the same spirit.

Prior to *Les Matelots'* opening, Massine had returned to London to choreograph and perform in C. B. Cochran's production of Noël Coward's *On with the Dance.* English music hall revues proved a good source of employment for Massine in ensuing years and gave him choreographic experience in another genre.

The *Cochran Revue 1926* enlisted Massine's services again as choreographer and principal dancer. For it, Massine revived *Gigue* and also created a new comic ballet, *The Tub.* The Ballets Russes came to London while Massine was with the revue, and Diaghilev and he made plans for the coming season. When the revue closed, Massine went to Monte Carlo to join the Ballets Russes, but he found a new young artist, George Balanchine, establishing himself as the company's major choreographer.

Diaghilev had decided that Massine should rechoreograph Bronislava Nijinska's *Les Fâcheux* and that the original Braque designs would be used again. Fortunately, Massine liked Auric's music and was invigorated by being able to dance the lead in the 1926 production.

Russian artists abroad in 1926 and 1927 did not ignore the newly formed Soviet regime. The Soviet influence began to permeate the Ballets Russes as the composer Sergei Prokofiev collaborated with Georgi Yakulov, a constructivist painter, on a ballet intended to represent the emerging industrialization of Soviet Russia. In later years, Massine spoke of his brief encounter with Prokofiev as a moment when he was able to remember his national heritage.

The new ballet resulting from this encounter was the very essence of the Russian collaborative spirit with Diaghilev at the helm; Massine choreographed and the young Prokofiev provided a bracing score; they worked closely to ensure a unity of movement, music, story line, and design. The result, *Le Pas d'Acier,* was rehearsed in Monte Carlo and introduced in Paris in June of 1927. The work was controversial, but Prokofiev's presence seemed to rouse the company's nationalistic Russian spirit.

Later that year, with the Ballets Russes on their tour of Europe, Massine started his last ballet for Diaghilev, *Ode.* It boasted a half-dozen collaborators, and Massine's task was to synthesize all the different ideas. The choreography was cleverly woven around props set about cumbersome and awkwardly placed scenery, though the choreography itself adhered to geometric formations. When *Ode* premiered in Paris in 1927, however, Massine realized that his working relationship with Diaghilev was coming to an end. Balanchine was a vigorous new talent, and Massine had become interested in another woman, the young dancer Eugénie Delarova, whom he had met during the Paris opening of *Le Pas d'Acier.*

Delarova was sympathetic to Massine's thoughts and goals; the two married in Paris in 1928 and left for America soon after. In New York the newlyweds were faced with the frustration of unemployment until Massine was offered a contract at the new Roxy Theater, New York's prime film showcase. He agreed to compose a new piece every week to be performed between film showings; both Massine and Delarova performed daily at the Roxy.

In New York, Massine established contact with artists such as Michel Fokine and Ida Rubinstein. Rubinstein invited Massine to create two new works for her company in Paris. The Massines willingly headed for Europe but returned to New York for the next season at the Roxy.

When the last Roxy contract expired in 1930, Massine restaged his version of *Le Sacre du Printemps* for a benefit at the Metropolitan Opera House. This was his first seri-

MASSINE. With sets and costumes designed by Christian Bérard, Massine's *Seventh Symphony* (1938) made a powerful impression and evoked critical controversy. His choreography produced a shifting series of sculptural effects as groups of dancers fell into formations representing air, water, earth, and fire. Some critics praised the choreography; others judged the work a failure; still others were simply uneasy with the notion of dancing to a Beethoven symphony. (Photograph by Raoul Barbà; from the Dance Collection, New York Public Library for the Performing Arts.)

ous ballet to be mounted in America, and he selected the young American dancer Martha Graham to perform in the leading role. After these performances, Massine began his work on analysis of movement and composition. He continued this theoretical study throughout the rest of his life.

In 1932, Massine created *Jeux d'Enfants* for Colonel Wassily de Basil's Ballets Russes de Monte Carlo, which had been formed around a nucleus of former Diaghilev dancers. Massine then went to London to create *The Miracle* but returned to Monte Carlo to work with the de Basil company.

Symphonic Ballets. Here Massine delved into the problem of interpreting symphonic scores. His symphonic ballets sparked the greatest controversy of his career, as musicians and music scholars disagreed as to whether a symphonic work should have movement created to it. Massine's first symphonic ballet, *Les Présages,* was to Tchaikovsky's Fifth Symphony. He felt that the theme was clearly suggested by the musical construction and choreographed the mood and emotions he instinctively felt were dictated by the music.

MASSINE. As Saint Francis, Massine is seen here with Nini Theilade as Poverty in a pose from his ballet *Nobilissima Visione* (1938). Later better known as *Saint Francis,* the work was more a dramatic and choreographic interpretation of the life of the saint than a ballet in the usual sense. Its goal was to create and sustain a sense of mystic exaltation. (Photograph © by Maurice Seymour; used by permission.)

In the ballet's first section, Massine gave Nina Verchinina an outstanding solo, emphasizing her expressive arms as they moved from soft curvilinear shapes into sharply angular patterns. The second section was a lyric and romantic pas de deux, followed by a sequence that embodied merriment. The final section depicted the chaos of war and was characterized by frenzied movements. The designs by André Masson were kept simple so as not to interfere with the choreography. The costumes were plain tunics reminiscent of classical Greece and Rome, initiating a design trend that came to be known as "symphonic costume."

Les Présages was well received by Monte Carlo audiences in April 1933, but the controversy it provoked had a direct influence on future choreography. Such choreographers as Balanchine and Frederick Ashton began to experiment with complete symphonic works as inspiration for interpretive creativity.

Although he still spent a good deal of time restaging earlier works, particularly *Le Beau Danube,* Massine continued to pursue his symphonic interest. A few smaller works, including *Beach* and *Scuola di Ballo,* were produced prior to his next major task—interpreting Johannes Brahms's Fourth Symphony. *Choreartium,* as the Brahms ballet came to be known, was more abstract than *Les Présages.* The male and female dancers followed the instrumentation that Massine associated with their gender: women danced to lighter, more delicate passages, and men to the heavier, percussive sections. Though *Choreartium* was much more readily received than *Les Présages* had been six months earlier, Massine's symphonic settings still had their deprecators.

Later in 1933, Massine and Delarova went to America with de Basil's Ballets Russes. There Massine choreographed a group of works on American themes, such as *Union Pacific.* He was still drawn to symphonies, however, and a particular fascination with Hector Berlioz's *Symphonie Fantastique* emerged into creative reality. Berlioz himself had written a detailed scenario for the symphony, so the libretto could not be disputed by music critics. Berlioz's theme, alluded to in the music by a use of leitmotif, revolved around a relationship between the characters of the Young Musician and his Eternal Beloved. Massine was faithful to that theme in his interpretive movement. The dramatic quality of Massine's choreography was now at its peak. At its 1936 premiere at the Royal Opera House in London, *Symphonie Fantastique* was highly acclaimed, as was Massine's realization of the Young Musician. The integration of the work's movement,

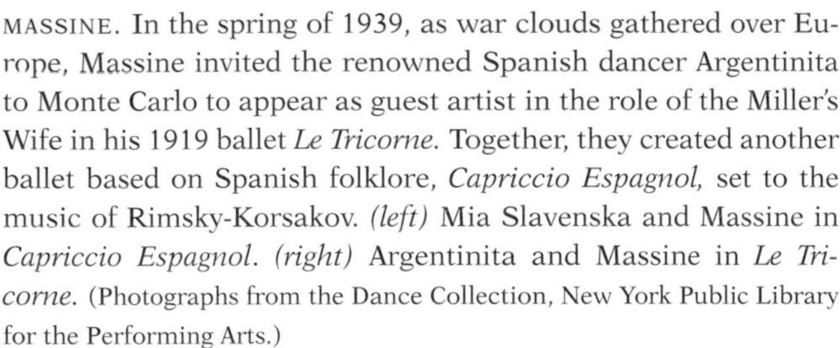

MASSINE. In the spring of 1939, as war clouds gathered over Europe, Massine invited the renowned Spanish dancer Argentinita to Monte Carlo to appear as guest artist in the role of the Miller's Wife in his 1919 ballet *Le Tricorne*. Together, they created another ballet based on Spanish folklore, *Capriccio Espagnol*, set to the music of Rimsky-Korsakov. *(left)* Mia Slavenska and Massine in *Capriccio Espagnol*. *(right)* Argentinita and Massine in *Le Tricorne*. (Photographs from the Dance Collection, New York Public Library for the Performing Arts.)

the early nineteenth-century designs by Christian Bérard, and the music's rich romanticism made this one of the greatest of Massine's symphonic ballets. It enjoyed remarkable success, and the term "symphonic ballet" now became part of the dance vocabulary.

Massine's association with Colonel de Basil was finally terminated in 1937. Massine was dissatisfied with the restrictions of his position and eventually turned to his own contacts and patrons for sponsorship. A new company, the Ballet Russe de Monte Carlo, was being formed, and Massine was appointed artistic director (a title he had never previously held), with Serge Denham as general director. Massine set about auditioning dancers and establishing a repertory, using some of Fokine's ballets and producing his own works.

For the new company Massine put together one of his most popular creations, *Gaîté Parisienne*, a lighthearted frolic set in a restaurant in Paris. The choreography was fanciful, though some critics thought the can-can sequence risqué. After the highly dramatic *Symphonie Fantastique*, this ballet demonstrated Massine's versatility in his choice of thematic material as well as his ability to conjure up a variety of atmospheres. The ballet premiered in April 1938 in Monte Carlo, and its success gave the young company a bright beginning. [*See* Gaîté Parisienne.]

Still fascinated with the symphonic ballet, Massine next took on Ludwig van Beethoven's Seventh Symphony, a work whose passion had long enraptured him. He translated that passion into four statements on the creation and evolution of the world, confining specific dramatic actions to each individual scene while eschewing overall thematic development throughout the ballet. Thus the work appeared to be a series of four independent choreographic essays on musical content and philosophical themes. Presented only a month after *Gaîté Parisienne, Seventh Symphony* was heavily criticized on thematic grounds, but Massine's choreography was praised.

On the suggestion of Paul Hindemith, Massine decided to create a ballet on the life of Saint Francis of Assisi. Hindemith composed the score and made important suggestions concerning the choreography. *Nobilissima Visione* (also known as *Saint Francis*) represented the completion of an idea that had remained with Massine for many years, ever since the aborted *Liturgie* of 1914. The movements and overall choreography were not particularly innovative, but dramatic intensity and symbolic movement were cleverly incorporated. Massine's outstanding musicality strengthened the work's choreographic structure. The ballet was a great success at its London opening in 1938 and was even praised by members of the clergy. Massine himself was lauded for his portrayal of Saint Francis. [*See* Nobilissima Visione.]

Later Career. Just before World War II erupted, Massine was at work on yet another symphonic ballet, *Rouge et Noir*. The title referred to the conflict between the spiritual and material worlds. The inspiration for the ballet was derived from Dmitri Shostakovich's First Symphony. Henri Matisse had designed the costumes to Massine's color specifications. Massine later reflected that the timing of the ballet's creation was precipitous, given the world political situation. *Capriccio Espagnol*, created for the Spanish dancer La Argentinita, premiered along with *Rouge et Noir* in Monte Carlo just before the war's advent.

MASSINE. A studio portrait in costume for *Aleko*, created for Ballet Theatre during Massine's guest engagement in 1942. (Photograph © by Maurice Seymour; used by permission.)

When hostilities broke out in 1939, the company fled to America and promptly commenced a tour, returning to New York for the 1940 season. By this time, Massine had created two new ballets—*Vienna 1814* and *The New Yorker*—though neither exhibited his choreographic skills to their best advantage.

Massine was asked by the Warner Brothers Studio in Hollywood to film two of his ballets, and in 1941 *Gaîté Parisienne* and *Spanish Fiesta* (Hollywood's title for *Capriccio Espagnol*) were produced for the screen. While the Massines were in Los Angeles for the filming, their daughter Tatiana was born.

The family returned to New York in 1941, and Massine found employment with Ballet Theatre. He and Marc Chagall collaborated on a work, *Aleko*, that Massine had devised to Tchaikovsky's Trio in A Minor. The theme was vaguely based on Aleksandr Pushkin's poem "The Gypsies." Chagall and Massine accompanied Ballet Theatre on its 1942 tour to Mexico City, where *Aleko* proved to be Massine's first major success in several years. The work went on to receive favorable response in New York. Massine's sojourn in Mexico inspired him to produce a ballet on a Mexican theme, *Don Domingo*, but between 1942 and 1944 he created only a few small ballets. In 1944 Massine's son Léonide (Lorca) was born.

Massine had always yearned to have his own company, and in 1945 he assembled several former Ballet Russe dancers, arranged excerpts from twenty-eight ballets, and formed the Ballet Russe Highlights. This small company toured more than twenty cities throughout the United States but was disbanded within a year. The series of one-night stands without a base residence had worn down the dancers as well as Massine, who had proved an adequate though not outstanding organizer.

The Massines decided to move to England, where they found work in a London play and later with the Sadler's Wells Ballet, for which Massine primarily did revivals of his early ballets. In the film *The Red Shoes*, Massine took the role of the Shoemaker, choreographing his own part as well as his duets with Moira Shearer. The film's release revitalized Massine's career and public appeal, and suddenly he was in demand again as a choreographer. [*See* Red Shoes, The.]

Massine went on to revive many of his ballets in theaters around the world. He spent two years traveling to Brazil, England, France, Monaco, and Italy before settling in Paris to choreograph a new work. He created several ballets over the next few years, most significantly *Laudes Evangelii* (1952), a deeply religious work based on the life of Christ. Massine's wife and children all danced in it.

MASSINE. In the film *The Red Shoes* (1948), Massine played a dual role, the choreographer Grisha Ljubov in the principal plot and the Shoemaker in the ballet within the film. The Shoemaker is one of his most memorable roles. He is seen here, at left, with Moira Shearer and Robert Helpmann, who was the titular choreographer of the ballet. Massine, in fact, created his own choreography within the context of Helpmann's work. (Photograph from the Dance Collection, New York Public Library for the Performing Arts.)

No longer attached to one company, and with the impetus of *The Red Shoes* having dissipated, Massine was working only sporadically now. In 1954, however, he was invited to return to the Ballet Russe de Monte Carlo as guest choreographer, and there he created his last symphonic ballet, to Berlioz's Symphony no. 2, "Harold en Italie," inspired by Lord Byron's *Childe Harold.* Massine felt that movement was a natural extension of expression for the score. When *Harold in Italy* premiered in Boston in October 1954, though, critics and audiences could not decide if the ballet was another masterpiece or merely a curious, if not meaningless, experiment.

By 1957, Massine was arranging lecture-demonstrations in which he and his son both performed. Revivals of some of his ballets also included his children's participation; young Tatiana, for example, danced with her father in *Le Tricorne* in Amsterdam in 1958. But opportunities to work were dwindling, and Massine turned his attention to research for a textbook on choreography.

When the book was completed, Massine arranged to have a course of study in choreography offered at the Royal Ballet Upper School. Students studied Massine's theories and choreographic analyses of harmonic progress and dynamic evolution in movement, as well as his own system of movement notation. The text, *Massine on Choreography,* was finally published in 1976; a second volume of notated choreographic studies was also prepared and edited in 1976 but was never published. In his last years, Massine considered these works his most important contribution to the world of dance. He also wrote an autobiography, *My Life in Ballet* (1968).

Massine traveled to America in 1976 to revive *Le Beau Danube* in California. The trip seemed to renew his spirit, and he returned the following year to explore some new choreographic ideas. *Bouquet* and *Parisiana,* the fruits of that exploration, appeared in 1977.

[*See also the entries on the principal figures mentioned herein.*]

BIBLIOGRAPHY

Anderson, Jack. *The One and Only: The Ballet Russe de Monte Carlo.* New York, 1981.

Buckle, Richard. *Diaghilev.* New York, 1979.

Chujoy, Anatole. "The Case against Massine." *Dance* (December 1936): 9.

Coton, A. V. "After Diaghilev: Massine." *Ballet* (September–October 1939).

Dorris, George. "Massine in 1938: Style and Meaning." In *Proceedings of the Fourteenth Annual Meeting of the Society of Dance History Scholars, Winston-Salem, North Carolina,* compiled by Christena L. Schlundt, pp. 200–211. Riverside, Calif., 1988.

Fusillo, Lisa A. "Léonide Massine: Choreographic Genius with a Collaborative Spirit." Ph.D. diss., Texas Woman's University, 1982.

García-Márquez, Vicente. *Massine, a Biography.* New York, 1995.

Gregory, John. "With Massine on Galli." *The Dancing Times* (October 1974): 24–25.

Lawson, Joan. *A History of Ballet and Its Makers.* New York, 1964.

Massine, Léonide. *My Life in Ballet.* New York, 1968.

Moore, Lillian. *Artists of the Dance.* New York, 1938.

Robert, Grace. *The Borzoi Book of Ballets.* New York, 1946.

Vitak, Albertina. "Ballet and Massine." *American Dancer* (September 1938): 15.

LISA A. FUSILLO

MATACHINS. [*To survey the figured sword dances known as* matachins, *this entry comprises three articles:*

Historical Overview
Danza de Matlachines
Matachines Dances in the Southwestern United States

The first article presents the history of these dances from the sixteenth to the eighteenth century; the second focuses on the dance as performed in the Mexican state of Aguascalientes; the third surveys characteristics of the dance as performed by Native Americans and members of the Hispanic diaspora living in the southwestern United States.]

Historical Overview

Matachins is the term for sixteenth- to eighteenth-century figured sword dance(s) for teams of armed men; they are still done today, especially in various parts of the Spanish-speaking world. The term may derive from the Spanish word *matar* ("to kill") or the Italian word *matta* ("buffoon"). In Spain the dances are called *mattachines* (*matachines* in Spanish America); in France, *matassins;* and in Italy, *mattaccino* or *mattaccinata.* Although battle dances are ancient and worldwide, Thoinot Arbeau's theory (*Orchésographie,* 1588) of a direct lineage between *matachins* and an ancient Greek pyrrhic dance is unsupported. Arbeau, who provides the only extant choreography, uses the French terms *matassins* and *bouffons* interchangeably. Further ambiguous usage during the Renaissance of other terms for simulated battle dances, such as *moresca,* or *Morris,* increases the difficulty of giving a comprehensive definition of *matachins.*

In the sixteenth century there seem to have been two main types of *matachins,* both of which were mock abstract battles (usually without narrative) and were frequently parts of spectacular events. One was a grotesque dance of "fools"; the other, a skilled sword dance performed by young noblemen before an aristocratic audience. A third type, particularly popular in parts of southern Europe, was a solemn ritual dance for religious occasions (e.g., dance of death), a *mattaccino* or *moresca* that apparently spread via the Spanish Conquest to Mexico and other parts of the Spanish Empire.

MATACHINS: Historical Overview. Four sword gestures for performance of the *matachins* as depicted by Thoinot Arbeau in his *Orchésographie* (1588). (Dance Collection, New York Public Library for the Performing Arts.)

References to the grotesque aspects of the *matachins* abound. John Florio (*A Worlde of Wordes,* 1598) calls the dance "a kind of antique [antic] moresco." Francisco Alcocer (in Corominas, 1599) refers to its ridiculous disguises and grimaces and Cesare Negri (*Le gratie d'amore,* 1602; 1604) terms a dance by dwarves with cudgels and shields (clearly grotesque) a *mattaccinata.* Randle Cotgrave (*Dictionarie of the French and English Tongues,* 1611) defines it as a Morris. In 1642 Juan de Esquivel Navarro refers to the bent knees of a *mattachino* as undesirable and awkward. Molière, in his *comédie-ballet Monsieur de Pourceaugnac* (1669), calls for six *matachins* "with syringes" and two grotesque doctors to attack the comic hero in a scatological ballet. Francisco del Hierro (*Diccionario de la lengua castellana,* 1732) mentions in his definition the bladders (traditionally water-, air-, or flour-filled) used by clowns.

The *matachins* as a skillful martial drill, performed by armed gentlemen with bells at their knees, is fully described only by Arbeau in his *Orchésographie* (1588). He depicts his four duelists with short swords and small bucklers and gives music and precise instructions for their simulated armor, step patterns, "passages" (in which the duelists pass and twirl rapidly from one to another in square formations), and virtuoso swordplay. Negri gives no choreography, but cites one *mattaccino* done by eight of his noble students, each armed with sword and dagger. He mentions another dance performed with spears and yet another danced by four noble pages with swords and bucklers.

In Arbeau's choreography, the constant swordplay and strong leaping kicks require coordination, strength, and stamina, especially if all the figures are done consecutively. The simple repetitive step pattern—large kick, small kick, small kick (all off the ground with alternating feet)—is rhythmically marked by the bells at the knees and the intricate interplay of clashing swords and also displays rapid turns to meet different combatants. (See Example 1.) Unfortunately, Arbeau's version appears to be inapplicable to other Renaissance battle dances, as well as to *matachins* of a later period: the style of the dance and the technique of swordplay would have had to vary with the weapons, as evidenced by many contemporary fencing manuals. Arbeau's dance calls for what is known as the English short sword, but the rapier was already the fashion in Spain and Italy and soon superseded the short sword altogether.

Arbeau's melody appears in some other European sources, where it is variously called *matassins, bouffons, antycke,* or *Totentanz* and is accompanied by the *passamezzo antico* or *passamezzo moderno* bass. Other musical evidence, however, indicates that this music was not uni-

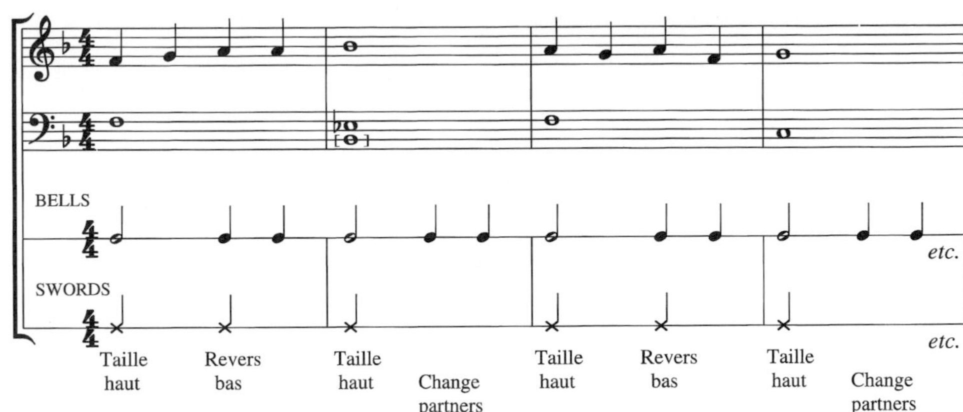

MATACHINS: Historical Overview. Example 1. Music example and the "three cuts" passage as described by Arbeau. The robust nature of the dance is enhanced by clashing swords, tinkling bells on the dancers' legs, and percussive footwork.

versal and that musical distinctions may have existed between *matachins* and *bouffons* for which there are, as yet, no documentation. If this is so, there may have been choreographic distinctions as well, all somehow confused by Arbeau. Later *matachins* music by, for example, Jean-Baptiste Lully and Christoph Willibald Gluck, appears unrelated to Arbeau's.

The ritual type of *matachins* and related sword dances were popular throughout the Spanish empire (Brooks, 1988). The dance, which does not always involve mock combat, is still a part of such solemn events as a village's patron saint's day in Mexico and Spanish-speaking communities in the southwestern United States. In these regional versions of *matachins,* teams of masked men may reenact the Aztec conversion to Christianity. The dances also intermingle several European and indigenous elements: costumes or headdresses are based on European models, such as the Christian bishop's miter; both dance and music are multisectional, although the rhythms are beaten with gourd rattles as European instruments (violin or guitar) play the melodies; and stock characters—the Bull, the Clown, or Montezuma's Bride—appear with the dancers. These characters closely resemble characters often connected with European male team dances (e.g., the Hobby-Horse, the Fool, and the Maid).

BIBLIOGRAPHY: SOURCES

Arbeau, Thoinot. *Orchésographie et traicte en forme de dialogve, par leqvel tovtes personnes pevvent facilement apprendre & practiquer l'honneste exercice des dances.* Langres, 1588, 1589. Facsimile reprint Langres, 1988. Reprinted with expanded title as *Orchesographie, metode, et teorie en forme de discovrs et tablatvre povr apprendre a dancer, battre le Tambour en toute sorte & diuersité di batteries, Iouët du fifre & arigot, tirer des armes & escrimer, auec autres honnestes exercices fort conuenables à la Ieunesse.* Langres, 1596. Facsimile reprint, Geneva, 1972.

Arbeau, Thoinot. *Orchesography.* 1589. Translated into English by Mary Stewart Evans. New York, 1948. Reprint with corrections, a new introduction, and notes by Julia Sutton, and representative steps and dances in Labanotation by Mireille Backer. New York, 1967.

Corominas, Juan. *Diccionario crítico etimológico de la lengua castellana* (1599). Facsimile reprint, Madrid, 1954.

Esquivel Navarro, Juan de. *Discursos sobre el arte del dancado* (1642). Facsimile reprint, Madrid, 1947.

Mancini, Giulio. *Del origine et nobiltà del ballo* (c.1623–1630). Facsimile reprint with introduction by Barbara Sparti, Freiburg, 1996.

Negri, Cesare. *Le gratie d'amore.* Milan, 1602. Reissued as *Nuove invenzione di balli.* Milan, 1604. Translated into Spanish by Don Balthasar Carlos for Señor Condé, Duke of Sanlucar, 1630. Manuscript located in Madrid, Biblioteca Nacional, MS 14085. Facsimile reprint of 1602, New York and Bologna, 1969. Literal translation into English and musical transcription by Yvonne Kendall. D.M.A. diss., Stanford University, 1985.

BIBLIOGRAPHY: OTHER STUDIES

Alford, Violet. *Sword Dance and Drama.* London, 1962.

Backman, Eugène Louis. *Religious Dances in the Christian Church and in Popular Medicine.* Translated by E. Classen. London, 1952.

Brooks, Lynn Matluck. *The Dances of the Processions of Seville in Spain's Golden Age.* Kassel, 1988.

Forrest, John. *"Morris and Matachin": A Study in Comparative Choreography.* London, 1984.

Galanti, Bianca Maria. *La danza della spada in Italia.* Rome, 1942.

Kenley, McDowell E. "Sixteenth-Century Matachines Dances: Morescas of Mock Combat and Comic Pantomime." Master's thesis, Stanford University, 1993.

Manfredi Cano, Domingo. *Bailes regionales.* 2d ed. Madrid, 1959.

Rey, Juan José. *Danzas cantadas en el renacimiento español.* Santiago de Campostela, 1978.

Sutton, Julia. "Matachin." In *The New Grove Dictionary of Music and Musicians.* London, 1980.

Tani, Gino. "Mattaccino." In *Enciclopedio dello spettacolo.* 9 vols. Rome, 1954–1968.

JULIA SUTTON
with Elizabeth Kurtz

Danza de Matlachines

The origin of the *danza de matlachines* (also called *matachines*) is not yet known, although it was documented in Europe in the sixteenth century. Colonial Spanish chroniclers in Mexico, including Bernal Díaz del Castillo, seem to have applied the term *matachines* to certain Mesoamerican dances that bore some resemblance to European dances. The dance may, however, have been introduced by the Spanish. Its present form is undoubtedly synergetic.

This dance is now performed, with regional variation, in the Mexican states of Veracruz, Tamaulipas, San Luis Potosí, Hidalgo, Jalisco, Aguascalientes, Zacatecas, and Coahuila, and among Native American groups of northern Mexico and the southwestern United States.

This entry discusses the dance as performed in the Mexican state of Aguascalientes, where it is sometimes referred to by the name of the district or locality in which it is performed or that of the patron saint venerated, instead of by the name *matlachines.* The historian Antonio Santos Rivera maintained that its original name was the *danza indígena Chichimeca,* referring to the peoples of north-central Mexico. In Aquascalientes, about two hundred miles (325 kilometers) northwest of Mexico City, the dance is performed at religious festivals. One of the most important is the Feast of the Assumption on 15 August, held in the cathedral of the city of Aguascalientes, where there are several dance groups.

The dance is performed in two lines consisting of an indeterminate number of male dancers. There are four captains, two ahead and two behind, who are generally selected from among the best dancers. The dancers who follow the forward captains are called *barriguillas.* Sometimes the group includes one or more *viejos* ("elders") whose job is to maintain order, keep a space open for the dance, and ward off competition; they often dress in women's clothes.

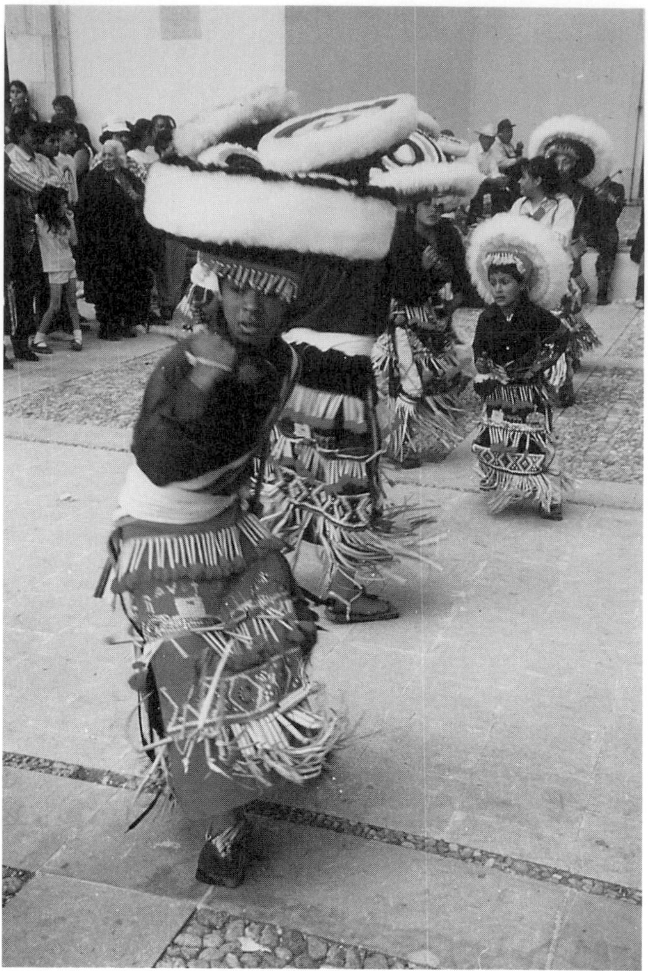

MATACHINS: Danza de Matlachines. In Zacatecas, the dancers wear the traditional fringed costume of the *matlachines* and hold *guajes* (rattles) in their right hands. (Photograph © by Roberto Ashentrupp; used by permission.)

The dance is usually accompanied by bass drum. Rarely, a violin is used; for example, of the fourteen dance groups that participated in the 1983 festival, only four had violinists. Canuto Santillán Ortiz, a violinist for one group, claimed that the more difficult melodies are not played because the dancers do not know how to perform to them. Older musicians disapprove of the inclusion of melodies that are not part of the tradition.

The costume consists of a flannel kilt, with borders, rows of reed decorations, and a fringe that may be of chamois or plastic; breeches; a shirt; a bodice similar to a vest, also with borders and reeds; crowfoot (thong) sandals; socks; and a plume. In their right hands the dancers hold rattles known as *guajes,* and in their left hands they hold arrows.

[For *related discussion, see* Mexico, *article on* Traditional and Indigenous Dance.]

BIBLIOGRAPHY

Champe, Flavia Waters. *The Matachines Dance of the Upper Rio Grande: History, Music, and Choreography.* Lincoln, Neb., 1983.

Díaz del Castillo, Bernal. *Historia verdadera de la conquista de la Nueva España* (1632). 2 vols. Edited by Joaquín Ramírez Cabañas. 7th ed. Mexico City, 1977.

Rodríguez, Sylvia. *The Matachines Dance: Ritual Symbolism and Interethnic Relations in the Upper Rio Grande Valley.* Albuquerque, 1996.

Romero, Brenda Mae. "The Matachines Music and Dance in San Pueblo and Alcalde, New Mexico." Ph.D. diss., University of California, Los Angeles, 1993.

Warman, Arturo. "Danza de los Matachines." In *Música indígena de México.* Mexico City, 1974.

CÉSAR DELGADO MARTÍNEZ

Matachines Dances in the Southwestern United States

In the southwestern United States, the *matachines* dances are choreographically related to, and almost certainly descendants of, those danced in northern and central Mexico. Performed in all parts of the greater Southwest, the most dense clusters occur along the border from Texas to Arizona and in the pueblos and Hispanic villages of the upper Rio Grande Valley of New Mexico. The dances of the border regions are closely related to their Mexican progenitors. Thus, for example, there is an active *matachines* tradition in Clint, Texas, which resembles in costume and choreography dances now performed primarily in central Mexico. Likewise the dances of the Yaqui people performed in Pascua, Arizona, are similar to those performed by Yaqui in Sonora, Mexico. *Matachines* at greater distances from the borders, particularly in formerly isolated regions such as the upper Rio Grande Valley, have evolved even further from their parent dances, into distinctive subgroups.

The New Mexico *matachines* are conventionally performed at village fiestas in the Christmas season—in paired traditions by both Tewa, Tiwa, and Towa peoples on the one hand and Hispanic villagers on the other. Thus, for example, the Tewa of San Juan pueblo perform a version of the dance that is very closely related to that performed in the neighboring Hispanic village of Alcalde. In the past these paired communities shared dancers, and they still share musicians.

The costumes of all the *matachines* traditions in the upper Rio Grande are variations on a theme. The main line dancers (called *matachines*) wear some form of holiday dress as their underlying outfit, ornamented with standard costume elements, so that the dancers' personal features are completely concealed. The *cupil* is similar to a traditional Aztec headdress, looking like a bishop's miter from the front, but with long colorful ribbons trailing over the head and down the back. From the front of the *cupil* hangs a beaded fringe that covers the wearer's eyes, and below the fringe is a large bandana that covers the nose, mouth, and neck. Pinned to the dancer's shoulders is a large rectangular piece of print fabric forming a flowing cape. The *matachines* wear gloves and carry a gourd rattle known as a *guaje* in the right hand and a decorated wooden trident called a *palma* in the left.

The *matachines* dance in double-column formation with anywhere from four to six dancers in each column. Dancers at the top and bottom of each column are known as *capitanes* ("captains") and have special roles in some of the dances. The other main characters include Monarca (The Monarch) who leads all the dancing. Monarca and the *capitanes* are dressed like line dancers, but wear *coronas* (decorated crowns) in place of *cupils.* Malinche is a young girl who generally dances with Monarca. She is usually dressed as a girl would be for first communion—all in white, with a white veil. But in some villages her costumes are of different colors for different days of the fiesta, and in a few pueblos she wears traditional buckskin and feathers. Abuelo (The Grandfather) serves as a fool as well as performing prescribed choreographic and mimetic actions. Conventionally he wears one-piece coveralls, a tall mask covers his head, and he carries a bullwhip. El Toro (The Bull), wears a horned headdress and a long tail and carries a wooden staff (sometimes two).

A complete performance of *matachines* consists of a number of dances called *bailes,* strung together in a sequence that is somewhat fixed, but open to modification according to circumstances. A great many of the particulars of performance vary from tradition to tradition, but the overall shape of the dance has a recognizable pattern. The dance sequence opens with a simple stepping dance by the *matachines* in double-column formation, and with Monarca at their head. Monarca then dances backward down the columns, dancing with each pair of *matachines* in turn. As Monarca moves back through the set the couples kneel at the conclusion of his performance with them, so that at the end of the *baile* all the *matachines* are kneeling, and Monarca is at the bottom of the set. The next *baile* is a solo by Malinche, who dances up to Monarca, takes one of his dancing implements, then dances away from him up the set. She returns to Monarca, takes the other implement, and dances up the set again. This is followed by a similar sequence in which she gives back the implements. Monarca then dances up the set, with Malinche following him. He again dances with the pairs of *matachines* in turn, who stand up and dance with him as he comes to their position in the set. Next is a *baile* usually called *La Cruz,* in which one column leads off in single file procession and forms a cross by dancing at right angles through the middle of the other column. El Toro is then brought out. The *capitanes,*

Monarca, and Malinche dance with him, in turn, before Abuelo wrestles him to the ground and castrates him.

One popular Hispanic interpretation of these *bailes* depicts them as enacting a sequence of events beginning with the courtship of Malinche (who represents the legendary Aztec mistress of Fernando Cortés) by Monarca (who represents Cortés himself) leading to their sexual union (which ultimately symbolizes both the physical and cultural synthesis of the Spanish and Indian peoples). This passage is followed by the conversion of the *matachines* (who represent Indians) to Christianity, but they are threatened by El Toro (symbolic of evil or the devil), who is first subdued by the *capitanes* (who represent Christianized Indian leaders) and then castrated by Abuelo. Thus, using this interpretation, the dances dramatically represent key components of the initial colonization of the New World by Spain.

By contrast, one Tiwa interpretation casts Monarca as the Aztec ruler Montezuma (not Cortés) and credits him with spreading the dance northward, as opposed to it being a Spanish colonial import. Under this analysis, Montezuma is cast as a pan-Indian culture hero, mitigating the harshness of Spanish imperialism with gifts of performances that incorporate his people's traditional symbols. Malinche is thus depicted as the ambassador of Cortés, bringing the message of Christianity to Montezuma (which he chooses to accept). In this interpretation, Spanish colonization required voluntary acceptance by Indians, and subsequent relations involved cultural exchange rather than forcible domination.

[*See* Mexico, *article on* Traditional Dances; *and* Yaqui Dance.]

BIBLIOGRAPHY

Champe, Flavia Waters. *The Matachines Dance of the Upper Rio Grande: History, Music, and Choreography.* Lincoln, Neb. 1983.

Forrest, John. *Morris and Matachin: A Study in Comparative Choreography.* Centre for English Cultural Tradition and Language Publications no. 4. Sheffield, 1984.

Kurath, Gertrude (with Antonio Garcia). *Music and Dance of the Tewa Pueblos.* Santa Fe, 1970.

Painter, Muriel Thayer. *With Good Heart: Yaqui Beliefs and Ceremonies in Pascua Village.* Tucson, 1986.

Robb, John D. *Hispanic Folk Music of New Mexico and the South West.* Norman, Okla. 1980.

Rodriguez, Sylvia. *The Matachines Dance: Ritual Symbolism and Interethnic Relations in the Rio Grande Valley.* Albuquerque, (forthcoming).

Romero, Brenda Mae. 1993. "The Matachines Music and Dance in San Juan Pueblo and Alcalde, New Mexico: Contexts and Meanings." Ph.D. diss. University of California at Los Angeles, 1993.

JOHN FORREST

MATISSE, HENRI (Henri-Émile-Benôit Matisse; born 31 December 1869 in Le Cateau-Cambrésis, France, died 3 November 1954 in Nice), French painter, sculptor, draftsman, graphic artist, book illustrator, occasional costume and set designer. Painter above all, and one of the major artists of the twentieth century, Matisse depicted dance as an elemental life force in one of his earliest important works, *Bonheur de Vivre* (1905–1906). Dance is also the subject of three of his large and well-known decorative paintings, all called *La Danse,* or *Dance* (1909–1910; 1931–1932; 1932–1933). Throughout his career, moreover, in paintings, in sculptures, and, later, in his vibrant cutouts, the luxuriant grace of many of his figures—standing, sitting, or reclining nudes; torsos; odalisques; acrobats; nymphs and satyrs—evokes the essence of dance, so rhythmic is the artist's line, so supple the bodies he represents.

Matisse's main concerns were color (sometimes violent, blinding color), line, and the creation of spatial ambiguity by combining two-dimensional patterns with perspective devices and three-dimensional modeling. After conservative beginnings, his palette lightened through the influence of impressionism and became more exuberant as he was exposed to the developing Fauvism. It was at this time that he painted *Bonheur de Vivre* (later retitled *Joie de Vivre;* now in the Barnes Foundation, Merion, Pennsylvania). In this giant canvas, nudes relax in an imagined pastoral landscape; deep in the distance, six women skip—or dance—in a circle. The sinuous line and lack of modeling emphasize a feeling of carefree abandon. With this work, Matisse announced another lifelong preoccupation: giving pleasure through purely visual means, regardless of subject. In his paintings, designs, and cutouts, surfaces have a life of their own.

In 1909, Sergei I. Shchukin, a Russian businessman who was the world's most important collector of twentieth-century French painting, commissioned from the artist two enormous decorative panels: *Dance,* perhaps Matisse's best-known work, and its companion, *Music,* both finished in 1910 (now in the Moscow Museum of Modern Western Art). In *Dance,* Matisse took the ring of six women from *Bonheur de Vivre* and monumentalized them by filling the surface with the figures—indeed, they almost burst out of it—and by using thicker, more deliberate outlines. The riot of Fauve color was replaced by intense vermilion skin tones and a deep blue and green background; a dancer who previously had had an open, casual position is now seen, twisted, from the back: Matisse turned the lighthearted group of 1905 into a dynamic, concentrated composition. (Shchukin's correspondence reveals that, despite his admiration for the artist, he hesitated before hanging the immense nudes in his dining room.) Matisse maintained that peasant dances were the inspiration for the work, and it is possible that Isadora Duncan was an influence as well, since the artist is known to have seen her perform. (Moreover, in 1909 they had studios at the same Paris address.) He also enjoyed watching dancing at the Moulin de la Galette, a popular music hall in the Montmartre section of Paris. Portions of the composition—truncated at unusual points—appear as backgrounds in *Still Life with the "Dance"* (1909) and in two treatments of *Nasturtiums and the "Dance"* (both 1912).

In 1930, Dr. Albert C. Barnes, who had the largest American collection of Matisse, commissioned a mural from him to decorate the great hall of the Barnes Foundation's museum in Merion, Pennsylvania. The difficulties were considerable: the painting was to occupy lunettes over three large French windows, above a gallery filled with distinguished paintings. After Matisse produced his mural it was discovered that the wrong measurements had been used, so he created a second one, reworking the design into two versions, *The Dance I* (1931–1932; now in the Musée d'Art Moderne de la Ville de Paris) and *The Dance II* (1932–1933; now in the Barnes Foundation museum). In both paintings a frieze of dancing figures is deployed across the wall. Again, the poses of 1905 are a point of departure, but, unlike those in earlier compositions, the figures no longer hold hands in a circle. In wild or exultant leaps, some are daringly cut off at the torso by the shape of the wall; others lunge and even fall, their size barely contained by the space. In the second version, the central duo might almost be combatants. The art historian Alfred Barr has described the action as "some frenzied, Dionysian game or tumbling act or perhaps a savage pyrrhic dance or gladiatorial miming." For once, Matisse turned away from voluptuous color: the figures are stone gray, with abstract, flat backgrounds of pink, black, and blue. In cutouts connected with designing Léonide Massine's ballet *Rouge et Noir* (1939) for the Ballet Russe de Monte Carlo and in creating designs for a cover of the magazine *Verve* in 1945, Matisse again based his figures on the seminal dancing poses of 1905.

In 1920, Matisse had created decors for *Le Chant du Rossignol,* choreographed by Massine to music of Igor Stravinsky for Diaghilev's Ballets Russes. The ballet was a failure and disappeared within the year, but in 1925 it was brought back with choreography by George Balanchine, one of his earliest assignments for Serge Diaghilev and a vehicle for the debut of fifteen-year-old Alicia Markova. Matisse was present for both the premiere and the revival. According to Buckle's description of the 1920 production:

> Against a background mainly white, outlined in black, with touches of sky-blue, the Chinese costumes stood out in the clear colors of Ming porcelain, green with pink as on a *famille verte* vase, saffron yellow or white barred with orange and black. The grotesque soldiers, whose armor Matisse sketched from originals in the Musée de Cluny, were sky-blue and white. Karsavina's costume as the Nightingale was not that of a bird . . . but of a white rose; Idzikovsky, as the Mechanical Nightingale, was encased in a globular carcase and had a long beak; as Death Sokolova wore scarlet tights, with a necklace of skulls and another on top of her head.

For Markova, the Nightingale in 1925, "Matisse decided that she was to wear white all-over tights with no skirt—a startling innovation" (Buckle, 1979).

In 1929, Diaghilev approached Matisse about decors for *The Prodigal Son* and a new *Schéhérazade,* but the artist

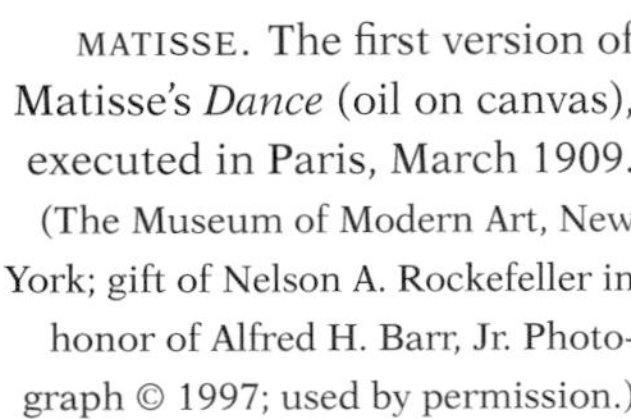

MATISSE. The first version of Matisse's *Dance* (oil on canvas), executed in Paris, March 1909. (The Museum of Modern Art, New York; gift of Nelson A. Rockefeller in honor of Alfred H. Barr, Jr. Photograph © 1997; used by permission.)

declined, maintaining that theater work was too strenuous and would take too much time from his painting. Matisse was, however, persuaded in 1939 when Léonide Massine proposed a "vast mural in motion" for his ballet *Rouge et Noir.* Taking a cue from his work for Barnes (triangles formed by the lunettes), Matisse produced a backdrop containing abstractions of pointed arches and flat planes of brilliant color. Around a central couple in white, Matisse dressed the dancers in leotards and tights (no longer shocking), a different color for each of four movements, and enlivened the severity of these uniforms with "flamboyant tongues" of black and white. Thus, the dancers moved in much-praised "color blocks," an ingenious translation to the stage of Matisse's essential artistic concerns.

BIBLIOGRAPHY

Anderson, Jack. *The One and Only: The Ballet Russe de Monte Carlo.* New York, 1981.

Barr, Alfred H., Jr. *Matisse: His Art and His Public.* New York, 1951.

Buckle, Richard. *Diaghilev.* New York, 1979.

Flam, Jack D. *Matisse: The Dance.* Washington, D.C., 1993.

Garafola, Lynn. *Diaghilev's Ballets Russes.* New York and Oxford, 1989.

Henri Matisse: Exposition du centenaire. 3 vols. Exhibition catalog, Grand Palais. Paris, 1970.

Henri Matisse: Paper Cut-Outs. Exhibition catalog, National Gallery of Art, Washington, D.C. Saint Louis, 1977.

Kochno, Boris. *Diaghilev and the Ballets Russes.* Translated by Adrienne Foulke. New York, 1970. Contains photos and sketches of *Le Chant du Rossignol.*

Matisse at the Ballet: Le Chant du Rossignol. Jerusalem, 1991.

NANCY REYNOLDS

MATSUI AKIRA (born 4 October 1946, Wakayama City, Japan), *nō* actor, teacher, choreographer, director, and playwright. Matsui's career has taken him to four continents, and both in Japan and abroad he has been instrumental in introducing non-Japanese actors, directors, composers, and dancers to the beauty and power of *nō* drama.

Matsui began studying *nō* chant as exercise for a weak physique; he showed such promise that he was eventually introduced to the head of the Kita school, Kita Minoru XVI. From the age of thirteen to twenty-one, Matsui was a live-in apprentice to Kita in Tokyo. He returned to Wakayama in 1967, where he continues to teach amateurs and to produce an annual professional recital, while still traveling to Tokyo most weekends for Kita-school recitals. Matsui's orthodox *nō* performances, which belie his small frame, display a rich, resonant voice, clear and delicate gestures, a strong stage presence, and a sharp dramaturgical sensibility.

A lover of movies and Broadway musicals from an early age, Matsui was naturally attracted to Europe and America. He began going abroad to give workshops in 1974. Since then Matsui has toured abroad almost annually to teach traditional *nō* in Australia, India, England, and the United States. "By seeing what non-Japanese find difficult or interesting about *nō* movement and vocalization, I learn more about its special power," he says.

In addition to his traditional teaching, Matsui is regularly requested to co-direct and choreograph "fusion" experiments that utilize *nō* techniques and spirit. In 1970 he choreographed *Saint Francis,* an English-language production based on the life of Francis of Assisi. He choreographed W. B. Yeats's *At the Hawk's Well* in Sydney in 1984 and in Kyoto in 1985. Matsui choreographed and played the role of the Ghost in *Ophelia,* a fusion piece based on Shakespeare's *Hamlet,* in Kyoto in 1987. He staged the original English-language *nō* play *Eliza,* concerning the alleged rape by Australian Aborigines of a ship-captain's wife, in Sydney in 1989; *A Forbidden Journey* in Denmark and Norway in 1990; and *A Midsummer Night's Dream* in Minneapolis, Minnesota, in 1991. In working with non-Japanese actors, Matsui focuses on teaching them the power expressed through stillness and the stillness present in action.

Matsui's choreography of his own dances, such as one set to Honda Toshio's jazz piece "Last Ballad" (1991) or the "There Is a Willow" dance from *Ophelia*'s death scene, employ *nō*'s graceful pace, circling turns, and simple hand gestures, combined with a flowing and explosive expressivity of his own. His choreography for fusion experiments, often with masked actors and cross-gender casts, is defined by asymmetrical chorus movements and a forceful theatricality full of poses, accelerating tempos, spirals, and foot stamping.

As a director or co-director, Matsui often finds the *nō*-inspired directors with whom he works too eager to maintain *nō*'s rigid forms. "I want to destroy *nō* and create a new beauty from what remains," he says. "*Nō* is restrictive, but those restrictions provide pressure to innovate. If you can't go to the right or left, you try to go down or up, and so are forced to explore directions you never would have otherwise." Matsui sometimes uses *nō*'s bridgeways and formality, but he can also depart into a more fantastic realm, using the abstract realism of *nō* to reinterpret Samuel Beckett's *Rockabye* (1990), Shakespeare's *A Midsummer Night's Dream,* Goethe's *The Sorcerer's Apprentice* (1985), and Mishima Yukio's modern *nō* play *Yuya* (1994).

Matsui is also an accomplished playwright, having adapted plays by Lafcadio Hearn to a fusion of Western and *nō* style. These have been translated into English and performed in the United States and Germany. *Hoichi* was produced in 1983 by Minneapolis's 21st Street Players; he also adapted *Rashomon*—Akutagawa Ryunosuke's *In a Grove*—with the 21st Street Players in 1985. *Reconcilia-*

MATSUI. A classically trained *nō* performer, Matsui has been involved in a number of innovative projects that combine elements of Japanese and European theater. In 1984, he staged his first version of W. B. Yeats's *At the Hawk's Well,* utilizing *nō* techniques. He is seen here performing the Hawk Dance in the Noho Theater Group's 1990 production. (Photograph by Osamu Muranaka; used by permission; courtesy of Jonah Salz.)

tion (1993) and *A Cup of Tea* (1994) were presented by Munich's Meta Theater.

Matsui has had long and fruitful collaborations with a number of theater companies and other artists: besides the 21st Street Players and the Meta Theater Group, he has worked with the Noho Theater Group in Kyoto and Joseph Houseal's Parnassus Dance-Theatre as well as with *biwa* (Japanese lute) composer and master Arai Shisui. He has also collaborated with American Richard Emmert in numerous "English *nō*" productions, singing the lead role or performing in the chorus, choreographing, and directing. At the same time, he has maintained his presence in the *nō* world by performing frequently in both Tokyo and Wakayama. No other *nō* actor has gone abroad as frequently or done such varied work, nor has any other contributed so much to Western artists' and scholars' knowledge of *nō.*

BIBLIOGRAPHY

Salz, Jonah. "Get Thee to a Noh Master: East Meets West Meets Hamlet." In *New Theatre Vistas,* edited by Judy Lee Oliva. New York, 1996.

Schaefer, Kerrie. "Reality and Fantasy: The Performing Body in an Australiannoh Play." *Tulane Drama Review* 35 (Winter 1991): 92–106

JONAH SALZ

MATSUMOTO KŌSHIRŌ, name used by nine generations of *kabuki* actors.

Matsumoto Kōshirō I (born 1674 in Omigawa, Shimōsa, Japan, died 25 March 1730 in Edo [Tokyo]), famous as an actor of mature male roles *(tachiyaku).* Kōshirō II and Kōshirō III were earlier names for Ichikawa Danjūrō IV (1778) and Ichikawa Danjūrō V, respectively.

Matsumoto Kōshirō IV (born 1737 in Kyoto, died 27 June 1802 in Edo), a versatile player who began his career in 1744. He held several names before becoming Kōshirō IV in 1772. In 1801, he gave this name to his son and became Omegawa Kyōjūrō.

Matsumoto Kōshirō V (born 1764 in Edo, died 10 May 1838 in Edo), debuted in 1770. A star in both Edo and the Kamigata (Osaka-Kyoto) region, he was widely known as Hanataka (High Nose) Kōshirō because of his most prominent feature. He became the most famous actor of villains' roles of his time. His son Matsumoto Kōshirō VI (born 1811 in Edo, died 3 October 1849 in Edo) died too young to make a significant mark.

Matsumoto Kōshirō VII (born 1870 in Tokyo, died 27 January 1949 in Tokyo), a great star, was the adopted son of the dancer Fujima Kan'emon II. He passed through three names before acceding to Kōshirō VII in 1911. Known for his dignity and composure, he came to be associated with the role of Benkei in *Kanjinchō,* which he played more than sixteen hundred times. His major contributions were in period-play *(jidaimono)* roles. This progressive artist starred in the first Japanese opera, *Roei no Yume,* in 1905. He formed the Shin Kabuki Kenkyū Kai, an actors' study group, with which he produced new plays and translations. His sons, Ichikawa Danjūrō XI (1909–1965), Kōshirō VIII, and Onoe Shōroku II (1913–1989) were among the greatest stars of *kabuki* after World War II.

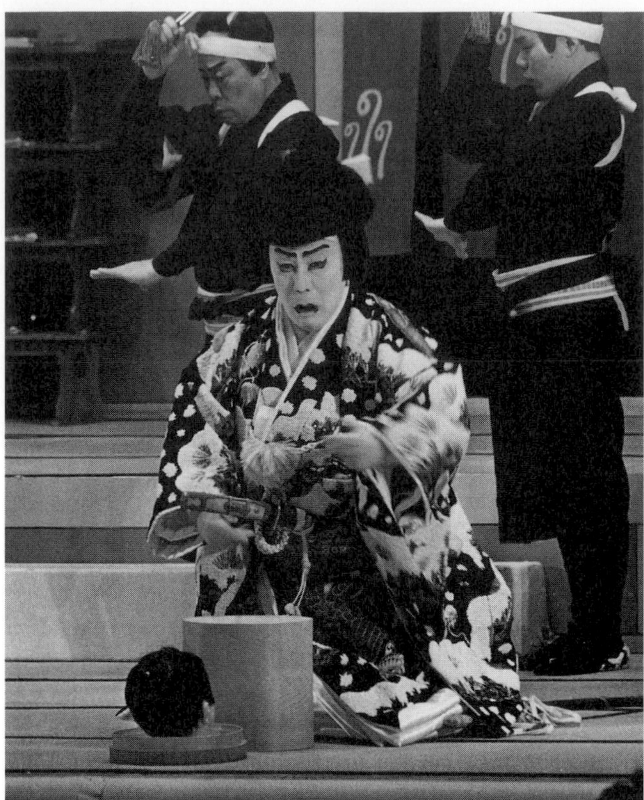

MATSUMOTO KOSHIRŌ. Matsumoto Koshirō VIII in a scene from the *kabuki* drama *Terakoya.* (Photograph courtesy of Samuel L. Leiter.)

Matsumoto Kōshirō VIII (born 7 July 1910 in Tokyo, died 11 January 1982 in Tokyo), debuted as Matsumoto Junzō in 1926. He was trained by Nakamura Kichiemon I, whose daughter he married. He was Ichikawa Somegorō V before becoming Kōshirō VIII in 1949. Kōshirō VIII's speciality was *tachiyaku* in *jidaimono* (history plays), such as *Chūshingura.* He also excelled in various domestic dramas *(sewamono).* His range extended to new Japanese works and to Western classics, including *Othello.* He also made several film appearances. In 1961, he created controversy by joining his sons, Ichikawa Somegorō VI (later Kōshirō IX) and Nakamura Mannosuke I (later Nakamura Kichiemon II) in leaving the Shōchiku company for the less classically oriented Tōhō. He returned to conventional *kabuki* in 1972. In 1975, he was named a National Living Treasure and a year later joined the Japan Arts Academy. In 1981, he surrendered his name to Matsumoto Somegorō VI, and took the name Matsumoto Hakuō I.

Matsumoto Kōshirō IX (born 19 August 1942 in Tokyo) debuted in 1946 as Matsumoto Kintarō. He and his brother formed a study group, Kinome Kai, in 1960, the same year he entered Waseda University, which he left in 1966. After joining the Tōhō company in 1961, this tall, handsome, and musically gifted star managed to perform in *kabuki* for Kinome Kai, in American musicals for Tōhō, and in commercial plays and foreign classics, including Shakespeare and ancient Greek tragedies. He even played on Broadway in the 1972 revival of *Man of La Mancha.* In 1979 he returned to Shōchiku *kabuki* and was soon starring in one classic role after another. His later non-*kabuki* work has included the leads in foreign musicals, such as *Sweeney Todd,* and in modern dramas, such as *Amadeus* and *Zeami.* The latter play toured North America in 1988.

[*See also* Japanese Traditional Schools *and* Kabuki Theater.]

BIBLIOGRAPHY

Akasaka Jiseki, ed. *Kabuki haiyū daihyakka.* Tokyo, 1993.
Engekikai (January 1994). Special issue on *kabuki* actors.
Fujita Hiroshi. *Kabuki handobukku.* Tokyo, 1994.
Nojima Jusaburō. *Kabuki jinmei jiten.* Tokyo, 1988.
Toita Yasuji, ed. *Kabuki kanshō nyūon.* 3d ed., rev. Tokyo, 1994.

SAMUEL L. LEITER

MATTHEWS, JESSIE (Jessie Margaret Matthews; born 11 March 1907 in London, died 20 August 1981 in London), British dancer. Matthews was a dancing star of both stage and screen. Her popularity in Britain rivaled that of Fred Astaire and Ginger Rogers; there was frequent talk of her being teamed with Astaire, but it never happened. She was born to a working-class family in the Soho district of London. Her talent for dancing was so obvious that as a youngster she was sent to study with Elise Clerc, who had danced at the Empire Theatre with Adeline Genée.

Matthews made her debut in 1919 in a children's play, *Bluebell in Fairyland,* at the Metropolitan Music Hall in London; she continued to dance in Christmas pantomimes in the following years. In 1923 she made her debut in the West End, London's main theater district, in Irving Berlin's *Music Box Revue* at the Palace Theatre. In the same year she joined the cast of André Charlot's revue *London Calling,* by Noël Coward, a version of which opened in New York in January 1924. Matthews understudied the leading lady, Gertrude Lawrence, and took over her part in the subsequent tour.

Returning to London, Matthews appeared in Charlot's 1925 and 1926 revues, then starred in C. B. Cochran's shows *One Damn Thing after Another* (1927), with songs by Richard Rodgers and Lorenz Hart; *This Year of Grace* (1928), by Noël Coward; *Wake Up and Dream* (1929), with songs by Cole Porter, which also played in New York; and *Ever Green* (1930), with songs by Rodgers and Hart. In these shows she worked with Buddy Bradley, the African-

American dance director who was to stage most of her numbers for both stage and screen. (Some she arranged herself, such as her most famous number, "Dancing on the Ceiling," in *Ever Green.*)

Matthews had made one or two silent films in the 1920s. In 1931 she made a not particularly auspicious sound-film debut in *Out of the Blue,* but her next movie, *There Goes the Bride* (1932), was a great success, and she was signed to a long-term contract. Her most successful films included a musical based on J. B. Priestley's novel and play *The Good Companions* (1932), in which she played opposite John Gielgud; *Waltzes from Vienna,* directed by Alfred Hitchcock (1934); *Evergreen* (1934); *First a Girl,* based on the play *Viktor und Viktoria* (1935); *It's Love Again* (1936); *Head over Heels* (1937); and *Gangway* (1938).

With her lissome figure, long legs, and beautiful line, Matthews would have been an ideal Balanchine dancer, and in fact, in 1941, by which time her film career had virtually come to an end, she went to the United States to appear in a Broadway musical, *The Lady Comes Across,* with choreography by George Balanchine. Among other things, she danced a ballet number with Marc Platt. She played the show in New Haven and Boston, but at the end of the Boston tryout she suffered a nervous breakdown (not her first), and for the (disastrous) New York opening she was replaced.

Matthews returned to London to star in a successful revival of Jerome Kern's *Sally,* retitled *Wild Rose,* in 1942, with choreography by Robert Helpmann. She was to appear in two more revues, *Maid to Measure* (1948) and *Sauce Tartare* (1949), for which Buddy Bradley again staged the dances. Thereafter she played in touring and repertory productions of straight plays and in a popular radio serial, *The Archers;* in 1958 she returned to the screen in *Tom Thumb.* Every so often she would appear in an all-star gala to sing one of the songs she had made famous, such as "Over My Shoulder" or "When You've Got a Little Springtime in Your Heart."

BIBLIOGRAPHY

Matthews, Jessie, with Muriel Burgess. *Over My Shoulder.* New Rochelle, N.Y., 1974.

Thornton, Michael. *Jessie Matthews.* London, 1974.

Vaughan, David. "Jessie Matthews." *Ballet Review* 24 (Summer 1996).

DAVID VAUGHAN

MAXIMOVA, EKATERINA (Ekaterina Sergeevna Maksimova; born 1 February 1939 in Moscow), dancer. After training with Elisaveta Gerdt, Maximova graduated from the Moscow Ballet School in 1958 and joined the Bolshoi Ballet as a soloist. In 1959 the young ballerina danced Katerina in Yuri Grigorovich's *The Stone Flower,* and in 1960 Galina Ulanova coached her for the role of Giselle. Maximova is known as a lyrical ballerina, as illustrated by her roles in Michel Fokine's *Chopiniana* and Rostislav Zakharov's *The Fountain of Bakhchisarai* and *Cinderella.* In the classical repertory, one of her finest achievements was Aurora in Petipa's *The Sleeping Beauty,* in which she conveyed in strictly academic style all the nuances of the choreography. Her lyricism and charm in depicting a child's character were exemplified by her portrayal of Masha in Grigorovich's 1966 version of *The Nutcracker,* and she blended the same lyricism with drama as Phrygia in his *Spartacus* (1968).

In 1973 Maximova danced Juliet in Leonid Lavrovsky's *Romeo and Juliet.* This first Juliet was gentler and more childish, at times even weaker, than her second, which she created in the Maurice Béjart–Hector Berlioz version for the Ballet du XXe Siècle in 1978. The latter was strong-willed, nervous, and serious. In Natalia Kasatkina and Vladimir Vasiliov's version, presented by the Moscow Classical Ballet company in 1981, her spirit and pathos were particularly impressive. Her role in both versions of

MAXIMOVA. In 1959 Maximova as Katerina was paired with Vladimir Vasiliev as Danila in their first created roles by Yuri Grigorovich, in his version of *The Stone Flower* for the Bolshoi Ballet. (Photograph from the Dance Collection, New York Public Library for the Performing Arts.)

Icarus (1971 and 1976), choreographed by her husband Vladimir Vasiliev, was full of drama, as was her Eve in *The Creation of the World,* staged by Kasatkina and Vasiliov for their Moscow Classical Ballet in 1984.

In 1960 Kasyan Goleizovsky had staged for Maximova a dance called *Mazurka,* to music by Aleksandr Skriabin. Goleizovsky was the first to appreciate her flair for comedy and her ability to draw airy, fanciful patterns on the stage with her filigree pointe technique. In this genre, in 1965 Maximova interpreted Kitri in Aleksandr Gorsky's *Don Quixote* with distinctive style. She also revived the style of Romantic ballet in *Natalie, ou La Laitière Suisse,* performed by the Moscow Classical Ballet company in 1980. Maximova's roles in the television ballets *Galatea, The Old Tango, Aniuta,* and others between 1978 and 1982 were important contributions to that genre.

Maximova graduated from the Choreography Department of the Lunacharsky Theater Technicum in 1980 and began teaching there two years later. In 1990 she also became a coach for the Kremlin Ballet company. In the early 1990s Maximova and Vasiliev formed a small company for worldwide tours. They returned to the Bolshoi in 1995, when Vasiliev was appointed director.

Maximova won first prizes at the national contest for ballet dancers in Moscow (1957) and the international ballet contests in Vienna (1959) and Varna, Bulgaria (1964). She received the Anna Pavlova Prize (1972), the Marius Petipa Prize for a duet with Vasiliev (Paris, 1972), and the State Prize of the USSR (1981). In 1973 she was named People's Artist of the USSR.

BIBLIOGRAPHY

Avaliani, Noi, and Leonid Zhdanov, comps. *Bolshoi's Young Dancers.* Translated by Natalie Ward. Moscow, 1975.

Demidov, Alexander P. *The Russian Ballet: Past and Present.* Translated by Guy Daniels. Garden City, N.Y., 1977.

Konstantinova, Marina E. *Ekaterina Maksimova.* Moscow, 1982.

Lvov-Anokhin, Boris. *Mastera Bolshogo Baleta.* Moscow, 1976.

Maximova, Ekaterina. "Dancing Is My Life." *Dance and Dancers* (August 1974): 630–631.

Smakov, Gennady. *The Great Russian Dancers.* New York, 1984.

Willis, Margaret E. "Ballerina à la Russe." *Dance Magazine* (October 1988): 48–49.

MARINA E. KONSTANTINOVA
Translated from Russian

MAY, PAMELA (Doris May; born 30 May 1917 in Trinidad), dancer and teacher. May began her training with Freda Grant in London and with Olga Preobrajenska, Lubov Egorova, and Matilda Kshessinska in Paris. She entered the Vic-Wells Ballet School—and Ninette de Valois's classroom—in 1933 and, with her company debut the following year in the *Swan Lake* pas de trois, began her swift conquest of the repertory. Almost at once she danced the Waltz and Prelude in *Les Sylphides,* the ghostly Alicia in *The Haunted Ballroom,* and the sultry Creole Girl in *Rio Grande.* In 1937 she created the weak Red Queen in *Checkmate,* Violet in *A Wedding Bouquet,* and one of the Red Girls in *Les Patineurs;* a year later, as the Moon in Frederick Ashton's *Horoscope,* she revealed the full beauty of her exquisite line.

She made a flirtatious Swanilda in *Coppélia* and created a moving Child of Light in *Dante Sonata* (1940), but the heart of her talent was neither coquettish nor dramatic. In early performances as Odette-Odile, Aurora, the Lilac Fairy, and Myrtha, she emerged as a superb classical dancer who, by 1946, was a ballerina equal in stature to Margot Fonteyn. That year May danced the Bluebird pas de deux in the company's opening performance at the Royal Opera House and Aurora on the second night and created one of the three female roles in Ashton's landmark work, *Symphonic Variations.* She was often credited with the most beautiful arabesque in English ballet.

Recurring knee injuries gradually restricted May to mime roles, such as Bathilde and the Queen Mother in

MAY. Known for the beauty of her line, May brought charm as well as dignity to her queenly roles. Here she portrays the Red Queen, a role she created, in Ninette de Valois's *Checkmate* (1937) for Sadler's Wells Ballet. (Photograph from the Dance Collection, New York Public Library for the Performing Arts.)

Swan Lake, which she graced with dignity and regal authority. From 1952 she appeared with the company as a guest artist, first frequently and then occasionally, until 1977. She also taught at the Royal Ballet School from 1954 to 1977, when she received the Royal Academy of Dancing's Queen Elizabeth II Award and retired.

BIBLIOGRAPHY

Anthony, Gordon. "Pamela May." In Anthony's *A Camera at the Ballet: Pioneer Dancers of the Royal Ballet.* Newton Abbot, 1975.

Clarke, Mary. *The Sadler's Wells Ballet.* London, 1955.

Percival, John. "Pamela May: A Study." *Ballet Today* (February 1952): 4–5.

Sinclair, Janet. "Thank You, Pamela May." *Dance and Dancers* (June 1982): 655–656.

BARBARA NEWMAN

MAYONG. A dance-drama genre of Kelantan and Kedah, northern provinces of Malaysia, *mayong* (also spelled *ma'yong* or *makyong*) was first noted in Patani (now part of Thailand). It appeared as court entertainment in Kelantan in the eighteenth century. By the 1920s it was performed as village theatrical entertainment; only after 1968 did it receive any international attention, but it was suppressed in 1994 by the Islamic government.

The word *mayong* may be related to a word for a female deity, or to the word for ancestor *(moyang).* Performances are used for magical healing or to celebrate a success. Today *mayong* may be produced purely for entertainment, but its magical aspect persists when *bomor* priests are called in to purify the stage before the drama can begin. Extensive use of slapstick comedy today often debases the repertory of myths about rajas (chiefs; rulers) and demons, but traditionalist performers still consider the stories to represent actual history.

Mayong troupes consist of female actor-dancers and male comedians and musicians. The sex of a character is expressed by costume; the women play male roles dressed in old courtly regalia. Comedians in Kedah reflect Thai influence by wearing red half-face masks, not found in Kelantan.

Mayong can be performed in any public facility but ideally uses a roofed outdoor stage some fifteen feet (5 meters) square and three feet (1 meter) above the ground. All or three sides may be open, although performers enter from the rear. The music is played by a *rebab* (bowed lute), two *gendang* (double-headed drums), and two *tawak tawak* (knobbed gongs). The musicians sit at the front left side of the stage, facing the performers. Actresses and comedians sit along the side railings and simply rise when they join the action.

Before a performance the musicians play a series of instrumental pieces based on *mayong* melodies. The *rebab* plays a free-rhythm melismatic introduction, followed by the gongs playing a time cycle (usually of eight beats), with the drums supplying interlocking patterns. This structure holds for most *mayong* vocal and dance music as well. The *barat* walking music brings the cast onstage. All performances begin with a *mendagap rebab* ("honor the *rebab*") dance. Only this dance begins on the floor. After a clasped-hands *sembah* movement, the lead singer begins. The chorus enters with ululating vocables (sound syllables without meaning) that seem to combine Islamic and Southeast Asian idioms. The most fluid hand and arm gestures of *mayong* are used during this dance, in which the dancers move to a kneeling position. The dance ends with the performers standing in a circle facing inward. This piece is followed by several standard dance songs. A play takes several evenings to complete, but each night begins with the required opening dance and others before the plot advances.

The standard *mayong* dances are all structurally similar. The performers stand in a circle, waiting for the end of the *rebab* introduction. One character then sings while vibrating the fingers of her right hand. The dancers move slowly counterclockwise, often pausing to move backward in individual clockwise circles. Hand gestures become more florid during these sections, but group movement stops during most solo text lines.

The story advances in dialogues, with the standard dances appearing throughout the play. These may include bathing songs, lullabies, fights, and laments. Pieces are named and identified by their melody or traditional function, but their text varies with the play. For example, there are different *sedayong* pieces whose full titles tell one whether the lead singer is a prince, a queen, or a clown. Other dance-music titles reflect cultural history, such as the popular *kijang emas* (golden mousedeer), a character from the Sanskrit epic of ancient India, the *Rāmāyana.* The *berjalan* ("walk and thinking") dance is a formal signal, which precedes the entrance of the *tari ragam* ("dance pattern"). The origins of this dance in Thai *manora* drama are evident in that a *serunai* oboe replaces the *rebab* and clacking bamboo sticks replace percussion, and in that the dance uses a figure-eight floor pattern and a fast finale. It seldom bears any relation to the plot.

Throughout the play comedians often jog behind the main dancer and mimic her movements, even in dramatically germane dances. These many plot distractions do not bother the audience who, until the introduction of Western media, felt no need for tightly structured drama. *Mayong* revivals and appearances on Malaysian national television have raised its standing and changed its structure. In either its folk or national forms it offers much information on the dance traditions of Malaysia.

[*See also* Malaysia.]

BIBLIOGRAPHY

Malm, William P. "Malaysian Ma'yong Theatre." *Drama Review* 15.3 (1971): 108–114.

Malm, William P., and Amin Sweeney. *Studies in Malaysian Oral and Musical Traditions: Music in Kelantan, Malaysia, and Some of Its Cultural Implications.* Michigan Papers on South and Southeast Asia, no. 8. Ann Arbor, 1974.

Nasuruddin, Mohamed. "Traditional Malaysian Dance and Music." In *Sixth Festival of Asian Arts.* Hong Kong, 1981.

WILLIAM P. MALM

MAYWOOD, AUGUSTA (Augusta Williams; born 1825 in New York, died 3 November 1876 in Lemberg, Austria-Hungary [now Lviv, Ukraine]), American dancer. Augusta Maywood, who began her career as a child prodigy in the United States, became the first American dancer to win a place among the top-ranking ballerinas of Europe, where she spent most of her adult life. Because she was a dynamic and virtuosic dancer, Maywood was often likened to the Italian ballerina Fanny Cerrito. She was also a talented mime and excelled in dramatic roles of the sort that had made Fanny Elssler famous. Much of her prime was spent in Italy, where her gifts as a dancer-actress earned her an enthusiastic following.

MAYWOOD. In this 1838 lithograph, "La Petite Augusta," aged twelve years, is costumed for the role of Zelica in *The Maid of Cashmere*. The original was rendered in watercolor and gouache by Edward Williams Clay and used for the only American print of the ballerina. (Photograph from the Dance Collection, New York Public Library for the Performing Arts.)

Maywood was born into a theatrical family. Her father and mother, Mr. and Mrs. Henry August Williams, were actors, as was her stepfather, Robert Campbell Maywood, whose name she assumed. While her elder sister Mary Elizabeth was trained as an actress, Augusta studied ballet at the school of Monsieur and Madame Paul Hazard in Philadelphia, where her stepfather was the manager of the Chestnut Street Theater. At the age of twelve she made her debut at that theater on 30 December 1837, playing the role of Zelica in *The Maid of Cashmere,* adapted from Filippo Taglioni's *opéra-ballet Le Dieu et la Bayadère.* Her youth, beauty, and talent caught the attention of the public, and she became known as "La Petite Augusta," a nickname that linked her with the popular foreign ballerinas of the time, in particular the German ballerina called Madame Augusta (Caroline Augusta Fuchs). Unfortunately, she was forced into a local rivalry with another gifted young pupil of the Hazards, Mary Ann Lee, who as a Philadelphia native had a competitive edge.

Augusta, however, soon left to seek her fortune in New York City. There she made her debut at the Park Theater on 12 February 1838, again in *The Maid of Cashmere,* following this up in April with the leading role in *The Dew Drop, or La Sylphide.* Reviews of the day commented upon her skillful miming as well as on her dancing: in the role of the Sylphide, wrote the *Albion,* "She moves tender feelings even while she delights us with her agile and lightly mischievous freaks" (Swift, 1980).

She did not remain long in New York. Accompanied by her mother, she sailed for Europe in May 1838. In Paris she honed her skills in the classes of Jean Coralli and Joseph Mazilier, and on 11 November 1839 she made her Paris Opera debut in a pas de deux inserted into act 1 of Coralli's *Le Diable Boiteux,* in which she was partnered by Charles Mabille. Her energy, virtuosity, and self-assurance were immediately noticed, and she was compared with two male dancers renowned for their elevation, Jules Perrot and Antoine Paul.

Théophile Gautier described her as being

> of medium height, supple-jointed, very young . . . with black eyes and an alert and wild little face that comes very near to being pretty. Add to that sinews of steel, legs of a jaguar, and an agility approaching that of circus clowns. . . . In two or three leaps she covered that great stage from the backcloth to the prompter's box, performing those almost horizontal *vols penchés* which made the reputation of Perrot *l'aérien*. . . . She has much elevation and dash, and her small legs, like those of a wild doe, make steps as long as those of Mlle. Taglioni.
>
> (Guest, 1980)

Maywood made steady progress at the Paris Opera, dancing in the ballets *La Tarentule, Nina,* and *Le Diable*

Amoureux. Her Opera career was cut short in the summer of 1840 by her elopement with Charles Mabille. Dancing under the name Madame Mabille, she appeared in Lyon and Marseille, then accepted an engagement with her husband in Lisbon in 1843. She spent two years there, dancing principal roles in *Giselle, La Gipsy, Le Diable Amoureux,* and other favorite Romantic ballets.

Her marriage came to an end in Lisbon in 1845 and she moved to Vienna, where she appeared for two years at the Kärntnertor Theater. During her stay in Vienna she worked with the choreographer Antonio Guerra, who further developed her dramatic gifts. She was partnered in *Giselle* by Gustave Carey and the Russian dancer Eraclito Nikitin; she also performed in Domenico Ronzani's restaging of Perrot's *Catarina*. In the winter season of 1847/48, she and Nikitin went to La Scala, Milan, where Perrot was mounting *Faust* for Fanny Elssler. Elssler, an Austrian, was poorly received at the first performance of *Faust* in February 1848 because of political tension between Italy and Austria, so at its second performance, Maywood replaced her in the leading role of Marguerite.

The ensuing twelve years, which Maywood spent almost exclusively in Italy, were her most fruitful. Her bravura technique and dramatic flair seemed ideally suited to Italian tastes, and she was so much in demand that she was able to choose the ballets she danced, her ballet master, her partners, and her supporting dancers. Accompanied by her own company, which possessed its own costumes and properties, she moved from city to city, performing in the opera houses of Milan, Venice, Trieste, Padua, Bologna, Ravenna, Genoa, Turin, and others. She danced in ballets by the leading Italian choreographers of the period, among them Pasquale Borri, Domenico Ronzani, and Giuseppe Rota.

One of her greatest successes of this period was *Bianchi e Negri* (La Scala, 1853), commissioned from Rota. Thinly based on Harriet Beecher Stowe's novel *Uncle Tom's Cabin* (1851–1852), the ballet presented Maywood in the role of the slave Dellay, a wife and mother whose adventures include the escape, pursuit, and ultimate rescue of her family.

Maywood's repertory also included several of Perrot's dramatic ballets, among them *Esmeralda* and *Catarina*. The role of Marguerite in *Faust* continued to be one of her favorites. Another Marguerite, the doomed heroine of the novel *La Dame aux Camélias* by Alexandre Dumas *fils*, inspired the very popular ballet *Rita Gauthier* (1856), choreographed by Filippo Termanini to music from Giuseppe Verdi's opera *La Traviata*.

In 1859 Maywood and her second husband, Carlo Gardini, opened a ballet school of ambitious scope in Vienna, teaching languages, history, and mythology in addition to dancing and acting. Although the school was highly successful, Maywood found time to choreograph as well as teach; little is currently known about her endeavors in this field. Having earned a large fortune in the course of her long career, she retired to a villa on Lake Como in Italy.

BIBLIOGRAPHY

Costonis, Maureen Needham. "'The Wild Doe': Augusta Maywood in Philadelphia and Paris, 1837–1840." *Dance Chronicle* 17.2 (1994): 123–148.

Farrell, Rita Katz. "Star-Spangled Giselles." *Ballet News* 6 (September 1984): 15–20.

Guest, Ivor. *The Romantic Ballet in Paris*. 2d rev. ed. London, 1980.

Maynard, Olga. "Barbara Weisberger and the Pennsylvania Ballet." *Dance Magazine* (March 1975): 45–60.

Migel, Parmenia. "Augusta Maywood." In Migel's *The Ballerinas*. New York, 1972.

Swift, Mary Grace. *Belles and Beaux on Their Toes: Dancing Stars in Young America*. Washington, D.C., 1980.

Winter, Marian Hannah. "Augusta Maywood." *Dance Index* 2 (January–February 1943): 4–19.

ARCHIVE. Walter Toscanini Collection of Research Materials in Dance, New York Public Library for the Performing Arts.

SUSAN AU

MAZILIER, JOSEPH (Giulio Mazarini; born 13 March 1797 in Marseille, France, died 19 May 1868 in Paris), French dancer. Although he was active in a period that idolized the ballerina at the expense of the male dancer, Joseph Mazilier enjoyed a long and distinguished career as a performer, dancing principal male roles opposite major ballerinas in some of the most important ballets of the time. He was, for example, the first James in *La Sylphide* (1832). As a choreographer he was competent, though not in the top rank, and he eventually earned the position of *premier maître de ballet* at the Paris Opera. His works were characterized by a strong dramatic quality that sometimes overshadowed the dance. Among his best-known ballets are *La Gipsy, Le Diable à Quatre, Paquita, Le Corsaire,* and *Marco Spada*.

Little is known about Mazilier's early life. He made his debut as a dancer in Bordeaux, then went to Paris in 1822 to dance at the Théâtre de la Porte-Saint-Martin, a boulevard theater famed for its innovations in Romantic-era drama and dance. There he performed in the works of the choreographer Jean Coralli in a company that included the gifted comic dancer Charles Mazurier as well as Jules Perrot, who became a great dancer and choreographer of the Romantic ballet. Mazilier played many leading roles in Coralli's ballets, including Alfred de Roseval in *La Visite à Bedlam* (1826), Edgard in *La Neige* (1827), and the choreographer Armand in *Les Artistes* (1829), suggesting that his face and physique must have filled the requirements for a ballet hero. He was also a skilled character dancer and earned special acclaim in the mazurka in the melodrama *Prisonniers de Guerre*.

In 1830 he joined the Paris Opera Ballet, making his debut on 3 March in Jean Dauberval's *La Fille Mal Gardée.* Coralli joined the Paris Opera in the following year and chose Mazilier to dance the leading male role in his first ballet for the company, *L'Orgie* (1831). Since this was a reworking of *Léocadie* (1828), which Coralli had first mounted at the Porte-Saint-Martin, Mazilier was probably quite familiar with the role of Don Carlos, a seducer who is ultimately united with the mother of his child. As at the Porte-Saint-Martin, Mazilier was to dance many leading male roles at the Paris Opera.

On 12 March 1832 he created the role of James Reuben in Filippo Taglioni's *La Sylphide,* partnering the choreographer's daughter Marie Taglioni, whose performance of the title role established her as the embodiment of the Romantic style. Although earlier works had used similar elements, *La Sylphide* is regularly cited as the first Romantic-era ballet, with its preponderance of unearthly heroines and their mortal lovers. Mazilier was fated to play the latter in many Romantic roles.

He again partnered Taglioni in *The Swiss Milkmaid* (1832), *La Révolte au Sérail* (1833), *Brézilia, ou La Tribu des Femmes* (1835), and *La Fille du Danube* (1836), all choreographed by Filippo Taglioni. The first two ballets represented another favorite genre of the Romantic period, the ballet of local color, while *Brézilia* gave Mazilier the unenviable role of a prisoner of a man-hating Amazonian tribe. *La Fille du Danube* returned to the supernatural world, with Mazilier as a hapless equerry who temporarily goes mad, then is put to the test of recognizing his true love among the water nymphs.

Mazilier also danced with Taglioni's rival, Fanny Elssler, who came to represent the sensuous, earthy qualities of the dance as opposed to Taglioni's purity and ethereality. He first danced with Elssler at her Paris Opera debut on 15 September 1834 in Coralli's *La Tempête.* In this loose adaptation of Shakespeare's play she danced the fairy Alcine, who tries to trick Fernando (Mazilier) by taking the place of his lover, Léa.

Elssler and Mazilier also danced the romantic leads in Louis Henry's *L'Île des Pirates* (1835); Coralli's *Le Diable Boiteux* (1836), *La Chatte Metamorphosée en Femme* (1837), and *La Tarentule* (1839); Thérèse Elssler's *La Volière* (1838); and Mazilier's own *La Gipsy* (1839).

By the time *La Gipsy* appeared, Mazilier's performing career was nearing its close. He danced his last romantic lead, Count Frédéric in *Le Diable Amoureux,* in the following year. His subsequent creations were all character roles: Beatrix's father in Monsieur Albert's *La Jolie Fille de Gand* (1842), the comic basketmaker Mazourki in his own *Le Diable à Quatre* (1845), and Elfrid's father in his *Griseldis* (1848). Although Mazilier did not attain the stature of Perrot or Arthur Saint-Léon, his achievements as a dancer were by no means petty. He had created the leading male role in almost every new ballet produced at the Paris Opera between 1831 and 1840. His partners had included, besides Taglioni and Elssler, Pauline Duvernay (whom he partnered in *Le Diable Boiteux* in London in 1836), Nathalie Fitzjames, Carlotta Grisi, Amélie Legallois, and Pauline Leroux.

La Gipsy, which had its premiere on 28 January 1839, was not Mazilier's first choreographic venture at the Paris Opera—he had previously arranged a *divertissement* for Jacques Halévy's opera *Guido et Ginevra* in 1838—but it was his first full-length ballet. Jules-Henri Vernoy de Saint-Georges, the librettist, set it in Edinburgh during the reign of Charles II, thus giving the ballet both historical and local color. Elssler played an aristocratic girl, Sarah, who is stolen by Gypsies. Stenio (Mazilier), a Roundhead who has taken refuge among the Gypsies, falls in love with her as she grows up, thus inciting the jealousy of the Gypsy Queen Mab (Thérèse Elssler), who loves him. Sarah is restored to her home, where she reveals to her father that she and Stenio are married. He gives them his blessing upon learning that Stenio, too, is of noble birth, but Mab and her followers rush in and shoot Stenio. Sarah stabs Mab in revenge.

Mazilier created for Elssler a Gypsy pas de deux, which she danced with her sister Thérèse, and a sprightly *cracovienne,* danced in military costume, which became one of her famous character solos. The role of Sarah also displayed the strength of her acting. This flair for drama was to be characteristic of Mazilier's ballets throughout his career.

By coincidence, the ballet's title resembled that of Filippo Taglioni's *La Gitana* (1838), which he had choreographed for his daughter in Saint Petersburg. Accusations of plagiarism were made, although the resemblance was actually superficial, and *La Gitana* was not seen in western Europe until June 1839.

Vernoy de Saint-Georges again supplied the scenario, based on a story by Jacques Cazotte, of *Le Diable Amoureux,* first performed on 23 September 1840. Count Frédéric (Mazilier) is a rake who pays court to three women, Phoebe (Lise Noblet), Janetta (Adèle Dumilâtre), and Lilia (Nathalie Fitzjames). Urielle (Pauline Leroux), a female demon, plots to steal his soul. When the Count decides to marry Lilia, Urielle takes her place at the wedding; meanwhile, Lilia is abducted and sold to the Grand Vizier of Ispahan. The Count signs away his soul in return for Urielle's help in rescuing Lilia, but when Urielle returns to collect the debt, she finds that she cannot, for she has fallen in love with the Count herself. She dies, but an angel restores her to life.

The ballet included scenes in a deserted Gothic tower, the caverns of the demons, and the Middle Eastern city of Ispahan, thus satisfying the public's taste for the medieval, the supernatural, and the exotic. Great versatility was also demanded of Leroux as Urielle. In male disguise, she danced a *pas de diable* with Phoebe, fascinating and inflaming her. She was equally irresistible in a *pas de bayadère* danced before the Grand Vizier. The ballet was lavishly mounted and won the public's favor. Mazilier's choreography was praised on the whole, although it was noted that he was more inventive with small groups than with large ensembles.

In the next three years Mazilier did not produce any ballets, but he did choreograph opera *divertissements* for Carl Maria von Weber's *Der Freischütz* in 1841, and the premiere of Jacques Halévy's *Charles VI* in 1843. In fact, he created opera *divertissements* throughout his career, notably for the Paris productions of Gioacchino Rossini's *Othello* in 1844 and *Robert Bruce* in 1846, Giuseppe Verdi's *Jérusalem* in 1847, and Félicien David's *Herculanum* in 1859.

Three composers collaborated on Mazilier's next ballet, *Lady Henriette, ou La Servante de Greenwich* of 21 February 1844: Friedrich Burgmüller, Édouard Deldevez, and Friedrich von Flotow, who later adapted the plot for his opera *Martha* (1847). Saint-Georges's libretto was set in England during the reign of Queen Anne. Lady Henriette (Adèle Dumilâtre) and her friend Nancy (Maria [Jacob]) impulsively hire themselves out as servants to two rich young farmers, Lyonnel (Lucien Petipa) and Plumkett (Jean-Baptiste Barrez). The servant's life soon palls on them and they escape. Lyonnel, who has fallen in love with Henriette, endures various trials for her sake, including a bout of temporary insanity, but the two are at last reunited.

The ballet's elaborate production included a court *divertissement,* in which Henriette plays Venus, and a visit to Bedlam, the notorious British lunatic asylum. The latter scene was singled out for special praise. In a sense, Bedlam was no novelty to Mazilier, who had danced in Coralli's *La Visite à Bedlam* at the Porte-Saint-Martin in 1826. As if to complete the circle, Coralli's son Eugène played a *dansomane* in Mazilier's Bedlam scene.

A greater success awaited Mazilier and his collaborators on 11 August 1845 in *Le Diable à Quatre.* This ballet had the advantage of a familiar story that had been seen in many adaptations, both English and French, since the 1686 premiere of the original play, *The Devil of a Wife.* Adolphe de Leuven, who wrote the ballet's libretto, gave it a Polish setting. The score was by Adolphe Adam, the composer of *Giselle* (1841). Mazilier played the basketmaker Mazourki, whose gentle wife Mazourka (Carlotta Grisi) magically exchanges places with a proud, quick-tempered Countess (Maria [Jacob]). Mazourki's roughness soon chastens the Countess, who learns a salutary lesson before she is restored to her true spouse.

Grisi was evidently not satisfied with Mazilier's choreography, for she interpolated two solos previously choreographed for her by Perrot in *La Esmeralda* (1844). Both she and Maria were much praised for their acting. Mazilier had hoped to employ in this ballet Les Danseuses Viennoises, a children's dance troupe that first appeared in Paris to great acclaim in 1845. Although he did not succeed in engaging them, he contrived to school the corps de ballet to an unusual degree of precision in its ensemble dances.

Grisi, the Paris Opera's reigning ballerina, also danced the title role of *Paquita* at its premiere on 1 April 1846, a ballet set in the ever-popular land of Spain. Paquita, a Gypsy girl, saves Lucien, a French officer (Lucien Petipa), from a murder plot and is ultimately rewarded by his hand in marriage. Mazilier's choreography contrasted the local color of the Spanish and Gypsy dances with a French ball of the Empire period. Grisi's dances could not have been very authentic, for the reviews reported that they contained an unusual amount of pointe work.

In demanding this of her, Mazilier may have been anticipating the imminent arrival of Sofia Fuoco, the Milanese ballerina who acquired the nickname of "La Pointue" because of her skill in pointe work. He choreographed *Betty* for her Paris Opera debut on 10 July 1846. *Betty* was criticized for its overcomplicated plot, but the choreography exploited Fuoco's pointe technique to the fullest and she achieved a personal success in the ballet.

Although Grisi's relations with the Paris Opera grew strained after 1847, she retained enough prestige with the public to be the logical choice for the title role of Mazilier's *Griseldis, ou Les Cinq Sens,* which had its premiere on 16 February 1848. Elfrid (Lucien Petipa) rejects the marriage that has been arranged for him, but his future wife Griseldis disguises herself and wins his love through successive appeals to each of his five senses. The ballet contained many novelties besides the dancing, among them a hypnotism scene and an appearance by Grisi on horseback. She also sang at the end of the ballet. *Griseldis* marked Mazilier's last created role, that of Elfrid's tyrannical father.

Performances of this ballet were curtailed by the outbreak of the 1848 European revolutions, which briefly closed the Paris Opera. Mazilier created no new ballets until 1851, when Arthur Saint-Léon became *premier maître de ballet,* replacing Coralli, who for many years had held the post in name only. *Vert-Vert* of 24 November 1851 was created for the debut of the fifteen-year-old Italian prodigy Olimpia Priora. The ballet had been in preparation for some time and Saint-Léon stepped in to complete and revise it. The story, adapted by de Leuven from a popular *vaudeville,* was a lighthearted romp set in eighteenth-century France. Blanche (Priora) falls in love with the page Vert-Vert (danced by Adeline Plunkett *en travesti*). The highlight of the evening was the ball scene, choreographed by Saint-Léon.

Mazilier's next ballet, first presented on 29 December 1852, was for Fanny Cerrito, the estranged wife of Saint-Léon. *Orfa* was set in Iceland under the dominion of the Norse gods. Orfa (Cerrito) is carried off by the evil god Loki, who takes her to his palace under the mountain. With the help of an old man who is actually Odin, the chief of the gods, in disguise, her fiancé (Lucien Petipa) rescues her. The ballet's elaborate scenery and Adolphe Adam's score were acclaimed, and Cerrito triumphed despite some difficulty in adjusting to Mazilier's as opposed to Saint-Léon's style of choreography.

When Saint-Léon resigned from the Opera in December 1852, Mazilier became *premier maître de ballet.* In the spring of 1853 he began work on a new ballet for Priora, but before its completion was ordered to add a second female lead for Marie Guy-Stéphan, a new dancer who hoped to display her expertise in Spanish dancing. The result, finally staged on 21 September 1853, was *Aelia et Mysis, ou L'Atellane,* considered one of Mazilier's finest ballets. It was set in ancient Rome at the time of Nero; Aelia (Priora) loves the dancer Euclio (Lucien Petipa). Guy-Stéphan, as the dancer Mysis, had plenty of opportunities to show off her skill, particularly in the Spanish-flavored *pas gaditan.* Priora took her turn in the spotlight as Venus in a mythological *divertissement.* In act 2, Aelia and Mysis, formerly rivals, join forces to save Euclio from the wrath of the Vestal Virgins when he intrudes on their sacred forest. Aelia's efforts end in her death.

This highly dramatic story, its second act reminiscent of Vincenzo Bellini's opera *Norma,* was well served by the acting of both Priora and Guy-Stéphan. Théophile Gautier, whose libretto for *Giselle* had helped to instill a love of Germanic legend into the Romantic ballet, found *Aelia et Mysis* a refreshing change.

Mazilier's *Jovita, ou Les Boucaniers,* also staged in 1853, on 11 November, introduced another new dancer, Carolina Rosati, to the Opera. Jovita, the daughter of a rich planter in seventeenth-century Mexico, daringly invades the camp of the brigands who have abducted her lover (Louis Mérante) and sets fire to their store of gunpowder. The ensuing explosion and collapse of the brigands' grotto was a much-admired special effect. The brigand theme was not new to Romantic ballet or opera, but it apparently retained its popularity; Mazilier himself used it again in *Marco Spada* (1857).

Rosati played the role of an eighteenth-century ballerina in *La Fonti* on 8 January 1855. Mazilier created for her a ballet within a ballet, *Flore et Zéphire,* titled after an actual ballet of 1796 by Charles Didelot. Rosati was also called upon to languish in prison, to don male attire, and finally to lose her reason and die in the middle of Rome's Carnival. Gautier criticized the emphasis on mime and compared the ballet to "a drama played by a troupe of deaf-mutes" (Guest, 1974). Other critics, however, declared *La Fonti* a success comparable to *Giselle.*

An even more ambitious undertaking was *Le Corsaire* on 23 January 1856. Vernoy de Saint-Georges and Mazilier adapted the libretto rather freely from Byron's poem. Domenico Segarelli, a famous Italian mime, was engaged especially for the role of the pirate Conrad. Medora (Rosati) is abducted and sold to an amorous Pasha (François Dauty), who captures Conrad when he tries to rescue her. As the price of Conrad's life, the Pasha forces Medora to marry him, but when he lifts the bride's veil he discovers instead his concubine, Gulnare (Claudina Cucchi). Conrad and Medora escape, only to be shipwrecked in a violent storm. All ends happily, however, with the lovers finding their way to land.

Proportionately, the ballet contained more mime than dancing, although the setting offered opportunities for orientalism in its choreography. The stage spectacle was highly praised, particularly the scene of the storm and shipwreck. The ballet was also notable for its score, which was the last composed by Adolphe Adam.

Vernoy de Saint-Georges and Mazilier next collaborated on a slighter work, *Les Elfes.* Amalia Ferraris made her Opera debut at its premiere on 11 August 1856 as Sylvia, a statue brought to life by the Queen of the Elves. After various love complications involving two men (Petipa and Segarelli), the statue is destroyed. This ballet was atypical of Mazilier in its emphasis on dancing. Ferraris's light, quick style evoked comparisons to Marie Taglioni.

Mazilier's last ballet, staged on 1 April 1857, was *Marco Spada, ou La Fille du Bandit.* It derived from Daniel Auber's 1852 eponymous comic opera. The complicated story revolved around two pairs of lovers. Federici (Petipa) loves Angela (Rosati), the daughter of the bandit Marco Spada (Segarelli). He is, however, betrothed to the Marchesa Sampietri (Ferraris), who loves Pepinelli (Mérante). Spada eventually resolves the conflict by kidnapping the Marchesa and Pepinelli and forcing them to marry. He is mortally wounded in an attack by soldiers, but before he dies he confesses that Angela is not really his daughter, thus freeing her to marry Federici.

The great spectacle of *Marco Spada* was the use of a split stage in the final scene, showing a forest above and the bandits' cavern beneath. The dance interest centered on the juxtaposition of Ferraris and Rosati in the two principal female roles, which contrasted the elevation and *ballon* of the former to the latter's *terre-à-terre* style. Both ballerinas joined in a *pas de leçon* in which the bandit's daughter is taught to dance. Much of the ballet, however, was filled with long passages of mime.

Although Mazilier did not formally retire as *premier maître de ballet* until 1859, he staged no more new ballets. He did, however, stage three more opera *divertissements,* the most notable of which was Félicien David's *Herculanum* (1859), led by the young ballerina Emma Livry, who became the protégée of Marie Taglioni. In 1867 Mazilier came out of retirement to revive *Le Corsaire* for Adèle Grantzow, rearranging much of its choreography and adding a *pas de fleurs,* danced by Medora and Gulnare, to interpolated music by Léo Delibes. He died in 1868 following an operation.

[Many of the figures and works herein are the subjects of independent entries.]

BIBLIOGRAPHY

Beaumont, Cyril W. *Complete Book of Ballets.* London, 1937.

Christout, Marie-Françoise. "Mazilier." In *Enciclopedia dello spettacolo.* Rome, 1954–.

Guest, Ivor. *The Ballet of the Second Empire.* London, 1974.

Guest, Ivor. *The Romantic Ballet in Paris.* 2d rev. ed. London, 1980.

Guest, Ivor. *Jules Perrot: Master of the Romantic Ballet.* London, 1984.

Wiley, Roland John, trans. and ed. *A Century of Russian Ballet: Documents and Accounts, 1810–1910.* Oxford, 1990.

SUSAN AU

MAZURKA. One of the most important Polish national dances, the mazurka (Pol., *mazur*) is performed in triple meter (3/4 or 3/8) in a quick tempo. Musical compositions in its characteristic rhythm have been traced back to the late fifteenth and sixteenth centuries, although it did not acquire its name until 1752. The term *mazur* derives from Mazovia, the central region of Poland, with which the dance is closely associated; the terms *mazur, mazurek* (its diminutive), *obertas,* and *oberek* are still used interchangeably by rural people to denote the same dance, although there are subtle differences among them (in melodic line, quality of movement, and manner of accentuation) in the different communities. Further variations were introduced when the *mazur* was adopted as a social dance by the gentry and the townspeople.

Like the polonaise (Pol., *polonez*) and the cracovienne (Pol., *krakowiak*), the other major Polish dances, the mazurka is led by the male partner of the first couple, with the other couples following in a circle. With his partner, the leading dancer moves around the room, cutting the *hołubce* (that is, striking his heels together in the air, twice in one beat), then moving through a dance figure that he often improvises, involving one or more other couples. The other couples then follow suit. Figures in the mazurka are not planned as in the quadrille but are freely improvised by the leader together with the other couples. Some typical figures include *krzyże* ("crosses"), *młyńce* ("whirls"), *dwa rzędy ku sobie tańczące* (two rows of dancers moving toward each other), *odbijany* (changing partners), and *zwodzony* or *wybierany* (the female dancer chooses one or two men out of a group, or tosses a handkerchief in the air for the nimblest man to catch). The dance may be concluded with another circle, whirling, or a "burst" of *hołubce.* In the twentieth century, hundreds of mazurka figures have been devised and published in special handbooks.

Although the folk *mazurek* was accompanied by singing, the social dance *mazur* was accompanied only by instrumental music; the term *mazur* or *mazurek* is thus also used to denote purely musical compositions, such as songs (the Polish national anthem is an example) or instrumental works. Beginning in the late eighteenth century (after the partitions of Poland by Prussia, Russia, and Austria), mazurkas were choreographed or composed for the stage as a conscious reference to Polish history, an expression of national pride and dignity. The musical *mazurek* is perhaps best known in the West through Polish pianist Frédéric Chopin's compositions, some of which are incorrectly called mazurkas.

The mazurka traveled from Poland to other European countries to become a fashionable ballroom dance. Introduced to Germany as early as the eighteenth century, it soon spread to France; it was highly popular in the cities of Vienna and Budapest, but it enjoyed only a limited vogue in England in the 1840s. It is said to have reached Russia in 1832, when the Russians annexed their partition of Poland, and it became a favorite dance there. With the exception of the Russian version, which could be danced by an indefinite number of couples, the ballroom mazurka was usually performed by four to eight couples, one serving as the leader. Like its Polish prototype, it allowed a certain amount of improvisation. Hybrid forms such as the polka-mazurka and the waltz-mazurka also appeared in European ballrooms. The dance spread as far as Mexico and the Philippines, where it was often combined with indigenous dances.

During the nineteenth century the mazurka also became popular as a character dance on the ballet stage. The first notable one appeared in Joseph Mazilier's *Le Diable à Quatre* in 1845. In 1870, Arthur Saint-Léon used a rollicking peasant mazurka in the first act of *Coppélia,* where it dramatically postpones an impending rift in the romance of the protagonists. For Marius Petipa's *The Sleeping Beauty* in 1895, Tchaikovsky composed a regal mazurka for the court to dance in the wedding-day finale. Then, in 1919, Léonide Massine's *La Boutique Fantasque* had four dolls, representing playing cards, dance a jolly mazurka for prospective buyers in a toyshop.

[*See also* Character Dancing.]

BIBLIOGRAPHY

Cellarius, Henri. *The Drawing-Room Dances.* London, 1847.

Gawlikowski, P. *Guide Complet de la Danse.* Paris, 1859.

Holden, Richard. "Character Dance for Ballet Students." *Dance Teacher Now* 8.6 (1986): 16–21.

Lange, Roderyk. "The Dance Folklore from Cuiavia." *Dance Studies* 12 (1988): 6–223.
Moreton, Ursula. "National Dances in Ballet" (parts 1–2). *The Dancing Times* (March–April 1935).
Pagels, Jürgen. *Character Dance.* Bloomington, 1984.
Sroka, Czesław. *Polskie tańce narodowe.* Warsaw, 1990.

SUSAN AU

MBUTI DANCE. In one of the first known references to the African Pygmies, the ancient Egyptians called them "dancers of God." Although the nature of their dance at that time is unknown, there seems to have been remarkable cultural continuity; today, in the Ituri Forest of Congo, the Mbuti Pygmies still use dance and song as their principal means of communicating with the supernatural.

The Mbuti are hunters, and their sacred dance forms have little in common with those of their non-Pygmy farming neighbors; nor do they use musical instruments as the surrounding agriculturalists do. The Mbuti dance in the depths of the forest, and their complex rhythms are established only by hand-claps, body percussion (giving added importance to the steps), and sometimes wooden sticks.

Youths, adults, and elders all participate in the dances. Children are expected to watch and, through imitation, involve themselves on the periphery. Besides this, in performing the ritual duty of lighting the daily hunting fire, children use freely improvised movements that often take on the form of a dance.

Mbuti dances reflect and reinforce the patterns of cooperation necessary in everyday life and serve to reduce potential conflict among different age levels and between the two genders by allocating to each group a specific yet equally important role. Certain basic steps and body movements are mandatory, but much room is left for individual improvisation. Thus in the *ekokomea,* a role-reversal dance, men and women imitate the other, with each dancer and each group trying to outdo the other in ridicule. The dancers proceed in a line from one chosen site to another, forming at each a circle in which single dancers improvise while the rest maintain the dance's fundamental setting step and the stylized body movements that depict role reversal. The object of the dance is a cumulative mutual ridicule, which culminates in hysteria and exhaustion, at which point the dancers collapse on the ground in recognition of the idiocy of supposing that one gender is superior to the other.

Other dances, usually performed during rites of passage and in times of crisis, also seek to forestall or reduce conflict by expressing it. Dance steps and complex vocal accompaniments utilizing counterpoint, canon, and hocket demand a form of cooperation that reflects social standards and expectations among the Mbuti.

Mbuti dance performs a dual function; it revitalizes the social norms of interdependence, equality, and cooperation, and it sacramentalizes the central activities of the tribe on all ritual occasions. During the Honey Dance, for example, women dancers act as bees, flying freely in search of honey and, with glowing embers from the fires, attack the plodding, earthbound men (who play drones); the sparks simulate bee stings. Only when the two sexes reach a point of harmony in the dance can they enjoy the world amicably, sharing the food of the forest. Similarly, in the *molimo* dance—performed every night for the month following the death of an adult—male and female cooperation is as essential as in the reproductive cycle, which is echoed in dance movements. As if to regenerate the cycle interrupted by the death, the *molimo* dance emphasizes the separate but equally necessary roles of male and female in creating life. The men build a sacred fire as they dance and then, with a movement imitating the act of copulation, fan it into a blaze. The women slowly and deliberately dance through the fire, scattering the burning logs, which the men once again build into a blaze. At any moment, the women can stop the activity of the men—"killing the hunt and killing the fire," as the Mbuti say—by taking over their roles as dancers and singers, rendering them immobile and useless until "life" is restored to them.

All Mbuti dances are characterized by improvisational movements built onto a structure of basic steps, body postures, and musical forms. The object is to create, through individual improvisation, a unity that makes all the dances a single entity with one belief and one purpose. When a dance reaches this stage, the participants are united not only with one another but also with the forest they consider sacred.

[*For related discussion, see* Central and East Africa *and* Sub-Saharan Africa.]

BIBLIOGRAPHY

Mark, Joan T. *The King of the World in the Land of the Pygmies.* Lincoln, Neb., 1995.
Philippart de Foy, Guy. *Les Pygmées d'Afrique centrale.* Roquevaire, France, 1984.
Schebesta, Paul. *Les Pygmées du Congo Belge.* Brussels, 1952.
Turnbull, Colin M. *The Forest People.* New York, 1961.
Turnbull, Colin M. *Wayward Servants.* New York, 1965.

COLIN M. TURNBULL

MCBRIDE, PATRICIA (born 23 August 1942 in Teaneck, New Jersey), American dancer. McBride studied dance as a child with Ruth Vernon, entering the School of American Ballet at thirteen. In 1959 she joined the corps of the New York City Ballet, where her gifts were quickly recognized. George Balanchine first made a solo for her, in *The Figure in the Carpet* (1960); by the next year she was a principal dancer, at the time the company's youngest.

MCBRIDE. With Edward Villella as her usual partner, McBride appeared several times at the Jacob's Pillow Dance Festival. She is pictured here in the late 1960s in a solo from Balanchine's *Raymonda Variations.* (Photograph from the archives at Jacob's Pillow, Becket, Massachusetts; used by permission. Choreography by George Balanchine © The George Balanchine Trust.)

Although she frequently appeared as a guest with other companies, McBride's career reflects a singular commitment to New York City Ballet and its master choreographers. She danced in more than seventy ballets, in every style and mood of the company's huge repertory, establishing herself as one of the authentic *prima ballerinas* of the climactic Balanchine years. She created roles in Balanchine's *A Midsummer Night's Dream* (Hermia), *Tarantella, Harlequinade* (Columbine), *Brahms-Schoenberg Quartet, Jewels (Rubies), Glinkiana, Who Cares?, Divertimento from "Le Baiser de la Fée," Coppélia, Pavane, The Steadfast Tin Soldier, Union Jack,* and *Vienna Waltzes.* Jerome Robbins created roles for her in such works as *Dances at a Gathering, In the Night, The Goldberg Variations, An Evening's Waltzes, Dybbuk, The Four Seasons,* and *Opus 19/The Dreamer.* In the 1960s McBride had a notable partnership with Edward Villella; later she danced with Helgi Tomasson, Ib Andersen, and Mikhail Baryshnikov. McBride retired in 1989.

Although her many-faceted repertory attests to her versatility, McBride excelled in allegro; in ballets such as *Jewels, Who Cares?,* and *Vienna Waltzes,* Balanchine used her speed and unique clarity and delicacy to extend the boundaries of female allegro dancing. Her technical mastery was matched by exceptional theatrical instincts, whether for comedy (Swanilda in *Coppélia,* perhaps her signature role) or for the mysterious, sinister, even macabre (Balanchine's *La Sonnambula* and *La Valse,* Robbins's *Dybbuk* and *The Cage*).

McBride married the French dancer-choreographer Jean-Pierre Bonnefous. They have two children.

BIBLIOGRAPHY

Ballet Review 17 (Spring 1989): 35–66. Special issue on McBride, with an introduction by Francis Mason.

Mazo, Joseph H. *Dance Is a Contact Sport.* New York, 1974.

Montague, Sarah. *The Ballerina.* New York, 1980.

Tracy, Robert, and Sharon DeLano. *Balanchine's Ballerinas: Conversations with the Muses.* New York, 1983.

ANNE MURPHY

MCKAYLE, DONALD (born 6 July 1930 in New York City), American dancer, choreographer, and teacher. Inspired by a dance concert presented by Pearl Primus, McKayle began his dance studies at the New Dance Group Studio in New York City. He made his professional debut in 1948. Since then he has performed in the work of Sophie Maslow and Anna Sokolow and as a guest performer with the companies of Martha Graham and Merce Cunningham, and he has established a diverse career as both dancer and choreographer in modern dance, musical theater, television, and film.

McKayle performed on Broadway in *House of Flowers* (1954) and *West Side Story* (1957). His numerous Broadway, television, and film choreography credits include Sammy Davis's *Golden Boy* (1964), *Raisin* (1974), *Sophisticated Ladies* (1981), the *Ed Sullivan Show* (CBS, 1966/67), *Minstrel Man* (CBS, 1977), Disney's *Bedknobs and Broomsticks* (1970), and the film version of *The Great White Hope* (1969).

McKayle has choreographed for modern and ballet dance companies in the United States, Canada, Europe, Israel, and South America. Three of his works inspired by American folklore, *Games* (1951), *Rainbow 'Round My Shoulder* (1959), and *District Storyville* (1962), exemplify his interest in examining the human condition. They became dance classics and brought him prominence as a modern dance choreographer. *Games,* based on his childhood memories, uses play songs and chants and explores how street games reflect children's attitudes about life. *Rainbow 'Round My Shoulder,* performed to songs of southern chain gangs, is about the misery of imprisonment, and *District Storyville* examines the New Orleans red-light district and the development of jazz.

McKayle has described his approach to choreography as visceral. He wants audiences to feel compassion for the

MCKAYLE. This photograph, taken c.1963, shows Carmen de Lavallade and McKayle in a scene from *Rainbow 'Round My Shoulder* (1959). A moving and artful portrayal of the hope and hardship of Southern Negro chain gangs, this dance became one of McKayle's signature works. (Photograph by Normand Maxon; used by permission of Donald McKayle.)

characters in his dances. Most of his work in concert dance examines real-life situations rather than abstract concepts. He is known for his inventiveness with movement and for his ability to evoke deep human emotions through his dances.

McKayle has also established a solid reputation as a teacher. He has served on the faculties of the Juilliard School of Music and the American Dance Festival, and he is professor of dance at the University of California at Irvine. He has been a major contributor to scholarship that examines both the work of black dance artists and the racial discrimination against African Americans in American dance.

McKayle received the 1963 Capezio Award, and in 1987 he was chosen as a featured choreographer for the American Dance Festival's preservation project the Black Tradition in American Modern Dance. In December 1991 the Alvin Ailey American Dance Theater recognized his contributions by dedicating an evening of their New York City season to a program of his works. In 1992 he received the Samuel H. Scripps/American Dance Festival Award for lifetime achievement in modern dance. His later work includes *House of Tears* (1992) and *Mysteries and Rapture* (1994) for the Cleveland–San Jose Ballet and *Gumbo Ya Ya* (1994) for the San Francisco Ballet, for which he received the prestigious John F. Kennedy American Ballet Commission.

BIBLIOGRAPHY

Cohen, Selma Jeanne, ed. *The Modern Dance: Seven Statements of Belief.* Middletown, Conn., 1966. See pages 53–61.

Dekle, Nicole. "Lyon Biennale de la Danse." *Dance Magazine* (February 1995): 66.

Emery, Lynne Fauley. *Black Dance from 1619 to Today.* Rev. ed. Princeton, 1988. See pages 293–297.

Hubbard, Karen. "Donald McKayle: Dance Is Movement That Lights the Soul." In *African American Genius in Modern Dance,* edited by Gerald Myers. Durham, N.C., 1993.

Mazo, Joseph H. "What Is Jazz Dance?" *Dance Magazine* (December 1990): 68–69.

MELANYE P. WHITE-DIXON

MÉDÉE ET JASON. Also known as *Médée, Medea und Jason.* Ballet in twelve scenes. Choreography: Jean-Georges Noverre. Music: Jean-Joseph Rodolphe (Johann Joseph Rudolph). Libretto: Jean-Georges Noverre. Scenery: Innocenzo Colomba. Costumes: Louis Boquet. First performance: 11 February 1763, Grand Ducal Theater, Stuttgart, Germany. Principals: Nancy Levier (Medea), Gaëtan Vestris (Jason).

As though to contradict the myth that great art is fostered by adverse conditions, *Médée et Jason* was created under a particularly happy set of circumstances. Choreographer Jean-Georges Noverre was at the peak of his creative powers, and since 1760 he had enjoyed the lavish and sympathetic patronage of Karl Eugen, duke of Württemberg. He had worked previously with both the composer and designer of the ballet and knew that they understood his aims. His dancers, too, were well equipped to put his precepts into practice. The role of Medea, with its strong but contrasting passions, was entrusted to Nancy Levier, who combined a strong dance technique with considerable acting ability. Gaëtan Vestris, who played Jason, was a leading male dancer of the time: tall and stately, he excelled in the noble style of dancing yet profited from Noverre's costume reforms. Noverre had eliminated the mask and the cumbersome tonnelet and expanded the dancer's dramatic range.

Médée et Jason proved to be worthy of its favorable portents. It justified Noverre's belief that ballet had the capacity to convey the grand and stark emotions required by tragedy without sacrificing or diminishing a work's formal and musical components. Revived throughout Europe, *Médée* did more than any of his other ballets to represent his achievement and give substance to the ideas he had published in his *Lettres sur la danse et sur les ballets* (1760).

The ballet was first produced for the duke of Württemberg's birthday celebration and performed between the acts of Niccolò Jommelli's opera *Didone Abbandonata.* In framing the action of the ballet, Noverre took into account the opera's libretto. The story derived from the ancient Greek myth of the Argonauts and their search for the Golden Fleece. Noverre's adaptation, like the plays by Euripides and Pierre Corneille that preceded it, focused on the tale's tragic ending.

The ballet opens in the palace of Creon, king of Corinth, who wishes to unite his daughter Creusa to Jason. Although married to Medea, Jason is not reluctant to respond to these overtures, particularly when Creon offers his throne as an additional enticement. The jealous and suspicious Medea casts off her pride and pleads pitifully with Jason, showing him their two children. He is briefly reconciled with her, but Creusa soon reclaims him, and he orders Medea from his presence.

In her wrath, Medea repudiates her children and invokes the elements. The palace is transformed into an infernal cavern, where the figures of Jealousy, Hatred, and Vengeance help Medea forge two deadly gifts: a diadem and a casket. Armed with these, she descends upon the nuptial feast of Jason and Creusa. She allays their fears by feigning resignation and good will, giving the diadem to Creusa and the casket to Creon. As soon as she withdraws, the gifts take their deadly effect: Creusa is poisoned and Creon is suffocated by noxious fumes. Medea returns in triumph as Jason tries to help them. One of her children already lies dead; she kills the other despite Jason's pleas, then hands him her dagger, with which he stabs himself. He dies in the arms of the expiring Creusa as Medea flees in her chariot.

Médée et Jason was revived repeatedly by Noverre and his followers. In 1780 the composer, Jean-Joseph Rodolphe, revised the score for Noverre's restaging at the Paris Opera. Vestris also revived it in Paris, as well as in Vienna, Warsaw, and London. Charles Le Picq revived it in Saint Petersburg in 1791, where it was acclaimed as the best ballet ever produced in that city. It fostered such interest in Noverre's ideas that a new edition of his *Lettres* was published there in 1803–1804 as *Lettres sur la danse, sur les ballets et les arts.*

[*See also the entry on Noverre.*]

BIBLIOGRAPHY

Guest, Ivor. "*Jason and Medea:* A Noverre Ballet Reconstructed." *The Dancing Times* (May 1992): 738–739.

Kirstein, Lincoln. *Movement and Metaphor: Four Centuries of Ballet.* New York, 1970.

Noverre, Jean-Georges. *Lettres sur la danse, sur les ballets et les arts.* 4 vols. St. Petersburg, 1803–1804.

Uriot, Joseph. *Description des fêtes donnés pendant quatorze jours à l'occasion du jour de naissance de son Altesse Serenissime Monseigneur le Duc Regnant de Wurttemberge et Teck . . .* Stuttgart, 1763.

RICHARD RALPH and SUSAN AU

MEDIEVAL DANCE. Dancing for recreation was popular among medieval aristocrats, city dwellers, and country people, and dance and dance music were part of every minstrel's repertory. Dances also enhanced sacred and profane theatrical events and religious services. Medieval theorists of music and medicine believed that dancing was good exercise, a healthful recreation, and a physical demonstration of rational and temperate behavior, organized in accordance with the temporal proportions of the musical notes. It also offered a means to increase the powers of concentration and thus a way to increase mental alertness.

If dance was capable of preserving health and increasing beauty and intellectual capacity, it was also capable of

MEDIEVAL DANCE. Two dancing figures from the fourteenth-century *Manessesche Minnesängerhandschrift,* published in Heidelberg, Germany. (Reprinted from Sachs, 1937.)

bringing on madness and death. The chronicles from the eleventh to the fifteenth century talk of the great waves of mass hysteria that swept periodically through central Europe, affecting everyone in their path, and causing hundreds of people at a time to dance for days on end to the point of total exhaustion, even death. Depending on the place or the day of their outbreak, these dance epidemics were called *chorea major, danse macabre,* Saint John's dance, or Saint Vitus's dance.

Information about the social and entertainment dances of the Middle Ages comes mainly from literary references and iconography. The history of dance music remains obscure until the thirteenth century. Medieval literature gives quite a number of terms for movement and gesture, names of dances, and descriptions of dance events (for example, see "Ruodlieb," quoted in Sachs, 1937; the dances in *Sir Gawain and the Green Knight*), and medieval art provides some pictures of dance performances. But the decisive connecting link—the choreographic description—is missing, and therefore whatever can be said about the dances of the Middle Ages is necessarily imprecise.

The key words from which much of the later terminology evolved were the Latin *saltare* (from which are derived *saltator/saltatrix,* and *saltarello,* with the Germanic counterparts *springen, springare, springan,* etc.); the Greek *ballein (ballare, ballatio, ballator/ballatrix, bal/bau/ballo)* and *choreare,* latinized from Greek *choros* and becoming *choreatio, chorea, choraula, carola,* and *carole* in medieval dance references.

MEDIEVAL DANCE. A procession of dancers led by a musician playing a *vielle,* from the fourteenth-century *Manessesche Minnesängerhandschrift.* (Reprinted from Sachs, 1937.)

Of these, *saltare* and its derivatives originally referred to dancing by professionals, including their skills of tumbling, vaulting, and tightrope walking. As late as the end of the sixteenth century the dancing master and "athletic director" of the Austrian and French courts, Arcangelo Tuccaro, had the title of *Hof-Springmeister.*

While *ballare* was used in the widest sense for dance activities of all kinds (*ballator/ballatrix* simply means "dancer"), *choreare* seems to refer more particularly to line and circle group dances, such as the *carole* (Ger., *Reien, Reihen*) in its many appearances in medieval literature and iconography.

Used in court epics of the high Middle Ages is the word group that includes *danzare, dancier, tantzen,* and their corresponding nouns. While these terms applied to dancing pastimes of the nobility in general, they seem quite soon to have acquired the more specific meaning of "couple dance" and may refer to early forms of processional dances. The juxtapositions of words from this group with terms designating linear choreographic shapes in literary formulae such as *danser et caroler, reien unde tantz,* and *carola and daunce* support this hypothesis.

Among the earliest of dance types mentioned are *tresca* ("La Passion de Sainte Foy," eleventh century) and *estampie* ("Kalenda Maya," twelfth century). *Tresque, trescone, estampie, istampita,* and *stantipes* also appear in dance and music of the thirteenth and fourteenth centuries. Contemporary are *nota, ductia, danse royale, saltarello, trotto,* and *rotta,* the last used as a contrasting after-dance to a main dance in two instances in a manuscript now in the British Museum in London (Add. 29987). The same source contains four *Chançonete tedesche,* dances either of German origin or reflecting a German variant of an unspecified dance type. The *bassedanse* is mentioned for the first time in 1340 by the troubadour Raimond de Cornet.

Contrary to the opinion of some twentieth-century dance researchers, we simply do not know what choreographic shapes are hidden behind the various dance names transmitted from the Middle Ages, including lower-class dances such as *Hoppaldei, Firlefanz,* and *Gofenanz.* The exception is the *carole,* which has been proved to be a line dance and appears to have been performed predominantly by lower- and middle-class citizens.

Line dances of the *carole* type could be danced by women alone to the singing and tambourine-playing of one of their group (as shown in the Ambrogio Lorenzetti fresco *The Good Government* in Siena, painted in the

1330s, and the Andrea de Firenze fresco in the Spanish Chapel of Santa Maria Novella, Florence, painted in 1365). Line dances for both men and women also occur, and sometimes aristocrats are shown in the leisurely enjoyment of line and circle dances.

A frequent figure in line dances is the "bridge": two stationary dancers face one another with hands clasped at shoulder or face level while the hand-holding line of the rest of the company passes underneath. Another figure repeatedly shown in the iconography is that of the first dancer ducking under the raised hands of the two that follow or under his own hand and that of the person next to him, possibly to pull the whole line along in one of the snaking patterns *(biscia* or *treccia)* for which ample documentation exists since the dance instruction manuals of the fifteenth century.

Movement terms reveal something of the speed and vigor of medieval dances. Lively motion is indicated by words such as *springen, sauter, tumer,* and *saillir; treten, gehen,* and *sliefen* ("to drag" or "glide") suggest slower steps; *swantzen* ("to strut"), *dancier, baler,* and *tantzen* fall somewhere in between, or indicate in a general way that people were dancing.

That some national movement styles existed in the Middle Ages is confirmed by a passage in a twelfth-century poem about the Tumbler of Ou r Lady *(Del tumbeor Nostre-Dame),* who performed his *saltatio* before the Virgin in the styles of Rome and Metz, Lorraine and Champagne, Brittany and Spain. Italian steps are mentioned in *Saelden Hort* (1298).

Hand and arm gestures are not infrequent in medieval dance iconography, but attempts at identifying their meaning and purpose (most recently by Busch, 1982) have not been entirely convincing. Foot positions in social dance representations include a pronounced turnout, crossed legs, and raised legs bent at the knee, with the last more pronounced in men's than in women's dances. The ideal lady, according to Dante, dances with the smallest possible steps, barely placing one foot ahead of the other. Salome's sinuous dancing is often depicted with a flexible torso and pliable arms; professional entertainers execute full backbends to the floor, deep *pliés,* leaps, handstands, and headstands, and other exaggerated motions that were excluded from the movement repertory of the upper classes.

The spaces for medieval dance activities were fields, city squares, and indoor halls in palazzos, town halls, guild houses, private mansions, and castles. In favorable weather, courtly dancing could take place outside, in the courtyard or in an enclosed formal garden. Of particular interest among specially constructed edifices is the *Tantz-Hauß,* also called "wedding house," which served as the civic center for the Jewish community in major European cities. The earliest securely dated *Tantz-Hauß* is the Domus Civium in Cologne, in active use since 1149. A social hall in Avignon and the Judentantzhaus in Mainz were established in the mid-thirteenth century; the *Tantz-Hauß* in Augsburg dates from 1290. Frankfurt, Speyer, and Ulm had similar buildings by the middle of the fourteenth century. Similarly, the Palazzo della Ragione in Padua (built 1172–1219, loggias added in 1306), a huge space 91 meters long, 27 meters wide, and 27 meters high with a free-floating, arched ceiling, served not only for legal proceedings, but also for civic banquets and dances. In addition, there were collapsible performance and dance halls that, after being used for a tournament or other court festival, could be dismantled and stored until the next occasion.

BIBLIOGRAPHY

Aeppli, Fritz. *Die wichtigsten Ausdrücke für das Tanzen in den romanischen Sprachen.* Beihefte zur Zeitschrift für romanische Philologie, 75. Halle, 1925.

Aubry, Pierre. *Estampies et danses royales.* Paris, 1907.

Barasch, Moshe. *Giotto and the Language of Gesture.* Cambridge, 1987.

Bédier, Jean. "Les plus anciennes danses françaises." *Revue des deux mondes* 31 (1906).

Böhme, Franz M. *Geschichte des Tanzes in Deutschland.* 2 vols. Leipzig, 1886.

Brainard, Ingrid. "The Role of the Dancing Master in Fifteenth-Century Courtly Society." *Fifteenth-Century Studies* 2 (1979):21–44.

Brainard, Ingrid. "Dance III: Middle Ages and Early Renaissance." In *The New Grove Dictionary of Music and Musicians.* London, 1980.

Busch, Gabriele C. *Ikonographische Studien zum Solotanz im Mittelalter.* Innsbruck, 1982.

Daffner, Hugo. *Salome: Ihre Gestalt in Geschichte und Kunst.* Munich, 1912.

Doob, Penelope Reed. "The Auxerre Labyrinth Ritual." In *The Myriad Faces of Dance: Proceedings of the Eighth Annual Conference, Society of Dance History Scholars, University of New Mexico, 15–17 February 1985,* compiled by Christena L. Schlundt. Riverside, Calif., 1985.

Doob, Penelope Reed. *The Idea of the Labyrinth from Classical Antiquity through the Middle Ages.* Ithaca, N.Y., 1990.

Gougaud, Louis. "La danse dans les églises." *Revue d'histoire ecclésiastique* 15(1914): 5–22.

Harding, Ann. *An Investigation into the Use and Meaning of Medieval German Dancing Terms.* Göppingen, 1973.

Hecker, J. F. C. *The Dancing Mania of the Middle Ages* (1837). Translated by B. G. Babington. New York, 1970.

Lacroix, Paul. *Moeurs, usages, et costumes au moyen âge et à l'époque de la Renaissance.* Paris, 1871.

Mandach, André de. "Contribution à l'histoire du théâtre en Rouergne au XIe siècle: Un Mystère de Sainte Foy?" In *La vie théâtrale dans les provinces du Midi: Actes du IIe Colloque de Grasse, 1976,* edited by Yves Girard. Tübingen, 1980.

Maynard, Susan W. "Dance in the Arts of the Middle Ages." Ph.D. diss., Florida State University, 1992.

McGee, Timothy J. "Medieval Dances: Matching the Repertory with Grocheio's Descriptions." *Journal of Musicology* 7 (1989): 498–517.

McGee, Timothy J. *Medieval Instrumental Dances.* Bloomington, 1989.

Mingardi, Maurizio. "Gli strumenti musicali nella danza del XIV e XV secolo." In *Mesura et arte del danzare: Guglielmo Ebreo da Pesaro e la danza nelle corti italiane del XV secolo,* edited by Patrizia Castelli et al. Pesaro, 1987.

Moser, Hans Joachim. "Stantipes und Ductia." *Zeitschrift für Musikwissenschaft* 2 (January 1920): 194–206.
Mullally, Robert. "Dance Terminology in the Works of Machaut and Froissart." *Medium Aevum* 59.2 (1990): 248–259.
Page, Christopher. *The Owl and the Nightingale: Musical Life and Ideas in France, 1100–1300.* London, 1989.
Randall, Lilian M. C. *Images in the Margins of Gothic Manuscripts.* Berkeley, 1966.
Records of Early English Drama (REED). Toronto, 1976–. Series of volumes covering regional and parish public entertainments, individual performers, and companies and their repertories, published by the University of Toronto Press.
Rimmer, Joan. "Dance Elements in Trouvère Repertory." *Dance Research* 3 (Summer 1985): 23–34.
Rimmer, Joan. "Medieval Instrumental Dance Music." *Music and Letters* 72 (1991): 61–68.
Rokseth, Yvonne. "Danses cléricales du XIIIe siècle." In *Mélanges 1945,* vol. 3, *Études historiques.* Paris, 1947.
Sachs, Curt. *World History of the Dance.* Translated by Bessie Schönberg. New York, 1937.
Salmen, Walter. *Der fahrende Musiker im europäischen Mittelalter.* Kassel, 1960.
Southworth, John. *The English Medieval Minstrel.* Woodbridge, Suffolk, 1989.
Switten, Margaret L. *Music and Poetry in the Middle Ages: A Guide to Research on French and Occitan Song, 1100–1400.* New York, 1995.
Wagenaar-Noltenius, Helene. "Estampie/Stantipes/Stampita." In *L'ars nova italiana del trecento: Secondo Convegno Internazionale, 17–22 luglio 1969,* edited by F. Alberto Gallo. Certaldo, 1970.
Weisheipl, James A. *Nature and Motion in the Middle Ages.* Washington, D.C., 1985.
Wickham, Glynne. *The Medieval Theatre.* 3d ed. Cambridge, 1987.
Wolf, Johannes. "Die Tänze des Mittelalters." *Archiv für Musikwissenschaft* 1 (1919): 10–42.

INGRID BRAINARD

MEI LANFANG (born 22 October 1894 in Beijing, died 8 August 1961 in Beijing), classical Chinese theater actor. A well-loved name in China, Mei was esteemed as the foremost actor of singing female roles in the classical Chinese theater. International recognition included the praises of Charlie Chaplin, Stark Young, and Sergei Eisenstein, as well as honorary doctorates from Pomona College and the University of Southern California.

Mei's versatility and artistry in singing, acting, dancing, and dramatic movement were considered without peer. He had an inquiring and creative mind, revising old plays and reviving ancient dances. He was a skilled painter and fluent speaker, and he wrote analytically about his film experiences and aesthetic theories; in the 1950s he wrote his autobiography. Although open to new concepts, he did not abandon the aesthetic and spirit of the classical theater, rendering his roles with impeccable fidelity.

Mei combined his superlative technique with empathy for the drama's content and the emotional nature of each character. He imparted to every role the force of his magnetic personality.

Mei was the first actor to perform the three different types of female roles with distinction, both technical and emotional. These types are *Ching-I,* the modest, virtuous woman—tragic, austere, or pathetic; *Hua Tan,* the flirtatious girl—lighthearted and humorous; and *Wu Tan,* the warrior woman of heroic calm—which requires acrobatic virtuosity.

Mei made the stage glow with his grace and his sculptural and rhythmic lines. His elegant hands and eloquent facial expressions, and especially his rich, pure singing voice, created an aesthetic harmony. He was the embodiment of his statement, "In solo dancing and singing, all the character's movements flow from the content of her singing, which in turn determines the changing rhythm of the dance."

Mei came from a theatrical family; his son too became an actor of female roles. His grandfather had been an actor in the Imperial Court. An uncle (his guardian after his father's early death) was a theater musician at whose daily musical sessions little Lanfang was always present. At seven he was a musician; at eleven he was presented at a Beijing tea-house theater, where he was judged to have an extraordinary voice and exceptional rhythmic grace. He thereafter concentrated on the study of dance, voice, acting, speech, costume manipulation, expressive characterizations, and the techniques of acrobatics and play of sword, spear, fan, and other properties. He was recognized as a virtuoso by the age of nineteen.

During the Japanese occupation of the 1930s and 1940s, he refused to act, going into "retirement." In 1950 he participated in the government of the newly established People's Republic of China as a vice-president. His profound interest in helping the women's struggle for equality in China developed from his study of the social and psychological nature of his female roles, as well as from his awareness of society's ills.

In his theater career, Mei listened with good grace to criticism of his innovative ideas, such as repositioning the orchestra to backstage and simplifying traditional costume. When being filmed, he acquiesced to directors' suggestions, perceiving that the aesthetics of Chinese symbolism did not harmonize with film's realism. After the establishment of the People's Republic of China in 1949, he wholeheartedly accepted changes in the content of old dramas, himself creating new and pertinent dialogue to suit the social ideals of the times while maintaining the traditional action.

[*See also* China, *article on* Classical Dance.]

BIBLIOGRAPHY

Eisenstein, Sergei. "The Enchanter from the Pear Garden." *Theatre Arts* (October 1935): 761–770.
Scott, A. C. *The Classical Theatre of China.* London, 1957.
Young, Stark. "Mei Lan-fang." *Orient et Occident* 1.9 (1935): 35–38.
Zung, Cecelia. *Secrets of the Chinese Drama.* Shanghai, 1930.

SOPHIA DELZA

MELANESIA. The geographical region of Melanesia lies in the Pacific Ocean west of the International Date Line and south of the equator, comprising New Guinea, New Ireland, New Britain, Manus (formerly known as the Admiralty Islands), the Solomon Islands, Vanuatu (formerly New Hebrides), and New Caledonia. Fiji is a transitional area between Melanesia and Polynesia, but its dance forms are more closely allied with Polynesia. The indigenous Melanesians are Oceanic peoples of various physical types who developed over thousands of years, with many diverse cultures, forming hundreds of small political groups and a variety of social structures with mutually unintelligible languages. Each sociopolitical group has its own dance tradition; this general discussion can only touch on the diversity of dance functions and movements in Melanesia.

Melanesian dance is essentially a visual enhancement of rhythm. It is primarily a group activity in which participation is more important than presentation for an audience. Traditionally, Melanesian dance has not been a form of entertainment; instead, it constitutes the movement dimension of important ritual activities often associated with rites of passage and secret societies. Large-scale ceremonies in which dance, or formalized movement, plays an integral role are traditionally held in conjunction with the erection of men's large ceremonial houses (New Guinea), the making and consecration of slit gongs (Solomon Islands), the purchase of higher grades in secret societies (Vanuatu), the sponsorship of ceremonies for the dead (New Ireland), the celebration of circumcision rites, or the reactivation of social relationships among groups.

In many Melanesian societies, the group leader is a self-made man (a "bigman"), and his social prestige is derived from amassing a following. The visual and performing arts are part of spectacular displays held or sponsored by bigmen to reaffirm the traditional, legendary, and social values of the society. The main performers often wear masks and unwieldy costumes, such as the six-foot-high *hevehe* masks of the Papuan Gulf of New Guinea, or the large barkcloth constructions of the Baining of New Britain. These performers enact (and spiritually become) mythical beings, birds and other animals, spirits of the sea or bush, or ancestors. In other cases, dance performances provide the occasion for a display of body decoration and ceremonial finery. Performers often carry and play hourglass-shaped drums, rattles, or panpipes.

Melanesian dance movements are done primarily with the legs and lower body. Usually a few motifs are repeated over and over. Often the function of the movements is to move the group from one place to another—for example, from the men's house to the beach, or from one side of a ceremonial ground to the other. The group may progress in single or multiple lines, in columns, or in circles (which usually move in a clockwise direction). Often the group moves in one direction and then turns and moves in the opposite direction. A stationary group may perform a movement sequence facing one direction and then repeat the same sequence facing the opposite direction.

MELANESIA. The segregation of the sexes is a prevalent feature of Melanesian culture. Traditionally, men and women live apart from each other, even after they are married. In performance contexts, men and women generally appear at the same event but form separate groups. Pictured here are women and girls from the Solomon Islands preparing for a dance, c.1927. (Photograph by H. S. Beck; from the archives of the American Museum of Natural History [no. 117413]; used by permission.)

MELANESIA. Men from Vanuatu (formerly called New Hebrides), carrying war clubs in a ritual line dance, 1918. (Photograph by Martin Johnson; from the archives of the American Museum of Natural History [no. 108178]; used by permission.)

Up-and-down bouncing movements are characteristic of Melanesian dance. The bouncing is created by bending and straightening the knees and rising onto the balls of the feet, by step-bend-step-bend movements progressing forward and back, or by a stamp of the foot followed by a quick backward lift of the lower leg while the opposite foot stamps. Other movements include leaps with the trailing leg thrust backward or bent upward toward the buttocks. A leader may begin the knee-bending and straightening, and others join in until the whole group moves up and down together. The trunk of the body or torso is usually held vertically, as a single unit, although occasionally women move their hips from side to side. Sometimes two or more groups perform different dances to different music, simultaneously.

In some areas, such as the Highlands of New Guinea, costumes are composed primarily of attachments that move as the dancer moves. Feathers, especially the tail feathers of the bird of paradise, are attached to a headdress, the back, a bustle, or the arms. Pieces of animal skin ripple like vertical waves, long aprons curl upward, shredded leaves cascade and bounce, and rattles made of seeds or shells are attached to the ankles or held in the hands. Penis sheaths made from gourd, shell, bark, or woven fibers curve forward and upward to emphasize the up-and-down movement of this part of the body. The movement of all these attachments, as the bodies move up and down to the beat of drums, creates a visual and aural rhythmic statement.

Some of the traditional functions of dance are still important parts of Melanesian culture. In Vanuatu, dance is an integral part of the ceremonies for boys' initiation into manhood and for the attainment of higher levels in secret societies. In the New Ireland *malanggan* ceremonies, masked spirits of the ancestors dance at funeral rituals. Among the Kaluli of New Guinea, the function of dance is to make those in attendance cry. Among the Umeda, dance is part of ritualized sexual antagonism in ceremonies concerned with the life cycles of humans and birds.

There are also innovative dance occasions and new dance forms. Today dancing is an important part of local festivals and large-scale *singsings,* events that combine singing, music, and dancing with the visual arts, especially body decoration. The best-known *singsing* takes place annually in the Highlands of New Guinea, alternating its venue between Mount Hagen and Goroka. Performing groups representing various tribes come from near and far to perform and take part in the festivities.

Local festivals are becoming increasingly important for the retention of ethnic identity and cultural diversity in some areas of Melanesia, especially for such occasions as independence celebrations. National theater and national dance groups are also becoming popular in some Melanesian areas. The Raun Raun Theatre, based in Goroka, New Guinea, has been successful in developing traditional movement concepts in ways that are appropriate both to modern New Guinea and to international theaters.

[*For general discussion, see* Oceanic Dance Traditions. *See also* Fiji; Papua New Guinea; *and* Music for Dance, *article on* Oceanic Music.]

BIBLIOGRAPHY

Coppet, Daniel de, and Hugo Zemp. *"Aré, Aré": Une peuple mélanesien et sa musique.* Paris, 1978.

Courlay, Ken G. *A Bibliography of Traditional Music in Papua New Guinea.* Port Moresby, 1974.

Feld, Steven. *Sound and Sentiment: Birds, Weeping, Poetics, and Song in Kaluli Expression.* 2d ed. Philadelphia, 1990.

Hesse, Karl. *Baining Life and Lore.* Port Moresby, 1982.

Kaeppler, Adrienne L. "The Performing Arts of Papua New Guinea." In *The Sixth Festival of Asian Arts.* Hong Kong, 1981.

ADRIENNE L. KAEPPLER

MENUET. *See* Minuet.

MÉRANTE, LOUIS (born 27 July 1828 in Paris, died 17 July 1887 in Courbevoie), French dancer, ballet master, and choreographer. Mérante, born into an Italian family of dancers (his father had danced at the Paris Opera), was originally destined for the priesthood. He first danced in public at the age of six in *Gustave III* in Liège, Belgium. In 1846 he appeared as a *premier danseur* in Marseille and at the Teatro alla Scala in Milan. He joined the Paris Opera in 1848 as an understudy to Lucien Petipa and made his debut in *La Jolie Fille de Gand.*

Mérante was well liked by the ballerinas he partnered. He danced the leading male role in Joseph Mazilier's *Jovita* (1853), opposite Carolina Rosati. Fanny Cerrito's *Gemma* (1854) gave him an opportunity to display his gifts as a mime; Théophile Gautier, who wrote the ballet's libretto, said in *La presse* that "he knew how to assume a sinister and fatal expression. His gestures have authority, his look, fascination." Although Mérante entered the profession at a time when the male dancer was overshadowed by the ballerina and was gradually being reduced to a *porteur,* his performance with Rosati in *La Fonti* (1855) caused the critic Pier-Angelo Fiorentino to declare in *Le moniteur universel* that "he gave proof of a most versatile talent rehabilitating the male." Mérante created the roles of Pepinelli in Mazilier's *Marco Spada* (1857) and Madhava, the king's favorite, in Lucien Petipa's *Sacountala* (1858). Raised to the status of a principal dancer, he created leading roles in Marie Taglioni's *Le Papillon* (1860), opposite Emma Livry; in Marius Petipa's *Le Marché des Innocents* (1861); and in Pasquale Borri's *L'Étoile de Messine* (1861).

After Lucien Petipa retired from dancing in 1862, Mérante became the only male principal dancer at the Opera, a distinction he retained almost until his death. In 1863 he danced the leading male role in Arthur Saint-Léon's *Diavolina,* and performed the role of Albrecht in *Giselle,* which Lucien Petipa (the original Albrecht) revived for the Russian guest artist Marfa Muravieva. He also partnered Muravieva in Saint-Léon's *Néméa* (1864) and created the role of the hunter Djémil in the same choreographer's *La Source* (1866).

His appointment as ballet master of the Paris Opera in 1869 required him to choreograph opera *divertissements* as well as ballets. Léandre Vaillat has noted that Mérante's dances in *Aïda* were Egyptian insofar as the viewer could recognize poses and movements derived from sculptures and paintings popularized by books on Egyptology. Vaillat also states that "in the *divertissement* of *Francesca da Rimini* (1882), Rosita Mauri leaped into the arms of Mérante, who had perfect visual judgment and unusual athletic strength" (Vaillat, 1947).

Mérante's first real ballet, *Gretna Green* (1873), was a failure. However, because Saint-Léon was dead and Jules Perrot in retirement, the Opera had no one else to whom it could turn. Mérante also choreographed *Sylvia* (1876), which is often revived, chiefly for its score by Léo Delibes; *Le Fandango* (1877), mounted for Léontine Beaugrand, the only important French dancer of the time; and *Yedda* (1879), set to music by Olivier Métra, with Rita Sangalli in the title role. The tragic ending of *Yedda,* which took place in Japan, was unusual for the time. In *La Korrigane* (1880), a ballet set in seventeenth-century Brittany, Rosita Mauri was much applauded as a peasant in wooden shoes. She also triumphed in Mérante's *divertissement* in

MÉRANTE. A cast photograph from the 1880s ballet *La Korrigane,* inspired by a legend from Brittany. Here, dancer-choreographer Mérante poses in Breton costume as Lilèz with his leading ladies Rosita Mauri as Yvonette the Tavern Maid and Mademoiselle Hottolini as Queen of the Korriganes. (Photograph by F. Lutton; from the Dance Collection, New York Public Library for the Performing Arts.)

Jules Massenet's opera *Le Cid* (1885), in which she and Mérante (who was then fifty-seven years old) danced a *catalane* and a *madrilène* that had to be encored.

Mauri also danced the leading role of Gourouli in Mérante's *Les Deux Pigeons,* based on a fable of Jean de La Fontaine. Created in 1886, the year before Mérante's death, this ballet allowed the whole troupe to shine. Wearing a blonde wig in the first act, and her own dark tresses in the second, Mauri showed off her gifts as a dancer and actress. Marie Sanlaville danced her lover, Pepio, *en travesti.* The ballet proved to be extremely popular at the Opera, and over the years a number of outstanding dancers have performed in it, among them Julia Subra, Carlotta Zambelli, Albert Aveline, Lycette Darsonval, Yvette Chauviré, Christiane Vaussard, and Michel Renault. André Messager composed the score, his first for ballet.

Mérante was still performing his duties at the Opera at the time of his death, and his loss was much regretted by his colleagues. The only reproach—an important one—that can be made against him is that he was unable to keep his predecessors' ballets in the repertory of the Opera. His own ballets have almost all disappeared.

BIBLIOGRAPHY

Beaumont, Cyril W. *Complete Book of Ballets.* Rev. ed. London, 1951.

Gautier, Théophile. *The Romantic Ballet.* Translated and edited by Cyril W. Beaumont. Rev. ed. London, 1947.

Guest, Ivor. "*Les Deux Pigeons:* The History." *The Dancing Times* (February 1961): 286–287.

Guest, Ivor. *The Ballet of the Second Empire.* London, 1974.

Guest, Ivor. *Le ballet de l'Opéra de Paris.* Paris, 1976.

Guest, Ivor. *Jules Perrot: Master of the Romantic Ballet.* London, 1984.

Vaillat, Léandre. *Ballets de l'Opéra de Paris (ballets dans les opéras—nouveaux ballets).* Paris, 1947.

MONIQUE BABSKY
Translated from French

MERENGUE. *See* Dominican Republic.

MERI, LA (Russell Meriwether Hughes; born 13 May 1899 in Louisville, Kentucky, died 7 January 1988 in San Antonio, Texas), dancer, writer, and teacher. La Meri was raised in San Antonio, Texas, where she was early exposed to Mexican and Spanish culture. She experimented in all the arts but was ultimately steered to a career in dance by Guido Carreras, who had introduced dancer Anna Pavlova and violinist Jascha Heifetz to Berlin, and actress Eleonora Duse to the United States. Carreras later became La Meri's manager and husband.

La Meri made her New York concert debut on 6 June 1928. Over the next twelve years she danced in Central and South America, Europe, North Africa, Australasia, India, Burma, Indonesia, the Philippines, China, Japan, and Hawaii. Wherever she performed, she studied the local dances with recognized masters. She also collected authentic costumes and recordings of native music, then made her own dances based on traditional steps, offering them for the approval of her teachers. In India she met a young dancer, Bassano Ramgopal, who danced with her on her tour of Asia and later performed on his own as Ram Gopal.

LA MERI. In La Meri's "Hindu version" of *Swan Lake* (1944), set to the Tchaikovsky score, Matteo (left) appeared as the Prince and La Meri (seated) portrayed the Swan Queen. (Photograph from the archives at Jacob's Pillow, Becket, Massachusetts.)

La Meri said, "Studying racial characteristics through the medium of dancing is one of my most lasting joys" (*New Zealand Radio Record,* 31 July 1936). She communicated that enjoyment not only through dancing but also through many lectures and books. In 1942 the dance critic Walter Terry wrote, "La Meri has long been welcomed for her ability to bring the world to one's door. Through magnificent costumes, authentic folk music and the movements of dance, she has taken her audiences on visits to the nations of the earth."

After the outbreak of World War II, La Meri settled in New York. There, at one of her lectures on Hindu dance, she met Ruth St. Denis; together they founded the School of Natya in 1940, to further interest in Asian cultures. When St. Denis returned to California in 1945, La Meri expanded her focus to all ethnic dance and opened the Ethnologic Dance Center. During this period she gave a series of ethnic dance concerts at the Museum of Natural

History. In 1945 she also opened the Ethnologic Dance Theater. In 1947 she inaugurated a Young Artists Series at which she presented young ethnic dancers from all over the world. She was also a frequent performer and teacher at Jacob's Pillow.

The two groups of national dances with which La Meri is most often associated are Spanish and Indian. She is particularly noted for her daring 1944 presentation—at Anatole Chujoy's suggestion—of *Swan Lake,* danced to Tchaikovsky's music but using Hindu gesture technique. She subsequently choreographed a suite of *bharata nāṭyam* dances to Bach's music (*Bach-Bharata Suite,* 1946), as well as *Indo-American Gesture Songs* (1946), American hymns and spirituals set in Hindu gesture technique. La Meri also choreographed "interpretive" dances, of which her early *White Peacock* was a perennial favorite.

Walter Terry, a devoted admirer, described her as "more of a recreative artist than a creative one" (*New York Herald Tribune,* 21 December 1941). Audiences loved not only her rich, varied costumes but also her expressive talents. Many critics noted that her face took on the personality of each dance she performed, so that she seemed to be many different women. She did not just present exotic dances but made them intelligible to her audiences with a salty, humorous running commentary. Her desire to educate as well as entertain is also evident in her many lecture-demonstrations and books, including *The Gesture Language of Hindu Dance* (1941) and *Spanish Dancing* (1948), as well as countless magazine articles.

During the early 1950s La Meri increasingly shifted her focus from performing to teaching ethnic dance. In 1959 she closed the Ethnologic Dance Center and retired to Cape Cod to raise show dogs. In 1970 she returned to dance to found Ethnic Dance Arts in Barnstable, Massachusetts, which sponsored yearly ethnic dance festivals and other educational activities and groomed a small company that toured New England. La Meri also served as contributing editor to *Arabesque,* the ethnic dance magazine.

BIBLIOGRAPHY

Dance Magazine (August 1978): 55–70. Section devoted to La Meri.

Fay, Anthony. "The Festival of '42: A History Making Summer at Jacob's Pillow." *Dance Magazine* (July 1976): 61–65.

Lahm, Adam. "La Meri: Ethnic Dance's Living Legend." *Dance Teacher Now* 4.6 (1982): 4–10.

Meri, La. *Dance as an Art-Form: Its History and Development.* New York, 1933.

Meri, La. *Dance Composition: The Basic Elements.* Lee, Mass., 1965.

Meri, La. *Spanish Dancing* (1948). Pittsfield, Mass., 1967.

Meri, La. *Dance Out the Answer.* New York, 1977.

Meri, La. *Total Education in Ethnic Dance.* New York, 1977.

ARCHIVE. The Dance Collection of the New York Public Library for the Performing Arts contains numerous files on La Meri's itinerary, productions, and publications, including "Tchaikovsky's *Swan Lake* in the Idiom of Indian Dance."

JUDY FARRAR BURNS

MESOPOTAMIA. The lands between the Tigris and Euphrates rivers have yielded archaeological finds that provide significant information about dance in the ancient Near East. This is the location of the earliest civilization, Sumer, which emerged as a theocracy about 3500 BCE. Dance was closely connected with the religions of ancient times. Drawings on pottery, minute ornamental sculptures, terra-cotta artifacts, and especially clay and stone cylinder seals (and seal impressions) yield a rich if incomplete picture of dance in ancient Mesopotamia.

Written evidence begins in the early third millennium BCE. Dance was depicted as arising from the lives of ordinary people, who used it in magic and worship. By means of the magical effects of dance, humans penetrated the world of the gods and other supernatural beings who controlled the forces of nature. In this way humans might win the gods' favor, avert the evil power of demons, become successful in hunting, bring rain for crops, or improve the conditions for life in the hereafter.

Dancers were usually male and probably magicians; later, they belonged to temple groups. Most often they danced unclothed, thus symbolizing the ritual purity of Mesopotamian priests.

In the earliest representations, however, women dancers also appear, usually clothed and most often performing circle dances. If nude, their pubic areas are marked with triangles.

Until approximately 3000 BCE the dancers' heads were covered. They often wore masks, usually representing animals or birds, which extended over the head and the upper torso. In dance, as in other art forms, symbolism predominated; different poses conveyed specific meanings, which may have changed over time.

Music and dance were linked from the earliest times by their roles in worship and magic. They were the main ritual components of the great Mesopotamian festivals and ceremonies recorded from 3000 BCE onward. In the second millennium BCE, dance began to incorporate foreign elements, a reflection of increased contact with the cultures and artistic styles of Egypt, Syria, and Persia (Iran).

The dancers were probably physically adept young men who trained with the musicians, wrestlers, and acrobats belonging to the temple. By 2000 BCE, dance had become so demanding that it could be performed only by professionals. Among imported dancers were African Pygmies, Nubians, and Libyans, who must have had special skills.

We have evidence of both solo and group dancing, as well as wrestling and acrobatics. There were dances performed by humans with animals and by trained solo animal performers. Dances can be further classified by the step techniques depicted, such as slapping dances and jumping dances—those in which both feet leave the ground. Musical accompaniment ranged from percussion (simple hand-clapping, sticks, drums, frame drums, and sistra, a kind of metal rattle) to stringed instruments (long-necked lute, lyre, and harp) and wind instruments (reed pipes). Wrestling and acrobatic performances might also be accompanied by drumming.

During the fifth millennium BCE, we know that circles of women had danced to bring rain, by lifting and lowering their joined hands. Such a scene is depicted on a neolithic ceramic sherd found in Samarra in northern Mesopotamia. On an Ubaid sherd from Tepe Gawra (also in the north), there is a nude man with knees bent and arms outstretched sideways and bent upwards at the elbow. This pose of the arms is also seen in later periods, for example, on a cylinder seal from the seventh century BCE.

We have only graphic documentation of rites incorporating dance for the earlier periods. As economies grew, artistic representations increased progressively through the Sumerian, the Old Babylonian, and the dynamic Mitanni periods. In addition, literary texts and economic documents contain references to temple dancers.

Ubaid Period. At the beginning of the Ubaid epoch, during the fourth millennium BCE, images of the genius-lord of animals, dancing with bent knees and surrounded by animals and snakes, appear on seals. A fragment of a vase (c.3000 BCE) from the Sumerian city of Tel Agrab depicts a group dance of naked women carrying frame drums; the women's pubic areas are indicated by triangles. Such scenes may represent a cult of fertility goddesses. Cylinder seals from the same period bear pictures of women clad in short garments, dancing around a feasting goddess. Another scene, from the decoration on the protruding end of a hairpin, shows a pair of female dancers in a pose that one can still see today. They dance face to face, each holding each other by one hand, with the other hand on the waist. A bronze sculpture in the round, astonishing for its artistic elaboration, shows two men balancing large pots on their heads while they wrestle, indicating the great skill of the performers.

MESOPOTAMIA. This drawing, taken from a cylinder seal dating from the Ubaid period, depicts dancing figures (at left) at a New Year festival. They are celebrating the ritual joining, or "holy marriage" (*hieros gamos*), of Sky Father and Earth Mother, enacted by the couple on the altar (at right). (Reprinted from Matoušová-Rajmová, 1993, fig. 7.)

Major religious and state festivals included dancing and singing. The New Year festival and the accompanying sacred marriage rites were enhanced by dances with music and song, which were performed to ensure fertility and prosperity in the coming year. Although male dancers were not at this time depicted as ithyphallic, all the dances were associated with the life cycle.

Akkad Period. The Akkad dynasty (c.2330–2150 BCE) brought forth a cult of political power and the high development of astrology. Wrestling and acrobatics were still popular and were now depicted in connection with flowing water. Kneeling standard-bearers depicting the lesser god Lahmu, accompanied by celestial symbols, appear to mark the advent of the new cult.

Isin-Larsa and Old Babylonian Periods. The Akkad dynasty was succeeded by the Isin-Larsa and Old Babylonian epochs (c.2000–1600 BCE), from which there survive many seals and terra-cotta plaques depicting elaborate rites and dances. Besides dances by women in circles, rows, or serpentines, there are also group dances by crowds of men, shown crossing one leg over the other. Both the solo and the pair jumping dance of older tradition are documented for the period 1000–1500 BCE. Widespread in Old Babylonian dance was the squat dance, in kneeling or half-kneeling position, which had appeared in earlier scenes of the taming of wild animals and in Akkadian scenes of standard-bearers performing rites. The step spread to neighboring countries in antiquity, and this kind of dance became the basis for the development of a certain style of Cossack dance. The male dancers in these depictions are never ithyphallic. Among the musicians and dancers were the temple prostitutes of the Ishtar cult, who wore bracelets, necklaces, and scant garments to cover the pelvic area, and sometimes carried timbrels or frame drums.

A dance of African Pygmies, the bent-knees or bobbing dance, spread to Mesopotamia; the dancers, who are almost always ithyphallic, performed grotesque movements of an erotic character. The dance with raised bent leg (often held by the hand at the ankle) called the foot-clutch appears in the third millennium in Mesopotamia; in the second millennium it was common in Egypt, but it appears rarely in other countries of the Near East at that time. Finds from the period provide evidence of great festivals, with a variety of dances, wrestling, acrobatics, dancing animals, and musical accompaniment.

Kassite Period. In the Kassite period (c.1550–1350 BCE), Old Babylonian dance scenes rarely appear. When northern Mesopotamia was annexed to the kingdom of Mitanni, the resultant Hurrian hegemony brought new

MESOPOTAMIA. In the top register of this drawing, from a cylinder seal of the Old Babylonian period, the central figure is performing a squat dance. He is shown in the pose typical of the "Russian dancer" in Mesopotamian art, so called because he is executing a movement similar to a *prisiadka*, a step in Russian folk dance. As he performs he raises his right arm in salute to the god seated on the throne (at left), who holds a ring and scepter as symbols of his power. Behind the dancer stands a bull-man holding a standard topped by a symbol for the sun. In the lower register of the drawing are shown animals in combat and a dragon swallowing a man. (Reprinted from Matoušová-Rajmová, 1978, fig. 6.)

dynamics to the arts. Numerous seals depict typically Mesopotamian dance scenes, now enriched by Egyptian, Syrian, and Elamite influences. The basic squat dance was performed solo and as a pair dance around a pole; it developed a complicated structure reminiscent of Egyptian dances. The ancient circle dances of women persisted, as they do today. A battle dance of men or demons was frequently performed. Acrobatics were enhanced by Elamite elements. The Mitannian dancers were usually nude but sometimes wore long, open kilts or short kilts with belt tassels.

Neo-Assyrian and Neo-Babylonian Periods. By Neo-Assyrian and Neo-Babylonian times (c.1000 BCE), the graphic arts ceased to depict dance. Sacred nudity appears to have been abandoned. On a cylinder seal from the seventh century BCE, a woman dancer with outstretched arms bent upward at the elbow chases bad spirits away from a sick man through the magical power of dance. This arm position is repeated through four millennia. In another representation, a male figure wearing a short decorated robe and supporting the winged Assyrian sun disk performs the squat dance.

Ancient Mesopotamian civilization came to an end during the eras of the Achaemenid Persians and the Seleucids. A Mesopotamian cylinder from the fourth century BCE heralds a new era; it depicts two dancers with clothes and movements showing Greek influence.

BIBLIOGRAPHY

Amiet, Pierre. *La glyptique mésopotamienne archaïque.* Paris, 1960.

Frankfort, Henri. *The Art and Architecture of the Ancient Orient.* 4th ed., rev. Harmondsworth, 1970.

Goff, Beatrice L. *Symbols of Prehistoric Mesopotamia.* New Haven, 1963.

Kilmer, Anne D. "Music and Dance in Ancient Mesopotamia." In *Civilizations of the Ancient Near East,* edited by Jack M. Sasson et al. New York, 1993.

Kramer, Samuel Noah. *The Sacred Marriage Rite.* Bloomington, 1975.

Matoušová-Rajmová, Marie. "Illustration de la danse sur les sceaux de l'époque babylonienne ancienne." *Archiv Orientální* 46 (1978).

Matoušová-Rajmová, Marie. "La position à génuflexion inachevée: Activité et danse." *Archiv Orientální* 47 (1979).

Matoušová-Rajmová, Marie. "Der Tanz bei magisch-medikalischer Behandlung eines Kranken." *Archiv Orientální* 55 (1987).

Matoušová-Rajmová, Marie. "Die Darstellung einer Krankenbeschwörung auf dem 'Grossen Aimlett.'" *Archiv Orientální* 57 (1989).

Matoušová-Rajmová, Marie. "Der Tanz auf kappadokischen Siegelbildern." *Archiv Orientální* 57 (1989).

Matoušová-Rajmová, Marie. "Die Tanzende Gottheit." *Archiv Orientální* 60 (1992).

Matoušová-Rajmová, Marie. "Die Tanzschulen im alten Orient." *Archiv Orientální* 60 (1992).

Matoušová-Rajmová, Marie. "Überlegungen zu Tanz, Kult und Magie." *Archiv Orientální* 61 (1993).

Parrot, André. *Tello: Vingt campagnes de fouilles, 1877–1933.* Paris, 1948.

MARIE MATOUŠOVÁ-RAJMOVÁ
Translated from Czech

MESSEL, OLIVER (born 13 January 1905 in Cuckfield, England, died 13 July 1978 in Bridgetown, Barbados), British scenery and costume designer. Although Messel did not design many ballets, his sets and costumes for the Sadler's Wells Ballet's landmark production of *The Sleeping Beauty* (1946) were lauded as "one of the great theater designs of our century" by the American designer Oliver Smith, who later commissioned him to revive his designs for American Ballet Theatre in 1976. Messel's flair for baroque magnificence and his painstaking attention to detail combined to create an effect of richness and elegance that was well suited to Marius Petipa's ballet to Tchaikovsky's music.

Educated at Eton and the Slade School of Art, Messel was initially interested in masks. One of his first professional jobs was making masks for Léonide Massine's *Zéphire et Flore* (1925) for its London performances by Diaghilev's Ballets Russes. Early in 1926 Messel received his first commission from the producer Charles B. Cochran, for whom he worked for several years. In

MESSEL. Costume design for the role of Bluebeard for the 1976 revival of *The Sleeping Beauty* by American Ballet Theatre. (Photograph by Vincent Miraglia; from the Dance Collection, New York Public Library for the Performing Arts.)

Cochran's *Revues* of 1930 and 1931, Messel designed sets and costumes for choreography by the young George Balanchine. His first full-length assignment was Cochran's production of *Helen* (1932), a new version of Jacques Offenbach's *La Belle Hélène,* choreographed by Massine.

Messel designed his first full-length ballet, David Lichine's *Francesca da Rimini,* in 1937. In 1942 he designed Robert Helpmann's *Comus.* For the 1946 London version of *The Sleeping Beauty,* his best-known work for ballet, he created what Richard Buckle called a "baroque Never-Never Land . . . seen through veils of rococo, Romantic, Edwardian and 1920s nostalgia." Although he revised some of these designs for American Ballet Theatre in 1976, his last work for ballet was Frederick Ashton's *Homage to the Queen* (1953). He also designed films, plays—including the Old Vic's *A Midsummer Night's Dream* (1937), with choreography by Ninette de Valois—operas, and architecture, and he painted portraits.

BIBLIOGRAPHY. Oliver Messel, *Stage Designs and Costumes* (London, 1933), contains sketches and production photographs of his work up to 1932, as well as a fine essay by James Laver. Arthur Boys, "Oliver Messel—English Designer," *Souvenirs de Ballet* 1 (1949), provides interesting details on Messel's working procedures. See as well Charles Castle, *Oliver Messel* (London, 1986), and the exhibition catalog *Oliver Messel,* edited by Roger Pinkham (London, 1983).

SUSAN AU

MESSERER, ASAF (Asaf Mikhailovich Messerer; born 6 [19] November 1903 in Vilnius, Lithuania, died 7 March 1992 in Moscow), dancer and teacher. Messerer studied at the Moscow School of Choreography from 1919 to 1921 under Aleksandr Gorsky. Upon graduation he joined the Bolshoi Ballet, in which he was a leading soloist until 1954. As an artist Messerer was one of the foremost champions of the realist principles of Soviet ballet. As a dancer he displayed a virility, virtuosic technique, refinement of classical dance forms, the finely honed skills of a creative artist, and a zest for life. He greatly refined the techniques of male dancing.

Having an extraordinarily broad artistic range, Messerer performed romantic, lyrical-comic, heroic, character, and grotesque roles in both the classical and contemporary repertories. These included the roles of Colas in *La Fille Mal Gardée,* Ziegfried in *Swan Lake,* and Basil in *Don Quixote,* all in versions choreographed by Gorsky; the title role in Michel Fokine's *Petrouchka;* Philippe in Vasily Vainonen's *The Flames of Paris;* the Little Chinese God and the Juggler in *The Red Poppy,* choreographed by Vasily Tikhomirov and Lev Lashchilin; the Fanatic in Igor Moiseyev's version of *Salammbô;* Nurali in Rostislav Zakharov's *The Fountain of Bakhchisarai;* and others.

Messerer began his career as a choreographer in 1925 when he produced the ballet *The Fairy Doll* at the Moscow School of Choreography. His later productions included *La Fille Mal Gardée* (1930, Bolshoi Theater, in collaboration with Moiseyev), *The Sleeping Beauty* (1936, 1952, Bolshoi Theater), *Swan Lake* (1937, Bolshoi Theater; 1951 and 1969, National Theater of Opera and Ballet, Budapest; 1967 and 1971, Belarussian Theater of Opera and Ballet, Minsk; 1981, National Theater of Opera and Ballet, Sofia), Yulus Yuzelyunas's *On the Seashore* (1953, Lithuanian Theater of Opera and Ballet, Vilnius), Léo Delibes's *Coppélia* (1974, Wielki Theater, Warsaw), and Yuri Ter-Osipov's *Spring in Tajikistan* (1972, Aini Theater of Opera and Ballet, Dushanbe).

In *Ballet Class* (also called *Class Concert*), a one-act ballet set to the music of Dmitri Shostakovich, Aleksandr Glazunov, and Anatol Liadov, Messerer artistically brought together the principles of the Soviet school of classical dance. *Ballet Class* was presented to audiences in 1960 on the stage of the Moscow School of Choreography, in 1961 at Brussels, in 1963 at the Bolshoi Theater, in 1972 in Dushanbe, and in 1973 in Kiev. Messerer also produced a cluster of concert numbers regularly performed by Bolshoi company artists: Mikhail Glinka's *Melody,* Sergei Rachmaninov's *Vernal Floods,* Gluck's *Melody,* and others. He was much involved in concert activities, going on frequent tours of the Soviet Union and abroad. *The Football Player,* a concert miniature that Messerer composed and performed to the music of Aleksandr Tsfasman, won general acclaim among theatergoers. In it he created the image of a contemporary idol, the Soviet athlete.

Active in teaching for more than sixty years, Messerer made a substantial contribution to Soviet choreographic studies. Between 1921 and 1923 he taught night courses at the Bolshoi Theater and at the Lunacharsky Theater Technicum, and from 1923 until 1960 he taught at the Moscow ballet school. He worked as a teacher and choreographer with the Théâtre Royal de la Monnaie in Brussels in 1961–1962 and lectured in Melbourne in 1977. From 1943 onward he directed the Class of Perfection at the Bolshoi Theater. In the 1980s and in 1990 Messerer was in the United States, teaching and staging some of his ballets in Pittsburgh and Chicago.

MESSERER. The athletic Messerer was a member of a family of great performing artists, including the ballerinas Sulamith Messerer (his sister) and Maya Plisetskaya (his niece). His exceptional virtuosity and elevation are evident in this photograph of his own choreography for the concert number *Football Player* (1924). (Photograph from the Dance Collection, New York Public Library for the Performing Arts.)

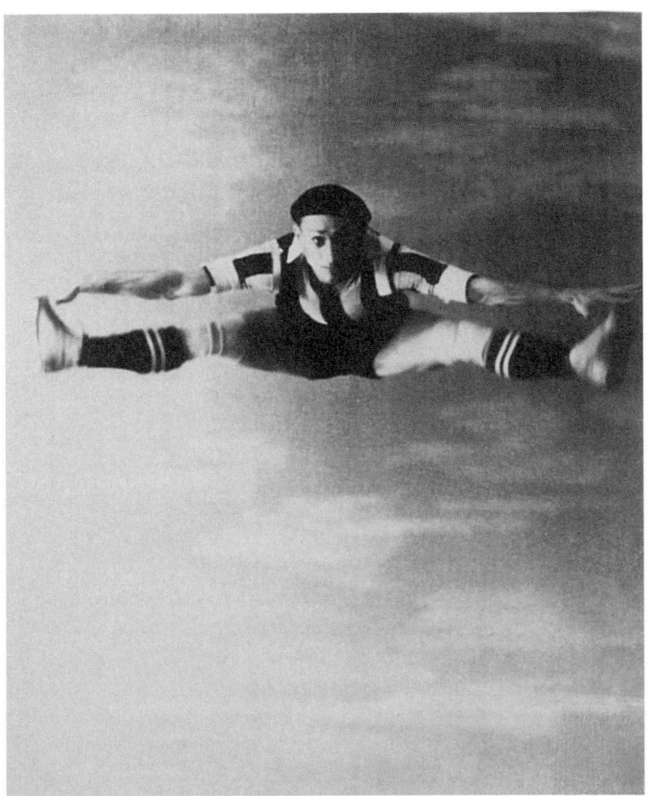

MESSERER. As Basil in the 1928 Bolshoi production of *Don Quixote,* Messerer displays his strong elevation. (Photograph from the Dance Collection, New York Public Library for the Performing Arts.)

Messerer's classes won international recognition. In response to demands by ballet artists, dance teachers, ballet scholars, and critics, during many of the Bolshoi Ballet's foreign tours he conducted open dance classes, in which he and his pupils demonstrated the special features and achievements of the Soviet school of classical dance. His classes were notable for their variety of instructive combinations, active use of *épaulement,* and small *terre-à-terre* movements combined with big jumps. At first, the technique did not seem problematic, but difficulties were introduced logically and sequentially. The class, which focused on developing choreographic themes, was remarkable for its steady pace and inner dynamics.

Messerer's pedagogical method resulted from a combination of his talents as a performer, choreographer, and teacher. He mixed fantasy, a broad and analytical knowledge of the systems of classical dance—its laws, principles, methods, and regulations—and personal perception in his teaching. His work contributed to the development of Soviet choreographic pedagogy. During his long career Messerer taught a great many of the foremost names in Russian ballet, among them, Galina Ulanova, Maya Plisetskaya, Mikhail Gabovich, Nikolai Fadeyechev, Maris Liepa, Ekaterina Maximova, Vladimir Vasiliev, Mikhail Lavrovsky, Yuri Vladimirov, Ludmila Semenyaka, Alla Mikhalchenko, Malika Sabirova, Viacheslav Gordeyev, Boris Akimov, Aleksandr Bogatyrev, Aleksei Fadeyechev, and Yuri Vasyuchenko. Messerer, who in 1976 was awarded the title of People's Artist of the Soviet Union, and in 1941 and 1947 won Soviet Union State prizes, wrote many articles on ballet and was the author of the 1967 textbook *Classes in Classical Ballet* (translated in 1975) and a book of memoirs, *Dance, Thought, and Times* (1979).

BIBLIOGRAPHY

Bocharnikova, Ella. "Asaf Messerer." In Messerer's *Uroki klassicheskogo tantsa.* Moscow, 1967.

Bocharnikova, Ella. "Fenomen Messerer." *Sovetskii balet,* no. 5 (1982).

Greskovic, Robert. "Ballet, Barre, and Center, on the Bookshelf." *Ballet Review* 6.2 (1977–1978): 1–56.

Messerer, Asaf. *Classes in Classical Ballet* (1967). Translated by Oleg Briansky. Garden City, N.Y., 1975.

Roslavleva, Natalia. *Era of the Russian Ballet* (1966). New York, 1979.

Swift, Mary Grace. *The Art of the Dance in the U.S.S.R.* Notre Dame, 1968.

Volkov, Nikolai D. "Asaf Messerer." In *The Soviet Ballet,* by Yuri Slonimsky et al. New York, 1947.

ELLA V. BOCHARNIKOVA
Translated from Russian

METHODOLOGIES IN THE STUDY OF DANCE.

[*To survey the uses of organized systems of study in examination and analysis of dance, this entry comprises articles focusing on sociology, cultural context, linguistics, anthropology, ethnology, and new areas of inquiry.*]

Sociology

The sociology of dance is concerned with the creation, performance, and meaning of all forms of dance in modern societies. Such societies are predominantly urban and metropolitan, with industrial economies whose main features are highly differentiated systems for the division of labor and socioeconomic stratification. Within these systems, considerable geographical and social mobility is typical. Their cultures are complex and heterogeneous, often with a variety of subcultures differentiated by generation, sex, class, and ethnicity. Among this variety of cultural traditions and practices verbal and literate modes predominate over the nonverbal and visual. One consequence of this is a pronounced tendency to marginalize the arts. Dance, as a nonverbal mode of communication and expression that inheres in body movement, has been even more marginalized than the other arts.

This is one reason why the sociology of dance has been a neglected area of study until recently; however, it has resources in better-developed related disciplines. The most significant of these is dance anthropology, in which a considerable amount of ethnographic research on dance in nonindustrial societies has been done. Initially this work resulted from the need to include analyses of the significance of dance in more general studies, which led in turn to the development of a subdiscipline concerned with classifying dance genres both within and across societies, and with discovering the meaning of dance through the application of models of human communication and movement. Although anthropology provides a clear model for the development of dance sociology, industrial societies are significantly different from the societies typically studied by anthropologists, and dance is usually a much less central social activity within the former. Exceptions to this generalization are found in certain subcultures, usually defined by generation, sex, or ethnic identity; for these groups, dance is a significant expression of their uniqueness and is sometimes a response to the difficulties that restrict their access to wealth and power.

There are four other disciplines that provide important resources for dance sociology. The first is dance history, which provides a basis for analyzing dance in the socioeconomic and political contexts of its creation and performance, together with an understanding of the development of its various forms in modern societies. Second is the study of the kinesic, proxemic, and linguistic components of human interaction, which provide analogues for the systematic analysis of the gestural and spatial dimensions of movement as a communicative form. This work derives from ethology (the study of animal behavior), social psychology, and cross-cultural anthropology, and has been mainly microsociological so far. The third discipline is the critical aesthetics of dance, which is specifically concerned with the meaning of dance as an art and is relevant to dance sociology inasmuch as it provides for an analysis of dance symbolism. Fourth, there is the practice of dance itself, which includes the work of dance thinkers and dance makers, who provide valuable insights into the structures of meaning in dance works.

The first three of these disciplines depend heavily on verbal models for studying human expression and communication, while dance is nonverbal body movement developed to a high degree of skill as a social activity and an art. Since the predominantly verbal cultures of industrial societies are crucial to the legitimation of their economic and political orders, the nonverbal character of dance may set it in opposition to the dominant order. It is therefore important to be aware of the danger of overdependence on linguistic models for the analysis of the relations between dance and society: to verbalize the nonverbal threatens the power of dance's expressive critique of the social order. Sociological analysis of dance needs to work with methods that are sensitive to dance's nonverbal character.

There is a further significant distinction within dance sociology between analytical and socio-institutional approaches. An analytical approach depends on an intrinsic, interpretive method. It seeks to analyze dance in terms of the symbolic and semiotic structures through which it generates meaning. We need critical aesthetic perspectives, especially in the study of modern Western dance, to understand the relation of dance to mundane human movement as a mode of communication.

By contrast, a socio-institutional approach to dance depends on an extrinsic and to some extent deterministic viewpoint. It seeks to explain dance in terms of the social backgrounds of creators, performers, and audiences, and the social conditions of dance productions, presentation, and performance. The distinction between the two approaches is itself analytical: an adequate dance sociology would contain elements of both, because the concepts and methods of each approach are rooted in the major traditions of classical and contemporary sociological inquiry. Within these traditions also lie the reasons for sociology's neglect of dance. The two problems, both central to sociocultural life, are art and the body.

Dance, like all the other arts, enacts symbolically the making of society itself in that it generates symbols that are meaningful in a specific cultural context and comprehensible to an audience. Dance is distinctive sociologically because of its medium, human body movement. Just as industrial society marginalizes art, it also marginalizes the qualities of human expression that it subordinates to its dominant rationalism, which values the conscious over the unconscious, the material over the ideal, the verbal over the nonverbal, and the mind over the body. In this sense, dance may be seen as doubly marginalized—as an art, and as an art of body movement. Dance thus presents a dual challenge to the sociocultural order, to both the dominance of scientific rationalism and the supremacy of verbal communication. In considering the role of the arts in contemporary culture, we may accordingly treat dance as centrally important. This also suggests why the everyday practice of dance is often so vital to the disadvantaged: it enables them to explore alternative ways of being through expressive modes not appropriated by the normative culture. Conversely, we can understand why certain forms of dance art are subsidized to sustain the exclusivity of their training and performance: they can be used to legitimate the hierarchy within the existing power structure. The difference between the two cases points up the central analytical significance of the body for dance sociology. In the first case, body movement is a means of asserting identity for groups with limited access to other forms of expression. In the second, the high degree of discipline and the lengthy dominance of elite groups can support formal training and the possibilities it generates. The disciplining of nonverbal movement actually reinforces the superiority of verbal expression.

The human body has thus become a vehicle for symbols that articulate the conditions of human existence; the human capacities for sociability and symbolism are interdependent. Realizing this, anthropology and sociology conceive of all bodily activities as socially regulated. The body can be seen unequivocally as a social rather than a natural phenomenon. Any natural activities or predispositions to activity in the body are significant only insofar as they are culturally controlled in order to articulate movements that express meaning. The body and its movements can be analyzed as semiotic and symbolic modes of social expression. From this point of view, the naturalistic conception of the body becomes less meaningful. Biological and physiological elements remain, but superimposed on them are the features of bodily activity controlled by the individual's socialization and education. More important are the body's social dimensions, which are encoded in the techniques for consciously articulating movement. These are related to the body's biology and physiology through human psychology, hence the role of consciousness. All articulation is initially conscious and creative, but from the earliest stages of movement it is converted through socialization into everyday habits. Everyday movement is learned; it carries encoded prescriptions for communicative movement specific to the individual's culture. The result is not conscious movement on which we can reflect, precisely because it is habitual and regular. On this basis we can generalize about movement sociologically and study it kinesically. The problem is, everyday movement is so deeply embedded in its culture that people tend to view their learned movement habits as innate or biologically determined.

This problem arises in dance analyses that rely too heavily on models derived from verbal language. Such models are tempting not only because of their analytical sophistication, but also because the critical interpretation of dance requires the use of language. To succumb to this temptation, however, is to miss the point of dance in two senses. First, in a straightforward sense, dance is nonverbal. Its very point is to explore and express the dimension of human communication and meaning that remains autonomous from words. Second, dance is a major and still largely unexplored route through the maze of cultural codes that constitute the body as a social phenomenon. Dance challenges the reduction of movement to a merely natural activity. Analysis of dance, therefore, should question the logical bias of Western culture manifest in the dominance of verbal over nonverbal expression and should examine its implications. Dance provides a double challenge to this dominance. As art it can propose alternatives to the existing sociocultural order; as body movement, practiced in conscious and creative ways, it celebrates nonverbal expressions of experience and thereby challenges verbal codings of culture.

Dance sociology has emerged during the past two decades in Britain as one of a number of responses to fundamental changes in the structure and culture of contemporary industrial society. The most important changes in relation to dance are the changing relation between work and nonwork; the increasing multicultural diversity of society due to immigration; and the widespread recognition of the body's significance as a medium of communication and expression. Dance sociology's most important task is to explain the significance of dance as a mode of communication in its sociocultural context. To accomplish this, we need a critical aesthetics of dance to differentiate dance as a performing art from mundane movement; we need anthropology to provide the ethnographic data from which we can draw cross-cultural comparisons between genres and contexts of dance; and we need history to locate the origins of the present significance of dance in society. Dance sociology also relies on the epistemology of dance techniques and on institutions of dance education and training to provide the conceptual apparatus for analyzing dance and movement at all levels of social interaction.

The first course in dance sociology was taught in 1978 at the Laban Centre for Movement and Dance in London. Its practical application has stimulated the development of other courses at the center, including a professional diploma in community dance launched in 1982 and undergraduate and postgraduate option (elective) courses in dance politics in 1992. The course has influenced interest in the application of dance in social, health, and community services, and studies of dance in contemporary society.

BIBLIOGRAPHY

Bateson, Gregory. *Steps to an Ecology of Mind.* New York, 1972.

Benthall, Jonathan, and Ted Polhemus, eds. *The Body as a Medium of Expression.* New York, 1975.

Birdwhistell, Ray L. *Kinesics and Context.* Philadelphia, 1970.

Blacking, John, ed. *The Anthropology of the Body.* London, 1977.

Boas, Franziska, ed. *The Function of Dance in Human Society.* 2d ed. Brooklyn, 1972.

Brinson, Peter. "Scholastic Tasks of a Sociology of Dance." *Dance Research* 1 (Autumn 1983): 59–68.

Brinson, Peter. *Dance as Education: Towards a National Dance Culture.* Falmer, 1991.

Brown, Jean Morrison, ed. *The Vision of Modern Dance.* Princeton, 1979.

Douglas, Mary. *Purity and Danger.* New York, 1966.

Douglas, Mary. *Natural Symbols.* New York, 1970.

Douglas, Mary. *Implicit Meanings.* London, 1975.

Featherstone, Mike, et al., eds. *The Body: Social Process and Cultural Theory.* London, 1991.

Filmer, Paul. "Durkheim, Jung, and Symbolism: The Necessity of a Sociology of the Unconscious." *Harvest* 23 (1977).

Foley, Catherine E. "Irish Traditional Step-Dance in North Kerry: A Contextual and Structural Analysis." Ph.D. diss., Laban Centre, London, 1988.

Foster, Susan Leigh. *Reading Dancing: Bodies and Subjects in Contemporary American Dance.* Berkeley, 1986.

Goodman, Nelson. *Languages of Art.* Indianapolis, 1968.

Hall, Edward T. *The Silent Language.* Garden City, N.Y., 1959.

Hall, Edward T. *The Hidden Dimension.* Garden City, N.Y., 1966.

Hanna, Judith Lynne. *To Dance Is Human.* Austin, 1979.

Hanna, Judith Lynne. *The Performer–Audience Connection: Emotion to Metaphor in Dance and Society.* Austin, 1983.

Hebdige, Dick. *Subculture: The Meaning of Style.* London, 1979.

Hertz, Robert. "La prééminence de la main droite." In Hertz's *Death and the Right Hand.* Translated by Rodney Needham and Claudia Needham. Glencoe, Ill., 1960.

Key, Mary Ritchie, ed. *The Relationship of Verbal and Nonverbal Communication.* The Hague, 1980.

Langer, Susanne K. *Feeling and Form.* New York, 1953.

Mauss, Marcel. "Techniques of the Body." *Economy and Society* 2.1 (1973).

McRobbie, Angela, and Mica Nava, eds. *Gender and Generation.* London, 1984.

Polhemus, Ted, ed. *Social Aspects of the Human Body.* London, 1978.

Prickett, Stacey. "Marxism, Modernism, and Realism: Politics and Aesthetics in the Rise of American Modern Dance." Ph.D. diss., Laban Centre, London, 1992.

Radcliffe-Brown, A. R. *The Andaman Islanders.* Cambridge, 1922.

Royce, Anya Peterson. *The Anthropology of Dance.* Bloomington, 1977.

Scheflen, Albert E. *Body Language and the Social Order.* Englewood Cliffs, N.J., 1972.

Sheets-Johnstone, Maxine. *The Phenomenology of Dance.* New York, 1966.

Spencer, Paul, ed. *Society and the Dance.* Cambridge, 1985.

Stokes, Adrian. *To-Night the Ballet.* London, 1934.

Thomas, Helen, ed. *Dance, Gender, and Culture.* New York, 1993.

Thomas, Helen. *Dance, Modernity, and Culture: Explorations in the Sociology of Dance.* London, 1994.

Turner, Bryan S. *The Body and Society.* Oxford, 1984.

Willis, Paul E. *Profane Culture.* London, 1978.

PAUL FILMER

Cultural Context

The element that broadly distinguishes dances among groups of humans, and human dancing from other animals' dancelike movements, is the impact of culture, or the cumulative values, beliefs, norms, and rules shared by a group and learned through communication. Culture is wider in scope than that embodied in any one person's competency. Each individual belongs to several overlapping subcultures, such as ethnic group, gender, socioeconomic class, and occupation; these share in the larger culture and also have their own particular values and beliefs. For example, in late nineteenth-century Poland, most people shared certain values, but low-income people enjoyed the polka while the elite preferred the polonaise. This pattern was perpetuated among Polish immigrants in the United States.

As humans evolved, the programmed-action sequences characteristic of other animals—for example, a bird's mating display—tended to be replaced by actions in which cultural learning and individual choice played a greater role than instinct. Through the action sequence called dance, humans have the capacity to communicate abstract concepts, to express emotion, to project experience beyond their own, to alter thought and feeling, and to transform them symbolically.

Through cultural communication, members of a group acquire mental "maps" that enable them to act correctly and to interpret what they observe. The textual and contextual dimensions of dance—who dances what, why, how, when, where, and with and for whom, as well as the audience's role—are part of a group's cultural heritage. Innovative dance that challenges the cultural norm either disappears quickly or becomes part of the culture.

The *textual* pattern of dance refers to the system of ordering movement (the cumulative set of rules or range of permissible gesture, locomotion, and posture with various body parts, performed in time and space with energy) and the associated meaning. *Contextual* pattern, by contrast, refers to the catalyst for dance—whether participation is required, expected, or voluntary; whether dancers are recruited through ascription (the position into which they were born) or achievement in some area; the process of dance production; whether the audience participates (with a significant or limited role) or keeps its distance from the dancer; and the social impact of performance. European classical ballet, for example, has a "map" that specifies five positions, pointed toes, years of training, distinctive movements for men and women, performance in a theater setting, voluntary paying viewers separate from the dancers, and an audience that shows appreciation through applause.

Some cultural maps, such as those of the Nigerian Igbo (Ibo) and the African-American, admit or even demand innovation and individual creative expression. Other cultures are more collectively oriented, and the transmission of unadulterated forms of dance take precedence. When cultures come into conflict, the traditional forms may be supplanted by challengers, the old and new may coexist or syncretistic forms may emerge from the blending of different concepts and expressive forms.

In considering the relationship between dance context and text, a key question is whether dance reflects what is, as a validation or criticism, or whether it suggests what might be, through reversing usual actions, mocking the status quo, or presenting innovation.

As a specific verbal language has culturally patterned words, sentences, and paragraphs, a specific dance has culturally patterned movement vocabulary, steps, and phrases. Because the meaning of movement is culturally patterned, dance is *not* a universal "language." A culturally mixed audience does not understand many of the dancers' intended messages; their perceptions of the same dance sequence onstage might sometimes be diametrically opposed.

Cognition is one dimension of dance, emotion is another. Both intertwine, for culture influences how to express and respond to feelings. Reciprocity of movement and emotion in dance varies—a performer may feel a particular emotion and express it through dancing. As a stimulus to dance, a dancer may recreate an emotion through remembering earlier situations in which it was experienced. A dancer may recollect emotion and express it symbolically, as the philosopher Susanne Langer argued. Dancing may induce emotion. And audience reaction to an ongoing dance may evoke the performer's emotions, which in turn affects the dancing.

Cultural patterns affect the status, purpose, and functions of dance in a society, whether it is an integral part of life, as in traditional non-Western societies, or is sequestered in the context of recreation, art, or religion, as in the West. A culture's views of mind and body, especially attitudes toward the display of emotions and sexuality, also determine whether dance is prominent in a society.

The dance's purpose may be determined by the dancers seeking social interaction in ethnic or folk genres, staged ethnic or folk, popular (common among the dominant culture of a society), or ritual dance genres. The dancer may try to affect the social or physical environment, to deal with power and authority, to work through individual or group problems therapeutically, to reach an altered state of consciousness for religious or secular goals, to earn a livelihood, or to acquire dance skills. Rather than initiating and doing a performance, a dancer may be acted upon by a supernatural entity in a state of becoming, or in another degree of altered state of consciousness such as supernatural possession.

Dance is often part of a culture's inventory of signs to identify and rank individuals and social groups (by ethnicity, gender, occupation, politics, or religion) and to maintain their boundaries. Humans create social taxonomies by using signs already in existence, producing new ones, or destroying old ones. Dance signs may promote self-identity, prescribe social values and roles, and evoke emotion that rallies people to action. Dancing is one of many media for educating both young and old about their sex roles and about patterns of dominance and submission in the economic, political, and spiritual realms.

Understanding a culture's dances usually requires several methods. Reliance on cultural members' verbal explanations alone may be inadequate because informants may not want to talk about certain topics or may lack knowledge. Performing the dances of an indigenous group to elicit the cultural group's aesthetic response may gain approval for an outsider but be an inadequate performance for an insider. Moreover, criteria for insiders often differ according to age, gender, or some other category. Many features of dance generally lie beyond the conscious awareness of dancers and viewers. Frequently in American and in African cultures, social dancers do not know the names of specific steps in such dances as the waltz, in rock-and-roll, disco, highlife, or *nkwa*. Just as grammarians and linguists name and define phenomena and syntax elements in verbal language, movement analysts name and describe comparable elements in dance. Even highly trained movement analysts, however, may describe the same dance differently; accurate and speedy notation of dance as it is performed may be difficult. Performers may present a dance only once during a research visit and may be unable or unwilling to replicate the performance for a notator. Because of such problems, researchers have preserved dancing on film and video; however, what is filmed and how it is filmed are culturally focused, selective processes.

Notation systems exist for analyzing the physical movement of dance—for example, Labanotation, Benesh notation, and Eskhol-Wachmann notation. One can probe for meaning in a culture's dance by using a semantic grid with devices and spheres of conveying meaning in movement (see Hanna, 1987). In probing meaning, the grid can be imposed on the whole dance and used to focus on smaller units to clarify informants' verbalizations and researchers' observations.

At least six symbolic devices exist for conveying meaning that may be used in dance.

1. A *concretization* is movement that produces the outward aspect of something, such as warrior dances displaying maneuvers of advance and retreat.
2. An *icon* represents most characteristics of something and is responded to as if it were what it represents; illustrative is a possessed person manifesting a deity through dancing and being revered as the god.
3. A *stylization* encompasses arbitrary and conventional gestures or movements, such as the Western dancer pointing to the heart as a sign of love.
4. A *metonym* is a motional conceptualization of one thing representing another of which it is a part, or with which it is associated; an example is a romantic duet representing a marriage.
5. The expression of one thought, experience, or phenomenon in place of another that it resembles in order to suggest an analogy is a *metaphor,* the bringing together of different domains in often unexpected and creative ways; thus, an animal fairy tale refers to analogous behavior among humans.
6. An *actualization* is a portrayal of one or several of a dancer's usual roles, such as a king dancing as king and being honored.

The devices for encapsulating meaning in dance seem to operate within one or more of eight spheres.

1. An example of the meaning of dance being in the dance *event* is found when people attend a dance to be seen socially, the dancing itself being incidental.
2. The meaning of dance may be in the sphere of the total human *body in action,* as in an individual's self-presentation.
3. The *whole pattern of performance,* which may emphasize structure, style, feeling, or drama, may be the locus of meaning.
4. Meaning may be centered in the *sequence of unfolding movement,* including who does what to whom, when, where, and how during the dance.
5. Specific *movements* and how they are performed may be meaningfully significant, as when a male dancer parodies a woman.
6. The *intermesh of movements* with other communication modes such as speech or costume may be where meaning lies.
7. Meaning may be in the sphere of dance as a *vehicle for another medium,* as when dance serves as a backdrop for a performer's poetry or rap recitation.
8. The sphere of meaning may be centered in *presence,* an emotional sensuality, raw animality, charisma, or "the magic of dance."

One can grasp a culture's conception of gender roles by observing the movements men and women perform. In most kinds of dance, for example, there was traditionally differentiated movements for each sex. Western ballet, for example, specified that only males support and lift females. Today, however, with challenges to male dominance, even in ballet men may also lift other men, and women may perform what were once considered men's movements. Within the global perspective, dance and gender are associated in a variety of ways that are not always mutually exclusive. Aphrodisiac dancing may promote courtship and fertility in the context of marriage. Alternatively, dance may lure a sexual partner in a licit premarital or extramarital situation, in a respectable or a disreputable vein, or it may entice illicitly.

Dance is frequently an element of the process by which people attract the power of the supernatural to the human world and reach out to the holy realm of ancestors, spirits, and gods. As a part of ritual constructions of reality, dance reenacts myths so that people can understand the world and operate in it. Social, political, and economic roles are often legitimated through divine sanction as the danced-out lives of anthropomorphic deities provide models. Dance is commonly part of worship, as illustrated by biblical-era dance that praised God. In some cultures, dance is the vehicle through which an individual as self or other (masked, possessed, or both) becomes a conduit of extraordinary power.

Dance may be a medium to reverse a debilitating condition caused by the supernatural or to prepare an individual or group to reach a religiously defined ideal state through rites of passage or rituals for death, curing, and prevention. Some cultures draw on dance as an activating agent to give oneself temporarily to a supernatural entity. Performance of a specific dance may indicate that the supernatural has invaded and overwhelmed the individual. A third kind of possession involves initiation, consecration, and the playing of a deity, during which time the dancer becomes deified, as in India's Rām Līlās, rituals honoring the god Rāma. Dancers may also be possessed by a supernatural essence. Some cultures spawn external transformations of the individual to embody the supernatural in masquerade dances. The Dogon of Mali have some seventy-eight different masks; the "Storied House" mask rises more than ten feet above the head of the dancer.

As a medium of political thought and action, dance empowers performers and beholders in various ways. Dance often validates and re-creates leadership. For example, the Swazi in Africa believe their own movements in the warrior dance keep their king alive and healthy; at certain times, the king himself must dance. Dance may also be a symbolic arena in which men compete for power: the Maring of Papua New Guinea, use massed dancing of visitors to convey information about the support the hosts might expect from them in later aggression. Competitive dance teams reflect their sponsors' power and authority among the Venda, Tutsi, and other groups in Africa. Some warriors prepare for war—psychologically and physically—through dance.

Many peoples use dance for social control. The Gikuyu (Kikuyu) of eastern Africa promulgated a new constitution through dance. Among the African Bakwele, masked dancers both communicate norms and enforce law and order as representatives of the spirits. Dance may serve to release and neutralize social tensions among those in a subordinated status (slaves, an underclass, migrant workers) and thereby perform a politically stabilizing function. Aggressive dance may express dangerous impulses in a comparatively harmless way. Veiled threats of power alternatives presented through dances that reverse roles of class, rank, and gender may help ameliorate or constrain the excesses of political leadership. Dance may also broadcast political concepts or incidents and lobby for redress and transformation. Stylistic choice may be a political statement, as in the postcolonial nationalist promotion of India's classical dance, which had fallen into disrepute during centuries of Muslim and Christian cultural imperialism.

The potency of dance in the political realm is exemplified by the banning of dances. For example, the *petro* was banned in Haiti because of its association with slave insurrections, and the high life was banned during the Nigerian war because of its commentary on current events. Totalitarian countries typically supervise both the occurrence and nature of dance performances.

How does a dance culture, with its distinctive genre, style, and aesthetics, come into existence? How is it transmitted? Some societies perpetuate their dance culture without self-conscious transmission effort, but others have intentional teaching programs. Informal learning occurs through observation and imitation; Inuit (Eskimo) hunters of the Arctic mimic their prey, and others imitate the hunters, who help them dance by using oral cues. Formal learning occurs through instruction by experts, teachers, tutors, and peers in schools, classes, groups, and by individualized instruction; ballet is a formal system, but here, too, observation and encouraged imitation serve the students. Not only is knowledge transmitted from adult to child or teacher to student, but children sometimes create their own dances.

In sum, the variety of dance manifestations depends on culture. Culture distinguishes human dance from other animals' dancelike behavior and shapes a society's use of dance in gender and other role socializations, in religious practice, and in political action. Both conservative and dynamic, culture develops in complex ways, often beyond individual awareness.

BIBLIOGRAPHY

Ager, Lynne Price. "Eskimo Dance and Cultural Values in an Alaskan Village." *Dance Research Journal* 8 (Fall–Winter 1975–1976): 7–12.

Cashion, Susan Valerie. "Dance Ritual and Cultural Values in a Mexican Village: Festival of Santo Santiago." Ph.D. diss., Stanford University, 1983.

Davies, J. G. *Liturgical Dance: An Historical, Theological and Practical Handbook.* London, 1984.

Dragu, Margaret, and A. S. A. Harrison. *Revelations: Essays on Striptease and Sexuality.* London, Ontario, 1988.

Gell, Alfred. *Metamorphosis of the Cassowaries: Umeda Society, Language, and Ritual.* London, 1975.

Hanna, Judith Lynne. "Toward Semantic Analysis of Movement Behavior." *Semiotica* 25.1–2 (1979): 77–110.

Hanna, Judith Lynne. "Is Dance Music? Resemblances and Relationships." *World of Music* 24.1 (1982): 57–71.

Hanna, Judith Lynne. *The Performer-Audience Connection: Emotion to Metaphor in Dance and Society.* Austin, 1983.

Hanna, Judith Lynne. "Dance and Religion." In *Encyclopedia of Religion.* New York, 1985.

Hanna, Judith Lynne. "Interethnic Communication in Children's Own Dance, Play, and Protest." *International and Intercultural Communication Annual* 10 (1986): 176–198.

Hanna, Judith Lynne. *To Dance Is Human: A Theory of Nonverbal Communication* (1979). Chicago, 1987.

Hanna, Judith Lynne. *Dance and Stress: Resistance, Reduction, and Euphoria.* New York, 1988.

Hanna, Judith Lynne. *Dance, Sex, and Gender: Signs of Identity, Dominance, Defiance, and Desire.* Chicago, 1988.

Hanna, Judith Lynne. "The Representation and Reality of Divinity in Dance." *Journal of the American Academy of Religion* 56.2 (1988): 501–526.

Hanna, Judith Lynne. "African Dance Frame by Frame: Revelation of Sex Roles through Distinctive Feature Analysis and Comments on Field Research, Film, and Notation." *Journal of Black Studies* 19 (June 1989): 422–441.

Hanna, Judith Lynne. "The Anthropology of Dance." In *Dance: Current Selected Research,* vol. 1, edited by Lynnette Y. Overby and James H. Humphrey. New York, 1989.

Hazzard-Gordon, Katrina. *Jookin': The Rise of Social Dance Formations in African-American Culture.* Philadelphia, 1990.

Johnston, Thomas F. "Alaskan Eskimo Dance in Cultural Context." *Dance Research Journal* 7 (Spring–Summer 1975): 1–11.

Jones, Betty True, ed. *Dance as Cultural Heritage.* Vol. 2. New York, 1984.

Royce, Anya Peterson. *The Anthropology of Dance.* Bloomington, 1977.

Vatsyayan, Kapila. *Classical Indian Dance in Literature and the Arts.* New Delhi, 1968.

JUDITH LYNNE HANNA

Linguistics

The use of linguistic analogies is a relatively recent theoretical and methodological approach to the study of dance. The main proponents of this methodological analogy are in the United States and Eastern Europe. Many of the ideas used in this approach are based on the Saussurian distinction between "acts and system," structural linguistics and Chomskyan transformational and generative linguistics. These methods and the ideas on which they are based are quite distinct from Ray Birdwhistell's kinesics, which studies "body motion as related to the nonverbal aspects of interpersonal communication," and Edward T. Hall's proxemics, which deals with spatial relationships between people. To understand the usefulness of employing linguistic analogies in the study of dance, one should have familiarity with the linguistic methodologies from which the analogies are drawn; this short entry can only introduce some of these concepts and how they have been used.

Etic/Emic Distinctions and Ethno-Scientific Analysis. The so-called etic/emic distinction can be traced to linguists who systematically applied Kenneth Pike's conceptualization of emic analysis, which was

> an attempt to discover and to describe the pattern of that particular language or culture in reference to the way in which the various elements of that culture are related to each other in the functioning of the particular pattern. (Pike, 1954, p. 8)

Using "contrastive analysis" and etic/emic distinctions, linguists evolved a method for deriving phonemic inventories and producing grammars that grouped morphemes into classes in a way that was inherent or natural to the languages themselves (that is, although the method could be used cross-culturally, the grammar was specific to that language alone). Such analysis is based on minimal contrastive units of sound and how they are combined, according to a particular group of people, into meaningful sequences (i.e., phonology and syntax). The "new ethnography," or ethno-scientific analysis, built on these concepts and applied contrastive analysis to cultural domains other than sound.

In 1964 Adrienne Kaeppler, starting with the assumption that only a small segment of all possible movement is significant in any single dance or movement tradition and that these significant units could be discovered, used ethno-scientific concepts and linguistic analogies to isolate minimal movement units. These movement emes were termed kinemes and were derived through contrastive analysis, in order to discover if kinetically different movements were considered by individuals of a specific group of people to be the same or different. Using Labanotation as a kinetic notation, the allokine variations were noted for each kineme, and an inventory of kinemes derived. Kinemes are minimal units of movement recognized as contrastive by people of a given dance tradition. Although having no meaning in themselves, kinemes are the basic units from which the dance of a given tradition is built. The next level of structural organization in this system was termed the morphokinemic level and is analogous to the morphemic level of linguistic structure. A morphokine is the smallest unit that has meaning as movement in the structure of a movement system (*meaning* here does not refer to narrative or pictorial meaning). Only certain combinations are meaningful, and a number of kinemes often occur simultaneously to form a meaningful movement. The resulting grammar groups morphokines into classes in a way that is inherent or natural to the specific movement system. As the first aim of this system is to derive dance "structure" and not dance "meaning," further analogies with language such as lexemes or sememes were not used. Morphokines, which have meaning as movement but do not have lexical meaning, were found to be organized into a relatively small number of motifs, which, when ordered simultaneously and chronologically (i.e., choreographed) form dances.

There are essentially two analytical processes involved in the analysis: (1) the derivation of the emic units or kinemes by observing movement behavior and questioning which etic behaviors are cognitively grouped or separated into emes (i.e., are they the same or different?—do they contrast?) and (2) to derive the movement system by observing and questioning how the emic units are structured or grouped into classes and what is the relationship between them. Kaeppler used this system to analyze the structure of Tongan dance (Kaeppler, 1967, 1972). This methodology was used by Irene Loutzaki (1989) to analyze style and by Frank Hall to analyze improvisation (1985).

Eastern European Linguistic Analogies. Meanwhile a group of Eastern European folk dance scholars organized a study group for folk dance terminology as part of the International Folk Music Council (now the International Council for Traditional Music). The precursors of this group were György Martin and Ernő Pesovár of Hungary, who had previously analyzed the morphology of Hungarian dance using principles from folklore research; they had found three important levels of analysis—"kinetic elements or parts" were combined into "motives or minor units," which by their succession, repetition, and fusion made up "major units." Building on this preliminary work, the folk dance terminology group added analogies from structural linguistics to derive minimal units similar to what Kaeppler had termed kinemes. In the Eastern European study (Study Group for Folk Dance Terminology, 1974), these minimal units were called "elements or dansemes." These minimal units were combined into "cells" (Kaeppler's morphokines) and organized into motives, phrases, stanzas, sections, and parts. This structural analysis was basically emic in that it was derived by Eastern Europeans analyzing their own dances from their own point of view. It is essential to note that the Eastern European system and Kaeppler's emic analysis were derived independently, but both used analogies from structural linguistics. The contributions of the Hungarian dance structuralists have been summarized in English and elaborated by László Kürti (1980).

Analogies with Transformational and Generative Grammar. Alice Singer, using Macedonian dance as an example, developed a theory of metrics "in which analogies to linguistic theory are as formalized and explicit as possible." Following Noam Chomsky and analyses of poetic meter, Singer developed a theory of metrics that proposed that dances are "generated by the encoding of abstract metrical patterns into an organized sequence of movements" and was working toward the derivation of a generative grammar of the metrical structure of dance. Unfortunately, Singer's untimely death has robbed the discipline of her further insights. A study based primarily on Chomsky's phrase-structure rules was carried out by Edward Myers in analyzing the fox trot to derive rules for grammatical performance in social dancing.

Semasiology. Semasiology owes its origins to Drid Williams's combination of analogies from Saussure, Chomsky, and semiotics but is different from all of these. Semasiology is concerned primarily with the semantics of body languages, and the focus is on meaning rather than structure. Whereas semiotics deals with communication and more specifically the doctrine of signs, semasiology is a theory and methodology that deals with the meanings of human body languages. According to Williams it is

> based on an application of Saussurian ideas to human movement and the result is a theory of human actions that is linguistically tied, mathematically structured and empirically based—but not "behaviourally-based." Semasiology is a form of semantic anthropology. (Williams, 1981, p. 221)

In semasiology, Chomsky's deep and surface structures have been transformed into "intransitive and transitive structures." Intransitive structures refer to invariant aspects of movement or space that are not created or produced by humans, whereas transitive structures are variable aspects of movement or space that can vary according to societies or individuals within them. Intransitive structures are based on the "semasiological body," which can make only a finite set of movements. Each part of the body has certain "degrees of freedom," which are the same everywhere and are therefore value-free and semantically null. These give the potential for describing and comparing body languages cross-culturally. Williams proposes seven basic transformational rules for sequential realization in space and claims that these meta-rules underlie all dance and ritual movement idioms anywhere in the world.

Another element of semasiology derives from Chomsky—the concepts of competence and performance. Chomsky noted that what a speaker of a language knows implicitly is his or her "competence," whereas what he or she does is "performance." A grammar is an account of competence and accounts for one's ability to understand a sentence that one has never heard before. Competence in semasiology, as in other theoretical systems using analogies from Chomsky, refers to an individual's ability to understand a grammatical movement sequence that he or she has never seen before.

The basic analytical steps of semasiology are two—the derivation of kinemes and kinesemes. Kinemes (like in Kaeppler's analysis) are based on the principle of contrastive analysis. Kinemes here are made up of kinetic elements based on Williams's "degrees of freedom" (whereas in Kaeppler's system kinemes are made up of allokines that can be referenced to Laban analysis). One or more kinemes make up a kineseme, which is analogous to a word or lexeme. Kinesemes are independent units of movement that convey meaning and include the element of time. This meaning can be augmented by analyzing the relationships of the various kinesemes to one another and to larger movement parts as well as the relationships of the parts to the whole. This methodology was used in the study of *hasta mudrā* in *bharata nāṭyam* by Rajika Puri (1983) and in the study of Plains Indian sign language by Brenda Farnell (1995).

Semasiologists share with structural analysts an interest in studying whole movement *systems* as well as movement competence as part of the social action in which they are embedded. Both are interested in human action and interaction as well as what is communicated by movement and to whom. The primary difference in the two systems is where meaning comes in. In both systems kinemes are significant movements that need not have meaning. In emic analysis the next step is derivation of the morphokine system. Morphokines have meaning as movement and are analogous to morphemes in language (the lexical meanings of which are not clear except in larger contexts). This level is not analyzed in semasiology. Morphokines are combined into motifs that have meaning in a similar manner to the way kinesemes have meaning. Kinesemes are larger than morphokines and smaller than motifs. The difference in terminology underscores the difference in emphasis between structure and semantics. The ultimate aim of both systems, however, is to understand structure and meaning just as analyses of language aim to understand structure and meaning. Linguists who deal with languages unknown to them probably feel more comfortable first analyzing structure and then trying to understand meaning, whereas linguists who incorporate meaning at a lower level are more likely to deal with languages that they already know. So it is with human movement. Emic analysis and the derivation of kinemes can be successfully carried out at the same time that the syntax is being learned in order to derive the system (i.e., how the emic units are structured at the morphokinemic level and what the relationships are among them). The derivation of kinesemes can be dealt with more easily in a body language with which one has a certain level of familiarity. Another basic difference is that emic analysis is more committed to analyzing each dance tradition in its own terms, especially in regard to syntax and grammar, whereas semasiology is more committed to the cross-cultural analysis of meaning at the kinesemic level. Finally, the derivation of kinemes in Kaeppler's system is referenced to kinetically different movements recognized by the kinetic alphabet of Labanotation, whereas the derivation of kinemes in semasiology is referenced to Williams's degrees of freedom. Both systems use Labanotation to render the results of analysis into written form.

These studies using linguistic analogies are currently being elaborated as theoretical bases for analyzing connections between spoken and movement languages and to overcome Cartesian mind/body dualistic thinking (Farnell, 1995).

BIBLIOGRAPHY

Birdwhistell, Ray L. *Kinesics and Context.* Philadelphia, 1970.

Farnell, Brenda. *Do You See What I Mean? Plains Indian Sign Talk and the Embodiment of Action.* Austin, 1995.

Farnell, Branda M., ed. *The Visible and the Invisible: Human Movement Systems in Cultural Context.* Metuchen, N.J., 1995.

Hall, Edward T. "A System for the Notation of Proxemic Behavior." *American Anthropologist* 65 (1963): 1003–1026.

Hall, Frank. "Improvisation and Fixed Composition in Clogging." *Journal for the Anthropological Study of Human Movement* 3.4 (1985): 200–217.

Kaeppler, Adrienne L. "The Structure of Tongan Dance." Ph.D. diss., University of Hawaii, 1967.

Kaeppler, Adrienne L. "Method and Theory in Analyzing Dance Structure, with an Analysis of Tongan Dance." *Ethnomusicology* 16.2 (1972): 173–217.

Kaeppler, Adrienne L. "Cultural Analysis, Linguistic Analogies, and the Study of Dance in Anthropological Perspective." In *Explorations in Ethnomusicology: Essays in Honor of David P. McAllester,* edited by Charlotte J. Frisbie. Detroit, 1986.

Kürti, László. "Hungarian Dance Structures: A Linguistic Approach." *Journal for the Anthropological Study of Human Movement* 1.1 (1980): 45–62.

Loutzaki, Irene. "Dance as a Cultural Message. A Study of Dance Style among the Greek Refugees from Northern Thrace. . . ." Ph.D. diss., Queen's University of Belfast, 1989.

Martin, György, and Ernő Pesovár. "A Structural Analysis of the Hungarian Folk Dance." *Acta Ethnographica Academiae Scientiarum Hungaricae* 10.1–2 (1961): 1–40.

Myers, Edward. "A Phrase-Structural Analysis of the Foxtrot, with Transformational Rules." *Journal for the Anthropological Study of Human Movement* 1.4 (1981): 246–268.

Pike, Kenneth. *Language in Relation to a Unified Theory of the Structures of Human Behavior.* Glendale, Calif., 1954.

Puri, Rajika. "A Structural Analysis of Meaning in Movement: The Hand Gestures of Indian Classical Dance." Master's thesis, New York University, 1983.

Singer, Alice. "The Metrical Structure of Macedonian Dance." *Ethnomusicology* 18.3 (1974): 379–404.

Study Group for Folk Dance Terminology. "Foundations for the Analysis of the Structure and Form of Folk Dance: A Syllabus." *Yearbook of the International Folk Music Council* 6 (1974): 115–135.

Williams, Drid. "Introduction to Special Issue on Semasiology." *Journal for the Anthropological Study of Human Movement* 1.4 (1981): 207–225.

Williams, Drid. "Semasiology: A Semantic Anthropological View of Human Movements and Actions." In *Semantic Anthropology,* edited by David Parkin. London, 1982.

ADRIENNE L. KAEPPLER

Anthropology

The anthropological study of dance is the application of the theories and methods of the discipline of anthropology to the understanding of dance as a cultural phenomenon. Contemporary anthropology in the United States consists of four subdisciplines, each of which is relevant to the study of dance: (1) physical anthropology is concerned with the evolution and biological diversity of the human species; (2) archeology deals with the reconstruction of human society based on the analysis of material evidence from the past; (3) linguistics covers the study of language as a crucial characteristic of human life and as a model for other communication systems; and (4) ethnology, social anthropology, or cultural anthropology encompasses the analysis of such elements of human culture as social organization, religion, economics, politics, art, and others. The term *anthropology* most often refers to ethnology. (Outside the United States, these four areas are not necessarily subsumed under one discipline, and in some countries the term *anthropology* is more likely to refer to physical anthropology.)

Although anthropology is generally considered to be a social science, it also shares many of the concerns of the biological sciences and the humanities. The anthropological study of dance, in particular, draws on the theories and methods of all these disciplines, as well as those of the arts and the behavioral sciences. Anthropology is thus inherently interdisciplinary. It is also empirical—it depends on gathering data through fieldwork in a particular society, using the method of participant observation. Anthropological theory and methods can also be applied to the study of historical data, literary sources, art works and other objects.

Anthropology has typically focused on the study of non-Western or nonindustrialized societies, but the discipline is defined not by the type of society it studies but by its perspective on the subject matter. Thus, the anthropology of dance can look at classical ballet or contact improvisation as well as any other type of dance.

A useful way of defining the goal of anthropological study has been suggested by the anthropologist Clifford Geertz. He feels that the analysis of culture is "not an experimental science in search of laws but an interpretive one in search of meaning" (Geertz, 1973, p. 5). The aim is to provide a "thick description," a multilayered analysis that considers social, psychological, and functional aspects. Certain key concepts in anthropology underlie the four subdisciplines and provide the foundation for the anthropological study of dance and for the construction of a thick description. The anthropological perspective is defined by the study of cultural phenomena in context and in a comparative framework. Although a study may focus on a specific case or on a cross-cultural comparison, data are gathered and analyzed with three questions in mind: How does the subject being studied relate to other aspects of that culture? How does this case compare with situations in other cultures? What does this information reveal to us about human life? By asking and trying to answer these questions, anthropology is thus holistic (dealing with the whole, or all relevant factors) and cross-cultural.

Although the anthropological study of dance emerged in the twentieth century, there were many precursor studies in comparative religion, sociology, and history. Because the history of anthropologically relevant dance studies has been described in detail elsewhere (Kurath, 1960; Royce, 1977; Kaeppler, 1991; Hanna, 1989; Williams, 1986; Giurchescu and Torp, 1991), only a few milestones will be discussed here.

Historical Overview. Throughout history, travelers to foreign countries have mentioned dance in their writings. This was especially true in the nineteenth century, when missionaries, early anthropologists, and colonial officials actively collected information. Most merely noted that dance activity occurred, but a few tried to relate dance to society or religion. Several major theorists—James Frazer, Jane Harrison, Ernst Grosse, E. B. Tylor, and others—incorporated data and theory about dance into their studies. Although many of their ideas about dance were speculative and assumed a false dichotomy between so-called civilized and primitive societies, they helped demonstrate that dance is often a very important aspect of society, needing to be studied.

In 1933, the musicologist Curt Sachs published *Eine Weltgeschichte des Tanzes* (translated in 1937 as *World History of the Dance*), an ambitious effort to construct a universal history of dance and to provide an analytical and comparative framework for the study of dance. The book was a pioneering attempt to analyze dance in relation to cultural factors. The data available to Sachs was, however, insufficient and often distorted, and his theories were based on the later discredited model of cultural evolution. The book was ground-breaking, but it is not now an appropriate model for the modern anthropological study of dance.

In the United States, many anthropologists working in the early part of the twentieth century—most under the direction of Franz Boas, the father of American anthropology—turned to the study of Native American cultures, where dance was often central to ceremonial life. Most of these researchers were not interested in dance itself, but because of the importance of dance in these societies, they could not ignore it and hence gathered much data about dance types and functions. A few analytical studies derive from this period, such as Margaret Mead's 1920s and 1930s studies in Samoa and Bali, of dance as an indicator of personality, and the research presented by leading anthropologists at two seminars (in 1944 and 1946) on the function of dance, organized by Boas's daughter, the modern dancer Franziska Boas.

Many British anthropologists in this period did fieldwork in Africa, the Pacific Islands, and other areas where dance could not be overlooked. Such notable workers as E. E. Evans-Pritchard and A. R. Radcliffe-Brown made contributions to our understanding of the value of dance within society. Nonetheless, despite the extraordinary significance that many cultures place on their dancing, most anthropologists have ignored dance entirely or have concentrated on its social significance alone.

Gertrude Prokosch Kurath is considered the pioneer of the American anthropological study of dance. Throughout a career of more than forty years she made many contributions to the development of methodology for the empirical and comparative study of dance. Her background was a career as a modern dancer, and for the most part, her research was not informed by anthropological theory and more appropriately may be called *dance ethnology*, a term she coined that is sometimes used alternatively to the "anthropology of dance." She defined the goal of dance ethnology as "an approach toward, and a method of, eliciting the place of dance in human life" (Kurath, 1960, p. 250). A growing body of dance ethnological studies emphasize the description of dance and its context; much of this research has been published by CORD, the Congress on Research in Dance, an international membership organization of dance researchers currently administered through the Dance Department of the State University of New York at Brockport.

In the 1960s, dance researchers began formally to study anthropology, some receiving doctorates in this subject. This small group can be credited with providing the foundation for an anthropological study of dance. Adrienne L. Kaeppler, Joann W. Kealiinohomoku, Judith Lynne Hanna, Drid Williams, Anya Peterson Royce, and John Blacking (in the United Kingdom) have published extensively in this field, helping to define the issues as well as making contributions in data collection, theory, and methods.

In general, European dance researchers have concentrated on the comparison of European dance types and on the description of dance contexts and functions within their own countries. European dance research with an anthropological focus has often overlapped with folklore studies, since the subject matter is frequently the same. Many of the researchers have collaborated in an ambitious study of dance types under the auspices of the International Council for Traditional Music (ICTM, formerly the International Folk Music Council), an international membership organization of music and dance researchers with administrative headquarters at Columbia University in New York.

It is misleading to dichotomize American and European research as there have been many approaches on both sides of the Atlantic as well in other countries, especially in Latin America, India, Japan, Africa, Australia, and New Zealand. In each country, the historical context in which the research has taken place affected the way in which the field of dance study developed, the issues raised, and the methodologies and theories applied to the collection and interpretation of the data. The growing interaction among scholars in different countries—facilitated through conferences and publications sponsored by CORD, ICTM, and other international dance organizations in the 1980s and 1990s—has led to increased sharing of perspectives and methodologies and even joint research projects.

Issues. If dance is to be studied in a comparative framework, one must first ask, What is the subject of study? What is dance? What is dance in this particular culture?

Many cultures have no generic word for *dance;* they may have many words for different types of movement genres, or they may include under the term *dance* some behavior not considered to be dance in European-American culture. Developing a cross-cultural definition of dance has been a basic issue in anthropological dance research. Anthropologists have discovered that they cannot expect to find the categories of their own culture exactly mirrored in other cultures. Our distinctions between art dance and non-art dance, religious and secular, or professional and amateur, for example, may be irrelevant in another society. Cross-culturally, trying to categorize dances into basic types such as primitive, ethnic, social, popular, folk, or classical is equally problematic. It must also be recognized that definitional problems are not merely academic issues; labeling dance types also implicitly labels the people who dance them.

The comparative perspective concentrates on discovering similarities and differences across cultures. Underlying this approach is the attempt to distinguish the universal from the culture-specific and from the idiosyncratic (specific to the individual). The issue of nature versus nurture is another dimension of this problem. Such questions arise as, What does human dance share, if anything, with the ritual movement of animals? Is there anything universal about how dance is structured, or about how emotions and thoughts are transformed into movement?

Many anthropologists of dance are now questioning whether "the concept of 'dance' may actually be masking the importance and usefulness of analyzing human movement systems" (Kaeppler, 1978, p. 47). Some favor calling this field the anthropological study of human movement rather than of dance to emphasize the focus on socially consructed movement systems.

One study that has called attention to the continuum between everyday movement and dance is the Choreometrics Project, a cross-cultural dance research undertaking begun in the early 1960s, conducted by Alan Lomax, Irmgard Bartenieff, and Forrestine Paulay. This study analyzed movement available on film from a cross-cultural sample. One of its hypotheses was that dance is a "patterned reinforcement of the habitual movement patterns of each culture or culture area" (Lomax, 1968, p. xv). In addition, the project sought to describe dance styles and to discover world stylistic areas; to find correlations between aspects of dance and certain cultural and ecological factors; and to uncover an evolutionary sequence based on the relationship between qualities of movement and the economic subsistence pattern of a culture. The project has been recognized as contributing to the methodology for describing style, but it has been severely criticized for its interpretation of the data.

There have been several major approaches to the study of dance in culture. The evolutionary framework was prevalent in the nineteenth century and underlies the analyses of both Sachs and Choreometrics. This perspective was built on the premise that some dances freeze in time while some more "civilized" forms evolve. The contemporary viewpoint, by contrast, is that all cultures and their dances have unique histories, and that broad categories of dance, representing progressive levels of complexity or stages of civilization, do not exist.

The functionalist approach has characterized much of the history of the anthropological study of dance. In brief, functionalism attempts to discern how the part contributes to the whole. In dance studies, the focus has been on studying the role or function of dance in society and, conversely, how culture is reflected in dance. Dance has been seen as promoting social solidarity, providing psychological safety valves for individuals (and thus contributing to social stability), and conveying social, religious, political, aesthetic, and other values. Functionalist studies have tended to reveal that dance is a conservative factor, acting to maintain social values, but they have also pointed out how dance can be a dynamic force that contributes toward shaping and changing society. From the opposite perspective, dance has been analyzed as a microcosm of a particular culture; studies have focused on how the social organization and belief system of a society are manifested in a dance event and thus on how a culture can be understood through its dance.

Functionalist studies are by definition contextual studies: they focus on the who, when, where, why, and how of dance. They also try to understand value systems and ask such questions as what should, could, cannot, and must be done relative to the dance.

In addition to the study of function and context, there have also been anthropological studies of the structures and styles of dance. Eastern European dance researchers have had a particular interest in analyzing dance types in a comparative framework, using a hierarchy of movement units analogous to the word–phrase–sentence structure of language. The studies of the Hungarians György Martin and Ernő Pesovár have been particularly influential and have been further developed by members of the ICTM dance study group.

Linguistic analogies have inspired other studies of dance, including research by Kaeppler, Williams, and Hanna. Their emphasis has been on how and what dance communicates; they often draw on the theories of semiotics, the study of symbols and signs.

Many dance studies have focused on specific circumstances or aspects of a dance or dance event. A major concern has been the documentation and analysis of the interrelationship between cultural change and changes in the form and function of a society's dance. The ways dance functions as a symbol of cultural identity or as a vehicle of political, religious, or economic meaning have been studied in many cultures. The relationship between dance and other art forms is also a frequent subject.

Although most studies have tended to focus either on dance movement or on the context of dance, discovering how form and function are integrated is an ultimate goal of analysis. The researcher asks how a particular dance form, its manner of execution, its sociocultural context, and its meaning are interrelated. A primary question becomes: how can we understand society through understanding movement systems?

Conclusion. It is often said that anthropology can make the strange familiar and the familiar strange. Thus, knowledge about the form and function of dance in other cultures can lead to greater understanding of how to perform, view, appreciate, and adapt these dances. At the same time, learning about dance in other cultures can make one look at and think about dance in one's own culture in a different light. For example, one might ask: Is ballet any less ethnic than any other dance form? Or, if dance is so important in many world religions, can it contribute something to contemporary Western religions?

Awareness of the diversity of human movement systems can lead to a greater realization of the scope of human variation and creative potential; such awareness can provide insight into what links human beings to nature and what distinguishes their humanity. Analysis of dance is a window into understanding the biological, social, and symbol-making dimensions of human life.

[*For related discussion, see* European Traditional Dance *and* Film and Video, *article on* Ethnographic Studies.]

BIBLIOGRAPHY

Adshead, Janet, ed. *Dance: A Multicultural Perspective.* Guildford, 1984.

Blacking, John. "Movement and Meaning: Dance in Social Anthropological Perspective." *Dance Research* 1 (Spring 1983): 89–99.

Boas, Franziska, ed. *The Function of Dance in Human Society* (1944). 2d ed. Brooklyn, 1972.

Comstock, Tamara, ed. *New Dimensions in Dance Research: Anthropology and Dance—The American Indian.* New York, 1974.

Dunin, Elsie Ivanchich, ed. *Dance Research: Published or Publicly Presented by Members of the Study Group on Ethnochoreology.* 2d ed. Los Angeles, 1991.

Geertz, Clifford. *The Interpretation of Cultures.* New York, 1973.

Giurchescu, Anca, and Lisbet Torp. "Preface" and "Theory and Methods in Dance Research: A European Approach to the Holistic Study of Dance." *Yearbook of the International Council for Traditional Music* 23 (1991): 1-10.

Grau, Andrée. "Intercultural Research in the Performing Arts." *Dance Research* 10 (Autumn 1992): 3–29.

Grau, Andrée. "John Blacking and the Development of Dance Anthropology in the United Kingdom." *Dance Research Journal* 25 (Fall 1993): 21–31.

Hanna, Judith Lynne. "Movements toward Understanding Humans through the Anthropological Study of Dance." *Current Anthropology* 20 (June 1979): 313–339.

Hanna, Judith Lynne. *To Dance Is Human*. Austin, 1979.

Hanna, Judith Lynne. "The Anthropology of Dance." In *Dance: Current Selected Research*, vol. 1, edited by Lynnette Y. Overby and James H. Humphrey. New York, 1989.

Kaeppler, Adrienne L. "Method and Theory in Analyzing Dance Structure, with an Analysis of Tongan Dance." *Ethnomusicology* 16 (May 1972): 173–217.

Kaeppler, Adrienne L. "Dance in Anthropological Perspective." *Annual Review of Anthropology* 7 (1978).

Kaeppler, Adrienne L. "American Approaches to the Study of Dance." *Yearbook of the International Council for Traditional Music* 23 (1991): 11–21.

Kealiinohomoku, Joann W. *Theory and Methods for an Anthropological Study of Dance*. Bloomington, 1976.

Kealiinohomoku, Joann W. "Review of *Dance and Human History*, a film by Alan Lomax." *Ethnomusicology* 23 (January 1979): 169–176.

Kealiinohomoku, Joann W. "An Anthropologist Looks at Ballet as a Form of Ethnic Dance." In *What Is Dance?*, edited by Roger Copeland and Marshall Cohen. New York, 1983.

Kurath, Gertrude Prokosch. "Panorama of Dance Ethnology." *Current Anthropology* 1 (1960): 233–254.

Kurath, Gertrude Prokosch. *Half a Century of Dance Research*. Flagstaff, Ariz., 1986.

Lange, Roderyk. "Anthropology and Dance Scholarship." *Dance Research* 1 (Spring 1983): 108–118.

Lomax, Alan, ed. *Folk Song Style and Culture*. Washington, D.C., 1968.

Ness, Sally Ann. *Body, Movement, and Culture: Kinesthetic and Visual Symbolism in a Philippine Community*. Philadelphia, 1992.

Novack, Cynthia J. *Sharing the Dance: Contact Improvisation and American Culture*. Madison, 1990.

Royce, Anya Peterson. *The Anthropology of Dance*. Bloomington, 1977.

Sachs, Curt. *World History of the Dance*. Translated by Bessie Schönberg. New York, 1937.

Spencer, Paul, ed. *Society and the Dance*. Cambridge, 1985.

Study Group for Folk Dance Terminology. "Foundations for the Analysis of the Structure and Form of Folk Dance: A Syllabus." *Yearbook of the International Folk Music Council* 6 (1974): 115–135.

Thomas, Helen, ed. *Dance, Gender, and Culture*. New York, 1993.

Williams, Drid. "Semasiology: A Semantic Anthropological View of Human Movements and Actions." In *Semantic Anthropology*, edited by David Parkin. London, 1982.

Williams, Drid. "(Non) Anthropologists, the Dance, and Human Movement." In *Theatrical Movement: A Bibliographical Anthology*, edited by Bob Fleshman. Metuchen, N.J., 1986.

Williams, Drid. *Ten Lectures on Theories of the Dance*. Metuchen, N.J., 1991.

Youngerman, Suzanne. "Curt Sachs and His Heritage: A Critical Review of *World History of the Dance* with a Survey of Recent Studies that Perpetuate His Ideas." *CORD News* 6 (July 1974): 6–19.

Youngerman, Suzanne. "Method and Theory in Dance Research: An Anthropological Approach." *Yearbook of the International Folk Music Council* 7 (1976).

SUZANNE YOUNGERMAN

Ethnology

Dance ethnology has been developed as a field primarily by North American researchers interested in understanding the cultural diversity of dancing. This approach is situated within scholarly institutions, including university departments, professional associations, and journals. Dance ethnologists also contribute to other domains of activity in interactions with performers, presenters, audiences, and other dance enthusiasts. In the United States, dance ethnology has tended, like ethnomusicology, to study non-Western dance genres abroad or among immigrant groups, and, like folkloristics, to examine the dances of the traditional rural and new urban folk groups. In Europe the parallel discipline of ethnochoreology developed much earlier from roots in folklore and musicology; its scholars have focused primarily on the study of their own national traditions, although this agenda has broadened in recent years to include the traditions of immigrant groups and urban contemporary dance.

Because of their interests, dance ethnologists have been challenged to conceptualize dance in a manner applicable across cultures and to develop theory and method able to generate insights into widely differing dance cultures. Their thinking owes much to anthropology and the other social sciences as well as to the arts and humanities. As a result, the understanding of dance has been much broadened from the narrow Eurocentric concepts that once dominated dance writing to embrace the wider domain of meaningful human action articulated through structured movement systems that formalize and intensify kinesthetic experience and communication; this is a perspective primarily developed by the anthropologists Adrienne Kaeppler and Drid Williams. Dance is increasingly being studied from an interdisciplinary perspective appropriate to its complexities.

The first full articulation of dance ethnology as a field is found in Gertrude Kurath's article "Panorama of Dance Ethnology" (1960). She acknowledged and tried to resolve some differences among people interested in the study of dance throughout the world in the following terms: "Any dichotomy between ethnic dance and art dance dissolves if one regards dance ethnology, not as a description of or reproduction of a particular kind of dance, but as an approach toward, and method of, eliciting the place of dance in human life." Although Kurath identified her proposed approach as a branch of anthropology, in fact her theory and method were much more influenced by European folklore studies, particularly those of Richard Wolfram, than by the American anthropologists with whom she collaborated in research on Native American dance. Her characterization of this nascent field was based on extensive correspondence with scholars from various countries and fields, including ethnomusicologists and anthropologists as well as dance teachers, performers, and theorists. Kurath's panorama, however, went well beyond a mere description of the fragmented research available at that time to formulate a powerful synthesis and to identify many issues still basic to dance ethnology. These include methods of documentation and movement analysis, processes of transmission and diffusion, stability and innovation in tradition, and dance's relations to other aspects of social and cultural organization, as well as consideration of the emergent qualities of dance performance, its communicative modes, and its experiential dimensions.

Joann Kealiinohomoku, among the most influential American dance ethnologists, was inspired by Kurath but pursued a more anthropologically oriented direction developed and shared by a small group of American dance researchers during the 1970s, including Judith Lynne Hanna, Kaeppler, Anya Peterson Royce, Suzanne Youngerman, and Williams. Their subdiscipline has been termed *anthropology of dance,* or *dance anthropology,* rather than dance ethnology, because it was explicitly informed by and addressed to prevailing anthropological theory. Anthropologists of dance begin with questions about culture and seek answers in the domain of movement. Dance ethnologists begin with questions about dance movement and seek answers through inquiry informed by interdisciplinary insights into the nature of human behavior. The two endeavors are not far apart, and the distinction, albeit genuine, characterizes a difference in perspective more than a radical disjuncture. The subject matter is much the same, and scholars in the two camps, often distinguished more by institutional affiliation and professional identification than by research interests, engage one another in lively exchanges. The 1972 Conference on Research in Dance, which produced *New Directions in Dance Research: Anthropology and the Dance—The American Indian* (1974), a second key document in the history of American dance ethnology, illustrates this interaction in an event that brought together many prominent researchers.

While some dance researchers became anthropologists, often moving away from their focus on dance, the orientation of dance ethnology—which kept the activity of dancing at the center of inquiry—continued in the European institutions which had informed its beginning and also became established in American academic departments of dance, most notably at the University of California, Los Angeles, during the 1970s. Here there was acknowledgment of the value of dance, the practice of dancers, and the kinesthetic knowledge of the dance researchers, that has been conspicuously absent in much of academia. Although some scholars have chosen to denigrate dance ethnology, others have struggled to assert its distinctive body of theory and method, developed over time from its choreologic material and in dialogue with closely related disciplines including anthropology, ethnomusicology, and folklore. In turn, dance ethnology has been instrumental in introducing theory and method to other subdisciplines of dance study and has enjoyed a long and productive interaction with choreography and performance on stage and beyond. Pearl Primus and Katherine Dunham are two figures who bridge the gap between theory and performance. Today, as some disciplinary boundaries become more porous, dance ethnologists increasingly situate themselves within an interdisciplinary framework, including such emerging areas of inquiry as performance and cultural studies, along with the more specialized fields such as women's, regional, and ethnic studies.

The intellectual heritage that informed Kurath's conception of dance ethnology, represented in her entry "Dance: Folk and Primitive" in the *Standard Dictionary of Folklore, Mythology, and Legend* (1949), was preoccupied with "folk" and "primitive" dance as an object for classification, as a communal expression, and as survival. A romantic conception of the music-making, dancing, and other folklore of village people as representative of the spiritual roots of a nation underlies this perspective and has colored much of European dance research. It grew out of the eighteenth- and nineteenth-century European preoccupation with nationalism, the social and intellectual milieu in which folklore studies and ethnochoreology developed. Their influence in the early twentieth century, when many European research archives were established, led to collections reflecting the effort of an educated elite to uncover and preserve what they believed to be the unadulterated folk expression of peasant bearers of tradition. Little attention was paid by these researchers and their institutions to either the people or the contexts in which they produced the songs, melodies, and dances collected. Following World War II, there was an increased sense of urgency in collecting materials from older informants, particularly in eastern Europe, in the face of rapid, radical social change. Despite their shortcomings, these archival collections provide a foundation and resource for the continuing study of vernacular dancing in Europe. The collections of the Institute of Musicology of the Hungarian Academy of Sciences in Budapest are particularly outstanding, housing extensive film documentation beginning in the 1930s. Important archives of various sizes exist in many other European countries.

The collection of dances by researchers associated with such institutions was guided by established principles of fieldwork emphasizing observation and documentation. Before film and video recording equipment became as available and portable, notation of collected dances was based on observation and informant questioning. Researchers in different countries, dealing with differing dance idioms, developed their own specialized notation systems. This hampered comparative research beyond national boundaries; however, since European researchers began to address this problem collectively in 1957, Kinetography Laban or Labanotation has gradually been adopted as a common method for recording material and communicating internationally.

Advances in technology to record the evanescent moments of dance performance have had a significant impact on the field. Alan Lomax's choreometric project is a significant, if much criticized, film-based study. Producers of the 1993 public television series *Dancing* utilized academic advisers from dance ethnology in developing episodes addressing several major themes that bring together a wide variety of dance idioms. New developments in interactive multimedia computer technology promise to make the quick and easy manipulation of moving images for analysis a practical reality.

The conception of dance as an expression of national and ethnic identities has also led to a close association between research and the conscious selection, manipulation, presentation, and practice of particular dances as symbols to serve ideological and political ends. This phenomenon has a long and complex history in Europe, in which researchers have always been complicit. Accessible to popular participation and amenable to theatrical manipulation, dance is an important element in what has been called *folklorism*—folklore which has been altered or even invented for specific purposes. In eastern Europe, where manipulation of dance and other folk culture was supported by communist governments as a means for altering societal patterns, scholars quickly began to build theoretical models for this phenomenon. Although each country has its own specific history and orientation to this issue, in general institutions for scientific research were charged with the task of discovering, investigating, documenting, and theorizing folk dance, while other institutions were responsible for its creation, alteration, and dissemination. The Folklore Section of the Institute of Music at the Bulgarian Academy of Sciences and its counterpart, the Department of Folk Creation at the Ministry of Education and Culture, provide one example. The downfall of communism is now reverberating through this system, and scholars are beginning to reexamine this history.

If the democracies of western Europe and North America saw less overt ideological manipulation of folk dance, they did experience extensive informal, participatory dance revival movements associated with the expression of national and ethnic identities. In America this impulse took the form of "international" recreational folk dancing, which began in the work of Elizabeth Burchenal in the New York schools and park systems in the early 1900s and spread throughout the United States. The California Folk Dance Federation was particularly important for its emphasis on documentation and notation of a standard dance repertory. This model of recreational international folk dancing was projected back into Europe through the work of such dance teachers as Ricky Holden.

Often coincident with but somewhat distinct from studies influenced by the intellectual heritage of romantic nationalism is a preoccupation with questions of geographical and historical diffusion. One approach, usually ascribed to Curt Sachs (1937) and his German anthropological school, posited processes of culture contact within a broad historical framework. Known as *Kulturkreislehre,* this aspect of ethnochoreology is best understood as a manifestation of a perspective that has always been central in folklore studies: a concern with processes of transmission that can account for observed patterns of stability and variation. Before such studies of the distribution and diffusion of types and variants comes analysis of form and structure. It is thus not surprising that European ethnochoreologists have been particularly concerned with formal structural analysis. Beginning in 1962, among eastern European researchers in particular, an effort was made to systematize methods of structural analysis to facilitate comparison, largely in the service of inquiry into origins and processes of diffusion, variation, and stability. This approach to research resulted in the delineation of geographical regions characterized by shared dance traits. Ivan Ivancan made a significant contribution in differentiating between political boundaries and what he termed *dance zones.* Suggested by the distribution of language and folklore traits, these were characterized by distinctive features of dance structure and movement style. His work and that of others of his generation, however, was hampered by insufficient data and a somewhat static view of dance practice in a pre–World War II "ethnographic present" that researchers endeavored to reconstruct from older informants. Elsie Ivancich Dunin has extended some of these methods to her investigation of change in the transmission of dance through time and space in South Slav communities in the former Yugoslavia, the United States, and Chile.

Dance context became an important element in dance ethnology in America as theoretical perspectives shifted to include a conception of dance as culture, resulting from the engagement with anthropology during the 1970s. Kealiinohomoku, for example, emphasized the importance of "dance culture" and the "dance event." The dance event was seen as a microcosm and means to discover the place of dance within the larger cultural context. Following the prevailing anthropological theory, questions were asked about the functions of dance within cultural systems. Allegra Snyder elaborated this concept, attempting to integrate the micro and macro levels within one model. Among European researchers, dance context was generally treated rather separately from dance form and structure. György Martin conceptualized context as "dance life" and utilized it as one factor in categorizing dance. Since the mid-1970s, European research has begun to integrate consideration of dancing contexts within a semiotic model, different from the American functionalist perspective. Informed by widespread disciplinary shifts, dance ethnologists have also moved toward a more dynamic conception of their subject, not as product but as performance and communication. This perspective gives attention to process and finds meaning in the emergent reality of performance. American concern with minority, ethnic, and gender issues across disciplinary boundaries has become important in dance ethnology and increasingly characterizes the work of a new generation trained in the theory and method established during the 1970s.

The gulf separating the European and American scholarly worlds of dance ethnology and ethnochoreology was definitively bridged at the Fifteenth Symposium of the ICTM Study Group on Ethnochoreology, which convened in Copenhagen in 1988 to discuss approaches to study of the dance event. The participants included dance ethnologists from the United States, among them Allegra Fuller Snyder, Elsie Ivancich Dunin, and Judy Van Zile; the anthropologist Adrienne Kaeppler and many others representing a new generation and an increasing diversity of national participation have since joined this group. Their work is represented in the Symposium proceedings, a bibliography of members' publications, and articles in the *Yearbook for Traditional Music.*

This new era of scholarship is now able to build on the literature developed since the work of Kurath and her predecessors. It is characterized by a greater presence of dance study in academia, increasing interest in embodied practice from the fields of feminist, performance, and cultural studies, and the increased ease of international communications. All this promises to yield new insights into the nature of dance in all its diverse manifestations.

[*For related discussion, see* European Traditional Dance *and* Film and Video, *article on* Ethnographic Studies.]

BIBLIOGRAPHY

Baier-Fraenger, Ingeborg. "Dance Notation and Folk Dance Research: The Dresden Congress 1957." *Dance Studies* 2 (1977): 64–75.

Bakka, Egil. *Springar, gangar, rull og pols: Hovudliner i eldre norsk folkedanstradisjon.* Trondheim, 1978.

Bakka, Egil. "Folk Dance Research in Norway." *Dance Studies* 5 (1981): 22–47.

Bakka, Egil. *Danstraditisjonar frå Vest-Agder.* Flekkefjord, Norway, 1990.

Boas, Franziska, ed. *The Function of Dance in Human Society* (1944). 2d ed. Brooklyn, 1972.

Bröcker, Marianne, ed. *Tanz und Tanzmusik in Überlieferung und Gegenwart.* Bamberg, 1992.

Buckland, Theresa Jill. "Traditional Dance Scholarship in the United Kingdom." In *Dance: A Multicultural Perspective,* edited by Janet Adshead. Guildford, 1984.

Buckland, Theresa Jill. "Traditional Dance: English Ceremonial and Social Forms." In *Dance History: An Introduction,* edited by Janet Adshead-Lansdale and June Layson. 2d ed. London, 1994.

Bucsan, Andrei. *Specificul dansului popular romanesc.* Bucharest, 1971.

Cardaro, Janice, and Elsie Ivancich Dunin. "Index: 1977–1992, Volumes 1–16." *UCLA Journal of Dance Ethnology* 16 (1992): 44–72.

Comstock, Tamara, ed. *New Dimensions in Dance Research: Anthropology and Dance—The American Indian.* New York, 1974.

Cowan, Jane K. *Dance and the Body Politic in Northern Greece.* Princeton, 1990.

Dąbrowska, Grażyna, and Kurt Petermann, eds. *Analyse und Klassifikation von Volkstänzen.* Cracow, 1983.

Dąbrowska, Grażyna, et al. *International Monograph on Folk Dance,* vol. 2, *Poland, Portugal, Sweden.* Budapest, 1987.

Dance Studies. Jersey, Channel Islands, U.K., 1976–.

Daniel, Yvonne. *Rumba: Dance and Social Change in Contemporary Cuba.* Bloomington, 1995.

Dunham, Katherine. *The Dances of Haiti* (1947). Los Angeles, 1983.

Dunin, Elsie Ivancich. "'Salonsko Kolo' as Cultural Identity in a Chilean Yugoslav Community, 1917–1986." *Narodna Umjetnost* 2 (1988): 109–122.

Dunin, Elsie Ivancich, ed. *Dance Research Published or Publicly Presented by Members of the Study Group on Ethnochoreology.* Los Angeles, 1991.

Dunin, Elsie Ivancich, ed. *Dance Research Published or Publicly Presented by Members of the Study Group on Ethnochoreology.* Zagreb, 1995.

Farnell, Brenda. *Human Action Signs in Cultural Context: The Visible and the Invisible in Movement and Dance.* Metuchen, N.J., 1995.

Felföldi, László, ed. *Proceedings of the Sixteenth Symposium of the ICTM Study Group on Ethnochoreology.* Studia Musicologica Academiae Scientarum Hungaricae, 33. Budapest, 1991.

Gere, David, ed. *Looking Out: Perspectives on Dance and Criticism in a Multicultural World.* New York, 1995.

Giurchescu, Anca. "La danse comme objet sémiotique." *Yearbook of the International Folk Music Council* 5 (1973): 175–178.

Giurchescu, Anca. "The National Festival 'Song to Romania': Manipulation of Symbols in the Political Discourse." In *Symbols of Power: The Esthetics of Political Legitimation in the Soviet Union and Eastern Europe,* edited by Claes Arvidsson and Lars Erik Blomqvist. Stockholm, 1986.

Giurchescu, Anca, and Lisbet Torp. "Preface" and "Theory and Methods in Dance Research: A European Approach to the Holistic Study of Dance." *Yearbook of the International Council for Traditional Music* 23 (1991): 1–10.

Giurchescu, Anca, and Sunni Bloland. *Romanian Traditional Dance: A Contextual and Structural Approach.* Mill Valley, Calif., 1995.

Hanna, Judith Lynne. *To Dance Is Human: A Theory of Nonverbal Communication.* Austin, 1979.

Hoerburger, Felix. "Once Again: On the Concept of 'Folk Dance.'" *Journal of the International Folk Music Council* 20 (1968): 30–32.

Ivančan, Ivan. "Folk Dances in Various Regions of Yugoslavia." In *The Folk Arts of Yugoslavia,* edited by Walter W. Kolar. Pittsburgh, 1976.

Kaeppler, Adrienne L. "Method and Theory in Analyzing Dance Structure, with an Analysis of Tongan Dance." *Ethnomusicology* 16.2 (1972): 173–217.

Kaeppler, Adrienne L. "Theoretical and Methodological Considerations for Anthropological Studies of Dance and Human Movement Systems." *Ethnographica* 8 (1992): 151–157.

Kealiinohomoku, Joann W. *Theory and Methods for an Anthropological Study of Dance*. Bloomington, 1976.

Kealiinohomoku, Joann W. "An Anthropologist Looks at Ballet as a Form of Ethnic Dance" (1969). In *What Is Dance?*, edited by Roger Copeland and Marshall Cohen. New York, 1983.

Kurath, Gertrude Prokosch. "Panorama of Dance Ethnology." *Current Anthropology* 1 (1960): 233–254.

Kurath, Gertrude Prokosch. *Half a Century of Dance Research*. Flagstaff, Ariz., 1986.

Lange, Roderyk. "The Development of Anthropological Dance Research." *Dance Studies* 4 (1980): 1–36.

Lange, Roderyk. "Semiotics and Dance." *Dance Studies* 5 (1981): 13–21.

Lange, Roderyk. "Guidelines for Field Work on Traditional Dance: Methods and Checklist." *Dance Studies* 8 (1984): 7–47.

Lange, Roderyk. "The Dance Folklore from Cuiavia." *Dance Studies* 12 (1988): 6–223.

Lomax, Alan, ed. *Folk Song Style and Culture*. Washington, D.C., 1968.

Loutzaki, Irene, ed. *Dance in Its Socio-Political Aspects/Dance and Costume: Proceedings of the Seventeenth Symposium of the Study Group on Ethnochoreology 1992*. Nafplion, Greece, 1994.

Martin, György, and Ernő Pesovár. "A Structural Analysis of the Hungarian Folk Dance." *Acta Ethnographica Academiae Scientiarum Hungaricae* 10.1–2 (1961): 1–40.

Martin, György. "A Survey of the Hungarian Folk Dance Research." *Dance Studies* 6 (1982): 9–45.

Martin, György, ed. *International Monograph on Folk Dance*, vol. 1, *Hungary, France*. Budapest, 1986.

Ness, Sally Ann. *Body, Movement, and Culture: Kinesthetic and Visual Symbolism in a Philippine Community*. Philadelphia, 1992.

Ness, Sally Ann. "Observing the Evidence Fail: Difference Arising from Objectifiction in Cross-Cultural Studies of Dance." In *Moving Words: Re-writing Dance*, edited by Gay Morris, pp. 245–269. London and New York, 1996.

Nor, Mohid Anis. *Zapin: Folk Dance of the Malay World*. Oxford, 1993.

Novack, Cynthia J. *Sharing the Dance: Contact Improvisation and American Culture*. Madison, 1990.

Quigley, Colin. *Close to the Floor: Folk Dance in Newfoundland*. St. John's, 1985.

Ronström, Owe. "Summary." In *Att gestalta ett ursprung: En musiketnologisk studie av dansande och musicerande bland jugoslaver i Stockholm*. Stockholm, 1992.

Royce, Anya Peterson. *The Anthropology of Dance*. Bloomington, 1977.

Sachs, Curt. *World History of the Dance*. Translated by Bessie Schönberg. New York, 1937.

Sklar, Deidre. "Can Bodylore Be Brought to Its Senses?" *Journal of American Folklore* 107.473 (1994): 9–22.

Snyder, Allegra Fuller. "Past, Present, and Future." *UCLA Journal of Dance Ethnology* 16 (1992): 1–28.

Spalding, Susan Eike, and Jane Harris Woodside, eds. *Communities in Motion: Dance, Community, and Tradition in America's Southeast and Beyond*. Westport, Conn., 1995.

Study Group for Folk Dance Terminology. "Foundations for the Analysis of the Structure and Form of Folk Dance: A Syllabus." *Yearbook of the International Folk Music Council* 6 (1974): 115–135.

Torp, Lisbet, ed. *The Dance Event, a Complex Cultural Phenomenon: Proceedings of the Fifteenth Symposium of the Study Group on Ethnochoreology*. Copenhagen, 1988.

Torp, Lisbet. *Chain and Round Dance Patterns: A Method for Structural Analysis and Its Application to European Material*. 3 vols. Copenhagen, 1990.

Traditional Dance. Vols. 1–6. Alsager, Cheshire, 1982–1988. Proceedings of the traditional dance conferences held at Crew and Alsager College of Higher Education, edited by Theresa Buckland.

UCLA Journal of Dance Ethnology. Los Angeles, 1977–.

Williams, Drid. *Ten Lectures on Theories of the Dance*. Metuchen, N.J., 1991.

Wolfram, Richard. *Die Volkstänze in Österreich und verwandte Tänze in Europa*. Salzburg, 1951.

FILM. Alan Lomax, *Dance and Human History* (Berkeley: University of California Extension Center, 1976).

VIDEOTAPE. Rhoda Grauer, "Dancing," eight-part series (WNET-TV, New York, 1993).

COLIN QUIGLEY

New Areas of Inquiry

The theoretical and methodological perspectives articulated in cultural theory had a substantial impact on dance research in the 1980s and continue to open up significant lines of inquiry. *Cultural theory* as used here is an umbrella term that encompasses developments within poststructuralist textual criticism, cultural studies, contemporary Marxist and postcolonial discourse analysis, feminist and gender studies, and interpretive and reflexive research strategies. These areas of inquiry share a common orientation toward the natural as a historical and cultural category deserving critical investigation. Inquiries into what has been construed as natural in a given cultural and historical context have influenced methods in all disciplines of the humanities.

The immediate relevance of this orientation for dance research lies in the fact that the body and its movement are typically construed as natural phenomena. The body has registered or conveyed but never participated in the manufacture of social forces. It has sometimes represented inexplicable phenomena such as the unconscious, desire, libidinal or sexual impulses, or irrational, whimsical, or perverse actions; otherwise, it has been regarded as merely decorative, pleasurable, or fashionable. In all these capacities, the body remains a natural object, incapable of agency or intelligence. Through its persistent interrogation of the natural, cultural theory has begun to overturn these assumptions about the body and to insist that nonverbal aspects of human experience deserve serious consideration in the humanities' inquiries into human identity and behavior.

The critical investigation of the natural, relevant to both cultural theory and dance research, can be traced to the examination of language initiated by Ferdinand de Saussure in the early twentieth century. De Saussure characterized the basic unit of meaning in language as the *sign*, a unit composed of a sound or acoustic element known as the *signifier* and a conceptual element (lexical meaning) known as the *signified*. De Saussure proposed that the relationship between these two elements is arbitrary in that it is based on cultural agreement rather than on any natural order. This theory of language was subsequently applied by researchers to a wide variety of cultural phenomena. This work, loosely referred to as the practice of *semiotics,* undertook to study all cultural objects and events as signs whose decipherment depended on the interpretation of the vast number of cultural codes and conventions through which the signs operate (Jameson, 1972; Silverman, 1983; Barthes, 1968, 1982; and works by Culler, Lotman, Eco, Matejka, and Titunik).

To see dance movement as sign is to assume that a nonnatural relationship obtains between movement, the signifier, and the concept to which it refers, the signified; therefore, one assumes that such a relationship can be constituted in varying ways. Dance's meaning becomes the product of cultural agreement, the result of a systematic use of various choreographic codes and conventions. Such an approach not only permits one to detect different kinds of meanings in dance, but it also focuses attention on how a dance means what it does.

Semiotic analysis of dance divides choreographic codes and conventions into two kinds: those that order the dance by giving it an internal coherence and structure; and those that organize the dance with respect to the world that surrounds it. Conventions that give dance its internal order include the vocabulary of movements that make up the dance, and the syntactical principles—such as repetition, reiteration, theme and variation, or algorithmic and aleatory techniques—that govern the selection and combination of these movements. Conventions through which the dance makes reference to the world include its frame, the aspects such as publicity and venue that set the dance apart from all other events; its style, including the specific use of space, body parts, and movement qualities that give the dance a signature; and its modes of representation, indexical, iconic, or symbolic, through which the dance summons up its subject matter.

As an illustration of the ways these conventions generate meaning, consider two distinct examples of theatrical dance, Marius Petipa's ballet *Swan Lake* and Martha Graham's solo *Lamentation.* The movement vocabulary for *Swan Lake* consists largely of the classical steps that define the ballet tradition, along with refinements in arm and head positions that iconically resemble the movements of swans. *Lamentation*'s vocabulary consists of original movement—contractions, reaches, twists, and collapses performed seated on a bench—which Graham developed specifically for this dance. The ballet's syntax derives from both the plot and the musical score; that is, the sequence of movement choices must show the Swan Queen and the Prince falling in love, discovering betrayal, and so forth, and they must also relate to the rhythmic and melodic patterns for phrasing specified in the music. The syntax for *Lamentation* follows the logic of emotional progressions through various stages of grief and mourning. The movement phrases build toward and fall away from climaxes which correspond to the experience of grieving and the struggle to express grief.

Swan Lake is framed not only by the proscenium stage but also by the specific auspices—company, season, and occasion—under which it is presented. *Lamentation* similarly takes place on a framed stage, but it first appeared as one of several solos performed by an emerging artist in her only concert of the season in New York.

Style in the two dances operates at many levels simultaneously. Balletic style differs from Graham's modern dance style in its emphasis on peripheral over core body parts; in its exploration of aeriality and effortless execution over sinuous, tensile, and restrained quality of movement; and in the symmetrical and painterly disposition of dancers in the space rather than the asymmetrical and sculptural treatment of the body in space. Each dance company and each individual dancer also develops a unique style which contributes to the overall impact of the work. For example, the Swan Queen's role can be performed with delicate fragility or assertive regality; similarly, each reconstructor of Graham's solo infuses it with a specific physicality and dynamism.

Modes of representation also work on several levels. In *Swan Lake* the crown worn by the Swan Queen is an index of her status, while her gestural dialogue with the Prince iconically represents pleading for the swans' lives; her wicked counterpart, Odile, functions as a symbol of evil forces at work within the enchanted world the characters inhabit. Taken as a whole, the ballet operates iconically to provide a visual likeness of a magical kingdom. In contrast, *Lamentation* functions primarily in a symbolic mode by presenting movement that shares essential qualities with certain psychological events. The information conveyed through these kinds of conventions crucially determines the overall significance and impact of the dance.

This kind of semiotic analysis forms the basis for each of the various interpretive strategies that constitute cultural theory. For example, poststructuralist textual criticism uses a semiotic analysis to map resonances between specific texts or traditions of text-making and the larger cultural context in which they occur (Barthes, 1974, 1978; Derrida, 1976, 1978; Harari, 1979). These inquiries have expanded the notion of the text to encompass cultural phenomena as diverse as film, television, advertisements, comics, computer-aided communication, and all forms of printed matter. As kinds of texts, each of these cultural events manifests a syntactic coherence, ways of referring to the world, and a theoretical orientation through which it comments on its position as a text among other texts. By extension, any given dance or dance practice embodies a theorizing of relationships between body and self and between body and society. Learning to choreograph, the choreographer learns to theorize; learning to dance, the dancer assimilates the body of facts and the structuring of discursive frameworks that permit theorization.

When applied to dance research, textual studies encourage examination of the relations among everyday patterns of behavior, other structured movement practices, and dance movement. They also advocate investigation of resonances between dance practices and other cultural practices in terms of genres, such as the solo and the large group work, or the intimate and informal event and the spectacular and grand event; modes of expression, such as the revelation of interior feeling or the display of virtuoso physical accomplishment; pedagogical practices that discipline the body to prepare it to participate in a given choreographic project; and conceptions of bodily identity and of bodily relationship to self. In each of these areas dance may mirror, contravene, or build on similar kinds of values articulated in other cultural practices. Investigating these kinds of relations yields a better understanding of a given dance's meaning and also of dance's participation in the construction of broader cultural values (Banes, 1994; Franko, 1993; Ness, 1992; Novack, 1990).

Resonances between a dance and other cultural practices often stabilize around values of race, class, or gender. Approaches to cultural criticism elaborated in the field of cultural studies have explored a variety of phenomena in an effort to comprehend their role in maintaining or redistributing power along racial, class, or gender lines (Bhabha, 1990; Foucault, 1978; Said, 1978; Spivak, 1987; Trinh, 1989). Their findings suggest treating dance as a form of cultural production infused with political and ideological implications for power relations (Attali, 1985; Martin, 1990). Dance's political and ideological messages are conveyed through both the subject matter of a given dance—as in the stereotypic depictions of Spanish and Hungarian dances in act 3 of *Swan Lake*—and in its choreographic form. For example, dances presented on a proscenium stage offer a hierarchy of optimal viewing locations, whereas dances performed in theaters-in-the-round imply egalitarian viewing conditions. In order to assess more fully the political values of which a dance is capable, cultural studies also advocate reexamination of traditional boundaries between and functions ascribed to dance genres classified as "high" art or "popular" culture. Whether the functions of edification and entertainment attributed to such events remain viable, and whether viewers' and participants' involvement at elite and mass-culture dance events is homogeneous, are questions to which cultural studies seek answers.

Economic theories add to these lines of inquiry by arguing for an assessment of dance as a kind of cultural production which entails certain forms of labor and compensation and which requires patronage, government funding, or other kinds of financial support (Jameson, 1971; Williams, 1958, 1981). Any practice or presentation of dance takes place within a given political and economic environment, and its success depends on its ability to interface with the legal requirements of the state and to draw potential viewers and participants (Garafola, 1989). Strategies for publicizing, marketing, and distributing dance can have an important effect on its overall conception and impact. Technologies of documentation and reproduction of dance forms, styles of moving and of dance-making, assist in establishing markets for dance practices on a global scale.

As a form of cultural production, dance can also participate in the global exchange of goods, serving as a symbol of regional or national identity and participating in projects of colonization and decolonization through which power relations among governments and businesses are articulated. For example, the European tradition of ballet has been adopted as a principal form of theatrical dance in Canada, Australia, and Hong Kong, all former British colonies; it also enjoys great popularity in the communist countries of Cuba and China. Similarly, the Argentine tango, taken up enthusiastically in Paris in the early twentieth century, has recently captured substantial public attention in Japan and Finland. Each instance of importation and exportation of dance forms results from complex relations among nations, conceptions of national identity—of the exotic and the marketable—which have begun to be elaborated in postcolonial discourse and in neo-Marxist analyses of capital (Savigliano, 1995).

Feminist theory, through its interrogation of the relationship between biological and cultural bodily constructions, has concerned itself with the category of gender, as well as with sexuality and sexual orientation, each of which can be encoded choreographically (Cowan, 1990; Manning, 1993). In order to ascertain how a dance performs roles of gender and sexuality, research focuses on all choreographic conventions through which masculine and feminine attributes and representations of physical intimacy and desire are expressed. These include the kinds of movements and movement qualities that are typically assigned to male or female dancers; conventions for touching and partnering same-sex and opposite-sex dancers; and codes of movement or of looking through which the dancer orients the viewer's gaze on the body. All techniques that exaggerate or otherwise satirize stereotypic comportment for male and female bodies are also relevant to an analysis of gender and sexuality (Butler, 1990; Case, 1988; De Lauretis, 1984; McClary, 1991; Sedgwick, 1985; Silverman, 1988).

Any given dance presents bodies gendered in a specific way, but a dance form or tradition can also embody gender attributes that signal a masculine or feminine approach to movement. Any dance tradition may also achieve a gendered identity within the culture as a masculine or feminine pursuit. The motivation within feminist theory to examine these constellations of gendered attributes stems from the unequal participation and representation of men and women in various cultural practices, from their unequal access to systems of power and governance, and from the pervasive tendency to allow masculine identity and conduct to stand both for male actions and for all human action. Masculine values thereby assume an unmarked status against which all other marked values are compared.

The emphasis in cultural theory on how events mean extends to an examination of the researcher's own role in determining that meaning. Cultural theory encourages awareness of the researcher's role in identifying, interpreting, and synthesizing evidence; it has experimented with an impressive array of devices designed to signal this awareness to the reader (Clifford, 1988; De Certeau, 1988; White, 1978). This reflexive understanding of the relationship between the subject of research and the process of research has special significance for dance scholarship, given the difficulties of documenting dance and of translating dance into written text. The fact that dance vanishes in the moment of its performance, leaving little evidence of its existence, and that its eloquence derives entirely from nonverbal action, illuminate the processes through which it is reconstituted for purposes of research. Dance scholars working to embody these processes in their writing contribute to cultural theory not only their invaluable insights into bodily practices, but also their profound understanding of the project of translating from one cultural domain to another.

The entry "Dance" in Diderot's *Encyclopédie* asserts confidently that dance consists of "regulated movements of the body, jumps, and measured steps performed to the sound of musical instruments or the voice." The entrance of cultural theories into dance research destabilizes such claims by demonstrating multiple, distinct approaches to the interpretation and even the definition of dance. Cultural theory facilitates an examination of a dance's cultural meanings and at the same time focuses attention on the research process itself. By recognizing in the body the ability to signify in different ways, cultural theory offers to dance research a broad repertory of strategies for analyzing dance and a new conception of the relationship between dance and the language that describes it. Applying cultural theory to various dance topics, scholars can elucidate a cultural identity for the dancing body, the dancing individual, and the dancing group. In undertaking such an inquiry, they also position their own bodies as participants in the process of making dance meaningful.

BIBLIOGRAPHY

Attali, Jacques. *Noise.* Translated by Brian Massumi. Minneapolis, 1985.

Banes, Sally. *Writing Dancing in the Age of Postmodernism.* Middletown, Conn., 1994.

Barthes Roland. *The Elements of Semiology.* Translated by Annette Lavers and Colin Smith. New York, 1968.

Barthes, Roland. *S/Z.* Translated by Richard Miller. New York, 1974.

Barthes, Roland. *Image/Music/Text.* Translated by Stephen Heath. New York, 1978.

Barthes, Roland. *Empire of Signs.* Translated by Richard Howard. New York, 1982.

Bhabha, Homi K., ed. *Nation and Narration.* London, 1990.

Butler, Judith. *Gender Trouble.* New York, 1990.

Case, Sue-Ellen. *Feminism and Theatre.* New York, 1988.

Clifford, James. *The Predicament of Culture.* Cambridge, Mass., 1988.

Cowan, Jane K. *Dance and the Body Politic in Northern Greece.* Princeton, 1990.

Culler, Jonathan D. *Structuralist Poetics.* Ithaca, N.Y., 1975.

De Certeau, Michel. *The Writing of History.* Translated by Tom Conley. New York, 1988.

De Lauretis, Teresa. *Alice Doesn't.* Bloomington, 1984.

De Lauretis, Teresa. *Technologies of Gender.* Bloomington, 1987.

Derrida, Jacques. *Of Grammatology.* Translated by Gayatri Chakravorty Spivak. Baltimore, 1976.

Derrida, Jacques. *Writing and Difference.* Translated by Alan Bass. Chicago, 1978.

Eco, Umberto. *The Role of the Reader.* Bloomington, 1979.

Foster, Susan Leigh. *Reading Dancing.* Berkeley, 1986.

Foster, Susan Leigh. *Choreography and Narrative.* Bloomington, 1996.

Foucault, Michel. *The Order of Things.* New York, 1971.

Foucault, Michel. *The Archaeology of Knowledge.* Translated by Alan Sheridan. New York, 1974.

Foucault, Michel. *Discipline and Punish.* Translated by Alan Sheridan. New York, 1978.

Foucault, Michel. *The History of Sexuality.* Translated by Robert Hurley. New York, 1978.

Franko, Mark. *Dance as Text: Ideologies of the Baroque Body.* New York, 1993.

Garafola, Lynn. *Diaghilev's Ballets Russes.* New York, 1989.

Harari, Josué V., ed. *Textual Strategies.* Ithaca, N.Y., 1979.

Jameson, Fredric. *Marxism and Form.* Princeton, 1971.

Jameson, Fredric. *The Prison-House of Language.* Princeton, 1972.

Jameson, Fredric. *The Political Unconscious.* Ithaca, N.Y., 1981.

Lotman, Jurij. *The Structure of the Artistic Text.* Translated by Ronald Vroon and Gail Vroon. Ann Arbor, Mich., 1977.

Manning, Susan A. *Ecstasy and the Demon: Feminism and Nationalism in the Dances of Mary Wigman.* Berkeley, 1993.

Martin, Randy. *Performance as Political Act.* New York, 1990.

McClary, Susan. *Feminine Endings.* Minneapolis, 1991.

Meglin, Joellen A. "Representations and Realities: Analyzing Gender Symbols in the Romantic Ballet." Ph.D.diss., Temple University, 1995.

Ness, Sally Ann. *Body, Movement, and Culture.* Philadelphia, 1992.

Novack, Cynthia J. *Sharing the Dance.* Madison, Wis., 1990.

Said, Edward W. *Orientalism.* New York, 1978.

Savigliano, Marta E. *Tango and the Political Economy of Passion.* Boulder, 1995.

Sedgwick, Eve Kosofsky. *Between Men.* New York, 1985.

Silverman, Kaja. *The Subject of Semiotics.* New York, 1983.

Silverman, Kaja. *The Acoustic Mirror.* Bloomington, 1988.

Spivak, Gayatri Chakravorty. *In Other Worlds.* New York, 1987.

Sturrock, John, ed. *Structuralism and Since.* Oxford, 1979.

Trinh T. Minh-ha. *Woman, Native, Other.* Bloomington, 1989.

White, Hayden. *Metahistory.* Baltimore, 1973.

White, Hayden. *The Tropics of Discourse.* Baltimore, 1978.

Williams, Raymond. *The Sociology of Culture.* New York, 1981.

SUSAN LEIGH FOSTER

METROPOLITAN BALLET. Based in London, the Metropolitan Ballet was active for only a few years (1947–1949) in the wake of World War II. Although it had a short life, it gave the stage to many young artists who later won international acclaim, and for this reason alone it has an important place in the history of British ballet.

The company, which opened at the Devonshire Park Theatre, Eastbourne, on 27 January 1947, was an amalgamation of two small companies, Letty Littlewood's Anglo-Russian Ballet and Leon Hepner's Fortune Ballet, both of which had been formed to work with the Entertainments National Service Association, organized to provide entertainment for military personnel during the war. The Metropolitan Ballet was run by Hepner alone during its initial season but was soon reorganized with Cecilia Blatch as director general and financial backer. A nucleus of dancers from the two former companies was strengthened by such artists as Sonia Arova and Henry Danton from the International Ballet, Eric Hyrst from the Sadler's Wells Theatre Ballet, and Colette Marchand and Serge Perrault from Paris.

As artistic adviser, George Kirsta designed most of the productions in the company's repertory. Victor Gsovsky, the first ballet master, was responsible not only for reviving the classics, such as *Swan Lake* (act 2), *Les Sylphides,* and various pas de deux, but also for creating original works. For the company's first season he made *Dances of Galánta,* set to a score by Zoltán Kodály, and *Pygmalion,* set to music by John Field. The remainder of the repertory was made up of works by Letty Littlewood: *The Marchaund's Tale,* set to music of Hubert Bath; *Caprice Viennois,* to the familiar piece by Fritz Kreisler; and *Picnic,* set to music of Arcangelo Corelli.

By the autumn of 1947, after the company's first tours, the Metropolitan Ballet was completely reorganized and the personnel changed considerably. Celia Franca became ballet mistress as well as a principal dancer. Nicholas Beriozoff was the company's *régisseur,* and his daughter, Svetlana Beriosova (then aged fifteen), was to become a principal ballerina. Of the original principals, only Arova and Hyrst remained. Others who joined the company as principal dancers were Poul Gnatt and Erik Bruhn, from the Royal Danish Ballet; Frank Staff, recently returned from South Africa (and who was first hired as resident choreographer); the Australians Peggy Sager and Paul Hammond; the Dutch Aart Verstegen; and the Canadian David Adams. John Lanchbery became musical director.

By the time the Metropolitan Ballet gave its first central London season, at the Scala Theatre in June 1948, the repertory had been considerably strengthened by two new ballets by Staff, *The Lovers' Gallery* and *Fanciulla delle Rose;* by Beriozoff's staging of Michel Fokine's choreography for the *Polovtsian Dances* from *Prince Igor;* and by John Taras's *Designs with Strings,* set to Tchaikovsky's Trio in A Minor. The Taras work, created for the company, was one of the highlights of the season, as was Beriozoff's production of Fokine's *Le Spectre de la Rose,* with Beriosova and Bruhn. The success of the season firmly established the company in the British dance scene. Immediately afterward, it appeared at the Royal Opera House, Covent Garden, in a musical version of John Bunyan's *Pilgrim's Progress,* for which Andrée Howard choreographed the dances.

A Scandinavian tour, followed by an English winter tour in 1948/49, saw more changes in personnel. Notably, Frank Schaufuss replaced Gnatt and Bruhn, who had to return to Copenhagen. In June 1949, the company gave a London season in the Empress Hall arena, with Alexandra Danilova, Léonide Massine, and Frederic Franklin as guest artists in a production of Massine's *Le Beau Danube.* A subsequent season at the Lyric Theatre, Hammersmith, gave London its first viewing of any work by August Bournonville, the pas de deux from *Flower Festival in Genzano,* staged by Elsa-Marianne von Rosen and danced by her with Henry Danton. The company's final creation, Rosella Hightower's *Pleasuredrome,* set to a score by Lanchbery, was shown in a London season at the People's Palace in November 1949, after which the company had to close because of lack of money.

[*See also the entries on the principal figures mentioned herein.*]

BIBLIOGRAPHY

Noble, Peter, ed. *British Ballet.* London, 1949.

Percival, John. "Backward Glances: The Metropolitan Ballet." *Dance and Dancers* (February 1960): 20–22.

PETER WILLIAMS

METROPOLITAN OPERA BALLET, the resident dance company of the Metropolitan Opera in New York City, dances the incidental ballets of opera. Throughout its history the Metropolitan Opera has presented ballet in the form of *divertissements* within operas or, during rare periods, in separate works on the same bill with short operas. Unlike the opera companies of Europe, it has never had separate ballet seasons at the Opera House or even regular separate performances of ballets during the opera season. These limited performing opportunities have prevented the Metropolitan Opera Ballet from rivaling the best American companies.

Established simultaneously in 1883 with the Metropolitan Opera, during its early years the Metropolitan Opera Ballet consisted of one or two *première danseuses* and a small corps of female dancers. The majority of the dancers came from Europe, since opportunities for serious ballet training in the United States were meager at that time. The first head of the Opera Ballet and its first *prima ballerina* was Malvina Cavallazzi, one of the many Italian artists from the Teatro alla Scala in Milan who dominated the upper echelons of the Opera Ballet until the 1930s.

Among the highlights of the first twenty-five years were the production of the *Walpurgis Night* ballet from Gounod's *Faust* during the 1885/86 season, with Italian ballerinas Marie Bonfanti and Bettina de Sortis as principals, and the staging of the Metropolitan's first self-contained ballet, *Vienna Waltzes.* The latter, staged by Giovanni Ambroggio after Louis Frappert, was a three-part spectacle that included an Austrian village scene, a wedding, and a final tableau. During the 1893/94 season the company brought the extravaganza *America* to its stage from the Chicago World's Fair. Patterned after Manzotti's *Excelsior,* which was first produced at the Teatro alla Scala in 1881, *America* traced the history of the United States from the landing of the Pilgrims to the dawn of the electric age.

METROPOLITAN OPERA BALLET. From 1883 to 1965, the Metropolitan Opera Ballet performed in productions at the opulent opera house located at Broadway and Thirty-ninth Street in New York. Here, in 1938, company members, spread downstage and up the stairs, take part in Boris Romanov's staging of Gluck's opera *Orfeo ed Euridice.* (Photograph by Wide World Studio; from the Dance Collection, New York Public Library for the Performing Arts.)

During its first decade the company functioned without men; women danced any male roles required *en travesti* (in masculine costume). The first important *premier danseur* was Luigi Albertieri, a protégé of Enrico Cecchetti. Albertieri made his debut in 1895 and held the post of ballet master intermittently for ten years. It was not until the 1920s that the first regular male corps members were engaged.

In 1909 Giulio Gatti-Casazza, the Metropolitan Opera's general manager, who had been director of La Scala, brought Cavallazzi to New York to start a ballet school. By 1914 enough pupils had graduated into the ballet company that it was no longer necessary to import dancers for the corps; a young pupil of Cavallazzi, Eva Swain, became the Metropolitan's first American *première danseuse.* Pauline Verhoeven succeeded Cavallazzi as director of the school and taught there until her death in 1917. Margaret Curtis, a pupil of Cavallazzi and Michel Fokine, then assumed the post, which she held until 1951. From 1951 until its closing in 1966 (when the Metropolitan moved to Lincoln Center), the school was headed by Antony Tudor and Margaret Craske. In its early years it was one of the few studios in New York where a dancer could obtain solid classical training, and it remained a respected institution throughout its history. Among its famous alumnae were Nora Kaye, Ruthanna Boris, and Sallie Wilson.

In February 1910, Anna Pavlova made her American debut with her partner Mikhail Mordkin in the Metropolitan Opera Ballet's production of *Coppélia*. The duo, with a corps they had assembled in Russia, performed at the Metropolitan during the next two seasons. Another renowned European ballerina, Adeline Genée, appeared in a production of *Coppélia* in 1912. Although Pavlova and Genée were both sensations with the public, their visits did little to elevate the status of ballet at the Metropolitan.

Of more lasting impact was the engagement in 1914 of the youthful Rosina Galli. A product of La Scala's school, Galli was *première danseuse* at the Metropolitan from 1914 until 1930, and ballet mistress from 1919 to 1935. The overall quality of ballet did not improve greatly under Galli, but she was an exceptionally gifted dancer and mime whose presence attracted attention from the press and the public. Galli's partner was Giuseppe Bonfiglio, also from La Scala, who arrived at the Metropolitan in 1897 and danced there for more than thirty years. Galli's most famous roles were in the *Polovtsian Dances* from Borodin's *Prince Igor*, choreographed by Ottokar Bartik in 1915 and *Le Coq d'Or* and *Petrouchka*, both staged by Adolph Bolm after Fokine, in 1917 and 1919, respectively.

During the reign of Galli and Gatti-Casazza, the Metropolitan Opera Ballet continued under a conservative nineteenth-century aesthetic. With Gatti-Casazza's departure in 1935, a new Metropolitan Opera management headed by Philip Johnson disbanded the resident ballet company to engage the fledgling company of George Balanchine, Lincoln Kirstein, and Edward M. M. Warburg.

The collaboration with Balanchine, which lasted only three seasons, was a failed opportunity for the Metropolitan to become home to a major national dance company. After Balanchine's departure, ballet at the Metropolitan generally reverted to old productions under directors Boris Romanov and Laurent Novikoff through the 1930s and 1940s. Nevertheless, stellar artists of the period danced there, including Felia Doubrovska, Ruth Chanova, Maria Gambarelli, and Marina Svetlova.

In 1950 the Metropolitan Opera Ballet initiated a brief collaboration with Ballet Theatre, during which Ballet Theatre contributed guest artists to the Opera Ballet and personnel to operate a joint school. Although the relationship proved unsatisfactory to both sides and was severed after one season, it had the lasting benefit of bringing Tudor and Craske to the Metropolitan Ballet School.

The 1951/52 season began the seven-year tenure of Zachary Solov as the Met's chief choreographer. Opinion about the quality of Solov's work is divided, but he did receive the first Capezio Award in 1951 for establishing "new standards of excellence within the area of the art which treats with opera ballet."

One of the most popular artists to dance in Solov's ballets was Janet Collins, the Metropolitan's *prima ballerina* from 1951 to 1954 and the first African-American principal to perform there. [*See the entry on Collins.*] Other ballerinas during Solov's time included Maria Karnilova, Mary Ellen Moylan, Carmen de Lavallade, and Alicia Markova. Solov organized a few all-ballet evenings, but they did not become a regular feature. Solov's successor, Alicia Markova (director from 1963 to 1969), also produced separate ballet evenings, but just once a year. During Markova's tenure, she also choreographed ballets for the opera and employed such guest choreographers as Katherine Dunham and Alexandra Danilova.

In 1976, while Norbert Vesak was the Metropolitan Opera Ballet's artistic director, a touring unit was established to keep members of the ballet troupe performing between opera seasons and thus maintain the quality of their dancing. In the early 1980s, twenty-three dancers under the directorship of Donald Mahler constituted both the touring and resident components of the company.

In 1983, for its one-hundredth birthday, the Metropolitan Opera presented an eight-and-a-half-hour celebration, which included the *Samson et Dalila* bacchanale, choreographed by Zachary Solov. In the spring of 1984, the Metropolitan's observance of one hundred years of nonoperatic performing arts included a distinguished roster of ballet and modern dance stars.

Since 1985, when Mahler resigned, the company has been led by its ballet mistress, Diana Levy; the Metropolitan's increased reliance on guest directors makes a resident choreographer unnecessary. The touring program was discontinued, since the opera's larger active repertory requires the dancers' full-time presence. Current production styles make greater use of the dancers than ever, and modern dancers and other specialists often supplement the Opera Ballet's fully contracted company of sixteen.

[*See also the entries on the principal figures mentioned herein.*]

BIBLIOGRAPHY

Moore, Lillian. "The Metropolitan Opera Ballet Story." *Dance Magazine* (January 1951): 20–29.

ARCHIVE. Metropolitan Opera Archives, New York.

TULLIA LIMARZI

MEXICO. [*To survey the dance traditions of Mexico, this entry comprises four articles:*

Traditional Dance
Theatrical Dance
Dance Companies
Dance Research and Publication

The first article explores the development of traditional dance as a fusion of indigenous and Spanish cultures; the second focuses on indigenous ceremonial dances and the introduction of European theatrical dance; the third discusses contemporary folkloric, modern, and ballet companies; the fourth provides a brief history of dance scholarship and writing.]

Traditional Dance

Mexico has the Pacific Ocean to the west and the Caribbean Sea to the east; it borders the United States to the north and Guatemala and Belize to the south. It was an important region of indigenous Mesoamerican civilizations before its early sixteenth-century contact with and conquest by the Spanish. Precolonial Mesoamerican peoples had lived throughout the deserts, plateaus, rain forests, and plains and along the seacoasts; some were hunters and gatherers at the time of contact; some were agricultural villagers—corn, beans, and squash had been domesticated here thousands of years ago; and some lived in and around the urban ceremonial centers of the Aztec, Toltec, Maya, Zapotec, Mixtec, and other civilizations.

Conquered in 1519–1521 by Christians whose country had in 1492 been won back from eight hundred years of domination by Islam, the Mesoamerican peoples experienced serious missionizing by Roman Catholics, slavery in agricultural and mining operations, and a series of epidemics—all of which resulted in the demise of the majority of the people and much of their cultures. Many of their ceremonial artworks (in gold, silver, and gemstones) were shipped to Europe. Made part of the viceroyalty of Nueva España (New Spain), Mexico fought for its independence, which was won in 1821. The indigenous cultures have survived in spite of those three hundred years of Spanish colonialism and the social and cultural predominance of a sector of the *mestizo* population.

Hundreds of traditional dances from all regions of Mexico form an essential part of the symbolic and value systems of marginalized social groups in Mexican society—indigenous peoples, poor peasants, and the unemployed. The social function of these dances is not to entertain foreign tourists but rather to express the point of view of these groups concerning their relationship to nature and to the society in which they live. Traditional Mexican dance is an important form of collective social practice. The social cohesion generated among the participants then plays a significant role in other aspects of communal life.

These dances may be characterized as traditional for two reasons. First, their form and content have been transmitted from generation to generation over a long period of time without undergoing major changes. Second, they learn these dances by observation and participation, rather than by formal training, spontaneously acquiring from childhood the fundamentals of style, design, meaning, and the other elements of the dance of their region.

MEXICO: Traditional Dance. Predating the Spanish conquest, "El Juego de los Voladores," with flying dancers dressed as birds, was an acrobatic and terrifying ceremonial spectacle. This print appears in Fray Javier Clavijero's *Historia antigua de México y de su conquista* (1844). (Reprinted from *Artes de México* 3 [March–August 1955], p. 15.)

Traditional Mexican dance is a choreographic form transmitted anonymously and spontaneously within a particular social group or region, by oral tradition and imitation. There are two major divisions, ceremonial dances *(danzas)* and secular dances *(bailes)*.

Ceremonial dances generally have a religious or magical function and are characterized by a formal choreography established in tradition, with rigid patterns of spatial distribution, steps, style, roles, costumes, and places of performance. Ceremonial dance performances require complex forms of social organization within the dance group—involving hierarchies, rights, duties, and sanc-

MEXICO: Traditional Dance. Mixing Spanish, Moorish, and indigenous Mexican elements, "Moros y Cristianos" (Moors and Christians) is a dance drama dating to the early sixteenth century. Its original purpose was to encourage the acceptance of Roman Catholicism and the supremacy of the Spanish empire. Here, two dancers engage in a mock battle with wooden swords. (Photograph by Luis Marquez; reprinted from *Artes de México* 3.8–9 [1955].)

tions—as well as close relations between the dance group and the civil and religious authorities.

There are some 225 Mexican ceremonial dances that have been described in the literature—and many more are currently performed but are not documented. Among the best-known examples of this genre are the dances of the Spanish conquest—"Moros y Cristianos" (Moors and Christians), and "La Pluma" (The Feather), for example—and others such as "Los Negritos" (The Blacks), "Los Voladores" (The Flyers), "El Venado" (The Deer), "Las Cintas" (The Ribbons), "Los Arcos" (Flower Arches), and "Las Pastoras" (The Shepherdesses).

Mexican secular dances are performed at nonritual festivals and private parties; they lack the religious or magical character of ceremonial dances. Their social function is generally to create a context for interaction between the sexes.

Although Mexican festive dances follow defined musical and choreographic patterns, they permit variations in design, steps, and interpretation. They are generally performed by couples, and their performance does not require complex forms of social organization or special costumes.

The majority of Mexican festive dances are derived from European court dances (such as the contradance, quadrille, galliard, mazurka, or waltz) or from popular Spanish dances (such as the *fandango, jota,* or *seguidillas*) which reached Mexico during the colonial period (sixteenth to nineteenth centuries), or after the War of Independence in 1810, when they were fashionable in Spain. In Mexico, these dances acquired a characteristically regional style and for that reason are also referred to as "regional dances."

The regional dances that have achieved the widest distribution in Mexico are the *jarabe* and *sone* (*chilena, jarana, cuadrilla, huapango,* and others). These developed different characteristics in the various regions, which are now rapidly disappearing. Every year there are fewer places in Mexico where the inhabitants remember these traditional dances, and even fewer where they are still performed.

Traditional Mexican dance has developed over the centuries as a fusion of indigenous pre-Christian and Spanish culture. Unfortunately, there are few historical studies of its evolution, and it is difficult to identify with certainty the origins of the majority of these dances. This entry therefore presents a general picture of what is known of the historical development of traditional Mexican dance.

The archeological and historical sources for reconstructing the traditional dance forms of the precolonial era consist of clay and stone figures, decorative temple images, codexes, and the texts of clerics and chroniclers. The following information refers only to Nahuatl culture, which was dominant in Mesoamerica. Fray Toribio de Benavente noted that in the precolonial period a distinction was drawn between *maceualiztli* (dances performed at festivals to honor the gods) and *netotiliztli* (dances of rejoicing or celebration). The Spaniards named these dances from a word in the Arawak language of the Caribbean Antilles, *areitos,* which the colonists used to refer to indigenous dances generically. The Spaniards also used *areitos* to refer collectively to the complex of dances, songs, and other activities associated with a ceremonial or festive occasion.

Fray Diego Durán described a *netotiliztli* performed by "unchaste women and libidinous men" that was known as the *cuecuechcuicatli* ("ticklish," or "itchy," dance). According to Francisco Javier Clavijero, the major dances *(macehualiztli)* were performed in three or more concentric circles, depending on the number of participants. The dancers in the smaller interior circles moved slowly; this was a choreographic space reserved for the nobility and the elderly. The dancers in the larger exterior circles had to move rapidly to maintain the straightness of the lines formed by the performers, which crossed each circle. The musicians were located in the center of the circles.

There were also dances performed by men and women who held hands and formed lines which moved in serpentine patterns; or they formed two lines led by two guides *(delanteros),* who were the best dancers or the bravest warriors.

Although all the chroniclers agree that the movements of the dancers were well coordinated, little information is provided about the specifics of the choreography. One of the few descriptions of these dances found in the chronicles is of one dedicated to the god Xilonen: "Some of the dancers joined hands, others threw their arms around their partner's waist; all in unison raised one foot, stepped forward and back, and performed turns in time to the music. They danced backsteps between the torches or bonfires."

The chroniclers state that before the Spanish conquest, three thousand to four thousand people would participate in the dances. By the middle of the sixteenth century, the number had dropped to one thousand and it continued to decrease rapidly.

The themes of the dances included wars and other historical or religious events. There were also dances based on economic activities such as hunting or agriculture. Dances were performed as part of the celebration of stages in the life cycle, particularly marriage. During festivals to honor a god, a slave was selected to play the part of that god and was sacrificed as part of the ceremony. A traditional character at the dances was a buffoon, dressed as an old woman or a clown, whose role was to make people laugh.

Considerable detailed information exists concerning the design of the dancers' costumes and the materials from which they were made. A great variety of costumes were employed in the dances, depending on the theme; some portrayed eagles, tigers, monkeys, dogs, hunters, or soldiers.

Sometimes the dancers' bodies were colorfully painted. It was common for a precolonial priest to dance wearing the skin of a slave who had been ritually sacrificed and flayed. The dancers were frequently adorned with colorful flowers, precious stones, gold or silver jewelry, or feathers. They often wore masks and carried cornstalk staffs. The dancers were supervised by officials to ensure that they maintained a serious and respectful attitude during the performance. According to Sahagún, if a singer or dancer made a mistake he or she would be seized and later executed.

Certain dances were performed only by the nobility; others were performed only by warriors or merchants. Women participated in almost all the dances. Some dances were only for maidens, while others—such as those to honor the men fallen in battle—were open to all women. There were dances performed only by women, but sometimes young boys would be allowed to join these.

According to Durán, in the ancient cities of Mexico, Texcoco, and Tabuba, there were large mansions called *cuicacalli,* where teachers of dance and song lived and taught. They were distinguished elders selected to dedicate themselves exclusively to teaching the traditional songs and dances. Their students were boys and girls between twelve and fourteen years of age. Durán provides various details concerning the teaching methods used, noting that dance and song were always taught together.

In the province of Tlalhuic, the people worshiped a god of dances from whom they would ask permission before dancing. The god was represented by a stone idol whose arms were spread wide in the attitude of a dancing figure. The idol was adorned with roses around its neck and

MEXICO: Traditional Dance. "La Danza de las Cintas" is a choral dance popular in the state of Tlaxcala (where it is also known as "La Garrocha" or "La Vara"). The dance is said to have roots in ancient harvest celebrations. The eight or ten pairs of men and women interweave multicolored ribbons as they dance around a pole nine and one-half feet (3 meters) tall. (Photograph by Luis Marquez; reprinted from *Artes de México* 3.8–9 [1955].)

hands and with feathers on its back, like the dancers themselves.

Benavente indicated that songs and dances were performed at the major festivals, which were celebrated at twenty-day intervals. The most important dances were presented in the town plaza, the patio of the lord's house, or at the houses of chiefs. Some dances occurred in the morning and afternoon; others began at sundown and ended about nine o'clock in the evening; still others began about nine o'clock in the evening and ended at midnight.

In 1521, the Spanish captured the city of Tenochitlan, the capital and ceremonial center of the Aztec Empire. The new culture that emerged destroyed many indigenous customs while it preserved or transformed others, fusing them with the Spanish culture of that time. The conquest of what the Spanish crown was to name Nueva España (New Spain) was based on a strategy of cultural and military confrontation, both justified on theological grounds.

The religious conversion of the original inhabitants of New Spain was the spearhead of a campaign to impose a wholly different economic, political, and social system. Various forms of artistic expression were utilized in carrying out the evangelization of the recently conquered. The introduction into Mexico of "Moros y Cristianos" (Moors and Christians) is one example of this tactic. This dance came into being in Spain during the period of the reconquest of the country from the Muslims (Moors). Its performance by the victims of the Spanish conquest in the New World encouraged an acceptance of the superiority of the Spanish Empire and its religion.

Bernal Díaz del Castillo mentioned "Moros y Cristianos" as first performed in Mexico in 1524, as part of the celebration by Spanish troops at the arrival of Fernando Cortés in the Port of Coatzacoalco, Veracruz. Díaz del Castillo also describes the performance of this dance (a mock battle) in 1538 in Mexico City, to celebrate the signing of the peace treaty between Spain's emperor, Carlos V, and the king of France. On this occasion the dance was performed by Mexica people and Spanish soldiers. Benavente says that a year later the same dance was performed in Tlaxcala, and it included a portrayal of the capture of Jerusalem; this performance used groups of dancers representing Spaniards, indigenous Mexicans, and Moors.

The anthropologist Arturo Warman (1972) suggests that the "Dance of Moors and Christians" is a Mexican variant of the Moorish dances *(moriscas)* of Spain. Other Mexican variants, incorporating figures and events from Mexican history, developed in the sixteenth to nineteenth centuries. According to Warman, these variants include the dances of the conquest such as "La Pluma" (The Feather) and "La Conquista de México" (The Conquest of Mexico); the *Santiagos* (various dances with different names, in all of which the main character is Santiago); and the *concheros,* various dances in which two groups of performers confront each other, such as "Los Caballeros" (The Horsemen), "Las Coloradas" (The Red-Colored Ones), "Los Espejos" (The Mirrors), "Los Indios" (The Indians), "El Paloteo" (The Fight with Sticks), and "Las Sonajas" (The Timbrels).

During the sixteenth century, not only were Spanish dances adopted by native Mexicans groups, but various genres of their own dance continued to be performed despite prohibitions decreed by the Roman Catholic church in 1524, 1550, 1555, and 1585. Perceiving the impossibility of eradicating traditional dance, some missionaries advocated a policy of tolerance for games and dances of rejoicing. They argued that it was good policy to permit recreation "when appropriate." The missionaries tried to transform the dances by purifying them of "superstitious" elements so that they could be performed "to do honor to God and the saints." Nonetheless, in 1775 and again in 1853 church authorities sought to prohibit these dances—whether of traditional or Spanish origin—on the grounds that they were superstitious and alien to Roman Catholic liturgy.

During Mexico's colonial period, European court dances and popular Spanish dances were introduced and were transformed; they acquired distinctively Mexican characteristics. These dances were brought to New Spain by dance teachers, who began to arrive relatively soon after the Conquest. The dances were presented by professional dancers during intermissions at theatrical performances.

The church also sought to prohibit these dances, as evidenced by hundreds of cases in the seventeenth and eighteenth centuries in which people were denounced to the Inquisition for participating in them. A number of these dances (for example, the *rumba, habanera, guarache,* and *chuchumbe*) show clear African influence by way of the Caribbean islands.

In the eighteenth century the dances called the *jarabe, jarana,* and *huapango* (dances derived from the Spanish *fandango* and *seguidillas,* and the *zapateado*) came to be referred to as *sones* or *sonecitos del pueblo* ("cute little popular dances"). According to Maya Ramos (1979), these dances were performed at religious as well as secular festivals—even before church altars.

At the beginning of the nineteenth century, during the War of Independence from Spain, the *jarabe* developed into an important national symbol. According to the musicologist Gabriel Saldivar (1937), the music from these dances was used to inspire and raise the spirits of Mexican soldiers in combat. *Jarabe* music also accompanied combat troops in the Mexican-American War of 1847, the War against the French Intervention in 1862, and the Revolution of 1910.

The great variety of traditional Mexican dances makes it impossible to elaborate a model applicable to all of them. Therefore, this entry will seek to describe only those features about which generalizations may be drawn. The following observations pertain primarily to the dances that formed part of the evangelization campaign of the sixteenth and seventeenth centuries—and that are still performed today.

A number of traditional dances—such as "La Conquista de México" (The Conquest of Mexico), "Los Cuchillos" (The Knives), and "La Culebra" (The Snake)—vary widely in regional choreography or interpretation. Other dances have different names in the different regions but are actually identical. For example, the dance called "Los Toreadores" (The Bullfighters) is known in various parts of Mexico as "Los Vaqueros" (The Cowboys), "Los Espueleros" (The Spur-Wearers), or "Los Vaqueritos" (The Cowhands). Almost all these dances are interpreted in choral form. The number of participants is also variable, with some involving as many as 150 dancers.

Traditional dances, which are generally referred to as *sones,* consist of various choreographic units because this is the musical genre they most frequently use. In many cases, each of these units also acquires a name referring to the role the unit plays in the dance (entrance, salute, and so on) or to the principal type of movement it employs (chains, twirling); the name may also be based on the title of the musical piece that accompanies it.

The basic geometric design of the majority of Mexican dances employs parallel lines or, less frequently, a circle. Variations of these two basic designs have evolved to include four parallel lines, diagonal lines, intertwined couples, and chains. The dancers are led into these choreographic patterns by one or two of the most experienced members, who are usually called *punteros* ("pointers"), *delanteros* ("forwards"), or *monarcas* ("monarchs"), depending on the type of dance and the region in which it is performed. The dancers' movements are generally confined to the legs and feet. The dance steps are simple but composite—tapping movements, slides, backsteps, small leaps and jumps, and numerous bows. The torso usually remains rigid; the body posture maintains a general rigidity. The dancers perform with little display of emotion or movement in space.

The majority of traditional Mexican dances have a ritual character and are performed for religious or magical reasons. When part of Roman Catholic rites, these dances constitute a form of worship. They serve as an offering to a venerated religious icon, to express gratitude, or to request favors, miracles, or merely everyday subsistence. The dances are not recreational, nor are they meant as spectacles for the entertainment of tourists.

MEXICO: Traditional Dance. Carnival is a popular occasion for dance in Mexico. Here, a street dancer at Pinotepa de Don Luis in Guerrero, dressed as a demon, menacingly waves an icon of a nude woman in his left hand. (Photograph © by Roberto Ashentrupp; used by permission.)

Although not all dances have themes, those that do tend to fall into two categories, those with and those without imitative and narrative images. A marked characteristic is their prolonged duration; some performances may last as long as two days. The imitative dances generally portray animals, personalities, groups, economic activities, or wars. Examples include "Los Jaguares" (The Jaguars), "La Tortuga" (The Turtle), "Los Caníbales" (The Cannibals), "Los Cañeros" (The Cane Cutters), "Los Hortelanos" (The Orchard Keepers), "Los Arqueros" (The Archers), and "Los Paloteros" (The Stick Fighters). The narrative dances depict religious events, biblical stories, historical events, economic activities, and labor relations. The dancers' movements are accompanied by the recitation of spoken texts. Examples include "Los Arqueros" (The Archers), "Las Tres Potencias" (The Three Powers), "La Conquista de México" (The Conquest of Mexico), "La Pluma" (The Feather), "Los Arrieros" (The Mule Drivers), "Las Mulas" (The Mules), and "Los Negritos" (The Blacks). The dances that do not employ images tend to express a particular relation to a natural or social phenomenon. Some of these dances, such as "Las Canacuas" and "La Muerte" (Death), celebrate a stage in the life cycle; others, such as "Los Arcos" (Flower Arches) and "Las Cintas" (The Ribbons) are related to nature. Still other express veneration for an icon, such as "La Guadalupana" and "La Santa Cruz."

MEXICO: Traditional Dance. Carnival dancers in Tlaxcala often utilize historical costume, as seen here on the character Catrín, in the *cuadrilla* ("quadrille"), a dance of European origin. Dressed in nineteenth-century European frock coat, top hat, and black pants, the dancers wear wooden masks that imitate European facial features. (Photograph reprinted by permission from Amparo Sevilla, Hilda Rodríguez, and Elizabeth Camara, *Danzas y bailes tradicimales del estado de Tlaxcala,* Mexico City, 1983, p. 147.)

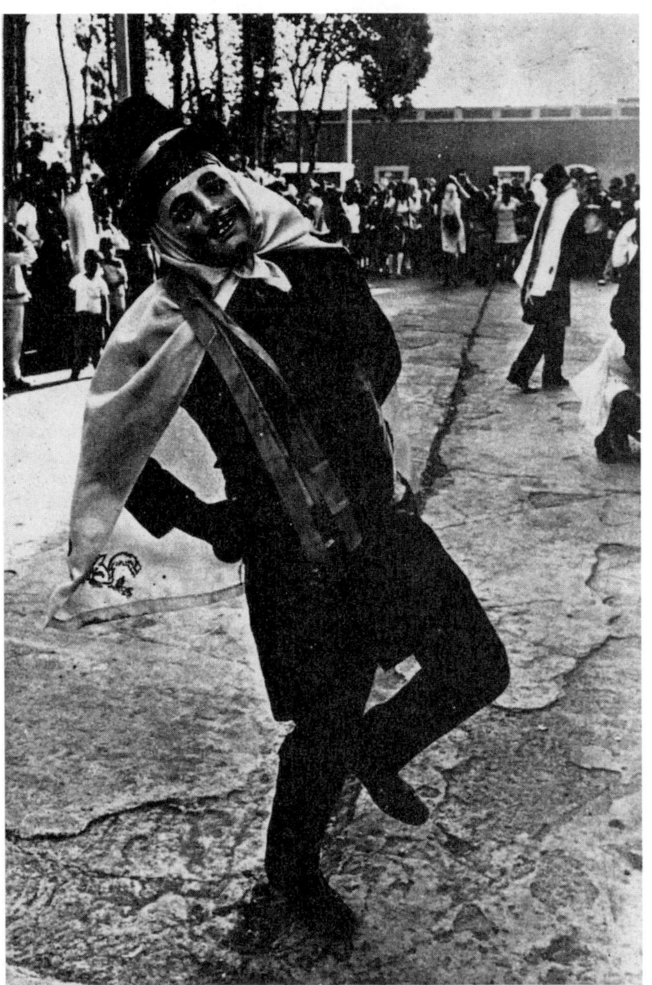

There are many character roles in traditional Mexican dances. Some are named for various military ranks, such as *mayor* ("major"), *capitan* ("captain"), and *alferez* ("ensign"). Others take their names from job titles in the *hacienda* (plantation) system, such as *caporal* ("foreman") or *capatáz* ("overseer"). Some are titles of nobility, such as *monarca* ("monarch") or *rey* ("king"). Others take their names from historical figures, such as Montezuma or Malinche, or from religious figures, such as Santiago or Mahoma (Muḥammad). At almost all dances there are individuals whose function is to circle around the dancers and tell jokes to entertain the audience; they also maintain space between dancers and spectators. These persons are called *gracejos* ("buffoons"), *chistosos* ("jokesters"), *corraleros* ("managers"), or *viejos* ("elders").

Most costumes show a marked Spanish influence in their materials—satin, velvet, sequins, and small mirrors and squares of glass—as well as in their design and embroidery. These elements are often combined with others of Mexican origin, such as feathers. Ornaments depicting national symbols also appear, such as the eagle perched on a nopal cactus, the Virgin of Guadalupe, or a peasant woman.

The organization of the dance performances generally forms part of the community's system of religious obligations. This system is embodied in the men's and women's religious organizations known as *hermandades* and *cofradías*. These organizations date from the colonial period and maintain close relationships with church authorities.

One or more people are given the responsibility to see that the dance performances take place. These individuals sometimes hold important offices in one of the religious organizations or work closely with them. They must obtain all the items necessary for the performance. They often provide the financing as well, although in some regions all the inhabitants make monetary contributions, in which case the persons responsible for the dance go door to door to solicit each family's contribution. They also bring the dancers together and assist in the teaching and rehearsal of the dances.

The dancers too assume a series of obligations as members of their dance group. These include learning roles, buying costumes, obeying the teacher, and, on occasion, helping to pay the musicians. Less frequent obligations include vows of silence and abstention from sexual activity, from certain foods, and from alcohol.

The dancers usually join the group because of a religious vow or promise they or one of their relatives has made. These vows may be in effect for several years or even a lifetime. Some dancers, however, join the group for pure enjoyment.

Most of the dances are open to participation only for men. Women have been barred from taking part in these dances since the Spanish conquest. The women's parts—

such as that of La Malinche, Cortés's Aztec interpreter, adviser, and lover—are played by young men or boys dressed as women. There are, however, certain dances performed exclusively by women, such as "Las Pastoras" (The Shepherdesses) and "Los Arcos" (Flower Arches). In some dances performed by certain Mesoamerican peoples, such as the Tarahumaras or the Zapotecs, the dancers are also women.

One of the principal characteristics of traditional Mexican dances is that they are not learned in schools or dance academies. Any member of the community, child or adult, who wishes to participate in a dance performance may, after observing the dances at community festivals for several years, attend rehearsals prior to the performance. The rehearsals are held in the home of the dance teacher, and there each participant is assigned his or her role in the performance. The newest members of the group are placed last in line.

The dances are performed at religious festivals dedicated to the patron saint of the community or to a venerated religious icon. At times they are done during pilgrimages, in sanctuaries, or at festivals in neighboring communities. The performance usually takes place in the atrium of the church, or sometimes in the sanctuary, with some dancers also going house to house through the community.

The accompanying music is diverse and depends on the type of dance and the region in which it is performed. Some indigenous dances use only a drum and a reed flute, such as "Los Voladores" (The Flyers) and "Los Quetzales" (The Quetzal Birds). Others use stringed instruments, generally a violin, a guitar, and a bass, or a combination of stringed and percussion instruments. Some may employ a band with brass instruments or even a full orchestra.

Although the Spanish conquistadors introduced stringed, wind, and percussion instruments into Mexico, some dances are still performed using only indigenous instruments such as the *teponaztli* and the *huehuetl* (drums made from tree trunks), round drums, water drums, reed flutes, timbrels, and rattles made of butterfly cocoons and seashells. The dancers themselves may play timbrels, castanets, small bells, the striker bow, canes, and tools or weapons such as sickles, machetes, knives, and whips.

The songs that accompany the dances have a structure of obvious Spanish origin and almost all express Christian religious themes. The songs are generally sung in Spanish, although some may be sung in indigenous languages. Narrative songs are called *relaciones;* they generally recount religious conflicts, such as those of the Moors and Christians cycle.

[*See also* Concheros; Ethnic Dance; *and* Matachins.]

BIBLIOGRAPHY

Acosta, José de. *Historia natural y moral de las Indias* (1590). Edited by Edmundo O'Gorman. 2d ed. Mexico City, 1962.

Benavente, Toribio de. *Memorias, o Libro de las cosas de la Nueva España y de los naturales de ella.* México City, 1971.

Benavente, Toribio de. *Historia de los indios de la Nueva España.* Porrúa, México, 1973.

Carmichael, Elizabeth, and Chloë Sayer. *The Skeleton at the Feast: The Day of the Dead in Mexico.* London, 1991.

Cashion, Susan Valerie. "Dance Ritual and Cultural Values in a Mexican Village: Festival of Santo Santiago." Ph.D. diss., Stanford University, 1983.

Clavijero, Francisco Javier. *Historia antigua de México* (1780–1781). Edited by P. Mariano Cuevas. 2d ed. Mexico City, 1964.

Delgado Martínez, César. "La danza folklórico en México." In *Proceedings of the Fourteenth Annual Conference, Society of Dance History Scholars, New World School of the Arts, Miami, Florida, 8–10 February 1991,* compiled by Christena L. Schlundt. Riverside, Calif., 1991.

Díaz del Castillo, Bernal. *Historia verdadera de la conquista de la Nueva España* (1632). 2 vols. Edited by Joaquín Ramírez Cabañas. 7th ed. Mexico City, 1977.

Durán, Diego. *Historia de las Indias de la Nueva-España.* 2 vols. Mexico City, 1967.

Florencia Pulido, Patricia del Carmen. *Crónica histórica del huapango huasteco veracruzano: Trovas, musica, danza y tradiciones.* Xalapa, 1991.

García Flores, Raúl. *Puro mitote! La música, el canto y la danza entre los chichimecas del Noreste.* Monterrey, 1993.

Lavalle, Josefina. *El jarabe.* Mexico City, 1988.

Lorenzana, Francisco Antonio. *Concilios provinciales.* Mexico City, 1769.

Mendieta, Gerónimo de. *Historia eclesiástica indiana.* Mexico City, 1945.

Motolinía, Toribio. *Memoriales* (1569). Edited by Edmundo O'Gorman. 2d ed. Mexico City, 1971.

Motolinía, Toribio. *Historia de los Indios de la Nueva España.* Edited by Edmundo O'Gorman. 2d ed. Mexico City, 1973.

Múzquiz, Rodolfo. *Bailes y danzas tradicionales.* Mexico City, 1988.

Olivera, Mercedes. *Las danzas y fiestas de Chiapas.* Fondo Nacional para el Desarrollo de la Danza Popular Mexicana, 1974.

Ramos Smith, Maya. *La danza en México durante la época colonial.* Mexico City, 1979.

Sahagún, Bernardino de. *Historia general de las cosas de Nueva España.* Edited by Angel María Garibay. 4 vols. Mexico City, 1956.

Saldívar, Gabriel. *El jarabe: Baile popular mexicano.* Mexico City, 1937.

Sevilla, Amparo. *Espresiones coreográficas y culturas subalternas,* 1984.

Sevilla, Amparo. *Danza, cultura y clases sociales.* Mexico City, 1990.

Smith, Deborah L. "Mexican Folk Dance in California." *UCLA Journal of Dance Ethnology* 15 (1991): 68–77.

Torquemada, Juan de. *Monarquía indiana* (1723). 7 vols. Edited by Miguel León-Portilla. 3d ed. Mexico City, 1975–.

Vélez Calvo, Raúl. *El baile y la danza en Guerrero.* 2d ed. Chilpancingo, 1992.

Warman, Arturo. *La danza de Moros y Cristianos.* Mexico City, 1972.

Warman, Arturo. "Danzas." In *Lo efímero y eterno del arte popular mexicano.* 2d ed. Mexico City, 1974.

AMPARO SEVILLA
Translated from Spanish

Theatrical Dance

Although Native American peoples and Mesoamerican civilizations had ceremonies and ceremonial dances that exhibited the magnificence of modern stage productions, the ingredients of theatrical dance as known today in

Mexico were introduced after the Conquest, when in the sixteenth century theatrical productions were organized to teach Roman Catholicism. The missionaries, in teaching, added small dance sequences, some inspired by native dances, to their theatrical works.

Theatrical dance in Mexico continued to develop in the seventeenth century, when professional theater companies included ballet dancers. Most of the famous actors and actresses counted dancing among their abilities. This was true of Ana María de Castro, Joseph Pisoni, and other performers who appeared at the Mexico City Coliseo, a theater built in 1671 and reconstructed several times.

European ballet masters visited the colonial region of New Spain toward the end of the eighteenth century, bringing spectacular staged allegoric, heroic, and pantomimic tableaux. Professional ballet was introduced in 1786 by Jerónimo Marani, a choreographer and dancer, although there is evidence that earlier some Italian dancers, such as Peregrino Turchi, Maria Rodríguez Turchi, and José Sabella Morali, had performed dances that could be called ballets. Between 1783 and 1786 there were eighty-nine performances with dancing, but only two of these were complete ballets—*El Jardin Encantado* and *Los Gitanos*. The prevailing idea that dancing was sinful (arousing the senses) affected not only dance's popular practice but also its theatrical performance; it was common for theatrical works containing dancing to be suspended by the authorities.

MEXICO: Theatrical Dance. During a visit to Mexico in 1919, Anna Pavlova and her company were taught several traditional Mexican dances by local teachers. Under the obvious title of *Mexican Dances*, three of them, classicized to include pointe work and set to music by Manuel Castro Padilla, entered her repertory in 1920. The authentic costumes and scenery, designed by Adolfo Best-Maugaro, were presented to her as a gift from the people of Mexico City. She is pictured here in *Jarabe Tapatio*, a "hat dance" characteristic of a region of Jalisco, near the city of Guadalajara. (Photograph by Ross Verlag, Berlin; from the Dance Collection, New York Public Library for the Performing Arts.)

Even with the support of certain governors, such as Count Bernardo de Gálvez (Intendent of New Spain, 1785–1786), ballet and other forms of theatrical dance did not flourish; yet boisterous popular dances performed during celebrations and festivities did. Nevertheless, there were efforts to make dance companies fully professional, so dancers were urged to aim for the highest standards. In the absence of professional ballet performances, popular dance genres developed and flourished onstage. In the last quarter of the eighteenth century, performers at the Coliseum danced to such popular tunes as "La Bamba Poblana," "Los Bergantines," "El Curritico," and "Los Chimistlanes."

In the last decade of the eighteenth century, the actor and dancer Jerónimo Marani lived and acted in Mexico and encouraged the taste for classical ballet. Another figure, Juan Medina, was in New Spain between 1796 and 1806; he widened the scope of professional ballet and *ballet d'action*, producing his own choreographies and structuring complete concerts of well-staged dance.

The independence movement of the early nineteenth century was paralleled by growing community support for professional dance. Many dance styles brought from Spain had taken root, and many dances original to New Spain had developed. European dance genres overlapped, mingled with native genres and attitudes, and united with popular versions of theatrical dance. After Mexico's political independence (1821), popular and theatrical dance genres harmoniously combined in the street during Carnival and civil festivities, and the theater continued to benefit from their influence.

During the Porfirian period (1877–1910), named for President Porfirio Díaz, Mexico City was visited by many European opera, ballet, and theater companies; particularly important was the 1897 visit of Loie Fuller, whose innovative fantasies influenced popular theatrical dance. Ballroom dancing, theatrical dance, and folk dance flourished in Porfirian Mexico, especially among the leisured classes, while traditional indigenous dances were performed mainly in indigenous communities. Nevertheless, the development of theatrical dance continued to be ham-

MEXICO: Theatrical Dance. A scene from *Circo Orrin,* a work produced by the Campobello sisters in the mid-1940s for the Ballet de Ciudad de México. (Photograph by Carlos Merida; reprinted from *Artes de México* 3.8–9 [1955].)

pered by traditional middle-class prudery concerning the human body; particularly among those middle-class segments affected by the currents of "moral renewal," there was strong opposition to dancing, regarded by many as sinful and physically unhealthy. Dance was therefore not part of public education, nor did it receive any official encouragement.

All this changed when Mexico's democratic and nationalistic 1910 revolution unleashed an artistic renaissance; it was characterized by a focus on uniquely Mexican (as opposed to Spanish or European) aspects of the country's culture. Theatrical revues gained freedom of expression, and the theatrical arts were adapted for popular presentation—for example, using puppet theater and masks. Visiting artists were soon swept up by the new artistic impulse; in 1919 Anna Pavlova paid homage to the Mexican nation by wearing the traditional China Poblana costume (wide hat, brightly sequined skirt, and white embroidered blouse) and dancing a *jarabe* (hat dance) on pointe.

Until the 1910 revolution there were no formal dance schools in Mexico. The new government began instituting programs to promote the arts, including the traditional dances of the indigenous peoples and the traditional popular and folk dances. In 1925 the Ministry of Education established the School of Physical Education to train dance teachers; in 1930 it established a school of classical dance in Mexico City under Hipólito Zybine, formerly of the Ballets Russes. In 1930, Nina Shestakowa founded a private dance academy. In 1931 the sisters Nelly and Gloria Campobello, two outstanding figures in Mexican dance, created the ballet *30–30* (named for the rifle commonly used by the Revolutionary army during the civil war), staged in the national stadium during festivities honoring the military and attended by a huge crowd of spectators.

The first official National Dance School was established in Mexico City in 1932 as a branch of the Ministry of Education's fine arts section; it was directed by the painters Carlos Orozco Romero and Carlos Mérida. From the start the new organization exhibited a healthy rebellion against established classical forms, however, it was difficult to find the right techniques to express Mexican or nationalistic feelings. Mérida's knowledge of the new modern dance trends in Europe may have helped to provide a fresh outlook for the new dance school, allowing experimentation with a variety of styles. Nelly Campobello taught classical ballet; Gloria Campobello taught Mexican folk dances; Zybine taught the art of choreography; Rafael Díez taught international folk dances; and Evelin Eastin was in charge of the theatrical dance department. Agustín Lazo and Carlos Orozco Romero were in charge of the scenography workshop, and Francisco Ramírez taught folk music. Excellent pianists provided accompaniment for the various groups, including Angelo Tercero, Consuelo Cuevas, and Jesús Durón.

In the late 1930s the National Dance School was dominated by the Campobello sisters. For scenography and libretto, several outstanding artists collaborated with them, notably the muralist José Clemente Orozco and the novelist Martín Luis Guzmán. They attempted to create a Mexican ballet based on classical discipline. There were some remarkable achievements after *30–30.* During subsequent seasons, the Ballet de la Ciudad de México, created in 1943 by the Campobello sisters, presented several works

MEXICO: Theatrical Dance. Waldeen was a pioneer of Mexican modern dance in the 1940s and 1950s whose work reflected her nationalistic ideals. Seen here is the "Dance of the Dispossessed" from her four-part *La Coronela* (The Lady Colonel; 1940). The suite was set to music by Silvestre Revuelta and designed by Gabriel Fernández Ledesma. (Photograph by Lola Álvarez Bravo; reprinted from *Artes de México* 3.8–9 [1955].)

with Mexican themes—*Alameda 1900, Fuensanta, Umbral,* and many others in a neo-Romantic style. This peculiar combination of styles still prevailed in the late 1940s, when programs included such a medley as *Presencia, Clase de Ballet, El Sombrero de Tres Picos* (The Three-Cornered Hat), *Obertura Republicana, Ixtepec, Circo Orrin,* and *Giselle.* This mixing of styles and techniques, and of new choreographies with the universal repertory, was followed even in the 1980s in some private academies.

Apart from a few private dance schools where the new Mexican art forms were adopted, younger dancers were drawn to the National Dance School where some of the best representatives of modern Mexican dance were trained. Students were also exposed to performances in Mexico by Anna Sokolow (1939) and Waldeen (1934 and 1939), who were invited by dance teachers to form Mexican modern dance groups. Modern dance, it was discovered, allowed the themes and images of Mexico to be united in a mode of expression that was up-to-date and effective. Thus in 1940 a Mexican modern dance movement emerged, renewing the nationalistic artistic orientation of post-revolutionary decades. Just as the muralists had, it grafted foreign techniques and procedures onto Mexican subjects.

By 1945 Waldeen's dance group (named after her) had traveled in the United States and had a large repertory of Waldeen's choreographies. For November and December 1945 a short season was organized at the Palacio de Bellas Artes in Mexico City, with a program consisting entirely of works by Waldeen *(Waltzes, Three Preludes, In the Wedding,* and *Elena la Traicionera).* The physical eloquence of her new dancers and works was evident. The participants included Guillermina Bravo, Lourdes Campos, Edmée de Córdoba, Gloria Mestre, Evelia Beristáin, Ricardo Silva, José Silva, and Alberto "Grishka" Holguín—artists who themselves would form new groups and movements later. [*See the entry on Waldeen.*]

As other dancers and choreographers went abroad, however, it was discovered that the professional teaching of modern dance was limited within Mexico; its success was attributable to the expressionist and theatrical bases matched by the original teachers to the natural talents of the participants, rather than to the excellence of their training. When the Academy of Mexican Dance was organized in 1947, its founders, Ana Mérida and Guillermina Bravo, made it their principal aim to produce excellently trained professionals who would preserve the uniquely Mexican character of their style and dances.

The path opened by Waldeen's *La Coronela* in 1940 led to the development of an aesthetic sensibility that included a break with classical ballet. Unlike the classical works presented by Nelly and Gloria Campobello, those sponsored by Waldeen effectively incorporated symbolic and expressionist elements. Skillfully taking its inspiration from the engravings of José Guadalupe Posada, *La Coronela's* four episodes were set to the music of Silvestre Revueltas. It attracted attention not only because it brought to the stage many nationalistic elements already known to audiences through the plastic arts but also because Waldeen was breaking away from the fallacy that Mexican dance could only express "the typically Mexican" through popular forms. Similarly, she was proposing a way to incorporate both narrative and a message without nineteenth-century allegories. Waldeen's dances mixed cosmopolitan and theatrical expressionism with the classical concept of structure.

When the Ballet Nacional de México was founded as an autonomous entity in 1948, its members considered the forms of classical ballet invalid, and they therefore rejected the technical preparation required by the genre. Their decision to use the term *ballet* in the name of the new organization demonstrated their desire to appropriate and socialize elements from elite art forms that were until this point remote from the lay performer and the general public.

Fortunately, Mexico's modern dance movement developed beyond the dogmatic artistic nationalism of its forerunners. It was able to incorporate urban subject in works such as Guillermo Key's *El Chueco* and Guillermina Bravo's *El Demagogo.* A rational trend appeared, oriented toward taking critical stances on political and artistic issues. The idea was not to transmit idyllic or didactic images of Mexican culture, but to act as political and social critics. Works such as Josefina Lavalle's *La Maestra Rural* and *Madres Polacas* and Bravo's *Braceros* and *El Dema-*

gogo clearly show the progressive political and artistic attitudes of the Ballet Nacional de México in that period. Such attitudes led to a crisis in 1954, when the authorities prohibited the opening of *Rescoldo,* a joint work by Bravo and Lavalle, which dealt with the "great turn" of the Mexican Revolution. [*See the entry on Bravo.*]

The movement as such gradually died out. José Limón and practically all Mexican dancers still performed on the enormous stage of the Palacio de Bellas Artes in Mexico City, but as important figures of the movement, particularly the women dancers, began to train the new generation, Mexico's dance technique was found lacking. As more affluent Mexicans traveled abroad, they compared Mexican dance with dance of the United States—clean, direct, simple, dehumanized, aseptic, and so severe that in some cases it approached the classical. The dancers of Mexico had not kept abreast of new trends in the world of dance.

A tour of China, the Soviet Union, and western Europe in 1957, in which most of the best Mexican dancers performed, helped them understand the weakness of their technique. The tour permitted them to see, study, and feel the results of rigid professionalism—a professionalism that the Mexican movement had been unable to offer because of its concentration on message, form, formula, popularity, and Mexican identity. Professionalism also implies knowledge of organization, teaching procedures, and world dance trends. Although Mexican dance was recognized all over the world, the Mexican dancers returned from abroad with the desire for something more. The Ballet Nacional de México entered a period of examining and questioning its work and learning new techniques; its members went to New York City to attend classes at the Martha Graham school, and foreign teachers were asked to give courses in Mexico. The Ballet Nacional de México then moved toward a new emphasis on contemporary artistic ideals, works, and techniques.

During the next thirty years, Mexico experienced a great expansion of dance choreography, pedagogy, and scholarship. While the Ballet Nacional de México and its associ-

MEXICO: Theatrical Dance. In 1951, the Instituto Nacional de Bellas Artes of Mexico invited José Limón to choreograph and perform in Mexico City. The works he created during this residency were influenced by Mexican themes. He incorporated local dancers into his choregraphy, creating, for the first time in his career, works for large casts of performers. Seen here are five dancers, including Limón (second from left), in his *Tonantzintla* (1951), which was set to music by Fray Antonio Soler (1729–1783) and the twentieth-century composer Rodolfo Halffter and which was designed by Miguel Covarrubias. (Photograph by Nacho López; reprinted from *Artes de México* 3.8–9 [1955].)

MEXICO: Theatrical Dance. A scene from Federico Castro's *La Vida Genera Danza,* with Eva Pardave (center). This dance, set to music by Antonio Russek, was designed by Jarmila Maserova. Castro danced with the Ballet Nacional de México from 1954 until 1980 and has been one of its chief choreographers since 1965. (Photograph by Christa Cowrie; courtesy of Frederico Castro.)

ated school continued to base their work in Graham technique, other companies emerged and began working in other styles and techniques, both modern and classical. During the 1960s and 1970s, teachers, choreographers, and directors—Waldeen, Bodil Genkle, Xavier Francis, Luis Fandino, Gloria Contreras, Raúl Flores Canelo, and others—contributed to the development of a distinctively Mexican contemporary dance style. Many dance professionals from the United States, Europe, Cuba, and elsewhere—among them Michael Lland, Enrique Martínez, and Job Saunders—influenced the dance scene. Meanwhile, Mexican talent flourished.

During those decades, the number of dance companies in Mexico City grew. A few of the more prominent were Ballet Independiente, Ballet Teatro del Espacio, Taller Coreografico de la Universidad Nacional Autónoma de México, and Ballet Clásico de México. New schools and dance troupes developed in the provinces at government-funded cultural centers (*casas de cultura*), at state universities, and as private or independent projects. In 1974, Xavier Francis and Rodolfo Reyes established the Ballet Contemporánea de la Universidad Veracruzana with some of the finest dancers in the country. Other university companies were formed in Puebla, Baja California, Guadalajara, Sonora, and elsewhere. Some of these groups explored experimental approaches to both training and choreographic production.

In the 1980s and 1990s, a so-called Mexican dance style—combining highly polished technique with a "content-oriented" approach that addresses political and social concerns—has begun to make itself known internationally. Today's Mexican avant-garde dance is led by dancers and choreographers, often based in independent and university groups, who strive to create and perform work that is not only technically excellent but also pertinent to Mexican audiences.

BIBLIOGRAPHY

Aulestia, Patricia, comp. *Testimony, 1934–1959: Twenty-five Years of Dance in Mexico.* Mexico City, 1984.

Aulestia, Patricia. *Cincuenta años de danza: Palacio de Bellas Artes.* 2 vols. Mexico City, 1986.

Castillo, Arturo. "How It All Began: Sowing Good Seed in Fertile Soil, Mexico, 1949–1995." *Dance Gazette,* no. 219 (1995): 19–21.

Cosío Villegas, Daniel, et al. *Historia moderna de México: El Porfiriato, vida social.* 3d ed. Mexico City and Buenos Aires, 1973.

Cosío Villegas, Daniel, et al. *Historia moderna de México: La república restaurada, vida social.* 2d ed. Mexico City and Buenos Aires, 1974.

Dallal, Alberto. *El "dancing" mexicano.* Mexico City, 1982.
Dallal, Alberto. *La danza en situación.* Mexico City, 1985.
Dallal, Alberto. *El aura del cuerpo.* Mexico City, 1990.
Dallal, Alberto. *La mujer en la danza.* Mexico City, 1990.
Dallal, Alberto. *La danza contra la muerte.* 3d. ed. Mexico City, 1993.
Dallal, Alberto. *La danza en México en el siglo XX.* Mexico City, 1994.
Dallal, Alberto. *La danza en México.* 3 vols. 2d ed. Mexico City, 1995.
Flores Guerrero, Raúl. *La danza moderna mexicana, 1953–1959.* Mexico City, 1990.
Garske, Rolf. "Dance in Mexico: Interviews with Mexican Choreographers." *Ballett International* 9 (March 1986): 14–29.
Luna Arroyo, Antonio. *Ana Mérida en la historia de la danza mexicana moderna.* Mexico City, 1959.
Maynard, Olga. "The Grand Plan for the State School of Dance in Mexico." *Dance Magazine* (October 1980): 67–71.
Ramos Smith, Maya. *La danza en México durante la época colonial.* Mexico City, 1979.
Ramos Smith, Maya. *El ballet en México en el siglo XIX: De la independencia al segundo imperio, 1825–1867.* Mexico City, 1991.
Segura, Felipe. *Gloria Campobello: La primera ballerina de México.* Mexico City, 1991.
Tibol, Raquel. *Pasos en la danza mexicana.* Mexico City, 1982.
"Una vida dedicada e la danza: Primer homenaje." *Cuadernos del CID-Danza,* no. 4–7 (1985): 5–41.
Vázquez Araujo, Salvador. *El diseño en la danza.* Mexico City, 1990.

Alberto Dallal

Dance Companies

Dance companies in Mexico can be organized by genre as well as by institution and geographical area. Genres such as folklore ballets, classical ballet, modern dance, dance theater, and contemporary dance are frequently combined within the diverse choreographic styles of the various companies and choreographers. Increasingly, folk dance or indigenous dance influences the contemporary scene, while ballet and modern styles continue to merge and overlap.

In the 1950s, most companies were centered in Mexico City. Today, they exist throughout Mexico. Often government support is available at state universities, at cultural centers (*casas de cultura*), from SEP (Secretary of Education), or at centers of fine arts. Dance groups thrive in almost all urban and rural, public and private secondary schools. Since the mid-1980s, the number of independent companies has also increased.

Folklore Ballets. Contemporary Mexican folk dance companies, also known as *danzas tipicas* or *costumbristas,* generally remodel and often invent folk or indigenous types of dances for theatrical presentation. Forerunners of these groups date back to the nineteenth century, when certain social dances of the period—now considered folk dances—were performed in theaters, private homes, and public places, such as the Coliseum in the center of Mexico City, a theater built in 1671 and since reconstructed several times.

The most famous folk dance company is the Ballet Folklórico de México, founded in 1952 by Amalia Hernández, who had studied Spanish dance with La Argentinita and participated in the Mexican modern dance movement. Hernández's group, which began with eight women

MEXICO: Dance Companies. Founded in 1952 by Amalia Hernández, the Ballet Folklórico de México presents theatricalized versions of Mexico's folk and regional dances. *The Tarascans,* choreographed by Hernández, is a work depicting the ages of man from birth to death. In this scene from "Childhood," villagers billow a fishing net in the Dance of the Fish. (Photograph from the Dance Collection, New York Public Library for the Performing Arts.)

dancers, at first presented a weekly television program and toured several countries in Europe sponsored by Mexico's Department of Tourism. In 1959, President Adolfo López Mateos helped the group achieve professional status and become a member company of the national theater, the Palacio de Bellas Artes. In 1962, representing Mexico, the company won several prizes at the Festival of Nations in Paris. Ballet Folklórico, now with more than two hundred members, has both a resident and a touring company.

To present Mexico's most important folk and regional dances, Hernández has created a large repertory drawn from various historical periods and from many of Mexico's states. She travels extensively to do research on original dances, costumes, and local cultures. Although concerned to retain the original meanings of the dances she discovers, Hernández reworks original material to sharpen its impact for the contemporary audience. This methodology of performance research and reconstruction is typical of most professional folklore groups.

MEXICO: Dance Companies. María Elena Anaya directs the Compañia de Danza Española in Mexico City. She is pictured here in her *Guajira,* a flamenco-style dance, in a 1992 performance at the Teatro Cervantes. (Photograph by Roberto Aguilar; courtesy of María Elena Anaya.)

With Hernández's success, other companies were established. Among these were the Compañía de Danzas y Bailes Méxicanos, by Josefina Lavalle in 1959; the Ballet Aztlan (later Ballet Folklórico Nacional), by Silvia Lozano in 1960; Ballet Folklórico de la Universidad Michoacana, by Salvador Prospero in 1963; Grupo Folklórico de Guadalajara, by Guillermina Galarza in 1974; and Ballet Folklórico de la Ciudad de México, by Hector Fink in 1977. Some of the more popular pieces performed by these companies are reconstructions of ancient Aztec and Mayan ceremonial rites, stagings of traditional festivals and celebrations, and scenes from Mexican history. An acknowledged masterpiece is *Deer Dance,* based on the Deer Dance of the Yaqui people, in which a man gracefully and powerfully portrays a deer pursued by two hunters.

Classical and Modern Dance Companies. Many fine ballet and modern dance companies exist in Mexico today as the distinctions between ballet and modern dance diminish. In an attempt to respond to both Mexican and international audiences, contemporary and complex techniques and artistic approaches have been used to create experimental and innovative choreographic works.

Of the companies established several decades ago in Mexico City, the Ballet Nacional de México is today a private modern and contemporary dance company that maintains its own school for dancers and teachers; it has toured throughout the world. In March 1991, the company established a school for daily work and rehearsals in Queretaro, near Mexico City. It sponsors the National Contemporary Dance Center, which provides professional dancers, choreographers, and teachers for the nation. Ballet Independiente, founded in 1966 by Raúl Flores Canelo (who died in 1992), always aims to unite Mexican and social themes with current trends in dance. Ballet Teatro del Espacio was established in 1979 by Gladiola Orozco and the French choreographer Michel Descombey, both former members of Ballet Independiente. Open to all creative possibilities, the company has experimented widely. The repertory has ranged from José Limón's *La Malinche* to Gladiola Orozco's attempt at psychotheater, *Icaro.* The group Alternativa was founded by Luis Fandino when he left the Ballet Nacional, where he had been principal dancer and choreographer until 1975. As a dancer, he had established his own technique based on the teaching of Xavier Francis, a U.S. citizen who went to live in Mexico in 1950. As a choreographer, Fandino's work is distinguished by its clear construction, careful abstraction, and balanced symbolism. The Forion Ensamble gave its first performance at the end of 1977. From the beginning, it was notable for the youth of its members and for its artistic innovation; these former members of the Ballet Nacional were ready to follow the trends of avant-garde dance in the United States. They presented

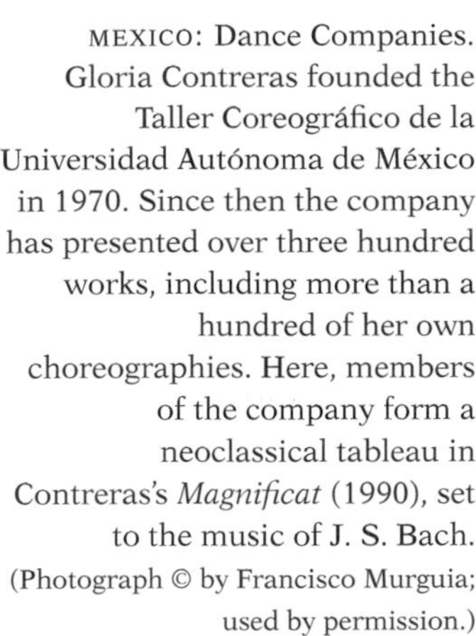

MEXICO: Dance Companies. Gloria Contreras founded the Taller Coreográfico de la Universidad Autónoma de México in 1970. Since then the company has presented over three hundred works, including more than a hundred of her own choreographies. Here, members of the company form a neoclassical tableau in Contreras's *Magnificat* (1990), set to the music of J. S. Bach. (Photograph © by Francisco Murguia; used by permission.)

such novel experiments as open-air dances and happenings in Mexico City's Museo de Arte Moderno, and they toured extensively abroad. The company disbanded in 1982.

The Taller Coregrafico de la Universidad Nacional Autónoma de México was formed in 1970 by Gloria Contreras. Contreras had worked with George Balanchine and tended toward a neoclassical style, but she has not been limited by it. In the company's repertory, Contreras has also incorporated works by experimental choreographers working with electronic and rock music. A splinter group, Danza Libre Universitaria, developed from the workshop (*taller*); its director, Christina Gallegos, won the 1980 National Prize for Dance for her choreographic work. Also, during these years, Raquel Vázquez and Valentina Castro founded modern dance companies in Mexico City.

In the 1980s, a number of independent contemporary dance groups presented experimental and postmodern works to Mexican audiences. Some of the new choreographers in these groups (Marco Antonio Silva, Rolando Beattie, Pilar Urreta, and Jorge Dominguez) offered interesting works and became professional dance producers. In 1986 in Mexico City, fifteen independent groups, such as Alternativa, Barro Rojo, and Contradanza, produced the First Encounter of Danza Callejera Contemporánea (Contemporary Street Dance), with choreographers Tania Álvarez, Alexander Schwartz, and Arturo Garrido among others. Other companies of note, Antares, Contempodanza, and Danza Estudio, have recently emerged to perform nationally and internationally.

Outside Mexico City, the Ballet Contemporánea de la Universidad Veracruzana has been led by a series of directors. Groups in Jalapa and San Luis Potosí have been directed by Onesimo González and Lila López, respectively. One of the leading companies outside the capital is that of Martha Bracho at the Universidad de Sonora in Hermosillo. As director of the dance department since 1954, she has taken dance groups to regions almost never reached by professional dance companies. The dance company is today named after Bracho. The universities of Puebla and Baja California also have companies; the Taller Coreográfico de la Universidad Autónoma de Puebla, founded in 1976 by Ann Axtmann and Patricia Estay, celebrated its fifteenth anniversary in 1991 by organizing a national encounter of independent and university dance troupes. Encounters and festivals are an integral part of the Mexican dance scene. Through the years, companies from both Mexico and abroad have participated in these events, thus creating forums for artistic exchange.

Some prominent Mexican dancers, including Lupe Serrano, Felipe Segura, Ana Cardus, Guillermo Keys Arenas, Laura Urdapilleta, Susana Benavides, and Nellie Happee, have promoted the establishment of a single major ballet company for Mexico. Since 1975, the Ballet Nacional de México has made an effort to accomplish this goal, succeeding for long and brilliant periods. In this effort, the

MEXICO: Dance Companies. The Taller Coreográfico de la Universidad Autónoma de Puebla was founded in 1976 by Ann Axtmann and Patricia Estay. In 1984, the company presented the first version of Axtmann's evening-length *Nunca Más* (Never More), a homage to Las Madres de la Plaza de Mayo—Argentinian women who protested the disappearance of their loved ones. Pictured here is the jail scene, with Antonio Moncada in the upper cell. (Photograph by Alain Cordier; courtesy of Ann M. Axtmann.)

counsel of the Ballet Nacional de Cuba and other non-Mexican organizations has been of great help.

BIBLIOGRAPHY

Aguirre Cristiani, Gabriela, et al. *El Ballet Folklórico de México de Amalia Hernández.* Mexico City, 1994.

Amaranto. Xalapa, 1991.

Anawalt, Sasha. "Mademoiselle de Monterrey." *Dance Magazine* (November 1993): 72–75.

Aranda, Verónica, and Patricia Aulestia. "Compañía Nacional de Danza." *Cuadernos del CID-Danza,* no. 12 (1986).

Artes de México, no. 88–89 (1967). Issue entitled "El Ballet Folklórico de México."

Ballet of the Five Continents. Mexico City, 1968.

Ballet Teatro del Espacio, México. Mexico City, 1990.

"Compañías subsidiadas: 3 compañías de danza contemporánea." *Cuadernos del CID-Danza,* no. 8 (1985): 1–17.

Dallal, Alberto. *La danza moderna en el mundo y en México.* Mexico City, 1975.

Dallal, Alberto. *La danza contra la muerte.* 3d ed. Mexico City, 1993.

Dallal, Alberto. *La danza en México.* 3 vols. 2d ed. Mexico City, 1995.

Danza contemporánea en Mexico. Mexico City, 1993.

Danza Et Al. Mexico City, c.1990.

Danza Libre Universitaria. Mexico City, c.1992.

Drama, Danza Contemporánea. Mexico City, 1990.

Duncan, Donald. "Doña Amalia's Ballet Folklórico de México." *Dance Magazine* (November 1963): 38–42.

Flores Martínez, Óscar. "Between Muslin and Mink." *Ballett International* 14 (November 1991): 15–18.

Gilbert, Pamela F. "Ballet Folclórico de Nacional de Mexico." *Viltis* 42 (September–November 1983): 24.

Hering, Doris. "Gloria Contreras Dance Group." *Dance Magazine* (April 1962): 52.

Hering, Doris. "Pilar Gómez Dance Company." *Dance Magazine* (June 1962): 64.

Hering, Doris. "Doña Amalia's at It Again." *Dance Magazine* (June 1971): 47–49.

Moreno, José Francisco. "Gloria Contreras." *Cuadernos CENIDI-Danza José Limón,* no. 21 (1989): 23–26.

Sloat, Susanna. "Ballet Folklorico de Mexico." *Attitude* 9 (Winter 1993): 22.

Taller Coregráfico de la UNAM: Vente años de existencia. Mexico City, 1992.

Tortajada, Margarita. "Lila López." *Cuadernos CENIDI-Danza José Limón,* no. 22 (1990): 9–16.

"Una vida dedicada e la danza: Primer homenaje." *Cuadernos del CID-Danza,* no. 4–7 (1985): 5–41.

ALBERTO DALLAL and CÉSAR DELGADO MARTÍNEZ
Amended by Ann M. Axtmann

Dance Research and Publication

With the arrival of Christopher Columbus in the Antilles (1492), a whole world became available for study, a world that included dance as an important expression of its culture. As far as Mexico is concerned, an enormous body of information is available for the study of the origin and development of pre-Columbian dance: legends, narratives, murals, glyph writing, codices, diverse archaeological remains (gold- and silverwork, tombs, pottery, and so forth), religious and lay documents, traditions preserved by the succeeding generations, and above all, the written testimony of the chroniclers—soldiers who became historians, friars of various Christian orders, and missionaries. Many left valuable descriptions of the new Spanish territories of the Americas.

Fray Bernardino de Sahagún speaks in 1547 of the "*areitos,* the dances used to delight the people, over which the lords took great care. . . . And when they were dancing, if some of the singers made a mistake in their singing, or if those who played the *teponaztli* and the *atambor* missed a beat, or if those who led the dance erred in the movements, then the lord ordered them to be killed." Sahagún also refers to the *mixcoalli* (the place where the singers and dancers met), the master drummers waiting to see what the lord might want, and what other writers, like Fray Diego Durán, call "the true academy specializing in learning to dance." Durán also says, "in all the cities there were close by the temples, great houses where the teachers of dance and singing lived."

Fray Toribio de Benavente, in his *Motolinía*, states that the Nahuatl word meaning "dance" or "ballet" was *maceualiztli,* since this word derives from *maceua,* "to dance," or "to do penance"; perhaps another root is *netotilitzi,* from *netolli*, "to dance," "to vow," or "to promise."

Gonzalo Fernández de Oviedo, Fray Gerónimo de Mendieta, Abbot Francisco Javier Clavijero, Antonio de Solís, Diego Muñóz Camargo, and others also wrote about the dances and ceremonies and the different styles and skills, providing further incidental information. Many texts still need to be studied for us to describe the dances of Mesoamerica before the Spanish conquest of the early sixteenth century.

With the arrival of the first Spaniards under the command of Fernando Cortés, who was from the province of Extremadura, Spanish dances were introduced. Bernal Díaz del Castillo mentioned the first teachers who arrived with Cortés: "Master Pedro of the Harp, Benito Bejel or de Vejel. Ortíz the musician, a great player of the viol and skilled at dancing, and a great Moorish fellow, a fine musician, who came from Colima." These teachers requested and obtained permission in 1526 to found "a school for dancing, as it would ennoble the city." They brought court dances: the *allemande;* the *alta* and the *baja;* the *spagnoletta*; the *zambra;* the *contrapás;* the contradances; the *moresca;* the torch dance; and others.

On a trip to Spain, Cortés brought dancers from Nueva España, complying with Carlos V's wish to see evidence of the skill of the natives in juggling and acrobatics. Later these performers probably traveled to Rome, to appear before Pope Clement VII and many Roman princes.

Mexico and its various regions have become enriched with dances from other places. Although some appear to have undergone few changes, others have today acquired fresh details and interpretive nuances. These are dances that need to be traced in ecclesiastical documents, dances that might be reconstructed from written descriptions and rudimentary choreographic notations. This job still needs to be done.

Dance in Mexico during the colonial period is recounted in the works of Enrique de Olavarría y Ferrari and Maya Ramos Smith. Both tell us how the missionaries used dance with music and songs for their evangelical work. They refer to dance representations such as the Conquests, the Pastoral Plays, the Oratories, and the Scapularians. They also mention ribbon dances, maypoles, the "Twelve Peers of France," the *voladores* (the dancers who fly from a tall pole), and the *saraos* (the fiestas of the *negros* and *mulattos*). Theatrical dance appears at the end of the sixteenth century as *entremeses* (between the acts) and *fines de fiestas* (at the end of the performance) in courtyards and playhouses performed by professional companies.

Maya Ramos Smith claims that ballet was introduced to Nueva España in the years 1778 to 1780. Both Olavarría y Ferrari and Ramos Smith give information about the teachers—Peregrino Turchi and José Sabella Morali (1778–1784), Jerónimo Marani (1786–1795), Juan Medina (1796–1806), Andres Pautret (1825–1840), and Giovanni Lepri (1880)—who led the companies of the Coliseo. There are also references to the ballets performed in this theater. Ramos Smith explores the social, moral, political, and economic situation of the dancer during this period, discusses the different ballet seasons, and tells the story of how the Coliseo assumed the name Teatro Principal. The work of Andres Pautret is of interest; in addition to founding a dance school, he gave scholarships to poor children with talent. He staged the ballet *La Fille Mal Gardée* in 1827, and we learn about his *prima ballerina,* Maria de Jesús Moctezuma (La Chucha), from Mexico. This information (and more) confirms the professionalism of the ballet in Mexico during the eighteenth and nineteenth centuries.

Around 1800, the social dances of the salon dominated theatrical dance. The waltz was king; the *jarabes* and the *toritos* were forbidden; and, the fashion of the *habaneras* arrived from Cuba. By 1869, as part of theatrical performances, the can-can dominated. It competed strongly against the opera companies, which brought eminent dancers from Italy, France, and Spain—performers like Loie Fuller, who appeared in Mexico much later than many of her imitators (1897).

In the twentieth century, dance activities have increased on a vast scale. This has meant that the number of critics, researchers, and historians is insufficient to attend and evaluate all that is taking place. Among the prominent writers we should recognize Miguel Covarrubias for his work on precolonial dance; Adolfo Salazar, Luis Bruno Ruiz, Raquel Tibol, Antonio Luna Arroyo, and Alberto Dallal for their biographies and general histories; Raúl Flores Guerrero, Patricia Cardona, and Matilde Koninsberg Aroeste for their books on the contemporary scene; and Amparo Sevilla for important work on the traditional dances of Mexico.

During the time of Miguel Covarrubias (1904–1957) there was noticeable support for the investigation of dance in Mexico. His students from the National Institute of Anthropology and History (Instituto Nacional de Antropología e Historia) in Mexico City are currently working throughout the country as self-nominated investigators of the folk dance and folklore of Mexico.

An important effort was the government's creation of the Fondo Nacional para el Desarrollo de la Danza Popular Méxicana (National Fund for the Development of Mexican Popular Dance, FONADAN), which investigated widely the popular dances of Mexico from 1972 to 1985.

In 1983, the Center for Dance Information and Documentation (Centro de Investigacion Informacion y Documentacion de la Danza) was established as a division of the National Institute of Fine Arts (Instituto Nacional de Bellas Artes); it is known as CID-Danza-INBA. Patricia Aulestia de Alba defined the center's goals as attempting to "rescue, compile, document, organize, investigate, preserve, and archive everything related to the dance; its history, its traditions, its theories and wealth in an institution that patronizes, foments, experiments, criticizes, informs, and diffuses the daily activities of dance and which makes them accessible to all the patrimony of the art of the dance, linked to the needs of national identity."

In addition to supervising the dance archive, the center has organized seminars on dance training, national meetings on dance and medicine, and a gathering called the Meeting of the Americas. Most important were the 1985, 1987, 1990, and 1995 International Conferences on Dance Research, whose participants considered such topics as reconstruction, notation, therapy, education, history, and cultural policies in the sixteen countries that were represented.

Lastly, the center has offered its knowledge in an advisory capacity to those countries that have asked for it. For example, the center has assisted Guatemala, Nicaragua, and Venezuela to consolidate their documentation centers. It has maintained contact with the Center for Documentation of the National Ballet of Cuba.

BIBLIOGRAPHY

Benavente, Toribio de. *Motolinía.* Memoriales (Cap. 27). Mexico City.

Covarrubias, Miguel. *Florecimiento de la danza.* Mexico City, 1952.

Covarrubias, Miguel. "La danza." *México en el Arte,* no. 12 (1952).

Covarrubias, Miguel. "La Danza Prehistórica." *México en el Arte,* no. 1 (1983).

Diaz del Castillo, Bernal. *Historia verdadera de la conquista de la Nueva España.* Mexico City, 1955.

Durán, Fray Diego. *Historia de la Indias de la Nueva España e las Islas de la Tierra Firme.* Mexico City, 1967.

Olavarría y Ferrari, Enrique de. *Reseña histórica del teatro en México (1538–1911).* Mexico City, 1961.

Ramos Smith, Maya. "La danza en México durante la época colonial." Mexico City, 1979.

Sahagún, Fray Bernardino de. *Historia general de las cosas de la Nueva España.* Mexico City, 1969.

Patricia Aulestia

MICRONESIA. The term *Micronesia* denotes a geographical and cultural area of Pacific islands that are west of the International date line and north of the equator. It comprises the Caroline Islands, which include the Federated States of Micronesia—including Pohnpei (formerly Ponape), Yap, Truk, and many small coral-based islands such as Kosrae, Ulithi, and Ifaluk—and Belau (formerly Palau); Kiribati (formerly the Gilbert Islands); the Marshall Islands; the Marianas Islands, including Guam; Nauru; and Banaba, or Ocean Island. There are at least twelve major Micronesian languages and many important cultural differences on the individual islands and among the island groups. Richness and diversity exists in traditional dances, which have been taught by one generation to the next, but there are few published studies of them. The most important early written sources are German ethnographic reports from the late nineteenth and early twentieth centuries. A few later anthropological and ethnomusicological studies also contain information on dance.

Micronesian dance is essentially a visual enhancement of poetry, with a strong rhythmic component. Rather than interpreting poetry as either actor or storyteller, the dancer performs movements that are often decorative or mimetic and that focus on the arms and torso, rather than on the lower body. In many areas frigate birds or other birds are imitated; an individual rises during a seated group dance to become a bird in flight. In many standing or seated dances, the arms are held outstretched to the sides or in various diagonal positions while the hands tremble and the torso turns. In Kiribati, small finger movements and subtle head facings and eye shifts combine with sharp hip movements that raise a heavy grass skirt to the shoulders. In Belau, women advance in long lines while performing side-to-side hip movements in a bent-knee position. In some dances, long or short sticks are manipulated to enhance the texts visually and rhythmically. Dances were traditionally and primarily a group activity, performed for the gods or for an audience assembled for an entertainment or a competition.

Although few in-depth studies of Micronesian dance have been carried out, much information on traditional forms still exists in the minds and bodies of older people, and versions of dances described in the following sections are still performed. Elders are passing on their knowledge to younger generations through cultural centers and other local organizations for performance at local celebrations and Pacific Arts festivals. Tourism has also encouraged the retention of traditional forms of dance as well as the blending of traditional with more recent forms.

Pohnpei. A 1902 account of Pohnpei dances describes the *uin* or *wen,* which consisted of graceful hand and arm movements in conjunction with rhythmic stamping on wooden boards; the *kapir* or *kepir,* performed on a platform built over a flotilla of canoes in which carved and painted dance paddles were manipulated and struck on a bar in conjunction with rhythmic stepping; and a dance now called *dukia,* in which a long board laid across the laps of seated girls is rhythmically tapped with short sticks that are also tapped against the sticks of the neighboring performers. These three dances—and a fourth, in which seated young women perform graceful head and hand movements—are now performed simultaneously with the dancers ranged in tiered rows. A European-inspired dance called *lehp* ("left") alternates traditional dance movements performed to a verse and a Pohnpei version of a military drill performed to a chorus.

Yap. A 1903 account of Yapese dance notes that men and women danced separately, and usually only in the presence of same-sex spectators. This may have been due to the sexual nature of many of the dances. Various dances were performed either standing or sitting, in lines or circular formations. When standing in lines, the tallest performers stood in the middle and the shortest on each end. The central performer stood opposite the highest-ranking person in the audience. The poetry and associated dance movements were often acquired as tribute payments from outlying islands in the Yap empire, so the Yapese dancers did not understand the meaning of the texts. The movements were gracefully decorative or sexually mimetic, with the focus on the pleasures of love. The range of performances included dances of welcome for visitors of the opposite sex and dances for the funeral of a young girl, expressing sorrow that she could no longer take part in lovemaking. Dances in which bamboo sticks were struck while the performers moved from one position to another were also important in Yap and its affiliated islands and are still performed today.

Marshall Islands. A 1906 account of Marshallese dance describes females dancing in a slow procession and in a stationary line with side-to-side hip and head movements, as well as lively dances in which the performers carried long sticks and turned in circles while standing in a row. There were also dances in which women squatted and rocked their torsos while trembling their hands, which were held out to the side. Seated women accompanied the dances with singing and played an hourglass-shaped drum, which they held on the left hip and struck with the fingers of the right hand. Seated dancers with arms stretched to the sides swayed and twisted their torsos. An 1893 account describes a dance in which the dancers sat on either side of a mat and struck wooden sticks together and on the mat while turning their heads and eyes from side to side. In other seated dances, the torso, arms, and eyes were twisted and turned in exhausting movements. The Marshallese stick dance *gjorrang* was performed by two rows of men, accompanied by the singing, hand clapping, and drumming by women. The varied floor pattern was enhanced by individuals who performed solos with trembling, vibrating, and twisting movements of various parts of their bodies.

Marianas Islands. The Chamorro people of the Marianas were influenced by Spanish culture beginning in the sixteenth century, so their dance has been primarily European since that time. Little is known of traditional Chamorro dance, but it is likely that the movements and contexts for performance were, precontact, similar to those in other areas of Micronesia.

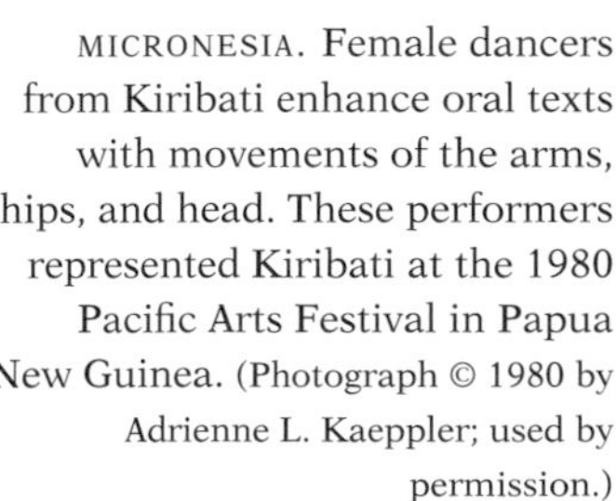

MICRONESIA. Female dancers from Kiribati enhance oral texts with movements of the arms, hips, and head. These performers represented Kiribati at the 1980 Pacific Arts Festival in Papua New Guinea. (Photograph © 1980 by Adrienne L. Kaeppler; used by permission.)

[*See also* Music for Dance, *article on* Oceanic Music; *and* Oceanic Dance Traditions.]

BIBLIOGRAPHY

Born, Regierungsarzt L. "Einige Bermerkungen über Musik, Dichtkunst und Tanz der Yapleute." *Zeitschrift für Ethnologie* 35 (1903).

Browning, Mary. "Micronesian Heritage." *Dance Perspectives,* no. 43 (1970).

Burrows, Edwin G. *Flower in My Ear: Arts and Ethos of Ifaluk Atoll.* Seattle, 1963.

Flinn, Juliana. "Pulapese Dance: Asserting Identity and Tradition in Modern Contexts." *Pacific Studies* 15.4 (1992).

Hahl, Albert. "Feste und Tänze der Eingeborenen von Ponage." *Ethnologisches Notizblatt* 3.2 (1902).

Krämer, Augustin. *Hawaii, Ostmikronesien und Samoa.* Stuttgart, 1906.

Petersen, Glenn. "Dancing Defiance: The Politics of Pohnpeian Dance Performances." *Pacific Studies* 15.4 (1992).

Pinsker, Eve C. "Celebrations of Government: Dance Performance and Legitimacy in the Federated States of Micronesia." *Pacific Studies* 15.4 (1992).

Adrienne L. Kaeppler

MIDDLE EAST. [*This entry surveys dance in the Islamic countries of Southwest Asia and North Africa. It comprises two articles. The first article provides a general overview of traditions; the second focuses on dance research and publication. For related discussion, see* North Africa *and entries on specific countries mentioned herein. See also* Israel.]

An Overview

Dancing in the countries of the Middle East is a favorite form of entertainment. It is considered indispensable at weddings and is frequently performed to celebrate circumcision, the harvest, and religious and national holidays; to honor important guests; and to welcome Muslim pilgrims returning from Mecca. This is a folk, rather than a classical, dance tradition. Although dances and appropriate contexts for dancing differ among communities, most people in a particular community can usually perform its dances. A large number of dances are performed throughout the region. At least thirty can be identified in the Gulf region (Kuwait, Bahrain, Qatar, United Arab Emirates); the small country of Yemen boasts at least twenty-five named dances; twenty Egyptian dances were documented by Magda Saleh (1979), who also mentions many more not included in her project. Some of these dances are associated with a particular country or community, while others are performed in several countries.

Among Muslims, religious dancing is confined to the mystical orders, such as the whirling dervishes, the Qādirī order and other Sufi sects, dissident groups such as the ʿAnṣārī Shīʿah of Syria and Iran, or the Yazīdī of northern Iraq. Dancing may be performed during visits to saints' shrines, although such visits are unorthodox in Islam and condemned by most religious scholars. Before the Islamic conquest of Egypt in the seventh century, religious dancing among Coptic Christians in Egypt was widespread, especially for a saint's day festival; afterward, dancers portrayed in Coptic inscriptions were less active and more modestly dressed than in earlier inscriptions. In general, dancing at funerals is rare, except among some rural groups in the Levant, Upper Egypt, and southern Yemen. Dancing also plays an important role in *zār,* a healing ceremony involving the exorcism of malevolent spirits.

Conflicting Attitudes toward Dance. The rich folk dance tradition in the Middle East has not been well documented because many of the urban elite consider dancing to be a frivolous activity, undignified and unworthy of scholarly attention. Paralleling this attitude is a lively debate in Islamic circles as to the permissibility of dancing and the playing of musical instruments. Some religious scholars maintain that these are permitted in Islam, and mystics often laud dancing and music as the ultimate expressions of divine ecstasy. Other, more conservative scholars, however, argue that dancing and music are forbidden. (*See* Islam and Dance.)

Singled out for condemnation are love songs, flirtatious dancing, and musical instruments that excite the emotions. Among these is a double-reed, oboelike instrument popular in rural areas; known as *mizmār, sorna, ghayṭa, surnāy,* or *zummāra,* depending on the country, it provides a favorite accompaniment to dancing. The instrument itself may have sexual connotations in the folk tradition. For example, in parts of Yemen, the *mizmār* is known as the "cock of Paradise," with an intended sexual pun. To the extent that dancing is associated with overt sexuality, it is frowned on by scholars and religious leaders.

Another factor that leads to ambivalence toward dancing is that many Middle Eastern dances focus attention on individual pleasures in a culture where cooperation and group cohesion are considered the most essential and noble values. Thus, dancing often highlights a tension found in the culture between the positive valuation of responsibility to one's group and a coexisting value on autonomy and individual expression (cf. Adra, 1982).

The major issue in the criticism of dancing, however, is that of context. Contexts defined as public are not considered appropriate for most dancing activity; yet gender-segregated contexts or those defined as informal and intimate are. In these informal contexts, Middle Eastern dancing flourishes. When a particular context appears to straddle the line between the public and the informal (e.g., a wedding celebration to which the whole commu-

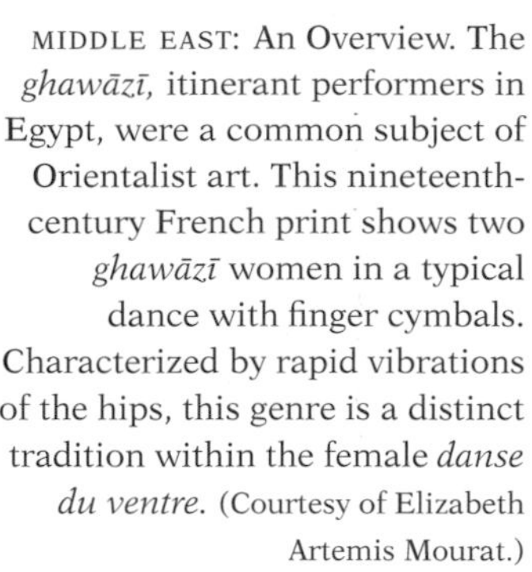

MIDDLE EAST: An Overview. The *ghawāzī*, itinerant performers in Egypt, were a common subject of Orientalist art. This nineteenth-century French print shows two *ghawāzī* women in a typical dance with finger cymbals. Characterized by rapid vibrations of the hips, this genre is a distinct tradition within the female *danse du ventre*. (Courtesy of Elizabeth Artemis Mourat.)

nity is invited), euphemisms may be used to refer to dancing. It may be glossed as *ghina'* ("song"), *ʿurs* ("wedding") or, in Yemen, *nafs* ("breath" or "freedom"). North African euphemisms for dancing include *bdd* ("to stand erect") and *hus* ("to turn") (Lortat-Jacob, 1980). It can be argued that dancing is an activity that almost everyone in the Middle East enjoys but does not advertise.

Urban-Rural Differences. Urban-rural differences in dance practice correspond to a general urban-rural split found throughout the Middle East. In rural areas, where men and women traditionally mixed freely, dancing may be performed by men and women together in the open air. The rule is that all those present be defined as members of the same community. Rarely will Middle Eastern women who are not professional dancers perform publicly in the presence of men defined as strangers. In urban areas, however, where the seclusion of women was traditionally a cultural ideal, dancing tends to be confined to intimate family gatherings or to gender-segregated contexts (i.e., parties of all men or all women). Dancing is not permitted at all in a small number of very conservative households. In those homes professional singers are hired to entertain guests at weddings and at other celebrations. Singers may be male or female, but women usually perform at women's parties.

In towns and cities only professional male and/or female dancers perform in contexts defined as public. Everywhere in the region, however, professional dancers (paid for their services) are considered to be of low social status. Some traditionally low-status groups, such as the Sulayb of central and southern Arabia, the *ghawāzī* of Egypt, and the Akhdam of Yemen, specialize in professional dancing as well as in other low-status service occupations. Historically, slave girls and concubines danced at royal courts; these were usually women captured in war, and their status was somewhat higher than that of other professional dancers. Some professional dancers are boys dressed as women. Dances performed by professionals may differ significantly in their movements from those performed by nonprofessionals in the same area, but not all. Nonprofessionals often learn dances by watching professionals and then practicing in intimate family contexts.

Location and Context. Dancing is performed in courtyards or other clear areas outdoors, or in small spaces indoors. The proscenium stage is an innovation used primarily by professional dancers in nightclubs, in large theatrical productions, or on televised programs. When dancing at a large gathering, dancers typically perform in their best clothes. Traditionally, they maintained serious facial expressions while performing; women were expected to keep their eyes lowered modestly or, in some cases, to veil their faces, thus conforming to culturally accepted standards of presentation. This is changing with regional access to television and videotapes. Dancers have begun to smile while performing, following the example of performers in Western films, television, and music videos.

At men's or at women's functions, members of the audience clap loudly or click their fingers, keeping time with the beat; make a rhythmic "sh, sh" sound meant to support the dancers; heap loud blessings on the dancers; and ululate and/or comment on the dancers' performances. It is usual for conversation to continue during dancing, but a true compliment to a dancer would be for the room to quiet down.

Identifying Characteristics. Characteristics of Middle Eastern dancing include lack of narrative content, the importance of improvisation, typical ways of shaping space, pelvic and shoulder isolations, and the division of dances into three segments. The vast majority of Middle Eastern dances are not mimetic, nor do they enact a story. Notable exceptions are *zār,* in which stereotypical figures are imitated, and the hobby-horse dance, once widespread but currently performed only in the Gulf region. Some but not all combat dances mimic duels. [*See* Zār.]

While Middle Eastern dances are characterized by a given range of movement or steps, improvisation is very important. Consequently, new steps are readily incorporated into traditional dances, and significant variation is found in steps or rhythm, even in neighboring communities. The major exception to the improvised nature of Middle Eastern dancing is found in theatrical and televised productions, which are carefully choreographed. These relative newcomers are appreciated for being well organized but are thought to lack the spontaneity and humor that characterize dancing in the region.

Space is shaped geometrically. Many dances are performed in lines, which may be either straight or curved. Often, two lines of dancers face each other, reciting poetry while they move. Solo and couple dances are performed between two lines of dancers or singers, facing a single line of dancers or singers (in the curve formed by a line of dancers or singers), or in a small space surrounded by spectators. Turns around the dancer's axis or in circles are very common in this tradition.

Feet are used for locomotion forward, backward, and sideways or to delineate shapes on the ground: figure eights, semicircles, and squares. Typical steps include walking, variations of the grapevine, skips, hops, jumping on two feet, and, for men, high leaps. Hands and arms may shape spirals, circles, and figure eights; be engaged in clapping; or hang loosely at the sides. They often hold a scarf, handkerchief, castanets, or a weapon. Pelvic, shoulder, and head isolations are common. The pelvis may be tilted, swayed, or shimmied, as may the shoulders. In some dances, however, the torso is held erect.

Lightness is a characteristic of almost all Middle Eastern dancing. Even when the dance calls for foot stamping, contact with the ground is not sustained. A step widespread in the region has the dancer propelling herself or himself forward and back by pressing the floor with the ball of one foot. This is sometimes done staccato and combined with a torso ripple, sambalike; in a different rhythm it can give the impression that the dancer is skimming the earth's surface. This step is frequently the basis of turning or whirling in place.

Although rapid level shifts are not normally associated with Middle Eastern dances, they are not uncommon. High vertical jumps and high leaps characterize many acrobatic and combat dances performed by men; dancing in a deep knee bend with rapid level shifts characterizes dancing in Yemen.

Dances are commonly divided into three segments, each with a different rhythm. There is usually a progressive increase in tempo with each segment. Yet, segments do not develop into each other; each stands on its own. As a rule, the dancers cue the musicians with respect to beginning and ending each segment. This may be done with a hand signal or by stopping or leaving the dance space.

Musical Accompaniment. Poetry is highly developed in the Middle East; traditionally, most men and women could compose rhymed couplets at the very least. Thus, song is an important accompaniment to dancing. The lyrics are important and appreciated as much as the dancers' movements. They may be love songs or have religious themes (although conservative Islamic and Christian religious scholars often lament the association of religion with dancing); they may relate to particular events in the life of the dancer; or they may contain political commentary. Singing is so closely related to dancing that the term *ghinā',* which denotes singing, also implies dancing.

Musical instruments that accompany dancing include varieties of lute, violin, single- and double-headed drums, single- and double-reed flutes, tambourines, cymbals, finger cymbals, and bagpipes. Currently, much informal dancing is accompanied by the radio or by audiotapes. [*See* Music for Dance, *article on* Arab Music.]

Classification. A number of classification systems have been suggested for Middle Eastern dances. The most commonly cited is that of Lois Lamya' al-Faruqi (1976–1977). Louis Mercier (1927) distinguishes three categories: women's dances, mixed dances, and men's dances, with the last subdivided into profane and religious. A classification more compatible with indigenous concepts of dancing would distinguish the following categories: combat dances, dances performed purely for entertainment, dances related to work activities (e.g., seafaring, hunting, and agriculture), and religious ecstatic dancing. Recently developed theatrical dances may form a fifth category. In each community, however, dances may be further classified and contrasted. Urban dances may be distinguished from rural dances. Professional cabaret dancing is classified differently from the more "respectable" dancing of nonprofessionals. In the Gulf region, dances associated with immigrant groups are distinguished from seafaring and agricultural dances.

Combat dances. The stigma generally attached to dancing is not shared by men performing combat dances because the dances are seen as demonstrations of skill, not frivolity. They represent the cooperation and unity of

MIDDLE EAST: An Overview. *Taḥṭīb* is the oldest extant Egyptian martial art. As seen here, a pair of opponents wield thick bamboo sticks, five to six feet long, with which they slash, feint, and parry, often to the accompaniment of *tabl baladi* (a large drum), *naqrazan* (a small kettledrum), and *mizmār* (a double-reed pipe). (Photograph from the collection of Metin And.)

the community or tribe—and, hence, its strength—and are associated with honor and chivalry. It is perfectly respectable even for heads of state to perform these dances in public. The close coordination of performers is very important in these dances, and there is an element of competition as well. Performers are judged on their agility, coordination, skill in wielding their weapons, and on how well they avoid injuring their partners. Spectators watch carefully, ready to separate the dancers if the mock combat threatens to become serious.

The *sharḥ al-sūr* of Oman involves two performers who sing while standing in front of a line of men carrying sticks (Stark, 1941). At the end of the song, the two men engage in a mock battle in which each attempts to trip the other by sweeping his sword (or stick) along the ground. His partner avoids injury by leaping away. The two partners may kneel opposite each other and fence. If they get too close to each other, a spectator carrying a stick leaps in between them. This also occurs when, at the end of the dance, the "victor" brandishes his dagger over his fallen victim. The *taḥṭīb,* an Egyptian stick dance described and filmed by Saleh (1979b, pp. 240–266) is a virtuoso performance of defensive and offensive moves by two men carrying large sticks. They are accompanied by drum and *mizmār,* with the drummer acting as a referee, ready to enter between the two dancers if their performance becomes too violent.

This pattern of mock battles, with built-in interference if the battle begins to get serious, reflects the traditional patterns of dealing with personal and community conflicts in the Middle East. In real life, arguments may get heated, with much shouting and brandishing of weapons, but outside mediators always step in before actual bloodshed occurs (Adra, 1982).

Combat dances may also be performed in lines, where strength in battle is implied rather than demonstrated. The emphasis in these dances is on the coordination and skill of the dancers and musicians. They represent the strength of the group through the ability of its members to work together. Among these is the Yemeni *barʿah,* which is performed in an open circle.

MIDDLE EAST: An Overview. This print depicts a row of well-armed Ansari men of northern Syria, clasping hands in a pyrrhic dance. (Collection of Metin And.)

MIDDLE EAST: An Overview. An Iranian hobby-horse dance depicting a mock combat. (Photograph from the collection of Metin And.)

The *ʿarḍah, ʿayyālah,* and *ḥarbīyah* (all variations of a combat dance popular in Saudi Arabia and in the Gulf countries) are similarly considered noble dances and are performed by men at official ceremonies and public festivities. Performing the *ʿarḍah* the men hold swords and stand in two or more lines, shifting their weight sideways, forward, and backward, while chanting poetry that deals with warfare, courage, and honor. This dance is accompanied by the beat of several drums. Small groups of men break off from the line to improvise their own movements, returning to the line when they wish. In the late nineteenth and early twentieth centuries, Western travelers (e.g., Burton, 1964; Doughty, 1921) observed dances in central Arabia in which a line of male dancers carried small weapons and executed small jumps with their arms raised overhead that may have been early versions of *ʿarḍah.*

A North African rifle dance consists of two lines of men facing each other and brandishing rifles or sticks (Brulard, 1958). Initially, these two lines advance toward each other and retreat. They then form a circle around the musicians in which they perform fast turns. The combat dances of Kurds are among the few Kurdish dances performed by men only (Kendal, 1979).

The *bayāḍīyah* of Yemen is considered a combat dance although no weapons are used in performing it. While spectators stand in a line, two men leave the line to dance. As one leads, the other must match his steps. Each tries to perform steps his partner cannot match. They weigh each others' movements, trying to trick one another. The two signal the end of their dance by dancing in unison before joining the spectators, to be replaced by two other dancers.

The hobby-horse dance is sometimes classified as a combat dance. In it, dancers simulate combat while "riding" a stick dressed to resemble a horse. This dance is called *cirit* (Kendal, 1979) when it is performed by Kurds. One variation of this is performed by women in the Gulf countries and another in Turkey. It appears to have been widespread in historical times (Gaudefroy-Demombynes, 1950; Shiloah, 1962).

Dances for entertainment. The broadest category of dances in the Middle East is those performed for entertainment. It includes weapons dances performed by women; varieties of line dances, such as the Levantine and Iraqi *dabkah* and the Yemeni *bālah;* solo and couple dances performed before a seated audience, like the Yemeni *luʿbah,* or a line of clapping dancers, such as the Egyptian *ḥajjālah.* It also includes numerous variations of the celebrated *danse du ventre* (belly dance). Women play important roles in these dances because they control the dancing, the music, and the event itself. The obvious exceptions are in the entertainment dances performed only by men.

Weapon dances performed by women have been observed in the Arabian Peninsula, the Levant, and in Egypt. The pattern is that of a woman dancing with sword or stick in her hand in the middle of a circle of men. The men will stretch their arms in attempts to touch her or impede her movements, while she keeps them at bay with her weapon. This dance is largely play, yet there is an element of danger: a man who actually touches the dancer is likely to be slashed with her sword, because he will have overstepped the bounds of decorum.

A variation of this genre of dancing has been observed among the Sulayb, professional dancers of central and northern Arabia (Dickson, 1951). They perform a couple dance in which the woman carries a stick. If the man approaches her too closely, she will tap him with her stick. A dance in which a dancer juggled a sword while her feet moved to music was observed by Philip Baldensperger (1913) in Palestine. When women carry a sword or stick while dancing, the combat portrayed is a teasing one between dancer and male spectators. Because of this playful quality, these dances are not classified as combat dances in the region. Other dances that imply competition between women and men include those in which a woman wears a veil while dancing that the men try to snatch away and dances in which a woman dancer provocatively takes an item of clothing, a turban or shawl, from male dancers or spectators.

Line dances. The best-known line dance in the Middle East is the *dabkah* (often pronounced *debkah*), performed in the Levant and parts of Iraq. *Dabkah*s vary with the region and village. The most common form involves a line of dancers moving to the right. A leader at the head of the line directs the movement and improvises variations on the basic steps. He or she may twirl a handkerchief in his/her right hand. Participants may be as few as four or five or as many as space will permit. A variation observed in Syria early in the century involved two facing lines of three dancers each. The two lines approached each other and retreated rather than follow each other in linear fashion (Mercier, 1927). Both men and women perform the *dabkah*. Originally associated with rural regions, the *dabkah* is now a favorite at the weddings and other parties of Middle Eastern immigrant groups in the United States.

Many Kurdish dances are similar to *dabkah*s. These are usually performed by men and women together. Typical of Kurdish dancing is the lifting of the shoulders straight up and down while the feet perform small locomotive steps.

MIDDLE EAST: An Overview. Performers at the Marrakesh Festival, an event sponsored by the Moroccan government to promote folkloric music and dance, presenting a Berber *ahwash*. (Photograph courtesy of Ibrahim Farrah, *Arabesque Magazine*, New York.)

Another line dance observed earlier in this century in Palestine by Baldensperger (1913) is the *saʿhjī*, performed by men only and involving responsorial poetry. In it the leader faced the dancers, singing a verse and directing the movement. The dancers repeated the verse as they moved to the right and left.

The *murādah* was originally performed by women in the Gulf while the men of the community were away on extended fishing and pearling expeditions. It involves two lines of dancers who move toward each other with small steps and then retreat while singing rhymed couplets. These couplets were largely laments for absent loved ones. Although seafaring is no longer economically important in the region, women continue to perform this dance at social gatherings.

The *ahwash* (Fr., *ahouache*) performed by Berber tribes of the Moroccan High Atlas Mountains, includes one or several curved lines of men and one or several curved lines of women, the whole forming a circle or ellipse around male drummers (Jouad and Lortat-Jacob, 1978;

Lortat-Jacob, 1980). One line recites a poem that the other line responds to with another poem; then all move to the beat of the drums. Customarily, the whole community participates. While performing, women dancers hold themselves very straight and move with staccato steps, holding onto the weaving rod of the house. Women as well as men compose the poetry that is recited. A similar dance reported for Morocco is the *dukkala*. In one variation a man and woman facing each other compete to see which one can dance the longest (Mercier, 1927).

The institution of *ay-aralla-buya* traditionally provided a context for unmarried women of the Moroccan Rif to voice their opinions about prospective husbands. While one woman recites a verse of her own composition that expresses her feelings, she and three others perform a slow walk in a circular path or a sideways shuffle. The women play small drums and tambourines to keep time. The tempo quickens after the verse has been recited to announce the second phase of the dance, which involves circular movements and shimmying of the hips, waist, and bust. Then the tempo slows again, and the first phase is repeated while a second woman sings her song. Men and married women of the community watch (Hart, 1976; Joseph, 1980).

MIDDLE EAST: An Overview. Men performing *luʿbah* at a wedding in 1978 in Al-Ahjur, Yemen. Musicians playing the *mizmār* (a double-reed pipe) and drum can be seen seated at right. (Photograph by Daniel Martin Varisco; courtesy of Najwa Adra.)

Elsewhere in the region, young unmarried girls perform the celebrated *nakhkh*, the *danse des cheveux* ("hair dance"). In Morocco it is performed to the sung poetry of male spectators. The unveiled dancers twirl their heads and upper bodies to swing their hair around. Dancers perform on their knees or standing, keeping their arms and bodies below the waist immobile. Older women ululate as they watch the dancing. They may also stop the dance when they decide that it has gone on long enough. This dance was performed traditionally by nomads of Tripolitania, southern Tunisia, and westward as far as the Algerian Souf. It was criticized by town dwellers of these regions, who disapprove of women dancing unveiled in the presence of men.

Women swinging their hair while dancing is fairly common elsewhere in the Middle East as well. It forms part of the Sulayb dance of the Arabian Peninsula and is the primary movement of a dance performed in the Ḥaḍramawt, in Yemen (where it is called *rīshī*), and in the Gulf countries, where it is known as *al-naʿīsh*. It forms an optional part of the North Yemeni *luʿbah*, is important to the Pigeon Dance of Sudan, and has been observed in Syria as part of a sword dance.

Mauritania is known for its *guedra*, in which a solo female dancer is seated on her knees with her body bent forward and her head touching the floor. Slowly she begins to raise her head, gesturing gracefully with her hands and arms, progressing to her shoulders and upper torso. Her movements accelerate and expand until she collapses in a trance. The dancer does not rise to her feet during her performance. Members of the audience clap their hands to the beat of a large drum, also called a *guedra* (Ferry, 1950). Saleh (1979, pp. 151–155) recorded a similar phenomenon in which a professional dancer performed while seated on a divan.

The *luʿbah* or *raqṣ* of North Yemen is performed by two men at all-male gatherings, by two women at parties attended only by women, or, within intimate family contexts (two women, two men, or a man and woman together). Traditionally, the rural version of this dance involved bending the knees and rising while shifting weight from one foot to another, while the torso was held more or less erect. In the urban version, weight shifts were tied to footwork in which designs were outlined on the floor. With the passage of time, the steps became progressively more elaborate, and men added shoulder and head movements. Until the late 1970s there was a certain lag between urban and rural versions of this dance, with the rural population tending to perform earlier versions of the urban dance. As transportation to cities improved and television provided instant access to what was going on elsewhere in the country, rural dances tended to match urban dances more closely. Today at social gatherings where *luʿbah* is performed by men, it is accompanied by song and the *oud* in towns and the *mizmār* in villages. Performances of women's *luʿbah* are accompanied by song, a brass cymbal hit by a metal ring, and a kettledrum in both urban and rural contexts. Rural villagers say that, in the past, male professional musicians would play the *mizmār* at women's wedding celebrations.

The Pigeon Dance is performed for guests at celebrations in northern Sudan by veiled young girls. The dancers, shoulders held back, thrust their breasts forward, bob their heads slowly up and down, and move forward with mincing steps, in imitation of courting pigeons (Cloudsley, 1983).

Perhaps the best-known Middle Eastern dance is the *danse du ventre* ("belly dance"), a flirtatious dance performed primarily by women, in which the pelvis, shoulders, and breasts are isolated and moved. This dance is probably of great antiquity, with some possible evidence for its performance both in pharaonic inscriptions in Egypt and on central Asian miniatures. It is performed today in most of the Middle East at gatherings of women for each other and by professional dancers for men in cabarets. [*See* Danse du Ventre.]

Pelvic and shoulder isolations are also important in many of the dances of the countries of Northwest Africa (the Maghreb). Professional dancers of the Ouled Naïl tribe have commanded a great deal of attention from travelers in the region, yet such movements are not limited to their dances. [*See* Ouled Naïl, Dances of the.] Differences between the *danse du ventre* performed in the Maghreb and in Egypt, the Levant, and Turkey include the way in which the pelvic area is moved. In the Maghreb, the pelvis is turned from side to side; to the east, it is tilted up and around in a motion initiated in the legs. With access to each other's dances through television, however, such differences are decreasing, as dancers incorporate steps and movements they see on television.

Throughout the Middle East, the bride entertains guests at her wedding by dancing. In northern Sudan, she performs the Pigeon Dance unveiled, while the groom plays an important supporting role (Cloudsley, 1983). *Tamghra*, performed in the Moroccan High Atlas Mountains, is danced by the veiled bride within a large circle formed by the men of her community (Jouad and Lortat-Jacob, 1978). She carries a long pole while dancing and covers the entire space in her movement.

Brides of al-Mukalla in southern Yemen traditionally danced in the procession that led from their house to that of the bridegroom. Now brides dance only from inside the front door of the bridegroom's house to the women's quarters on the upper stories of the house (Serjeant, 1961). Dancing in bridal processions between the house of the bride and that of the groom is very common in the Middle East. In some communities the bride dances; in others, relatives and friends do so; and in still others, professional dancers perform.

MIDDLE EAST: An Overview. An international style of belly dance, or *danse du ventre*, related to Egyptian forms, has gained popularity throughout the Middle East. Here, a belly dancer from Morocco is surrounded by male musicians. Although a similar kneeling posture can be seen in the *guedra* of the Berber tribes in Morocco, this professional entertainer, wearing the conventional brassiere and low-slung skirt, is clearly costumed for an international Oriental-style dance. (Photograph from the collection of Metin And.)

At northern Yemeni weddings the bride dances with her sister or a close friend in the presence of the assembled women guests. The dance is similar to that performed by the guests, but special songs accompany it. In one traditional Palestinian bridal dance, the bride brandishes a sword; in another she moves slowly, holding a lighted candle in each hand. Both candles and swords are seen as symbols of protection from malignant forces. It is traditional in many parts of the Middle East for the bride's mother to dance at her daughter's wedding carrying a tray of lit candles on her head. Other items designed to bring the bride good luck and keep away malevolent spirits—incense, eggs, or rue—may also be placed on the tray.

Work-related dances. A number of dances in the region are performed in conjunction with subsistence activities or other work. The seafaring and pearl-diving traditions of the Gulf region are associated with numerous

MIDDLE EAST: An Overview. A whirling dance is characteristic of the devotional rituals of the Mevlevi order of Sufis. With arms outstretched and heads tilted to the right, these Muslim mystics revolve at steady pace to achieve a higher plane of consciousness. Pictured here is a group from Turkey in a performance at the Cathederal Church of Saint John the Divine, New York. (Photograph © 1994 by Jack Vartoogian; used by permission.)

dances. Each stage of pearling activity was punctuated by song and movement. Although women did not fish or dive for pearls, a ship's maiden voyage always included young girls who sang and danced. This practice was thought to bring good fortune to the ship and its crew.

Customarily, the crew of pearling ships was divided in half: while one half worked, the other sang and danced. The dancing provided the crew with rest and served to encourage the workers. The two halves switched roles at regular intervals. Distinct songs and dances were performed when the anchor was lowered; others when fish were brought on board; and still others when the ship was on its way home. A song-dance leader, called *nahhām* was the only member of the crew who did not work; he spent his entire time on the ship singing and leading dances. This was considered an important position, and ships competed with each other for the best *nahhāms*. Drumming and clapping in cross rhythms were also important in these dances. Currently, these dances are performed during holidays by those who still remember them.

The Yemeni *bara*ʿ, which is classified as a combat dance, was also performed during communal work projects to encourage workers. While one half of the workers applied themselves to the project at hand (building a mosque or cleaning a cistern), the other half performed the equally strenuous *bara*ʿ. The rhythmic step pattern used to tamp down newly sown seed in rural Yemen is considered a dance, as is the rhythmic grinding of grain in the Gulf region.

Religious dancing. In the Middle East, religious dancing is performed primarily among the mystical orders and the less orthodox sects of Islam; it is frowned on by conservative religious leaders. The dancing of mystics ranges from a mild side-to-side movement of the head and upper torso while reciting the name of God *(dhikr)* to the well-known whirling of dervishes. Some religious dancing is accompanied by feats of self-immolation, such as stabbing oneself with a dagger or walking on burning coals. The rituals of some women's mystical orders in Tunisia includes dancing and trance, while male mystics in the same orders do not dance (Ferchiou, 1972). The Yazidi of northern Iraq traditionally performed a dance that appears to be an ecstatic version of the *dabkah*. Kurdish theological students, who consider themselves to be of elevated social status, perform a dance called *behete*, which serves to distinguish them from the common people (Kendal, 1979).

There is also religious dancing among Christians and Jews in the Middle East. For example, Christian pilgrims dance ecstatically before the Church of the Holy Sepulcher in Jerusalem, and Jews in Yemen and Israel participate in a variety of dances whose significance is religious.

New Influences. Although the Middle Eastern dance tradition is ancient, and many currently performed genres are portrayed in pre-Islamic inscriptions, it is a flexible tradition in which new steps, costumes, and musical instruments are easily incorporated. There is a keen interest in learning the dances of others. When a person returns from a trip, he or she is expected to teach the dances learned abroad to those at home. Dances seen on television and in films are watched closely and imitated. Eventually, these dances are added to the repertory of dances performed in a region, or aspects of new dances become incorporated into traditional dances.

For example, there is a lively trade in dances in Yemen, with dances from the south being performed in the north and vice versa. Meanwhile, urban dances are continually evolving to include more intricate rhythms and complicated steps. The development of cinema and the theater in Egypt did much to enhance the status of professional "belly dancers," and the *danse du ventre* has spread to all parts of the Middle East. It continues to spread to rural areas at the same rate as television transmission reaches those areas. Professional dancers are frequently hired to perform *danse du ventre* at weddings, even in localities where this form of dancing is not traditional. Performances seen in night clubs and on television tend to be more choreographed, with greater correspondence between specific movements and musical phrases than was the case traditionally.

In the colonized areas of the Middle East in the early twentieth century, ballroom dancing was adopted by Western-educated Middle Easterners and became a favorite form of at-home and evening entertainment. At times, traditional folk dances have been incorporated into ballroom-dance events (e.g., the performance of a *dabkah* between performances of the fox trot; see Mercier, 1927). This trend has continued in urban contexts. Currently, the latest Western dances are performed regularly in conjunction with, and sometimes instead of, local dances.

To accommodate mixed-gender parties and the fact that respectable women attend nightclubs, a new dance has evolved in urban areas. This dance combines footwork reminiscent of the *dabkah* with the arm and hand movements of the *danse du ventre*. Pelvic movement is, however, restrained. Women and men may perform this dance in semipublic contexts without risking their reputations.

A fascinating case of adoption and adaptation of the Charleston has been described and documented by Saleh (1979, pp. 87–93). This dance, called *bambūṭīyah*, is performed along the Suez Canal. It combines Charleston-like movements of the legs with arm movements related to boating.

In the twentieth century there has also been a growing interest in adapting folk dances to the proscenium stage. The *raqṣ al-samāḥ*, originally a religious dance, was adapted to the stage and accompanied by a popular genre of song called *muwashshaḥāt* (Ibn Dhurayl, 1970). The mystical dancing of the Mevlevi dervishes has also been adapted to the stage and commercialized.

A number of women residing in Casablanca perform a staged version of the Moroccan *ahwash*, accompanied by men playing musical instruments. In this version one man will sing verses while the dancers respond in chorus. The performers are all immigrants from the town of Sous. In 1950 the dancers were veiled and kept their backs to the

MIDDLE EAST: An Overview. The *raqṣ al-sham ʿeddan* (candelabrum dance) is a traditional solo genre, in which a dancer balances a heavy, lighted candelabrum on her head as she performs a variety of tricks. Here, women of the Reda troupe, founded in Egypt by Mahmoud Reda in 1958, wear candelabrum headdresses in a choreographed ensemble interpretation of the genre. (Photograph courtesy of Ibrahim Farrah, *Arabesque Magazine*, New York.)

men and other members of the audience, but by the early 1970s the dance was performed on stage in Casablanca by unveiled, bare-armed women, before audiences of mixed gender. It has come to symbolize the Sous migrant community in Casablanca, helping Sousis maintain a consciousness of their community and presenting the community to others in the city (Waterbury, 1972). The Iraqi *darjah* has also changed since the 1960s. Once exclusively a women's dance, it is currently performed by men, women, or mixed groups (Aḥmad, 1978). *Ṣawt,* one of the most popular dance forms currently performed in the Gulf, has roots in traditional Yemeni music and dance forms (al-Qāsimī, 1988).

In Egypt in 1958, Mahmoud Reda formed a folk dance company that performed choreographed dances inspired by Egyptian folk dances (Saleh, 1979b). His example has been followed by several of the ministries of culture that have formed folk dance troupes in their respective countries to perform on stage and television.

Staged and televised dance and musical performances by the Reda troupe and those at the annual Lebanese Baalbek Festival (held in Jordan since the Lebanese civil war) have renewed urban interest in traditional dances. Usually, improvisation is sacrificed for highly choreographed, often mimetic presentations, and control of the dance events is in the hands of professionals. Because Russian or western European consultants are employed to help develop large pageants, European themes are often incorporated into the dances of national folk dance troupes. The degree of audience appreciation of these changes depends largely on the background of the spectators. Urban audiences tend to consider these to be improvements and signs of the "evolution" of folk genres, while more traditional rural folk may be heard to complain about the inauthenticity of the changes.

Whether the dances are old or new, however, Middle Easterners tend to perceive their dances as essential to life, as the following Yemeni proverbs attest: "Al-shaʿb lā yughannī li-yamūt" (A population that does not sing/dance would die) and "Li-kull ḥālah maqālah wa li-kull daqqa barʿah" (There is a proverb for every situation and a dance for every beat).

[*For related discussion, see* Aesthetics, *article on* Islamic Dance Aesthetics; *and* Bedouin Dance.]

BIBLIOGRAPHY

Adra, Najwa. "Qabyala: The Tribal Concept in the Central Highlands of the Yemen Arab Republic." Ph.D. diss., Temple University, 1982.

Adra, Najwa. "Achievement and Play: Opposition in Yemeni Tribal Dancing." In *Proceedings of the Consulting Seminar on the Collecting and Documenting of the Traditional Music and Dance for the Arabian Gulf and Peninsula, 15–19 December 1984.* Doha, Qatar, 1984.

Adra, Najwa. "The Concept of Tribe in Rural Yemen. In *Arab Society.* Social Science Perspectives, edited by Nicholas S. Hopkins and Saad Eddin Ibrahim. Cairo, 1985.

Adra, Najwa. "Tribal Dancing and Yemeni Nationalism: Steps to Unity." *Revue du Monde Musulman et de la Méditerranée* 67 (1993).

Aḥmad, Ibrāhīm Farḥān. "Al-darjah." *Al-Turāth al-Shaʿbī* 9 (1978).

And, Metin. *A Pictorial History of Turkish Dancing: From Folk Dancing to Whirling Dervishes, Belly Dancing to Ballet.* Ankara, 1976.

ʿArḍāwī, ʿĀdil al-. "Lamaḥāt fī aghānī wa raqaṣāt al-ṣayd al-Khalījīyah." *Al-Turāth al-Shaʿbī* 9 (1978).

ʿArif, ʿArif al-. *Bedouin Lore, Law, and Legend.* London, 1922.

Atiya, A. S. "Mythological Subjects in Coptic Art: Dancers." In *The Coptic Encyclopedia.* New York, 1991.

Awhān, Fārūq. "Al-iḥtifāl al-masraḥī fī taqālīd al-raqṣ al-shaʿbī (raqṣat al-ʿayyālah)." *Al-Maʾthūrāt al-Shaʿbīyah* 3 (1988).

Ayyūb, Ayyūb Ḥusayn al-. *Maʿa dhikrayātinā al-Kuwaytīyah.* Kuwait, 1972.

Bakewell, Anderson. "Music on the Tihāmah." In *Studies on the Tihāmah,* edited by Francine Stone. Harlow, 1985.

Baldensperger, Philip J. "Peasant Folklore of Palestine." *Palestine Exploration Fund Quarterly Statement* (1893).

Baldensperger, Philip J. "Song and Dance in the East." In Baldensperger's *The Immovable East.* London, 1913.

Bāshī, Ḥasan al-. *Al-ughniyah al-shaʿbīyah al-Falasṭīnīyah.* Damascus, 1987.

Berger, Morroe. "A Curious and Wonderful Gymnastic: The Arab Danse du Ventre." *Dance Perspectives,* no. 10 (Spring 1961): 4–41.

Berger, Morroe. "The Belly Dance." *Horizons* 8.2 (1966): 41–49.

Blanco Izaga, Emilio. "Las danzas rifeñas." *Africa* (Madrid) 5 (1946).

Brulard, M. "La musique et la danse à Ghat." *Bulletin de Liaison Saharienne* 9 (1958).

Buonaventura, Wendy. *Serpent of the Nile: Women and Dance in the Arab World.* London, 1989.

Burckhardt, John L. *Notes on the Bedouins and Wahābys, Collected during His Travels in the East* (1831). Vol. 1. New York, 1967.

Burton, Richard F. *Personal Narrative of a Pilgrimage to al-Madinah and Meccah.* 2 vols. New York, 1964.

Çelik, Zeynep, and Leila Kinney. "Ethnography and Exhibitionism at the Expositions Universelles." *Assemblages* 13 (1990).

Cloudsley, Anne. *Women of Omdurman: Life, Love, and the Cult of Virginity.* Rev. ed. London, 1983.

Dawkhī, Yūsuf Farḥān. *Al-aghānī al-Kuwaytīyah.* Doha, Qatar, 1984.

Deaver, Sherri. "Concealment vs. Display: The Modern Saudi Woman." *Dance Research Journal* 10 (Spring–Summer 1978): 14–18.

Dickson, H. R. P. *The Arab of the Desert.* London, 1951.

Doughty, Charles M. *Travels in Arabia Deserta.* 3d ed. New York, 1921.

DuRy, Carel J. *Art of Islam.* Translated by Alexis Brown. New York, 1972.

Duwayb, Rifʿat Muḥammad Khalīfah. *Aghānī al-aʿrāqṣ fī Dawlat al-Imārāt al-ʿArabīyah al-Muttaḥidah.* Abu Dhabi, U.A.E., 1982.

Ettinghausen, Richard. "The Dance with Zoomorphic Masks and Other Forms of Entertainment as Seen in Islamic Art." In *Arabic and Islamic Studies in Honor of Hamilton A. R. Gibb,* edited by George Makdisi. Leiden, 1965.

Farrah, Ibrahim. "Impressions of Marrakesh." *Arabesque* 2 (September–October 1976): 11–15.

Faruqi, Lois Lamya' al-. "Dances of the Muslim Peoples." *Dance Scope* 11.1 (1976–1977): 43–51.

Faruqi, Lois Lamya' al-. "Dance as an Expression of Islamic Culture." *Dance Research Journal* 10.2 (1978): 6–13.

Ferchiou, Sophie. "Survivances mystiques et culte de possession dans le maraboutisme tunisien." *L'Homme* 12 (1972).

Ferry, J. "La danse des cheveux: Contribution à l'éthnographie du Souf." *Travaux de l'Institut de Recherches Sahariennes* 6 (1950).

Gaudefroy-Demombynes, Maurice. "Sur le cheval-jupon et al-kurraj." In *Mélanges offerts à William Marçais.* Paris, 1950.

Gharīb, Khālid ibn Jābir al-. "Al-ʿarḍah wa-al-ahāzīj al-ḥarbīyah." In Gharīb's *Kitāb manṭaqat al-Aḥsā' ʿabr aṭwār al-ta'rīkh.* Al-Ahsa, Saudi Arabia, 1986.

Graham-Brown, Sarah. *Images of Women: The Portrayal of Women in Photography of the Middle East, 1860–1950.* New York, 1988.

Ḥaddād, ʿAbdallāh Ṣāliḥ. "Raqṣah sahʿbīyah: Al-ʿidda." *Al Turāth al-Shaʿbī* 9 (1978).

Hart, David Montgomery. "The Cultural Role of Ay-aralla-buya: Poetry, Music, and Dancing." In Hart's *The Aith Waryaghar of the Moroccan Rif.* Tucson, Ariz., 1976.

Hickmann, Hans. "Quelques considérations sur la danse et la musique de danse dans l'Égypte pharaonique." *Cahiers d'histoire égyptienne* 5 (1953).

Hilton-Simpson, M. W. *Algiers and Beyond.* London, 1906.

Hilton-Simpson, M. W. *Among the Hill-Folk of Algeria.* London, 1921.

Hunter, Frederick M. *An Account of the British Settlement of Aden in Arabia.* London, 1877.

Ḥusayn, Muṣṭafā. "Al-ghinā' wa al-raqṣ ʿind ʿashā'ir al-ʿIrāq." *Jarīdat al-Balad* 70 (1963).

Ibn Dhurayl, ʿAdnān. *Muʿjam raqṣ al-samāḥ.* Damascus, 1970.

Ibn Khaldūn. *The Muqaddimah.* Translated by Franz Rosenthal. New York, 1958.

Ibrahim, Hamada. "Les chansons de la mer *(al-nihām)* au Kuwait." *Annali Instituto Orientale di Napoli* 36 (1976): 351–357.

Ingrams, Harold. "A Dance of the Ibex Hunters in the Hadramaut: Is It a Pagan Survival?" *Man* 37 (1937).

Isfahānī, al. *Kitāb al-Aghānī.* Cairo, 1979.

Joseph, Terri. "Poetry as a Strategy of Power: The Case of Riffian Berber Women." *Signs* 5 (1980).

Jouad, Hassan, and Bernard Lortat-Jacob. *La saison des fêtes dans une vallée du Haut-Atlas: Textes et photographies.* Paris, 1978.

Kamāl, Ṣafwat. "Al-raqṣ al-shaʿbī." In Kamāl's *Madkhal li-dirāsāt al-fūlklūr al-Kuwaytīyah.* Kuwait, 1986.

Katabī, Muḥammad Mūkh al-Kannānī al-. "Ghina' al-Chūb'yah fī Manṭaqat al-Furāt al-Awṣaṭ." *Al-Turāth al-Shaʿbī* 5 (1974).

Kendal, Nezan. "Kurdish Music and Dance." *World of Music* 21.1 (1979): 19–28.

Kerbage, Toufic. *The Rhythms of Pearl Diver Music in Qatar.* Doha, Qatar, n.d.

Khādim, Saʿd al-. *Al-raqṣ al-shaʿbī fī Miṣr.* Cairo, 1972.

Khulayfī, ʿĀ'ishah al-. "Al-murādah: Raqṣat al-nisā' fī al-Khalīj al-ʿArabī." *Al-Ma'thūrāt al-Shaʿbīyah* 1 (1986): 104–129.

Lāmī, Majīd al-. "Fī Abū Ḍabī: Raqaṣāt ʿArabīyah Qadīmah." *Al-Turāth al-Shaʿbī* 4 (1973).

Lāmī, Majīd al-. "Al-Yaman wa-al-turāth al-shaʿbī. *Al-Turāth al-Shaʿbī* 5 (1974).

Lane, Edward W. *Manners and Customs of the Modern Egyptians* (1836). Vol. 2. New York, 1966.

Lexová, Irena. *Ancient Egyptian Dances.* Translated by Karel Haltmar. Prague, 1935.

Lortat-Jacob, Bernard. *Musique et fêtes au Haut-Atlas.* Paris, 1980.

Maṭar, Būlus Anṭūn. *Khalīj al-aghānī.* Beirut, c. 1980.

McPherson, J. W. *The Moulids of Egypt.* Cairo, 1941.

Mercier, Louis. *La chasse et les sports chez les Arabes.* Paris, 1927.

Meri, La. "Learning the Danse du Ventre." *Dance Perspectives,* no. 10 (Spring 1961): 43–47.

Molé, Marijan. "La danse extatique en Islam." In *Les danses sacrées,* edited by Jean Cazeneuve. Paris, 1963.

Monty, Paul. "Serena, Ruth St. Denis, and the Evolution of Belly Dance in America, 1876–1976." Ph.D. diss., New York University, 1986.

Murray, G. W. *Sons of Ishmael.* London, 1935.

Muslimānī, Muḥammad al-. "Ḥawl al-mūsīqa wa-al-raqṣ al-shaʿbī fī Qaṭar." *Al-Ma'thūrāt al-Sha'bīyah* 1 (1986): 88–103.

Myers, Oliver C. "Little Aden Folklore." *Bulletin de l'Institut Français d'Archéologie Orientale* 44 (1947).

Najah, Ahmed. "De l'étymologie du 'nakh' ou danse des cheveux dans le Souf." *Bulletin de Liaison Saharienne* 11 (1960).

Nieuwkerk, Karin van. *"A Trade Like Any Other": Female Singers and Dancers in Egypt.* Austin, Texas, 1995.

Osgood, J. B. F. *Notes of Travel, or, Recollections of Majunga, Zanzibar, Muscat, Aden, Mocha, and Other Eastern Ports.* Salem, Mass., 1854.

Qāsimī, Khālid al-, and Nizār Ghānim. *Judhūr al-ughniyah al-Yamanīyah fī aʿmāq al-Khalīj.* Damascus, 1987.

Qāsimī, Khālid al-, and Nizār Ghānim. "Al-mūsīqā al-ḥumāsīyah fī al-khalīj wa-al-Yaman." *Al-Ma'thūrāt al-Shaʿbīyah* 2 (1987).

Qāsimī, Khālid al-. *Awāṣir al-ghinā'īyah bayna al-Yaman wa-al-Khalīj.* Beirut, 1988.

Rezvani, Medjid K. *Le théâtre et la danse en Iran.* Paris, 1962.

Rihani, Amin. "The Dance." In Rihani's *Around the Coasts of Arabia.* London, 1930.

Saleh, Magda. "Dance in Egypt: A Quest for Identity." In *Dance Research Collage,* edited by Patricia A. Rowe and Ernestine Stodelle. CORD Dance Research Annual, 10. New York, 1979a.

Saleh, Magda. "A Documentation of the Ethnic Dance Traditions of the Arab Republic of Egypt." Ph.D. diss., New York University, 1979b.

Salem, Lori Anne. "'The Most Indecent Thing Imaginable': Race, Sexuality, and Images of Arabs in American Entertainment, 1850–1990." Ph.D. diss., Temple University, 1995.

Sāmarā'ī, ʿAbd al-Jabbār al-. "Maṣādir wa-marājiʿ fī fūlklūr al-Khalīj al-ʿArabī wa-al-Jazīrah: Al-raqṣ al-shaʿbī." *Al-Turāth al-Shaʿbī* 9 (1978).

Sammakia, Najla. "Dances from Arab Lands." *Arab Perspectives* 5 (1984).

Scott, Hugh. *In the High Yemen.* London, 1942.

Serjeant, R. B., ed. *Prose and Poetry from Ḥaḍramawt.* London, 1951.

Serjeant, R. B. "The Ma'n 'Gypsies' of the West Aden Protectorate." *Anthropos* 56 (1961).

Serjeant, R. B. *South Arabian Hunt.* London, 1976.

Shay, Anthony V. "Traditional Music and Dances of Lebanon." *Viltis* 35 (December 1976): 6–10.

Shiloah, Amnon. "Réflexions sur la danse artistique musulmane au moyen âge." *Cahiers de civilisation médiévale* 6 (October–November 1962): 463–474.

Shukrī, Ibrāhīm al-. *Al-raqaṣāt al-shaʿbīyah al-Kuwaytīyah: Dirāsah fannīyah.* Kuwait, 1978.

Sinclair, Albert Thomas. "The Oriental Gypsies." *Journal of the Gypsy Lore Society* 1 (1907–1908).

Skene, R. "Arab and Swahili Dances and Ceremonies." *Journal of the Royal Anthropological Institute* 47 (1917): 413–434.

Stark, Freya. *A Winter in Arabia.* London, 1941.

Stone, Francine. "Saints and Saints' Days." In *Studies on the Tihāmah,* edited by Francine Stone. Harlow, 1985.

Suwaydā', ʿAbd al-Raḥmān ibn Zayd al-. *Najd fī al-ams al-qarīb.* Riyadh, 1983.

Ṭayyāsh, Fahd ʿAbdallah al-. "Ḥawl irtibāṭ aghānī al-zār bi-raqaṣāt al-sāmirī." *Al-Ma'thūrāt al-Shaʿbīyah* 2 (1987).

Uzayzi, R. Z., and Joseph Chelhod. "L'amour et le mariage dans le désert." *Objets et Mondes* 9 (1969).

Waterbury, John. *North for the Trade: The Life and Times of a Berber Merchant.* Berkeley, 1972.

Wood, Leona, and Anthony V. Shay. "Danse du Ventre: A Fresh Appraisal." *Dance Research Journal* 8 (Spring–Summer 1976): 18–30.

Yūnus, ʿAbd al-Ḥamīd. "Al-raqṣ al-shaʿbī." In Yūnus's *Muʿjam al-fūlklūr.* Beirut, 1983.

VIDEOTAPE. Magda Saleh, "Egypt Dances" (1979).

NAJWA ADRA

Dance Research and Publication

Although there are some valuable sources on Middle Eastern dancing, most of the information available in English and the Romance languages comes from passing mention in travelogues and ethnographies. These descriptions vary according to the interests and perceptions of the authors. Some simply mention that dancing occurred; others describe the dance steps and/or the event at which they were performed. A major obstacle to adequately documenting Middle Eastern dances is that most foreign scholars and travelers have been men, with limited access to the intimate family settings in which most urban dancing occurs. Furthermore, dancing is more likely to be performed outdoors in rural areas, where foreign visitors are few.

A number of sources written in Arabic, Turkish, and Persian since the 1960s have been devoted to dancing, reflecting a renewed local interest in folklore; other local scholars discuss dancing as an integral part of local customs and ceremonies. Because dancing is so often used as a metaphor in Middle Eastern proverbs and aphorisms, collections are a good source of information on dancing. Middle Eastern dancing often accompanies sung poetry, and singing is not necessarily distinguished from dancing as a separate genre. Thus, a number of musical analyses contain information about dancing, and most descriptions of dancing in Arabic include the lyrics of the songs that accompany dances. Journals with a significant number of articles on Middle Eastern dancing include *Al-ma'thūrāt al-shaʿbīyah,* published by the Gulf Cooperation Council Folklore Centre, and *Al-turāth al-shaʿbī,* published in Iraq. The former includes articles in both Arabic and English, but the latter is written entirely in Arabic. Both journals include English abstracts of articles in Arabic. *Arabesque* is a publication based in New York that is written in English and devoted to Middle Eastern dance and culture.

Visual documentation of Middle Eastern dancing is scattered: few photographs or drawings of dancing exist, and although some authors have notated the dances they describe, no systematic attempt has been made to notate regional variety. A valuable contribution is Magda Saleh's film *Egypt Dances;* the accompanying monograph with line illustrations was her doctoral dissertation at New York University in 1979: "A Documentation of the Ethnic Dance Traditions of the Arab Republic of Egypt." It provides clear visual documentation of Egyptian ethnic dances. In her lengthy survey of dance in Egypt, Saleh selected more than twenty dances from different sections of the country, which she described, notated, and filmed. Furthermore, she summarized the literature on Egyptian dancing, including works in Arabic. The documentation of the research and filming process is also offered in detail, providing useful information for future researchers.

Metin And's *A Pictorial History of Turkish Dancing* (Ankara, 1976) traces the historical roots of Turkish dancing and discusses the ecstatic and sacred dancing and the variety of folk and entertainment dancing in Turkey; it concludes with the introduction and establishment of classical ballet in Turkey. Medjid Rezvani's *Le théâtre et la danse en Iran* (Paris, 1962) discusses the history of Iranian dancing and documents the development of theatrical dance and classical ballet in Iran.

Major works in Arabic include Būlus Anṭūn Maṭar's *Khalīj al-aghānī* (The Gulf of Songs) (Beirut, c.1980), a detailed and well-illustrated study of dances in the Gulf region. Other important works are Yūsuf Farḥān Dawkhī's *Al-aghānī al-Kuwaytīyah* (Kuwaiti Songs) (Doha, 1984); Rifʿat Duwayb's *Aghānī al-aʿraqṣ fī Dawlat al-Imārāt al-ʿArabīyah al-Muttaḥida* (Wedding Songs in the United Arab Emirates) (United Arab Emirates, 1982); Ibrāhīm al-Shukrī's *Al-raqaṣāt al-shaʿbīyah al-Kuwaytīyah: Dirāsah fanniyah* (Kuwaiti Folk Dances: A Technical Study) (Kuwait, 1978); Ḥasan al-Bāshī's *Al-ughniyah al-shaʿbīyah al-Falasṭīnīyah* (Palestinian Folk Songs) (Damascus, 1987); and Sa'd al-Khādim's *Al-raqṣ al-shaʿbī fī Miṣr* (Folk Dance in Egypt) (Cairo, 1972).

Shorter, but no less valuable, surveys include Louis Mercier's chapter on dancing in *La chasse et les sports chez les Arabes* (Paris, 1927); Nezan Kendal's "Kurdish Music and Dance," *The World of Music* 21 (1979); Anthony Shay's "Traditional Music and Dances of Lebanon," *Viltis* 35 (1976); and M. Brulard's "La musique et la danse à Ghat," *Bulletin de Liaison Saharienne* 9 (1958). Works in Arabic include Muḥammad al-Muslimānī's "Ḥawl al-mūsīqā wa-al-raqṣ al-shaʿbī fī Qaṭar" (Traditional Folk Music and Dance in Qatar), *Al-ma'thūrāt al-shaʿbīyah* 1 (1986); and Muṣṭafā Ḥusayn's survey of song and dance among the tribes of Iraq, "Al-ghinā' wa al-raqṣ ʿind ʿashā'ir al-ʿIrāq," *Jarīdat al-balad* 70 (1963). Considerable information on dancing can be found in 'Abd al-Raḥmān al-Suwaydā"s *Najd fī al-ams al-qarīb* (Najd in the Recent Past; Riyadh, 1983).

The literature on southern Yemen contains a wealth of information on a variety of dances. Among these are R. B. Serjeant's *Prose and Poetry from Ḥadramawt* (London, 1951); R. Skene's "Arab and Swahili Dances and Ceremonies," *Journal of the Royal Anthropological Institute* 47 (1917); Oliver C. Myers's "Little Aden Folklore," *Bulletin de l'Institut Français d'Archéologie Orientale* (Cairo) 44 (1947); Frederick M. Hunter's *An Account of the British Settlement of Aden in Arabia* (London, 1877); and Harold Ingrams's "A Dance of the Ibex Hunters in the Hadramaut: Is It a Pagan Survival?" *Man* 37 (1937). The dancing of Gypsies in the Middle East is discussed by Albert Thomas Sinclair in "The Oriental Gypsies," *Journal of the Gypsy Lore Society* 1 (1907–08), and given passing mention elsewhere.

Other scholars have provided detailed descriptions of particular dances or dance genres. For example, H. R. P. Dickson describes the *sulubba* dance on the Arabian Peninsula in his *The Arab of the Desert* (London, 1951). Anne Cloudsley discusses the Sudanese Pigeon Dance in the context of a wedding in *Women of Omdurman* (London, 1983). Hamada Ibrahim's "Les chansons de la mer *(al-nihām)* au Kuwait," *Annali Instituto Orientale di Napoli* 36 (1976), and Toufic Kerbage's *The Rhythms of Pearl Diver Music in Qatar* (Doha, n.d.) provide useful information about dances associated with traditional pearling activities in the Gulf.

Studies in Arabic of particular dances include ʿAdnān Ibn Dhurayl's in-depth analysis of the Syrian *samāḥ* dance in his *Muʿjam raqṣ al-samāḥ* (A Concordance of the Samāḥ Dance; Damascus, 1970); Muḥammad al-Katabī's discussion of the Iraqi *chūbīyah* in *Al-turāth al-shaʿbī* 5 (1974); Fahd al-Ṭayyāsh's analysis of the link between *zār* and the *sāmirī* dance in *Al-ma'thūrāt al-shaʿbīyah* 2 (1987); ʿĀ'ishah al-Khulayfī's work on the *murādah* of the Gulf in *Al-ma'thūrāt al-shaʿbīyah* 1 (1986); and ʿAbdallāh Ṣāliḥ Ḥaddād's description of the Hadrami *ʿidda* in *Al-turāth al-shaʿbī* 9 (1978).

Some dances have received greater attention and a fuller discussion in the literature than others. One of the best known is the Palestinian sword dance of the Beersheba bedouin, sensitively described by ʿArif al-ʿArif in his *Bedouin Lore, Law and Legend* (London, 1922); and by Philip J. Baldensperger in *The Immovable East* (London, 1913) and R. Z. Uzayzi and Joseph Chelhod's "L'amour et le mariage dans le désert," *Objets et mondes* 9 (1969). *Al-ʿardah*, the combat dance performed in Saudi Arabia and the Gulf region, and its variations are discussed in some depth in the literature in Arabic: in Majīd al-Lāmī's "Fī Abū Ḍabī: Raqaṣāt ʿArabīyah Qadīmah" (In Abu Dhabi: Ancient Arabic Dances), *Al-turath al-shaʿbi* 4 (1973); and Khālid ibn Jābir al-Gharīb's "Al-ʿarḍah wa-al-ahāzīj al-ḥarbīyah" (The *Arḍa* and Martial Poetry), in his *Kitāb manṭaqat al-Aḥsā' ʿabr aṭwār al-ta'rīkh* (The Book on the Ahsa Region across the Stages of History; Al-Ahsa, Saudi Arabia, 1986). A short description in English of one version of this dance can be found in Sir Richard Burton's *Personal Narrative of a Pilgrimage to al-Madinah and Meccah* (New York, 1964).

The North African *ay-aralla-buya* has been described in detail by ethnographers David Hart in "The Cultural Role of Ay-aralla-buya: Poetry, Music and Dancing," in his *The Aith Waryaghar of the Moroccan Rif* (Tucson, Ariz., 1976), and by Terri Joseph in her "Poetry as a Strategy of Power: the Case of Riffian Berber Women," *Signs* 5 (1980). Earlier versions of the dance were observed and described by Colonel Emilio Blanco Izaga in "Las Danzas Rifeñas," *Africa* (Madrid) 5 (1946). Hassan Jouad and B. Lortat-Jacob provide an extensively illustrated study of the *ahwash* (Fr. *ahouache*), which may be a variant of the *ay-aralla-buya*, in their *La saison des fêtes dans une vallée du Haut-Atlas: Textes et photographies* (Paris, 1978). Further discussions of *ahwash* are found in Lortat-Jacob's *Musique et fêtes au Haut-Atlas* (Paris, 1980) and in André Adam's "La maison et le village dans quelques tribut de l'Anti-Atlas," *Hespéris* 37 (1950).

Nakhkh, another North African dance, has also received much attention. Nicknamed *"la danse des cheveux"* (the hair dance) because dancers fling their hair from side to side and around, it is described by J. Ferry in his "La danse des cheveux: Contribution à l'éthnographie du Souf," *Travaux de l'Institut de Recherches Sahariennes* 6 (1950); Ahmed Najah in his "De l'étymologie du 'nakh' ou danse des cheveux dans le Souf," *Bulletin de Liaison Saharienne* 11 (1960); and Frank E. Johnson in "Here and There in North Africa," *National Geographic Magazine* 25 (1912). Al-Lāmī (1973) discusses young girls swinging their hair in the Gulf region.

Among Western scholars the *danse du ventre* (the belly dance) has received the greatest amount of attention. Studies have been published by La Meri: "Learning the Danse du Ventre," *Dance Perspectives* 10 (1961); Morroe Berger: "A Curious and Wonderful Gymnastic: The Arab Danse du Ventre," *Dance Perspectives* 10 (1961) and "The Belly Dance," *Horizons* 8.2 (1966); and Leona Wood and Anthony Shay: *"Danse du Ventre:* A Fresh Appraisal," *Dance Research Journal* 8 (1976). Wendy Buonaventura's *Serpent of the Nile: Women and Dance in the Arab World* (London, 1989) is a well-illustrated history dealing extensively with Orientalist depictions of, and their influences on, belly dancing. Sherri Deaver writes about the belly dance as it is most often performed, among friends in private homes, in her "Concealment vs. Display: The Modern Saudi Woman," *Dance Research Journal* 10 (1978). North African forms of dancing that also make use of pelvic tilts and rotations, most notably the performances of professional dancers of the Ouled Naïl, were described by M. W. Hilton-Simpson in his *Algiers and Beyond* (London, 1906) and *Among the Hill-Folk of Algeria* (London, 1921), and by Johnson (1912). Karin van Nieuwkerk followed the careers and lives of professional Egyptian dancers, documenting their place in society and attitudes toward their craft, in her ethnography, *"A Trade Like Any Other": Female Singers and Dancers in Egypt* (Austin, Texas, 1995).

The Orientalist fascination with *danse du ventre* has been the subject of much scholarly writing. Buonaventura (1989) provides an illustrated history of orientalist depictions of Middle Eastern dancing. Zeynep Çelik and Leila Kinney argued in "Ethnography and Exhibitionism at the Expositions Universelles," *Assemblages* 13 (1990), that the export of *danse du ventre* to European expositions in the nineteenth century fed Orientalist stereotypes of an erotic, feminine Middle East, stereotypes that still influence relationships between West and East. Similar arguments are made by Sarah Graham-Brown in her *Images of Women: The Portrayal of Women in Photography of the Middle East 1860–1950* (New York, 1988). Two doctoral dissertations have been concerned with belly dancing in America: Paul Monty's "Serena, Ruth St. Denis, and the Evolution of Belly Dance in America, 1876–1976" (New York University, 1986) traces its history in America, and Lori Anne Salem's "'The Most Indecent Thing Imaginable': Race, Sexuality and Images of Arabs in American Entertainment, 1850–1990" (Temple University, 1995) discusses belly dancing in the context of American notions of race and sexuality.

Evidence of Middle Eastern dancing throughout history is provided by a variety of sources. Pharaonic inscriptions are analyzed for evidence of dancing by Irena Lexová in *Ancient Egyptian Dances* (Prague, 1935) and by Hans Hickmann in "Quelques considérations sur la danse et la musique de danse dans l'Égypte pharaonique," *Cahiers d'histoire égyptienne* (Cairo, 1953). One of the most important sources on dancing in pre-Islamic Arabia is *Kitāb al-aghānī* (Cairo, 1979), which contains poetry and anecdotes collected by al-Isfahānī (died 967). Carel DuRy describes a stucco sculpture of a dancer dated to 1342 as "one of the oldest examples of free-standing sculpture in Islamic art" in his *Art of Islam* (New York, 1972). Richard Ettinghausen speculates on dancing in the Middle Ages in his "The Dance with Zoomorphic Masks and Other Forms of Entertainment as Seen in Islamic Art," in *Arabic and Islamic Studies in Honor of Hamilton A. R. Gibb,* edited by George Makdisi (Leiden, 1965). Hobbyhorse dancing during the Abbasid period is discussed by the late fourteenth-century scholar Ibn Khaldūn in *The Muqaddimah,* translated by F. Rosenthal (New York, 1958), and elaborated on by Maurice Gaudefroy-Demombynes in his "Sur le cheval-jupon et al-kurraj" in *Mélanges offerts à William Marçais* (Paris, 1950). Arab historians and early Muslim travelers sometimes mention dancing in their works, including the Yemeni al-Khazrajī, who died in 1410, and Ibn Bāṭṭūṭah, who wrote of his own travels in the fourteenth century. The history of Turkish dancing is outlined in an amply illustrated volume by And (1976). Amnon Shiloah's "Réflexions sur la danse artistique musulmane au moyen âge," *Cahiers de civilisation médiévale* 6 (1962) reviews the evidence of artistic dancing in Islamic history in an attempt to understand why it is largely neglected in scholarly historical treatises that deal extensively with music.

Western ethnographers and travelers to the Middle East have witnessed and written about dance events since the 1830s. Notable among them is Edward Lane, who provides a wealth of information about dancing in nineteenth-century Egypt in his *Manners and Customs of the Modern Egyptians* (New York, 1966), first published in 1836. Others include Philip J. Baldensperger in his "Peasant Folklore of Palestine," *Palestine Exploration Fund Quarterly Statement* (1893) and "Song and Dance in the East," in *The Immovable East: Studies of the People and Customs of Palestine* (London, 1913); John L. Burckhardt's *Notes on the Bedouins and Wahābys, Collected during His Travels in the East,* vol. 1 (New York, 1967); and J. B. F. Osgood, who wrote *Notes of Travel, or, Recollections of Majunga, Zanzibar, Muscat, Aden, Mocha, and Other Eastern Ports* (Salem, Mass., 1854). Amin Rihani wrote extensively about dancing in Saudi Arabia and Yemen in his *Around the Coasts of Arabia* (London, 1930), and G. W. Murray's *Sons of Ishmael* (London, 1935) includes photographs of dancing. Most examples of this genre are not informed discussions of dancing, but they provide the researcher with a sense of the extent and variety of the dances performed in the region.

Regarding religious dancing Marijan Molé's "La danse extatique en Islam," in *Les danses sacrées,* edited by Jean Cazeneuve (Paris, 1963), is a thorough study of ecstatic dancing in Islam and of the Mawlawī dervish *dhikr* ceremony (*dhikr* is the repeated invocation of God's name, basic to all Muslim Sufi ritual, whether or not it involves dancing). Molé's article also analyzes in detail the polemic on the permissibility of dancing by religious scholars. A more recent study of the whirling dervishes is Talat Halman and Metin And's *Mevlana Çelal Eddin Rumi and the Whirling Dervishes* (Istanbul, 1992). Other Sufi orders are also discussed in the literature: Sophie Ferchiou's "Survivances mystiques et culte de possession dans le maraboutisme tunisien," *L'homme* 12 (1972), compares the movements that accompany *dhikr* in two religious associations. Rihani (1930) describes in detail a ceremony of the Qādirī order in Hodeida, Yemen, in the 1920s. Religiously motivated dancing in Hodeida in the 1980s is described by Francine Stone and Anderson Bakewell in Stone's *Studies on the Tihāma* (Harlow, 1985). In J. W. McPherson's *The Moulids of Egypt* (Cairo, 1941) a wealth of information is included on dancing during religious holidays in Egypt; some dances form an integral part of *dhikr* ceremonies and some are performed purely for entertainment. Magda Saleh (1979) and M. A. Murray in "Ancient and Modern Ritual Dances in the Near East," *Folklore* 46 (1955), also provide considerable information on *dhikr* and dancing during religious holidays.

Several scholars address the relationship between dancing and culture. Lois Lamya' al-Faruqi argues in her "Dance as an Expression of Islamic Culture," *Dance Research Journal* 10.2 (1978), and in "Dances of the Muslim Peoples," *Dance Scope* 11.1 (1976–1977), that the abstract and improvisatory nature of dancing by Muslims corresponds to Islam's view of monotheism and the concept of the unity of God *(tawḥīd).* Ferchiou (1972) argues that cultural gender differences underlie differences in the movements that accompany *dhikr* in the two orders studied. Joseph (1980) also relates dancing to gender roles.

The only ethnographic study of dancing in the Middle East to date is Najwa Adra's 1982 Temple University doctoral dissertation, "Qabyala: The Tribal Concept in the Central Highlands of the Yemen Arab Republic." Adra analyzes the contextual and stylistic elements of two genres of dancing performed in the highlands of Yemen, *bara*ʿ and *luʿbah.* Her thesis is that the opposition between these genres replicates two opposite value emphases in Yemen's traditional tribal society. Adra argues that tribal values must be understood in order to recognize the significance of the dancing and that understanding the dancing helps to elucidate the tribal concept. She summarizes this argument in "Achievement and Play: Opposition in Yemeni Tribal Dancing," *Proceedings of the Consulting Seminar on the Collecting and Documenting of the Traditional Music and Dance for the Arabian Gulf and Peninsula 15–19 December 1984* (Doha, Qatar, 1984) and in her "The Concept of Tribe in Rural Yemen," in *Arab Society,* edited by N. S. Hopkins and S. E. Ibrahim (Cairo, 1985). As a consequence of major societal changes in Yemen in the 1970s and 1980s *bara*ʿ has become more a national than a tribal dance. These changes are described in Adra's "Tribal Dancing and Yemeni Nationalism: Steps to Unity," *Revue du monde musulman et de la Méditerranée* 67 (1993).

In other examples of changes in Middle Eastern dancing, John Waterbury's *North for the Trade* (Berkeley, 1972) documents the adaptation of Moroccan Sousi rural folk dances to the urban stage, performed for the immigrant Sousi community in Casablanca. The Iraqi *darjah* has also changed since the 1960s. Once exclusively a women's dance, it is currently performed by men, women, or in mixed groups. These changes are described in Ibrāhīm Farḥān Aḥmad's "Al-darja," *Al-turāth al-shaʿbī* 9 (1978). One of the most popular genres of dance and music currently performed in the Gulf region has roots in traditional Yemeni music and dance forms. This phenomenon is documented in Khālid al-Qāsimī's *Awāṣir al-ghināʾīyah bayna al-Yaman wa-al-Khalīj* (Musical Links between Yemen and the Gulf) (Beirut, 1988).

Some scholars have addressed issues related to the importation of Western aesthetic forms. Saleh's "Dance in Egypt: A Quest for Identity," in *Dance Research Collage,* edited by Patricia A. Rowe and Ernestine Stodelle (New York, 1979), considers attempts in Egypt to form a viable and authentic Egyptian ballet. The formation of national ballet companies in Turkey and Iran are discussed, respectively, in And (1976) and Rezvani (1962). Fārūq Awhān's "Al-iḥtifāl al-masraḥī fī taqālīd al-raqṣ al-shaʿbī (raqṣat al-ʿayyālah)" (The Theatrical Celebration of Folk Dance Traditions—The ʿAyyālah Dance), *Al-maʾthūrāt al-shaʿbīyah* 3 (1988), considers the value of developing an indigenous theatrical form, arguing that the *ʿayyālah* dance of the United Arab Emirates is eminently suited to adaptation to the stage.

Middle Eastern researchers have renewed their interest in documenting and preserving their traditional dance and music. Mahmoud Reda in Egypt pioneered this trend in 1958, starting a dance company that performed choreographed "folk" dances. His example was followed by others in Egypt (see Saleh, 1979), Lebanon, and Jordan. In some cases Russian choreographers were invited to help "develop" theatrical forms, resulting in "folk" dances that had little resemblance to indigenous forms.

National dance companies have been formed in several Middle Eastern countries. Television coverage of local folk dancing has also maintained public interest in dance traditions. Fears that imported popular culture will replace traditional expressions of a rapidly disappearing local heritage also serve to encourage the documentation and airing of indigenous art forms. In 1984, the Arab Gulf States Folklore Centre (since renamed the Gulf Cooperation Council Folklore Centre), based in Qatar and funded by a number of Gulf countries, sponsored a consulting seminar to explore research needs in the classification and documentation of music and dance in the region. While dance research in the Middle East is still in its infancy, attempts have been made to document indigenous dances; a systematic program to collect and notate traditional dances has yet to be developed, however. Researchers have so far only touched on issues of similarity and difference among Middle Eastern traditions and of change and adaptation, opening a fertile field for future research.

NAJWA ADRA

MILHAUD, DARIUS (born 4 September 1892 in Aix-en-Provence, France, died 22 June 1974 in Geneva), composer. Born of a distinguished Provençal Jewish family, Milhaud excelled in music at an early age. After studying with local teachers, he entered the Paris Conservatoire, where he first concentrated on the violin. In time, however, composition became his primary interest. His early works, which were influenced by Claude Debussy, were performed for the public and attracted critical attention.

Milhaud soon met one of his literary idols, Paul Claudel, who was destined to exert considerable personal and artistic influence on him. Medically exempt from military service in World War I, in 1916 Milhaud was offered the post of secretary to Claudel when the poet-dramatist-diplomat was appointed minister to Brazil. The indigenous music Milhaud heard in Brazil attracted him profoundly and became a permanent part of his vocabulary; he joined polytonality and the folk *melos* of his native Provence as one of the cornerstones of his music. Although Milhaud spent fewer than two years in South America, Brazilian rhythms and melodic turns of phrase remained indelibly within him to be used throughout his career. The intoxicating blandishments of American jazz were similarly to stimulate his creative energies.

Upon his return to Europe, Milhaud became associated with the group known as Les Six, thus entering a period of enormous productivity and increasing renown. This period of good fortune continued through the 1920s and 1930s. Music of every category came readily from his pen, as it was to do throughout his life; he was also in demand as conductor, lecturer, and performer.

In 1940, with World War II raging in Europe and France fallen to Germany, Milhaud with his wife and son fled to the United States; there, he became a music-faculty member at Mills College in Oakland, California. He resigned this post in 1971 and returned permanently to Europe, where he continued to work despite increasing illness. With his final work, a quintet for winds, he reached his opus 443, which qualifies him as one of the twentieth century's most productive composers.

Milhaud was a theater man to his fingertips, and he composed opera, dance works, film scores, and incidental music for the stage. His first ballet, the 1918 *L'Homme et Son Désir,* composed in Rio de Janiero, was premiered in Paris on 6 June 1921 by Les Ballets Suédois; the choreography was by Jean Börlin. Claudel provided the scenario for this mystical *poème plastique,* set in a Brazilian forest. The music, for various instruments, vocal quartet, and a battery of percussion, preserves melodic, rhythmic, and tonal independence among several separate performing groups, with the percussion hypnotically summoning the nocturnal sounds of the forest. It is a haunting score, evocative in the extreme, with the ability to say more than it intends, and to suggest more than it says.

Le Boeuf sur le Toit, composed in Paris in 1919, is subtitled *Cinema-Fantasy on South American Airs.* Originally conceived by Milhaud as possible musical accompaniment to a Charlie Chaplin silent film, the lively score was taken over by dramatist Jean Cocteau, who employed it as the basis for a theatrical extravaganza starring the Fratellinis, the celebrated clowns of the Cirque Médrano. Set in an American bar that never saw the light of day, other than in Cocteau's creative imagination, the theater piece shows a covey of disreputable characters doing their best to thwart the enforcement of Prohibition. *Le Boeuf sur le Toit* was mounted in Paris on 21 February 1920, with decor by Raoul Dufy. This good-natured divertissement became one of Milhaud's most popular works as a concert piece. In 1921 he also worked with Les Six on the one-act Cocteau–Börlin collaboration *Les Mariés de la Tour Eiffel,* a ballet-farce; the piece was considered the manifesto of the composers.

La Création du Monde, composed in Paris in 1923, was set to a scenario by Blaise Cendrars. It depicts the world's beginning as imagined by African aborigines and was called a *ballet nègre*. The music presents the tones and gestures of jazz as filtered through the sophisticated technique of a European intellectual—an astonishing amalgam of transformations and attitudes. With decor by Fernand Léger and choreography by Börlin, this influential score was first presented by Les Ballets Suédois in Paris in October 1923. For many it remains Milhaud's most successful composition.

Salade (with choreography by Leónide Massine) and *Le Train Bleu* (with choreography by Bronislava Nijinska) were composed for rival companies in rapid succession, from February to March 1924, one for Etienne de Beaumont's Soirées de Paris and the other for Serge Diaghilev. The first was inspired by the *commedia dell'arte;* the second invokes the spirit of Jacques Offenbach. The scores represent Milhaud in his most engaging light manner. *Les Songes,* written for George Balanchine and Les Ballets 1933, has the charm of French operetta.

Of the later Milhaud ballets, three deserve special mention: *Moïse, The Bells* (after Edgar Allen Poe), and *'Adame Miroir* (from a book by Jean Genet). *Moïse* (1940) was commissioned but never staged by Ballet Theatre. It was finally produced at the Rome Opera Theater in 1950. Musically, it is a work of weight and gravity, reflecting Milhaud's deeply felt religious convictions. *The Bells* (1946), choreographed by Ruth Page, closely follows the shifting moods of Poe's celebrated poem; it is a composition symphonic in scope. *'Adame Miroir* (1948), with a Genet book reminiscent of Cocteau in its mirror imagery, was produced in Paris by Roland Petit, with choreography by Janine Charrat. There is a febrile quality to the music, set for chamber orchestra, that sharply underlines the wiry dramatic insistencies of the story. Milhaud's composition *Jeux de Printemps* (1944), was choreographed and danced by Martha Graham as *Imagined Wing.* His *La Rose des Vents* was choreographed as a ballet by Roland Petit in 1958.

BIBLIOGRAPHY

Beck, Georges. *Darius Milhaud: Étude suivie du catalogue chronologique complet de son oeuvre.* Paris, 1949.

Häger, Bengt. *Ballets Suédois.* Translated by Ruth Sharman. London, 1990.

Milhaud, Darius. *Notes sans musique.* Paris, 1949. Translated as *Notes without Music* (New York, 1953). Enlarged as *Ma vie heureuse* (Paris, 1974).

Milhaud, Madeleine. *Darius Milhaud.* Translated and edited by Jane H. Galante. San Francisco, 1988.

JAMES RINGO

MILLER, ANN (Johnnie Lucille Collier; born 12 April 1923 in Chireno, Texas), tap dancer, singer, actress. One of Hollywood's top female tap-dancing stars, Ann Miller was known for dances filled with robust energy, bursting with joy, vigor, and wild excitement. She was accurately described by a New York critic as an eye tonic, a personality who whirls with hurricane force across the footlights.

As a child, Miller showed signs of rickets and was enrolled in ballet classes in the hope of strengthening her legs. She loathed the lessons, however, and it was only after seeing Bill "Bojangles" Robinson perform at the Majestic Theater in Houston that she became enamored with the idea of becoming a dancer—a tap dancer.

After a series of amateur stints, she and her mother headed to Hollywood in the summer of 1934, where Miller studied at the Fanchon and Marco dancing school. Her parents' marriage collapsed shortly thereafter, and a two-year financial struggle ensued for mother and daughter. Miller was discovered in San Francisco's popular Bal Tabarin supper club, where she had become a dancer. She received a screen test (she lied about her age by several years, as she was still only fourteen), which resulted in appearances in *New Faces of 1937, Life of the Party,* and *Stage Door,* all in 1937. She played the lead in her next film, *Radio City Revels* (1938), her first contact with dance director Hermes Pan, who was Fred Astaire's assistant at RKO.

Miller left Hollywood briefly to strengthen her career by appearing on Broadway in *George White's Scandals of 1939.* She remarked, "I left RKO at a $150 a week, and came back to RKO at $3,000 a picture—that's what one Broadway show did for you!" (Frank, 1994). She then worked in a string of B pictures at RKO and Columbia: *The Hit Parade of 1941* (1940), *Melody Ranch* (1940), *Time Out for Rhythm* (1941), and *Reveille with Beverly* (1943). Miller finally landed a good role in a glossy Metro-Goldwyn-Mayer (MGM) musical, *Easter Parade* (1948), starring Judy Garland and Fred Astaire, in which Miller dazzled audiences with her number "Shakin' the Blues Away." It was her first work with Astaire. Miller next joined Gene Kelly, Vera-Ellen, Frank Sinatra, and Jules Munschin in the film version of Leonard Bernstein's 1944 musical *On the Town* (1949).

Miller is perhaps best remembered for "I've Gotta Hear That Beat" in *Small Town Girl* (1953). Dance director Busby Berkeley thought of the concept for the number: musicians' hands and instruments come through the floor as Ann ricochets through and past them. However, the dance was the uncredited work of tap legend Willie Covan (of the Four Covans), who, together with Miller, created one of the most riveting tap dance numbers on film. Miller's other films include *Kiss Me, Kate* (1953), *Deep in My Heart* (1954), and *Hit the Deck* (1955). After an active film career, and numerous television and nightclub appearances, Miller again appeared on Broadway in the long-running *Mame* (1966), in a revival of the 1934 Cole Porter musical *Anything Goes,* and in the hit show *Sugar Babies* (1979), in which she and Mickey Rooney entertained packed houses until 1986.

ANN MILLER. Known for her fast-paced, "machine-gun" style of tapping, Miller danced in many Hollywood films. In *Small Town Girl* (MGM, 1953), directed by Busby Berkeley and choreographed by Willie Covan, she performed "I've Gotta Hear That Beat," tapping her way through a forest of trombones held by musicians' hands springing from the floor. (Photograph from the collection of Rusty E. Frank.)

[*See also* Tap Dance.]

BIBLIOGRAPHY

Connor, Jim. *Ann Miller: Tops in Taps.* New York, 1981.

Frank, Rusty E. *Tap! The Greatest Tap Dance Stars and Their Stories, 1900–1955.* Rev. ed. New York, 1994.

Thomas, Tony. *That's Dancing.* New York, 1984.

RUSTY E. FRANK

MILLER, MARILYN (Mary Ellen Reynolds; born 1 September 1898, in Evansville, Indiana, died 7 April 1936 in New York City), American musical comedy dancer. After her parents, Edwin Reynolds and Ada Thompson, were divorced when she was an infant, Miller lived with a grandmother in Memphis, Tennessee, until she was four, at which time she joined her mother, an actress, and her stepfather, Carlo Miller, in their vaudeville act. Miller made her stage debut on 20 August 1903 at Lakeside Park in Dayton, Ohio, billed as "Mademoiselle Sugarplum," one of the "Columbian Trio," subsequently called "The Five Columbians" when her sisters were added to the act. The Millers became adept on tour at avoiding the Gerry Society, a national organization determined to invoke child labor laws and keep youngsters from performing until they were sixteen.

The family was appearing in "The Dresden Doll" at London's Lotus Club in 1913, when American producer Lee Shubert spotted Miller doing a series of impersonations, including one of Adeline Genée. Shubert hired her for the Winter Garden Company in New York. Because her mother had divorced her second husband, legal difficulties arose over his negotiations on Miller's behalf, but she was sixteen (and thus legally responsible for her contracts) when she made her Broadway debut on 10 June 1914 as Miss Jerry in the *Passing Show of 1914.* She appeared in the annual edition of the Shuberts' revue through 1917. The following season she played Betty Pestlewaite in *Fancy Free* at the Astor Theater and was hired by Florenz Ziegfeld.

Miller sang and danced in Ziegfeld's *Follies of 1918* and, under his tutelage, became a star in the title role of Jerome Kern's *Sally,* which ran for five hundred and seventy performances. During this period Miller's husband, Frank Carter, was killed in an automobile crash. Shortly thereafter she was diagnosed as having a heart condition, and she broke with Ziegfeld. These may be reasons why she chose the mildly less strenuous breeches role of Peter, with Leslie Banks as Captain Hook, in Charles Dillingham's 1924 production of *Peter Pan* at the Knickerbocker Theater. Miller had married Jack Pickford (Mary Pickford's brother), but their union was dissolved in Paris in 1927.

As the circus-riding heroine in Dillingham's *Sunny* (1925), the first collaboration between Kern and Oscar Hammerstein II, Miller began a dazzling dance partnership with Jack Donahue. In 1927 she returned to Ziegfeld to play the lead in *Rio Rita,* and in 1928 she played the princess in Ziegfeld's *Rosalie,* partnered again with Donahue. Their dances were staged by the Dallas-based Theodore Koslov, who described Miller as "quick to learn and businesslike rather than pleasant to work with." Clifton Webb also danced in this production.

Like many Broadway celebrities, Miller was lured to Hollywood, where in 1929 she was paid $100,000 to star in the film version of *Sally.* Soon thereafter she appeared on Broadway with Fred and Adele Astaire in *Smiles* (1930). Vincent Youmans had created the score from a story suggested by Noël Coward. Miller's last Broadway role was in *As Thousands Cheer* (1933), in which Clifton Webb was again featured as a dancer. In 1934 she married Chester L. O'Brien, a chorus singer in *As Thousands Cheer* who was five years her junior. When O'Brien was fired from the show, Miller quit in protest.

Called "A Degas turned American" by the critic John Mason Brown, the dimpled blond also was heralded as "Titania of the jazz age" and as "the smiling embodiment of grace." She died at Doctors' Hospital in Manhattan at the age of thirty-seven from complications following a sinus and jawbone infection. After her burial at Woodlawn Cemetery, an ugly lawsuit ensued over her will, which designated her mother as principal heir and made no provision for either her stepfather or O'Brien, who, her sisters attested, had abandoned and neglected her. June Haver played the adulated star in *Look for the Silver Lining* (1949), a film biography of the dancer.

Miller was one of the most beloved stars in the early days of musical comedy. Her incandescent stage presence and lyrical dancing captivated audiences and enamored the jazz age. Realizing both her personal goal and, to a degree, the ideal of her era, she soared high and died young.

BIBLIOGRAPHY

Bordman, Gerald. *American Musical Theatre: A Chronicle.* 2d ed. New York and Oxford, 1992.

Harris, Warren G. *The Other Marilyn.* New York, 1985.

CAMILLE HARDY

MILLOSS, AURELIO (Urel de Miholy; born 12 May 1906 in Ozora, Hungary, died 21 September 1988 in Rome), Hungarian-Italian dancer, choreographer, and ballet director. Milloss took lessons in academic dance as a youth from Nicola Guerra and Cesare Smeraldi in Budapest, Jelena Poljakova in Belgrade, and Anton Romanovsky in Bucharest. He furthered his training with Olga Preobrajenska in Paris, Enrico Cecchetti in Milan and Turin, and Victor Gsovsky in Berlin. In addition, he studied modern dance with Rudolf Laban in Berlin and attended university courses in the humanities.

In 1928 Milloss made his debut as a dancer, performing his own compositions at Der Sturm gallery in Berlin. He then spent brief seasons with the Berlin State Opera and other municipal opera companies in Germany, where his attention turned primarily to choreography. In the mid-1930s he returned to Budapest and staged works for the Budapest Opera, including Robert Schumann's *Carnaval,* Zoltán Kodály's *Kuruts Tale* (1935), Igor Stravinsky's *Petrouchka* (1933), and Beethoven's *Creatures of Prometheus* (1942). In consultation with Béla Bartók he began to choreograph *The Miraculous Mandarin,* but the production never reached the stage; it finally premiered at Teatro alla Scala in Milan in October 1942. Like Bartók, Milloss researched folk performances in Hungarian villages, and together with Béla Paulini he created folklore-inspired ballets presented under the title of *Csupajáték* in

MILLOSS: (*right*) A scene from *Le Creature di Prometeo* (The Creatures of Prometheus), mounted by Milloss at the Teatro alla Scala, Milan, in 1952. He had staged earlier productions in Augsburg (1933) and Rome (1940). Set to Beethoven's famous ballet score, the work was modeled on Salvatore Viganò's original production of 1801. (*below*) Milloss mounted *Fantasia Brasileira* to music by Jacques Ibert for the Ballet do IV Centenario de São Paulo in 1954. Decor and costumes were designed by Noemia Mourão. (Photograph at left by Marka; photograph below from a private collection.)

the Operetta Theater in 1938, and as *Just a Play* in London in 1939.

In the late 1930s Milloss settled in Italy, where he became a naturalized citizen in 1960. He served as ballet director and choreographer at the Rome Opera from 1938 to 1945 and at La Scala from 1947 to 1977. During the same period he was active at theaters in Palermo, Turin, Genoa, and Bologna as well as at the Biennale in Venice, the Festival of Sacred Music in Perugia, the Two Worlds Festival in Spoleto, and above all the Musical May Festival in Florence.

After World War II Milloss's international career resumed. Significant assignments included ballet master for the Ballet do IV Centenario de São Paulo (1953–1954), for the Ballett der Bühnen der Stadt Köln (1960–1963), and for the Vienna State Opera (1963–1966, 1971–1974). He also worked in Buenos Aires with the Teatro Colón, in Stockholm with the Royal Opera, in Brussels with Les Ballets du XXe Siècle, and in Paris with Les Ballets des Champs-Élysées, Théâtre National au Palais de Chaillot, and Le Grand Ballet du Marquis de Cuevas.

Milloss occupied a significant place in contemporary ballet, particularly in Italy, which owes much of its ballet renaissance to his guidance. He created a repertory of modern Italian ballets in collaboration with the best-known musicians, painters, and sculptors of his generation. His musical collaborators included Alfredo Casella, Gian Francesco Malipiero, Goffredo Petrassi, Luigi Dallapiccola, Roman Vlad, and Nino Rota. His scenic collaborators included Giorgio de' Chirico, Gino Severini, Enrico Prampolini, Filippo de Pisis, Felice Casorati, Mario Mafai, Toti Scialoja, Renato Guttuso, Léonor Fini, Fabrizio Clerici, Corrado Cagli, Afro and Mirko Basaldella, Giacomo Manzù, and Umberto Mastroianni.

In addition to staging about twenty lyric operas, Milloss choreographed a total of 175 ballets. His works evidence a universality of poetic intent. They originate in elemental forces, sensed in the internal tensions of his subjects, perhaps inspired by values that can be intuited only as mysterious abstractions. These spiritual references clearly reflect his humanistic, cultural, and philosophic interest.

[*See also* Italy, *articles on theatrical dance.*]

BIBLIOGRAPHY

Arout, Georges. *La danse contemporaine.* Paris, 1955.

Ballett-Journal/Das Tanzarchiv 34 (December 1986): 30–37. Special section on Aurelio Milloss.

Bentivoglio, Leonetta. "Aurel von Milloss: Interview." *Ballett International* 9 (May 1986): 14–21.

Bentivoglio, Leonetta. "L'opera fiorentina di Milloss." In *Aurelio M. Milloss: 35 anni di balletto al Maggio Musicale Fiorentino,* edited by Moreno Bucci and Caterina D'Amico de Carvalho. Florence, 1987.

Carones, Laura. "Milloss e la critica anglosassone." *La danza italiana* 4 (Spring 1986): 109–117.

D'Amico, Fedele. "Ciò che gli dobbiamo." In *Aurelio M. Milloss: 35 anni di balletto al Maggio Musicale Fiorentino,* edited by Moreno Bucci and Caterina D'Amico de Carvalho. Florence, 1987.

de Zoete, Beryl. "Aurel Milloss." In de Zoete's *The Thunder and the Freshness.* New York, 1963.

Guatterini, Marinella, and Michele Porzio. *Milloss, Busoni e Scelsi: Neoclassico, danza e musica nell'Italia del Novecento.* Milan, 1992.

Koegler, Horst. "Aurel von Milloss zwischen den Proben." *Melos* 4 (April 1960): 112–115.

Michaut, Pierre. *Le ballet contemporain, 1929–1950.* Paris, 1950.

Milloss, Aurelio. "Zur Aktualität der Ballettklassik." *Österreichische Musikzeitschrift* (November 1963): 501–506.

Milloss, Aurelio. "Das Erbe des Expressionismus im Tanz." *Maske und Kothurn* 11 (1965): 329–343.

Milloss, Aurelio. "Il balletto nel propio labirinto: Confessioni di un coreografo" (1963). *Terzo occhio* 14 (December 1988): 27–31.

Pinzauti, Leonardo. "A colloquio con Aurelio Milloss." *Nuova rivista musicale italiana* (1968).

Regner, O. F. "Milloss und die grosse Synthese." In Regner's *Das neue Ballettbuch.* Frankfurt am Main, 1962.

Tani, Gino. "Il balletto e l'opera di Aurelio M. Milloss." In *Il balletto e l'opera di Aurelio M. Milloss, al Maggio Musicale Fiorentino,* edited by Stelio Felici. Florence, 1977.

Tegeder, Ulrich. "Testaments from the Past." *Ballett International* 9 (November 1986): 24–29.

Testa, Alberto. "Il Maudarino meraviglioso." Programe, Teatro dell'-opera di Roma, no. 13 (1978–1979): 830–861.

Testa, Alberto. "Ritorno di Milloss all'opera di Roma. Infelice destino oli 'un Marino." In *Il dramma* 7–8 (July–August 1979): 2–7.

Testa, Alberto. "Bartók nell'estetica del balletto moderno in generale e nell'opera di Milloss in particolare." *Nuova rivista musicale italiana,* no. 2 (1981): 227–240.

Testa, Alberto. *Discorso sulla danza e sul balletto.* 3d ed. Rome, 1981.

Testa, Alberto, et al. *Il balletto nel Novecento.* Turin, 1983.

Testa, Alberto. *Storia della danza e del balletto.* Rome, 1988.

Testa, Alberto. *I grandi balletti: Repertorio di quattro secoli del teatro di danza.* Rome, 1991.

Veroli, Patrizia. "The Choreography of Aurelio Milloss" (parts 1–4). *Dance Chronicle* 13.1–3 (1990): 1–46, 193–240, 368–392; 14.1 (1991): 47–101.

Veroli, Patrizia. "Der besessene Tänzer Aurel v. Milloss, von 1928 bis 1938." *Tanzdrama Magazin* (October 1995): 19–25.

Veroli, Patrizia. *Milloss: Un maestro della coreografia tra expressionismo e classicità.* Lucca, 1996.

ALBERTO TESTA
Translated from Italian

MILON, LOUIS (Louis-Jacques Milon; born 18 April 1766 [possibly 1765 or 1769] in Saint-Martin de Caux, died 26 November 1849 [possibly 1845] in Neuilly), French ballet dancer, choreographer, and teacher. Having studied at the Paris Opera Ballet School, Louis Milon made his debut with the company in 1790. He was made a "replacement" in 1793 and a principal *(grand sujet)* soon afterward. He became a very popular dancer, noted as an excellent mime as well as a *danseur noble,* but he was destined to make as great a mark as a choreographer as a performer.

Milon produced his first ballets outside the Paris Opera. *Pygmalion,* created at the Théâtre de l'Ambigu-Comique in 1799 and starring his young sister-in-law, Émilie Bigottini, was so successful that he was invited to restage it at the Opera the following year. Before the end of 1799, however, Milon had produced *Héro et Léandre* at the Opera and had proved that he could compete with Pierre Gardel in the use of mythological love affairs as subject matter. He was named assistant ballet master to Gardel at this time, and they thereafter worked harmoniously together.

This collaboration enabled Milon to create *Les Noces de Gamache* in 1801, based on episodes in *Don Quixote,* the great novel by Miguel Cervantes. For this ballet Milon based his libretto on the most comic passages in the novel and demonstrated that he was completely at ease in the genre of comedy. [*See* Don Quixote, *article on* Early Productions.] This ballet remained in the repertory until 1841. By contrast, *Lucas et Laurette* was quickly withdrawn after its presentation in 1804 because it displeased Napoleon, who was aware of everything done on the stage of the imperial theater. In 1807, *Le Retour d'Ulysse,* set to a score by Louis-Luc de Persuis, found favor with Jean-Georges Noverre, who wrote that

> M. Milon gave four pantomime ballets at the Opera; these productions were well received and revealed the creator's expertise. . . . To succeed next to Gardel, to win public support without the help of political intrigues and cabals is to have shown a combination of delicacy, modesty, and ability.
> (Noverre, [1807] 1950, no. 32)

In 1813, Milon's ballet *Nina, ou La Folle par Amour,* also set to a score by Persuis and danced by Biggottini, Monsieur Albert (François Decombe), and Milon himself, was highly praised by the critics and the public. It remained in the repertory of the Opera until 1837 and was produced in London in 1821, with Lise Noblet in the title role, and in Saint Petersburg by Charles-Louis Didelot in 1828. More than a hundred years later, the British ballet historian Cyril Beaumont noted that

> *Nina* is a well-constructed dramatic ballet that might be revived with advantage. Based on the comedy first produced by Marsollier in Paris in 1786 . . . the first act is of particular interest for certain dramatic scenes which have much in common with those of *Giselle.* (Beaumont, 1937)

Depicting the story of a woman driven mad by love, *Nina* was followed by *L'Épreuve Villageoise, ou André et*

Denise (1815), a peasant ballet; *L'Heureux Retour* (1815), an *opéra ballet* created (with Gardel) especially to mark the return of the Bourbons; and *Le Carnaval de Venise, ou La Constance à l'Épreuve* (1816). All these works had music by Persuis. Milon's *Les Sauvages* (1816) attracted attention as the first ballet to evoke the local color of South Seas islands.

Another ballet that made a favorable impression several years later was *Clari, ou La Promesse de Mariage* (1820), with Bigottini and Albert in the principal roles. "It was a typical example of pre-Romantic ballet," said Ivor Guest (1980), "with characters drawn from everyday life and its action evincing a rather naive sympathy with the common people." A contemporary French critic, François Castil-Blaze, thought it was too long but noted that Bigottini's outstanding interpretation was unlikely to be excelled by others later on (*Journal des débats,* 22 June 1820).

Milon was still dancing and acting in his own ballets and in works by other choreographers. He created roles in *Les Pages du Duc de Vendôme* (1820) and *Alfred le Grand* (1822), both by Jean-Louis Aumer, and in *Zémire et Azor* (1824), the sole ballet done by André Deshayes for the Paris Opera. Like Gardel, Milon staged *divertissements* for various operas, including *La Mort du Tasse* and *Blanche de Provence* in 1821, *Florestan* in 1822, and a revival of Gluck's *Armide* in 1825. Having begun to teach at the Paris Opera Ballet School as early as 1799, Milon continued to direct the mime class until his retirement in 1826.

[*See also the entry on Bigottini.*]

BIBLIOGRAPHY

Beaumont, Cyril W. *Complete Book of Ballets.* London, 1937.

Chazin-Bennahum, Judith. *Dance in the Shadow of the Guillotine.* Carbondale, Ill., 1988.

Guest, Ivor. *The Romantic Ballet in Paris.* 2d rev. ed. London, 1980.

Guest, Ivor. *Jules Perrot: Master of the Romantic Ballet.* London, 1984.

Michel, Marcelle. "Apothéose et décadence de la danse classique sous la Révolution et l'Empire." Ph.D. diss., Sorbonne, 1955.

Noverre, Jean-Georges. *Lettres sur les arts imitateurs en général et sur la danse en particulier* (1807). Edited by Lieutier. Paris, 1950.

MONIQUE BABSKY
Translated from French

MIME. *Mime* and *pantomime* are terms used almost interchangeably today to describe theatrical presentations that rely greatly on the actor's movements and gestures. While definitions are difficult to formulate and change with speed and ease, there are certain elements with which mime and pantomime are associated throughout most of their varied histories. These elements are amplified gesture; mask or masklike makeup; acrobatics, juggling, and clowning; satire and improvisation; and puppets and marionettes. During a few notable periods in the history of these arts they were completely silent, but from Greek times forward many mime and pantomime performances have been accompanied by music as well as by speech, either of the mime actor, a narrator, or a chorus.

Classical references indicate that mimes and pantomimes were as popular in the marketplaces as they were in the palaces of Greece and Rome. Their art, derived perhaps from religious ceremonies and popular entertainments of Egypt and Mesopotamia, continued in the mystery plays of medieval Europe, the work of wandering minstrels, court masques, and the players of the *commedia dell'arte.*

The muteness today associated with mime and pantomime was historical fact for brief periods only. Legend has it that the mime Livius Andronicus lost his voice in 240 BCE and hired an actor to speak for him; during periods of state censorship, however, mimes were silenced by law. An eighteenth-century French decree limited speaking theaters, which were seen to compete with the officially sanctioned Comédie-Française and the Paris Opera. This restriction, although lifted for a short time following the French Revolution (1789), was reestablished by Napoleon in 1807, and indirectly gave rise, in 1819, to the career that was to mark European pantomime for the next century. Jean Gaspard Deburau (1792–1846) performed his mute Baptiste character at the Théâtre des Funambules to public and critical acclaim. His image of Pierrot, white-faced and in long, flowing garments, served as a model for generations of followers. Deburau's career was the subject of Marcel Carné's classic film *Les Enfants du Paradis* (1945), in which feature roles were performed by two of the twentieth century's leading mime figures, Étienne Decroux and Jean-Louis Barrault.

The art of pantomime suffered a decline with the death of Deburau, as decrees limiting speech in theaters were lifted during Deburau's lifetime, reducing silent pantomime to a charming period piece; the popular theater form of the day became melodrama. Although Deburau had a long line of successors, none of them flourished in artistic freedom as Deburau had under censorship.

Asian theater forms have often woven speech, instrumental music, singing, dance, and mime into one fabric. Each of the great theater dance forms of the East—*nō, kyōgen, kabuki, bunraku,* Chinese opera, *kathakaḷi,* and *bharata nāṭyam,* as well as the rich Indonesian dance dramas—have all included mime in an inseparable whole.

This wholeness impressed European theater reformers of the early twentieth century, who longed to overthrow what they perceived as the decadent theater of the late nineteenth and early twentieth centuries and replace it with a revitalized form worthy of the great periods of theater history. One of the most prominent of these revolutionaries was Jacques Copeau (1878–1949), who founded L'École du Vieux-Colombier in Paris. Although short-lived as an institution (1920–1929), the Vieux-Colombier continues still as a seminal idea. Copeau advocated a redis-

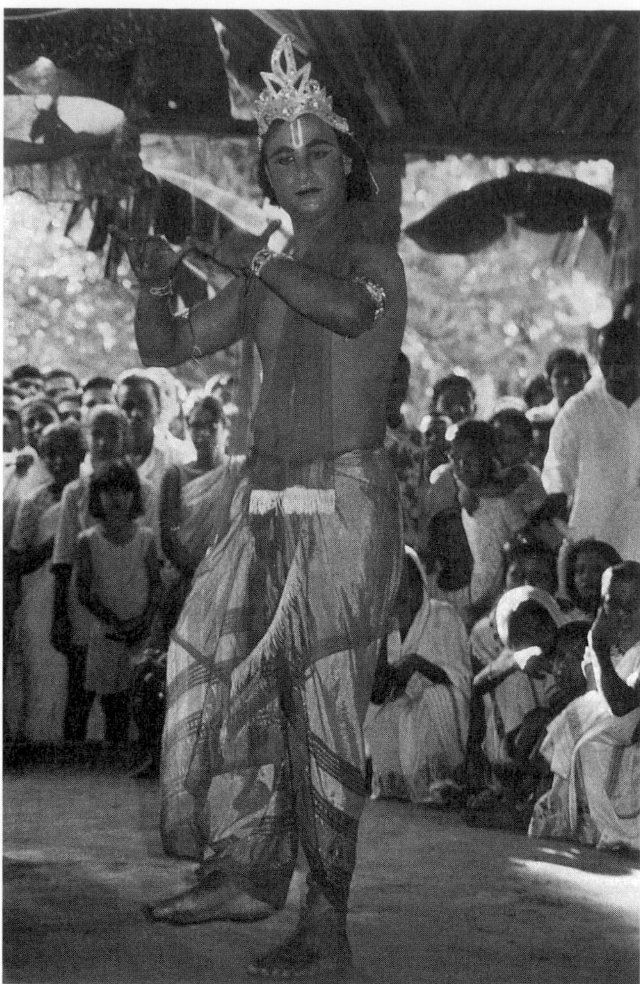

MIME. Making the gesture of the flute, this actor portrays the young Kṛṣṇa (Krishna) in a performance of *ankiya nat,* a devotional dance drama from Assam, in northeast India. This familiar gesture connects the deity to his youth among humble villagers. (Photograph by Farley Richmond; used by permission.)

covery of the actor's body, made supple by gymnastics, ballet, and improvisation, a body given new freedom and expressiveness through the use of the neutral and expressive mask in training and performance. Copeau's curriculum included studies of language, history, philosophy, theater crafts, and music as well. Central to Copeau's vision was the idea of a communal way of life that would foster ensemble acting. The qualities Copeau admired in Greek theater, *commedia dell'arte* and Asian theater he found remarkably absent in the theater of his day. His reforms are now taken for granted, and many contemporary theaters, forty years and more after his death, use the mask in training and performance, study Asian theater techniques and mime, and value improvisation and physical training to produce the whole, liberally educated actor-creator.

Étienne Decroux (1898–1991) enrolled in an evening course at the Vieux-Colombier to study diction to prepare himself for a career in politics. There Decroux saw improvisations with veiled or masked face, improvisations that placed the burden of communication on the actor's body rather than primarily on the face or speech. These exercises so captivated Decroux that he turned from his original intention and began more than half a century of work in what he called corporeal mime, so named to distinguish it from the nineteenth-century pantomime of face and hands, which he detested. Eugenio Barba wrote in *The Drama Review* (1982) that Decroux was "perhaps the

MIME. Marcel Marceau is perhaps the best-known exponent of modem mime. The characteristic whiteface makeup accentuates the display of a variety of mute emotions. (Photograph © 1975 by Fred Fehl; used by permission.)

only European master to have elaborated a system of rules comparable to that of an Oriental tradition." Decroux worked daily, for more than fifty years, unearthing a mountain of technical discoveries that are only now beginning to filter into performance. He trained or influenced hundreds of students and lived long enough to see his work go in and out of fashion several times. His book *Words on Mime* (1985) is an eloquent treatise on corporeal mime.

Jean-Louis Barrault (1910–1994) was Decroux's first student. As members of Charles Dullin's Atelier theater company in Paris, Decroux and Barrault spent every hour (when not rehearsing or performing speaking theater under Dullin's direction) innovating corporeal mime. Decroux proposed a theme or movement; Barrault improvised as Decroux observed and took notes; Decroux refined the concept; Barrault continued the improvisation. This work continued for two years, culminating in a performance sponsored by Dullin. Barrault subsequently left Decroux to make his own mime pieces, and eventually, with his wife, Madeleine Renaud, became one of the leading forces in postwar French theater. His acting is marked by an extraordinary aptitude for and training in movement, and his *mise-en-scène* owes a debt to Copeau's vision of an open stage and a highly visual approach to unusual scripts as well as theater classics.

Marcel Marceau (born in 1923) also apprenticed with Decroux. Marceau's unique synthesis of corporeal mime with nineteenth-century pantomime and makeup have captured the public imagination in much the way that Jean Gaspard Deburau must have done in the nineteenth century. For decades Marceau has performed three hundred times a year throughout the world, for full houses of enthusiastic adults and children. His phenomenal success has spawned imitators, mini-Marceaus who lack the original's genius and dedicated professionalism. In copying Marceau's work without understanding its source in life—or the simplification, amplification, and counterweights of corporeal mime—these opportunists mimic what is already a profound mimesis, much to their own detriment. The irony for Decroux was that his best-known student, Marceau, performs a variation of the nineteenth-century pantomime against which corporeal mime reacted and which Decroux worked to move beyond for so many years.

Jacques Lecoq (born in 1912) is, with Decroux, Barrault, and Marceau, among the four most important influences on contemporary Western mime. As a young man, Lecoq studied and taught physical education and learned mask work from Jean Dasté, the son-in-law of Jacques Copeau and a faculty member of L'École du Vieux-Colombier. Beginning in 1948, Lecoq lived in Italy for eight years, where he discovered the spirit of the *commedia dell'arte* and the *commedia* masks of Sartori. Lecoq has

MIME. Bill Irwin, often called a new-style vaudevillian, is a unique performer who creates innovative theater pieces drawing on conventional mime techniques and music-hall traditions. (Photograph from the archives at Jacob's Pillow, Becket, Massachusetts.)

taught in Paris since 1956, where his school attracts one hundred first-year students of twenty nationalities, from whom only thirty-five second-year students are selected. Among the subjects taught in Lecoq's school are the neutral mask, the larval mask, the expressive mask, *commedia dell'arte,* tragic chorus, clowns, buffoons, and melodrama. Lecoq's work has been largely responsible for the revival of interest in the twentieth century in the clown, *commedia dell'arte,* and vaudeville.

While greatly different, the approaches of Decroux, Barrault, Marceau, and Lecoq are known as modern mime. The developments of the past decade, however, are often referred to as postmodern mime. Postmodern mime's advent coincides with and is perhaps a product of the national and international festivals held since the 1970s in North America and Europe. At these festivals performers were able, for the first time, to see a cross section of their art and to discuss it among themselves. Festival audiences perceived that there was something more to mime than the one aspect so ably represented by Marceau. As a result of these germinal gatherings, performers more readily found acceptance for new work that easily included text, music, real props, and contemporary themes. As geographical and cultural barriers were more frequently crossed, so were those between art forms, as new syntheses replaced old paradigms. The festivals marked a beginning of a break in the impasse of ideas that seemed to have stopped somewhere around the image of the white-faced Pierrot popularized by Deburau in the 1820s, as resuscitated by Marceau in the 1950s.

The major trends in postmodern mime were adumbrated by the curriculum of L'École du Vieux-Colombier in the early twentieth century. Copeau's vision of a revitalized theater became a reality as theater once more ventured boldly beyond text in the later twentieth century, placing a renewed emphasis on the actor's art, on the ensemble, and on recognizing the importance of Asian theater forms and mask work in training and in performance. Modern and postmodern mime helped rouse the theater as a whole into a more vital mode; toward the end of the twentieth century, movement theater, new vaudeville, and new mime became important theater forms.

[*See also* Commedia dell'Arte *and* Pantomime.]

BIBLIOGRAPHY

Decroux, Étienne. *Words on Mime.* Claremont, Calif., 1985.

Leabhart, Thomas. *Modern and Post-Modern Mime.* New York, 1989.

Leigh, Barbara Kusler. "Jacques Copeau's School for Actors." *Mime Journal* (1979).

Nicoll, Allardyce. *Masks, Mimes, and Miracles: Studies in the Popular Theatre.* London, 1931.

Rolfe, Bari, ed. *Mimes on Miming.* London, 1979.

THOMAS LEABHART

MIMUS. The term *mime* (Latin *mimus* from Greek *mimos*, "actor," akin to *mimesthai* "to imitate") referred both to the type of play that dealt with imitations of all aspects of life and to the actor who performed in these plays. Romans were first introduced to mime during the First Punic War (264–241 BCE) when Roman soldiers fighting in southern Italy and Sicily had the opportunity to sample various forms of Greek entertainment, including mime, which the Doric Greeks had introduced to the area some two centuries earlier. This form of theater appealed to the Romans because the performances depended on mimicry and gesture more than language.

The Roman mime, unlike its Greek counterpart, included both male and female players from the beginning, a feature without precedent in the ancient world. By contrast it was only late in the Roman Empire that women occasionally appeared in pantomimes. The inclusion of women may have been one of the reasons for the popularity of mimes. The talents of the Roman mime actor and actress were many: dancing, singing, acrobatics, juggling, rope dancing, conjuring, walking on stilts, sword swallowing, fire eating, fire spitting, mind reading, performing with animals, and buffoonery of all kinds. An ancient painting shows mime rope-dancers dressed as bacchanals, satyrs, and other imaginary beings in various graceful attitudes, while others play lyres and flutes, and still others balance themselves with poles as they dance along the rope. Improvisation, learned from the Greeks, in whose theater it played a subsidiary role, soon began to dominate in Roman mime.

People from all levels of society associated with mime actors and enjoyed their performances. The dictator Sulla (138–78 BCE) was on friendly terms with Norbanus Sorex, an *archimimus* (actor-manager), and also with Metrobius, a female impersonator. Julius Caesar patronized the mimes, and in 45 BCE he forced Decimus Laberius (106–43 BCE), an elderly Roman knight and mime writer, to perform in a competition against the mime writer-actor Publilius Syrus. Because Laberius had never performed before (acting was beneath the dignity of an equestrian), Publilius won. The speech given by Laberius so moved Caesar, however, that he generously rewarded Laberius as compensation for the disgrace. And in *De oratore* Cicero comments on how entertaining he found a performance of *The Tutor,* "an old mime, that was exceedingly funny." Just as the themes of mime encompassed both lower and upper class characters, so also its audience included people from all levels of Roman society.

Aspects of Performance. In contrast to the Atellan farces, mimes included only a couple of stock characters—the fool and the parasite. The actors did not wear masks and therefore had the opportunity to add to their performances through facial expressions. The improvised nature of the plays also allowed the actors to take advantage of current events to increase the humor of the performance. Mimicry and parody of important people of the times dominated performances; frequently high officials and even the emperors were criticized. Favor, a mime actor during the reign of Vespasian (69–79 CE), imitated the emperor himself and played upon Vespasian's well-known miserliness to draw laughter from the audience. William Beare attributes the popularity of the mime to its ever-changing form and content, which ranged from the ridiculous to the sententious—a match for the tastes of the Roman populace.

Mimes gradually began to replace Atellan farces as afterpieces, or as performances given between plays. Sometimes mimes were performed in the orchestra areas while the scenes for a play were being prepared onstage. When this happened the mimes played in front of the *siparium* (either a curtain or folding screen) in the orchestra. Although this use of mimes to fill in between other performances may appear to have relegated the mime to the status of mime played during an intermission, in the case of festivals, during which it was a *vitium* (an affront to the god) to allow the performances to pause even briefly, the mimes served the valuable purpose of continuing the celebration and therefore ensuring the favor of the gods. Sextus Pompeius Festus (late second century CE) recorded that in 211 BCE the Ludi Apollinares (Apollonian Games) were interrupted by an alarm to which both the audience and the performers responded. When everyone returned, they found an elderly mime dancer who had performed continuously during the interruption, thereby saving the state from having to restart the games and ensuring the favor of the gods for Rome. H. J. Rose says that this incident provided the origin of the proverb "Salva res est dum saltat senex" (All is well while the old man dances).

When mimes eventually replaced tragedies and comedies in the imperial period, they once again resumed their original status as independent productions and were performed on the stage proper. The staging was simple because the players did not depend on props: their actions and words served to set the scene. Performances of mimes were not, therefore, confined to the theaters. There is evidence that mime actors performed in circuses, amphitheaters, and private homes. In Pompeii one private home has been uncovered that was equipped with a small outdoor theater.

Performers. In addition to individual actor-writers who made Rome their home, groups of mimes traveled the countryside performing wherever there was an audience. The mime troupe or *collegium* varied greatly in size, ranging from groups with fewer than ten to larger companies with as many as sixty actors. At the head of each company was an *archimimus* (actor-manager) or an *archimima* (actress-manager). The archimimus might be the leading actor or he might play the secondary role of the clown or buffoon who parodied the leading actor. The archimimus Gaius Norbanus Sorex (c.50 BCE–50 CE)—perhaps a descendant of Sulla's friend—was noted for playing secondary parts. Other members of the players included a parasite—a character also prevalent in literary comedies—who gained favors, mostly food, by flattering his master. The *stupidus* or *sannio* always appeared bald and barefoot; on his head he wore a long, pointed, cone-shaped hat. His distinctive costume was the *centunulus* (a cloaklike garment of colored patches), tights, and a phallus. The rest of the company wore costumes suitable for the roles they played. All mime performers played in bare feet, a feature that distinguished them from tragedians, who wore *cothurni* (elevated shoes), and comedians in literary drama, who wore *socci* (slippers).

A few mime actors (Norbanus Sorix, Publilius Syrus, Matius, Favor, Damasippus, Lentulus, Vitalis) are known by name, but little is known about their acting style or the specific parts that they played. Of the exceptions, Juvenal mentions that Lentulus played the role of the crucified bandit in *Laureolus,* and Vitalis' epitaph brags that "many women whom I imitated on the stage blushed and were overcome with confusion" (Friedländer, 1965). Mime actresses gained more notoriety; poets wrote about their charms, merits, and private lives. They were a novelty in a largely male-dominated theater, and the most successful made handsome salaries. Among those who were greatly admired was the singer Antiodemes; Arbriscula was another whose performances were praised as delightful and pleasing. Julia Bassilla won fame for her excellence in dance and acting; in addition, she was praised for her wisdom and virtue. The actress Volumnia Cytheris seems to have been more noted as a mistress of famous men, including Mark Antony, than as a skilled mime. Arete and Claudia Herminone were two famous actress-managers.

Two of the most famous mime actresses were Pelagia and Theodora. Pelagia was a leading dancer in ancient Antioch who, because she converted to Christianity and gave up her career in the theater—was praised by members of the church. Theodora, who was born in the early years of the sixth century CE, either in Cyprus or Constantinople, achieved her greatest fame first as mistress and later wife of the emperor Justinian I (483–565 CE). According to the Byzantine historian Procopius, in her younger years Theodora was a courtesan and mime actress noted as a skilled performer, witty and clever, and as a woman without any sense of shame. After her marriage to the emperor, she proved by all accounts to be an excellent empress. She took an active part in ridding the city of Constantinople of vice and prostitutes.

Two recurring complaints lodged against the mimes were the lewdness of the actresses in their public performances and private lives, and the coarse and indecent themes of some of the plays. There is no question that the presence of women onstage was shocking to the early Romans, who considered acting to be suitable only for slaves and freedmen, and mime actresses were regarded by most Romans as no better than prostitutes. Many were upset with some of the dances performed by women at the Floralia, an annual festival instituted in 173 BCE to honor the goddess Flora, an ancient Italian deity of fertility and flowers: female dancers often undressed and danced or wrestled in the nude at the request of the spectators. The greatest excesses happened at private performances given by mimes before the emperor's court and at wealthy citizens' homes, but there is no doubt that at some public performances nudity, torture, and other questionable acts occurred, especially in the late empire.

Subjects of Mime. An examination of the extant titles and fragments of lines from mimes written in the first century BCE indicates they covered a wide variety of subjects, and in some cases encroached upon the subjects of literary comedies. Among the standard offerings were plays that dealt with adultery or attempted adultery: an old man jealous of his young wife and her suspected lover; a mistress who desires her stepson; a woman who poisons her husband. Another category focused on a master having trouble with his slaves. In a mime written by one Catullus (not the great lyric poet), *Laureolus*, a bandit leader was captured and quite realistically crucified, the artificial blood flowing freely from the cross. The biographer Suetonius remarks that this mime was particularly popular during the reign of Caligula (37–41 CE). Martial (40–104 CE) writes in *Libellus spectaculorum* 7 about a condemned prisoner who was forced to take the part of the robber and was actually put to death on a cross during performance. Other titles such as *The Ghost, The Bean, The Guardian,* and *The Silphium Vendor* suggest some of the situations exploited by mime actors.

Church Opposition and the End of Mime. The newly converted Christian fathers, such as Tertullian (155–222), who so violently opposed all forms of theater, vehemently criticized mime, especially those pieces that dealt with adultery. The church waged a constant war against the theater through its edicts and councils, which followed one after the other for almost five hundred years. During this time, the mimes fought back, openly ridiculing certain church practices. By 568, following the Lombard invasion, all theatrical performances had ceased in Rome. The mimes continued in the Eastern Roman Empire until 692 however, when they were finally stopped by the church, although there are doubts concerning the complete effectiveness of the interdiction.

[*See also* Music for Dance, *article on* Western Music before 1520; Pantomimus; *and* Roman Empire.]

BIBLIOGRAPHY

Arnott, Peter D. *The Ancient Greek and Roman Theatre.* New York, 1971.

Beare, William. *The Roman Stage: A Short History of Latin Drama in the Time of the Republic.* 3d ed. New York, 1963.

Bieber, Margarete. *The History of the Greek and Roman Theatre.* 2d ed., rev. and enl. Princeton, 1961.

Butler, James H. *The Theatre and Drama of Greece and Rome.* New York, 1972.

Cicero. *De oratore.* Vols. 1–2. Translated by Harris Rackham. Loeb Classical Library. Cambridge, Mass., 1948.

Conte, Gian Biagio. *Latin Literature: A History.* Translated by Joseph B. Solodow. Baltimore, 1994.

The Context of Ancient Drama. Ed. by Eric Csapo and W. J. Slater. Ann Arbor, Mich., 1995.

Friedländer, Ludwig. *Roman Life and Manners under the Early Empire.* Vol. 2. Translated by Leonard A. Magnus. 7th ed., rev. and enl. New York, 1965.

Jory, E. J. "Publilius Syrus and the Element of Competition in the Theatre of the Republic." In *Vir bonus discendi peritus: Studies in Celebration of Otto Skutsch's Eightieth Birthday,* edited by Nicholas Horsfall. Institute of Classical Studies, Bulletin Supplement, 51. London, 1988.

Juvenal. *The Sixteen Satires.* Translated by Peter Green. New York, 1967.

Kehoe, Patrick H. "The Adultery Mime Reconsidered." In *Classical Texts and Their Traditions: Studies in Honor of C. R. Trahman,* edited by David F. Bright and Edwin S. Ramage. Chico, Calif., 1984.

Martial. *Libellus Spectaculorum.* In *Martial: Epigrams.* Vol. 1. Translated by D. R. Shackleton Bailey. Loeb Classical Library. Cambridge, Mass., 1993.

McKeown, J. C. "Augustan Elegy and Mime." *Proceedings of the Cambridge Philological Society* 25 (1979): 71–84.

Nicoll, Allardyce. *Masks, Mimes, and Miracles: Studies in the Popular Theatre* (1931). New York, 1963.

Reich, Hermann. *Des Mimus,* vol. 1, *Ein litheras-entwichelungsgeschichtlicher Versuch;* vol. 2, *Entwichelungsgeschichte des Mimus.* Berlin, 1903.

Reynolds, R. W. "Verrius Flaccus and the Early Mime at Rome." *Hermathena* 61 (1943): 56–62.

Rose, H. J. *A Handbook of Latin Literature.* New York, 1960.

Suetonius. *The Twelve Caesars.* Translated by Robert Graves. New York, 1957.

T. DAVINA MCCLAIN

MINKUS, LÉON (Aloisius Ludwig Minkus; born 28 March 1826 in Vienna, died 7 December 1917 in Vienna), Austrian-Russian composer. Minkus achieved renown as a ballet composer in Russia, where he spent most of his professional life between 1855 and 1886. Uncertainties abound in Minkus's biography. It is unclear, for example, whether his birthplace was actually Vienna; some scholars believe he might have been born near Brno, in the Moravian town of Grossmeseritsch. The date and place of his death vary even more than his birth. He is reputed to have died in Russia, in Berlin, and in Vienna anywhere between 1890 and 1917, the last being the official date in Vienna's municipal records. Even the credited number of his complete ballet scores ranges from fourteen to twenty-three; the most painstaking count places the number at twenty.

Minkus studied at the Vienna Conservatory and began to compose seriously while in his teens. As a student, he wrote five pieces for violin that were published in 1846 or 1847. In 1844, he had made a successful recital debut in Vienna, repeating his program later in Pest (Budapest). The Viennese newspaper *Der Humorist* noted that on 18 October 1845 "Louis Minkus" was one of the most talented young violinists of the previous season, combining a conservative style with a glittering performance.

Among Minkus's few known nonballet pieces are Twelve Études for Solo Violin, *Chante d'Été, Romance sans Paroles* for violin with piano accompaniment, and *March Kanli* (Fast March) for piano and wind ensemble. Also during the mid-1840s Minkus began to compose light music for dancing, briefly conducting an orchestra that competed with that of the younger Johann Strauss.

According to some sources, Minkus performed in Paris in 1846, where he is credited with contributing to Édouard Deldevez's score for *Paquita,* produced in April with choreography by Joseph Mazilier. Press notices of the premiere, however, do not mention Minkus's contribution. Yet when the ballet was revised by Marius Petipa for the Maryinsky Theater in Saint Petersburg in September 1847, the score was listed as having been composed by Léon Minkus, with interpolated music by Deldevez. [*See* Paquita.]

In 1853, Minkus's reputation as both violinist and cellist led to an invitation by Prince Nikolai Yusupov for Minkus to conduct the prince's serf orchestra. Minkus filled this position for two years before joining the orchestra of the Italian Opera theater in Saint Petersburg, where one account noted that he "has a broad, singing bow and an extremely graceful performance."

In 1861, Minkus was appointed concertmaster at the Bolshoi Theater in Moscow, and the next year he was named inspector of the music of the Imperial Theaters. In 1864, he was named ballet composer at the Bolshoi, with responsibilities also for composing incidental dance music for opera and dramatic productions. His contract stipulated annual payment of two thousand rubles.

By this time, Minkus had three ballets to his credit. The first, *Paquita,* is still among his most popular ballets. This was followed by *Fiammetta,* which was composed with the twenty-eight-year-old Léo Delibes and choreographed by Arthur Saint-Léon to be presented in Saint Petersburg in February 1864. The Paris version, presented at the Paris Opera on 14 July that year, was titled *Némea, ou L'Amour Vengé;* it contained additional music and a reworking of some of the previous material. Minkus's third score, written in 1862, was for the one-act *Two Days in Venice.*

Minkus continued to earn praise as a concert artist. One reviewer noted that his

> playing is very precise. The left hand and the bow strokes are beautifully worked out. He always plays with classical calm, without any gymnastics or tricks favored by most young violinists. (*Moscow Herald,* February 1863)

His skill as an instrumentalist in turn played a role in the way he orchestrated. Minkus was superior in this respect to Cesare Pugni, whom he was to succeed in Saint Petersburg. Both knew, however, that the orchestral musicians were generally of high quality. Many were foreigners imported to boost the level of the Russian players. Thus Minkus, like Pugni, wrote extensive solos for them. Henri Wieniawski, who was a young violinist in the Bolshoi Orchestra at the time, programmed Minkus's music when he was a renowned violin virtuoso.

In 1866, Minkus became a professor of strings at the Moscow Conservatory, where he served until 1872. He was also asked in 1866 by the Paris Opera to collaborate with Delibes again, as insurance against the younger man's relative inexperience. Minkus was assigned the opening and closing tableaux of Saint-Léon's ballet *La Source,* which premiered in Paris on 12 November 1866. Minkus's contribution proved inferior to that of Delibes (which has remained in the repertory). Thereafter, Saint-Léon arranged versions of *La Source* that primarily used Delibes's music. (In 1869 in Saint Petersburg it was renamed *The Lily;* in 1878 it was known as *La Sorgente* in Italy and as *Naïla* in Vienna.)

Pugni died during the 1869 season, after nineteen years as staff composer for the Russian Imperial Theaters. Minkus was appointed to the vacant position and was transferred to Saint Petersburg, where he was also in charge of the Bolshoi Library and musical instruments.

On 26 December 1869, Petipa's ballet *Don Quixote,* to an engaging Minkus score, premiered at the Bolshoi in Moscow. Taken to Saint Petersburg two years later, it marked the beginning of a long association between Petipa and Minkus, who collaborated on fourteen more ballets. Minkus's imagination flowered in *Don Quixote.* Despite numerous changes, additions, and patchwork in the music before the ballet took the stage, his lively and colorful melodies, often reflecting Spanish rhythms and local color, were put together so effectively that the ballet never left the repertories of the Imperial and later Soviet ballets. [*See* Don Quixote, *articles on* Petipa Production *and* Gorsky Production.]

The Adventures of Peleus and Thetis, with choreography by Petipa, was given its first performance at the Maryinsky on 18 January 1876. Some sources list this as a collaboration between Minkus and Delibes, but it is more likely that music by Delibes was interpolated.

When Petipa made *A Midsummer Night's Dream* to Felix Mendelssohn's music (staged on Olgin Island at Peterhof on 14 July 1876), the famous score was rearranged and shaped by Petipa to suit his intentions. This included having Minkus write bridging music and various interpolated themes, for which he received no official acknowledgment. This was typical of the way in which the Imperial Theater worked. Thus, Petipa's 1888 version of *Giselle* contained a Minkus pas de deux and Minkus fragments in acts 1 and 2 that are still performed. Minkus also wrote the score for Saint-Léon's *The Goldfish,* which premiered at the Bolshoi Theater in Saint Petersburg on 28 September 1867.

Minkus's second-most familiar work, *La Bayadère,* premiered on 23 January 1877. Although little in the music supports its setting, in India, Minkus's score is notable for its arching melodies—above all, in the opening of the Kingdom of the Shades scene—and charming variations, providing the choreographer with many opportunities for both spectacle and virtuoso display. [*See* Bayadère, La.]

During the 1869/70 season in Saint Petersburg, the director of the Imperial Theaters, Stepan Gedeonov, had suggested that Aleksandr Borodin, César Cui, Modest Mussorgsky, and Nikolai Rimsky-Korsakov collaborate to write an *opéra-ballet* to be called *Mlada,* from a libretto by Gedeonov, with ballet music to be composed by Aleksandr Serov. Gedeonov considered Minkus (who was then occupied in Moscow) for the non-Russian ballet music, but the entire project was soon shelved and the composers put the music already written to other uses. The administration was still interested in the idea, however, and Minkus was asked to compose the ballet with Petipa; *Mlada* was first performed on 2 December 1879. Eventually, Rimsky-Korsakov composed an *opéra-ballet* of his own with the same name, also with choreography by Petipa, but it was not performed until 1892. The Minkus ballet was a success while the Rimsky-Korsakov *opéra-ballet,* initially, was not.

Thereafter, Minkus was occupied mainly with the ballet stage. He wrote five more scores for Petipa; the final one, *Kalkabrino,* received its first performance on 13 February 1891. By then, however, the winds of change had stirred; critics and balletomanes began to be dissatisfied with ballets that they regarded as little more than set pieces for reigning ballerinas and the occasional *danseur noble.* The public wanted more coherent ballets, each a unified whole, with music that was more "symphonic" in character. These desires may not always have been articulated so specifically, but the mood was growing even before the scores of the great reformers, Petr Ilich Tchaikovsky and Aleksandr Glazunov.

Pugni, more prolific and talented than Minkus, might have weathered the gathering storm. Late in 1886, Ivan Vsevolozhsky, director of the Imperial Theaters from 1881 to 1899, ordered the post of ballet composer abolished. (Minkus was thus effectively dismissed, although with an offer to continue composing, in the event of necessity, for additional compensation; under this arrangement *Kalkabrino* [1891] was written.) Shortly after Vsevolozhsky's decision, on 9 November 1886, Minkus was given a benefit in Saint Petersburg. The program featured a performance of *Paquita,* with Virginia Zucchi, and act 3 of *The Magic Pills.* Minkus then retired on an annual pension of five hundred and seventy rubles, which was about the same then given to the lowliest corps dancer. (A newspaper writer of the period placed the pension at 1,140 rubles per year.)

Minkus stayed on in Russia until 1891. At age sixty-five, he then returned to Vienna; embittered, he is not known to have composed again. He did spend much time in the company of an old friend, Theodor Leschetizky, the great piano pedagogue, with whom Minkus shared an affinity for playing pool.

Official records show that Minkus's wife Marie had died and that he then owned very little, moving from one unfashionable address to another. Minkus died in Vienna of pneumonia on 7 December 1917, aged ninety-one, and was buried in Döblinger Cemetery.

A writer for the fifth edition of *Grove's Dictionary of Music and Musicians* judged Minkus to be a third-rate hack. To be sure, both Minkus and Pugni were responsible for a fair share of turbid music. But Minkus also wrote music that has endured the test of time. Western audiences know the captivating melodies of *Don Quixote, La Bayadère,* and *Paquita,* but there is equally ingratiating music in *La Camargo, Zoraya,* and *Daughter of the Snow,* none of which is produced any longer. Despite his detractors, Minkus's music is so graceful, pliable, and melodious that it has been mined, repeatedly, by modern choreographers.

More of Minkus's music would be heard today if choreographers could decide how best to use it; nineteenth-century ballets have become unacceptable because of their improbable plots. Their music, however attractive, is not easily arranged for contemporary use, barring the expense and effort needed to do so. Although he apparently wrote no symphonies, concertos, or operas, Minkus was a serious and disciplined musician who worked without complaint under subservience to the choreographer; he was a conscientious craftsman and a consummate melodist. As a man of his time, his misfortune was to be working at the end of an era, when the conventions he had mastered were becoming passé.

A writer for the *Moscow Herald* said of his ballet *Zoraya* in 1882 that the music "is extremely melodious and is gracefully and elegantly orchestrated." A year earlier, the critic for the *Petersburg Gazette* wrote that Minkus's music "is at times beautiful, graceful, and full of color, and its masterful orchestration reveals the great talent of the composer."

BIBLIOGRAPHY

Bakhrushin, Yuri. *Istoriia russkogo baleta.* 3d ed. Moscow, 1977.

Borisoglebskii, Mikhail. *Proshloe baletnogo otdeleniia Peterburgskogo teatral'nogo uchilishcha, nyne Leningradskogo gosudarstvennogo khoreograficheskogo uchilishcha: Materialy po istorii russkogo baleta.* Vol. 1. Leningrad, 1938.

Chujoy, Anatole, and P. W. Manchester, eds. *The Dance Encyclopedia.* Rev. and enl. ed. New York, 1967.

Fétis, François-Joseph. *Biographie universelle des musiciens.* Paris, 1875.

Krasovskaya, Vera. *Russkii baletnyi teatr vtoroi poloviny deviatnadtsatogo veka.* Leningrad, 1963.

Lifar, Serge. *A History of Russian Ballet.* Translated by Arnold L. Haskell. New York, 1954.

Mannoni, Gérard. "Minkus et la danse." *La saisons de la danse* (May 1981): 42–43.

Petipa, Marius. *Russian Ballet Master: The Memoirs of Marius Petipa.* Edited by Lillian Moore. Translated by Helen Whittaker. London, 1958.

Saint-Léon, Arthur. *Letters from a Ballet Master: The Correspondence of Arthur Saint-Léon.* Edited by Ivor Guest. New York, 1981.

Scherer, Barrymore. "Maligned Minstrel." *Ballet News* 1 (May 1980): 22–23.

Scherer, Barrymore. "Three Composers Who Knew What Dance Needed." *New York Times* (27 March 1983).

Slonimsky, Nicolas. *Baker's Biographical Dictionary of Musicians*. 8th ed. New York, 1992.

Spencer, Jennifer. "Minkus, Léon." In *The New Grove Dictionary of Music and Musicians*. London, 1980.

Studwell, William E. "The Choreographic Chain: Seventy Years of Ballet Music." *Dance Scope* 10.2 (1976): 51–55.

Vazem, Ekaterina. "Memoirs of a Ballerina of the St. Petersburg Bolshoi Theatre." Translated by Nina Dimitrievich. *Dance Research* 3 (Summer 1985): 3–22; 4 (Spring 1986): 3–28; 5 (Spring 1987): 21–41; 6 (Autumn 1988): 30–47.

JOSEPH GALE

MINSTRELSY. *See* United States of America, *articles on* African-American Concert Dance *and* African-American Social Dance.

MINUET. The term *minuet* (Fr., *menuet*) usually denotes a French court and theater dance in moderate or slow meter, but it can also refer to a musical composition or a symphonic movement. The origin of the minuet is obscure, but the scores of Jean-Baptiste Lully (1632–1687), which contain some ninety pieces titled *menuet,* indicate that the rhythm was used increasingly during the 1600s and soon predominated. The *menuet ordinaire* superseded Louis XIV's favorite dance, the *courante,* and remained the most popular ballroom *danse à deux* (couple dance) in aristocratic society until the years following the French Revolution in 1789. Michael Praetorius wrote in *Terpsichore* (1612) that the minuet was a descendant of the dance called "Branle de Poitou," and Pierre Rameau expressed the same opinion in *Le maître à danser* (1725).

Supporting this theory is the structure of the triple-meter "Branle de Poitou" and the "Branle à Mener de Poitou," in three-measure phrases, and the existence of similar early minuet music (in the Philidor manuscript). Lully wrote one or two minuets of this type, but almost all minuet music has phrases of two 3/4 measures, sometimes notated as one measure of 6/4. According to Gottfried Taubert (1717), the *menuet* was the daughter of the *courante*. The two dances have the structural similarities of rhythmic interplays of two against three, and step-units of unequal length within a 3/2 measure of courante and a 6/4 measure of minuet. Without further knowledge of the development of the early minuet and how it compared with other dances, the often expressed theory that it is so called because of the smallness of its steps cannot be substantiated.

After 1700, in treatises describing dance during the reign of Louis XIV (1643–1715), considerable space was devoted to the minuet. The clearest descriptions of the dance, including its steps and rhythms, occur in Rameau's *Le maître à danser* and *Abbrégé de la nouvelle méthode* (1725) as well as in Kellom Tomlinson's *The Art of Dancing* (1735). Tomlinson gives an earlier version of the dance with an S shape as the main figure, while Rameau describes modifications made by Louis Pecour—primarily the regulation of the S into a Z—a shape to which the two dancers could more readily conform.

The minuet had enormous social significance. Even those who did not particularly enjoy dancing were expected to practice the minuet until they could dance it with ease and, as Rameau constantly stresses, without affectation. Thus, the English statesman and writer on manners Lord Chesterfield (1694–1773) wrote to his son:

> As you will be often under the necessity of dancing a minuet, I would have you dance it very well. Remember that the graceful motion of the arms, the giving of your hand, and the putting on and pulling off your hat genteelly are the material parts of a gentleman's dancing. But the greatest advantage of dancing well is that it necessarily teaches you to present yourself, to sit, stand and walk genteelly; all of which are of real importance to a man of fashion.

Tomlinson indicates moments in the dance where the hat can be most appropriately removed and replaced.

Technically, the minuet is the easiest of the *danses à deux*. It incorporates only a few steps and the main arm motions are an unaffected taking of hands. Yet, as Tomlinson writes, this very simplicity renders it the hardest to perform, "through the Plainness of the Step and the Air and Address of the Body that are requisite to its Embellishment."

For the two dancers alone on the ballroom floor, the minuet was all-revealing; the quality of their air, poise, and presence while dancing was held to reflect their breeding, education, and character. As Sarah, duchess of Marlborough, observed, "I think Sir S. Garth is the most honest and compassionate, but after the minuets which I have seen him dance . . . I can't help thinking that hee may sometimes bee in the wrong."

The minuet consists of an introduction and four figures: the S or Z figure; the presentation of right hands; the presentation of left hands; the S or Z figure and the presentation of both hands. The dance is preceded and concluded by Honours to the Presence (the person or persons of highest social rank) and by partners to each other.

While other *danses à deux* are choreographed to specific music, the minuet can be danced to any suitable minuet air. Its unique characteristic among the baroque dances is flexibility. The S or Z figure may be repeated as often as the gentleman chooses; the dance may be performed throughout with the same *pas de menuet;* certain other steps may sometimes be substituted as embellishments; the Z may be lengthened by one *pas de menuet,* and the gentleman may choose to circle more than once when presenting hands. The choices made can greatly alter the length of the dance. Rameau suggests that five or six Zs be danced the first time and three or four the second, which means that the dance will last for about seven minutes. Tomlinson says that the shortest option is to dance one S or Z each time.

Whatever its origin, the minuet is a refined expression of ritualistic courtship. The dancers face each other almost continually; they approach, pass, and retreat, and their only physical contact is holding hands at arm's length while circling.

When dancing the minuet, a gentleman must lead with consideration. Tomlinson explains that the speed at which the man performs the Honours will dictate where the couple begins the dance, within the music; it is also the man's responsibility to see that he and his partner commence on the first beat of a pair of 3/4 measures, whether during a musical strain or at its beginning. He must indicate in advance his intention to change from the Z figure to the presentation of hands lest the lady dance past him—and, while holding both hands, circling, and looking at the lady, he must keep sight of the top of the room for fear of opening out in the wrong direction, and thus bowing with his back to the Presence.

MINUET. The male dancer in this highly stylized depiction of a ballroom scene, called *Le Menuet de Strasbourg* (1682), is reputedly Louis XIV. (Bibliothèque Nationale, Paris.)

According to Tomlinson, it was preferable to begin in the middle of a strain: "Instead of standing to wait the Close or Ending of a Strain of the Tune, begin upon the first Time that offers, in that it is much more genteel and shows the Dancer's Capacity and Ear in distinguishing of the Time, and from thence begets himself a good Opinion from the Beholders."

In general, minuets composed either to accompany dancing or for purely instrumental purposes have strains of an even number of 3/4 measures. Dance music has most frequently strains of eight or sixteen measures or an eight-measure strain followed by one of twelve, the length of Pecour's Z figure.

The various *pas de menuet* consist of four changes of weight and different numbers of *mouvement* (movements). A *mouvement* is a *plié*, a bending of the knees, which is followed by an *élevé*, a rise, a straightening of the knees usually extended onto *[demi]-pointe*. The *mouvements* provide the rhythmic accents within the dance—the *pliés* leading to the *élevés*, which give the accents that usually coincide with the musical downbeats. *Pas de menuet* always begin with the right foot. Both Rameau and Tomlinson describe the two most commonly used steps: the *pas de menuet à deux mouvements* and the *pas de menuet à trois mouvements*. Each *pas de menuet* takes two measures of 3/4 time. The most characteristic relationship between steps and music has the cross-rhythm:

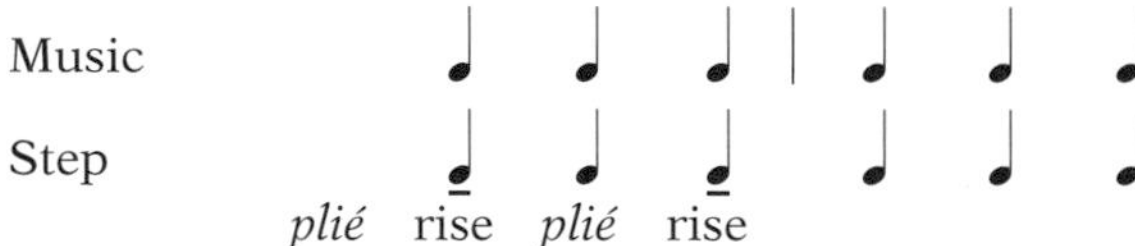

Some masters give rhythms for these *pas de menuet* in which the cross-rhythm is avoided, the two rises coinciding with the two downbeats.

In appropriate places, certain other steps can be substituted for *pas de menuet*. Rameau names the *contretemps de menuet*, which contains three small springs and one step, and is performed without a cross-rhythm; the *pas balancé*, which marks both downbeats; and the *temps de courante* and *demi-jeté*, which is danced so that the *demi-jeté* coincides with that of a *pas de menuet à trois mouvements*. Tomlinson gives other step-units from the common step vocabulary, such as two *pas de bourrées*, each danced to one 3/4 measure.

One other frequently used step, the *pas de menuet à la bohemienne*, is found in English scores of individual minuets. According to Tomlinson, this step was no longer danced in the *menuet ordinaire* "through Alteration of Fashion which varies in this respect as in Dressing, etc." He writes that the *pas de menuet à trois mouvements* was fashionable in England, whereas in France it had largely been replaced by the *pas de menuet à deux mouvements.* The minuet figures were danced with little variation throughout the eighteenth century, but steps of embellishment were introduced, thus giving the dance an individual flavor in different locales.

In addition to the *menuet ordinaire,* ballroom minuets were choreographed to specific airs. For instance, "Le menuet d'Alcide," Pecour's new *danse à deux* for the year 1709, is composed to a minuet from *Alcide* by Louis de Lully and Marin Marais. Some ballroom *menuets à quatre* combine the S-figure with country dance figures. Country dance minuets for "as many as will" are also documented.

Edmund (or Edward) Pemberton's *An Essay for the Further Improvement of Dancing* (1711) contains minuets by various masters, including Josias Priest, for three to twelve young ladies. The spatial figures of the dances are given but, for the most part, the step sequences are left to the discretion of the interpreter. They are followed by a "Chaconne/Minuet" for a woman by Mr. Isaac. The minuet is particularly attractive, with various *pas de menuet,* the *contretemps de menuet,* and other steps from the general vocabulary which are danced to one 3/4 measure.

Several minuets performed by famous dancers are extant: Pecour's "Entrée pour un Homme et une Femme," published in 1704; a *menuet rondeau* from *Omphalle,* by Destouches, danced by Ballon and Subligny; "The Submission" by Tomlinson (1717), performed in London by "Monsieur and Mademoiselle Salle, the two French Children"; and Anthony L'Abbé's "Menuet performed by Mrs. Santlow," published c. 1725. A solo for a man, "Le Menuet de Mr. Ballon," contained in an undated manuscript, begins with one basic minuet step and then uses other, more complex theater steps.

The minuet was danced with slight variations in different locales and times. Some changes in use by 1779, at least in Italy, are given by Gennaro Magri in his *Trattato teorico-prattico di ballo.* The responsibility for initiating the Honours, starting correctly with the music, and taking hands, had passed to the lady. Discreet arm motions might be introduced. The step used, the *pas de menuet à deux mouvements,* danced without the cross rhythm, had slight, yet stylistically significant differences. Magri advised his amateur pupils to study at various schools to avoid being surprised in public by a partner dancing with a different style.

Magri's instructions toward an impressive performance of the minuet echo those of earlier masters. A dancer should have a languid eye to display humility, a slightly smiling mouth, unaffected hands, and "a majestic carriage . . . with an easy air above all devoid of anything false."

Among professional dancers, Magri singles out Monsieur Lepieg *(sic),* whose performance of a theater minuet had the "quintessence of good taste."

During the nineteenth century, new minuets were composed in the style and technique of the time. With their more sentimental air, high arm positions, pointed toes, and tilted heads, these minuets, while at their best very beautiful dances, have nothing in common with the seventeenth- and eighteenth-century minuets. It was these later dances that served as the models for the twentieth-century choreographic corruptions offered in motion pictures and in the productions of period plays.

[*See also* Ballet Technique, History of, *article on* French Court Dance; *and* Social Dance, *article on* Court and Social Dance before 1800.]

BIBLIOGRAPHY

Bickham, George. *An Easy Introduction to Dancing.* London, 1738.

Dukes, Nicholas. *A Concise and Easy Method.* London, 1752.

Gallini, Giovanni. *A Treatise on the Art of Dancing.* London, 1762.

Green, David. *Sarah, Duchess of Marlborough.* New York, 1967.

Hilton, Wendy. *Dance of Court and Theatre: The French Noble Style, 1690–1725.* Princeton, 1981.

Little, Meredith Ellis. "The Dances of J. B. Lully." Ph.D. diss., Stanford University, 1967.

Magri, Gennaro. *Trattato teorico-prattico di ballo.* Naples, 1779. Translated by Mary Skeaping as *Theoretical and Practical Treatise on Dancing.* London, 1988.

Pasch, Johann. *Maître de danse, oder, Tanz-meister.* Frankfurt, 1705.

Praetorius, Michael. *Terpsichore.* London, 1612.

Rameau, Pierre. *Abbréé de la nouvelle méthode, dans l'art d'écrire ou de traçer toutes sortes de danses de ville.* Paris, 1725.

Rameau, Pierre. *Le maître à danser.* Paris, 1725. Translated by Cyril W. Beaumont as *The Dancing Master.* London, 1931.

Taubert, Gottfried. *Rechtschaffener Tantzmeister, oder Gründliche Erklärung der frantzösischen Tantz-Kunst.* Leipzig, 1717.

Tomlinson, Kellom. *The Art of Dancing Explained by Reading and Figures . . . Being the Original Work First Design'd in the Year 1724, and Now Published by Kellom Tomlinson, Dancing-Master.* 2 vols. London, 1735.

WENDY HILTON

MIRANDA, CARMEN (Maria do Carmo Miranda da Cunha; born 9 February 1909 in Marco de Canavezes, Portugal, died 5 August 1955 in Hollywood, California), singer, dancer, actress. This diminutive, highly energetic performer was raised in Rio de Janeiro, Brazil. Although she had little formal training in singing or dancing, she became a star of local nightclubs before her twentieth birthday and the manager of her own club by 1935. She developed a unique, larger-than-life personality by donning elaborate headdresses, wearing exaggerated gowns, and dancing in platform shoes with very high heels, to make her look taller. She adapted the *samba, maxixe,* and *marcha* to fit her hyper-theatrical style and included intri-

MIRANDA. Wearing her signature costume—a flashy gown and a fruit-laden headdress—Miranda dances with Hermes Pan in *That Night in Rio* (1941), the film that generated her most famous song, "I Yi Yi Yi Yi (I Like You Very Much)." (Photograph from the collection of Rusty E. Frank.)

cate arm gestures, animated facial expressions, and sensual hip movements to capture the audience's attention. Her Broadway debut was in the Shubert 1939 revue *The Streets of Paris,* where she introduced "South American Way," a number she repeated in her film debut, *Down Argentine Way* (1940).

Between 1940 and 1946, when she was under exclusive contract to Twentieth Century–Fox, Miranda quickly established herself as "the Brazilian Bombshell" (and one of the highest paid women in Hollywood) by playing comic supporting roles to Betty Grable or Alice Faye. In these films she inevitably fractured the English language, changed from one outrageous outfit to another, and was showcased in elaborate production numbers generally set in Latin-themed nightclubs where she was surrounded by a bevy of chorus boys and girls dancing in surreal technicolor costumes. Most of her numbers were staged by either Hermes Pan or Busby Berkeley. Although she mainly performed solo, she was occasionally partnered by Hermes Pan, once by Tony DeMarco, and twice by Cesar Romero—in *Weekend in Havana* (1941) and *Springtime in the Rockies* (1942).

Her most famous number is probably "The Lady in the Tutti-Fruitti Hat," which Berkeley staged for her in *The Gang's All Here* (1943). Miranda arrives in a cart at a banana plantation and, after singing about how she received the name referred to in the song title, plays a circular marimba of bananas. This dissolves into overhead shots of chorus girls lofting up giant bananas to form kaleidoscopic patterns. The end of the number shows Miranda in front of a backdrop of hundreds of bananas made to look as if it were one of the tallest headdresses in the world.

After 1946 Miranda became a freelance artist and appeared at various studios. Her most important films during this later period were probably MGM's *A Date with Judy* (1948), where she performed with Xavier Cugat and his orchestra, and *Nancy Goes to Rio* (1950), where she introduced "Cha Bomm Pa Pa," a variation on her most famous song, "I Yi Yi Yi Yi (I Like You Very Much)," which she had sung and danced to in *That Night in Rio* (1941). Her last film was with Jerry Lewis and Dean Martin in 1953, *Scared Stiff.* She died suddenly of a heart attack after rehearsing a strenuous dance routine for the Jimmy Durante television show.

Carmen Miranda was probably one of the most imitated performers of the 1940s and 1950s. Some notable renditions include Imogene Coca's "Souse American Way" for her nightclub act, Betty Garrett singing "South America, Take It Away" in *Call Me Mister,* which opened on Broadway in 1946, as well as countless male imitators of stage, screen, and cabaret such as Mickey Rooney and Jerry Lewis.

[*For related discussion, see* Film Musicals, *article on* Hollywood Film Musicals.]

BIBLIOGRAPHY

Green, Stanley. *Encyclopedia of the Musical Film.* New York, 1981.
Hirschhorn, Clive. *The Hollywood Musical.* New York, 1981.
Korbal, John. *Gotta Sing, Gotta Dance.* Rev. ed. New York, 1983.

VIDEOTAPE. "Carmen Miranda: Bananas Is My Business" (WNET-TV, New York, 1995).

FRANK W. D. RIES

MISKOVITCH, MILORAD (born 26 March 1928 in Valjevo), Yugoslavian dancer, ballet director, and choreographer. With his athletic but slender body and his blond good looks, Milorad Miskovitch seemed to have been created to embody Romantic princes and legendary heroes. He also succeeded in allying the nobility of the classical tradition with powerful dramatic expression. He made his dancing debut in his native country at the age of sixteen as a soloist with the Belgrade Opera. In 1946 he went to Paris to study with Olga Preobrajenska and Boris Kniasseff.

After engagements with the International Ballet in London and Colonel de Basil's Ballets Russes, Miskovitch brought his gifts to the Marquis de Cuevas's Grand Ballet de Monte Carlo, where he danced *Giselle* in 1947 with Rosella Hightower. His rise to fame began in 1948 in Roland Petit's Ballets de Paris troupe; his interpretation of *Le Combat* (choreography by William Dollar, 1949) won him an award as the best dancer of the year when he danced the role in New York. He then became the regular partner of Alicia Markova, touring with her in England, Italy, France, and the United States.

In 1956 Miskovitch formed his own company, Les Ballets 1956 de Miskovitch, which made its debut at the Lyon Festival, with Veronika Mlakar, Tessa Beaumont, Claire Sombert, Vassili Sulich, and Milko Šparemblek. The troupe did international tours for about ten years and also had several seasons in Paris with a repertory of new ballets. At the same time, Miskovitch was appearing as a guest star with the Chicago Opera Ballet (1962), the London Festival Ballet, and the Belgrade Opera (1968), where he triumphed in Dimitrije Parlič's *Joan of Zarissa*. For several years he partnered Carla Fracci in Italy, dancing *The Gull* (1970) and staging *The Creatures of Prometheus* and other ballets.

In 1972 Miskovitch began his American career by becoming ballet master in Dallas, director of the dance section at the High School of Fine Arts in Birmingham, Alabama, and assistant artistic director to Willam Christensen in Ballet West. He returned to Europe in 1974 and staged *Giselle* and then *The Nutcracker* at the Verona Arena, with Fracci. In Yugoslavia he choreographed *Veritas* (1977), *Tancredo*, and *Korak* (both 1980). His most remarkable performances included *Giselle, Les Sylphides, Le Beau Danube, Le Combat, Promethée*, created for him by Maurice Béjart, *Señor de Manara*, and *Le Jugement de Pâris*. In 1982 he began a new career as an artistic advisor to UNESCO Information Service in Paris, remaining for eight years. In 1989 he was elected president of the International Dance Council of UNESCO.

BIBLIOGRAPHY

Lidova, Irène. *Dix-sept visages de la danse française*. Paris, 1953.
Lidova, Irène. "Milorad Miskovitch." *Saisons de la danse*, no. 85 (June 1976): 16–21.
Lidova, Irène. *Ma vie avec la danse*. Paris, 1992.
Swinson, Cyril. *Great Male Dancers*. London, 1964.

IRÈNE LIDOVA
Translated from French

MISZCZYK, STANISŁAW (born 25 April 1910 in Warsaw, died 2 July 1976 in Warsaw), Polish dancer, choreographer, and company director. After training at the Warsaw Ballet School with Bonifacy Śliwiński, Adam Blancard, and Piotr Zajlich, Stanisław Miszczyk joined the Wielki Theater Ballet in Warsaw in 1927. From 1929 to 1939 he was a soloist in companies in Katowice, Lwów, Poznań, and Warsaw, and from 1938 to 1939 he was one of the soloists of the Ballet Polonais, a touring company under the direction of Bronislava Nijinska. After World War II he danced in the ballet companies of opera houses in Poznań (1945), Bytom (1946–1949), Warsaw (1949–1952), and again in Poznań (1952–1954). From 1945 to 1971 he was ballet director or choreographer for operas in Poznań, Bytom, Warsaw, Wrocław, and Szczecin. He retired in 1972.

One of the most active participants in the reconstruction of Polish ballet after World War II, Miszczyk was a choreographer of great imagination. Unfortunately, Poland's postwar isolation from western Europe prevented him from fully realizing his talents, as he was obliged to work within the official aesthetic imposed on theatrical artists during the period of Soviet hegemony over Poland. Nevertheless, he made a major contribution to Polish culture.

Miszczyk's preferred form for choreography was the full-evening story ballet. For a number of years, his version of *Swan Lake* was the only one presented on Polish stages (Poznań, 1953; Warsaw, 1956, Wrocław, 1961). He staged the popular national ballet *Pan Twardowski* no fewer than five times (Bytom, 1948; Warsaw, 1951, 1957, and 1965; Wrocław, 1962), each time somewhat differently. Among his other ballets were *Swantewit* (Bytom, 1949), *Serenade* and *The Highlanders* (both Warsaw, 1952), *The Peasant King* and *The Festival in Lipiny* (both Poznań, 1954), *Mazepa* (Warsaw, 1958), *The Amber Maiden* (Poznań, 1961), and *Coppélia* (Szczecin, 1963).

BIBLIOGRAPHY

Chynowski, Paweł, and Janina Pudełek. *Almanach baletu warszawskiego, 1785–1985 / Le ballet de Varsovie, 1785–1985*. Warsaw, 1987.
Mamontowicz-Łojek, Bożena. *Terpsychora i lekkie muzy*. Kraków, 1972.
Neuer, Adam, ed. *Polish Opera and Ballet of the Twentieth Century: Operas, Ballets, Pantomimes, Miscellaneous Works*. Translated by Jerzy Zawadzki. Kraków, 1986.
"Notes sur le Ballet Polonais." *La revue musicale* (December 1952–January 1953): 151–157.
Pudełek, Janina. *Two Hundred Years of Polish Ballet, 1785–1985*. Warsaw, 1985.
Turska, Irena. *Almanach baletu polskiego, 1945–1974*. Kraków, 1983.
Williams, Peter. "Paschal Contrasts in Monaco." *Dance and Dancers* (June 1959): 11–15.
Wysocka, Tacjanna. *Dzieje baletu*. Warsaw, 1970.

ARCHIVE. Wielki Theater Museum, Warsaw.

PAWEŁ CHYNOWSKI

MITCHELL, ARTHUR (born 27 March 1934 in New York City), dancer, teacher, choreographer, and founder and artistic director of the Dance Theatre of Harlem. Mitchell was the first black to gain prominence as a classical ballet dancer with the New York City Ballet. The eldest of five children born to Arthur and Willie Mae Mitchell, he showed an aptitude for the arts at an early age. Encouraged by a junior high school counselor to study tap, Mitchell attended New York's High School of Performing Arts, majoring in modern dance. In 1952 he got leave to appear in a revival of *Four Saints in Three Acts* in Paris. On graduation that same year, he was awarded the annual dance award of High School of Performing Arts—the first male student to achieve that honor.

Offers of two scholarships followed: to Bennington College, Vermont, and, on Lincoln Kirstein's invitation, to the School of American Ballet. Mitchell accepted the latter, though he kept a foothold in modern dance by continuing to perform with various modern dance companies. In 1954 he made his Broadway debut, dancing in the musical *House of Flowers.* The following year, while touring with the John Butler Company in Europe, Mitchell was invited to join the New York City Ballet, making his debut on 9 November 1955 in *Western Symphony.* During fifteen years with the company, Mitchell rose to prominence as a *premier danseur* of classical style; he was also very effective in jazz and modern ballets, such as Jerome Robbins's *Interplay,* John Taras's *Ebony Concerto,* and John Butler's *The Unicorn, The Gorgon and the Manticore.* George Balanchine created several ballets with prominent roles for Mitchell. Notably, he danced the pas de deux in *Agon;* he danced it first in 1957 with Diana Adams. Balanchine also furnished Mitchell with his most successful original role, Puck in *A Midsummer Night's Dream* in 1962.

MITCHELL. A publicity photo of Mitchell as a soloist in the New York City Ballet, 1959, showing his characteristic elegance and purity of line. (Photograph by Martha Swope © Time, Inc.; used by permission.)

Between seasons with the ballet, Mitchell appeared as a guest artist with various dance companies, in musicals, and occasionally on television. In 1966 he organized the short-lived American Dance Company. At the behest of the U.S. government, he then took the assignment of creating the National Ballet of Brazil. In 1968, learning of the assassination of Martin Luther King, Jr., Mitchell determined to found a black classical dance school and company in New York, and he invited Karel Shook to join him as co-director. With grants from the Ford Foundation and other donors, the Dance Theatre of Harlem was established in 1969, making its official debut in 1971.

In 1988 Mitchell and the Dance Theatre of Harlem went to the Soviet Union, the first ballet company to be invited as part of the U.S.–USSR Cultural Exchange initiative. In 1990 their touring schedule encompassed Cairo and other cities in Egypt, and in 1992 Mitchell led the company in a highly successful tour of South Africa, performing to integrated audiences.

Mitchell made it a priority to emphasize community outreach and education. For this and among other accolades, he received thirteen honorary doctoral degrees, including those of Havard and Princeton universities, and was inducted into the National Association for the Advancement of Colored People Image Awards of Fame. In 1993 he was the recipient of an award for lifetime contributions to American culture from the John F. Kennedy Center for the Performing Arts. In 1996 he was awarded the National Medal of Arts by President Bill Clinton.

[*See also* Dance Theatre of Harlem.]

BIBLIOGRAPHY

Emery, Lynne Fauley. *Black Dance from 1619 to Today.* 2d rev. ed. Princeton, 1988.

Estrada, Ric. "Three Leading Negro Artists and How They Feel about Dance in the Community: Eleo Pomare, Arthur Mitchell, and Pearl Primus." *Dance Magazine* (November 1968): 45–60.

Goodwin, Noël. "Arthur Mitchell: An Interview." *Dance Gazette* (October 1984): 15–17.

Gruen, John. *People Who Dance: Twenty-Two Dancers Tell Their Own Stories.* Princeton, N.J., 1988.
Latham, Jacqueline Q. M. "A Biographical Study of the Lives and Contributions of Two Selected Contemporary Black Male Dance Artists—Arthur Mitchell and Alvin Ailey—in the Idioms of Ballet and Modern Dance, Respectively." Ph.D.diss., Texas Woman's University, 1973.
Lyle, Cynthia. *Dancers on Dancing.* New York, 1977.
Maynard, Olga. "Arthur Mitchell and the Dance Theater of Harlem." *Dance Magazine* (March 1970): 52–64.
Mitchell, Arthur, et al. "NYCB and DTH: Anniversary Reflections." *Ballet Review* 22 (Fall 1994): 14–28.
Tobias, Tobi. *Arthur Mitchell.* New York, 1975.

HILARY B. OSTLERE

MLAKAR, PIA AND PINO, husband and wife team of choreographers important for their contributions to theatrical dance in the former country of Yugoslavia. Students of Rudolf Laban in Berlin and Jelena Poljakova in Belgrade, the work of **Pia Mlakar** (Pia Scholz; born 28 December 1908 in Hamburg, Germany) and **Pino Mlakar** (born 2 March 1907 in Novo Mesto, Yugoslavia), represents a bridge between the traditions of ballet and modern dance. In 1932 the Mlakars' work *Un Amour du Moyen Age,* to music by Antonio Vivaldi and Johann Sebastian Bach, won second prize at the choreographic competition in Paris sponsored by the Archives Internationales de la Danse. The Mlakars held a succession of joint ballet directorships during the 1930s and early 1940s, at Darmstadt (1929), Dessau (1931–1933), Zurich (1934–1938), and Munich (1939–1943). Important works from this period include *The Devil in the Village* (1935), *The Ballad of Medieval Love* (1937), and *The Arc* (1939).

After World War II the Mlakars settled in Yugoslavia, where they restaged their earlier works and created many new ones for the major ballet companies in Belgrade, Zagreb, and Ljubljana. Among those they staged were *The Little Ballerina* (1947), which included their daughter Veronika in its representation of the life of itinerant performers, and *Danina, or Jocko the Brazilian Ape* (1950), an attempt to reconstruct a Taglioni-Lindpaintner work from the nineteenth century. They created about forty ballets, of which the last was *The Legend of Ochrid* (Belgrade, 1978). The Mlakars were among the first choreographers to use Labanotation to record their works.

BIBLIOGRAPHY

Jovanović, Milica. *Balet narodnog pozorišta u Beogradu izmedju dva rata.* Belgrade, 1976.
Jovanović, Milica. *Pia and Pino Mlakar.* Ljubljana, 1985.
Mlakar, Pino. *Balet na slovenskem odru.* Ljubljana, 1967.
Vogelnikova, Marija. *Sodobni ples na Slovenskem.* Ljubljana, 1975.

MILICA JOVANOVIĆ

MLAKAR. *The Devil in the Village* (1935), one of the Mlakars' best-known works, was mounted for several ballet companies. At the National Theater in Belgrade in the late 1940s, Dušanka Sifnios and Dušan Trninić danced the leading roles of Jela and Mirko. (Photograph by Marka.)

MODERN DANCE. *See* Genres of Western Theatrical Dance.

MODERN DANCE TECHNIQUE. [*This entry is limited to discussion of modern dance traditions in the United States, which has been particularly fertile ground for the development of techniques of expressive movement. For related discussions, see* Bodenwieser Technique; Chladek Technique; *and* Wiesenthal Technique.]

From the outset, the formulating and teaching of technique figured prominently in the development of American modern dance. In the world of ballet, the most renowned teachers have tended to be retired performers, uninterested in choreography. However, Martha Graham, Doris Humphrey, Charles Weidman, and many of their colleagues and followers taught modern dance classes at the peak of their careers, directing companies that performed only their choreography and featured them as leading performers. In this they resembled the German choreographer-dancer-pedagogue Mary Wigman, who had preceded them into modernism.

The early modern dancers had various reasons for teaching. Having seen some of the "free" dance drifting across America in the wake of Isadora Duncan, or that espoused by educators who encouraged individual creativity tinged with Hellenism, they were aware of the dangers of vaunting self-expression over discipline. In their classes, students acquired techniques and in turn helped to forge styles that often entailed new conceptions of how the dancer should look and move. To the early modernist teachers, a class was a laboratory in which to test choreographic ideas, a place to discover and train dancers with the commitment necessary to embark on a life of hard work and scant financial reward as well as a way to earn money to help defray the expenses of performances.

The early American modernists assumed a certain intellectual acuity on the part of their disciples; it was assumed that many of them would also wish to be choreographers. Some teachers taught composition (such as Louis Horst at the Graham studio), and some, such as Humphrey and Weidman, encouraged a degree of individuality even in technique classes.

Modern dance techniques are as idiosyncratic as the styles they support, and the generic term *modern dance,* which began to appear in college catalogs and school brochures during the 1930s, reflects the eclectic training of many who began to teach it. Some studied under a pioneering dance educator, like Margaret H'Doubler at the University of Wisconsin, who combined expressive dancing with a sound and thorough approach to movement training. Some would-be physical-education teachers, as well as would-be performers, went to Germany to study. (News of Wigman's experiments had reached America long before her first American tour in 1930). Others worked with German dancers who came to America, such as Jan Veen (Hans Wiener), who arrived in the late 1920s and eventually settled in Boston.

Bennington School of the Dance. In the 1930s many New York studios offered summer courses that attracted teachers. Once the Bennington School of the Dance was founded in 1934, many teachers spent their summers there, studying with the major (or "in") choreographers of the day: Graham, Humphrey, Weidman, and Hanya Holm, a former Wigman dancer who started a Wigman School in New York City in 1931. Many of these student-teachers returned to their college jobs and taught a modern dance blended to suit their individual taste and skills.

Different as the four Bennington stars were, they did share certain beliefs, which their classwork, like their dances, reflected. All wished to avoid prettiness, undue glamor, and displays of virtuosity. The three Americans, former Denishawn dancers, were particularly interested in paring movement down to the bone. All wanted to discover the impact of emotion on the human body—ugly though the result might be—without recourse to previous academic traditions. Holm gradually adapted her Wigman training to suit the American temperament and physique.

Generally speaking, the early modern dance classes emphasized weight in ways that ballet did not. The pull of gravity was not something to be denied or escaped with an illusion of ease. Effort was to be emphasized rather than played down. The teachers acknowledged the floor, devising exercises to be done in sitting, kneeling, or lying positions. The sequences they made often stressed force or weightiness in the thrust and swing of gestures or the solid advance of the foot. The classwork featured many ways of falling and rising; whether the dancer fought the pull of gravity or yielded to it, she or he always rose victorious. Big jumps, when executed without traveling steps to link them, created an illusion of emphatic rebound.

The modern dancers were also at odds with the balletic notion of almost constant equilibrium and the perpetually erect spine. Instead of keeping their hips aligned over their legs and bending only their upper body, the modernists often canted their pelvis out, using their hips to initiate turns or to counterbalance extreme bends. The so-called hinge, in which the dancer leans backward toward the floor, the body a straight line from head to knees, was common to all the principal techniques. Most emphasized the center of the body as a motivating force: often the limbs followed what the torso initiated.

These first modern dance classes laid down a format that has, with some notable exceptions, become traditional: exercises on the floor, exercises standing in place, and sequences across the floor. Some teachers (Weidman, for one; later, Graham) occasionally used the barre for stretches or a few other exercises that could be facilitated by a support. The traveling sequences often developed as increasingly strenuous or complicated variations on natural forms of locomotion: walking, running, skipping, leaping. Indeed, the concept of thematically related material molded early modern dance classes. "All exercises are in the form of theme and variations," wrote Martha Graham (Rogers, 1941). From a simple core, an exercise could enlarge in scope, alter its rhythms, and evolve by the addition of new material. It could be made to grow or diminish, speed up or slow down, by the addition or subtraction of counts: a Graham fall, for instance, or a Weidman push-up might first be performed in eight-count divisions, then in groups of four, then two, then one (or fewer), the increasing speed altering the look and feel of the action. In class, piano or percussion accompaniment emphasized the crucial rhythmic component. [*See* Bennington School of the Dance.]

Martha Graham. Probably beginning in the late 1920s, Martha Graham conceived of the dancer as one poised for action, charged both physically and emotionally. Even in stillness, there was to be no relaxation. As the underpinning of her technique, she developed her well-known theory of contraction and release. The body, with percussive force, empties of breath, as if a blow to the midriff or a powerful sob has knocked the wind out of the dancer. As a consequence, the pelvis may tip, the spine curl, the head fall back, and the hands cup in miniature contractions of their own. But there is no collapse. No sooner is the contraction at its deepest than the release brings a straightening out, an expansion, a new taking in of breath. (The basis is breath; in practice, the student may only imply the pattern of breathing described above.)

This principle informs much of the classwork. The remarkable Graham falls are shaped by a series of contractions and releases; and this closing and opening action in the center of the body also shapes many of the stretching and strengthening exercises performed on the floor as well as standing and traveling movements. Notable in the floorwork are several sequences—almost like small dances—that begin with the dancer sitting, one leg folded in front, one bent in back. Within this base, the dancer twists to the back of the room—hips leading, followed by the upper body and shoulders, finally the head, and sometimes the arms—and then turns to face front again. This spiral through the back also figures in exercises standing in place or traveling. Some of the traveling steps are unique to the final third of the hour-and-a-half class. An example is the "triplet," whose rhythm and basic down-up-up steps resemble those of the waltz (although the dancer, instead of melting into it, strides through space). Other sequences across the floor link movements already done in place by means of one or more steps. Still others, such as the prances, can be performed either in place or traveling.

The best-known of the modern dance techniques have adapted over the years to their creators' changing concerns and the dancers with whom they worked. What was being taught in the Martha Graham School of Contemporary Dance at the time of her death in 1991 was less lean, raw, and percussive that what Graham herself was teaching in 1930, at which time she was formulating some of her most crucial theories. Initially Graham used very little turnout; the parallel stance, like the flexed foot, was more in keeping with the deliberate primitivism of her dances. Later, movements created for her "Greek" dance dramas—many of them based on archaic or Asian styles—entered the classwork and gave it a new complexity. [*See the entry on Graham.*]

Doris Humphrey and Charles Weidman. By nature a more lyrical dancer than Graham, Humphrey also formulated a theory of movement on which she built her technique. "My entire technique," she said, "consists of falling away from and returning to equilibrium" (Humphrey, 1959). She drew her idea in part from Friedrich Nietzsche's theory about the intertwined Apollonian and Dionysian aspects of art. What she saw as humans' dual needs—for stability and peace on one hand, risk and progress on the other—she translated into her theory of fall and recovery. The drama of motion, with all its shifting tensions, dynamic changes, rhythms, and designs, took place between two possible extremes, or "deaths": the state of perfect equilibrium and that of total collapse.

Shaped by the fall-and-recovery principle, classes taught by Humphrey, or by Weidman, her partner, co-director of the Humphrey-Weidman Company, involved a variegated use of swinging motion, the body or limbs describing large arcs, circles, and figure eights, with a drop of the weight, a rebound, and a momentary suspension of breath and motion just before equilibrium was reached. Humphrey's circular fall spun the dancer through 360 degrees on the descent and again on the ascent. The rhythm of breathing was as intimately connected with Humphrey's work as it was with Graham's, but instead of emphasizing the in–out motion of breathing, Humphrey concentrated on its rise and fall.

Probably influenced by her exposure, while with the Denishawn school and company, to the theories of François Delsarte, Humphrey classified movements as occurring in unison, opposition, or succession. [*See* Delsarte System of Expression.] She built some of her most memorable class exercises on the notion of successional movement: a gesture would flow through the torso and/or limbs, animating each part as it passed, producing the illusion of a wave or a wind-induced ripple.

Dances in the Humphrey-Weidman repertory presented men and women as equals, but not as indistinguishable from each other in movement style, and Weidman took particular interest in developing the male dancer. His classes featured some very vigorous exercises, utilizing a more percussive swing, clenched fists, leaps, and steps designed to build and display strength. (Students remember grimly having to put one leg on a barre and lift it repeatedly from that position.)

Crippled by arthritis and forced to retire as a performer in 1944, Humphrey did not codify her technique to the extent that Graham did—nor did she teach technique after her retirement, although her composition classes continued to stimulate young dancers. The technique classes she had taught before retiring stimulated creativity, too. Former students recall that Humphrey often built an entire class around a phrase she was developing for a dance, first giving a warm-up, then introducing elements of the phrase in a variety of ways, and finally putting the parts together.

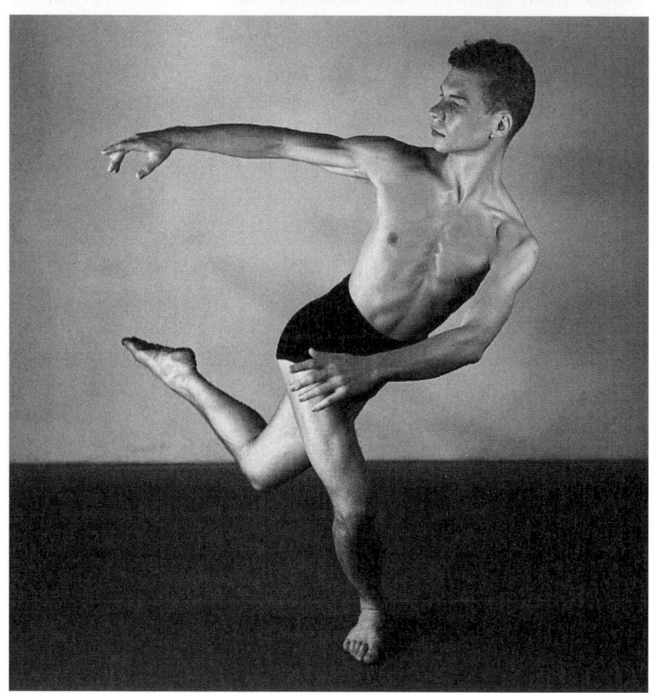

MODERN DANCE TECHNIQUE. Merce Cunningham demonstrates a sitting fall-and-recovery sequence from the Graham technique, 1942: *(above, left)* preparation; *(above, center)* sinking to the floor, the working leg tucked under the standing leg in a yogalike position; *(above, right)* twisting toward the standing knee to complete the fall's spiral motion; *(right)* continuing the spiral to recover in a low parallel attitude position. The hands never touch the floor in the fall, a principle shared by all the early modern choreographers. Cunningham's own approach to floorwork remained strikingly similar, but he replaced the spiral with a simple twist at the waist, and he eliminated Graham's contraction-and-release initiations. (Photographs © 1991, 1994 by Barbara Morgan; used by permission of the Barbara Morgan Archives, Hastings-on-Hudson, New York.)

Some of the classwork developed by Humphrey and Weidman has been passed on through the teaching of former company members such as Ernestine Stodelle (Henoch) and Nona Schurman. José Limón, trained by Humphrey and Weidman, and a dancer in their company for ten years, taught a technique shaped by the dynamic of drop and rebound, although much of his classwork emphasized the powerful attack and weightiness that his dances featured. Limón's classes often began with the students standing in place; exercises at the barre, stretches on the floor, and traveling steps followed. Limón technique, as it is taught by former Limón dancers and their pupils, still owes much to Humphrey. [*See the entries on Humphrey, Limón, and Weidman.*]

Hanya Holm. While a member of Wigman's company, Hanya Holm learned about dance and the teaching of dance from Wigman and, through Wigman, from the German theoretician Rudolf Laban. Therefore, the technique she taught was less intimately connected to her choreographic style than those of Humphrey, Graham, or Weidman. This may also be attributable in part to the Laban heritage—to his brilliant analysis of movement and its expressive powers in terms of the elements of space, time, weight, flow, and effort. In her class, dancers were made aware of the ways in which emotions affect the human body; they also learned how, even in the most basic warm-up exercises, their gestures and postures relate to the space around them. For instance, standing with the feet apart affirms width as a dimension in space, while standing with the feet slightly crossed (in a modified ballet third position) points out two opposing diagonals. Holm once said that the idea of space as "an emotional element, as active partner in the dance" was one factor that distinguished the German modern dancers from the American ones (Sorell, 1969).

Among the elements of Wigman's technique that Holm continued to use and develop were a great variety of circular patterns. The dancer would walk the perimeter of a circle, shifting the hips either toward or away from the imagined center; he or she might combine a circle with a plane by tracing circles or figure eights with the feet, while the body continued to face one direction. Dervish spins would make the dancer the axis of a whirling circle. In articulating the polarities of tension and relaxation, Holm, like Humphrey, taught a variety of swings.

Holm's teaching has served such dissimilar artists as Don Redlich and Alwin Nikolais, the former interested in human drama, the latter in creating patterned universes of color, light, and motion. In training dancers to the needed flexibility of mind and body, Nikolais used some of the techniques learned from Holm in his own teaching; his pupil and colleague, choreographer Murray Louis, continues to do so.

Holm and Nikolais considered technique inseparable from theory and composition classes. An idea introduced in a technique class could be taken apart by students in theory class and improvised on until many variants had been wrung from it and the core made plain. The understanding thus gained could then be used in the students' own composition studies. [*See the entry on Holm.*]

Erick Hawkins. Although many who performed with Martha Graham—Jane Dudley, Bonnie Bird, and Pearl Lang, among others—have used her technique as a base from which to develop teaching methods of their own, some, like May O'Donnell, teach classes that bear little resemblance to Graham's. However, no former Graham dancers repudiated Graham's approach to technique as thoroughly as Erick Hawkins and Merce Cunningham.

Inspired by Duncan's theory about the prevalence of wave motion in nature as well as by ideas gleaned from Mabel Ellsworth Todd's *The Thinking Body* (1937), Hawkins developed a system of training intended to banish the unnecessary tension and strain responsible for so many dancers' injuries. He stressed relaxation of muscles (or "decontraction"—an example of the vocabulary he has developed to describe his theory) and the contracting only of those necessary to perform a particular action. Gravity is a force to be played with and complied with, rather than fought against. Among the images he asked his students to imagine is that of the limbs and head moving like tassels in response to an impulse begun in the pelvis or spine. Even a simple shift of weight he conceived as in a curve (the "undercurve" or the "overcurve"). His technique classes, unlike those of most others, focused on the mastery of individual movements rather than sequences, although these might be taken up in improvisation or composition classes. Everything Hawkins taught was aimed at producing dancers who appear to be fluidly in harmony with nature and with the nature of their own bodies—fit inhabitants for his delicate, impressionistic dances. [*See the entry on Hawkins.*]

Merce Cunningham. Although Merce Cunningham's non-narrative dances posit a world in flux, a complex field in which individual decisions may at any minute be short-circuited by accidents or chance events, his training methods have always produced dancers who appear calm, alert, quick on their feet, and able to achieve a state of equilibrium in almost any position. Some writers have characterized Cunningham's style as balletic because of his use of the erect spine, controlled weight, complex footwork, and attenuated lines. Yet his dancing, subject as it is to distortions of shape, timing, and sequence, is as far from academic ballet as it is from Graham's Dionysian passion.

Cunningham (1985) has said that in formulating his technique he wished to give equal emphasis to the feet, which he felt modern dance ignored, and to the torso, which he felt ballet ignored. A Cunningham student spends no time sitting on the floor. The first class exercises, done standing in place without the support of a barre, work the back, then the legs, and then the two together. Distinctions are made between the action of the upper back, the middle back, and the lower back. The general sequence and types of exercises are set, but the exercises themselves may vary. Eventually, bending, tilting, and twisting of the spine may be set against very rapid, complicated leg gestures and steps, performed in place or across the floor, or used in smooth sequences stressing balance, as in ballet's adagios. Whether the technique is taught by Cunningham himself, by dancers formerly or currently in his company, or by others he has trained, the simple, clear, almost dry warm-ups contrast with the more freely "choreographed" material that appears later in the class. Often, Cunningham's classwork features long and rhythmically complex phrases, instead of the short, repeated phrases shaped by musical meter that are a feature of much modern dance training. [*See the entry on Cunningham.*]

Lester Horton. Working in Los Angeles from the 1930s until his death in 1953, Lester Horton developed classes that trained many important dancers and choreographers: Carmen de Lavallade, Alvin Ailey, Joyce Trisler, James Truitte, and Bella Lewitzky (who has created her own training method, based on a sane and systematic approach to anatomy and musculature). Horton, emphasizing power and flexibility, did not base his technique on any single vision of dance or the body. According to Lewitzky, he began building the technique through experiment, asking his students to discover, for example, all possible ways of going down to the floor and of rising. He often worked with dramatic motivation or ethnic styles in class.

Lewitzky has mentioned his idiosyncratic use of throwing or flinging movement as well as his isolation exercises for every part of the body, including eyes and fingers. The warm-up that developed as he formalized his teaching features slow, smooth stretching and strengthening exercises performed from a standing position; these extend the body in all directions, into extreme positions and canted balances. A vital ingredient is the "flatback" position, in which the dancer's body bends at the hips until the torso is parallel to the floor. Horton devised unusual ways of working the muscles within a single exercise: as the dancer bends his or her knees in a *plié,* the foot is clenched, then the toes are flexed, then the foot contracts again. His technique, like his choreographic style made notable use of level changes—sometimes drastic ones, such as from a jump to a fall. [*See the entry on Horton.*]

Modern Dance Technique Today. Beginning in the 1950s, modern dancers became less prone to discipleship, more eager to study a variety of techniques—especially ballet. Because training became more eclectic, the tracing of influences is tricky and perhaps inadvisable. A dancer who studied with José Limón, or even performed with his company, may not teach exactly the same material he taught. Teachers tend to be choreographers themselves, and, whether attached to a university or school or offering classes independently, they reassess, add to, and subtract from their heritage in order to arrive at a technique that suits their aesthetic and pedagogical concepts. However, the influence of that heritage may be enduring, even if subtle. Like his mentor Hanya Holm, Nikolais made improvisation, composition, and pedagogy vital ingredients of his training system; many former company members—such as Phyllis Lamhut—whose own choreographic styles may differ considerably from that of Nikolais, have in turn become noted for their expertise in directing composition classes.

Some prominent choreographers today do not patent training systems, and some do not teach technique at all. Many teach only intermittently, offering master classes while on tour, or giving workshops lasting a short period of time. During the time Twyla Tharp maintained the company she disbanded in 1988, her dancers taught ballet classes in residencies across the United States, but, more importantly, they gave classes in which they dissected and manipulated phrases from her repertory in terms of content, rhythm, dynamics, spatial design, and other factors. As of 1997 former Tharp dancers Sara Rudner and Jennifer Way were still giving classes structured in this way; the point is to give students a deeper understanding of the phrase in question and to foster facility of body and mind.

The Martha Graham Technique has been copyrighted, and official teachers must be approved by the New York studio that bears her name. In contrast, Paul Taylor has never proclaimed a Paul Taylor Technique; he established a school in 1983, after having been a leading choreographer and the director of a company for more than twenty years. With his input and guidance, company members and school graduates have built training techniques related to his distinctive style, and incorporate phrases from his repertory into the classes. [*See the entry on Taylor.*]

Trisha Brown, originally one of the radical choreographers associated with Judson Dance Theater in New York in the 1960s, has often taught workshops, but only in 1995 did she open a school—a school that two years later was still defining itself. (Her previous reluctance perhaps related to a belief nourished in the anti-elitist 1960s that training systems such as Graham's, which promulgated a choreographer's strongly defined style, tended to rob the student dancer of individuality.) At the school, company members past and present offer various technical approaches that complement and even help to define for students the bases of Brown's complex, virtuosic, yet tension-free style; no one, however, speaks of "Brown Technique." [*See the entry on Brown.*]

Many modern dancers study ballet, yoga, or one of the martial arts, such as aikido or *taijiquan,* which began to attract dancers during the artistic and political upheavals of the 1960s. Some take workshops in contact improvisation, a two-person form developed by Steve Paxton, or acquaint themselves with one of the various techniques that promote body awareness.

Originally, modern dance technique imparted the aesthetic of the teacher as firmly as it trained bodies. Most who teach today consider technique more dispassionately than did their predecessors. Their classes aim at building strong, versatile, correctly aligned bodies, without attempting to instill a particular vision of dance.

BIBLIOGRAPHY

Brown, Beverly. "Training to Dance with Erick Hawkins." *Dance Scope* 6.1 (1971–1972): 7–30.

Cunningham, Merce, in conversation with Jacqueline Lesschaeve. *The Dancer and the Dance.* New York, 1985.

Humphrey, Doris. *The Art of Making Dances.* New York, 1959.

Lewis, Daniel. *The Illustrated Dance Technique of José Limón.* New York, 1984.

Rosen, Lillie F. "A Conversation with Bella Lewitzky." *Ballet Review* 10.3 (Fall 1982): 81–94.

Rogers, Frederick R., ed. *Dance: A Basic Educational Technique.* New York, 1941.

Selden, Elizabeth. *The Dancer's Quest: Essays on the Aesthetic of the Contemporary Dance.* Berkeley, 1935.

Sorell, Walter. *Hanya Holm: The Biography of an Artist.* Middletown, Conn., 1969.

Stewart, Virginia, comp. *Modern Dance. New ed.* New York, 1991.

Stodelle, Ernestine. *The Dance Technique of Doris Humphrey and Its Creative Potential.* Princeton, 1978.

Warren, Larry, et al. "The Dance Theater of Lester Horton." *Dance Perspectives,* 31 (Autumn 1967).

Warren, Larry. *Lester Horton, Modern Dance Pioneer.* New ed. New York, 1991.

FILMS. *The Modern Dance (Humphrey Technique)* (c.1930), Dance Collection, New York Public Library for the Performing Arts. Betty Lind, *Dancers at Bennington School and Mills College* (1938–1939), Dance Collection, New York Public Library for the Performing Arts. Helen McGehee et al., *Graham's Technique* (1967). Dawn Lille Horwitz, *Dance Techniques an.d Movement Patterns of May O'Donnell* (1978). *Lester Horton Technique: The Warm-Up* (1990).

INTERVIEWS. Bonnie Bird (1973) and Jane Dudley, collection of Selma Jeanne Cohen. Dorothy Bird and Claudia Moore Read, Oral History Archives, Columbia University.

DEBORAH JOWITT

MŌHINIĀṬṬAM. This dance style is indigenous to Kerala, a state on the southwestern coast of India. The word *mōhiniāṭṭam* means "dance of the enchantress," *mohini* meaning a "charming, seductive woman," and *āṭṭam* meaning "dance" in the local language, Malayalam. The style was evolved by the women of Kerala around the middle of the nineteenth century, because they were not allowed to participate in the dance drama *kathakaḷi*. Denied the privilege of taking part in this male-dominated tradition, they amalgamated the dramatic elements of this style, which they had seen the men perform but had not studied themselves, with the rhythmic elements of the *bharata nāṭyam* style from the neighboring state of Tamil Nadu. This style had filtered into Kerala through an interchange of dancers and musicians between the royal courts.

The result was a charming, graceful, and feminine style, appearing almost naive and artless next to the splendor of *kathakaḷi* and the architectural grandeur of *bharata nāṭyam*. The metrical complexities of *bharata nāṭyam* were replaced by simple, almost elementary rhythms; its rigid angularity of line and precise, well-defined positions gave way to softer, more supple movements. In *mōhiniāṭṭam* the torso is kept flexible, and the body bends from side to side like a resilient bow. The arms are fluid and graceful.

In its expressive acting, *mōhiniāṭṭam* uses hand gestures from both earlier styles, shifting from one to the other whenever the occasion demands. The gestures borrowed from *kathakaḷi* are performed without the accompanying eye movements or stylized facial expressions that are a unique feature of *kathakaḷi*. They are seldom performed at the three prescribed speeds of single, double, and quadruple, a repetitive pattern which greatly slows the dramatic movement in *kathakaḷi*. Some hand gestures have also strayed in from *bharata nāṭyam*, but there is much less emphasis on holding the hand in a prescribed manner; the hands are held more softly and loosely.

The basic stance of *mōhiniāṭṭam* calls for *kathakaḷi*'s wide turnout of the knees. The feet are kept flat; in *kathakaḷi*, they are rolled to the sides. In static positions, the hands are clenched and are usually kept on the stomach, or they may be held on the left side of the waist, the left fist held at the wrist by the right forefinger and thumb. The eyebrows flutter throughout, and the eyes flash seductive messages.

The *mōhiniāṭṭam* style reached its zenith in the court of Maharajah Swathi Thirunal, who ruled over Travancore state in Kerala in the nineteenth century. He was a great poet, musician, and composer, and the arts flourished during his reign. Many of his songs are interpreted by the *mōhiniāṭṭam* dancer. The repertory closely follows that of *bharata nāṭyam*, except that instead of *allarippu*, the invocatory dance is *cholkettu*. This segment begins with an invocation to the goddess Bhagavatī, flowers into a series of rhythmic passages, and concludes with verses glorifying the gods Śiva and Rāma. This is followed by segments called *jātīśvaram, śabdam, varṇam, padam,* and *tillānā*. The costume is usually ivory-white with a gold border. A six-yard length of fabric is pleated and tied around the lower half of the body, crossing at the back. One end is then taken across the chest and over a blouse, and tucked in at the side. The hair is tied in a topknot and decorated with flowers and jewels. A gold waist ornament completes the picture.

[*See also* Asian Dance Traditions, *overview article;* India, *article on* History of Indian Dance. *For related discussion, see* Bharata Nāṭyam *and* Kathakaḷi.]

BIBLIOGRAPHY

Bharati, Shivaji. *The Art of Mohiniyattam*. New Delhi, 1986.
Chatterjee, Ashoke. *Dances of the Golden Hall*. New Delhi, 1979.
Jones, Betty True. "Mohiniyattam: A Dance Tradition of Kerala, South India." In *Dance Research Monograph One*. New York, 1973.
Massey, Reginald, and Jamila Massey. *The Dances of India: A General Survey and Dancer's Guide*. London, 1989.
Ragini Devi. *Dance Dialects of India*. 2d rev. ed. Delhi, 1990.
Rele, Kanak. *Mohiniattam, the Lyrical Dance*. Bombay, 1992.

RITHA DEVI

MOISEYEV, IGOR (Igor' Aleksandrovich Moiseev; born 8 [21] January 1906 in Kiev, Ukraine), dancer and choreographer. Igor Moiseyev was the son of a lawyer and spent his childhood and adolescence traveling around Russia with his father and becoming acquainted with the cultures of various ethnic groups. At age twelve he began dance training with Vera Mosolova and two years later entered the Moscow School of Choreography. He graduated from the school in 1924, where he studied under Aleksandr Gorsky, whose pedagogical and professional experience played a key role in the development of Moiseyev's talent. Upon graduation, Moiseyev was invited to join the Bolshoi Theater troupe, with which he danced from 1924 to 1939 as a soloist in numerous roles. At the Bolshoi Experimental Theater in 1925 he appeared in Kasyan Goleizovsky's ballets—Raoul in *Theolinda* and Joseph in *Joseph the Beautiful*—and with the Bolshoi Ballet in the well-known ballets *The Red Poppy, International Sailors,* and others.

The young dancer possessed a good feel for style and fluid plastique, and a penchant for heroic roles. Moiseyev's concert work, in partnership with the famous ballerina Ekaterina Geltser, played a significant role in the making of the dancer. Moiseyev was also greatly influenced by Michel Fokine's *Chopiniana.*

Five years after Moiseyev joined the Bolshoi he began to choreograph. His first ballets—*The Football Player* (1930, in collaboration with Lev Lashchilin to music by Oransky), *Salammbô* (1932, to music by Arends), and *Three Fat Men* (1935, to music by Oransky)—were marked by brilliant choreography that incorporated eurhythmic gymnastics and crowd scenes. Moiseyev mounted his own version of Aram Khachaturian's *Spartacus* at the Bolshoi in 1958, about which the conductor Yuri Fayer wrote, "The Circus scene was particularly good—the gladiators' fight, which gave the impression of a dynamic pageant, building up to a tragic climax" (cited in Inozemtseva, 1979, p. 275).

MOISEYEV. Soon after joining the Bolshoi Ballet, Moiseyev choreographed a version of *The Football Player* (1930). In this moment, the men are displaying athletic prowess, a characteristic of Moiseyev's works. (Photograph reprinted from Faubion Bowers, *Broadway U.S.S.R,* New York, 1959.)

Under Moiseyev's direction, a Festival of Folk Dances of the USSR was held in Moscow in 1936. This coincided with the dawn of amateur theatricals, a time of dynamic interaction between folk art and professional art. The following year, Moiseyev formed the State Folk Dance Ensemble of the USSR, drawn from participants in the festival and a group of professional artists. Moiseyev set the dancers a number of creative objectives that amounted to an aesthetic program. The basic goal was to develop and perfect traditional folk dances using the combined experience of classical and modern dance. The very first concert performances proved that Moiseyev's quest had not been in vain. Because of his keen perception of different cultures, their ethnographic and psychological characteristics, Moiseyev became a genuine composer of dance. In his works folk dance traditions underwent complex transformations, enriched by professional art and imbued with an expressive contemporary flavor. Dances such as the Russian *Polyanka* (1937), the Ukrainian *Gopak* (1945), and the Belarussian *Lyavonikha* (1937) formed the core of the ensemble's concert programs. In these dance numbers the choreographer made use of national traits that had developed over centuries, setting them in solos and group dances. Moiseyev reinterpreted folk dances, integrating them into a single choreographic scheme. As well as using folklore, Moiseyev added a new dimension with artistic elements drawn from various domains of dance. Turning to work rituals and harvest time, he created a new Belarussian dance, *Bulba* (1937), which subsequently joined the repertories of many folk dance companies.

The leader and members of the ensemble moved to a new stage of creative activity when individual choreographed miniatures were arranged into integrated suites, such as *The Four Seasons* (1949–1950) and *Pictures from the Past.* Seeking artistic excellence and variety, Moiseyev introduced into his dance compositions seemingly heterogeneous elements: lyrics, jokes, grotesqueries, and heroics. These elements were interwoven into a homogeneous dance spectacle, fascinating and dynamic, with its own dramaturgy and design. Moiseyev also focused attention on individual characters who performed solos within the larger dance work. The traditions of Moldovan folklore and vivid theatricality are manifest in the character of Mokanu in Moiseyev's production of *The Clever Mokanu* (1961). Moiseyev constructed a number of his compositions—for example, *A Labor Festival* (1976)—on contemporary themes. The dance suite *A Day on a Ship* (1944–1945) conveyed the everyday routine on board ship: cleaning detail, work on deck during emergencies, and free time. The individual segments of the suite were presented in pantomime and dance. *The Partisans* (1950), steeped in the heroic spirit of World War II, received wide acclaim; Moiseyev described the life of guerrilla fighters in the vivid language of dance and captured the thunder-

MOISEYEV. The large cast of the Moiseyev Dance Company watches as three dancers execute *prisiadkas*, a signature step of Russian folk dance, performed by kicking out the feet from a squatting position. (Photograph from the Dance Collection, New York Public Library for the Performing Arts.)

ing charge of the cavalry. In the *Ukrainian Suite* he altered the traditional lyrical plot to portray lovers separated by war.

Extensive use of his own experience as a teacher, and his personal assistance in the formation of an entire array of other dance companies have been activities of Moiseyev throughout his creative career. He searched not only for new artistic forms but also for effective organizational structures. In 1966 Moiseyev founded the Concert Dance Ensemble of the USSR (later known as the State Concert Ensemble), setting it the task of encouraging the development of talented youth through concert ballet works. A key aspect of Moiseyev's work was popularizing the folk arts of the peoples of the USSR through frequent foreign tours by his dance company. Beginning in 1945 Moiseyev and his company appeared in most countries of the world to great acclaim. While on tour, Moiseyev continued to work intensively. His ensemble was a creative laboratory in which new dance numbers were born out of folklore observed in various parts of the world. Thus the ensemble's repertory acquired an international flavor in numbers such as the manly dance of the Argentine herdsmen, *Gaucho,* marked by an austere beauty and built on sharp staccato rhythms, or the temperamental *Jota Aragonesa* (1965), performed at a whirlwind tempo.

Moiseyev's work on a given dance was not confined to the time of its creation but evolved over years, beginning with the impressions from his travels in the Caucasus Mountains during his youth, which colored his interpretation of the Adzharian war dance *Khorumi* (1937). In the 1970s Moiseyev turned to larger theatrical dance types and created one-act ballets to the music of Russian classical composers. Among them is the well-known *Polovtsian Dances* (1971) from Aleksandr Borodin's opera *Prince Igor.* In this version Moiseyev reinterpreted the musical score, imparting to the historical plot a contemporary passion, temperament, and colorful, explosive rhythmic design. *Polovtsian Dances* enjoyed tremendous success all over the world. Moiseyev's work on the beautiful *Night on the Bare Mountain,* to the music of Modest Mussorgsky (1983), enjoyed similar success. The production synthesized classical music and ballet traditions with the rhythm and imagery of modern dance. Moiseyev has made a truly outstanding contribution to Soviet and world choreography.

Moiseyev was named People's Artist of the USSR (1953) and winner of the Lenin (1966) and State (1942, 1947)

MOISEYEV. The combination of folk dance traditions and professionally trained dancers is evident in Moiseyev's choreographies and company. Here, the women from the Moiseyev Dance Company perform an exuberant line dance. (Photograph © 1986 by Jack Vartoogian; used by permission.)

Prizes, and received the title of Hero of Socialist Labor (1976).

BIBLIOGRAPHY

Acocella, Joan. "Moiseyev Dance Company." *Dance Magazine* (December 1986): 35–36.

Brinson, Peter, ed. *Ulanova, Moiseyev, and Zakharov on Soviet Ballet.* Translated by E. Fox and D. Fry. London, 1954.

Chudnovskii, Mikhail. *Ansambl Igoria Moiseeva.* Moscow, 1959.

Farah, Ibrahim. "Center Stage: The Ethnic Dancer." *Arabesque* 12 (November–December 1986): 4–5.

Greskovic, Robert. "Moiseyev Dance Company." *Ballett International* 9 (December 1986): 2–14.

Inozemtseva, Galina V. "Igor Moiseev." In *Mastera stseny: Geroi Sotsialisticheskogo truda,* edited by N. A. Abalkina. Moscow, 1979.

Mason, Edward C. "Dance Lectures: Moiseyev on Folk Dance as Theatre." *Dance and Dancers* (January 1956): 36–37.

Moiseyev, Igor. "Ballet and Reality." *Dance Magazine* (May 1953): 28–31.

Moiseyev, Igor. *Ya vspominaiu.* Moscow, 1996.

Moiseyev's Dance Company (in English and Russian). Moscow, 1966.

Moore, Lillian. "Class with Igor Moiseyev." *Dance Magazine* (August 1958): 19–22.

Roslavleva, Natalia. "Twenty-Five Years of Moiseyev." *Dance and Dancers* (May 1962): 18–21.

MARGARITA I. ISAREVA
Translated from Russian

MOLDOVA. The present-day state of Moldova is surrounded by Ukraine to the north, east, and south, and by Romania on the west with which it shares an eastern Romance language and culture. Originally inhabited by the Bessi (thus, the area called Bessarabia), Moldova became part of the Dacian area of the Roman Empire in the second century CE. After being overrun by successive invasions, it became an independent principality in the fourteenth century, ruling over Bessarabia and Bukovina until the early nineteenth century, when it was ruled alternately by the Russian and Ottoman empires. In 1918 Romania annexed all the Bessarabian portion of Moldova; in 1924 the remainder became an autonomous republic of the USSR within the territory of the Ukrainian SSR. In 1940 Bessarabia was retaken by the USSR, and the Moldavian Soviet Socialist Republic was established. During World War II, it was occupied by combined fascist Romanian and German forces but was retaken by the USSR in 1944. Moldova has been an independent state since the dissolution of the USSR in 1991.

Folk Dance. Of all the Moldovan arts, folk dance is one of the oldest and most popular genres. Among the common dances is the *khora.* In the early eighteenth century, the *khora*—a name derived from a Greek noun, meaning "dance"—was applied not only to a kind of round dance often accompanied by singing but also to folk festivals. By the end of the nineteenth century, however, dances accompanied by singing had become almost extinct. In most of Moldova today the *khora* is a type of round dance performed at a moderate tempo with the dancers holding hands.

In the first half of the nineteenth century, the original *khora* was replaced by the dance called *zhok.* The word comes from the Latin *jocus,* meaning "play" or "amusement," but in the Moldovan language it also means "dance." Often a modifier is added: *zhok bytrynesk* is an ancient dance; *zhok glumesk* is a jocular dance. In the broadest sense *zhok* means a complete dance scene, such as a festival or a ball. Traditionally such events occurred in each village at a designated place—in a field, near a flour mill, or on a square.

Traditional Moldovan folk dances were of two types: ritual and everyday. Ritual dances included "Kelushari," "Dragaika," and the wedding dances "Ostropetsul," "Zestrya" (Dowry), and "Dansul Miresey" (Bride's Dance). There were two kinds of wedding dances. There were also dances that had no distinct plot, although they did express emotions, such as the *khora* and the *invertita* (dance with spin). Everyday dances were thematic. Some were dances of work, such as "Poama" (Grapes) and "Jokul Ferarirol" (Dance of the Blacksmiths). There were heroic dances, dances for women, and satirical dances, such as "Shokilku" (Mischievous Boy). Some dances were devoted to natural phenomena, like "Vyntul" (Wind), and to flowers and animals, like "Trandaferul" (Rose) and "Ratsa" (Duck).

The movement patterns of Moldovan folk dance fall into four main groups: round dances, line or semicircle dances, *invertita*-type dances performed by couples or small groups, and dances with mixed patterns. The dances are usually performed to the accompaniment of an orchestra, called *tarafa,* that consists of violins, cymbals, a clarinet, trumpet, drum, and sometimes other instruments. The most common rhythms are 2/4, 3/8, 6/8, and 7/16.

Theatrical Dance. Professional dance began in Moldova after 1917. In 1936 a theatrical folk dance company was established, which was later named Doima. In 1945 it became the official folk dance company of Moldova, and in 1958 was renamed Zhok. Since then its chief choreographer has been Vladimir Kurbet, although guest choreographers, including Igor Moiseyev and Leonid Yakobson, also contributed dances based on Moldovan folklore. In 1970 a company was founded in conjunction with the Fluerash folk orchestra. [*See the entry on Kurbet.*]

The first national ballet, *An Ancient Story,* choreographed by Yuri Sidorenko to music by Valery Poliakov, was produced in 1938. In 1957 Aleksandr Protsenko choreographed his own version of *The Fountain of Bakhchisarai* for the newly established Moldovan Opera and Ballet Theater. From its earliest years the company gave considerable attention to national ballets. In 1960 Vladimir Varkovitsky choreographed *The Dawn* to music by V. Zagorsky and a libretto by G. Gelovani, which recounted the Moldovan people's battle for reunification of Bessarabia with the Soviet Union. The music was notable for its use of folk melodies. The brightest moments are the scenes of folk festivals on the banks of the Dnestr River, which feature the men's dances "Briul" and "Betuta," along with the rushing, energetic circle dance "Cirba." This act 1 finale not only unites everyone in merriment but also protectively conceals a political fugitive, whose assailant tries in vain to breach the circle. The ballet concludes with a triumphal festival.

Other national ballets have been based on native legends, poetry, and fairy tales. Music by Moldovan composers is regularly used. The company's repertory includes both classical ballets and new works by Moldovan and commonwealth choreographers.

BIBLIOGRAPHY

Golubeva, Elvira. *Iz istorii baleta v Moldavii.* Kishinev, 1979.

Golubeva, Elvira. *Baletnaia muzyka kompozitorov Sovetskoi Moldavii.* Kishinev, 1988.

Korkina, Alla. *Petr Leonardi.* Kishinev, 1980.

Koroleva, Elfrida. *Khoreograficheskoe iskusstvoe Moldavii.* Kishinev, 1970.

Koroleva, Elfrida. *Spektakl, baletmeister, tantsovshchik.* Kishinev, 1977.

Koroleva, Elfrida. *Tvorchestvo artista baleta.* Kishinev, 1983.

Koroleva, Elfrida. *Moldavskii narodnyi tanets.* Moscow, 1984.

Koroleva, Elfrida. *Moldavskii baletyni teatr.* Kishinev, 1990.

"Lippovan Folk-Lore." *Rosin the Bow* 5 (Autumn 1955): 13–19.

Oshurko, L. V. "Moldavian Folk Dances." *Rosin the Bow* 6 (Autumn 1957): 4–8.

Protsenko, Aleksandr. *Vladimir Tikhonov.* Kishinev, 1981.

Roslavleva, Natalia. "How Large Is Soviet Ballet?" *Dance Magazine* (November 1963): 35–37, 58–61.

Roslavleva, Natalia. "Back to the Bard." *Dance and Dancers* (December 1966): 21–23.

Tkachenko, Tamara. *Narodnyi tanets.* 2d ed. Moscow, 1967.

ELFRIDA A. KOROLEVA
Translated from Russian

MOLIÈRE (Jean-Baptiste Poquelin; born January 1622 in Paris, died 17 February 1673 in Paris), French playwright, actor, and dancer. One of the greatest names of French theater, Molière was influenced by the comedy of gestures current in France and Italy and by the ballets put on at the Jesuit Collège de Clermont in Paris, where he was a student. A founder of the Illustre Théâtre in 1643, he based his pseudonym—Molière—on the name of Louis de Mollier, a librettist and musician with the royal ballet. He hired the professional dancer Daniel Mallet and Mademoiselle du Parc, the actress and dancer. His early comedies abounded in stage business.

Molière himself danced two *entrées* in the ballet *Les Incompatibles* in Montpellier in 1655. After touring in the provinces, he appeared in Paris, performing a burlesque courante in *Les Précieuses Ridicules* (1659). Like Scaramouche, with whom he initially shared the Louvre theater, in his performances he moved imperceptibly from words to rhythmic gestures, and then into dance.

For a royal festival at Vaux, organized by Nicolas Fouquet for Louis XIV (1661), Molière and the choreographer Pierre Beauchamps designed a new genre, the *comédie-ballet,* using both actors and dancers in *Les Fâcheaux.* In this piece Lisandre teaches the courante to Erastus, while the Fâcheaux (pests) disturb him with their dancing and playing. *Les Fâcheaux* was among the three plays by Molière that were most often performed during his lifetime.

After this, all the works commissioned from Molière by Louis XIV were comic ballets. *Le Mariage Forcé* (1664) was known as "the king's ballet." The *entrées* had a dramatic structure, because Molière believed that ballets were "comedies without words." At Versailles, Molière participated in *Les Plaisirs de l'Île Enchantée,* and he danced and played the role of the clown Moron in *La Princesse d'Élide,* which was even more popular than *Tartuffe.* He produced *L'Amour Médecin* (1665) in five days, declaring that comedy, music, and dance are the greatest doctors. Audiences in Paris and the court delighted in his comedies of character *(Le Misanthrope),* his comic ballets (*Mélicere, La Pastorale Comique,* and *Le Sicilien,* 1667; *Georges Dandin,* 1668; *Monsieur de Pourceaugnac,* 1669), and his burlesques (the sumptuous *Les Amants Magnifiques* and *Le Bourgeois Gentilhomme,* undoubtedly the best work of the genre). With Thomas Corneille's assistance, Molière composed *Psyché*—which involved seventy professional artists—*La Comtesse d'Escarbagnas,* and *Les Fourberies de Scapin* (1671). He was involved in a lengthy rivalry with Jean-Baptiste Lully, which Molière lost when he failed to persuade the king to retain his company of twelve dancers and twenty-two musicians. Symbolically, he died while dancing in his last comic ballet, *Le Malade Imaginaire.*

Prefiguring the *ballet d'action* (plotted ballet), this man of the theater combined a feeling for gesture as expression in drama, plastic animation, and physical grace. In *Les Amants Magnifiques* Molière evokes "those dancers who express every emotion so well." Beauchamps, Louis XIV, and such famous dancers as Marie Camargo and Auguste Vestris interpreted his work, which has also inspired such modern choreographers as Bronislava Nijinska *(Les Fâcheaux),* George Balanchine *(Le Bourgeois Gentilhomme),* Serge Lifar *(Fourberies),* and Maurice Béjart *(Le Molière Imaginaire* and *Les Plaisirs de l'Île Enchantée).*

Molière was aware of the importance of theatrical gesture: "Without dance," he said, "a person would be capable of nothing."

[*See also* Ballet de Cour *and the entry on Lully.*]

BIBLIOGRAPHY

Bray, Raymond. *Molière, homme de théâtre.* Paris, 1954.

Chazin-Bennahum, Judith. *Dance in the Shadow of the Guillotine.* Carbondale, Ill., 1988.

Christout, Marie-Françoise. "L'exemple Molière." *Saisons de la Danse,* no. 265 (February 1995): 38–43.

Chumbley, Joyce A. "The World of Molière's Comedy-Ballets." Ph.D. diss., University of Hawaii, 1972.

Copeau, Jacques. *Registre Molière.* Paris, 1976.

Fleck, Stephen H. *Music, Dance, and Laughter: Comic Creation in Molière's Comedy-Ballets.* Paris, 1995.

Garwood, Robert E. "Molière's 'Comedies-Ballets.'" Ph.D. diss., Stanford University, 1985.

Mazouer, Charles. *Molière et ses comédies-ballets.* Paris, 1993.

McBride, Robert. "Ballet: A Neglected Key to Molière's Theatre." *Dance Research* 2 (1984): 3–18.

McBride, Robert. *The Triumph of Ballet in Molière's Theatre.* Lewiston, N.Y., 1992.

Pellisson, Maurice. *Les comédies-ballets de Molière.* Paris, 1914.

MARIE-FRANÇOISE CHRISTOUT
Translated from French

MOLNÁR, ISTVÁN (born 17 September 1908 in Kolozsvár [now Cluj], Romania; died 2 June 1987 in Budapest), Hungarian dancer and choreographer. Molnár created a style of theatrical folk dance, pioneered scientific folk dance research, and was a theoretician and teacher. In the 1930s he started his career as a modern dancer with solo recitals and worked with Valéria Dienes's School of Orchestics. He first used modern music and concertos for his expressionistic choreographies but later shifted in the 1940s to Hungarian folk dance music, working with amateur dancers selected from youth associations and colleges.

Molnár attempted to evolve an autonomous and self-expressive Hungarian art of stage dance, using not only characteristic folk dances and the dances of Hungarian ethnic minorities, but also adapting ballads and folk tales, dances to music by Hungarian and foreign composers, and dance plays with historical and topical themes. For this purpose he collected and began to classify Hungarian dance folklore and developed his own training method.

Molnár created a rich body of choreography as head of professional folk ensembles between 1950 and 1971—the Folk Ensemble of the Trade Unions, the Folk Army, and the Budapest Dance Ensemble. His works included *Hungarian Picture Book, Verbunk and Czardas of Kapuvár, Czardas from Doboz, Love Dance,* Béla Bartók's *Hungarian Scenes,* and Zoltán Kodály's *Dances from Marosszék,* all lasting productions expressing the Hungarian art of dance.

Molnár made a permanent impact on dance chiefly through his sensitivity to problems, his vocabulary, and his reliance on vanishing folk art as a pure source of artistic renewal. Many theatrical and television films were made of his works, and Hungarian television produced programs about him and his work in 1968 and 1980. He was named Merited Artist (1953) and Eminent Artist (1980). He received the Kossuth Prize posthumously in 1990.

BIBLIOGRAPHY

Dance Ensemble of Budapest, 1958–1978. Budapest, 1978.

Falvay, Károly, et al. "Studies on István Molnár." *Tánctudományi tanulmányok* (1978–1979).

Koegler, Horst. "Molnár, István." In *Ballettlexikon.* Budapest, 1977.

Körtvélyes, Géza. "Táncművészet és táncfolklór térben, időben." *Kritika* 4 (1982).

Molnár, István. *Koreografiak.* Budapest, 1983.

Táncszók: Molnár István különszám (1983). Special issue on Molnár.

GÉZA KÖRTVÉLYES

MOMMERIE. A *mommerie* (Ger. *Mummenschanz, Maskerada;* Eng., *mummery*; It., *mascherata*) is a spectacle or event of disguises, usually of a gay, grotesque, amusing, or frivolous nature, executed or performed with masks. The term has been used to designate masquerades, fancy dress balls, mummings, large Carnival celebrations, dumb shows, skits, and court ballets; it is said to be derived from the name of Momus, the mocking and censorious prankster among the gods of classical antiquity. In a fifteenth-century English glossary, the *Promptorum parvulorum, mummynge* was translated as "murmuring or keeping silence," emphasizing the soundless manner of the performance (as in the word *mum* in modern English). The Low German *Mumme,* a mask, has also been suggested as the root of the term. All three aspects are present, jointly or severally, in the various shapes that *mommeries* assumed over the centuries. In different places and times, *mommeries* had religious overtones, were vehicles for social and political satire, or were simply a means of introducing uninhibited fun into high and holy days or organized festive events.

Especially in the joyous days of Christmas and the Carnival season, *mommeries* flourished. Though vigorously persecuted by civic and church authorities, neither the crowds of masquers swarming through the streets nor the Fêtes des Fous (Feasts of Fools), in which clerics themselves participated wearing monstrous masks or disguised as women, could be suppressed.

Mommeries were incorporated into fourteenth-century mystery plays and formed one of their principal attractions. German popular plays contained elements of the mommerie, as did Italian theatrical pantomimes. In England the mummers' plays to this day combine ancient fertility rites, dancing, and broad comedy, the identity of the performers hidden under masks and fantastic human and animal guises.

At court the *mommerie,* antecedent of the *mascarade,* served as *entremet,* a dramatic *divertissement* of relatively small dimensions, mimed and danced, with or without instrumental or vocal accompaniment. The silence preserved by the masked performers was one of the trademarks of the genre.

One of the most famous *mommeries* of the fifteenth century concluded the spectacles at the allegorical banquet *La Fête du Faisan* (Feast of the Pheasant) in Lille in 1454, given by Philip III, duke of Burgundy, on the occasion of the establishment of the Order of the Golden Fleece. It was a mixture of *cortège*, musical entertainment, and verse, culminating in a dance "en guise de mommerie" executed by twelve torchbearing knights in gilt masks and their ladies in transparent face veils. From such events a direct line leads to the formation of the *ballet de cour* of the sixteenth and seventeenth centuries.

A series of pictures from the court of emperor Maximilian I illustrates the entertaining *mommeries* that ended each day of the cavalier's tour of the Knight Freydal (*nom de clé* for Maximilian). The performers, all gentlemen of the court, sometimes wear animal or bird masks, sometimes the padded costume, stringy hair, and grotesque features of the clown; they dance circle dances, battle and free-form *morescas*, or, disguised as giants, perform processional dances with tiny lady partners (children?) before the court, whose members look on from dais, balcony, or elevated benches.

Documents attesting to the intrusion of disguised mummers into the banquets of kings and nobles of England exist since the 1370s. The maskers came either to dice, drink, and dance with the company or to entertain them with a dumb show. Because of the dangers inherent in such visits to great houses, an act of Parliament (1511) forbade them and made even the sale of masks illegal. Nevertheless, the medieval practice continued, and visits by "guisers" or "geese dancers" remained part of English Christmas customs into the twentieth century.

Similarly, the carefully planned and strictly organized sequences of events during balls in the Renaissance and the seventeenth century were sometimes interrupted by the entrance of a *mommerie*, a group of masked dancers who introduced an element of disorder and comedy into the well-regulated, stately proceedings in much the same way that the antimasque provides a thematic and choreographic contrast to the English masque. [*See* Masque and Antimasque.]

Mommeries also developed into shortened versions of the court ballets. Called *mascarades* in the seventeenth and eighteenth centuries, they became independent theatrical spectacles with themes taken from fables, history, and mythology, costumes to match, and were choreographed from the beginning to the final *grand ballet*. [*See* Masquerades.]

While the dramatic *mommerie* became absorbed into the *ballet comique* and related choreographic spectacles, the raucous progress of masquers in fantasy costumes, on foot, on floats, or wagons, to this day forms an integral part of the great Carnival celebrations of Cologne, Basel, New Orleans, Trinidad, and South America.

BIBLIOGRAPHY

Chambers, E. K. *The Mediaeval Stage* (1903). 8th ed. Oxford, 1978.

Compan, Charles. *Dictionnaire de danse.* Paris, 1787.

Lacroix, Paul, ed. *Ballets et mascarades de cour de Henri III à Louis XIV.* 6 vols. Geneva, 1868–1870.

Malherbe, Paul. *Encyclopédie de musique.* Paris, 1930.

McGowan, Margaret M. *L'art du ballet de cour en France, 1581–1643.* Paris, 1963.

Petit de Julleville, Louis. *Les mystères.* 2 vols. Paris, 1880.

Prunières, Henry. *Le ballet de cour en France avant Benserade et Lully.* Paris, 1914.

Reyher, Paul. *Les masques anglais.* Paris, 1909.

Sachs, Curt. *World History of the Dance.* Translated by Bessie Schönberg. New York, 1937.

Savaron, Jean. *Traicté contre les masques.* Paris, 1608.

Sharp, Cecil J., and Herbert C. Macilwaine. *The Morris Book.* 5 vols. London, 1909–1913. 2d ed. London, 1912–1924.

Sharp, Cecil J. *The Sword Dances of Northern England.* 3 vols. London, 1912–1913. 2d ed. London, 1951.

Smith, A. William. "Dance in Early Sixteenth-Century Venice: The *Mumaria* and Some of Its Choreographers." In *Proceedings of the Twelfth Annual Conference, Society of Dance History Scholars, Arizona State University, 17–19 February 1989,* compiled by Christena L. Schlundt. Riverside, Calif., 1989.

Sumberg, Samuel L. *The Nuremberg Schembart Carnival.* New York, 1941.

Tiddy, R. J. E. *The Mummer's Play.* Oxford, 1923.

INGRID BRAINARD

MONCION, FRANCISCO (born 6 July 1918 in La Vega, Dominican Republic; died 1 April 1995 in Woodstock, New York), American ballet dancer, choreographer, and painter. Moncion's family emigrated from the Dominican Republic to the United States in 1922 or 1923, when he was four years old. He did not begin his dance training until 1938, when, as a young man of twenty, he accepted the offer of a scholarship at the School of American Ballet in New York and became a pupil of George Balanchine, Pierre Vladimiroff, Anatole Oboukoff, and Muriel Stuart. In 1942, while still a student, he appeared in the New Opera Company production of Balanchine's *Ballet Imperial.* Following two years of military service during World War II, he performed in a Broadway production of *The Merry Widow* with dances choreographed by Balanchine. After this engagement ended in 1944, he danced with the marquis de Cuevas's Ballet International, creating the title roles in Léonide Massine's *Mad Tristan* and Edward Caton's *Sebastian,* among others, and he performed as a soloist with Colonel de Basil's Original Ballet Russe during the 1946/47 season.

Moncion was an original member of Ballet Society, founded by Balanchine and Lincoln Kirstein in 1946, and later of its successor, the New York City Ballet. In the four

MONCION. A studio portrait in costume for the title role in Edward Caton's *Sebastian* (1944), created by Moncion during the first season of the marquis de Cuevas's Ballet International in New York. (Photograph by Carl Van Vechten; used by permission of the Estate of Carl Van Vechten.)

decades he spent with these companies (he became a U.S. citizen in 1947), he participated in many historic performances and created a number of major roles. At Ballet Society's first performance on 20 November 1946 he danced with Gisella Caccialanza to the third theme in the opening section of *The Four Temperaments*. Thereafter, Balanchine created many roles for Moncion to utilize his exceptional partnering ability and strong dramatic presence. Among them were the principal man in *Divertimento* (1947), the Dark Angel in *Orpheus* (1948), Prince Ivan in *The Firebird* (1949), the death figure in *La Valse* (1951), the Ricercata in *Episodes* (1959), Theseus in *A Midsummer Night's Dream* (1962), and the principal man in *Emeralds*, the opening section of *Jewels* (1967). Other important roles created by Moncion include King Mark in Frederick Ashton's *Picnic at Tintagel* (1952), the Boy in Jerome Robbins's *Afternoon of a Faun* (1953), the principal man in Robbins's *In the Night* (1970), and the Devil in *Pulcinella* (1972), co-choreographed by Balanchine and Robbins.

Early in his career it was evident that Moncion would never become a true *danseur noble*, yet it was equally clear that he was capable of dancing many different roles as a *premier danseur*, from the dashing figure in Balanchine's dances for a Broadway production of *The Chocolate Soldier* (1947) to the attentive partner of the ballerina in the second movement of *Symphony in C* (1948). Edwin Denby, writing about Moncion at this time, noted that "his exceptional gift is his intense imaginative sincerity. He creates a character completely, and he has power, musicality, and humor." Denby's observations remained true throughout Moncion's long career. He was as effective in the comic role of the Husband in Robbins's *The Concert* as he was in the dramatic title roles of Balanchine's *Prodigal Son* and *Don Quixote*. In 1983, he was the only charter member of the New York City Ballet still performing with the company, adding character roles such as Herr Drosselmeyer and Doctor Coppélius to his repertory. He retired from the stage in 1985.

The New York City Ballet has performed four works choreographed by Moncion: *Jeux d'Enfants* (1955), a collaborative work with Balanchine and Barbara Milberg to music by Georges Bizet; *Pastorale* (1957), set to music by Charles Turner; *Choros No. 7* (1959), to music by Heitor Villa-Lobos, which formed part of another collaborative work, entitled *Panamerica;* and *Les Biches* (1960), to the score by Francis Poulenc, part of a program called *Jazz Concert*. The Boston Ballet and the Pennsylvania Ballet have also performed *Pastorale*. Moncion choreographed *Honegger Concertino* for the Pennsylvania Ballet in 1965 and *Night Song*, set to music by Harold Shapero, for the Washington Ballet in 1966. In addition to choreography, Moncion also had a strong interest in the visual arts. He was a painter of considerable talent whose works were seen in several New York exhibitions.

BIBLIOGRAPHY

Boroff, David. "Group Portrait of a Ballet Dancer." *The Dancing Times* (May 1957).

Chujoy, Anatole. *The New York City Ballet*. New York, 1953.

Denby, Edwin. *Looking at the Dance* (1949). New York, 1968.

Hunt, Marilyn. "Balanchine's *Divertimento:* A New Life." *Ballet Review* (Fall 1985).

Kirstein, Lincoln. *The New York City Ballet*. With photographs by Martha Swope and George Platt Lynes. New York, 1973.

Reynolds, Nancy. *Repertory in Review: Forty Years of the New York City Ballet*. New York, 1977.

WILLIAM JAMES LAWSON

MONK, MEREDITH (born 20 November 1942 in New York City), American composer, choreographer, filmmaker, and performance artist. Monk has created an innovative brand of dance-music-theater. Raised in Connecticut, she began composing at the age of sixteen. After receiving a bachelor of arts degree from Sarah Lawrence

College in 1964, she moved to New York City. She was briefly associated with Judson Dance Theater, where in 1966 she performed her solo *16 Millimeter Earrings;* it foreshadowed later pieces in its use of film sequences, the taped vocalisms of Monk, and a variety of props.

Monk soon began creating large interdisciplinary events for nontraditional spaces. These early works include *Juice* (1969), subtitled a "theater cantata," which was performed over a period of four weeks in three locales of diminishing size: the Guggenheim Museum, Minor Latham Playhouse at Barnard College, and Monk's own loft, where spectators watched videotapes of the performers. This progressive reduction in scale, wrote Deborah Jowitt, "involved an intensification of focus, a zeroing in on intimate details, and gradual lessening of formality" (*New York Times,* 14 January 1974).

Vessel (1971), an "opera epic" about Joan of Arc, reversed this sequence, in this case in the course of a single evening. The performance began in Monk's loft, continued at The Performing Garage, and concluded in a nearby parking lot, so that the epic dimensions of the piece were continually enlarged.

Education of the Girlchild (1973), an "opera," was structured in two parts; the second was a solo for Monk showing the stages of a woman's life, starting with old age and moving backward in time through womanhood to girlhood. One of her most enduring and influential works, it won first prize for musical theater at the 1975 Venice Biennale.

In 1968 Monk formed a company known as The House, augmented in 1978 with the separate Meredith Monk Vocal Ensemble, dedicated to the performance of her musical compositions. Her careers as composer and choreographer have run parallel, with recordings sharing equal importance with live and film productions.

Her imagistic, nonlinear theater evokes a tantalizingly recognizable but never precisely definable dreamworld. Her strongest creations have focused on personal catastrophe within the larger cataclysm of war: the martyrdom of Saint Joan in *Vessel,* a child's experience of World War II and the Holocaust in *Quarry* (1976), two families in the American Civil War in *Specimen Days* (1981), or survivors in a postnuclear future in *The Games* (1983). The last, created for the Schaubühne Ensemble in Berlin, was a collaboration with the performance artist Ping Chong.

Between 1972 and 1976, Monk and Chong collaborated on four pieces collectively known as *The Travelogue Series.* One of these, *Paris,* was filmed in 1982 by KCTA in Minneapolis. A half-hour section of *Turtle Dreams* (1981) was produced by WGBH in Boston. In 1980 Monk made a film version of *16 Millimeter Earrings,* and her 1981 film *Ellis Island* won prizes at the Atlanta and San Francisco film festivals. She is the subject of one of four hour-long documentaries on contemporary American composers made by the British filmmaker Peter Greenaway in 1982 and 1983.

In 1989 Monk completed a feature film, *Book of Days.* Her full-length opera *Atlas* was first performed by the Houston Grand Opera in February 1991. Dealing with spiritual quest as reflected in the life of a single woman, the opera showed its heroine and her companions immersing themselves in remote cultures and undergoing personal ordeals that led to transfiguration.

Monk also continued to make site-specific works, such as *American Archeology No. 1: Roosevelt Island,* where, on an island in New York's East River, the actors/dancers/singers (and the audience as well) moved from a spacious park to the ruins of a smallpox hospital, ending on a lighted hilltop—a symbol of hope.

For "Archeology of an Artist," the 1996 exhibition of her work at the New York Public Library for the Performing

MONK. Composer-choreographer Meredith Monk as Alexandra in one of her largest-scale music-theater works, *Atlas: An Opera in Three Parts* (1991), inspired by the life of explorer Alexandra David-Neel. In its themes—family, comradeship, community, travel, woman's life-journey, the myths hidden within everday experience—and in its multimedia staging and extended vocal techniques, the opera was a *summa* of Monk's work to date. The costume was designed by Yoshio Yabara. (Photograph © 1991 by Michael O'Neill; used by permission.)

Arts, Monk wrote that she thought of herself as a vocal archaeologist, "trying to dig down to the most fundamental human utterances. . . . I combine forms weaving together music, movement, film object, light and ambiance. This multi-dimensional approach hopefully creates a poetry of sound, image and movement that increases the luminosity and radiance of the experience."

BIBLIOGRAPHY

Anderson, Jack. "Entering a World Only Meredith Monk Can Map." *New York Times* (16 June 1996).

Banes, Sally. *Terpsichore in Sneakers: Post-Modern Dance.* Boston, 1980.

Finkelstein, David. "The Films of Meredith Monk." *Ballet Review* 19 (Summer 1991): 60–67.

Foster, Susan Leigh. *Reading Dancing: Bodies and Subjects in Contemporary American Dance.* Berkeley, 1986.

Goldberg, Marianne. "Transformative Aspects of Meredith Monk's *Education of a Girlchild.*" *Women and Performance* 1 (Spring–Summer 1983): 19–28.

Jowitt, Deborah. "Ice Demons, Clicks, and Whispers." *New York Times Magazine* (30 June 1991).

Kreemer, Connie, ed. *Further Steps: Fifteen Choreographers on Modern Dance.* New York, 1987.

Lynch, Joan Driscoll. "*Book of Days:* An Anthology of Monkwork." *Millennium Film Journal,* nos. 23–24 (Winter 1990–1991): 38–47.

Marranca, Bonnie. "Meredith Monk's Atlas of Sound: New Opera and the American Performance Tradition." *Performing Arts Journal* 14 (January 1992): 16–29.

McNamara, Brooks. "*Vessel:* The Scenography of Meredith Monk." *Drama Review* 16 (March 1972): 87–103.

Monk, Meredith. "*Vessel:* An Opera Epic." *Drama Review* 16 (March 1972).

Monk, Meredith. "Ages of the Avant-Garde." *Performing Arts Journal* 16 (January 1994): 12–15.

Siegel, Marcia B. "Evolutionary Dreams: Meredith Monk." *Dance Theatre Journal* 4 (Autumn 1986): 2–5.

FILM. *Making Dances* (Blackwood Productions, 1979).

ALLEN ROBERTSON
Amended by Selma Jeanne Cohen

MONOTONES. Two pas de trois. Choreography: Frederick Ashton. Music: Erik Satie. Costumes: Frederick Ashton. First performances: 24 April 1966 *(Monotones I),* 24 March 1965 *(Monotones II),* Royal Opera House, Covent Garden, London, Royal Ballet. Principals: Antoinette Sibley, Georgina Parkinson, Brian Shaw *(Monotones I);* Vyvyan Lorrayne, Anthony Dowell, Robert Mead *(Monotones II).*

The first to be performed of the two pas de trois that make up *Monotones* was choreographed to Erik Satie's *Trois Gymnopédies,* orchestrated by Claude Debussy and Roland Manuel. It later came to be called *Monotones II* when a second pas de trois was choreographed to be performed before it. This second creation was set to Satie's *Trois Gnossiennes,* orchestrated by John Lanchbery, and is referred to as *Monotones I.* Lanchbery's orchestration of Satie's *Préludes d'Eginhard* was played as an overture. The *Gymnopédies* pas de trois is still sometimes performed by itself.

These works are Frederick Ashton's most sustained and extreme exposition of adagio classicism. No subject matter is implicit. The dancers of each trio remain onstage throughout, as in his *Symphonic Variations.* Unusually for Ashton, they are revealed amid encompassing darkness by side and top lighting. In *Gymnopédies,* this effect, combined with the remote calm of Satie's music and the dancers' white leotards and tights, suggest astronauts in space. That Ashton's more specific concerns were the changing geometries described by the dance and the forms of classical ballet was apparent in *Trois Gnossiennes.* Both *Monotones I* and *II* feature unison adagio work and complex partnering.

The dances demonstrated the Royal Ballet's mastery and development of the Cecchetti method in ballet, its control in adagio, its precision, and its *épaulement.* Both parts of *Monotones* refer to motifs from *Symphonic Variations,* and *Trois Gnossiennes* echoes George Balanchine's *Apollo.* Remarkable in both are the lack of climax, the changing rhythms of the dance set on or against the rhythms of the music, and the long, seamless phrasing.

BIBLIOGRAPHY

Croce, Arlene. "How to Be Very, Very Popular." In Croce's *Afterimages.* New York, 1977.

Hall, Fernau. "*Monotones.*" *Ballet Today* (May–June, July–August 1966).

Vaughan, David. *Frederick Ashton and His Ballets.* London, 1977.

ALASTAIR MACAULAY

MONPLAISIR, HIPPOLYTE AND ADÈLE (Hippolyte Georges Sornet; born 1821 in Bordeaux, France, died 10 June 1877 in Besana, Italy; and Adèle Bartholomin; *fl.* 1840s–1860s), French dancers. As the leading dancers of the first large-scale European ballet company to visit the United States, Hippolyte and Adèle Monplaisir, who were husband and wife, played a major role in bringing the Romantic ballet to American audiences. Their greatest single success was their restaging of Jules Perrot's masterpiece *La Esmeralda* (1844). Their many tours spanned the country, and they often played return engagements in cities such as New York and New Orleans, where they were always warmly received. In later life they separated and concluded their careers in Europe.

As dancers, the Monplaisirs were known for their technical virtuosity and vigorous attack. They excelled in balleticized national dances, following the precedent set by Fanny Elssler. Many of their ballets included folk-flavored pas de deux, which they also performed, like Elssler, as independent dances. Otherwise, their choreography was typical of the era.

Some of the most vivid evocations of their dancing have come from the New Orleans journal *L'Abeille de la Nouvelle Orléans.* On their first season there in January 1848, "A. F." wrote of Adèle,

> Rien n'égale la grâce, l'abandon, la fougueuse *morbidezza* de tous ses mouvements, la souplisse de ces corps qui ploie et se tord comme un serpent, le nerf et l'incomparable vigueur de ces deux pieds.
> (Nothing can equal the grace, the freedom, the spirited "softness" of all her movements, the suppleness of her body, which bends and writhes like a snake, the nerve and incomparable vigor of her feet.)

In 1849 "Jacques de R" described her dancing as

> vive, petulante, et quelque peu désordonnée. . . . Les tours de force lesplus audacieux, les poses les plus provocantes, les pirouettes les plus rapides et les plus interminable, mme Monplaisir les exécute en se jouant et *con amore.*
> (lively, impetuous, and a bit untidy. . . . The most audacious tours de force, the most provocative poses, the fastest and most endless pirouettes Mme Monplaisir executes playfully and lovingly.)

He found Hippolyte less satisfactory:

> Sa danse manque de moelleux, elle est trop virile; mais opposée à celle de sa femme, elle se complète et alors le défaut disparait.
> (His dancing lacks softness; it is too virile; but opposite that of his wife it is made whole and thus the fault disappears.)

The ballets mounted by the Monplaisirs in the United States were frequently lavish in scenery and costumes; as one reviewer noted of their production of *Le Diable à Quatre,* "No miserable economy marks the ballet in any respect." This attention to the production, which paralleled European trends, helped to draw in audiences and introduce more Americans to the art of ballet.

Little is known about the Monplaisirs' early lives in Europe. Hippolyte began his career in Brussels, where he studied with Guillemin, the *premier danseur* of the Théâtre de la Monnaie, and made his debut in 1839. It is not known where he met Adèle Bartholomin, whose father, Victor, was a dancer, mime, and ballet master at La Monnaie until 1836. In 1844 the Monplaisirs were engaged as leading dancers at the Teatro alla Scala, Milan, where they probably studied with Carlo Blasis. Their first season was shared by two illustrious ballerinas, Fanny Elssler and Lucile Grahn. Hippolyte partnered Elssler in Antonio Cortesi's three-act version of *Giselle,* in which they made the ill-fated experiment of interpolating the *cracovienne* from *La Gipsy* into the first act; it was eliminated after one performance. Elssler restaged Perrot's *La Délire d'un Peintre,* which under different titles became a staple of the Monplaisirs' repertory in the United States.

MONPLASIR. The Monplaisirs dancing "La Zingarilla" in *L'Almée,* billed as a "grand Asiatic ballet" and performed under the direction of V. Bartholomin at the Broadway Theater, New York, in the 1840s. Lithographed music cover after R. de Trobriand (New York, 1847). (Courtesy of Madison U. Sowell and Debra H. Sowell, Brigham Young University.)

The Monplaisirs danced at La Scala until 1846, laying the foundation for much of their later work. In 1845 Perrot restaged *La Esmeralda* there for Elssler, one of the greatest interpreters of the ballet's title role. Marie Taglioni was a guest artist in 1846, for a season that included a revival of Joseph Mazilier's *Le Diable à Quatre,* which the Monplaisirs also took to America. The couple went to Trieste for the 1846/47 season and also danced in Barcelona and Lyon. Hippolyte's first ballet, *Azelia, or The Syrian Slave,* was first produced in Barcelona.

The Monplaisirs and Victor Bartholomin then formed a ballet company that made its U.S. debut on 21 October 1847 at the Broadway Theater in New York City. The company also included Madame Bartholomin; Anna Bulan, a ballerina from Trieste; A. Grossi, a mime from the Paris Opera; and the comic dancer Corby from Bordeaux, who became the most popular member of the troupe after the Monplaisirs themselves. He was apparently small in stature, for the Monplaisir libretti for *L'Almée* and *Esmer-*

alda describe the characters he played as dwarfs. Two Americans, Sallie St. Clair and Celeste Williams, who went by the name Mademoiselle Celeste, also joined the company.

The opening performance featured Bartholomin's *L'Almée,* an Oriental fantasy reminiscent of Perrot's *La Péri* (1843). In it, Zuliska (Bulan), a harem girl, yearns for the young sultan Nadhir (Hippolyte), who is in turn obsessed by a woman he has seen only in dreams, the *almah* (dancing-girl) Haydée (Adèle). When he meets her at last, the frustrated Zuliska plots against them with El Kebir (Bartholomin), who lusts after her. A fire breaks out as Nadhir and Haydée are celebrating their wedding; they escape, only to confront Zuliska, who tries to stab Haydée. However, Zisco (Corby), a musician who loves Haydée, intercepts the fatal blow.

The ballet included a *pas des bayadères* for the ladies of the harem; a dream scene similar to that in *La Péri,* in which Nadhir sees a vision of Haydée; and the pas de deux "La Zingarilla," which became the Monplaisirs' most frequently performed dance.

L'Almée was followed on 2 November by Bartholomin's *La Jeune Dalmate, ou Le Retour au Village* (first produced in Lyon in 1838). This was a more complex version of the much-used theme of a peasant girl who loves a nobleman: Elina (Adèle) is torn between her love for Eric (Hippolyte) and her guilt and remorse at allowing him to carry her off to his castle. The ballet skillfully contrasted the folk-flavored dances in act 1—in which Eric, like Albrecht in *Giselle,* appears in disguise to dance a Polka National with Elina—with a glittering court ball in act 2. Like La Zingarilla, the Polka National was often performed independently.

Hippolyte's *Azelia,* presented in New York on 24 November 1847, had a Middle Eastern setting like that of *L'Almée.* In this rather slender story of harem intrigues, the Syrian slave Azelia (Adèle) is pursued by old Isouf (Corby), abetted by the keeper of the harem (Madame Bartholomin). She prefers, however, the young Selim (Hippolyte), who is actually a prince disguised as a slave to test her love. The dances included a *pas de séduction* for Azelia and Isouf, a *pas tartare* danced by Mademoiselle Yates and the mime Grossi—and, testifying to the artistic license permitted in nineteenth-century ballet, a pas de deux from *Giselle,* danced by the Monplaisirs.

The company's first season in New York was rounded out by Perrot's *La Folie d'un Peintre,* Bartholomin's *Les Deux Roses,* and the pas de deux *Le Contrabandier Espagnole.* At the close of the season, the company embarked on a U.S. tour that included Boston, Charleston, New Orleans, Louisville, and Philadelphia.

Upon their return to the Broadway Theater in July 1848, the Monplaisirs presented Mazilier's *Le Diable à Quatre,* with Adèle, Hippolyte, Bulan, and Corby as the enchanted quartet. The company then moved to the Park Theater, where on 18 September it presented Perrot's *Esmeralda* for the first time in the United States. The libretto closely followed Perrot's. Adèle played the title role, first danced by Carlotta Grisi, while Hippolyte played Perrot's own role of Pierre Gringoire. The cast also included Grossi as the villainous Claude Frollo, Corby as Quasimodo, Cornet as the handsome Phoebus, and Bulan as his fiancée, Fleur-de-Lys.

Adèle's Esmeralda was rapturously received. "Each time she spurned the earth," wrote the *Spirit of the Times,* "and sought a midaerial position, we experienced a tendency to leave the soles of our boots; at each rattle of the tambourine we fell victims to a palpitation of the heart, and the execution of a prolonged *tour de force* induced an equally lasting fit of mental delirium tremens." More sedately, the *New York Herald* declared her "worthy of the highest rank as a *danseuse* and *comédienne,*" and noted that Hippolyte "rendered his part . . . with a *naiveté,* a *bonhomie,* which proved that he deeply knew the character of his part; his dancing was as wonderful as it was difficult." The supporting cast and the elaborate costumes and scenery were also highly praised.

Esmeralda proved to be so popular that it displaced the English tragedian William Charles Macready, who had been scheduled to follow it. Two other novelties were given during the season. *Love! Despair! and Champagne!* (later titled *Spleen and Champagne*) was a comic vehicle for Corby. *Liberty, or The Four Quarters of the World* featured personifications of America (Adèle), Europe (St. Clair), Asia (Mademoiselle Waldegrave), and Africa (Bulan). On 16 December, catastrophe struck—a fire caused by a gas jet burned down the Park Theater, destroying most of the company's sets and costumes. Fortunately all the performers escaped unhurt.

Victor Bartholomin probably left the company sometime in 1848, perhaps to return to Europe. Neither he nor Madame Bartholomin is listed among the large cast of *Esmeralda.* Hippolyte became the sole head of the company.

February 1849 found the company in New Orleans, where it danced in the operas *Robert le Diable* and *La Muette de Portici* as well as in ballets. Hippolyte's *Les Follets des Alpes* (later titled *The Goblin of the Alps*) was presented on 26 February; this was a *grand pas fantastique* danced to Gioacchino Rossini's *William Tell* overture. A more topical theme was danced by Corby as part of *Un Bal Travesti:* as the man who returns in 1850 from the 1849 California gold rush, he wore clothes covered with gold.

After a season in Mobile, Alabama, the company returned to New York. The major offering of the season, presented at the Broadway Theater on 28 May 1849, was Hippolyte's *Folletta, or The Enchanted Bell.* In this elaborate *ballet-féerie* set in China, the genie Folletta (Adèle) helps Yanko (Hippolyte), an Indian prince disguised as a peasant, to win the hand of the princess Tshingka (Bulan). The company also danced that year in Philadelphia and New Orleans, where it performed the seminal Romantic ballet *La Sylphide.*

The Monplaisirs' movements in the United States and Europe are not yet fully documented. The historian Lillian Moore's pioneering research indicates that they may have visited Mexico in late 1849. In October and November 1850 they were in Charleston, restaging the Romantic ballets *L'Ombre, The Judgment of Paris,* and *Catarina,* possibly learned during an intervening trip to Europe. A year later they were again in New Orleans, where they danced from November 1851 to May 1852; their extensive repertory included restagings of *La Tentation,* the *opéra-ballet La Bayadère,* and ballets by Hippolyte, such as *Ketly, or The Mountain Rose, The Carnival of Rome,* and the *Grand Pas de Kossuth,* a tribute to the Hungarian hero Lajos Kossuth, then visiting the United States. Hippolyte also appeared as an actor during this engagement.

In 1854 the company was in California, dancing the "grand Chinese fantasy" *Kim-Ka* and a tribute to the gold rush, *The Female Forty Thieves, or The Daughters of the Golden West* (Cohen, 1976).

It is not yet known when the company disbanded or when Adèle and Hippolyte separated. In November 1855 Hippolyte, alone, appeared in New York, dancing in Giacomo Meyerbeer's opera *Le Prophète* at the Academy of Music. He was still in the city in January 1856, staging dances for Laura Keene's Varieties Theater.

Adèle returned to New Orleans in March 1856, on her way back from California, accompanied by Émile Gredelue and her new partner Léon Espinosa. On 26 November she and Espinosa danced with the company of Antoine and Jerome Ravel in a new production of *Esmeralda* at Niblo's Garden in New York. In the title role, reported *Frank Leslie's Illustrated Newspaper,* she "displayed all that graceful and elegant ability for which she is so famed. The finished beauty of her poses, and the dashing vigor of her tours de force, were the themes of general comment and admiration." Her supporting cast included Espinosa as Pierre Gringoire, Antoine Ravel as Claude Frollo, and Jerome Ravel as Quasimodo.

She continued to dance with the Ravels for at least another year. *Esmeralda* was revived for a second season at Niblo's Garden in February and March 1857. When the company returned in August, a more varied repertory was introduced. Adèle danced in and may have staged her father's ballet *L'Almée,* in addition to dancing her other principal roles.

Hippolyte was engaged as first dancer by the Teatro São Carlos in Lisbon for the 1856/57 season, but a foot injury forced him to turn to choreography. Although his ballets were considered inferior to those of his predecessor, Arthur Saint-Léon, he was reengaged as choreographer for the 1859/60 season.

Meanwhile Adèle and Espinosa returned to Paris to dance at the Théâtre de la Porte-Saint-Martin. Espinosa choreographed at least two ballets there, *Le Jockey du Diable* and *Le Carrousel* (both 1859); they also danced in plays there and at the Théâtre de l'Ambigu-Comique. They last appeared at the Porte-Saint-Martin in the *féerie* called *Le Pied de Mouton,* which opened on 8 September 1860; they subsequently took this play on a European tour that included Vienna, Berlin, Stockholm, and Copenhagen. To date, little is known of Adèle's later life. Like her husband, she began to choreograph: her *divertissement* called *L'Amour Vaincu* was given at the Théâtre du Vaudeville in Paris on 8 May 1871.

Hippolyte returned to La Scala, Milan, and mounted his first ballet for that theater, *Benvenuto Cellini,* on 24 August 1861. Inspired by the life of the raffish sixteenth-century sculptor and raconteur, the ballet ended by acclaiming Italy as queen of the arts. Hippolyte created or restaged some fourteen ballets for La Scala and also worked in Genoa, Naples, Rome, and Turin. Approximately one-third of his Italian works were composed by Costantino Dall'Argine. The titles of the ballets—*La Devâdâcy* (1866), *Brahma* (1868), *Le Figlie di Chèope* (1871), and *L'Almea* (1872)—reflect his attraction to Asia and the Middle East, first revealed in *Azelia. Brahma,* his most enduring ballet, depicted the quest of the Hindu god (danced by Efisio Catte) "for a pure and disinterested love, through which he can gain readmittance to Paradise" (Guest, 1977); this was achieved through the self-sacrifice of the slave girl Padmana (Amalia Ferraris). Set in China, India, and the Dutch East Indies, the ballet provided plenty of opportunities for exotic spectacle. It included a nautch dance and the character dance "La Mogolienne," named for the Mughal rulers of India. Hippolyte revived the ballet in 1873 for Virginia Zucchi, who restaged it in Saint Petersburg in 1884. It was revived in Paris as late as 1912.

Hippolyte found a second major source of inspiration in historical characters like Cellini. His ballets in this genre include *Cristoforo Colombo* (1861), *Nostradamus* (1862), *La Camargo* (1868), and *Giulio Cesare* (1874). Despite the prestige of his leading ballerinas (who included Caterina Beretta, Claudina Cucchi, Ferraris, Olimpia Priora, and Zucchi), Hippolyte's works are little known today. His final years, like Adèle's, are shadowy. His last ballet, *Loreley,* was created in 1877, the year of his death.

BIBLIOGRAPHY

Cohen, Selma Jeanne. "The Fourth of July, or, The Independence of American Dance." *Dance Magazine* 50 (July 1976): 49–53.

Guest, Ivor. *The Divine Virginia: A Biography of Virginia Zucchi.* New York, 1977.

Moore, Lillian. "Esmeralda in America." *Dance Magazine* 28 (October 1954): 31–32. Reprinted in Moore's *Echoes of American Ballet*. Brooklyn, 1976.

Moore, Lillian. "Monplaisir, Ippolito Giorgio." In *Enciclopedia dello spettacolo*. Rome, 1954–.

Odell, George C. D. *Annals of the New York Stage*. Vols. 5–7. New York, 1931.

SUSAN AU

MONTENEGRO. *See* Yugoslavia.

MONTH IN THE COUNTRY, A. Ballet in one act. Choreography: Frederick Ashton. Music: Frédéric Chopin, arranged by John Lanchbery. Libretto: Frederick Ashton, based on the play by Ivan Turgenev. Scenery and costumes: Julia Trevelyan Oman. First performance: 12 February 1976, Royal Opera House, Covent Garden, London, Royal Ballet. Principals: Lynn Seymour (Natalia Petrovna), Anthony Dowell (Beliaev), Denise Munn (Vera), Wayne Sleep (Kolia), Marguerite Porter (Katia), Derek Rencher (Rakitin), Alexander Grant (Yslaev).

A MONTH IN THE COUNTRY. Lynn Seymour as Natalia Petrovna and Anthony Dowell as Beliaev. (Photograph from the Dance Collection, New York Public Library for the Performing Arts.)

For his choreographic account of Ivan Turgenev's play *A Month in the Country,* Frederick Ashton selected three of Chopin's works for piano and orchestra: Variations on "Là ci darem la mano" from Mozart's *Don Giovanni* (op. 2), Fantasy on Polish Airs (op. 13), and Andante Spianato and Grande Polonaise in E-flat Major (op. 22). Ashton worked with Martyn Thomas in constructing the action of the ballet "to accord with the music."

The original program synopsis is as follows:

> The action takes place at Yslaev's country house in 1850. Beliaev, a young student, engaged as a tutor for Kolia, disrupts the emotional stability of the household. Finally Rakitin, Natalia's admirer, insists that he and the tutor must both leave in order to restore a semblance of calm to Yslaev's family life.

John Lanchbery arranged the score with minor adjustments to suit this scenario.

Ashton concentrated on the characters of Natalia Petrovna and Beliaev, eliminating several of Turgenev's characters and reducing Rakitin's significance. Also given prominence are Natalia's ward Vera, her young son Kolia, and the maid Katia.

Ashton described the structure of the ballet as operatic, with dance arias and interludes of mime or more naturalistic movement serving the same function as recitative. The work demonstrates his talent for characterization, as in the opening, when, to the first variations on "Là ci darem," the characters of the household are established by dance solos and mime passages.

The action accompanying the Fantasy on Polish Airs demonstrates Ashton's ability to encapsulate complex narrative in concise choreography. Natalia confesses her affection for Beliaev to her admirer Rakitin; Beliaev has quite different duets with Vera and Katia; and in a swiftly moving mime scene, Natalia rebukes Vera for her indiscreet behavior, Vera confesses her love for Beliaev, and Natalia explains that such a relationship can lead to nothing. In the dances to the Andante Spianato, Natalia's own more powerful passion becomes apparent in a duet with Beliaev, as she draws him into reciprocating it. Vera, discovering them, summons the household; Natalia laughs off the situation; Rakitin suggests to Beliaev that his presence has caused quite enough trouble; and Beliaev departs, leaving Natalia alone at curtain fall.

In the two decades since its premiere, *A Month in the Country* has been performed well over a hundred times at Covent Garden as well as numerous times on tour. Lynn Seymour and Antony Dowell always enjoyed particular success in the leading roles. Other important performers who have played them include Merle Park, Natalia Makarova, Antoinette Sibley, Altynai Asylmuratova, Sylvie Guillem, and Genesia Rosato as Natalia and David Wall and Mikhail Baryshnikov as Beliaev. The role of Natalia is unusual in ballet in that it portrays the complex emotions and character of a mature woman living within the strictures of her social class.

BIBLIOGRAPHY

Anderson, Jack. *Choreography Observed.* Iowa City, 1987.

Jordan, Stephanie. "*A Month in the Country:* The Organization of a Score." *Dance Research Journal* 11.1–2 (1978–1979): 20–24.

Vaughan, David. *Frederick Ashton and His Ballets.* London, 1977.

ALASTAIR MACAULAY

MOORE, LILLIAN (born 20 September 1911 in Chase City, Virginia, died 28 July 1967 in New York City), American dancer, teacher, historian, and author. Moore received her dance training at Peabody Conservatory (1923–1928); with Charles Weidman (1931–1933); at the Metropolitan Opera Ballet School, under Boris Romanov, Rosina Galli, Margaret Curtis, and Laurent Novikoff; at the School of American Ballet, under George Balanchine, Pierre Vladimiroff, Anatole Vilzak, Ludmilla Schollar, and Muriel Stuart; in Europe, under Hedy Pfundmayer, Lubov Egorova, and Tamara Karsavina; and with Aleksandra Fedorova in New York City. She also attended Goucher College (1927–1928). In 1935 she married David Craine Maclay.

Moore danced with the Metropolitan Opera from 1928 to 1934 and from 1939 to 1942, becoming a soloist in 1931. From 1935 to 1938 she danced with Balanchine's American Ballet in concerts, operas, and the film *Goldwyn Follies.* Her first article, "When Fanny Danced: New York in the [Eighteen] Forties as seen by Fanny Elssler," was published in the 29 November 1938 issue of *Theatre Guild Magazine,* and her first book, *Artists of the Dance,* was published in 1938.

From 1940 to 1946 Moore was *première danseuse,* choreographer, and ballet mistress for the Cincinnati Summer Opera Company; she was a soloist with several opera companies between 1941 and 1945; and she toured with the stars of the Metropolitan Opera from 1943 to 1947. During World War II she performed with the United Service Organizations (USO) Camp Shows Pacific Tour (1945–1946), and after the war she danced with the U.S. Army Special Services in Europe (1947–1948). In November 1948, after a stint as the American participant at the International Music Festival held that June in Vienna, she gave solo recitals in Vienna, Budapest, and Italy.

Moore was a dancer for Jacob's Pillow Dance Festival from 1950 to 1952, and she went on U.S. solo tours from 1951 to 1953. After teaching ballet and dance history at the New York High School of Performing Arts (1950–1958), she went on to teach at Robert Joffrey's American Ballet Center (1958–1967). There she was especially noted for classes completely devoted to the execution of various forms of pirouettes, for her staging of dances from August Bournonville's ballets, and for her role, beginning in 1966, as director of the apprentice and scholarship program.

Moore assisted Walter Terry as an associate dance critic at the *New York Herald Tribune* (1950–1965), and she was acting curator of the Dance Collection of the New York Public Library for the Performing Arts in 1954. Also in 1954 she retired from performing to devote herself to teaching, research, and writing.

By the 1950s Moore was acknowledged as the leading dance historian in the United States. That reputation soon became international as her writings appeared in, among other publications, *The Dancing Times* (1930–1967), *Encyclopaedia Britannica* (1959) and its *Book of the Year* (1951–1959 and 1965–1966), *Enciclopedia dello spettacolo, Ballet Annual,* the *New York Times, Opera News, Musical Courier, Ballet Today, Dance News,* and *Dance Magazine.*

Moore received a Rockefeller grant (1955–1957) to produce a history of theater dance in the United States, but she never completed the project. She was adjudicator for the National Association for Regional Ballet from 1959 to 1966 and was a member of the President's Advisory Commission on the Arts from 1960 to 1967.

A self-taught dance historian, Moore was one of the first American dance scholars. Her writing was characterized by relentless research, accuracy, and thoroughness. She also had an insatiable curiosity when it came to unexplored subjects, and this led her to publish monographs on "The Petipa Family in Europe and America" (May 1942), "John Durang, the First American Dancer" (August 1942), "Mary Ann Lee: First American Giselle" (May 1943), "George Washington Smith" (June–August 1945), and "Moreau de Saint-Méry and Dance" (October 1946), all in *Dance Index,* and "The Duport Mystery" (1960) and "Prints on Pushcarts" (1962) in *Dance Perspectives.*

Moore's writings have become invaluable standard sources for the history of dance in the United States, Romantic ballet, and Bournonville technique. Her interest in the Danish choreographer led to *Bournonville and Ballet Technique* (1961), with Erik Bruhn as her coauthor, and her monograph *Bournonville's London Spring* (1965). *Images of the Dance* (1965) was published by the New York Public Library to celebrate the opening of its Dance Collection at Lincoln Center. *Echoes of American Ballet* (1976), an anthology of selected essays, was published posthumously. Her personal collection, including books, prints, statuettes, scrapbooks, correspondence, notebooks, manuscripts, and memorabilia, was bequeathed to the Dance Collection of the New York Public Library for the Performing Arts and to the Harvard Theater Collection.

ARCHIVES. Dance Collection, New York Public Library for the Performing Arts; Harvard Theater Collection, Harvard College Library, Cambridge, Massachusetts, the Lillian Moore File, Goucher College, Towson, Maryland; and the Peabody Conservatory, Baltimore.

CHRYSTELLE TRUMP BOND

MOOR'S PAVANE, THE. Choreography: José Limón. Music: *The Gordian Knot Untied* and *Abdelzar Suite* by Henry Purcell, arranged by Simon Sadoff. Costumes: Pauline Lawrence. First performance: 17 August 1949, American Dance Festival, Connecticut College, New London, Connecticut. Principals: José Limón (The Moor), Betty Jones (The Moor's Wife), Lucas Hoving (His Friend), Pauline Koner (His Friend's Wife).

The Moor's Pavane is considered José Limón's signature work and masterpiece. Subtitling the work *Variations on the Theme of Othello,* he sought not simply to create a dance version of Shakespeare's play but also "to bring forth all the passion, grandeur, all the tragedy" (Limón Papers). The pavane, a court dance, serves as a structure within which the plot and the characters' emotions are given a formal, understated expression. The story unfolds through stylized gesture, facial expression, and the spatial patterning of the dancers. As dramatic episodes alternate with the stately pavane, elegance and control are juxtaposed with passionate intensity, building the tension to its inevitable climax.

THE MOOR'S PAVANE. The original cast of José Limón's signature work. Limón (The Moor) clutches the all-important handkerchief as he bows to Betty Jones (The Moor's Wife); onlookers Lucas Hoving (His Friend) and Pauline Koner (His Friend's Wife) kneel in the background. (Photograph from the archives at Jacob's Pillow, Becket, Massachusetts.)

The dance opens as the two couples, facing each other, join hands to begin the pavane. The Moor gives his wife a lace handkerchief and, as they dance, the friend insinuates himself between them. He then turns to his own wife and draws her into his plot as the other two stand frozen at the side of the stage. They all return to the pavane; the friend's wife seizes the handkerchief when it is accidentally dropped. The two women stand unmoving at the side of the stage as the friend tells the Moor slanderous tales about his wife. The Moor's disbelief translates into a stylized fight between the two men. The handkerchief is produced and the Moor's rage at his wife explodes. Stepping downstage, the friend and his wife veil the murder, then draw aside in horror as the Moor despairingly reveals his wife's body.

In 1950, José Limón received a *Dance Magazine* Award for *The Moor's Pavane.* Major companies that have performed *The Moor's Pavane* are American Ballet Theatre, Compañía Nacional de Danza (Mexico City), Dresden Ballet, English National Ballet, Hamburg Ballet, Joffrey Ballet, Maggio Danza (Florence), Miami City Ballet, Nureyev and Friends, Oakland Ballet, Pacific Northwest Ballet, Paris Opera Ballet, Pennsylvania Ballet, Royal Danish Ballet, Royal Swedish Ballet, and the National Ballet of Canada. It also remains in the repertory of the Limón Company.

BIBLIOGRAPHY

Horst, Louis. "The Moor's Pavane Seventh Premiere of Dance Festival." *Evening Day* (New London, Conn.) (18 August 1949).

Koner, Pauline. "The Truth about *The Moor's Pavane.*" *Ballet Review* 8.4 (1980): 386–396.

Krasovskaya, Vera. "Ballet Changes, Shakespeare Endures." *Ballet Review* 19 (Summer 1991): 71–80.

Loveless, Robert C. "Limón Exquisitely Revered in Dance." *Honolulu Star-Bulletin* (4 December 1972).

Martin, John. "Limón Work Given at Dance Festival." *New York Times* (21 August 1949).

McDonagh, Don. *The Rise and Fall and Rise of Modern Dance.* Rev. ed. Pennington, N.J., 1990.

Mindlin, Naomi. "José Limón's *The Moor's Pavane:* An Interview with Lucas Hoving." *Dance Research Journal* 24 (Spring 1992): 13–26.

Reynolds, Nancy, and Susan Reimer-Torn. *Dance Classics.* Pennington, N.J., 1991.

ARCHIVE. José Limón Papers, Dance Collection, New York Public Library for the Performing Arts.

DANIEL LEWIS and LESLEY FARLOW

MORDKIN, MIKHAIL (Mikhail Mikhailovich Mordkin; born 21 December 1880 [2 January 1881] in Moscow, died 15 July 1944 in Millbrook, New Jersey), Russian dancer and choreographer. Mordkin graduated from the Moscow Theater School in 1900, after studying with Vasily Tikhomirov, and joined the Bolshoi Ballet. In school he had created leading classical, character, and mime roles in ballets. In 1898 he danced the Subaltern in *La Halte de Cavalerie;* in 1899 he danced Colin in *La Fille Mal Gardée,* Yuri in *The Magic Mirror,* and the Spirit of Fire and the Spanish variation in *The Magic Shoes.* Upon graduation Mordkin performed Ivan Clustine's role in *Stars* and created the leading roles in Aleksandr Gorsky's versions of *Swan Lake, Giselle,* and *The Sleeping Beauty.*

Mordkin and Gorsky forged a distinct Moscow school centered in plastique, drama, and characterization. For his mime dramas Gorsky found in Mordkin an ideal interpreter who based his roles on improvisation and psychological insight. Mordkin rebelled against the stereotyping of roles and included angular and awkward movements if he thought them appropriate. Refusing to serve as a mere *porteur,* Mordkin insisted that male and female roles receive equal treatment. His muscular physique and emotive vigor became the paradigm for the Moscow school. This conception also became the standard by which male dancing was judged in America after Mordkin's pioneering tours there.

Mordkin created many roles in Gorsky's ballets: Phoebus in *Gudule's Daughter,* Conrad in *Le Corsaire,* Jean de Brienne in *Raymonda,* King Hitaris in *La Fille du Pharaon,* Mato in *Salammbô,* Nur in *Nur and Anitra,* Solor in *La Bayadère,* the Norwegian Fisherman in *Love Is Quick!,* Sonnewald in *Schubertiana,* the Khan in *The Little Humpbacked Horse,* Espada and later Basil in *Don Quixote,* Petronius in *Eunice and Petronius,* and Colin in *La Fille Mal Gardée.* A teacher in the Bolshoi school, he was also appointed *régisseur* in 1904 and an assistant ballet master in 1905. He gave independent concerts at other Moscow theaters and in 1905 inaugurated a course in plastique at the Adashev Art Theater.

Mordkin performed in Serge Diaghilev's first Paris season in 1909 in *Le Pavillon d'Armide.* He and Anna Pavlova then formed a partnership, dancing in revues at London's Palace Theatre and on tours across the United States. They made their Metropolitan Opera debut in February 1910 in *Coppélia.* Their repertory consisted mostly of *divertissements,* including Mordkin's Glazunov *Bacchanale,* and one-act ballets like his *Legend of Aziade,* one of his best-known works, choreographed to a pastiche score and apparently inspired by Michel Fokine's Orientalism. When the partnership dissolved in 1911 in professional jealousies, Mordkin embarked on a tour of the United States with his All-Star Imperial Russian Ballet, a group that included Ekaterina Geltser, Julia Sedova, Carlotta Zambelli, Lydia Lopokova, Vera Karalli, Alexandre Volinine, and Lydia Sokolova. Internal dissension caused the principals to leave, and the tour ended prematurely. Mordkin went into the Broadway show *Vera Violetta,* performing his own *divertissements.* He and his wife, Bronislava Pozhitskaya, also established a ballet school at the Winter Garden in New York City.

MORDKIN. Known for his strong characterization and sense of drama, Mordkin struck a pensive pose for this 1916 studio portrait of Solor, the leading male role in *La Bayadère.* (Photograph from the Dance Collection, New York Public Library for the Performing Arts.)

Mordkin returned to the Bolshoi in 1912; there his repertory turned to plastique and mime. He also choreographed, and his popular *Italian Beggar,* to music by Camille Saint-Saëns, entered the repertory in 1916. A version of his *Legend of Aziade* was performed in 1917/18 in a Moscow circus, and a film of the ballet with Mordkin and Margarita Froman was released in 1918. He choreographed interludes for Molière's *Le Malade Imaginaire* for Konstantin Stanislavsky's Moscow Art Theater in 1913, performed and choreographed for the Moscow Free Theater, and taught dance and plastique in his home and in private schools.

In 1918 Mordkin left the Bolshoi to tour across Russia. In 1919 he set dances for a production of Lope de Vega's *Sheep Spring* in Kiev. He settled in Tiflis in 1920 to teach and produce ballets and *divertissements,* including Schumann's *Le Carnaval* and *Flowers of Granada* to music by Moritz Moszkowski (both 1922), and *The Pearl of Seville* to music by Cesare Pugni (1924). He briefly returned to the Bolshoi as dancer and director in 1922, but conditions there forced him to leave again.

In 1923 Mordkin, Viktorina Kriger, and a troupe of dancers left for an American tour, and Mordkin remained in the United States. Under the direction of Morris Gest he danced in the 1924 *Greenwich Village Follies* and toured for two years with Ksenia Makletsova and Vera Nemchinova. His Studio of Dance Arts opened in New York City in 1924. From 1926 to 1928 the Mordkin Russian Ballet, a company founded as a performance outlet for his students, toured the United States with Vera Nemchinova, Pierre Vladimiroff, and Hilda Butsova. By the early 1930s Mordkin had five schools in the New York City area, and in 1935 he mounted a full-length version of *The Sleeping Beauty* with his students. Haphazard in matters of technique, Mordkin was nonetheless an inspirational teacher of emotive, demonstrative dancing.

Mordkin's last company, the Mordkin Ballet, was the basis of Ballet Theatre. Formed in 1937 it had Mordkin as choreographer and director, Rudolph Orthwine as managing director, Mordkin's son Michael as business manager, and ballerina Lucia Chase as principal backer. Its first performances were given in April 1937 at the Majestic Theater in New York, with Mordkin's versions of *Giselle* and *The Goldfish.* The company included Patricia Bowman, Lucia Chase, Viola Essen, and Dimitri Romanoff. The repertory consisted of Mordkin's choreography and his versions of the classics, including *La Fille Mal Gardée, Giselle, The Sleeping Beauty, Voices of Spring* to music by Johann Strauss, *Trepak* and *The Goldfish,* both to music by Nikolai Tcherepnin, and *Swan Lake.* Mordkin returned to the stage as the Old Fisherman in the premiere of *The Goldfish* and as Marcelina in *La Fille Mal Gardée,* the General in *Voices of Spring,* and the Devil in *Trepak.*

In 1939 Mordkin lost a power struggle to the company's manager, Richard Pleasant, who reformed it as a repertory company with multiple choreographers and renamed it Ballet Theatre. Mordkin's association with Ballet Theatre ended in December 1939, a month before the premiere performances; only one of his works, *Voices of Spring,* remained in the repertory. He returned to teaching until his death in 1944.

BIBLIOGRAPHY

Krasovskaya, Vera. *Russkii baletnyi teatr nachala dvadtsatogo veka,* vol. 2, *Tantsovshchiki.* Leningrad, 1972.

Mordkin, Mikhail, and Vera Caspary. "The Story of My Life" (parts 1–4). *Dance Magazine* (December 1925–March 1926).

Payne, Charles, et al. *American Ballet Theatre.* New York, 1977.

Relkin, Abbie. "In Pavlova's Shadow." *Ballet News* 2 (January 1981): 26–29.

Smakov, Gennady. *The Great Russian Dancers.* New York, 1984.

Souritz, Elizabeth. *Soviet Choreographers in the 1920s.* Translated by Lynn Visson. Durham, N.C., 1990.

Suzanne Carbonneau

MORESCA. The *moresca* (Fr., *mourisque, moresque;* Eng., *Morris, Morris dance*; Ger., *Moriskentanz, Maruschka-Tanz*) has been performed as a court dance, ballroom dance, folk dance, dance spectacle, and *entrée de ballet* with exotic, bizarre, foreign, comic, and grotesque traits, frequently involving bells and masks or the blackening of the face. Documented since the twelfth century, it flourished in the Renaissance and is still practiced in Europe and Latin America and in the American Southwest.

The *moresca*'s history is complicated. Through the centuries, as it spread geographically, the dance assumed many different shapes, merged with existing local and folk dance traditions, absorbed ritualistic motifs from Christianity and local religious traditions, and was part of courtly entertainments as well as of civic and popular festivals. It overlapped with other dances, including "Les Bouffons" (in Thoinot Arbeau's *Orchésographie,* 1588), "Les Mattachins" (in Jacques Callot's *Balli di Sfessania* c.1621/22), the *canario,* and the *folía,* as well as with folk tales and their dramatizations (such as Robin Hood plays).

Mercurialis, in *De arte gymnastica* (1572) mentions the use of the name *morisca* for the sword dance in Europe. Any investigation of the *moresca* is further complicated by the fact that in literary references through the centuries the term is often used as a synonym for the unusual, the strange, the mysterious, and the wild in dance spectacles of all kinds.

From the masses of literary and pictorial documents, however, three fundamental choreographic types emerge: the mock-battle *moresca,* either in the form of a mass choreography whose participants imitate two fighting armies or in a more dancelike longways formation in which two lines of participants confront one another; the linear *moresca* with its variants of circle and free-form patterns; and the solo *moresca* for the single performer or, at most, two or three participants.

Of these three, the mock-battle *moresca,* or confrontation *moresca,* is probably the oldest. It reflects the battles between Christians and Moors that took place in Spain during the Middle Ages, the reenactments of which began the tradition and gave the genre its name. One of the earliest such spectacles was the performance of "Moros y Cristianos" (Moors and Christians) at Lérida, Spain, in 1150 on the occasion of the marriage of Queen Petronila of Aragon and Count Ramón Berenguer IV of Catalonia (Capmany, 1934, p. 384). From then on, mock battles were a part of tournaments, jousts, banquets, and other courtly entertainments (see those cited in Brainard, 1981; Chambers, 1978; Domokos, 1968; Heartz, 1960; Pirro, 1940). At times such mock battles were fought with real weapons, at others they were danced with sticks (as in Basque dances), castanets, or kerchiefs (as in the English Morris dance). Genuine battle *morescas* flourished in all areas that were subject to invasion by foreign armies: they appear in Italy in the wake of the conquests of Ottoman sultan Mehmet II in the fifteenth century; in eastern Europe following the attacks of the Turks in the fourteenth, sixteenth, and seventeenth centuries; and in Mexico after the defeat of the French in 1860.

The subject of most confrontation *morescas* is the victory of good over evil, whether the *morescas* are religious in emphasis (as in "Moros y Cristianos" performances) or seasonal ritual celebrations in which the powers of spring defeat the armies of winter and darkness (as in the English May Day Morrises). Subsidiary themes include the liberation of a beautiful princess (as in the *moresca* from the island of Korčula, off the coast of Croatia), the storming of a tower or a citadel, and so on.

According to ancient folk belief, evil spirits can be expelled with noise. The clashing of swords and sticks fulfilled this function, as did the bells that were an essential accessory of *moresca* costumes in all the regions where the dance was performed. Bells might be sewn into pads (as in the English Morris); jingle from strings around wrists, ankles, or knees; serve as buttons on tunics or jackets; or be attached to belts or the points of fools' caps (as appear in German woodcarver Erasmus Grasser's *Maruschkatänzer* figurines of 1480, the Betley Window [see E. J. Nicol], the reliefs on the Goldenes Dachl in Innsbruck, Austria, and so on).

Bells are an especially important feature of the second category of *morescas*—the circle, linear, and free-form morescas. In these the choreographic emphasis is on the acting and dancing skills of the individual performers. In circle *morescas* the participants, all men in masks suggestive of their assumed roles (Dandy, Old Man, Hunchback, Moor, Fool, as in the Grasser figurines), dance around a center person who bears the prize to be given to the performer who most convincingly portrays his chosen character. The technique, as shown in the iconography and confirmed in written comments (see Chambers, 1903; Baskervill, 1929), is powerful, the gestures exaggerated, even—especially those of fools—obscene. Steps are large, kicks high, kneebends deep, the torso flexible and active; tumbling and vaulting are also used.

Linear *morescas* allow progression of the group of performers from one location to another. German guild dancers (e.g., Nuremberg *Schembart,* the bakers of Strasbourg) and English Morris dancers (e.g., Oxfordshire Morris dancers) frequently make use of this pattern, taking the dance through city streets at Carnival time, on the feast of Corpus Christi, at Easter, and on May Day. John Taylor, in *A Navy of Land Ships* (1630) speaks of capering a "Morisca . . . of forty miles long" (Baskervill, 1929, p. 302). Supernumeraries such as the Fool, the Maiden (Maide Marian), the Horse (Hobby-Horse), wild men, and giants were part of such cortèges; their function was to clear the way and to interact with the spectators, staining them with tar, touching or embracing them, distributing candies among them, or sprinkling them with fragrances—all remnants of ancient fertility and good-luck rituals.

Both the circle and the linear formation can temporarily lose their shape and turn into an improvised free-for-all, held together rhythmically by the accompanying music and dramatically by the theme of the event. The *choreas saracennicas* danced by a group of wild men, all members of the French nobility and including the king himself, on 29 January 1393 at the Hotêl Saint-Paul—and known as the "Ballet des Ardens" (Ballet of the Burning Men) because the costumes accidentally caught fire during the performance—appears to have been such a spectacle (Prunières, pp. 2ff.). The "Moresque des Singes" (Moorish Dance of the Monkeys) performed in Bruges in 1468 (cf. Claude-François Ménestrier, *Traîté des tournois,* Lyon,

MORESCA. A grotesque circle dance from a fifteenth-century engraving by Israhel van Meckenen. The character in the lower left has bells on the end of pointed sleeves, and the group is accompanied by a musician playing a pipe and tabor. (Photograph from Lily Grove, *Dancing,* London, 1895, p. 295.)

1669, p. 79, and also Heartz, 1960, and Brainard, 1981) is another example, as are the *mommeries* depicted in the Freydal Manuscript of emperor Maximilian I (1502). The absence of formality and courtly restraints that the nobles enjoyed in performing *morescas* led the fifteenth-century arbiter of courtly manners Baldassare Castiglione to issue a warning: ranking personages, he wrote in *Il cortegiano,* should dance *moresche* only in "in camera privatamente" ("in chambers, privately"), not in public.

The solo *moresca* appears to have been closely connected with the professional theater. In late medieval mystery plays, the dances performed by the characters Miriam and Salome—dances that had gyrating, seductive motions described by the thirteenth-century Minnesänger of Sachsendorf as "writh[ing] like a willow-wand"—were probably *morescas* (Salmen, 1977, p. 20). These motions may also have been used in the *morescas* for the two Sirens that preceded the great mock battle at the conclusion of the sixth banquet of the "Pas d'Arbre d'Or" (Spectacle of the Golden Tree) festivities in Bruges in 1468. A solo *moresca* for a male entertainer—his face blackened, bells on his legs, yellow and white streamers floating from his costume—is described by Thoinot Arbeau in his *Orchésographie* (1588). In 1600 William Kempe danced his Morris jig "The Nine Daies Wonder" from London to Norwich, sharing his dance with a Maide Marian only at brief moments. The Fool in an English Morris dance must likewise be a skillful solo performer.

As ballroom dances, *mouriscas* were taught in special schools in Lisbon during the sixteenth century (Sasportes, 1970). It is impossible to say whether these were stylized versions of battle dances like the *battaglias* and *barrieras* described in Fabritio Caroso's *Il ballarino* (1581) and Cesare Negri's *Le gratie d'amore* (1602). England, too, besides its traditional Morris dances for six men and supernumeraries, knew social Morris dances for one of more couples. A less joyful, social couple-*moresca* appeared twice in Nicolaus Manuel's *Berner Totentanz* (Bern Dance of Death). That fresco, now lost, was painted between 1516 and 1520 (for details, see Beerli, 1956); its depiction exemplifies the close connections between the blackfaced Moor, Death, the *Schwartz Knab* (Black Boy), and the Black Rider of Renaissance literature and folklore.

[*See also* Morris Dance.]

BIBLIOGRAPHY

Alford, Violet. "Ceremonial Dances of the Spanish Basques." *Musical Quarterly* 18 (1932).

Alford, Violet. "Morris and Morisca". *Journal of the English Folk Dance and Song Society* 2 (1935): 41–48.

Alford, Violet. *The Hobby Horse and Other Animal Masks.* London, 1978.

Baskervill, Charles R. *The Elizabethan Jig and Related Song Drama.* Chicago, 1929.

Beerli, C.-A. "Quelques aspects des jeux, fêtes et danses à Berne pendant la première moitié du XVIe siècle." In *Les fêtes de la Renaissance,* vol. 1, edited by Jean Jacquot. Paris, 1956.

Brooks, Lynn Matluck. *The Dances of the Processions of Seville in Spain's Golden Age.* Kassel, 1988.

Brainard, Ingrid. "An Exotic Court Dance and Dance Spectacle of the Renaissance: *La Moresca.*" In *Report of the Twelfth Congress, International Musicological Society [Berkeley 1977],* edited by Daniel Heartz and Bonnie C. Wade. Kassel, 1981.

Capmany, Aurelio. "El baile y la danza." In *Folklore y costumbres de España,* vol. 2, edited by Francisco Carreras y Candi. Barcelona, 1934.

Carrasco Urgoiti, María Soledad. "Aspectos folkloricos y literarios de la Fiesta de Moros y Cristianos en España." *Publications of the Modern Language Association of America* 78 (1963).

Chambers, E. K. *The Mediaeval Stage* (1903). 8th ed. Oxford, 1978.

Champe, Flavia Waters. *The Matachines Dance of the Upper Rio Rio Grande. History, Music, and Choreography.* Lincoln, Neb. 1983.

D'Ancona, A[lessandro]. *Origini del teatro italiano.* 2 Vols. Torino, 1891.

Dean-Smith, Margaret. "Morris." In *Die Musik in Geschichte und Gegenwart.* Kassel, 1949–.

Domokos, Paul P. "Der Moriskentanz in Europa und in die ungarischen Tradition." *Studia Musicologica Academiae Scientiarum Hungaricae* 10 (1968).

Emmerson, George S. *A Social History of Scottish Dance. Ane Celestial Recreation.* Montreal and London, 1972.

Engel, Hans. "Moresca." In *Die Musik in Geschichte und Gegenwart.* Kassel, 1949–.

Ferrari Barassi, Elena. "La tradizione della moresca e un sconosciuto ballo del cinqueseicento." *Rivista italiana di musicologia* 1 (1966); 5 (1970).

Forrest, John. *"Morris and Matachin": A Study in Comparative Choreography.* London, 1984.

Galanti, Bianca Maria. *La danza della spada in Italia.* Rome, 1942.

Galanti, Bianca Maria. "Ancore sulla Moresca." In *Lares* 15 (1949): 42–58.

Gallop, Rodney. "The Origins of the Morris Dance." *Journal of the English Folk Dance and Song Society* 1.3 (1934): 122–129.

Gilchrist, Anne G. "A Carved Morris-Dance Panel from Lancaster Castle." *Journal of the English Folk Dance and Song Society* 1.2 (1933).

Gombosi, Otto. "The Cultural and Folkloristic Background of the *Folía.*" *Papers of the American Musicological Society* (1940): 88–95.

Guglielmo Ebreo da Pesaro. *On the Practice or Art of Dancing* (1463). Translated and edited by Barbara Sparti. Oxford, 1993.

Halm, Philipp M. "Der Moriskentanz." *Bayrischer Heimatschutz* 23 (1927).

Halm, Philipp M. *Erasmus Grasser.* Augsburg, 1928.

Harris, Max. *The Dialogical Theatre: Dramatizations of the Conquest of Mexico and the Question of the Other.* New York, 1993.

Harris, Max. "The Arrival of the Europeans: Folk Dramatizations of Conquest and Conversion in New Mexico." *Comparative Drama* 28 (1994): 141–165.

Harris, Max. "Muhammed and the Virgin: Folk Dramatizations of Battles Between Moors and Christians in Modern Spain." *The Drama Review* 38.1 (1994).

Heaney, Michael, and John Forrest. *Annals of Early Morris.* Sheffield, 1991.

Heartz, Daniel. "Un divertissement de palais pour Charles Quint à Binche." In *Les fêtes de la Renaissance,* vol. 2, edited by Jean Jacquot. Paris, 1960.

Kenley, McDowell E. "Sixteenth-Century Matachines Dances: Morescas of Mock Combat and Comic Pantomime." Master's thesis, Stanford University, 1993.

Kurath, Gertrude Prokosch. "Mexican Moriscas: A Problem in Dance Acculturation." *Journal of American Folklore* 62 (1949): 87–106.
Lowe, Barbara. "Early Records of the Morris in England." *Journal of the English Folk Dance and Song Society* 8 (1957).
Mansanet Ribes, José Luis. *La fiesta de moros y cristianos de Alcoy y su historia*. Alcoy, 1990.
Nettl, Paul. "Die Tänze Jean d'Estrées." *Die Musikforschung* 8.4 (1955): 437–445.
Nettl, Paul. "Die Moresca." *Archiv für Musikwissenschaft* 14.3 (1957): 165–174.
Nicol, E. J. "Some Notes on the History of the Betley Window." *Journal of the English Folk Dance and Song Society* 7.2 (1953): 59–67.
Nicoll, Allardyce. *Masks, Mimes, and Miracles: Studies in the Popular Theatre*. London, 1931.
Pirro, André. *Histoire de la musique de la fin du XIVe siècle à la fin du XVIe*. Paris, 1940.
Pontremoli, Alessandro, and Patrizia La Rocca. *Il ballare lombardo: Teoria e prassi coreutica nella festa di corte del XV secolo*. Milan, 1987.
Prunières, Henry. *Le ballet de cour en France avant Benserade et Lully*. Paris, 1914.
Ricard, Robert. "Les fêtes de *Moros y cristianos* en Mexique." *Journal de la Société des Américanistes* 24 (1932): 51–81, 287–291.
Rodriguez, Sylvia. "The Taos Pueblo Matachines: Ritual Symbolism and Interethnic Relations." *American Ethnologist* 18.2 (1991).
Sachs, Curt. *World History of the Dance*. Translated by Bessie Schönberg. New York, 1937.
Salmen, Walter. "Ikonographie und Choreographie des Reigens im Mittelalter." *RIdIM/RCMI Newsletter* 2 (1977).
Sasportes, José. "Feasts and Folias: The Dance in Portugal." *Dance Perspectives*, no. 42 (1970).
Sharp, Cecil, and Herbert C. Macilwaine. *The Morris Book*. 5 vols. London, 1909–1913. 2d ed. London, 1912–1924.
Sharp, Cecil. "Dances, Sword, Morris, and Country." In *Encyclopedia and Dictionary of Education*. 1921–1922.
Shergold, N. D. *A History of the Spanish Stage from Medieval Times until the End of the Seventeenth Century*. Oxford, 1967.
Sparti, Barbara. "Antiquity as Inspiration in the Renaissance of Dance: The Classical Connection and Fifteenth-Century Italian Dance." *Dance Chronicle* 16.3 (1993): 373–390.
Sumberg, Samuel L. *The Nuremberg Schembart Carnival*. New York, 1941.
Wangermée, Robert. *Flemish Music and Society in the Fifteenth and Sixteenth Centuries*. Translated by Robert Erich Wolf. New York, 1968.
Warman, Arturo. *La danza de Moros y Cristianos*. Mexico City, 1972.
Welsford, Enid. *The Fool: His Social and Literary History*. London, 1935.
Wolfram, Richard. "Neue Funde zu den Morisken und den Moristänzen." *Zeitschrift für Volkskunde* 50 (1953).

INGRID BRAINARD

MORETON, URSULA (born 13 March 1903 in Southsea, England, died 24 June 1973 in London), British dancer and teacher. Moreton's career as a dancer, teacher, and administrator closely parallels the development of English ballet. While studying ballet with Enrico Cecchetti and mime with Francesca Zanfratti, she made her debut, at the age of sixteen, in J. M. Barrie's fantasy for Tamara Karsavina, *The Truth about the Russian Dancers* (1920). She next danced corps and solo parts, including a Porcelain Princess in *The Sleeping Princess* (1921) for Serge Diaghilev, took leading roles in ballets by Michel Fokine and Nikolai Legat in London's West End, and appeared briefly with Léonide Massine's company.

Moreton first met Ninette de Valois in Cecchetti's classes and in 1926 became her assistant and a teacher at de Valois's Academy of Choreographic Art. In 1931, Moreton was one of the original six dancers of the embryonic Vic-Wells Ballet, and then both its ballet mistress and a teacher at its school. After World War II, she helped launch the smaller touring company, then known as the Sadler's Wells Theatre Ballet; as de Valois's assistant director, she assumed complete day-to-day responsibility.

Teaching and administrative duties forced Moreton to give up dancing in 1949, but she is still remembered in romantic roles—particularly the Prelude in *Les Sylphides* and the Girl in *Le Spectre de la Rose*—and in such *demi-caractère* roles as Bathilde, the Queen Mother in *Swan Lake*, and her most memorable creation, the Dancer in *The Rake's Progress*, to which she brought exceptional gifts of mime and characterization.

She was named principal of the Royal Ballet Lower School in 1952 and of the entire Royal Ballet School in 1956. She held this position, while also teaching mime classes, until 1968, when she retired and began conducting regional auditions for the school. She received the Royal Academy of Dancing's Queen Elizabeth II Coronation Award in 1961; she was named a Commander of the Order of the British Empire in 1968; and she was elected a fellow of the Royal Academy of Dancing in 1973.

BIBLIOGRAPHY

Anthony, Gordon. "Ursula Moreton." In Anthony's *A Camera at the Ballet: Pioneer Dancers of the Royal Ballet*. Newton Abbot, 1975.
Woodcock, Sarah C. *The Sadler's Wells Royal Ballet*. London, 1991.

BARBARA NEWMAN

MORLACCHI, GIUSEPPINA (born 10 October 1836 in Lainate, Italy, died 23 July 1886 in Billerica, Massachusetts), musical theater dancer and choreographer. Morlacchi studied ballet at the Teatro alla Scala, Milan, with Carlo Blasis, and made her debut in 1856 at the Teatro Carlo Felice, Genoa, in Jules Perrot's ballet version of *Faust*. After engagements in major European cities and several seasons at Her Majesty's Theatre in London, she went to the United States to star in *The Devil's Auction*, a musical spectacle.

On 23 October 1867, Morlacchi made her debut at Banvard's Opera House in New York City. Critics agreed she was a superb technician with quick, weightless pointe work, an elastic jump, and an aptitude for pirouettes. After a short engagement in New York, Morlacchi and *The Devil's Auction* company, under the management of John De Pol, moved to the Theatre Comique in Boston, where

MORLACCHI. This 1868 lithographed music cover, by E. Baker after a photograph by Burnham, depicts Giuseppina Morlacchi and Leopoldina Baretta in a pas de deux from a can-can number, performed with John De Pol's Grand Ballet Troupe, at the Theatre Comique in Boston. (Courtesy of Madison U. Sowell and Debra H. Sowell, Brigham Young University, Provo, Utah.)

they opened on 23 December 1867. While in Boston, De Pol's choreographer, Domenico Ronzani, became ill and Morlacchi assumed his duties. She restaged repertory from La Scala and devised several new dances, the most popular of which was a can-can.

Morlacchi formed her own company in November 1868, hired Major Tom Burke, a former bit actor turned publicist, as her business manager, and opened in Boston's Theatre Comique with a production of *Lurline*. For the next four years she maintained her company, traveling as far west as the mining towns in Nevada and as far south as New Orleans. In 1869 her company performed *Esmeralda*, *L'Almée*, and *The Nymphs of the Forest* at Wood's Museum in New York. They also performed incidental dances in Shakespeare's *The Tempest* at the Grand Opera House and Jacques Offenbach's *La Perichole* at the Fifth Avenue Theater.

Morlacchi established a reputation as a champion of dancers' rights, walking out of engagements in which dancers were treated unfairly and impounding scenery when managers were late in paying salaries. In 1869, she bought a forty-acre farm in Billerica, Massachusetts. Between engagements she took members of her company there to rest and rehearse.

In December 1872, while in Chicago, Morlacchi was asked to join Buffalo Bill (William Cody) and Texas Jack (John Omohundro) in a new drama, *Scouts of the Prairie*, and to play her first speaking role, the Native American maiden Dove Eye. The incongruity of Morlacchi's Italian-accented dialogue did not detract from the production's success at the box office. As the prototype for the Hollywood Western, *Scouts of the Prairie* presented live American heroes onstage, with Morlacchi, on pointe, in buckskins, dancing "Invocations to the Great Spirit."

On 31 August 1873 Morlacchi and Omohundro married in Rochester, New York. They continued to perform in dramas about the American West with Cody each winter until 1875. Each summer, Omohundro returned to the West, and Morlacchi reassembled her ballet company for engagements on the East Coast. They performed in *La Bayadère*, *The Black Crook*, *The French Spy*, and *Masaniello*. From 1875 to 1880 the couple performed together as well as independently.

In June 1880, while both were appearing in Leadville, Colorado, Omohundro caught pneumonia and died. Inconsolable, Morlacchi retired from the stage and returned to the home she and Texas Jack had purchased in Lowell, Massachusetts, not far from Billerica. She lived quietly with her sister, Angelina, and taught ballet to the local mill girls. A much loved member of her community, Morlacchi died of cancer at the age of forty-nine. She left the bulk of her estate to the Actors' Fund. In her thirteen-year American career she had managed her own company, presenting restaged European repertory and her own choreography in opera, variety, melodrama, burlesque, and Wild West shows, successfully adapting her La Scala training to a growing American theater.

BIBLIOGRAPHY

Barker, Barbara. *Ballet or Ballyhoo: The American Careers of Maria Bonfanti, Rita Sangalli, and Giuseppina Morlacchi.* New York, 1984.

Logan, Herschel C. *Buckskin and Satin: The Life of Texas Jack (J. B. Omohundro).* Harrisburg, Pa., 1954.

Moore, Lillian. "Ballerina and Plainsman." *Dance Magazine* (September 1942): 14–15.

Moore, Lillian. "George Washington Smith." *Dance Index* 4 (June–August 1945): 88–135.

Odell, George C. D. *Annals of the New York Stage.* Vols. 8–10. New York, 1936–1938.

ARCHIVE. Dance Collection, New York Public Library for the Performing Arts.

BARBARA BARKER

MOROCCO. A North African country of geographic and climatic contrasts, Morocco encompasses desert, snowcapped mountains, Mediterranean and Atlantic beaches, green valleys, and ancient forests. Its population includes Arabic-speaking urban and rural Islamic peoples, desert nomads, sedentary tribespeople, and black peoples (who live primarily in the southern region). Morocco thus has a greater variety of traditional dances than any other North African country.

Berber Dances. In the relatively inaccessible High Atlas Mountains, many Berber tribes live much as they did centuries ago, having accepted only the smallest amount of Arabo-Islamic culture. Although Berber dances exist in every major region of Morocco, it is among these sedentary (as opposed to nomadic) tribes that the distinctive Berber style is best preserved.

The song dance is probably the quintessential Berber form. Both song and dance are performed simultaneously, in a line or circle that nearly always moves counterclockwise. Often, a leader dances alone and directs the group. Just as there is no separation between singing and dancing, there is often no clear distinction between musician and dancer. As they play, musicians invariably move to the music, often dancing with the dancers; dancers sing and chant, play sophisticated rhythms on percussion instruments, and perform syncopated, interlocking, clapping patterns while dancing.

The controlled resilience of the steps lends a softened grace to the dancers' excellent carriage. In many dances this springy quality, combined with a relaxed upper body, produces a rapid rebounding of the shoulders. Many Berber dances are characterized by rapid percussive footwork, leaps, stamps, and a pliant, reciprocal bending and flexing of the upper torso.

The Tuareg, a nomadic Berber people, possess a music-and-dance tradition completely distinct from that of the sedentary tribes. It has more in common with the traditions of other Saharan nomads, whether Berber or Arab (bedouin). The dances of the nomads of Algeria, Libya, Chad, Niger, Mali, and Mauritania are also performed in southernmost Morocco. The dances generally involve the use of weapons—daggers, swords, or staves—and the men glide over large areas, make subtle shoulder and torso movements, and leap into smooth fast turns or squats.

The dances of the sedentary Berber tribes account for the vast majority of Moroccan dance styles, however. Each Berber village has its own special dance.

Guedra. The dance called the *guedra* is seen primarily in the caravan center of Goulimine. On market day, the marketplace is full of Tuareg nomads, who have crossed the Sahara from Timbuktu to trade and who often attend performances of the *guedra.*

The men form a circle around the dancer, a woman, who kneels, completely shrouded in a blue veil. Clapping their hands to the beat of the *guedra*—the cooking-pot drum from which the dance takes its name—the men accompany the dancer with the repetitious phrases of a simple song.

The dancer's upper body rocks gently to the beat, or sometimes in syncopation to it, as she leans forward, back, or to the side, now beckoning, now retiring. All the while her tensed fingers are pointing, opening, closing, and fanning to a regular beat. These movements resemble modern sign language and seem to be remnants of a mimetic language whose meaning has been lost.

The dance begins slowly; it gradually accelerates. At one point the dancer removes her veil. Her facial expression is sometimes flirtatious, sometimes introverted and involved in the music's hypnotic character. Suddenly, the

MOROCCO. (*above*) *Guedra* dancers, gesturing and swaying, in characteristic kneeling position. The headdresses are fashioned from elaborately coifed braids. (*below*) In Berber dances there is often no clear distinction between musician and dancer. Here, tribesmen play *tarijas* (small clay drums) and *bendirs* as they dance. (Photographs from the collection of Mardi Rollow.)

drummer shifts into a new rhythmic pattern, the music accelerates rapidly, and the singers begin antiphonal chanting. At this point, the dancer's upper body and arm movements become stronger and more repetitive, her hand movements much simpler. She dances forward a little on her knees. Later, she whips her head around and around in small, rapid circles (her hair is elaborately braided into a headdress). The dance can go on for hours until the dancer collapses from exhaustion.

Guedra dancers sometimes perform a similar dance standing, which they call *tbila*. They step slightly to one side, then the other, while executing arm and hand movements closely resembling those of the *guedra* dance. Some *guedra* dancers now perform abbreviated, uninspired versions of their dance for tourists and at festivals in many parts of Morocco.

The rapid head movement of the *guedra* dance is also found in the *zār*, a trance dance performed in healing ceremonies in Egypt and parts of South Arabia. If the *zār* is an exorcistic dance performed mainly for women, the *guedra* is basically entertainment for men, performed by professionals—a dance of seduction that also includes a trance element.

Ahouache. The *ahouache* (Ar., *ahwash*) is found in the High Atlas Mountains and in the valley of Ouarzazate, between the western foothills of the High and the Anti-Atlas ranges, southeast of Marrakesh. It is a class of song dances performed in a circle by the female members of Shleuh (Berber) tribes. During the performance, several men stand in the middle of the circle near the fire, playing in pentameter on their *bendirs* (circular frame drums). One of them begins a song in a high shrill voice and a second echoes it. In the *ahouache* from Imintanout, the women begin to sing with the men, swaying from side to side with their arms at their sides and their hands clasped. After the song begins, they commence to dance in place, moving their forearms in a forward, circular motion while rapidly flexing their knees, which causes the coins of their necklaces to move up and down. Soon the women advance and retreat, sometimes bent at the waist and seemingly propelled by the movements of their arms. When the rhythm changes, the melody becomes simpler and the women begin to move to the right, swinging their arms, their hands still clasped. After a time, the men stop singing and repeat the original drum pattern. The circle of women divides into two arcs that drift apart but continue to face each other. The women in one arc sing the refrain, and the women in the second repeat it. At a signal from the leader, all participants kneel: the men continue to clap and both men and women bend from the waist, the women still swinging their arms. After the leader signals the lines to rise, the women resume moving to the right. At the end of the dance, the men sing the last refrain, followed by a five-beat pattern on the *bendirs*.

MOROCCO. This dance from Imintanout is an example of the *ahidous*. (Photograph from the collection of Mardi Rollow.)

Another dance from the High Atlas region northeast of Ouarzazate is that of the Kelaa M'Gouna people. Their song dance begins in two lines, one of which is composed of women only, the other of men playing *bendirs*. Standing shoulder to shoulder, the women holding hands, the lines move smoothly and rapidly toward each other and back again. Then they approach very near and swing past each other at the last moment. The line of women divides into two, each repeating the original figure. The men's line also divides into two, and all four lines face inward, roughly forming the sides of a square. At first, opposite pairs advance and retreat as before; soon, all of the lines travel rapidly toward the center, timing their arrivals so that they quickly rotate and pass through the center, one after the other, to the opposite sides of the square.

Ahidous. The *ahidous*, another example of the song dance, is found in the northwest of the central Atlas Mountains. It is performed outdoors, especially at festivals and fairs. Some types of *ahidous*, called *tamhawst*, are accompanied by footwork and clapping, while others, *tamseralit*, are not. In the *ahidous*, the lines or circles are formed alternately of men and women, standing elbow to elbow. The *amessad* (poet-singer), who leads them, first sings a very short phrase of a poem, which is immediately repeated by the group as a refrain. The dancers sing in place, their lower arms loosely extended, palms up. As they sing, the dancers rock gently back and forth and make subtle tossing movements with their hands. The music changes, and the dancers and musicians begin antiphonal chanting as they move around the circle. When the leader so indicates, the dancers accent the music with stamping patterns.

Dances from the Sous. In one of the Shleuh tribes, a group of male adolescent professional dancers and musicians lives solely from their art. They are from the Sous valley, south of the port city of Agadir. Members of this group no longer perform in the Sous; they are sent to Marrakesh to sing and dance in cafés and the Djemaa el-Fna (the central square). The boys perform in a female style, preserving a tradition formerly more widespread in North Africa.

The performance begins when the flutist plays a call on his *'awwade* (a Berber flute). The dancers promenade for a while and then sing, all in a line, the orchestra seated beside them. The song leader, who faces the others, begins an arrhythmic song, and the boys sing and play the *guimbri* (three-stringed lute) in response. The percussion instruments join in for the second, rhythmic, song and the dancers begin to sway to the music. Their singing grows merrier, and the song gradually becomes a dance.

They dance in different formations—two rows that approach, retreat, and pass through each other, as well as variations on a circle. As they walk, their lower torsos swing forward and back easily. Their style also includes the pervasive bending and flexing of the upper torso; fast, springy footwork; kneeling bows; and backbends. The dance is followed by more Shleuh airs or Arabic and European tunes. The culmination of the performance is the *shtih* (dance), a rapid trembling of the shoulders considered by the Shleuh to be the high point of the performance.

The dancers are accompanied by the *bendir,* the *nagus* (a small iron bowl struck with two metal rods), and the *rabāb* (a bowed viol). The dancers themselves play the *guimbri* and the *nuiqsat* (finger cymbals). Their method of playing the cymbals is unique: two are worn on the left thumb and middle finger, as is customary, but there is only one on the right middle finger. The dancers brush the right cymbal against the two in the left hand—the hands move up and down in opposite directions—in patterns whose beats always total five per measure, regardless of the music's time signature.

In the heart of the Berber-speaking Sous valley an Arabic-speaking Berber tribe, the Houara, performs a couple dance. At the beginning of the dance the man, holding his robe, leaps forward from the line of performers, almost as if on tiptoe; he then stops still with a comic expression on his face. After several of these playful false starts, both the man and the woman dance toward each other from opposite sides of the line with graceful, light steps. As they advance, they move their forearms in a forward, circular motion with their palms pressed together. When they have come part of the way, they execute rapid footwork patterns (their dignified bearing is unaffected by the speed of the footwork). The woman then grasps the lower edges of the front panels of her outer dress and she and the man, leaning toward each other, approach with a series of jumps. When they are very close, they turn suddenly, arching back toward each other; they then pass close by each other to rejoin the line of performers. Small groups of men then dance, alternating with the couple, performing the footwork patterns but not the jumps and turns.

Rif dancing. The Rif is the extreme northern region of Morocco, comprising the mountains along the Mediterranean between Tetouan and Melilla. The anthropologist Carleton Coon (1931) described the dancing at a Rifian marriage ceremony as a song dance in pentameter, in which all the young women of the clan "form two opposing and equal lines in the courtyard, each line with a leader. The two parallel lines, each girl with her hands on the shoulders of the one in front of her, move up and down the courtyard, and sometimes swing at angles to each other." They make rapid, isolated movements with their abdomens, hips, and shoulders, "stamping their feet in time to the music. . . . The leaders of the lines sometimes carry shallow, open-based drums."

Coon also describes an unusual dance from the central Rif, in which all the unmarried girls dance in the usual style in a circle; the two leaders, however, dance in the middle: "they wear short skirts, and hold in their hands . . . wooden clickers, or castanets. These two dance side by side, moving their hips in opposite directions, and from time to time kicking their legs high in the air, clicking their castanets beneath their raised thighs and striking them on their buttocks. When the spirit of the dance has sufficiently aroused them, they pick up and swing each other's shoulders, standing for a moment on them."

Martial dances. Berber martial dances performed in Morocco are typically noncombative. A familiar type is the rifle dance, which is found in Chouen, Taza, and Oujda in the north. Typically, the leader dances facing the rest of the group, shouting directions to them. The men of Oujda dance in lines with springy steps and corresponding shoulder movements to the music of *bendirs* and *ghayṭahs* (folk oboes). Now and then the dancers match special rhythmic sections of the music with short, stamping figures and shimmying shoulders. Their guns (old-fashioned muzzle-loading muskets) function as important paraphernalia in the dance. Much of the dance centers around various maneuvers with the rifles. The men promenade with guns on their shoulders for a time, then lift them to firing position. At the very end, they all face inward and fire the muskets in the air in a final salvo.

Arab Morocco. Although Morocco is an Arabic-speaking country, Moroccan dancing reveals very little that comes from the Arabs (who brought Islam to all North Africa in the seventh century). It is in music that Arab influence has had some impact. The classical music brought back to Morocco from Andalusia (by the expelled Moors in the fifteenth century), *ʿala,* is still a purely Arab style. The popular city music called *griha* is also an Arab style, but it has Berber elements; it is usually in syncopated 6/8 time and often includes interlocking drum or clapping patterns. In the *griha,* even the oud (Arab lute) is played in a markedly different style than in other Arab countries; its percussive character is unmistakably Moroccan.

One strong Arab influence is that of the *shikhat,* female professional entertainers found in Arabic-speaking areas of Morocco. In Morocco, the role of the professional dancer is still connected to that of the courtesan; thus the *shikhat* are not considered respectable. Theirs is primarily an urban tradition—they dress in caftans, the traditional city attire, and sing and dance to the popular Moroccan urban music style, *griha.* In the past, they were patronized by a cultivated audience. Today, they perform at various festivals and celebrations. Many travel from town to town, performing in tent theaters at celebrations of local saints' days.

Their performance traditionally begins with the *lmaìt,* a long, high, drawn-out note or call that is immediately followed by a song, sometimes of a scandalous nature. The performance consists of solo and unison response sections. The *shikhat* often play interlocking rhythmic patterns on *tarijas* (very small goblet drums) and clap in rhythmic patterns during the orchestral interludes. The short repetitive phrases of the song, often more rhythmic than melodic, are delivered in a passionate style.

MOROCCO. A woman and man spinning in the Tuareg marriage ritual in which a dagger on a long cord is placed around the woman's neck. These performers were part of the Moroccan contingent at the 1977 FESTAC Nigeria. (Photograph © by Folklore Film; courtesy of Ibrahim Farrah, *Arabesque Magazine*, New York.)

After they have sung, the *shikhat* begin to dance, taking turns doing improvised solos or, occasionally, duets. The dance is a combination of smooth, pelvic undulations, hip accents, shimmies, and percussive, syncopated footwork, stamps, and jumps. Accordingly, the drums often alternate between the typical Moroccan 6/8 pattern and a double-time variation in which all the beats of the measure are played—a pattern especially suited to the footwork. The dance sometimes includes syncopated false-stop figures. The performance often ends with an ensemble finale of fast footwork followed by a short, rhythmic pattern consisting of five stamps. The pattern is the same as the *bendir* pattern at the end of the Moroccan Berber *ahouache.*

The *shikhat* perform in groups of four to eight. They are accompanied by several male musicians, who play the *bendir,* the violin (replacing the older folk instrument), the *guimbri,* and sometimes the oud. When not dancing, the *shikhat* accompany the solo dancer of the moment on the *bendir,* the *tarija,* the *sanuj* (finger cymbals) and the *guimbri.* Whether dancing or playing, they are at ease and even careless of the presence of an audience, adjusting their clothing or sharing private jokes.

Sub-Saharan Morocco. Some of the blacks in Morocco have acculturated to the Berber and Arab communities in which they have settled, while others retain their sub-Saharan customs. An example of the former is found in Tissint, where the black inhabitants perform a duet in which the man circles the woman while holding aloft a dagger suspended from a cord. Ultimately, he uses the cord and dagger as a necklace, placing it around the woman's neck. This dance is drawn from a marriage ritual, similar to many in Islam, in which a sword or dagger is a symbol of protection.

The black ecstatic brotherhoods, in contrast, have preserved some of their sub-Saharan rituals. Perhaps the best known of these is the brotherhood of the Gnawa. It was once established in many regions of Morocco but is now located primarily in Marrakesh. Members are called in to homes to cure the sick, who are believed to be possessed by spirits; they perform a *derba,* an exorcism ceremony, consisting of incantations, music, and dancing, during which they urge the afflicted person to dance, to exorcise the spirits. The dance is now also performed as a secular entertainment at the Djemaa el-Fna in Marrakesh and at such events as the National Folklore Festival.

The dance of the Gnawa is characterized by fast drops to push-up position, high jumps with scissorlike leg splits, squats, and fast spins with sudden stops. They dance to a *ganga* (large two-headed drum played with two curved sticks) and accompany themselves on *chakchakas,* iron

MOROCCO. Accompanying themselves with metal *chakchakas,* these dancers of the Gnawa brotherhood perform a secular version of a *derba,* at the Marrakesh Festival, c.1965. (Photograph by Claude Melin; from the collection of Mardi Rollow.)

percussion instruments consisting of two concave disks connected by a flat bar. A Gnawa dancer plays a pair of *chakchakas* in each hand.

Traditional Arts. Moroccans continue to value their cultural heritage. Morocco is the only country in North Africa that still produces a large variety of traditional handicrafts of the high quality once common throughout North Africa. Traditional music and dancing are also thriving, with folk music and dance an integral part of village life. Each spring Morocco's government sponsors the popular National Folklore Festival in Marrakesch, at which groups from every region of the country perform in a grand exhibition of folk music and dance. The festival is usually booked months in advance.

These arts are not only being preserved—they are growing and evolving. For example, the "new" music of a group called Naas el-Ghiwan is popular throughout Morocco. They play on traditional Moroccan instruments, such as the *tbila* (a connected pair of clay drums), *guimbri,* and *rabāb.* Their style of music derives from Moroccan folk music. It is a continuation of the living tradition of music and dance in Morocco.

[*See also* North Africa.]

BIBLIOGRAPHY

Chottin, Alexis. *Tableau de la musique marocaine.* Paris, 1939.
Coon, Carleton. *Tribes of the Rif.* Cambridge, Mass., 1931.
Westermarck, Edward A. *Marriage Ceremonies in Morocco.* London, 1914.
Westermarck, Edward A. *Ritual and Belief in Morocco.* London, 1926.
Wrage, Werner. *Frühlings Fahrt in die Sahara.* Radebeul, 1959.

RECORDINGS. *Music of the Shikhat and Dance Music of Tunisia* (Disques Maghrébins 5001). *Songs and Rhythms of Morocco* (Lyrichord 7336). *Vacances au Maroc* (Pathe PTX 40906).

VIDEOTAPE. *Dances of North Africa: Vol. 1, Morocco and Tunisia* (Araf, 1995).

AISHA ALI, MARDI ROLLOW, and LEONA WOOD

MORRICE, NORMAN (born 10 September 1931 in Agua Dulce, Mexico), dancer, choreographer, and director. Morrice was studying geophysics at the University of Nottingham when a performance of *Symphonic Variations* and *Hamlet* by the Sadler's Wells Ballet convinced him to give up science for a career in ballet. He began his dance training at the Rambert School in 1952 and joined Ballet Rambert the following year, eventually attaining principal status. Usually remembered as a character dancer—as Doctor Coppélius, Hilarion, or The Man She Must Marry in *Jardin aux Lilas*—Morrice also danced James in *La Sylphide,* the Scottish Rhapsody in *Façade,* and the Poet in *Night Shadow* and acquitted himself well in the classical repertory.

In 1958 he choreographed his first ballet, *The Two Brothers,* in which he also appeared as the Younger Brother. This ballet marked an important transition in his career. Although he continued to dance for several years, Morrice concentrated largely on choreography, mixing modern steps and shapes with the classical ballet vocabulary and emphasizing personal relationships and contemporary situations. *Hazana* (1959), for example, presented the dramatic tale of the construction and raising of a huge cross in a small Latin American town; in *A Place in the Desert* (1961), Western engineering threatened the existence of a primitive Middle Eastern village.

In 1961, a fellowship in choreography from the Ford Foundation enabled Morrice to study for four months in the United States with Martha Graham and other modern choreographers. Inspired by their work, he returned to Ballet Rambert in 1962 as its principal choreographer. Increasingly adept in the modern idiom, he was perfectly suited to become its associate director in 1966. That year, in large part through his guidance, the company abandoned its classical repertory and image and adopted a more contemporary approach. He was named joint artistic director with Marie Rambert in 1970, by which time he had choreographed eighteen ballets of great emotional immediacy (although less than lasting power), several of them for the Batsheva Dance Company in Israel and one, *The Tribute* (1965), for the Royal Ballet's touring company.

In 1974, the Royal Academy of Dancing awarded Morrice its Queen Elizabeth II Coronation Award for his contribution to dance. He resigned from Ballet Rambert the same year and embarked on a three-year stint as a freelance teacher and choreographer in Britain, Canada, Australia, and Israel.

In 1977 Morrice was appointed director of the Royal

MORRICE. A scene from the Ballet Rambert's 1977 production of Morrice's *Smiling Immortal,* set to music by Jonathan Harvey, with Zoltán Imre, Lucy Burge, and John Chesworth. (Photograph by Alan Cunliffe; used by permission.)

Ballet, the first from outside the company. By barring guest artists for two entire seasons, he clearly established his staunch commitment to discovering and encouraging young talent within the company. Although faithful to the classical tradition—he supervised new productions of *Swan Lake* in 1979 and *Giselle* in 1980—he maintained the same commitment toward choreographers. He commissioned new ballets not only from Glen Tetley and Rudolf Nureyev but also from dancers within the company, such as David Bintley, Michael Corder, Ashley Page, and Wayne Eagling, as well as from Richard Alston. He served annually as a judge of the choreographic competition at the Royal Ballet Lower School. In 1986 Morrice relinquished his role as director to Anthony Dowell; a year later he succeeded Leslie Edwards as director of the Royal Ballet Choreographic Group.

[*See also* Royal Ballet.]

BIBLIOGRAPHY

Bland, Alexander. *The Royal Ballet: The First Fifty Years.* London, 1981.

Clarke, Mary. *Dancers of Mercury.* London, 1962.

Garske, Rolf. "The Range of the Guard." *Ballett International* 6 (October 1983): 22–30.

Morrice, Norman. "Pioneering in Beijing." *Dance and Dancers* (September 1987): 14–16.

Prichard, Jane, comp. *Rambert: A Celebration.* London, 1996.

Vaughan, David. "The Evolution of Ballet Rambert: From Ashton to Alston." *Dance Magazine* (October 1982): 74–77.

BARBARA NEWMAN

MORRIS, MARK (born 29 August 1956 in Seattle, Washington), American dancer and choreographer. At age eight, at a José Greco concert, Mark Morris decided to become a dancer. He studied Spanish dance with Verla Flowers and ballet with various teachers, including Perry Brunson. (He had almost no training in modern dance.) As a teenager, Morris performed for three years with the Koleda Folk Ensemble, a semiprofessional Balkan folk dance group whose communal ideals and rhythmic bravura were to influence his later work. Morris first danced professionally (that is, for pay) at age eleven and first choreographed professionally at fourteen. He made his first classical ballet at fifteen.

Morris graduated from high school in 1973 and spent part of 1974 in Madrid, studying Spanish dance. In 1976 he moved to New York, where, over the next seven years, he danced with the troupes of Eliot Feld, Lar Lubovitch, Hannah Kahn, and Laura Dean. In 1980 he rented the Merce Cunningham Studio for two nights and with ten dancer friends mounted a show of five of his works. With this unpretentious event, of which there is a surviving videotape, the Mark Morris Dance Group was born.

MORRIS. Members of the Mark Morris Dance Company in *Soap-Powders and Detergents* (1986), part of the evening-length suite of dances entitled *Mythologies,* inspired by French literary theorist Roland Barthes's 1957 essay collection of the same name. The score, by Hershel Garfein, is a cantata in praise of laundry detergent, loosely modeled on J. S. Bach's *Coffee Cantata.* The choreography includes rapturous mimicry of the wash, spin, and rinse cycles couched in a fall-and-recovery vocabulary that honors early modern dance. (Photograph © by Beatriz Schiller; used by permission.)

Morris's talent was quickly recognized. By 1984 his company was invited to perform at the Next Wave Festival of the Brooklyn Academy of Music, and the concert that he presented there, consisting of *Gloria* (1981), *O Rangasayee* (1984), and *Championship Wrestling after Roland Barthes* (1984), made him famous. Meanwhile, his verbal intelligence and wit endeared him to interviewers. By 1986, the year he turned thirty, he was being reviewed in national magazines, major ballet companies were premiering works by him, and the Public Broadcasting Service had aired an hour-long special on him. In that year, too, the company began touring extensively; its administration, under Barry Alterman and Nancy Umanoff, solidified; and Morris, who until then had still regarded himself as a freelance choreographer, committed himself decisively to the Mark Morris Dance Group.

In 1988 the company underwent a beneficent but traumatic change. Invited to replace Maurice Béjart as dance director of Belgium's national opera house, the Théâtre Royal de la Monnaie, Morris doubled the number of his dancers (from twelve to twenty-four) and moved the troupe to Brussels, where it was renamed the Monnaie Dance Group/Mark Morris. Working with richer resources than ever before, Morris rose to a new level of mastery, notably in the grand-scaled, large-hearted *L'Allegro, il Penseroso, ed il Moderato* (1988), his first full-evening work, set to George Frideric Handel's oratorio of the same name, and in the dark *Dido and Aeneas* (1989), a danced version of Henry Purcell's opera. (In the latter, both Dido and the Sorceress were played by Morris—the greatest role of his dancing career.) Much of Morris's work at the Monnaie received damning reviews, for the Belgian dance press was unaccustomed to American modern dance.

In Brussels, Morris's choreography became precise and more balletic. With this shift, and with the grafting of a second, younger generation of performers onto the first, the company's dancing, which had formerly had a lovably shambling quality, became tidier and more virtuosic. In 1990, while still in Belgium, Morris helped Mikhail Baryshnikov to found the White Oak Dance Project, and he supplied the repertory for that troupe's first two seasons (1990–1991). Morris's farewell to La Monnaie was *The Hard Nut* (1991), his pop version of *The Nutcracker.* In 1991, the company, with seventeen dancers including Morris, returned to New York. Before his departure for Europe, Morris had been a controversial figure in the United States. Now, on the basis of his Belgian works, he was recognized as one of America's foremost artists.

◀ MORRIS. In *O Rangasayee* (1984), a virtuosic twenty-three-minute solo to classical South Indian music by Sri Tyagaraja sung by M. S. Subhalakshmi, Morris performed in a white *dhoti* (loincloth) with his hands and feet stained red in the manner of Indian dancers. The solo was hailed by critics as a sublime and daring re-imagination of the Denishawn-era formulaic "Oriental solo." (Photograph © 1984 by Beariz Schiller; used by permission.)

Through the mid-1990s Morris's work did not change notably, but it grew in assurance and subtlety. He remained prolific, averaging five to six works a year. His most remarkable dances since his return to the United States have been *Beautiful Day* (1992, to Georg-Melchior Hoffmann), a severe duet about human and divine love; *Bedtime* (1992), a dream/nightmare interpretation of three songs by Franz Schubert; *Grand Duo,* a thundering, primitivist work to a score by Lou Harrison; *The Office* (1994, to music by Antonín Dvořák), a Balkan-flavored dance suite with a subtext about death; and *Somebody's Coming to See Me Tonight* (1995, to songs by Stephen Foster), a cross between a charming genre piece and a gray reverie.

What strikes most spectators immediately in Morris's work is its unforced directness, the combined result of his elastic rhythms, his refusal to conceal effort, his lack of self-consciousness about dancing, and his preference for down-to-earth dancers. An equally important quality of his work is its musicality. From childhood, he has been as absorbed in music (in which he is largely self-taught) as in dance. His dances are inspired by their music; their structure mirrors that of the music (he choreographs with score in hand); their emotions are those evoked in him by the music. Morris's musical taste is broad—he has used scores by more than fifty composers—but he has clear preferences. About half his works have been set to vocal music, which he loves for its physicality, and many of his most ambitious pieces have been set to Baroque music, which he favors for its structural clarity and emotional directness. Whenever possible, the company performs to live music.

Morris's work is forthrightly humanistic. He addresses the "great themes": love, death, grief, fellowship. His company looks like a community, and it stands for the world. A few of his dances tell stories; most are quasi-narrative. A piece by Morris typically uses a fixed vocabulary of gestures, some mimetic ("flying," crawling), others less translatable but nevertheless emphatic. Morris weaves the dance out of these gestures, using musical logic (variation, development, recapitulation). Thus, though the movements may begin as story, they end as dance, with the poignant ambiguity of emotion so common to dance. Still, the audience can normally tell what a dance by Morris is "about," and this readability is a key element in his success.

Morris's work is a cross. In its musicality, danciness, and humanism, it is traditional, a continuation of the main line of American modern dance. But others of Morris's qualities—his scabrous wit, his fondness for high style, his repudiation of gender-typing, and (especially in his early work) his taboo-breaching—mark him as an artist of the so-called postmodern period. His emotional logic is also double-sided. On the one hand, his work is accessible, "sincere," even wholesome. (Morris is one of few contemporary choreographers to deal with religious feeling.) On the other hand, he has pursued emotion into its darkest corners—violence, monstrousness, desolation—and, to add to the trouble, has often laced these terrors with comedy. He habitually deals in mixed moods, in spiritual strife. His desire to communicate, which is very strong, has not caused him to simplify.

As of this writing, Morris is probably the most popular choreographer in American modern dance. He has also created classical ballets for the Boston Ballet, the Joffrey Ballet, the American Ballet Theatre, the Paris Opera Ballet, Les Grands Ballets Canadiens, and the San Francisco Ballet. He has directed three operas (*Die Fledermaus,* 1988; *The Marriage of Figaro,* 1991; Christoph Willibald Gluck's *Orfeo ed Euridice,* 1996) in addition to *Dido and Aeneas,* and he has made dances for other operas, notably Peter Sellars's productions of John Adams's *Nixon in China* (1987) and *The Death of Klinghoffer* (1991). He received a Guggenheim fellowship in 1986 and a MacArthur fellowship in 1991.

BIBLIOGRAPHY

Acocella, Joan. *Mark Morris.* New York, 1993. Includes a detailed chronology of Morris's works to 1993. The paperback reprint (New York, 1995) extends the chronology to 1995.

Brazil, Tom. *Dances by Mark Morris.* New York, 1992.

Croce, Arlene. "Mark Morris Comes to Town," "Championship Form," and "Choreographer of the Year." In Croce's *Sight Lines.* New York, 1987.

Croce, Arlene. Reviews. *The New Yorker* (8 June 1987, 16 January 1989, 23 July 1989, 31 July 1989, 8 January 1996).

Greskovic, Robert. "A Classic Nut Case." *The Village Voice* (15 December 1992).

Keefe, Maura, and Marc Woodworth. "An Interview with Mark Morris." *Salmagundi* 104–105 (Fall 1994–Winter 1995): 218–240.

Kisselgoff, Anna. "Divining the Mystique of Mark Morris." *New York Times* (11 November 1990).

Macaulay, Alastair. Reviews. *The New Yorker* (20 June 1988, 11 May 1992).

Singer, Thea. "Mark Morris: Beautiful Dances." *Stuff* (Boston) (June 1992).

Temin, Christine. "The Triumph of Mark Morris." *Boston Globe Magazine* (19 February 1989).

Tobias, Tobi. "Mark Morris." *New York* (11 December 1995).

Vaughan, David. "A Conversation with Mark Morris." *Ballet Review* 14 (Summer 1986): 26–36.

VIDEOTAPES. "Mark Morris," *Dance in America* (WNET-TV, New York, 1986). "Nixon in China," *Great Performances* (WNET-TV, New York, 1988). "The Hidden Soul of Harmony," *South Bank Show* (London Weekend Television, 1990). "The Hard Nut," *Dance in America* (WNET-TV, New York, 1992). "Mark Morris, Choreographer," *Adrienne Clarkson Presents* (CBC, Toronto, 1992). "Falling Down Stairs" (Sony Classical, Rhombus Media, 1995). "Dido and Aeneas" (BBC, Channel 4, 1995).

ARCHIVES. Monnaie Dance Group, Mark Morris Archives, Brussels. The Mark Morris Dance Group, Archives, 225 Lafayette Street, New York, N.Y.

JOAN ACOCELLA

MORRIS DANCE. The term *morris* has been applied indiscriminately by folk and folklorists alike to all manner of male ceremonial dances in Europe. Consequently, accurate tracing of the dance types subsumed under the name has been difficult. In England the name is best applied to ceremonial dances performed in double-column longways formation. This distinguishes one broad class of dances from the linked, circular, hilt-and-point sword dances, which form a choreographically and historically distinct class.

The word *morris* means "Moorish"; it is related etymologically to other European dance names such as *moresca, morisco,* and *moros y cristianos.* [*See* Moresca.] The European fashion for Moorish dancing—that is, dances that had some connection, however slight, with the Moors (Muslim invaders from North Africa who ruled much of the Iberian Peninsula from 711 to 1492)—began in 1149 at Lérida, at the betrothal of Petronilla, queen of Aragon, to Ramón of Barcelona. At the festivities, court dancers performed a feigned combat between Moors and Christians *(moros y cristianos)* in commemoration of the expulsion of the Moors from Lérida in the previous year. As the Moors were pushed southward in the Iberian Peninsula during the Reconquest, the *moros y cristianos* custom spread until it was common throughout Spain. Subsequently it became popular in parts of Italy and France and was taken by the conquistadors to the New World, where its message of military evangelism was not lost on the native population.

Dances called *morris, morisco,* or *morisk* did not appear in England until the mid-to-late fifteenth century, by which time the putatively Moorish characteristics were, at most, incidental to the dance proper. Two quite distinct Morris dances were recorded at that time: the ring dance and the processional.

The ring dance was performed at the royal courts by well-paid professional dancers wearing elaborate, specially constructed costumes. Of the four to six male dancers, one was clothed as a fool and the rest wore fancy coats, matching headgear, and pads of bells at the knees. A female character wore a brightly colored dress lined with sharply contrasting material. The female stood at the center of the circle of dancers holding a ring, apple, or some other favor to be awarded to the man who danced most grotesquely. The dance involved considerable gesticulation and use of hands and fingers. The prize was conventionally awarded to the fool. This dance was exceedingly popular across Europe, as is attested to by the variety of contemporary drawings, paintings, and sculptures of it.

The processional Morris was performed by the craft guilds as part of state and local parades. Although there is no record of how the dance was performed, it was probably based on a double-column formation.

The next substantial references to Morris dancing in England comes from the eighteenth century. Three points are generally emphasized. First, the dance was characterized by the rhythmic clashing of stout staves. Second, the performers all wore bells strapped to their knees. Third, the dance was performed by the lower classes only. An explanation of how this great change came about between the sixteenth and the eighteenth centuries may be furthered by analyzing the detailed choreographic accounts (provided by Cecil Sharp and his co-workers) of what the dance became in the nineteenth and twentieth centuries.

The contemporary Morris since the early 1800s is a nonprogressive, double-column, longways dance. It can be subdivided into set dances and processionals. The set dances of the Cotswold regions of Oxfordshire and Gloucestershire are by far the best known, because they were the first ceremonial dances to be discovered and popularized by Sharp and because they are immensely popular with revival dancers. Related dance forms are found to the east in Cambridgeshire and to the west in the Welsh border counties of Shropshire, Herefordshire, and Worcestershire.

Each Cotswold team has its own distinctive, uniform costume. But all costumes are variations on a theme. The basic outfit consists of a white shirt and white or dark trousers, or knee breeches, with pads of bells strapped under the knees. To this, various teams add their own livery of ribbons, rosettes, and sashes. Headgear has varied with fashion, but top hats have had a long vogue.

With some exceptions each team has four types of dances: stick, hand-clapping, handkerchief, and solo jigs. The first three types are performed in longways sets of six. Each dance can be divided into common and distinctive figures. The common figures are those that occur in most, or all, of the dances of a particular village and are similar or identical to country dance figures; they include Back to Back, Gypsy, Cross Over, Hands Around, and Hey. Distinctive figures differentiate dances and are alternated with the common figures. These figures may combine to act as a repeated chorus or may change progressively through the dance. Most stick and hand-clapping dances are of the chorus type, involving a fixed sequence of clashings or clappings. Handkerchief dances often have progressive, distinctive figures that require contrary corners to take turns in executing increasingly complex leaps and capers.

Each village tradition has a basic phase of stepping, for use in the common figures, and having a corresponding arm movement made up of a synchronized up-and-down or circular motion. The peculiarities of stepping and common figures can be said to make up a village style, and while styles vary considerably across the Cotswolds, the villages have many dances in common. A handkerchief dance with a Side-Step-plus-Half-Hey distinctive figure, for example, is known virtually everywhere.

Each team has one or more extra characters, the most common of which is the Fool. He is generally dressed incongruously and carries a stick with an inflated pig's bladder attached to one end and a cow's tail to the other. He amuses the crowd and also keeps its numbers from encroaching on the dancing space.

The Cotswold Morris is performed mostly for festivities in May and at Whitsuntide. Church-sponsored Whitsun "ales" (country festivals) were very popular until a prudish element in the nineteenth-century Anglican hierarchy outlawed them as conducive to drunkenness and riotous behavior. The best-known ale was the Lamb Ale at Kirtlington, where many teams met and competed for prizes. Such competitions may well be the reason for both the core of universally known dances and the substantial stylistic variations from village to village.

The Morris of the Welsh border country is similar to the Cotswold Morris but is less elaborately developed. Most of the dances are stick dances, and there are only one or two per village as opposed to five or more in the Cotswolds. The Molly dances of Cambridgeshire are essentially country dances performed by men only. Usually there is only one dance per village.

The most highly developed processional Morris dances come from Lancashire and Cheshire. They were for many years associated with the custom of "rushbearing," that is, carrying a decorated load of commercial rushes to church around harvest time or during Wakes Week. The dancers wear flowered hats, white shirts decorated with sashes and ribbons, dark breeches, and laced shoe clogs, and they carry colored sticks or slings. Dancers line up in a two-column longways set of eight or more and alternate marching or stepping down the street with figures called at the discretion of the leader. Some of the processional forms have been converted into set dances by eliminating the marching element and running the figures together in a fixed sequence. Because many of the figures are like country-dance figures, the overall choreography of the set dances is reminiscent of country dancing, although the costumes, clogs, and modes of stepping give the dance a singular air.

If the scant historical sources are to be trusted, the contemporary Morris achieved its form between the sixteenth and eighteenth centuries. It is amply documented that during this period the country dance was extremely popular with all classes and that the longways-set formation came to dominate. Morris dances that largely or entirely comprise country-dance figures could well have developed out of this fad. There seems no question that this is how Molly dancing developed. The Cotswold and border traditions probably have a more complex origin, however. Stick-clashing is a novelty that must have had an origin other than in country dance. One interesting speculation is that it comes from the *matachin,* a courtly dance fad of the sixteenth century. This dance was a mock combat that emphasized the rhythmic clashing of swords interspersed with a stepping chorus. Known descendants of the *matachin* still exist in North America, and they are strikingly

MORRIS DANCE. The Bampton Morris Dancers from Oxfordshire, dressed in white, wearing bells on their legs, and waving handkerchiefs, perform in typical double-column formation. During the nineteenth century the dancers were accompanied by a pipe and tabor. Here the dancers are accompanied by an accordian player. (Photograph © by Derek Schofield; used by permission.)

similar to Cotswold dances in many ways. Thus a fusion of the *matachin* with country-dance figures could well have produced the border and Cotswold traditions.

[*See also* Jig; Matachins; *and* Sword Dance. *For general discussion, see* Great Britain, *article on* English Traditional Dance.]

BIBLIOGRAPHY

Bacon, Lionel. *A Handbook of Morris Dances.* London, 1974.

Cawte, E.C., Alex Helm, R.J. Marriott, and Norman Peacock. "A Geographical Index of the Ceremonial Dance in Great Britain" *Journal of the English Folk Dance and Song Society* 9 (1960):1–41.

Chandler, Keith. *"Ribbons, Bells and Squeaking Fiddles": The Social History of Morris Dancing in the English South Midlands, 1660–1900.* London, 1993a.

Chandler, Keith. *Morris Dancing in the English South Midlands, 1660–1900: A Chronological Gazeteer.* London, 1993b.

Forrest, John. *"Morris and Matachin": A Study in Comparative Choreography.* London, 1984.

Forrest, John. *The History of Morris Dancing.* Toronto, 1997.

Heaney, Michael, and John Forrest. *Annals of Early Morris.* (Bibliographical and Special Series #6), Sheffield, England, 1991.

Sharp, Cecil, and Herbert C. Macilwaine. *The Morris Book.* 5 vols. London, 1909–1913. 2d ed. London, 1912–1924.

JOHN FORREST

MORT DU CYGNE, LE. *See* Dying Swan, The.

MOSCOW CLASSICAL BALLET. *See* Russia, *article on* Secondary and Provincial Dance Companies.

MOURET, JEAN-JOSEPH (born 11 April 1682 in Avignon, died 20 December 1738 in Charenton), French composer. After receiving his musical education in Avignon, Mouret left his native city by 1707 and shortly thereafter entered the service of the duke and duchess du Maine. In 1714 he became the organizer for the duchess for the "Grandes Nuits" festivals that were held at Sceaux. For this purpose he composed all his intermezzi, including *Apollon et les Muses,* which contained what may have been the ancestor of the *ballet d'action,* a *danse caracterisé* ("characterized dance") performed by Claude Ballon and Françoise Prévost as a pantomime. Based on Pierre Corneille's *Les Horaces,* it was designed to show Horace's murder of his sister Camille.

In 1714 Mouret also provided an *opéra-ballet* for the Paris Opera, *Les Fêtes, ou Le Triomphe de Thalie,* which was to enjoy great success. He composed other works for this theater, including two *tragédies lyriques* ("lyric tragedies"), *Ariane* (1717) and *Pirithoüs* (1723); three *opéra-ballets, Les Amours des Dieux* (1727), *Le Triomphe des Sens* (1732), and *Les Grâces* (1735); and a one-act pastorale, *Le Temple de Gnide,* which was not presented until 1741, after the artist's death. In 1716 he began writing *divertissements* for the Théâtre Français, and in 1718, for the Comédie Italienne. For the latter he provided the music for more than 140 pieces, including several by Pierre Carlet de Chamblain de Marivaux. He also created parodies of the famous *opéra-ballets Les Éléments,* by Michel-Richard de Laland and André Cardinal Destouches, and *Les Indes Galantes,* by Jean-Philippe Rameau.

In 1722 Mouret participated in the celebrations held at Villers-Cotterets for the coronation of Louis XV, for which he composed all the dances (the choreography was done by Guillaume-Louis Pecour). He reached the peak of his career in 1728 when he took over the artistic direction of the Concert Spirituel, a prestigious post that he was obliged to give up in 1734. In 1737 he lost his post with the Comédie Italienne, after which he went mad and had to be hospitalized at the asylum of Charenton, where he died.

His four *opéra-ballets* made him, together with André Campra and Rameau, one of the best illustrators of this genre during the first half of the eighteenth century. In *Les Fêtes, ou Le Triomphe de Thalie* he set a new tone that was noticed by his contemporaries. This was the first treatment for the Paris Opera of such a realistic subject, with characters taken from daily life and "dressed in French clothes." The confidantes spoke in the tones of the soubrettes of the Comédie, and the comic element, which Campra had already introduced in *Les Fêtes Vénitiennes,* was revealed here with greater freedom. Along with conventional dances, such as *menuets, rigaudons,* and a very merry and greatly applauded *contredanse,* ballet airs provided humorous descriptions of the character of Folly and that of the peasants at the village wedding. Mouret also exploited this light, bubbly vein in the *divertissements* he created for the Théâtre Italien. He was thus one of the principal precursors of the French comic opera.

BIBLIOGRAPHY

Anthony, James R. *French Baroque Music from Beaujoyeulx to Rameau.* Rev. ed. London, 1978.

Jean Joseph Mouret et le théâtre de son temps: Actes des journées d'études consacrées à Jean Joseph Mouret pour le tricentenaire de sa naissance, organisées à d'Aix-en-Provence, les 28 et 29 avril 1982. Paris, 1983.

Masson, Paul-Marie. "Le ballet héroïque." *La revue musicale* 9 (June 1928): 132–154.

Viollier, Renée. *Mouret: Le musicien des grâces, 1682–1738.* Paris, 1950.

JÉRÔME DE LA GORCE
Translated from French

MOVEMENT CHOIR. The concept of movement choir, or *Bewegungschöre,* was developed by Rudolf Laban in Germany during the early 1920s. Laban considered dance to be an integral part of life experience, and he wanted lay people to enjoy dance, not only as spectators but also as participants. Movement choir was perceived as a communal movement form for those who were not technically trained dancers but who wanted to have the "shared experience of the joy of moving" (Laban). The main emphasis was on the collective expressiveness of the group. Guided by trained leaders, simple group compositions were created and then molded into performances for community festivals. The performance was not to be judged as a professional artistic event but to be seen as a cultural and educational force in society.

Movement choir emerged from the social and political atmosphere that developed from 1918 to the early 1930s in Germany, during which the end of World War I, the social influence of the Russian Revolution, the toppling of the German monarchy, and the establishment of the Weimar Republic resulted in a loosening of many of the rigid structures of German society. Among the young people, there was a real sense of building and contributing to a new society. There was also a general receptiveness to all kinds of art forms. People participated in many collective activities such as adult extension courses, craft guilds, youth organizations, and political clubs. The new cultural and political organizations revived the tradition of celebrations to evoke a common spirit through group participation. This social climate provided the opportunity for a layman's communal dance form to flourish.

When Laban was sixteen years old, he helped design *tableaux vivants*. He soon decided to show these statically held positions in a moving sequence. Laban used this idea again when he directed city festivals in Munich (1911–1914). Many of the elements of Movement Choir developed from Laban's work at Ascona, Switzerland (1910–1913), during the open-air summer festivals where spectators would join the dance events.

When Laban was in Hamburg in 1922, he experimented with combining speech choirs and choric dance. He collaborated with Vilma Mönckeberg-Kollmar, a lecturer who was working with a speech choir for lay people, and Laban produced six choric dances for this theater event. He also used speech and movement choirs to be used in scenes for Goethe's drama *Faust* and Aeschylus's *Prometheus*. In 1923, the term *movement choir* came into existence when one of the participants of a community movement session in Hamburg mentioned, "We are a moving choir." These sessions produced the first performance, *Solstice,* by a lay choir of eighty people.

Throughout Germany and other parts of Europe, Laban schools were established, and each school provided a place for the lay person to join others and dance. Movement choir courses were given at adult-education academies and community centers. Weekly classes were led by trained Laban teachers who instructed the students in body training based on the Laban theories of movement; these utilized such concepts as natural movement, dynamic qualities, and spatial patterns. In these sessions people were divided into groups of high, medium, and deep movers, based on the natural tendencies of the individual. The high mover favored light, buoyant, and rising movements; the medium mover particularly liked swinging and flowing movements; and the deep mover felt at home with strong, energetic and earthbound movements. These divisions helped to create a distinctive group character. Group movement exercises, using both improvisational and structured material, were conducted to promote sensitivity to group rhythm and shape. Groups gathered, divided, and surrounded each other, they moved in opposition and in harmony. Themes would develop or be suggested by a member of the group. Through improvisation and repetition, movement sequences were formed into a *saltata,* or group dance composition. Many of these themes reflected the urban life and work experiences of the participants.

Simplicity and clarity of movement were emphasized in these *saltatas*. Mary Wigman, who studied with Laban, was also experimenting with the elements of choric dance. Wigman wrote in her book, *The Language of Dance* (1966): "The most inexorable demand of the choric principle is simplicity in space structure, in rhythmic content in movement, posture and gesture in their dynamic tensions, solutions and crescendi. Anything too complicated is an offense against the choric idea."

Festivals helped to disseminate the concept of movement choir. Lisa Ullmann, a renowned colleague of Laban, said, "It is the festive occasion when the movement choir comes most fully into its own; when choral movement works are created and danced for the purpose of making a special event" (Ullmann, 1956). As Laban's reputation grew, he was commissioned to organize and direct movement choirs for festivals. Large-scale festivals required the leader to provide a more structured framework that involved advanced planning of floor patterns and group formations. At times, Laban would orchestrate a movement score, record it in an early form of his notation system, and then teach it to a group. An example of his structured form was *Titan,* a choral work that premiered at the First Dance Congress in Magdeburg in 1927. Laban gave the notated score to Albrecht Knust, a skilled leader, who reproduced this work in Hamburg (1928) for the celebration of the fifth anniversary of movement choir.

Laban's largest pageant was for the Vienna Festzug des Handwerkes und der Gewerbe (Pageant of Crafts and Craft Guilds). This event took place through the city streets of Vienna in 1929 and included over twenty-five hundred dancers. Laban involved the craft and trade guild workers by using their work movements and rhythms, weaving them into a simple dance form.

Martin Gleisner, one of the most prominent leaders of movement choir, led choirs for the labor and socialist communities. He organized festivals that integrated singing, speaking, and moving choirs. Gleisner's book, *Tanz für Alle* (*Dance for All,* 1928), spoke of movement Choir as a contemporary folk dance that had cultural and educational significance.

In 1936, Laban prepared a choir for the Berlin Olympic games, which was to include one thousand performers. This production never took place, for the Nazi government declared it to be against the state. Laban was banished to the village of Staffelberg and his books were banned. Instead, Mary Wigman was chosen to stage *Lament for the Dead* for the Olympic festival. The ordeal deeply affected Laban's health, and in 1938 he joined Kurt Jooss and other friends at Dartington Hall in England. His later years were spent writing and teaching in England assisted by Lisa Ullmann.

Ullmann was a major force in establishing movement choir in England. In 1935, Ullmann founded the first movement choir in Plymouth, England, under the auspices of the Workers Educational Association. Ullmann and Sylvia Bodmer, a former Swiss student of Laban, formed the Manchester Dance Circle in 1943, a recreational dance group. Soon dance circles were formed throughout England. In 1970, at the Albert Hall in London, fifteen dance circles came together under the direction of Geraldine Stephenson to celebrate the twenty-fifth anniversary of the Laban Art of Movement Guild. In 1979, directed by Joan Russell, seven hundred people came together at the Coventry Sports Centre for the centennial celebration of Laban's birth. In England, the focus of movement choir has been its recreational appeal for the community and its use in modern dance education for the schools.

Irmgard Bartenieff introduced the concept of movement choir to the United States through her workshops and courses. Bartenieff stressed the interactional process of moving together, for in movement choir each member can be part of a group yet still maintain his or her individuality. She saw the choir as a therapeutic and a restorative resource that could help provide relief from the stresses of today's life.

Each society will interpret and adapt movement choir according to the mores and needs of the prevailing culture. One society might formalize the structure, another might utilize its ritualistic nature, while yet another might accent the group unifying and supportive nature of movement choir. As Laban stated, "The main aim of movement choir must always be the shared experience of the joy of moving. It is to a great extent an inner experience and, above all, a strengthening of the desire for communion" (Laban, 1975).

[*See also the entries on Laban and Wigman.*]

BIBLIOGRAPHY

Arnold, Joan, and Carole Crewdson. "The Twilight Ritual." *Contact Quarterly* 9 (Spring–Summer 1984).

Bartenieff, Irmgard, and Dori Lewis. *Body Movement: Coping with the Environment.* New York, 1980.

Bodmer, Sylvia. "Memories of Laban." *Laban Art of Movement Guild Magazine* (November 1979).

Crewdson, Carole. "Festival of Freedom." *Laban/Bartenieff Institute Newsletter* (February 1982).

Gleisner, Martin. "On Movement Choirs." *Laban Art of Movement Guild Magazine* (November 1979).

Laban, Rudolf. *A Life for Dance: Reminiscences.* Translated and edited by Lisa Ullmann. New York, 1975.

Matalon, Leah. "An Interview with Irmgard about Movement Choirs." *American Association of Laban Analysts Newsletter* (October 1983).

Thornton, Samuel. *Movement Perspective of Rudolf Laban.* Boston, 1971.

Ullmann, Lisa. "Recreative Dancing in the Movement Choir." *Physical Recreation* (January 1956).

Wigman, Mary. *The Language of Dance.* Translated by Walter Sorell. Middletown, Conn., 1966.

Willett, John. *Art and Politics in the Weimar Period: The New Sobriety, 1917–1933.* New York, 1978.

CAROLE CREWDSON

MOVIES. *See* Film Musicals.

MOZAMBIQUE. *See* Central and East Africa; Southern Africa. *See also* Shangana-Tsonga Dance.

MUDRĀ. The hand gestures in Indian classical dance are commonly known as *mudrā,* although the term used by dancers is *hasta.* The gestures form part of the system of *aṅgīkabhinaya* (body movement used to convey meaning and expression). The *Nāṭyaśāstra* treatises treat the topic of *hasta*s in detail. They are classified in three categories: *asamyuta* (single), *samyuta* (double), and *nṛtta* (pure dance). Their number varies according to different texts: the *Nāṭyaśāstra* enumerates twenty-four single, thirteen double, and twenty-seven *nṛtta hasta*s; the *Abhinayadarpaṇa* lists twenty-eight single, twenty-three double, and thirteen *nṛtta hasta*s. Similarly, there are differences in the usage of the *hasta*s. In the oral tradition the gurus teach the usage and placement of the *hasta*s. Facial expressions also help to convey the meaning of the song, along with the *hasta-mudrā*s.

The *hasta*s cover almost all aspects of human life. They are capable of expressing abstract concepts such as truth, beauty, and time; they scale distances between two objects; they can be used to command, reject, admonish, or make love; they suggest castes and relationships; and they enable a dancer to interpret, narrate, and describe many things. A dancer can employ the *hasta*s in the way a poet would use a simile or metaphor, so that the same gesture can express a wide range of objects and events and the conceptual relations among them.

MUDRĀ. The twenty-four root *mudrā*s (or *hasta*s) of *kathakaḷi* dance. Although these hand positions are essentially the same across all forms of Indian dance, each organizes them differently. *Kathakaḷi* has the most elaborate system, dividing the *mudrā*s into three categories (one hand, same *mudrā* in both hands, different *mudrā*s in each hand) with a total vocabulary of about nine hundred words. The mimetic meaning of the positions varies enormously: in *kathakaḷi,* the first *mudrā* (top left), called *pataka,* can have fifty-one different meanings, from "sun" to "anthill" to "tender leaf." (Drawing used by permission of Nicola Savarese.)

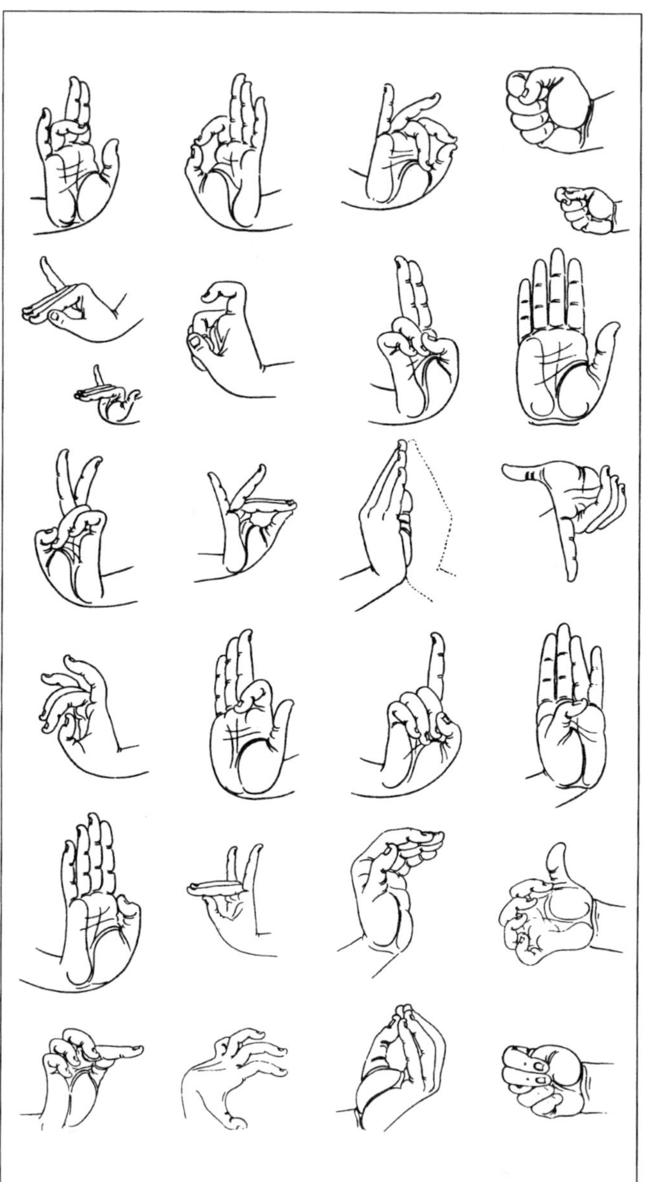

BIBLIOGRAPHY

Banerji, Projesh. *Art of Indian Dancing.* New Delhi, 1985.

Center for the Promotion of Traditional Arts. *Mudras, in Symbols.* Madras, 1988.

Coomaraswamy, Ananda K. "Notes on Indian Dramatic Technique." *The Mask* 6 (October 1913): 109–128.

Kavi, Manavalli Ramakrishna, ed. *Nāṭyaśāstra of Bharatamuni.* Vol. 2. Gaekwad's Oriental Series, no. 68. Baroda, 1926–. See chapter 9.

Kothari, Sunil, ed. *Bharata Natyam: Indian Classical Dance Art.* Bombay, 1979.

La Meri. *The Gesture Language of the Hindu Dance.* New York, 1941.

Puri, Rajika. "The Family of Rama." *Journal for the Anthropological Study of Human Movement* 1 (Spring 1980): 20–35.

SUNIL KOTHARI

MUMMENSCHANZ. *See* Mommeries.

MUNICH STATE OPERA BALLET. *See* Bavarian State Ballet.

MURDMAA, MAI-ESTER (born 31 March 1938 in Tallinn), Estonian ballet dancer and choreographer. Murdmaa completed her studies at the Tallinn Ballet School in 1956 and began to dance with the Estonia Ballet that same year. From 1959 to 1964, she studied choreography with Rostislav Zakharov at the Moscow State Institute for Theatrical Art, producing her first significant work, *Ballet Symphony,* to music by Eino Tamberg, in 1963. In 1965 she became artistic director of the Estonia Theater Ballet in Tallinn; since 1973 she has been its chief choreographer. She toured with the company, showing her ballets in Bulgaria, Germany, Poland, Sweden, Italy, and Finland. Among her important productions are *The Miraculous Mandarin* (1968), to music by Béla Bartók; *The Prodigal Son* (1973), to music by Sergei Prokofiev; *The Woman* (1986), to music by Luciano Berio; *Cry and Silence* (1986), to music by Kuldar Sink; and *Crime and Punishment* (1991), to music by Arvo Pärt.

Murdmaa has also staged works for companies abroad. In the United States she choreographed for the Colorado Ballet (1990) and the Indianapolis Ballet (1992). She has worked with such international artists as Mikhail Baryshnikov and Natalia Makarova. She has also created works for film and television in various cities of the former Soviet Union.

In interviews with the Western press, Murdmaa spoke of her work as being a kind of response to what she considered to be the excesses of Soviet ballet. Refusing to rely on the classical vocabulary, Murdmaa sought a language of stylized expression. She liked to say that she found the movements inside herself. Most of her works are tensely dramatic. About *Cry and Silence,* she remarked that it was about hope and lack of hope, about suffering as she had witnessed it in her troubled country.

[*See also* Estonia.]

BIBLIOGRAPHY

Dunning, Jennifer. "Dance in Review." *New York Times* (6 April 1992).

Shulgold, Marc. "Estonian Speaks with Eloquence." *Rocky Mountain News* (22 March 1991).

SELMA JEANNE COHEN

MURPHY, GRAEME (born 1950 in Melbourne, Australia), dancer and choreographer. Most of Murphy's childhood was spent in rural Tasmania. He auditioned for the Australian Ballet School at the age of fourteen and began his career as a dancer with the Australian Ballet.

Murphy created his first ballet, *Ecco,* for a choreographic workshop in 1971. Soon after, he studied at the Joffrey School and performed with the Australian Ballet on its 1971 Nureyev tour in New York before joining the Sadler's Wells Royal Ballet and later the Ballets Félix Blaska. In 1975 Murphy returned to Australia and worked as a freelance choreographer. He was appointed artistic director of The Dance Company of New South Wales, with his partner and muse Janet Vernon as his associate, in November 1976 and began to build a repertory of original works by Australian choreographers. In 1978 Murphy created his first full-length work, *Poppy,* which is about the life of French author Jean Cocteau. In 1979 Murphy changed the company's name to the Sydney Dance Company, and the following year he led it on its first tour of Europe. The Sydney Dance Company has since presented new Australian dance works to audiences in the United States, Europe, and parts of South America, Asia, and the Middle East.

Murphy has choreographed more than forty original works for his own company and has been regularly commissioned by other performing arts organizations. For the Australian Ballet his choreography includes *Beyond Twelve* (1980), *Gallery* (1987), and a new version of *The Nutcracker* (1992). For the Australian Opera he directed *Metamorphosis* (1985), *Turandot* (1990), *Salome* (1993), and *The Trojans* (1994). Other commissioning organizations include the Royal New Zealand Ballet, the Canadian Opera Company, and the ice skaters Torvill and Dean. In 1988 the Australian Bicentennial Authority commissioned Murphy to create *Vast,* a landmark work reflecting the senses and aesthetics of the various Australian environments—sea, coast, cities, and the outback. For this work he brought together the dancers of Australian Dance Theatre, the Queensland Ballet, the West Australian Ballet, and the Sydney Dance Company.

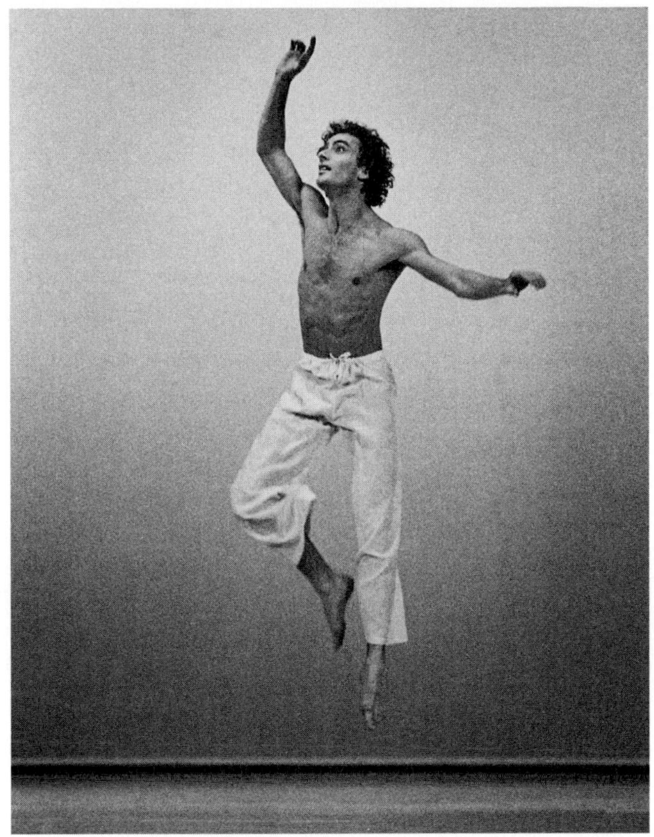

MURPHY. In his three-act ballet *Poppy* (1978), Murphy appeared in the role of Jean Cocteau. In act 2, he is hospitalized to undergo a cure for opium addiction. (Photograph © by Branco Gaica; used by permission.)

Murphy's choreography is very theatrical and often gimmicky, but it is also varied in style and thematic material, ranging from narrative full-evening works such as *Poppy* (1978), *After Venice* (1984), and *King Roger* (1990) to plotless works such as *Kraanerg* (1988), *Soft Bruising* (1990), and *Piano Sonata* (1992) to collaborations such as those with Iva Davies's rock group Icehouse, in *Boxes* (1985) and *Berlin* (1995), and with Michael Askill's contemporary percussion group Synergy, in *Synergy with Synergy* (1992). In the program notes Murphy described the latter as a "concerto for music, muscle, and machine"; it is a good example of his dynamically sophisticated work and of his skill in presenting visually and musically fulfilling dance that is always energetic.

Murphy champions contemporary music and has commissioned new scores from Australian composers such as Carl Vine, Graeme Koehne, Barry Conyngham, and Iva Davies. He has created new dance works to existing scores by Luciano Berio, Steve Martland, Gavin Bryars, Olivier Messaien, and Iannis Xenakis. In 1982 Murphy was made a Member of the Order of Australia for services to dance; in 1988 he was voted Australian of the Year by the national newspaper *The Australian.* Both Murphy and Vernon were among the honorees of the first Sydney Opera House Awards in 1993 and at the International Dance Day celebrations in Sydney in 1995.

[*See also* Australia, *article on* Modern Dance.]

BIBLIOGRAPHY

Grove, Robin. "Silent Stories." *Brolga* (December 1994): 9–16.

Pask, Edward H. *Ballet in Australia: The Second Act, 1940–1980.* Melbourne, 1982.

Potter, Michele. *A Passion for Dance.* Canberra, 1997.

ARCHIVE. Sydney Dance Company.

VALDA L. CRAIG

MURRAY, ARTHUR (Moses Teichman; born 4 April 1895 in East Harlem, New York City, died 3 March 1991 in Honolulu), American dance instructor and businessman. Savvy business acumen enabled Murray to build an international dance-instruction empire through mail-order courses, studio lessons, and television entertainment. Known as much for his inventive and relentless use of advertising as for his dance abilities, Murray began dancing when a high school girlfriend saved him from becoming a wallflower by teaching him a few steps. He decided to become a dance instructor after winning a waltz contest at age seventeen. After studying with Vernon and Irene Castle, he taught for them and at a high-society hotel in South Carolina. In an unexpectedly practical move, he entered Georgia Tech at age twenty-four to major in business administration. While there he continued to teach dance and hit upon the idea of selling dance instruction by mail order. He built a highly successful business featuring follow-the-footsteps directions, his own innovation. It was during this period that Murray began to develop his almost scientific use of advertising. By trial and error he developed advertising techniques featuring testimonials that promised social and even business success by developing confidence through dance skills.

MURRAY. A portrait of Murray and a dancing partner, elegantly poised. (Photograph reprinted from Murray, 1947.)

Shortly after 1923, with the decline of his mail-order business, Murray opened a dance studio on East Forty-third Street in New York City. Occupying six floors and employing approximately 150 teachers at the height of its success, the studio had a highly structured internal organization. A student was handed from receptionist to evaluator to instructor and encouraged to sign a long-term contract. Teachers were stringently trained and monitored. Instruction focused on established dances with occasional fad offerings. All details were carefully managed according to Murray's directions. Sending teachers to resorts and hotels developed into what is purported to have been the first franchise operation ever. Depending on the source consulted, Murray's franchise emporium grew to between 350 and 500 branches in the United States and Europe.

Murray married Kathryn Kohnfelder, a student who became his dance and business partner. For seven years, in the 1950s, the Murrays produced, hosted, and danced on *The Arthur Murray Party,* a television show featuring dance displays and guest entertainers. Murray claimed that the show boosted annual studio revenues from $20 million to $50 million.

Murray's sales technique was considered too hard sell by some, and his advertising misleading by others. In 1957, he was sued by a blind man who had invested $6,000 in lessons without developing the social graces that had been promised. In 1960, the Federal Trade Commission issued a complaint against Arthur Murray, Inc., for deceptive sales practices. Murray blamed individual franchisees but claimed to have already addressed the infractions.

In 1964, Murray resigned as president of the Arthur Murray Dance Studios but remained as a consultant. (He had sold controlling interest in 1952.) He and his wife retired to their homes in Rye, New York, and Honolulu.

[*See also* Social Dance, *article on* Twentieth-Century Social Dance to 1960.]

BIBLIOGRAPHY

Murray, Arthur, and Kathryn Murray. *The Arthur Murrays' Dance Secrets.* New York, 1946.

Murray, Arthur. *How to Become to Good Dancer.* New York, 1947.

Murray, Arthur. *Let's Dance.* New York, 1953.

Murray, Kathryn, and Betty Hannah Hoffman. *My Husband, Arthur Murray.* New York, 1960.

VIDEOTAPE. "The Arthur Murray Party" (WNBC–TV, New York, 16 November 1953), available at the Museum of Broadcasting and Radio, New York.

ARCHIVES. Dance Collection, New York Public Library for the Performing Arts.

CYNTHIA R. MILLMAN

MUSE OF DANCE. *See* Terpsichore.

MUSETTE. A small French bagpipe, the musette was descended from the Eurasian and Celtic forms and was popular in French court circles during the seventeenth and eighteenth centuries. It was bellows-blown and had four or five drones enclosed in a cylinder. It gave its name (from Old French *muser,* "to make music") to both a musical genre and a type of dance.

In the eighteenth century, the instrument was a symbol of the fashionable fad among the upper classes with the notion of Arcadia—an elusive mythic ideal of pastoral innocence and rustic pleasures. Jean Antoine Watteau (1684–1721) captured this concept in his *fêtes galantes* paintings; his earlier works sometimes portray dance accompanied by a *musette.* Along with the *vielle* (various medieval stringed instruments including the hurdy-gurdy) the *musette* is an *instrument champêtre* (country instrument). It was liked for its sweet, delicate sound, its small drones, and its relative ease of playing; it could be played by court ladies, who often affected elegantly pastoral costumes in pastel shades.

Musical pieces were composed in imitation of the sound of the *musette.* Their chief characteristic was a drone bass *(basse de musette);* they have been variously described as pastoral, innocent, rustic, caressing, gentle, naive, or serene. These musical pieces called musettes were composed in duple, triple, and compound meters, and their melodies often employed intervals of a second. They were sometimes combined with other dance forms, such as *gavottes* and *menuets,* creating *gavottes en musette, menuets en musette,* and so on.

In opera and ballet, these compositions were used to accompany dances of a pastoral character. The danced or theatrical use of the *musette* occurs most frequently among French composers, although Handel (*Il Pastor Fido,* 1734) and Mozart (*Bastien und Bastienne,* 1768) also used them. Rameau wrote the greatest number—many of his *opéra-ballets* contain *musettes* in various meters—but musettes also appear in Destouches and Lalande's *Les Éléments* (1721); Destouches's *Callirhoé* (1712); Montéclair's *Les Fêtes de lÉté (1716);* and Campra's *Les Muses* (1703) and *Les Âges* (1718).

No choreographies for Rameau's ballets and operas are known to survive. Indeed, only three choreographies of *musettes* survive, and only two are identified as such. The first *musette* to appear in Beauchamps-Feuillet notation is "La Muszette à Deux," choreographed by Guillaume-Louis Pecour for Destouches's *Callirhoé.* The dance was published by Michel Gaudrau in his collection of court and theater dances by Pecour (Paris, 1712). Choreographed for two women, this *musette* was danced at the Opera by performers named Prévost and Guiot. The four figures employ much of the standard Baroque theater dance vocabulary, including *pirouettes, tombés, changements,* a full-turn *contretemps,* and other steps. The music, *gavotte,* is in cut time (2/2), in the key of G, and in AB form. The choreography, which begins with an unusual step-unit *(pas composé),* is characterized by rather rapid, delicate, skimming footwork, supported by calm, leisurely, dreamlike music with a fairly slow pulse. The dance starts with a brief echo sequence, continues mostly with mirror-image figures, and includes a passage toward the end with one dancer making unhurried half-pirouettes while the other circles around her. An exquisite choreography, it is full of turnings, shadings, delicate bendings and risings, finely wrought floor patterns, and suspended balances dropping into *tombés.* Perhaps the *pas composé* that begins this dance (and is found in only one other) was a characteristic of *musette* theater choreographies, but without more surviving examples a definitive judgment cannot be reached.

The only other surviving theater choreography that employs this unusual step and can be identified as a *musette* is found in the same collection of dances as "La Muszette à Deux" and is therefore also by Pecour. Entitled "Entrée pour un Berger et une Bergère," it is a couple dance from *Sémélé* (1709) by Marin Marais. The title page of this notation indicates that Guiot performed this dance at the Opera with her male partner Dumoulin. This *entrée* has four figures and an overall character and step vocabulary not unlike Pecour's *musette* for two female dancers. The music appears only in Marais's *Troisième livre* (1711), containing *Pièces de Violes,* as "La Muzette."

One more *musette* choreography survives, this one a ballroom dance for a couple published in the annual collections *(Petits recüeils annuels)* in Paris in 1724. Titled "La Musette par M. Pécour," it consists of three figures.

The subtitle, given under the tune at the top of the first page, is "Premier Rigaudon"; "2e (second) Rigaudon" appears halfway through the dance. Typically, the first *rigaudon* is in a major key (G), and the second in a minor (g). Despite the subtitle, this tune, in 2/2 time, could be called a *gavotte* rather than a *rigaudon*, as the phrases begin with the half-bar upbeat common to *gavottes*. Each *rigaudon* is in ABA form. The choreography is fairly typical of ballroom choreographies found in the annual collections around 1720 and similar to other *gavotte* choreographies, frequently employing the *pas de gavotte*.

[*See also*, Ballet Technique, History of, *article on* French Court Dance.]

BIBLIOGRAPHY

Bricqueville, Eugène de. *Les musettes*. Paris, 1894.

Girdlestone, Cuthbert. *Jean-Philippe Rameau: His Life and Work*. Rev. ed. New York, 1969.

Lindenmann, F. B. "Pastoral Instruments in French Baroque Music: Musette and Vielle." Ph.D. diss., Columbia University, 1976.

MARGARET DANIELS

MUSEUMS. *See* Libraries and Museums.

MUSICAL OFFERING. Choreography: Paul Taylor. Music: Johann Sebastian Bach. Designer: Gene Moore. Lighting: Jennifer Tipton. First performance: 8 April 1986, City Center, New York City, Paul Taylor Dance Company. Dancers: Kate Johnson, Christopher Gillis, Cathy McCann, David Parsons, Linda Kent, Kenneth Tosti, Karla Wolfangle, James Karr, Raegan Wood, Douglas Wright, Sandra Stone, Mary Cochran, Joao Mauricio, Jeff Wadlington.

Paul Taylor presented two contrasting new works in 1986: *Ab Ovo usque ad Mala (From Soup to Nuts)* to music by P. D. Q. Bach (a pseudonym used by the contemporary American composer Peter Schickele) and *Musical Offering* to music as titled by the eighteenth-century composer J. S. Bach. Where the former parodied dance conventions in general and Taylor's own work specifically, *Musical Offering* revealed Taylor at his most sophisticated and solemn. Moreover, it marked the culmination of twenty-five years of his choreography to music by J. S. Bach and other Baroque composers.

His first work to music by Bach was *Junction* in 1961 and it is significant that, in working closely with two of the composer's cello suites, Taylor's main aim was to develop his musicality. Subsequently, he has used the rich textural and rhythmic structures of Baroque music as accompaniment for several of his dances, most notably for *Esplanade* and *Brandenburgs* (Bach); *Aureole* and *Airs* (George Frideric Handel); and *Arden Court* (William Boyce). What is so intriguing about Taylor's musicality is that it is an aural response. He cannot read a score, so listening closely to music has been of ongoing importance in his choreographic process. For Taylor, musicality is a dialogue between choreography and accompaniment; a two-way conversation in which there are many types of interaction between the two forces. This dialogue is particularly remarkable in *Musical Offering*. The music inspired Taylor's subject matter and it also provided the structural framework for him to create many contrapuntal relationships between movement and accompaniment. That Taylor retained Bach's original title is indicative of this correlation.

Though Bach's *Musical Offering* is considered to be one of the finest exercises in counterpoint, this did not deter Taylor from using it; more likely, it was because he was unaware of its historical importance that he was able to interpret the score in such a consummate way. He first heard the music on a tape that had been sent to him from Germany. (Within a year of its premiere, *Musical Offering* was taken into the repertory of the Berlin Opera Ballet.) Initially, Taylor thought that the music was by a contemporary minimalist composer, such as Philip Glass or Steve Reich, because the entire score is developed from a single *ostinato* theme: "I was amazed at how many times that damned tune could play over and over again and still work. It was a revelation."

Like Bach, Taylor used the theme as the leading imitative voice. Alone on stage, a female soloist (Kate Johnson) begins the work, outlining the theme in the opening measures of the first *ricercare*. As the theme becomes embellished musically, her movements become fuller; then other dancers enter in canon upstage and repeat the soloist's opening phrase.

In rehearsals, however, Taylor began tracing and developing the theme, not with the main female soloist, but with the more complex dances for other soloists and ensemble groups, thus layering his movement immediately against the music's densely orchestrated inner sections. Even when the theme is intentionally hidden by Bach through fugal and canonic accumulations, Taylor has discerned its most subtle manipulations. He uses almost the complete score (omitting only the Largo and second Allegro from the Trio Sonata) and has structured his choreography in sixteen movements, in an alternating pattern of solo and group dances. As well as the main female protagonist, *Musical Offering* features several of Taylor's senior dancers as soloists. Most often, the solos occur downstage of a unison group or groups of dancers and, throughout the work, the latter either form still linear tableaux or they delineate the upstage area as a corridor by their cumulative entrances and exits.

Taylor's soloist/ensemble structure and his creation of spatial corridors across the stage are two important devices used to convey the quasi narrative woven through the work. Bach himself inspired it: *Musical Offering* was one of his last compositions, and Taylor saw the score as a farewell. Furthermore, he interpreted the music as a requiem, a mysterious ritual, mourning either the loss of one person from a group or the isolation of an individual through the departure of an entire community. Taylor provided many clues about his subject matter in interviews prior to the premiere and in these he also referred to a series of New Guinea wood sculptures in the Metropolitan Museum, New York. (Gene Moore's flesh-colored leotards, dark loincloths, and backdrop also suggest an archaic context, and soon after the premiere, Taylor added a subtitle: "a requiem for gentle primitives.")

This curious combination—Bach's score and the museum sculptures—inspired Taylor to discover a new movement style for *Musical Offering*. The main motif is a W-shape that, like the theme, is augmented as the work progresses. It is introduced by the soloist as a flat, angled arm position in the opening section. Initially, it accompanies her side-to-side rocking motion before being developed in side hops, knee hinges, and stiff-kneed *chainé* turns. The major influence on Taylor's movement vocabulary was undoubtedly the wood sculptures, a collection of finely carved, thin-limbed figures and two-dimensional skull racks. Some of the exhibits are double figures in which two angular forms sit one on top of the other; Taylor makes particular reference to these in the ninth movement of *Musical Offering*. This section recalls part of George Balanchine's *Ivesiana*, in which a woman is lifted and carried, sphinxlike, without ever touching the ground. Tellingly, in Taylor's choreography, the position of the woman (Karla Wolfangle) as she is carried aloft by four men is the same as the squatting, W-shaped upper figure in some of the New Guinea sculptures.

The W-motif was also inspired by the alternatively ascending and descending lines in Bach's music. The motif becomes inverted in deep *pliés* and headstands, with the most obvious inversion occurring in the closing ricercare. Here, during the protagonist's last solo, the whole ensemble lies on the floor in a group tableau forming an M-shape across the back of the stage. Thus, the motif is stated literally (and collectively) as the letter *M*, Taylor's final tribute to the formal logic and complexity of Bach's music.

In *Musical Offering* the visual and aural correspondences between choreography and accompaniment are uncanny. So, too, are the extended movement phrases that Taylor developed from the most minimal of material, his Reichian manipulation of "that damned tune."

BIBLIOGRAPHY

Berman, Janice. "Paul Taylor Takes a Step into the Past." *Newsweek* (30 March 1986).

Kisselgoff, Anna. "Taylor's Musical Offering." *New York Times* (10 April 1986).

Mazo, Joseph. "Paul Taylor's Troupe: Dancing Bach to Bach." *The Record* (28 March 1986): 7.

Tobias, Tobi. "Taylor's More Lasting Shapes." *New York* (5 May 1986): 8.

Ulrich, Allan. "Taylor-made." *San Francisco Examiner* (23 October 1986).

ANGELA KANE

MUSICAL THEATER IN THE UNITED STATES. *See* United States of America, *article on* Musical Theater.

MUSIC FOR DANCE. [*To demonstrate the variety of relationships between music and dance, this entry comprises nine articles:*

African Music
Arab Music
Asian Music
Oceanic Music
Western Music before 1520
Western Music, 1520–1650
Western Music, 1650–1800
Western Music, 1800–1900
Western Music since 1900

The first four articles focus on specific areas of world cultures; the remaining articles discuss music for European-based social and theatrical dance.]

African Music

Music in sub-Saharan African societies is so closely bound with dance that one can speak of music-dance cultures. Music and dance usually share a common or overlapping vocabulary and are often parts of the same social institutions. In fact, the same performer often supplies both music and dance, or the musician's movements are choreographically stylized.

Africans structure dance in at least three orders of relationship to music. Dance may accompany music, in that performers emphasize the sounds they produce rather than their movements. Music may accompany dance in performance, in which case the movements themselves are foregrounded. Finally, performers may strive for a parity through which one should "see the music and hear the dance." Any order of relationship may characterize an entire dance, or only a phase of the dance in combination with the others.

Music-making is primarily a group activity, although African societies also cultivate solo traditions. If dance consists minimally of structured movements of the body, then one observes that for many solo traditions dance is *melogenic*—that is, it grows out of melodic contours and rhythm. This may be the unaccompanied solo line of a Fon child in Benin, singing to commemorate the loss of its first tooth; eventually, the child begins to move to the rhythm of the song. Another example is the monophonic lullaby of the mother's sister among the Nzakara of the Central African Republic, who customarily cares for her older sister's child. Her melodic contours and rhythm conform to those preferred by the Nzakara, and she sways while singing to the child. Since the texture is monophonic, there is no sound accompaniment. Instead, like the Fon child, she visually punctuates the melody. Both forms of melogenic dance serve as accompaniment to the music.

Dance may sonically accompany music in at least two ways. First, the percussive sounds produced by the dance movements themselves may serve this purpose. Tanzanian Masai men's characteristic prancing movements, interspersed by jumps, are an example, as are the leaps in Zulu warriors' dances, the springing movements of Samburu clan dances, and the Kikuyu's vertical springing followed by running movements. The dancers' feet produce loud, percussive sounds, especially when several move simultaneously; these beats outline the basic pulse of the song and contribute to its overall sonority.

There is a rich array of drums, wind, string and percussion instruments for the dance. Some societies, however, use only a few portable instruments or none at all for their musical forms; these societies have large dance repertories and complex vocal genres. For most Zulu dances, handclapping and sounds made with body ornaments provide the principal accompaniment, although the Zulu have one indigenous drum. Igbo dancers in Nigeria prefer bells to drums as accompaniment in their Igogo festivals. The !Kung (Bushmen) and BaMbuti of Congo (formerly Zaïre) have no indigenous drums. Several African societies proscribe the use of the principal dance instruments by certain classes, particularly women; these groups have responded by using alternative instruments or body ornaments worn by dancers.

Second, sound devices may be attached to dancers' bodies. Dancers' costumes may include ornaments constructed and attached so that any movement produces a sound. The dance movements temporally accord with the song rhythms and indirectly produce an accompaniment for song.

Such sound devices include strings of beads joined in ladderlike fashion with small chains. Strings of metal and shells cross-garter the legs, or strings of small bells are wound crosswise around the body. Dancers may wear corncob ornaments, iron knee bells containing loose balls, heavy bracelets, iron and brass armlets, or ostrich-eggshell girdles. Iron banana-shaped bells strapped above the knee and bean-shaped ankle bells containing pellets are not uncommon. Metal, bark, or cowrie-shell ankle rings are also worn. Dancers carry millet stalks, swords, shields, or dancing sticks; the last resemble walking sticks covered with brass which dancers clash or strike against the ground as they move. All are instruments played by the dancer as part of the music. Some cultures where masking is important have "sound masks" played by musicians.

Most music-dance performances are group activities and integral parts of public occasions. At public performances Africans dance the identities of individuals or groups. On these occasions they recognize the forms of social action associated with different groups. African movement with music creates, articulates, and recreates age, gender, and class identities.

Africans dance new identities at rites of passage. Societies usually reserve a specific category of music for each rite. Performances of both may be generically referred to as dances, with the music at least conceptually backgrounded. For instance, the Luo at Kenya perform praise songs and prayers at naming ceremonies. Luo movements at these times announce the purpose of the occasion, highlight natural features that the Nuer consider most important, and bring a child into contact with the environment destined to become an important aspect of his or her identity. Dancers, rather than musicians, wear the symbols of these priorities—vine necklaces and belts, goatskin dresses, and clay smeared on the body.

Funeral dances may emphasize human relationships, interaction with the supernatural environment, and ideas about the person. Many societies view death as an event that transforms rather than terminates life. At Congo BaMbuti Molimo death ceremonies, the surviving mortals form a circle and, seated, swing in unison from side to side. Their song opens the dance by awakening the benevolent forces of the life-giving forest and calling their attention to the dancers. The high point of the ceremony is dance, including one by an elder woman. Funerals end with a foot dance to extinguish the symbolic Molimo fire.

The principal actors dance their own changed identities at puberty and wedding ceremonies as musicians accompany them. When Shilluk boys dance their new identities as men, they salute the drum, encircling it before their puberty ceremony officially begins. This gesture establishes the relationship between the drummers and dancers, which foregrounds the dance.

Weddings are often ceremonial outgrowths of puberty ceremonies. Flutes and drums accompany Bambara brides' dances, but the focal point is the bride and her female friends, who form a long line for her wedding dance. Other wedding dances, such as those of the Samburu of Kenya, feature both women and men. Again music, in this case songs and the sounds of their elaborate costumes, serves simply as accompaniment.

Among the types of dance accompanied by music are those performed to highlight membership in particular social groups. Rather than marking changing identities, they mark stable ones. Certain musical elements may be prescribed. For instance, Dogon priests in Mali must dance to handclapping and hourglass drum accompaniment when a chief priest dies. Shilluk begging dances, exclusively for women, are performed to accompanying songs. Only men who are members of the warrior's company may perform the *asafu* dance, accompanied by drumming, in Fante society.

Music is subordinate to dance not only in forms marking identity changes or those exclusive particular social categories; it is also mere accompaniment to dance in forms that articulate status differences. A Zambian Bemba man or woman may perform solo dances and sing for another out of respect, fulfilling social obligations to those of higher status.

In most African cultures, music and dance have a relationship of parity, neither subordinate to the other. Their practical interdependence begins with basic spatio-temporal orderings. African music-dance performances take place outdoors or in open courtyards. A vacant lot, a town square, an open dance plaza, or the area around a large shade tree are usual sites. Performances may occur in places where people conduct special activities such as worship, healing, or commerce. It is unusual to find permanent structures built exclusively for music or dance. Some societies proscribe certain places for music-dance performance: when the Shilluk install a king, people may drum and sing inside the fence surrounding the former king's tomb, but they must not dance there.

Dance formations, the arrangement of the musicians, the spatial orientation of specific ritual acts and objects, and custom are among the factors that determine the shape of the arena. "Front" for a dancer is usually the principal musical instrumentalist. This facilitates the dialogue in which they engage throughout the performance.

According to some African belief systems, sound–movement forms associated with religious and medical practices themselves have power. African physicians customarily use both music and dance as part of their therapies. !Kung healing practices illustrate the interactive dynamic between music and dance. !Kung believe that a malevolent force enters the body and causes disease; treatment centers on driving it out. !Kung women's songs accompanied by handclapping incite men to dance. Wearing rattles around their legs, the men stamp the ground. Kindled by the songs, trance follows in both dancers and physician. Entranced, the physician can summon and make efficacious the healing power that drives out disease. [*See* !Kung San Dance.]

Dogon healing ceremonies, similarly, display a relationship of parity between music and dance. The Dogon define disease as a loss of forces of vitality within the soul. Music and dance together are curative. Only healers can manufacture the musical instrument, a *gingiru* or four-stringed lute, used as part of the treatment. The *gingiru* puts rhythm into the patient and into the descent of the spiritual being. This establishes unity between them. Once the spirit is inside them, patients dance to the rhythm. The spiritual being brings new life to Earth and reinvigorates the patient's soul. [*See* Dogon Dance.]

Music-dance performances may occur regularly on an annual, seasonal, or diurnal schedule. The Gurri dances of Egypt and Ethiopia are performed to restore or maintain balance in the cosmic order. Musicians perform prophetic and moralizing songs accompanied by hand-

MUSIC FOR DANCE: African Music. The concertina player (left) and whistler player (right) lead the *umteyo* (shaking dance), a double-file line dance performed by young men (called *amakwenkwe*) of the Xhosa tribe in southern Africa. Introduced to the Xhosa in the 1820s by European settlers, the concertina emits squeaky-sounding melodies that provide the tempo for the dance. The whistle player is called the *idraiva*, after the English word *driver*. Rippling actions of the spine and weight-shifting actions of the feet set the bells strapped to the performers' chests and rattles attached to their calves jangling and clattering for additional accompaniment to the dance. (Photograph by Merlyn Severn; reprinted by permission from Hugh Tracey, *African Dances of the Witwatersrand Gold Mines*, Johannesburg, 1952.)

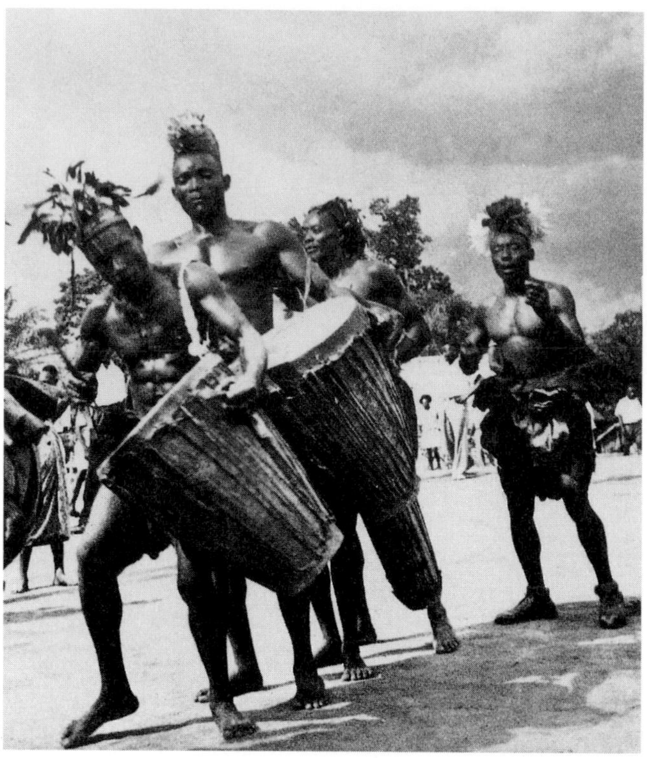

MUSIC FOR DANCE: African Music. Mangbetu drummers from northern Congo. (Photograph from the Department of Library Services, American Museum of Natural History, New York [no. 322900]; use by permission.)

clapping. Their songs signal the arrival and departure of the gods, who are mobilized to possess entranced mediums. Once possessed, the mediums dance convulsive movements, and the deities communicate with the participants through them. Annual and seasonal performances associated with subsistence may employ specific musical forms. After the Nuer harvest millet, they perform a nonceremonial couple dance around an earthenware zither. Bambara women dance to the *mouso denou* (women's drum) for an entire night on the occasion of each new moon.

A regular grouping of beats, called the *time span*, governs the temporal organization of a composition or music-dance corpus. One hears the time span (often six, eight, or twelve beats, or multiples of these) by listening to the combination of all performing parts. Frequently the orienting part is that of a bell, rattle, or other musical instrument with high carrying power (sonority rather than amplitude). Its pattern articulates the temporal boundaries to which all must adhere. The instrument does not simply "beat time," as in 1–2–3–4–5–6–7–8 in a time span of eight. Rather it may play 1—3–4—6—, or another interesting pattern. Other musicians and dancers must carefully place their patterns and steps against this orienting pattern. They either maintain this placement throughout the performance or improvise on it.

Only certain performers improvise. Instrumental and vocal improvisers have the freedom to construct any pattern within the boundaries of the time span. Nonetheless, they strive to create patterns that will combine with the others so that the ensemble sounds every beat. They strive to create variety in the accentual scheme. Vocal improvisers must also craft new texts with innovative and socially appropriate ideas. If these are possible for the instrument, an improvising instrumentalist may switch from the dance mode to the speech or signaling mode. In the speech mode, the musician may "talk" to the dancers, to inspire, encourage, direct, follow, praise, or even chide them. He or she may also "talk" to other participants in the same ways. Such messages may be conveyed through the signaling mode, although this does not correspond to spoken words. Dancers' basic movements should fit within the time span and be unvarying; improvisations are also temporally bounded by the time span.

Africans themselves classify music-dance by occasions of performance. This was also important to functionalist ethnographic interpretations concentrating on institutions and context. Functionalism was the dominant paradigm in reports of African music and dance during the mid-twentieth century, and much of the data currently available reflect this viewpoint.

Attention then turned to interpretive studies. Music theories and aesthetic systems, microsocial studies of individual composers, choreographers, and performers, gender issues, and performance practices are some of the topics investigated. Popular music and dance forms in cities have received attention. New methods for probing meaning are producing deeper insights into an African-centered understanding of expressive culture. The notion that meaning in African dance is bound up with indigenous, culture-specific concepts of the body, body movements and the person shaped new questions.

Today, Africans perform music-dance at schools, universities, state functions, nightclubs, ballrooms, concert halls, and even churches. Both music and dance continue to serve instructive purposes for children and to communicate the feelings most important to the community. Both are a feature of African television dramas, film documentaries, and theatrical plays.

Spatiotemporal conditions have changed. Staged performances on elevated platforms pose new choreographic problems. Audiences no longer determine the shape of the space as they surround dancers and musicians. "Front" for the dancers has become the edge of the stage. Musicians, then, must find other ways to engage in dialogue with dancers.

Music may no longer be live, but rather recorded. This has created a new relationship between dancers and musicians. Often music borrowed from distant cultures of the African diaspora, such as reggae or rap, comes with its own distinctive dance forms. People use recorded versions of locally created musical styles (Afro-disco, juju, Afro-rock, highlife, and Afro-beat) as dance accompaniment. Popular recording artists—notably Kofi Ghanaba, Fela Anikulapo-Kuti, Sonny Ade, Ignace de Souza, and Luambo Makiadi (Doctor Franco)—and female vocalists (including M'Pongo Love, Miatta Fahnbulleh, Pinise Saul, Princess Audrey, and Aicha Koje) have generated new dances or dance variations.

Changes in contexts, meanings, and purposes do not necessarily affect African music–dance vocabularies and processes. Improvisation continues to be a requirement of both African musicians and dancers. Meanings and the feelings vested in music-dance forms change, but the basic processes by which content is constructed endure. Identities change, but the identification with certain music-dance forms that nurture a sense of selfhood and belonging has not. Ethnomusicologists and dance ethnographers constantly discover fresh material in new patterns of relationship generated by the urbanization of sub-Saharan Africa.

[*For related discussion, see* Sub-Saharan Africa.]

BIBLIOGRAPHY

Blacking, John. *How Musical Is Man?* Seattle, 1973.

Blacking, John, ed. *The Anthropology of the Body.* London, 1977.

Blacking, John, and Joann W. Kealiinohomoku, eds. *The Performing Arts: Music and Dance.* The Hague, 1979.

Gell, Alfred. "On Dance Structures: A Reply to Williams." *Journal of Human Movement Studies* 5 (1979): 18–31.

Hanna, Judith Lynne. "African Dance and the Warrior Tradition." *Journal of Asian and African Studies* 12 (1977): 111–133.

Hanna, Judith Lynne. "African Dance: Some Implications for Dance Therapy." *American Journal of Dance Therapy* 2 (1978): 3–15.

Hanna, Judith Lynne. *To Dance Is Human: A Theory of Nonverbal Communication.* Austin, 1979.

Kubik, Gerhard. "Pattern Perception and Recognition in Dance Music." In *The Performing Arts: Music and Dance,* edited by John Blacking and Joann W. Kealiinohomoku. The Hague, 1979.

Langer, Susanne K. *Feeling and Form.* New York, 1953.

Mitchell, J. Clyde. *The Kalela Dance: Aspects of Social Relationship among Urban Africans in Northern Rhodesia.* Livingstone, 1956.

Ranger, T. O. *Dance and Society in Eastern Africa, 1890–1970: The Beni Ngoma.* London, 1975.

Rouget, Gilbert. "Music and Possession Trance." In *The Performing Arts: Music and Dance,* edited by John Blacking and Joann W. Kealiinohomoku. The Hague, 1979.

Royce, Anya Peterson. *The Anthropology of Dance.* Bloomington, 1977.

Spencer, Paul, ed. *Society and the Dance: The Social Anthropology of Process and Performance.* Cambridge, 1985.

Williams, Drid. "Deep Structures of the Dance." *Yearbook of Symbolic Anthropology* 1 (1978): 211–230.

Witkin, Robert W. *The Intelligence of Feeling.* London, 1976.

BARBARA L. HAMPTON

Arab Music

The Arab people generally identify with a common historical legacy, based on desert life, of literature, art, and science; they share the Arabic language and traditions influenced by a long-standing (since the seventh century CE) Islamic religious and social framework. The Arab world—extending from Morocco in western North Africa east to the Arabian Peninsula and Iraq—is also a region of significant ethnic, religious, and political contrasts. The artistic heritage and the social life of this vast area, however, share traits with the cultures of neighboring non-Arabs in the Middle East, Asia, and Africa.

In the Arab world, dance and music constitute two well-recognized traditions. Aspects of body movement considered to be "dance" include *raqṣ,* a term largely applied to the professional dancing encountered in the cities. The manifestations of sound accepted as "music" incorporate the notions of *mūsīqá* (literally, "music"); *ghinā'* (literally, "singing"); and *ṭarab* (literally, "enchantment", or "entertainment"); all these terms refer to the secular music typical of the cities. Yet the two broadly conceived phenomena of movement and sound acquire various folk, urban, secular, and sacred manifestations and are historically, contextually, and aesthetically linked.

Background. Arab dance and music are rooted in antiquity and predate Islam. Since the emergence of Islam in the seventh century, music and dance are known to have existed as essential components in folk rituals, including weddings, funerals, preparation for war, celebration of religious holy days, and entertainment at the gatherings of patrons and connoisseurs. In the early centuries of Islam, several theological treatises expressed suspicion toward both dance and music—an attitude that appears to have continued in various places, degrees, forms, and contexts during later eras. The background of this historical posture may be related to the morally dubious settings in which dance and music were or might be performed; it may also stem from the generally humble backgrounds of professional dancers and musicians, including female slave entertainers who performed at the courts during the early Islamic era. By the nineteenth and early twentieth centuries, however, negative attitudes and social restrictions were applied only to members of certain professional guilds, particularly those incorporating dancers and musicians.

Despite such a background, Arab dance and music remain ubiquitous and indispensable. Throughout Arab history, the vitality and momentum of the dance and music traditions have been enhanced by underlying conceptual, economic, and political developments. Officially expressed denigration usually focused on *raqṣ* and *mūsīqá* (or *ghinā'*), categories that usually exempted the folk manifestations of sung poetry, wedding celebrations, camel songs, and war dances and chants. Similarly, this sentiment did not apply to revered religious expressions, such as Qur'ānic chanting and the call to prayer.

Meanwhile, since the thirteenth-century emergence of the Sufi orders of Islam, sound and body movement have been recognized as essential means for the mystical experience and have been granted special spiritual and symbolic significance. Some Sufis have either expounded the special significance of the music and dance combination (*samāʿ*) or were composers, performers, and singers themselves. The image of the arts was also shaped by medieval court life, by various non-Arab and non-Islamic cultures, and by the trends toward humanism and secularization among influential patrons in Syria, Iraq, and Muslim Spain (711–1492). These factors were to further the importance and economic status of accomplished dancers and singers (particularly singers).

Contact between the Islamic world and ancient Greek philosophy and scholarship became an important factor during the ʿAbbasid dynasty (750–1258) in Baghdad. As a result, music emerged as a speculative science distinct from the practical art of *al-ghinā'*—and, for that matter, dance. Thus, whereas musical science was pursued by such notable philosophers as Abū Yūsuf Yaʿqūb al-Kindī and Abū Naṣr al-Fārābī, dancing seems to have remained within the realm of practice, possibly with the exception of Sufi writings on the *samāʿ* ritual. In Arab history, there has been a wealth of writing about music, and some about calligraphy, but little about dance.

Today's Arab dance and music embody aspects of tradition and modernity. The emergence of the theatrical play—incorporating elements of song, dance, and drama—in Egypt during the late nineteenth and early twentieth centuries led to the creation and popularization of new dance and music forms. The appearance of motion pictures in Egypt, largely after the early 1930s, also bestowed a celebrity status on numerous dancers and singers. Consequently, the names of dancers such as Sāmyah Jamāl and Taḥiyyah Karyūkah (Carioca) began to vie in fame with those of celebrity singers such as Farīd al-Aṭrash and Asmahān.

The recognition of local dancers and musicians has been increasing because of an emulation of Western cultural attitudes toward dance and music. Of some bearing on the dancers' local image has been a growing interest in Middle Eastern arts and culture (particularly urban dance) by researchers, dance students, and audiences worldwide, but especially in the United States and Europe. Meanwhile, the profile of an educated urban dancer from a reputable upper-middle-class family has been greatly promoted by newly formed government-sponsored dance troupes. So-called national folk ensembles exist in almost all Arab countries; they comprise young, systematically trained dancers as well as musicians, choreographers, costume designers, and stage directors. Some ensembles perform in theaters throughout the world.

In social settings throughout the Arab world, the influence of the West is evidenced by the increasing prevalence of European and American popular and rock music, song, and dance. Especially among the urban population, the latest Western performers quickly appear on audio and video cassettes, to be emulated and adapted by Arab youths. Ballroom dancing was in vogue in the twentieth century until disco became popular in the 1970s; the 1980s included such fads as break dancing, punk, and new wave.

Context and Performance Technique. Arab dance and music exist within broad ethnic, social, and religious contexts. Traditionally, the domains of men and women are separate. Genres such as the *taḥṭīb* (stick-dance duels) of Egypt, and the *ʿardah* (war dance) of the Arabian Peninsula are performed by men. In contrast, the *zār* (a possession-healing dance of Egypt and Sudan) is essentially performed by women.

Performance genres in exclusively male or exclusively female gatherings tend to exhibit certain differences. In the somewhat spontaneous solo dance of wedding parties in Egypt and in the Levant (the coastal region east of the Mediterranean Sea), choreographic subtleties may distinguish male from female dancers. For example, characteristic of female solo dancers are lateral head movements, hip and shoulder isolations, and fluid curvilinear arm and hand configurations. Conversely, the male solo dancer often presents strong, contained energy; a predominantly vertical (straight) torso; angular hand and arm gestures; and, occasionally, intricate, rhythmic footwork.

Male-female contrasts can be observed in the division of performance roles. As a rule, certain instruments are played by males, particularly the dance-accompanying *al-ghayṭah* (a double-reed type of oboe) in Morocco, the *mizwid* (bagpipe) in Tunisia, and the *mijwiz* (double clarinet) in Lebanon. In some folk rituals, female performing groups appear to emphasize vocal music and use musical instruments somewhat sparingly.

In many cases, a division of labor appears in the same ensembles. In a number of traditions, only male instrumentalists accompany dancers who are either female, male, or groups of both. In Egypt, male musicians accompany the *ghawāzī* female dancers. Similarly, male musicians play for performance genres of the Gulf region, namely the African-derived *laywā* performance in which rows of dancers perform with a *surnāy* (an oboe type of wind instrument), large elongated drums, and a stick-beaten tin can. Another example from the Gulf region is the *ṭanbūrah* in which the dancing of just men, just women, or groups of both may be accompanied by several drums and a large African-derived lyre.

In Arab dance and music, the distinction between male and female domains may coincide with other criteria, such as manual labor and professional specialization. In Kuwait, Bahrain, and Qatar, a highly complex repertory of dance and music was historically connected with male ensembles and attributed to the now-discontinued profession and lifestyle of pearl fishing. Also in the Gulf region, a performance genre such as *daqq al-ḥabb* (pounding grain) consists of women's chanting while they grind grain in large wooden bowls and move together in a rhythmically synchronized manner.

Aesthetics. In Arab dance and music, certain aesthetic phenomena recur with some consistency. It is widely maintained that, in general, Islamic arts are highly abstract. Traditional Arab music and dance performances usually have no explicit programmatic purpose, concrete literary message, or dramatic plot. This tendency may appear quite distinct if Arab dances are compared with their counterparts in India, where *mudrā*s (hand gestures) are linked with specific meanings, or with Polynesian dances in which hand gestures convey poetic interpretations. Further contrasts come from Asian cultures, in which dance and dance dramas portray and dramatize mythical or historical scenes, battles, and stories. In the Arab world, however, there are cases in which a folk dance may be recognizably connected with a certain sentiment, mood, or image. Two examples are the almost true-to-life Lebanese mountain sword duels that represent a display of masculine vigor and the frantic movements of the sheepskin-garbed mythical character Bū Jlūd, whose dance at a Moroccan folk festival brings to life the role of a magically transformed person.

Similarly, Arab music exhibits a strong tendency toward abstraction. In Turkish and Arab musical traditions, no connection with a concrete program or visual depiction is sought in a wealth of instrumental pieces (including the *peşrev* and the *saz semai* in Turkey and the *dūlāb* and *taḥmīlah* in Egypt). Improvisatory genres (such as the vocal *layālī* and the instrumental *taqāsīm*)—which are based on a system of *maqāmāt* (melodic modes)—also have an abstract quality, although occasionally an individual *maqām* (mode) may be loosely linked to a type of sentiment or mood. In Arab song, too, particularly in urban, professional domains, the texts are typically stylized, lyrical, and sentimental. The theme of love (with the lover typically addressed in the masculine gender) may be symbolic of divine love, especially when Sufi poetry is used.

Exceptions exist. In Egypt there are narrative song types, such as the folk ballad "Ḥasan and Naʿīmah" and the old epic "Abū Zayd al-Hilālī," commonly performed by poet-singers. In Egypt, programmatic depictions are also encountered (e.g., in the use of Western ballroom dance rhythms) as interpolations within longer love songs. There are also many programmatic instrumental pieces by such Arab composers as ʿAbd al-Wahhāb and Farīd al-Aṭrash. These pieces have titles depicting old bazaars, caravans, historic ruins, and others (often reflecting the influence of Europe's romanticized views of the Middle East).

MUSIC FOR DANCE: Arab Music. A print depicting a dancing girl of Damascus, Syria, performing to the accompaniment of a *qānūn* (zither). (Collection of Metin And.)

Emphasis on programmatic depiction became a major twentieth-century trend in Arab music. In Lebanon during the late 1950s, the government and upper classes of Beirut made systematic efforts to create a new form of Lebanese "folklore." Although based on village dance and music, the newly conceived art was expected to present a modern and Europeanized image of the country. Thus, the new folklore evolved under the initial influence of Russia's Igor Moiseyev, who was invited to Lebanon for a brief visit and subsequently asked to "improve" the quality of Lebanese folk dance. During the 1960s and early 1970s, Lebanese folklore presented line dances, programmatic dances, and songs within elaborate musical plays inspired by Lebanon's mountain life. The repertory developed in the hands of such Lebanese composers as the Raḥbānī brothers, such singers as Fayrūz and Wadīʿ al-Ṣāfī, and some Soviet-trained choreographers (especially Lebanese Armenians).

The new Lebanese folkloric tradition essentially emerged as an urban popular art form. It combined Arab elements with some from Europe, the Balkans, and the Soviet Union and became a vehicle for various programmatic devices. Not only did the background music, or *mūsīqá taṣwīrīyah,* depict certain events within the plot, but there was also *raqṣ taʿbīrī,* or descriptive dance (e.g., two flirtatious girls teasing a male shepherd). Similarly included were narrative songs often presented in the form of dialogues among actors.

In other Arab countries, there have been comparable forms in which dramatic depiction is an essential component. In Egypt, the Reda Troupe (established in 1959) has presented choreographies based on regional and national folk dances as well as orchestral arrangements inspired by the music of Egypt's countryside. Influenced by elements from Western balletic technique, the dances present abstract formations and various programmatic sketches. The dancers may represent interactions among folk characters (e.g., a young, playful woman and a licorice-juice vendor).

MUSIC FOR DANCE: Arab Music. Two Lebanese folk dancers perform outdoors, to the music of two male singers, who also provide a rhythmic accompaniment of handclapping and the pounding of a mortar and pestle used to grind coffee, a traditional folk instrument in many parts of the Arab world. (Photograph from the collection of Metin And.)

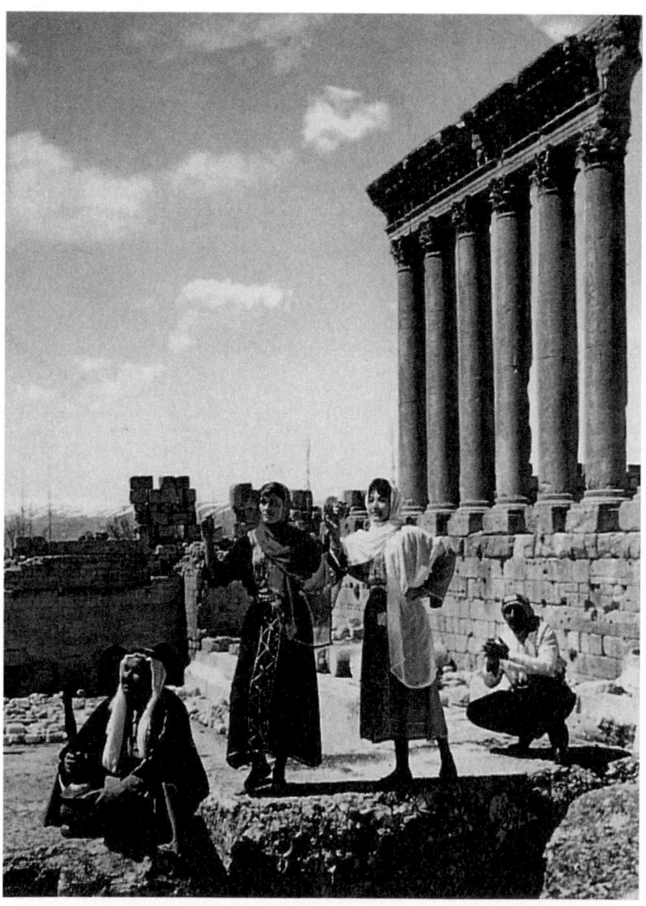

Structure. Arab dance tends to rely on spontaneously created formations, flexibility in performance length and in details of choreography—including the movements of certain segments of the body and hand and facial gestures, which all vary from one dancer to another and from one dance interpretation to another. Dance flexibility exists within traditionally prescribed frameworks. In the *dabkah,* the line dance of the Levant, recognizable step formations are found that identify its ethnic or geographic origins. The *dabkah* consists of repeated cycles or connected climactic episodes. Each of these cycles begins with a passage in which the accompanying wind instrument plays the tune of a dance song. It is followed by verses of the song sung by one of the dance participants, with choral responses from the rest of the dancers. This exchange then leads to the *zakhkhah* phase, which features repetitions of highly accentuated musical motifs and animated and virtuosic dancing that build to a climax. The sequence is repeated again and again.

In the *qidrah* (*guedra*) performed in Morocco, and in *dhikr* performances among certain Sufi orders in North Africa, a climactic buildup occurs gradually through the entire performance "set." The form of each self-contained performance set may be organized as a multisectional compound form. As such, gradual acceleration in the tempo and level of animation in the overall music and dance content is the norm.

For the *sharqī,* the "Eastern" female solo dance of the cities, there are numerous performance formats. Consistent with the musical structure of the accompaniment, the dance usually incorporates animated sections, typically at the beginning and end of the dance performance; at a point in the middle, it also includes slower, fluid undulations of the torso and arms accompanied by *taqāsīm,* the solo instrumental improvisation. A "question-and-answer" section between the *ṭablah* (hand-drum) and the dancer emphasizes rapid hip movements punctuated by sharp drum strokes; it occurs toward the end, in the dance's climactic phase.

Structured flexibility in the dance has parallels in the music. Indeed, several central forms, including the *layālī* and *mawwāl,* are improvised in accordance with modal rules and aesthetic criteria. However, a good portion of Arab music is precomposed rather than spontaneously created. Examples include Turkish-Arab instrumental compositions such as the *samāʿi* and *longa,* and the Hispano-Arab vocal form known as the *muwashshaḥ.* In numerous Islamic cultures, improvisatory and nonimprovisatory genres are linked in suitelike compound genres. Each single example may share the same *maqām* but incorporate several pieces that illustrate various types of rhythm and gradually become faster and livelier. Compound forms include the Moroccan *nūbah*, the Egyptian pre–World War I *waṣlah*, and the modern *sharqī* dance suite.

In the Arab world today, partly from the rise of large ensembles and the influence of sound recording, there is a growing interest in fixed compositional formats. In Lebanese "folklore" and its counterparts in Iraq and Jordan, the music, as in most urban popular songs, is largely precomposed and prearranged. Instead of the flexible and loosely strophic folk songs in which the singer renders countless variations, the new compositions represent a functional separation between composer and performer. Similarly, instead of maintaining the traditional aspect of coordinated spontaneity, the line-dance choreographers design special dance steps for each song and use a wide vocabulary of movements.

Similar patterns of precomposition in dance and music exist in some recent performances of the *sharqī* dance. Among the more balletic and Western-conscious dancers, there have been attempts to preset body movements in formations that exactly match the (often specially composed) musical accompaniment. Instead of the flexible latitude of parallelism between the dance and musical accompaniment, a fixed and literal correspondence is encountered between movement structure and musical accent, phraseology, and form, with less room for personal interpretation.

Generally, in both Arab dance and music, performance and improvisation occur in a context of collective participation and active involvement on the part of the audience. Dancers and musicians frequently speak about the necessity of having a responsive audience in order to develop a mental framework and ambince suitable for artistic excellence. It is this intense relationship between the dancers, singers, and musicians as well as the impact of an emotionally involved audience that imbues Arab dance and music with its soul and vitality.

Conclusion. Arab dance and music contribute to the structure and coherence of Arab social life. They also reflect the aesthetic principles and cultural complexities of a large area of the world. Contacts with other areas (more recently Europe and the United States) have influenced Arab dance and music in substance, meaning, and in the manner in which the two expressions are related.

BIBLIOGRAPHY

Arabesque: A Magazine of International Dance. New York, 1975–.

Berger, Morroe. "The Belly Dance." *Horizons* 8.2 (1966): 41–49.

Farmer, Henry George. *A History of Arabian Music.* London, 1973.

Faruqi, Lois Lamya' al-. "Dance as an Expression of Islamic Culture." *Dance Research Journal* 10.2 (1978): 6–13.

Racy, Ali Jihad. "Music." In *The Genius of Arab Civilization: Source of Renaissance,* edited by John R. Hayes. 3d ed. London, 1983: 149-171.

Racy, Barbara T. "Dance." In *The Cambridge Encyclopedia of the Middle East and North Africa,* edited by Trevor Mostyn. Cambridge, 1988: 252-253.

Wright, Owen, et al. "Arab Music." In *The New Grove Dictionary of Music and Musicians.* London, 1980.

BARBARA T. RACY and ALI JIHAD RACY

Asian Music

Within each Asian country there are many different styles of music and dance, so one cannot deal with characteristics common even to a single country, much less to all dance genres of Asia. Therefore, this article addresses general relationships between music and dance that are applicable to all cultures, including those of the West, using selected East, Southeast, and South Asian dance traditions as the basis for a broader understanding.

Conventions and Communication. For music and dance to function in a society, they must incorporate repertory-wide conventions that communicate with an audience of a specific culture. Because dance and music have different systems of communication, a first step toward understanding music and dance from other cultures is to seek out their basic sonic and movement conventions. The term *gesture* is used here to denote either physical or sonic events. In traditional arts, Eastern or Western, the conventional music–dance gestures are the glue that holds performances and audiences together. Their possible relationships and ability to communicate are best understood through the following examples.

The dance section of a *mayong* folk drama from Kelantan Province of Malaysia begins with the cessation of dramatic action; the dancers stand in a circle while the *rebab* (spiked fiddle) plays a free-rhythm, ornamented solo. The solo contains enough melodic conventions to tell the dancer which dance music will be performed. When two gongs and two drums join the fiddle in time cycles, the main dancer begins singing a text. She is immobile except for small finger gestures. The entire group moves only after the poem is completed and a cadencing gong is heard. While they heterophonically sing an abstract syllable (a vocable, an utterance without lexical meaning), they move through a prescribed floor pattern and sequence of hand gestures. Once these are completed within the proper number of gong time cycles, the next solo verse is sung; the dancers then stop, and the cycle begins again (without the instrumental introduction of the fiddle).

In this example, the music first guides the dancers into the piece, and then the dancers guide the musicians to the end of a dance sequence. At the same time, both guide the audience. Music and dance exist in a time continuum, and audiences participate in the logical progression of the performance by anticipating the events implied by the signals given within a predetermined time frame.

MUSIC FOR DANCE: Asian Music. In *kabuki* plays, music is performed by musicians both on stage and off stage. One typical onstage arrangement has singers and players of the *shamisen*—a three-stringed plucked instrument—seated on a dais at the back of the stage, with flute or drummer seated below. In this scene from *Yakko Dōjōji* (The Footman at the Dōjō Temple), musicians play for a dance performed by Ichikawa Ennosuke II. (Photograph courtesy of Samuel L. Leiter.)

Different signals produce different expectations. For example, in *mayong* the use of bamboo clappers and a *serunai* (oboe) instead of the *rebab* tells the audience that the dancers will move in a figure-eight pattern and use gestures derived from the *Manōhrā* tradition of Thailand.

Both the dance and the music of *mayong* folk drama consists of standard pieces. The plot determines the sequence of music and events in a given play. However, it is this very sameness in many Asian traditional arts that allows them to communicate so well. Originality in both music and dance of Asia generally has a different meaning than in the West. Because the audience does not have to struggle to comprehend an array of novel sonic or gestural signals, they are able to concentrate on the artistic way in which the performers combine established conventions.

Time and Rhythm. The direct relation of music to dance rhythm is essential to most folk and work dances of the world. In Asian theatrical dance, musical rhythms seldom differ greatly from those of the dance movements. An example of this close relationship is the singing of rhythmic mnemonics *(bol)* in the accompaniment of many South Asian dances. The singer is often the dance teacher, and the mnemonics are guides to both the dance movements and the drum part. In Bali the lead drummers of accompanying gamelan ensembles play direct rhythmic signals for both the dance and music gestures, while small cymbals underline dance movements. Javanese drum leaders maintain a similar role; in Java the sounds of a wooden box *(keprak)* may be used to guide only the dance movements. Its rhythmic patterns are often signals for the rhythmic flow of the dance, which in turn moves without specific relation to the melodic part of the accompanying music.

The temporal orientation that holds most South and Southeast Asian music and dance together is the time cycle. The South Asian *tāla* (rhythm) cycles and the gong time markers of both continental and island Southeast Asia are important reference points for both music and dance. The dance movements tend to change at predictable points in such cycles, although the first beat of the music and of the dance time cycle often are not the same.

East Asian music and dance are fundamentally different from South and Southeast Asian in their time orientation, in that they tend to be linear rather than cyclic. This is implied, for example, in the teaching of dancing for the Japanese *nō* drama. Sung mnemonics of the flute rather than of drums are used to memorize the dance. The flute part consists of a sequence of melodic patterns that are generally eight beats long. There are four basic repertory-wide phrases that are mixed in a different order for each dance. A few other special patterns are used to signal a progression to a new section of the dance. The drum parts also consist of named, stereotyped patterns generally of eight beats. The combination of these flute and drum patterns produces a strong linear motion toward a cadence quite different from that of the time cycles mentioned earlier.

In Japanese *kabuki* or *buyō* (classical dancing), the rhythmic relationships are more direct. One example is the use of foot rhythms *(ashibyōshi)* in which drums and the dancer may perform a call-and-response version of the pattern. In Japan there is a tripartite concept of form called *jo ha kyū* (introduction, scattering, and rushing toward the end). Throughout this formal progression, sonic or movement signals are seldom repeated; neither cyclic organization nor the Western theme-and-variation system are applicable. In the *kabuki* dance an audience is moved through time by the use of changes in orchestration and melodic or dance styles that signal progression to a new section of a piece. It is often difficult, however, to predict what will happen next, because *kabuki* is flexible in outline, subject to choreographic or compositional imagination.

Word Orientation. A majority of Asian music and dance is word-oriented. Even if no singing is used, the arts tend to depict something descriptive of a place, person, mood, or event. When there is singing in dance accompaniment, the words themselves are usually closely related to gestures. The *mudrā*s or hand positions of South Asian dance are often specifically related to sung text, although gestures with such meanings can also be combined into purely abstract series. Similar gestural combinations are found in Southeast Asian dance.

The relationship between music and dance is clearest in battle dances related to specific character types. Warriors, clowns, refined persons, and songs and recitations about them usually have specific musical instrumentation or set musical pieces. This is particularly true if the dance becomes acrobatic, as in Chinese opera and the battle scenes *(tachimawari)* of Japanese *kabuki* plays. While the movements of a given battle may change, the use of standard music gives the dancers an important frame of reference for the performance of complicated ensemble movements. When text describes a character in greater detail, both the music and dance signals may become more subtle though still accessible to knowledgeable viewers.

Pantomimic gesture is found in some form of theatrical dancing in every Asian culture, but the degree to which the music responds to the gestures is not well studied. It is known that in *kabuki* and the related concert dance *buyō,* nearly every tune or percussion signal from the offstage ensemble relates to a stage action or setting. Signals before a dancer appears may tell the audience where the dancer will enter (via a trap door, or down a ramp), the location of the scene (a temple, a palace, or the sea), the season, the time of day, or the nature of the character being portrayed. For example, the sound of a small xylophone *(mokkin)* playing an erratic melody offstage means that the dancer will soon appear as a blind man or an animal, with appropriate pantomimic movements. If a large drum plays a "sound of the waves" *(nami no oto)* pattern and the song "Eight Miles to Hakone" is sung, an audience knows before the curtain opens that the scene is set along the Tokaido road near the sea. A different song and different percussion patterns might tell them that the scene will be at a geisha house on the Sumida River in Tokyo, while another will place the scene in a house in Kyoto.

Correlations among music, dance, costume, and text can also be found in Japanese *kabuki*-based dance. For example, the mention of butterflies in a text often triggers bell sounds in the music. Wing gestures may be used in the dance, or there may simply be butterfly patterns on the costume, which may be held out for view at the moment the butterflies are mentioned. Fan and musical gestures relating to text are equally common.

Abstract Music and Dance. As music and dance become more refined, meaningful gestures tend to lose their

MUSIC FOR DANCE: Asian Music. Players of the *gamelan semar pegulingan* from the village of Teges Kanginan, Bali. (Photograph © by Edward Herbst; used by permission.)

specific communicative ability. The Javanese *bedaya* court dances are a good example of such abstraction. The dancers are thought originally to have represented the psychic centers of energy in the spiritual body, and the floor patterns their relationships. The dance's slow, elegant gestures may once have had meaning, but now both they and the choreography are viewed more as Western ballet movements are. This abstraction is enhanced by the accompanying poem, which is in a dialect unknown to most native listeners and is sung in elongated syllables.

A similar distancing of dance events from meanings can be found in most contemporary interpretations of ancient Japanese and Korean court dances. The dance movements are drawn mostly from a set of named conventions (as in ballet), and the music can be performed with or without the dance (again as with ballet). The accompaniment and dance relate in mood and tempo, but one cannot successfully state that a given passage of music is shaped to the movement it accompanies. The music and the dance have changed radically over the centuries, making them in a sense abstractions—stylistically new creations based on what may have been pantomimic performances centuries ago. For example, the flightlike gesture in *bugaku* (Japanese court dance) is called "pattern of the bird" *(torite)*, but it is so called in order to help remember it rather than to use it in a bird dance. The music that accompanies a passage in which such a gesture appears is equally unrelated. Likewise, the dance and music of four winged dancers in the *bugaku* piece *Kochōmai* are truly abstract. Historically, this dance was derived from the magic bird tradition of Indian Hinduism, but under the influence of Buddhism the bird became a butterfly. The dance movements relate to neither creature, nor does the music. The use of four dancers may reflect Confucian influence, raising the question of the relationship among music, dance, ritual, and religion.

Sacred Dance, Magic Dance, and Music. The relationship of music and dance to the supernatural or metaphysical is still strong in many Asian genres. Confucian influence is obvious in Korean and Taiwanese genres in which the "correct" (the balanced) number of dancers perform the correct number of dances in the correct order, while an accompanying ensemble uses the correct instruments, some of which are not used for any other function. The relation of the music to the dance in such cases is more the creation of a balanced, common texture than a sonic or rhythmic response.

There are many Asian sacred or magic performances that require dance accessories, movements, or musical accompaniment unique to that event; these adjuncts often tell us much about the ritual's nature or possible origin. For example, the flat gong used by the Korean *mudang* shaman dancers bears a fascinating similarity to the pan drums used by shamans in Siberia, central Asia, and the entire Subarctic. Similarly, the head motions of the *putri* shamans of Malaysia, and the brass bowl beaten in accompaniment to their dance, are reminiscent of features of the dervish ecstasies of the Near East and North Africa, which may have influenced Malaysian practice when introduced with Islam.

Another factor that can influence both music and dance in Asia is the concept of magic numbers. For example, in many Japanese folk festivals a dance is repeated three times with the same music and mask, while the internal repetitions of both the music and the dance are also in threes. The entire set can be repeated a second time with a new mask, and a third time with yet a different mask. The movements and repetitions in old Chinese and Japanese court dances often occur in patterns of four (four times, four sides, four corners). These numerical features may have similar magical origins, although they also serve as an aid in memorizing choreographic and musical patterns.

Balance and Control. Unlike ballet, dance in Asia seems to control an event more often than the music does. Some of the music may even be generated by the dancers themselves—for example, in the frequent use of bells or jingles attached to South Asian dancers. In some Sri Lankan and Manipuran dance genres, the drummers become as physically active as the dancers so that they belong to both the music and dance of the event. Similarly, the large circle of chanting, gesticulating men that surround young female dancers in the Balinese "monkey dance" *(kécek)* constitute a kind of rhythmic chorus in motion. Dancers who also sing are found in several Asian traditions, such as Japanese *nō* drama, Indian Kuchipudi, Malaysian *mayong*, and the *lakhọn*, *likay*, and *Manōhrā* forms that appear throughout the Southeast Asian region from Thailand to Laos.

Control of a performance in Asian theatrical arts, as in the West, often depends on who is the "star." *Kabuki* dance pieces can be rearranged to the taste of a given actor, and a *nō* drama actor-dancer's interpretation of a role may cause a considerable adjustment in the accompaniment. In contrast, *wayang golek* dancers in Sunda, Indonesia, may have to interrupt the drama if the singer who accompanies them receives a paid request for some other song. In many Indian dance genres, the balance of music to dance is complicated; whereas the dancers' teacher normally leads the music ensemble with music and dance mnemonics, in professional Indian performances the dancer may lead the ensemble.

[*See also* Film Musicals, *article on* Bollywood Film Musicals]

BIBLIOGRAPHY

Ananya. "Training in Indian Classical Dance: A Case Study." *Asian Theatre Journal* 13.1 (1996): 68-91.

Barnett, Elise B. "Special Bibliography: Art Music of India." *Ethnomusicology* 14.2 (1970): 278–312.

Becker, Judith O. *Gamelan Stories: Tantrism, Islam, and Aesthetics in Central Java.* Tempe, Ariz., 1993.

Bethe, Monica, and Karen Brazell. *Dance in the Nō Theater.* Ithaca, N.Y., 1982.

Brandon, James R., et al. *Studies in Kabuki.* Honolulu, 1978.

Chopyak, James D. "Music in Modern Malaysia." *Asian Music* 18.1 (1987): 111–138.

De Danaan, Llyn. "The Blossom Falling: Movement and Allusion in a Malay Dance." *Asian Theatre Journal* 3 (1986).

de Zoete, Beryl, and Walter Spies. *Dance and Drama in Bali.* London, 1938.

Higgins, Jon B. *The Music of Bharata Natyam.* New Delhi, 1993.

Jones, Betty True, ed. *Dance as Cultural Heritage.* 2 vols. Dance Research Annual, 14–15. New York, 1983–1985.

Klens, Deborah S. "*Nihon Buyō* in the *Kabuki* Training Program at Japan's National Theatre." *Asian Theatre Journal* 11.2 (1994): 231–241.

Malm, William P. *Nagauta: The Heart of Kabuki Music.* Rutland, Vt., 1963.

Mohd Taib Osman, ed. *Traditional Drama and Music of Southeast Asia.* Kuala Lumpur, 1974.

Togi, Masataro. *Gagaku: Court Music and Dance.* Translated by Don Kenny. New York, 1971.

Van Zile, Judy, and Jon B. Higgins. "Balasaraswati's 'Tiśram Alārippu." *Asian Music* 18.2 (1987).

WILLIAM P. MALM

Oceanic Music

In the Pacific Islands, composite named performing genres are composed of structured sound, structured movement, and poetry—all of which are integrally related. Thus, to speak of music for dance is to bring in Western categories, but this is useful for analytical purposes. Music–dance relationships in the three large cultural areas of the Pacific can be characterized as follows: Polynesian dance is primarily sung poetry made visual by allusion; Micronesian dance is often a visual enhancement of sung poetry; and Melanesian dance is a visual enhancement of rhythm. Within these large cultural areas, however, the variation is overwhelming. This entry will include generalized statements about music for dance for each area and four specific examples, to illuminate a variety of relationships between music and dance in the Pacific: Tonga from West Polynesia; Hawai'i from East Polynesia; Kiribati from Micronesia; and the Kaluli of New Guinea, from Melanesia.

Polynesia. Polynesian music/dance is based on poetry conveyed through indirectness ("to say one thing but mean another") in the sung poetry itself as well as in the movements that accompany it. The sound component of music is primarily the vehicle for conveying the poetry and the resulting melodic/rhythmic motifs and phrases are often stereotypic and repetitious. The lower-body movement motifs primarily keep the time, while the hand/arm motifs convey the poetry.

Tonga. Tongan performances include a number of genres with a variety of music and dance relationships. *Lakalaka,* usually a village-based performance, can best be characterized in English as a sung speech with choreographed movements, but in Tongan it is simply a *lakalaka,* which by definition includes three elements—poetry that is sung and moved—and excludes musical instruments. The basic element is poetry, through-composed in stanzas, which are usually repeated. The poetry is set into a polyphonic musical setting consisting of *fasi* (melody or leading part), *laulalo* (bass or underlying part), and one or more additional parts—a tenorlike part *(lalau* or *tenoa)* that may cross the melody in either direction, another low part *(ekenaki)*—all sung by men—and usually high and low women's parts. The composer of the poetry is called *pulotu ta'anga,* who may also compose the musical setting as *pulotu hiva,* or one or more specialists may be brought in for this purpose. The choreographer, *pulotu haka,* adds two sets of movements for men and women. An individual who can compose all three of the basic elements is a *punake,* a most elevated term. The performers, often one hundred or more, stand in two or more long lines facing the audience, the men on the right (from the observer's point-of-view) the women on the left. The dancers also sing and a chorus of men and women stands behind them to augment the sound; the poetry must be heard clearly by the audience in order to understand how the movements enhance or hide the meaning of the poetry.

Another Tongan genre, *mā'ulu'ulu,* often draws its participants from a school or church. The poetry is structured in verse–chorus alternation, and it is usually sung in two or three parts. The poetry is conveyed visually by one set of arm movements. The performers may be all female, all male, or both—seated in curved lines (or the second and consecutive lines may be raised by kneeling, standing, or elevated on benches)—the number of participants ranging from ten to five hundred. Sung poetry is preceded by a long introduction of complicated drumming on one or more *nafa* membranophones (at the side of the performance space) and elaborate hand/arm movement motifs; next a verse of poetry is sung without movement or drum accompaniment; then the rest of the verses and choruses are sung with hand/arm movements that make allusions to the poetry and with (less complicated) drum accompaniment; finally, the introduction is repeated—sometimes in a shortened version—the whole performance lasting some twenty to thirty minutes.

Another performance type combines *tau'olunga* movements—hand/arm movements similar to those above but with a wider variety of lower-body movement motifs—with *hiva kakala,* sweet songs, accompanied by stringbands, composed of ukulele and guitars (and sometimes banjos, one-string bass, etc.). Structured in verse–chorus alternation, the melodic line and harmony are more Western, but unmistakably Tongan. The poetry is topical about places, people, and Tonga as a paradise. The movements may be pre-set or spontaneous and may be performed as a solo or by a number of women. These principal dancers may be accompanied by one or more secondary dancers (male or female), who spontaneously join in with virile movements to emphasize the graceful movements of the women.

A men's club-dance, *kailao,* imported from Uvea, has no singing—its complex movements are structured according to rhythmic motifs struck on an empty biscuit tin with additional sounds from ankle rattles. The *sōkē* combines sung poetry, with the striking of short and long sticks in complex patterns. It is performed by a large number of male and/or female participants in sets of four that combine into larger and larger groupings.

The *me'etu'upaki,* a traditional dance in which paddle-like implements are twirled and manipulated, is performed by men from the village of Lapaha on special occasions as an identity marker of their association with the highest line of kings and the fertility rituals of old. Sung in a poetic idiom no longer understood, it is accompanied by a slitdrum and chorus that face the dancers. One section divides into three parts, each of which has a different poetic length, different melody, and different movements.

A traditional women's dance, *fa'ahiula,* begins seated in a curved row *('otu haka);* then one or more female dancers stand and perform *(ula).* The singing is accompanied by a percussion instrument consisting of a rolled mat or lengths of bamboo rolled in a mat.

Hawai'i. The basis of Hawaiian music/dance is also chanted/sung poetry *(mele hula)* that is integrated with movements and (usually) musical instruments. *Hula* are categorized according to the musical instrument with which the sung poetry is integrally related. Thus, poetry for *hula pahu* is performed in conjunction with a *pahu* drum (a single-headed cylindrical membranophone that stands vertically and is covered with a tightly stretched sharkskin that is struck with the left hand) and sometimes a secondary drum, *pūniu* or *kilu* (a coconut-shell drum covered with fish skin that is struck with a braided coconut-fiber beater held in the right hand). *Hula pā ipu* is performed in conjunction with a gourd idiophone, *hula kāla'au* with *kāla'au* rhythm sticks and sometimes a treadle board *(papa hehi); hula 'ulī'ulī* with a gourd rattle; *hula pū'ili* with a slit-bamboo rattle; *hula 'ili'ili* with stone clappers; and *hula pa'iumauma* with striking the chest and thighs with open palms.

Music/dance is in duple time (2/4 or 4/4) and rhythmic motifs are named. There are three ways to strike the *ipu:* with the thumb followed by the fingertips; with the whole palm; and on the ground. These are combined into named motifs and phrases that are related to the rhythm of the poetry. The musician/chanter *(ho'opa'a)* may perform in conjunction with one or more standing dancers *('ōlapa);* or a performer may be a musician/chanter and a dancer simultaneously. Rhythmic patterns are important dimensions and two instruments are sometimes used together to create contrasts in rhythm as well as contrasts in sound. Structure varies from through-composed in sections (with movements alluding to words of the text with

MUSIC FOR DANCE: Oceanic Music. Asmat dancers from Irian Jaya perform a men's dance at Baird Auditorium at the Smithsonian Institution, 1991. The dancers wear headdresses of feathers and marsupial fur, shell-and-dog-teeth necklaces, and elaborate face and body makeup. Some sing and play small double-headed log drums, while others carry typical Asmat dance shields. (Photograph © 1991 by Adrienne L. Kaeppler; used by permission.)

one or a few allusions per line) to compositions in couplets (with more pantomimic movements interpreting the text, performed first to the right side of the body and repeated on the left side of the body).

Polyphonic singing was not indigenous to the Hawaiian Islands, but was introduced by Protestant missionaries in the early nineteenth century. Also introduced were stringed instruments, which were adapted to Hawaiian taste as ʻukulele, steel guitar, and more recently as slack-key (slackened-string tunings). This combining of new instruments with traditional sounds in the 1880s was also enjoyed in movement as *hula kuʻi,* joining of old and new.

Since the 1960s additional categories have been introduced and are used especially for competitions: *hula kahiko* (old hula) dances performed in conjunction with traditional musical instruments and less melodic vocal contours; and *hula ʻauana* (modern hula) dances performed with introduced musical instruments and Western harmony.

Micronesia. The music/dance of Micronesia is also based on poetic phrases, but the movements do not necessarily interpret or allude to the poetry. Instead, movements enhance the poetry and in some areas texts are not understood by the performers or audience. Music/dance was traditionally associated with tattooing, seafaring, and fertility; many movement motifs were, and are, linked mimetically with frigate birds.

In sitting or standing positions, group singing and moving is associated with rhythmic striking of the body, ground, concussion sticks, or lap boards tapped with small sticks. Drums were not characteristic of most Micronesian islands. Performances using sticks as sound and visual design components are common. Indigenous vocal polyphony consisted of singing parallel contours or a melodic contour sung against a sustained note. Limited pitches in a narrow range, acceleration through a piece, and shouted exclamations were common. Today, imported stringed instruments are used for many dances.

Kiribati. Formerly the Gilbert Islands, Kiribati dance is integrally related to sung poetry and, except for dancing sticks, no instruments were used traditionally. Today, a percussion box struck with the palm and tins struck with sticks have been imported from Polynesia and stringed instruments have been imported from the Western world.

Traditional Kiribati performances consist of one or more principal dancers of the same sex and similar age, located at the front of a chorus who sing and clap. Precisely choreographed movement sequences are performed by the principal dancers, while the chorus's singing, clapping, foot stamping, and body percussion are also choreographed. Movement and sound must be exactly coordinated.

The most traditional music-dance form is *ruoia,* a series of texts usually sung in unison with a small number of pitches—men and women an octave apart and occasionally with parallel harmonies—except for the male song leader who decorates the text by singing around the melody and adding texture. The principal dancers enhance the texts with a series of poses with slow movements between them or abrupt arm, head, and hand movements. Besides singing, the chorus executes clapped percussion patterns and for some sections performs dance movements in parallel with the principal dancers.

Newer traditional music/dance forms are based on Samoan and Tuvaluan prototypes, such as the *batere,* which combines old and new movements with more "Polynesian" sounds and the percussion box drum. In addition there are dance forms imported from the Cook Islands, Tonga, New Zealand, and Hawaiʻi along with skin drums, wooden slitdrums, and stringed instruments.

Melanesia. Music/dance among Melanesians, although having some elements in common, differs significantly from island to island and from group to group. A common feature throughout much of the area is a basis in rhythm.

Many movement systems, especially those concerned with ritual are primarily the province of men, although women might move independently or "participate" as observers. Whether part of ritual or social activities, dance is mainly participatory and not presented for an audience. The dancing group is often a moving group and may function to take participants from one part of the dance ground to another or from the menshouse to the beach. Some performers carry a *kundu,* the generic term for the hourglass-shaped drum. *Kundu* have one end open and the other is covered with a skin membrane to which wax pellets are added to fix the drum note by reducing vibration and raising the pitch. Often carved and/or painted, the open end may be carved in the form of an open jaw or with whimsical designs based on a human face. Sometimes the drum represents a mythical animal with sacred characteristics, with a sound all its own. When the performers are masked, they too may represent ancestral or totemic spirits. Accompanying singing may be simply vocables or short texts that may or may not convey narrative meaning.

A leader begins by starting a knee-bending-and-straightening movement motif. Others join in, usually in a line or circle, until the whole group moves up and down together in place or in the prearranged choreographed pattern. The rhythmic environment of drumming and singing is made visual by the massed human bodies as they move together to create an aesthetic elaboration of rhythm. Costumes, composed primarily of attachments that move, emphasize this visual rhythm. Bird of paradise plumes and other feathers extend from headdresses, back, bustle, or arms. Hanging rattles of seeds or shells are attached to legs or costumes or are held in the hand. Cuscus skin ripples like vertical waves, and shredded leaves and fibers cascade and bounce. Penis coverings of gourd, shell, or bark are curved forward and upward to emphasize the up-down movement of this part of the body. It is difficult to discern if the costume is aimed at emphasizing rhythm or if the rhythm is a way of showing off the costume—together they create a mass rhythmic statement.

In many cases dance is realized as movement after the introduction of a regular rhythm, set by the beating of a kundu or occasionally a slit gong or rattles. In some areas melodic instruments such as flutes and panpipes, or today stringed instruments, furnish the aural dimension.

Kaluli. The importance of rhythm in Melanesian music/dance can be seen in Steven Feld's characterization of the Kaluli of New Guinea as "a visual image set in sonic form and a sonic form set in visual imagery" (1988, p. 78). Sounds from shells, streamers in motion, drums, rattles, and stamping feet combine with vocal solo, duet, or chorus—sometimes in overlapping parts, known as "lift-up-over sounding." The primary movement motif is up-and-down bouncing, which re-creates the movement of the Giant Cuckoodove that taught the Kaluli to dance. The performer represents this bird singing and dancing at a waterfall and his movements are accentuated by the bouncing of feathers, streamers, and rattles attached to his costume. The high frequency sounds of the streamers and shells evoke the sound of the waterfall while the drums and the performers' voices evoke the voices of birds.

Everywhere in Oceania, new forms of music and dance—ranging from waltz to disco, from fox trot to punk, from reggae to wave dancing and beyond—coexist with more traditional forms. Having their roots in the past, they are performed in a variety of contexts that reveal cultural and ethnic identity as well as their appropriation of the modern world.

[*See also* Oceanic Dance Traditions.]

BIBLIOGRAPHY

Feld, Steven. "Aesthetics as Iconicity of Style, or, 'Lift-up-over sounding': Getting into the Kaluli Groove." *Yearbook for Traditional Music* 20 (1988): 74–113.

Feld, Steven. *Sound and Sentiment: Birds, Weeping, Poetics, and Song in Kaluli Expression.* 2d ed. Philadelphia, 1990.

Kaeppler, Adrienne L. "Polynesian Music and Dance." In *Musics of Many Cultures,* edited by Elizabeth May. Berkeley, 1980.

Kaeppler, Adrienne L. "Movement in the Performing Arts of the Pacific Islands." In *Theatrical Movement: A Bibliographical Anthology,* edited by Bob Fleshman. Metuchen, N.J., 1986.

Kaeppler, Adrienne L., and Elizabeth Tatar. *Hula Pahu: Hawaiian Drum Dances,* vol. 1, *Ha'a and Hula Pahu: Sacred Movements.* Honolulu, 1993.

Kaeppler, Adrienne L. *Poetry in Motion: Studies in Tongan Dance.* Nukuʻalofa, Tonga, 1993.

Lawson, Mary E. "Tradition, Change, and Meaning in Kiribati Performance: An Ethnography of Music and Dance in a Micronesian Society." Ph.D. diss., Brown University, 1989.

ADRIENNE L. KAEPPLER

Western Music before 1520

Documentation attesting to musical performance practices in the West begins in the fourth millennium BCE. Music was first and foremost connected with worship: prayers were intoned or sung and at times were accompanied by instruments, which became sanctified in the process.

Mesopotamia and Egypt. No instruments survive from ancient Mesopotamia, but in written texts, letters shaped like harps and illustrations of lyres on tablets and cylinder seals attest to the presence of these instruments in the third millennium BCE. Prehistoric Egypt knew rudimentary aerophones, pipes, and long flutes besides the *sistrum* and a multitude of clappers *(badari),* rattles *(merimde),* bells, and drums. The long-necked lute *(tanbūr)* first appeared in Mesopotamia during the second half of the third millennium, was soon accepted in Egypt, and attained the height of its popularity in the second millennium. Sacred drums and double-reed double-pipes from Babylon likewise belong to this period, as do the clarinet- and oboe-type wind instruments from Egypt. Played by themselves or in concert with singers, these instruments provided music for every kind of ritual and ceremony, including the dances that were performed in honor of deities and departed souls in temples, burial chambers, and royal courts.

The traditional accompaniment of ritual and funerary dancing, however, was the human voice in conjunction with percussion of all kinds: hand clapping, body slapping, clappers, rattles, *sistra,* bells, jingling ornaments on the dancers' bodies and clothing, drums of various sizes and playing techniques. Depictions of dance scenes on tablets, papyri, frescoes, and reliefs show solo and group dances—some involving professional performers, others performed by elite members of society and priests.

In Egypt, the god Ihy was the protector of music, but other deities, including Amun, Hathor, Isis, and Osiris, also were associated with the art. Songs saluting the rising sun, hymns, and recitations of mythological epic tales were simultaneously sung, mimed, and danced to the accompaniment of individual singers and instrumentalists or orchestra-like ensembles of musicians, often guided by chironomists whose hand signs give us some idea of the intervals and pitches involved (see Hickmann, 1953, 1954, 1970, 1975).

Singers and instrumentalists in large numbers belonged to the households of the pharaohs and the Assyrian kings, to the temples of Sumeria, Babylon, and ancient Egypt, and to the necropolises of the entire region. All played at one time or another for dancing, but because of the absence of musical notation, the kinds of music used for the purpose largely elude any attempt at definition.

Greece. Although the dances of ancient Greece are well documented, as are the physical and spiritual disciplines they represented, their choreographic shapes, and their functions in social, ritual, and theatrical situations, we know very little about the music that accompanied the various choreutic activities. Neither the tonal nor the rhythmic substance of dance music employed in the cults of Dionysus and Apollo, in the choral dances of Spartan virgins *(parthenia),* in the wrestling dances of boys and men *(gymnopaidiai),* in the ball-dance at Phaiakia, or in the accompaniment of choral movement in the theater can be defined with any certainty. It is probably a safe commonplace to say that the rhythm of Greek dance music was as intimately connected with the meters of classical verse as that of the music associated with poetic recitation, and that the mood of a given dance piece corresponded to the dramatic or social situation in which it was employed.

We are on slightly more solid ground with respect to the music-making bodies that provided the accompaniment for dancing. Greek dance music was either sung (and rhythmically reinforced by handclapping) or played on instruments. Voices accompanied the *emmeleia* (a restrained, serious dance, especially the dance of tragedy) and the processional *kōmoi* (some raucous, some joyful and civilized), for which many of Pindar's odes were written. Choral songs combined with instruments underlined the motions of a solo dancer in the *kordax.*

Among the instruments, the one most frequently mentioned is the *aulos,* a double-pipe reed instrument (not a flute) with a shrill, piercing tone that was closely associated with the cult of Dionysus and, as a consequence, with Greek drama; the *aulos* accompanied the *pyrrhikhē,* a choral dance for men and boys that was performed with weapons, shields, and helmets and that was understood as a preparation for as well as a representation of actual battle.

In the cult of Apollo, the *phorminx* (a kind of lyre) was the customary instrument. Like the larger *kithara,* it was a stringed instrument, with five to seven strings, later with as many as eleven. Mainly used to accompany epic poetry and hymns, the *phorminx* was also played for dances such as the processional *paian.* (A *paian* to Apollo on a papyrus now in Berlin is one of the few pieces of Classical Greek music extant today.) *Phorminx* and *aulos* could be employed separately and jointly, as in the wedding dance described in the *Iliad* (18.490–496), in several of Pindar's odes (Mullen, 1982, p. 22), probably playing heterophonic improvisations. To these, a hand drum (tympanum) could be added, as in the ritual dance of women from Cyprus depicted on a bronze bowl now in the New York City Metropolitan Museum (Lawler, 1964, plate 17).

Panpipes *(syringes;* singular, *syrinx),* castanets, cymbals, hand drums, and *sistra* appear in vase paintings and sculpture from Greece, Sparta, Crete, and Cyprus, showing dancing maenads, women, professional dancing girls, actors, men, and boys in diverse choreographic activities, group and solo dances, mimed and masked dances, sacred and profane dances, and work and entertainment dances that are documented from the Classical period. [*See* Greece, *article on* Dance in Ancient Greece.]

Rome. Dances of ritual (cults of Cybele, Isis, Dionysus) and representation *(mimus, pantomimus)* continued in the repertory of ancient Rome, as did processions; weapon dances by the priests of Mars *(salii);* street and tavern dances performed by professional women dancers *(saltatrices)* from Egypt, Syria, and Spain; and theatrical dances performed by outstanding actor-dancers *(pantomimi)* at games and during interludes at comedies and tragedies. Despite the protests of writers such as Cicero, Quintilian, and Seneca and the devastating satire of Juvenal, and despite condemnation by early Christian moralists, dancing was cultivated at all levels of Roman society. The nobility employed dancing and music teach-

MUSIC FOR DANCE: Western Music before 1520. A detail from a Greek vase (fourth century BCE) showing a female dancer carrying a hand drum (*tympanum*). (Photograph from a private collection.)

ers, and dancing schools sprang up in cultural centers throughout the Roman empire.

The music that accompanied these various activities consisted of *cantica,* sung pieces for one to three voices, and music for a large variety of instruments, some inherited from conquered nations and left intact (the Oriental long-necked lute, the old Egyptian long flute), some modified in the new Roman environment *(kithara).* Comparable to the Greek *aulos* in construction and function was the *tibia,* of Etruscan origin. As the most important nonmilitary instrument, the *tibia* was played, singly or in groups of several, in the theater, at festivals, and for dancing. It is frequently shown in the hands of a player who also gives the rhythm with the *scabellum,* a foot-activated clapper. Such a player was called *scabillarius* and seems to have functioned as the leader of instrumental ensembles, notably in the theater. Other percussion instruments shown in Roman dance iconography are *tympana* (tambours), *kymbala* (hand-activated elongated clappers), *krotala* (long, narrow castanets, made of ivory or wood), bells, and bronze cymbals.

Toward the end of the western Roman Empire (476 CE) official recognition of and support for music declined, but itinerant dancers, musicians, and actors continued to enjoy public favor. They became the link between the musical practice of antiquity and that of the *joculatores* of the Middle Ages. [*See* Roman Empire.]

Middle Ages and Early Renaissance. Emerging at least in shadowy outline from medieval literature and iconography are various kinds of dance, dance settings, and performance occasions, public and private. But the music that accompanied these activities eludes definition until the thirteenth century. The presence of the rhythmic modes in liturgical music and in song and epic poetry has generated scholarly speculation regarding the rhythms of medieval dance, but it is dangerous to assume that merely because a medieval secular song maintains a steady rhythmic pulse throughout, it would automatically have been danced. The exceptions, of course, are pieces from the secular vocal repertory that were genuine dance songs—including some of the *lais,* early forms of *ballades, virelais,* and *rondeaux*—and, in the liturgical repertory, the *conductus-caudae,* which almost certainly accompanied choral movement. Instrumental passages in the late thirteenth-century "Cantigas de Sancta Maria" of King Alfonso X of Spain and in later dramatic works such as the *Jeu de Robin et de Marion* (c.1284) and *Roman de Fauvel* (1310–1314) also seem to relate to dance. But the large repertory of dance music for all kinds of occasions that must have circulated among the minstrels and *jongleurs,* the *trouvères, troubadours,* and *Minnesinger* of the Middle Ages was transmitted orally and is largely irrecoverable.

It is probably safe to assume, however, that refrain structures and repeats of sections, so frequent in the later Middle Ages, were present early in the music for dancing. The leader of the dance might intone a segment of the music, and the dancing company would respond as chorus, either repeating the solo line or interjecting a brief response, like the "eiya" in the twelfth-century *estampie, Kalenda maya* (text by Raimbaut de Vaqueiras, 1156–1207). Prior to the beginnings of early polyphony in the late twelfth century, dance music, like "composed" music, was performed monophonically by voices or on the many-stringed or wind instruments that a good *joculator* was required to know how to play.

Three of the earliest two-part instrumental dance pieces on record are contained in the thirteenth-century manuscript Harley 978 in the British Museum. Their form is clear and symmetrical, and their rhythm is a natural 6/8 pulse. Although they bear no titles in the source, the first has been identified as a *stantipes,* the second as a *nota* or *ductia,* the third, tentatively, as a *stantipes imperfecta.* The music theorist Johannes de Groccheo (*fl.* 1275) includes *stantipes* and *ductia* in his discussion of instrumental music *(musica vulgaris),* stressing the rhythmic precision of the *ductia* that the wealthy danced at festivals and games, and the intellectual challenge of the *stantipes,* which requires concentration and keeps the thoughts of the dancers from straying toward vulgar amusements.

Two main fourteenth-century sources of monophonic instrumental dance music (one in the British Library in London, the other in the Bibliothèque Nationale in Paris) demonstrate a method of composition that continues a practice already present in some thirteenth-century dance pieces: each individual piece consists of four to seven sections *(puncta),* each of which is repeated. The first statement of the *punctum* ends with an "open" *(ouvert)* half-cadence, the repeat with a "closed" *(clos)* full cadence. The repertory of the French document consists of eight *estampie royal,* two *dansse real,* and one untitled opening number; the famous London collection contains eight *istampite,* four *saltarelli,* one *trotto,* four *chançonete tedesche,* the *Lamento di Tristano* with *Rotta* and *La Manfredina,* also with *Rotta.* The latter two demonstrate the coupling of a main dance with a rhythmically contrasting after-dance using related musical material; in such pairs lie the origins of the later *bassedanse-saltarello,* pavane-tordion, passamezzo-galliard combinations.

Contemporary with these rare instrumental dances are the sung *ballades* and *rondeaux* whose names and often whose texts associate them with dance and whose structures are described in terms that at least in part suggest their relationship to the movement arts. *Volta* ("turn") is used as the equivalent of refrain or *ripresa; pes* ("foot") stands for verse *(versus)* or section. Andrea da Tempo describes the *ballata* for dancing as consisting of four sections (A-B-B-A).

The manner of performing late medieval dance music receives some clarification from the iconography and imaginative literature. The musical documents cited above do not describe the required instruments. Pictures, however, show the social setting and connect certain instruments with specific choreographic shapes.

The line dance *par excellence* of the Middle Ages and through the fourteenth century was the *carole.* It was danced in courtly and civic settings, by angels at the Nativity, by the dead in the Dances of Death, and by peasants, shepherds, and mummers. Depictions of *carole* (for example, the Ambrogio Lorenzetti fresco in Siena's Palazzo Publico, painted c.1330) frequently show a tambourine, a custom to which Giovanni Bocaccio also refers in the *Decameron* (days five and eight). Line dances shown in the margins of fourteenth-century manuscripts of stories such as the *Roman d'Alexandre* or the *Roman de la Rose* tend to be accompanied by a single instrumentalist, frequently a fiddler playing *rebec* or *vielle,* sometimes a musician playing a wind instrument or a portable organ; from time to time a tambourine, nakers, and bells appear. When a lutenist, ghittern (a guitar-type stringed instrument), or harp player is shown, the melody of the dance piece might be accompanied by a rudimentary kind of polyphony, a drone or chords. The bagpipe, which mainly plays for peasant dances, also offered that possibility.

Combinations of instruments such as the fiddle with lute, harp, crwth, and psaltery are also documented, as are single and double recorders and *organetto,* in addition to the stringed instruments. Such combinations suggest an increase in polyphonic playing for dance toward the end of the fourteenth century, a practice natural also for the performance of dance music by loud wind bands, consisting of shawms and trumpets, with an occasional percussion instrument, which appear in increasing numbers during this period as accompaniment for courtly couple dances.

From such instrumental groupings, it is but a small step to the "loud" and "soft" bands that performed the dance music of the fifteenth century. Ensembles of three, later five, wind players *(pifari)* who worked together on a daily basis belonged to the musical establishments of cities and courts since the 1370s (Polk, 1968); it was the duty of the *haults menestrels* to play for grand and outdoor occasions, while *les instrumens bas*—harp, lute, fiddle, flute, *organetto,* and the individual pipe-and-tabor player—performed for more intimate events and accompanied informal dancing.

In all cases, extempore ensemble improvisation was the prerequisite of proper musical performance. The training of his musical memory was part of any practicing musi-

MUSIC FOR DANCE: Western Music before 1520. A woodcut by Michael Wolgemut and/or Wilhelm Pleydenwurff depicting musicians playing a flute and a drum for four dancing couples, from Hartmann Schedel's *Liber chronicarum*, Nuremberg, 1493. (Courtesy of Madison U. Sowell and Debra H. Sowell, Brigham Young University, Provo, Utah.)

cian's apprenticeship. He knew the favorite dance tunes of his time by heart and could play them, fully embellished, as they were needed.

When a *cappella alta* played, the main melody (tenor) was sounded by the lower of the two shawms, while the higher shawm and the sackbut would play the improvisations above and below the tenor. This was the manner of performance for the *bassesdanses* preserved in the fifteenth-century dance treatises (the Brussels manuscript, Michel Toulouze, Antonio Cornazano). A similar musical texture would also have been required for the realization of the monophonic Italian *ballo* tunes in the works of Domenico da Piacenza, Antonio Cornazano, and Guglielmo Ebreo, which, although singable, are notated at tenor pitch and, at least in their *bassadanza* sections, are quite similar to the *bassadanza tenores* proper.

There is, however, an important difference between the *balli* and the *bassedanze* of fifteenth-century Italy: although the *bassedanze* are notated choreographically only, without music, and could be danced to any tenor melody of the right length, the *ballo* tunes were composed to fit only the choreography to which they belong. *Bassedanze* remain in one musical meter throughout; *balli* are composed in sections of changing meters and speeds, going back and forth between *saltarello, piva, quadernaria,* and *bassadanza* in accordance with the requirements of the choreographic plan. Only a very few of the *balli* remain solely in one meter, the *quadernaria,* also known as *saltarello tedescho* (C = 4/4). It is not too farfetched an idea to see in these the earliest beginnings of the *allemande.*

Besides the improvised accompaniments for the elegant dances of the aristocracy and the upper middle classes and the *cantus-firmus* dance pieces preserved in musical sources (Gombosi, 1955; Crane, 1968; Heartz, 1966), the vocal repertory of the fifteenth century abounds in pieces that may have served to accompany simpler dance types such as early forms of the branle, first mentioned, but not described, in Antonius de Arena's manual. Strophic forms such as early *villanelle, frottole, chansons* and *canzonette, ballate,* and certain part-songs in collections such as the *Lochamer Liederbuch* and the *Glogauer Liederbuch* all contain elements that make them suitable for dancing: clear sections, repeated if or when needed, a steady rhythmic pulse, and a relatively uncomplicated musical texture.

With the invention of the printing press, a wider distribution of music (including music for the dance) became possible. Through the printed volumes of part-music, intabulations of songs and dances for lute, viols, and keyboard instruments, the expansion of the dance repertory can be shown.

The first music publisher of international renown was the Venetian Ottaviano Petrucci, whose *Harmonice musices odhecaton* (first edition, 1501) contains the dancelike "Dit le Bourguygnon"; the "Bassadanza La Spagna" appears in his *Motetti* (1502) and, together with "Le Hault Dalemaigne," in his *Canti C*—in fact, the famous "Spagna" remains in the repertory of music printed by Petrucci and later publishers up to 1576 (see listings in Brown, 1965).

The first examples of *pavane* music appear in Joan Ambrosio Dalza's *Intabulatura de lauto* (published by Petrucci in 1508); the same collection contains several *pive* and *saltarelli,* in continuation of the dance practice of the preceding century, and thirteen *calate.*

Appearing more and more frequently in the early sixteenth century are pairs of main dance and livelier afterdance *(Hupf-auff, Proportz, Nach-Tantz).* Hans Judenkunig published a *Hoff Dantz* with *Nach Tantz* (i.e., *bassedanse* with *saltarello*) in the first edition of his lute tablatures and expanded the repertory by several more such pairs in the 1523 edition, which also contains adaptations for the lute of an Italian dance *(Rossina ain welscher Dantz* with *Nach Tantz);* dances with the same title also appear in several German manuscript lute tablatures from the same period.

In 1529 the Parisian music publisher Pierre Attaingnant printed his first collection of songs intabulated for the lute, among them the "Bassesdanses Dou Vient Cela" (called *bergerette* in T. Susato 1551) and "Jouissance Vous Donneray," a *chanson* by Claudin de Sermisy used by Thoinot Arbeau as the main example for his version of the sixteenth-century *bassedanse.* The transition to the dance repertory of the sixteenth century is practically completed in Attaingnant's *Dixhuit basses danses garnies de/Recoupes et Tordions, avec dixneuf Branles, quatre que Sauterelles que/Haulberroys, quinze Gaillardes, & neuf Pavennes"* (1530).

Although the types of dances fashionable in the first half of the sixteenth century, their rhythmic properties, phrase structure, and harmonic texture become clear from the intabulations, the part-books, "scores," and mode of performance do not. The choice of instruments, now as earlier, depended on the occasion and the place—city or court, grand spectacle or private gathering. The loud wind band was as active as ever; among the soft instruments, the viols were in the ascendant, as was the harpsichord. Lutes could be used by themselves or in combination with one or more melody instruments such as recorder and/or flute. A fine example for various instrumental colors used in the course of one major theatrical event is the music for the wedding of Cosimo de' Medici and Leonora of Toledo (1539) printed by Antonio Gardano in Venice that year. The table of contents lists the instruments played for songs and dances on this occasion (see Brown, 1965, entry 1539_1): twenty-four voices, four *tromboni,* and four *cornetti* play for the entry of the *Illustrissima Duchessa,* followed by several pieces for four to nine voices. From here to the end, all the music is for the *comedia* that took place on the second day of the festivities. The *comedia* begins with a four-part vocal number, and music played by one *grave cimbalo,* and several *organetti* with different registers. Six shepherds sing a cantata, on the repeat accompanied by unspecified instruments. Three transverse flutes and three lutes "all together" play the music for sirens and sea monsters. *Violone* and soprano, four *tromboni* together with voices accompany the next numbers; the final "Ballo di Satiri et Baccante" requires sixteen voices and *varii strumenti tutti ad un tempo* (various instruments all in time)—a rich and beautiful sound on which to end the celebration.

[*See also* Social Dance, *article on* Court and Social Dance before 1800.]

BIBLIOGRAPHY: MESOPOTAMIA AND EGYPT

Anderson, Robert. "Egypt §I." In *The New Grove Dictionary of Music and Musicians.* London, 1980.

Brunner-Traut, Emma. *Der Tanz im alten Ägypten.* Gluckstadt, 1938.

Galpin, Francis W. *The Music of the Sumerians and Their Immediate Successors, the Babylonians and Assyrians* (1937). 2d ed. Strasbourg, 1955.

Hickmann, Hans. "Quelques considérations sur la danse et la musique de danse dans l'Égypte pharaonique." *Cahiers d'histoire égyptienne* 5 (1953).

Hickmann, Hans. "Le métier de musicien au temps des Pharaons." *Cahiers d'histoire égyptienne* 6 (1954).

Hickmann, Hans. *Altägyptische Musik.* Handbuch der Orientalistik, vol. 1.4. Leiden, 1970.

Hickmann, Hans. *Musikgeschichte in Bildern,* vol. 2.1, *Ägypten.* 2d ed. Leipzig, 1975.

Lexová, Irena. *Ancient Egyptian Dances.* Translated by Karel Haltmar. Prague, 1935.

Sachs, Curt. *The Rise of Music in the Ancient World: East and West.* New York, 1943.

Stauder, Wilhelm. "Mesopotamia." In *The New Grove Dictionary of Music and Musicians.* London, 1980.

BIBLIOGRAPHY: CLASSICAL ANTIQUITY, MIDDLE AGES, AND EARLY RENAISSANCE

Aeppli, Fritz. *Die wichtigsten Ausdrücke für das Tanzen in den romanischen Sprachen.* Beihefte zur Zeitschrift für romanische Philologie, 75. Halle, 1925.

Arlt, Wulf. "Zur Aufführungspraxis der Musik des 15. Jahrhunderts und zum Stand ihrer Reflexion." *Basler Jahrbuch für Historische Musikpraxis* 14 (1990): 9–12.

Baratz, Lewis Reece. "Improvising on the Spagna Tune." *American Recorder* 29.4 (1988): 141–146.

Behn, Friedrich. *Musikleben im Altertum und frühen Mittelalter.* Stuttgart, 1954.

Blackburn, Bonnie J. "On Compositional Process in the Fifteenth Century." *Journal of the American Musicological Society* 40.2 (1987): 184–210.

Blades, James, and Jeremy Montagu. *Early Percussion Instruments: From the Middle Ages to the Baroque.* London, 1976.

Borthwick, E. Kerr. "Dance: Western Antiquity." In *The New Grove Dictionary of Music and Musicians.* London, 1980.

Brainard, Ingrid. "Dance: Middle Ages, Early Renaissance." In *The New Grove Dictionary of Music and Musicians.* London, 1980.

Brown, Howard M. *Music in the French Secular Theater, 1400–1550.* Cambridge, Mass., 1963.

Brown, Howard M. *Instrumental Music Printed before 1600: A Bibliography.* Cambridge, Mass., 1965.

Brown, Howard M. *Embellishing Sixteenth-Century Music.* London, 1976.

Brown, Howard M. "Dance and Dance Music in Fourteenth-Century Italy." Presentation, Smith College, Northamptom, Mass., 5 October 1983.

Busch, Gabriele C. *Ikonographische Studien zum Solotanz im Mittelalter.* Innsbruck, 1982.

Caroso, Fabritio. *Nobiltà di dame* (1600). Translated and edited by Julia Sutton. Oxford, 1986.

Chew, Geoffrey. "Emmeleia." In *The New Grove Dictionary of Music and Musicians.* London, 1980.

Crane, Frederick. *Materials for the Study of the Fifteenth-Century Basse Danse.* Brooklyn, 1968.

Cummings, Anthony M. *The Politicized Muse: Music for Medici Festivals, 1512–1537.* Princeton, 1992.

Daniels, Véronique, and Eugen Dombois. "Die Temporelationen im Ballo des Quattrocento: Spekulative Dialoge um den labyrinthische Rätselkanon *De la arte di ballare et danzare* des Domenico da Piacenza." *Basler Jahrbuch für Historische Musikpraxis* 14 (1990): 181–247.

Daniels, Véronique. "Tempo Relationships within the Italian *Balli* of the Fifteenth Century: A Closer Look at the Notation." In *The Marriage of Music and Dance: Papers from a Conference Held at the Guildhall School of Music and Drama, London, 9th–11th August 1991.* Cambridge, 1992.

Dieckmann, Jenny. *Die in deutscher Lautenabulatur überlieferten Tänze des 16. Jahrhunderts.* Kassel, 1931.

Emmanuel, Maurice. *La danse grecque antique d'après les monuments figurés.* Paris, 1896.

Fenlon, Iain. *Music and Patronage in Sixteenth-Century Mantua.* Cambridge, 1980.

Ferand, Ernst. *Die Improvisation in der Musik.* Zurich, 1938.

Fleischhauer, Günter. *Musikgeschichte in Bildern,* vol. 2.5, *Etrurien und Rom.* Leipzig, 1964.

Fleischhauer, Günter. "Rome §I." In *The New Grove Dictionary of Music and Musicians.* London, 1980.

Gatiss, Ian. "Realizing the Music in the Fifteenth-Century Italian Dance Manuals." In *The Marriage of Music and Dance: Papers from a Conference Held at the Guildhall School of Music and Drama, London, 9th–11th August 1991.* Cambridge, 1992.

Gombosi, Otto. "About Dance and Dance Music in the Late Middle Ages." *Musical Quarterly* 27 (July 1941): 289–305.

Gombosi, Otto, ed. *Vincenzo Capirola Lute Bok, circa 1517.* Chicago, 1955.

Guglielmo Ebreo da Pesaro. *On the Practice or Art of Dancing* (1463). Translated and edited by Barbara Sparti. Oxford, 1993.

Heartz, Daniel. "Hoftanz and Basse Dance: Towards a Reconstruction of Fifteenth-Century Dance Music." *Journal of the American Musicological Society* 19 (1966): 13–36.

Heartz, Daniel. *Pierre Attaingnant: Royal Printer of Music.* Berkeley, 1969.

Hill, Simon R. "Improvising Accompaniments to the Burgundian *bassedanse.*" In *The Marriage of Music and Dance: Papers from a Conference Held at the Guildhall School of Music and Drama, London, 9th–11th August 1991.* Cambridge, 1992.

Hudson, Richard. *The Allemande, the Balletto, and the Tanz.* Cambridge, 1986.

Jones, Pamela. "The Relation between Music and Dance in Cesare Negri's 'Le gratie d'amore' (1602)." 2 vols. Ph.D. diss., University of London, 1988.

Kahrstedt, Ulrich. *Kulturgeschichte der römischen Kaiserzeit.* 2d ed. Bern, 1958.

Kendall, Yvonne. "Rhythm, Meter, and *Tactus* in Sixteenth-Century Italian Court Dance: Reconstruction from a Theoretical Base." *Dance Research* 8 (Spring 1990): 3–27.

Kinkeldey, Otto. "Dance Tunes of the Fifteenth Century." In *Instrumental Music: A Conference at Isham Memorial Library, May 4, 1957,* edited by David G. Hughes. Cambridge, Mass., 1959.

Latte, Kurt. *De saltationibus Graecorum capita quinque.* Giessen, 1913.

Lawler, Lillian B. *The Dance in Ancient Greece.* Middletown, Conn., 1964.

Lockwood, Lewis. *Music in Renaissance Ferrara, 1400–1505.* Cambridge, Mass., 1984.

Marcuse, Sibyl. *Musical Instruments. A Comprehensive Dictionary.* New York, 1975.

Marrocco, W. Thomas. *Inventory of Fifteenth-Century Bassedanze, Balli, and Balletti in Italian Dance Manuals.* New York, 1981.

McGee, Timothy J. *Medieval and Renaissance Music: A Performer's Guide.* Toronto, 1985.

McGee, Timothy J. "Medieval Dances: Matching the Repertory with Grocheio's Descriptions." *Journal of Musicology* 7 (1989): 498–517.

McGee, Timothy J. *Medieval Instrumental Dances.* Bloomington, 1989.

McKinnon, James. "Scabellum." In *The New Grove Dictionary of Music and Musicians.* London, 1980.

McKinnon, James. "Tibia." In *The New Grove Dictionary of Music and Musicians.* London, 1980.

Merian, Wilhelm. *Der Tanz in den deutschen Tabulaturbüchern* (1927). Hildesheim, 1968.

Meylan, Raymond. *L'énigme de la musique des basses danses du quinzième siècle.* Bern, 1968.

Meylan, Raymond. "Migration et transformation des polyphonies à armatures (Basse Danse et Hoftanz)." In *Le concert des voix et des instruments à la Renaissance: Actes du XXXIVe colloque international d'études humanistes Tours [1991],* edited by Jean-Michel Vaccaro. Paris, 1995.

Miller, James. *Measures of Wisdom: The Cosmic Dance in Classical and Christian Antiquity.* Toronto, 1986.

Mingardi, Maurizio. "Gli strumenti musicali nella danza del XIV e XV secolo." In *Mesura et arte del danzare: Guglielmo Ebreo da Pesaro e la danza nelle corti italiane del XV secolo,* edited by Patrizia Castelli et al. Pesaro, 1987.

Mullen, William. *Choreia: Pindar and Dance.* Princeton, 1982.

Page, Christopher. *Voices and Instruments of the Middle Ages.* London, 1987.

Palisca, Claude. *Humanism in Italian Renaissance Thought.* New Haven, 1985.

Pirrotta, Nino, and Elena Povoledo. *Music and Theatre from Poliziano to Monteverdi.* Translated by Karen Eales. Cambridge, 1982.

Polk, Keith. "Flemish Wind Bands in the Late Middle Ages: A Study in Improvisatory Performance Practices." Ph.D. diss., University of California, Berkeley, 1968.

Pontremoli, Alessandro, and Patrizia La Rocca. *Il ballare lombardo: Teoria e prassi coreutica nella festa di corte del XV secolo.* Milan, 1987.

Reese, Gustave. *Music in the Middle Ages.* New York, 1940.

Rimmer, Joan. "Dance Elements in Trouvère Repertory." *Dance Research* 3 (Summer 1985): 23–34.

Rimmer, Joan. "Medieval Instrumental Dance Music." *Music and Letters* 72 (1991): 61–68.

Sachs, Curt. *World History of the Dance.* Translated by Bessie Schönberg. New York, 1937.

Sachs, Curt. *The Rise of Music in the Ancient World: East and West.* New York, 1943.

Salmen, Walter. *Der fahrende Musiker im europäischen Mittelalter.* Kassel, 1960.

Séchan, Louis. *La danse grecque antique.* Paris, 1930.

Smith, A. William, trans. and ed. *Fifteenth-Century Dance and Music: The Complete Transcribed Italian Treatises and Collections in the Tradition of Domenico da Piacenza.* 2 vols. Stuyvesant, N.Y., 1995.

Southern, Eileen. *The Buxheim Organ Book.* Musicological Studies 6, Institute of Medieval Studies. Brooklyn, New York, 1963.

Southern, Eileen. "Some Keyboard Basse Dances of the Fifteenth Century." *Acta musicologica* 35 (1963): 114–124.

Southern, Eileen. "Basse-Dance Music in Some German Manuscripts of the Fifteenth Century." *Aspects of Medieval and Renaissance Music. A Birthday Offering to Gustave Reese.* Edited by Jan LaRue. New York, 1966: 738–755.

Southworth, John. *The English Medieval Minstrel.* Woodbridge, Suffolk, 1989.

Sparti, Barbara. "Music and Choreography in the Reconstruction of Fifteenth-Century Balli: Another Look at Domenico's *Verçepe.*" *Fifteenth-Century Studies* 10 (1984): 177–194.

Sparti, Barbara. "The Fifteenth-Century *Balli* Tunes: A New Look." *Early Music* 14.3 (1986): 346–357.

Straeten, Edmond Vander. *Les ménestrels aux Pays-Bas du XIIIe au XVIIIe siècle.* Brussels, 1878.

Sutton, Julia. "Triple Pavans: Clues to Some Mysteries in Sixteenth-Century Dance." *Early Music* 14.2 (1986): 174–181.

Treitler, Leo. "Oral, Written, and Literate Process in the Transmission of Medieval Music." *Speculum* 56.3 (1981).

Ward, John M. "A Dowland Miscellany." *Journal of the Lute Society of America,* vol. 10 (1977).

Ward, John M. "The English Measure." *Early Music* 14.1 (1986): 15–21.

Weege, Fritz. *Der Tanz in der Antike.* Halle, 1926.

Welker, Lorenz. "Bläserensembles der Renaissance." *Basler Jahrbuch für Historische Musikpraxis* 14 (1990): 249–270.

Wiora, Walter, and Walter Salmen. "Die Tanzmusik im deutschen Mittelalter." *Zeitschrift für Volkskunde* 50 (1953): 164–187.

Wright, Craig. *Music at the Court of Burgundy, 1364–1419: A Documentary History.* Musicological Studies, no. 28. Henryville, Ottawa, 1979.

INGRID BRAINARD

Western Music, 1520–1650

From 1520 to 1650, the qualities peculiar to social and theatrical dance music (then closely related) had an ever-increasing influence on all other genres of vocal and instrumental music. This may have been because dancing was so immensely popular in all walks of life that people wished to be reminded of it even outside the ballroom, or perhaps because dance music was radically different from, and seemingly newer and simpler in style than, the rhythmically fluid, complex, and polyphonic style that dominated sixteenth-century madrigals and motets. Renaissance "dancelike" music, then, whether truly for dancing or inspired by dance, served as one of the key feeders into some of the newer aspects of early Baroque music (c.1600–1650): Claudio Monteverdi's sacred *Exulta filia sion,* for example, begins with a clear statement of a galliard rhythm (see below).

In this period, music for dancing, whether for formal couple dances, figured two-couple dances, or group circle dances generally had clear metric organization and incisive, often-repeated rhythmic motives that frequently characterized a specific dance type, and regular phrasing (usually four or eight bars in a strain); it was also often tuneful (or treble dominated), with a tendency toward tonality rather than modality, and with simple basses. All these characteristics were held together by a homophonic texture in mostly functional harmony and conventional chord schemes (sometimes these were on well-known ostinatos, such as the *passo e mezzo antico*). [*See* Passo e Mezzo.] Single dances were commonly made up of two to three strains of music, each strain marked off by repeat signs, and each as well as the whole clearly intended to be repeated as often as necessary for the dance. Dances grouped together (e.g., *pavane-galliarde-saltarello*) often were in variation suites called *balletti*—that is, they used the same musical material, transforming it in meter and character according to the dance type designated.

All these traits, especially some of the specific rhythmic patterns common to popular dance types (e.g., C 𝅗𝅥 ♩ ♩ | 𝅗𝅥 ♩ ♩ | for the *pavane,* and 3 𝅗𝅥 𝅗𝅥 𝅗𝅥 | 𝅗𝅥. ♩ 𝅗𝅥 | for the *galliarde*), dominate such major northern instrumental ensemble collections as Claude Gervaise's *Danceries* (1550–1556), Tylman Susato's *Danserye* (1551), Antony Holborne's *Pavans, Galliards, Almains* (1599), and Michael Praetorius's *Terpsichore* (1612). Among southern ensemble publications, Giovanni Gastoldi's *Balletti* (1591, 1594), whose title pages carry the rubrics *per cantare, sonare, & ballare* ("to sing, to play, and to dance"), contain delightful music that surely influenced such English composers as Thomas Morley (*Balletts,* 1595). Although all the foregoing are called dance collections, it cannot be known with certainty whether all the music in them was intended to be danced, or even whether it was intended to be played by educated amateurs rather than professional dance musicians. (Iconography of the period almost always shows professional musicians playing by memory.) [*See the entry on Praetorius.*]

Dance music was heavily represented in manuscripts and printed instrumental collections of the time that were clearly intended to be played by the educated amateur. Some of these collections are either attached to musical-instruction manuals, such as those printed for various instruments by Adrian Le Roy, or the huge lute collection by Jean-Baptiste Besard, *Thesaurus harmonicus* (1603). Non-instructional collections include those for ensemble (e.g., Giorgio Mainerio, *Il primo libro de balli,* 1578) or for solo instrument (e.g., *Fitzwilliam Virginal Book,* c.1609–1619). The music may vary from very simple pieces in two or three strains with emphasis on melody and bass, to huge sets of virtuosic variations. Again, it is not known how much of this music might have been intended for dancing, but the large part "dance" music played in the instrumental and vocal repertory of this time is incontrovertible.

A microcosm of dance music within the wealth of instrumental music of the period is to be found in the large lute music repertory. Collections by Giulio Abondante, Alessandro Piccinini, and Giulio Cesare Barbetta in Italy; Pierre Attaingnant, Adrian Le Roy, and Ennemond Gaultier in France; Hans Newsidler and Conrad Gerle in Germany; Luis de Milán and Alonso Mudarra in Spain; John Dowland and Antony Holborne in England; and the Phalèse family in the Low Countries, all contain music from dances that were popular then. Other instrumental publications of importance were those by Antonio Gardane and Giacomo Gorzanis in Italy; Claude Gervaise, Guillaume Morlaye, Estienne Du Tertre, Jean d'Estrée, and Anthoine Françisque in France; Hans Jacob Wecker, Bernhard Schmid, Elias Nikolaus Ammerbach, and Matthäus Waissel in Germany; Tylman Susato in the Low Countries; William Barley and Thomas Morley in England; and Antonio de Cabezón and Diego Ortiz in Spain.

By the end of the sixteenth century, dance, music, and spectacle were often united in the opulent productions of the Italian *intermedio,* the French *ballet de cour,* and the English masque. The interconnections among the three types of entertainment were many, for the Neoplatonism of the time was universal; in addition, musicians and dancing masters from Italy and France were everywhere. All such theatrical spectacles were designed to glorify the event they celebrated and the nobility or monarchy that produced them, and many were composed by a number of contributors. Included among the large performing forces were musicians, on stage and in costume, playing a multitude of instruments according to the standard conventions of the scenes they accompanied. The most noticeable aspects of theatrical versus social dance music at this time seem to be the greater complexity of musical structures and the more irregular phrase lengths in the specially choreographed theater pieces. [*See* Ballet de Cour; Intermedio; *and* Masque and Antimasque.]

Although the relationships among the Italian *intermedio,* the French ballet, and the English masque are known to have been close, and those types of entertainments contributed generously to the development of opera, the only extant detailed stage choreographies with music are Italian—four by Cesare Negri (1602) and one by Emilio de' Cavalieri (1589). It can only be surmised from literary descriptions that northern choreographies may have been similar: it is not certain, for example, that such dances as "Gray's Inn Masque," in John Playford's *The English Dancing Master* (1651), were choreographed on Italian or French models. Only one of Negri's four *balli,* "Brando Alta Regina," is in a complex musical and choreographic form. His other three stage choreographies and their music are comparatively simple, but all of them, and Cavalieri's *ballo* as well, open with or include a half-moon figure facing the audience that apparently occurred only in staged *balli.*

Cavalieri, a nobleman and diplomat, composed the music and created the choreography for the final *gran ballo* of the great Florentine *intermedi* of 1589 (printed by Cristofano Malvezzi in 1591). His attractive *ballo* for a large onstage group, supported also by offstage musicians, and sung and played by an alternating full chorus and solo trio, consists of different dance types in a complex variation suite whose rhythms are partly governed by a highly organized poetic scheme; the *ballo* calls for twenty-four changes in meter and tempo in about eight minutes, danced by seven deities and a chorus of mortals. It is undoubtedly the most complicated and sophisticated surviving choreography (the melody and bass became famous throughout Europe as *Il Ballo del Gran Duca*). Unfortunately, the correlation of choreography with music is ambiguous, and although many different accompanying instruments are listed in the verbal description, the exact parts they played in the three- to six-voice *ballo* are also unclear.

At that time Claudio Monteverdi, one of the giants of early Baroque music, wrote some of the most beautiful music known to be for stage *balli,* notably *Il Ballo delle Ingrate* (published in 1638), *Volgendo il Ciel* (published in 1638), and *Tirsi e Clori* (published in 1619); they are similar in musical structure to Negri's and Cavalieri's multisectional stage dances, but there are no choreographies.

MUSIC FOR DANCE: Western Music, 1520–1650. A late sixteenth-century engraving by Crispin de Pas, after a painting by the Flemish artist Martin de Vos, depicting a lively social dance scene: a couple dances by torchlight, to the accompaniment of three female musicians, who play a keyboard instrument, a lute, and a tambourine. (Courtesy of Madison U. Sowell and Debra H. Sowell, Brigham Young University, Provo, Utah.)

Tirsi e Clori, for example, begins with a dialogue between the two lovers in which Tirsi, in a lilting triple-meter aria, invites Clori to join the dancing nymphs and shepherds; Clori responds in monody in duple meter until she finally accedes to Tirsi's wishes. She then joins him musically in the triple-meter duet "Balliamo" (Let Us Dance). The *ballo* continues with multisectional music in various dance types chosen to suit the text, with chorus and instruments participating equally and delectably. Much of Monteverdi's other music also suggests and celebrates dance (e.g., *Alle danze,* 1619, which may well have been a *ballo,* and his lively *Scherzi musicali,* 1607). In his great opera *L'Orfeo* (1607), the music for the joyful moments is frequently in dance styles and rhythms (e.g., the second chorus of nymphs and shepherds). The final triumphant ensemble *bergamasca* puts a fitting and typical close to the first operatic masterpiece.

The French ballets—also combining poetry, music, and dance, and designed to glorify the reigning monarch—have much sparser choreographic clues than the Italian *balli,* although it is known that they ranged from intimate indoor presentations within the court to grand outdoor *carousels* and brilliant water shows. For example, the first *ballet de cour* based on a single narrative, *Circé, ou Le Balet Comique de la Royne* (1581), combined poetry, music, decor, and dance to support its dramatic action. The "book" of the show includes multisectional dance music for a five-part instrumental ensemble, but provides too little of it to fit the textual references to more than sixty different figures without seemingly endless repetitions. Nevertheless, without choreography this grand show cannot be reconstructed. The large repertory of ballet music from this period and the seventeenth century in, for example, the Philidor Collection, was most often notated simply as melody and bass, rather than in the ampler scoring of *Circé, ou Le Balet Comique.* [*See* Balet Comique de la Royne, Le.]

While no complete score exists for any English court masque, this aristocratic spectacle of the Elizabethan, Jacobean, and Caroline eras provided a large amount of dance music identified with masques in collections by both continental and English composers, including Alfonso Ferrabosco, Thomas Campion, and Henry and William Lawes. Much of this music is also in melody-bass notation. Some of the dance types that might have been used are known from this music and the texts to the masques: for the antimasques there were jigs and *morescas,* anonymous popular music, and other vigorous or specially composed bizarre dances—often with fermatas at irregularly placed cadences to indicate, perhaps, special action; and for the general revels there were standard measures, *allemandes, pavanes, galliardes, courantes,* and other popular dance types. For the three grand masquing dances of the masque proper, however, it is known chiefly that they were specially composed and choreographed for the event and were danced in many, various, and complex formations (e.g., the initials of newlyweds at a nuptial masque). The music for these dances consisted in the simplest form of two strains in duple, with an occasional third strain in triple, but it could also be considerably more complex. [*See* Allemande; Galliard; *and* Pavan.]

Despite much additional evidence of the importance of dance and dance music at the time, it is neither in the accounts of spectacle nor in the dance music collections that most surviving examples of music with specific choreographies are found, but rather in the dance manuals themselves. The four important printed manuals that include music are *Il ballarino* (1581) and *Nobiltà di dame* (1600) by Fabritio Caroso, *Orchésographie* (1588) by Thoinot Arbeau, and *Le gratie d'amore* (1602) by Cesare Negri. The form in which the music appears in these manuals and what the dancing masters have to say about music and its performance yield many clues as to how this functional music was used (its tempos, articulations, affects), presumably by professional musicians, to accompany the dances at a ball. [*See the entries on Arbeau, Caroso, and Negri.*]

The least problematic method of performing the music for dances in the manuals of Caroso, Arbeau, and Negri is, of course, to use the given music for each specific dance; however, the music as it appears (either in score or in lute tablature) probably was often only the basis for arrangements by professional dance musicians, who did not record them and who improvised freely on the skeletal melodies and chord schemes. It is thus vital that musicians (and dancers) today be knowledgeable about the performance practices of this music. Here the dancing masters themselves are helpful. For each dance, for example, Arbeau provides the tune in white notation as part of his tabulation, correlating it with the choreography so that steps and music are lined up. He does, however, provide one four-part setting of the graceful pavan "Belle qui Tiens Ma Vie" (complete with rhythm notated for the tabor). It can be seen as a model for realizing the one-line music in the rest of his manual, especially when considered in the light of such statements as the following:

> In our fathers' time, the tabor, accompanied by its long flute [i.e., the pipe and tabor] . . . was used because a single musician could play them both together in symphony without necessitating the additional expense of other players. . . . Nowadays there is no workman so humble that he does not wish to have hautboys and sackbuts at his wedding.
>
> (Arbeau, 1967, p.51)

Concordances with some of the tunes in *Orchésographie* appear in multipartite settings such as Jean d'Estrée's *Premier livre de danseries* (1559). They suggest that the melodies provided for the other choreographies in Arbeau's manual might be arranged similarly to accommodate the ensembles that were in vogue in the 1580s.

In the manuals of Caroso and Negri, the music is always notated in Italian lute tablature, some of it with melody and bass lines in white notation (Negri always includes the melody in this form). A wide variety of discrete dances appear (e.g., the vigorous *passo e mezzo,* the light and lively *cascarda,* the stamping mock-angry *canario*) as well as *balletto* suites in variation form, and are of primary interest in the manuals. [*See* Ballo and Balletto; Cascarda.]

While three strains (usually of eight semibreves to a strain) are typical of most individual dance movements, music for an entire dance also may consist of one strain only (e.g., Caroso's "Ballo del Fiore") or of many more (e.g., Negri's "La Battaglia"). Repetitions depend on the choreographies and are often specified, sometimes calling for a far more complex musical structure than meets the eye. As with Arbeau's tunes, the lute tablatures in Caroso and Negri can be considered skeletal arrangements of this music (or cheat sheets, as they would be termed today) for larger ensembles when desired; for example, the first eight dances in *Nobiltà di dame*—notated in score for lute, plus melody, and bass—illustrate how the tablature may be expanded for the subsequent dances provided with lute tablature only. Multipartite settings also exist of some music from the Italian manuals in such publications as Gasparo Zanetti's *Il scolaro* (1645).

The tremendous production of dance music in the seventeenth century is further exemplified by the publication in Germany alone of more than one hundred large collections in the first quarter of the century (e.g., Praetorius's *Terpsichore*). The instrumental suite received a particularly strong impetus here with Johann Hermann Schein and Paul Peuerl, was given its basic classical format by Johann Jakob Froberger and Johann Erasmus Kindermann, and was conceptually completed later in the seventeenth century by such composers as Johann Kuhnau. That there was dance activity throughout the seventeenth century is clear, and that dance music was composed for it is also clear.

It is certain that dance continued to have a powerful influence on "abstract" dance music. What is not yet determined is exactly which music, whether of individual dances or of suites, was intended truly for dancing and which was truly abstract. There is still a frustrating paucity of precise information on dance from about 1610 until 1650, despite all the accounts in memoirs and letters, despite all the iconography, and even despite the existing manuals of F[rançois] de Lauze (1623) and Juan de Esquivel Navarro (1642). (These two authors give no music, for example, and are highly enigmatic in their directions.) So far, it does not seem possible to know with certainty the step patterns or figures to most dance music of that time. Recognizable dance basses (such as the *passacaglia*), recognizable dance rhythms and meters (such as those of the *galliarde, courante, canarie,* and *sarabande*), and recognizable dance forms (whether standard binary, three-strain, or *ostinato* variations) all appear in that music, however. [See Canary; Chaconne and Passacaglia; *and* Sarabande.]

BIBLIOGRAPHY: SOURCES

Arbeau, Thoinot. *Orchesographie et traicte en forme de dialogve, par leqvel tovtes personnes pevvent facilement apprendre & practiquer l'honneste exercice des dances.* Langres, 1588, 1589. Facsimile reprint, Langres, 1988. Reprinted with expanded title as *Orchesographie, metode, et teorie en forme de discovrs et tablatvre povr apprendre dancer, battre le Tambour en toute sorte & diuersité de batteries, Iouët du fifre & arigot, tirer des armes & escrimer, auec autres honnestes exercices fort conuenables à la Ieunesse.* Langres, 1596. Facsimile reprint, Geneva, 1972.

Arbeau, Thoinot. *Orchesography.* 1589. Translated into English by Mary Stewart Evans. New York, 1948. Reprint with corrections, a new introduction, and notes by Julia Sutton, and representative steps and dances in Labanotation by Mireille Backer. New York, 1967.

Beaujoyeulx, Balthazar de (Belgioioso, Baldassare de). *Le Balet Comique de la Royne* (1581). Facsimile reprint, Turin, 1965. Translated by Carol and Lander MacClintock, the music transcribed by Carol MacClintock. Rome, 1971.

Caroso, Fabritio. *Il ballarino* (1581). Facsimile reprint, New York, 1967.

Caroso, Fabritio, *Nobiltà di dame.* Venice, 1600, 1605. Facsimile reprint, Bologna, 1970. Reissued with order of illustrations changed as *Raccolta di varij balli.* Rome, 1630. Translated into English with eight introductory chapters by Julia Sutton, the music transcribed by F. Marian Walker. Oxford, 1986. Reprint with a step manual in Labanotation by Rachelle Palnick Tschor and Julia Sutton, New York, 1995.

Cavalieri, Emilio de'. "Intermedio VI". In Cristofano Malvezzi's *Intermidii Et Concerti, fatti per la Commedia rappresentata in Firenze nelle Nozze del Serenissimo Don Ferdinando Medici et Madama Christiana di Loreno, Granduchi di Toscana.* Venice, 1591. Transcribed and edited by D.P. Walker as *Les Fêtes de Florence: Musique des intermédes de "La Pellegrina."* Paris, 1963.

Mersenne, Marin. *Harmonie universelle* (1636–1637). Facsimile reprint, Paris, 1963. English translation of Book 2 by J.B. Egan. Ph.D. diss., Indiana University, 1962.

Manuscripts of the Inns of Court. Located in Bodleian Library, Rawl.Poet.108, ff.10v-11r; British Library, Harley 367, pp. 178–179; Bodleian, Douce 280, ff.66av-66bv (202v-203v); Bodleian, Rawl.D.864, f.199v, ff.203r-204; Royal College of Music, MS 1119, title page and ff.1-2, 23v-24r; Inner Temple, Miscellanea vol. 27. Some MSS have music.

Negri, Cesare. *Le gratie d'amore.* Milan, 1602. Reissued as *Nuove invenzione di balli.* Milan, 1604. Translated into Spanish by Don Balthasar Carlos for Señor Condé, Duke of Sanlucar, 1630. Manuscript located in Madrid, Biblioteca Nacional, MS 14085. Facsimile reprint of 1602, New York and Bologna, 1969. Literal translation into English and musical transcription by Yvonne Kendall. D.M.A. diss., Stanford University, 1985.

Playford, John. *The English Dancing Master.* London, 1651. Facsimile reprint with introduction, concordances, and lists of references by Margaret Dean-Smith, London, 1957.

BIBLIOGRAPHY: OTHER STUDIES

Aldrich, Putnam. *Rhythm in Seventeenth-Century Italian Monody.* New York, 1966.

Bank, J.A. *Tactus, Tempo, and Notation in Mensural Music from the Thirteenth to the Seventeenth Century.* Amsterdam, 1972.

Brown, Howard M. "Sixteenth-Century Instrumentation: The Music for the Florentine Intermedii." *Musicological Studies and Documents* 30 (1973).

Esses, Maurice. *Dance and Instrumental Diferencias in Spain during the Seventeenth and Early Eighteenth Centuries.* Stuyvesant, N.Y., 1992.

Heartz, Daniel. "Sources and Forms of the French Instrumental Dance in the Sixteenth Century." Ph.D. diss., Harvard University, 1957.

Heartz, Daniel. *Preludes, Chansons, and Dances for Lute Published by Pierre Attaingnant, Paris, 1529–1530.* Neuilly-sur-Seine, 1964.

Hilton, Wendy. *Dance and Music of Court and Theater: Selected Writings of Wendy Hilton.* Stuyvesant, N.Y. 1997.

Jones, Pamela. "Spectacle in Milan: Cesare Negri's Torch Dances." *Early Music* 14.2 (1986): 182–198.

Jones, Pamela. "The Relation between Music and Dance in Cesare Negri's 'Le gratie d'amore' (1602)." 2 vols. Ph.D. diss., University of London, 1988.

Jones, Pamela. "The Editions of Cesare Negri's *Le Gratie d'Amore:* Choreographic Revisions in Printed Copies." *Studi musicali* 21(1991): 21–33.

Matteo (Vittucci, Matteo Marcellus), with Carola Goya. *The Language of Spanish Dance.* Norman, Okla., 1990.

Moe, Lawrence H. "Dance Music in Printed Italian Lute Tablatures from 1507 to 1611." Ph.D. diss., Harvard University, 1956.

Sutton, Julia. "Reconstruction of Sixteenth-Century Dance." *Council on Research in Dance* 2(1969): 56–63.

Sutton, Julia. *Renaissance Revisited: Twelve Dances Reconstructed [in Labanotation] from the Originals of Thoinot Arbeau, Fabritio Caroso, and Cesare Negri.* New York, 1972.

Sutton, Julia, and Charles P. Coldwell. Review of Helmut Mönkemeyer's *Fabritio Caroso: "Il ballarino." Notes* 30 (1973): 357–359.

Sutton, Julia. "Dance: I. Introduction," "Dance: IV. Late Renaissance and Baroque to 1700." In *The New Grove Dictionary of Music and Musicians.* London, 1980.

Sutton, Julia. "Triple Pavans: Clues to Some Mysteries in Sixteenth-Century Dance." *Early Music* 14.2 (1986): 174–181.

Sutton, Julia. "Musical Forms and Dance Forms in the Dance Manuals of Sixteenth-Century Italy: Plato and the Varieties of Variation." In *The Marriage of Music and Dance: Papers from a Conference Held at the Guildhall School of Music and Drama, London, 9th–11th August 1991.* Cambridge, 1992.

Sutton, Julia, and Sibylle Dahms. "Ballo, Balletto." In *Die Musik in Geschichte und Gegenwart.* 2d ed., vol. 1, 1994. Kassel, 1994–.

VIDEOTAPE. Julia Sutton. *Il Ballarino (The Dancing Master).* A teaching videotape featuring a glossary of steps and three sixteenth-century Italian dances by Caroso and Negri (Pemmington, N.J.: Princeton Book Co., 1991).

JULIA SUTTON
with David Hahn

Western Music, 1650–1800

By about 1600, France had gradually acquired its leadership in the realm of European dance music. From about 1650 until the French Revolution of 1789, France maintained this preeminence. French theatrical dance had begun as a part of the carefully rehearsed court social dance performances before royalty; this custom was diminished, though never completely lost, through the efforts of the Académie de Danse and the seventeenth-century French court composer and choreographer Jean-Baptiste Lully's demanding dance productions. For theatrical dance, Lully's *airs de vitesse* and *entrées caractérisées* started the differentiation between balletic virtuoso *airs dansants* and the genres that long remained social dancing.

In France, dance and theater owe their special social status to their inclusion in education. Every educated person was capable of participating in both dancing and theatrical events at court, in the salons, and at the learned societies. This educational ideal exerted considerable influence throughout both France and the rest of Europe. Even after the mid-eighteenth century, for example, practicing the minuet was understood not only to further dance posture, elegance, and grace but to provide good training for presentation and behavior in society. At a time when dance fulfilled such an important function, dance music was consequently of very high quality.

French Court Dance and Early Ballet. Lully was an extraordinary musician—a dancer, composer, teacher, and grand organizer—and he considered danced pantomime a significant art form, one worthy of support by his musical compositions. The *airs dansants* were danced expressions that differed from other dance structures, through accelerated movement and virtuosic and dramatic performance. Like marches and corteges, the *airs dansants* were particularly suited to the staged productions called *tragédie lyrique;* there, they were essential to the section called the *divertissement.* Although the specifically choreographed ballet scenes in the first French opera, Robert Cambert's *Pomone* (1671), had no connection with the action, ballets in Lully's operas that followed (after he was granted a court monopoly in 1672) were generally integrated into the dramatic events (for example, the *pompe funèbre* in *Alceste, ou Le Triomphe d'Alcide,* act 3, or the underworld scene in act 4; and the combat in *Amadis,* act 1), although they are often a point of rest during the dramatic performance. André-Cardinal Destouches and Jean-Philippe Rameau soon individualized the dance types even more strongly than did Lully.

Much documentation exists to suggest that many of the early theatrical dances then in favor were more or less identical to those still danced socially. During Lully's period of influence (from 1653 when he entered the service of Louis XIV until his death in 1687) for example, permission was granted to the noncourtly Associations de Joueurs d'Instruments to include in its balls and festivities, after a respectful interval of one month, the latest repertory of court dances as well as the dances performed at the Paris Opera. In the theater, however, dances often remained in use long after they had gone out of fashion as social dances (for example, the *gigue*). Some social dances never found their way into the theater (various *branles,* the *polonaise,* and the mazurka of the eighteenth century are cases in point). [*See the entry on Lully.*]

During the period of renewal of the *ballet d'action,* Rameau (Lully's successor in French opera and ballet, whose theater dances rank among the best of the eighteenth century) succeeded in dramatizing many of his compositions. Like Lully's, Rameau's dance music was known throughout Europe. According to contemporary sources, it was used even in Italy (the early home of theatrical music and opera) for a variety of purposes, including as entr'acte music in the theater. [*See the entry on Rameau.*]

Eighteenth-century choreographers continued to contribute to the wide dissemination of the French ballet, as did the guest appearances of famous Parisian stars and ensembles in the cultural centers of Europe. Thus, when a French ballet troupe under the direction of Marie Sallé visited London for the 1733/34 season, George Frideric Handel created for her his most significant ballet music in *IL Pastor Fido* (1734, with the one-act *opéra-ballet Terpsichore* as prologue), *Arianna in Creta,* and *Oreste* (both, 1734), and *Ariodante* and *Alcina* (both, 1735).

Christoph Willibald Gluck created his first ballet masterpiece with *Don Juan, ou Le Festin de Pierre,* (1761; choreography by Gasparo Angiolini). Characterized by extraordinary passion and tragic depth, this work left visible traces in Mozart's opera *Don Giovanni* (1787). Gluck also used dance—the Dance of the Furies to a set of variations in D-minor—in the Paris version of his opera *Orfeo ed Euridice,* performed in 1774. Along with *opéras comique,* numerous ballets were performed in Vienna's French theater (for example, *Les Aventures de Serail,* 1762, with music by Giuseppe Scarlatti and choreography by Angiolini). For the Paris Opera, Mozart composed his *ballet-divertissement Les Petits Riens* (1778), which was choreographed by

MUSIC FOR DANCE: Western Music, 1650–1800. A small stringed instrument, the *pochette* (Eng., kit) is the signature instrument of the dancing master. This engraving, c.1760, by Rennoldson after John Collett's humorous painting entitled *Grown Ladies Taught to Dance,* shows a dancing master holding his *pochette* as he instructs an elderly lady, to the amusement of the young onlookers at right. (Courtesy of Madison U. Sowell and Debra H. Sowell, Brigham Young University, Provo, Utah.)

Parisian ballet master Jean-Georges Noverre. Individual movements from Franz Joseph Haydn's symphonies were frequently used as ballet music by the Paris Opera.

Social Dance. Immensely varied dance genres and immensely popular music for solo instruments, chamber ensembles, and orchestras had been developed in the second half of the seventeenth century. After 1700, however, the variety of social dance types was greatly reduced, enough so that the eighteenth century might be called the age of the minuet and the contradance, the former continuing the older dance aesthetic and the latter representing the new spirit of playfulness, freedom, and daily life. During the second half of the seventeenth century, not all theater dances had been recorded in notation; but those found in archives often included several versions. Of the social dances that were included in collections, only a few are extant. Many of these survived only outside the major European centers (such as Germany or Sweden) or were assembled at a much later date.

The Philidor collection contains the repertory surviving from the period of Louis XIII to the early years of Louis XIV's reign. Especially in France, but also in Germany and England, dances were printed with texts: Ballard annually published a *Livre de chansons pour danser et pour boire* (Book of Songs for Dancing and Drinking). In the eighteenth century such collections as *Menuets chantants* (Sung Minuets), *Rondes* (*contredanse* parodies), and others also were available. The *Livre de chansons* (twenty-two volumes until 1663) and others contain a substantial repertory of fashionable social dances—*branles*, *sarabandes*, *courantes*, *gavottes*, *menuets*, and *gigues* composed by François Chancy and others—that, like manuscript collections of suites abstracted from the stage works of Lully, André Campra, and others, should be subjected to scholarly scrutiny.

In Germany, England, the Netherlands, the Scandinavian countries, and Spain, these French dances were widely popularized by French dance masters, French court orchestras, and the many journeys taken by European royalty and aristocracy to the court at Paris and Versailles. In these countries many dances were composed, the majority of them preserved only in manuscript (for example, the anonymous 1689 suites for the Hofkapelle in Hanover and some by Telemann, Graun, Bach, Düben, and others). Even in Vienna—a city with a strong, independent tradition of music for the dance and a long-time resistance toward French music—the ballet music for Pier Francesco Cavalli's *Ercole Amante* (Paris, 1662) was introduced as early as 1667 during a festivity hosted by the French ambassador. Johann Heinrich Schmelzer (c.1621–1680) composed many dances for seventeenth-century Viennese court balls; these are gathered in one hundred fifty suites, with free introductory and final movements *(aria ad ingressum* and *ad egressum).* Still missing among Schmelzer's dances is the minuet.

This fascination exerted by the dance music of this period can be gauged by the rapidly increasing production of dances in compositions intended for chamber ensembles and chamber orchestras—and also by the large number of published dance instruction books that were sold in France, Germany, and England after 1700. Dance suites were created by combining the favorite numbers from stage works with newly composed dances. Besides the established dance genres, many contained *airs dansants* in addition to free introductory, descriptive movements as well as others that belonged to the realm of nondance music (for example, the *caprice*, *fantasie*, *sinfonie*, or fugue).

At the time of Louis XIII and Louis XIV, court balls began with the *branle de cortège,* which, according to Madame de Sévigné, was followed by a *chaconne*, *passepied,* and then by a *gavotte*, *sarabande*, *courante*, *bourrée*, and *menuet*. In 1699 the French oboist André Philidor included many *branles* in his *Suite de Triode Différents Auteurs,* but the *menuet* had by then replaced the introductory *branle*. Until approximately 1700 the *courante* was the favorite social dance at French court balls; the king himself performed it even on short visits to festive gatherings. The *gavotte* lasted for several decades in the ballroom, although as an adaptable theater-dance it remained in use up to the Napoleonic Empire. After the English country dance was introduced at the French court in 1685, Raoul-Auger Feuillet's *Recüeil de contredanses* (1706) helped to increase its popularity, and it soon became the favorite social dance of French urban society. In simplified form, it retained its attractiveness even during the French Revolution and later. Besides the *menuet* and *contredanse*, balls in the eighteenth century also featured the *passepied*, *musette*, *rigaudon*, *polonaise*, and after 1750 the *allemande* in either 3/4 or 2/4 meter. In the Australian-Bavarian regions, the *Ländler* and *Langaus* dances were the immediate predecessors of the waltz, which developed in the second half of the eighteenth century (it appeared onstage in Vienna for the first time in Martín y Soler's *Una Cosa Rara,* 1786).

Following the model set by the French court, public dance events began in Paris in 1715, the most famous of these being the balls at the Paris Opera and at the Comédie Française. After 1750, large segments of French citizenry became interested in balls through local dance halls, such as the Vauxhall (1768) and later the Ranelagh, after English models. The English dance books published by John Playford also contain dance instructions; his *The Dancing Master* (editions from 1651 to 1728) is the most important source for the early country dance. [*See the entry on Playford.*] Most such books of the seventeenth century contain a colorful mix of dances; in the dance instruction books that appeared after 1700, the dance masters attempted to explain the widest possible variety. Early examples are J. H. Mittel, *Neuer Allemanden, gigues, balletten, couranten . . .* (Strasbourg, 1658), and Maurizio Cazzati, *Corenti, balletti, galiarde, a 3 e 4* (Venice, 1659). Innumerable collections, frequently with anonymous dances, were published in all musically inclined nations during the eighteenth century. During this period, collections containing a variety of dance genres become rare (for example, Walsh and Hare's *Collection of Minuets, Rigadoons, & French Dances*), although still relatively frequent were the combinations of *menuets* with *contredanses, cotillons, rigaudons, polonaises* (or marches), as well as those with *allemandes* and *anglaises.* During the second half of the eighteenth century, collections devoted to one dance type only predominated, such as the *Menuets tant anciens que noveaux qui se dansent aux bals de l'Opéra* with more than one hundred minuets and the *Recüeils de contredanses* for the balls at the Paris Opera.

Composers mentioned occasionally in the collections from the seventeenth century include Guillaume Dumanoir and Giovanni Battista Vitali. Most pieces, however, can be identified only with the help of concordances. Composers' names appear with far greater frequency in collections of the eighteenth century. Among those mentioned are the early opera composers: Campra, Colin de Blamont, Blaise, Antoine Dauvergne, Jean-Joseph Cassanea de Mondonville, Handel, Telemann, Rameau, Egidio Duni, and others. Lesser masters and dancing masters—Cupis, Benaut, Kellom Tomlinson, Senallié, Duval, Carpentier, Exaudet, Azais, Rodolphe, and Audinot—are also represented. Often, the minuet movements for symphonies composed by Anton Filtz, Karl Stamitz, and Haydn, were printed separately in simplified or solo versions and advertised as dance music.

In the seventeenth and eighteenth centuries the practice of transforming popular melodies into social dances was widespread. Mozart affirmed with satisfaction that the people of Prague danced to tunes from his *Marriage of Figaro* (1786). From this tradition comes the custom, prevalent also in the nineteenth century, of making use of the most successful melodies from the latest theatrical works for quadrilles to be danced during balls at the opera house. Great composers of the Baroque (for example, Telemann, *Sept fois sept et un menuets* [1728]) and of the classical period composed ballroom dances (Haydn [Hoboken IX], *Minuets, German Dances,* and *Contredanses;* Mozart, *Minuets, German Dances, Ländler,* and *Contredanses* for Prague; Beethoven, *Minuets, German Dances,* and *Ländler*). In the first finale of his opera *Don Giovanni* (1787), Mozart united the three characteristic dance genres of his time: minuet, contradance, and German dance. In Vienna, as opposed to Paris, the minuet was danced in the urban dance halls until the early twentieth century—and until World War II in the countryside.

If one considers that social dances are characterized by symmetrical, evenly measured movements that are defined by specific, final formulas and cadences, then one must ask whether these obvious formal principles apply to all dance types. For the early balletic *airs dansants* and *entrées,* the answer is no: Lully's dances were in general much less regularly constructed and less standardized than those of his successors, the only exception being his student, Rameau. In Lully's works, the minuet (which in the eighteenth century was seen as the prototype of regular, periodic construction) acquires the later norm of 8 + 8 or 8 + 16 measures only rarely (for example, in *Atys* and *Phaéton*). Quite frequently Lully arranges his phrases into 6 + 6 or 6 + 8 measures and subdivides the six-measure phrases into 2 + 2 + 2 or 3 + 3 measures. His *Thésée* even has a minuet with a seven-measure division. Only the rondos tend to have sections with an even number of measures. In contrast to the structure of Lully's minuets, those in the *Recüeils de chansons pour danser et pour boire* feature the eight-measure phrase more frequently than the six-measure one.

Among Lully's immediate successors Desmartes and Collasse were already employing the standardized eight-measure phrase, while Rameau preferred more strongly heterogeneous structures. Outside France (as in the anonymous orchestra suites of the Hanover Hofkapelle), composers such as J. C. Fischer, Muffat, Lambranzi, and Bach hardly ever depart from the eight-measure organization. (One exception appears in Fischer's *Journal de printemps:* the minuet of the eighth suite consists of 8 × 5 measures.) From the late seventeenth century onward, dance music intended for listening likewise gives preference to regular periodic structures, specifically in the minuet—although the six-measure phrase, as, for example, in Haydn, still occurs. Lully's *gavottes* are more regularly built than his minuets. *Gavottes,* like *rigaudons,* usually begin with a four-measure phrase. *Musette, tambourin, contredanse,* and *bourrée* belong to the evenly constructed movements, whereas the *courante, sarabande,* and *gigue*—particularly in chamber music—usually are not given a periodic shape. The majority of the *courantes* created for court balls (Ballard 1665, Philidor 1669) are, however, subdivided in eight-measure phrases. The *gigue, canarie,* and *loure* (less often than the *passepied*) show a tendency to considerably extend the second reprise. Purely musical compositional elements such as polyphony, rich ornamentation, fugal entrances of the voices, and canons are evident in *allemandes, courantes, gigues,* and *menuets.* No further relationship exists between the standard movement sequence of the suite and the practice of theatrical and ballroom dancing.

In France, the minuet retained its important role in dance education until the end of the *ancien régime.* It did so as well in the theory and teaching of composition until the end of the Mozart era. According to Joseph Riepel, theory postulates that "even measures . . . are required especially for a Minuet," that its "melodic parts . . . [must have] an even-numbered rhythmic relationship" to each other. The internal structure of the individual reprises also belongs to Riepel's teaching syllabus and thus to the foundation of the development of form in the Viennese classical period. Since Kirnberger (1757), the minuet served as a fundamental composition exercise by means of which the composition of musical periods and the placement of cadences could be learned. This confirms the extraordinary importance of dance music for classical symphonies and chamber music.

[*For related discussion, see* Ballet Technique, History of, *article on* French Court Dance. *See also the entries on the principal figures and dance types mentioned herein.*]

BIBLIOGRAPHY

Anthony, James R. *French Baroque Music from Beaujoyeulx to Rameau.* Rev. ed. London, 1978.

Beck, Hermann. *The Suite.* Cologne, 1966.

Brown, Bruce Alan. *Gluck and the French Theatre in Vienna.* Oxford, 1991.

Chujoy, Anatole, and P. W. Manchester, eds. *The Dance Encyclopedia.* Rev. and enl. ed. New York, 1967.

Coeyman, Barbara. "Theatres for Opera and Ballet during the Reigns of Louis XIV and Louis XV." *Early Music* 18 (February 1990): 22–37.

Danchin, Pierre. "The Foundation of the Royal Academy of Music in 1674 and Pierre Perrin's *Ariane..*" *Theatre Survey* 25 (1984): 55–67.

Échorcheville, Jules. *Vingt suites d'orchestre du XVIIe siècle.* Berlin and Paris, 1906.

Eggebrecht, Hans Heinrich. *Versuch über die Wiener Klassik: Die Tanzszene in Mozart's "Don Giovanni."* Wiesbaden, 1972.

Flotzinger, Rudolf. "Und walzen umatum: Zur Genealogie des Walzers." *Österreichische Musikzeitung* 30 (1975): 505–573.

Goldmann, Helmut. "Das Menuett in der deutschen Musikgeschichte des 17. und 18. Jahrhunderts." Ph.D. diss., University of Erlangen, 1956.

Guilcher, Jean-Michel. *La contredanse et les renouvellements de la danse française.* Paris, 1969.

Harris-Warrick, Rebecca. "Contexts for Choreographies: Notated Dances Set to the Music of Jean-Baptiste Lully." In *Jean-Baptiste Lully: Actes du colloque, Saint-Germain-en-Laye, Heidelberg, 1987,* edited by Jérôme de La Gorce and Herbert Schneider. Laaber, 1990.

Harris-Warrick, Rebecca, and Carol G. Marsh. *Musical Theatre at the Court of Louis XIV: Le Mariage de la Grosse Cathos.* Cambridge, 1994.

Heyer, John, ed. *Jean-Baptiste Lully and the Music of the French Baroque.* New York, 1989.

Hilton, Wendy. *Dance of Court and Theater: The French Noble Style.* Princeton, New Jersey, 1981.

Isherwood, Robert M. *Music in the Service of the King: France in the Seventeenth Century.* Ithaca, N.Y., 1972.

Jordan, Stephanie. "The Role of the Ballet Composer at the Paris Opera, 1820–1850." *Dance Chronicle* 4.4 (1982): 374–388.

Junk, Victor. *Handbuch des Tanzes.* Stuttgart, 1930.

La Gorce, Jérôme de. "L'Académie Royale de Musique in 1704." *Revue de Musicologie* 64 (1979): 160–191.

Little, Meredith Ellis. "The Dances of J. B. Lully." Ph.D. diss., Stanford University, 1967.

Little, Meredith Ellis. "Problems of Repetition and Continuity in the Dance Music of Lully's 'Ballet des Arts.'" In *Jean-Baptiste Lully: Actes du colloque, Saint-Germain-en-Laye, Heidelberg, 1987,* edited by Jérôme de La Gorce and Herbert Schneider. Laaber, 1990.

Mráček, Jaroslav J. S., ed. *Seventeenth-Century Instrumental Dance Music in Uppsala University Library, Instr. Mus. hs 409.* Monumenta Musicae Svecicae, 8. Stockholm, 1976.

Nettl, Paul. "Die Wiener Tanzkomposition in der zweiten Hälfte des 17. Jahrhunderts." *Studien zur Musikwissenschaft* 8 (1921): 45.

Nettl, Paul. *The Story of Dance Music.* New York, 1947.

Nettl, Paul. *Mozart und der Tanz.* Zurich and Stuttgart, 1960.

Otterbach, Friedemann. *Die Geschichte der europäischen Tanzmusik.* Wilhelmshafen, 1980.

Petermann, Kurt. *Tanzbibliographie: Verzeichnis der in deutscher Sprache veröffentlichten Schriften und Aufsätze zum Bühnen-, Gesellschafts-, Kinder-, Volks- und Turniertanz sowie zur Tanzwissenschaft, Tanzmusik und zum Jazz.* 4 vols. Leipzig, 1966–1982.

Reichert, Georg, ed. *The Dance* (1965). Translated by William Pistone. Cologne, 1974.

Rice, Paul F. *The Performing Arts at Fontainebleau from Louis XIV to Louis XVI.* Ann Arbor, 1989.

Sachs, Curt. *World History of the Dance.* Translated by Bessie Schönberg. New York, 1937.

Salmen, Walter, ed. *Mozart in der Tanzkultur seiner Zeit.* Innsbruck, 1990.

Schneider, Herbert. *Die Rezeption der Opern Lullys im Frankreich des ancien régime.* Tutzing, 1982.

Schwandt, Erich. "L'Affilard on the French Court Dances." *Musical Quarterly* (July 1974): 389–400.

Seefrid, Gisela. *Die Airs de danse in den Bühnenwerken von Jean-Philippe Rameau.* Wiesbaden, 1969.

Smith, Marian E. "Music for the Ballet-Pantomime at the Paris Opéra, 1825–1850." Ph.D. diss., Yale University, 1988.

Steinbeck, Wolfram. *Das Menuett in der Instrumentalmusik Joseph Haydns.* Munich, 1973.

Taubert, Karl Heinz. *Höfische Tänze: Ihre Geschichte und Choreographie.* Mainz, 1968.

Thomas, Günter. "Haydns Tanzmusik." *Haydn-Studien* 3 (1973): 5.

Witherell, Anne L. "Pierre Rameau's French Menuet." Ph.D. diss., Stanford University, 1973.

Wynne, Shirley S. "The Charms of Complaissance: The Dance in England in the Early Eighteenth Century." Ph.D. diss., Ohio State University, 1967.

HERBERT SCHNEIDER
Translated from German

Western Music, 1800–1900

A split between music for social and theatrical dancing, which had begun in the middle of the eighteenth century, grew wider throughout the nineteenth. The development of the *ballet d'action* in the first thirty years of the new century attracted varying musical approaches, of which Ludwig van Beethoven's *The Creatures of Prometheus* (op. 43) is perhaps the most outstanding. He composed the overture, introduction, and sixteen dance numbers for this ballet by Salvatore Viganò at Vienna's Burgtheater in 1800–1801. Although it had some success, Beethoven commented in a letter that the "ballet master has not done his share very well." The pas de deux music for the fifth dance has Beethoven's only orchestral writing for harp, and the theme of the finale recurs in his 1802 Piano Variations (op. 35, now called the *Eroica* Variations), and in the finale of his 1804 *Eroica* Symphony (no. 3, op. 55).

Beethoven's score was an exception to the prevailing European custom for ballet music to be delegated to a staff musician at a theater or opera house. The musician, who would usually be expected to shape what he wrote to the rhythms and sequence of dances already worked out by the ballet master, would have no compunction in supplementing his own ideas, often improvised at rehearsals, with themes from operas and popular songs that were well enough known to reinforce the sentiment of the stage action. [*See the entry on Beethoven.*]

Among those so engaged in Paris was Rodolphe Kreutzer (dedicatee of Beethoven's *Kreutzer* Sonata, op. 47, for violin and piano), who wrote at least eight ballet scores in addition to operas and other theater music. In the lowly position of second chorus master was Jean Schneitzhoeffer who, with his superior, Ferdinand Hérold, and Hérold's successor, Fromental Halévy, made attempts during the 1820s at writing more homogeneous scores for dance. Hérold's music for *La Fille Mal Gardée* in 1828, the basis for most present-day productions, still had operatic borrowings, mostly from Gaetano Donizetti. Halévy's *Manon Lescaut*, choreographed by Jean-Louis Aumer in 1830, is thought to be the first work to identify character in musical themes. [*See the entries on Hérold and Schneitzhoeffer.*]

Similar conditions obtained both in London, where the principal ballet composers included the French-born Nicholas Bochsa, music director at the King's Theatre, and in Saint Petersburg, where the Russian ballet was principally influenced by the French choreographer Charles-Louis Didelot until his death in 1837. Didelot was said to be more concerned with music than most choreographers of his time and often worked with Catterino Cavos, an Italian-born composer who was more successful with his ballet music—which was composed to a structure supplied to him—than with his several operas.

The ballet revolution initiated by Filippo Taglioni and his daughter Marie in Paris brought limited changes in music composition. Schneitzhoeffer's music for *La Sylphide* (1832) had fewer borrowings from others. In fact, some reviews criticized him for not making more use of this device. His music sought to engage the audience's sympathy by its expressive character in relation to mood and situation. The need to emphasize a ballerina's lightness and grace, however, became more desirable than the illustration of drama and incident.

Perhaps the most successful in reconciling these demands was Adolphe Adam in *Giselle* (1841), which was written in the cantilena style of Vincenzo Bellini and Donizetti. While little musical difference exists between the two acts—between illustration and illusion—it made further, although inconsistent, use of leitmotif and of musical reminiscence for dramatic effect. [*See the entry on Adam.*] Adam's otherwise homogeneous score was, however, supplemented by the peasant pas de deux music composed by Friedrich Burgmüller, who was to compose *La Péri* for Jean Coralli two years later.

In Copenhagen, when August Bournonville directed the Royal Danish Ballet from 1830 until 1877, a lack of time seems to have been the basic feature governing ballet music. When Bournonville staged his own *La Sylphide* based on the 1832 Paris model, the resulting pressures led to new music by Herman Løvenskjold and to the frequent engagement of more than one composer to collaborate on other ballets. A typical example is *Napoli* (1842), for which the central Blue Grotto act was composed by Niels Gade, the leading Danish composer of the century. The rest, for reasons of time, was parceled out among three theater staff musicians—Edvard Helsted, Holger Simon Paulli, and Hans Christian Lumbye—who were asked to make use of the same thematic motifs when the action required it. Bournonville often asked the three to write for his ballets, and Lumbye even became something of a specialist in writing finales, including those for *Far from Denmark* and *The King's Volunteers on Amager.* [*See* Bournonville Composers.]

Elsewhere in midcentury western Europe and Russia, music for ballet was linked with two specialist composers: the Italian-born Cesare Pugni and the Viennese Léon Minkus. Pugni learned his craft in western Europe and Great Britain, chiefly with Coralli in London, where he composed more than twenty ballet scores in the 1840s. He then went to Russia and was appointed in 1851 as ballet composer to the Imperial Theater at Saint Petersburg. Minkus reached Russia at about the same time, finding work as a violinist and conductor. Moscow's Bolshoi Theater first engaged Minkus in this capacity in 1861, and he succeeded Pugni at Saint Petersburg after Pugni's death in 1870. Their musical idioms had close similarities and methods. They wrote to match the narrative, to illustrate mood and situation with abundant melody and unforced harmony, and to give rhythmic support to the dancers. They sought to be decorative without distracting attention from the stage. There was no conscious attempt at novelty, although Pugni's "Valse à Cinque Temps" in *Catarina* (1846), with a bell struck at the end of each bar, is now the earliest known example of a 5/4 meter in ballet, and Minkus made much of the new taste for national dances in the stage spectacle. [*See the entries on Minkus and Pugni.*]

By the nineteenth century the waltz had become the pivot of dancing as a social pastime, extending from the aristocracy to the professional, merchant, and working classes. Much of the music came from Vienna, where Joseph Lanner, followed by the two Johann Strausses, father and son, perfected a flexible waltz form, derived from the previous century's German dance and *Ländler.* Waltzes were played for both audiences and dancing, and they soon became a regular ingredient of theater dance, where patrons eagerly watched a man and woman dance face to face in an embracing posture. Until the end of the century, the waltz as social dance was closely rivaled in popularity by the polka, which originated in Bohemia. The Strausses composed prolifically in both categories, as did a great many lesser composers. [*See the entry on the Strauss family.*]

From Vienna, interest in the waltz rapidly spread to other European centers and to North America, where the "Boston waltz" emerged as a variant in slower tempo. In general, the waltz had as profound an effect on social customs and conventions in the nineteenth century as the minuet did in the eighteenth. Other prevalent dance forms included the simpler galop and the quadrille—originally *quadrille de contredanses,* which often relied on arrangements from popular operatic music.

Stage spectacle of the time required that ballet was a desirable, and in some instances essential, ingredient of opera, drawing varied responses from the leading composers. In some respects, *La Sylphide* was anticipated by more than twenty years in Carl Maria von Weber's early opera *Silvana* (1810), involving a mostly mute woodland spirit who expressed herself in dance. Weber's *Oberon* (1826) also had dances woven into the musical fabric. By that time Paris audiences had come to expect ballet as a regular feature in opera, acknowledged by Gioacchino Rossini in *Guillaume Tell* (1829) with two dance scenes, including the Tyrolean dance that featured Marie Taglioni.

Most operatic ballets were *divertissements,* which had no organic part in the musical drama, although the ballet of spectral nuns in Giacomo Meyerbeer's *Robert le Diable* (1831), again featuring Taglioni, played a crucial part in tempting the hero from the path of honor. Other Meyerbeer ballets were diversionary spectacles, as were those Donizetti added to his 1840s operas *Les Martyrs* (the French version of *Poliuto*), *La Favorite,* and *Dom Sébastien.* In Russia, Mikhail Glinka's fondness for ballet, in which he had been schooled in his youth, led him to include dance scenes that grew out of the dramatic action in both *Ivan Susanin* (1836) and *Ruslan and Ludmila* (1842).

Some operas became ballets, and vice versa. When Friedrich von Flotow collaborated with Burgmüller and Édouard Deldevez in 1844 for Joseph Mazilier's Paris ballet *Lady Henriette, ou La Servante de Greenwich,* Flotow was prompted to write his opera *Martha,* which premiered in Vienna in 1847, on the same subject. When André-Ernest-Modeste Grétry's *Zémire et Azor* (1771) became a ballet in 1824, Schneitzhöffer kept much of the opera's music in his score, but when Daniel Auber's 1852 opera *Marco Spada* likewise was turned into a ballet five years later, the composer put together a quite different score using themes from his other operas, including *Fra Diavolo* (1830).

By then the Romantic ballet, already in decline, was being replaced by display and spectacle for its own sake, whether in association with opera or not. French composers such as Hector Berlioz, Charles Gounod, and Jules Massenet ensured that their operas met the continuing demand for ballet. When Richard Wagner learned that a ballet was required before *Tannhäuser* (1845) could be staged in Paris in 1861, he added one at the start of act 1. Members of the Jockey Club, however, arrived too late to witness the ballet and caused a disturbance that wrecked the opera's prospects, leading Wagner to withdraw it after three performances.

Giuseppe Verdi took note of the situation in his arrangements with Paris. He added new ballet music to *I Lombardi alla Prima Crociata* (1843), *Il Trovatore* (1852), and *Macbeth* (1847) for their respective Paris productions and composed ballet scenes as integral parts of *Les Vêpres Siciliennes* (1855) and *Don Carlos* (1867), which were both commissioned for Paris. He refused to add ballet to *Rigoletto* (1851), but did so for *Otello* (1887), the last ballet music he composed, in 1894.

Some composers worked successfully in both opera and ballet. The leading figure in this category was Léo Delibes, who first found himself paired with Minkus, then a guest composer from Saint Petersburg, in writing the music for Arthur Saint-Léon in *La Source* (1866). Delibes was thought to be the more successful of the two and alone composed a ballet that became a universal classic, *Coppélia* (1870), followed by *Sylvia* six years later. These ballets signaled a trend for the better in their melodic invention, harmonic richness, and skill in orchestration, and *Sylvia* made a deep impression on Tchaikovsky just when he was finishing his first ballet commission in 1877, *Swan Lake.* [*See the entry on Delibes.*]

In musical terms, *Swan Lake* has to be considered in relation to the almost universal situation prevailing at the time of its Moscow premiere in 1877. The Russian ballet was under the musical sway of Minkus and was performing works by the recently deceased Pugni. The few native composers for ballet, such as Yuri Gerber, whose score for Sergei Sokolov's *The Fern* in 1867 was a step toward a more Russian musical element, were, like their European counterparts, theater musicians, usually violinists or conductors. Ballet elsewhere chiefly consisted of local versions of the European Romantic ballets brought by touring ballerinas and expatriate managers, which meant bringing the music that was part of them.

The musical fate of *Swan Lake* is well documented. The first conductor was unable to obtain a satisfactory performance, and during the next few years nearly one-third of Tchaikovsky's score was progressively replaced by other composers' music for repertory performances at the Bolshoi Theater. Tchaikovsky nevertheless demonstrated that a higher standard of musical imagination was not incompatible with dance, although it presupposed a corresponding level of imagination and musical sensibility on the part of the choreographer. [*See the entry on Tchaikovsky.*]

A significant step was taken by Ivan Vsevolozhsky, who, on his appointment as director of the Russian Imperial Theaters, abolished the post of staff ballet composer and sought the collaboration of more distinguished musicians. Tchaikovsky, of course, was the most notable, and his subsequent ballets at the instigation of Vsevolozhsky, *The Sleeping Beauty* (1889) and *The Nutcracker* (1892), reflect the composer's heightened awareness of balletic needs. Also pointing to the future were the *Polovtsian Dances* from Aleksandr Borodin's opera *Prince Igor* (1890), which were first choreographed by Lev Ivanov. Aleksandr Glazunov's music for Marius Petipa's *Raymonda* (1898) and *The Seasons* (1900) suggests that he could have further developed the content of his dance music if he had been less concerned with his symphonic aspirations. [*See the entry on Glazunov.*]

By this time, four years after her New York debut, Isadora Duncan had reached London and Paris with an entirely new concept of dance and its relation to music. The merits of her approach remain a matter of scholarly debate; however, Duncan's use of music by the great composers of the nineteenth century, the examples set by Tchaikovsky and Glazunov, and the new stylistic changes that were beginning in Russian ballet, all led to the more organic partnership between music and dance.

BIBLIOGRAPHY

Fiske, Roger. *Ballet Music.* London, 1958.

Guest, Ivor. *The Romantic Ballet in England.* London, 1972.

Guest, Ivor. "Cesare Pugni." *Dance Gazette* (February 1979): 22–24.

Guest, Ivor. *The Romantic Ballet in Paris.* 2d rev. ed. London, 1980.

Guest, Ivor. "Cesare Pugni: A Plea for Justice." *Dance Research* 1 (Spring 1983): 30–38.

Lanchbery, John, and Ivor Guest. "The Scores of *La fille mal gardée*" (parts 1–3). *Theatre Research* 3.1–3.3 (1961).

Roslavleva, Natalia. *Era of the Russian Ballet.* London, 1966.

Schiørring, Nils. "Bournonville and the Music to His Ballets." In *Theatre Research Studies.* Vol. 2. Copenhagen, 1972.

Warrack, John. *Tchaikovsky Ballet Music.* London, 1979.

Wiley, Roland John. *Tchaikovsky's Ballets.* London, 1985.

Wiley, Roland John. *A Century of Russian Ballet: Documents and Eyewitness Accounts, 1810–1910.* London, 1990.

NOËL GOODWIN

Western Music since 1900

The twentieth century has witnessed a series of liberating changes in the relationship of music and dance. Composers, long governed by the assumption that music was necessarily subordinate to choreography, have been freed to follow their creative impulses more or less independently, and their experiments with new rhythms and sonorities have invigorated both art forms. Choreographers, likewise emancipated from the constraints of nineteenth-century convention, have discovered new ways to juxtapose movement with music. The very concept of "music for dance" has expanded to include all kinds of music, not just that composed to accompany movement, and indeed all kinds of sounds, "musical" or otherwise.

Diaghilev and His Composers. Ballet's modern era began in 1909 with the first Paris season of Serge Diaghilev's Ballets Russes. Diaghilev believed that a ballet should be an artistic unity to which all elements—movement, music, decor, and costumes—contribute equally; in this and many other respects, he represented a break with the past. A devotee of novelty, Diaghilev welcomed into his fold avant-garde artists such as Jean Cocteau, Erik Satie, and Pablo Picasso and encouraged them to be audacious: his celebrated advice to Cocteau—"Astonish me!"—epitomizes a principle to which he was unswervingly true.

Diaghilev's impact on ballet music can scarcely be exaggerated. He was the first ballet director to insist that the composers he engaged be no less able than the choreographers with whom they worked. He was the first to accord composers a significant degree of independence, and the commissions he offered were invariably stimulating. Moreover, his championship of avant-garde music established a precedent that evolved into common practice—especially in the U.S. modern dance community, which became (and remains) an important patron of new and experimental music.

Although he never attended a conservatory, Diaghilev could read complicated scores with ease, his tastes were those of a connoisseur, and he was a remarkably astute judge of talent; accordingly, he engaged as collaborators many of the leading composers of the day, among them Maurice Ravel (*Daphnis et Chloë,* 1912); Claude Debussy (*Jeux,* 1913); Richard Strauss (*Die Josephslegende,* 1914); Manuel de Falla (*Le Tricorne,* 1919); Francis Poulenc (*Les Biches,* 1924); Darius Milhaud (*Le Train Bleu,* 1924); and Sergei Prokofiev (*The Prodigal Son,* 1929). None was more influential, however, than Igor Stravinsky. Diaghilev's interest in Stravinsky was sparked by a 1909 performance in Saint Petersburg of Stravinsky's concert piece *Scherzo Fantastique,* and he engaged the twenty-six-year-old composer to produce the score for *The Firebird. The Firebird* was Stravinsky's first masterpiece and, as choreographed by Michel Fokine, the hit of the Ballets Russes's 1910 season.

The Firebird launched a memorable series of major works composed by Stravinsky for the Ballets Russes: *Petrouchka* (Fokine, 1911); *Le Sacre du Printemps* (Vaslav Nijinsky, 1913); *Le Chant du Rossignol* (Léonide Massine, 1920); *Pulcinella* (Massine, 1920); *Le Renard* (Bronislava Nijinska, 1922); and *Les Noces* (Nijinska, 1923). *The Firebird* is notable for its brilliant orchestration and stirring evocation of Russian folk music; *Petrouchka* for its novel sonorities, including a particularly astringent chord generated by the simultaneous sounding of two incompatible keys, C major and F-sharp major, thereafter known as the "Petrouchka chord." *Pulcinella,* based on themes then attributed to Giovanni Battista Pergolesi, presages Stravinsky's neoclassical period, which reached full flower with the ballet *Apollon Musagète* (1928).

The most controversial of these works was *Le Sacre du Printemps,* a score of such ferocious intensity that its first performance touched off a riot in the theater; with its pounding, jagged rhythms and brutal percussive energy, it resembled no dance music the world had ever heard. Although Stravinsky had merely taken his cue from the ballet's subject—a pagan fertility rite culminating in a human sacrifice—the result was a landmark in the relationship of music and dance: by demonstrating the power of rhythm to whip a cosmopolitan Parisian audience into a frenzy, Stravinsky liberated music from its nineteenth-century role as handmaiden to the ballet and made composer and choreographer equal partners. [*See the entry on Stravinsky.*]

After Stravinsky, the most influential of the composers who worked with the Ballets Russes were Claude Debussy, Erik Satie, and Maurice Ravel. Debussy devised a new musical language free of traditional tonality and structural development. Impressionism, the term generally applied to it (despite Debussy's objection), aptly suggests its capacity to conjure musical visions of atmosphere and mood. *Jeux* is noteworthy for its free-flowing form, in which the various musical subjects float in and out of the listener's perception. Although Debussy composed only a handful of works for the dance, his concert music has long appealed to choreographers—none more so than *Prélude à l'Après-midi d'un Faune* (1892–1894), adapted by Nijinsky in 1912. [*See the entry on Debussy.*]

Satie was an eccentric prodigy whose witty iconoclasm and strikingly modern style—plain, direct, and intentionally artless—made a tremendous impression not only on his younger French colleagues but on a subsequent generation of American composers, most notably John Cage. His music for *Parade* (1917), a collaboration with Massine, Cocteau, and Picasso, might be described as the musical embodiment of cubism: the sounds of typewriters and steam whistles contribute to its colorfully urban mood. Satie also composed the music for the ballets *Mercure* (Massine, 1924); *Relâche* (Jean Börlin, 1924); and *Jack in the Box* (George Balanchine, 1926); his concert music, like Debussy's, has frequently been put to use by choreographers—half a dozen different works by Merce Cunningham alone. [*See the entry on Satie.*]

Daphnis et Chloë, Ravel's first composition for the Ballets Russes, reached the stage in 1912. The ballet owed its success in no small measure to its lyrical, delicately hued score—a "choreographic symphony" (Ravel's term) that evoked Greece as it might have been portrayed by French landscape painters of the late eighteenth century; two instrumental suites drawn from the score have become concert hall favorites. No less famous is *Boléro* (Nijinska, 1928), a piece comprising nothing more than two alternating melodies, repeated ad infinitum at the same slow tempo but with ever-increasing volume. Ravel regarded it as a sort of parlor trick. [*See the entry on Ravel.*]

Every French composer of the Diaghilev era was influenced by Stravinsky, Debussy, Satie, and Ravel. After the hardships of World War I, however, composers were less inclined toward impressionism, and the perfumed exoticism typified by *L'Après-midi d'un Faune* yielded to music that captured the flavor, pace, and complexity of urban life in the machine age. Composers increasingly used the dance stage as a platform for their own political and social views; *Les Mariés de la Tour Eiffel* (Börlin, 1921), a satire of French bourgeois values presented by Rolf de Maré's Ballets Suédois, served in part as a manifesto for the group of composers known as Les Six, five of whose members—Georges Auric, Arthur Honegger, Darius Milhaud, Francis Poulenc, and Germaine Tailleferre—contributed numbers to it.

Both music and dance were stimulated by contemporary developments in painting, such as cubism and surrealism, by the activities of the Dadaists, and by the increased exposure of many composers to music of foreign cultures. Darius Milhaud, an eclectic who borrowed freely from many sources, employed Brazilian melodies and rhythms in *Le Boeuf sur le Toit* (Cocteau, 1920) and American jazz in *La Création du Monde* (Börlin, 1923). [*See the entry on Milhaud.*] Albert Roussel was similarly influenced by a voyage to India; his "ballet opera" *Padmâvatî* (Léo Staats, 1923) is based on a story from Indian mythology.

European Ballet Music since 1930. The Ballets Russes died with Diaghilev in 1929, and periodic efforts to rekindle its glories ended in failure: its moment had passed.

The vacuum was partly filled, however, by the Paris Opera, which experienced a renaissance after Serge Lifar was appointed ballet master in 1930. Lifar adopted Diaghilev's practice of commissioning scores from prominent contemporary composers; as a consequence, most of the leading French composers of the day—Albert Roussel,

Jacques Ibert, Arthur Honegger, Francis Poulenc, Georges Auric, Henri Sauguet, André Jolivet, Jean Françaix—wrote for the Opera at one time or another. Many wrote for other companies as well: Sauguet, the most prolific of the group, produced no fewer than twenty-five ballet scores, including *Les Mirages* (1947) for Lifar, *La Chatte* (1927) and *Fastes* (1933) for Balanchine, *La Nuit* (1930) for Massine, *Les Forains* (1945) for Roland Petit, and *Die Kameliendame* (1957) for Tatjana Gsovska. A disciple of Satie, Sauguet strove to write sophisticated, unpretentious music. [*See the entry on Sauguet.*] Scarcely less productive was Milhaud, who produced scores for seventeen ballets. While individual styles vary widely, modern French ballet music generally is typified by refinement, clarity, expert craftsmanship, and economy of means.

Although Germany produced its share of important composers in the early 1900s, various circumstances—including the enormous popularity of modern dance during the 1920s and the brutally repressive policies of the Third Reich—stifled the development of a national ballet. Significantly, the most celebrated German ballet to reach the stage between the wars, Kurt Jooss's *The Green Table* (1932), received its premiere in Paris. Its two-piano score, a masterpiece of ironic understatement, was composed by Frederick Cohen, who also wrote or adapted the music for several other Jooss ballets. Ballet activity was not completely extinguished by the Nazis, however; noteworthy scores from the war years include Werner Egk's *Joan von Zarissa* (Maudrik, 1940) and Gottfried von Einem's *Prinzessin Turandot* (Victor Gsovsky, 1942). [*See the entry on Egk.*]

After World War II, a divided Germany moved in divergent directions: the ballet companies of East Germany adopted Soviet models while those of West Germany became more international. Of the German composers who came to prominence after the war, Hans Werner Henze has been especially interested in dance as an integral element of music-theater performance; many of his scores specify choreographic activity. Those classified as ballets include *Jack Pudding* (von Pelchrzim, 1949), *Ballett-Variationen* (Erich Walter, 1949), *Die Schlafende Prinzessin* (Paolo Bortoluzzi, 1954), *Der Idiot* (Gsovsky, 1952), *Ondine* (Frederick Ashton, 1958), *Tancredi* (Rudolf Nureyev, 1966), and *Tristan* (Glen Tetley, 1974). [*See the entry on Henze.*] Although several leading twentieth-century German and Austrian composers—including Arnold Schoenberg, Anton Webern, Alban Berg, Carl Orff, and Karlheinz Stockhausen—composed little or no ballet music, many of their concert pieces have been used by choreographers; a few, such as Schoenberg's sextet *Verklärte Nacht* and Orff's secular cantata *Carmina Burana,* have been used repeatedly.

British ballet music received an early impetus from Diaghilev, who chose the young English composer Constant Lambert to write the score for Nijinska's *Romeo and Juliet* (1926); Lambert went on to become one of the principal architects of modern British ballet. He subsequently composed scores for four Ashton ballets—*Pomona* (1930), *Rio Grande* (1932), *Horoscope* (1938), and *Tiresias* (1951)—and provided arrangements for several others. The vitality of British ballet may be measured, in part, by the stature of the composers who composed for it. Ralph Vaughan Williams wrote the music for Ninette de Valois's masque *Job* (1931). Arthur Bliss composed scores for *Checkmate* (de Valois, 1937), *Miracle in the Gorbals* (Robert Helpmann, 1944), and *Adam Zero* (Helpmann, 1946), among others. Benjamin Britten's *The Prince of the Pagodas* (John Cranko, 1957) was the first full-length ballet score by a modern British composer. [*See the entries on Bliss and Lambert.*]

In Western Europe, full-evening ballets became the exception rather than the rule. In the Soviet Union, however, where the *ballet d'action* never fell from favor, composers continued to turn out scores designed to amplify stories of heroism, noble passions, and poetic love. While Sergei Prokofiev's *Romeo and Juliet* (Váňa Psota, 1938; Leonid Lavrovsky, 1940) and *Cinderella* (Rostislav Zakharov, 1945) are universally regarded as the Soviet Union's two finest contributions to the genre, they are but two of many: Boris Asafiev alone produced the music for twenty-seven, including Vasily Vainonen's *The Flames of Paris* (1932), Zakharov's *The Fountain of Bakhchisarai* (1934), and Lavrovsky's *Prisoner in the Caucasus* (1938). Other Soviet composers who wrote for the ballet include Reinhold Glière, Aram Khatchaturian, and Dmitri Shostakovich, all of whose works were characterized by rousing vigor, bright instrumental colors, and a liberal use of folk tunes or melodies derived from them. Individual numbers—such as the "Russian Sailors' Dance" from Glière's *The Red Poppy* (1927) and the "Saber Dance" from Khatchaturian's *Gayané* (1942)—have become popular as concert pieces. [*See the entries on Asafiev, Glière, Khatchaturian, Prokofiev, and Shostakovich.*]

In terms of their effect on the relationship of music and dance, the most significant ballet productions of the 1930s were Massine's "symphonic ballets," large-scale ballets set to symphonies by Beethoven, Berlioz, Brahms, Tchaikovsky, and Shostakovich. Although Massine was not the first to employ concert music in this fashion—Deshayes had choreographed a ballet to Beethoven's Sixth Symphony as early as 1829—symphonic ballets such as *Les Présages* (1933, to Tchaikovsky's Fifth), *Choreartium* (1934, to Brahms's Fourth), and *Le Rouge et Noir* (1939, to Shostakovich's First) were perceived as innovations and widely admired. They did much to popularize the use of concert music for the dance.

In the last half of the twentieth century the practice of setting ballets to music intended for the concert hall has become standard. The foremost practitioner was George Balanchine, several of whose ballets adhere rigorously to the formal organization of their music. Representative is *Symphonie Concertante* (1947, to Mozart's Sinfonia Concertante in E-flat, K. 364), in which the entrances and exits of the two ballerinas correspond precisely to those of the solo violin and viola. The long list of Balanchine ballets includes many set to concert works by Mozart, Mendelssohn, Brahms, Tchaikovsky, Chabrier, Glazunov, Schoenberg, Ives, and Stravinsky.

The increased popularity of concert music in the ballet theater has undoubtedly worked to the disadvantage of many modern composers, only a handful of whom have enjoyed extended working relationships with major choreographers. Preeminent among those who have done so was Stravinsky, a close associate of Balanchine, for whom he composed *Jeu de Cartes* (1937), *Orpheus* (1948), and *Agon* (1957).

Modern Dance and Modern Music. Of the American dancers who, around the turn of the century, rejected the established traditions of European ballet, it was Isadora Duncan whose musical ideas exerted the greatest influence. She conceived her dances as responses to the emotional sweep of works by classical composers, thereby establishing a clear, complementary relationship between the two art forms. Her phenomenal impact throughout Europe is well documented; Fokine's *Les Sylphides* (1907–1909, to music by Chopin), the first plotless ballet, and Massine's symphonic ballets were direct descendants of her approach.

The seeds planted by Duncan and Ruth St. Denis, who made her own successful European tour in 1906–1909, bore fruit of a different kind in Germany, where Mary Wigman launched the *Ausdruckstanz*—literally, "expressive dance"—movement in the years immediately after World War I. Wigman's dark, introspective solo works dispensed with all the trappings of ballet, including its musical embellishments; she typically performed either to the accompaniment of percussion instruments or to no music at all. The austerity of her approach did not lend itself to the creation of a significant body of musical works; among her disciples, however, Yvonne Georgi choreographed many dances to commissioned music—including several to electronic scores by Dutch composer Henk Badings.

In its more severe manifestations, American modern dance, like its German counterpart, rejected conventional music as a corset that imposed unacceptable restrictions on a dancer's freedom of movement. During the late 1920s, dancers routinely drafted their works without reference to music and then submitted an outline of their rhythmic requirements to a willing composer. By the mid-1930s, however, Martha Graham and others had begun to take an interest in the musical possibilities inherent in their medium.

Graham's musical tastes were to a large extent shaped by Louis Horst, who was music director of the Denishawn company when she joined it in 1916. Horst encouraged Graham to embark on an independent career and became her mentor, musical adviser, and closest friend. He taught her the importance of stylistic consistency—the need for choreography, music, costumes, and decor to share a common dramatic purpose—and he composed scores for three of her most famous works, *Primitive Mysteries* (1931), *Frontier* (1935), and *El Penitente* (1940). Horst instilled in Graham a lasting appreciation for contemporary music; the list of composers from whom she commissioned scores reads like a *Who's Who* of modern music: Samuel Barber, Carlos Chávez, Norman Dello Joio, Paul Hindemith, Gian-Carlo Menotti, Milhaud, William Schuman, and Carlos Surinach, among others.

In one vital respect, however, Horst was a conservative; he viewed music as subordinate to choreography. Their proper relationship, he argued, was that of a frame to its picture; music should help focus the viewer's attention on the dance. This may account for the fact that, of all the scores composed for Graham's dances, only Aaron Copland's *Appalachian Spring* (1944) has found a life of its own in the concert hall. [*See the entry on Horst.*]

Copland, the acknowledged leader of the generation of American composers who reached maturity after World War I, produced five dance scores. Orchestral suites extracted from three of them—*Billy the Kid* (Eugene Loring, 1938), *Rodeo* (Agnes de Mille, 1942), and *Appalachian Spring*—are among the best-known and most popular of all works by modern American composers; that of *Appalachian Spring* received the 1945 Pulitzer Prize. In his music Copland strove for a Whitmanesque accessibility and directness: music with "a largeness of utterance," as he put it. His works are brightly orchestrated and rhythmically complex, for he intended his music to reflect vernacular American speech rhythms. He made liberal use of popular tunes; for example, cowboy songs are sprinkled throughout *Billy the Kid,* and a Shaker hymn figures prominently in *Appalachian Spring.* [*See the entry on Copland.*]

Many of Copland's peers composed for the dance. Nicolas Nabokov's *Union Pacific* (Massine, 1934), Paul Bowles's *Yankee Clipper* (Loring, 1937), and Virgil Thomson's *Filling Station* (Lew Christensen, 1938) were, with *Billy the Kid,* the first "Americana" ballet scores. Wallingford Riegger composed the music for Doris Humphrey's *New Dance* (1935), *Theatre Piece* (1936), and *With My Red Fires* (1936), among others. Elliott Carter wrote the music for *Pocahontas* (Christensen, 1939) and *The Minotaur* (John Taras, 1947). Leonard Bernstein contributed scores for Jerome Robbins's ballets *Fancy Free* (1944), *Facsimile* (1946), and *Dybbuk Variations* (1974).

The Avant-Garde since 1930. The angularity of early modern dance was particularly well served by percussion music. Although the pioneers in this realm were Henry Cowell and Edgard Varèse, it was Cowell's protégé John Cage who achieved the most noteworthy results. His early works for percussion, many written to accompany dances, utilize both conventional and found instruments such as automobile brake drums; they tend to be vigorous and ebullient. In 1940, for a dance by Syvilla Fort, Cage invented the prepared piano; he subsequently composed more than a dozen works for it.

In 1942 Cage began working with Merce Cunningham, then a member of Graham's company, in what became the longest continuous artistic partnership of modern times. As Horst had served Graham, so Cage served Cunningham, encouraging him to strike out on his own, acting as friend and adviser, and generally influencing his aesthetic outlook. For many years Cage held the position of music director in Cunningham's company, commissioning works by many eminent avant-garde composers, among them Earle Brown, Morton Feldman, and Christian Wolff.

From the early 1950s Cage composed by chance methods, and Cunningham, too, introduced an element of chance into some of his dances. Together they demonstrated that movement and music need not share a common objective and, indeed, need not be related at all except by the circumstance of their being simultaneously performed. This concept, which enlivened their presentations, became a cornerstone of postmodern dance. [*See the entry on Cage.*]

The Judson Dance Theater, the loose alliance of independent choreographers to whom the term *postmodern* most specifically applies, evolved out of a composition course taught by Robert Ellis Dunn, a Cage disciple. Relieved of the necessity of finding appropriate sounds (because all sounds were deemed equally relevant) to accompany their presentations, the Judson choreographers experimented freely. Many of their dances were performed in silence; others used sounds ranging from classical music to that of a vacuum cleaner. An extreme example of aural eclecticism was Yvonne Rainer's *Three Seascapes* (1962), a solo in three parts; the first part was accompanied by music of Rachmaninov, the second by the sound of a chair being scraped across a wood floor, and the last by screams from Rainer herself. [*See the entry on Dunn.*]

Although only marginally successful in the concert hall, electronic music has been employed with more satisfactory results by many choreographers. One of the first ballets set to electronic music was Tatjana Gsovska's *Paean* (1960), performed to a taped score by Remi Gassmann and Oskar Sala; Balanchine used the same music for his 1961 ballet *Electronics.* The sounds used to accompany Cunningham's *Variations V* (1965) were generated by the dancers themselves, whose movements were read by sensors placed at various points on the stage and transformed electronically into audible signals. Alwin Nikolais, who viewed dance as a theatrical form integrating form, movement, color, and sound, has composed electronic accompaniments for all of his works since the mid-1950s.

Popular and Ethnic Music. Popular music has played an increasingly prominent role in the recent history of dance. Ragtime, the first vernacular music to capture America's fancy after the turn of the century, was also the first to generate a best-selling phonograph record ("Alexander's Ragtime Band," 1911) and the first to inspire a ballroom dance (the fox trot, introduced by Harry Fox in the 1914 Ziegfeld Follies). Although ragtime found its way into a few works by serious contemporary composers—Stravinsky's *Piano-Rag Music* dates from 1920—choreographers remained oblivious to it until the ragtime revival of the 1970s inspired a rash of ragtime ballets, including James Waring's *Eternity Bounce* (1973), Kenneth MacMillan's *Elite Syncopations* (1974), and Gray Veredon's *The Ragtime Dance Company* (1974).

Ragtime was superseded in the 1920s by jazz, which spawned its own set of social dances—notably the Charleston, the Black Bottom, and the Shimmy—and an endless wave of jazz ballets, beginning with *La Création du Monde* and continuing to the present day. Among the finest was Robbins's *New York Export: Opus Jazz* (1958), set to a lively score by Robert Prince. During its 1960/61 season, the New York City Ballet offered two jazz evenings, one of which included *Modern Jazz: Variants,* a new Balanchine ballet with music composed by Gunther Schuller. However, its main attraction was the onstage presence of the Modern Jazz Quartet.

Rock, the most pervasive form of popular music since the 1950s, has generated dozens of social dances, most of them short-lived. Many choreographers have created rock ballets, using rock music and appropriate steps as metaphors for the fast pace and high energy level of contemporary life; a celebrated example was Robert Joffrey's *Astarte* (1967) with music by Crome Syrcus, a multimedia assault on the audience's senses. The finest such work, however, was Twyla Tharp's 1973 *Deuce Coupe,* a witty, entertaining juxtaposition of classical ballet and pop dance set to a medley of hits by the Beach Boys. In 1992 the Joffrey Ballet premiered *Billboards,* danced to a score by the rock musician Prince.

African-American music has made significant contributions to the dance theater. Both ragtime and jazz were originally black music forms, and early rock music was strongly influenced by black rhythm and blues. Since the mid-1930s, black choreographers such as Katherine Dunham, Pearl Primus, Donald McKayle, Alvin Ailey, and Carmen de Lavallade have effectively used spirituals, gospel songs, and blues. Famous examples include McKayle's *Rainbow 'Round My Shoulder* (1959), set to traditional prison songs, and Ailey's *Revelations* (1960), set to spirituals and gospel tunes.

Since Paris discovered the tango in 1910, Latin American music and dance have been popular in both Europe and the United States. The conga, rumba, and samba became fashionable during the 1930; successive decades witnessed crazes for the mambo, cha-cha, bossa nova, and lambada. Many serious composers have incorporated Latin rhythms into their scores; the tango, for example, figures prominently in William Walton's *Façade* (1922) and Samuel Barber's *Souvenirs* (1952), both of which have been made into ballets.

Musically speaking, the late-twentieth-century dance scene is characterized by kaleidoscopic variety. At one extreme are those choreographers who prefer setting dances to concert music; at the other are Cunningham and his followers, who commission new scores for every dance and are entirely flexible in their musical requirements. All would agree, however, that the music of dance—whatever pedigree—should have its own life and vitality.

BIBLIOGRAPHY

Anderson, Jack. *Dance.* New York, 1974.

Arvey, Verna. *Choreographic Music: Music for the Dance.* New York, 1941.

Calvocoressi, M. D. *Musicians Gallery: Music and Ballet in Paris and London.* London, 1933.

Chujoy, Anatole, and P. W. Manchester, eds. *The Dance Encyclopedia.* Rev. and enl. ed. New York, 1967.

Emerson, Isabelle, ed. *Twentieth-Century American Music and Dance: A Bibliography.* Music Reference Collection, no. 53. Westport, Conn., 1996.

Griffiths, Paul. *A Concise History of Avant-Garde Music.* New York, 1978.

Hodgins, Paul. *Relationships between Score and Choreography in Twentieth-Century Dance.* Lewiston, N.Y., 1992.

Jordan, Stephanie. "Dance Style and Study: The Contribution of Music and Musicality." *Cairón,* no. 1 (1995): 37–47.

Kelkel, Manfred. *La musique de ballet en France de la belle époque aux années folles.* Paris, 1992.

Koegler, Horst. *The Concise Oxford Dictionary of Ballet.* New York, 1977.

Nestiev, I. V. *Diagilev i muzykalnyi teatr XX veka.* Moscow, 1994.

Preston-Dunlop, Valerie, and Susanne Lahusen, eds. *Schrifttanz: A View of German Dance in the Weimar Republic.* London, 1990.

Vasina, Vera. "Music of the Soviet Ballet." In *The Soviet Ballet,* by Yuri Slonimsky et al. New York, 1947.

Yates, Peter. *Twentieth-Century Music.* New York, 1967.

ROY M. CLOSE

MUSIC HALL. [*This entry discusses the tradition of dance in music halls in the urban centers of Great Britain and France, two countries where this tradition flourished.*]

British Traditions

The British music hall originated in concert saloons and public house singsongs; with the Licensing Act of 1843, which compelled publicans to convert their taverns to places of amusement or to end entertainment entirely, the music hall proper began to develop. In accordance with its origins, the music hall featured individual singers and comedians; the shallow stages provided little space for dancing, and the lower-middle-class audiences had no taste for it. However, at the Alhambra Palace of Varieties, London (opened 1860), which catered to a predominately masculine and moneyed audience, Frederick Strange introduced ballets under the catchall designation *divertissements* at a time when they were being eliminated from the opera. The ballet girls entertained their admirers in the theater's canteen, and for many years the Alhambra's shows, with their spectacular effects, expensive costumes, straightforward plot lines, and display of feminine legs, defined ballet for the average Englishman.

In the ordinary music hall, dance meant either the rudimentary steps that accompanied a singing team or the acrobatics practiced by the Majiltons and the Clodoches. J. H. Stead gained ephemeral stardom in the 1850s by jumping up and down as, clad in a conical cap and striped pajamas, he sang "The Perfect Cure." This eccentric sensation was copied and perfected by The Nerves (Taylor and Bryant). In the provinces, clog dancing retained favor in the halls, usually in a competition. Dan Leno (George Galvin, 1860–1904), the most popular comedian of Victorian England, won a gold and silver belt as Champion Clog-Dancer of the World at the Princess's Music Hall, Leeds, in 1880. It is significant, however, that when Leno made his London debut at Forester's, only his songs were cheered, for the Cockney audiences knew little and cared less about the clogger's art.

Leno himself lamented that there were few "extempore dancers" left, other than W. J. Ashcroft and Lottie Collins (1866–1910). Collins had begun her career in 1877 as a skipping rope dancer and from 1886 to 1890 was billed as "The Kate Vaughan of the Music Halls." Fame arrived in 1891, when Collins first sang "Ta-ra-ra-boom-de-ay" at the Tivoli, London: adopting a demure pose for the stanzas, she would explode during the chorus into the most authentic can-can yet seen in a respectable English theater. It was interpolated into the burlesque *Cinder-Ellen Up to Date* and the pantomime *Dick Whittington.* Holbrook Jackson has viewed it as a symbol of the new spirit of freedom that emerged in the 1890s.

The best-known music-hall dancers of the time were Nellie Navette, Ida Heath, Kate Seymour, and Clara Wieland, who performed a fire dance. The blackface "coon singers" G. H. Elliott and Eugene Stratton introduced soft-shoe dancing or "light dancing" in shoes with special buff leather soles. A standard music-hall turn might consist of a schottische, soft-shoe, or, later, tap-dance opener followed by a hornpipe and ending with a lively exhibition dance to stir up applause.

In the 1880s, the dwarfish clown Little Tich (George Relph, 1868–1928) won popularity by concluding his act with a big-boot dance: on the toes of his ski-like boots, which were as long as he was tall, he would precariously overbalance himself parallel to the stage—without toppling over. As popular in Paris as he was in London throughout the next decades, Tich excelled in "drag" parodies of *danseuses,* among them a Spanish Carmen entangled in her lace mantilla and Miss Turpentine (a shaft aimed at Loie Fuller), who would spiral about in swirling gowns, pause, look annoyed, catch up yards of muslin, and finally scratch her leg.

By the turn of the century the music hall had become a lucrative business, and developers, to attract middle-class

MUSIC HALL: British Traditions. The Alhambra (successively named Palace, Music-Hall, and Theatre) was the venue for the London debut of the French trapeze artist Jules Léotard, in 1861, an event depicted in this contemporary engraving. (Photograph used by permission of the Board of Trustees of the Victoria and Albert Museum, London.)

family audiences, were constructing elaborate "palaces of variety" featuring miscellaneous bills. The Empire Theatre of Varieties, London, opened in 1887 and like its Leicester Square rival, the Alhambra, staged spectacular ballets. Music-hall ballets were kept brief—a prologue and four scenes lasted under three-quarters of an hour—and as costumer C. Wilhelm (William Pitcher) complained in the *Daily Telegraph* in 1908, audiences demanded that it be "based to some extent on the principles of musical comedy." Adeline Genée, who danced at the Empire from 1897 to 1900, noted that "the English public knows little of the technique of dancing. . . . The male dancer has quite disappeared from England, I believe" (*Sketch*, 17 January 1900).

Acrobatic high kicks, somersaults, Catherine wheels, and handsprings, the bases of music-hall dance acts, were supplemented by American innovations. Billy Farrel, a black American, introduced the cakewalk at the Alhambra in the late 1880s. My Fancy (Mrs. E. Bawn, 1878–1933), billed as "The Finest Sand Dancer in the World," was a hit at the London Pavilion and the Oxford Music-Hall in 1894 and 1895. Marie Leyton, originally part of a pas de quatre, saw Loie Fuller's *Serpentine Dance* in New York City in 1892 and brought it to the London Tivoli two years later. Fuller herself also appeared on the halls with some success.

In a perhaps misguided pursuit of sophistication, the Edwardian music hall introduced culture. Maud Allan made her London debut at the Palace Theatre in 1908; she performed barefoot to Chopin and Mendelssohn and elicited a sandalous frisson with *The Vision of Salomé,* to a waltz by Archibald Joyce. Seemingly unclad beneath her diaphanous draperies, she cuddled a *papier-mâché* head of John the Baptist for an unprecedented eight-month run; later she was banned in Manchester. Ruth St. Denis appeared at the Scala and the Coliseum in 1906; Anna Pavlova and Mikhail Mordkin, at the Palace in 1911. John Tiller, a cotton broker, began a school to train precision dancers; the high-kicking Tiller Girls Dancing Troupe first performed at the King's Theatre, Manchester, in 1890, and they participated in the first Royal Command Performance of Variety in 1912.

The clog dancing tradition was carried on by John W. Jackson's Eight Lancashire Lads, whose personnel changed as members aged; Charlie Chaplin, as part of the original troupe, danced a cellar flap. Well into the 1930s the group maintained its popularity by shifting to tap dance and using a cinematic decor. During the craze for exhibition ballroom dancing, Mr. and Mrs. Jack Carlton introduced it at the Coliseum, performing a simple fox trot, waltz, and two-step against black drapes. Gaston and Andrée (Jimmy Wood, died 1966; Rosemary Andrée, died 1974) adapted the male partner's gymnastic prowess to the first adagio dancing seen in British variety. Kitty Albert and Harry Baroux initiated an *apache* dance in Percy Honri's musical act *Concordia* as early as 1911.

The American influence continued strong with the Du Four Brothers (London debut, Tivoli, 1911); Eddie Ready (1907–1974), an adagio dancer with the Four Malinoffs; and Harland Dixon (1891–1978), a tap, rhythm, and eccentric dancer who topped touring bills in the 1920s.

According to the music-hall agent Don Ross, the "class" dance acts on the modern halls were the Ganjou Brothers and Juanita, an acrobatic adagio team who made their debut in 1933 in *Romance in Porcelain;* the Sherry Brothers (Dan, Harry, Jim, Peter, and Sam Conroy), who performed birdcalls and acrobatic tap dancing immaculately dressed in white tie and tails; and Wilson, Keppel, and Betty (Jack Wilson, 1894–1970; Joe Keppel, 1895–1977; Betty Knox). Starting in the United States, in 1928 they developed a comic sand-dancing act called *Cleopatra's Nightmare*, the two spindly men in fezzes partnering a shapely brunette before a backdrop of the Great Sphinx. The act caused a sensation at the Palladium in 1932 and subsequently played every variety theater in the United Kingdom as well as in pantomime, revue, command performances (1934, 1945, 1947), and on the Continent before the group disbanded (having changed Bettys several times) in 1963.

Competition from other media severely reduced the music-hall public by the late 1920s, and many performers who had begun in variety went on to other things. Victor Silvester (1900–1978), a champion ballroom dancer whose textbook on dancing ran into fifty-seven editions, became a leading dance-band conductor in 1935. Jack Buchanan rapidly moved from the halls, where he had started in 1911, to revue and musical comedy. A typical career was that of Harry Dennis, who before 1914 had been a member of the great tap-dance team the Four Kemptons. In 1927 he formed a double act with his wife and then quit performing to become an agent and dance producer, creating more than fifty acts for the Palladium. In the 1950s, television siphoned off the remaining music-hall audience, and most of the older halls were then demolished or converted into cinemas.

[*For related discussion, see* Vaudeville.]

BIBLIOGRAPHY

Allan, Maud. *My Life and Dancing.* New York, 1908.

Alltree, George W. *Footlight Memories: Recollections of Music Hall and Stage Life.* London, 1932.

Barker, Kathleen M. D. "Dance and the Emerging Music Hall in the Provinces." *Dance Research* 5 (Autumn 1987): 33–42.

Bratton, J. S., ed. *Music Hall: Performance and Style.* Milton Keynes, 1986.

Busby, Roy. *British Music Hall: An Illustrated Who's Who from 1850 to the Present Day.* London, 1976.

Cooper, Johnny. "Fifty Years in Variety at Home and Abroad." *The Call Boy* (Spring 1981).

Senelick, Laurence, et al. *British Music-Hall, 1840–1923: A Bibliography and Guide to Sources, with a Supplement on European Music-Hall.* Hamden, Conn., 1981.

Sherry, Sam. "'Actual Stepdancing': Sam Sherry, an Autobiography." *The Call Boy* (Spring 1980).

Vernon, Doremy. *Tiller's Girls*. London, 1988.

Wilmut, Roger. *Kindly Leave the Stage! The Story of Variety, 1919-1960*. London, 1985.

FILMS. *Dancing Girls* (British Film Institute [BFI], 1895). *First a Girl*, with Jessie Matthews (1936). Alberto Cavalcanti, *Champagne Charlie* (1944). *Little Tich and His Big Boots* (BFI). "The Rodney Hudson Victoria Girls," in *Two Typical Numbers of the Late Twenties* (BFI). *Sam Sherry, Stepdancer* (British Arts Council). *Wilson, Keppel and Betty in Cleopatra's Nightmare, Sand Dance* (BFI).

LAURENCE SENELICK

French Traditions

By the seventeenth century, various kinds of musical, comic, and acrobatic acts could be seen in popular entertainments in France, appearing at venues such as principal fairs. By 1764 the Théâtre du Nicolet, a rival of the Opéra-Comique, assembled a troupe of tightrope dancers and tumblers. The small theaters on the "Boulevard du Crime"—a nickname given to the Boulevard du Temple during a period when bloody melodramas were the main theater fare—welcomed dancers, mimes, acrobats, and miscellaneous acts with orchestral accompaniment. Madame Saqui, the daughter of a Nicolet company actor, performed on the tightrope until the age of seventy; she staged pantomimes and slapstick comedies rivaling those of the Théâtre des Funambules, even during the days of Jean-Charles Deburau.

The cafes of the boulevards and the Palais-Royal had small stages for the mounting of song-and-dance acts and short plays. Singing predominated in these cabarets. During the mid-nineteenth century these establishments proliferated, especially on the Champs-Élysées and in Montparnasse and Montmartre. Not until the end of the nineteenth century, however, was the modest cabaret transformed into a real music hall.

The most popular Parisian music halls included the Eldorado (founded in 1858), La Scala (1874), the Folies-Bergère, Casino de Paris, Ambassadeurs, Ba-ta-Clan, Eden-Concert, and Mayol. These music halls presented spectacular revues, in which dancing alternated with the singing and impersonations that were often the main attractions. Previously, apart from visits by foreign troupes (usually Spanish), dancing had been presented mainly in public dance halls such as the Moulin Rouge, Bal Rochechouart, or Bal de la Reine Blanche.

The inexpensive entertainments attracted an enormous audience. In 1867 the government director of theaters authorized the use of sets, costumes, dialogues, dances, and pantomimes in music halls. By 1890 there were one hundred and fifty such establishments. The Folies-Bergère and the Casino de Paris soon became famous. Their revues over the ensuing decades included song-and-dance

MUSIC HALL: French Traditions. A lithographed music cover, published in 1908, for Charles Dubourg's *Valse Chaloupée*, presented at the Moulin Rouge, Paris. In the upper left corner are portraits of the show's stars, Mistinguett and Max Dearly. Mistinguett, noted for her vivacity, also appeared frequently at the Casino de Paris and the Folies-Bergère. (Dance Collection, New York Public Library for the Performing Arts.)

acts by Dranem, Paulus, Polin, Mistinguett, Maurice Chevalier, and Yvette Guilbert, who were rivals of Mayol, Fragson, and Polaire. The writer Colette staged mime acts with Paul Franck and Georges Wague. The Cigale featured Gaby Deslys and Yvonne Printemps, surrounded by a chorus who were often very scantily clad.

In 1893 the striptease arrived, with such alluring titles as "Yvette Goes to Bed" and "The Parisienne Gets out of Bed." Carolina Otéro displayed her sensual physique in these entertainments, and Jane Avril's can-can alternated with quadrilles, belly dances, and the tap dances of Norman French, who was Chevalier's teacher.

Jacques Charles, a producer of famous revues during the 1920s and 1930s, took his inspiration from the music halls of New York and adapted ideas from the Ziegfeld Follies. The rhythm, discipline, and beauty of the eighteen Hoffmann Girls enhanced the "American" revue at the Moulin Rouge. Mistinguett moved from the Casino de Paris to the Eldorado with her chorus boys and girls, in-

MUSIC HALL: French Traditions. Renée (Zizi) Jeanmaire, ballet dancer turned music-hall performer, is thronged by men from the Ballet National de Marseille in this 1995 show choreographed by her husband, Roland Petit. (Photograph by Colette Masson; used by permission of Agence Enguerand/Iliade, Paris.)

cluding Harry Pilcer, who also partnered Jane Auber. The Folies-Bergère featured Loie Fuller, the Hanlon-Lees, the mime Séverin, Liane de Pougy, and Cléo de Mérode. The designers Erté, Zinoviev, Gesmar, Zamora, and Gyarmathy created costumes for the stars. The Tiller Girls and the Bluebell Girls appeared at the Lido cabaret. Paul Derval hired Josephine Baker to lead revues that included Cécile Sorel, Tino Rossi, Line Renaud, Lisette Malidor, and Zizi Jeanmaire. Other famous music halls included the Tabarin, Alhambra, A.B.C., Palace, Bobino, Empire, and Olympia; their successors were the Lido, the Paradis Latin, and the Alcazar.

[*See also* Can-Can *and the entries on Baker and Bluebell.*]

BIBLIOGRAPHY

Boris, Jean-Michel, and Marie-Ange Guillaume. *28, boulevard des Capucines.* Paris, 1991.

Bost, Pierre. *Le cirque et le music-hall.* Paris, 1931.

Castle, Charles. *The Folies Bergère.* London, 1982.

Coquatrix, Paulette. *Les coulisses de ma mémoire.* Paris, 1984.

Damase, Jacques. *Les folies du music-hall.* Paris, 1960.

Fréjouville, Gustave. *Au music-hall.* Paris, 1922.

Weill, Alain, comp. *One Hundred Years of Posters of the Folies Bergère and Music Halls of Paris.* London, 1977.

MARIE-FRANÇOISE CHRISTOUT
Translated from French

MYANMAR, formerly called Burma (1886–1989), is the westernmost country in Southeast Asia. It is bounded on the west by the Bay of Bengal, Bangladesh, and India, on the north and east by China, Laos, and Thailand, and on the south by the Andaman Sea. The Burman people probably migrated into the region from the Tibetan Plateau in the second to third century CE, but they were not united until the eleventh century, when King Anawrahta established his capital city at Pagan around 1050. The Pagan dynasty, which flourished until 1298, was the formative period of Burmese culture. Strongly influenced by neighboring India, the Burman people adopted many Indian cultural forms: a political system based on semidivine kingship; Theravada Buddhism and its characteristic architectural feature, the pagoda; and the written form of the Burmese language. Influenced since the twelfth century by China, and since the sixteenth by traders and missionaries from Europe, Burma became part of the British Empire in 1886. The country gained independence in 1948, but a strong political unity failed to develop because of ethnic pluralism. Decades of civil war ensued, with military governance in the 1970s, 1980s, and 1990s.

The inhabitants of the country now known as the Union of Myanmar include a number of culturally and linguistically distinct peoples. In the highland regions of the western, northern, and eastern parts live a number of groups often called collectively "hill tribes." These include such groups as the Shan, the Kachin, and the Chin. In the lowlands live the Burmese, who, along with their cultural and linguistic neighbors the Arakanese, form the single largest cultural group. Many Burmese follow an agrarian way of life, although one-fourth of the modern population resides in urban areas, chiefly in the cities of Rangoon (Yangon) and Mandalay.

Nat Pwe Ceremony. Although nominally Buddhist, the country actually has two important and distinct religions; coexisting with Buddhism is the ancient religion centered around the worship and propitiation of the *nat*, a pantheon of spirits honored with offerings and entreaties through the activities of mediums (male and female). Dance has no place in formal Buddhist worship or ceremony here, but it plays a prominent role in the *nat* ceremonies. The propitiation ceremony is known as *nat pwe,* which literally means "Nat theater," or "the drama of the Nats."

The ceremony consists of a ritual offering of food (most often bananas and green coconuts) to the spirits, followed by the performance of special music and dance for these spirits, and finally the possession in a trance state of the spirit mediums by the *nat* who has been enticed to the ceremony by these offerings. A complete performance of the spirit possession ceremony may last several hours. The pantheon of *nat* spirits comprises thirty-seven nats, each of whom has his own special music and dance and must receive offerings of food, music, and dance before consenting to appear through the medium.

The dance of propitiation can function as a ritual purification in association with an event other than a *nat pwe,* or it can establish an auspicious atmosphere before some other event. Thus, the opening *nat* dance, the propitiation by the *nat* votaress, *Apyu Do,* is regularly used as the ceremonial opening dance on the first night of a series of secular theatrical performances, or it may be the first dance in a performance of the puppet theater. In both contexts the opening *nat* dance has nothing to do with the story of the drama to follow.

Folk Dance. Numerous forms of folk dancing have provided an important source for Burmese dance movement, which are usually performed in the context of village festivals. The song and the dance together are identified with the name of the characteristic drum type that dominates the accompanying ensemble; the name denotes the characteristic rhythm, melodic type, song genre, and dance. Characteristic Burmese folk dances of this type include the *ouzi, doupat, byo,* and *boungyi.* They often become incorporated into the context of dramatic forms—the theater with live actors *(pwe)* or the puppet theater, *you thei.*

Court Dances. Another important facet of Burmese dance was the vast repertory of court dances that existed during the days of the monarchy. With the dissolution of the royal court by the British in the early twentieth century, the tradition of court dancing largely waned. What did survive were dances that were preserved in dramas as stylized representations of court scenes. Today it is difficult to determine which dances actually preserve the movements used in the court and which are based on later reconstructions drawn from written or oral historical descriptions of dance; nor can we be sure to what degree pure imagination has played a part in these reconstructions.

MYANMAR. The opening dance of propitiation of a *nat* votaress, the medium through which the *nat* (spirit) appears. (Photograph © by Jukka Miettinen; used by permission.)

Theatrical Dance. *Pwe* is a Burmese term denoting theater in general. Although the term *pwe* is also applied to the Nat spirit possession ceremonies, this usage represents something of an exception, because *nat pwe* is more ritual than theater. The terms *pwe* and *zat pwe* are used almost interchangeably to mean "theater." By extension, the Burmese puppet theater, properly called *you thei,* is also referred to as *pwe:* it is in fact another form of *pwe.*

The *pwe,* or theater with live actors, and the *you thei,* or theater with puppets, both follow the same general theatrical conventions. Each usually begins with a ritual performance of the dance of the *nat* votaress and then moves on to the presentation of the story itself, which may infrequently be drawn from the Hindu epics *Rāmāyana* or *Mahābārata,* but more often from Burmese history and tradi-

MYANMAR. U Po Sein, one of the greatest Burmese *pwe* dancers, as a prince character, c.1920. (Photograph from the Dance Collection, New York Public Library for the Performing Arts.)

tions. During the unfolding of the story, dances are introduced wherever they are appropriate to the story line; a village scene may incorporate a folk dance or a palace scene a court dance. Dance may also be included in contexts outside the situation depicted onstage; for example, when a young prince returns from study at a Buddhist university in India, the princess comes forth to greet him, and they dance the *myaing ta* or some other love duet.

One important convention observed in all types of Burmese *pwe* is the performance of an interlude known as the *hnapa thwa*. This usually occurs well into the night of the performance, often at about midnight or later. The action of the main story stops, usually at a convenient point in the story line, and the *hnapa thwa* begins. Traditionally the *hnapa thwa* was designed to show off the particular talents of the main actors of the troupe and in particular of the star and leader. The *hnapa thwa* was initially performed as a formal dance and song duet in the old court style by the leading male and female actor-dancers of the troupe. Gradually, a chorus of supporting female dancers was introduced, as well as the troupe of clowns now standard in any Burmese theatrical performance. The clowns engage in dialogue on virtually any subject and serve as commentators on the skill and grace of the performers. Following the performance of the *hnapa thwa,* the main story line is reintroduced, or a new play begins. In either case, the performance of the *pwe* then continues for several more hours.

The *pwe* was a kind of repertory dance and drama troupe that depended for its livelihood and existence on its uniqueness and superiority, so virtuosity quickly became a hallmark of *pwe* dance style. Amazing leaps, rapid turns, and even quick rolls along the floor of the stage, all timed to end in perfect synchronization with the final rhythmic beat, have become part of the accepted style of *pwe* dance. In recent times, some of the most famous Burmese *pwe* dancers to add their original stamp to Burmese dancing have included U Po Sein (also known as "the Great Po Sein"), his son Kenneth Sein, and, most recently, Shwei Maung Htin Aung. Today, numerous *pwe* troupes travel and perform throughout the country. The tradition remains strong, but it is in a state of continual development.

The traditional Burmese theater continues to thrive, with numerous troupes of dancer-actors traveling about the country performing for the many pagoda festivals, novitiate celebrations, and other observances. Although Burmese theater has experienced gradual and continuous changes over the years, it maintains significant elements from its origins. All actors in the troupe are expected to be singers as well as dancers. The context, style, and period setting of any particular play determines the degree to which dance is incorporated. Some plays, particularly those in a modern setting, rely more heavily on dialogue, with little or no dancing. Others, in particular the period plays, may consist of many colorful scenes with almost continuous dancing. The style of the play also affects the type of dances included. In plays that depict the life of the king and his court, the dances, however stylized, attempt to portray dances that might actually have occurred in the court. In other plays, more allegorical or mythological in nature, certain stock characters—for example, the demons *(balu)* or the magician Zogyi—dance onto the stage to specific music associated with their characters. The entering character is not dancing as part of the story, but rather his appearance onstage conventionally takes the form of dance.

Anyein Dance Theater. *Anyein* is another form of Burmese dance theater, separate from and yet related to *pwe*. The form takes its name from the solo or main female dancer, the Anyein, who is frequently also the leader of the little band of dancers, clowns, and musicians. The *anyein* genre may have originated as a lighter type of dance entertainment outside the court, gradually becoming increasingly formalized, until today some *anyein* troupes resemble small *pwe* troupes. In the days of the court, the songs and dances of the *anyein* were accompanied by the sounds of the Burmese thirteen-stringed harp, the *saung gauk*. Soon, however, as in all other forms of Burmese dance, the *saing* ensemble of drums and gongs became the usual accompaniment.

The performance of the *anyein* troupe centers around the talent of the Anyein herself. In the more traditional style as it survives today, the Anyein is introduced by a group of clowns, or *lu bye,* who take over the stage, joking about anything and everything. At a certain point in the proceedings, the Anyein is introduced, sings a short song in a characteristic style, and then dances a short but complex dance based on the same melody before leaving the stage to another clowning segment. This alternation of the Anyein with the clowns may occur several times during the course of one performance.

Rāmāyana. Completely outside the traditional Burmese *pwe* context is the masked dance drama performance of the Hindu epic the *Rāmāyana.* The tradition of this performance comes not directly from India, but from Thailand, whence it is believed to have been introduced following the sixteenth-century Burmese military destruction of Ayutthaya, a Thai kingdom. It is probable that the dance-drama version of the *Rāmāyana* was never very well known outside the Burmese court. The tradition survives today largely through the efforts and tenacity of a single group of performers. Even after centuries, the Burmese *Rāmāyana* performance has a distinctly foreign quality to its costumes, dance, and music. The music used falls into a special category of the classical Burmese song repertory called *yodaya* songs. Although many of the *yodaya* have been popular elements in the repertory, they nonetheless retain a Thai flavor.

Puppet Theater. *You thei* is the Burmese puppet theater. Like the puppet theaters of Japan, China, and Indonesia, *you thei* is not an entertainment for children; instead, it is a classical drama performed by puppets rather than human actors and dancers. Burmese puppets are actually marionettes from one to one-and-one-half feet (0.3 to 0.4 meter) in height, operated with strings from above. Like Burmese *pwe,* the *you thei* makes use of a number of stock characters. These number around twenty-eight and include a king, prince, princess, ministers, ogres, astrologers, hermits, and buffoons. The stories are drawn from the tales of the early life of the Buddha and from *jātaka* tales ("birth" stories, which are also the source of *zat pwe*). In addition, as in *pwe,* the *you thei* draws heavily on Burmese historical chronicles and mingles the ordinary concerns of daily life into improvised sections of dialogue.

A *you thei* performance usually begins with the dance of the *nat* votaress. The same ensemble of gongs and drums used for the *pwe* accompanies the *you thei.* Although the number of dances in a performance of *you thei* may be somewhat fewer than in *pwe,* dancing by the puppets nonetheless forms an important aspect of the tradition. Some believe that Burmese puppet theater may have preceded *pwe.* In any case, it is clear that the performance style of the puppets has influenced the style of live actors. In particular, in *pwe* dance the actors often consciously imitate the movement style of puppets.

State Theater. Another context in which dance survives in Burma is in the State Fine Arts Schools of Mandalay and Rangoon and in the Burmese State Theater Troupes. Both institutions resulted from renewed national conciousness after World War II and Burma's 1948 independence from Britain. The Fine Arts Schools train young dancers for about three years in Burmese basic dance exercises (the traditional method of teaching dance) as well as in the major dance types. After training, the best dancers are taken into the State Theater Troupe of Rangoon or Mandalay. Some may join one of the established traveling *pwe* troupes, at which time their real training

MYANMAR. There is a close relationship between Burmese music, dance, drama, and poetry. Folk dances, often incorporated into larger dramatic contexts, are generally identified by the characteristic drum that leads the accompanying ensemble. The man seen here plays the *ouzi*—a goblet-shaped drum worn suspended from the shoulder—and the woman accompanies with cymbals. (Photograph courtesy of Sylvia Frazer-Lu.)

MYANMAR. Dancers of the Burmese State Theater pose as royal characters. (Photograph from the archives of The Asia Society, New York.)

may be said to begin. In the *pwe* troupe the young dancers are expected to learn all the techniques of the stage.

The State Theater Troupes are an important element in the future of Burmese dance. The State Theater versions of traditional dances are adapted specifically for performance on a large stage and for international audiences. Dances that originated in the stage tradition of the *pwe* can be adapted to the modern stage without much difficulty. The State Troupes also perform other dances that are largely new creations, based on written historical materials rather than on continuous performance tradition.

[*See also* Costume in Asian Traditions.]

BIBLIOGRAPHY

Ba Han. "Evolution of Burmese Dramatic Performances and Festive Occasions." *Journal of the Burma Research Society* 49 (June 1966).

Ludu Daw Amah. *Anyein.* 2 vols. Rangoon, 1973.

Maung Htin Aung. *Burmese Drama.* London, 1937.

Maung Thein Nin. *Myanmar You Soun Thabin.* Rangoon, 1971.

Miettinen, Jukka O. *Classical Dance and Theatre in South-East Asia.* New York, 1992.

Pe Hla, ed. and trans. *Konmara Pya Zat: An Example of Popular Burmese Drama in the XIX Century by U Pok Ni.* London, 1952.

Sein, Kenneth, and J. A. Withey. *The Great Po Sein: A Chronicle of the Burmese Theatre.* Bloomington, Ind., 1965.

Singer, Noel F. *Burmese Dance and Theatre.* New York, 1995.

Strachan, Paul. *Mandalay: Travels from the Golden City.* Gartmore, 1994.

U Hla Tin, ed. *Myanmar You Thei Thabin.* Rangoon, 1968.

U Lu. *Myanmar Thabin Lo Ka.* Rangoon, 1967.

ROBERT GARFIAS

N

NÁDASI, FERENC (born 16 October 1893 in Budapest, died 20 February 1996 in Budapest), Hungarian dancer, choreographer, and ballet master. As a child in Budapest, Nádasi was a pupil of Henrietta Spinzi, formerly a ballerina of La Scala Ballet. He first danced on stage at the age of ten and after five years of study became a member of the company of the Metropolitan Orpheum in Budapest. In 1909 he joined an itinerant company to tour Europe. He also danced in Russia and studied intermittently for three years at Enrico Cecchetti's private school in Saint Petersburg.

Returning to Hungary in 1912, Nádasi became solo dancer at the Opera House on 1 February 1913, continuing his training there under Nicola Guerra and dancing leading roles in Guerra's ballets. In 1914 he partnered Serafina Astafieva, a visiting dancer. He began touring the variety stages of Europe in 1921 with his partner Aranka Lieszkovszky and from 1928 with his second wife, Marcelle Vuillet-Baum, dancing in twenty-two countries in the 1930s. He continued his studies under Lubov Egorova, Olga Preobrajenska, and Evgenia Eduardova, eventually evolving his own teaching method. In Budapest in 1936 he opened a private school with his wife; in 1937 he became the ballet master responsible for exercises and training for the Budapest Opera. He retired in 1963.

With Gyula Harangozó, the great Hungarian choreographer, Nádasi laid the foundations for the work of the Budapest Opera House's ballet company. He created a repertory with a typical national style of performance that is characteristic of the Budapest ballet to this day. Nádasi borrowed from the Russian and Italian schools but always considered the temperament and physical qualities of Hungarian dancers. He evolved a specific teaching method under which the technical standards of the company rose rapidly within a few years. This was the first time in the history of Hungarian ballet that a choreographer and a ballet teacher had cooperated for an extended period. In the 1940s Nádasi also created ballets for the Budapest Opera, including his versions of the one-act *Sylvia* (1941), *The Birthday of the Infanta* (1945, 1949), set to music by Miklós Radnai, *Le Spectre de la Rose* (1948), and the Bluebird pas de deux in 1949.

In 1950 the new State Ballet Institute synthesized its teaching methods from those of the Soviet teacher Agrippina Vaganova and the Hungarian Nádasi. Nádasi was a leading teacher at this institute from 1950 to 1961, ballet director of the opera in 1960/61, and president of the Association of Hungarian Dance Artists from 1955 to 1963. He also published several articles in the Hungarian monthly *Táncművészet* in the early 1950s. His best-known pupils include Nóra Kováts (Kovach), Dóra Csinády, Gabriella Lakatos, Zsuzsa Kun, Adél Orosz, István Rab, Viktor Fülöp, Ferenc Havas, and Viktor Róna. Nádasi's honors included the Merited Artists Award (1955) and the Kossuth Prize (1958).

BIBLIOGRAPHY

Imre, Zoltán. "Wayfaring Hungarian." *Dance and Dancers* (February 1977): 28–31.

Körtvélyes, Géza, and György Lőrinc. *The Budapest Ballet: The Ballet Ensemble of the Hungarian State Opera House.* 2 vols. Translated by Gedeon P. Dienes and Éva Rácz. Budapest, 1971–1981.

Kun, Zsuzsa. "Ferenc Nádasi." *Muzsika* (April 1966).

Lőrinc, György, et al. *A balettművészet felé.* Budapest, 1961.

Major, Rita. "Ferenc Nádasi the Teacher." *Hungarian Dance News,* no. 1–2 (1984): 3–4.

Nádasi, Myrtill, ed. *Nádasi Ferenc, 1893–1966.* Budapest, 1993.

Szechy, Klari. "The Sensational Teaching of Ferenc Nadassy." *Ballet Today* (December 1953): 12–15.

Vályi, Rózsi, et al. *A magyar balett történetéből.* Budapest, 1956.

GÉZA KÖRTVÉLYES

NADEZHDINA, NADEZHDA (Nadezhda Sergeevna Nadezhdina; born 21 May [3 June] 1908 in Vilnius, Lithuania, died 11 October 1979 in Moscow), dancer, choreographer, art director, and teacher. Nadezhdina graduated from the Second State Ballet School in Saint Petersburg, where she studied under Nikolai Legat, Agrippina Vaganova, A. A. Gordova, and others. Between 1925 and 1934 she danced with the Bolshoi Ballet in Moscow. She performed in *Swan Lake* (Spanish and Hungarian dances and the mazurka), *The Little Humpbacked Horse* (Slav and Ukrainian dances), *Don Quixote* (the *fandango*), *The Red Poppy* (Malayan dance and the Boston), *La Bayadère* ("dance with lilies"), *Raymonda* (the *panaderos*), and others. From 1931 onward she also performed on the variety stage. In 1941 Nadezhdina began her career as a choreographer in the companies of the Siberian military district and the Karelian frontline district. Starting in 1943 she was choreographer and from 1946 to 1948 artistic director of the ballet department of the Moscow variety agency; concurrently, starting in 1945, she was artistic director of the Russian folk choir of the Karelian philharmonic.

Nadezhdina founded the Berezka Academic Choreographic Company in 1948 and was the artistic director and producer of all its programs, which revealed her significant talent. She created a new style in choreography by synthesizing Russian dance folklore and classical dance. "Nadezhdina developed her own original style whose most vivid attributes are the close link of dance images with the people's life; . . . Russian dance of the Berezka company has absorbed what is most poetical in the wealth of folk art," Marina Semenova wrote in the 3 February 1963 edition of *Pravda.* Nadezhdina sought to express the many-sided nature and generosity of the Russian character: its heroic spirit and subtle lyricism, romanticism and sense of humor, outward restraint and inner passion, pride and modesty, courage and bravery. The age-old, deep-rooted foundations of the life of the people and the poetical traditions associated with them provided an inexhaustible source of themes and content for her dance narratives. "The dance image created by her is elevated to high poetical generalization which is the secret of the depth and force of Nadezhdina's art," critic Natalia Arkina wrote in the 19 April 1976 edition of *Pravda.* Her art was dominated by specimens of lyrical poetry, as seen in her round dances "Berezka" (Birch Tree), "Lebedushka" (Swan), "Tsepochka" (Chain), "Uzory" (Lace), "Vesenny Khorovod" (Spring Round Dance), "Pryalitsa" (Spinner), and "Severnoe Siyanie" (The Northern Lights).

Nadezhdina was not only a choreographer of rich fantasy, but also a teacher and an artistic director. "Every dance of the Berezka dance company amazes one with its clarity of conception, neat dramaturgical proportions, artistic perfection. These are not simply dances but veritable novellas with a highly interesting approach to choreography and art direction," wrote Konstantin Sergeyev in the 25 May 1965 issue of *Sovetskaia kultura.*

Nadezhdina retired in the early 1980s. She was the author of the book *Russian Dances* (1951) and many articles. Honors awarded her include the State Prize of the USSR (1950), the Joliot-Curie Gold Medal of Peace (1959), and the Order of "The Lebanese Cedar," the supreme award of Lebanon.

BIBLIOGRAPHY

Chizhova, Aleksandra. *Beryozka Dance Company: Russian Folk Dance Company Directed by Nadezhda Nadezhdina.* Translated by R. Flaxman. Moscow, 1968.

Chizhova, Aleksandra. *Berezka.* Moscow, 1972.

Peters, Kurt. "Nadiejka Nadiejdina." *Das Tanzarchiv* 27 (1979): 681.

ALEKSANDRA E. CHIZHOVA
Translated from Russian

NAGAUTA. The major genre of lyrical music used in Japan's *kabuki* theater, dance concerts, and *shamisen* recitals is *nagauta,* which means "long song." The term was used in the eighteenth century to distinguish this from the shorter songs performed by courtesans. It began in the Kamigata (Kyoto–Osaka) area of Japan but it was the Edo (Tokyo) area's *nagauta* that dominated *kabuki* and dance music. In the nineteenth century, nondance concert pieces *(ozashiki nagauta)* were composed. Today the genre is heard frequently in all three settings. Nineteenth-century compositions predominate, but new pieces appear. *Nagauta* may be studied at Tokyo National University as well as privately.

Nagauta performances require only a singer and a player of the three-stringed, plucked *shamisen* lute, but a full ensemble has several singers and *shamisen* plus a group known as the *hayashi.* This consists of two hourglass-shaped hand drums *(ko tsuzumi, ō tsuzumi),* a *taiko* stick drum, and one flutist who uses either the *nō* drama flute *(nōkan)* or a bamboo flute *(takebue* or *shinobue).* An obbligato *(uwajōshi) shamisen* may also be used.

The standard compositional structure is the six-sectioned *kabuki* dance form. The *oki* is a prelude, and the *michiyuki* is used for the dancer's entrances, while the *kudoki* is lyrical. Tempo and orchestration brighten at the *odori ji* (literally, "basic dance") and maximum density occurs in the *chirashi,* followed by a retard and *dangire* cadence.

The repertory is large, so there is great flexibility in form and orchestration. Composition is a communal effort. The "composer" provides the *shamisen,* the vocal line, or both, while the rest of the orchestration is done by members of the *hayashi.* Thus the sound of a piece may vary greatly from one performance to another. This gives *nagauta* coherence and constant creativity.

[*See also* Kabuki Theater.]

BIBLIOGRAPHY

Brandon, James R., et al. *Studies in Kabuki: Its Acting, Music, and Historical Context.* Honolulu, 1978.

Malm, William P. *Nagauta: The Heart of Kabuki Music.* Rutland, Vt., 1964.

Malm, William P. *Six Hidden Views of Japanese Music.* Berkeley, 1986.

WILLIAM P. MALM

NAGRIN, DANIEL (born 22 May 1917 in New York City), American dancer and choreographer. Nagrin achieved fame as a dancer in American musical theater in such Broadway productions as *Up in Central Park* (1945) *Annie Get Your Gun* (1946), *Touch and Go* (1949), and *Plain and Fancy* (1954); his work in *Plain and Fancy* was recognized by the Donaldson Award "for all that is finest in theatrical achievement" (*Billboard,* July 1955). He had studied modern dance with Helen Tamiris and Martha Graham and ballet in various New York City studios.

A performer and choreographer of American modern and jazz concert dance since 1940, Nagrin was noted for his "Dance Portraits," solos that were both biting and gentle. Spare elegant posturings dominated *Spanish Dance* (1948); the mannerisms of the American gangster filled *Strange Hero* (1948); the frenzy of the always-late businessman characterized *Man of Action* (1951); and the twitches of the angst-ridden citizen made up *Indeterminant Figure* (1957). In the 1960s and 1970s Nagrin presented solo concerts throughout the United States and in Canada, Europe, Guam, and the Philippines. His full-evening solo *The Peloponnesian War* (1968) was a raw, vital, and confrontive attack on war in the late 1960s. All of his choreographies are studies in human behavior; they present the dancer Nagrin as taut, spare, powerful, and no-nonsense, with a continual awareness of the contemporary world, provoking audiences to share and ponder. Thus jazz dance and its music received respect in his concerts.

As a teacher—carrying forward many of the Konstantin Stanislavsky–inspired ideas gleaned from his wife, Helen Tamiris, and from Joseph Chaikin's Open Theater—Nagrin continued structured improvisations in dance technique and choreography, the purest statements appearing in his "Workgroup" performances between 1970 and 1973. Then Nagrin toured with retrospectives of his solo dances, acted off-Broadway, and continued to teach. From 1982 to 1992, he was Professor of Dance at Arizona State University, where he lives and writes books on his art. In 1992 he was awarded a Distinguished Teaching Chair, American Dance Festival, Durham, North Carolina, and in 1993 he received the Master Teacher/Mentor award from the National Endowment for the Arts.

BIBLIOGRAPHY

Nagrin, Daniel. "War Diary." *Dance Perspectives* 38 (Summer 1969): 18–23.

Nagrin, Daniel. *How to Dance Forever: Surviving against the Odds.* New York, 1988.

Nagrin, Daniel. *Dance and the Specific Image: Improvisation.* Pittsburgh, 1994.

Nagrin, Daniel. *The Six Questions: Acting Technique for Dance Performance.* Pittsburgh, 1997.

Schlundt, Christena L. *Daniel Nagrin: A Chronicle of His Professional Career.* Berkeley, Calif., 1997.

FILM AND VIDEOTAPE. *Dance in the Sun* (1953). *The Dancer Prepares* (1958). *Strange Hero* in *A Time to Dance* (1959). *Nagrin: "Path" and "A Gratitude"* (1967). "Nagrin Videotape Library of Dances" (1984).

ARCHIVE. Daniel Nagrin Collection, New York Public Library for the Performing Arts. Daniel Nagrin Theatre, Film, and Dance Foundation, Tempe, Ariz.

CHRISTENA L. SCHLUNDT

NAHARIN, OHAD (born 22 June 1952 in Israel), dancer, choreographer, and musician. Naharin's initial contacts with dance and theater were at home; his father was an actor and his mother a music and dance teacher. After completing army service, he became an apprentice with Tel Aviv's Batsheva Dance Company. When Martha Graham arrived in Israel to create a new work for Batsheva, *The Dream* for the 1973/74 season, she gave Ohad Naharin an important role in it and invited him to become a student and, later, a dancer in her company.

Naharin also auditioned for Maurice Bejart's Ballet du XXe Siècle in Brussels and danced with the company for two seasons before returning to Israel, to dance as a guest artist with the Bat-Dor Company in Tel Aviv and marry Mari Kajiwara. After completing his studies in New York at the Juilliard School of Music and the Graham School, he began choreographing. His first work, the solo *Pas de Pepsi*, is a witty and whimsical "duet" for a soft-drink addict and a supermarket cart. He performed with his own small company in New York and held residencies at universities. His *Interim*, a group dance created in New York and transferred to Batsheva in 1981, deals with Jewish history as an ongoing, perhaps eternal process; it was set

NAHARIN. The choreographer with Mari Kajiwara in a 1984 performance of his *Dancing Ink.* (Photograph © 1984 by Johan Elbers; used by permission.)

to music by the modern *kleizmer* Giora Feidman and to pieces by Leonard Bernstein.

In 1983, Naharin choreographed *Innostress* to music by Brian Eno; it was his comment on Israel's war with Lebanon and its aftermath. In 1984, he created *Black Milk,* to music by Paul Smadbeck, for the Kibbutz Dance Company. It was originally a ritual with a milking pail for five women, which in 1992 he transferred to Batsheva, making it an all-male dance. In 1987, he choreographed *Tabula Rasa,* to music by Arvo Pärt, a composer whose music he often uses.

In the late 1980s, Naharin worked repeatedly for Batsheva, until in 1990 he was asked to become its artistic director. One of his important works of that period was *Kyr,* which marked a further refinement of his eclectic, energetic, sensuous style, full of fantastic images. For it, he collaborated with a group of rock musicians and also contributed his own musical material. *Anaphase* (1993) was an important, all-evening event. It became a hit with the public in Israel, and audiences usually wary of modern dance flocked to see it.

Naharin has been commissioned by the following companies to create or stage his works for them: the Netherlands Dance Theater, Sydney Dance Company, Pittsburgh Ballet Theater, Ballet du Grand Théâtre de Geneve, Bavarian State Ballet, Lyon Opera Ballet, Cullberg Ballet, Frankfurt Ballet, and other companies.

Naharin's work with the Batsheva Dance Company radically changed and modernized the company's look and style. As a native-born Israeli, Naharin speaks in an instinctive Israeli dance vocabulary within the contemporary universal dance idiom.

BIBLIOGRAPHY

Eldor, G. "Ohad Naharin Talks to Gabi Eldor." *Israel Dance Quarterly* 4 (October 1994): 105.

Manor, Giora. "Batsheva—the Flagship of Modern Dance in Israel." *Israel Dance Quarterly* 4 (October 1994): 111.

Servos, Norbert. "A Place of Storms Which Speaks of Calm." *Ballet International/Tanz Aktuell* 10 (1996): 51.

GIORA MANOR

NAKAMURA GANGIRŌ. A leading Kamigata-style actor and *onnagata,* Nakamura Gangirō III appears here as Shizuka Gozen in *Yoshitsune Senbon Zakura.* (Photograph courtesy Samuel L. Leiter.)

NAKAMURA GANJIRŌ, name used by three generations of *kabuki* actor-dancers.

Nakamura Ganjirō I (born 6 March 1860 in Osaka, died 1 February 1935 in Osaka), the son of Nakamura Ganjaku III (1841–1881), debuted in 1863 but soon after was separated from his father and raised by his mother's nontheatrical family. He returned to *kabuki* at twelve, however. Known variously in *kabuki* as Jitsukawa Tamatarō and Jitsukawa Ganjirō, he spent part of the period from 1875 to 1880 working as a puppet-theater handler, using the name Yoshida Tamatarō. In 1877, he and his father were reunited, and in 1878 he became Ganjirō I.

In 1890, he was a success in Tokyo. He formed his own company and returned to the Osaka-Kyoto (Kamigata) region, but he went back to Tokyo in 1906, thereafter splitting his career between Tokyo and Kamigata. He was outstanding in both male and female roles, but his special abilities were in domestic dramas *(sewamono),* where he epitomized the gentle *wagoto* style of young lovers. Ganjirō I's greatest roles were included in the family repertory called *Ganjirō Jūnikyoku* (Twelve Ganjirō Plays), which includes such characters as Kamiya Jihei in *Shinjū Ten no Amijima.* His great period-play *(jidaimono)* roles included Yuranosuke in *Chūshingura.*

Nakamura Ganjirō II (born 17 February 1902 in Osaka, died 13 April 1983 in Tokyo), the youngest son of Ganjirō I. Like his father, he typified the Kamigata style, but he became equally famous as a female impersonator *(onnagata)*. He debuted in Kyoto as Hayashi Yukio in 1907 but went through several name changes, becoming Nakamura Senjaku I, then Nakamura Ganjaku IV, and finally in 1946, Ganjirō II. During his teens, he had led a few young actors' troupes. In the mid-1950s, he enjoyed a fling as a movie actor, also appearing on television and on the non-*kabuki* stage. Because of Kamigata *kabuki's* travails in the mid-1950s, he worked mainly in Tokyo, where he was the quintessential Kamigata-style actor. In 1967 he was designated an Important Intangible Cultural Property, and in 1972 he was made a member of the Japan Arts Academy. Although mainly recognized for his *sewamono* roles, such as Tokubei in *Sonezaki Shinjū*, he was also adept at various *jidaimono* characters.

Nakamura Ganjirō III (born 31 December 1931 in Kyoto), Ganjirō II's son, follows his predecessors' traditions and is present-day *kabuki*'s major Kamigata-style actor. He debuted in 1941 as Nakamura Senjaku II. A major advancement came in 1949 when he and Bandō Tsurunosuke (later Nakamura Tomijūrō V) gained fame as the Sen–Tsuru combination in the experimental Takechi Kabuki run by director-critic Takechi Tetsuji. His roles, all female, included Fuji no Kata in *Kumagai Jinya* and Osome in *Toribeyama Shinjū*. When he played Ohatsu—his signature female role—opposite his father in *Sonezaku Shinjū* in 1953, a "Senjaku boom" followed. In the mid-1950s, he made several films. From 1963, he has concentrated on classic roles, such as Danshichi in *Yadonashi Danshichi*, and a multi-role performance in *Chūshingura*, in which he plays seven parts, male and female. A master dancer, his dance name is Fujima Kansuke.

In 1981, he formed the Chikamatsu-za, a company created to study and produce plays by Chikamatsu Monzaemon. Ganjirō III, who took that name in 1990, has toured in the West (1988) and has received numerous important honors, including designation as a National Living Treasure. His sons, Nakamura Tomotarō and Nakamura Hirotarō, are both *kabuki* actors.

[*See also* Japanese Traditional Dance *and* Kabuki Theater.]

BIBLIOGRAPHY

Akasaka Jiseki, ed. *Kabuki haiyū daihyakka*. Tokyo, 1993.
Engekikai (January 1994). Special issue on *kabuki* actors.
Fujita Hiroshi. *Kabuki handobukku*. Tokyo, 1994.
Nojima Jusaburō. *Kabuki jinmei jiten*. Tokyo, 1988.
Toita Yasuji, ed. *Kabuki kanshō nyūmon*. 3d ed., rev. Tokyo, 1994.

SAMUEL L. LEITER

NAKAMURA KANKURŌ, name used by five generations of *kabuki* actor-dancers. The name dates to the Edo theater manager Nakamura Kankurō I (flourished 1699).

The first star performer of the name is Nakamura Kankurō V (born 30 May 1955 in Tokyo), son of Nakamura Kanzaburō XVII. This actor, also known by the dance name of Nakamura Kanchō, debuted at Tokyo's Kabuki Theater in 1959 under his present stage name. He was recognized early on as a brilliantly promising actor and received a rigorous artistic education. He was given one important child's role after another, performed in films, and appeared as one of the children in a Japanese staging of the musical *The King and I*. He inherited two great acting traditions, that of his grandfather Onoe Kikugorō VI (1885–1949) and that of his uncle Nakamura Kichiemon I (1886–1954).

Like his versatile father, he plays every type of role and moves with surprising ease between leading male and female characters. He first co-starred with his father in the paired lion dance *Renjishi* in 1969, proving so able that they revived the piece several times. Also in 1969, he joined Sugi no Kai, a study group of boy actors, for which he played a succession of classic roles. In 1974, at age nineteen, Kankurō acted Benkei, one of *kabuki's* most demanding roles, in *Kanjinchō*. A major career milestone came in 1988, when Kankurō replaced his ailing father during the run of *Shunkan* and demonstrated remarkable power. Several months later, he was playing, for the first time, one of his father's greatest roles, the title character in *Kamiyui Shinza*, when Kanzaburō XVII died; despite his grief, Kankurō continued to give superlative performances, strikingly reminiscent of the late actor.

His major period-play *(jidaimono)* roles include that of Lord Ōkura in *Ichijō Ōkura Monogatari*, Gonta and Tadanobu in *Yoshitsune Senbon Zakura*, Matsuōmaru in *Sugawara Denju Tenarai Kagami*, Kanpei in *Chūshingura*, Omiwa in *Imoseyama*, and Otoku in *Domo no Matahei*, where Kichiemon's influence is felt. Kankurō's domestic-drama *(sewamono)* roles include Danshichi in *Natsu Matsuri*, Benten Kozō in the play of that name, and Oiwa in *Yotsuya Kaidan*, where Kikugorō's traditions are often reflected. His "new" *kabuki (shin kabuki)* characters include Chūtarō in *Mabuta no Haha*, and his main dance plays include *Kagamijishi*, *Musume Dōjōji*, and *Funa Benkei*, also embodiments of the Kikugorō style.

Kankurō is almost possessed by the inner depths of his roles. He is noted for his expert management of emotional transitions and his ability to alter his interpretation of a role according to the style of the actor playing opposite him. Kankurō's work has extended to the *shinpa* genre and even to Shakespeare's *Othello*, in which he has played Iago. His talent and diligence have been recognized on numerous occasions by the granting of prestigous awards. He toured in the West in 1982, 1983, and 1991. Kankurō is also the author of several books on acting. He is married to the daughter of the famous female impersonator Nakamura Shikan VII, and his children are the young actors Nakamura Kantarō II and Nakamura Shichinosuke II.

[*See also* Japanese Traditional Schools; Jidaimono; *and* Kabuki Theater.]

BIBLIOGRAPHY

Akasaka Jiseki, ed. *Kabuki haiyū daihyakka.* Tokyo, 1993.
Engekikai (January 1994). Special issue on *kabuki* actors.
Fujita Hiroshi. *Kabuki handobukku.* Tokyo, 1994.
Nojima Jusaburō. *Kabuki jinmei jiten.* Tokyo, 1988.
Toita Yasuji, ed. *Kabuki kanshō nyūmon.* 3d ed., rev. Tokyo, 1994.

SAMUEL L. LEITER

NAKAMURA KANZABURŌ, name used by seventeen generations of *kabuki* actors and theater managers. Dating from the early sixteenth century, the line was associated with the Nakamura-za, one of the three main *kabuki* playhouses in Edo (Tokyo), until the end of the Tokugawa shogunate (1603–1868). Most members of the line combined acting and managing careers, the only exceptions being Kanzaburō IX and Kanzaburō X, who were strictly managers. The three actors from Kanzaburō XIV through Kanzaburō XVI are counted in the succession although they never publicly took the name.

Nakamura Kanzaburō I (born 1598 in Kyoto, died 9 June 1658 in Edo), also known as Saruwaka Kanzaburō, is considered one of the founders of Edo *kabuki.*

Nakamura Kanzaburō XVII (born 29 July 1909 in Tokyo, died 16 April 1988 in Tokyo) was the most distinguished actor in the line. Kanzaburō XVII was the youngest son of actor Nakamura Karoku III (1849–1919) and the brother of the famous actors Nakamura Tokizō III (1895–1959) and Nakamura Kichiemon I. His adoptive father and main teacher was the great Onoe Kikugorō VI. Kanzaburō debuted in 1916 and held the names Nakamura Yonekichi III and Namakura Moshiho IV before acceding to Kanzaburō XVII in 1950. Although most of his career was with the Shōchiku production company, he spent several years in the 1930s with the breakaway group sponsored by the Tōhō firm.

Despite frequent illness, he had an unusually productive career and was one of the most versatile modern players, acting roles of every age, both male and female, for a remarkable total of more than eight hundred roles. He combined Kikugorō VI's style with that of his own brother, Kichiemon I, giving him an unusually wide approach. Kikugoro's traditions were especially visible in Kanzaburō's domestic-drama *(sewamono)* roles, such as the title character in *Kamiyui Shinza,* while Kichiemon's influences were seen in Kanzaburō's period-play *(jidaimono)* performances, such as the role of Lord Ōkura in *Ōkura Kyō* or Shunkan in the play of that name. In addition, he inherited certain unique traditions of the Kyoto-Osaka area from his father, allowing him to master such roles as Heisaku in *Igagoe.* Although known for being moody and selfish, his stage charm was strong enough to cover his personal shortcomings.

He was also an outstanding dancer, excelling in such pieces as *Kagamijishi, Migawari Zazen,* and *Ukare Bōzu,* while making significant contributions in "new" *kabuki (shin kabuki)* roles, such as *Saigo to Buta-hime,* in which he played Otama, and *Ippon Gatana,* in which he played Mohei. His range even extended to Shakespeare, with roles such as Richard III. He was also a revered acting teacher, handing on the venerable traditions to which he was heir.

The recipient of many prestigious awards and prizes, he became a member of the Japan Arts Academy in 1969 and in 1987 was awarded an honorary doctorate from the University of Illinois. He was a major player in postwar *kabuki's* first Western tour (1960) and subsequently acted abroad on several other occasions, making him one of the best-known *kabuki* actors internationally. His son is the current star Nakamura Kankurō V.

[*See also,* Japanese Traditional Schools *and* Kabuki Theater.]

BIBLIOGRAPHY

Leiter, Samuel L. *Kabuki Encyclopedia: An English-Language Adaptation of "Kabuki Jiten."* Westport, Conn., 1979.
Noguchi Tatsuji, ed. *Kabuki haiyū meikan.* Tokyo, 1970.
Nojima Jusaburō. *Kabuki jinmei jiten.* Tokyo, 1988.
Toita Yasuji et al. "Nakamura Kanzaburō o shinobu." *Engekikai* (June 1988): 133–148.

SAMUEL L. LEITER

NAKAMURA KICHIEMON, name used by two generations of *kabuki* actors.

Nakamura Kichiemon I (born 24 March 1886 in Tokyo, died 5 September 1954 in Tokyo) was the son of Nakamura Karoku III (1849–1919) and the brother of *kabuki* stars Nakamura Tokizō III (1895–1959) and Nakamura Kanzaburō XVII. He debuted in Tokyo in 1897 and rose to fame early in the twentieth century as the acting partner and rival of Onoe Kikugorō VI. Working together at Tokyo's Ichimura-za, these stars were responsible for the golden age of brilliant young actors known as the Ichimura-za period, which lasted into the 1920s. In 1943, Kichiemon founded his own troupe, which became a dominant force in postwar *kabuki.* He was especially gifted at playing leading men in period plays *(jidaimono),* but he was not especially versatile or skilled at dancing.

Nakamura Kichiemon II (born 22 May 1944 in Tokyo) is the younger son of the late Matsumoto Hakuō I (better

NAKAMURA KICHIEMON. In this scene from the *kabuki* drama *Benten Kozō,* the title character (Matsumoto Kōshirō IX, right) restrains Nango Rikimaru (Nakamura Kichiemon II, center) from fighting with a local fireman (Nakamura Matagorō II, left) who interferes on behalf of the shop's owner. The conflict begins after Benten, disguised as a woman, purposely allows himself to get caught stealing a piece of fabric, as part of a scheme to extort money from the shopowner. Benten assumes that he will be assaulted when the theft is discovered. When Nango, impersonating Benten's samurai retainer, demands reparation for the insult to his "mistress," the fireman intercedes, threatening violence. (Photograph courtesy of Samuel L. Leiter.)

known as Matsumoto Kōshirō VIII) and brother of Matsumoto Kōshirō IX. Adopted by his grandfather, Kichiemon I, he debuted in 1948 as Nakamura Mannosuke. When he co-starred with his brother and the future Ichikawa Ennosuke III in *Kuruma Biki* in 1958, their performances were advertised as "teen *kabuki.*" In 1960, he and his brother (then called Ichikawa Somegorō VI) created a study group, the Kinome Kai. A year later, they left the Shōchiku company to play for Tōhō, where they were joined by their father and his company. With Tōhō, they frequently acted in commercially appealing modern plays. For their study group, Mannosuke played a series of great parts, including Genzō in *Terakoya,* Danshichi in *Natsu Matsuri,* Naosuke in *Yotsuya Kaidan,* and Higuchi in *Hiragana Seisuiki.* He studied literature at Waseda University but did not complete a degree.

In 1966, he became Nakamura Kichiemon II. He continued playing both in popular drama and *kabuki,* starring in the latter genre in a series of great roles associated with his namesake: Kumagai in *Kumagai Jinya,* Rokusuke in *Keyamura,* and others. His non-*kabuki* work extended to *shinpa,* but he inclined increasingly toward *kabuki,* playing the title role in *Ishikiri Kajiwara,* Takatsuna in *Kamakura Sandaiki,* and Heiemon in *Chūshingura,* while also playing in "new" *kabuki (shin kabuki).* He continued to assume difficult old roles, including Yuranosuke in *Chūshingura,* Jirōzaemon in *Kagotsurube,* and Moritsuna in *Moritsuna Jinya.*

Kichiemon, who is tall for a *kabuki* actor, plays only male roles and is prized for his excellent speaking skills, essential to the period roles that have made him the leading star in this genre. He is equally adept at domestic dramas *(sewamono),* and he has done well playing the title role in *Murai Chōan,* Yosaburō in *Yowa Nasake Ukina no Yokogushii,* and Naozamurai in *Kumo ni Magō Ueno no Hatsuhana.* He is a conservative actor and is not especially noteworthy in physically flamboyant roles, such as the fox-Tadanobu, in *Yoshitsune Senbon Zakura.*

This much-honored actor has also appeared in television and films. Writing under the name Matsu Kanshi, he was responsible for a 1985 play called *Saikai Zakura Misome no Kiyomizu.* Among his many accomplishments was his participation in reviving *kabuki* at Shikoku's old-style Kanamaru-za.

[*See also* Japanese Traditional Schools *and* Kabuki Theater.]

BIBLIOGRAPHY

Akasaka Jiseki, ed. *Kabuki haiyū daihyakka.* Tokyo, 1993.
Engekikai (January 1994). Special issue on *kabuki* actors.
Fujita Hiroshi. *Kabuki handobukku.* Tokyo, 1994.
Nojima Jusaburō. *Kabuki jinmei jiten.* Tokyo, 1988.
Toita Yasuji, ed. *Kabuki kanshō nyūmon.* 3d ed., rev. Tokyo, 1994.

SAMUEL L. LEITER

NAKAMURA TOMIJŪRŌ, name used by five generations of *kabuki* actor-dancers.

Nakamura Tomijūrō I (born 1719 in Osaka, died 3 June 1786 in Osaka), a female impersonator *(onnagata)* and the son of the famous female impersonator Yoshizawa Ayame I (1673–1729), was mainly associated with the Kyoto-Osaka region (Kamigata) *kabuki.*

Nakamura Tomijūrō II (born 1786 in Osaka, died 13 February 1855 in Osaka) was also a famous Kamigata *onnagata.*

Nakamura Tomijūrō III (born 10 May 1859 in Osaka, died 21 February 1901 in Tokyo), although originally from Kamigata, became a well-known Tokyo female impersonator.

Nakamura Tomijūrō IV (born 11 June 1908 in Tokyo, died 17 October 1960 in Tokyo), originally known as Bandō Tsurunosuke III, began his career as a female impersonator in Tokyo but achieved his greatest fame in Osaka.

Nakamura Tomijūrō V (born 4 June 1929 in Tokyo), the son of Tomijūrō IV and the dancer Azuma Tokuhō, plays both men and women with ease. Raised in Tokyo, he made his debut in Osaka in 1943 as Bandō Tsurunosuke IV. Most of his teenage career focused on dance concerts rather than *kabuki* childrens' roles. In 1949, he and Nakamura Senjaku II (later Nakamura Ganjirō III) rose to fame as the "Sen–Tsuru" combination in the experimental Takechi Kabuki troupe run by director-critic Takechi Tetsuji. At the same time, he received training from the leading puppet theater and *kyōgen* masters. He starred opposite Senjaku in such roles as Kumagai in *Kumagai Jinya* and Benkei in *Kanjinchō.* Despite the venture's success, Kamigata *kabuki* floundered, and in 1954 he left the Shōchiku company to act in films and dance in his mother's Azuma Kabuki company for an American tour. He then joined a Kamigata troupe run by Kataoka Nizaemon XIII (1904–1993) and Ichikawa Jūkai III (1886–1971). Under the latter's instruction, he learned many important "new" *kabuki (shin kabuki)* roles.

NAKAMURA TOMIJŪRŌ. Nakamura Tomijūrō V as Umeō in the *kabuki* drama *Kuruma Biki.* (Photograph courtesy of Samuel L. Leiter.)

In 1957, he joined Tokyo's Kikugorō Geludan troupe but was cast mainly in supporting roles. He imbibed the special techniques and atmosphere associated with the troupe's specialty, domestic drama *(sewamono).* He changed his name to Ichimura Takenojō in 1964 and, after leaving the Kikugorō troupe and working freelance, in 1972 altered it to Nakamura Tomijūrō V. His talent was recognized and he was given support by the leading *kabuki* stars, especially Onoe Shōroku II, who trained him in many classic roles. He thus became outstanding in *sewamono, shin kabuki,* and period plays *(jidaimono);* in the last of these genres he gave exceptional performances as Heiemon in *Chūshingura,* Hachiemon in *Fuingiri,* and the title role in *Narukami,* among others, and he performed brilliantly in such dances as *Funa Benkei, Kagamijishi, Yoshino Yama,* and *Musume Dōjōji.* In 1978, he formed Yasha Kai, a group for which he produced dances such as *Kasuga Ryūjin* and *Seki no To.*

Although short and stocky, Tomijūrō V is revered for his versatility, his tremendous stage enthusiasm and energy, his exceptional dancing skills, his passion for artistic perfection, and his remarkable vocal powers and precise diction. A Living National Treasure, he is considered present-day *kabuki*'s most technically skilled player of male roles. His brother is Nakamura Kikaku I.

[*See also* Japanese Traditional Schools *and* Kabuki Theater.]

BIBLIOGRAPHY

Akasaka Jiseki, ed. *Kabuki haiyū daihyakka.* Tokyo, 1993.

Engekikai (January 1994). Special issue on *kabuki* actors.

Fujita Hiroshi. *Kabuki handobukku.* Tokyo, 1994.

Leiter, Samuel L. "Four Interviews with Kabuki Actors." *Educational Theatre Journal* (December 1966): 391–404.

Nojima Jusaburō. *Kabuki jinmei jiten.* Tokyo, 1988.

SAMUEL L. LEITER

NAKAMURA UTAEMON, name used by six generations of *kabuki* actors. The first four actors in the line were players of male roles *(tachiyaku),* but the fifth and sixth were brilliant female impersonators *(onnagata).*

Nakamura Utaemon I (born 1714 in Kanazawa, died 29 October 1791 in Kyoto), a provincial physician's son, joined a troupe of strolling players at seventeen and developed into an outstanding player of both leading men and villains. He was adopted by Nakamura Genzaemon II and took the name Nakamura Utanosuke I but switched to Utaemon I in 1741. He developed his career in the Kamigata (Kyoto-Osaka) area. From 1757, he was also popular in Edo (Tokyo). He passed his name on to his disciple, Nakamura Tōzō I, in 1782, and became Kagaya Kashichi I. He also dabbled in playwriting as Nakamura Kashichi.

Nakamura Utaemon II born 1752 in Kyoto, died 22 March 1798 in Kyoto), the line's only undistinguished actor, first called himself Mizuki Tōzō but became Nakamura Tōzō I. In 1782, when Utaemon I became Kashichi, he assumed his master's name as Utaemon II, but he gave the name up in 1790 to Utaemon I's son, Kagaya Fukunosuke, and resumed as Tōzō I.

Nakamura Utaemon III (born 3 March 1778 in Osaka, died 13 July 1813 in Osaka), son of Nakamura Utaemon I, disobeyed his father's wishes that he become a doctor and, after gaining good notices in a children's *kabuki* company, received his father's training. He took the name Kaga before acceding to Utaemon III in 1790. He changed to Nakamura Shikan I in 1818 but resumed Utaemon III in 1819. In 1837, he gave the name Utaemon III to his adopted son Shikan II and took the name Nakamura Tamasuke. This Osaka star was extremely versatile, playing *tachiyaku, onnagata,* and villains as well as being an outstanding dancer. Despite his physical shortcomings, his skill, invention, and cleverness were widely honored. His rivalry with the great Edo actor Bandō Mitsugorō III in quick-change dances *(hengemono),* and with fellow Osakan, Arashi Kichisaburō (later Arashi Rikan I), was legendary. He founded the methods still used in playing many classic puppet-theater *(bunraku)* roles, such as Higuchi in *Sakaro* and Umeomaru in *Sugawara.* He also wrote plays under the name Kanazawa Ryūgyoku.

Nakamura Utaemon IV (born 1796? in Edo [Tokyo], died 17 February 1852 in Osaka), son of a teahouse proprietor, became the disciple of his adoptive father, choreographer Fujima Kanjūro I, and began his career as Fujima Kamesaburō. He moved back to Edo in 1811 and entered the household of Utaemon III, becoming Nakamura Fujitarō. In 1813 he changed his name to Nakamura Tsurusuke, then became Nakamura Shikan II in 1825. In 1836 he was adopted by Nakamura Utaemon III, who changed his name to Tamasuke, and later elevated him to Utaemon IV. A great dancer, his major rival was Bandō Mitsugorō IV. Large and imposing, he excelled in period-play *jidaimono* roles such as that of Matsuōmaru in *Sugawara,* but he also sometimes played females.

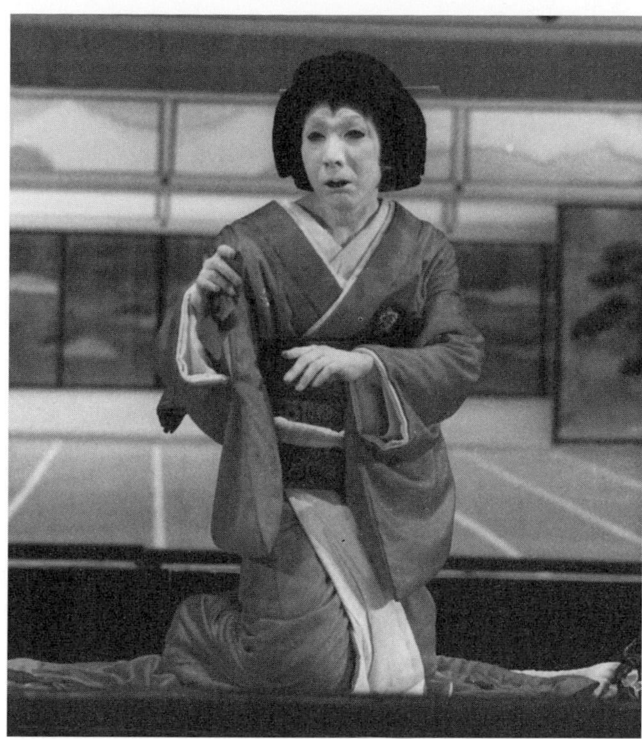

NAKAMURA UTAEMON. A great *onnagata,* Nakamura Utaemon VI appears here as Masaoka in the *kabuki* drama *Sendai Hagi.* (Photograph courtesy of Samuel L. Leiter.)

Nakamura Utaemon V (born 29 December 1865 in Edo [Tokyo], died 12 September 1940 in Tokyo), the son of a shogunate official and, from 1875, adopted son of Nakamura Shikan IV, debuted as Nakamura Kotarō, and took the names Nakamura Fukusuke IV and Nakamura Shikan V before becoming Utaemon V in 1911. Although he often played *tachiyaku,* he was famous as one of the finest *onnagata* of his time. After the deaths of Onoe Kikugorō V and Ichikawa Danjūrō IX, he became the leader of the *kabuki* world, which was unusual for an *onnagata.* His good looks and intelligence aided him immeasurably in such important princess roles as Yaegaki in *Honchō Nijūshikō* and in the roles of older court ladies, such as Masaoka in *Meiboku Sendai Hagi.* Despite disabling lead poisoning, he he still managed to amaze his audiences. One of his great characters was the historical Yodogimi in Tsubouchi Shōyō plays such as *Kiri Hitoka.* Utaemon V founded the Japan Actors' Association.

Nakamura Utaemon VI (born, 20 January 1917 in Tokyo), son of Utaemon V, debuted in 1922 as Nakamura Kotarō III, and became Nakamura Fukusuke VI in 1933. After his influential father died in 1940, he was taken into the house of Nakamura Kichiemon I, against whom he often played female leads. In 1941, he took the name Nakamura Shikan VI, and he succeeded to Utaemon VI in 1951. From then until the early 1990s, he competed with Onoe Baikō VII as the greatest *onnagata* of their generation. His acting is detailed, colorful, and imaginative, and he maintains a traditional attitude toward the *onnagata*'s life. Apart from occasional performances as handsome youths, his career has been marked by his devotion to female characters. He has excelled as young city women, princesses, courtesans, and court ladies. His great roles include Sadaka in *Imoseyama,* Onoe in *Kagamiyama,* Tamate in *Gappō,* and Agemaki in *Sukeroku.*

One of the finest dancers of his age, he is associated with such works as *Dōjōji, Seki no To, Sumidagawa,* and *Masakado.* Utaemon VI is an outstanding musician of the three-stringed *shamisen,* the *koykyū* (the single stringed chinese fiddle), and the *koto* (a horizontal harp with thirteen strings); he is also an avid dance experimentalist, having formed the Tsubomi Kai study group in 1955. His achievement was so substantial that he was inducted into the Japan Arts Academy in 1963, at the unusually young age of forty-six. He was subsequently presented with Japan's other most prestigious awards, including being designated a National Living Treasure. In later years, illness restricted his movement and he focused on directing, but he made a comeback in April 1995. His adopted sons are Nakamura Baigyoku IV and Nakamura Matsue V.

[*See also* Japanese Traditional Schools; Kabuki Theater; *and* Onnagata.]

BIBLIOGRAPHY

Akasaka Jiseki, ed. *Kabuki haiyū daihyakka.* Tokyo, 1993.

Fujita Hiroshi. *Kabuki handobukku.* Tokyo, 1994.

Engekikai 52.2 (1993). Special issue: *kabuki* actors' directory.

Leiter, Samuel L. "Four Interviews with Kabuki Actors." *Educational Theatre Journal* (December 1966): 391–404.

Mishima Yukio, ed. *Rokusei Nakamura Utaemon.* Tokyo, 1959.

Nakamura Utaemon and Yamakawa Shizuo. *Utaemon no Rokujunen.* Tokyo, 1986.

Nojima Jusaburō. *Kabuki jinmei jiten.* Tokyo, 1988.

Toita Yasuji, ed. *Kabuki kanshō nyūmon.* 3d ed., rev. Tokyo, 1994.

Samuel L. Leiter

NATHALIE. *See* Swiss Milkmaid, The.

NATIONAL BALLET OF CANADA. Founded in 1951 and based in Toronto, Ontario, the National Ballet of Canada is the country's largest classical ballet company, currently boasting a roster of some seventy dancers. It is the only Canadian troupe to perform most of the full-length works surviving from the nineteenth-century European repertory. These ballets—*Giselle, Coppélia, La Sylphide, The Nutcracker, The Sleeping Beauty, Swan Lake,* and others—are central to the company's artistic personality and have come to define its public image. In addition, the company has accumulated a large and varied repertory of shorter works by foreign and Canadian choreographers. The mixed programs in which these are presented have been given increasing prominence in recent years.

Considering its size and importance as one of the country's oldest professional performing arts institutions, it is remarkable that the National Ballet of Canada has only recently come to have the advantages of adequate accommodations in its home city. Until 1996 its studios and offices occupied most of a historic but cramped nineteenth-century public building in downtown Toronto. Its newly constructed headquarters are now, however, among the largest and best-equipped in North America, although its usual performance venue still leaves much to be desired. Its major Toronto seasons have, since 1964, been given in the unsuitable 3,200-seat Hummingbird Centre (formerly the O'Keefe Centre), and there is as yet no sign that often-discussed plans to build a proper opera-ballet theater in the city will be ever realized.

The company offers its Toronto audiences ballet seasons totaling twelve to thirteen weeks and comprising more than a hundred performances each year. The remainder of each season is occupied with cross-Canada tours as well as visits to the United States and occasional overseas tours. Since 1969 the company has also presented a number of choreographic workshops in smaller Toronto theaters.

Origins and Background. Despite the word *National* in its name, the National Ballet of Canada has never been officially mandated to assume any form of national responsibility for ballet in Canada. Rather, the name reflects the ambition of a small group of Toronto ballet enthusiasts, backed by a number of prominent local business executives, to establish a classical ballet company that would draw its personnel from all parts of the country. The interest of this group had been spurred early in 1949 by the appearance in Toronto of a number of small semi-professional and amateur troupes from various cities for the second annual Canadian Ballet Festival. The ten-year-old Winnipeg Ballet was among these companies, and its popular success is said to have given rise to a degree of envy among the Torontonians, whose civic pride was offended by the thought that Winnipeg might well become Canada's ballet capital.

Toronto was not, at the time, completely deprived of ballet performances. Boris Volkoff, a Russian-born dancer who had settled in Toronto in 1929 and had become one of the city's leading ballet teachers, already had a small company of his own. In 1936 it had been favorably received during its performances at the Internationale Tanzwettspiele of the XIth Olympiad in Berlin, and it had thereafter continued to present dance performances in Toronto throughout the 1940s. Volkoff's students earnestly looked forward to the formation of a fully professional national ballet company, but some observers harbored doubts concerning his capacity to head such an enterprise.

In November 1949, a visit to Toronto by the Sadler's Wells Ballet, then on its first North American tour, clarified and reinforced the aspirations of local ballet enthusiasts. They were impressed by the accomplishments of the British company, which had been achieved in such a remarkably short time. They approached the company's director, Ninette de Valois, and asked how they should go about forming a similar company for Canada. Having urged them to look outside Canada for an artistic director of experience and proven talent, de Valois later specifically recommended the British dancer and choreographer Celia Franca.

Franca accepted an invitation from the Toronto group to attend the third Canadian Ballet Festival in Montreal in November 1950. Well aware that many of the dancers she saw had been inadequately schooled but impressed by the high level of enthusiasm, Franca agreed to return to Canada in February 1951 to conduct a fuller survey. Her presence in Toronto generated considerable interest and speculation. Franca and her newly formed provisional board of directors of the "Canadian National Ballet" (a name soon abandoned) were swept forward on a wave of public expectation. Rather than delay and allow this interest to subside, they resolved to proceed and launch a company.

The Franca Regime: 1951–1975. Although Franca knew that such action was in many respects premature, she accepted the appointment as artistic director of the company and undertook her new duties with typical energy and single-minded determination. In the summer of 1951 she organized a number of trial performances with a small group of dancers for a "Promenade Concert" given in Toronto and Montreal. With the success of these performances, and the satisfactory completion of a special intensive summer school in Toronto, the recently formed Canadian Dance Teachers Association offered to sponsor Franca and her group in an audition tour of western Canada, which they promptly undertook. She and her board considered this tour an important opportunity to dispel the misgivings of those who feared that the new company would become just another locally oriented troupe.

The National Ballet of Canada made its official debut in Toronto's Eaton Auditorium on 12 November 1951. Despite the limitations of the largely inexperienced company assembled for that first season, Franca presented a program that included *Les Sylphides,* the peasant pas de deux from *Giselle,* the *Polovtsian Dances* from *Prince Igor,* a revised version of Franca's own *Salome* (first choreographed for BBC television in England), and *Études,* a work by Kay Armstrong of Vancouver. The program was warmly received and was taken to several nearby cities and to Montreal in January 1952.

Franca's ambitious goals for the company no doubt reflected those of her governing board. The company was to be firmly rooted in the classical tradition and modeled on a developmental pattern not unlike that used by de Valois in Great Britain. In an article for Arnold Haskell's seventh *Ballet Annual* in 1953, Franca set forth her ideas:

> My policy with regard to the repertoire is to present the classical ballets together with new Canadian works. Emphasis has been on the classics this year in order to set a standard for both dancers and the public; I believe that only from a firm foundation of the classical repertoire can Canadian Ballet develop its own style of choreography.

These principles were to guide Franca throughout her twenty-three years as the company's artistic director. [*See the entry on Franca.*]

In the beginning, Franca's goal was doubly daunting: not only had she to create a new repertory and direct a new company, but she had to build an audience to support its performances. Despite the pioneering efforts of a number of talented teachers across Canada and the educational effect of appearances by foreign touring companies, the population at large had little appreciation of ballet. The new National Ballet of Canada thus had much pioneering work of its own to do.

Franca's vision of mounting the classics for her company was eventually realized, although her stated ambition to foster native choreographic talent met with only mixed results. There was no Canadian equivalent of Frederick Ashton or George Balanchine on hand to give the company a personal style of movement, nor was Franca able to attract notable foreign choreographers to create a body of original works for the company. Chronic difficulties in raising enough money to operate the company on a fully professional basis during its early years compelled Franca to stage her own versions of the classics. The English artist and writer Kay Ambrose, Franca's artistic adviser from 1952 to 1961, designed the majority of the company's productions during that period. Franca often depended on others' generosity to contribute works to the repertory for meager remuneration. Financial difficulties had a direct effect on the company's repertory, for they limited the company's freedom to take artistic risks. Although the company was slow to build its national audience, Franca's stagings of the classics proved increasingly popular, and the company's willingness to satisfy public taste only served to entrench it.

To some concerned Canadians, Franca's development of the National Ballet appeared to be an exercise in cultural imperialism: the company looked to them like a weak offshoot of the Sadler's Wells Ballet. They questioned the seriousness of Franca's commitment to promoting Canadian creativity. Their criticisms, which continued for many years, reflected to a degree the sensitivities common to former colonial societies. Many areas of Canadian life were dominated by British leadership during the 1950s, and fervent nationalists saw Franca and her National Ballet as yet another manifestation of a disagreeable trend. Franca's own forceful personality, at times abrasive and undiplomatic, did little to mollify her critics.

Nevertheless, Franca did from the start try to foster the development of Canadian choreographers. Ballets by the gifted Albertan Grant Strate, by the company's Winnipeg-born *premier danseur* David Adams, and by several other Canadians were added to the repertory during the 1950s and 1960s. These new works, however, especially when choreographed in a contemporary idiom to modernistic scores, proved less popular than traditional ballets and works by choreographers of international renown.

Important among these foreign choreographers was Antony Tudor, with whom Franca had worked in England. His *Jardin aux Lilas* was presented during the company's second season in 1952 and was followed in subsequent years by *Gala Performance, Offenbach in the Underworld,*

NATIONAL BALLET OF CANADA. A scene from Antony Tudor's *Jardin aux Lilas,* staged for the company in 1952. From left to right: Celia Franca, Colleen Kenney, Grant Strate, Lilian Jarvis, Earl Kraul, Judie Colpman, Glenn Gibson, Robert Ito, Diane Childerhose, David Adams, Lois Smith, and James Ronaldson. Although Franca danced many leading roles during the company's early years, she was, by her own admission, "no technician." She did, however, excel in the dramatic and comic roles in the Tudor repertory. (Photograph by Ken Bell; used by permission of the National Ballet of Canada.)

NATIONAL BALLET OF CANADA. Celia Franca as the Operetta Star and David Adams as the Artist in Tudor's *Offenbach in the Underworld,* created for the company in 1955. Their costumes were designed by Kay Ambrose, artistic adviser to the company. (Photograph by Ken Bell; used by permission of the National Ballet of Canada.)

and *Dark Elegies. The Judgment of Paris* was acquired in 1962 and *Fandango* in 1971. The best of these Tudor ballets enhanced the company's artistic image and satisfied even its severest critics. Works by other foreign choreographers, including Frederick Ashton *(Les Rendezvous),* John Cranko *(Pineapple Poll),* George Balanchine *(Concerto Barocco* and *Serenade),* and Andrée Howard *(The Mermaid* and *Death and the Maiden),* supplemented Canadian ballets and Franca's stagings of the classics during the company's first decade.

The self-appointed mission to be a national company required costly tours to Canada's widely dispersed communities. Tours abroad began in 1953 with a visit to the Jacob's Pillow Dance Festival in western Massachusetts, and a United States touring agreement was signed with the William Morris Agency of New York in 1955.

Although she had not originally intended to do so, Franca continued to dance until 1959, when she announced her official retirement from the stage at age thirty-seven. (She returned to dance several character roles in later years.) The company's undisputed stars in its early years were the Canadians David Adams and Lois Smith. Apart from the consideration of financial constraints, Franca resisted on principle the idea of stocking the company's upper ranks with foreign dancers. The Russian Galina Samsova was, in 1960, the first foreign dancer to be hired as a soloist, and it was not until 1963 that an outsider was invited to headline the company as a guest artist. Even then, the occasion was due to an injury sustained by Smith, and the guest artist invited to replace her was Melissa Hayden, a native Canadian.

By 1959 Franca had achieved her objective of establishing a school for the company. The National Ballet School of Canada was founded with the English-born teacher Betty Oliphant as director and principal teacher. Oliphant, who had moved from London to Toronto in the late 1940s, was the company's first ballet mistress, a post she held from 1951 until 1962, and was associate artistic director from 1969 to 1975. She continued to direct the school until 1989, when she relinquished her duties to Mavis Staines, formerly a soloist with the company.

After the mid-1960s, the school, by then independently constituted but still strongly linked to the performing

NATIONAL BALLET OF CANADA. David Adams as Franz and Lois Smith as Swanilda in the final pose of the pas de deux in act 3 of *Coppélia,* c.1960. The complete ballet, with choreography credited to Arthur Saint-Léon, was staged by Franca in 1958. (Photograph by Ken Bell; used by permission of the National Ballet of Canada.)

company, began to produce an increasing number of the National Ballet's dancers. Martine van Hamel, Veronica Tennant, Vanessa Harwood, and Nadia Potts were among the first of this new generation of excellently trained dancers. They were followed by Karen Kain, Frank Augustyn, and many others. By the early 1970s it became clear that the training of a majority of the company's dancers in the National Ballet School had given the company something approaching a recognizable style: technically clean, unmannered, and precise. This was noted when the National Ballet made its first visit to London and other European cities in 1972. Critics remarked that the dancers had something of the elegant bearing and strong footwork associated with the Royal Ballet, with an additional measure of vitality characteristic of North American stage performers.

The company's image changed significantly during its second decade. In 1964 it shifted its Toronto seasons from the small stage of the Royal Alexandra Theatre, an architectural gem of Edwardian elegance, where it had appeared since January 1953, to the vast stage of the four-year-old O'Keefe Centre. As other large, all-purpose theaters were being built or planned in several of Canada's major cities, Franca judged that the company was ready to expand to fill Toronto's main performance facility.

Because of an improvement in the company's financial circumstances during the later 1960s, thanks to government grants and expanded fundraising activities, Franca was able to enlarge the repertory with ballets by internationally celebrated choreographers, including Roland Petit, John Neumeier, Kenneth MacMillan, Eliot Feld, and others. Lavish productions of full-length ballets were added to the repertory, beginning with John Cranko's *Romeo and Juliet* in 1964. Later that year Erik Bruhn staged North America's first production of *La Sylphide,* and Franca restaged her own production of *The Nutcracker.* In 1967 Bruhn mounted his controversial *Swan Lake,* and Franca staged a full-length *Cinderella.* Peter

NATIONAL BALLET OF CANADA. Members of the ensemble in *Kraanerg,* commissioned from Roland Petit and first performed at the opening of the National Arts Centre, Ottawa, in 1969. With mobile scenery by Victor Vasarely and Yvaral, it was set to music by Iannis Xenakis. (Photograph by Ken Bell; used by permission of the National Ballet of Canada.)

Wright staged a new production of *Giselle* in 1970, and, with momentous consequences, Rudolf Nureyev mounted his version of *The Sleeping Beauty* for the National Ballet in 1972. As Bruhn had done in *Swan Lake,* Nureyev attempted to make the premier danseur the dramatic and dancing focus of his production. The company thus acquired eccentric versions of the two most important Tchaikovsky ballets.

Both Bruhn and Nureyev had important effects on the National Ballet. Their charismatic presences were inspirational, stimulating the company to higher levels of artistry. With Nureyev (who had first danced with the company in January 1965, replacing Bruhn in *La Sylphide*) came a contract with Sol Hurok for a large-scale U.S. tour culminating in an appearance at New York's Metropolitan Opera House. (In later years the company paid repeated visits to New York, both with and without Nureyev as a guest artist.) Nureyev's influence and encouragement significantly advanced a number of the dancers' careers, notably those of Kain and Augustyn. Nureyev also danced with the company in Canada and joined its second tour to Europe in 1975.

The association with the great Russian dancer undoubtedly brought the company international celebrity, but it also generated criticism. In a *New York Times* article of 27 July 1975, the Canadian journalist and critic John Fraser suggested that Nureyev's involvement with the National Ballet had become a liability; he said that the Russian superstar overshadowed the company's male principals and claimed that he used the company merely as a convenient backdrop for his own performing career. Although Fraser's remarks were denounced by the company's dancers and by such other leading figures as Martha Graham, they permanently soured Nureyev's relations with the National Ballet.

Erik Bruhn's relationship with the company was, arguably, more fundamental in effect than that of Nureyev. After 1964, his work as a frequent guest teacher in the school contributed to marked improvement among the dancers, particularly the men. As a guest artist with the company, dancing the leading roles in the classics, his high technical standards and personal emphasis on stylistic purity were also beneficial. Finding his work with the National Ballet particularly congenial, he served as resident producer from 1973 to 1976.

In 1973, Franca announced that she was stepping aside as artistic director at the end of the 1973/74 season to leave David Haber, her co–artistic director since 1972, in sole command. Her intention then was not to sever links with the company she had founded but to devote more time to work with the dancers in the studio. Her plans were scuttled, however, when Haber was forced to resign as artistic director in June 1975. The company's board thus effectively ended the Franca regime.

NATIONAL BALLET OF CANADA. Karen Kain as the Sylphide and Frank Augustyn as James in a 1975 performance of August Bournonville's *La Sylphide,* first staged for the company by Erik Bruhn in 1964. (Photograph © 1975 by Linda Vartoogian; used by permission.)

The Grant Years: 1976–1983. After an extensive international search, the company appointed Alexander Grant as the new artistic director in July 1976. The New Zealand–born Grant had spent thirty years in England with the Royal Ballet, where he had risen to become one of the century's greatest *demi-caractère* dancers. [*See the entry on Grant.*] He had known Franca since his earliest days in England, and his outlook was not dissimilar to hers. He planned no immediate changes to the company's artistic policy, nor did he deviate from it significantly during the seven years he stood at its head. His directorship was nevertheless notably impressive.

Grant's long personal and professional association with Frederick Ashton enabled him to acquire several of the great choreographer's ballets. The company's production of *La Fille Mal Gardée,* first presented in Toronto in November 1976, supervised by Ashton himself, was a triumph. Over the next three years the company presented *Monotones II, The Dream, Les Patineurs,* and *The Two Pigeons.* The wealth of solo parts, many of them character roles, in these Ashton works helped extend the company's

NATIONAL BALLET OF CANADA. Frederick Ashton's *Monotones II* entered the company's repertory during the 1976/77 season. James Kudelka, Nadia Potts, and Miguel Garcia formed the original cast. Subsequently, Kudelka himself would become an important contributor of new choreographies to the repertory and, in 1996, the artistic director of the company. (Photograph © by Andrew Oxenham; used by permission.)

performing and dramatic talents. Ashton's musical and technical demands also enlarged the dancers' stylistic capabilities, which had a positive effect on the performance of many other ballets in the repertory.

Grant increased the number of annual performances and urged the dancers, whom even Franca had sometimes accused of being too complacent and dependent, to accept greater responsibility for their own artistic growth. By programming more mixed bills, Grant opened up leading roles to more of the company's emerging artists, and, although he took considerable risks in casting relatively unproven talents in important roles, he was mostly rewarded with success. The company, sometimes charged by both foreign and domestic critics with being too prim and restrained on stage, gained a new vitality. The general level of performance rose measurably, and while the dancers sometimes looked less meticulously prepared than in earlier years, this effect was offset by a heightened spontaneity.

Aware of weakness in the company's male ranks, Grant paid special attention to raising the level of technical proficiency among the men, to broadening their performing abilities, and to encouraging their growth as artists. By the end of his directorship, observers remarked favorably on his achievements in developing such young artists as Raymond Smith, Peter Ottmann, Kevin Pugh, and David Roxander, among many others.

Like Franca before him, however, Grant was often criticized for his failure to attract a major choreographer to work on a continuing basis with the company and to contribute a significant body of original works to its repertory. Lacking a resident choreographer of recognized stature, the company had become better known for the opulence of its full-length productions and the excellence of its dancers than for presentation of major new works. Grant's failure on this score, if such it can be termed, was not for want of trying, for he did his best to encourage the work of choreographers within the company, notably Ann Ditchburn, James Kudelka, and Constantin Patsalas.

Kudelka, who had begun to choreograph for the company while he was still a student at the school, made a number of works during the 1970s, notably *Washington Square* (1977, revised 1979). The Greek-born Patsalas, too, made several works for the company, including *Black Angels* (1976) and *Rite of Spring* (1979). These works showed such promise that both Kudelka and Patsalas were appointed company choreographers in 1980. Kudelka, however, defected to Les Grands Ballets Canadiens in Montreal in 1981, claiming that the National Ballet lacked commitment to creative activity. The same complaint had also caused the earlier departure of Ditchburn. Patsalas continued to contribute to the repertory through the 1980s.

Grant also introduced works by Glen Tetley, Vicente Nebrada, Maurice Béjart, Jerome Robbins, and other notable choreographers. Setting off a flurry of publicity, he

NATIONAL BALLET OF CANADA. Gregory Osborne as Prince Siegfried and Gisella Witkowsky as Odile in an early 1980s performance of the Black Swan pas de deux from act 3 of *Swan Lake,* mounted for the company in 1967 by Erik Bruhn. Bruhn's staging retained most of the familiar choreography from the classic Petipa-Ivanov version but radically altered the emphasis of the story to give greater prominence to the role of the prince. (Photograph © by Andrew Oxenham; used by permission.)

invited Peter Schaufuss, a company principal since 1977, to mount North America's first full-length production of Bournonville's *Napoli,* which was generally acclaimed both by local critics and by the many foreign reviewers who attended its premiere in Toronto in November 1981. A full-length *Don Quixote,* staged by Nicholas Beriozoff, was added to the repertory a year later.

All Grant's efforts earned him, finally, little praise and less support. Despite his achievements, which were clearly evident in the company's performances, he was accused of failing to provide strong artistic leadership and for causing a decline in company morale. His contract was prematurely terminated in 1983.

The Bruhn Years: 1983–1986. Grant's successor was Erik Bruhn, who took over the artistic directorship of the National Ballet of Canada in July 1983 amid hopes that he would push the company into the kind of international prominence that his predecessors had never managed to achieve. Like them, however, Bruhn had to accommodate a governing body obliged to deal with perennially difficult financial conditions and consequently sensitive to the impact of artistic policy on box-office revenues. Circumstances seemed to dictate that the company would remain true to its relatively conservative heritage.

NATIONAL BALLET OF CANADA. Kimberley Glasco and John Alleyne in Tetley's *La Ronde,* set to music by Erich Korngold. Tetley created this work for the company in 1987. (Photograph © by Andrew Oxenham; used by permission.)

NATIONAL BALLET OF CANADA. Rex Harrington as Oedipus in *The Sphinx,* created for the company by Glen Tetley in 1982. A dancer of considerable power and expressiveness, Harrington was also something of a "matinee idol" during the 1980s. (Photograph © by Andrew Oxenham; used by permission.)

Almost from the beginning of his directorship, however, Bruhn struck out in new directions. He sought to enrich the repertory with works by Canadian choreographers, but he looked especially for works by choreographers, of whatever nationality, whose vocabulary of movement combined both the idiom of modern dance and the lexicon of classical ballet. Chief among these was the American choreographer Glen Tetley, from whom Bruhn commissioned several major works. The first of these ballets, *Alice,* set to a score by David del Tredici, was presented in 1986, shortly before Bruhn's untimely death.

Bruhn's leadership, though tragically brief, was inspirational for the dancers and invigorating for audiences. He had clearly articulated ideas about the place of classical ballet in the wider realm of dance and about what ballet needed to secure its survival into the twenty-first century. Notably, Bruhn made the National Ballet more emphatically part of the Canadian dance community. He went out of his way to attend performances by local companies and to commission works from such Canadian modern dance choreographers as David Earle (*Realm,* 1985), Robert Desrosiers (*Blue Snake,* 1985), and Danny Grossman (*Hot

House: Thriving on a Riff, 1986). Bruhn continued to support new work by his friend Patsalas, who had held the title of resident choreographer since 1982, and he encouraged the early choreographic careers of company soloists David Allan and John Alleyne. Bruhn also supervised the staging in 1984 of a popular addition to the company's repertory of full-length works, one planned by Grant, John Cranko's *Onegin.*

Over the years, Bruhn made invaluable contributions to the artistic life of the National Ballet of Canada, and his accomplishments as the company's director were many. His death, in Toronto on 1 April 1986, was thus much lamented and a severe blow to the company.

Interim Period: 1986–1989. Following Bruhn's wishes, the board of directors left the company's artistic direction and administration in the hands of Valerie Wilder and Lynn Wallis, who had been, respectively, Bruhn's artistic administrator and artistic coordinator. Patsalas continued as resident choreographer, as well as assuming a role as artistic adviser, but he resigned later in 1986 as a result of acrimonious and irreconcilable differences with Wilder and Wallis concerning the company's leadership. In 1987, Glen Tetley was officially appointed artistic associate and became an influential member of the artistic team.

The emphasis in company programming continued Bruhn's shift toward a more contemporary repertory and included two important creations by Tetley, *La Ronde* (1987) and *Tagore* (1989). John Alleyne began to emerge as a choreographer with *Have Steps, Will Travel* (1988), *Trapdance* (1988), and *Blue-Eyed Jack* (1989). Also, David Allan created his first full-company work, *Masada* (1987), but he left soon after to pursue his choreographic career in the United States. Ronald Hynd's *The Merry Widow* was also acquired in 1986. The Wilder-Wallis regime, with Tetley's prestige as support, also won the company return engagements at New York's Metropolitan Opera House in 1986 and 1988.

Although Tetley regretted the move, the National Ballet's board of directors, apparently with Wallis and Wilder's concurrence, resolved to search for a new artistic director. Reid Anderson was eventually appointed, and he assumed the post in July 1989, with Wilder continuing as associate director.

The Anderson Years: 1989–1996. Born and initially trained in Canada, Anderson had spent the bulk of his career in Germany, working with the Stuttgart Ballet as a dancer and ballet master. He returned to Canada in 1986 and was soon involved with Ballet British Columbia, taking over as its artistic director from Annette av Paul in 1987. Anderson thus came to Toronto as, in many respects, an outsider to the National Ballet's traditions, yet he quickly established himself as an effective and popular leader.

Anderson's directorship came during a particularly intense period of economic recession and declining govern-

NATIONAL BALLET OF CANADA. Members of the ensemble in the "Waltz of the Snowflakes" in James Kudelka's production of *The Nutcracker,* mounted for the Christmas season in 1995. (Photograph © by Andrew Oxenham; used by permission.)

ment grants. One of his early disappointments was the collapse in 1990 of an ambitious plan for construction of a suitable ballet-opera house in Toronto to be shared with the Canadian Opera Company. Despite this, Anderson committed himself to sustaining the National Ballet artistically and materially. By general consensus, he is judged to have succeeded admirably. He made important additions to the repertory, staged well-balanced seasons, took the company on ambitious overseas tours, and reaffirmed the company's essentially classical roots while simultaneously commissioning important new works.

One of Anderson's early moves was to appoint John Alleyne as resident choreographer in 1990. When Alleyne left two years later to become artistic director of Ballet British Columbia, Anderson scored a major coup by coaxing the choreographer James Kudelka back into the National Ballet fold. Kudelka, by then a famous artist much in demand by the leading North American ballet companies, was given broadly defined responsibilities and the title artist in residence.

Kudelka had already created *Pastorale* for the company in 1990. While continuing to choreograph for other companies, Kudelka added a number of new works to the National Ballet's repertory: *Musings* (1991), *The Miraculous Mandarin* (1993), *Spring Awakening* (1994), *The Actress* (1994), and an ambitious and well-received restaging of *The Nutcracker* (1995). His 1977 dramatic ballet *Washington Square* was also successfully revived in 1995. Kudelka's knowledge of modern dance, combined with his deep respect for ballet classicism and innate, sensitive musicality, had a positive impact on dancers and audience alike. [*See the entry on Kudelka.*]

Anderson also introduced new works by other major choreographers, including William Forsythe, Jiří Kylián, Paul Taylor, Antony Tudor, and Jerome Robbins. A notable commission was Forsythe's *The Second Detail* (1991), and notable additions to the Ashton repertory were *A Month in the Country* and *Symphonic Variations.* John Neumeier returned to the company after a long absence to create *Now and Then* in 1992. Anderson also commissioned works from the rising young Canadian choreographers Christopher House (*Cafe Dances,* 1992) and Jean Grand-Maître (*Frames of Mind,* 1994). Nor were evening-length ballets neglected. Anderson acquired Ben Stevenson's *Cinderella* and Kenneth MacMillan's *Manon;* he restaged John Cranko's *The Taming of the Shrew* and had Cranko's *Romeo and Juliet* completely redesigned.

Exasperated by continuing cuts in government grants despite the company's indisputable success, Anderson decided to resign his post at the end of the 1995/96 season. Recognized as an artistic director of rare accomplishments, he was soon chosen as the new head of the Stuttgart Ballet, where he took up his duties at the beginning of the 1996/97 season.

NATIONAL BALLET OF CANADA. Robert Tewsley as Des Grieux and Martine Lamy in the title role of Kenneth MacMillan's *Manon,* staged for the company in the spring of 1996. (Photograph © by Cylla von Tiedemann; used by permission.)

Prospects for the Future. The National Ballet's board of directors then selected Kudelka as Anderson's successor, nominating him as artistic director to serve in equal partnership with Valerie Wilder as executive director. Kudelka's acceptance of the appointment came as a surprise to many, who believed that his main interest lay in choreography. Nevertheless, his appointment was generally seen as an encouraging commitment on the company's part to artistic growth. Apart from being the first truly homegrown artistic director the company has had, Kudelka is also the first well-established choreographer to assume its direction. Soon after beginning his new job, Kudelka expressed a desire to rework some of the company's aging productions of full-length classics and to introduce into the repertory some of the works he has created for other companies. He also seemed ready to deal with the continuing threat of declining public subsidies, which by 1996 threatened to undermine much of what the company had accomplished during the previous four decades.

[*See also* Canada, *article on* Theatrical Dance, *and the entries on the principal figures mentioned herein.*]

BIBLIOGRAPHY

Bell, Ken, and Celia Franca. *The National Ballet of Canada: A Celebration.* Toronto, 1978.

Crabb, Michael. "Getting There: The National Ballet of Canada Turns Thirty." *Ballet News* 3 (November 1981): 10–18.

Macdonald, Brian. "The Impact of British Ballet on the Canadian Dance Scene." *The Dancing Times* (April 1963): 415–421.

Maynard, Olga. "Idea, Image, and Purpose: Ballet in Canada Today." *Dance Magazine* (April 1971): 32–65.

Neufeld, James. *Power to Rise: The Story of the National Ballet of Canada.* Toronto, 1996.

Odom, Selma Landen, and Penelope Reed Doob. "The National Ballet of Canada." *Dance Magazine* (March 1977): 59–67.

Oliphant, Betty. *Miss O: My Life in Dance.* Winnipeg, 1996.

Whittaker, Herbert. *Canada's National Ballet.* Toronto, 1967.

Wyman, Max. *Dance Canada: An Illustrated History.* Vancouver, 1989.

MICHAEL CRABB

NATIONAL BALLET OF SENEGAL. A country of approximately 76,124 square miles, Senegal is situated on the Atlantic coast, at the westernmost point of West Africa. Through the Partition Treaties of the Conference of Berlin (1884–1885), the continent of Africa was divided into colonial segments by the European powers—France, Great Britain, Spain, Italy, Belgium, Germany, the Netherlands, and Portugal. After the segmentation, with the exception of five English-speaking colonies, France ruled all of West Africa, including what is now Senegal. Senegal has fifteen to seventeen language groups, with the Wolof (30 percent), Serers (17 percent), and Peuls (12 percent) constituting the majority. Senegal has a rich and diverse population, with separate and distinct groups, each having its own musical culture. They are bound together by a common language, Wolof, which approximately 95 percent speak regardless of their indigenous language; this is not the case in other nations of West Africa. Senegal was predominately animistic until the eleventh century, when a Peul chief was converted to Islam. Today Senegal is primarily a Wolof and French-speaking Muslim nation. Senegal therefore has a triple heritage: traditional animism; an Arabic heritage through conversion to Islam; and a European heritage imposed by French colonialism.

Senegal gained its independence from France on 4 April 1960, and Leopold Sedar Senghor, an intellectual artistic man, became its president. The National Dance Company of Senegal was also formed in 1960; the man who inspired and created the company was Maurice Sonar Senghor, nephew of the president. Although officially created in 1960, the company's founding began in the 1950s, with Maurice Sonar Senghor's nightclub act in Paris. Originally in France to follow a family tradition of politics, he soon succumbed to the lure of the theater. His aristocratic family immediately disinherited him, but, undaunted, he pursued his career. He formed his first artistic troupe with African actors, singers, and dancers. He also read poetry that gave audiences an insight into Africa's poets, such as Leopold S. Senghor, Damas, and Birago Diop. Audiences

NATIONAL BALLET OF SENEGAL. Men and women of the ensemble performing a theatrical version of traditional dance in New York, 1981. (Photograph © 1981 by Johan Elbers; used by permission.)

applauded his act, and this was during a period of great strife for his people, who were still living under colonial rule in Senegal. He soon decided to become a spokesman against colonial rule, using his nightclub act as a platform. Often the police would enter, drag him off the stage, and shackle him in handcuffs before a stunned, horrified, and bewildered audience. He was taken to the dungeons of the police station where he was beaten for expressing his views against colonialism. This happened several times, only serving to embitter him and lead him to further protest.

Senghor had as a goal to establish the first modern African theater in Senegal. He returned to Senegal in 1954 and there became the director of Théâtre du Palais, which gave him the opportunity to create a company of Senegalese performers. To create a national dance company, he visited approximately two hundred villages to view more than two thousand singers and dancers; he shot yards of film and taped many hours of songs from various parts of the country. With the advant of independence in 1960, he founded the first National Ballet of Senegal, which had its European debut in the Théâtre des Nations in Paris. The troupe would later perform in London, Brussels, Stockholm, Berlin, and several cities in Australia. A new theater was constructed in Dakar, called Théâtre National Daniel Sorano. In 1964, Senghor became the first director of the theater, the realization of his dream.

The National Dance Company of Keita Fodeba is also linked to the brilliance of Maurice Senghor. In 1950, Keita Fodeba, who went to France to study to be a magistrate, also succumbed to the lure of the theater. He joined Maurice Senghor's troupe, then created his own company while in Senegal, and later returned to Guinea, where his company Les Ballets Africains de Keita Fodeba became the National Ballet of Guinea. The National Dance Company of Senegal made its New York debut under favorable circumstances—the tail end of the cultural-awakening movement of the late 1960s. African Americans were then shedding their poor self-image and creating positive new images. Essentially, the audience that greeted the National Dance Company of Senegal was largely one of black Americans with mighty Afro hairstyles who came with an eagerness and a desire to share in their ancestry, which had been brutally stripped from them.

In 1974, auditions were held in Dakar for new artists. Although many were hired, the most exciting ones were Taco, a thirteen-year-old accomplished dancer, and Samba Diallo Fula, a Peul acrobat. In 1984, Maurice Senghor retired from his post as director-general of Théâtre National Daniel Sorano and was replaced by Pathe Gueye, whose background was not rooted in theater arts. Today, the National Dance Company has second- and third-generation dancers as well as new artists. Many performers from the first dance company are scattered throughout the United States and Paris. These artists have made more than twenty-two world tours and, exposed to a different way of life, have essentially outgrown the opportunities of Senegal. Senghor was director-general for twenty years. During that time he established the company and, with his great vision, created four theater troupes, including a dramatic troupe, a second dance company, and an instrumental ensemble. In 1985 he created the Organisation pour la Promotion des Échanges Artistiques Internationaux, which houses a performing group and a center for the study of oral sub-Saharan African traditions. For his thirty years of theater work he was awarded Senegal's highest distinction of honor, La Dignité de Grand-Croix de l'Ordre du Mérite Senegalais; he is referred to as the "Father of African Theater."

BIBLIOGRAPHY

Bonner, Jeanne, and Leif Stahl. *Senegal, Mali, The Gambia*. Dakar, Senegal, 1977.

Goss, Wade Tynes Pretlow, and Julinda Lewis Williams. "A Call for Valid Black Dance Criticism." *Congress on Research in Dance, Dance Research Annual* 10 (1979).

Green, Doris. *Sangba, the Origin of the Djimbe*. New York, 1986.

Knight, Roderic. "Mandinka Drumming." *African Arts* 7.4 (1994): 24–35.

Ministry of Information and Cultural Affairs. *Musical Instruments of Liberia*. Monrovia, 1968.

Nikiprowetzky, Tolia. *Trois Aspects de la Musique Africaine: Mauritanie, Senegal, Niger*. Paris, 1963.

Remy, Mylene. *Senegal Today*. Paris, 1974.

Senghor, Leopold Sedar. *Négritude, Arabite et Francite: Réflexions sur le problème de la culture*. Beyrouth, 1969.

INTERVIEWS. Maurice Sonar Senghor and Mamadou Ly, by Doris Green, 1972.

ARCHIVE. Private collection of Doris Green.

VIDEOTAPE. *Djembefola* (the man who makes a *djembe* speak), France, 1991. The story of Mamady Keita, featured drummer of National Djoliba Ballet of Guinea, West Africa.

DORIS GREEN

NATIVE AMERICAN DANCE. [*This entry comprises nine articles to discuss dance traditions of indigenous peoples in various regions of North America and the scholarship of and writing about these practices:*

For discussion of specific topics and peoples, see Ghost Dance; Hopi Dance; Navajo Dance; Powwow; Pueblo Dance; Tigua Dance; *and* Yaqui Dance.]

An Overview

During the several glaciations of the Pleistocene epoch, Eurasia and North America were one vast paleoarctic land area on which plants, animals, and humans lived. When the last glaciation melted back, from fifteen thousand to ten thousand years ago, the meltwater caused a worldwide sea level rise that covered much of the land area between the Siberian and Alaskan peninsulas, forming the Bering Strait. Those peoples who continued to live on the North American continent were therefore culturally related to the peoples of Eurasia, and they continued to practice similar social and ceremonial traditions while developing others. Some remained related by language, kinship, trade, or treaty; others became isolated by ecological features.

Today their descendants are collectively called Native Americans in North America, or American Indians. For thousands of years they successfully migrated throughout the Western Hemisphere, developing all types of societies in every ecological region. Since the 1500s, colonizing and Christianizing Europeans have settled the Americas, recording much about the Native American cultural life they experienced—even while, as an alien culture, causing its change or demise in many instances, whether on purpose or not. The accounts, the persistence of many Native American peoples, and the reconstructions from ceremonial and oral tradition provide a base for understanding the features of the various dance traditions.

Native Americans danced to ask the supernatural for sustenance, to celebrate human relationships, to mark life stages, and to heal. They invoked and appeased the spirits of the elements, the plants, and the animals, as well as the Great Spirit. Often wearing masks, they impersonated or embodied spirits.

Regional Features. The subsistence patterns of the various ecological regions of North America influenced the dances to some extent. The paleolithic hunters and gatherers followed game animals throughout the hemisphere, and some were able to continue this lifestyle successfully in areas of abundance until European contact. Others became specialized collectors, farmers, and herders. Native American agricultural societies hold dance ceremonies for their most important crops—corn, beans, and squash—just as plant gatherers hold ceremonies for wild rice, acorns, pine nuts, or maple sap. Those living near water may focus on fish, waterfowl, or whales. Some revere totemic animals from the mythological past, such as the raven, turtle, or bear in their dances; some dance to attract and appease the spirits of game, such as deer, walrus, or buffalo. On the Great Plains, the celebration of the buffalo has continued long after the demise of the great herds.

Within their diverse North American habitats, Native Americans developed some distinctive dance patterns; some dances have also been adopted or adapted from other groups during visits or migrations. Sometimes psychoactive plants, such as tobacco, jimson weed, the peyote cactus, or hallucenogenic mushrooms have been used to enhance the ceremonial or trance effect for either the shaman (medicine man or woman) or for all the participants. The characteristic dances can be grouped in large geographic regions, albeit with imprecise boundaries.

The ceremonial dances of the woodlands east of the Mississippi River were influenced by hunting and harvesting rites, the medicine societies, and the interactions of the social divisions called clans or moieties. Clowns were often featured wearing wooden masks; open dance circles move counterclockwise; antiphony and improvisation are important. In the southern part of this region, spiral dances were common; in the northern, solo peace-pipe (tobacco) dances were common.

On the Great Plains, ceremonial dance was important to the age-grade societies, to male societies, to the buffalo and hunt cults, and to agricultural rites for crops planted seasonally along river banks. Some features of Plains dances include clowns with hide masks; closed clockwise circles; the sacred number four (referring to the cardinal directions); the sacred peyote cult introduced from Mexico. Sun dances were also performed.

Most Native Americans of the Southwest became agriculturalists, so seasonal ceremonies focus on corn in summer and on animals in winter. Their sacred societies perform dances by both sexes, featuring clowns in hide masks or paint, single- or double-file dances, circles, elaborate formations, the number four, and symbolic gestures. Tribes that were formerly nomadic emphasize medicine rites, girls' puberty celebrations, dancers in hide masks impersonating spirits, single file, and social circles.

Peoples from the western plateau to the Pacific coast perform dances for mortuary rites, trance cults, wild fruit rites, and spirit impersonations for boys' initiations, employing parallel lines, circles, and solos by masked dancers.

In the Pacific Northwest, masked spirit impersonations are performed for initiates and the community. These societies also hold ostentatious gift-giving feasts (called potlatches in English). Raven and salmon cults are important in this area. Dances are characterized by vibration, ecstatic frenzy, mime gesture, and solo displays by high-caste men or women.

Some characteristics of dances from the subarctic and boreal regions of Canada are the bear cult, mortuary rites, trance cures by shamans, figure eights, and closed circles. The Arctic coastal peoples have bear and whale cults, trance cures by shamans, comical animal mime in wooden masks, and social gatherings featuring solo improvisational song and/or dance performances and contests by both men and women. These last are held during the long-awaited, fun-filled weeks of visiting, feasting, and trading by related Eskimoan groups during the six-month-long Arctic winter night.

There are many exceptions to these general patterns. In the eastern woodlands, the Algonkians of the western Great Lakes share features with their eastern neighbors, but they also share with the Great Plains in having pipe dances, the ritual number four, and clockwise circling. In Wisconsin, wild rice ceremonialism replaces that associated with corn. The Mesquakie of Iowa (formerly of Michigan) developed an important buffalo cult. The Plains Ojibwe, in their migration to Manitoba and North Dakota, kept their medicine society and Dream Dance but adopted the Sun Dance and the Grass Dance.

These relatively recent historical shifts after myriad prehistoric events have blurred any regional boundaries, dispersing linguistically related groups while enriching and complicating myth and choreography.

Dance Styles. A characteristic Native American dance-movement style involves a slight forward tilt in posture, forward raising of the knee, flatfooted stamping, toe–heel action, muscular relaxation, and restraint in gesture. In its details, the style varies from area to area, from group to group, from dance to dance, and even from one individual to another. In agricultural dances, the body is even held generally upright, with an easy carriage. Male war dances may include gyrations and flexions of the torso. Women's dances are more subdued, with smaller movements. In vision dances, the body tends to become distorted.

Generally the dancing contains a pulsation, a vertical bounce in the knees that is sometimes a double bounce, and occasionally there may be an accent placed on every second step. In some dances the arms execute improvised or codified gestures that are specialized for men or for women. For example, Pueblo clowns and singers in the Corn Dance invoke the four rain gods for their crops with symbolic gestures that are fitted to the words. Onondaga and Cayuga women of northern New York and Canada mime harvest work in a dance borrowed from the refugee Tutelo tribe.

Dance and Music. The pulsation of the body in Native American dance binds the movement to the accompaniment of percussion and song. The identification is complete in self-accompanied dances, such as the stationary Deer Dance of the Tewa and the progressive Snake Dance of the Cherokee. The singer-dancers accent every second beat with rattles and jingles on their bodies. This beat also prevails in separate accompaniments by a team or a chorus. Other types of stress meters are less common, and a break in the beat is a rarity. In some southwestern traditions, the performers change beat temporarily, but they then return to the usual beat. The tempo is generally

NATIVE AMERICAN DANCE: An Overview. Some of the earliest European portrayals of the New World were sketched by explorers and then reinterpreted and published by others. This engraving of Native Americans in Florida, "dancing for their new queen," was made by Theodore de Bry (1528–1598), a Flemish German. His depiction of the dance formation as a circle is probably correct, but all other details in his engraving are suspect. The "new queen" on the dais is a European concept, and the dancers certainly look more like plump, flaxen-haired Dutch maidens than Native American women. (Photograph from the Department of Library Services, American Museum of Natural History, New York [no. 324279]; used by permission.)

NATIVE AMERICAN DANCE: An Overview. The American artist and author George Catlin (1796–1872) devoted himself to the study of American Indians, making many drawings and paintings during his visits among tribal peoples. This oil sketch from the 1830s shows the Green Corn Dance of the Minataree (later called the Hidatsa), a Siouan-speaking people of the northern Great Plains. A first-fruits ceremony and rite of thanksgiving, the Green Corn Dance was performed as soon as ears of young, green corn could be picked, roasted, and eaten, well before the corn crop was mature and ready for harvest. This ceremony was also performed in other Native American agricultural societies. (Photograph from the Department of Library Services, American Museum of Natural History, New York [no. 15149]; used by permission.)

steady, whether slow or fast, but at times it accelerates. Often a suite contains both a slow and a fast dance; as another binary device, some song types have two parts. During a percussion tremolo the dancers shake or amble; during the duple beat in the second half, they engage in rhythmic footwork.

Often the human voice pulsates, either with the relaxed, deep tone of woodland Iroquois and southwestern Pueblo men or the strident tension of Plains singers. Pulsation is evident among the southwestern Navaho and, more intensely, among the Dogrib of Canada's Northwest Territory. The stress accents of the voices synchronize with those of the instruments, but the tunes have their own rhythmic structure, which is not interpreted by the dancers.

The most common instruments are hide drums of many kinds, from the small light-toned woodland water drums, to the tall Pueblo drums, to the huge booming powwow drums. Rattles are made of available materials—gourds, turtle shells, claws, horns, and, recently, tin cans. The Yaqui of Arizona and Mexico's state of Sonora use the indigenous scraper with gourd drum, *sistrum,* and cane flute, as well as the European violin, guitar, or harp.

Role of Women. Men predominate as musicians, but sometimes women join the singing. They also sing in their own mortuary or medicine societies and often compose songs for them.

During dances, the prestige of women varies. In the Great Plains, women traditionally played a secondary role, but today young women may even don feathered headdresses and join in war dancing. Along the northwest coast of the United States and Canada, and among Native American agriculturalists, women enjoy considerable prestige. They perform in a subdued manner, sometimes with their own special steps, but they often join men in the line or circle. Sometimes they partner with men, but the partnering usually has little erotic connotation.

Among the Iroquois—a matrilineal society—matrons are honored in their longhouses. They cook the ceremonial feasts and manage the summertime first-fruit ceremonies. They also manage some male ceremonies, like the False Face (or Wooden Face) Dance. In their *enskanye* dance, they symbolize the life-giving spirits of corn, beans, and squash. In the ritual of the women planters, they walk in a circle, shake tortoise rattles, and sing to bring about ripening crops and healthy children.

Animal Mime. Animal dances are usually a male prerogative, but graceful creatures like swans may be assigned to women. The mimetic rounds of the Iroquois are shared by both sexes, although men provide the music.

Since Native Americans had originally depended on wildlife for their subsistence, they respected the spirits of animals. They danced in supplication or in appeasement to the spirits, as well as in thanks for hunting success. Some of these dances continue to be performed. The enactments may be realistic in movement and costume, as in the Buffalo Dance of the Plains and the Fox Dance of the Inuit (Eskimo). Sometimes they are stylized but retain the essence of the creature, as in the Game Animals Dance of the Pueblo and the Buffalo Dance of the Cherokee. The dances may be comical, like the Raccoon Dance of the Ojibwe, or terrifying, like the Raven Dance of the Kwakiutl.

The animals depicted are usually those native to the area, but introduced animals sometimes appear, such as the horses, goats, bulls, and chickens that came with Europeans. The hobby-horses of Santa Ana Pueblo are derived from the horses brought to Mexico from Spain—from the Spanish mounted expeditions that explored northward from Mexico into their territory.

NATIVE AMERICAN DANCE: An Overview. George Catlin entitled this elaborate painting *War Dance of the Apaches against the Navajos* (1855). The circling Apache warriors wield weapons and shields in ceremonial preparation for attacks on the farm villages of the Navajo, where stored food and supplies might be raided and where wives and slaves might be captured. The six Apache tribes—the Chiricahua, Jicarilla, Kiowa Apache, Lipan, Mescalero, and Western Apache—ranged widely over the American Southwest. (Photograph from the Department of Library Services, American Museum of Natural History, New York [no. 324939]; used by permission.)

Male Ceremonial Clowns. Native American male ceremonial clowns can be in animal form or ghostly, funny, awesome, chthonic (possessed of power drawn from the Earth), or celestial; they may also have mixtures of some of these qualities. By identification with the spirits of the dead and with animals, fire, or clouds, clowns possess powers for fertility, weather control, and cures. They often sprinkle ashes or water as they dance. Their reversed actions and speech-echo reversals are found in rites for the dead. The Iroquois False Faces wiggle their hips, straddle their legs, and turn out their toes, while shaking turtle rattles. In a modern vein, Pueblo *koshare* may parody the Roman Catholic mass, or Cherokee *boogers* may ridicule lascivious white traders.

The dramatic effectiveness of the clowns is heightened by their disguise, which may consist of white body paint with black stripes and a face-concealing headdress. Depending on natural resources, grotesque masks may be carved out of wood, as for the False Face society, the Yaqui *pascola*s, and the Inuit walrus masks. The Yaqui *chapayeka,* Papago *djidjur,* and Tewa *tsaviyo* fashion hide into helmets with big ears and noses. Other materials used for masks include cornhusks, feathers, gourds, and stiffened cloth. The garments may consist of furs, rags, women's skirts, shawls, or even European work clothing.

Borrowing and Diffusion. Borrowing and diffusion have affected Native American dances for centuries, and this process continues today. For example, the Comanche Dance of the southwestern Pueblos is an example of relatively recent borrowing from the Great Plains; it involves poking fun at the Pueblo people's former enemy, who rode into the settlements and raided. In double file, the men bounce back and forth wearing Plains war bonnets and using a Plains war-dance hop. The women shuffle demurely in place with a gentle Pueblo step. Other borrowing may be from popular social dances, such as the twist, which may also be incorporated into traditional dances—often for satiric purposes.

A dance that became widely popular in the East is the Snake Dance of the Cherokee, originally perhaps a fertility dance but now a social group dance. A male leader guides a long line of miscellaneous participants in a counterclockwise run, winding into a spiral and then unwinding. In the South, the leader gestures with a song phrase and the followers echo; the Seminole of Florida have a quadruple spiral at the four corners of the grounds; the Penobscot of Maine line up in a double file; Wisconsin Algonkians conclude with a double-file bridge and run-through, as in the Virginia reel; the Flathead of Montana use a separate drum and song, thus avoiding the Snake Dance's unfamiliar antiphony; and the Cherokees, both in their southeastern homeland as well as those relocated to Oklahoma, retain their agricultural symbolism in the Snake Dance. Most groups consider this dance great fun.

Another dance spread to many tribes by the waterways, for political relations—the Calumet Dance or Pipe-of-Peace Dance for expert youths. It originated near the pipestone (soapstone) quarry in Minnesota as a swaying dance performed by successive soloists with a feathered pipe. During its spread down the Mississippi River and along the Missouri and Yellowstone, it became a duet and then a foursome. On the Platte, it fused with the Eagle Dance of the Pawnee *hako,* a possible borrowing from Mexico. In that form it reached the Iroquois east on the

NATIVE AMERICAN DANCE: An Overview. This engraving by Charles Geoffrey, made from a sketch by Carl Bodmer (c.1832), shows a group of Mandan women performing a religious dance using a sacred robe made from the skin of a rare white buffalo. The Great Plains cultures developed around the buffalo hunt. The huge herds provided food, utensils, and socioreligious meaning to the Plains peoples, who venerated the animals and appeased their spirits in ceremonies for abundance. (Photograph from the Department of Library Services, American Museum of Natural History, New York [no. 3119820]; used by permission.)

Ohio River, where it survives as a rite performed by four youths. The Eagle Dance became famous on the Rio Grande as a showy duet. In intertribal shows it survives as a contest in which pairs of youths confront each other to a song with a binary beat. The eighteenth century had been a period of burgeoning political alliances, when northern and southern dance patterns met.

During the nineteenth century, eastern traditions met western in the Oklahoma Territory, where relocated groups, forced into exile by the U.S. government, shared dances and developed pan-Indianism; there the Snake Dance was introduced from the southeast and the War Dance or Grass Dance for male experts from the Great Plains. The dancers in the latter, usually older men, perform toe–heel steps and prance with a proud bearing. The so-called fancy dancers of the present-day powwow can flex, twist, shake, and whirl, but they do not kick or leap. Nowadays they may, however, insert jazz steps. The music is provided by four or five men seated around a kettle drum, shouting with high-pitched voices. War mime is no longer observed in these dances.

Women are subsidiary in most powwow performances, treading or meekly bouncing on the fringe of the eddy or helping the singers. In social round dances, descended from scalp dances, women join the men, lock arms as they face the singers in the center, and limp to the left. They may also join in the song, with either native or silly English words. In the Indian swing dance, pairs progress clockwise and pivot on command; the dancing may continue monotonously for hours. It is popular because of the opportunity it provides for interaction between the sexes.

Pan-Indian dances have spread across North America; they are performed outdoors as summer tourist shows or in community centers and auditoriums as theatrical performances for urban dwellers. Variations and new songs have evolved, and the repertory also varies. For example, in Manitoba and the Dakotas the Grass Dance prevails; usually round dances are included; Midwesterners enrich the program with the Calumet Dance, the Hoop Dance, the Eagle Dance, and the Swan Dance; in the North, a light-footed, sinuous style is used.

The shows range in size and atmosphere from intimate to superpowwows. The big events have stridently modern features, such as deafening loudspeakers, dance contests, beauty and baby contests, and food and souvenir concessions. Nonetheless, they have social value, especially if they are enhanced by Native American spectator participation.

New Developments. Despite the new powwow's social and entertainment values, both rural and urban, it does not satisfy all Native Americans. Some search for more meaning and structure in dance; some attempt the reconstruction of old dances and the creation of new ones in traditional molds. Generally, older tribal members provide continuity of customs, and young people provide innovations and renewal of enthusiasm for the entire group.

The reconstruction of extinct rites takes research and ingenuity, as exemplified by the achievements of Mary Redwing Congdon. After 1935 she tried to revive Narragansett ceremonies; she trained young girls in dances for August festivals at Charlestown, Rhode Island, and for programs in schools and museums. On the model of the ancestral calendar, she produced monthly ceremonies at the Tomaquog Museum in Ashaway, Rhode Island.

Rosalie Jones, a Blackfoot-Welsh dancer, has successfully created solos and coherent dance dramas that combine modern dance with tribal concepts and legends. Using the name Daystar, she tours extensively with solo programs of original creations, such as *Lament: A Prayer for the Land.* In master classes she inspires young people to create in this kind of new hybrid style.

Museums are providing a context for the continuation of old dances and for the creation of new ones. The museum in Uncasville, Connecticut, for example, was started in the 1930s by a brother and sister, Harold and Gladys Tantaquidgeon, descendants of four Mohegan (Mohawk) chiefs. They encouraged camping and native dancing on their grounds. The Native American Center for the Living Arts opened in Niagara Falls in June 1981 under Iroquois management but with intertribal displays. It offers craft exhibits and instruction, powwows, and art and dance programs. Dance artists have included Daystar and the Solaris/Lakota group. The latter is a company of modern dancers who have collaborated with dancers from the Lakota Rosebud Reservation in South Dakota to create a synthesis of Native American and modern concert dance.

[*For related discussion, see also* Ethnic Dance *and* Matachins, *article on* Matachines Dances in the Southwestern United States.]

BIBLIOGRAPHY

Burton, Bryan. *Moving within the Circle: Contemporary Native American Music and Dance.* Danbury, Conn., 1993.

Buttree, Julia M. [Moss, Julia Seton]. *The Rhythm of the Redman.* New York, 1930.

Densmore, Frances. *Chippewa Music.* 2 vols. Washington, D.C., 1910–1913.

Densmore, Frances. *Teton Sioux Music.* Washington, D.C., 1918.

Densmore, Frances. *Menominee Music.* Washington, D.C., 1932.

Densmore, Frances. *Cheyenne and Arapahoe Music.* Los Angeles, 1936.

Fenton, William N., and Gertrude Prokosch Kurath. *The Iroquois Eagle Dance: An Offshoot of the Calumet Dance.* Washington, D.C., 1953.

Fletcher, Alice C. *The Hako.* Washington, D.C., 1904.

Frisbie, Charlotte J., ed. *Southwestern Indian Ritual Drama.* Albuquerque, 1980.

Heth, Charlotte, ed. *Native American Dance: Ceremonies and Social Traditions.* Washington, D.C., 1992.

Herzog, George. "Plains Ghost Dance and Great Basin Music." *American Anthropologist* 37 (1935): 403–419.

Kealiinohomoku, Joann W. "Dance." *Native America in the Twentieth Century: An Encyclopedia.* Edited by Mary B. Dairs. New York, 1996.

Kurath, Gertrude Prokosch. *Iroquois Music and Dance.* Washington, D.C., 1964.

Kurath, Gertrude Prokosch. *Michigan Indian Festivals.* Ann Arbor, Mich., 1966.

Kurath, Gertrude Prokosch. *Dance and Song Rituals of the Six Nations Reserve, Ontario.* Ottawa, 1968.

Kurath, Gertrude Prokosch, and Antonio Garcia. *Music and Dance of the Tewa Pueblos.* Santa Fe, 1970.

Kurath, Gertrude Prokosch. *Tutelo Rituals on Six Nations Reserve, Ontario.* Ann Arbor, Mich., 1981.

Mason, Bernard S. *Dances and Stories of the American Indian.* New York, 1944.

McAllester, David P. *Enemy Way Music: A Study of Social and Esthetic Values as Seen in Navaho Music.* Cambridge, Mass., 1954.

Merriam, Alan P. *Ethnomusicology of the Flathead Indians.* New York, 1967.

Morgan, Lewis H. *League of the Ho-dé-no-sau-nee, or Iroquois.* 2 vols. Rochester, N.Y., 1851.

Speck, Frank G. *Ceremonial Songs of the Creek and Yuchi Indians.* Philadelphia, 1911.

Speck, Frank G. *Penobscot Man.* Philadelphia, 1940.

Speck, Frank G., and Leonard Broom. *Cherokee Dance and Drama.* Berkeley, 1951.

FILMS. Franz Boas and Bill Holm, *The Kwakiutl of British Columbia* (University of Washington, 1918, 1931). *Hupa Indian White Deerskin Dance* (Barr Films, 1958). *Circle of the Sun* (National Film Board of Canada, 1960). *Northwestern Indian War Dance Contest* (University of Washington, 1960). *Kashia Men's Dance: Southwestern Pomo* (University of California, Berkeley, 1963). *Totem Pole, Kwakiutl* (University of California, Berkeley, 1963). *Dream Dance of the Kashia Pomo* (University of California, Berkeley, 1964). Hugh Dempsey and Bill Marsden, *Okan: Sun Dance of the Blackfoot* (Glenbow-Alberta Institute, 1966). *Introduction to American Indian Dance* (Philadelphia Dance Academy, 1967). *Filmstrips of Michigan Indians* (Philadelphia Dance Academy, 1969).

ARCHIVES. Field collections of recordings, films, photographs, paraphernalia, manuscripts, and publications are held by the American Philosophical Society, Philadelphia; Cross-Cultural Dance Resources, Inc., Flagstaff, Arizona; Milwaukee Public Museum; National Museum of Canada, Ottawa, Ontario; New York State Museum, Albany; Smithsonian Institution, Washington, D.C.; and Wenner-Gren Foundation for Anthropological Research, New York.

GERTRUDE PROKOSCH KURATH

Northeastern Woodlands

The dances of the Native Americans in the region northeast of the Mississippi River are by no means homogeneous, but they share many common traits. These forest-dwelling hunting, collecting, and agricultural peoples paid great attention to the seasonal rituals devoted to thanksgiving, harvesting, honoring nature, and both healing and preventive medicine—and most of their rituals incorporated dance. Most of the dances were communal, conducted by the various clans, moieties, special societies, or tribal towns. Many northeastern Native American dances are still performed.

All but a few dances are performed in circular formations moving counterclockwise. Some dances are exclusive to one sex, some alternate between the sexes or intermingle them, and some are danced by partners. There are several prescribed body postures, steps, and ground plans.

One of the primary differences between northeastern and southeastern dances is the place of performance. In the North, perhaps because of the colder weather, dances have been traditionally performed indoors, in longhouses or council houses; in the South, they are performed outdoors at ceremonial or "stomp" grounds. As a result, the sound is different: although the instruments are smaller in the North, the voices echo and sound louder. The smoother floor surfaces may also account for some of the more elaborate northern steps and movements.

The Cherokee of North Carolina are an exception to the general southern (Muskogean) pattern; some Cherokee indoor winter dances share traits with those of the northeastern Iroquois, to whose language family they belong. A rich repertory of music and dance still exists in New York, North Carolina, Oklahoma, Mississippi, and Florida, where Native Americans are concentrated. The most communal and most easily learned social dances should survive the twentieth century. The less communal and more specialized ceremonial dances may not survive after the lifetimes of their elderly specialist practitioners.

Northeastern Tribes. The northeastern culture area originally extended south from Maine to the Carolinas and west to the Great Lakes and the Ohio Valley. There are historical accounts of dances among the coastal tribes—such as the Virginia and Carolina Algonkians, and the Nanticoke, Abnaki, Maliseet, Passamaquoddy, Micmac, and Beothuk—but little traditional dance survives there. The peoples of the Great Lakes, while retaining their languages and customs to some extent, have adopted dances from the neighboring Great Plains as well as maintaining some of their own. Most of the Iroquois Six Nations (Seneca, Cayuga, Mohawk, Tuscarora, Onondaga, and Oneida) were able to stay in their New York State and Canadian homelands and have retained many of their traditional ceremonies. The Delaware and the Seneca-Cayuga nations, who were relocated by the U.S. government in the nineteenth century to the Indian Territory (now Oklahoma), have also perpetuated many of their ancient dances. The Shawnee, another displaced Algonkian people, maintain a full ceremonial calendar in Oklahoma. Each of these tribes has also adopted a few dances from its new neighbors.

The nations of the northeast dance to vocal music, performed mostly by men accompanying themselves with hand-held horn rattles and sometimes a water drum. The singers set the dance meter, a steady two-beat pulse with the first beat accented. The northern Iroquois dancers frequently wear bells, while the Shawnee and Seneca-Cayuga women in Oklahoma may wear terrapin-shell or tin-can rattles. Although men are the primary singers, some songs require women's voices; in others, women are allowed to join the chorus if they desire. The songs are sung in unison, in leader–chorus response, or in antiphony (two men in unison with the chorus answering).

Most social and some ceremonial dances are song cycles. Because each performance can vary in the selection of songs, number of repetitions, and length, the dancers need aural cues in the music to anticipate the prescribed changes in choreography.

The dances of the northeast include the mixed dances of alternating women and men, couple dances, dances with parallel lines of men and women, and dances exclusive to one sex or the other. In general, the execution of the whole dance or ceremony is more important than the individual dance steps. There are many more body movements and gestures with the arms in the northeast than in the southeast, along with a greater variety of dance formations and ritual paraphernalia. In part, this may be accounted for, since the Iroquois of the north have remained in their original homelands. Although they had a long history of interaction with European settlers—mainly French, British, Dutch, Scandinavian, and German—they retained much of their religion and social organization.

In Iroquois society and ceremonial dance, clan and sex roles are clearly defined. The clans are divided into two color-identified moieties (such as red and white) that have set roles in daily life, politics, and ritual. These patterns of duality are visible in Iroquois dance; for example, if a dance or music leader belongs to moiety one, the leader's helper must belong to moiety two. Men and women also interact, each sex having special functions and separate, prescribed seating arrangements. Each song is repeated and often divided into two sections. If partners cross over during the end of the first verse, they return to their original positions during the song's repeat. Spectators and performers interact; spectators can leave their benches and join the dance circle at an appropriate place.

Iroquoian ceremonials follow a yearly cycle. Principal events are the midwinter rites, the summer first-fruit festivals, the Green Corn Festival, and spring and fall ceremonies of the medicine society *kakosa* (the False Face or Wooden Face society). Grotesquely masked clowns perform to the accompaniment of horn or turtle-shell rattles. All religious ceremonials also include social dances such as the Stomp Dance. The Eagle Dance is a virtuosic ceremony for four youths from the Eagle Medicine society; it combines elements of the Calumet Dance, or Pipe Dance.

Women also have an important ceremonial role. In their crisp, sawfooting dance, the *enskanye,* they symbolize the life-giving spirits of corn, beans, and squash. In their ritual, the women planters walk in a circle, shake turtle-shell rattles, and sing about ripening crops and healthy children.

NATIVE AMERICAN DANCE: Northeastern Woodlands. Members of the Iroquois False Face society pose in carved and painted masks. Even today, the False Face society presents the ancient medicine ceremonies to assembled clans and honored guests. Dancers carry staffs and rattles made from the shells of turtles and horseshoe crabs. (Photograph from the Department of Library Services, American Museum of Natural History, New York [no. 13561]; used by permission.)

Unlike the culture of the Iroquois, the culture of the Algonkians around the Great Lakes, was greatly transformed by Europeans. After 1621, the Algonkians were unwilling hosts to the French Jesuits, but they gradually accepted European tales, morality plays, processionals, and plainchants. After 1800, Native American leaders helped Austrian Franciscans translate hymns and establish cultural centers, such as Arbre Croche on Lake Michigan. At the same time, Methodist missionaries were condemning Native American dances while making converts, especially among the unwanted offspring of Europeans and Native Americans. They replaced Native American summer gatherings with evangelistic camp meetings and Native American songs with Wesleyan hymns in Ojibwe

(Chippewa). By the twentieth century, both Roman Catholics and Protestants were sponsoring theatrical performances with fragments of the animistic ceremonies of the Native Americans.

Some Native Americans have attempted to keep the traditional dances and ceremonies alive. In Arbre Croche, David Kenosha of Cross Village was the last custodian of Ottawa traditions. He led the August Sun ceremony in Cross Village and taught the dances for Harbor Springs pageants with the aid of Susan Shagonaby. He sang native songs and hymns, and his Sun, Pipe, Bear, and Eagle dances were filmed by the lakeshore.

Christianity reached the Wisconsin tribes mainly in the twentieth century. In the 1920s some Wisconsin tribes still held wild rice festivals and medicine rites, but pan-Indian round dances were beginning to be adopted. In the 1950s the Menomini held the Dream Dance, a ceremony for intertribal harmony, yet Native American elders in the Great Lakes region retained many of their own traditions. In Wisconsin in the 1980s, there was increasing participation in the Dream Dance, and the Medicine Lodge Ceremony was revived.

Tourist programs thrive in the Great Lakes region. The Siouan Winnebago of Black River Falls invite the public to social dancing on the Red Cloud Memorial Grounds during Memorial Day and Labor Day afternoons and evenings. Winnebagos and Algonkians have also camped at Charlton Park, contributing to the colorful events held there in the August gatherings. They serve to attract the scattered members of many local Native American nations to the area.

BIBLIOGRAPHY

Ballard, William L. *The Yuchi Green Corn Ceremonial: Form and Meaning.* Los Angeles, 1978.

Densmore, Frances. *Seminole Music.* Washington, D.C., 1956.

Draper, David E. "Occasions for the Performance of Native Choctaw Music." *Selected Reports in Ethnomusicology* 3.2 (1980): 147–173.

Fenton, William N., and Gertrude Kurath. *The Iroquois Eagle Dance: An Offshoot of the Calumet Dance.* Washington, D.C., 1953.

Fogelson, Raymond D. "The Cherokee Ballgame Cycle: An Ethnographer's View." *Ethnomusicology* 15 (1971): 327–338.

Herndon, Marcia. "The Cherokee Ballgame Cycle: An Ethnomusicologist's View." *Ethnomusicology* 15 (1971): 339–352.

Heth, Charlotte, "The Stomp Dance Music of the Oklahoma Cherokee." Ph.D. diss., University of California, Los Angeles, 1975.

Heth, Charlotte. "Stylistic Similarities in Cherokee and Iroquois Music." *Journal of Cherokee Studies* 4.3 (1979): 128–162.

Howard, James H. "Bringing Back the Fire: The Revival of a Natchez-Cherokee Ceremonial Ground." *American Indian Crafts and Culture* 4 (January 1970): 9–12.

Howard, James H. *Shawnee!* Athens, Ohio, 1981.

Howard, James H. *Oklahoma Seminoles.* Norman, Okla., 1984.

Hudson, Charles. *The Southeastern Indians.* Knoxville, 1976.

Kurath, Gertrude. "Antiphonal Songs of the Eastern Woodland Indians." *Musical Quarterly* 42 (1956): 520–526.

Kurath, Gertrude. "Effects of Environment on Cherokee-Iroquois Ceremonialism, Music, and Dance." In *Symposium on Cherokee and Iroquois Culture,* edited by William N. Fenton and John Gulick. Bureau of American Ethnology, Bulletin 180. Washington, D.C., 1961.

Kurath, Gertrude. *Iroquois Music and Dance.* Washington, D.C., 1964.

Kurath, Gertrude. *Dance and Song Rituals of the Six Nations Reserve, Ontario.* Ottawa, 1968.

Kurath, Gertrude. *Tutelo Rituals on Six Nations Reserve, Ontario.* Ann Arbor, Mich., 1981.

Laubin, Reginald, and Gladys Laubin. *Indian Dances of North America.* Norman, Okla., 1977.

Mason, Bernard S. *Dances and Stories of the American Indian.* New York, 1944.

Mooney, James. *Myths of the Cherokee.* Washington, D.C., 1900.

Morgan, Lewis H. *League of the Ho-dé-no-sau-nee, or Iroquois.* 2 vols. Rochester, N.Y., 1851.

Speck, Frank G. *Ceremonial Songs of the Creek and Yuchi Indians.* Philadelphia, 1911.

Speck, Frank G., and Leonard Broom. *Cherokee Dance and Drama.* Berkeley, 1951.

Swanton, John R. "Aboriginal Culture of the Southeast," "Religious Beliefs and Medical Practices of the Creek Indians," and "Social Organization and Social Usages of the Indians of the Creek Confederacy." *Annual Report of the Bureau of American Ethnology* 42 (1928).

Trigger, Bruce G., ed. *Handbook of North American Indians,* vol. 15, *Northeast.* Washington, D.C., 1978.

GERTRUDE PROKOSCH KURATH
and CHARLOTTE HETH

Southeastern Woodlands

The southeastern woodlands of North America included present-day western North Carolina, South Carolina, Georgia, Florida, Alabama, Mississippi, Louisiana, southern and eastern Arkansas, Tennessee, and the portions of Missouri, Illinois, and Kentucky that border the Mississippi River. The Native American peoples who inhabited this area about whose dances we know anything were the Cherokee, Choctaw, Chickasaw, Creek, Seminole, Catawba, Yuchi, Caddo, Chitimacha, Tunica, Natchez, Alabama, and Koasati. Many were speakers of the widespread southern Muscogean language family.

Although a large number of Native Americans still live east of the Mississippi, forced relocations by the U.S. government in the 1830s marched most of the region's peoples into Oklahoma, where many still remain. In this relocation, known as the Trail of Tears, some groups were placed on the same reservation because of linguistic and cultural similarities or because of a former geographical proximity. Thus, the Creek of today descend from all the Muskogee, some Natchez, Yuchi, Alabama, Hitchiti, Koasati, and a few Seminoles who were relocated to Oklahoma. Besides the Creek, the Choctaw and Chickasaw are the largest groups of Muskogean language speakers. Similarly, the Cherokee adopted some northeastern members of the Shawnee and Delaware nations. Another northeastern group, the Seneca-Cayuga, also settled near the Cherokee in Oklahoma.

Dance still pervades the life of these people. Its occasions include stately ceremonial dances, traditional ball games, animal dances, and lively social dances. The midsummer Green Corn Ceremony (Busk) encompasses most styles of dance and is the highlight of the year for many communities. Its major dances—the Feather, Ribbon, and Buffalo dances—occur in the daytime, along with ceremonies for renewal and purification. Nighttime stomp dancing and social dances accompany the Green Corn Ceremony but are also held from spring to fall at most ceremonial grounds, variously called *stomp grounds, square grounds,* or *tribal towns.* Most dances take place outdoors in the center of the ground, around a sacred fire with four logs pointing to the cardinal directions. The dances are performed primarily in circles or spirals, counterclockwise, in follow-the-leader fashion.

Most southeastern dances are performed by mixed groups of men, women, and children. While the stately Feather Dance of the Green Corn Ceremony is exclusive to men, the corresponding Ribbon Dance is the domain of women and girls. For these dances, two male singers provide the music, accompanying themselves with a water drum and a shell or gourd rattle.

The most common dance, the Stomp Dance, proceeds as follows. A male song-dance leader begins by walking counterclockwise around the sacred fire, followed by his male helpers. On a musical cue, they begin to dance, using a flat-footed running step. Next the female shell shakers, wearing terrapin or tin-can leg rattles, enter in alternate positions behind the men, using a touch-step or stamp-step. The rest of the male and female dancers then join in, alternately, executing the dance steps initiated by the leader. Several songs then follow, punctuated with shouts and slower steps between the songs in the cycle. At certain high points in each song, the leader addresses the fire—with a quarter turn toward the fire, he bends over at a forty-five-degree angle from the waist and moves his arms alternately up and down in time to the music.

In most tribes, the other men and women follow the leader's example, but in Cherokee dances, the women continue dancing forward using the same trotting manner. The men use four dance steps—a natural run, a natural walk, a flat-footed stomp, and a flat-footed hopping in place. Women not wearing leg rattles also use the last three steps and add a succession of flat-footed forward jumps. The shell shakers use three steps in addition to walking: a touch step or stamp-step for major portions of most dances; a flat-footed double stamp for beginnings and endings of songs and song cycles; and, as a special ending, a forward series of jumps with both feet hitting the ground together. Except for the Buffalo Dance and the Stomp Dance, when the dancers bend forward from the waist, the body postures used are primarily upright, with hands at the sides. Emphasis is placed on excellence in executing steps rhythmically, following the leader, and participating fully.

Dance music of all the southeastern peoples is primarily vocal and monophonic, accompanied by rattles and sometimes by a water drum. The rattles worn on both legs by

NATIVE AMERICAN DANCE: Southeastern Woodlands. The Choctaw of the Mississippi Valley were members of the so-called Five Civilized Tribes (Cree, Seminole, Cherokee, Chickasaw, and Choctaw). They lived in towns with streets and a central square that was often used for ritual dance. George Catlin depicted their Ball-play Dance, a ceremony that probably originated in Mesoamerica and was brought north as trade relationships were formed, centuries before European contact. (Photograph from the Department of Library Services, American Museum of Natural History, New York [no. 250517]; used by permission.)

women dancers therefore provide the primary instrumental accompaniment. In general, the dance songs are either sung in unison by the men or are in leader–chorus response (sometimes both). The songs are integrated with shouts, animal cries, and opening and closing formulas as cues for the dancers and singers. The Stomp, Friendship, and Buffalo dance songs are cycles, but most animal dances and other ceremonial songs are strophic. For example, four Buffalo Dance songs of the Seminole or Creek—with various prescribed introductions, transitions, responses, and endings—comprise a Buffalo Dance that makes possible the enaction of the necessary choreographic changes and ceremonial aspects.

The various dance meters are based on a steady accented-unaccented pulse, as provided by the female dancers with their leg rattles. The number of pulses in a phrase varies from four to twelve. Although both duple and triple meters are used, the most important organizing principle is isorhythm, a device that serves as a mnemonic aid in oral transmission. It is not unusual for every phrase in a song to follow the same rhythmic pattern while to some degree the melody, words, and dance movements change.

A rich repertory of music and dance still exists where the eastern nations are concentrated—New York, North Carolina, Mississippi, Florida, and Oklahoma. The most communal and most easily learned social dances have survived the twentieth century, yet the least communal and most specialized ceremonial dances may not survive after the lifetimes of their specialist practitioners (unless they are taught to younger performers and/or captured in motion pictures).

BIBLIOGRAPHY

Ballard, William L. *The Yuchi Green Corn Ceremonial: Form and Meaning.* Los Angeles, 1978.

Densmore, Frances. *Seminole Music.* Washington, D.C., 1956.

Draper, David E. "Occasions for the Performance of Native Choctaw Music." *Selected Reports in Ethnomusicology* 3.2 (1980): 147–173.

Fenton, William N., and Gertrude Kurath. *The Iroquois Eagle Dance.* Washington, D.C., 1953.

Fogelson, Raymond D. "The Cherokee Ballgame Cycle: An Ethnographer's View." *Ethnomusicology* 15 (1971): 327–338.

Herndon, Marcia. "The Cherokee Ballgame Cycle: An Ethnomusicologist's View." *Ethnomusicology* 15 (1971): 339–352.

Heth, Charlotte. "The Stomp Dance Music of the Oklahoma Cherokee." Ph.D. diss., University of California, Los Angeles, 1975.

Heth, Charlotte. "Stylistic Similarities in Cherokee and Iroquois Music." *Journal of Cherokee Studies* 4.3 (1979): 128–162.

Howard, James H. "Bringing Back the Fire: The Revival of a Natchez-Cherokee Ceremonial Ground." *American Indian Crafts and Culture* 4 (January 1970): 9–12.

Howard, James H. *Shawnee!* Athens, Ohio, 1981.

Howard, James H. *Oklahoma Seminoles.* Norman, Okla., 1984.

Hudson, Charles. *The Southeastern Indians.* Knoxville, 1976.

Kurath, Gertrude. "Antiphonal Songs of the Eastern Woodland Indians." *Musical Quarterly* 42 (1956): 520–526.

Kurath, Gertrude. "Effects of Environment on Cherokee-Iroquois Ceremonialism, Music, and Dance." In *Symposium on Cherokee and Iroquois Culture,* edited by William N. Fenton and John Gulick. Bureau of American Ethnology, Bulletin 180. Washington, D.C., 1961.

Kurath, Gertrude. *Dance and Song Rituals of the Six Nations Reserve, Ontario.* Ottawa, 1968.

Kurath, Gertrude. *Tutelo Rituals on Six Nations Reserve, Ontario.* Ann Arbor, Mich., 1981.

Laubin, Reginald, and Gladys Laubin. *Indian Dances of North America.* Norman, Okla., 1977.

Mason, Bernard S. *Dances and Stories of the American Indian.* New York, 1944.

Mooney, James. *Myths of the Cherokee.* Washington, D.C., 1900.

Speck, Frank G. *Ceremonial Songs of the Creek and Yuchi Indians.* Philadelphia, 1911.

Speck, Frank G., and Leonard Broom. *Cherokee Dance and Drama.* Berkeley, 1951.

Swanton, John R. "Aboriginal Culture of the Southeast," "Religious Beliefs and Medical Practices of the Creek Indians," and "Social Organization and Social Usages of the Indians of the Creek Confederacy." *Annual Report of the Bureau of American Ethnology* 42 (1928).

Trigger, Bruce G., ed. *Handbook of North American Indians,* vol. 15, *Northeast.* Washington, D.C., 1978.

CHARLOTTE HETH

The Great Plains

From the perspective of dance as well as other cultural domains, the Great Plains region of North America may be divided into northern and southern areas, with an imaginary line running through the state of Nebraska. The dances of the northern and southern extremes were at one time quite disparate, tending to overlap and diffuse toward the central plains, in southern South Dakota.

Diffusion and borrowing took varied paths. Dance songs sung in unison by male and female singers, to the accompaniment of drums, tended to diffuse southward from the Canadian plains toward Oklahoma. Specific dances, however, moved northward mainly from Oklahoma, the heart of the southern plains, toward the Canadian plains. Both music and dance underwent some stylistic changes as they passed through the South Dakota reservations; today, however, these stylistic differences are amalgamating into the generalized form of Plains dance typically seen in powwow performances.

The well-known buffalo-hunting, tipi-dwelling, equestrian nomads of the Great Plains, popularly regarded as the stereotype for all Native Americans, flourished for only a short time—from the acquisition of horses that escaped from or were traded by the Spanish colonizers and explorers in the 1600s and 1700s. Plains culture changed abruptly in the mid-nineteenth century with the establishment by the U.S. government of reservations, fewer than two hundred years after the introduction of the horse had brought it into being. What we know about Plains dance before the mid-1800s is sparse and comes almost exclusively from the observations of early travelers, such as the artist George Catlin (1796–1872), who painted and wrote about the dances of the Plains vividly in his book *O-kee-pah,* about the Mandan Sun Dance.

Plains dance as we know it today is strongly influenced by the reservation system. The dance styles are related to both regions and unique tribal traditions. There are hundreds of genres of songs on the Plains, but fewer types of dances; dance style is often dictated by musical style, drum tempo and rhythm, and costume. The different styles can be distinguished by region and tribe only on the basis of melody, rhythm, tempo, and choreographic patterns.

In the northern Plains region, the Blackfeet style is performed by the Blackfeet proper, Piegan, Blood, and Sarsi (Sarsee). The North Dakota style includes the Arikara, Assiniboine, Gros Ventre (or Atsina), Hidatsa, Mandan, Plains Cree, Plains Ojibwe, and the Lakota and Dakota of Canada, Montana, and North Dakota. The Crow style is limited to the Crow. The South Dakota style includes the Northern Arapaho, Northern Cheyenne, and the Lakota and Dakota of South Dakota and Nebraska.

In the southern Plains region, the Western Oklahoma style is performed by the Chiricahua Apache, Caddo, Comanche, Kiowa, Kiowa Apache, Southern Arapaho, Southern Cheyenne, and Wichita. The Northern Oklahoma style includes the Iowa, Kansa, Omaha, Osage, Oto, Pawnee, Ponca, Quapaw, and Tonkawa.

Plains dances are still viable, particularly in the context of the powwow. They also continue to influence the song and dance styles of Native Americans from other parts of North America, who adopt Plains styles in order to compete in powwow dance contests.

Secular Dances. Most Plains secular dances are performed by groups of males and females. In some dances, men exhibit highly individualistic combinations of basic steps while women dance more conservatively; examples include the Omaha Dance of the Lakota, the Chicken Dance of the Blackfeet, and analogous dances commonly called War Dance. In the Round Dance and Forty-Nine Dance performed by nearly all Plains tribes, men and women dance in a clockwise-moving circle. Men and women dance in lines in the Stomp Dance, which came to the Plains from the southeast, and there are occasional linear configurations of men related through their mother's family in the War Dance of the Crow. Men and women dance as partners in the Two-Step of the southern Plains and the Rabbit Dance and Owl Dance of the northern Plains, in which dancers hold hands in "skater's" position (arms crossed) and all the couples dance in a circular formation. Partner dances generally are a twentieth-century innovation, imitating or parodying European-American couple dancing. Solo dancing by males or by females exists only in some recently innovated show dances, such as the Hoop Dance imported from the American Southwest.

NATIVE AMERICAN DANCE: The Great Plains. In full ceremonial dance regalia, these Plains hunters carry bows and arrows and wear buffalo-horned headdresses, to gain the attention and appease the spirits of the animals who sustained their traditional lifestyle. Even after the herds had been overhunted and decimated by whites, the Buffalo Dance was performed. (Photograph 1934 by H. S. Rice, from the Department of Library Services, American Museum of Natural History, New York [no. 282544]; used by permission.)

Generally, songs are sung in a higher pitch and dance tempos are slower in the northern Plains; while songs are pitched lower and dance movements are faster in the southern Plains. Individual dances last longer in the north, and come to a more abrupt halt in the south. The Blackfeet style is more subdued than the North Dakota style, which is characterized by bouncy steps, frequently accompanied by shoulder shaking and trick steps performed by both men and women. The Crow style is similar to the Blackfeet, but the Crow wear unique costumes.

The South Dakota style is generally regarded as the traditional Plains style, exhibiting both reservedness and athletic body movements, with little attention paid to footwork. The northern Oklahoma style is extremely reserved, while western-style dancers are vigorous and gymnastic in their fancy footwork and sudden body whirls. The popularity of the powwow has tended to blur the lines between tribal styles, particularly in competitive dances.

Sacred Dances. The most sacred dance of the Great Plains is the Sun Dance, performed by most tribes. As in secular dance, there is no single Plains style. Rather, each tribe applies unique movements and choreographic patterns to this annual religious ceremony. Originating with the Mandan of North Dakota in the 1800s, the best-known version is one in which ritual specialists insert skewers of wood or bone into incisions made in the male dancers' chests. The skewers are then tied to a rope connected to a center pole. The dancers dance for hours, gazing at the sun and tugging at the rope to tear their flesh free from the skewers. Skewers are also inserted into the flesh over the shoulder blades, and some dancers drag buffalo skulls on ropes attached to the skewers until they are freed. Women may offer flesh from their arms.

Although officially banned by the U.S. government in the 1880s, the Sun Dance, complete with self-mortification, was resumed by some of the northern Plains tribes in 1959. It continues to be one of the most important sacred ceremonies, although most of the tribes no longer pierce the flesh. Instead, those who have pledged to perform the dance fast for several days and dance from dawn to dusk. One of the most traditional Sun Dances, admired by other tribes, is performed without piercing by the Northern Arapaho at Wind River, Wyoming.

In 1888, the Ghost Dance achieved a short-lived popularity on the Plains and adjacent areas. It was believed that if the people adopted this particular dance, European settlers would disappear and deceased Indians and the buffalo herds would return. Holding hands and dancing in a circle without accompaniment, the dancers fell into trances and dreamed that they conversed with their dead relatives. In 1890 the U.S. government, fearful that the Ghost Dance movement would provoke an uprising, ordered it halted. On 29 December 1890, therefore, Ghost dancers were massacred by federal troops in South Dakota near a frozen creek called Wounded Knee, thus ending what was essentially a pacifistic movement.

[*See also* Ghost Dance.]

BIBLIOGRAPHY

Densmore, Frances. *Teton Sioux Music.* Washington, D.C., 1918.

Densmore, Frances. *Pawnee Music.* Washington, D.C., 1929.

Lewis, Thomas H. *The Medicine Men: Oglala Sioux Ceremony and Healing.* Lincoln, Neb., 1990.

Mooney, James. *The Ghost-Dance Religion and the Sioux Outbreak of 1890* (1896). Chicago, 1965.

Powers, William K. *War Dance: Plains Indian Musical Performance.* Tucson, Ariz., 1990.

Spier, Leslie. *The Sun Dance of the Plains Indians: Its Development and Diffusion.* New York, 1921.

WILLIAM K. POWERS

The Southwest

Dance is at the heart of the religious culture of the Pueblo peoples who have inhabited what is now the southwestern United States for more than two thousand years. As early as c.500 BCE, they lived in small autonomous villages, surviving on hunted game and cultivated corn, beans, and squash. Today the Pueblo groups live in New Mexico and Arizona and have several distinct linguistic affiliations. The Hopi reside in northeastern Arizona and speak a Uto-Aztecan language. The Zuñi language has no known relatives; these people live in New Mexico close to the Arizona border, just south of the city of Gallup. The Rio Grande Valley Pueblos are divided into Keresan and Tanoan Pueblos. The Keresan-speaking Pueblos include Acoma, Laguna, Cochiti, Santo Domingo, San Felipe, Santa Ana, and Zia; the Tanoan-speaking Pueblos are Sandia, Isleta, Jemez, Picuris, Taos, Nambé, Tesuque, San Ildefonso, Santa Clara, and San Juan. The last five speak Tewa, a branch of Tanoan.

In many Native American cultures, all objects are seen as having spirits; they are believed to be related to one another, and all their actions interrelate; each has a function that contributes to maintaining a balance in the universe. Humans are only one component of the schema, regarded in Pueblo thought as having neither less nor more importance than any other animal or natural element. This philosophy is reflected in the relationships between tribes; each tribe does not consider its practices to be superior to those of other groups, thus ceremonial traditions are commonly shared and borrowed.

Among the Pueblo peoples, religion is at the core of all life functions. Philosophical concepts about sustenance, longevity, aesthetics, space, relationships, communication, and honor are woven into ceremony and ritual. Symbols and designs on artworks such as pottery, rugs, and costumes also represent these religious themes. Pueblo peoples believe in supernatural spirits and beings who can use their power in either constructive or destructive ways. Participation in religious rituals is a necessity to ensure consistent blessings from and for the supernaturals, members of the community, and all of nature. The regular enactment of the ceremonies reinforces connections within the community and continues traditional legacies. Many Pueblo people pray every morning, facing and throwing cornmeal in seven directions—north, west, south, east, heaven, earth, and to oneself.

Native Americans, like people elsewhere in the world,

believe that through prayer and ceremonies humans help to encourage the continuance of natural cycles, such as the proper course of the seasons or plentiful rain and sunshine for crops. Respect for animals is paramount in game dances and this respect is shown by hunting only what is needed and then using every part of the animal. From early childhood individuals are trained to participate in communal rituals. The ceremonial prayers climax in a ritual dance which combines song, poetry, dance, drama, and symbolic costumes. Each dance is performed for a specific purpose, and always with the subtext of pleasing the supernaturals and promoting long life, health, and happiness.

The song is the key to each Pueblo dance, and each dance step is created to fit the musical rhythm and reinforce the drumbeat. The drumbeat represents the Earth Mother's heartbeat. There are always an entrance song, a main song, and an exit song. Each verse is played twice: first to call up the spirits, then to give them blessings. The musical patterns are composed to emulate natural sounds such as wind or thunder, rain hitting the earth, the flapping of an eagle's wings, or the stomping of buffalo hooves. Sometimes there is use of poetry, while at other times vocal sounds mimic natural sounds. In some modern songs, English words are interwoven with the native language. Vocal tones vary from tribe to tribe. Other musical instruments often accompany drumming, including bells and turtleshells—attached to costumes or strung around ankles, arms, or waists—flutes, and rattles made from gourds.

An entrance song brings Pueblo performers into the dance space. A village usually has a large plaza, unpaved to maintain connection with the earth. A *kiva* is the sacred ceremonial chamber; it may be either square or circular, under or above ground; it is used as a place for private meetings or sacred ceremonies. Dancers often practice for a ritual performance inside the *kiva*. To symbolize the emergence myth—in which the first people emerged from a world below the present one—the participants in a community celebration often begin a ritual in the *kiva* and then move to the plaza outside.

Pueblo dancers often enter a dance space in single file, with unison steps danced in rhythm to a drumbeat. Many of the main dance sections are performed in long parallel lines, the dancers moving together in unison, facing the cardinal directions. Simple floor patterns are inscribed into the earthen dance floor by the dancers; these may take the form of zig-zag or S-shaped lines. A few dances, such as the Friendship Dance, first inscribe a circular pattern, with the participants holding hands and facing into the center. An exit song allows the participants to leave the dance space. After a song is finished, each individual takes a deep breath to inhale the air of the spirits who have been called on in the dance.

Most of the Pueblo dance movement is upright, with rhythmic hops that travel vertically or horizontally but remain relatively close to the ground. In many dances, the torso is held in an erect position while the arms, bent slightly at the elbow, move just a few inches back and forth, from the body outward. Each movement casts a blessing in the direction indicated. When the dancer imitates an animal, however, the arms move outward, away from the torso and outstretched, as in the Eagle Dance.

In general, attention is not targeted at individual virtuosity but rather toward communal connection. Eyes are often cast down toward the earth with a concentrated focus. This intense dedication allows the participants to connect with the energy and power of supernatural forces. A sense of balance and control, with much repetition, permeates the aesthetic style of most Pueblo dances.

Some variations in Pueblo dance movement styles are associated with gender, while others are tribal. Men may lift their feet a little higher off the ground and with more force than do women. Tewa dancers always initiate dance sequences with the right foot, while Hopi dancers begin with the left.

Pueblo dance steps include permutations of rhythmic stepping such as light hops, weight shifts, deep knee bends, or shuffle-like movements that accent a step with one foot that then sends the other out. Other dances utilize stylized walks and movements that imitate a specific animal, the most common being deer and buffalo. The deer walk usually includes two sticks which the dancer uses like walking sticks, leaning forward on them to give the appearance of a four-legged animal. The upper body inclines forward and the knees remain lightly bent as the individual slowly roams about in imitation of the deer. In the buffalo walk, dancers stand on both feet with the body leaning slightly forward as they shift their weight from side to side with the knees deeply bent. There is a heavy, grounded quality to the buffalo walk as the performers stride with their legs separated, feet outside the pelvis width.

Most articles of Pueblo dance costume are made from animal skins, fur, and feathers. Various materials have also been used for spinning and weaving, such as cotton, milkweed fiber, and hair from dogs, mountain sheep, bears, beavers, rabbits, and humans. Costumes are adorned with natural elements that have multidimensional meanings. In general, branches and twigs from evergreen spruce trees symbolize everlasting life. Balls of cotton represent rain clouds, and long tassels represent raindrops. A feathered fan may represent the sun. A basket may signify both the womb and the sun. Additional decorations on costumes include beadwork, embroidery, and yarn dyed, stained, or painted in various colors to represent the ideas, objects, and cardinal directions for the various groups.

Male dancers use body painting to set an individual apart from his physical human body and to empower him as immortal while he is wearing colors in ceremony. During this time he is charmed, and no one may touch him for he is not of this world. After the ceremony, the painted individual ritualistically washes his body and hair to return to his human body.

There are two distinct types of Pueblo dance performances—ceremonial or private dances, and the social or public productions. Religious rituals combine music, poetry, dance, drama, and costumes in sacred prayers and are intended only for the participants. Dances performed away from a Pueblo's traditional spaces are not considered as important as the sacred rituals, so may be witnessed by outsiders.

Pueblo dances are performed regularly during specific seasons, on fixed dates, throughout the year. The exact number of dances performed annually differs among villages (see Bahti, 1971, for a calendar of approximate dates of the annual cycle). Although some dances start at noon, most begin just before dawn and continue until dusk. Winter ceremonies generally center around hunting rituals and animal dances, while spring, summer, and fall performance rituals focus on agriculture.

Hunting used to be a very important activity for the Pueblo peoples. Deer were most commonly hunted for meat and hides, as were antelope, elk, and mountain sheep. The buffalo was seldom hunted since Plains buffalo-hunting groups were known to guard their territories aggressively and would attack trespassers. A successful hunt required not only the skills of an individual but also the consent of the animals. Pueblo hunting dances continue the rituals necessary to ensure success and at the same time to pay homage to the animals. The two beings, man and animal, work together in an understanding that the animal is giving itself in order to sustain human life. Through these dances the performers thank the animals and ask their cooperation and assistance in being hunted. Today Pueblo hunting rituals are still performed before, during, and after a hunt.

In the Rio Grande Pueblos, animal dances are performed mostly during winter. Sometimes the dance has only a few participants, such as two Buffalo dancers with a Buffalo woman; the single female represents the Mother of All Game. At other times the dances are performed by a large number of dancers dressed as the animal being represented—deer, elk, eagle, or antelope. Often the animal ceremonials begin the night before the actual dance day.

Many Pueblo versions exist of the Buffalo Dance, still performed in honor of buffalos who gave themselves to keep humans alive. In some tribes the Buffalo Dance is thought to help bring the onset of winter. In addition, after a Buffalo Dance, the headdress used was thought to have curative powers.

Many agricultural dances are performed during the spring, summer, and fall that ask the supernaturals to bless the village with plentiful rain and sun, for crops to flourish. Their themes reflect regenerative cyclical life forces and celebrate the female. Highly revered are the

NATIVE AMERICAN DANCE: The Southwest. Standing before the ceremonial stepped platform are three drummers who accompany the two dancers in feathered costumes performing the Eagle Dance at Pueblo San Ildefonso, near Santa Fe, New Mexico, one of the Tanoan-speaking pueblos. Although this pueblo is in the Southwest, by 1934, when this photograph was taken, traditional Great Plains feathered headdresses had been adopted for public ceremony by two of the three drummers. (Photograph by Clyde Fisher, from the Department of Library Services, American Museum of Natural History, New York [no.282740]; used by permission.)

Corn Dances, which are performed at various times of the year but mostly during spring and summer. They may also be performed to mark political events, such as an installation of new tribal officers. As the cultivation and propagation of corn has been the basis of southwestern Pueblo life, there are many versions of the Corn Dance, as well as various meanings associated with these dances. In all versions, the Corn Dance is primarily associated with the life force and the female. Sometimes this dance is called the Cloud Dance or the Corn Maiden Dance, because of its associations with fertility, growth, and weather control.

The atypical Corn Grinding Dance features young girls who gather to grind corn as young men sing and play flutes. Amid the giggling and flirting, a special food is created. More than a fertility ritual, this dance is about the generation of life and power.

The Blue Corn Dance resembles the Butterfly Dance of the Hopi. During the early spring when butterflies are first emerging, young women dance in the cornfields. Young men follow in pursuit of the women. The unification represents a cyclical life force and a power to attract generative blessings.

The Basket Dance also represents the female, the womb, growth cycles, and fertility. The dance begins slowly with the dancers standing and singing, each woman holding a basket in one hand. The tempo then accelerates, and the women kneel as they add to the musical accompaniment by scraping notched sticks over the baskets.

Other regenerative rituals include the *kachina* (*katsina*) ceremonies, performed by all Pueblo groups, but the Zuñi and Hopi participate in the greatest number. *Kachinas* are the symbolic representations of the spirits in human form. They are exaggerated and abstracted figures who signify the spirits of animals, plants, places, and ancestors. While wearing a *kachina* mask, the impersonator is thought to receive the spirit of whatever entity the costume symbolizes. The *kachina* becomes a channel through which the villagers can communicate with powerful deities. The *kachina* dances usually take place outdoors during spring and summer.

Other dances have a public theatrical function. An example is the Hoop Dance, primarily performed in the Rio Grande Valley Pueblos by boys at public exhibitions. In acrobatic style, the dancer manipulates a number of hoops, weaving limbs and body into, around, and over them as they spin. The hoops constantly metamorphose into visual patterns around the dancer, appearing to become the wings of an eagle or a rainbow in the sky. The costumes are usually derived from Great Plains dance costume—a feathered headdress and a breechcloth. One Tewa hoop dancer said that through the Hoop Dance a person learns that all the actions committed by an individual will come back to him. Another interpretation, by anthropologist Tom Bahti, claims that the Hoop Dance was originally created as a symbolic reenactment of humans' emergence from the underworld into this world.

Many other dances take place throughout the year in each Pueblo. All of them are performed for specific purposes: to unify and reaffirm traditional values, to seek and find new regenerated life, and to bless and thank the deities and all participants in order to maintain balance and harmony within the universe.

[*See also* Pueblo Dance; Navaho Dance; Tiwa Dance; *and* Yaqui Dance.]

BIBLIOGRAPHY

Allen, Paula Gunn. *Grandmothers of the Light: A Medicine Woman's Sourcebook.* Boston, 1991.

Bahti, Tom. *Southwestern Indian Ceremonials.* Las Vegas, 1971.

Evans, Bessie, and May G. Evans. *American Indian Dance Steps.* New York, 1931.

Fewkes, Jesse Walter. *Hopi Snake Ceremonies* (1894–1898). Albuquerque, 1986.

Forrest, Earle R. *Missions and Pueblos of the Old Southwest.* 2 vols. Cleveland, 1929.

Frisbie, Charlotte J., ed. *Southwestern Indian Ritual Drama.* Albuquerque, 1980.

Garcia, Andrew. "Indian Social Dances." Paper Presented at the University of Mexico, Spring 1995.

Kurath, Gertrude Prokosch, and Antonio Garcia. *Music and Dance of the Tewa Pueblos.* Santa Fe, 1970.

Ortiz, Alfonso. *The Tewa World: Space, Time, Being, and Becoming in a Pueblo Society.* Chicago, 1969.

Roediger, Virginia More. *Ceremonial Costumes of the Pueblo Indians.* Berkeley, 1961.

Rushforth, Scott, and Steadman Upham. *A Hopi Social History: Anthropological Perspectives on Sociocultural Persistence and Change.* Austin, 1992.

Sweet, Jill D. *Dances of the Tewa Pueblo Indians: Expressions of New Life.* Santa Fe, 1985.

Underhill, Ruth M. *The Papago Indians of Arizona and Their Relatives the Pima.* Washington, D.C., 1940.

ADRIENNE CLANCY

California and the Intermountain Region

Before contact with Europeans, California was densely populated by peoples of more than sixty linguistic groups. Most were hunters or specialized collectors in localized ecological habitats of the mountains, lakes, rivers, valleys, and seashore. Their various religious systems were animistic, so their dance rituals were aimed mainly at affecting spiritual entities governing the physical environment and the course of human life. Californian dances contained aspects of spectacle, magic, drama, and initiatory ordeal, and they often had an element of clowning or comic relief. Formalism and abstract symbolism were less developed than among other Native Americans, perhaps because both the shaman's and an individual's religious experiences were expressed by individualistic innovations within dance rituals.

The dance paraphernalia and costumes were regarded as sacred, awe-inspiring, or even dangerous among nearly all Californian groups. In many instances the display of these items appears to have been the central purpose of ritual dance.

With a few important exceptions, communal dance was the province of men; there was widespread belief that the female menstrual cycle might undermine or corrupt the spiritual dimensions of ritual. There were absolute prohibitions against women's dancing in or even witnessing certain dances.

Although some dances featured male soloists whose actions were vigorous, movement in dance was otherwise limited. The characteristic step for males involved rhythmic stamping of the feet, with the body held in a half-crouching posture. This might be done by a line or circular formation of men standing in place, or the dancers might move over a definite course during the dance. When allowed to participate, females generally danced in place, twisting or perhaps only swaying, with little or no motion of the feet.

Dance was always accompanied by singing, which it matched in tempo. Songs were brief, generally less than two minutes in duration; after a pause a song was repeated or followed by another song. Dance rituals were episodic, and a nightlong event consisted of repeated bursts of activity rather than continuous dancing.

Almost all tribes observed some form of girls' puberty ceremony, in which dance was prominent. Various forms of war dances were performed throughout the California area. Some form of shamanistic dance featuring a vision-inspired soloist also existed among nearly all groups. Dance types otherwise differed greatly in the major cultural subregions.

Northeastern and Southeastern California. Dances among the Achumawi and Atsugewi of northeastern California were few, and little is known about them; only a female puberty dance has been briefly described. Among the Mohave of the southeastern Californian sector, ritual consisted of the performance of lengthy song cycles in which the element of dance was evidently negligible. Dance culture is more elaborated, however, among the Native Americans of three distinct California provinces—the northwestern, the central, and the southern below the Tehachapi Range. Some dances of these three provinces are still being performed.

Northwestern California. Most important among the northwestern California groups (Yurok, Hupa, Karok, and others) are dances of the world-renewal cult, especially the White Deerskin Dance and the Jump Dance. These dances are still performed to renew or purify the landscape, assure bountiful wild crops and abundance of salmon, and prevent sickness or catastrophe. Both are performed outdoors by men standing in line formation, and both feature the display of sacred and valuable objects, including albino deerskins, large flaked blades of obsidian (volcanic glass), dentalium-shell money, otter skins, and scarlet woodpecker scalps.

NATIVE AMERICAN DANCE: California and the Intermountain Region. The Hupa people of northwestern California were visited by the Christian missionary H. C. Meredith from c.1889 to 1895. These men donned the sacred dress required to perform their ritual dances of renewal, stood in line, and posed for Meredith's camera. Here, they are dressed to perform the Woodpecker Dance. (Photograph from the Department of Library Services, American Museum of Natural History, New York [no. 124359]; used by permission.)

Another enduring northwestern Californian ceremony is the Brush Dance, performed to cure or ensure the well-being of a small child. It now takes place in a pit that represents the semisubterranean dwelling of precontact times. While the medicine woman (a shaman) works on the child in the center, men and young girls line the perimeter of the pit. Their singing and dancing in place is believed to assist in the ritual therapy. Dances that are rarely performed today include the Flower Dance (girls' puberty dance) and the Kick Dance (doctor-making dance)—this last performed to assist a female shaman in controlling her special abilities. Others that probably were not performed after 1890, and about which nothing is known, include the War Dance, the Death-Purification Dance, and the Fish Dam Dance.

Central California. The central California groups include the Yuki, Pomo, Wintun, Maidu, Costanoan, Miwok, Yokuts, and Mono. Except for the dance of the southerly Yokuts and Mono, which reflected their proximity to Great Basin and southern California cultures, dance rituals of the central tribes featured impersonation of supernatural beings. These rituals were typically held in large, semisubterranean ceremonial chambers and lasted for several nights. Some of the dances were named after animals and involved imitation of the animal itself, but more important impersonations featured abstract beings such as the Yuki creator figure Taikomol or the widely revered deity Kuksu, who was impersonated in dance among the Wintun, Maidu, Pomo, and Miwok.

Impersonators often wore the "bighead" costume, an enormous headdress of feathers attached to radiating sticks. Otherwise the dancers might wear feathered capes, fastened to a network, that entirely covered their heads and bodies. Their dance movements were vigorous, acrobatic, and sometimes menacing to the onlookers. In some instances they handled rattlesnakes, swallowed burning coals, or performed other feats of magic. Although such events clearly were intended to inspire awe rather than simply to entertain, dance performances generally included clown figures who improvised amusing antics and managed the audience between sacred segments.

The spirit impersonation dances were conducted by members of a male secret society; generally, the rituals included elements of initiation or instruction for boys. The boys progressed from lesser to more important impersonations as they grew older. These dance rituals varied greatly from group to group, each having its own annual cycle of ceremonies that included sacred or dangerous impersonations and lesser dances performed by men and women or by women only.

During the 1870s the Ghost Dance cult swept through northern California and transformed the aboriginal cults. Whether known as the Earth Lodge cult or the Maru (Dreamer) cult, the new religions combined the older aboriginal practices with the ideas of new "prophets." The details of dance ritual, the design of bighead costumes, and some other aspects of ceremony came to be determined

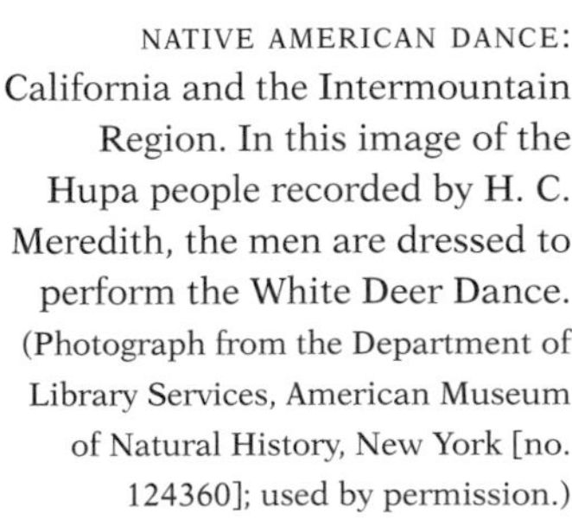

NATIVE AMERICAN DANCE: California and the Intermountain Region. In this image of the Hupa people recorded by H. C. Meredith, the men are dressed to perform the White Deer Dance. (Photograph from the Department of Library Services, American Museum of Natural History, New York [no. 124360]; used by permission.)

by the dream experiences of the major *maru* of each community.

Southern California. In general, mourning ceremonies and initiatory rituals were the most important contexts for the dances of southern California tribes such as the Luiseño, Diegueño, and Cahuilla (the so-called Mission Indians). The annual mourning ceremony, held for all tribal members who had died within a given year rather than upon the death of an individual, was also known among the Yokuts, Maidu, and Miwok of central California; however, this type of ritual was more specialized among the southern tribes and included several ritual elements. In the Image Ceremony, effigies of the dead were burned; this spectacle included a solo performance known in English as the Whirling Dance. In the Eagle Dance, one of the sacred animals was ritually killed; the Fire Ceremony also included dancing.

The main initiatory rite was the Toloache ceremony, in which jimson weed *(Datura stramonium)*, a psychoactive substance of the nightshade family, was ritually administered to boys. After taking the drug, the boys were marched around a fire until they dropped from the intoxication, in a dance known among the Luiseño as the *tanish*. Their adult attendants then danced the *tanish* until dawn. Dance was also part of the girls' puberty ceremony.

European Settlement. The Spanish first reached California in 1542, and Native American societies in southern California were severely disrupted by continuous European settlement and by the Christian missionization that took place over the next three hundred years. California was ceded to the United States in 1848 after Mexico's defeat in the Mexican War; in that year gold was discovered, bringing thousands of new settlers; it became the thirty-first state in 1850. Native Americans of the northern and Sierra Nevada areas were spared general contact with Europeans before the gold rush of 1849–1850.

BIBLIOGRAPHY

Barrett, Samuel. *Ceremonies of the Pomo Indians.* Berkeley, 1917.

Barrett, Samuel. "The Jump Dance at Hupa, 1962." *Kroeber Anthropological Society Papers* 28 (1963): 73–85.

Du Bois, Constance Goddard. *The Religion of the Luiseño Indians of Southern California.* Berkeley, 1908.

Du Bois, Cora Alice. *The 1870 Ghost Dance.* Berkeley, 1939.

Gifford, E. W. *Central Miwok Ceremonies.* Berkeley, 1955.

Goldschmidt, Walter R., and Harold E. Driver. *The Hupa White Deerskin Dance.* Berkeley, 1940.

Handbook of North American Indians, vol. 8, *California.* Washington, D.C., 1978.

Keeling, Richard. "Songs of the Brush Dance and Their Basis in Oral-Expressive Magic." Ph.D. diss., University of California, Los Angeles, 1982.

Kroeber, A. L. *Handbook of the Indians of California.* Bureau of American Ethnology, Bulletin 78. Washington, D.C., 1925.

Loeb, Edwin M. *The Western Kuksu Cult.* Berkeley, 1932.

Loeb, Edwin M. *The Eastern Kuksu Cult.* Berkeley, 1933.

Meighan, Clement W., and Francis A. Riddell. *The Maru Cult of the Pomo Indians.* Los Angeles, 1972.

Waterman, T. T. *The Religious Practices of the Diegueño Indians.* Berkeley, 1910.

RICHARD KEELING

The Northwest Coast

Among the native peoples of the Northwest Coast—the Pacific coastal region of North America from southeastern Alaska to the State of Washington—individuals of high rank established and maintained their position in the community by holding feasts and displaying material and intellectual property, called *privileges* in the anthropological literature. These privileges might include songs, stories, dances, personal names, totem poles, house carvings, and ritual objects. The people who participated in and witnessed these displays were given gifts to remember the occasion. The individual who thus displayed and dispersed his wealth assumed higher status in the community; in this way the social order of the village and beyond was modulated and maintained. The ceremonies are generally called *potlatches* in English. Dances take different forms in the various regions of the coast, but in all groups both men and women dance.

Southern Region. In the southern coastal region, the sacred dances of the Salish are personal in nature. A dancer acquires a dance by going on a vision quest involving isolation and fasting. It is customary not to reveal to anyone the exact nature of a vision; instead, a general feeling of the encounter with a spirit is expressed in the dance. Such dances are performed in longhouses fifty feet wide (15 meters) and up to four hundred feet (130 meters) long, with benches along the sides and back for the audience. One or more fires burn down the center of the packed-earth floor. When it is a male solo dancer's turn to perform, he rises from his seat and begins to dance, making a complete counterclockwise circuit of the fires. He is accompanied around the house by several musicians playing drums and singing. Each dancer has his own dance, combining movements taken from a standard repertory, always including an emphasis on movement of the upper torso. Here, and along most of the coast, the ability to shake the hands and fingers continually in a nonspasmodic way is considered the sign of a good dancer.

Central Region. In the central coastal region, the sacred dances of the Kwakiutl, Bella Coola, and Northern Wakashan (Bella Bella) are usually inherited; they enact the story of an individual encountering a supernatural being. In earlier times the dancer left the village, supposedly spirited away by his supernatural patrons. When the dancer returned after hours, days, or even months, he was considered "wild." The dancer appeared here and there around the beachfront village, dancing in a frenzied manner. Attendants performing a role assigned by privilege rushed about trying to capture and subdue the wild dancer, accompanied by eerie sounds played on whistles and drums.

Later that night, when all the people were assembled in one of the large plank houses, the dancer reappeared at the back of the dance floor and danced around the large central fire. The audience sat across the front and along the sides of the house and the singers across the back. The details of the dance varied with the specific dance being performed and the individual dancer.

The dancer is almost always considered to be dangerous, either because he has received special powers from a supernatural being, or, as with the Bella Coola, because this is considered to be a reenactment of ceremonies of the supernatural beings in their own realm. Attendants accompany the dancer to aid him, but they usually attempt to make it appear that they are working to protect the audience from the dancer. As the dances progress, the dancer becomes increasingly tame, but even at the end of the dance sequence he is still seen as dangerous.

In the most common dance step the dancer alternates feet, bending both knees as he raises one foot parallel to the floor. He straightens each leg as he steps, causing his body to rise on the beat. The arms are bent and extended from the body in various positions. The Bella Coola men dance with both hands at head height slightly forward of the line of the shoulders, while the Kwakiutl often hold one hand near the hip while the other arm is extended in front with the hand slightly above the head.

The principal dancer is often followed by masked dancers. The masks are usually made of wood and range from simple humanoid face masks little larger than a human face to large bird and animal masks up to six feet (2 meters) long. Such masks are heavy and awkward, requiring the utmost in strength and skill to manage in a dance. Experienced dancers are usually hired to perform these dances.

The Vancouver Island people use fewer formal dance steps, instead giving a more naturalistic presentation of the supernatural being. These dances are accompanied by fast drumming. Though sometimes lacking in rhythm, they have a special kind of energy that strongly suggests the presence of the supernatural.

In dances that depict an episode of family history or a founding ancestor, the sequence usually begins with a headdress dance. The headdress consists of an elaborately carved mask seven or eight inches (twenty centimeters) high, attached to the front of a crown of swan skin with the down left on, and surmounted by a ring of sea-lion whiskers. On the back of the headdress is a canvas trailer covered with about fifty ermine skins, which hangs down the dancer's back and moves freely during the dance. The dancer usually wears an intricately decorated dance blanket, and sometimes matching leggings.

The headdress dance is performed with the torso bent slightly forward and the hands on the hips with fingers pointing toward the floor. The dancer hops to the beat, with both feet and knees apart, moving his head about in time to the music. Down, which has been placed inside the ring of sea-lion whiskers, floats out and around the dancer, creating a magical effect.

Sometimes the attendants, who are at first always careful to help, begin to harrass the dancer, who eventually becomes too disturbed to continue and rushes from the

NATIVE AMERICAN DANCE: The Northwest Coast. A studio portrait of a Kwakiutl man dressed for the Hamatsa Dance. Of all the winter ceremonies performed by the "dance societies" of the Northwest Coast, the Hamatsa Dance of the Kwakiutl was the most famous and, according to the Kwakiutl, the most powerful. The *hamatsa* was a human who had been abducted by supernatural creatures and imbued with a wild desire to consume human flesh. When he returned to his people, they gradually tamed his wildness and ferocious energy through a long series of ritual dances in which they pledged to sacrifice their wealth and, upon death, their souls to feed the spirits so that the world would remain in balance. (Photograph taken at the Columbian Exposition in Chicago, 1894; from the Department of Library Services, American Museum of Natural History, New York [no. 2A12823]; used by permission.)

NATIVE AMERICAN DANCE: The Northwest Coast. A studio portrait of a dancer bearing a wooden mask of a "killer whale" *(Orcinus orca)*, a large black-and-white dolphin still common in the waters off the Northwest Coast. Such heavy, elaborate masks required considerable strength and skill on the part of the dancer. Animal-mask dances were performed by the Bella Coola, the Kwakiutl, and other peoples of the central Northwest Coast. (Photograph attributed to Charles Carpenter, taken at the Columbian Exposition in Chicago, 1894; from the Department of Library Services, American Museum of Natural History, New York [no. 337927]; used by permission.)

house. The attendants follow and soon return to report that the dancer has vanished, and all that could be found was the headdress. Soon strange noises are heard outside. When the attendants investigate they find a supernatural being, who is carefully ushered in behind a curtain of dance blankets and then revealed to the audience. This dancer wears a mask depicting a being significant in the headdress dancer's family history, such as a bear, whale, crane, raven, or eagle. Some masks are quite remarkable—for example, echo, a mask with many interchangable mouths to imitate different sounds, or eagle, a mask that transforms into a man-sized sun. The dancers try to move in a way suggestive of the creature represented, so the performance is as much a pantomime as a dance.

Northern Region. In the northern coastal region, the Haida, Tsimshian, and Tlingit perform dances depicting family histories. These reach their most elaborate form among the Tlingit. Many dancers, some wearing headdresses of the type described above, some wearing small forehead masks, and others who are without masks dance together, led by a chief carrying a dance baton. The baton is usually about six feet (2 meters) long, with half this length being a round handle and the rest a flattened paddle blade decorated with clan symbols. Often one edge of the paddle has tufts of human hair set into it, imparting a sinuous quality when in motion. The chief holds the baton in various positions, sometimes parallel to the floor or at a steep angle, and moves it vigorously in time to the music. Each dancer takes a part in the story being acted; thus a variety of dance genres are represented simultaneously.

These dances are still performed today, though much abbreviated from former times. Usually the religious aspects of the dances are now omitted, but the dramatic elements remain. Community organizations, often with government funding, are working to preserve the elders' knowledge of dance traditions and to help children learn them. Many Northwest Coast towns now have well-trained dance troupes that participate in regional festivals as well as potlatches. The major function of the potlatch today is as a memorial to a deceased person.

BIBLIOGRAPHY

Amoss, Pamela. *Coast Salish Spirit Dancing.* Seattle, 1978.

Boas, Franz. *The Social Organization and the Secret Societies of the Kwakiutl Indians.* Washington, D.C., 1895.

McIlwraith, T. F. *The Bella Coola Indians.* 2 vols. Toronto, 1948.

Swanton, John R. *Contributions to the Ethnology of the Haida.* Leiden, 1905.

HARRY J. CALKINS

The Far North

The native peoples of Alaska belong to four language families: Eskimo-Aleut, Na-Dene, Haida, and Tsimshian. The last two and the Tlingit and Eyak peoples (who are part of the Na-Dene group) are culturally associated with the Northwest Coast. The Athabaskans—widespread peoples of the northwestern plains and woodlands of Alaska, Canada, and the northern tier of the United States—are the major branch of the Na-Dene family. Alaskan Eskimos comprise two main branches, subarctic Yupik and coastal arctic Inupiaq (they live in Alaska, Canada, and Greenland; by Canadians they are known as Inuit). The Aleuts of the Aleutian Island chain have a distinctive arctic maritime culture. Most Alaskan native peoples still inhabit, and largely own, their ancestral territories. Ceremonial culture faded by the mid-twentieth century but by the 1970s began to return and by the 1990s is vigorous throughout the state; traditional dances remain integral in the lives of many Alaska Natives.

Eskimo-Aleut. The Inupiaq Eskimo, numbering about twelve thousand, reside mostly in coastal communities above the Arctic Circle. Hunting, especially of sea mammals, and fishing were the main source of their traditional subsistence. The central Yupik Eskimo number about twenty thousand and reside in southwestern Alaska, on the seacoast, along rivers, and on Nunivak and Nelson islands. Subsistence was primarily fishing and sea-mammal hunting but reindeer herding, land game hunting, and trapping were also important. Today subsistence is supplemented by imported goods.

Traditional Inupiaq dance is now performed by rehearsed and uniformed teams at festivals in which pairs of neighboring villages alternate at hosting and feasting guest teams. This practice is derived from ancient festivals, such as the Messenger Feast. Motions, primarily mimetic, enact significant events in cultural history, such as hunting adventures.

Inupiaq dance is classified as either *sayuun* (unison fixed motions) or *atuutipiaq* (free motions, at will). Yupik dance tradition classifies motions according to gender—for example, the men's stomping dance *(puallassuutnek)*, the men's kneeling dance *(arulassuutnek)*, or the women's rhythmic knee-bend dance *(putuluteng)*.

In some villages, dance participation is based partly on membership in a ceremonial whaling lodge and contributions to whaling crew labor. Drumming ensembles wielding light frame drums accompany dance teams, with an experienced drummer often composing dances and songs. Dancing is prestigious and is led by the most skilled and respected elders, although the most spectacular solos tend to be danced by young men.

The well-organized team aspect of Alaskan Eskimo dancing contrasts with dance in Canada, where subsistence is sparser and ceremonialism less prominent, and where small nomadic groups of inland Eskimos once followed the caribou herds. In Canada, dance is restricted mainly to the solo drum dance, with one male dancer wielding the large, heavy frame drum, encircled by singers.

Eskimo dance utilizes many male-based subsistence-derived motifs, such as scanning the horizon, harpooning, and sledding; but women mime carcass-cutting, meat-hauling, and skin-sewing. Any motion performed to the left is usually repeated to the right. In the *sayuun,* the feet rarely leave the ground, but trunk, arm, and head movements are vigorous. The neck projects rapidly in and out, turkey-style. The palms of the hands are used expressively, turning this way and that like the fins of a swimming seal. The knees bend rhythmically in time with the drumbeat, which is mainly in 5/8 time. Drummers sing but do not dance. Dancers do not sing or drum. The surrounding audience may sing with the drummers. Both Yupik and Inupiaq dance are characterized by movements using limited ground area and seated or crouching body positions, characteristics dictated by performance in low-ceilinged semisubterranean winter houses.

Yupik female dancers kneel and wave circular dance fans of beaded woven grass, decorated with fur or feathers. They may wear crownlike headdresses of wolverine or other fur. There are numerous stanzas, cycles, or sections in each Yupik dance. Male dancers are more mobile but often dance in a bent-knee position; they frequently employ elaborate masks.

Inupiaq dancers stand; they often wear loonskin headdresses with the beak projecting in front, symbolizing the shaman's dive to communicate with ocean spirits. Each dance is performed twice—once slowly with minimal movement, and once fast with energetic movement.

In both societies, dance humor is prominent, manifested in comic masks, parody of personalities, and antics such as scratching or sneezing. Humor helps people crowded together for long periods of time indoors to get along with minimal hostility. Broadly comical performances are given by men and older women.

Numerous Eskimo ritual dances survive. These include the whalers' Puppet Dance, the whalers' Masquerade (transvestite) Dance, the Walrus-skin Toss, the Northern Lights Dance, the Box-Drum Dance, and the Spinning-Top Dance. In the last, a spun top throws off flying feathers that must be caught in order to ensure good fortune in the forthcoming whale hunt.

Movements for cultural preservation and revival began in the 1970s, stimulating the formation of many village dance troupes and the teaching of traditional dance to children. A coincident pan-Inuit movement brought Alaskan, Canadian, and Greenlandic dancers into contact at conferences and at festivals, such as the Arctic Winter Games. In the early 1980s a company led by Yupik dancer-composer Chuna McIntyre combined traditional dance and costume with theatrical and modern dance techniques, touring internationally. Extensive video documentation of dance events has been largely supported by government arts organizations.

Aleut. The people of the Aleutian Islands have suffered more from European and Russian incursion than has any other Alaskan group. They were decimated by disease, warfare, and slavery in the nineteenth-century Russian period; they were relocated by the Americans and Japanese during World War II. Their traditional religious culture was largely replaced by conversion to the Russian Orthodox church, so our knowledge of native Aleut dance comes mostly from reports of early explorers.

Shamanistic performances to contact the deities for good hunting or for healing included singing, dancing, and drumming, in common with shamanism over much of the Arctic. [*See* Shamanism.] The villages, some of which were quite large, held public ceremonies at which both men and women danced in groups. The dances were said to begin with subtle movements, accelerating to violent ones. The women shook rattles made from inflated sea-mammal stomachs filled with pebbles. One important festival was held in association with whaling and featured masked dancers representing spirits and mythic people.

NATIVE AMERICAN DANCE. The Far North. At a 1940 whaling feast at Point Hope, Alaska, neighboring groups of Eskimos celebrate the joy of friendship and give thanks for their survival in the perilous Arctic. *(left)* Two women dance on long boards while men sing and accompany them on flat, hand-held drums. *(below)* A traditional "blanket-toss," the *nalukatuk*, a competitive game in which contestants are tossed higher and higher, literally "dancing in air." (Photographs by F. Rainey, from the Department of Library Services, American Museum of Natural History, New York [no. 338431; no. 2A3833]; used by permission.)

According to Lantis (1984), the men's dances mimed hunting and mockery, while women danced in unison; the men's dances were more individualistic.

Tlingit. In southeastern Alaska the Tlingit peoples number about ten thousand and are the northernmost of the Northwest Coast societies. This culture is distinguished by its rich maritime and forest resources, abundant game, skilled woodcarving, stylized art, elaborate social stratification (traditionally divided into nobles, commoners, and slaves), and its potlatch ceremonies, featuring oratory, theatrics, and dance.

Tlingit dances are considered the property of specific clans or moieties. A dance is performed by one group, addressed to a second group, in honor of a third group. The privilege of presenting a certain dance may be given in honor or conciliation, or even sold. Such privileges are inherited through matrilineal clans.

Dance staffs and dance costume indicate rank. Chiefs' hats consist of carved wooden bears' ears mounted with ermine tails, sea-lion whiskers, and swansdown. The down floats from the bobbing hat across a screen during dancing, bringing "peaceful feelings" to rivals. Patriarchs and matriarchs wear conical, woven-grass dance hats, upon the peak of which is affixed a stack of flattened cylinders of woven straw; these indicate the number of potlatches the dancer has given. Clan crests are depicted in fabric, paint, or buttons on colorful dance tunics.

Dance costume includes beaded dyed tunics, bibs, button blankets (large shawls of red wool decorated with white buttons), and the unusual octopus dance apron with four dangling "legs." Best known is the heavy Chilkat dance blanket, of mountain-goat wool woven onto shredded cedar bark. Called "the dancing fringe" by the Tlingit, it is woven with pictorial display in the round, and it features long, swinging fringes.

Leaders carry carved and painted wooden dance paddles bearing tufts of human hair. With these they demonstrate their office, keep the dancers in line, and direct masked dancers away from the fire.

Formal Tlingit dance is usually performed in a crouch, using short stiff jumps, during which both feet leave the ground. One dancer may move to the circle's center and mime the movements of a mythic protagonist, such as Master Raven the Trickster. In the Spirit Dance, a shaman, stripped and painted, shakes a rattle bearing the carved wooden figure of a medicine-man sucking power from a frog. He circles the patient, dancing and sniffing out the illness. In other dances, participants wear enormous flapping wings and painted dance masks with movable jaws.

Within the context of the social potlatch, Tlingit dance is a visible and audible sign of social hierarchy, formal clan relationships, and property rights. It symbolizes and embodies elaborate social etiquette, helps to validate status and seniority, and demonstrates the clan's corporate capacity to spend time ceremonially and to muster and exhibit wealth.

NATIVE AMERICAN DANCE. The Far North. Tlingit dancers and spectators at a 1901 potlatch in Sitka, Alaska. In this ceremonial challenge feast, goods were given away and destroyed to emphasize the wealth and abundance enjoyed by the participants. They wear long-fringed Chilkat blankets decorated with symbolic images and patterns; carved and painted dance staffs are held by three dancers. (Photograph by Blankenberg; from the Department of Library Services, American Museum of Natural History, New York [no. 338431]; used by permission.)

Athabaskan. The Alaskan Athabaskan Indians number about fifteen thousand with most residing in villages of a few hundred people in the interior of the state. Subsistence consists mainly of fishing in the large rivers such as the Yukon and the Tanana, maintaining traplines for fur, caribou and moose hunting, and berry gathering. The Northern Athabaskan language group also includes peoples of the Yukon and British Columbia, where they are known collectively as Déné.

Traditional dance is performed primarily at community gatherings, now called *potlatches* in English, but not as elaborate as those of the Tlingit. Alaskan Athabaskan dances are mostly done in a circle. The trunk is bent forward and sways to the fast steady quarter-note beat of a single moosehide frame drum. Feet barely leave the ground, and there is minimal floor pattern. Women usually shuffle in a progressing or stationary line, often with a syncopated step. In some traditions they hold and gesture with objects—nowadays, purchased scarves are usual. Men, both old and young, step out to perform strenuous solos in front of the lines of dancers, who encourage them with calls and laughter.

At the week-long Feast for the Dead, held every two or three years at Nulato or Kaltag on the lower Koyukon

River, dancers ceremoniously circle a decorated spruce pole erected in the center of the community hall, distribute large quantities of gifts, and formally honor a nucleus of guests who temporarily symbolize the deceased. These individuals are treated to delicacies once favored by the deceased, ritually dressed in new clothing, and silently thanked for having dressed the deceased for burial and carried the casket. The end of the event is marked by the Mask Dance, during which Yupik music and dance are humorously imitated. After this, the spruce pole is formally broken and thrown onto the frozen river, the lie of its pieces determining the next venue for the dance. The Feast for the Dead (also known as the *hi'o,* or Stick Dance) has six main functions: to repay the pallbearers; to symbolize the deceased; to aid the departed on their journey to the spirit world; cathectic release after the confining winter; charitable distribution of goods; and reaffirmation of social and kinship alliances, including trading partners, hunting partners, and in-laws.

Canadian and eastern Alaskan Athabaskans also adopted dance styles from the Scottish trappers and traders who founded in 1847 the Hudson's Bay Company trading post at Fort Yukon. Local festivities usually include line, round, square, and couple dances, including jigs, reels, and old-fashioned ballroom dances, accompanied by Shetland-style fiddling performed by old men, many of whom make their own instruments.

Alaskan Athabaskan dance costume consists of fringed and beaded brown hide tunics, circular feathered headdresses, and beaded fur moccasins. Dancers vigorously sing the accompanying dance songs. Dance songs often come to the composers in dreams or on vision quests. They are passed down in oral tradition; some songs are borrowed from other linguistic groups.

Athabaskan dance requires little material preparation, as might be expected of small nomadic bands. Formerly an important part of the food quest and of spirit placation, dance today reinforces community pride and ethnic identity.

[*For related discussion, see* Russia, *article on* Siberian Dance Traditions.]

BIBLIOGRAPHY

De Laguna, Frederica. *Under Mount Saint Elias.* 3 vols. Washington, D.C., 1972.

Hawkes, Ernest W. *The "Inviting-in" Feast of the Alaskan Eskimo.* Ottawa, 1913.

Hawkes, Ernest W. *The Dance Festivals of the Alaskan Eskimo.* Philadelphia, 1914.

Johnston, Thomas F. "Alaskan Eskimo Dance in Cultural Context." *Dance Research Journal* 7 (Spring–Summer 1975): 1–11.

Johnston, Thomas F. *Eskimo Music: A Circumpolar Comparative Survey.* Ottawa, 1976.

Johnston, Thomas F. "The Eskimo Songs of Northwestern Alaska." *Arctic* 29 (March 1976).

Johnston, Thomas F. "The Social Background of Eskimo Music in Northwest Alaska." *Journal of American Folklore* 89 (October–December 1976): 438–448.

Johnston, Thomas F. "Tlingit Indian Music and Dance." *Viltis* 36 (September–November 1977).

Johnston, Thomas F. "Humor, Drama, and Play in Alaskan Eskimo Mimetic Dance." *Western Canadian Journal of Anthropology* 8.1 (1978).

Johnston, Thomas F. "Cognitive Patterns in Eskimo Dance." *Inter-Nord* 16 (1982).

Koranda, Lorraine D. *Alaskan Eskimo Songs and Stories.* Seattle, 1972. Includes a recording.

Lantis, Margaret. *Alaskan Eskimo Ceremonialism.* Seattle, 1971.

Lantis, Margaret. "Aleut: In *Handbook of North American Indians,* vol. 5, *Arctic,* pp. 161–184. Washington, D.C., 1984.

Murdoch, John. *Ethnological Results of the Point Barrow Expedition.* In *9th Annual Report of the Bureau of American Ethnology for the Years 1887–1888,* pp. 19–441. Washington, D.C., 1892.

Nelson, Edward William. *The Eskimo about Bering Strait.* Washington, D.C., 1899.

Spencer, Robert F. *The North Alaskan Eskimo.* Washington, D.C., 1959.

THOMAS F. JOHNSTON

Dance Research and Publication

Writing on Native American dance ranges from descriptive surveys of the dances of various groups to analyses of the symbols, structures, and social meanings of particular dances. Since Native American peoples comprise many different groups, studies of specific areas are more numerous, and usually more informative, than general descriptions of Native American dance. Furthermore, because both dance forms and the perspective of the writers continue to change, works of different historical periods often present contrasting images and points of view.

In the nineteenth century, journalists, adventurers, and amateur anthropologists described Native Americans largely as curiosities or, following then-current theories of cultural evolution, approached them as fascinating but savage precursors of civilized humanity. Nevertheless, much of this work is historically important. Lewis Henry Morgan, for example (1954, first published in 1851), observed ceremonies of the Iroquois nation that are no longer performed, providing descriptions often rich in detail and in insight into the social and religious significance of the dances.

As anthropology developed in the late nineteenth and early twentieth centuries, descriptive emphasis was placed on the ethnographic and historical aspects of certain rituals, such as the Ghost Dance, part of a millennial religious movement (Spier, 1927). In other cases, emphasis was placed on dance as evidence of the diffusion of cultural traits (Gatyon, 1930), as the structural reflection of an entire way of life (Boas, [1944] 1972), or as manifestations of psychocultural themes (Benedict, 1934). Still other researchers emphasized the aesthetic and dramatic content of the ceremonies, presenting Native American dance as both religion and art, while describing the ceremonies and dances in great detail (Fergusson, 1931).

Ethnomusicologists studying Native American music also made substantial contributions to the literature. The most influential of them was Gertrude Prokosch Kurath, a modern dancer who studied ethnomusicology independently. She created a system for notating Native American dance and music in order to do research and to create a record for Native Americans themselves, working with them as collaborators. Her work marks an important shift of attention to the events and characteristics of the dance itself as subject matter for observation, notation, and analysis.

Most researchers in the first half of the twentieth century assumed that they were recording the remnants of almost extinct cultures. Yet many Native American cultures have survived, often adapting their traditions to emerging circumstances while maintaining key elements of their former cultures. Increasingly, writers are treating Native American dances less as historical artifacts and more as examples of ways of art and life that continue to endure and evolve. Studies have proliferated, including some by Native Americans, such as Alfonso Ortiz and Jamake Highwater.

The dance literature on the American Southwest, where Native American ceremonial life continues more vitally than in any other region of the United States, constitutes the most significant body of material. Vincent Scully's 1972 account of Pueblo dance and architecture attempts to define the aesthetic concepts of what the author sees as religious theater. Alfonso Ortiz's 1969 book on the Tewa (a Pueblo group) provides an anthropologist's structural and symbolic account of the Tewa worldview, which is embodied in the dance. Jill D. Sweet's 1985 book on Tewa dance presents an anthropological discussion of the structure and characteristics of the dances, as well as contextual analyses of their meanings and symbols.

The Congress on Research in Dance, in the periodicals *CORD Research Annual* and *Dance Research Journal,* have published many articles and reviews on Native American dance since the late 1960s. Further examples of contemporary research by both Native American and other writers are collected in anthologies edited by Charlotte Frisbie (1980) about theater, music, and dance, and by Charlotte Heth (1992), which include discussions of Native American modern dancers, powwows for political reasons and for tourism, and the American Indian Dance Theater.

BIBLIOGRAPHY

Benedict, Ruth. *Patterns of Culture.* Boston, 1934.

Boas, Franz. "Dance and Music in the Life of the Northwest Coast Indians of North America (Kwakiutl)." In *The Function of Dance in Human Society,* edited by Franziska Boas. 2d ed. Brooklyn, 1972.

Fergusson, Erna. *Dancing Gods: Indian Ceremonials of New Mexico and Arizona.* Albuquerque, 1931.

Frisbie, Charlotte J., ed. *Southwestern Indian Ritual Drama.* Albuquerque, 1980.

Gayton, A. H. *The Ghost Dance of 1870 in South-Central California.* Berkeley, 1930.

Heth, Charlotte, ed. *Native American Dance: Ceremonies and Social Traditions.* Washington, D.C., 1992.

Highwater, Jamake. *Ritual of the Wind: North American Indian Ceremonies, Music, and Dance.* Toronto, 1984.

Morgan, Lewis H. *League of the Ho-dé-no-sau-nee, or Iroquois.* 2 vols. Rochester, N.Y., 1851.

Ortiz, Alfonso. *The Tewa World: Space, Time, Being, and Becoming in a Pueblo Society.* Chicago, 1969.

Scully, Vincent. *Pueblo: Mountain, Village, Dance.* Chicago, 1972.

Spier, Leslie. *The Ghost Dance of 1870 among the Clamath of Oregon.* Seattle, 1927.

Sweet, Jill D. *Dances of the Tewa Pueblo Indians.* Santa Fe, 1985.

CYNTHIA J. NOVACK

NĀṬYAŚĀSTRA. The most ancient extant text on Indian dramaturgy, the *Nāṭyaśāstra* is believed to have been written sometime between the second century BCE and the second century CE; it is in Sanskrit, the classical Indo-European language of India. Ascribed to the sage Bharata, it is a monumental work covering dance, drama, music, and related arts and crafts. Its thirty-six chapters deal exhaustively with practically every aspect of the performing arts—their techniques, presentation, and appreciation. Among its subjects are theater architecture, scenery, costume, and properties; the religious rites to be observed at performances; music, dance, movements, and gestures, and the modes of delivery; the classification of roles; dramatic genres; the general characteristics of dramatic poetry; and the theory of *rasa,* the emotions which form a vital element in drama.

The *Nāṭyaśāstra* is not, contrary to some writers' belief, a manual of dance, nor is it an instruction manual for producing dramas. The principles that govern Indian classical dance can, however, be culled from its pages, since dance was integral to classical Sanskrit drama. In the fourth chapter, *Tāṇḍavalakṣaṇam,* there is a list of 108 dance sequences called *karaṇa*s, composed from various movements of the parts of the body. Other chapters associate these sequences with the expression of specific emotions. There are chapters dealing with the movements of the hands and of the feet, with seated and standing positions, and so on.

The text also deals with the types of *abhinaya,* or dramatic expression. It categorizes this into *lokadharmi,* or naturalistic acting, and *nāṭyadharmi,* or stylized movement.

Its painstaking observation of contemporary practice, conventions, and the tradition of the time gives the *Nāṭyaśāstra* a unique place in the literature of the performing arts. Remarkably, too, the principles detailed in it are still reflected in the neoclassical Indian dance of today.

[*See also* Asian Dance Traditions, *overview article.*]

BIBLIOGRAPHY

Gaston, Anne-Marie. *Śiva in Dance, Myth, and Iconography.* Delhi, 1982.

Hema Govindarajan. *The Nāṭyaśāstra and Bhārata Nāṭya.* New Delhi, 1992.

Iyer, Alessandra. "A Fresh Look at *Nṛtta.*" *Dance Research* 11 (Autumn 1993): 3–15.

Kale, Pramod. *The Theatric Universe: A Study of the Natyasastra.* Bombay, 1974.

Kavi, Manavalli Ramakrishna, ed. *Nāṭyaśāstra of Bharatamuni.* 4 vols. Gaekwad's Oriental Series, nos. 36, 68, 124, 145. Baroda, 1926–1964.

SUNIL KOTHARI

NAULT, FERNAND (Fernand Noël Boissonneault; born 27 December 1921 in Montreal), French Canadian dancer, choreographer, ballet master, and teacher. Nault received his early training in Montreal, studying ballet at the school of Maurice Lacasse-Morenoff, which he attended for six years, and modern dance with Elizabeth Leese. He first appeared on stage at Les Variétés Lyriques in shows choreographed by Morenoff. In 1944, Nault was chosen to replace an injured Todd Bolender during a local engagement by Ballet Theatre and was subsequently invited to join the company. As a professional dancer he was an avid student of the leading teachers in New York, London, and Paris, rarely missing an opportunity to take class with such luminaries as Edward Caton, Margaret Craske, Vera Nemchinova, Anatole Vilzak, Aubrey Hitchins, Valentina Pereyaslavec, Vera Volkova, Olga Preobrajenska, and Luigi. He was to remain with Ballet Theatre (later American Ballet Theatre) for twenty-one years, until 1965, distinguishing himself first as an outstanding character dancer and then as a respected ballet master and director of the company's school.

In 1965, Nault was invited by Ludmilla Chiriaeff to return to his hometown and join Les Grands Ballets Canadiens as co–artistic director and resident choreographer. In these roles he helped the fledgling company establish an international reputation within a very few years by creating a body of work of notable diversity, ranging in style from classical to neoclassical to contemporary. His first productions for Les Grands Ballets Canadiens were works that he had originally staged in the United States: *La Fille Mal Gardée* (1960), *Carmina Burana* (1962), and *The Nutcracker* (1963). Nault's production of *The Nutcracker*, incorporating innovative staging and dazzling spectacle, quickly became an annual event of the Christmas season in Montreal, and his imaginative choreography for *Carmina Burana* so successfully captured the power and lyricism of Carl Orff's compelling score that the ballet was a highlight of Expo 67 and a resounding success, making possible the company's first European tour the following year.

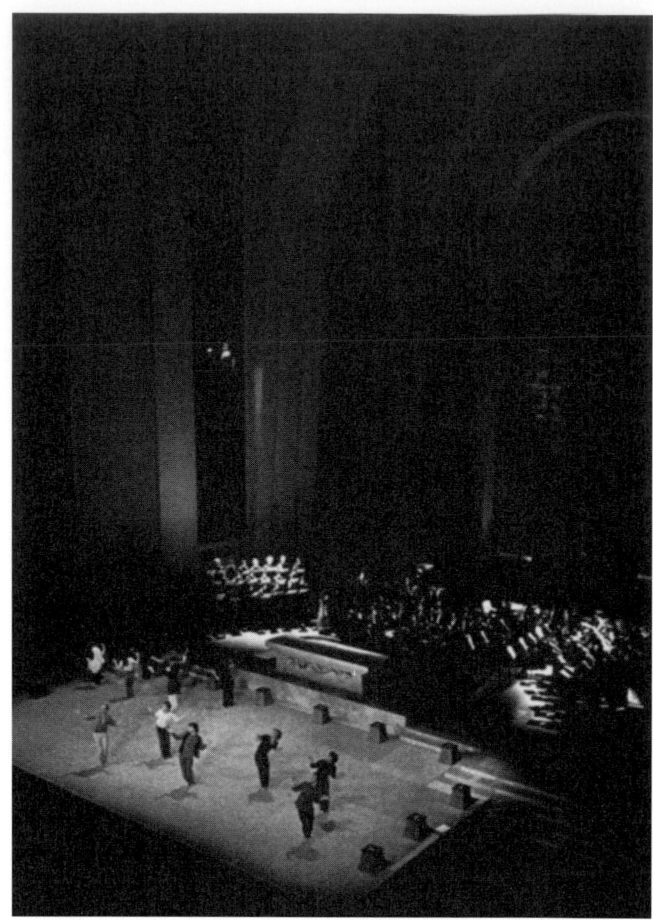

NAULT. The huge nave of Saint Joseph's Oratory in Montreal was the setting for this performance of Nault's *Symphony of Psalms* during Holy Week in the spring of 1970. Members of Les Grands Ballets Canadiens danced on a platform in front of the high altar; the Montreal Symphony Orchestra was seated at the rear. (Photograph from the archives of Les Grands Ballets Canadiens; courtesy of Ludmilla Chiriaeff.)

During the 1969/70 season, Nault created two extraordinary works. His production of *Tommy,* a rock opera by The Who, became the kind of megahit that ballet impresarios dream about. Although its choreography was unremarkable, its psychedelic production values, hippy symbolism, and message of love, peace, and flower power led to hundreds of performances before audiences of enthusiastic youths in many cities in North America and Europe. Almost at the other end of the artistic spectrum is Nault's choreography for Stravinsky's *Symphony of Psalms.* Presented for the first time in the nave of Saint Joseph's Oratory, Montreal, during Holy Week, this moving work and the occasion of its premiere did much to heal the breach between the performing arts and the largely Roman Catholic public of the province of Quebec. With the blessing of the church, dancing could be viewed not as occasion for sin but as a source of devotion and spiritual renewal.

Other notable works choreographed by Nault for Les Grands Ballets Canadiens include *Hip and Straight* (1967), *Cérémonie* (1972), *Incohérence* (1976), *Liberté Tempérée* (1976), *La Scouine* (1977), *Aurkhi* (1978), and *Les Sept Péchés Capitaux* (1978). Some of these ballets have been mounted for local companies in the United States and Canada, including the Denver Civic Ballet, the Atlanta Ballet, the Washington Ballet, the Colorado Ballet, and the Alberta Ballet. Throughout his career Nault has taken a special interest in the regional ballet movement in North America, serving not only as guest choreographer for several companies but as artistic director of the Louisville Civic Ballet (1959–1964) and the Colorado Ballet (1981–1982). In recent years, his works have been staged in countries as far afield as France and Korea.

Without question, however, Fernand Nault has made his most significant contribution to dance during his many years of association with Les Grands Ballets Canadiens. After resigning the post of co–artistic director in 1974, he remained as resident choreographer while serving also as choreographer and ballet master at the École Supérieure de Danse du Québec, the school established by Madame Chiriaeff in 1966. His special place in Canadian dance history has been recognized by two awards from the Canadian government, the Centennial Medal in 1967 and the Order of Canada in 1977. He was honored with the Prix Denise-Pelletier for the Performing Arts in 1984, and in 1990 he was made a Chevalier de l'Ordre National du Québec and was named choreographer emeritus of Les Grands Ballets Canadiens, a post he retains to the present day.

[*See also* Grands Ballets Canadiens, Les.]

BIBLIOGRAPHY

Citron, Paula. "The French Canadian Experience: Montreal's Les Grands Ballets Canadiens." *Dance Magazine* (April 1982): 62–69.

Crabb, Michael F. "Les Grands Ballets Canadiens." *Dancing Times* (July 1982): 744–745.

NAULT. The Christmas season in Montreal has been marked by performances of Nault's production of *Casse-Noisette* (The Nutcracker) every year since 1965. Here, the ensemble of Les Grands Ballets Canadiens is seen in a 1991 performance. Clara is seated in a swan-shaped boat at left, at the beginning of her journey to the Kingdom of the Sugarplum Fairy; a host of angels forms a semicircle as she departs. (Photograph by David Street; courtesy of Fernand Nault.)

Leddick, David. "Conversation with Fernand Nault." *Dance Magazine* (April 1960): 16–17.
Tembeck, Iro Valaskakis. *Dancing in Montreal: Seeds of a Choreographic History.* Studies in Dance History, vol. 5.2. Madison, Wis., 1994.
Thom, Rose Anne. "Fernand Nault and Les Grands Ballets Canadiens." *Dance Magazine* (July 1968): 54–57.
Wyman, Max. *Dance Canada: An Illustrated History.* Vancouver, 1989.

CLAUDE CONYERS

NAUTCH. The Anglo-Indian term *nautch,* derived from Hindi and Urdu *nāc,* and ultimately from Sanskrit *nāṭya,* was used in the eighteenth and nineteenth centuries to refer to Indian dance in very broad terms. Usually it denoted some variety of northern Indian *kathak,* but it could also refer to much simpler "light dances," such as those performed at wedding receptions or state banquets in the palaces of Rajasthan. The term could also refer to the dances of the female performers of Tamasha from Maharashtra, or it could indicate the dances of the *hijra,* bands of traditional transvestite performers of northern India. In the early decades of the twentieth century, the term *nautch* was also popularly used to denote a dance concert, as in the phrase *nautch kaccēri.* The term *nautch girl* usually indicated a female performer belonging to the class of courtesans, who were often practitioners of the performing arts. Although the word originated in northern India, its use by foreigners spread it throughout the subcontinent.

There are a number of pertinent illustrations in late nineteenth-century paintings, especially those made for sale to Europeans, which included such subject matter as architectural monuments, temples, bazaars, and portraits of the various castes showing their costumes and occupations. Among these are to be found quite detailed paintings of concerts arranged by British officials or by merchant princes to entertain Indian and European guests. Details of costumes and accompanying musicians and their instruments, as well as a variety of styles of presentation, can be derived from these documents.

The term *nautch,* in popular use into the late 1920s, became known in the United States through the choreographic impressions of *nautch* created by Ruth St. Denis. The term is not much used today in India; greater sophistication in knowledge of the varieties of dance, and the concomitant use of more specific terms, have rendered *nautch* too generalized a term for dance.

BIBLIOGRAPHY

Ruswa, Mirza Mohammad Hadi. *Umrao Jan Ada: Coutesan of Lucknow.* Translated by Khushwant Singh and M. A. Husaini. Bombay, 1961.

CLIFFORD REIS JONES

NAVAJO DANCE. The Navajos form the largest of the Native American nations in the United States. They speak an Athabaskan language, related to those of western Canada, and are thought to have migrated to the Southwest, assimilating with the Shoshone and the Yuma but remaining a distinct people with more than fifty clans. Today, the Navajo reservation lands of Arizona, New Mexico, and Utah comprise some 16 million acres, with lumbering, mining, and farming enterprises. The Navajo hold three major ceremonies that require dancing. The Blessing Way and the Mountain Way (the Fire Dance) are performed during the winter; the Enemy Way (the Squaw Dance) is performed in the summer and autumn. The majority of Navajo religious ceremonies are performed for individuals when they are ill, in contrast with the other major people of the American Southwest, the Pueblo, whose religious rituals are performed as part of a ceremonial calendar.

In Navajo culture, it is believed that there have been several epic migrations from other worlds to the present world. The migration into this world brought disease, sickness, poverty, and lice. These things were allowed to exist by twin gods, Child of the Water and Monster Slayer, as a check to keep people honest and striving for a good life. It is believed that if the people are out of harmonious contact with the forces of life, a disequilibrium occurs that results in illness.

A Navajo traditional believer who is ill consults a diagnostician, either a crystal gazer or a hand trembler, who prescribes a remedy, usually a ceremony. The patient then engages the suggested practitioner (usually male but sometimes female; sometimes called a *shaman* by outsiders) to conduct the appropriate ceremony. [*See* Shamanism.] The healer performs numerous activities during the days of the ceremony, including prayers, chants, purification rites, and sand painting. The dancing takes place at night, ending at dawn.

The dancers perform on the last two nights of the nine days and nights of the ceremony. On the last night, masked and fully costumed, the dancers represent the *Yei* (the holy people), and the lead dancer becomes Grandfather Talking God. While moving in a clockwise direction, in accord with the way the universe is perceived to turn, the dancers perform stomping steps that exorcise evil and sickness and send them back into the earth. The success of the ceremony and the dance depends on the healer's ability to manage the event properly and on the attitudes of the dancers and other participants; there must be unity among all involved. The dance team is contracted by the relatives of the patient. The team establishes a reputation based on the number of times it has participated in successful healing ceremonies.

Among the Navajo, one does not have to receive a vision to become a dancer, nor is dancing inherited. Learning to dance is voluntary and involves storing within the mind the abstracts of the myth complex. There are no Navajo secret societies or clan restrictions for the dancers. Similarly, a Navajo healer makes a decision to learn this role; there is no supernatural calling, vision, or inheritance of the office. By becoming apprenticed to an established healer, one eventually becomes a ritual specialist with a lifelong commitment to perform healing services.

Dancers participate in Navajo ceremonies for several reasons. They anticipate both direct and indirect rewards for their services; often they are paid with sheep, cattle, horses, or jewelry. By virtue of their participation they are also blessed with good health, long life, prosperity, and protection for their families. Transformed into beings of the mythical past, they are part of the cure in a healing ceremony.

Dance is important in Navajo society because it helps reinforce the whole mythical complex. Dance provides a bridge for the return of the mythical past that aids in curing. Without dance the Navajo universe would be incomplete, and there would be no hope of overcoming evil or reestablishing harmony with the elements of nature.

[*See also* Native American Dance.]

BIBLIOGRAPHY

Frisbie, Charlotte J. *Kinaaldá: A Study of the Navaho Girls' Puberty Ceremony.* Middletown, Conn., 1967.

Haile, Berard. *The Navaho Fire Dance.* Michaels, Ariz., 1946.

McAllester, David P. *Enemy Way Music: A Study of Social and Esthetic Values as Seen in Navaho Music.* Cambridge, Mass., 1954.

STEVE DARDEN

NEGRI, CESARE (born c.1535 in Milan, died c.1604 in Milan?), prominent Italian dancing master and author. Cesare Negri, called Il Trombone, is the author of an important dance manual, *Le gratie d'amore* (1602), reissued as *Nuove inventioni di balli* (1604). Dedicated to the ruler of Milan, Philip III of Spain, most of it was written during the long reign of Philip II (died 1598). The book is divided into three sections, or treatises: the first provides information about Negri's professional life, his colleagues, students, and productions; the second describes typical galliard steps and galliard variations of varying lengths, with a broad spectrum of technical demands; and the third gives definitions of steps and step patterns for dancing, with forty-three complete choreographies and their music (in Italian lute tablature and mensural notation). Illustrated throughout by Leon Pallavicino, *Le gratie d'amore* is perhaps the richest and most varied primary source of information available on social and theatrical dance at the courts of Italy in the latter half of the sixteenth century.

Negri apparently spent his entire career in Milanese service; he is unique among sixteenth-century dancing masters in the quantity of autobiographical information he provides on his fifty-year career, although it has not yet been confirmed by other sources. By his own account, he was highly successful. His sobriquet, Il Trombone, suggests both that he may have played the instrument and/or been known as a braggart, however. When his dancing master, Pompeo Diobono, was called to the court of France in 1554, Negri took his place, serving the Spanish governors of Milan until at least 1599 (he lists them in chronological order, along with his distinguished male and female students during the tenure of each governor). Indeed, his clientele comprised the cream of Italian aristocracy, including members of the Visconti, Medici, Gonzaga, and Este families. He seems also to have been connected to one of the humanist academies so popular with the nobility at that time, the Academico Inquieto di Milano. He participated in numerous official events as performer and/or director between 1555 and 1600, among them various kinds of celebrations for royalty or important dignitaries—for example, for Admiral Andrea Doria, during and after his triumph against the Turks in 1560, and for the visit of Queen Margaret of Spain to Milan in 1598. Negri accompanied Milanese notables on official journeys such as military campaigns and danced for them at Malta, Genoa, Naples, Florence, Mantua, and Saragossa. According to his accounts, some of the celebratory processions and spectacles under his direction comprised hundreds of participants and required considerable choreographic and theatrical skills of their director.

Negri resembles two of his most important contemporaries, Thoinot Arbeau of France and Fabritio Caroso of Rome. He, as they, sums up the practices of half a century: his dance style and choreographies are compatible with what is known of the international dance language of the time, and he employs a kind of dance notation (via terminology, punctuation, and musical notation) that permits a reasonable correlation of figures and steps with music. Despite these aspects in common, however—most especially those between Negri and Caroso—there are differences in terminology, favored dance types, formal structures, and details of steps, that await more examination. The subtitles of a number of Negri's dances (e.g., "adapted to the manner of Milan") indicate, furthermore, that he recognized a distinctive Milanese style yet to be studied in detail. For example, he gives both a "Pavaniglia alla Romana" (in Roman style) and a "Pavaniglia all'uso di Milano" (as done in Milan).

From a historical perspective, Negri's unique listing of the students in his classes, with information on when they were his pupils, may enable the dating of his dances, for each dance is dedicated to a lady, and most of his dedicatees are in the class lists he provides early in his book. If, indeed, his dance dedications reflect the years when each lady was his student, then his collection can be dated inclusively from 1563 to 1599. Intimations that he was using preexistent materials, however, suggest an even earlier validity for some aspects of a number of dances (e.g., "Balletto detto 'l Cesarino messo in uso dell' Autore" [Balletto called Cesarino arranged in the author's style"]). Such a long time span would effectively broaden the perspective on his book to include the entire second half of the sixteenth century in Italy (and perhaps elsewhere in Europe, wherever Italian dancing masters worked).

Negri is unique among his contemporaries in the extent of biographical detail he supplies for forty-four of his colleagues (including his teachers, peers, and professional pupils). He thus documents a well-established class of dancing masters, citing the kinds of occasions on which they showed their skills, the cities in which they taught, and the patrons they served. Indeed, his generous list reflects his awareness that he was part of a strong tradition of Italian dance. He takes further care to mention the particular specialties of the masters he names, whether in horsemanship, gymnastics, swordsmanship, music, dance technique (*prestezza della gamba* [speedy legs]), or in the invention of galliard and canary variations. He vividly demonstrates that dance was recognized in his time as one of the standard manly arts to be mastered by young gentlemen (closely related to horsemanship and swordsmanship) and as a performing art whose full panoply of skills required dedicated professionals. Negri, like Caroso, includes several dances by other masters in his manual (e.g., M[aestro] Stefano), which do not differ noticeably from his own. Furthermore, Negri and Caroso clearly share their awareness of a body of popular tunes or chord progressions (in the case of "Il Tordiglione," set by both masters, their music is in fact the same).

NEGRI. A dancing figure from Negri's 1602 treatise *Le gratie d'amore,* which contains directions for a series of virtuoso galliard variations involving pirouettes and *tours en l'air.* (Dance Collection, New York Public Library for the Performing Arts.)

The number, precision, and technical virtuosity of the galliard instructions that comprise the second section of *Le gratie d'amore* reveal the vaunted male techniques possessed by Negri and his colleagues. In sixty-three pages, he makes a major contribution to what is known of sixteenth-century dance technique; many of his virtuosic galliard steps or variations for men employ techniques that are still the basis for male showmanship in traditional ballet: rapid and successive multiple turns in the air, pirouettes on the ground, and various kinds of capers of up to six *intrecciati/entrechats;* there is just one page of much simpler variations for women. While Prospero Lutii (1587/1589) and Livio Lupi (1600/1607) published similar lists of variations, here (and in the galliard movements of his *balletti* in section three) Negri gives for each variation its exact number of leg gestures *(botte)* and exact total of six-beat measures *(tempi),* thus making close correlation possible with galliard music: for example, "Questa mutanza ha 25. botte, e cinque tempi di suo suono" (This variation has twenty-five strokes and takes five bars of music). Despite the detail, Negri nevertheless makes it abundantly clear that skilled improvisation in dance was expected and taught (just as it was in music and fencing). [*See* Galliard.]

In his third section, Negri gives rules for standard step patterns and then verbal descriptions with music for twenty-three *balletti* (normally in sets of variation or in multimovement variation suites); variation sets of two *pavaniglie,* a canary, and a *tordiglione* (tordion); three *basse,* four *alte,* two longways "for as many as will," and dances miming aspects of the tournament ("Barriera," "Torneo Amoroso," "La Battaglia"); except for "La Battaglia," the same types appear in Caroso's manuals. As in Caroso, couple dances predominate, and there are dance trios and dances for three couples. Negri, however, includes as well the only examples in sixteenth-century Italian sources of various types of two-couple dances (he gives thirteen). He also gives the first and only examples of Italian *brandi (branles),* a *nizzarda,* and the first Italian *alemana (allemande)* and *corrente (courante).*

Negri's manual is, furthermore, the only one of the time to give choreographies specified as theatrical for amateurs: among them two torch dances—one for six ladies and the other for six gentlemen "dressed as Hungarians."

He also refers to, but does not give in detail, some types of mock combat for males only that are clearly display dances: *mattaccino, mattaccinato,* and *combattimento.* Other dance types Negri only briefly describes or mentions include the *piantone* and *zoppa,* both types of galliard.

All the choreographies in *Le gratie d'amore* designate precisely which step patterns to do and when to do them. However, in a few instances Negri names steps he does not describe (e.g., *segnate*), thereby adding to the problems of reconstructing his dances. The step vocabulary Negri defines is highly concordant with Caroso's and with the other sixteenth-century Italian sources. The existence of a fairly large and highly varied step vocabulary regularly in use throughout Italy makes it clear that the dancers would have taken lessons in order to learn it. Also concordant with other sources are the figures in Negri's one-couple dances (see Caroso, 1967, 1986).

The figures of Negri's two-couple dances are danced either simultaneously by all or alternately (e.g., the two men dance simultaneously and then the two women); they include changes of partner, "Turns Single," partner turns by hands or arms, Heys for four with or without hands, and other two-couple figures; some of these figures, such as the Heys, appear first in the Italian *balli* of the fifteenth century, and most of these figures appear next in primary sources in the first edition of John Playford's *The English Dancing Master* (1651). Playford's book contains eight two-couple country dances, among which some titles, such as "Heartsease," can be traced back to the sixteenth century. All these figures exist today in the popular two-couple folk dances of France, Portugal, Spain, and Italy and in the United States in New England contradances and Appalachian running sets.

Some of Negri's figures in the group dances for three, six, or "as many as will" occur also in Caroso's group dances (e.g., heys with or without hands, both in circles or down a line, casting off, or changes of partner). Unique in sixteenth-century sources, however, although well known in group folk dances today, are such figures as *in foggia di lumaca* (in the shape of a snail; from Negri's "La Catena d'Amore"), known today in America as "winding up the ball of yarn."

Of the purely social dances in Negri's third section, the largest group is the nineteen dances for one couple; next in frequency come the thirteen two-couple dances cited above, and then a variety of other combinations for three dancers (two men and a women), three couples, or any number of couples. There is a range of dance types, variants of the pavane and galliard (e.g., "So Ben My Chi Bon Tempo"), virtuosic displays of memory and footwork in canary or *tordiglione* variations or in group dances similar to but more complex than the Virginia reel (e.g., "La Caccia d'Amore"), mock combat between the sexes (e.g., "La Battaglia"), dances in which the partners move through a series of formal figures that bring them no closer than a handhold (e.g., Cortesia Amorosa), and dances in embrace position whose steps and figures are largely improvised (e.g., La Nizzarda).

Negri's dances in his third section, although similar to Caroso's, are often more difficult, less symmetrical, and more varied choreographically. On the other hand, Negri's galliard movements that are part of *balletti* are more likely than Caroso's to call for basic galliard patterns *(cinque passi).* It is in his third section, however, that Negri reveals closest ties with Caroso's first book, *Il ballarino* (1581); Negri seems not to have known of Caroso's second book, *Nobiltà di dame* (1600), despite the fact that Negri's *Le gratie d'amore* was published two years later. Negri and Caroso compare quite closely in their versions of some dances (e.g., "Barrieras"). Negri not only praises Caroso highly in his first section but, most significantly, appears to plagiarize him directly in the step descriptions in his third section. Although some scholars have surmised, therefore, that Caroso was Negri's teacher, there is no evidence that they were even acquainted. In fact, the early date at which Negri began teaching and the probable dates of his dances render him and Caroso exact contemporaries. The issue of plagiarism cannot now be resolved; certainly such borrowing was not seen as a breach of morals or of law at that time. One explanatory theory suggests that both Negri and Caroso used an earlier source, now lost. The present significance of the strong resemblances in step definitions, however, lies not in the question of plagiarism but in the fact that in *Nobiltà* Caroso corrects errors he says he made in *Il ballarino.* Those very corrections may well apply also to the reconstruction of Negri's step patterns.

Negri's four choreographies designated as theatrical provide strong evidence of dance performance by noble Italian amateurs of the period. Together with Cavalieri's large-scale *ballo* for the Florentine *intermedi* of 1589, the dances presently constitute the entire corpus of precise choreographies (as distinguished from general descriptions) of this important genre of sixteenth-century Italy and may also contribute to what is known of stage choreographies at French and other courts. They include the presentation torch dance for six ladies, that for six "Hungarians," one for four shepherds (two couples), and a dance for four shepherds and four shepherdesses. The last named ("Brando detto Alta Regina"), the most complex of this group, follows a description of a set of *intermedi* of 1599 that, significantly, includes the tale of Orpheus—the same tale told by the first operas in about 1600 by Jacopo Peri and Claudio Monteverdi. Because early operas included dances whose choreographies are lost, and because some of the dance music in those operas and staged *balli* (e.g., Monteverdi's *Tirsi e Clori*) seems to have been conceived in the same tradition as that found in *Le gratie d'amore,* the small repertory Negri supplies is of utmost importance in any attempts at authentic revival of those works.

Like the dances, Negri's music also resembles Caroso's in its derivation from a large body of traditional material or popular "hits" (e.g., both use the same tune and chord scheme for "Il Tordiglione"; see Moe, 1956) and in its formal structures (variation sets, variation suites, refrain forms), skeletal and homophonic nature, expectations of performance practice, mysteries of notation, and problems of correlation with the dances. While these problems are beginning to yield to intensive systematic study in Negri as well as Caroso, they appear to be equally severe: for example Negri's unique rubrics heading each piece seem to give precise instructions regarding repetitions or returns of sections; though certainly useful, they often require modification for the dance to fit the music.

How far outside Italy Negri's and Caroso's style of dance extended in the sixteenth and early seventeenth centuries is unknown. It is known, however, that many sixteenth-century Italian dancing masters joined renowned Milanese armorers, swordsmen, and makers and players of musical instruments in spreading Italy's culture to major courts in Europe. Some of the dancing masters Negri lists (e.g., Virgilio Bracesco, in France) are documented in preserved court records of payment.

How late into the seventeenth century the style persisted is also uncertain. Negri and a number of his dances are mentioned specifically by Felippo degli Alessandri in 1620, and *Le gratie d'amore* was translated into Spanish in 1630 for the Duke of Sanlúcar. Nevertheless, it seems that by the 1620s, in northern Europe and England at least, the strength of the Italian style was giving way to one that was distinctly French, for in 1623 F[rançois] de Lauze disapproves of the showy tricks Negri espouses.

[*See also* Ballo and Balletto; *and the entries on the principal dance types mentioned herein. For related discussion, see the entry on Caroso.*]

BIBLIOGRAPHY: SOURCES

Alessandri, Filippo degli. *Discorso sopra il ballo.* Terni, 1620.

Anonymous. Four "balletti" from Tuscany c.1555, and a "Battaglia" (1559). In Gino Corti's "Cinque balli toscani del cinquecento." *Rivista Italiana di Musicologia* 12 (1977): 73–75.

Arbeau, Thoinot. *Orchesographie et traicte en forme de dialogve, par leqvel tovtes personnes pevvent facilement apprendre & practiquer l'honneste exercice des dances.* Langres 1588, 1589. Facsimile reprint, Langres, 1988. Reprinted with expanded title as *Orchesographie, metode, et teorie en forme de discovrs et tablatvre povr apprendre a dancer, battre le Tambour en toute sorte & diuersité de batteries, Iouët du fifre & arigot, tirer des armes & escrimer, auec autres honnestes exercices fort conuenables à la Ieunesse.* Langres, 1596. Facsimile reprint, Geneva, 1972.

Arbeau, Thoinot. *Orchesography.* 1589. Translated into English by Mary Stewart Evans. New York, 1948. Reprint with corrections, a new introduction, and notes by Julia Sutton, and representative steps and dances in Labanotation by Mireille Backer. New York, 1967.

Caroso, Fabritio. *Il ballarino* (1581). Facsimile reprint, New York, 1967.

Caroso, Fabritio. *Nobiltà di dame.* Venice, 1600, 1605. Facsimile reprint, Bologna, 1970. Reissued with order of illustrations changed as *Raccolta di varij balli.* Rome, 1630. Translated into English with eight introductory chapters by Julia Sutton, the music transcribed by F. Marian Walker. Oxford, 1986. Reprint with a step manual in Labanotation by Rachelle Palnick Tsachor and Julia Sutton, New York, 1995.

Cavalieri, Emilio de'. "Intermedio VI." In Cristofano Malvezzi's *Intermedii et concerti, fatti per la Commedia rappresentata in Firenze nelle Nozze del Serenissimo Don Ferdinando Medici et Madama Christiana di Loreno, Granduchi di Toscana.* Venice, 1591. Translated and edited by D.P. Walker as *Les Fêtes de Florence: Musique des intermèdes de "La Pellegrina."* Paris, 1963.

Cavalieri, Emilio de'. *La rappresentazione di anima e di corpo* (1600). Facsimile reprint, Bologna, 1967.

Compasso, Lutio. *Ballo della gagliarda.* Florence, 1560. Facsimile reprint with introduction by Barbara Sparti, Freiburg, 1995.

Davies, John. *Orchestra, or A Poem of Dancing.* London 1596.

Gardano, Angelo. *Balletti moderni facili per sonar sopra il liuto.* Venice, 1611.

Jacobilli, Ludovico. *Modo di ballare.* Circa 1615. Manuscript located in Foligno, Biblioteca Jacobilli, AIII.19, ff. 102–104.

Lauze, F[rançois] de. *Apologie de la danse, 1623.* Translated by Joan Wildeblood, and with original text, as *A Treatise of Instruction in Dancing and Deportment.* London, 1952.

Lupi, Livio. *Libro di gagliarde, tordiglione, passo e mezzo, canari e passeggi.* Palermo, 1600. Rev. ed., Palermo, 1607.

Lutti, Prospero. *Opera bellissima nella quale si contengono molte partite, et passeggi di gagliarda.* Perugia, 1589.

Mancini, Giulio. *Del origine et nobiltà del ballo* (c.1623–1630). Facsimile with introduction by Barbara Sparti, Freiburg, 1996.

Negri, Cesare. *Le gratie d'amore.* Milan, 1602. Reissued as *Nuove inventioni di balli.* Milan, 1604. Translated into Spanish by Don Balthasar Carlos for Señor Condé, Duke of Sanlucar, 1630. Manuscript located in Madrid, Biblioteca Nacional, MS 14085. Facsimile reprint of 1602, New York and Bologna, 1969. Literal translation into English and musical transcription by Yvonne Kendall. D.M.A. diss., Stanford University, 1985.

Thibault, Girard. *Académie de l'Espée.* Antwerp, 1628.

BIBLIOGRAPHY: OTHER STUDIES

Aldrich, Putnam. *Rhythm in Seventeenth-Century Italian Monody.* New York, 1966.

Bank, J.A. *Tactus, Tempo, and Notation in Mensural Music from the Thirteenth to the Seventeenth Century.* Amsterdam, 1972.

Brainard, Ingrid. "Ballo." In *The New Grove Dictionary of Music and Musicians.* London, 1980.

Brown, Alan. "Galliard" and "Pavan." In *The New Grove Dictionary of Music and Musicians.* London, 1980.

Brown, Howard M. "Alta." In *The New Grove Dictionary of Music and Musicians.* London, 1980.

Chew, Geoffrey. "Notation: III, 4. Mensural Notation from 1500." In *The New Grove Dictionary of Music and Musicians.* London, 1980.

Chilesotti, Oscar, ed. *Biblioteca di rarità musicali,* vol. 1, *Danze del secolo XVI trascritte in notazione moderne dalle opere: "Nobiltà di dame" del Sig. F. Caroso da Sermoneta; "Le gratie d'amore" di C. Negri, Milanese, detto il Trombone.* Milan, 1884.

Collins, Michael B. "The Performance of Coloration, Sesquialtera, and Hemiolia, 1450–1750." Ph.D. diss., Stanford University, 1963.

Collins, Michael B. "The Performance of Sesquialtera and Hemiolia in the Sixteenth Century." *Journal of the American Musicological Society* 17 (Spring 1964): 5–28.

Dalhaus, Carl. "Zur Theorie des Tactus im 16. Jahrhundert." *Archiv für Musikwissenschaft* 17 (1960): 22–39.

Dalhaus, Carl. "Zur Entstehung des modernen Taktsystems im 17. Jahrhundert." *Archiv für Musikwissenschaft* 18 (1961): 223–240.

Dieckmann, Jenny. *Die in deutscher Lautentabulatur überlieferten Tänze des 16. Jahrhunderts.* Kassel, 1931.

Gudewill, Kurt. "Courante." In *Die Musik in Geschichte und Gegenwart.* 1st ed., vol. 2, 1952. Kassel, 1949–1979.

Heartz, Daniel. "Tourdion." In *Die Musik in Geschichte und Gegenwart.* 1st ed., vol. 13, 1966. Kassel, 1949–1979.

Heartz, Daniel. "Branle." In *The New Grove Dictionary of Music and Musicians.* London, 1980.

Hudson, Richard, and Suzanne G. Cusick. "Balletto." In *The New Grove Dictionary of Music and Musicians.* London, 1980.

Hudson, Richard. "Canary" and "Pavaniglia." In *The New Grove Dictionary of Music and Musicians.* London, 1980.

Hudson, Richard. *The Allemande, the Balletto, and the Tanz.* Cambridge, 1986.

Jones, Pamela. "Spectacle in Milan: Cesare Negri's Torch Dances." *Early Music* 14.2 (1986): 182–198.

Jones, Pamela. "The Relation between Music and Dance in Cesare Negri's 'Le gratie d'amore' (1602)." 2 vols. Ph.D. diss., University of London, 1988.

Jones, Pamela. "The Editions of Cesare Negri's *Le Gratie d'Amore:* Choreographic Revisions in Printed Copies." *Studi musicali* 21 (1991): 21–33.

Kendall, Yvonne. "Rhythm, Meter, and *Tactus* in Sixteenth-Century Italian Court Dance: Reconstruction from a Theoretical Base." *Dance Research* (Spring 1990): 3–27.

Little, Meredith Ellis, and Suzanne G. Cusick. "Allemande" and "Courante." In *The New Grove Dictionary of Music and Musicians.* London, 1980.

Little, Meredith Ellis. "Saltarello." In *The New Grove Dictionary of Music and Musicians.* London, 1980.

Meyer, Ernst Hermann. "Ballo" and "Galliarde." In *Die Musik in Geschichte und Gegenwart.* 1st ed., vol. 1, 1949–1951; vol. 4, 1955. Kassel, 1949–1979.

Meyer, Ernst Hermann. "Concerted Instrumental Music." In *The New Oxford History of Music.* New York, 1968.

Moe, Lawrence H. "Dance Music in Printed Italian Lute Tablatures from 1507 to 1611." Ph.D. diss., Harvard University, 1956. See for further concordances in the music of Negri and Caroso.

Mönkemeyer, Helmut, ed. *Cesare Negri: "Nuove inventioni di balli."* 2 vols. Rodenkirchen, 1970. Music only, transcribed for guitar.

Nettl, Paul. "Ballett." In *Die Musik in Geschichte und Gegenwart.* 1st ed., vol. 1, 1949–1951. Kassel, 1949–1979.

Pirrotta, Nino, and Elena Povoledo. *Music and Theatre from Poliziano to Monteverdi.* Translated by Karen Eales. Cambridge, 1982.

Sutton, Julia. *Renaissance Revisited: Twelve Dances Reconstructed [in Labanotation] from the Originals of Thoinot Arbeau, Fabritio Caroso, and Cesare Negri.* New York, 1972.

Sutton, Julia. "Negri, Cesare." In *The New Grove Dictionary of Music and Musicians.* London, 1980.

Sutton, Julia. "Triple Pavans: Clues to Some Mysteries in Sixteenth-Century Dance." *Early Music* 14.2 (1986): 174–181.

Sutton, Julia. "Musical Forms and Dance Forms in the Dance Manuals of Sixteenth-Century Italy: Plato and the Varieties of Variation." In *The Marriage of Music and Dance: Papers from a Conference Held at the Guildhall School of Music and Drama, London, 9th–11th August 1991.* Cambridge, 1992.

Sutton, Julia, and Sibylle Dahms. "Ballo, Balletto." In *Die Musik in Geschichte und Gegenwart.* 2d ed., vol. 1, 1994. Kassel, 1994–.

Sutton, Julia. "Canario." In *Die Musik in Geschichte und Gegenwart.* 2d ed., vol. 2, 1995. Kassel, 1994–.

Tani, Gino. "Allemanda," "Alta," "Balletto," "Ballo," "Brando," "Canario," "Corrente," "Gagliarda," "Mattaccino," "Nizzarda," and "Tourdion." In *Enciclopedio dello spettacolo.* 9 vols. Rome, 1954–1968.

Walker, Thomas. "Ciaccona and Passacaglia: Remarks on Their Origin and Early History." *Journal of the American Musicological Society* 21 (1968): 300–320.

VIDEOTAPE Julia Sutton. *Il Ballarino (The Dancing Master),* a teaching videotape featuring a glossary of steps and three sixteenth-century Italian dances by Caroso and Negri (Pennington, N.J., 1991).

JULIA SUTTON

NĚMEČEK, JIŘÍ (born 12 April 1924 in Říčany u Prahy, Czechoslovakia, died 29 July 1991 in Prague), Czech dancer and choreographer. Němeček's most important ballet teacher was Jelizaveta Nikolská, who gave him the firm basics of the Russian classical school. At the age of fifteen, Němeček was apprenticing as a dancer at the National Theater in Prague. His first engagement (1940–1942) was with the operatic Tyl Theater in Prague-Nusle. The following season he was a member of the ballet corps in the National Theater, and during the 1943–1944 season he was a soloist in Wrocław, Poland.

After World War II, from 1945 to 1948, Němeček was again a soloist, this time in Opava, where he was named director of ballet in 1946. Over the course of his next engagement, in Brno under Ivo Váňa Psota from 1948 to 1951, Němeček polished his craft and gained professional rigor and discipline. From 1951 to 1957 he fully developed as a choreographer in Pilsen, where under his leadership a young, ambitious, and homogenous company soon was formed. Even though it was at Pilsen that Němeček's career as a dancer reached its peak, by then his central activity had already become choreography. He knew how to give his ballets a clear dramatic ground plan and how logically, effectively, and clearly to unfold the narrative of each ballet; he also knew how to build a clear plot and to give plasticity to individual characters. His production of *Youth* by Soviet composer Michail Tchulaki was chosen as the best theater performance of 1956.

Němeček's successes in Pilsen led to his being named ballet director of the Prague National Theater Ballet, a post he held from 1957 to 1970. At the National Theater also Němeček demonstrated his organizational abilities: He restructured the company, dividing it into the ballet proper and smaller groups for use in opera; he gradually expanded the corps to 150 dancers; and he consistently attended to the quality of not only premieres but also all reprises. His high expectations, which he insisted on emphatically, soon led to the creation of such peak productions as *The Servant of Two Masters,* to the music of Jarmil Burghauser, in 1958; *Othello,* set to music by Jan Hanuš, in 1959; Sergei Prokofiev's *Romeo and Juliet* in 1962; and *Conscience,* to music by Viliam Bukový, in 1964.

Němeček also was guest choreographer in Sofia, Amsterdam, and Havana. From 1971 to 1977 he was choreographer as well as director of ballet for the Musical Theater in Karlín and Prague-Nusle, a theater for operetta and musicals. Also in this period, from 1974 to 1977, he served simultaneously as director of ballet in Brno, where he staged a successful production of the Soviet ballet oratorio *Mother's Field* by Kalyi Moldobasanov. In 1977, Němeček returned to the National Theater in Prague as a choreographer, where he served as ballet director from 1979 to 1989. [*See* Prague National Theater Ballet.]

Němeček created more than seventy ballets as well as choreographies for opera, operetta, musicals, television, and films. The dominating aspects of his personality, rationality, discipline, and earnestness, were qualities that animated such socially committed and politically relevant works as *Youth, Conscience,* and *Mother's Field.* He was outstanding as a narrator of dramatic ballets but was less successful in plotless choreographies. More an epic dramatist than a lyricist, he embraced a hierarchy of values in which theater stood above dance, content above form, "what" above "how." He was the holder of several titles and distinctions. In 1972 the International Ballet Competition in Varna, Bulgaria—where Němeček often served as a member of the jury—awarded him a prize for contemporary choreography.

BIBLIOGRAPHY

Rey, Jan. "Change and Growth in Czechoslovakia." *Dance and Dancers* (October 1960): 14–17.

Schmidová, Lidka. *Československý balet.* Prague, 1962.

Vašut, Vladimír. *Jiří Němeček.* Prague, 1974.

VLADIMÍR VAŠUT
Translated from Czech

NERINA, NADIA (Nadine Judd; born 21 October 1927 in Cape Town, South Africa), dancer. Nerina's first dance studies were in Durban. In 1945 she arrived in London and was accepted at the Rambert School. She transferred to the Sadler's Wells Ballet School and joined the newly formed Sadler's Wells Theatre Ballet in 1946. For this company she premiered the Circus Dancer in Andrée Howard's *Mardi Gras,* winning immediate critical attention with the buoyancy of her technique and the charm of her manner.

In December 1947 she was transferred to the Sadler's Wells Ballet at Covent Garden and within three days was dancing the mazurka in *Les Sylphides.* Her progress thereafter was swift: principal roles (the Can-Can Dancer in *La Boutique Fantasque,* the premiere of Fairy Spring in Frederick Ashton's *Cinderella*) were followed by her first full-length interpretations, Cinderella and Swanilda, in 1951. In January 1952 she made her debut as Aurora, a role with which she was subsequently to be especially associated, through the joyous clarity and assurance of her dancing. Her first Sylvia (in Ashton's production), in November 1952, and her first Odette-Odile a month later confirmed that she was a ballerina of wide range.

With the assumption of Giselle in 1956, Nerina's repertory became the most extensive of any of her contemporaries of ballerina rank. Other roles included the Ballerina in *Petrouchka,* the Firebird (in which her superb jump lent a magic power to the role), principal dancer in George Balanchine's *Ballet Imperial,* and creations in Ashton's *Homage to the Queen, Variations on a Theme by Purcell,* and *Birthday Offering,* in which Ashton made a dazzling solo for her, with soaring jumps and double *tours;* she also created the Faded Beauty in Kenneth MacMillan's *Noctambules.*

She went on a British concert tour, with Alexis Rassine and two pianists, and performed a six-week season at the Palace Theatre, London, in 1958, in a variety bill. Twice nightly Nerina danced the Black Swan pas de deux (with Veit Bethke) and *The Dying Swan.* Between 1957 and

NERINA. As Lise, one of her most famous roles, Nerina strikes an exuberant arabesque in Frederick Ashton's *La Fille Mal Gardée* (1960). (Photograph by Houston Rogers; used by permission of the Board of Trustees of the Theatre Museum, London.)

1965, Nerina appeared in seven major programs for BBC-TV, including the landmark *Giselle,* broadcast live on 23 November 1958, with Nikolai Fadeyechev of the Bolshoi Ballet as Albrecht. In the autumn of 1960 Nerina was invited to dance in the Soviet Union, giving performances of *Swan Lake* at the Bolshoi Theater, Moscow, with Fadeyechev, and dancing *Giselle* at the Kirov Theater in Leningrad, partnered by Konstantin Sergeyev.

By that time Nerina had acquired the role that sums up the joyful brilliancy of her dancing: Lise in Ashton's *La Fille Mal Gardée,* partnered by David Blair. She was to dance this role and several others with great success during the Royal Ballet's visit to the Soviet Union in 1961. In the spring of 1962 Nerina was joined by Erik Bruhn for a series of performances at Covent Garden. In March 1963 she created the title role in Robert Helpmann's *Elektra.* For a guest appearance with Western Theatre Ballet, Peter Darrell created *Home* for her in February 1965. Her last major role before her retirement in 1969 was in Ashton's 1968 revival of *Sylvia.*

BIBLIOGRAPHY

Crisp, Clement, ed. *Ballerina: Portraits and Impressions of Nadia Nerina.* London, 1975.

Newman, Barbara. *Striking a Balance: Dancers Talk about Dancing.* Rev. ed. New York, 1992.

Swinson, Cyril. *Nadia Nerina.* London, 1957.

CLEMENT CRISP

NETHERLANDS. [*To survey the dance traditions of the Netherlands, this entry comprises seven articles:*

Folk and Traditional Dance
Social Dance
Theatrical Dance before 1900
Theatrical Dance, 1900–1945
Theatrical Dance since 1945
Dance Education
Dance Research and Publication

For further discussion of theatrical dance, see entries on individual companies, choreographers, and dancers.]

Folk and Traditional Dance

Neither the domination of Calvinist reform Christianity nor the development of industry, towns, and communication favored dance traditions in the Netherlands. Yet even with the general disinterest of medieval and Renaissance Dutch authorities, dances from the common western European dance culture were performed. Town archives from the fourteenth through sixteenth centuries, for example, listed either payments by guilds for "Moressen dancers" and sword dance teams, or decrees forbidding such dances. Period drawings, engravings, and paintings show line dances, couple dances, sword dances, and dances performed over eggs or clay tobacco pipes.

Because the Netherlands is a small country, urban influences easily extend into the rural regions, especially in the western provinces. And through their seafaring and trade, the Dutch have always shown a keen interest in the ways of foreigners, including their languages and dances.

Research. Research into Dutch dance traditions was not undertaken by folklorists until the early twentieth century. Concerned about vanishing folk traditions, they registered all kinds of folklore facts, including dances that were often mentioned only briefly or described poorly. The first book on Dutch folk music and dance, *Terschellinger volksleven* (Folklife in Terschelling), by musicologist Jaap Kunst, was published in 1915. Not until 1942 was there a summary of existing essays on folk dance subjects, the work of D. J. van der Ven.

The most important and useful collection of Dutch folk dances was made by A. Sanson-Catz and A. de Koe, two volumes of *Oude Nederlandse volksdansen* (Old Dutch Folk Dances), published in 1927 and 1929 and containing thirty-one dances. Their impetus for research was the revival of folk dancing by the post–World War I Dutch youth movement that opposed the new mass culture and the alcoholism, jazz music, and modern society dances that went with it. These young people were looking for their own means of expression through dress, song, and dance, and old folk dances met this need for group awareness and the resurrection of "natural" ways. Lacking a Dutch collection then, the dances were chosen from English, German, and Scandinavian collections.

Because the principal aim of Anne Sanson-Catz was to provide material for the youth movement's folk dance revival, she did not accentuate authenticity in form and style and thus often adapted or extended the dances with the addition of new forms. By teaching these mostly rural dances to city youths, she hoped to develop a new Dutch dance folklore. She found a fierce opponent in Elise van der Venten Bensel, who also was interested in a new dance folklore but who wanted to find a starting point for such a development in the seventeenth-century dances published in England by John Playford.

The Dances. One village in the eastern region of the Netherlands still has the tradition of everyone joining at Easter Sunday in the remains of an ancient carol-type chain dance, with the dancing reduced to a solemn walk. They call it "Vlöggelen." Also an ancient ritual dance uncovered by the earliest researchers is the "Zevensprong" (Seven Jumps), which probably dates as far back as Teutonic times.

All other folk dances clearly show the foreign influences of several fashions of social dance. In the northern regions, the Island of Terschelling and the province of Friesland, Scottish influences are recognizable in names such as "Skotse Fjouwer" and "Skotse Trije" (Scottish Four and Scottish Three) and also in steps and figures such as the reel. This Scottish influence may have come not only from Dutch sailors trading with Scotland but also from the Scottish brigades stationed as mercenary troops in the Netherlands from the early 1570s to the early 1780s.

The figure dances of the eastern and southern provinces show influences from the French quadrille. The "Vleegert" and the "Peerdesprong" (Horse Jump) resemble the quadrille only in their use of the square formation, whereas the "Mie Katoen" and "Overijsselse Kontradans" have a sequence of several quadrille figures. In the *horlepiep* (Dutch degeneration for *hornpipe*), one of the most interesting of Dutch dances, both French and Scottish influences meet.

Residents of all Dutch provinces also knew many of the dances common to and popular in the rest of nineteenth-century northwestern Europe, such as the waltz, polka, and mazurka. Variations on these included the "Hakke Tone" (Heel and Toe), a polka *piqué*; "De Slaapmuts" (The Nightcap), which was known as "La Sept" in France and "Siebenschritt" in Germany and Austria; "Driekusman"; and "Jan Pierewiet," a *varsovienne*. However, it was only on the island of Terschelling that these dances developed their distinct style of movement and variations.

Contemporary Practice. Contemporary folk dancing in the Netherlands began with the pioneering work of folk dance researchers after World War I and accelerated after World War II. There are two kinds of folk dance groups now: folkloric groups who perform dances from their own regions in authentic costumes and hobby folk dance groups, which developed during the Nazi occupation when the Germans forbade youth movements and allowed young people to meet only in folk dance groups. Today groups still meet and perform international folk dances simply for the pleasure of dancing.

In about 1950, local groups united into national organizations that changed the pre–World War II repertory of Dutch, German, English, and Scandinavian dances by dropping the German dances and adding French, American, Scottish, Israeli, Yugoslavian, and other Balkan dances. Today, African, Asian, and Pacific Island dances have been added. The organizations have done much to organize the training of teachers and improve dance techniques. Many demonstration groups and folk dance orchestras also have been formed.

Since 1972, there exists in the Netherlands a professional company, the International Folkloristisch Danstheater (International Folklore Dance Theater), which presents artistic performances of many countries' folk dances. Also, since that time, research into traditional Dutch dances has been renewed, and the discovered remnants have been adapted and integrated with new forms to suit the taste of modern folk dancers and audiences. In this way, folk dance has remained a living form as the Netherlands has moved to a modern society.

BIBLIOGRAPHY

Allenby Jaffe, Nigel, and Margaret Allenby Jaffe. *The Netherlands*. Skipton, England, 1982.

Bos, Marco, and Kees Notenboom. *Dansen uit Noord-Holland*. Hilversum, 1983.

Doorn-Last, Femke van. *Nederlandse volksdansen in de volksdansbeweging*. Neerlands Volksleven, 1980.

Doorn-Last, Femke van. *Leren lesgeven in volksdansen*. Winschoten, 1990.

Geael, Tineke van. "Folk Dance in the Netherlands." *Viltis* 51.5 (1993): 4–11.

Kloetstra, Jan. *Friese volksdansen*. Winschoten, 1980.

Korf-Schröder, Elsche H. E. *Terschelling danst*. Hilversum, 1983.

Korf-Schröder, Elsche H. E., and Frans Tromp. *Op goede voet*. De Bilt, 1991

Kunst, Jaap. *Terschellinger volksleven*. The Hague, 1951.

Olderaan, Elly. *Dansen uit de zuidelijke lage landen*. The Hague, 1985–.

Olderaan, Elly. *Dansen uit de zuidelijke lage landen*. 10 vols. Vught, 1985–1994.

Rimmer, Joan. *Two Dance Collections from Friesland*. Groningen, 1978.

Rimmer, Joan. *Sociale aspecten van enkele oudere Nederlandse dansen; enige muziekhistorische gegevens*. Nederlands Volksleven, 1980.

Sanson-Catz, A., and A. de Koe. *Oude Nederlandse volksdansen*. 2 vols. Amsterdam, 1927; Rotterdam, 1929.

Sanson-Catz, A., and A. de Koe. *Nederlandse volksdansen*. Rotterdam, 1971.

Tempel, Cees. *Muziek en dans uit Oost Nederland*. Hilversum, 1986.

Ven-ten Bensel, Elise van der, and D. J. van der Ven. *De volksdans in Nederland*. Naarden, 1942. Reprinted as *Volksdansen vroeger en nu* (Arnhem, 1981).

Ven-ten Bensel, Elise van der. *Dances of the Netherlands*. London, 1949.

Verberk, Marita. *Hopsa en 25 andere oude en gereconstrueerde Nederlandse dansen*. Winschoten, 1882.

FEMKE VAN DOORN-LAST

Social Dance

Social dance has always held a solid if disputed place in Dutch society. The few remaining seventeenth- and eighteenth-century treatises on dance show the strong Calvinist prejudice against dancing. Still, there were dance masters who taught privately and inconspicuously, as well as regular dance institutes that were approved and sometimes even initiated by city councils.

In many other countries, social dances had their origins in folk dance. In the Netherlands, however, the upper classes had no interest in their own country's culture, including dance, and frequently spoke a language other than Dutch among themselves. Courtiers and well-to-do merchant families danced whatever was the European fashion of the time. As a consequence, not a single social dance originated from a native Dutch folk dance.

At the beginning of the twentieth century, as manners and morals changed, social dancing began to spread through the different social classes, and the private dance

NETHERLANDS: Social Dance. This seventeenth-century etching by Cornelis Koning depicts dancers and musicians at an upper-class social gathering. (Courtesy of Madison U. Sowell and Debra H. Sowell, Brigham Young University, Provo, Utah.)

master became rare. The introduction of lively and often more informal dances from North and South America provoked controversy among the long-established dance institutes. Some refused to include these dances in their programs, while others saw that their exuberant, often provocative, appeal could not be stopped. Social dancing no longer was the product of a good education alone; it had become a favorite Dutch pastime.

The random growth of dance instruction brought the bona fide dance institutes together in 1921 to form the Nederlandse Vereeniging van Dansleraren (Dutch Association of Dance Teachers), an organization that still exists. The association established dance programs and mandated the awarding of teaching certificates. Today there are several other social dance organizations as well.

Since this more formal approach to instruction began, social dance has become ever more popular with the Dutch public. Even now the examinations for dance instructors are administered by a government-appointed civil servant. Thomas Bus in particular has been a great advocate of social dance and of high standards for organized teaching. All these efforts have paid off, and regular national and international dance competitions now attract not only many participants but also large audiences.

[*For related discussion, see* European Traditional Dance.]

BIBLIOGRAPHY

Brooks, Lynn Matluck. “Dancing at a Dutch University: The Franekar Dancing Master.” *Dance Chronicle* 9.2 (1986): 157–176; 9.3 (1986): 356–385.

Brooks, Lynn Matluck. “Court, Church, and Province: Dancing in the Netherlands, Seventeenth and Eighteenth Centuries.” *Dance Research Journal* 20 (Summer 1988): 19–28.

Holst, Johannes van. *Missive aan een vriend: Tegens de Antwoordt op een missive wegens een boekje genaamt de Dansmeester van Franeker geheekelt ende geholpen.* Leeuwarden, 1683.

Huber, Ulrik. *Dansmeester van Franequer geheekelt ende geholpen, nevens het Antwoordt op denselven.* Amsterdam, 1683.

Le Roy, Daniel. *Oordeelkundige aanmerkingen over de dansseryen, zoo der oude als latere volkeren, uit haar vornaamste grondbeginselen en in haar wezentlykste byzonderheden betoogt, met betrekking tot ons hedendaagsche Christendom.* Rotterdam, 1722.

INE RIETSTAP

Theatrical Dance before 1900

Dutch theatrical dance in the seventeenth, eighteenth, and nineteenth centuries was based on both French and, to a lesser degree, Italian theatrical dance. It was not influential internationally, and its national prominence was limited in that period as well, since theatrical dance was considered inferior to Dutch drama.

NETHERLANDS: Theatrical Dance before 1900. Carolina and Charlotta Frédéric were child performers who had distinguished careers in the Netherlands as they grew up. They were daughters of the actor-manager Frédéric Sluyter and grandnieces of François-Duval Malter, who was their teacher and dancing master at the Paris Opera. Their grandfather Malter ("the Englishman") had partnered Marie Sallé in her 1734 production of *Pygmalion* in London. This 1759 engraving, by Jan Punt after G. van der Myn, shows the two sisters, aged seven and nine, in a 1758 performance of that ballet in Amsterdam. (Courtesy of Madison U. Sowell and Debra H. Sowell, Brigham Young University, Provo, Utah.)

Few theatrical performances took place at the Dutch court in the seventeenth and eighteenth centuries. The only example of a court ballet, the *Ballet de la Paix* (Ballet of the Peace), was performed in The Hague on 7 and 13 February 1668 at the court of Prince William III of Orange. The seventeen-year-old prince danced in it as a Pastor, a Peasant Woman, and the god Mercury, who makes peace allegorically between the Netherlands and England.

The first public theater building, the Amsterdam Schouwburg (Theater), was opened in 1638. The first theatrical dance performed in it was the *Ballet van de Vijf Zinnen* (Ballet of the Five Senses), in 1645. The first dancing master paid by the Amsterdam Schouwburg was Joan Dutan in 1681. During the second half of the seventeenth century and the whole eighteenth century, ballet pieces were used as a prologue or as an afterpiece for a drama. Only the titles and in some cases the principal roles of these ballets are known. A few eighteenth-century printed libretti have been preserved. Dancing was also featured in some dramas, as in *Het Eeuwgetyde van den Amsteldamschen Schouwburg* (The Centenary of the Amsterdam Schouwburg), in 1738.

Among the ballet masters in the eighteenth century were Jan de Bruyn, Bernard Le Roy, Pietro Nieri, Antonio Busida, Giuseppe Monterossi, and Bernard Le Boeuf. According to a theatrical almanac from 1786, twelve dancers were employed by the Amsterdam Schouwburg. A special attraction in Amsterdam from 1758 to 1763 were the child dancers Carolina and Charlotta Frédéric, the elder of whom usually danced a boy's role.

Ballet at the Amsterdam Schouwburg reached its first peak under the direction of the French ballet master Jean Rochefort from 1801 until 1811. Thirteen printed libretti of his ballet-pantomimes and four of his manuscripts with notes about roles, costumes, and props have been preserved. His ballet-pantomimes were always performed after a drama, and the repertory featured about twelve per season. Two French ballet-pantomimes that were well known in his versions were *La Dansomanie* in 1807 and *La Fille Mal Gardée* in 1809. During Rochefort's period, about forty dancers were employed by the Amsterdam Schouwburg. The French Polly de Heus-Cuninghame was the most popular solo dancer, praised in reviews from 1801 until 1823. Her qualities were reflected in her high salary.

From Rochefort's departure in 1811 until 1828, the Schouwburg's ballet masters were Antoine Corniol, Louis Lachapelle, Pieter Greive with Jan van Well, Charles Soisson with Achille Soulier, and Michel Rives. The Dutch actor and visual artist Johannes Jelgerhuis made four sketches of the Viennese dancers Jeannette and Nanette Köbbler, who were performing at the Amsterdam

Schouwburg in 1812. One of these illustrations is an early depiction of a dancer on pointe. Jelgerhuis published *Theoretische lessen over de gesticulatie en mimiek* (Lessons on the Principles of Gesticulation and Mimic Expression; 1827–1830), an illustrated textbook for actors. Lesson twelve discusses the significance of ballet classes for actors.

In the nineteenth century, the Royal Schouwburg in The Hague, which opened in 1804, occasionally employed ballet dancers. Among the most memorable performances there was the 1836 staging of *La Sylphide* by guest choreographer Appiani (first name unknown).

Ballet at the Amsterdam Schouwburg reached its second peak under the direction of Andries van Hamme, ballet master from 1826 to 1868. The names of sixty dancers employed by the Amsterdam Schouwburg in the 1842/43 season are known, and more than 120 printed libretti of van Hamme's ballets have been preserved. The vast majority are fairy tales and adventures of Harlequin. Van Hamme also staged his own versions of French ballets, such as *La Gypsy* in 1840, *Esmeralda* in 1848, *La Sylphide* in 1848, and *Giselle* in 1853. Many printed libretti of guest choreographers from van Hamme's period have been preserved, among them Jean Rousset's first Amsterdam versions of *La Sylphide* in 1843 and of *Giselle* in 1844. Of the well-known French solo dancers, only Arthur Saint-Léon danced in Amsterdam and in The Hague, performing his *Tartini il Violinista* in 1853.

After van Hamme's death in 1868, his choreographies disappeared, and the tradition of the ballet at the Amsterdam Schouwburg was lost. By that time ballet was no longer considered a serious art genre by Dutch audiences and the press. Clearly, van Hamme did not have the enduring influence that August Bournonville had in Copenhagen.

The Viennese ballet master Franz Opfermann worked at the Amsterdam Schouwburg from 1870 to 1872. Then the ballet company was dissolved. In the 1880s Eduard Witt created some ballets for the Paleis voor Volksvlijt (Palace for People's Industry) and the Grand Théâtre, both popular theaters in Amsterdam.

By 1890, ballet had almost disappeared from the Netherlands. The performances of Loie Fuller in Amsterdam in the 1890s, however, presaged the gradual rise of modern dance in the country after 1900.

BIBLIOGRAPHY

Aken, Lucie J. N. K. van. *Catalogus: Nederlands toneel.* 3 vols. Amsterdam, 1954–1956.

Albach, Ben. "De Amsterdamse geschreven bronnen van de Nederlandse toneelgeschiedenis." *Scenarium* 1 (1977): 92–113.

Albach, Ben. "De geschreven bronnen buiten Amsterdam van de Nederlandse toneelgeschiedenis." *Scenarium* 3 (1979): 89–101.

Albach, Ben, and Paul Blom. "Uit in Amsterdam: Van schouwburgen en kermissen tussen 1780 en 1813." Paul Blom, Editor. *La France aux Pays-Bas: Invloeden in het verleden* (Vianen, 1985): 89–151.

Brinson, Peter. *Background to European Ballet: A Notebook from Its Archives.* Leyden, 1966.

Erenstein, Rob, Editor. *Een theatergeschiedenis der Nederlanden: Tien eeuwen drama en theater in Nederland en Vlaanderen.* Amsterdam, 1996.

Groot, Hans de. "Bibliografie van in Nederland verschenen 18de- en 19de-eeuwse toneeltijdschriften (1762–1850) en toneelalmanakken (1770–1843)." *Scenarium* 4 (1980): 118–157.

Jelgerhuis, Johannes. *Theoretische lessen over de gesticulatie en mimiek.* Amsterdam, 1827–1830. Reprint, 1970. Translated by Alfred Golding as *Classicistic Acting: Two Centuries of a Performance Tradition at the Amsterdam Schouwburg, to Which Is Appended an Annotated Translation of the "Lessons on the Principles of Gesticulation and Mimic Expression" of Johannes Jelgerhuis* (Lanham, Md., 1984).

Oey-de Vita, Elisa, and Marja Geesink. *Academie en schouwburg: Amsterdams toneelrepertoire, 1617–1665.* Amsterdam, 1983.

Paquot, Marcel. "Une fête politique à la française en 1668 chez le prince d'Orange." *Revue belge de philologie et d'histoire* 15 (1936): 23–45.

Rebling, Eberhard. *Een eeuw danskunst in Nederland.* Amsterdam, 1950.

Tuin, H. van der. "Gautier en Hollande: L'accueil fait à *Giselle,* 1844–1885." *Revue de littérature comparée* 44 (1970): 356–366.

Uitman, Hans. "Ein holländisches Hofballett." *Maske und Kothurn* 11 (1965): 156–163.

Uitman, Hans. *Toen de Parijse benen de Moerdijk passeerden! De invloed van de Parijse boulevardtheaters op het Amsterdamse ballet (1813–1868).* Leyden, 1996.

Van Aelbrouck, Jean-Philippe. *Dictionnaire des danseurs, chorégraphes et maîtres de danse à Bruxelles de 1600 à 1830.* Liège, 1994.

Veen, Henk T. van. "Ein italienischer Augenzeuge eines holländisches Balletts." *Maske und Kothurn* 27 (1981): 123–134.

Winter, Marian Hannah. *The Pre-Romantic Ballet.* London, 1974.

VIDEOTAPE. Dekker, Jellie, and Jessica Voeten. *De danswoede, of Episoden uit de Nederlandse dansgeschiedenis vanaf 1645 tot heden.* Nederlandse Omroep Stichting, 21 September 1993.

ARCHIVES. Gemeente Archief Amsterdam (Amsterdam Municipal Archives), Haags Gemeentemuseum (The Hague Municipal Museum), Koninklijke Bibliotheek (Royal Library), The Hague, Theater Instituut Nederland (Theater Institute of the Netherlands), Amsterdam, Universiteits Bibliotheek Amsterdam (Amsterdam University Library).

NANCY DE WILDE

Theatrical Dance, 1900–1945

Foreign pioneers and local enthusiasts helped to strengthen Dutch theatrical dance in the first years of the twentieth century. Between 1900 and 1921, Isadora Duncan and Émile Jaques-Dalcroze visited the Netherlands several times. Among their Dutch followers were Jacoba van der Pas and Lili Green, who both lived in The Hague. They opened studios and gave recitals and demonstrations based generally on the Dalcroze method.

For several years Green worked in London, where she visited ballet schools and performed with a Dutch partner, Henk van Dorp de Weyer. As was typical of ballet in those years, they called themselves Russian dancers, and they took the theatrical names Vallya Lodowka and Andreas

Pavley. Back in The Hague, with the support of Margareth Walker, Green opened a new school to give lessons in ballroom dance, modern dance, and ballet. In addition to touring abroad, Green produced many open-air spectacles with students and amateurs. In 1929 she published, in German, an explanation of what she called "plastic dancing" and her own dance notation. She founded another dance company in 1936, but it ceased existence with the German occupation of 1940.

In the first half of the twentieth century, Dutch theatrical dance was dominated by the German and Austrian modern dance developed by Rudolf Laban and Mary Wigman. Dancers seeking classical ballet training generally had to go to Paris.

In the 1920s the German dancers Angèle Sydoff and Gertrud Leistikov settled in The Hague and Amsterdam, respectively; they became the gatekeepers of the new dance for Dutch dancers who wanted to become professionals. Among their pupils were Corrie Hartong, Florrie Rodrigo, and Darja Collin, the founders of Dutch modern dance. Hartong was a true disciple of Mary Wigman's *absoluter Tanz* ("absolute dance"); she worked to reestablish dance as a full-fledged art. Rodrigo occupied an almost isolated place in Dutch dance history; her social involvement, political pugnacity, and affinity with communist ideals put their stamp on her dance career. [*See the entry on Hartong.*] Collin was the first Dutch dancer and choreographer to become an international star. She founded schools in Amsterdam and The Hague, started her own company, and introduced classical ballet with the support of the Russian ballet master Igor Schwezoff.

Schwezoff also led his own ballet group in Amsterdam. With Collin and Schwezoff, Iril Gadeskov (the stage name of Richard Vogelesang) became the third of this group that would be responsible for the spread and gradual acceptance of classical ballet by twentieth-century Dutch audiences. After a brilliant career as a "Russian dancer" in major Euopean cities, Gadeskov opened a ballet school in The Hague.

Before World War II, ballet performances were given sporadically in the Netherlands but often employed distinguished guest artists, as a list of those invited by the impresario Ernst Krauss shows: La Argentina, Vicente Escudero, Sent M'Ahesa, Uday Shankar, Alexander Sakharoff, Clothilde von Derp, Harald Kreutzberg, Yvonne Georgi, Nini Theilade, and Anna Pavlova, as well as the Ballets Russes de Serge Diaghilev. (Following Pavlova's sudden death in The Hague in 1931, Krauss organized an annual memorial performance for several years.)

In this period before the war, the followers of classical ballet and modern dance were implacable opponents. Kurt Jooss and Yvonne Georgi were among the few choreographers who lamented this situation and wanted to reconcile the two forms into one new genre of dance. Their impact on Dutch theatrical dance proved to be of great importance. Following his success with *The Green Table* in Paris in 1932, Kurt Jooss and his group visited the Netherlands—first with scarcely any response but later to enormous success. Among the Dutch dancers who went to his school or joined his company were Hans Snoek, Attie van den Berg, Noëlle de Mosa, Lucas Hoving, Darja Collin, Lou van Yck, and Evert Compaan.

Yvonne Georgi settled permanently in Amsterdam in 1936 and had a more direct influence. Showing a highly developed feeling for dramatic visual effects, she produced many dance spectacles in which she combined modern and classical principles. She started the Yvonne Georgi Ballet and opened her own school in Amsterdam, where she worked with Dutch composers, designers, and dancers. She offered dancers the chance to work under highly qualified guidance and also cultivated a broad public for new dance. Her entrance into the Dutch dance world had a stimulating effect and led to great artistic productivity until 1945. Her dominance, however, also led to the departure of other dance companies, including those led by Leistikov, Collin, Green, and Rodrigo. Opposed to Georgi's activities, some dancers in The Hague tried to form a new ensemble and dance union with the help of civil servants who favored the Nazi ideology. [*See the entry on Georgi.*]

The German occupation in 1940 had far-reaching consequences for the Dutch art world. In 1942 all artists, including dancers, had to become members of the Cultuur Kamer (Culture Chamber), which excluded Jewish artists; it prohibited compositions, books, and paintings of Russian, American, French, or English origin; and it exerted direct censorship. The dancers in The Hague, with their newly founded Netherlands Ballet (Nederlandsche Ballet; not the Nederlandse Ballet of 1954–1961), refused to work in Germany. As a consequence, they were forbidden to perform.

Georgi's almost bankrupt group became the ballet department of the Amsterdam Municipal Theater Institution, an organization controlled by the Germans. After the war, Georgi was punished for her collaboration by a one-year banishment from the stage. Bitter and disillusioned, she left the Netherlands in 1950.

BIBLIOGRAPHY

Buning, J. W. F. Werumeus. *De wereld van den dans.* Amsterdam, 1922.

Buning, J. W. F. Werumeus. *Dansen en danseressen.* Amsterdam, 1926.

Green, Lili. *Einfuhrung in das Wesen unserer Gesten und Bewegungen.* Berlin, 1929.

Schaik, Eva van. *Op gespannen voet: Geschiedenis van de Nederlandse theaterdans vanaf 1900.* Haarlem, 1981.

Westra, L. "Dans." In *Winkler Prins Encyclopedie van de Tweede Wereldoorlog.* Amsterdam, 1980.

EVA VAN SCHAIK

Theatrical Dance since 1945

After World War II, modern dance virtually disappeared in the Netherlands; anything of German origin or association—including prewar Dutch modern dance—was regarded with suspicion. This attitude allowed classical ballet to gain popularity quickly as artists turned to ballet after training in modern dance. In this climate, many foreign companies that toured the Netherlands set an example for Dutch ballet dancers and choreographers.

One of the first Dutch leaders was Hans Snoek. In 1945 she became artistic director of the new Scapino Ballet in Amsterdam (now known as Scapino Rotterdam), which is now the oldest dance group in the Netherlands. The company was the first to specialize in performances and demonstrations for schoolchildren, a project that was abandoned in 1992. Snoek was one of the so-called ballet matriarchy, the strong, authoritative women who dominated the Dutch dance world from the 1940s until the end of the 1960s. [*See* Scapino Rotterdam *and the entry on Snoek.*]

Another matriarch was Sonia Gaskell, who was both famous and notorious for the drill-like manner in which she professionalized Dutch ballet. She was more concerned with the craftsmanship of pure dance than with theatrical presentation. In her first companies from 1945 to 1954—Studio '45 and Ballet Recital I and II—Gaskell showed preferences for Russian ballet technique and the Diaghilev repertory as exemplified by the early ballets of Michel Fokine. [*See the entry on Gaskell.*]

The third matriarch was Mascha ter Weeme. She directed the Ballet of the Lowlands (Ballet der Lage Landen) in Amsterdam from its founding in 1947. Emphasizing the theatrical aspects of dance, ter Weeme demonstrated a preference for story ballets, especially those by English choreographers. [*See* Ballet der Lage Landen *and the entry on Weeme.*]

Immediately after the war, Amsterdam's opera, to which Yvonne Georgi's ballet company had been attached, was disbanded because of its collaboration with the German invaders. A new company, the Ballet of the Netherlands Opera, was founded in 1947 with Darja Collin as artistic director. Collin gave her dancers firm training in classical technique, but her own ballets were so unsuccessful that she was replaced in 1951 by Françoise Adret from Paris.

Like the Russian-oriented Gaskell, Adret stirred controversy because her transplantation of foreign traditions, such as annual examinations of all dancers taken into the Ballet of the Netherlands Opera. The repertory also took a distinctly French flavor, displaying the sensual charm found in the ballets of Adret's teacher, Serge Lifar, together with the eroticism of Roland Petit.

The companies of Adret, Gaskell, Snoek, and ter Weeme were all established in Amsterdam. Other smaller, short-lived companies included the Rotterdam Ballet Ensemble,

NETHERLANDS: Theatrical Dance since 1945. Members of the Netherlands Dance Theater in Benjamin Harkarvy's *Recital for Cellist and Eight Dancers* (1964), set to the music of J. S. Bach. (Photograph © 1965 by Hans van den Busken; used by permission.)

NETHERLANDS: Theatrical Dance since 1945. Dancers from the Netherlands Dance Theater in a 1981 performance of Jiří Kylián's *Symphony of Psalms* (1978), set to the score by Igor Stravinsky. (Photograph © 1981 by Jack Vartoogian; used by permission.)

directed by Netty van der Valk; the Residence Ballet of Peter Leoneff, which operated in The Hague; and the Ballet Marjo, also in The Hague, directed by Puck Goekoop.

In the 1940s and 1950s almost every Dutch company fared poorly because of a dearth of state financial support; the lone exception was the Ballet of the Netherlands Opera, which was subsidized by the city of Amsterdam. Dancers thus were badly paid and often earned their living by working in other jobs; most of the money available had to be spent in mounting productions.

The companies of Gaskell, Snoek, and ter Weeme also traveled extensively, performing in theaters, gymnasiums, and public halls. Through this pioneering work, these companies made ballet known to a new public and increased its popularity.

In 1945 the Netherlands Professional Association of Dance Artists (Nederlandse Beroepsvereniging van Danskunstenaars) was founded to promote theatrical dance. The task of promoting dance in general—from folk dance and ballroom dance to theatrical dance—has been carried out by the advisory, organizational, and documentary Central Dance Council (Centraal Dansberaad), founded in the Hague in 1957.

Ballet's increasing popularity also attracted the attention of the Dutch government, which in 1957 decided to establish and subsidize one large national ballet company. Thus began a bitter "ballet war" among the advocates of the three artistic leaders and their companies—ter Weeme of the Ballet of the Lowlands, Adret of the Ballet of the Netherlands Opera, and Gaskell of Ballet Recital II. This financial and political struggle brought several major changes.

First, in 1954 Gaskell became the leader of the first national company when her Ballet Recital II was transformed into the Netherlands Ballet; it was subsidized by the Dutch government and the municipal government of The Hague, the company's new home town. With this company Gaskell was able to follow her artistic principles and produce and perform standard pieces of the world repertory, both historical and modern, in addition to contemporary ballets created especially for the company's dancers. [*See* Netherlands Ballet.]

Second, in 1959 the Ballet of the Lowlands and the Ballet of the Netherlands Opera merged to become the Amsterdam Ballet under ter Weeme's direction. This new company then fused with the Netherlands Ballet in 1961 to become the Dutch National Ballet, which was based in Amsterdam and directed initially by Gaskell and ter Weeme, the latter withdrawing in 1962. [*See* Dutch National Ballet.]

Third, also in 1959, many of Gaskell's collaborators, colleagues, and leading principals and soloists left the Netherlands Ballet to form the Netherlands Dance Theater. These dissidents had three leaders: Gaskell's administrative director, Carel Birnie; ballet master Benjamin Harkarvy, whom Gaskell had invited to come to the Netherlands from the United States; and soloist Aart Verstegen. The new company was established in The Hague and was directed by Harkarvy for its first two years, and then by Hans van Manen from 1961. [*See* Netherlands Dance Theater.]

Thus the end of the ballet war in the 1960s resulted in two companies dominating the scene—Gaskell's Dutch National Ballet and the Netherlands Dance Theater of Harkarvy and van Manen. To some extent, the repertories of these companies are comparable in that they both perform contemporary ballets created for them. Both also have been influenced by American modern dance. This influence was greater in the Netherlands Dance Theater, which has had many American dancers as guest choreographers and, in the 1960s, Glen Tetley as a resident choreographer. The Dance Theater has been extremely successful in combining classical and modern dance techniques and in concentrating exclusively on chamber ballets with individualized roles for the dancers. The main distinction between the two companies is that the Dutch National Ballet focuses more on the standard pieces of the world repertory, from nineteenth-century Romantic ballets to Balanchine classics.

The smaller Scapino Ballet stayed out of the fray between the large companies because it had different and more educational aims. In 1970 Snoek withdrew as the Scapino's artistic director, a year after Gaskell retired as director of the Dutch National Ballet. The Dutch ballet matriarchy thus came to an end. For their respective companies, the 1960s had been years of consolidation.

Although the 1970s showed the public's growing interest in modern dance, most attention still was focused on the ballet scene represented by the Dutch National Ballet and the Netherlands Dance Theater. In 1968 the former came under the artistic direction of Rudi van Dantzig, who continued Gaskell's principles. Toer van Schayk and Hans van Manen joined van Dantzig as resident choreographers in 1971 and 1973, respectively. Thanks to their different approaches, Dutch ballet has an attractive variety—van Dantzig's heavy, tormented expressionism, the controlled and poised eroticism of van Manen, and the socially inclined, mild-tempered expressionism of van Schayk. [*See the entries on van Dantzig, van Manen, and van Schayk.*]

Following van Manen's departure in 1970 the Netherlands Dance Theater entered a period of decline, from which it recovered with the ballets of artistic director Jiří Kylián (from 1975). Kylián quickly developed into one of Europe's foremost choreographers with ballets that demonstrated his preference for the elegant and polished expression of emotions. Nils Christe, director of the Scapino Ballet from 1986 to 1992, stood out among the dancers who tried their hand at choreography under Kylián. Christe was succeeded in 1992 by Ed Wubbe, who also came from the Netherlands Dance Theater. Wubbe's athletic and energetic choreographic style has been influenced by Kylián, William Forsythe, and Hans van Manen. His ballets include *Rameau* (1990), set to music by Jean-Philippe Rameau; *Kathleen* (1994), set to music by Godflesn and Ruben Stern; and *Romeo and Julia* (1994), set to music by various composers. [*See the entry on Kylián.*]

Modern Dance. In the 1960s modern dance in the Netherlands underwent a strong revival with a decidedly American influence. This revival began in a company with educational aims, the Rotterdam Dance Center (Rotterdams Dans Centrum), which operated for two periods (1961–1964 and 1969–1975). Its director was Ineke Sluiter, a Graham-oriented choreographer. The two foremost representatives of Dutch modern dance in the 1960s were Pauline de Groot and Koert Stuyf (with his wife, the American dancer Ellen Edinoff); they may be considered the spiritual parents of postwar modern dance in the Netherlands. The development of modern dance was further stimulated by Lucas Hoving, who directed the Rotterdam Dance Center from 1971 to 1978.

At the beginning of the 1980s, more than thirty small modern dance companies were active in the Netherlands, the result of the seminal work begun in the 1960s. The most important were Foundation Contemporary Dance,

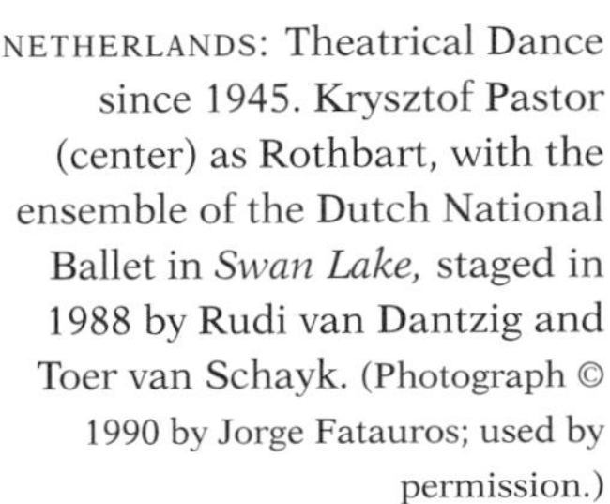

NETHERLANDS: Theatrical Dance since 1945. Krysztof Pastor (center) as Rothbart, with the ensemble of the Dutch National Ballet in *Swan Lake,* staged in 1988 by Rudi van Dantzig and Toer van Schayk. (Photograph © 1990 by Jorge Fatauros; used by permission.)

Pauline de Groot's company, Movement Company, Introdans, Penta Theater, Work Center Dance, Foundation Dance Production, and Krisztina de Châtel's company.

One of the first of these companies was Foundation Contemporary Dance (Stichting Eigentijdse Dans), which Koert Stuyf (born in Amsterdam, 6 June 1938) began with Edinoff in 1961. Following training in classical technique, Stuyf debuted with the Ballet of the Lowlands and then studied in New York with Merce Cunningham, Martha Graham, and Lucas Hoving, among others.

Stuyf and Edinoff's 1960s productions had much in common with Cunningham's happenings because of their interests in experimentation, pop art, and the composition principle of "planned change." The most sensational productions were *Focus I to V* (1966); *Visibility by Chance* (1967), created for the Dutch National Ballet; and *Mutation* (1968). The company explored abstract movement in relation to space, time, and light, and made often playful use of various objects. For example, one spectacular project was *Trottoir* (Sidewalk; 1970), in which ordinary passersby were taken by surprise when they walked on springy rubber tiles.

In the 1970s Foundation Contemporary Dance shifted its emphasis to pure dance, expressing feelings concordant with the music of Erik Satie. One highlight was the melancholic *Autumn* (1962). But the company kept its characteristic orientation toward the plastic arts, especially by its sophisticated use of props. In this respect, Stuyf has influenced the artistic approaches of many later dance and mime companies. In all productions Edinoff, who studied the techniques of Graham and Cunningham, excelled because of her magnetic stage personality and virtuosity.

Other works by Stuyf include *Two for Yesteryears* (1964), set to music by Anton Webern; *Reflections on Pale Silence* (1964), set to music by Karlheinz Stockhausen; and five with music by Erik Satie: *Cantos* (1972), *Seesaw* (1973), *Fuzz* (1973), *Tinge* (1974), and *Calico* (1974). Both the company and its school were reorganized in 1975 as Foundation Contemporary Dance Bis, although no performances have been given since that year.

Pauline de Groot (born in Renkum, 5 February 1942) followed her education in classical ballet technique with studies under Merce Cunningham, Martha Graham, and José Limón; she also danced in the companies of Limón (1960–1962), Pearl Lang (1961), and Erick Hawkins (1962–1965), the last as a soloist. She developed a relaxed style most notable for its light, free-flowing movements and serene quality. Her most important technical principles have concerned the conscious experience of gravity, or the "bounce," and respiration as inspired by work with yoga and the Chinese discipline of *taijiquan*. Improvising, especially contact improvisation, also has become important. She considers live music essential for her choreographies, most of which she has created in close collaboration with musicians.

Since 1965 de Groot has directed her own company in Amsterdam, and from 1972 to 1980 she was one of the most influential teachers at the department of modern dance at the Amsterdam Theater School. In 1986 she or-

NETHERLANDS: Theatrical Dance since 1945. Rachel Beaujean (center) as the Bride, with the ensemble of the Dutch National Ballet, in a 1991 revival of Bronislava Nijinska's *Les Noces* (1923). (Photograph © 1991 by Jorge Fatauros; used by permission.)

ganized the first Dutch Festival of Improvisation, Dance, and Music. De Groot has toured in England, France, Norway, Sweden, the United States, and Australia. Her works include *Canticle* (1963, music by Lou Harrison), *Sea Sand, Sanderlings* (1965, music by Simeon ten Holt), *Regenmakers* (Rainmakers; 1968, music by Henk Barendrecht), *Monkey and His Shadow* (1975, music by Henry Nagelberg), *Yellow Whale* (1981, music by Matthieu Keyser and Bart Fermi), *Stone Work Fragments* (1989, music by Malcolm Goldstein), and the 1995 *V.O.I.D. (Velocity of Interfering Data)*, set to music by Joost Buis.

In 1969 Koert Stuyf's brother, Bart Stuyf (born in Amsterdam, 26 October 1944), founded Multi Media, a company devoted to combining modern dance and plastic arts. The name was later changed to Movement Company (Bewegingsgroep) Bart Stuyf. Stuyf was trained in classical ballet technique, danced with the Scapino Ballet from 1962 to 1964 and with his brother's company from 1965 to 1967, and studied at the Graham school from 1967 to 1969. His movement theater is comparable to the earlier work of Alwin Nikolais in being mainly emotionless and highly objective. In his first productions, ingenious costumes often turned the dancers into objects.

Since the latter half of the 1970s, Movement Company's productions have been dominated by huge objects that sometimes cover the entire stage and are integral to the performance's movements. For example, *Spiegels* (Mirrors; 1978) was spectacular, with huge rotating mirrors that had a disorienting effect on the spectators. The atmosphere of the choreographies is mainly cool and sometimes humorous; lithe, athletic, and acrobatic movements characterize the dances. Other Bart Stuyf works include *Reuzenturbine* (Giant Turbine; 1972), *Makake* (1973, choreographed with F. Vogels), *Squeeze* (1975, music by John Cage, Mauricio Kagel, and Karlheinz Stockhausen), *Eventails* (Fans; 1976, music by György Ligeti), *Kluft* (Declivity; 1979, music by J. Armagnac, Edward Elgar, and Ligeti), and *Grey* (1980, music by Steve Reich and Cromshaw).

In 1971 Studio L.P. was formed, with a concentration on classical dance. Ton Wiggers was its artistic director and main choreographer. In 1979, however, the company changed its name to Intro-dans and adopted a more eclectic approach, combining classical and modern styles. With Arnhem as its home town, the company offers dance education to schoolchildren as well as regular dance performances in the eastern regions of the Netherlands.

In 1972, five dancers—Hannie Keesmaat, Hennie Konings, Ton Lutgerink, Daniel Nieman, and Maria Weinstock—left the Rotterdam Dance Center to help found the Penta Theater, the first Dutch dance collective whose participants shared in making both artistic and organizational decisions. The Penta Theater also was the first Dutch dance company that aimed to synthesize dance with other theatrical forms such as acting and mime. Its productions have often been ironic or satirical.

NETHERLANDS: Theatrical Dance since 1945. Andreas Jüstrich as the title character in the Scapino Ballet's 1992 production of *Pulcinella*, choreographed by Nils Christe to Stravinsky's score. The Scapino Ballet, founded in 1945 in Rotterdam, is a state-sponsored ballet company dedicated to presenting dance works for children. (Photograph © 1992 by Jack Vartoogian; used by permission.)

The Penta Theater's creations have all been choreographed by the collective and include *Kiek (Snapshot)* (1973), *Hooggeëerd Publiek* (Highly Honored Audience; 1973), *Den Vaderland Getrouwe* (Loyal to the Fatherland; 1974), *Uw Nederige Dienaar* (Your Humble Servant; 1977), *Trevira Rood* (Trevira Red; 1977), *Roffel en Touché* (Ruffle and Touché; 1978), *E Pericolloso Sporgersi* (Dangerous to Lean Outside; 1978), and *Penta Danst* (Penta Dances; 1979). In 1977 Ton Lutgerink left the Penta Theater to work as a freelance choreographer, combining dance and mime with text and often working with the American-Dutch dance artist Amy Gale.

Work Center Dance (Werkcentrum Dans), now called Rotterdamse Dansgroep, was founded in 1975 by the city of Rotterdam to fill the gap left by the Rotterdam Dance Center, which operated from 1961 to 1964 and from 1969 to 1975. Work Center Dance teaches children about dance by using *dansexpressie* (educational dance). By performing special programs in theaters, the company also contributes in general to the development primarily of modern dance.

From Work Center Dance's start, Käthy Gosschalk (born in Amsterdam, 30 August 1941) has been its artistic director; this followed a career from 1961 to 1972 as one of the most expressive soloists of the Netherlands Dance Theater. As a choreographer since 1964, she has combined classical and modern dance techniques. Her company also aims to develop its dancers' choreographic talents (for example, Ton Simons later worked in the United States) and is noteworthy as a platform for many American and English guest choreographers.

Work Center Dance has offered Robert North's *Ogenblikken* (Moments; 1976, music by B. Dowes); Gosschalk's *Canapé* (Sofa; 1976, music by Duke Ellington and Debussy) and *Zijwind* (Sidewind; 1980, music by Henryk Górecki); Kate Flatt's *Foto-album* (1977, music by Hot Club de France); Hans Tuerlings's *Harem* (1977, music by H. Nilsson), *Tutto Liscio* (1979, music by Bernard van Beurden), and *Wasteland* (1980, music by Jean Sibelius); Ton Simons's *Ikoon* (1978, music by Louis Toebosch and Michael Waisvisz) and *Commonplace Quintet* (1980, music by Waisvisz); Charles Czarny's *Tafelmanieren* (Table Manners; 1979, music by Steve Reich); and Ian Spink's *Cloud Cover* (1980, music by Brian Eno).

Among those who began their careers at Work Center Dance is Hans Tuerlings, who later became a popular freelance choreographer, particularly through his combination of dance and mime. In sober pieces, he uses angular and abrupt gestures and postures that are emotionally controlled but have nervous undertones. He sometimes demonstrates a dry sense of humor.

One of the first Dutch advocates of minimal dance was Bianca van Dillen (born in Amsterdam, 5 December 1947), who followed her classical training with stints in the Scapino Ballet (1965–1967) and in Pauline de Groot's company (1968–1969). In 1977 van Dillen was among those who helped to start Foundation Dance Production (Stichting Dansproduktie). The other founders were Truus Bronkhorst, Pauline Daniels, Patrice Kennedy, and Margie Smit. By the end of the 1970s, van Dillen abandoned the principles of minimal dance and adopted a style that is more free and more emotionally expressive. In 1983 she became the company's sole artistic director until its demise in 1992.

The company, which favored the Cunningham technique, also was noteworthy because of the participation of Pauline Daniels, one of the most outstanding modern dancers in the Netherlands. Some of Foundation Dance Production's works have been Daniels's *Come Out* (1978, music by Steve Reich); Margie Smit's *Huis* (House; 1979,

NETHERLANDS: Theatrical Dance since 1945. The ensemble of the Dutch National Ballet in a 1994 revival of *Collective Symphony* (1975), a collaborative work by Rudi van Dantzig, Hans van Manen, and Toer van Schayk, choreographed to Igor Stravinsky's Symphony in C. (Photograph © 1994 by Deen van Meer; used by permission.)

music by Dirk van der Horst); and the collective *Lopen* (Walk; 1979, music by Henk van der Meulen).

Van Dillen's other choreographies have included *109* (1977, music by Reich); *Hexa* (1984, music by Henk van der Meulen), *Parlando* (1990, music by van der Meulen), and *Gratis* (For Free; 1997, music by Reich and David Dramm). She is now experimenting with computer-assisted choreography with Stamina, a foundation begun in 1992. Stamina is also responsible for the archives of Foundation Dance Production, including the music scores created for the company's works.

The most dedicated adherent of minimal dance has been the Hungarian-Dutch artist Krisztina de Châtel (born in Budapest, 3 August 1943). She studied with Kurt Jooss and Hans Züllig, and in Amsterdam with Koert Stuyf and Ellen Edinoff, in whose company she also danced in 1973 and 1974. In 1977 de Châtel founded her own company, for which she developed her own distinctive version of minimal dance, with a severe and closed character. The most remarkable pieces were two featuring decor of neon tubes, designed by Jan van Munster: *Lines* (1979, music by Philip Glass) and *Light* (1980, music by W. van Es and T. Willems). Other works by de Châtel are *Kompositie voor Twee Dansers* (Composition for Two Dancers; 1977, music by Glass), *Kompositie voor Drie Dansers* (1977, music by Glass), and *Voltage Controlled Temperaments* (1978, music by L. de Boer).

Other notable companies and performers have included the North Netherlands Dance Group, established in Groningen in 1970 by choreographer Wanda Grendel; the Dancers' Collective, the first company to be founded in the south (in Tilburg, 1980); Amy Gale and Ton Lutgerink, who combined dance with other theatrical means of expression; and Beppie Blankert and Kim van der Boon, who practiced improvisational dance.

Most of these and other modern dance companies have performed in small theaters or in museums or cultural centers. A few smaller theaters—in particular, the Blue Hall in Utrecht, the HOT-theater in The Hague, The Lantern in Rotterdam, the Shaffy Theater in Amsterdam, and the Little Hall in Arnhem—stimulated the public's interest in modern dance by organizing demonstrations and annual dance festivals. These have complemented the dance promotion of the large annual Holland Festival.

Since the 1980s, modern dance and avant-garde choreography have been promoted by smaller theaters that hold biannual festivals, including the Spring Dance Festival held in Utrecht and the Holland Dance Festival held in The Hague. Cuts in funding during the 1990s have, however, led to the closing of several dance companies and dance work centers, such as the Netherlands Institute for Dance and the Central Dance Council. *Notes,* the only Dutch dance magazine for professionals, ceased publication in 1997.

NETHERLANDS: Theatrical Dance since 1945. Anna Seidl (kneeling, in front) with the ensemble of the Dutch National Ballet in *The Sleeping Beauty,* staged for the company in 1995 by Peter Wright. (Photograph © 1995 by Jorge Fatauros; used by permission.)

BIBLIOGRAPHY

Boswinkel, Willem, et al. *Het Nederlands Ballet*. Haarlem, 1958.

Dantzig, Rudi van. "The Dutch Inheritance." In *Ballet and Modern Dance*. London, 1974.

Dekker, Keso. *Hans van Manen + Modern Ballet in Nederland*. Amsterdam, 1981.

Hense, Peter, and Luuk Utrecht. *Het Nederlands Dans Theater en de balletten van Jiří Kylián*. Amsterdam, 1981.

Mannoni, Gérard. *Kylián*. Arles, 1989.

Schaik, Eva van. *Op gespannen voet: Geschiedenis van de Nederlandse theaterdans vanaf 1900*. Haarlem, 1981.

Schaik, Eva van. "The Dutch Dilemma." *Ballett International* 5 (April 1982): 36–41.

Sinclair, Janet. *Ballet der Lage Landen*. Haarlem, 1956.

Utrecht, Luuk. *Het Nationale Ballet 25 jaar: De Geschiedenis van Het Nationale Ballet van 1961 tot 1986*. Amsterdam, 1987.

Utrecht, Luuk. *Rudi van Dantzig: A Controversial Idealist in Ballet*. Zutphen, 1992.

Weetering, Conrad van de, and Luuk Utrecht. *Sonia Gaskell*. Zutphen, 1976.

Weetering, Conrad van de. *Kijk, een ballerina*. Utrecht, 1991.

LUUK UTRECHT

Dance Education

Until the twentieth century, Dutch education in dance was limited to instruction in the social dances fashionable among the upper class. But the new century's new ideas about life, society, and the individuality of human beings—the intellectual ferment in Germany, France, and the United States—slowly found their way into Dutch intellectual and artistic circles to heighten awareness, acceptance, and appreciation of the human body as an instrument of expression.

A few Dutch dancers were inspired by the performances and ideas of Isadora Duncan, Émile Jaques-Dalcroze,

Mary Wigman, Rudolf Laban, Anna Pavlova, and the Ballets Russes de Serge Diaghilev. Unfortunately, if they wished to pursue professional careers as dancers, teachers, or choreographers, they had to study abroad. If they returned, they brought unlimited enthusiasm, even if their training was a bit limited; in this way, many private schools began to offer instruction in theatrical dance.

Because the Netherlands lacked a firm theatrical dance tradition and because the Dutch people are staunch individualists, the dance styles that found their way into those schools were primarily the modern dance styles of Laban, Wigman, and Kurt Jooss. Well-known teachers included Jacoba van der Pas, Lili Green, Gertrud Leistikov, Corrie Hartong, and Florrie Rodrigo. A few individuals—Iril Gadeskov, Igor Schwezoff, and Peter Leoneff among them—were lonely defenders of the classical dance tradition.

In 1931, the first professional all-around dance school was established in Rotterdam by Corrie Hartong, who attached her academy to the Royal Conservatory. In 1936, official dance examinations were established at her urging. However, the German occupation of World War II temporarily ended any further growth of dance.

New enterprises exploded after 1945. Guest performances by great classical companies such as the Sadler's Wells Ballet, American Ballet Theatre, New York City Ballet, and Le Grand Ballet du Marquis de Cuevas combined with an aversion toward anything German to arouse a new interest in classical ballet at the expense of modern dance. Ballet schools sprang up, led by people who still had to go abroad to learn their craft.

While theatrical dance rapidly developed higher standards through the importation of well-trained dancers, choreographers, and teachers, dance instruction grew far more slowly. In Amsterdam, Rotterdam, Tilburg, and Arnhem, vocational dance academies based on the classical dance technique grew out of private schools headed by the former dancers Karel Poons, Nel Roos, Corrie Hartong, Eeke Thomee, and Winja Marova. In The Hague, a dance department under the direction of Sonia Gaskell was added to the Royal Conservatory.

To curb the alarming increase in the number of unskilled dance teachers, the government established a certification program in 1958 and took over professional schooling in the arts in 1968. By 1996 there were eight fully subsidized dance academies across the country, with curricula approved and controlled by government inspectors. These academies offer classes in classical ballet; modern, jazz, and folk dance; dance and music history and theory; anatomy; composition and improvisation; and teaching methods and analysis.

Dance education includes both performing and instruction; the latter until recently has been limited to the teaching of amateurs. Branches of other institutions, including the English Royal Academy of Dancing and the Cecchetti Society, also are found in the Netherlands.

From the start, some teachers were convinced that classical technique is not the only route to a real dance education. They kept their eyes open for new ways to teach dance to children and adults, not for a future professional career but as an important facet of total education. To meet this challenge, in the early 1960s Corrie Hartong and Kit Winkel introduced *dansexpressie* as a form of educational dance suitable for all ages; it was modeled on the work of Laban movement centers in England that included dance as part of general education. In 1975 a government committee began to design an educational program for dance, mime, and drama for the Dutch general school curriculum; such a program, however, has yet to be realized.

Visiting folkloric groups from around the world also have sparked interest in folk dance. All over the country, well-attended courses are given in a wide variety of folk dances by both guest and native teachers. These instructors' schooling is certified by the National Center of Folk Dancing (Landelijk Centrum Volkdans) and by the dance academies in Rotterdam and Tilburg, the result of work by folk dance pioneer and specialist Femke van Doorn.

Several dance companies also provide dance education through introductory performances, dance demonstrations, and lectures before young audiences in both theaters and schools. The Scapino Rotterdam (formerly the Scapino Ballet) introduced this type of program; today Work Center Dance, Intro-dans, and International Folklore Dance Theater have educational departments and special programs for children. For this work they receive subsidies from government, municipal, and provincial councils.

BIBLIOGRAPHY

Beumkes, Yvonne. "Nederland en de balletsyllabus 1: De Cecchetti Society." *Dansbulletin* 12 (September 1980): 3–7.

Hartong, Corrie. *Over dans gesproken*. Rotterdam, 1982.

Hougée, Aat. "Responsible Anarchy." *Ballett International/Tanz Aktuell* (March 1994): 42–45.

Leroy, Dominque. "La relation formation-emploi dans le secteur de la danse." In *Recherche en danse*, no. 3 (June 1984): 111–130.

Schaik, Eva van. *Op gespannen voet: Geschiedenis van de Nederlandse theaterdans vanaf 1900*. Haarlem, 1981.

Weetsering, Conrad van de, and Luuk Utrecht. *Sonia Gaskell*. Zutphen, 1976.

INE RIETSTAP

Dance Research and Publication

For many centuries in the Netherlands, dance was prohibited or disapproved of but never researched. The scholarly study of dance and its history did not develop in the Netherlands until after Isadora Duncan and other soloists appeared on the country's stages at the beginning of the twentieth century. Initially, newspapers drafted music critics to comment on ballet, and many became intrigued by the art form through the music used by Diaghilev's Ballets Russes. Other writers became interested in dance, and the first books began to appear; among these authors were the poet J. W. F. Werumeus Buning, the painter J. Tielens, the theologian G. van der Leeuw, and the musicologist E. Rebling, who was the first researcher of nineteenth-century Dutch dance. The first researchers of folk dance were A. Sanson-Catz, D. J. van der Ven, E. van der Ven, and the musicologist J. Kunst. A. Bus investigated the history of court and ballroom dance.

Only after World War II did dance specialists begin to publish their research. *Danskroniek* (1946–1959) was the first magazine devoted solely to dance. Soon performers also became interested in writing, among them Indra Kamadjojo, an Indonesian dancer, and Corrie Hartong, who had studied with Mary Wigman. Hartong also founded the Centraal Dansberaad (Central Dance Council) in 1954 to initiate general research and documentation projects and organize conferences. [*See the entry on Hartong.*]

The scientific and dance worlds did not communicate with one another until the end of the 1960s. As interest grew in dance generally and in Dutch theater dance specifically, academic scientists and dance devotees began to share their interests and to develop a scientific approach to dance. Although it was only a modest beginning, dance was now the subject of serious inquiry.

Academic Studies. In 1971, an interdisciplinary faculty of physical education was established at the Vrije Universiteit of Amsterdam and linked to the existing social science and medical departments. Five subdepartments were developed—functional anatomy, effort physiology, psychology, movement studies, and history and philosophy—with the last three offering a rich field for dance research.

Specialized research was done from 1972 to 1983 at the Dr. E. Boekman Foundation (Amsterdam), an institute for social research on the arts. The sociologist A. Schrijnen-Van Gastel produced several reports: *Survey of the Dance in the Netherlands* (1973), *Dance and the Public* (1974), *Social Problems of the Ex-Dancer* (1975), *Bibliography of Dance and Social Scientific Research* (1981), and *Dance Politics, Decentralized?* (1983).

In 1973, the Ministry of Culture, the theater-studies department of the University of Utrecht, the Centraal Dansberaad in The Hague, and the Amsterdam Theater School established a postgraduate course in dance history at Utrecht; seventeen students, some of them students and teachers at dance academies, participated in the first offering. The classes and guest lectures stimulated a new generation of students who were interested in the history and theories of dance. In 1983 the newly created Institute for Theater Studies commissioned the psychologist and dance critic Luuc Utrecht to teach dance history as part of its introduction to theater history. Eighty students took the course that year; by 1987, 120 students were enrolled.

From 1974 to 1984 the audiovisual department of the Amsterdam Theater School produced fifteen video programs on dance in the Netherlands from 1900 to 1970, including specific programs on production (by Wilbert Bank), research (by Eva van Schaik and Louki van Oven), and general guidance (by Jan Kassies). Intrigued by the video series and an accompanying cycle of ten readings by Eva van Schaik, the University of Amsterdam student cultural society Crea sought the establishment of specific programs on dance within the theater studies program; the request resulted in the establishment of a dance work group and in several short papers on theater dance during Germany's Weimar Republic.

Since 1975 increasing numbers of students have written papers on dance in relation to art history, theater, musicology, anthropology, literature, or physical education. Except for work done at the University of Utrecht, all scholarly research in dance (at the universities at Amsterdam, Leiden, Groningen, Tilburg, and Nijmegen) is undertaken on the initiative of interested students with the help of faculty members from various departments.

At the beginning of the 1980s dance could be studied at several universities, but nowhere did an autonomous dance science department exist. Six state-subsidized dance academies could be found in the country, but none had formal ties to Dutch universities and none gave dance research the same priority as dance instruction. Only in Amsterdam and Rotterdam were possibilities for cooperation between universities and dance academies even discussed.

Through the 1980s sundry courses in dance theory and history were available at various universities, including the Institute of Theater Studies, the Free University of Amsterdam (through the human movement studies department), the Catholic University of Nijmegen (through the film and performing arts department), the University of Groningen (through the art program of the human movement studies department), and the Rotterdam Erasmus University (through the art and cultural sciences department). In addition, nonacademic studies were possible at the Netherlands Institute for Dance, the Rotterdam Dansacademie, the Laban-Bartenieff Institute of Movement Studies, the Instituut voor Theateronderzoek, and the Amsterdam Theater School.

Nonacademic Studies. In late 1979 the Centraal Dansberaad in The Hague, the only state-subsidized service and documentation center for dance, amateur as well as professional, sought to establish more focused and structured dance research methodologies. This proposal, however, was at odds in many ways with the Ministry of Culture's proposal to abolish the Centraal Dansberaad to form a new Central Dance Institute. Still, the Dansberaad concluded that dance research was needed in three specific and yet interdependent areas: the practical artistic, the methodologically didactic, and the theoretical scientific.

Recent Dance Literature. Only a handful of scholars published work on dance in the years immediately after World War II. Corrie Hartong published her first book, *The Art of Dance,* in 1948 (her latest, *Speaking about Dance,* was published in 1982). Among the scholars who now regularly write on dance are Ine Rietstap, Eva van Schaik, Luuk Utrecht, Conrad van de Weetsering, and Nancy de Wilde. Journals that publish dance research include *Dans, Etcetera, Muziek en Dans, Notes,* and *Toneel Theatraal.*

In 1985 the Netherlands Dance Institute took over the Centraal Dansberaad's dance literature collection and became the primary research center for the country. The Institute now holds some five thousand books, twenty international dance magazines, twenty Dutch daily and weekly journals, and a broad collection of reference works, many of them catalogs of foreign collections. The archives also hold collections from the Nederlands Ballet (1954–1961), Dutch National Ballet (1961–1975), and private collections from ex-dancers, choreographers, dance teachers, and dance critics. Approximately five thousand photographs of dance in Holland as well as an extensive bibliography of ethnic African dance (compiled by the anthropologists Feri de Geus and Kees Epskamp) are also in the collection. In cooperation with the Nederlands Theater Institute, the Netherlands Dance Institute also has developed an extensive video collection of historic and contemporary dance, containing more than 375 videotapes.

CORRIE HARTONG and EVA VAN SCHAIK

NETHERLANDS BALLET. The Netherlands Ballet was founded in 1954 with Sonia Gaskell as artistic director and Arnold Haskell and Kurt Jooss as official advisers to the Dutch government, which wanted to establish a single state-subsidized national ballet company. The new company was headquartered in The Hague but can be regarded as the continuation of Gaskell's former Amsterdam company, Ballet Recital (1949–1951, 1952–1954). Some dancers from the latter company were among the first soloists of the Netherlands Ballet, including Willy de la Bije, Milly Emmer, Jaap Flier, Marianne Hilarides, Maria Huisman, Louki van Oven, Janine van Thor, Aart Verstegen, Conrad van de Weetering, and Johanna Zuiver; Joan Cadzow and Linda Manez were regular guest soloists. The state subsidy improved Gaskell's financial possibilities: she now had a company of more than thirty-five dancers, twice the size of Ballet Recital, and she could also engage guest choreographers. [*See the entry on Gaskell.*]

Thanks to the funding and Gaskell's artistic interests, the company worked purposefully and systematically to establish a repertory of the historical and contemporary highlights of international ballet. Considerable attention was given to works by Michel Fokine *(Les Sylphides, Petrouchka)* and Léonide Massine *(Les Présages);* the base was laid for the Balanchine tradition in the Netherlands with *La Sonnambula, Concerto Barocco, The Four Temperaments,* and *Serenade.* Ballets originally made for French companies were also popular, especially those by David Lichine *(La Rencontre, La Création),* Serge Lifar *(Suite en Blanc, Les Mirages),* George Skibine *(Annabel Lee),* and John Taras *(Designs with Strings).* Harald Lander set the oldest surviving ballet, *The Whims of Cupid and the Ballet Master,* and his own *Études.* The Netherlands Ballet was also experimentally inclined, as demonstrated by the presence of young guest choreographers such as Maurice Béjart and Paul Taylor. Dutch dancers could also develop their choreographic interests with the company, among them Peter Appel, Willy de la Bije, Rudi van Dantzig, Jaap Flier, Marianne Hilarides, and Aart Verstegen.

In 1959 the company lost almost half of its dancers, including many soloists; they were dissatisfied with Gaskell's authority and her emphasis on a repertory that had not been created especially to suit the available dancers. On the initiative of administrative director Carel Birnie, American ballet master Benjamin Harkarvy, and leading soloist Aart Verstegen, sixteen dancers left the company to found the Netherlands Dance Theater. The most talented of the remaining dancers were rapidly promoted to soloists—Peter Appel, Sonja van Beers, Andrea Jungen, Leonie Kramar, Ronald Snijders, and Irène de Vos. Another American, Karel Shook, then became ballet master; later he was joined by the Russian teachers Abderachman Kumuznikov and Natalia Orlovskaya.

In 1961 the Netherlands Ballet became part of the newly formed Dutch National Ballet, according to the original plan of the government. [*See* Dutch National Ballet.]

Some creations of the Netherlands Ballet are *De Stoelen* (The Chairs; 1955), choreographed by Sonia Gaskell to music by Rudolf Escher, *Het Proces* (1955), choreographed by Jaap Flier to music by Jan Mul; *Nachteiland* (Night Island; 1955), choreographed by Rudi van Dantzig to music by Claude Debussy; *Le Cercle* (1956), choreographed by Maurice Béjart to music by J. S. Bach and Pierre Schaeffer; *Disgenoten* (Table Fellows; 1958), choreographed by Rudi van Dantzig to music by Béla Bartók; and *De Witte Salamander* (The White Salamander; 1960), choreographed by Paul Taylor to music by Jaap Stokkermans.

[*See also* Netherlands, *article on* Theatrical Dance since 1945.]

BIBLIOGRAPHY

Boswinkel, Willem, et al. *Het Nederlands Ballet*. Haarlem, 1958.

Schaik, Eva van. *Op gespannen voet: Geschiedenis van de Nederlandse theaterdans vanaf 1900*. Haarlem, 1981.

Weetering, Conrad van de, and Luuk Utrecht. *Sonia Gaskell*. Zutphen, 1976.

LUUK UTRECHT

NETHERLANDS DANCE THEATER. Sixteen disaffected dancers left the Netherlands Ballet in 1959 and formed a company of their own. The nucleus of the new Netherlands Dance Theater was formed by the soloists Aart Verstegen, Jaap Flier, Willy de la Bije, Hannie van Leeuwen, Rudi van Dantzig, and Marianne Hilarides. The sixteen dancers shared a desire to express their personal qualities in a more satisfying way and to explore contemporary influences. They opened their studio to American modern dance, jazz, and even musicals; along with classical ballet they introduced classes in modern dance.

Ballet master and artistic director Benjamin Harkarvy was the inspiring force in this artistic adventure. To attain their goal of becoming a qualified contemporary company, the dancers had only their self-confidence, will power, and idealism. They bypassed the usual hierarchy and repertory of a classical company and focused on ballets of drama and atmosphere. Despite the group's early financial problems and a hostile press, they slowly grew popular. Most of their ballets were created by Harkarvy, van Dantzig, Flier, Sanders, and Hans van Manen, who joined the company in 1960 and became joint artistic director with Harkarvy.

After two years Netherlands Dance Theater received governmental subsidies and was accommodated in the former studios of the Netherlands Ballet, in an old school building in The Hague. The company steadily expanded.

NETHERLANDS DANCE THEATER. *(above)* Jaap Flier and Willy de la Bije, founding members of the company, in Glen Tetley's *Sargasso* (1964). *(right)* Members of the company in Jiří Kylián's satirical ballet *Symphony in D* (1981), set to the music of Franz Joseph Haydn. (Photograph above © by Hans van den Busken; used by permission. Photograph at left © 1981 by Linda Vartoogian; used by permission.)

Among the dancers were Gerard Lemaitre, Marianne Sarstädt, Anne Hyde, Alexandra Radius, Han Ebbelaar, Charles Czarny, Martinette Janmaat, and Mea Venema. The company became a platform for modern choreographers; the first ones invited from abroad were Anna Sokolow, John Butler, and Glen Tetley. Sokolow choreographed *Rooms* and *Opus '58;* Butler, *Carmina Burana;* and Tetley, *Pierrot Lunaire, Anatomical Lesson, Arena, Ricercare, Embrace Tiger and Return to Mountain,* and *Mythical Hunters.*

The company's artistic policy aimed to integrate the classical and modern dance vocabularies. Its lack of traditional ties within Dutch theatrical dance simplified this refreshingly openminded approach. Examples of Dutch choreography that resulted from this marriage of different schools are Flier's *The Process, Réjouissance, Intérieur,* and *Nouvelles Aventures,* and Sanders's *Valkuil, Danses Concertantes, Pop Beat, Entrata, Screenplay,* and *Choreostruction.* In particular, Hans van Manen became very productive; in ten seasons he produced twenty-five ballets and many television shows.

In spite of its successes abroad and at home, Netherlands Dance Theater met its first crisis of identity after its tours in Israel, Germany, Great Britain, and the United States. Harkarvy left in 1968 and was replaced by Glen Tetley. He and van Manen did not continue collaboration after their coproduction of *Mutations.* Van Manen left in 1969, and Tetley one season later; however, their ties with the company remained, and both continued to choreograph for the company. Jaap Flier, the newly appointed director, tried a new wave of experiments that were not welcomed, and he left in 1973.

With the departure of many members of the original company, the inner ties of Netherlands Dance Theater slowly loosened. Inviting a new generation of American and Australian choreographers and dancers, the company tried to consolidate its position with works by Cliff Keuter, James Waring, Don Asker, and Peter Dockeley. Louis Falco and Jennifer Muller gave the dancers a fresh dynamism, and Muller's evening-long ballet *Strangers* became a smash hit. Nevertheless, the crisis within the artistic directorate endured until 1975, when Carel Birnie was appointed administrative director, while Hans Knill and Jiří Kylián became artistic leaders. After two years Knill became *régisseur,* and Kylián became the sole artistic leader and agreed to create two new ballets every season. Kylián had entered the company in 1973 as guest choreographer for *Stoolgame* and *Viewers.* Within a decade he augmented his share of the company's repertory with twenty-three new ballets. He defined its new artistic policy, bringing the company huge success at home and abroad. Among his most performed ballets are *Cathédrale Engloutie, Elegia, Ariadne, Verklärte Nacht, Novembersteps, Psalmen Symphonie, Soldatenmis,* and *Dream Dances.*

In the 1970s many Dutch dancers and choreographers left Netherlands Dance Theater. Kylián, with the help of his dancers (among them Jeanne Solan, Alida Chase, Arlette van Boven, Joke Zijlstra, Sabine Kupferberg, Marly Knoben, Gerald Tibbs, Ric McCullough, Glen Eddy, Leigh Warren, and Gérard Lemaître), created an ideal instrument for his atmospheric ballets. Walter Nobbe and John MacFarlane designed most of his ballets.

In 1977 the company expanded with a group called Springplank (Springboard), made up of talented but inexperienced dancers who prepared for possible admission to the parent company by performing on a small alternative-theater circuit.

Nacho Duato, a Spanish dancer in the company, made his choreographic debut with *Jardi Tancat* in 1981, becoming the first of a new generation of house choreographers. In September 1987 the company celebrated the opening of its new theater in The Hague. On this occasion its company of twelve juniors, directed by Arlette van Boven, were renamed Netherlands Dance Theater II.

[*See also the entries on the principal figures mentioned herein.*]

BIBLIOGRAPHY

Dekker, Keso. *Hans van Manen en Modern Ballet in Nederland.* Amsterdam, 1981.

Elsken, Ed van der. *Nederlands Dans Theater.* Amsterdam, 1961.

Fatauros, Jorge. "Choreographic Portraits." *Ballett International* 11 (June–July 1988): 18–27.

Garske, Rolf. "At the Crossroads: NDT 1989." *Ballett International* 12 (May 1989): 14–20.

Hense, Peter, and Luuk Utrecht. *Het Nederlands Dans Theater en de balletten van Jiří Kylián.* Amsterdam, 1981.

Koegler, Horst. "Pledged to the Spirit of Our Times: Nederlands Dans Theater, 1959–1989." *Ballett International* 12 (May 1989): 11–13.

Mannoni, Gérard. *Kylián.* Arles, 1989.

Nugent, Ann. "Scions of Kylián." *Dance Now* 4 (Summer 1995): 17–21.

Schaik, Eva van. *Op gespannen voet: Geschiedenis van de Nederlandse theaterdans vanaf 1900.* Haarlem, 1981.

Sinclair, Janet. "Company with a Difference." *Dance and Dancers* (July 1989): 29–31.

Versteeg, Coos. *Nederlands Dans Theater: Een revolutionaire geschiedenis.* Amsterdam, 1987.

EVA VAN SCHAIK

NEUMEIER, JOHN (born 24 February 1942 in Milwaukee, Wisconsin), American ballet dancer, choreographer, teacher, and company director, active in Germany. John Neumeier began his dance training with Sheila Reilly in his hometown of Milwaukee. During his years as a student at Marquette University in Milwaukee, from 1957 to 1961, he traveled to Chicago to study ballet with Bentley Stone and Walter Camryn at the Stone-Camryn School and to attend classes in modern dance given by Sybil Shearer. After his graduation from Marquette, with a bachelor of arts degree, he went to London in 1962 to study at the Royal Ballet School and later to Copenhagen to study with the famed Russian teacher Vera Volkova.

In 1960, while still a university student in Milwaukee, Neumeier choreographed his first ballet, *The Hound of Heaven,* to music by Sergei Prokofiev, and he began to perform with the Sybil Shearer Company in Chicago. He continued to appear with Shearer's troupe until 1962. The following year, in 1963, he joined the Stuttgart Ballet as a soloist and remained with this company until 1969. In 1966 and 1967 he staged several ballets at the Noverre Society matinees for aspiring choreographers, earning not only critical acclaim but two important commissions: in 1968 he made *Separate Journeys,* to music by Samuel Barber, for the Stuttgart Ballet and *Stages and Reflections,* to music by Benjamin Britten, for the Harkness Ballet. The success of these works solidified his reputation as an unusually gifted choreographer.

Neumeier left Stuttgart in 1969 to accept an appointment as ballet director and chief choreographer at the Frankfurt State Opera, where he remained until 1973, when he moved on to Hamburg to take up the same positions with the Hamburg State Opera. He has remained in Hamburg ever since, creating a large body of work for the Hamburg State Opera Ballet as well as staging works for companies in other cities in Germany and abroad. He has been a guest choreographer for the Vienna State Opera Ballet, the Royal Ballet (London), the Paris Opera Ballet, the Royal Danish Ballet, the Royal Winnipeg Ballet, the National Ballet of Canada, and American Ballet Theatre, among others.

Neumeier has built the Hamburg Ballet into one of Germany's top companies, performing not only at the opera house and its workshop opera but also at the Hamburg Theater am Spielbudenplatz and at the central parish church of Saint Michael. He has thus created a large following of ballet patrons who frequent both regular performances and regular introductory matinees as well as the Hamburg Ballet Weeks, which are offered at the end of each season and which always finish with a Nijinsky Gala. He has also completely overhauled and restructured the associated Opera Ballet School, housed since 1989 in the newly acquired and completely rebuilt Balletzentrum Hamburg–John Neumeier.

A highly articulate man, Neumeier has had his own television series in which he lectures about the essentials of ballet. As a choreographer, he works from a classical base, enriching the dance vocabulary by borrowing liberally from various contemporary schools and styles. All his ballets have firm dramaturgical structures, even his plotless concert works, but he is at his best with full-length productions, whether from the classical repertory (distinctive versions of *The Nutcracker,* 1971; *Swan Lake,* 1976; and *The Sleeping Beauty,* 1978; his *Giselle* of 1983, however, is more traditional) or from the standard reper-

NEUMEIER. The ensemble of the Hamburg Ballet with Gamal Gouda (center) in one of Neumeier's best-known works, *The Third Symphony of Gustav Mahler* (1975). (Photograph © by Holger Badekow; used by permission.)

tory (such as Prokofiev's *Romeo and Juliet,* 1971), or adapted from classical literature (*A Midsummer Night's Dream,* 1977; *The Lady of the Camellias,* 1978; and *King Arthur,* 1982). A specialty has been his ballets set to Mahler's music—*Third Symphony* (1975), *Fourth Symphony* (1977), *Lieb und Leid und Welt und Traum* (the First and Tenth symphonies, 1980), *Sixth Symphony* (1984), and *Zwischenräume* (Ninth Symphony, 1994). His range of taste extends from Bach's *Saint Matthew Passion* (1981) through Leonard Bernstein's *West Side Story* (1978).

In programs of multiple works Neumeier always finds and establishes a common denominator that holds the individual works together and creates a strong entity. For example, he explored various approaches to love and sex in combining Gluck's *Don Juan* with Stravinsky's *Le Sacre du Printemps* (1972), and the summer-winter relationship in opposing Ravel's *Daphnis and Chloe* to Stravinsky's *Le Baiser de la Fée* (1972); he dealt with two different sorts of dreamers in following Strauss's *Die Josephslegende* with the same composer's *Don Quixote* (1979).

Neumeier's recent major ballet creations include *Amleth* (1985, music by Michael Tippett), *Shall We Dance?* (1986, music by George Gershwin), *Fratres* (1986, music by Arvo Pärt), *Magnificat* (1987, music by J. S. Bach), *Peer Gynt* (1989, music by Alfred Schnittke), *Medea* (1990, music by Schnittke and others), *Requiem* (1991, music by Mozart), *On the Town* (1991, music by Leonard Bernstein), *A Cinderella Story* (1992, music by Sergei Prokofiev), *Now and Then* (1993, music by Ravel), *Serenade* (1993, music by Bernstein), *Trilogie M.R.* (1994, music by Ravel), and *Ondine* (1994, music by Hans Werner Henze).

Undoubtedly one of today's foremost intellectual choreographers, Neumeier has been attacked mainly by certain U.S. critics, who find his ballets void of choreographic substance; European critics, although not blind to his limitations, generally have admired his intelligent and spirited theatricality. He received a *Dance Magazine* award in 1983.

[*See also* Hamburg Ballet.]

BIBLIOGRAPHY

Albrecht, Christoph, ed. *Zehn Jahre John Neumeier und das Hamburger Ballett, 1973–1983.* Hamburg, 1983.

Dauber, Angela. *Matthäus-Passion.* Hamburg, 1983.

Jeschke, Claudia. "American Theatricality in Contemporary German Dancing: John Neumeier and William Forsythe." In *Proceedings of the Fifteenth Annual Conference, Society of Dance History Scholars, University of California, Riverside, 14–15 February 1992,* compiled by Christena L. Schlundt. Riverside, Calif., 1992.

Koegler, Horst. "John Neumeier's Expatriate Gains." *Dance Magazine* (June 1993): 34.

Koegler, Horst, and Monika Schlösser. *John Neumeier unterwegs.* Darmstadt, 1972.

Loney, Glenn. "Ballet's Freethinker: John Neumeier." *Dance Scope* 11 (Spring-Summer 1977): 24–33.

Merrett, Sue. "John Neumeier and the Hamburg Ballet." *The Dancing Times* (October 1988): 39–40. Interview with Neumeier.

Neumeier, John. *Traumwege.* Hamburg, 1980.

Neumeier: Photographien und Texte zum Ballett der Matthäus-Passion von Johann Sebastian Bach. Munich, 1983.

Odenthal, Johannes. "The Self-Controlled Romantic: John Neumeier in Conversation." *Ballet International/Tanz Aktuell* (March 1996): 52–55. Interview with Neumeier.

Willaschek, Wolfgang, ed. *Zwanzig Jahre John Neumeier und das Hamburg Ballett, 1973–1993.* Hamburg, 1993.

FILMS. Neumeier served as ballet director of films of several of his major works, including *Rondo, Third Symphony of Gustav Mahler, Othello,* and *Die Kameliendame* (The Lady of the Camellias).

ARCHIVES. Numerous interviews with Neumeier, from 1975 onward, are recorded in the voluminous program books of the Hamburg Ballet. These and other materials pertinent to Neumeier's career can be found in the archives of the Hamburg State Opera.

HORST KOEGLER

NEW BRITAIN. *See* Melanesia.

NEW CALEDONIA. *See* Melanesia.

NEW DANCE GROUP was designed "for the purpose of developing and creating group and mass dances expressive of the working class and its revolutionary upsurge," according to John Martin of the *New York Times,* 26 March 1933. Founded in 1932, it was formed in New York City by six Wigman School students including Miriam Blecher and Nadia Chilkovsky, with Estelle Parnas as music director. The school offered classes in the Wigman/Holm technique at low fees to many who then spread an appreciation of if not an active participation in modern dance throughout the country.

By 1935, Martha Graham's technique was added, followed by Doris Humphrey's; by the late 1930s, branch schools were opened in other cities; and by 1940, a range of ballet, modern, ethnic, and composition classes were taught to multiracial students, some on scholarships, thus forming the curriculum that continues to the present. Lester Horton's and Merce Cunningham's techniques were also introduced. It was estimated by B. Gottlieb in *Theatre Arts,* February 1952, that "there is hardly a dancer in New York who has not at one time or another taken classes at New Dance Group."

Onstage, New Dance Group was one of the many left-wing companies in the 1930s that became part of the Workers Dance League (later called the New Dance League), which in trade union halls and theaters sponsored concerts and spartakiades (annual concerts) that promoted social protest. New Dance Group won first prize in the first two contests (4 June 1933, with 3 dances: *Hunger, Charity,* and *Awake;* 2 June 1934, with *Van Der Lubbe's Head*).

NEW DANCE GROUP. A scene from Sophie Maslow's *Folksay* (1942), a dance based on Carl Sandburg's long, free-verse poem *The People, Yes* and set to songs by Woody Guthrie. (Photograph from a private collection.)

In 1934, Jane Dudley had joined New Dance Group; her solo works were acclaimed and she became its first president, remaining in that post until the mid-1960s. In 1935, Sophie Maslow first taught Graham technique; she later was dancer, chief choreographer, and president.

On 10 March 1942, the Dudley-Maslow-Bales Trio debut, with students from the school, began a new wave of activity (to mid-1950s) which continues to the present with the Sophie Maslow Dance Company. Festivals have also included works by Pearl Primus, Donald McKayle, Anna Sokolow, Talley Beatty, Jean Erdman, Joyce Trisler, and Jean-Léon Destiné, among many others.

From 1939 to 1966, Judith Delman served as executive director of the New Dance Group; she saw its identity change from one of social protest to one that was purely educational. She saw it through incorporation (1944), dance festivals (of special note were 1945, 1948, 1953, 1962, 1963, and 1964), and the securing of its present home in 1954 at 254 West Forty-seventh Street, New York City.

[*See also the entries on Dudley and Maslow.*]

BIBLIOGRAPHY

Delman, Judith. "The New Dance Group." *Dance Observer* (January 1944): 8.

Lloyd, Margaret. *The Borzoi Book of Modern Dance.* New York, 1949.

Maskey, Jacqueline. "The Group." *Dance Magazine* (January 1965): 44–49.

Ocko, Edna. "New Dance Group." *New Theatre* (November 1934).

DAVID SEARS

NEW DANCE TRILOGY. A dance work in three parts: *Theatre Piece*, *With My Red Fires*, and *New Dance.* Choreography: Doris Humphrey. Music: Wallingford Riegger.

- *Theater Piece.* Choreography for "In the Theater" section by Charles Weidman. First performance: 19 January 1936, Guild Theater, New York City. Dancers: Doris Humphrey, Charles Weidman, and Concert Group.
- *With My Red Fires.* First performance: 13 August 1936, Bennington Armory, Bennington, Vermont. Dancers: Doris Humphrey, Charles Weidman, Katherine Litz, and Concert Group augmented by members of the Bennington School of Dance Workshop.
- *New Dance* (first six parts). Choreography for Third Theme by Charles Weidman. First performance: 3 August 1935, College Theater, Bennington, Vermont. Dancers: Doris Humphrey, Charles Weidman, and Concert Group. *New Dance* (variations and conclusion). Choreography for Variations by José Limón, Beatrice Seckler, Letitia Ide, and Sybil Shearer. First performance: 27 October 1935, Guild Theater, New York City. Dancers: Doris Humphrey, Charles Weidman, and Concert Group.

In the extended work, *New Dance Trilogy,* probably the most ambitious Doris Humphrey ever undertook and certainly one of the most sweeping achievements the modern dance had seen, the choreographer wished to make an indictment of society's evils and propose a utopian remedy. Each of the trilogy's parts took a different theatrical style, though movement themes recurred to tie them together. Wallingford Riegger wrote the music for each part after it was choreographed. His lean dissonances and spirited rhythms gave support to the vitality of the dance.

Theater Piece was a satirical view of competitiveness in business, sports, and the theater. Using a half-literal, half-abstract performing style that probably derived from Charles Weidman's kinetic pantomime, Humphrey offered a wry view of modern life. Moving among the large boxes that were the basic elements of all Humphrey-Weidman sets, the characters appeared and disappeared, sometimes in surrealistic, disembodied form. As they struggled and raced about, Humphrey, an outsider, danced a more reasoned and harmonious theme, foreshadowing the positive resolution of *New Dance.*

With My Red Fires showed a dramatic confrontation between a young girl and her lover and a possessive matriarch. The mother's unsuccessful attempts to prevent her daughter from leaving with the man are posed against a larger theme, that of the ritualistic powers of the community. In a great nuptial ceremony, the chorus selects and blesses the lovers; then, coerced by the fury of the matriarch, it brutally punishes them and expels them from membership.

The forces of reason and love exert a positive influence on society in *New Dance.* Humphrey, now a benevolent matriarch, persuasively draws the group of women together, and later the men, led by Weidman. United, they dance the variations and conclusion, a contrapuntal celebration in which the group lends constant rhythmic support to a succession of solo dancers. *New Dance* is a superb affirmation of Humphrey's view that the group's strength lies not only in its ability to act in concert but also in its capacity to foster the individual's creative talents.

Because of its size and length, *New Dance Trilogy* was never performed on a single evening. With a smaller cast than the original forty-seven dancers, *With My Red Fires* was periodically revived. Almost all the sections of *New Dance* were shown as separate dances at one time or another, and the variations and conclusion remained in active repertory until after Humphrey's death. Notation was begun during a repertory class of Humphrey's in the late 1940s, and the whole of *New Dance* was reconstructed by Weidman in 1972 with the help of several former company members. *With My Red Fires* was notated in 1954 under Humphrey's supervision. *Theater Piece* has been lost.

BIBLIOGRAPHY

Humphrey, Doris. "New Dance." In *Doris Humphrey, an Artist First: An Autobiography.* Edited by Selma Jeanne Cohen. Middletown, Conn., 1977.

Kriegsman, Sali Ann. "New Dance." In Kriegsman's *Modern Dance in America: The Bennington Years.* Boston, 1981.

Siegel, Marcia B. *The Shapes of Change: Images of American Dance.* New York, 1979.

Siegel, Marcia B. *Days on Earth: The Dance of Doris Humphrey.* New Haven, 1987.

MARCIA B. SIEGEL

NEW GUINEA. *See* Papua New Guinea *and* Indonesia, *article on* Dance Traditions of the Outlying Islands.

NEW IRELAND. *For discussion of dance traditions in New Ireland, see* Melanesia.

NEW YORK CITY BALLET. [*To survey the institutional and stylistic history of the New York City Ballet, this entry comprises two articles. The first article considers the origins of the company and its development until the death of George Balanchine; the second focuses on the company as it continues under new leadership.*]

Origins to 1983

In 1946 choreographer George Balanchine and critic and arts patron Lincoln Kirstein formed the Ballet Society, a nonprofit subscription organization "for the encouragement of lyric theatre by the productions of new works." The fifth program of the Ballet Society's second season presented a brilliant premiere, *Orpheus,* a collaboration between Balanchine and Igor Stravinsky. *Orpheus* attracted the attention of Morton Baum of the City Center of Music and Drama, a New York City commission founded to provide concerts, plays, and operas at popular prices. Baum approached Kirstein to invite the Ballet Society to join City Center; the offer was accepted, and the New York City Ballet (NYCB) came into existence. [*See the entry on Kirstein.*]

The company began on a small scale, with fourteen performances in October and November 1948, ten in January 1949, eighteen in November and December 1949, and thirty-two in February and March 1950. In 1951 the company danced four seasons totaling fifteen weeks, and in 1952, two seasons totaling ten weeks. In 1954 *The Nutcracker* was premiered; by 1959/60, when the month-long Christmas run of that ballet had become established, the New York seasons consisted of eight weeks before and after Christmas, and a month in the spring. By 1966/67, after the company had moved to the New York State Theater in Lincoln Center and had developed a subscription plan, the New York schedule had grown to eleven weeks before and after Christmas, and six weeks in the spring;

by 1982/83, it had grown to fourteen weeks before and after Christmas and nine weeks in the spring. In 1956 the company numbered about fifty dancers; in 1963, sixty; in 1966, seventy; in 1975, ninety; and in 1983, one hundred ten. By 1956 the dancers were paid for a twelve-week rehearsal period and twenty-four weeks of performance. The rehearsal period remained constant, but the performance period varied according to touring schedules. Principal dancers in 1956 earned an average weekly salary of $50 for rehearsal and $90 for performance; by 1983 these figures were $400 for both rehearsal and performance.

The New York City Ballet was conceived as an essentially residential company, but in 1951 it began dancing short seasons (three days to six weeks) on a fairly regular basis in a few other large American cities. In Chicago the company danced ten seasons between 1951 and 1980; in Washington, fourteen seasons between 1953 and 1982 (after the opening of Kennedy Center in 1971, the seasons lengthened and became annual); in Los Angeles, eight seasons between 1953 and 1964; in San Francisco, five seasons between 1953 and 1962; and in Philadelphia, five seasons between 1957 and 1974. Shorter and less frequent appearances were made in Baltimore, Boston, Detroit, Seattle, and other smaller cities, including university towns in the Midwest. Through 1983, the company had danced in Canada on three occasions, and it made frequent appearances at summer arts festivals, including those at Stratford, Connecticut; Ravinia, Illinois; Columbia, Maryland; Blossom, Ohio; and Wolf Trap Farm in Virginia. In 1966 the company began annual seasons in July at the Saratoga Performing Arts Center in Saratoga Springs, New York.

A boldly early foreign appearance established the New York City Ballet as an international institution. David Webster's invitation to present a five-week season at London's Covent Garden in 1950 led to great success, despite British press criticism of the company's athleticism and its emphasis on undecorated abstract ballets. Many foreign tours followed: to England in 1952, 1979, and 1983 and to Europe in 1952, 1953, 1955, 1956, 1962, and 1965. In 1958, the company danced in Japan, Australia, and the Philippines. In 1962 it paid its first visit to Russia, from which Balanchine had emigrated in 1924. Both company and choreographer were given a predictably mixed reception but excited great interest; as in England in 1951, there was much critical questioning of the Balanchine style. The company returned to Russia in 1972. The New York City Ballet participated in leading European arts festivals, including Edinburgh and the Maggio Musicale in Florence in 1952 and Spoleto in 1965. Trips with special resonance for ballet history were those to Monte Carlo in 1969 and to Copenhagen in 1978, 1980, and 1983. In 1976, 1980, and 1983, the company took part in the International Festival of Dance in Paris.

NEW YORK CITY BALLET. *Orpheus,* created by Balanchine for Ballet Society in 1948, was the work that led to formation of the New York City Ballet. In this photograph, Eurydice (Maria Tallchief) clings to Orpheus (Nicholas Magallanes), beseeching him to look at her, as he struggles, with eyes blinded by a mask, to lead her out of Hades to the surface of the upper world. At right, the hand of the Dark Angel (Francisco Moncion) holds the lyre of Orpheus as a guide. The score for this ballet was written by Igor Stravinsky; scenery and costumes were designed by Isamu Noguchi. The lyre of Orpheus became the identifying icon of the New York City Ballet. (Photograph © by George Platt Lynes; used by permission. Choreography by George Balanchine © by the New York City Ballet.)

By the end of the 1950s, the New York City Ballet had become one of the world's leading classical ballet companies. Several subsequent developments further secured its survival, power, and prestige. In 1963 the Ford Foundation gave $2 million to the company and $3,925,000 to the Balanchine-directed School of American Ballet; and in 1964 the company moved into the newly constructed New York State Theater at Lincoln Center, a state-subsidized theater expressly designed for dance according to Balanchine's specifications. This move to Lincoln Center coincided with the inauguration of an extremely successful subscription system. By the winter season of 1982/83, the company was playing to a 92.3 percent capacity audience of 279,674 paid admissions.

In 1972 the company mounted a Stravinsky festival, followed by a Ravel festival in 1975, a Tchaikovsky festival in 1980, and a second Stravinsky festival in 1982. These extravaganzas were offered to support a claim that no other company had the creative resources and morale needed to produce such torrents of originality, quick study, and stamina; however, only the euphoric first Stravinsky festival,

NEW YORK CITY BALLET. Balanchine's *Concerto Barocco* (1941) was the first ballet danced by the New York City Ballet in its inaugural performance, 11 October 1948. Seen here are Diana Adams, Tanaquil Le Clercq, and members of the ensemble, c.1950. (Photograph © by Roger Wood; used by permission. Choreography by George Balanchine © by the New York City Ballet.)

which yielded four important new Balanchine works (*Stravinsky Violin Concerto, Symphony in Three Movements, Divertimento from "Le Baiser de la Fée,"* and *Duo Concertant*), can be said to have been successful.

Kirstein had brought Balanchine to America in 1933, to establish classical ballet there, so it was inevitable that Balanchine ballets, style, and technique would dominate the New York City Ballet's operations. Although Balanchine was always listed in the program under more modest titles, he was actually the company director until the onset of his final illness in 1982, making decisions in all areas of the company's operations and supervising its day-to-day workings. Jerome Robbins and Peter Martins later contributed significantly to the repertory and the development of dancers, but Balanchine himself shaped the company almost entirely according to his own conceptions. Kirstein played a primary role in arranging financial support, both through his own contributions and through influence on other patrons and institutions of public philanthropy. His role in the artistic activity of the company was advisory. [*See the entries on Balanchine, Martins,* and *Robbins.*]

Despite Balanchine's predominance, the New York City Ballet has always shown the work of other choreographers, and in its first years an effort was made to acquire a varied repertory. Certain choreographers associated with Balanchine and Kirstein in earlier companies—such as Todd Bolender, Ruthanna Boris, Lew Christensen, Fred Danieli, and William Dollar—were asked to restage earlier ballets and to mount new ones, many of them not in the Balanchine mode. Two eminent choreographers from quite different traditions, Frederick Ashton and Antony Tudor, staged ballets in the first years. Tudor restaged his 1941 *Time Table* in 1949 and choreographed *The Lady of the Camellias* in 1951 and *La Gloire* in 1952, but these ballets did not remain in the repertory. Of his earlier ballets, *Lilac Garden* (*Jardin aux Lilas,* 1936) was revived in 1951, *Dim Lustre* (1943) in 1964, both remaining in the repertory briefly. Ashton's *Illuminations,* choreographed to a Benjamin Britten score for the New York City Ballet in 1950, became a staple of the repertory until the early 1970s and was successfully revived thereafter; his *Picnic at Tintagel* (1952) survived only a few seasons. In 1958 Birgit Cullberg restaged her 1950 *Medea.* Martha Graham was invited in 1959 to choreograph the first section of *Episodes,* to the music of Anton Webern, but her part of the work was soon dropped. Another leading modern dance choreographer, Merce Cunningham, who had made *The Seasons* for the Ballet Society in 1947, staged *Summerspace* in 1966, but this ballet also failed to survive. The policy of using outside choreographers was pursued with less and less energy as the New York City Ballet developed, and none of these works were in the company repertory in the early 1980s.

In 1949 Jerome Robbins, who had built a major reputation as choreographer at Ballet Theatre and for Broadway musicals, joined the New York City Ballet as choreographer, dancer, and later associate artistic director. His company ballets of this period include *The Guests, Age of Anxiety, The Cage, The Pied Piper,* a revival of *Interplay, Afternoon of a Faun, Fanfare,* and *The Concert.* Robbins left the company in the late 1950s, returning in 1969 to choreograph the immensely successful *Dances at a Gathering.* After 1969, resuming the title of ballet master (which he shared with Balanchine), he choreographed with great fertility; in 1983 his active ballets formed about one-fifth of the repertory and a higher percentage in number of performances. Through 1983 various company dancers, including Todd Bolender, John Taras (who became one of the company's ballet masters in 1960), Jacques d'Amboise, Francisco Moncion, Edward Villella, John Clifford, Richard Tanner, and Lorca Massine had each mounted one or more ballets, though without much critical and popular success. Only a few ballets of Taras and d'Amboise were still being performed in 1983. Peter Martins, the company's leading male dancer from 1974, began choreographing with *Calcium Light Night* in 1976, and by 1983 he had choreographed fifteen ballets.

Despite the use of other choreographers—including, in the period preceding Balanchine's death, Joseph Duell and Helgi Tomasson—it was clear from the beginning that Balanchine himself proposed to construct a full repertory. Its extraordinary richness and variety has led to Balanchine's being likened to William Shakespeare and Wolfgang Amadeus Mozart as that rare kind of genius who is also a realistic man of the theater. Balanchine first revived important past works: *Serenade* and *Concerto Barocco* in 1948, *The Prodigal Son* and *Le Baiser de la Fée* in 1950, *Apollo, Jeu de Cartes* and *The Four Temperaments* in 1951, *La Sonnambula* and *Theme and Variations* in 1960, and *Ballet Imperial (Tchaikovsky Piano Concerto No. 2)* in 1964. To these Balanchine gradually added other masterpieces, notably abstract ballets to serious concert music, such as *Divertimento No. 15* (1956), *Episodes* (1959), and *Mozartiana* (1981).

Balanchine saw himself not only as an individual artist expressing himself, but also as the heir of a tradition and as the director of a theater. There is thus a special importance in the less personal ballets through which he endowed the New York City Ballet with a genuine repertory and not merely a collection of his ballets. The premiere of *Firebird* (1949) made clear his intention to arrange a balanced menu of ballets for his new company, to use his own culinary metaphor. In resetting this exotic narrative work, the first and most popular of the Stravinsky-Diaghilev ballets and an emblem of Russian ballet to the general audience, Balanchine was responding to his company's and audience's needs—and those of Maria Tallchief, his brilliant prima ballerina—rather than his own. His aim was to enlarge and correct popular taste as well as to please it. It was probably Stravinsky's 1945 revision of the 1910 ballet that made the revival conceivable. Stravinsky's revision, though perhaps primarily undertaken to bring his immensely popular work under copyright protection, tightened up the 1910 score, pruning its diffuse repetitions, particularly in the opening section, while retaining its contrasts of theatrical mood and its narrative momentum. Balanchine followed this lead by

NEW YORK CITY BALLET. *Serenade,* created in 1935 for students at the School of American Ballet, was the first work Balanchine choreographed for American dancers. Mounted for the New York City Ballet in October 1948, it soon came to be considered the company's signature work. Patricia Wilde is pictured here with members of the ensemble, c.1955. (Photograph © by Fred Fehl; used by permission. Choreography by George Balanchine © The George Balanchine Trust.)

fashioning a suite of boldly contrasting dances that told the familiar story with high theatrical legibility but little mime.

This innovative approach aroused controversy at the time; the English found *Firebird* outrageously "streamlined." A similar condensation and distillation characterized all the remountings of narrative ballets through which Balanchine gradually built the popular repertory necessary to acquire patronage, and these works eventually received critical as well as popular acceptance. Act 2 of *Swan Lake* was mounted in 1951, *The Nutcracker* in 1954, *Harlequinade* in 1965, and *Coppélia* in 1974. Similar stylistic norms govern Balanchine's original narrative works, *A Midsummer Night's Dream* in 1962 and *Don Quixote* in 1965. These thoroughly modern narratives are clear and economical, though often elliptical, in story line. Along with important formal classical choreography, they contain passages of great dramatic power and resonance, as in act 2 of *Coppélia,* the wandering-bed episode in *The Nutcracker,* the finale of *Swan Lake,* act 1 of *A Midsummer Night's Dream,* and Don Quixote's dream of beautiful women and his windmill delusion in act 3 of *Don Quixote.*

In other works Balanchine caught the essence of earlier styles in order to give the New York City Ballet repertory a full historic and generic view of classical ballet. A series of works inspired by Aleksandr Glazunov's music for *Raymonda* remains true to the spirit and often to the actual steps of Marius Petipa's 1898 full-evening narrative ballet while discarding the narrative and enlarging Petipa's mode into the far greater complexity, power, and depth of the Balanchine style. In 1946 Balanchine and Alexandra Danilova had staged an abbreviated *Raymonda* for the Ballet Russe de Monte Carlo, but this premature attempt had failed. In 1955 Balanchine composed *Pas de Dix* for Tallchief, mainly to the *pas classique hongrois* music from the second act of *Raymonda;* he used a different selection of music for *Raymonda Variations* (1961); still later, *Cortège Hongrois* (1973), another version of the *pas classique hongrois,* was mounted as a farewell gesture to the ballerina Melissa Hayden. In *Cortège Hongrois* Balanchine paid respect to national dances prominent in the Russian tradition, but in *Pas de Dix* and *Raymonda Variations,* much more significantly, he explored and developed the variation form, a prime inheritance from Petipa's classicism.

Another historical reference may be found in *Donizetti Variations* (1960), with its evocation of Italian opera ballet and perhaps of the idealization of Italian dancing in the ballets of August Bournonville. *Scotch Symphony* (1952) may allude to Bournonville's *La Sylphide.* Balanchine may have come to know this work during his brief stint as bal-

NEW YORK CITY BALLET. Balanchine mounted *The Prodigal Son* for the company in 1950. During the company's first London season that summer, Francisco Moncion appeared in the title role, with Yvonne Mounsey as the Siren. (Photograph © by Roger Wood; used by permission. Choreography by George Balanchine © The George Balanchine Trust.)

let master of the Royal Danish Ballet in 1930, or a more general, literary romanticism may underlie the narrative, which drifts elusively through the slow movement.

The French ballet tradition probably came to Balanchine's attention through his admiration for the composer Léo Delibes, whom Petr Ilich Tchaikovsky had also admired. In 1950 he made an exhibition pas de deux to music from *Sylvia;* in 1965, *Pas de Deux and Divertissement* to music from both *Sylvia* and *La Source;* and the 1968 *La Source* used a different arrangement of some of the same music. The full-length narrative *Coppélia* followed in 1974. *Ballo della Regina* (1978) and *Walpurgisnacht Ballet* (1980) evoked the spirit of the Paris Opera Ballet, the first seriously and the second half in parody. *Ballade* (1980) hybridized the refined arabesque of Gabriel Fauré's Chopinesque score with the energy of the company's allegro style, specifically that of ballerina Merrill Ashley.

Beginning with the 1950 *Sylvia* pas de deux, Balanchine composed several independent pas de deux to fill out the range of styles in his repertory and to serve as exhibition vehicles for dancers. These cover a wide range of tone and emotion, owing in part to the nature of the dancers for whom they were composed. The *Tchaikovsky Pas de Deux* (set for Violette Verdy and Conrad Ludlow to the recently rediscovered original "Black Swan" music from *Swan Lake*) appeared in 1960, *Meditation* (for Suzanne Farrell and Jacques d'Amboise) in 1963, *Tarantella* (for Patricia McBride and Edward Villella) in 1964, *Valse Fantaisie* (for Mimi Paul and John Clifford) in 1967, Maurice Ravel's *Sonatine* (for Verdy and Jean-Pierre Bonnefous) in 1975, and *The Steadfast Tin Soldier* (for McBride and Peter Schaufuss) in 1975.

Their emphasis on style identifies these ballets as primarily repertory works, but all of them show Balanchine's high taste and workmanship, with no hint of cynicism or the perfunctory. Other ballets are harder to categorize. The decor and scenario of *La Valse* (1951) seem to locate it in the demi-monde of "camp" rather than the world of serious art, yet the ballet's structural strength enlarges and purifies its dance imagery. Balanchine said of *Allegro Brillante* (1956), set to Tchaikovsky's unfinished third piano concerto, that it contained "everything [he knew] about the classical ballet—in thirteen minutes"; this unusual condensation brings a small piece to major intensity. *Square Dance* was cheapened in 1957 by the loud, tasteless rhymes of a square-dance caller imposed on the music by Antonio Vivaldi and Arcangelo Corelli; after its reworking in 1976, without the caller and with a superb, new melancholy male solo, this ballet took its place near the highest rank of Balanchine's masterpieces. *Who Cares?* (1970), set to orchestrated versions of sixteen Gershwin show tunes, was a crowd-pleaser that was also recognized as a masterpiece by the critics. In setting Gershwin as seriously as he would set Mozart, Balanchine showed his sure intuition about the range of tone possible in serious classical ballet.

NEW YORK CITY BALLET. *Apollo, Leader of the Muses* entered the company repertory in November 1951. André Eglevsky danced the title role; Diana Adams, Maria Tallchief, and Tanaquil Le Clercq appeared as the Muses: Calliope, Terpsichore, and Polyhymnia, respectively. (Photograph © by George Platt Lynes; used by permission. Choreography by George Balanchine © The George Balanchine Trust.)

Toward the end of his career, in *Union Jack* (1976) and *Vienna Waltzes* (1977), Balanchine made more ambitious blends of repertory needs and personal expression. Both were big, richly costumed showpieces that displayed the whole company to advantage; both were divided into sections of strongly contrasting theatrical atmosphere; and both patently aimed for the popularity they enjoyed. Nevertheless, because of their unusual length and format, both ballets explored and deepened their popular material. The three sections of *Union Jack* (timed to coincide with the bicentennial of the American Revolution) paid tribute to Great Britain in a record of Balanchine's touristic and professional encounters with British ways of moving. The hypnotic marching drills reminiscent of the Changing of the Guard or of military tattoos, followed by country dances, the low music-hall comedy of the Costermonger Pas de Deux, the smart revue-style Tars and Gals finale (which may have been meant to evoke the Cochran revues Balanchine worked on in the late 1920s)—all came together in an original theatrical unity. *Vienna Waltzes* traces waltz movement from the ingenuous romance of the younger Johann Strauss's *Tales from the Vienna Woods,* through the café sophistication of Franz Lehár, to the sumptuous reveries of *Der Rosenkavalier.* Both ballets showed personal expression most clearly in using key dancers, particularly Suzanne Farrell, whose evocation of the secret dreaming of late adolescence in the *Rosenkavalier* section touched the highest art.

Western Symphony (1954) and *Stars and Stripes* (1958) were works of popular appeal that unpretentiously represented an important development in American ballet classicism. In the 1930s Kirstein had composed several narrative scenarios that led to a series of Americana ballets, one of which, *Billy the Kid,* remained in the general repertory. Although Balanchine had been involved in one such venture, *Alma Mater* (1935), this way of making ballet American never caught his imagination. He found his own approach to American themes in the mode of *Western Symphony* and *Stars and Stripes*—suites of dances with American decor and atmosphere but completely classical in structure and faintly though affectionately parodistic in style.

The full-evening, plotless *Jewels* (1967)—three ballets, entitled *Emeralds, Rubies,* and *Diamonds*—is perhaps the best example of Balanchine's habits as a maker of repertory, showing his imaginative and pragmatic use of dancers, both the responsibility he felt toward them and the inspiration he took from them. In *Emeralds* he seemed to count on Violette Verdy to give dramatic power point, and nobility of style to Fauré's chic textures. In *Rubies* he played off Edward Villella's electric American vitality and charm against the wit and dry lyricism of Stravinsky's Capriccio for Piano and Orchestra. Villella had formed a popular partnership with Patricia McBride for which *Rubies* provided a new vehicle, and the new role for McBride released an unexpected nervous energy. *Diamonds,* created at the height of Balanchine's concentration on Suzanne Farrell, publicly idealized this dancer as his embodiment of the most advanced classicism. *Emeralds* gave Mimi Paul her great Balanchine role in a pas de deux with the gravely eloquent Moncion, which is the most intimate moment in the whole evening. *Jewels* delighted in the depth of the company's resources: *Emeralds* showed off the elegance of three young soloists, Sara Leland, John Prinz, and Suki Schorer, in a delicate and brilliant pas de trois; *Rubies* gave the formidable Patricia Neary an alternately menacing and wittily exuberant role. *Emeralds* showed the lyricism of the corps, and *Rubies* its jazzy piquancy and drive, with particularly visible roles for four men; *Diamonds* brought virtually the whole company onto the stage in a crowded final polonaise that would have been unbearably "noisy" were it not for the speed and lightness that had become characteristic of the New York City Ballet.

Balanchine's abstract ballets to serious concert music form the heart of his personal work because of their mu-

NEW YORK CITY BALLET. Using music by Vivaldi and Corelli, Balanchine created *Square Dance* in 1957, adapting patterns from American folk dance to classical ballet. Patricia Wilde and Nicholas Magallanes led the original cast. (Photograph from the Dance Collection, New York Public Library for the Performing Arts. Choreography by George Balanchine © The George Balanchine Trust.)

sicality—their special relation with their scores. Music was central to the conception of the New York City Ballet. The uniquely high level of the music in the Ballet Society continued in the company not only in the form of an excellent permanent orchestra, conducted by such distinguished musicians as Leon Barzin and Robert Irving, but in the venturesomeness of the music chosen for choreography, including works as advanced, as difficult to play and listen to, as the serial compositions of the later Stravinsky, Webern, and Arnold Schoenberg and the experimental music of Charles Ives, Iannis Xenakis, Pierre Henry, and others. (The company was less enterprising in commissioning music: apart from *Agon,* there is nothing but the mediocre Nicolas Nabokov score for the three-act *Don Quixote.*)

Balanchine's professional musical education at the Saint Petersburg conservatory no doubt gave him the exceptional musical facility that distinguishes him from other choreographers, but his musicality and the centrality of music at the New York City Ballet came from a deeper source. Some critics see Balanchine's choreography in works such as *The Four Temperaments* or *Divertimento No. 15* as forming a line of quasi-musical counterpoint, while others see it as a visualization of the music. Stravinsky's tribute to Balanchine's setting of his *Movements for Piano and Orchestra* used an illuminating comparison: "The performance was like a tour of a building for which I had drawn the plans but never explored the result." Balanchine's most musical ballets are greater than the sum of their parts, creating a new medium and a new kind of theater.

This centrality of music may have been responsible for the sparing use of stage decoration at the New York City Ballet. Despite fine work by Esteban Francés, Barbara Karinska, and a few others, the company paid little attention to decor. There can be theatricality without decor, however, and the use of space and, in particular, lighting in *Symphony in C* or *Mozartiana* were among the great visual achievements of modern art.

Balanchine's relation with Stravinsky started at the beginning of Balanchine's career and continued until Stravinsky's death, and the surviving Balanchine-Stravinsky ballets constitute a monumental achievement: *Apollo* (1928), *Orpheus* (1948), *Firebird* (1949), *Agon* (1957), *Monumentum pro Gesualdo* (1960), *Movements for Piano and Orchestra* (1963), *Rubies* (1967), *Violin Concerto* (1972), *Symphony in Three Movements* (1972), *Duo Concertant* (1972), and *Divertimento from "Le Baiser de la Fée"* (1972). Up to *Agon,* Stravinsky independently made all the musical and theatrical decisions in these ballets, creating a "scenario" to which Balanchine then gave choreographic embodiment. In the composition of *Agon,* composer and choreographer worked out every aspect of the scenario together, and this ballet was actually their first

NEW YORK CITY BALLET. *Agon,* set by Balanchine to a score commissioned from Stravinsky, was given its premiere on 1 December 1957. Jonathan Watts, Melissa Hayden, and Roy Tobias danced the *bransle double (de poitou).* In a later performance, pictured here, Richard Rapp danced in place of Tobias. (Photograph from the Dance Collection, New York Public Library for the Performing Arts. Choreography by George Balanchine © The George Balanchine Trust.)

genuine collaboration. It was also the last, for with *Monumentum pro Gesualdo* Balanchine began to set Stravinsky scores not composed for dance, as he did with the works composed for the 1972 festival commemorating Stravinsky's death. Balanchine had followed this procedure with concert music of the past since 1934 *(Serenade),* and it is arguable that setting concert music to dance was the method of his greatest works: *Concerto Barocco, Tchaikovsky Piano Concerto No. 2, The Four Temperaments, Symphony in C, Divertimento No. 15, Episodes, Liebeslieder Walzer,* and *Mozartiana.*

The high prestige of Balanchine's abstract ballets gave rise to the idea that he and his company were hostile to ballet narrative, but this is not certain. Balanchine's decision to mount four full-evening narrative ballets—*Coppélia* as late as 1974—suggests at least a practical respect for narrative ballet as part of repertory. The mastery of narrative in *The Prodigal Son, La Sonnambula, A Midsummer Night's Dream,* and *Don Quixote* hardly came from distaste for the mode. Yet there were very few short narrative ballets in the repertory, and Balanchine's truncation of the narrative opening of *Apollo* in 1978, destroying the symmetry of the score, suggested at least a temporary revulsion against narrative. As early as *Cotillon* (1933) and *Serenade* (1934), Balanchine had created a mixed mode of plotless ballets with imagery resonant enough to imply a dramatic situation without actually representing it. Balanchine's pas de deux suggest indefinable love relation-

NEW YORK CITY BALLET. Birgit Cullberg's *Medea,* mounted for the company in 1958, provided dramatic roles for Violette Verdy as Creusa, Jacques d'Amboise as Jason, and Melissa Hayden as Medea. Costumes for this production were designed by Lewis Brown. (Photograph by Martha Swope, © Time, Inc.; used by permission.)

ships, often more evocative than whole evenings of narrative by other choreographers. His last two major works developed this mixed mode subtly: *Robert Schumann's "Davidsbündlertänze"* (1980) was a suite of dances that contained but was not wholly concerned with portraits of Robert and Clara Schumann and a narrative of Schumann's growing insanity; *Mozartiana* (1981), essentially abstract and with an entirely nondramatic relation between the ballerina and her cavalier, nevertheless opened with a dance of prayer based on everyday arm and hand gestures.

Jerome Robbins's ballets fit into the repertory because they followed Balanchine's practice in handling music and narrative. Robbins's enduring early masterpieces *Fancy Free* (1944) and *Afternoon of a Faun* (1953) are admirably musical works, though not quite Balanchinian in their relation to their scores. *Faun* is sensual and lyrical and at the same time a profound parody of the Nijinsky original. One of the great vehicles for dancers in the modern repertory, this ambiguous encounter between narcissistic dancers in a dance studio always shows new aspects of its dancers, qualities of temperament of which the dancers themselves seem barely aware, yet without embarrassing self-exposure. Many would rank Robbins's *The Cage* (1951) as a masterpiece, and it surely retains great power as a work of private fantasy and public theatricality, but it was from the beginning coarsened by thematic insistence and a melodramatic mishearing of its music, Stravinsky's Concerto in D for Strings.

When he returned to the New York City Ballet in 1969 with *Dances at a Gathering,* a nonnarrative suite of dances set to Frédéric Chopin's piano music, Robbins's conception of ballet seemed in line with Balanchine's. Actually, his version of American classicism was very different, a difference enthusiastically welcomed by many for the variety it contributed to the company's repertory. *Dances at a Gathering* exhibited the clarity, speed, openness, and elegance of School of American Ballet style, but Robbins spiced this style with acrobatic thrills and with stylizations of the way American young people behave. The tremendous popularity of Robbins's ballet showed how exactly he had matched the imagination and sensibility of a large portion of the New York City Ballet audience. A minority faulted him for the faintly meretricious charm of his picture of American behavior and for false sentiment.

Robbins followed *Dances at a Gathering* by three shorter ballets in the same mode—*In the Night* (1970) and *Other Dances* (1977), to Chopin, and a night-piece to music by Sergei Prokofiev, *An Evening's Waltzes* (1973). *The Goldberg Variations* (1971) certified Robbins's dedication to serious music and restated his contrast between American vernacular behavior and American classical dancing, which became the theme of the ballet, structurally articulated in the two halves of the work. A few brilliant passages, however, could not redeem the constant straining for invention and the lack of natural breathing rhythm and of emotional depth. *Watermill* (1971) was a long, pretentious, empty experiment in new kinds of theatrical time and space. *The Dybbuk Variations* (1974), to an original Leonard Bernstein score, attempted unsuccessfully to render the essence of the story without narrative structure. Robbins's repertory ballets, particularly his contributions to company festivals, were highly professional works, however, skillfully contrived to exhibit dancers—

Farrell and Martins in *In G Major,* or Ib Andersen and Kyra Nichols in *Piano Pieces. The Four Seasons* (1978), *Gershwin Concerto* (1982), and *Glass Pieces* (1983) were equally effective theatrically and structurally but seldom fine in taste or true in feeling.

Peter Martins's choreography, like Robbins's, emulated Balanchine's musicality. His wittily inventive first ballet, *Calcium Light Night* (1976), set to some orchestral pieces by Ives, suggested a capacity to make nonnarrative dance images of the relations between men and women, Balanchine's great theme. Martins afterward choreographed competent classical pas de deux in *Sonate di Scarlatti, Tchaikovsky Symphony No. 1, Delibes Divertissements* and other works, but these were emotionally neutral, with little structural power.

In his last years Balanchine, having chosen Martins to succeed him as director, began giving him the specific assignments a master gives an apprentice. One was *The Magic Flute* (1980), a one-act story ballet to Riccardo Drigo's music, based on the scenario of an 1893 Maryinsky ballet in which Balanchine himself had danced; another was the Stravinsky *Concerto for Two Solo Pianos* (1982). For both assignments, Martins produced solidly built ballets that demonstrated devotion and skill but were not very interesting. Apart from *Calcium Light Night,* the most truly musical of his ballets through 1983 were the charmingly witty *Eight Easy Pieces* (1978), a setting for three young ballerinas of Stravinsky's four-hand piano pieces, and *Capriccio Italien,* a fluent setting for a large cast of Tchaikovsky's broad score.

In addition to creating a repertory for his new company, Balanchine proposed to create its style and technique of dancing. At the beginning this was visible chiefly in the dancing of the principals, whom he had coached in roles expressly made for them. By the mid-1970s this style was consistent throughout the company; most of the dancers had been trained at Balanchine's School of American Ballet and reflected the stylistic and technical standards and even the conception of the ideal dancer's body that informed the training there. The Balanchine dancer was caricatured as a very young ballerina with a small head and long legs. There were in fact many physical types at the New York City Ballet, but there was unquestionably a distinctive Balanchine look, movement, and carriage. Under Balanchine, company technique fostered speed, variety of attack, and continuity in phrasing and changing direction, rather than the careful preparations, correctness, and conventional legato of academic dancing.

The consistency and depth of the dancing at the New York City Ballet owed much to the special nature of Balanchine's company class. As the twentieth century's major innovator in ballet style and technique, he made company class a laboratory rather than a warm-up, working with his dancers to explore and expand the vocabulary of classical ballet and to increase the scale and dynamic range of classical dancing. As he taught his dancers to know classi-

NEW YORK CITY BALLET. Created in 1960 to the well-known music of Johannes Brahms, Balanchine's romantic *Liebeslieder Walzer* is danced by four couples to two sets of waltzes written for piano duet and vocal quartet. Dancers, pianists, and singers in period costumes, designed by Karinska, are on stage together. Here Suzanne Farrell (seated at left) watches as Frank Ohman and Patricia McBride swirl across the floor in a 1963 performance. (Photograph © by Fred Fehl; used by permission. Choreography by George Balanchine © The George Balanchine Trust.)

cal ballet vocabulary with unprecedented depth and precision, he constantly monitored their progress in order to create roles that would show their individual skills and personalities. This consistency of style did not suppress the dancers' individuality of style and temperament, despite criticism to the contrary.

When the Ballet Society became the New York City Ballet, its two ballerinas were great stars who embodied Balanchine's training without sacrificing their individuality. The vivid and powerful Maria Tallchief, for whom Balanchine made dazzling roles in *Firebird, Swan Lake, Pas de Dix,* and *Scotch Symphony,* reigned as *prima ballerina* until 1956, returning for a brief period with much diminished powers in the 1960s. In partnership with André Eglevsky, she handled the bravura repertory with the highest taste. The sophisticated elegance and fluidity of Tanaquil Le Clercq inspired diverse roles in *The Four Temperaments, La Valse,* and *Bourrée Fantasque,* as well as in Robbins's greatest ballerina role in *Afternoon of a Faun.*

NEW YORK CITY BALLET. In 1959 Toshirō Mayuzumi was invited by the New York City Ballet to compose a ballet score in the spirit of traditional Japanese court music *(bugaku).* Upon its delivery, Balanchine choreographed a stunning ballet in three movements, *Bugaku* (1963), for Allegra Kent and Edward Villella, suggesting ceremonial rites of courtship and marriage. (Photograph © by Bert Stern; used by permission. Choreography by George Balanchine © The George Balanchine Trust.)

NEW YORK CITY BALLET. *A Midsummer Night's Dream* (1962), in two acts and six scenes, was Balanchine's first wholly original full-length ballet. Seen here are Suki Schorer, Anne Burton, Linda Yourth, and (barely visible) Judith Friedman as Butterflies, surrounding Arthur Mitchell as Puck. (Photograph © by Fred Fehl; used by permission. Choreography by George Balanchine © The George Balanchine Trust.)

She danced the first great performances of one of the greatest Balanchine roles, the adagio in *Symphony in C.* Her career was tragically ended by polio in 1956, when she was twenty-seven years old.

In its first years, several ballerinas were invited into the company to form a full contingent of principals, including Diana Adams, Melissa Hayden, Jillana, Nora Kaye, Yvonne Mounsey, Janet Reed, and Patricia Wilde. Balanchine had used Adams, Hayden, and Reed at Ballet Theatre, and Mounsey and Wilde at Ballet Russe de Monte Carlo, so these dancers fit into the company style immediately. Nora Kaye had danced in Balanchine's *Waltz Academy* at Ballet Theatre, but her specialty was Tudor's psychological expressionism; although she made a strong impression in Robbins's *The Cage* and Tudor's *Lilac Garden,* she was unable to take a place in the regular repertory. Diana Adams's large-scale lyricism struck one of the keynotes of company style in the 1950s, with central roles in *Agon, Episodes,* and *Monumentum pro Gesualdo.* The tiny Janet Reed was delectable in *Bourrée Fantasque* and *Jeu de Cartes,* and Yvonne Mounsey's Siren in *The Prodigal Son* combined power and beauty to a degree rarely seen since. Melissa Hayden and Patricia Wilde, abundantly gifted in force and intelligence, were dependable dancers for whom Balanchine made memorable roles: for Hayden, most notably the second pas de trois in *Agon;* for Wilde, the Highland Girl in *Scotch Symphony* and the virtuosic ballerina roles in *Square Dance* and *Raymonda Variations.* Jillana, richly womanly, danced a softly malicious Coquette in *La Sonnambula,* rivaling Tallchief's fiery original.

Two new ballerinas of the late 1950s, Allegra Kent and Violette Verdy, had contrasting styles not unlike the earlier Le Clercq and Tallchief. Kent, delicately pliant, brought electrifying power to *La Sonnambula* and a rare wit to Robbins's farcical *The Concert, Gounod Symphony,* and *Stars and Stripes* and to the paradoxical off-balances of the Concerto in *Episodes;* her suppleness in *Bugaku* almost surpassed belief. The chic, powerful, and musical Verdy, trained in France, had from the beginning a fruitfully ambiguous relation with the company style. She danced repertory roles with rich detail; her *Firebird* was a masterwork of theatrical calculation. Her Balanchine roles, in *The Figure in the Carpet* (1958), *Liebeslieder Walzer* (1961), *Emeralds* (1966), *La Source* (1968), and *Sonatine* (1975), all showed Balanchine delighting in, deepening, and refining her dramatic gift. Robbins used this gift wittily in the single appearance of the Girl in

NEW YORK CITY BALLET. First mounted in 1954, when the New York City Ballet was a resident company at the City Center for Music and Drama, Balanchine's version of *The Nutcracker* was given a new production in 1964, after the company had moved to the New York State Theater at Lincoln Center. New scenery was designed by Rouben Ter-Arutunian, and some new costumes were made by Karinska. Seen here is Melissa Hayden (at center) as the Sugarplum Fairy, leading the entire ensemble in the finale to act 2. (Photograph © by Fred Fehl; used by permission. Choreography by George Balanchine © The George Balanchine Trust.)

NEW YORK CITY BALLET. Balanchine's *Jewels* (1967) is a full-evening program of three independent works: *Emeralds,* set to romantic music by Fauré; *Rubies,* set to a jazzily astringent score by Stravinsky; and *Diamonds,* set to the grand strains of two movements of Tchaikovsky's Third Symphony. Seen here in *Emeralds* are Violette Verdy and Conrad Ludlow, who were the principal dancers in the original cast. (Photograph © by Fred Fehl; used by permission. Choreography by George Balanchine © The George Balanchine Trust.)

Green at the strategic center of *Dances at a Gathering,* and more literally as one of the tormented lovers in *In the Night.*

In the 1960s there emerged a widely publicized group of young dancers, including Suzanne Farrell, Gloria Govrin, Patricia McBride, Marnee Morris, Patricia Neary, Mimi Paul, and Suki Schorer. From 1965 to 1969, and after her reappearance in 1975, Farrell reigned supreme in the company. Her perfect athlete's physique, her beauty, and her dance genius—in particular, the coherence of her body configuration at extremes of speed and changing direction—made her the most highly gifted dancer the company had known. Balanchine's roles marked her as the embodiment of both his private and his public vision. *Meditation, Don Quixote,* and *Pithoprakta* revealed a fantasy of ideal womanhood. In *Diamonds, Chaconne, Walpurgisnacht Ballet,* and *Mozartiana,* Farrell was the instrument of Balanchine's final experiments in the expansion of classical dancing. Robbins gave her cool smoothness a handsome vehicle with *In G Major.*

Patricia McBride had an ideal dependability, giving herself unfalteringly to her roles exactly as she learned them. Her power in the theater was the more remarkable for the neutrality of her temperament and dance style. At her best she was a uniquely pure dancer who commanded attention by dance energy. In using her in *Harlequinade, Coppélia, Divertimento from "Le Baiser de la Fée,"* and *The Steadfast Tin Soldier,* Balanchine counted successfully on that energy to take the curse of cuteness off these soubrette roles. An exciting personal identity appeared in *Rubies,* in *Brahms-Schönberg Quartet* and, most beautiful of all, in "Fascinatin' Rhythm" and "The Man I Love" in *Who Cares?*

The statuesque Govrin, uniquely powerful, was often used half-comically, as in the role of the Good Fairy in *Harlequinade.* She and Neary made a thrilling entrance in a high-flying twin routine in the finale of *Raymonda Variations.* Paul's concentration was almost alarming in *Bugaku,* and her vision of Romantic ballet, which later led her to leave the company to dance the classics at American Ballet Theatre, made her early *Swan Lake* authoritative. Schorer, small for ballerina roles, nevertheless acquired the power necessary for the first movement of *Symphony in C;* she was exactly right in such soubrette roles as Pierette in *Harlequinade* or the lead Butterfly in *A Midsummer Night's Dream.* Morris's perfectionism made her *fouettés* in "My One and Only" in *Who Cares?* brilliant, and her personality made them unexpectedly winsome.

Farrell's departure from the company in 1969, leaving key roles temporarily empty, led to the ascendancy of Kay Mazzo, Sara Leland, and Karin von Aroldingen, limited dancers who performed loyally but inadequately in Farrell's roles. Balanchine repaid Mazzo's and von Aroldingen's dedication with roles that fitted them beautifully: in *Stravinsky Violin Concerto* and *Duo Concertant* Mazzo's brittle delicacy was set off against Peter Martins's velvety power; in *Stravinsky Violin Concerto, Who Cares?* and *Robert Schumann's "Davidsbündlertänze,"* von Aroldingen became a strong, beautiful, and affecting stage presence. Leland was less handsomely treated, but her Polka in *Vienna Waltzes* was a charming tribute, and she brought real conviction to the role she inherited from Mazzo in *Davidsbündlertänze.* Robbins used her excitingly in *Dances at a Gathering.* From 1970 to 1974 Gelsey Kirkland emerged as a major talent, with a notable Robbins role in *The Goldberg Variations* and memorable appearances in Balanchine ballets such as *Monumentum pro Gesualdo* and *Concerto Barocco,* but her career in the company came to an end when she left in 1974 to join Mikhail Baryshnikov at American Ballet Theatre.

The new ballerinas of the 1970s were Merrill Ashley, Colleen Neary, Kyra Nichols, and Heather Watts; of the early 1980s, Darci Kistler and Maria Calegari. Ashley attracted attention by her exact, plucked-string style even before her 1974 triumph in *Tchaikovsky Concerto No. 2.* Her buoyancy and brio were prime resources for Balanchine's major reworkings of *The Four Temperaments* (1975) and *Square Dance* (1976); and Balanchine paid her fleet accuracy elegantly tailored tributes in *Ballo della Regina* (1978) and *Ballade* (1980). Neary was often powerful in demanding roles, such as the second lead in *Rubies;* Balanchine made an unusually interesting role for her in *Kammermusik No. 2* (1978), but she left the company soon after.

Nichols had by 1983 become a mainstay of company repertory and a prime exemplar of its style. Her *Square Dance* and *Tchaikovsky Piano Concerto No. 2* were equal to Ashley's in verve and power and superior in elegance and flow. Although Balanchine made no roles for her, Robbins gave her effective vehicles in *The Four Seasons* (1978) and *Piano Pieces* (1981). Watts was Martins's earliest leading ballerina, with powerful and original, though charmless, roles in *Calcium Light Night* (1976) and *Concerto for Two Solo Pianos* (1982). Her specialties were strong drive coupled with a wonderfully light jump. The young Kistler's amazing suppleness, united to her appealing pleasure in being onstage, promised a great future. Calegari's strength was in purity and perfection of style and line; Robbins gave her the witty and imaginative gift of a sexy role in *Gershwin Concerto* (1982). Lourdes Lopez's strength and style in the second lead in *Tchaikovsky Piano Concerto No. 2* and other roles were of ballerina quality, while Stephanie Saland's ample beauty and musicality were a major company resource; her first movement of *Symphony in C* stood out.

At the beginning, the company's men were not strong classical dancers, although Nicholas Magallanes, Jonathan Watts, and Herbert Bliss partnered capably, and Magallanes's *Orpheus* was completely right in its soft vulnerability. Francisco Moncion's dramatic gift led to some memorable roles: his remote grandeur in *La Valse,* in *Afternoon of a Faun,* and as the Dark Angel in *Orpheus* set the standard for these roles, and his Prodigal Son, though lacking the virtuosity Villella and Baryshnikov were to bring, had a vulnerable dignity no less effective than the boyishness of later conceptions. Todd Bolender's easy wit and charm in the first pas de trois in *Agon* seem unrecapturable. In the late 1950s two important American male dancers emerged, Jacques d'Amboise and Edward Villella. They were followed in the 1960s by Anthony Blum, Con-

NEW YORK CITY BALLET. *Dances at a Gathering,* created by Jerome Robbins in 1969 to piano music by Frédéric Chopin, became an "instant classic." The original cast was composed of these ten dancers: (from left to right) Anthony Blum, John Clifford, Patricia McBride, John Prinz, Allegra Kent, Edward Villella, Violette Verdy, Kay Mazzo, Robert Maiorano, and Sara Leland. The costumes were designed by Joe Eula. (Photograph © by Fred Fehl; used by permission.)

rad Ludlow, and Arthur Mitchell, and in the 1970s by Bart Cook, Daniel Duell, Robert Weiss, and Sean Lavery.

In 1951 André Eglevsky was invited to join the company, the first of many foreign male dancers. Trained in the European tradition but experienced with American companies, Eglevsky found the New York City Ballet congenial and remained for nine years. Hugh Laing had come to the company with his wife, Diana Adams, but his style was out of place and he soon left. Two more promising recruits of 1959, Paul Taylor and Erik Bruhn, found company rehearsal procedures unacceptably casual. The French-trained André Prokovsky came in 1963, adapted well, and remained three years. In 1969 the company initiated a regular importation of male dancers, many trained in the Danish tradition—Peter Martins, Peter Schaufuss, Adam Lüders, and Ib Andersen—and others from different traditions, such as Jean-Pierre Bonnefous, Helgi Tomasson, and Leonid Koslov. By the mid-1970s the male contingent was in satisfactory balance with the women. In 1978 Mikhail Baryshnikov joined the company; in a year and a half he learned more than fourteen roles, most of which he danced with notable success. But he was not ideally suited, physically or temperamentally, to the New York City Ballet methods, and in 1979 he accepted the directorship of American Ballet Theatre.

NEW YORK CITY BALLET. Balanchine's *Who Cares?*, set to a medley of show tunes by George Gershwin, had its premiere in February 1970. Its infectious gaiety, high spirits, and cheerfulness made it an audience favorite. Seen here in "That Certain Feeling" are Earle Sievling and Bettijane Sills, who were members of the original cast. (Photograph © by Bob Mayette; from the Dance Collection, New York Public Library for the Performing Arts. Choreography by George Balanchine © The George Balanchine Trust.)

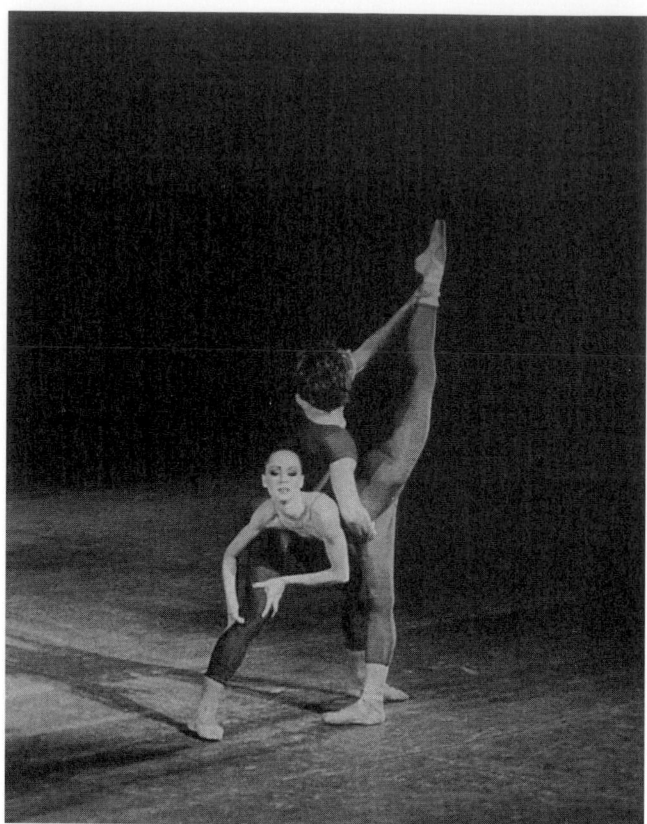

NEW YORK CITY BALLET. *Calcium Light Night* (1977), set to music by Charles Ives, was the first work by Peter Martins to enter the company's repertory. Heather Watts and Daniel Duell were the original performers. (Photograph from the Dance Collection, New York Public Library for the Performing Arts.)

Balanchine's famous remark, "Ballet is woman," is not apocryphal; his primary attention went to teaching and choreographing for women. As a practical man of the theater, however, he accepted Serge Lifar's centrality in the Serge Diaghilev company in the late 1920s, creating two superb roles for him in *Apollo* and *The Prodigal Son*. Balanchine built a repertory to exhibit Eglevsky's virtuosity, yet these brilliant roles seem not to have called forth any deep interest or inspiration from Balanchine. Taylor's inventive role in *Episodes* proved that he had interested Balanchine, but the oddity of the role perhaps indicates only a momentary fascination. Villella, however, visibly and permanently caught Balanchine's imagination, inspiring a group of *demi-caractère* roles that are among the glories of the repertory: *Tarantella, Rubies,* Oberon in *A Midsummer Night's Dream, Harlequinade,* and others. Balanchine gratefully used d'Amboise's height for partnering; he clearly enjoyed d'Amboise's easy American charm and made memorable use of it in *Who Cares?* For the supremely gifted Peter Martins, Balanchine composed a supreme repertory, expanding male classical dancing only

NEW YORK CITY BALLET. Balanchine's quintessential work of Americana is *Stars and Stripes,* created in 1958 to music by John Philip Sousa, adapted and orchestrated by Hershey Kay. Rarely absent from the company's repertory, it never fails to rouse audiences to cheers and prolonged applause. Seen here in a 1979 performance of the "Fourth Campaign," a pas de deux danced to "Liberty Bell" and "El Capitan," are Merrill Ashley and Peter Martins. (Photograph © 1979 by Linda Vartoogian; used by permission. Choreography by George Balanchine © The George Balanchine Trust.)

slightly less spectacularly than Farrell's 1970s roles had expanded the range of the ballerina. Martins's greatest roles were *Stravinsky Violin Concerto* and *Chaconne,* but his charmingly lecherous Chief-Mate in *Union Jack* was great comic dancing. Helgi Tomasson's solo in *Divertimento from "Le Baiser de la Fée"* (1972) and Bart Cook's solo in the 1976 *Square Dance* were richly moody dances, and Ib Andersen's role in *Mozartiana* gave elegance a wholly new look.

Balanchine's death in 1983 cast the shadow of uncertainty on the company's future, though Martins and Robbins, both named ballet master in chief, strove to preserve the Balanchine inheritance, uniquely rich in ballet history.

[*Many of the figures and works mentioned herein are the subjects of independent entries.*]

BIBLIOGRAPHY

Chujoy, Anatole. *The New York City Ballet.* New York, 1953.

Kirstein, Lincoln. *The New York City Ballet.* New York, 1973.

Kirstein, Lincoln. *Thirty Years: The New York City Ballet.* New York, 1978.

Kirstein, Lincoln, et al. *Choreography by George Balanchine: A Catalogue of Works.* New York, 1983.

Reynolds, Nancy. *Repertory in Review: Forty Years of the New York City Ballet.* New York, 1977.

Taper, Bernard. *Balanchine: A Biography.* New rev. ed. New York, 1984.

ROBERT GARIS

History since 1983

Balanchine's last public appearance took place during a curtain call at the New York State Theater at Lincoln Center on 4 July 1982, closing night of the spring season. The choreographer accepted a warm ovation but reportedly felt so dizzy that he feared being unable to stand without support. By November he became so incapacitated that he entered the hospital, where he died on 30 April 1983, of complications from the neurological disorder Creutzfeldt-Jacob disease.

Though shocked and saddened, the company continued dancing strongly under the guidance of Jerome Robbins and Peter Martins—the team who shared the title "co–ballet master in chief." It was a likely and expected transfer of leadership, with Martins assuming virtually all the responsibility for day-to-day administration and casting. Though Balanchine himself had questioned whether his work could survive him, the New York City Ballet's administration insisted, before and immediately after he died, that his vision was sacrosanct. Not only would his canon be preserved by the company, but it would also enhance its image and avoid the un-Balanchinean role of "museum" by continuing to present worthy new repertory. In the years that followed, this ideal came to be understood as a goal rather than a guarantee, and a difficult one at that.

Peter Martins concluded his dancing career in December 1983. Almost from the beginning of his administration, marketing in general and attracting new audiences in particular loomed ever larger in shaping the company's evolution. New means of promotion increasingly influenced what the company danced. Themed subscription series offered introductions to ballet (the "Discovery" and "Next Step" series), to modern choreography (the "Next Generation" series), to the "Classics," and more. The proportion of programs devoted to Balanchine's works declined. In fall 1995 the company reduced its number of weekly performances from eight to seven and dropped a pre-*Nutcracker* week of November repertory.

The Balanchine Repertory. Beginning in 1984 with a restaging of the *Liebeslieder Walzer,* which had not been danced for more than a decade, the New York City Ballet's set about reviving long-absent Balanchine ballets that by now had virtually the cachet of being "new." In spring 1985 the solo and pas de deux created by Balanchine for Maria Tallchief in *Firebird,* which had been superseded by a number of inferior versions, were restored. *Gounod Symphony* was revived in 1985, as was *La Sonnambula. The Prodigal Son* was restored in 1986 and the 1972 *Danses Concertantes* in 1989. For the 1988 American Music Festival, the long-discarded third movement scherzo was restored to *Western Symphony,* as was a solo originated by Paul Taylor in *Episodes.*

NEW YORK CITY BALLET. *The Sleeping Beauty,* mounted by Peter Martins in 1991, includes the "Garland Waltz" choreographed by Balanchine in 1981. This streamlined version of the Petipa classic has proved a popular springtime favorite with New York audiences. Pictured here are Darci Kistler as Aurora and Damien Woetzel as the Prince. (Photograph © 1991 by Costas; used by permission.)

Several "lost" works were revived for an eight-week Balanchine Celebration in 1993. Among them were *Haieff Divertimento* (1947); *Minkus Pas de Trois* (1948); *Sylvia Pas de Deux* (1953); the 1953 *Valse-Fantaisie; Glinka Pas de Trois* (1955); *Pavane* (1975); and *Le Bourgeois Gentilhomme* (1978). The prologue was also returned to *Apollo,* as was the birth scene.

The Balanchine Celebration, which devoted the entire spring season to a recapitulation of seventy-three works in roughly chronological order, provided a focus for controversy about the direction of the company. Arlene Croce, the *New Yorker*'s dance critic, defined the event as "marking the tenth anniversary of [Balanchine's] death and the catastrophically swift decline of his repertory under Peter Martins." The chief *New York Times* dance critic Anna Kisselgoff later responded, "Balanchine is dead. . . . [T]hose who still cannot come to terms with [his] death . . . remain completely subjective in their appraisal, . . . speaking less to what is on stage than to their own private vision of what the City Ballet should be." The question of Martins's stewardship and the survival of the Balanchine legacy continued, nevertheless, as the context for ongoing seasons of the New York City Ballet.

New Choreography. Robbins's major new works of the period were *Antique Epigraphs,* for eight of the company's women (to music by Claude Debussy, 1984); *Brahms/Handel,* a collaboration with Twyla Tharp (1984); *In Memory Of . . . ,* for Suzanne Farrell (to music by Alban Berg, 1985); and *Ives, Songs,* an elegiac look back at life from the perspective of old age (1988). In 1995, his *2 + 3 Part Inventions* (to music by Johann Sebastian Bach), created the previous year for the School of American Ballet, was danced by the New York City Ballet, which also staged a new Robbins work, *West Side Story Suite.* A festival of Jerome Robbins ballets was given in June 1990.

In addition to carrying out the day-to-day administrative responsibilities of the company, Martins choreographed two or three new works a year. He returned most often to dances of stark abstraction combined with alienated, often hostile sexual conflict. Among the most notable were *Ecstatic Orange* (1987); *Tanzspiel, Black & White,* and *The Waltz Project* (all three 1988); *Ash* (1991); and *Jazz* (1993). *Ecstatic Orange* was set to music by the young minimalist composer Michael Torke, with whom Martins worked again on *Black & White, Echo* (1989), and *Ash.* He also set many scores by John Adams. In a more romantic vein, he showcased individual ballerinas, such as Merrill Ashley, Kyra Nichols, and Darci Kistler in, respectively, *Barber Violin Concerto* (1988), *Beethoven Romance* (1989), and *Symphonic Dances* (to music by Sergei Rachmaninoff, 1994). In 1991 Martins staged a complete production of *The Sleeping Beauty,* incorporating Balanchine's own setting of the "Garland Waltz." A popular success, the staging, which featured Kistler as Aurora, confirmed Martins's commitment to an aspect of Balanchine's vision and established the company's connection to the nineteenth-century tradition of Russian classicism inherited from Petipa.

Choreographic Festivals. A major response to the challenge of developing new repertory took the form of festivals in which large groups of choreographers were commissioned to produce clusters of new works. The trend began in 1988 with the American Music Festival (AMF), which unleashed twenty-two new works. AMF's sense of hipness was also augmented by an array of commissioned paintings and musical scores. Past and present New York City Ballet dancers invited to participate as choreographers included Jean-Pierre Bonnefous, Robert Weiss, and Miriam Mahdaviani. Martins himself contributed eight new ballets. Five choreographers outside the company also took part: Lar Lubovich (*Rhapsody* *in Blue,* to music by George Gershwin); Eliot Feld (*The Unanswered Question,* to Charles Ives); Laura Dean (*Space,* to Steve Reich); William Forsythe (*Behind the China Dogs,* to Leslie Stuck); and Paul Taylor (*Danbury Mix,* to Ives).

The AMF struck many observers as excessive; future events were more modest. A 1992 grant from the Aaron Diamond Foundation and other sponsors launched a biannual "Diamond Project" to fund the creation of new works making use of the ballet vocabulary. Of the eleven ballets premiered in 1992, the strongest were Richard Tanner's *Ancient Airs and Dances* (to Ottorino Respighi) and William Forsythe's *Herman Schmerman* (to Thom Willems). The second event, held in spring 1993, presented twelve new ballets, with the stand-outs being Robert LaFosse's *Danses de Cour* (to Strauss), Lynne Taylor-Corbett's *Chiaroscuro* (to Francesco Geminiani), and Kevin O'Day's *Viola Alone* (to Paul Hindemith).

Personnel. Key events involving changes of leadership and guidance included Robbins's resignation as co-ballet master in chief in 1989; the retirement to emeritus status of general director Lincoln Kirstein in 1990; the death in 1991 of Robert Irving, who had been musical director from 1958 to 1989; and Kirstein's death in January 1996.

Inevitably, dancers who had worked with Balanchine retired, and new talent emerged. Jacques d'Amboise and Karin von Aroldingen retired in 1984, Helgi Tomasson in 1985. Sean Lavery experienced a career-ending injury in 1986 and disappeared from the roster in 1989. Patricia McBride stepped down in 1989, a few months before Suzanne Farrell, whose chronic hip injury forced her prematurely from the stage. (In 1993, Farrell's connection with the New York City Ballet was terminated when a magazine profile implied she was critical of Martins's directorship.) Ib Andersen retired in 1990, Bart Cook and Stephanie Saland in 1993, Maria Calegari and Adam Lüders in 1994, and Heather Watts in 1995.

Kyra Nichols evolved into the most important dancer of the period. Long distinguished in bravura roles such as *Square Dance* and *Theme and Variations,* she also won acclaim for her interpretation of parts originated by Farrell and for her handling of Violette Verdy's expressive role in *Liebeslieder Walzer.* However, her classical precision was never effectively deployed by post-Balanchine choreographers.

Darci Kistler, who returned from a long injury in 1985, experienced a gradual fading of the rapturous reception that had gilded her first years when, singled out by Balanchine, she symbolized the end of his era. While some observers continued to express admiration, others noted a pattern of technical weakness that undercut her artistic authority. In 1991 she married Peter Martins and devoted much of her energy to serving as the ballerina in many of his works.

The era's new principals were Margaret Tracey, Wendy Whelan, Peter Boal, Jock Soto, Ethan Stiefel, and Damian Woetzel. In 1992 Nikolaj Hübbe of the Royal Danish Ballet and Igor Zelensky of the Kirov both joined. Each worked successfully with the New York City Ballet; Hübbe, especially, found a comfortable home in the reper-

NEW YORK CITY BALLET. Members of the female ensemble in *Jazz—Six Syncopated Movements,* choreographed by Peter Martins in 1993 to a commissioned score by trumpet virtuoso Wynton Marsalis. (Photograph © by Paul Kolnik; used by permission.)

tory. In 1995 a generation of rising young women included Yvonne Borree, Maria Kowroski, Jenifer Ringer, and Miranda Weese.

[*See also entries on the principal figures mentioned herein.*]

BIBLIOGRAPHY

Barnes, Clive. "NYCB: State and Status." *Dance Magazine* (April 1991).

Daniels, Don. "Collaborators: The File on NYCB." *Ballet Review* 15 (Spring 1987): 21–25.

Finkel, Anita. "The Golden Bough." *New Dance Review* 5 (Summer 1993): 3–13.

Gradinger, Malve. "Faith in the Power of Classical Ballet." *Ballett International/Tanz Aktuell* (December 1995): 32–35.

Hardy, Camille. "Breaking Down Barriers." *Dance Magazine* (May 1994): 58–59.

Mason, Francis, et al. "NYCB and DTH: Anniversary Reflections." *Ballet Review* 22 (Fall 1994): 14–28.

Mejias, Jordan. "The End of an Era: New York City Ballet Settles Balanchine's Succession." *Ballett International* 6 (May 1983): 6–7.

Moss, Howard. "The New York City Ballet: Balanchine, Martins, Robbins." *Boulevard* 1 (Fall 1986): 1–15.

Newman, Barbara. "Doubrovska's Eyes: NYCB 1986." *The Dancing Times* (February 1987): 404–405.

Newman, Barbara. "Returning for Balanchine." *Ballet Review* 21 (Winter 1993): 74–81.

Parry, Jann, et al. "Portrait of a Company: NYCB." *Dance and Dancers* (November 1983): 16–23.

Reiter, Susan. "New York City Ballet's Segmented Season." *Dance View* 10 (Autumn 1992): 48–55.

Siegel, Marcia B. "A Ballet's Best Friend." *Dance Ink* 3 (Fall 1992): 22–28.

ANITA FINKEL

NEW ZEALAND. [*To survey professional dance in New Zealand, this entry comprises two articles. The first article provides a general overview of theatrical dance; the second discusses dance scholarship and writing. For discussion of indigenous dance traditions, see* Maori Dance.]

Theatrical Dance

Physical vitality and an awareness of an ancient and highly varied natural landscape have been claimed as qualities that contribute to a New Zealand identity in professional dance and choreography. At the heart of the profession is the national ballet company, the Royal New Zealand Ballet, formed in 1953 by Poul Gnatt, a former soloist with the Royal Danish Ballet. The company, arguably the oldest professional ballet company in the Southern Hemisphere, has earned an international reputation through inviting guest performers, releasing several leading dancers for periods abroad, and making company tours to Australia, China, Europe, and the United States.

Ballet. Soloists and companies have visited New Zealand since the early 1900s, among them Adeline Genée (1913), Anna Pavlova with her company (1926), Colonel W. de Basil's Ballets Russes (second company, 1936), the Covent Garden Russian Ballet with Michel Fokine and Anton Dolin (1939), Ballet Rambert (1947), Borovansky Ballet (between 1947 and 1960), soloists from the Bolshoi Ballet (1955), the Royal Ballet with Margot Fonteyn, Robert Helpmann, and Lynn Seymour (1960), the Kirov Ballet (1960s), and Sadler's Wells Royal Ballet (since the 1970s). A biennial international festival established in the capital, Wellington, in 1986 presented the Sydney Dance Company (1986), the Paris Opera Ballet with Rudolf Nureyev (1988), and several modern dance companies, including the Netherlands Dance Theater, Garth Fagan Dance, Rosas, the Frankfurt Ballet, and the Lyon Opera Ballet.

Ballet was also made known in New Zealand through several private studios. The Repertory Theatre, formed from the Nettleton-Edwards studio in Auckland, New Zealand's largest city, toured in the 1940s and 1950s and supported the Auckland productions by Poul Gnatt, who had remained in New Zealand after visiting with the Borovansky Ballet in 1951. Gnatt sensed that New Zealanders would support their own professional company and, with backing from Beryl Nettleton, Bettina Edwards, and the Community Arts Service at the University of Auckland, he founded the New Zealand Ballet Company in 1953. The company transferred to a Wellington base, where Gnatt remained artistic director for ten years, touring extensively. In 1984 a royal charter was awarded; the Royal New Zealand Ballet has toured nationally for a large portion of each year but maintains an international standard and a repertory of traditional and contemporary commissioned works.

From 1953 to 1962, Gnatt produced works from the Danish repertory, including *Napoli, La Sylphide, Coppélia, Le Spectre de la Rose,* and *Les Sylphides.* Kirsten Ralov (Gnatt's sister) and her husband, Fredbjørn Bjørnsson, were guest performers in 1962; Nora Kovach and Istvan Rabovsky were guests in a season that included *Schéhérazade* (1961); and a special season in 1962 involved guests Rowena Jackson, Philip Chatfield, Sara Neil, and Walter Trevor from the Royal Ballet in a revival of Frederick Ashton's *Les Patineurs.* An elegant neoclassical choreography, *Prismatic Variations*—the collaboration between Gnatt and Russell Kerr to music of Brahms—was a hallmark work of these early years.

The director from 1962 to 1968, New Zealand–born Russell Kerr, drew on his experience with London's Festival Ballet and Ballet Rambert to mount several new productions. The most outstanding were a moving *Petrouchka* with renowned New Zealander Alexander Grant (1964) and *Giselle* with Svetlana Beriosova (1965).

After a return caretaker period by Gnatt, subsequent directorships were held by Bryan Ashbridge (1971) and

Rowena Jackson and Philip Chatfield (1975–1978), all of whom had worked with Britain's Royal Ballet. Una Kai, director from 1973 to 1975, had worked with George Balanchine and the New York City Ballet, and she added Balanchine works to the repertory. Patricia Rianne, a New Zealander returning after a career with Ballet Rambert and Scottish Theatre Ballet, has been guest director on several occasions.

Artistic director from 1982 to 1992 was the Australian-born Harry Haythorne, who came to New Zealand after a performing and teaching career in Britain and Europe. Haythorne has developed the repertory to include *Konigsmark* (André Prokovsky), *No Exit* (Ashley Killar, to the music of Dmitri Shostakovich), *Mélodrame* (Jack Carter, to the music of Kurt Weill), *The Witch Boy* (Carter, to the music of Carlos Salzedo), *The Rake's Progress* (Ninette de Valois, to the music of Gavin Gordon), *'Tis Goodly Sport* (Jonathan Taylor, to traditional Elizabethan music), *Sweet Sorrow* (Taylor, to the music of Robert Schumann), and *Orpheus* (Graeme Murphy, to the music of Igor Stravinsky). The above works all required dramatic performance, which became a strength of the repertory; the traditional classics were meanwhile maintained.

Haythorne designed new productions of *Swan Lake, Giselle,* and *Coppélia.* Imaginative ballets for children—*Terrible Tom* and *Te Maia,* choreographed by Russell Kerr—proved extremely popular. Mary Jane O'Reilly choreographed an intriguing work, *Jean,* based on the life of pioneering New Zealand aviatrix Jean Batten, a work also produced as a commercial film.

A number of commissioned works by New Zealand choreographer Gray Veredon include *Ragtime Dance Company,* a new version of *The Firebird,* the autobiographical *Tell Me a Tale,* and the *commedia*-inspired *Servant of Two Masters.* Veredon produced *Wolfgang Amadeus* (which had premiered in Poland) in 1991. Douglas Wright choreographed *The Decay of Lying* (using various musical sources), a work that was both striking and controversial. Ashley Killar (English born, formerly at the Royal Ballet and Stuttgart Ballet) directed from 1993 to 1995, leading the company out of financial straits with popular programs, including his own *Dark Waves* (to music of Maurice Ravel), *No Exit, A Midsummer Night's Dream* (Peter Scholes). Douglas Wright performed the title role of *Petrouchka* in an acclaimed production by Russell Kerr in 1994. In 1996 Matz Skoog, Danish born and trained, was appointed artistic director. Poul Gnatt died in September 1995 and was bid farewell in a moving public tribute held in the empty theater currently awaiting refurbishment to become the Royal New Zealand Ballet's permanent home.

The company's *premier danseur* has been Jon Trimmer, whose performance career spans almost the entire existence of the company. Trimmer's technique, musicality, and dramatic skills have made him an inspiration to several generations of dancers. In recognition of this outstanding career, which could well have been spent internationally, Trimmer was awarded the Turnovsky Fellowship for achievement in New Zealand arts and has continued a career of remarkable longevity with outstanding character and comic roles. Another longstanding company member is ballet master and choreologist Peter Boyes, formerly with the Dutch National Ballet.

Ballet Training. The New Zealand School of Dance is affiliated with the Royal New Zealand Ballet and also trains dancers for freelance careers. A three-year training course with classical and modern dance options includes opportunities to choreograph. There is also a teacher-training course and a dance-in-education program whereby younger students continue an academic education at an affiliated college in tandem with their dance training.

NEW ZEALAND: Theatrical Dance. The Royal New Zealand Ballet's 1986 production of *Tell Me a Tale* with choreography by Gray Veredon, set to music by Matthew Fisher. Here, Jon Trimmer as the Teller of Tales and Kim Broad (seated) as the Boy. (Photograph by Martin Stewart; courtesy of Jennifer Shennan.)

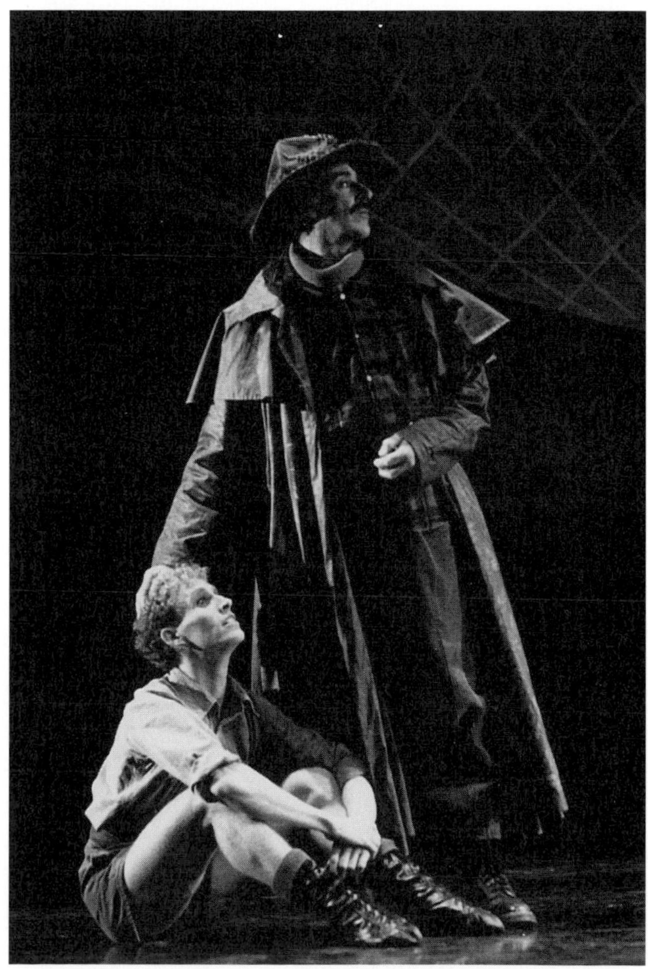

Founded in 1967 as the National School of Ballet, the school changed its name in 1983 to mark the broadening of the curriculum to include modern dance. The school came under the direction of Anne Rowse in 1970, with Patricia Rianne the senior classical tutor. Louis Solino, formerly with the Limón Dance Company, joined the staff in 1989 and taught works by José Limón and Doris Humphrey. Poul Gnatt, recognized as a world authority on Bournonville style, produced *Konservatoriet* in 1991.

The school, with approximately sixty students, is government-funded; entry is by audition, and almost all attendance is by scholarship, but a few foreign students are accepted on a fee-paying basis. The curriculum includes dance studies with components of anatomy, history, notation, dance anthropology, music, and historical dance. Graduates include Mary Jane O'Reilly, who directed Limbs Dance Company for ten years, Sherilyn Kennedy of the Royal Ballet, Martin James of the English National Ballet, Shona McCullagh, and Taiaroa Royal. The school has been directed since 1993 by Rochelle Zide-Booth.

NEW ZEALAND: Theatrical Dance. Ashley Killar's *Dark Waves* was first performed by the Royal New Zealand Ballet on a tour of the United States in 1992. Here, Jon Trimmer is pictured as the Husband, Sonya Behrnes as the Wife. (Photograph by Martin Stewart; courtesy of Jennifer Shennan.)

The Southern Ballet Theatre in Christchurch, New Zealand's third-largest city, was directed from 1973 to 1990 by Russell Kerr, who developed an extensive repertory of classics as well as his own highly musical choreographies. Southern Ballet Theatre is the only dance company in New Zealand resident in its own theater. Kerr's full-time training course recruited a number of dancers from Japan. *Scripting the Dreams* was an abstract choreography in which Kerr took as subject his own lifetime and prolific choreographic output. *Mr. Scrooge* was his acclaimed final production for Southern Ballet Theatre, and for it he played the title role. Kerr continued as a freelance choreographer and producer in New Zealand, with productions for The Royal New Zealand Ballet of *Petrouchka* (1944) and *Swan Lake* (1996).

Modern Dance. Introduced to New Zealand in the 1940s and 1950s by European teachers (Austrian and Dutch) modern dance developed a small but faithful following owing to the efforts of independent teachers. The success of Limbs Dance Company for a decade, in the mid-1970s to mid-1980s, lifted the profile of modern dance enormously. The demise of Limbs in 1989 has been followed by a number of single-season companies formed by independent choreographers.

Margaret Barr, who taught at Dartington College in Britain until the arrival of Kurt Jooss, moved to New Zealand in the 1930s. She taught in Auckland and choreographed music-poetry collaborations. She later moved to Sydney, Australia, where she continued to teach and choreograph for many years. Harold Robinson then continued to teach her distinctive dance-drama technique in Auckland until the 1970s. An Austrian teacher, Gisa Taglicht, had worked in Wellington with the New Dance Group in the 1940s. Rona Bailey and Tup Lang, members of this group, have remained active in drama teaching and dance therapy ever since. Another Austrian, Olive Mendel, formed a national creative dance society in the 1940s, which continues today.

Théo Schoon, a Dutch sculptor and painter renowned for his experiments with Maori art motifs, also pioneered with solo dance performance in the 1950s. Boujke van Zon from Holland taught creative dance in her Auckland schools beginning in the 1950s. Deborah McCulloch, Rozeane Worthington, and Carla van Zon are among her most successful pupils.

Liong Xi, of Dutch and Indonesian background, has performed and taught Rudolf Laban–based modern dance as well as Balinese classical dance in secondary schools throughout the country beginning in the 1950s.

Shona Dunlop MacTavish, after early years with the Bodenwieser Company in Europe and Australia, later formed the Dunedin Dance Theatre. Bronwyn Judge, Jan Bolwell, and Carol Brown are among her successful pupils. She also wrote *An Ecstasy of Purpose,* the definitive biography of Gertrud Bodenwieser, a leading figure in the Ausdruckstanz movement in Germany and Austria in the 1930s.

The mime artist Francis Batten, after dance studies in New Zealand, attended École Jacques Lecoq in Paris, then returned to New Zealand with colleagues in 1971 to form Theatre Action. For four years the company presented choreographed theater of dramatic and poetic originality, including collaborations with composer Jack Body. Theatre Action later moved to Sydney, Australia, and opened Drama Action Centre, which continues to offer full-time theater training.

Jamie Bull formed Impulse Dance Company (1976–1982). Footnote Dance Company performed in schools under the direction of Deirdre Tarrant. Philip Smithells, foundation professor of Physical Education at the University of Otago, established a modern dance course in the 1950s. Its directors have included Margaret H'Doubler, Annette Golding, John Casserley, Gaylene Sciascia, Helen Langford, and Suzanne Renner.

Michael Parmenter, director of the Commotion Dance Company, studied with Shona Dunlop, then with Erick Hawkins in New York and with Min Tanaka in Japan. Between 1982 and 1996, he choreographed *Between Two Fires,* an impressive collaboration with composer Jack Body, *Insolent River, Gravity and Grace, The Race, The Dark Forest,* and *A Long Undressing.*

Paul Jenden, a choreographer-designer, often uses surreal and fantastic costumes and masks. He performs in partnership with Louis Solino and regularly tours in New Zealand and Europe. From the late 1980s to 1996, their repertory includes *Dead Ballerinas, Cheek to Cheek, Seven Deadly Sins, Hansel and Gretel,* and many successful productions from popular children's books.

Susan Jordan uses pacifist and feminist themes with a strong autobiographical thread, allowing atmosphere to become an intrinsic part of the composition. *Unknowing Steps, Holy Women,* and *Stone the Crow* are theater works; *Face Value* was memorably set in an abandoned but once grand building. In 1996 Jordan was appointed lecturer in dance studies at the University of Aukland.

Limbs Dance Company, formed in Auckland in 1977 by Chris Jannides, was directed by Mary Jane O'Reilly and Susan Paterson from 1979 to 1988. A large and enthusiastic audience responded, enabling Limbs to secure a dance style confidently built on both contemporary and classical techniques under the guidance of ballet teacher Dorothea Ashbridge. Limbs toured New Zealand extensively and also visited the United States, Mexico, Japan, Hong Kong, Papua New Guinea, and Australia. In 1989 its Arts Council subsidy was withdrawn and Limbs Dance Company ceased performing. Ambivalence in Council policy makes it difficult to predict whether another modern dance company will be established on a contract basis, or whether only project funding will be available. Limbs's prominent dancers included Mark Baldwin (later with the Rambert Dance Company), Brian Carbee, Joanne Kelly, Deborah McCulloch, Shona McCullagh, Felicity Molloy, Kilda Northcott, Taiaroa Royal, Marianne Schultz, Susan Trainor, and Douglas Wright. Wright, an extremely athletic dancer and highly imaginative choreographer, left Limbs to join the Paul Taylor Dance Company in New York City for four years. Wright then worked with DV-8 in London in *Dead Dreams of Monochrome Men.* He returned to New Zealand to mount two full-length works on Limbs—*Now Is the Hour* (1988) and *How on Earth* (1989)—during Cath Cardiff's term as director.

NEW ZEALAND: Theatrical Dance. Paul Jenden (left) and Louis Solino (right) of the Fandango Company perform *Cheek to Cheek,* a piece choreographed and designed by Jenden in 1986. (Photograph by Jocelyn Carlin; courtesy of Jennifer Shennan.)

In 1990 Wright independently choreographed an uncompromising *Passion Play* for himself and Kilda Northcott, and, for a company of seven, an ecstatic *Gloria* to music by Antonio Vivaldi. Cath Cardiff formed Dance Pacific, a dancer-actor cooperative of former Limbs members. Taiaroa Royal, who choreographed *Te Po* for Dance Pacific in 1990, was in the same year invited to join Garth Fagan Dance in Rochester, New York. Wright has enjoyed meteoric success and much appreciation for his full-length works *As It Is Forever* and *Buried Venus* (1996).

Shona McCullagh choreographed *Flare-Up,* a festive yet satirical revue in collaboration with Six Volts, a popular New Zealand music group. Mary Jane O'Reilly designed a mammoth dance pageant depicting the various immigrations in the peopling of New Zealand for the opening ceremony of the 1990 Commonwealth Games in Auckland.

Early modern dancers and companies to visit New Zealand included La Meri, Katherine Dunham, Gertrud

NEW ZEALAND: Theatrical Dance. Members of the Douglas Wright Dance Company, including Wright (standing), Marianne Schultz, Kilda Northcott, and Glen Mayo, perform Wright's *How on Earth* (1989). (Photograph by Jane Ussher; courtesy of Jennifer Shennan.)

Bodenwieser, Beth Dean, and Emily Frankel. Later, Mary Fulkerson from Dartington College made an impact with marathon performances in the late 1970s; Australian Dance Theatre from Adelaide and Human Veins from Canberra also toured. The 1988 International Festival brought Twyla Tharp and Marie Chouinard, to mixed reception, but Sankai Juku, Garth Fagan, and The Kosh had enormous success in 1990.

Dance Education. A full-time training program in dance and related arts is taught at Wellington Performing Arts Centre, under the direction of Jenny Stevenson; another is taught at the Performing Arts School in Auckland, under the direction of Alison East, and a Maori- and Polynesian-oriented training and repertory was established in a performing arts course at Whitireia Polytechnic near Wellington, under the direction of Gaylene Sciascia. The only university dance studies are taught at Victoria University of Wellington within the school of music as Music and Dance of the Pacific, plus supervised graduate work. Dance studies, including dance notation, are taught in an outreach program of the Centre for Continuing Education of Victoria University.

European historical dance of the fifteenth through the eighteenth centuries has been taught by Helga Hill of Melbourne, Australia, as part of a series at the Early Music School. Jennifer Shennan has taught and performed Baroque dance with the Sonnerie & Concordance music ensemble since 1984, and Wendy Hilton taught Baroque dance in 1990 and 1992. Flamenco dance is taught and performed by Jane Luscombe and by Miriama Lange in Auckland, and by Faye-Theresa in Wellington.

Indian classical dance is taught and performed in Auckland by Kanan Deobhakta and in Wellington by Vivek Kinra. Indian dance visitors to New Zealand have included Sivaram in the 1950s, Charka in 1978, and Chandrabhanu in 1988 and 1989. Two troupes of *kathakaḷi* dancers from the International Centre for Kathakali came in 1984, and a troupe from Kerala Kalamandalam in 1990.

[*For discussion of indigenous dance, see* Maori Dance.]

BIBLIOGRAPHY

Ashton, Beatrice. *The New Zealand Ballet: The First Twenty-Five Years.* Wellington, N.Z., 1978.

Brinson, Peter. *Dance in New Zealand.* Wellington, N.Z., 1981.

The New Zealand Ballet, 1953–1983. Thirtieth anniversary program. Wellington, N.Z., 1983.

JENNIFER SHENNAN

Dance Research and Publication

Dance studies in New Zealand are just beginning and as yet dance researchers lack a central organization to disseminate information about studies already done and to develop ideas for future research. In interdisciplinary contexts, encompassing anthropology, music, film, and drama, teachers have a chance to include an aspect of dance in their work and thus contribute to a developing awareness of dance studies in the wider community. For example, an architect has written a thesis on the parallels between Baroque architecture and dance, and there have been profiles of several prominent New Zealand choreographers in *Film Studies.*

Mervyn McLean's *Annotated Bibliography of Music and Dance in Oceania* (1977) and *Supplement* (1981) are invaluable sources for existing published materials on dance in Oceania. The Archive of Maori and Pacific Music, established by McLean at the University of Auckland, has some audio and video holdings of dance materials. The music analysis in Richard Moyle's studies of the traditional musics of Samoa and Tonga is well developed, but their dance analysis is only introductory. Adrienne Kaeppler's extensive work on Tongan dance is exemplary. Kaeppler's work, Shumway's work on Tongan *lakalaka,* and Futa Helu's publications and lectures at the Atenisi Institute in Nukuʿalofa on the Tongan perspective on their dance traditions, make Tongan dance well studied. *Dance in Tahiti* by J. F. Moulin is also splendidly researched and presented. Timoti Karetu has written on Maori dance, both *haka* and *waiata-a-ringa,* with extensive discussion of the significance of song-texts.

Music and Dance of the Pacific is a course taught jointly by Allan Thomas and Jennifer Shennan at Victoria University. Students view videotapes, some made by Shennan and Thomas, and others issued from South Pacific festivals held in Fiji (1972), Rotorua, New Zealand (1976), Papua New Guinea (1980), and Tahiti (1985). Students also view *Movietone News* programs of the 1940s, 1950s, and 1960s that contain footage of fragments of ceremonial dances. Students have written theses on such topics as the compilation of the music and dance vocabularies of Futuna; a profile of Ngati Pooneke, the oldest established cultural group in Wellington; a study (using Labanotation) of *pōkeka,* a form of traditional Maori dance chant; and a translation of dance-song texts of Tokelau dance. Tongan social and political history has been researched using historical accounts of dance performances.

Other dance traditions and dance pioneers invite research. Shona Dunlop MacTavish has written a book on Gertrud Bodenwieser, *An Ecstasy of Purpose* (1987); Jan Bolwell has written *Susan Jordan—The Making of a New Zealand Choreographer.*

The National Dance Archive, Nga Kaitiaki Taonga Kanikani o Aotearoa, has no established funding but is pursuing an oral-history project by commissioning interviews with prominent New Zealand dance personalities. These taped interviews are deposited in the National Library of New Zealand, which also holds an important collection of dance manuscripts owned by a New Zealand family for many generations. Known as the Lowe collection, this includes hitherto unpublished material by an eighteenth-century English dance master, Kellom Tomlinson, and a nineteenth-century Scottish dance master, Joseph Lowe. Two of these rare manuscripts were published by Pendragon Press of New York in 1992 and several more are planned for publication.

Dance Literature and Criticism. Dance critics include Shona Dunlop MacTavish, Bernadette Rae, Ann Hunt, Raewyn Whyte, and Jennifer Shennan. *Dance News,* a national magazine founded by Tup Lang in 1972 and later edited by Raewyn Whyte, ceased publication in 1988. In 1988 the Royal New Zealand Ballet began publishing a national bimonthly newsletter, also called *Dance News. Tirairaka,* a bimonthly publication, has since 1996 been absorbed into the newsletter of D.A.N.Z. (Dance Aotearoa New Zealand).

JENNIFER SHENNAN

NICHOLAS BROTHERS. Jazz tap dancers, singers, and musical theater artists. **Fayard Nicholas** (born 20 October 1914 in Mobile, Alabama) and **Harold Nicholas** (born 17 March 1921 in Winston-Salem, North Carolina), created an exuberant style of American theatrical dance melding jazz rhythm with tap, acrobatics, ballet, and black vernacular dance. Most often remembered for the daredevil splits, slides, and flips in their routines, they were labeled "acrobatic" and "flash" dancers. But their rhythmic brilliance, musicality, eloquent footwork, and full-bodied expressiveness are unsurpassed, and their dancing represents the most sophisticated refinement of jazz as a percussive dance form.

At a young age, at the Standard Theater in Philadelphia, where his parents conducted a pit band orchestra, Fayard was introduced to the jazz of Louis Armstrong and the best tap acts in black vaudeville, such as Reed and Bryant, Buck and Bubbles, and the Four Covans. Fayard then proceeded to teach young Harold basic tap steps. The Nicholas Kids made their professional debut in Philadelphia (1930/31); in New York City in 1931/32, at the Lafayette Theater, they billed themselves as "The Nicholas Brothers." Fayard was eighteen and Harold eleven when in 1932 they opened at the uptown Cotton Club, in Harlem, which became their home base for the next few years. Dancing with the orchestras of Cab Calloway and Duke Ellington, the brothers, without formal training, developed a classy and swinging musical performance in which comic quips and eccentric dance combined with precision-timed moves and virtuosic rhythm tapping.

Alternating between stage and screen throughout their career, the Nicholas Brothers made their first film, the 1932 Vitaphone short *Pie, Pie, Blackbird,* with Eubie Blake, and their first Hollywood movie, *Kid Millions,* for Samuel Goldwyn in 1934. On Broadway in *Ziegfeld Follies of 1936* and in *Babes in Arms* in 1937, they worked with choreographer George Balanchine; during the same period they performed at the newly opened downtown Cotton Club and starred in the London West End production of *Lew Leslie's Blackbirds of 1936.* At the Harlem Opera House and the Apollo, Palace, and Paramount theaters in the 1930s and 1940s, they danced with the big bands of Jimmie Lunceford, Chick Webb, Count Basie, and Glen Miller.

Collaboration with Hollywood dance director Nick Castle on seven musical films for Twentieth Century–Fox added flashy embellishments to the brothers' dancing. In *Down Argentine Way* (1940), they moved in perfect synchrony: arms and wrists circling, they slipped and slid along the floor, dipping into splits and whipping into one-legged wings. They tapped on suitcases in *The Great American Broadcast* (1941), jumped off walls into back flips and splits in *Orchestra Wives* (1942), and in *Stormy Weather* (1943), jumped over each other down a flight of stairs, landing into a split on each step. These dazzling feats were delivered with a smooth effortlessness.

By the late 1940s, the high-speed and rhythm-driven style of the Nicholas Brothers was fast and fluent enough

NICHOLAS BROTHERS. An extraordinary tap-dancing duo, Fayard and Harold Nicholas won acclaim for their rhythmic virtuosity and energetic flash acts. During their careers, the brothers danced in more than fifty Hollywood films. Here, they leap side by side in the "Chattanooga Choo Choo" number from *Sun Valley Serenade* (Twentieth Century–Fox, 1941). (Photograph from the Film Stills Library, Museum of Modern Art, New York; used by permission.)

to endure the radical musical shift from jazz to bebop. The brothers headlined "The Hepsations of 1945" on a southern tour with Dizzy Gillespie's big band and worked with bop composer-arranger Tadd Dameron, but they were irresistibly drawn to the steady and danceable rhythms of swing and continued to work in that musical tradition. In 1946 both danced, and Harold sang, in the musical *St. Louis Woman,* with songs by Harold Arlen and Johnny Mercer.

While also working as solo artists in the 1950s and early 1960s—Harold in Europe and Fayard in the United States—the brothers were reunited for three *Hollywood Palace* television specials in 1964 and continued to perform as a team. Musicality and an insistent exploration of rhythm within an elegant form were the distinctive features of their performance style. Harold's later theatrical roles included the lead in the national touring companies of Duke Ellington's *Sophisticated Ladies* in 1982, *The Tap Dance Kid* in 1986, and *My One and Only* in 1989. Fayard's choreography for "Butter and Egg Man," in the Broadway musical *Black and Blue* in 1989, demonstrated how the jazz tap style of the Nicholas Brothers has been embodied by dancers of later generations and evolved into a classical American jazz dance form. The brothers received the Kennedy Center Honors for their extraordinary contribution to American culture in 1991 and the following year were the subject of the award-winning documentary *The Nicholas Brothers: We Sing and We Dance.*

[*See also* Tap Dance.]

BIBLIOGRAPHY

Bogle, Donald. *Blacks in American Film and Television: An Illustrated Encyclopedia.* New York, 1988.

Frank, Rusty E. *Tap! The Greatest Tap Dance Stars and Their Stories, 1900–1955.* Rev. ed. New York, 1994.

Jefferson, Margo. "An Era for Movement." *Dance Ink* (September 1993): 18–24.

Pomerance, Alan. *Repeal of the Blues: How Black Entertainers Influenced Civil Rights.* Secaucus, N.J., 1988.

Stearns, Marshall, and Jean Stearns. *Jazz Dance: The Story of American Vernacular Dance.* Rev. ed. New York, 1994.

FILM AND VIDEOTAPE. *Pie, Pie, Blackbird* (Vitaphone short, 1932). *Kid Millions* (Samuel Goldwyn, 1934). *The All-Colored Vaudeville Show* (Vitaphone short, 1935). *The Big Broadcast of 1936* (Paramount, 1935). *Down Argentine Way* (Twentieth Century–Fox, 1940). *Sun Valley Serenade* (Twentieth Century–Fox, 1941). *Orchestra Wives* (Twentieth Century Fox, 1942). *Stormy Weather* (Twentieth Century–Fox, 1943). *Carolina Blues* (Columbia, 1944). *The Pirate* (MGM, 1948). *History of American Tap: Fayard Nicholas* (1978), held in the Dance Collection, New York Public Library for the Performing Arts. *Tap* (Hoofer Films/Tri-Star, 1988). *The Nicholas Brothers: We Sing and We Dance* (Picture Music International with Channel Four, London, 1992). *Let's Tap* (Editing Productions, 1994).

CONSTANCE VALIS HILL

NICHOLS, KYRA (born 2 July 1958 in Berkeley, California), American ballet dancer. Nichols received her first training from her mother, Sally Streets, who had danced with the New York City Ballet in the 1950s, and from Alan Howard, one of her mother's dance partners trained in the Ballet Russe style. By age thirteen, Nichols was dancing in Howard's Pacific Ballet. She entered the School of American Ballet in New York in 1972 and joined the New York City Ballet in the autumn of 1974, when she was sixteen years old.

As a member of the corps de ballet, Nichols caught the attention of Jacques d'Amboise, a principal dancer, who made a point of demonstrating and explaining to her the technical and stylistic qualities that George Balanchine wanted to see. Her first leading role was in d'Amboise's ballet *Irish Fantasy,* but it was her dancing in *Tchaikovsky Suite No. 2,* one of Balanchine's own works, that brought her to his attention. Her first featured part in a Balanchine ballet, the fourth movement of *Symphony in C,* soon followed, as did a series of progressively more important solo and leading roles.

Nichols began to attract critical attention in the late 1970s for the qualities that define her distinct gifts: her clarity, precision, awe-inspiring technical command, and musicality. A tall ballerina at five feet, seven inches, and not especially flexible, she is characterized by strength combined with delicacy: an incorruptibly secure center softened by a gracious, regal presence. Among the early roles in which she distinguished herself were Jerome Robbins's *Other Dances* (1976) and the pas de trois from *La Ventana* in Stanley Williams's staging of *Bournonville Divertissements* (1977). In the Balanchine repertory she shone as the Russian Girl in *Serenade* (1979), as Polyhymnia in *Apollo* (1980), in a version of *Firebird* reworked for her by Balanchine (1980), and in the central roles in *Tchaikovsky Piano Concerto No. 2* (1979) and *Theme and Variations* (1980). She was named a principal dancer in 1979.

For several years Nichols was married to New York City Ballet principal Daniel Duell, with whom she had an important professional partnership. Jerome Robbins featured the couple in *Verdi Variations* in 1978 and again when the work was put in final form as *The Four Seasons* in 1979. Besides Duell, Nichols has had several other significant partners, among them Sean Lavery, Joseph Duell, Adam Lüders, Damian Woetzel, and Philip Neal. But her nearly Amazonian ability to accomplish technical feats unsupported led to many important solos and roles where, as a woman alone, she suggested mystery and strength.

After Balanchine's death in 1983, Nichols emerged as one of the outstanding inheritors of his legacy and a superb interpreter of roles he had created for Suzanne Farrell. As an archetypal classicist in ballets such as *Stars and Stripes, Allegro Brillante,* and *Divertimento No. 15,* she was unquestionably standard-setting. Reviewing her performances of *Raymonda Variations* and *Cortège Hongrois,* Arlene Croce called her "the consummate Raymonda." But she also triumphed in Violette Verdy's lyrical, tragic part in the 1984 revival of the romantic *Liebeslieder Walzer.* The Farrell roles she danced included those in *Walpurgisnacht Ballet, Diamonds, Chaconne, Mozartiana,* and the "Rosenkavalier" section of *Vienna Waltzes.*

Peter Martins and other contemporary choreographers at times attempted to create works suited to Nichols's gifts, but her formal classicism resisted expression in dance vocabularies largely inspired by jazz and modern dance, and her aristocratic, sunny temperament was unsuited to the atmosphere of antagonism and anomie that often accompanied these works. She concentrated her energies on the Balanchine repertory and, especially in the Balanchine Celebration of 1993, consolidated her reputation as the outstanding Balanchine ballerina of the post-Balanchine era.

BIBLIOGRAPHY

Croce, Arlene. *Going to the Dance.* New York, 1982.
Croce, Arlene. *Sight Lines.* New York, 1987.
Finkel, Anita. "In Her True Center." *Ballet News* (July 1985).
Kelly, Patrick. "Diamonds Are Forever." *Dance Magazine* (October 1988).

ANITA FINKEL

NIELSEN, AUGUSTA (born 20 February 1822 in Copenhagen, died 29 March 1902 in Copenhagen), Danish dancer. Nielsen had a short but illustrious career with the Royal Danish Ballet under August Bournonville's guidance. She was among his first pupils, and she made her debut as the protagonist in *La Sylphide* on 6 September 1839, after the company's leading ballerina, Lucile Grahn, had left Denmark. Nielsen was promoted to soloist in 1841. She was tall and slender, with blue eyes and dark hair. According to Bournonville, she was "synonymous with grace and ladylike elegance," which she expressed most convincingly in Bournonville's solos "Cracovienne" and "La Lithuanienne." Bournonville created the role of the French ballerina Celeste for Nielsen in his 1840 ballet *The Toreador.* What Nielsen lacked in technique onstage, she compensated for with mimic liveliness. She was praised for her distinguished charm when she danced in the theaters of Stockholm, Christiania (now Oslo), Berlin, and several other German cities.

Nielsen was also applauded with enthusiasm when she appeared at the Paris Opera. Here she took daily classes with Jules Perrot, who helped her refine her technique and style. Her debut in Paris was delayed because she refused to sign a contract with the Opera, but she eventually made her debut on 20 May 1842 in a pas de deux in Fromental Halévy's opera *La Juive* and in a pas de deux in Gioacchino Rossini's opera *William Tell.* Her success was compared with that of Lucile Grahn, and a critic for *Siècle* wrote, "These girls from the north seem to dance on snow, frightened of leaving footprints."

Back in Copenhagen, Nielsen met her nemesis in the person of King Christian VIII's nephew, Prince Frederick of Hesse, who admired her with great passion. When their intimate relationship became public knowledge, the audience reacted strongly and condemned the ballerina, hissing her in the theater. In February 1849, she danced for the last time; she left the Royal Theater in June 1851 with a pension. She married Prince Frederick, but he soon cast her aside with some property for her support. She lived remote from the theater world and public life in a suburb of Frederiksberg, after a short and unhappy second marriage to the Swedish poet A. A. Afzelius. The portraitist Edvard Lehmann did several paintings of her in her stage roles, most notably as Celeste in *The Toreador,* a work now in the Danish Theater Museum, Copenhagen.

BIBLIOGRAPHY

Bournonville, August. *My Theatre Life* (1848–1878). Translated by Patricia McAndrew. Middletown, Conn., 1979.

Neiiendam, Robert. *En danserinde.* 2d ed. Copenhagen, 1965.

EBBE MØRK

NIEVES AND COPES, Argentine dance team that has generated international interest in theatrical performance of the tango.

María Nieves (born 193? in Buenos Aires), dancer. The daughter of Spanish immigrant parents, Nieves began to go to the *milongas* (dance halls) of the neighborhood when she was very young. In 1951, while still in her teens, she won the local dance competition known as the Concurso de Tango del Luna Park, dancing with Juan Carlos Copes. Copes's ideal dance partner, Nieves has interpreted his choreography with mastery, helping him to renew the dance. Art, grace, versatility, creativity, and distinction mark Nieves's style. As she has said, "Dance for me is life, love, death, hatred." Nieves is considered to be one of the best dancers in the history of the tango, following in the tradition of Edith Peggy, Olga San Juan, and Carmencita Calderón, among others.

Juan Carlos Copes (born 31 May 1931 in Buenos Aires), dancer and choreographer. As a young man, Copes studied engineering at night and went to the *milongas* (dance halls) straight from school. Then, in his third year, he dropped out to dedicate himself to tango. Copes "graduated" as a *milonguero* in 1948/49. Dancing with María Nieves, he won first prize at the 1951 Concurso de Tango del Luna Park, a local dance competition in which more than three thousand dancers participated. From then on, Copes and Nieves were professional dance partners. In the 1950s, the couple worked in Buenos Aires and toured Latin America. During the final year of that decade, they performed on Broadway as well as in Washington, D.C., and Chicago. They continued to tour the Americas in the 1960s, appearing on the *Ed Sullivan Show* more than once, and adding Europe, Japan, and the Middle East to their performance itinerary. From 1983 to 1987 Copes and Nieves "brought flamboyance and stylistic perfection to [the Broadway hit] *Tango Argentino.*" They were named the best in dance by the *New York Times* (1985) for their performance in the show, which Copes also choreographed. They have also been featured in various films, including the documentaries *Tango mío* (British Broadcasting Corporation, Jana Bokova, 1985) and *Tango* (National Geographic Society, 1992).

Copes has taught in Argentina and elsewhere and has been a visiting professor at both the Juilliard School (1985) and Stanford University (1993/94). His many students have included Mikhail Baryshnikov, Robert Duvall, Bob Fosse's assistants, and teachers from Arthur Murray's and Fred Astaire's dance schools. In 1986 Copes won the ACE prize in New York and was nominated for a Tony Award (1986) for best choreographer. He has been a great force in stage tango. Not only is his choreographic interpretation of Astor Piazzolla's *Verano Porteño* a masterpiece, but by bringing the tango from the dance halls to the stage, Copes has created a new style of tango dancing. [*See also* Tango.]

BIBLIOGRAPHY

Azzi, María Susana. *Antropología del tango: Los protagonistas.* Buenos Aires, 1991.

Bialor, Perry G. "Tango." *Ballet News* 7 (January 1986): 10–15.

Copes, Juan Carlos. *Let's Dance: Bailemos tango.* Buenos Aires, 1984.

Ferrer, Horacio. *El libro del tango.* Buenos Aires, 1980.

Hanna, Gabriela. *Así bailaban el tango.* Berlin, 1993.

MARÍA SUSANA AZZI
Translated from Spanish

NIGERIA. *See* Sub-Saharan Africa *and* West Africa. *See also* Hausa Dance; Tiv Dance; Ubakala Dance; *and* Yoruba Dance. *For discussion of Gelede masquerades, see* Mask and Makeup, *article on* African Traditions.

NIGHT JOURNEY. Choreography: Martha Graham. Music: William Schuman. Scenery: Isamu Noguchi. Costumes: Martha Graham. First performance: 3 May 1947, Cambridge High and Latin School, Cambridge, Massachusetts, Martha Graham Dance Company. Principals: Martha Graham (Jocasta), Erick Hawkins (Oedipus), Mark Ryder (The Seer).

A prime example of Graham's dance plays based on Greek myth and drama, *Night Journey* shares with other of her works a nonlinear narrative form predicated on the device of memory. In these dances, Graham presents a contemporary view of antiquity, abstracting and intensifying personal feeling into archetypal dimensions.

The events of *Night Journey* take place in the heroine's

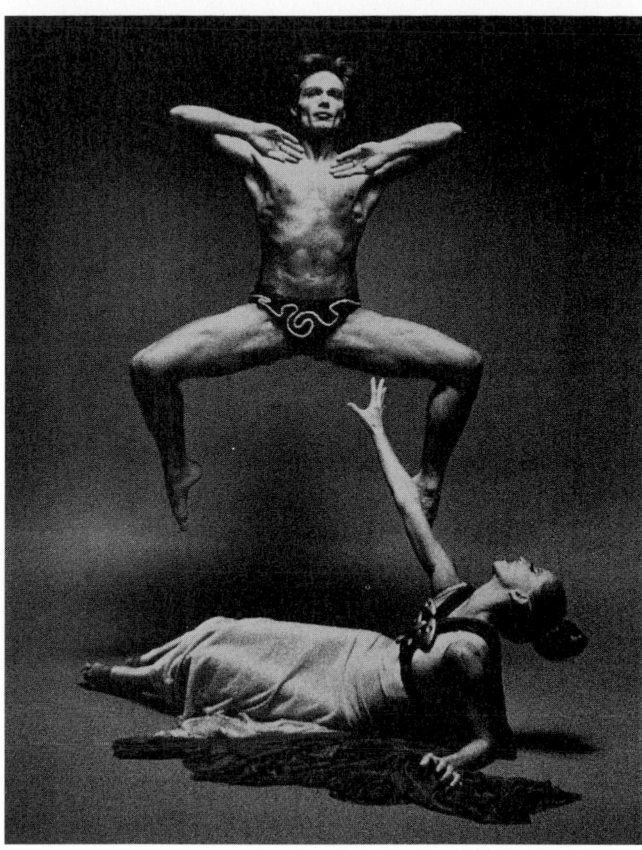

NIGHT JOURNEY. Tim Wengerd as Oedipus and Diane Gray as Jocasta in a 1978 revival. (Photograph © 1978 Max Waldman; used by permission.)

mind, in the moments before her suicide. Queen Jocasta relives the entry into Thebes of the conquering Oedipus, and her seduction by this man who, unbeknownst to her, is her son. The choreography for their duet subtly reveals to the audience the dual nature of their relationship, as erotic embraces dissolve into gestures of cradling. Throughout the piece a chorus of six women, one designated as "leader," comments on the action and predicts the tragic end with dancing that is ceremonious in design and violent in energy. The Seer (Tiresias) makes several fateful entrances, once using his staff as a pogo stick—its ominous thuds contrasting with the inherent playfulness of the image. Finally, he breaks the symbolic white cord that binds the protagonists.

Graham revised *Night Journey* before its New York premiere in February 1948. She later rechoreographed Oedipus's solo after Erick Hawkins left her company in 1950 and Bertram Ross took over his role.

BIBLIOGRAPHY

Jowitt, Deborah. *Time and the Dancing Image.* New York, 1988.

Oswald, Genevieve. "Myth and Legend in Martha Graham's *Night Journey.*" *Dance Research Annual* 14 (1983): 42–49.

Sears, David. "Graham Masterworks in Revival." *Ballet Review* 10.2 (1982): 25–34.

Siegel, Marcia B. *The Shapes of Change: Images of American Dance.* New York, 1979.

FILM AND VIDEOTAPE. Nathan Kroll, *Night Journey* (1961). "Martha Graham: An American Original in Performance," a Nathan Kroll Production; Contains *A Dancer's World* (1957) and *Appalachian Spring* (1958), both directed by Peter Glushanok, and *Night Journey* (1961), directed by Alexander Hammid.

DEBORAH JOWITT

NIGHT SHADOW. *See* Sonnambula, La.

NIJINSKA, BRONISLAVA (Bronislava Fominichna Nizhinskaia; born 8 January 1891 [27 December 1890] in Minsk, Russia, died 21 February 1972 in Pacific Palisades, California), dancer, choreographer, and teacher. Nijinska is a key figure in the development of twentieth-century choreography. A product of the school of the Maryinsky Theater of Saint Petersburg, she was strongly influenced by Michel Fokine's reform ballets. Her first works, created in her native Russia, reflect a turning away from classical ballet and toward experimentation around the time of the revolution. The first ballets she choreographed for the Ballets Russes of Serge Diaghilev are entirely in the new style and also contain evocations of the groundbreaking works of her brother Vaslav Nijinsky.

Work on Marius Petipa's *The Sleeping Beauty* in 1921 marked the turning point in Nijinska's career. In almost all the works she created after this epochal encounter, the classical school is the starting point of her creation, but the vocabulary of steps is used in a new way—curved and broken. *Les Biches* (1924) is the keystone of the new style that came to be called neoclassicism; but Nijinska was traveling through more than a stylistically new territory. Her ballet *Chopin Concerto* (1937), set to the Piano Concerto in E Minor, was one of a handful of experiments in abstract form created in the late 1930s, in which she was concerned exclusively with the interaction of music and choreography. Later, in her new home in California, she concentrated on teaching. An article about her by Jack Anderson (1963) heralded her comeback. Taken to England by her student, Frederick Ashton, in 1964 and 1966 she produced *Les Biches* and *Les Noces*. These revivals familiarized a new generation with her work.

Nijinska was the youngest child of Foma Nijinsky and Eleonora Bereda, both dancers. After private study with her father, in 1900 she entered the Imperial Ballet School in Saint Petersburg, where she studied with Enrico Cecchetti, Victor Gillert, Michel Fokine, and Klavdia Kulichevskaya. After her graduation in 1908, she was accepted into the corps de ballet of the Maryinsky Theater.

By her second year with the corps, the brilliant dancer was already being given small parts. Her repertory of roles was limited only by her modern looks, which did not match the prevailing notion of beauty. She participated as a member of the corps in the first Russian season organized by Serge Diaghilev in Paris in 1909. In 1910 she was made a *coryphée* (principal dancer). After her brother Vaslav was dismissed from the Maryinsky Theater Association in 1911, Nijinska also terminated her contract with the Imperial Theaters and joined the Ballets Russes. By the time she left the Ballets Russes in 1913, in connection with her brother's termination, she had created a number of roles in Fokine ballets, the most important being the Butterfly in *Carnaval,* the Bacchante in *Narcissus,* the Street Dancer in *Petrouchka,* and a Nymph in Nijinsky's *L'Après-midi d'une Faune.* These were followed by the Mazurka in Fokine's *Les Sylphides,* the Ballerina in *Petrouchka,* and Myrtha in *Giselle.*

After the birth of her daughter Irina in Saint Petersburg in October 1913, Nijinska joined her brother and her husband, Aleksandr Kochetovsky, in founding a ballet company that lasted only for a two-week guest appearance at the Palace Theatre in London. Just after the outbreak of World War I, Nijinska returned to Saint Petersburg, where she danced at the Narodni Dom as first ballerina from 1915 to 1916. Here, in 1915, she created her first choreographic work, her own solo *La Tabatière,* set to music by Anatol Liadov. Between 1915 and 1916 she was a ballerina with the Kiev Opera. In 1919, after the birth of her son Léon, she established her own studio, which she called École de Mouvement.

NIJINSKA. In Michel Fokine's *Petrouchka* (1911), Nijinska (at left) created a role as a Street Dancer. She is pictured here with K. Kobelev as the Organ Grinder and Ludmilla Schollar as a Gypsy. (Photograph by Bert; reprinted from Nijinska, 1981, fig. 89.)

Nijinska's choreographies during this period are characterized by a search for new means of expression. At her studio she taught classical and character dance according to her own method, as well as expression through movement. Based on her teaching she developed a movement vocabulary, on which she based her choreography. Works like her *Chopin Prelude no.* 7 (1919), for which Alexandra Exter created the sets, are typical of a choreographic orientation turning away from classical ballet. Vsevolod Stalinsky, one of her students, reported that at this period Nijinska was already beginning to experiment with the classical vocabulary of steps, which she bent and broke and sometimes executed *en dedans;* he noted that this exercise was of great help to him in his later work with Kasyan Goleizovsky. Another student, Oleg Stalinsky, compared the style developed by Nijinska in Kiev to that of Kurt Jooss.

With her children and her mother, Nijinska left Russia in the fall of 1921. She met her brother in Vienna and returned to the Ballets Russes. Her first work for that company was decisive for her subsequent choreographic career. Asked to improve on several weak spots in Petipa's *The Sleeping Beauty,* Nijinska was forced to come to terms with Petipa's school and aesthetics. The alterations and additions she made were altogether in the Petipa mode. For act 2, she created the *pas d'action* and hunting dances, and for act 3, the "Three Ivans," an enduring favorite. The next two works she produced as the official choreographer of the Ballets Russes do not reflect her encounter with Petipa; the music of Igor Stravinsky's *Le Renard* and *Les Noces* is much more appropriate to the choreographic style Nijinska had begun to develop in Russia. Her choreography corresponds exactly with Stravinsky's intentions. The premiere of *Le Renard* on 18 May 1922 was followed on 13 June 1923 by the Paris premiere of Nijinska's first masterpiece, *Les Noces,* and her second, *Les Biches,* on 6 January 1924. During this period she was also one of the group's leading ballerinas. She demonstrated her versatility as a choreographer with *Les Tentations de la Bergère,* to music by Michel Pinolet, Monteclair, and Henri Casadesus, *Les Fâcheaux,* to music by Georges Auric, and *Le Train Bleu,* to the score by Darius Milhaud. As a ballerina Nijinska's principal roles were the Buffoon in *Chout,* the Witch Kikora in *Contes Russes,* the Elect in *Le Sacre du Printemps,* the Fox in *Le Renard,* the Hummingbird Fairy and the Lilac Fairy in *The Sleeping Beauty,* the Hostess in *Les Biches,* and the Tennis Champion in *Le Train Bleu.*

After several disputes with Diaghilev, Nijinska left the Ballets Russes in January 1925 and founded her own small company, the Théâtre Choréographique, in Paris. After staging a work for the Paris Opera, *La Naissance de la Lyre* set to music by Albert Roussel, she took her company on a tour of the spas in southern England. The group consisted almost exclusively of Nijinska's Kiev dancers: Czeslaw and Jan Hoyer, Eugen Lapitzki, and Serge Unger. Among the female soloists was Hélène Woizikowska. The group performed only Nijinska's works. The most important item on the program was *Holy Etudes,* set to music by Bach. This work formed the nucleus for the later ballet *Étude,* which is concerned chiefly with the relationship between music and dance, with overtones of earlier choreography and influences evident in its architectonics and its color symbolism.

From her home in Paris, Nijinska now worked on a wide variety of projects; although some of them were merely odd jobs, they were all interesting. In November 1925 she created *Les Rencontres,* to music by Jacques Ibert for the Paris Opera and Olga Spessivtseva. This was followed early in 1926 by *Un Estudio Religioso,* a revised version of *Holy Etudes* for the Teatro Colón of Buenos Aires, with which Nijinska was loosely connected until 1946. During this period her principal dancers were Ludmilla Schollar and Anatole Vilzak. With Constant Lambert's *Romeo and Juliet,* Nijinska returned to the Ballets Russes in 1926. In April 1927 she created *Les Impressions de Music-Hall,* set to music by Gabriel Pierné for the Paris Opera, in which the Opera's last Italian prima ballerina, Carlotta Zambelli, danced for the last time. In Buenos Aires in 1927, Nijinska produced Alfredo Casella's *La Giara,* Lambert's *Pomona,* and Sergei Prokofiev's *Ala y Lolly.*

Late in the summer of 1928, Nijinska was invited to put together a company sponsored by Ida Rubinstein. The dancers she recruited included Schollar, Vilzak, Roman Jasinski, Yurek Shabelevsky, David Lichine, and Frederick Ashton. The group had all the advantages and disadvantages of a troupe maintained by a sponsor who also dances. The intrinsically valuable creations that Rubinstein proposed were rendered dubious by her performances as principal dancer. A few, however, became permanent features of the international repertory. On 22 November 1928, Nijinska's *La Bienaimée,* to music by Liszt and Schubert, arranged by Darius Milhaud, with sets by Alexandre Benois, a ballet about an artist's muse, failed in its premiere at the Paris Opera. (When it was restaged in 1937 and 1941, it was more successful, thanks to different dancers.) *Boléro,* based on Maurice Ravel's

NIJINSKA. In Nijinsky's *L'Après-midi d'un Faune* (1912), Nijinska danced the sixth nymph to make an entrance. Here, she confronts her brother in the title role of his first ballet, danced to the tone poem by Claude Debussy. (Photograph by Baron de Meyer; from the Dance Collection, New York Public Library for the Performing Arts.)

work, had its premiere on the same evening, also with sets by Benois, and was more successful. Its scenic concept—the male corps de ballet is assembled around a table on which a girl (originally Rubinstein) is dancing—survives chiefly in Maurice Béjart's version. On 27 November 1928 Nijinska premiered her next ballet for the company, *Le Baiser de la Fée,* Stravinsky's homage to Tchaikovsky, commissioned by Rubinstein. Rubinstein again danced a leading role, and her incompetence destroyed the equilibrium of the ballet. *La Princesse Cygne,* to the music of Nikolai Rimsky-Korsakov's *Czar Sultan,* with sets and costumes by Benois, had its premiere on 29 November 1928 at the Paris Opera, with no better success.

A group tour resulted in Nijinska's most demanding choreographic work for the company, Ravel's *La Valse,*

NIJINSKA. A rehearsal for Nijinska's *Les Noces*, photographed on the roof of the Théâtre de Monte-Carlo in the spring of 1923. The sculptural grouping reflects Nijinska's interest in the modern Russian movement of constructivism, which she married with a neoclassical technique and a story of a peasant wedding in Old Russia. Felia Dubrovska as the Bride appears at the apex of the pyramid; Lubov Tchernicheva and Léon Woizikowski, the leading dancers among the wedding guests, stand on either side. (Photograph by J. Enrietty; from the Dance Collection, New York Public Library for the Performing Arts.)

which had been commissioned and then rejected by Diaghilev. It had its premiere in Monte Carlo on 15 January 1929. In her first version of the ballet, instead of translating the music into a piece for waltzing couples, Nijinska choreographed a series of dances without a story line; the French critic Pierre Michaut commented that this anticipated the symphonic ballets of Léonide Massine. At Ravel's urging, Nijinska prepared new choreography of the ballet for the Paris season. It was agreed that the second version, presented on 23 May 1929, succeeded in conveying and intensifying the atmosphere created by Ravel. Rubinstein's company dissolved early in the summer of 1929. When it was reestablished in 1931 and 1934, the Nijinska works were retained in the repertory.

In June 1930 Nijinska began working for the newly founded Nijinska Ballets, under the auspices of Ballet de l'Opéra Russe à Paris. The first evening of ballet by the group was presented late in 1931. The most important work was *Étude*, in which, according to an interview given by Nijinska, the dance complemented instead of merely translating the music. At a time when the abstract ballet had not yet come into existence, this venture into new territory was inevitably controversial. André Levinson (1929) declared that mathematics had become the subject of ballet; he was particularly disturbed by the depersonalization of the dancers, a factor that upon *Étude's* revival in 1944 was mentioned unfavorably in a *New York Times* review by John Martin. Levinson also disliked the classical virtuoso middle section of the ballet, which he thought was not expressive; Martin, however, found some of its passages "stunningly composed" and "stunningly danced" by Nathalie Krassovska and Maria Tallchief (Nijinska had added a solo for the ballerina).

In 1931 Nijinska worked in Berlin for Max Reinhardt. In January 1932 in Paris she founded another company, which she called Théâtre de la Danse Nijinska. The heart of the program she presented on 10 June at the Opéra-Comique was *Les Variations,* which Nijinska put together from thirty-two piano pieces by Beethoven orchestrated by Vladimir Pohl. The rest of the program consisted chiefly of revivals of her ballets. The "composition for dance," as Nijinska called *Les Variations,* had three sections, each organized around a theme that had more influence on the sets than on the choreography. Nijinska resisted the later view that *Les Variations* anticipated the symphonic ballets of Massine. "I did not care to bind myself to the already fixed ideas and forms of the musician," she wrote. In her opinion, a symphony was a complete and independent composition, and it was dangerous to try to give choreographic expression to a work of music or literature. This opinion, however, did not prevent Nijinska from endeavoring to do precisely that. Her *Hamlet,* set to music by Liszt, Giovanni Pierluigi da Palestrina, and Modest Mussorgsky, premiered on 23 June 1934, with Nijinska herself dancing the title role. It was not a simple translation of a drama into dance, but her interesting dramaturgy of a breakdown of the protagonist into the various aspects of his character; unfortunately, it could not be effectively executed.

Nijinska's next creation, *Les Cent Baisers,* set to music by Frédéric d'Erlanger, was more successful. She produced it in July 1935 for Colonel W. de Basil's Ballets Russes, with Irina Baronova in the leading role. This was the first Nijinska ballet seen in the United States, where the company danced it on tour, and it enjoyed general acclaim. A. V. Coton (1938) marveled at the economical construction of the ballet's story and the choreographic vocabulary, which reminded him of *Les Biches*. In connection with this ballet, Arnold Haskell (1928) sought to characterize the Nijinska style. "La Nijinska is intensely personal in all her work so that before she can settle down to production she must educate her dancers in her own type of movement," he wrote. "Every step devised is demonstrated and carefully analyzed by her . . .

NIJINSKA. In 1924, Nijinska created two major works, *Les Biches* and *Le Train Bleu,* based on the jazz-age antics of high society in the South of France. *(right)* Lydia Sokolova in a bathing costume as Perlouse and Léon Woizikowski as Le Joueur de Golfe in *Le Train Bleu,* golden youth cavorting on the Côte d'Azur. *(below)* Members of the Ballets Russes in a 1927 performance of *Les Biches,* which takes place at a chic house party. The three Athletes showing off their muscles are (from left to right) Serge Lifar, Léon Woizikowski, and Tadeo (Thadée) Slavinsky. (Photographs from the Dance Collection, New York Public Library for the Performing Arts.)

explained both choreographically and in its dramatic and emotional context."

During the second half of the 1930s Nijinska was associated chiefly with two companies. For the Markova-Dolin Company she produced mainly revivals of her own works. With her *Chopin Concerto,* based on Chopin's Piano Concerto in E Minor and introduced on 20 November 1937 at the Théâtre de Mogador in Paris by the Polish Ballet, she made another major contribution to the still youthful genre of abstract ballet. *Chopin Concerto,* wrote A. V. Coton in 1938, "will easily justify its position within the first half dozen experiments in abstract form." John Martin noted in his *New York Times* review on 20 October 1942 that "a more beautiful work it would be difficult to find or one which moves so directly to its goal with such easy command of form." He added, "Abstractions are frequently not popular with the public, but if this one proves not to be, the public will be missing a notable ballet." *Chopin Concerto* was danced in 1970 by the Niagara Frontier Ballet. It was pronounced dated, but the flow of the choreography and the romantic mood were admired.

Nijinska left Europe in 1939 and opened her own studio in Hollywood in 1941. *La Fille Mal Gardée* in 1940 was her first work for Ballet Theatre (later American Ballet Theatre). In 1942 she created *Snow Maiden,* set to music by Aleksandr Glazunov, for the Ballet Russe de Monte Carlo. Immediately after the end of World War II, she began working with Le Grand Ballet du Marquis de Cuevas as ballet mistress, choreographer, and specialist in classical productions. The company's 1960 production of *The Sleeping Beauty,* on which Nijinska ceased working before the premiere, was her last work for the Marquis. Her most important ballet of this period was *Brahms Variations,* set to Brahms's variations on themes by Handel and Paganini, for the International Ballet. Her last creation was *Rondo Capriccioso* (1952), to music by Camille Saint-Saëns, which she created for dancer Rosella Hightower. Her other late creations do not approach her important works of the 1920s and 1930s.

When Nijinska retired to California in 1940, she began to be forgotten, but Frederick Ashton called her back out of retirement. With the revival of *Les Biches* in 1964, the Royal Ballet began a Nijinska renaissance.

[*See also* Biches, Les *and* Noces, Les.]

NIJINSKA. Members of Ida Rubinstein's company in Nijinska's first production of *Boléro* (1928), set to the hypnotic music of Maurice Ravel. This was only one of a number of works commissioned from Nijinska by Rubinstein in 1928 and 1929. Among others were *La Bien-Aimée,* to music by Schubert and Liszt; *Le Baiser de la Fée,* to the Stravinsky score; and *La Princesse Cygne,* to music of Rimsky-Korsakov. Rubinstein, a commanding presence on stage, although not an accomplished dancer, created the leading roles in all these works. (Photograph by J. Enrietty; from the Dance Collection, New York Public Library for the Performing Arts.)

BIBLIOGRAPHY

Acocella, Joan. "Nijinska: The Survivor's Story." *Dance Magazine* (April 1986): 50–58.

Anderson, Jack. "The Fabulous Career of Bronislava Nijinska." *Dance Magazine* (August 1963): 40–46.

Arkin, Lisa C. "Bronislava Nijinska and the Polish Ballet, 1937–1938: Missing Chapter of the Legacy." *Dance Research Journal* 24 (Fall 1992): 1–16.

Ashton, Frederick. "A Word about Choreography." *The Dancing Times* (May 1930): 124–125.

Baer, Nancy Van Norman. *Bronislava Nijinska: A Dancer's Legacy.* San Francisco, 1986.

Ballet Review 18 (Spring 1990): 15–35. Special section entitled "Bronislava Nijinska: Dancers Speak."

Coton, A. V. *A Prejudice for Ballet.* London, 1938.

Garafola, Lynn. "Bronislava Nijinska: A Legacy Uncovered." *Women and Performance* 3.2 (1987–1988): 78–89.

Garafola, Lynn. *Diaghilev's Ballets Russes.* New York, 1989.

Garafola, Lynn. "Bronislava Nijinska's *Bolero.*" In *Proceedings of the Fourteenth Annual Conference, Society of Dance History Scholars, New World School of the Arts, Miami, Florida, 8–10 February 1991,* compiled by Christena L. Schlundt. Riverside, Calif., 1991.

Garafola, Lynn. "Choreography by Nijinska." *Ballet Review* 20 (Winter 1992): 64–71.

García-Márquez, Vicente. *The Ballets Russes: Colonel de Basil's Ballets Russes de Monte Carlo, 1932–1952.* New York, 1990.

Haskell, Arnold L. *Some Studies in Ballet.* London, 1928.

Huber, Andrea G. "A Conversation with Irina Nijinska." *Ballet Review* 20 (Spring 1992): 36–60.

Levinson, André. *La danse d'aujourd'hui.* Paris, 1929.

Meisner, Nadine. "Nijinska: The Making of a Choreographer." *Dance and Dancers* (June–July 1991): 17–21.

Merrett, Sue. "Bronislava Nijinska Remembered." *The Dancing Times* (May 1991).

Michaut, Pierre. *Le ballet contemporain, 1929–1950.* Paris, 1950.

Nijinska, Bronislava. "Von der Schule und der Schule der Bewegung." *Der Schrifttanz* 3.1 (April 1930).

Nijinska, Bronislava. "Reflections about the Production of *Les Biches* and *Hamlet* in Markova-Dolin Ballets." *The Dancing Times* (February 1937): 617–620.

Nijinska, Bronislava. *Early Memoirs.* Translated and edited by Irina Nijinska and Jean Rawlinson. New York, 1981.

Nijinska, Bronislava. "On Movement and the School of Movement." *Ballet Review* 13 (Winter 1986): 75–81.

Oberzaucher-Schüller, Gunhild. "Bronislava Nijinska." Ph.D. diss., University of Vienna, 1974.

Severn, Margaret. "Dancing with Bronislava Nijinska and Ida Rubinstein." *Dance Chronicle* 11.3 (1988): 333–364.

Sorley Walker, Kathrine. *De Basil's Ballets Russes.* New York, 1983.

GUNHILD OBERZAUCHER-SCHÜLLER
Translated from German

NIJINSKY, VASLAV (Vatslav Fomich Nizhinskii; born 12 March 1889 [1890?] in Kiev, Ukraine, died 8 April 1950 in London), foremost male dancer of and choreographer for the early Ballets Russes de Serge Diaghilev. Nijinsky was the second of three children. The eldest was Stanislav (1886–1917), who lived from adolescence in a sanitorium, probably as the result of a severe fall on the head in early childhood. The youngest was Bronislava (1891–1972), who, like her brother Vaslav, became one of the pioneers of twentieth-century choreography.

Nijinsky received his early dance training from his parents, Tomasz Lavrentievitch Nijiński (1862–1912) and Eleonora Nicolaevna Bereda (1856–1932), both of whom had studied ballet at the Wielki Theater school in Warsaw. Tomasz (Russ., Foma) and Eleonora earned their living on the touring circuit, mounting and performing dances in state opera houses, summer theaters, and other enterprises throughout Russia and their native Poland, and their children toured with them. At an early age Nijinsky learned elementary ballet, a bit of tap and acrobatics, and many folk and character dances. He made his first professional appearance at age seven, in a pantomime for children and animals staged by the celebrated Russian clown Vladimir Durov for Albert Salamonsky's circus in Vilna (now Vilnius, Lithuania). Nijinsky played a chimney sweep who rescued a piglet, a rabbit, a monkey, and a dog from a burning house and then extinguished the fire.

In 1897 Nijinsky's parents separated, and Eleanora settled with the three children in Saint Petersburg. The following year, Nijinsky was admitted to the Imperial Theater School, where in the course of his nine years' training he was taught by Sergei Legat, Mikhail Obukhov, and Nikolai Legat. After graduation he studied with Pavel Gerdt and in private classes with Enrico Cecchetti, who was also his teacher during the years with the Diaghilev company.

From 1899 to 1906 Nijinsky appeared in children's parts in the regular repertory of Saint Petersburg's Imperial Ballet: the mazurka in *Paquita,* a Page and then one of Tom Thumb's brothers in *The Sleeping Beauty,* a Mouse and then the Mouse King in *The Nutcracker,* among others. As his remarkable virtuosity came to be noted, he was given increasingly demanding roles in ballets mounted for student performances at the Maryinsky Theater by Nikolai Legat, Klavdia Kulichevskaya, and Michel Fokine. In 1906, in his first major appearance with the Imperial Ballet, he partnered company ballerina Vera Trefilova in the ballet *Roses and Butterflies* (N. Legat), inserted into Wolfgang Amadeus Mozart's opera *Don Giovanni.* Also in 1906 he appeared with the Imperial Ballet in certain soloist roles, such as the Mulatto in Marius Petipa's *King Candaule.*

Accounts of his graduation performance in 1907 differ, though he seems to have been the featured dancer of the program. According to one review, he appeared in the Lightning variation from *The Magic Mirror* and in a selection from *Paquita,* probably the pas de trois. Nijinska records that in this program Nijinsky took the leading role in Kulichevskaya's *Salanga* and created a sensation with his huge leaps in his solo variation in Fokine's *The Animated Gobelin,* an early, one-act version of what was to become *Le Pavillon d'Armide.* On his graduation in 1907, he

NIJINSKY. As Armida's Page in Fokine's *Le Pavillon d'Armide,* a studio portrait taken in Paris in 1911. Nijinsky first danced this role (also known as the White Slave or the Favorite Slave) at the Maryinsky Theater in Saint Petersburg in 1907. For opening night of Diaghilev's first Saison Russe in Paris, 19 May 1909, at the Théâtre du Châtelet, Alexandre Benois designed a new costume for the Page. Although it was correct in every historical detail of eighteenth-century French court dress, some thought it overly ornate. Nijinsky's sister Bronislava said bluntly that it looked like a lampshade. Nijinsky nevertheless managed to amaze the Parisian audience with his performance. (Photograph by Bert; from the Dance Collection, New York Public Library for the Performing Arts.)

was named an Artist of the Imperial Theaters with the rank of *coryphé,* one grade higher than the usual starting rank of corps de ballet.

Nijinsky's debut at the Maryinsky as a member of the Imperial Ballet in 1907 was in *La Source,* where he danced an interpolated pas de deux, "Jeux des Papillons" (Kulichevskaya), with Julia Sedova. He was immediately sought as a partner by the company's leading female dancers, including *prima ballerina assoluta* Matilda Kshessinska, with whom he starred in *La Fille Mal Gardée* less than two months after the beginning of his first season with the company. Also in 1907 he danced the prized role of Bluebird (with Lydia Kyasht) in *The Sleeping Beauty.* Other important roles in which he appeared during his three and a half years with the company were (dates indicate Nijinsky's first appearance) a pas de deux (probably the peasant pas de deux) in *Giselle* (1907); Ivanushka in *The Little Humpbacked Horse* (1908); Hurricane in *The Talisman* (1909); the Prince in *The Blood-Red Flower* (N. Legat, 1909); and Albrecht in *Giselle* (1911). At the Maryinsky and elsewhere, he created roles in most of Fokine's early Saint Petersburg ballets, including the Favorite Slave in *Le Pavillon d'Armide* (1907); the Slave in *Eunice* (1907); the Slave in *Une Nuit d'Égypte* (1908); the male lead in the revised *Chopiniana* (1908); and Florestan Harlequin in *Le Carnaval* (1910).

In 1907 Nijinsky became the companion of Prince Pavel Dmitrievich Lvov, a wealthy court official. In 1908 Lvov introduced him to Sergei Pavlovich Diagilev (Serge Diaghilev), who at that time was planning a season of Russian ballet in Paris. Soon thereafter Nijinsky became Diaghilev's lover, and the following spring he was the featured male dancer in the first season of what was to become Diaghilev's Ballets Russes.

In Saint Petersburg, Nijinsky had been a locally celebrated young dancer; with the Ballets Russes he became an international star. He danced in the Diaghilev seasons from 1909 to 1913 and from 1916 to 1917. His roles included the following (asterisks [*] indicate roles created for Nijinsky; choreography is by Fokine unless otherwise indicated; dates indicate Nijinsky's first appearance in the role in the Diaghilev seasons):

*Favorite Slave, *Le Pavillon d'Armide* (1909); "L'Oiseau de Feu" pas de deux (M. Petipa) in *Le Festin* (1909); *male lead, *Les Sylphides* (1909); *Slave, *Cléopâtra* (1909); *Golden Slave, *Schéhérazade* (1910); Albrecht, *Giselle* (Coralli, Perrot, Petipa, rev. Fokine; 1910); *"La Danse Siamoise" and *"Kobold" (Fokine [Nijinsky]) in *Les Orientales* (1910); *"Lezghinka" (Fokine after M. Petipa) in *Le Festin* (1910); *Spirit of the Rose, in *Le Spectre de la Rose* (1911); Harlequin (1911 [1910?]), *Le Carnaval* (1911); *Narcissus, *Narcisse* (1911); *Petrouchka, *Petrouchka* (1911); Prince, *Aurore et le Prince* (M. Petipa; 1911); Siegfried, *Swan Lake* (M. Petipa and L. Ivanov, rev. Fokine; 1911); *Blue God, *Le Dieu Bleu* (1912); *Faun, *L'Après-midi d'un Faune* (Nijinsky; 1912); *Daphnis, *Daphnis et Chloé* (1912); *male lead, *Jeux* (Nijinsky; 1913); *Till, *Till Eulenspiegel* (Nijinsky; 1916).

In 1909 and 1910 the participants in Diaghilev's ballet seasons were not a permanent troupe, but a collection of

Russian Imperial dancers on vacation. Then, in January 1911, Nijinsky was dismissed from the Imperial Theaters after a dispute over the propriety of the costume he chose to wear in a performance of *Giselle* at the Maryinsky. The incident may or may not have been engineered by Diaghilev. In any case, with his foremost male dancer now available full time, Diaghilev in early 1911 organized a permanent troupe, with Fokine as chief choreographer, and began seeking year-round engagements. In March 1911, Nijinsky, age twenty-two, left Russia with Diaghilev, bound for Monte Carlo. He was never to return to his homeland.

Shortly before this, Nijinsky had begun choreographing his first major ballet. He had had some prior experience. In 1906, while still in school, he had arranged the dances for a privately performed children's opera, *Cinderella,* composed by Boris Asafiev. In 1907 (1908?) he created the dances for Asafiev's *The Snow Queen,* another children's opera. In 1910, according to Nijinska, he set the arm movements for her Papillon in Fokine's *Le Carnaval.* He may also have created his solo, "Kobold," in *Les Orientales* of the 1910 Diaghilev season. Whatever the precedents, in the winter of 1910 Nijinsky, with Diaghilev's encouragement, began work on a ballet to Claude Debussy's "Prélude à l'Après-midi d'un Faune," setting the movements on himself and his sister. [*See* Après-midi d'un Faune, L'.]

First performed at the Théâtre du Châtelet in Paris on 29 May 1913, *L'Après-midi d'un Faune* had a cast of eight—a Faun (Nijinsky), a Principal Nymph (Lydia Nelidova), and six other Nymphs—and a libretto suggested by Stéphane Mallarmé's eponymous poem. A faun, from his perch on a rock, watches a nymph bathing, attended by her sister nymphs. He accosts her, but she flees, forgetting her veil. The faun takes the veil up to his rock and lies down on it, ending with a convulsive movement like that of orgasm.

In direct contrast to Claude Debussy's rich and fluid music, Nijinsky's choreographic style was austere and angular. Moving in fixed lines across the stage, with their feet flexed and their limbs and heads in profile, the nymphs resembled an antique frieze—a similarity enhanced by the long pauses that broke the movement. There were no classical steps, no virtuosity, no charm, expansiveness, or "personality." The total impression, despite the flowing lines of the music, decor, and costumes, was one of true archaism: meaning compacted into mysterious, ritualistic forms.

Nothing in the descriptions of Nijinsky's earlier dancing or choreography prepares one for the utterly radical break represented by this movement style—a break not only with classicism but also with the anticlassical experiments of Fokine. Here the academic canon was not just adapted; it was truly inverted. And "period" style was used not so much for decorative as for psychological value, the archaism of the movement underlining the intimate nature of the subject: the discovery of sexuality. Above all, movement was treated not as a pantomimic means but as an end in itself: a mystery to be analyzed and a potent metaphor of emotion.

NIJINSKY. As Albrecht in act 2 of *Giselle,* performed in Paris in 1910 with Karsavina in the title role. (Photographic print by L. Roosen; from the Dance Collection, New York Public Library for the Performing Arts.)

L'Après-midi d'un Faune precipitated a break within the troupe. Fokine, angered at the preferential treatment Diaghilev had given to Nijinsky's ballet over Fokine's own new "Greek" ballet *Daphnis et Chloé,* resigned from the company, leaving in early June. Thus Nijinsky became the chief choreographer of the Ballets Russes at age twenty-three.

His two new projects for the 1913 season were *Jeux,* to newly commissioned music by Debussy, and *Le Sacre du Printemps,* to a new score by Igor Stravinsky. The two ballets were choreographed in the same time period, from the fall of 1912 through the spring of 1913, work on one alternating with work on the other. Nijinsky was apparently less interested in *Jeux* than in *Le Sacre du Printemps.*

While the latter was to have been performed first, program changes forced the rescheduling of *Jeux* for the opening night of the Paris season, so that Nijinsky reluctantly had to set aside his work on *Sacre* and return reluctantly to *Jeux*. These circumstances, as well as artistic considerations, may help to explain the somewhat inconclusive character of *Jeux* in contrast to *Faune* and *Sacre*. Nijinsky referred to the choreography as "my experiments in stylized gesture," and the ballet apparently had the look of an experiment.

First performed on 15 May 1913 at the Théâtre de Champs-Élysées (Paris), *Jeux* was a self-declaredly modern ballet. To begin with, it was one of the first ballets to deal with athletics, a new enthusiasm in Europe. (The Olympic Games had been revived in 1896.) The theme was tennis, and the cast—two young women (Tamara Karsavina and Ludmilla Schollar) and a young man (Nijinsky)—was costumed accordingly. The women wore sports outfits by Maison Paquin: white knit tops and short white skirts. Nijinsky carried a tennis racket and wore white stylized practice clothes that looked generally sporty. But the *Jeux*, or games, of the title were erotic as well as athletic. The characters, in their three-way courtship, suggested a ménage à trois. (Later, in his *Diary*, Nijinsky claimed that this grouping actually symbolized a sexual encounter involving a man and two boys, a fantasy of Diaghilev.) In all, *Jeux* embodied a new, light, experimental attitude toward life, a reaction to the solemnities of the nineteenth century. In this, it anticipated the 1920s. (The prescient Diaghilev wrote to Debussy in 1912 that the ballet was set in 1920.)

NIJINSKY. As the Golden Slave in Fokine's *Schéhérazade* (1910), Nijinsky was a spectacular success. During the orgy scene, his lusty leaping and writhing reminded some people of a panther, others of a snake. His costume, designed by Léon Bakst, was predominantly golden; his facial and body makeup an odd shade of bluish-gray, suggesting Ethiopian or Nubian origins. (Photograph by Bert; from the Dance Collection, New York Public Library for the Performing Arts.)

The backdrop, designed by Léon Bakst, showed a dense bank of trees lit by circles of electric light and surmounted, in the background, by a white house. Across the green floorcloth, painted with flower beds, a white ball comes flying, and flying after it comes a young man with a tennis racket. Then the two women arrive, apparently seeking a private conversation. They are interrupted by the youth, who has been spying on them. He dances with one, then with the other, each time provoking the jealousy of the excluded one. Finally, the three dance together. Suddenly another ball falls on the stage, and the young people scatter.

There are differing reports on the relationship of the movement to the score—Debussy's rich, surging symphonic poem, its main theme a waltz in 3/8 time. At times, it seems, Nijinsky followed the score closely; at other times, as in *Faune,* he appeared to ignore it.

The choreography had some of the same intermediate character. After the great break in *Faune,* Nijinsky now reverted to some classical maneuvers. The women wore shoes that were stiffened at the tips (though apparently they were not fully blocked pointe shoes), and they danced much of the time on three-quarter pointe, performing some basic classical steps, such as *pas de bourrée.* Yet on the evidence of the few remaining photographs and a series of pastels by Valentine Gross, Nijinsky's chief interest in *Jeux* was the mass of the bodies and their relation to one another. At this time, according to Nijinska, he was greatly excited by his recent discovery of Paul Gauguin, and the careful sculptural groupings of the three dancers, preserved in the pictorial evidence, resemble the psychologically reverberant groupings in Gauguin's Tahitian paintings. Also Gauguin-like is the compact quality of the bodies. Presumably in emulation of sports postures, the

NIJINSKY. In costume for "La Danse Siamoise," one of the suite of dances billed by Diaghilev as *Les Orientales* (1910). Nijinsky did his own choreography to music by Christian Sinding. The elaborate costume was designed by Léon Bakst. (Photograph by Druet; from the Dance Collection, New York Public Library for the Performing Arts.)

dancers through much of the ballet held their arms bent, with the hands in a loose fist ("as one maimed from birth," wrote Karsavina, who did not like *Jeux*). The result was far removed from the expansive beauties of classicism, though in its application of freer postures to the academic technique, it pointed toward late twentieth-century classicism. Like *Faune, Jeux* was a bravely unpretty work—an act of research, an exploration of movement, in the service of a complicated emotional truth.

Jeux was cooly received—Debussy, too, disliked it—and was discarded after only five performances. The ballet is now lost, though Kenneth MacMillan reassembled parts of it for Herbert Ross's movie *Nijinsky* (1980).

Almost equally brief is the performance history of *Le Sacre du Printemps,* which was probably Nijinsky's masterpiece, as well as Stravinsky's. The idea of the ballet first came to Stravinsky in 1910: "I saw in imagination a solemn pagan rite: wise elders, seated in a circle, watch a young girl dance herself to death. They were sacrificing her to propitiate the god of spring." Stravinsky enlisted the collaboration of his friend Nikolai Roerich, who was both a painter and an archaeologist, specializing in ancient Slavic culture. (He had designed the sets and costumes for the *Polovtsian Dances* in Diaghilev's 1909 production of *Prince Igor.*) In the summer of 1911, Stravinsky and Roerich worked out a final scenario, and Stravinsky began to compose the music. By March 1913 the score was finished: An utterly revolutionary work whose combined innovations of rhythm and orchestration permanently altered Western music.

Originally Fokine was to have choreographed *Sacre.* With his departure, the job fell to Nijinsky. Nijinsky began his work in late 1912, in Germany, first creating the ballet's one solo, the Sacrificial Dance of the Chosen Victim, on Nijinska. (Nijinska was to have danced this role, but she became pregnant and was replaced by Marie Piltz.) In

NIJINSKY. (*below*) In costume for "Lezghinka," one of the suite of dances billed by Diaghilev as *Le Festin*. This dance, a theatricalized version of a traditional dance of the Caucasus, was set by Fokine to music by Mikhail Glinka and was performed by Nijinsky in 1910. It may have had special meaning for him, as his parents, Foma and Eleonora Nijinsky, had once been well known for their performances of the *lezghinka* when they toured Poland and Russia as itinerant dancers. His father had taught him some steps when he was a child. (Photograph by Bert; from the Dance Collection, New York Public Library for the Performing Arts.)

alternation with *Jeux, Sacre* was gradually choreographed between November 1912 and May 1913, with Stravinsky often present at rehearsals.

Aside from the score, there were apparently two important influences on Nijinsky's choreography for this ballet. One was the primitivism and incipient abstraction of contemporary painting, particularly that of Gauguin and Roerich. The second influence was Émile Jaques-Dalcroze's eurhythmics, a system for inculcating musical sensitivity through the translation of rhythm into bodily movements. In 1912 Diaghilev and Nijinsky made two visits to Jaques-Dalcroze's school outside Dresden. On the second visit, Diaghilev hired one of Jaques-Dalcroze's pupils, Marie Rambert, to help Nijinsky with the complicated rhythms of Stravinsky's score.

Le Sacre du Printemps, with sets and costumes by Roerich, had its premiere at the Théâtre des Champs-Élysées in Paris on 29 May 1913. The ballet is one of the purest examples of the primitivism that so pervaded the art and thought of the early twentieth century (cf. Freud, Conrad, D. H. Lawrence). Superficially a portrait of precivilized society, it was also, by extension, an exploration of primitive impulses in the heart of civilized man. In addition, it was a tribute to the origins of dance in ancient fertility rituals. Above all, the ballet seems to have been an attempt to capture in movement the sheer driving force of nature, irrational and amoral—nature understood as including man.

NIJINSKY. A rare onstage photograph of Nijinsky in the title role of Fokine's *Le Spectre de la Rose* (1911), with Karsavina as the dozing Girl, just returned from a ball. As the Spirit of the Rose, Nijinsky displayed spectacular elevation. His final leap through the open window was said to cause women in the audience to faint with astonishment. (Photograph by Bert; from the Dance Collection, New York Public Library for the Performing Arts.)

The choreography was as drastic as the theme. Except for the solo of the Chosen Victim and the brief maneuvers of the Old Woman and the Wise Elder, *Sacre* was an ensemble ballet. But here, in violation of centuries of theatrical dance tradition, ensemble groupings were deployed asymmetrically, their movements "hatched in isolation," wrote Jacques Rivière, "like those spontaneous fires that break out in haystacks." The symmetry of the individual body was also abandoned, the postures and movements "almost bestial" (Nijinska), with knocked knees and turned-in feet—a complete inversion of classical form. With some intervals of serene lyricism, the choreography consisted largely of shudders, jerks, stamps, and thudding runs, culminating in the violent hurlings of the Chosen Victim's sacrificial dance.

In keeping with Jaques-Dalcroze's system, the dance followed the music very closely. Eyewitness accounts indicate that in some parts it was very nearly music visualization: "The dancers thin out into a straggling line, while the orchestra dwindles to a trill on the flutes; then a little tune begins in the woodwind two octaves apart, and two groups of three people detach themselves from either end of the line to begin a little dance" (the London *Times,* quoted in Macdonald, 1975). Yet there is strong evidence that much of the choreography was in counterpoint to the musical accents.

The premiere of *Sacre* provoked a riot, colorful accounts of which have been left by Jean Cocteau *(Cock and Harlequin)* and Valentine Gross (Buckle, 1971). The French reviews were generally harsh; the English reviews, generally dismissive. This tumultuous premiere is now regarded by many as the final birth spasm of modernism, and Stravinsky's score has become the most celebrated composition of twentieth-century Western music. Nijinsky's ballet, meanwhile, was lost, for it was dropped from repertory after nine performances and was soon forgotten by the dancers, most of whom loathed it. In 1987 Millicent Hodson created for the Joffrey Ballet a version of *Sacre,* though her choreographic evidence, most of it drawn from scores annotated by Stravinsky and Rambert, was apparently too sparse for this version to be called a reconstruction. [*See* Sacre du Printemps, Le.]

In August 1913, after the London season, the company

departed by ship, without Diaghilev, for a South American tour. Before they reached their first port, Nijinsky had proposed to Romola de Pulszky (1891–1978), a young Hungarian woman (daughter of Emilia Markus, Hungary's foremost actress) who had attached herself to the company in the hope, she later claimed, of capturing Nijinsky. The couple were married on 10 September 1913, in Buenos Aires, and three months later the aggrieved Diaghilev dismissed Nijinsky from the Ballets Russes.

Refusing offers from other companies, Nijinsky, with the help of the loyal Nijinska, formed a seventeen-member company for an eight-week engagement at the Palace Theatre, a London music hall, beginning in March 1914. Because Nijinsky became ill, and because of disagreements between him and the management, the season was canceled after two weeks. Among the works shown were Fokine's *Le Spectre de la Rose,* a *Les Sylphides* rechoreographed by Nijinsky, and a few other short dances by Nijinsky.

Soon thereafter Nijinsky and Romola traveled to Vienna, where Romola gave birth to a daughter, Kyra, on 19 June 1914. From Vienna they went to Budapest, where they found themselves detained as prisoners of war until 1916. Nijinsky used this time to work on a dance notation system that he had been devising and on a new ballet, *Till Eulenspiegel,* to Richard Strauss's tone poem. In the meantime, Diaghilev had arranged an American tour, for which he had promised to reengage Nijinsky. With much difficulty, the dancer's release was obtained, and in April 1916 Nijinsky made his American debut with the Ballets Russes at New York's Metropolitan Opera House, dancing his old Fokine repertory.

There followed a second American tour, coast to coast, from October 1916 to February 1917. This time, at the insistence of the tour's impresario, Otto Kahn, the company was to be directed by Nijinsky. (Diaghilev meanwhile returned to Europe.) Because of Nijinsky's lack of administrative skills, together with his growing absorption in Tolstoyan philosophy, the tour was chaotically directed. It is notable, however, for its inclusion of Nijinsky's fourth and last major ballet, *Till Eulenspiegel,* which premiered at the Manhattan Opera House in New York on 23 October 1916.

The least discussed of Nijinsky's major works, *Till* is said to have represented a retrenchment from the radical aesthetic that Nijinsky had advanced in the three ballets of 1912–1913. Like a Fokine ballet, it had a picturesque setting (medieval Brunswick, captured in handsomely stylized sets and costumes by Robert Edmond Jones), numerous character roles (portly burghers, a rosy-cheeked apple-seller), a naturalistic rather than symbolic movement style, and a fairly detailed plot: the mischief making of the legendary Till, ending in his hanging. At the first performance, the choreography was unfinished, necessitating some improvisation. Yet the premiere was enthusiastically received by both audience and press. The ballet was apparently given twenty-two performances, all during the 1916/17 American tour. It was then dropped, making it the sole Ballets Russes production that Diaghilev never saw. As with *Le Sacre du Printemps,* Millicent Hodson attempted a reconstruction of *Till* (Paris Opera Ballet, 1944), on what was apparently even sparser choreographic evidence than in the case of *Sacre.*

NIJINSKY. A studio portrait in the title role of Fokine's *Petrouchka* (1911). This ballet-burlesque, devised by Igor Stravinsky and Alexandre Benois, was originally entitled, by Stravinsky, *The Cry of Petrouchka.* Nijinsky's moving portrayal of the suffering of the ill-fated puppet, depicted in photographs such as this and described in the memoirs of his colleagues, has influenced the interpretation of every subsequent performer of the role. (Photograph by Elliott & Fry, London; from the Dance Collection, New York Public Library for the Performing Arts.)

The remainder of Nijinsky's artistic career can be briefly told. In the summer of 1917 he again joined the Diaghilev company, for a series of performances in Spain and South America. On 30 September 1917, in Montevideo, he danced in a Red Cross gala that he had arranged. This was his last public performance. He was twenty-nine years old.

In December 1917 the family settled in Saint-Moritz to wait out the war. There, in 1918 and 1919, according to

NIJINSKY. For his second ballet, *Jeux*, created in 1913 to music by Claude Debussy, Nijinsky cast Tamara Karsavina and Ludmilla Schollar as his partners in a flirtatious game among three tennis players. Such "anticlassical" poses as this, with arms bent, hands cupped, and feet turned inward, were linked by purely classical dance steps. (Photograph by Gerschel; from the Dance Collection, New York Public Library for the Performing Arts.)

Romola, Nijinsky continued refining his notation system and also worked on three ballets: a tale of Sapphic love, to Debussy's *Chansons de Bilitis;* a "Renaissance" ballet about a young painter's love first for his master, then for a woman; and a ballet entitled *Les Papillons de Nuit*, set in a brothel. (The list of Nijinsky's unfinished and/or unperformed works should include, in addition, two earlier projects: a "Japanese" ballet inspired by the woodblock prints of Hokusai, sketched in 1915; and *Mephisto Valse*, to music by Franz Lizst, a Faust ballet that Nijinsky worked on in 1916, intending it for the New York season in late 1916.)

Nijinsky now showed increasing signs of mental instability, evidenced in two further projects of the period: a series of drawings based on circles and arcs, often taking the form of staring eyes, and the remarkable diary that he wrote in 1918 and 1919. One of the most direct and poignant documents of Western confessional literature, the diary has as its theme the Tolstoyan dichotomy of intellect versus feeling. It records Nijinsky's conviction of his visionary status ("I am His present. I am God, in a present") and, at other times, his anguished knowledge that he is going mad ("I cannot restrain my tears. . . . I feel that I am going to be destroyed"). In 1934 Romola published a severely abridged version of the diary, translated from Russian into English. In 1995 a far more complete text was published in French, as *Cahiers*. A correspondingly complete English version was published in 1998.

In 1919 Nijinsky was diagnosed as schizophrenic by the eminent Swiss psychiatrist Eugen Bleuler. In 1920 Romola gave birth to a second daughter, Tamara. The last thirty years of Nijinsky's life were spent partly in sanatoriums and partly in the various homes that Romola was able to make for him when her work and his condition permitted. Though he suffered hallucinations and was occasionally violent, for the most part he was silent and withdrawn. He died of kidney failure in 1950 in London.

In his brief time, Nijinsky was the most famous male dancer in the world, a preeminence due in part to his extraordinary virtuosity. His body was not beautiful by conventional standards. ("He looked more like a factory-worker than a demi-god," wrote Alexandre Benois.) He was short (five feet, four inches) with a small head, Tatar features, a very long neck, and a powerfully muscled body. His thigh muscles in particular were so heavily developed that in *développé devant* he could not raise his leg higher than ninety degrees. But owing in part to this rare endowment, he was able to achieve remarkable technical feats, such as triple *tours en l'air*, twelve pirouettes (onstage—in the studio, according to Nijinska, he often executed fourteen and sixteen), and *entrechat huit*. (Nijinska reports his doing *entrechat dix* as well, both at the Maryinsky and in Paris.) Above all, Nijinsky was famous for his great *ballon* and elevation, the latter made more impressive by the fact that he took an almost imperceptible preparation for his leap and that at the apex of the leap he seemed to pause in the air. Astonishing descriptions of his dancing, step by step, can be found in Nijinska's *Early Memoirs*. These marvels were achieved, moreover, at no expense of clarity or musicality. Of his musical sensitivity, Cyril Beaumont wrote, "He did not so much dance to the music, he appeared to issue from it. His dancing was music made visible."

But it was not his virtuosity alone that made him such a powerful stage presence. As contemporary reports make clear, Nijinsky was a great and unusual actor. The ideal Fokine interpreter, he was able to expand a simple choreographic design into a rich dramatic portrait, using, in keeping with Fokine's dicta, the whole body as an expressive instrument. Yet his acting style apparently went beyond Fokine's principles; it was not so much realistic as classical, aimed at the portrayal of universalized states of the soul. As Beaumont remarked in 1913, "He does not seek to depict the actions and gestures of an isolated type of character he assumes; rather does he portray the spirit or essence of *all* the types of that character." He thus seemed to pass through the psychological into the metaphysical.

In this he was probably helped by the fact that many of the characters he depicted were something other than human: a puppet, a god, a faun, the specter of a rose. Or, if human, they inhabited some strange and special sphere, as in the case of the numerous slaves and androgynes he portrayed. Such roles, of course, were tailor-made by Fokine for Nijinsky's own personality, which seemed strange and special to many. But Nijinsky, in turn, knew how to use them as a route to emblematic truth.

Such portrayals at the same time dovetailed neatly with the tastes of Nijinsky's audiences, tastes formed by the *fin de siècle* and specifically by literary and pictorial symbolism. The primitivism, exoticism, mysticism, Platonism, and perversity that marked the arts of the late nineteenth century were not yet forgotten by European audiences of the prewar period, and Nijinsky (indeed, the early Ballets Russes as a whole) seemed to offer a revival of these pleasures. His androgyny was celebrated, and exaggerated, in numerous and tasteless popular drawings. His Tatar face and passionate dancing were interpreted as expressions of the "Slavic soul," mysterious and barbaric. His seemingly indeterminate nature and abstract style were seen as incarnations of symbolist metaphor—vague, radiant glimpses of noumenal truth. Such adaptability to prevailing tastes increased Nijinsky's popularity, as did the atmosphere of scandal that surrounded this shy and modest man throughout his career.

The symbolic approach that Nijinsky adopted on the level of characterization in Fokine's ballets became, in his own ballets, the foundation of dance design. Building on Fokine's achievements—costume reform, the one-act format, the fusion of dance and drama, the de-emphasis of the academic vocabulary and particularly of virtuosity—he nevertheless rejected the leading points of Fokine's style: the period charm, the reliance on character dance, the fluidity of line, and above all, the descriptive use of gesture. Like Fokine, he sought expressiveness in dance, but through nonrealistic means. For each of his ballets of 1912/13, he established a general mode of movement—light, flat, and sharp in *Faune*, knotted and crossed in *Jeux*, rugged and heavy in *Sacre*—and for each mode certain characteristic postures: the profiled limbs in *Faune*, the bunched fists in *Jeux*, the turned-in feet in *Sacre*. On this foundation he built his dances, largely in angular and asymmetrical patterns. Through their cumulative force, such dances served to suggest emotion, but in an indirect, emblematic fashion, unlike the stylized pantomime of Fokine. They were less a story than a vision.

In adopting this nondiscursive, nonmimetic approach, Nijinsky brought dance into alignment with modernism in the other arts—his primary achievement as a choreographer. His kinship with the framers of early modernism (e.g., Picasso, Joyce) can also be read in his treatment of the medium as an absolute, a thing expressive in itself, without need of pretext; in his analytic approach to the medium; in his consequent breaking through to radically new styles, as opposed to fashioning adaptations of established styles; and in his willingness to make something that looked genuinely ugly. "Nijinsky (with Rodin, Cezanne, Picasso . . .) for his generation murdered

NIJINSKY. *Till Eulenspiegel*, a dramatic comedy-ballet set to the music of Richard Strauss, was premiered at the Manhattan Opera House, New York, on 23 October 1916. In the title role, Nijinsky performed a number of "merry pranks," including this impersonation of a pompous professor wearing a mortarboard hat and an academic gown. (Photograph by Karl Strüss; from the Dance Collection, New York Public Library for the Performing Arts.)

beauty," wrote Lincoln Kirstein. Finally, in his subject matter—above all, the exploration of sexuality as a means of self-discovery *(Faune)* and as the engine of social survival *(Sacre)*—he was at one with modernism.

Nijinsky's influence as a dancer was immediate and huge. That ballet, nearly extinguished artistically in western Europe, was revived in this century is due to him and other great dancers of his generation, such as Anna Pavlova and Karsavina, as well as to Diaghilev. That male ballet, utterly extinguished, was also revived is due to him preeminently. Nijinsky was the first real ballet star of the male sex that Europe had seen since the retirement of Auguste Vestris nearly a century earlier. He initiated a renaissance.

The influence of Nijinsky's choreography is harder to assess. Inded, it was not until recently that he was accepted as a major choreographer by more than a few scattered voices (e.g., Kirstein, Rambert) in dance history, and by then all but one of his ballets, *L'Après-midi d'un Faune,* were lost. Certain experts on his work, such as Richard Buckle and Kirstein, have claimed that it had a decisive influence on early modern dance. More easily established and possibly more important is the effect his ballets had on the artistic development of Nijinska, who in turn influenced Frederick Ashton and probably George Balanchine as well. What Nijinska says of *Jeux* may be true of Nijinsky's work in general: that it was a crucial forerunner of the new classicism of twentieth-century ballet.

[*See also the entry on Diaghilev.*]

BIBLIOGRAPHY

Acocella, Joan. "After the Ball Was Over." *New Yorker* (18 May 1992): 91–100.

Beaumont, Cyril W. *Bookseller at the Ballet: Memoirs, 1891 to 1929.* London, 1975.

Buckle, Richard. *Nijinsky.* London, 1971.

Buckle, Richard. *Diaghilev.* New York, 1979.

Denby, Edwin. "Notes on Nijinsky Photographs." In Denby's *Looking at the Dance.* New York, 1949.

Garafola, Lynn. *Diaghilev's Ballets Russes.* New York, 1989.

Harris, Dale. "Elusive Genius." *Ballet News* 2 (March 1981): 18–25.

Hodson, Millicent. "Ritual Design in the New Dance: Nijinsky's Choreographic Method." *Dance Research* 4 (Spring 1986): 63–77.

Kirstein, Lincoln. *Movement and Metaphor: Four Centuries of Ballet.* New York, 1970.

Kirstein, Lincoln, et al. *Nijinsky Dancing.* New York, 1975.

Macdonald, Nesta. *Diaghilev Observed by Critics in England and the United States, 1911–1929.* New York, 1975.

Nijinska, Bronislava. *Early Memoirs.* Translated and edited by Irina Nijinska and Jean Rawlinson. New York, 1981.

Nijinsky, Romola. *Nijinsky.* New York, 1934.

Nijinsky, Romola. *The Last Years of Nijinsky.* New York, 1952.

Nijinsky, Vaslav. *Cahiers: Le Sentiment.* Translated by Christian Dumais-Lvowski and Galina Pogojeva. Paris, 1995. French translation of Nijinsky's diary.

Nijinsky, Vaslav. *The Diary of Vaslav Nijinsky.* Translated by Kyril Fitz-Lyon, edited by Joan Acocella. New York, 1998.

Ostwald, Peter. *Vaslav Nijinsky: A Leap into Madness.* New York, 1991.

Rambert, Marie. *Quicksilver: The Autobiography of Marie Rambert.* London, 1972.

Stanciv-Reiss, Françoise, and Jean-Michel Pourvoyeur, eds. *Ecrits sur Nijinsky.* Paris, 1992.

Whitworth, Geoffrey. *The Art of Nijinsky.* London, 1913.

JOAN ACOCELLA

NIKOLAIS, ALWIN (born 26 November 1910 in Southington, Connecticut, died 8 May 1993 in New York City), American choreographer, composer, stage and lighting designer, teacher, and theatrical innovator. Nikolais's works were characterized by an interaction of light, sound, color, time, shape, props, and moving bodies in which the dancer was used as a motor force. The conflict of his dances was often built through an accumulation of abstract designs that dissolved and changed to form the dramatic meaning. The image by itself was not as important as its being a catalyst that elicited reverberations within the onlookers. Nikolais was unique among his peers in that he was responsible for the complete production of his work. In addition to the choreography, he designed the sets, lights, props, and slides, created the costumes (which were primarily executed by Frank Garcia), and composed most of the music. Nikolais's dancers often were disguised by props acting as extensions of the body, costumes that distorted the human figure, or slides that created a particular atmosphere. For this reason he was accused of dehumanization, which he preferred to label as "decentralization," whereby humans are merely part of their environment, not its central focus.

Son of a Russian father and a German mother, Nikolais grew up in Southington, Connecticut. As a teenager, he played the organ for silent movies in Westport. His first introduction to acting and designing for the theater was in a drama center that he helped to form in his hometown. With his brother he had also created marionette shows in his attic, and this combined experience led in 1935 to his appointment as director of the Hartford Parks Marionette Theatre, a post he held until 1937. At that time Hartford was a vital community for the arts, and Nikolais became involved with many productions. In addition to his work with the marionette theater, during 1936 and 1937 he led the successful movement to establish the Gilpin Players, an all-black federal theater project.

Also while he was in Hartford, Nikolais studied dance with Truda Kaschmann, a former student of Mary Wigman. Nikolais had seen a performance by Wigman in 1933 and had been particularly struck by her use of percussion, a kind of music that he studied and practiced. His work during this period included, in 1936, choreography for Leonid Andreyev's *Sabine Women* (Nikolais's first dance work to be staged) and the choral-speaking and tap-dancing sequences for Karel Čapek's *World We Live in* (or *The Life of the Insects*). While still working with Kaschmann, Nikolais started his own small company. The year 1939 saw the premiere of their jointly choreographed work, *Eight Column Line*, which was commissioned by the Friends and Enemies of Modern Music to a score by Ernst Krenek. The warm reception to this work encouraged Nikolais to continue. During this time he also worked for Anne Randall Productions, directing and helping with speaking parts that included works performed to the poetry of William Carlos Williams and Archibald MacLeish. Following the success of *Eight Column Line*, the Hartt School of Music engaged Nikolais to teach dance, and he also worked for the Hartford Opera Guild, choreographing, among other works, *Martha* and *The Barber of Seville*.

During the summers of 1937 through 1939 Nikolais attended the Bennington School of Dance. While there he danced in José Limón's *Danza de la Muerte*, and he was fascinated with the percussion work in Franziska Boas's class, but he was most taken with the work of Hanya Holm: "It was motional stuff, much of which I then went on from because I had new thoughts about time and space. But I never had to forget what Hanya taught me. All I had to do was expand and go on" (quoted in Kriegsman, 1981, p. 255). In the summer of 1940 Nikolais performed on a coast-to-coast tour with Dancers En Route, a small group led by Elizabeth Waters.

NIKOLAIS. *Sanctum* was choreographed, designed, and scored by Nikolais in 1964. In this scene from a 1976 revival, Gerald Otte, Karen Sing, and Jim Teeters stretch their bodies against loops of fabric to create an architectural tableau. (Photograph © 1976 by Max Waldman; used by permission.)

With the onset of American involvement in World War II, Nikolais joined the army and served as an agent in the Criminal Investigation Division. His army years were the only time of his life when he was not creating for the theater, although he did work on his own form of dance notation—always fearful that someone might see the work and think he was a spy!—which he called Choroscript. After the war Nikolais went to live and work in New York City. He danced with Holm's workshop group and, through her, took a teaching job at the Henry Street Playhouse in 1948. The next year he was appointed codirector with Betty Young. There, over the next twenty-two years, he produced his unique theater-dance, first under the name of the Playhouse Dance Company, later renamed the Nikolais Dance Theatre.

Two important things happened to Nikolais in the early 1950s, at the beginning of his playhouse years. First, through his teaching he began to develop a corps of dedicated young dancers, including Murray Louis, Phyllis Lamhut, Gladys Bailin, Beverly Schmidt, and Coral Martindale. Second, he started to break away from psychological dance drama and storytelling as such and to explore abstract possibilities of dance. At the playhouse, students learned percussion and notation, and through the dance plays that Nikolais created for children, his students gained additional training in performance.

Nikolais's first abstract dance, *Kaleidoscope*, was eight minutes long; it was premiered in May 1953. Also in 1953 *Forest of Three*, an abstract fairy tale, was produced, as was *Masks, Props and Mobiles*, a longer work, parts of which continue to be performed. In his next major work, *Village of Whispers* (1955), the young company was pushed by Nikolais into a joint choreographic effort in the new "decentralized" way. Nikolais described this work as an "entire flip into abstraction." This dance was followed by a second *Kaleidoscope* (1956), in which the dancers manipulated objects such as disks and poles that seemed to become part of their bodies. This work scored a major success at the American Dance Festival in Connecticut that summer and brought Nikolais national recognition.

Asked to describe his investigation of decentralization, Nikolais explained that it began with the realization that motion imparts meaning to movement. It was a conclusion he reached by working with marionettes: the face of a marionette shows no emotion; it is the nature of its movements that imparts the emotion. This insight led him to decide that "dance is the art of motion" and that "if you could not get your intelligence into motion, then you lacked the basic substance and quality of dance." Further thinking about the intelligence of motion elicited the idea of decentralization: "If intelligence can exist in motion, it can impart whatever it wants to impart; it can be any kind of state of nature or anywhere at all." At the same time,

NIKOLAIS. The Women's Trio section from Nikolais's *Vaudeville of the Elements* in a performance on 10 December 1965 at the Walker Arts Center, Minneapolis, which had commissioned the work. (Photograph by Susan Schiff-Faludi; courtesy of the Nikolais/Louis Foundation for Dance, Inc.)

Nikolais began to de-emphasize sexuality and to tear down barriers between male and female, dressing his dancers in unisex costumes for the first time in the 1956 *Kaleidoscope.* "These were ideas that had not been stressed, if they had been done before."

When Nikolais became an abstractionist he had to redesign the structure of stage lighting. No longer concerned with the realism of the sun, the moon, and the stars but with lighting the human figure, he began the process of lighting the dancing figure from all directions. Later he worked with the effect of design projected on the body as a kinetic distortion, that is making the body seem to move more quickly or slowly or in a manner entirely different from the one that people were accustomed to seeing.

In December 1956 Nikolais presented *Prism,* which marked his first exploration of light in and around the dancers and which was also his first manipulation of light projected directly on the dancer. He remembered working very carefully to create a striped light on Murray Louis's face so that it would look as if it were fragmenting. In *Allegory* (1959) Nikolais used elastic costumes and created a sophisticated sound score based on his theory that unfamiliar music allows listeners to have their own imaginative responses. As electronic music developed, Nikolais incorporated it into his scores. He was one of the first to use the Moog synthesizer, for example.

During the 1960s Nikolais continued to work at expanding and innovating, producing *Totem* (1960), *Imago* (1963), and *Vaudeville of the Elements* (1963; his first major work to be premiered anywhere other than Henry Street). With the advent of government support for dance touring, the company became widely known throughout the United States and in 1968 went on a major tour of Europe that culminated with an enormous success in Paris, particularly with *Imago* and *Tent.* The overwhelming response of the Parisian audience was one of the high points in Nikolais's career, and it began a relationship between him and the French that led to two decorations from the French government. In 1978 Nikolais was asked to form the Centre Nationale de Danse Contemporain in Angers, France, which he led for three years, and in 1980 he created *Schema* for the Paris Opera; this work featured Murray Louis, a twenty-four-foot-high marionette, twelve circus acrobats, and dancers from the Paris Opera.

After Nikolais left the Henry Street Playhouse in 1970, he remained in Manhattan, where he taught and collaborated with Murray Louis. Holm taught at his school until 1985. In 1989 the Nikolais and Louis companies were incorporated into a ten-member group with the name Nikolais and Murray Louis Dance Company, which performed works by both men. Some of Nikolais's dancer/pupils have made distinctive contributions as choreographers and dancers; they include Phyllis Lamhut, Carolyn Carlson, Tandy Beal, Beverly Blossom, Gladys Báilyn, and Susan Buirge. Nikolais's later creations released his dancers from a heavy theatrical environment and allowed them to be more visible than in earlier works. Among them were *The Mechanical Organ* (1980); *Persons and Structures* (1984), in which the dancers climbed and crawled into lucite boxes; and *Contact* (1985). He also experimented with gamelan music and worked with rock groups.

Four pages of a company biography are taken up with Nikolais's awards and accomplishments, which included honorary doctorates from the University of Utah and the University of Illinois, the *Capezio* and *Dance Magazine* awards, the Samuel H. Scripps American Dance Festival Award, the National Medal of Arts, the Kennedy Center Honors List, and the Grande Medaille-de-Vermeille de la Ville de Paris. He received commissions from all over the world, including Japan, Venezuela, and Germany. His work was filmed many times. In 1987 the Public Broadcasting Service *American Masters* series produced the documentary "Nik and Murray."

[*See also* Scenic Design.]

BIBLIOGRAPHY

Blossom, Beverly, et al. "Dancers' Roundtable." In *Dance Reconstructed,* edited by Barbara Palfy. New Brunswick, N.J., 1993.

Diénis, Jean-Claude. "Alwin Nikolais." *Danser* (March 1987): 42–49.

Feinman, Jane M. "Alwin Nikolais, a New Philosophy of Dance: The Process and the Product, 1948–1968." Ph.D. diss., Temple University, 1994.

Finkel, Anita. "Looking Backward." *New Dance Review* 6 (Fall 1993): 3–6.

Gilmore, Bob. "'A Soul Tormented': Alvin Nikolais and Harry Partch's *The Bewitched." Musical Quarterly* 79 (Spring 1995): 80–107.

Hardy, Camille. "The Road Less Traveled." *Dance Magazine* (November 1993): 106–107.

Hines, Thomas Jensen. "The Sacred and the Profane: *Triad.*" In Hines's *Collaborative Form.* London, 1991.

Kriegsman, Sali Ann. *Modern Dance in America: The Bennington Years.* Boston, 1981.

Lamhut, Phyllis. "Alwin Nikolais, 1912–1993." *Ballet Review* 21 (Fall 1993): 8–9.

Louis, Murray, and Ruth E. Grauert. "Alwin Nikolais's Total Theater." *Dance Magazine* (December 1979): 56–69.

Mazo, Joseph H. "The Nik of Time." *Dance Magazine* (July 1993): 28–31.

NIKOLAIS. In Nikolais's *Scenario,* patterned circles of light and shadow intersect on a screen and over the dancers' moving bodies. This work premiered at the ANTA Theater, New York, on 25 February 1971. (Photograph © by Milton Oleaga; used by permission.)

McDonagh, Don. *The Rise and Fall and Rise of Modern Dance.* Rev. ed. Pennington, N.J., 1990.

Rogosin, Elinor. *The Dance Makers.* New York, 1980.

Siegel, Marcia B. "Nik: A Documentary." *Dance Perspectives,* no. 48 (1971).

Zupp, Nancy T. "An Analysis and Comparison of the Choreographic Process of Alwin Nikolais, Murray Louis, and Phyllis Lamhut." Ph.D. diss., University of North Carolina, Greensboro, 1978.

INTERVIEW. Alwin Nikolais, by Kitty Cunningham (1986).

KITTY CUNNINGHAM

NŌ. One of the major classical dance genres of Japanese theater, *nō* originated in the late fourteenth century in Japan, flourished through the sixteenth century, and survives substantially unaltered to the present as a living testimony to the spiritual dimensions and understated aesthetic splendor of the samurai culture. *Nō* holds a central position among Japanese dance-drama genres, following in time the aristocratic *bugaku* but preceding the popular *kabuki. Nō* features a variety of plays, haunting music, and stylized singing and acting, intertwined with dance patterns of rigorous simplicity, which have a profound impact on discriminating audiences.

Repertory and Play Structure. Today, the *nō* repertory includes more than two hundred plays, which can be categorized according to two basic types: *geki nō* (dramatic *nō*), which are rich in dramatic content; and *furyū nō* (dance *nō*), in which the plot is little more than an excuse for elegant dance. *Nō* plays are further distinguished as belonging to *genzai nō* (present-life *nō*), in which the main role is that of a living human being, and *mugen nō* (dreams and phantasms *nō*), in which the protagonist is a ghost or other supernatural being. A common classification scheme also divides the plays into five categories: *kami mono* (god pieces), *shura mono* (warrior pieces), *katsura mono* (wig pieces, or woman pieces), *kurui mono* (madness pieces), and *kiri nō mono* (final pieces, or goblin pieces).

Compared with Western drama, *nō* plays are short, sometimes more like simple one-act plays than full-length works. A typical dramatic *nō* of the *mugen nō* type is built in two acts *(ba)* and an interlude *(ai)*. The first act consists of five scenes: the entrance of the supporting actor *(waki)*, often as a wandering monk; the entrance of the protagonist *(shite)* in disguise; a confrontation between *shite* and *waki;* the *shite*'s revelation of his true identity; and the exit of the *shite.* While the *shite* changes costume and mask, a *kyōgen* actor recites the interlude, which is related to the plot of the *nō* play. The second act is also divided into five scenes: the *waki* chants in expectation; the *shite* reenters in his true appearance; a dialogue between *shite* and *waki* ensues; the *shite* performs the climax of the play, a long dance that relives the past event; and both make their final exit.

Mise-en-Scène. *Nō* stages were originally built within temple or palace compounds for open-air performances. At present, however, most professional *nō* performances take place in modern, air-conditioned theaters, where stages are built according to the style and measurements that became standard around 1700. Elements of the *nō* stage include a templelike stage roof that rests on four pillars, about fifteen feet (4.5 meters) high. These pillars define the square main dance platform (*honbutai,* measuring about 325 square feet, or 30 square meters) and are important for the orientation of the masked dancers and their positioning. The stage, including the bridgeway (*hashigakari,* about thirty three feet, or 10 meters, long) that connects the greenroom to the main stage, is built in unpainted but highly polished *hinoki* wood (Japanese cypress). The only decor consists of a majestic pine tree painted on a permanent wooden backdrop and a few shoots of bamboo painted on the short, side panel. Large earthenware jars are half-buried under the high stage to enhance acoustically the song, music, and the stamping of the dancers.

The *nō* orchestra *(hayashi)* consists of three or four musicians. They sit on the *atoza,* a continuation of the bridgeway behind the main dance floor, and play a flute, two hand drums, and a stick drum. Short guttural shouts uttered by the musicians, which have the function of regulating the beat, can also be considered part of the music.

The chorus *(jiutai)* usually consists of eight singers, whose main function is to continue the singing of the *shite* while he is dancing, without taking on any specific role. Throughout the play the chorus members squat stage left on a side extension of the main dance floor.

In most *nō* plays, masks are worn by the *shite* and his companions *(shitezure). Nō* masks—whose characterizations range from fierce demons to elegantly aloof young court ladies—are remarkable for their beauty and include old masterpieces of central importance in the history of Japanese sculpture. *Nō* costumes are splendid but not garish. Often woven of precious silks and gold in stunning patterns and colors, the costumes are always elegant, even when representing simple robes for pilgrims and old servants. Props are simple, almost skeletal, and used sparingly.

Influences on Nō's Development. Major influences on the formation of *nō* were shamanistic traditions and Buddhist spirituality, and both of these sources are responsible for the intensity and depth of the *nō* experience. Shamanism influenced aspects of *nō* drama's content and structure, including the importance in many *nō* plays of the apparitions of ghosts and other supernatural beings as well the functions of the two major roles: the *waki* as conjurer and the *shite* as appearing spirit. The structure of the ghost plays follows that of a shaman's journey: conjuration, encounter, and revelation by the apparition from the "other dimension." The gliding, ghostlike dance movement, the haunting atmosphere created by the music, and the guttural vocal sounds are also probably of shamanic origin.

Zen Buddhism inspired *nō* to express spiritual ideals by the simplest means, a goal achieved through emphasis on spiritual energy over actual movement—resulting in the deliberate restriction of dance vocabulary. Buddhist spirituality in general is the major source of the extraordinary inner energy required for the highest degrees of achievement by the *nō* master.

Other important influences on *nō* were the heroic *epics* of the samurai wars and the tenets of samurai ethics, which provided the subject matter and morals of many *nō* plots. The idealized elegance of the aristocratic military court around the shogun set the highest standard of taste for costumes, masks, and stage architecture and determined the literary-aesthetic principles embodied in *nō* performance.

Nō presented the first developed dramatic plots in Japanese literature, and the first "realistic" acting—as the mimetic dance was then perceived, in contrast to abstract, almost plotless dance—and this accomplishment it owes to the influence of popular taste during its formative years in the provinces, far from the capital. *Nō*'s development can therefore be said to have been influenced by all strata of Japanese society and by the synthesis of Shinto-shamanic and Buddhist-mystic approaches to the "other dimension."

Movement in Nō Dance. Extraordinary power of concentration and a kind of freedom that results from meticulous self-control are necessary to project the "spirit of *nō*." In the basic standing position *(kamae)* for *nō* dance, the torso is "in one piece," slightly bent forward, with the back forming a straight line; the head is held erect with the chin pulled back; the arms are curved downward and slightly toward the front of the body, with the elbows lifted and the hands kept at the sides; the knees are slightly bent, and the feet are parallel. This position, enhanced by the long, wide sleeves of the costume, furthers the appearance of a powerful flow of energy. A gathering of energy is required to unify body and spirit in the control of the "center point" in the lower abdomen, which roughly corresponds to the center of weight of the human body. The concentration of energy in this spot reinforces the pull of gravity and gives the dancer an appearance of more substance and weight. To acquire this awareness of gravity and feeling of weight, the dancer is taught to lower his hips without much bending of the knees and to maintain a counterbalance of energy forward and away from gravity's pull. To project energy, the dancer imagines lines of force emanating from the center of his body in all directions. Contrary to the expectation that this effort would require a high level of tension, the dancer is taught to be relaxed, breathing calmly and evenly and avoiding any excitement or rigidity of the body.

As basic as the standing position is the movement of walking *(hakobi)*, which pervades the overall performance, tying the various dance patterns together. From the hips up, the dancer's body keeps the standing position unchanged, and the dancer moves through space like a statue gliding on air. Among the energy lines emanating from the center of the dancer's body, the forward direction is usually the strongest—the dancer moves as if drawn by this force. As he turns, the body changes direction "in one piece," rotating on the feet and redirecting the sagittal focus of the energy line that pulls him. He glides on his heels, which continuously touch the polished wooden

NŌ. Komparu Yasuaki as the deity Sumiyoshi Myōjin promising peace and prosperity, in the final dance of *Takasago*, a *nō* drama by Zeami. (Photograph by Morita Toshirō; used by permission; courtesy of Stephen Comee.)

floor, while the toes, curving slightly backward, are rhythmically lifted, after which the whole foot rests for a moment on the floor.

Nō's limited number of dance patterns *(kata)* were formed through a process of stylization and simplification. This process reached the point that the original imitative or indicative meanings of various movements were lost, giving way to abstract, pure dance. Although some *kata,* such as the *shiori* (imitation of weeping), still preserve their primitive functions and are used to illustrate the text, others are now generic patterns applied to various occasions and often interwoven with other *kata* solely for their beauty. In *nō,* there is no complex body language, as in classical Indian dance. With rare exceptions, the *kata* are not complicated and do not require extraordinary virtuoso skills for their execution.

Nō Dramaturgy. The word *nō* is written with a Chinese ideogram indicating ability or talent, thus signifying the polished art of a skilled performer. Central to the understanding of *nō* performance are a number of aesthetic concepts—*monomane, yūgen, hana, kokoro*—formulated by Zeami, the greatest playwright, choreographer, dancer, and theoretician of the art. [*See* Zeami.]

Monomane (roughly, "mimesis") involves the actor's effort to imitate his object realistically. The identification at which the *nō* actor aims is not with a specific character but rather with the character's interior essence *(hon-i),* that is, with the essential traits of a universalized type, for example, an old man, a graceful lady, or a warrior. Perfect imitation leads to nonimitation, that is, to an identification oblivious of the original effort to imitate. There are limitations on the objects that should be imitated, because anything that can break the spell of elegant beauty is to be avoided.

Yūgen is a concept with a long history of variations in meaning. Originally, in China, it referred to hidden meanings beneath the surface texts of the Buddhist sutras. It later came to be applied to the criticism of poetry and, eventually, by Zeami, to performance, as the supreme criterion of beauty. In his earliest writings, Zeami used *yūgen* as an equivalent for grace and elegance; he later deepened its meaning to include the hidden power of interior, essential beauty, adding in his old age a touch of cosmic truth and the sad realization of human fate.

Hana (the "flower") indicates the effect of a successful performance. The "flower" is the main goal of a performer, because its presence determines audience success. The "temporary flower" *(jibun no hana)* results from the natural, though passing, fascination of youthful charm. The "true flower" *(makoto no hana)* is the real aim of *nō* training and results only from long years of rigorous dedication to the art. Two conditions are required for the true flower's appearance: first, the actor's capacity to bewitch the audience, moving it deeply and fascinating it;

NŌ. Performers from the Kanze school of *nō* in *Daihannya* (The Sutra of Great Wisdom), a drama that was revived in 1983, after four hundred years of obsolescence. This photograph was taken during a 1993 performance in the forecourt of the Temple of Dendur, Metropolitan Museum of Art, New York. (Photograph © 1993 by Jack Vartoogian; used by permission.)

second, his capacity to surprise the audience with novelty and originality, that is, to be perceived as fresh and unique even when repeating familiar patterns. The great performer always performs as if for the first time. In different contexts, Zeami proposed that the "seed" of the "flower" lies in technique and *yūgen*.

Kokoro (the "heart" or "mind") is a multilevel concept rooted in Buddhist speculation about the Buddha-nature of all things. *Kokoro* indicates both the foundation of the *nō* art and the ultimate source of energy for the actor's impact on the audience. Zeami distinguished among *kokoro's* various levels of meaning: first, at the origin of emotions and feelings, *kokoro* gives birth to *yūgen;* second, *kokoro* is the source of the self-conscious, judging mind, which is aware of good and bad in performance; third, *kokoro* is the source of unconscious, spontaneous performance, when the art becomes *mushin,* a "nothingness-heart", and all division is overcome in the unity of the source. At this level, the performance becomes sublime *(myō),* mysterious, indescribable—that is, it reaches the highest level of *hana.* The fourth level includes all the other levels and is rooted in the true essence of all things: the all-encompassing, unchanging Buddha-nature. The various facets of *kokoro* appear and work in the artist at different stages of his artistic development: emotional, rational, and prerational (intuitive, spontaneous, and sublime), but they all point to one supreme source of interior energy. *Kokoro* conceals the secret of secrets, which takes a lifetime of dedication to grow into, until the master becomes like a puppet moved by the strings of the primordial energy, being relaxed while fascinating the audience as a powerful manifestation of the mysterious "other dimension."

Training the Performer. Professional *nō* training traditionally occurs within a family. The art is transmitted from father to son (natural or adopted) and from "body to body"—that is, the master gives concrete demonstrations to the student, who rehearses under his continuous surveillance. Zeami related the phases of a *nō* performer's training to the various stages he passes through as he matures, and Zeami's scheme reveals a deep pedagogical wisdom. The teacher must first win the child's heart, inculcating a love of *nō* at a tender age; must encourage the adolescent during the crises of frustration and the time of voice change; and must guide the young adult, helping him to avoid the dangers of complacency and self-indulgence that might result from first successes. Zeami recommended realistic evaluation of any ephemeral success at this stage, when the actor is in his twenties; he insisted on serious commitment to continuous, hard, humble exercise. Total dedication to *nō* should bear the fruit of highest achievement when the performer is in his early thirties. As he continues to age, the true genius compensates for the loss of exterior glamour with an increasing closeness to the essential.

NŌ. In this scene from Akira Matsui's solo version of the *nō* play *Yuya,* Matsui appears as Yuya, reading a letter from his sick mother. This photograph was taken during a 1993 performance at Franklin and Marshall College, Lancaster, Pennsylvania. (Photograph by John Herr; used by permission; courtesy of Jonah Salz.)

The process of growth manifests itself at different ranks of achievement in a variety of performance styles, described by Zeami in his *Kyū-i* (The Nine Levels). The child's playful beginning embodies the style of shallowness and loveliness. A novice, after some disciplined training, advances to a style of versatility and exactness. Only after the craft is thoroughly mastered can a further, decisive step be made to the style of the "flower of truth." This stage is attainable through a combination of natural talent and much labor. The next three ranks belong, however, only to the great master and to different degrees reveal the performer's connection with the ultimate source of energy. In the language of Zeami, such *kokoro* performances communicate purity like snow in the flower of stillness, depth like the invisible roots of high mountains in the style of supreme profundity, and the transparency of indescribable, numinous mystery in the sublime style of the flower of the miraculous.

[*For related discussions, see* Asian Dance Traditions, *overview article;* Costume in Asian Traditions; Japan, *overview article; and* Mask and Makeup, *article on* Asian Traditions. *See also the entries on the five schools of* nō: *Hōshō, Kanze, Kita, Kongō, and Konparu.*]

BIBLIOGRAPHY

Bethe, Monica and Brazell, Karen. *Dance in the Nō Theatre.* 3 vols. Ithaca, N.Y., 1982.

Hare, Thomas B. *Zeami's Style: The Noh Plays of Zeami Motokiyo.* Stanford, Calif., 1986.

Keene, Donald. *Nō: The Classical Theatre of Japan.* New York, 1966.

Komparu, Kunio. *The Noh Theatre: Principles and Perspectives.* New York and Tokyo, 1983.

Ortolani, Benito. *The Japanese Theatre: From Shamanistic Ritual to Contemporary Pluralism.* Rev. ed. Princeton, 1995.

Rimer, Thomas and Yamazaki, Masakazu, trs. *On the Art of the Nō Drama: The Major Treatises of Zeami.* Princeton, 1984.

Smethurst, Mae J. *The Artistry of Aeschylus and Zeami: A Comparative Study of Greek Tragedy and Nō.* Princeton, 1989.

Thornhill, Arthur H. *Six Circles, One Dewdrop: The Religio-Aesthetic World of Komparu Zenchiku.* Princeton, 1993.

Tyler, Royall, tr.. *Japanese Nō Dramas.* London, 1992.

Zobel, Günther. *Nō-Theater: Szene und Dramaturgie, volks- und völkerkundliche Hintergründe.* Tokyo, 1987.

BENITO ORTOLANI

NOBILISSIMA VISIONE. Ballet in one act, five scenes. Choreography: Léonide Massine. Music: Paul Hindemith. Libretto: Paul Hindemith and Léonide Massine. Scenery and costumes: Pavel Tchelichev. First performance: 21 July 1938, Theatre Royal, Drury Lane, London, Ballet Russe de Monte Carlo. Principals: Léonide Massine (Francesco Bernadone), Simon Semenoff (Pietro Bernadone), Frederic Franklin (The Knight), Vladimir Dokoudovsky (The Poor Man), Nini Theilade (Poverty), Jeannette Lauret (Obedience), Lubov Rostova (Chastity).

Nobilissima Visione, called *Saint Francis* after its New York premiere, was one of the best received of Léonide Massine's religious ballets. It represented a choreographic transition for Massine, in that many critics felt this endeavor was more in the modern dance idiom.

The idea for *Nobilissima Visione* was presented by Paul Hindemith, who collaborated with Massine on the libretto. *Nobilissima Visione* is a dramatization through dance of the life of Saint Francis of Assisi. The narrative begins in a house, from which Francis is lured away by dreams of military adventures evoked by a visiting Knight. In the second scene, Francis joins the Knight and his soldiers and is soon disillusioned by their unscrupulous behavior. At this point Francis meets the personifications of Poverty, Chastity, and Obedience. On returning home, he is appalled by his father's treatment of some beggars, so he leaves for the last time. In another change of scene, Francis has retreated to the country, where he tames a wild wolf. He meets with the vision of Poverty and ritualistically declares their union. The final scene is a gathering of the faithful (monks and nuns) to celebrate the marriage of Francis and Poverty.

The choreography resembled danced mime, and the dancers were not given steps of virtuosic magnitude. Bravura technique was not the purpose of the ballet for Massine; rather, choreographic emphasis was placed on dramatic impact.

The ballet opened with the dancers moving in archaic poses, creating a sense of the period. Massine incorporated Russian folk steps into the choreography, appropriately modified to lend continuity to the movement patterns. Intricate groupings of the dancers evoked religious symbolism, such as the use of three groups signifying the Holy Trinity. Dances by solo performers and larger groups were all reverently created and portrayed.

Arm movements were very important to the choreography. For example, Massine had the dancer's hands in prayer position held high above their heads. Some critics speculated that this reflected the Gothic arches in architecture. The costumes by Pavel Tchelichev allowed the dancers the freedom necessary for this type of arm movement.

Ecclesiastically oriented shapes and formations were used throughout the ballet, and particularly in the final scene, when the entire group was on stage with Saint Francis like the gathering of a flock. The group faced the audience and moved their arms in unison, forming crosses and praying with dynamic impetus, making the theater a universal church.

Massine was praised by clergy and press alike for his dramatic and moving performance as Saint Francis.

[*See also the entry on Massine.*]

BIBLIOGRAPHY

Beaumont, Cyril W. *Supplement to Complete Book of Ballets.* London, 1942.

Fusillo, Lisa A. "Léonide Massine: Choreographic Genius with a Collaborative Spirit." Ph.D. diss., Texas Woman's University, 1982.

Lawrence, Robert. *The Victor Book of Ballets and Ballet Music.* New York, 1950.

LISA A. FUSILLO

NOBLET, LISE (born 24 November 1801 in Paris, died September 1852 in Paris), French ballet dancer. Having been a student at the Académie Royale de Danse, Lise Noblet joined the Paris Opera Ballet in 1816. Soon attaining soloist rank, she danced as a guest artist at the King's Theatre in London from 1821 to 1824. She became a principal dancer at the Paris Opera in 1824, upon the retirement of reigning ballerina Émilie Bigottini, and she remained with the company until 1841. The historian Ivor Guest has noted that

> her perfect figure and the vivacious sparkle in her eyes gave the illusion of greater beauty than she actually possessed; her style was marked by a voluptuous quality in her movements, great lightness and elegance in her poses. (Guest, 1980)

Noblet's ambition was to become Bigottini's successor in every respect. She had scored a success when she appeared with Bigottini in 1823 in Jean-Louis Aumer's *Aline, Reine de Golconde,* and she had a most flattering reception when she appeared in London in 1824 in Aumer's new version of Jean Dauberval's *Le Page Inconstant.* At the Opera, Noblet followed Bigottini in the leading role in Louis Milon's *Clari* in 1824 and successfully replaced Amélie Legallois in the production of *Cendrillon* (Cinderella) mounted by Monsieur Albert (François Decombe). In 1826 she appeared in *Mars et Vénus,* the sole ballet of Jean-Baptiste Blache to be mounted at the Paris Opera. The *Journal des débats* (1 June 1826) reported that "the honor of creating the role of Venus had fallen to Lise Noblet, whose piquant graces and expressive mime had earned her a considerable triumph."

Noblet again won praise for the eloquence of her miming when she created the title role of Fenella in the opera-ballet *La Muette de Portici* (1828), which had music by Daniel Auber, a libretto by Eugène Scribe, and choreography by Aumer. Another ballet by Aumer, mounted in 1829, *La Belle au Bois Dormant* (The Sleeping Beauty), gave her an opportunity to share the public's affection with Marie Taglioni, who created the role of a Naiad. She also danced a minor role in Aumer's *opéra-ballet Le Dieu et la Bayadère* (1830), with Marie Taglioni in the starring role and choreography by Filippo Taglioni. Of all her roles, Noblet will perhaps be best remembered as Effie, the Scottish girl abandoned by her sweetheart, in the original production of Filippo Taglioni's *La Sylphide,* with Marie Taglioni in the title role. With these works, Romanticism on the ballet stage reached its peak.

The otherworldliness of most Romantic heroines did not, in fact, come naturally to Noblet, for she was by nature possessed of a fiery temperament. As a performer of Spanish dances, she became a rival of Fanny Elssler, specializing in *El Jaleo de Jerez,* which she often danced with her sister. Much admired for her dramatic expressiveness, she was, throughout her career, frequently cast in *divertissements* in operas, appearing in numerous original productions, including Giacchino Rossini's *The Siege of Corinth* (1826) and *Moses* (1827), both with choreography by Pierre Gardel; Rossini's *William Tell* (1829), with choreography by Aumer; Giacomo Meyerbeer's *Robert le Diable* (1831), Auber's *Gustave* (1833), and Fromental Halévy's *La Juive* (1835), all with choreography by Filippo Taglioni; and Gaetano Donizetti's *La Favorite* (1840), with choreography by Monsieur Albert. Her last major role at the Opera was in Joseph Mazilier's *Le Diable Amoureux* in 1849.

BIBLIOGRAPHY

Ces demoiselles de l'Opéra. 2d ed. Paris, 1887.

Guest, Ivor. *The Romantic Ballet in England.* London, 1972.

Guest, Ivor. *Le ballet de l'Opéra de Paris.* Paris, 1976.

Guest, Ivor. *The Romantic Ballet in Paris.* 2d rev. ed. London, 1980.

Martel. "Some Lesser Stars of the Victorian Era" (parts 1–4). *The Dancing Times* (July 1917–October 1917).

Perugini, Mark E. "How Ballet Began." *The Dancing Times* (February 1941): 257–260.

MONIQUE BABSKY
Translated from French

NOCES, LES. Choreographic scenes in four tableaux. Choreography: Bronislava Nijinska. Music and libretto: Igor Stravinsky. Scenery and costumes: Natalia Goncharova. First performance: 13 June 1923, Théâtre de la Gaîté-Lyrique, Paris, Ballets Russes de Serge Diaghilev. Principals: Felia Doubrovska (The Bride), Nikolai Semenov (The Groom), Lubov Tchernicheva, and Leon Woizikowski.

Soon after the premiere of *Le Sacre du Printemps* (The Rite of Spring) in 1913, Igor Stravinsky began thinking about composing a cantata on the theme of a peasant wedding. In selecting folk songs from a Kiev collection, the composer was guided chiefly by considerations of the picturesque. The young Léonide Massine began the choreography but soon abandoned it to work instead on *Le Soleil de Nuit* (Midnight Sun). Stravinsky did not complete the piano arrangement until late 1917 or early 1918. In 1921, Serge Diaghilev decided to produce *Les Noces* (The Wedding). The final orchestration was not completed until shortly before the premiere of the ballet. In 1922 Natalia Goncharova submitted the first costume designs, done in a lush folkloric style. Bronislava Nijinska, who was doing the choreography, rejected them. Like the composer, she did not want to put a saccharine Russian peasant wedding on the stage. She invited Goncharova to the rehearsals in Monte Carlo. The dancers' practice clothes became the model for Goncharova's white and earth-colored costumes, which resembled the everyday dress of the Russian people. The bare, empty room of the set, which in the fourth scene was divided into two levels, harmonized with the style of the garments.

The premiere was a triumph for the composer, the choreographer, and the Ballets Russes. In addition to the principals cited above, Ernest Ansermet directed, while the four pianos, positioned like singers in the orchestra pit, were played by Georges Auric, Édouard Flament, Hélène Léon, and Marcelle Meyer.

Usually even masterpieces are part and parcel of their artistic environment, but Nijinska's *Les Noces* stood and still stands alone as an original work of art. Even today, *Les Noces* is disturbing and almost stunningly modern. In 1923 the composition and structure and the use of the choreographic media in *Les Noces* were mostly new and certainly unique. The ballet subgenre itself was new. Nijinska called *Les Noces* a "choreographic concerto," a work in which the story was secondary to pure choreography. The relationship between choreography and music, which Edwin Denby called "separate, but inseparable," is also prophetic.

Influences from numerous sources are obvious in the conception of *Les Noces*. The composition and structure of the ballet are reminiscent of Vaslav Nijinsky's choreography for *Le Sacre du Printemps*. Nijinska, like her brother, used the corps de ballet as a mass. All dressed alike, all dancing in unison, they are the counterpoint of the soloists, but at the same time they are also a commenting voice. In this way Nijinska succeeded in representing a ritual to which the human being has been delivered up. She was always interested in plasticity and expressiveness, and in *Les Noces* she actually acted as a sculptor. The more the corps de ballet is compressed into architectural or sculptural forms, the greater is their distance from the bridal pair, who become increasingly isolated and solitary.

The vocabulary of steps was also new. Nijinska did not ignore the repertory of folk dance steps, but she linked it with an extraordinary use of pointe dancing, through which the religious component of a wedding is emphasized. The upward-stretching lines of the young women dancing on pointe is reminiscent of representations in Russian icons and symbolizes reaching toward God.

An essential element of the choreography is the deliberate contrast of almost ecstatic dance and pure forms in which the dancers remain in architectonically structured groups that pulsate mysteriously with movement. This element of the choreography is most unambiguously used at the end of the ballet, characterized by Denby as "a cli-

LES NOCES. A Royal Ballet production with Svetlana Beriosova as the Bride and Robert Mead as the Bridegroom. (Photograph from the Dance Collection, New York Public Library for the Performing Arts.)

max of genius." Organized into a gigantic pyramid, the ensemble listens to the pealing of bells rendered by the four pianos, which ends the work.

Les Noces has been revived regularly since its premiere. In 1926 it was presented by Teatro Colón, Buenos Aires, with Ludmilla Schollar and Anatole Vilzak. In 1933 Nijinska mounted the work for Théâtre de la Danse Nijinska, with Tatiana Lipkovska and Boris Kniaseff in the leading roles. Colonel de Basil's Ballets Russes de Monte Carlo performed the ballet at the Metropolitan Opera House in 1936, with Tamara Grigorieva and Roman Jasinski. It was brought to the stage by the Royal Ballet at Covent Garden in 1966, where it was danced by Svetlana Beriosova and Robert Mead. Since then, *Les Noces* has been added to the repertories of numerous companies, among them the Balletto di Teatro La Fenice, Venice; the Stuttgart Ballet; the Paris Opera Ballet; and the Oakland Ballet in California. It was revived by the Joffrey Ballet in New York in 1989 and by the National Ballet in Amsterdam in 1991.

[*See also the entry on Nijinska.*]

BIBLIOGRAPHY

Baer, Nancy Van Norman. *Bronislava Nijinska: A Dancer's Legacy.* San Francisco, 1986.

Brown, Tom. "Documenting Bronislava Nijinska's *Les Noces.*" In *Dance Reconstructed,* edited by Barbara Palfy. New Brunswick, N.J., 1993.

Dance Research Journal 18 (Winter 1986–1987). Issue entitled "Stravinsky's *Les Noces.*"

Denby, Edwin. *Looking at the Dance.* New York, 1949.

Garafola, Lynn. *Diaghilev's Ballets Russes.* New York, 1989.

Goncharova, Natalia. "The Metamorphoses of the Ballet *Les Noces.*" *Leonardo,* no. 12 (1979): 137–143.

Haskell, Arnold L. *Some Studies in Ballet.* London, 1928.

Johnson, Robert. "Ritual and Abstraction in Nijinska's *Les Noces.*" *Dance Chronicle* 10.2 (1987): 147–169.

Nijinska, Bronislava. "Appendix D: The Creation of *Les Noces.*" In *Making a Ballet,* by Clement Crisp and Mary Clarke. New York, 1975.

Oberzaucher-Schüller, Gunhild. "Bronislava Nijinska." Ph.D. diss., University of Vienna, 1974.

Sullivan, Lawrence. "*Les Noces:* The American Premiere." *Dance Research Journal* 14.1–2 (1981–1982): 3–14.

Weinstock, Steven. "The Evolution of *Les Noces.*" *Dance Magazine* (April 1981): 70–75.

Williams, Peter. "Les Noces." *Dance and Dancers* (May 1966): 14.

GUNHILD OBERZAUCHER-SCHÜLLER
Translated from German

NOGUCHI, ISAMU (born 17 November 1904 in Los Angeles, died 30 December 1988 in New York), sculptor and set designer. Noguchi was educated in Japan until the age of thirteen. He spent two years at Columbia University before enrolling at the Leonardo da Vinci School in Greenwich Village, where he learned the basic principles and mechanics of sculpture from its director, Onorio Ruotolo. After only three months the school gave him a solo show, and he was elected to the National Sculpture Society. In 1926 he was transfixed by his first viewing of the work of Constantin Brancusi and only a year later was working in Brancusi's studio in Paris on a Guggenheim Foundation fellowship.

Noguchi's first experience with dance was in 1926 when he made papier-mâché masks for the Japanese dancer Michio Ito. In 1929, at the beginning of a lifelong friendship, he sculpted two heads of Martha Graham and often watched her in classes evolving her new approach to dance. Their first collaborations in the theater were *Frontier* (1935), *Chronicle* (1936), and *El Penitente* (1940), in which he attempted in settings to "wed the total void of theater space to form and action [so that] space became a volume to be dealt with sculpturally" (Noguchi, 1968). Noguchi has stated that it was in 1943 that his major work with Graham commenced, their partnership apparently having developed to the point that the choreographer placed nearly unlimited trust in Noguchi's inspiration:

> In our work together, it is Martha who comes to me with the idea, the theme, the myth on which the piece is to be based. There are some sections of music perhaps, but usually not. She will tell me if she has any special requirements—whether, for example, she wants a "woman's place." The form then is my projection of these ideas. (Noguchi, 1968)

In *Appalachian Spring* (1944) he used the image of Shaker furniture to eliminate all the nonessentials and arrive at an architectural essence of the stark American pioneer spirit. His set for *Herodiade* (1944) was more specifically sculptural—a chair, a mirror, a clothes rack, forms suggesting Salome's skeletal framework laid bare. Altogether Noguchi designed twenty settings for Graham, from 1935 to 1967, many of which included props and pieces of jewelry that she blended into her choreographic symbolism. Among the most successful were *Dark Meadow* (1946), *Cave of the Heart* (1946), *Errand into the Maze* (1947), *Night Journey* (1947), *Diversion of Angels* (1948), *Judith* (1950), *Voyage* (1953), *Seraphic Dialogue* (1955), *Embattled Garden* (1958), *Clytemnestra* (1958), *Acrobats of God* (1960), *Alcestis* (1960), *Phaedra* (1962), *Circe* (1963), and *Cortege of Eagles* (1967).

The effectiveness of the Noguchi designs derived in part from his belief in "the activity of sculpture—actual or illusory," that "sculpture moves," and his concern with gravity as a vital element. In Graham he found a compatible sensibility who could live among his forms as if they were her natural environment, endowing the controlled elegance and austerity of his shapes—which, like her costumes, resonated both high sophistication and primitivism—with potent dramatic symbolism.

Noguchi also created sets for Graham dancers Erick Hawkins and Yuriko; for Ruth Page's ballet *The Bells*

NOGUCHI. Martha Graham in her solo *Frontier* (1935). For his first stage collaboration with Graham, Noguchi designed a spare, elegant set evoking the vastness of landscapes in the American West. (Photograph © 1980 by Barbara Morgan; used by permisssion of the Barbara Morgan Archives, Hastings-on-Hudson, New York.)

(1944); and for George Balanchine's *Orpheus* (1948), for which he also designed costumes and properties.

[*See also* Scenic Design *and the entries on the Martha Graham works* Appalachian Spring; Clytemnestra; *and* Dark Meadow.]

BIBLIOGRAPHY

Leatherman, LeRoy. *Martha Graham*. New York, 1966.
Noguchi, Isamu. *A Sculptor's World*. New York, 1968.
Tracy, Robert. "Noguchi: Collaborating with Graham." *Ballet Review* 13 (Winter 1986): 9–17.

MALCOLM MCCORMICK

NOMURA MANSAKU II (Jirō; born 1931 in Tokyo), *kyōgen* dancer-actor of the Izumi school. The second child of Nomura Manzō VI, he made his stage debut at age three in the role of the monkey in *Utsubo-Zaru* (The Monkey-Skin Quiver). In 1950, he made his first performance of the ceremonial dance *Sanbasō* and took his father's childhood name, Mansaku. In 1953, he performed the monologue narrative *Nasu no Yoichi no Katari* (The Tale of Yoichi of Nasu) and in 1956 he performed *Tsuri-Gitsune* (Fox Trapping), thus completing the four plays required as rites of passage in *kyōgen* training.

Following in his father's footsteps, Mansaku is known for his strictly classical, precise, and powerful acting style—giving him a range of expression that brings pride, dignity, and pathos to even the most foolish of *kyōgen*'s comic characters. His intense concentration and attention to detail create a vortex of energy into which audiences are irresistably drawn. He has the ability to create the illusion of changing size, shape, and all other aspects of physical appearance and vocal effect in accordance with a given role. He is deservedly regarded as the most versatile and expressive *kyōgen* actor today.

Working with his father to introduce *kyōgen* to the rest of the world, in 1957 Mansaku made his first overseas appearances as part of a *nō* and *kyōgen* group that participated in the Paris International Theater Festival. In 1963 he was appointed visiting professor in the drama department at the University of Washington at Seattle (his father had earlier given a three-month intensive workshop there). At the end of that year, Mansaku directed his students in a *kyōgen* performance in English—the first time *kyōgen* had ever been performed in a language other than Japanese.

From 1965 through the mid-1990s Mansaku toured extensively in North America, Europe, India, China, Australia, and New Zealand. Teaching during this period included another workshop at the University of Washington; workshops at the University of Hawaii, the University of California at Los Angeles, and in San Francisco; and an exchange workshop with the Chinese Opera Company in Beijing. Notable performances included one in 1983 for First Lady Nancy Reagan at the National Nō Theater of Japan during U.S. president Ronald Reagan's visit to Tokyo. Mansaku's twenty-one overseas tours make him the most traveled *kyōgen* performer in the six-hundred-year history of the art.

Aside from his work in the classical *kyōgen* repertoire, Mansaku has shown a vigorous interest in the experimental theater form known as fusion. His first venture into the avant-garde was a 1953 performance of the Kinoshita Junji play *Yūzuru* (Evening Crane) in *kyōgen* style, followed in 1955 by the same playwright's *Hikoichi-Banishi* (The Tale of Hikoichi). Also in 1955, he performed with a modern dancer to Arnold Schoenberg's *Pierrot Lunaire.* In 1969, he began working with Tamamoto Yasue, a *shingeki* (modern, Western-style theater) actress, as a member of her choral-reading group that presented staged readings of classical Japanese literature, beginning with *Tomomori* from *Heike Monogatari* (Tales of the Heike). In 1970 he was one of the founding members of Mei-no-Kai, a group organized by *nō, kyōgen, kabuki,* and *shingeki* actors to perform classical Greek drama; their productions included Sophocles' *Oedipus the King* (1970), Aeschylus' *Agamemnon* (1971), and Euripides' *Medea* (1975).

In 1979, Mansaku played the leading role of the legendary general Yoshitsune in Kinoshita Junji's adaptation of *Heike Monogatari,* entitled *Shigosen no Matsuri* (The Fêting of the Meridian), in a lavish production that featured renowned actors from all styles of Japanese theater. Mounted at the National Kabuki Theater of Japan, the production proved so popular that it was broadcast twice on Japanese television in its full five-hour form. *Shigosen no Matsuri* subsequently made three nationwide tours of Japan and had four extended, sold-out runs in Tokyo.

More recent and highly acclaimed forays into fusion theater include Mansaku's own production of a *kyōgen* adaptation of Shakespeare's *The Merry Wives of Windsor* entitled *Hora-Zamurai* (The Braggart Samurai), written by Takahashi Yasunari, in which Mansaku played the role of Falstaff. Originally prepared for the 1991 Japan Festival in the United Kingdom, the production has been subsequently performed in Japan, Wales, England, Australia, and New Zealand.

[*See also* Kyōgen.]

BIBLIOGRAPHY

Furukawa Hisashi, et al. *The Kyogen Encyclopedia.* Vol 2 (Kyogen Jitan Jikohen). Tokyo, 1976.

Kenny, Don. *The Kyogen Book: An Anthology of Japanese Classical Comedies.* Tokyo, 1989.

Nomura Mansaku. *Living Taro Kaja* (Taro Kaja o Ikiru). Tokyo, 1984.

DON KENNY

NOMURA MANZŌ VI (Mansaku; born 1898 in Tokyo, died 1978), *kyōgen* dancer-actor of the Izumi school. The eldest son of Nomura Manzō V, he made his stage debut in 1903, at age five, in the role of the monkey in *Utsubo-Zaru* (The Monkey-Skin Quiver) and his first performance of *Tsuri-Gitsune* (Fox Trapping) in 1917, at age nineteen. In 1922, he succeeded his father as the official head of the Nomura family and the following year took the name Manzō (his father becoming Mansai).

Manzō VI was known for the precision and power of his acting style, which stressed both the humanity and the nobility of *kyōgen*'s characters—especially the servant Tarō Kaja (the "Everyman" character in *kyōgen*). He brought pure, classical *kyōgen* to life in the contemporary context, and he worked assiduously throughout his career for the spread of *kyōgen* in Japan and abroad.

He made his first overseas tour—to China and Korea—in 1922. In 1963 he held an intensive *kyōgen* workshop at the University of Washington at Seattle, followed, in 1964, by an extended tour of the United States. In 1965, he toured Germany and Italy; in 1968, North America; and in 1971 he opened a tour of the United States and Central America with a lauded performance at New York's Carnegie Hall. The international exposure he received was unprecedented for his generation.

Manzō was the first to perform *kyōgen* on radio (1925) and the first to make a commercial recording of *kyōgen* (1952). He was the recipient of almost every honor bestowed on artists in Japan: a command performance for the emperor and empress in 1917, designation (along with his family) as an Important Intangible Cultural Property, and induction into the Japan Nōgaku Society in 1957. He received the Ministry of Education Arts Award in 1958 and the third Hirose Award and the National Arts Festival Award in 1962, among many other prizes. In 1967 he was designated a National Living Treasure—the second *kyōgen* actor ever to receive this honor.

At age thirteen, Manzō began training in traditional *nō* and *kyōgen* mask carving—the only *kyōgen* actor ever to have made a name for himself in this field. His masks are renowned for their delicacy of execution and power of expression. In addition, he was a proficient haiku poet, and he wrote a number of books on the art of *kyōgen,* which together cover all aspects of *kyōgen* acting, staging, and philosophy—another unprecedented achievement. All his literary work was republished in a 1982 memorial volume, *The Complete Writings of Nomura Manzō.*

Manzō's three sons—Mannojo (who became Manzō VII in 1994), Mansaku, and Mannosuke—carry on the traditions of the Nomura family, as do their sons, grandchildren, and professional students.

[*See also* Kyōgen.]

BIBLIOGRAPHY

Furukawa Hisashi, et al. In *The Kyogen Encyclopedia. Vol. 2* (Kyogen Jiten, Jikohen). Tokyo, 1976.

Kenny, Don. *The Kyogen Book: An Anthology of Japanese Classical Comedies.* Tokyo, 1989.

Nomura Manzō VI. *The Complete Writings of Nomura Manzō* (Nomura Manzō Chosaku Shu). Tokyo, 1982.

DON KENNY

NORTH AFRICA. [*This entry focuses on the dance traditions in the nations of the Maghreb, in northwestern Africa, extending from Libya to Morocco. For discussion in a broader context, see* Middle East.]

Most of North Africa's political boundaries were drawn in the twentieth century by European nations that had colonized in the eighteenth and nineteenth centuries, during their era of empire-building. Some of the boundaries, drawn arbitrarily, are in dispute. North Africa is inhabited mainly by ethnic groups whose intermingling and coexistence have, since the seventh century CE, been fostered by a commonly held faith—Islam. The dominant religion of North Africa, including the sub-Saharan savanna, was brought by newly Islamized Arab cavalry who conquered and converted in the name of the Prophet Muḥammad. A pilgrimage *(ḥajj)* to Muḥammad's birthplace, Mecca, in Saudi Arabia, is expected of each Muslim who can do so, and this journey to the center of Islam has kept far-flung coreligionists in contact over the centuries.

Dance in North Africa is traditional but also reflects a history of foreign cultural presences that considerably predate Islam. To a greater or lesser extent, many of these influences were absorbed by the indigenous Berbers. The first documented foreigners to arrive in North Africa were the ancient Phoenicians of the northeastern Mediterranean coast, who had become sea-going traders. They brought their culture to island populations in the eastern Mediterranean and established their own colonies along the western coasts. Their settlements dotted the shores of North Africa and the Iberian Peninsula, even on the Atlantic. One such town, Gades (now Cádiz in Spain), figures importantly in the history of dance because, after the Carthaginian Empire (the Phoenicians of northern Africa with a capital at Carthage built in the ninth century BCE) had fallen to Rome in 146 BCE, the town's dancing girls (known in Latin as *gaditanae*) attracted the attention of the Roman writers Martial and Juvenal. They recorded their performances, and their descriptions reveal the dancers to have been practitioners of a style similar to what is now called belly dance *(danse du ventre).* Many of the dances of North Africa fall into this category. Graphic

NORTH AFRICA. A nineteenth-century photograph of a group of itinerant Ouled Naïl dancers and musicians. A confederation of tribes in Algeria, the Ouled Naïl occupy a large area of the country's mountainous desert region. Traditionally, unmarried women were expected to earn their dowries through dancing and the associated art of prostitution. Under French colonial rule, the dance arts of the Ouled Naïl flourished, thanks to the steady patronage of French military personnel. (Photograph from the collection of Mardi Rollow.)

NORTH AFRICA. *(left)* The cane is a ubiquitous prop for dances in Libya, Egypt, and the Sudan. This mid-nineteenth-century print depicts professional entertainers at Darfur. *(right)* A depiction of *dalloukah,* one of several dance genres performed at weddings in towns of the eastern Sahara. (Both prints reproduced from *Les moeurs et costumes de tous les peuples: Afrique,* edited by Casimir Henricy, under the direction of Frédéric Lacroix, Paris, 1847; collection of Mardi Rollow.)

evidence first appeared in ancient Egypt, where an Eighteenth Dynasty painting shows several female musicians and dancers performing at a feast in an atmosphere suggestive of a modern cabaret.

The widespread distribution of this kind of dancing is further evidenced by a second-century CE Roman tomb built near Ariccia, in northern Italy. It is decorated with a frieze in high relief, depicting black musicians and dancers, the latter in the unmistakable postures of this Afro-Oriental style. The Roman poet Horace (65–8 BCE) had earlier described a similar style of Ionian dancing; this seems to confirm that, in antiquity, dancing expressed through movement of the torso was common throughout the circum-Mediterranean world. Thus it becomes difficult to determine how much of North Africa's dance is a legacy shared with the rest of the Mediterranean region, and how much is attributable to more recent stylistic accretions, and how much is unique.

Berbers. The most widespread inhabitants of North Africa, the Berbers, also constitute its original population and the demographic majority. Although Arabic is today the dominant language in North Africa, large numbers of Berbers still speak one of the traditional main Berber dialects. The nomadic Tuareg (Berbers of the western and central Sahara) speak their ancient dialect and even use their original Numidian (now eastern Algeria) alphabet.

Berber musical idioms bear little resemblance to the Arabic modes that dominate their urban music. In addition, both the modal structure and the manner of singing differ greatly for the two main Berber divisions. The first are those who live in the fortified towns of the Atlas Mountains; they sing their choral dance songs in a manner that more closely resembles rural Spanish unison singing or Andaluz (classical music of the western Arabs) singing than it does modern Arabic singing. It bears little or no resemblance to the art music of the nomadic Berbers—the Tuareg and other Saharan tribes. With a modal structure and highly ornamented vocal style (like the one that accompanies the *guedra* and similar dances of the northwestern Sahara), it resembles no neighboring culture.

Western Sahara. In the western Sahara, professional musicians are called *griots* and occupy a lowly social position. In Mauritania, *griots* are a repository for the music of some desert peoples, including the Tuareg, Tekna, Berabish, and others. This music, like the dancing of Tuareg men, prevails across thousands of miles—a dramatic dispersion that allows western Saharan dances—whether in Libya, Algeria, Niger, Chad, Mali, or Mauritania—to be included in North African national folklore.

The people of Senegal (in West Africa) are black and Senegalese *griots* were often attached to the court of a North African ruler. They now perform a singularly eclectic repertory, in the midst of which emerge striking examples of medieval Hispano-Arabic music. Their music is a reminder that to group them with the black cultures of equatorial and southern Africa is to overlook a thousand years of Islam and their northward acculturation. En-

NORTH AFRICA. *(above)* Women of the Tunisian National Folklore Troupe balance jugs on their heads in a performance of "Raqṣ al-Juzur," a dance from the islands of Djerba and Kerkennah off the eastern coast of Tunisia that celebrates the making of pottery, the chief industry of the region. This dance is also a popular amateur dance performed at weddings and social gatherings. *(below)* A woman performing a characteristic Tunisian solo dance. (Photographs © by Folklore Film, Stockholm; courtesy of Ibrahim Farrah, *Arabesque Magazine,* New York.)

claves of this Senegalese population are also well distributed in some North African countries bordering the Mediterranean. Many belong to religious brotherhoods famed for their dancing.

Al-Andaluz. The relationship between Andalusian dance and that of North Africa was noted by Edward Lane in 1835 in his author's preface on the *ghawāzī,* the public dancing girls in Egypt. Speculating on the similarity between the Spanish fandango and the dancing of the *ghawāzī,* Lane cited descriptions of the ancient Roman *gaditanae* to refute the proposition that Arabs brought voluptuous dancing into Spain.

In the seventh century CE, when the bearers of Islam swept away the remains of Christianity in North Africa, bringing the Moors (Muslim North Africans) to the Iberian Peninsula in 711 CE, the great period of Arab civilization in the West began. Until the final reconquest of the peninsula by Spain in 1492, most of the peninsula was a cultural continuum of North Africa; thus, the gradual passage of Jenkanes (Gypsies) into Spain's Andalusia went unnoticed in the Christian north, where the reconquest began. Not until the middle of the fifteenth century, when Gypsies from France arrived in Barcelona, did any mention of them appear in Spanish annals.

The Gypsies, wanderers from India, had been migrating for a long time, going to Asia, Europe, the Middle East, and thence to North Africa; these Jenkanes appeared as far south as Agades in present-day Niger. A uniquely Indian drum, unusual in Africa, even today, accompanies the dancing women of Zouar in Chad.

Because Gypsies often assimilate the music and dance of the countries they inhabit, usually bringing a heightened emotional and sensual character to their performance, it is difficult to establish how much they have contributed to the fusion of the Punic (Phoenician), Berber, and Arab traditions danced today by Spanish Gypsy women and the Moroccan female entertainers called *shikhat.*

After the expulsion of the Moors from Spain at the end of the fifteenth century, the reemergence of anything Moorish was forbidden by both church and crown. As the Spanish Inquisition began—to reestablish a zealous form of Roman Catholicism—the *zarabanda* (a saraband) was denounced by church authorities for its erotic dance movements and for the lewd texts of its accompanying songs. [*See* Christianity and Dance.]

The "Zambra Mora"—perhaps the only dance of Andalusia that frankly exhibits its Moorish origins, although considered a dance in its own right today—was originally a festival named after the *zimr,* the folk oboe that still accompanies similar festivities in North Africa. It is danced with small brass cymbals on each hand—an eastern practice uncommon to North Africa west of Egypt, except among the boy dancers of a Shleuh tribe.

While the Moorish choral dances with their stamping and leaps are unquestionably indigenous to North Africa, highly complicated and syncopated footwork appear only in the professional dancing of the *shikhat* and *gitanas*. Characteristics shared by these dances are also found in the dances of isolated villages of the Rif (the extreme northern region of Morocco), where young women of the villages, not professional entertainers, perform with swinging hips and high kicks in an acrobatic style.

Ottoman Rule. As Moorish power in Spain was gradually reduced, until only the kingdom of Granada remained under Arab rule, a new Islamic power—Ottoman Turkey—was rising in the east. After the fall of Granada in 1492 and the subsequent Spanish military adventures in North Africa, it was to the Muslim Turks that the Algerians applied for help, thus bringing the Ottoman presence into North Africa.

Even before the taking of Constantinople in 1453, the Turks had already conquered the remains of the eastern (Byzantine) Roman Empire in Anatolia and had gradually absorbed much of its culture, including the Ionian dance eventually incorporated into the voluptuous Turkish style. In the Ottoman provinces of North Africa, music, dance, and costume soon acquired a distinctive Turkish flavor. Eastern taste also established a dance tradition for transvestite boys—one that still lingers in Morocco; their female costume is appropriate because the voluptuous movements of their dancing are those of female dancing. Transvestite performances were still seen in the early 1980s in the Djemaa el-Fna, the great square of Marrakesh, along with acrobats, snake charmers, and other public entertainers.

Balancing feats are often performed by men in North Africa while dancing. Brass trays filled with glasses are piled tier upon tier and balanced on the dancer's head as he makes sinuous movements that are not at all feminine. Similar pelvic movements are included in a Tunisian musicians' dance, but the *fustanella* worn by these players is a nineteenth-century military garment, not a female costume. The dancing boys of Jebala and the Shleuh youths who dance in some of the restaurants in Morocco's larger modern cities wear male clothing, even though they dance in a female style.

Music, Paraphernalia, and Costume. Dance cannot always be defined in terms of movement alone. Music, musical instruments, and costumes sometimes indicate patterns of cultural distribution, are integral to the style of dance, and function as dance paraphernalia. Dances are commonly named for the music to which they were performed. Particularly among the Berbers, a dance can

NORTH AFRICA. Members of the Aman folkloric company performing a staged version of a Tuareg dance from the central Sahara. (Photograph by S. Pleitez; from the collection of Mardi Rollow.)

be performed only to its own special song; in other instances, lyrical improvisation on the part of the musicians is expected.

Most North African and Middle Eastern dance performances feature the shrill celebratory ululation called *zaghareet* in Arabic, *tillilau* by many Berbers, and *irrintzi* in northern Spain. Elements external to movement or music are sometimes definitive in categorizing a dance: for example, a sword dance, if performed using a stick instead of a sword, will be called a stick dance.

Special dance costumes, other than women's clothing, are rare in North Africa. An exception is found at Ouargla, an oasis in north-central Sahara. At Muslim festivals such as the ʿĪd al-Kabīr and ʿĀshūrāʾ, the boys used to take part in rude masques, dressing up as various animals and as Europeans, both male and female; their tight-fitting clothes made them figures of fun. Most North African male dances are martial, however, and are often performed with weapons.

In the Berber-speaking regions of Morocco, men and women participate in a great many choral dances. Among the Berbers choral dancing with mixed sexes is traditional, whereas among the Arab population separation of the sexes is enjoined, unless the dancing takes place within a family unit or where female dancers are considered prostitutes. Dancing is separated into categories—by ethnic group, religion, class, and occupation.

Exorcistic dancing also appears widely throughout North Africa. This includes dancing associated with religious and healing rituals such as the *zār* in Egypt and the dances of the Hamadsha of Morocco. [*See* Zār.]

Contemporary Dance. The national folk troupe, a phenomenon that arose in North Africa shortly after 1945, represents an attempt to raise the status of indigenous dance forms. Nationalistic pride sometimes transcends artistic judgment, and the programs presented often consist of naively choreographed folk dances, interspersed with storytelling episodes about, rather than from, the culture. At another extreme, sophisticated choreographies are performed by imaginatively costumed dancers whose ballet training obscures the unique character of regional dance styles. In the most successful and polished of these companies, the dances and costumes are the least authentic. The intent has been to produce a conventional performance for export to showcase national pride rather than genuine native dances. The pervasive Western influence that has affected many aspects of North African life has altered attitudes toward exhibition dancing insofar as the dancers belong to a state-sponsored organization that can be useful for cultural and political diplomacy.

In Libya, where the chief folkloric dance is the *kaska*, a stick dance done by men only, much of the repertory necessary to fill a two-hour program consists of creative variations on a limited number of themes. Many dances are unsuitable for stage presentation, such as a traditional dance of Fezzan, in southwestern Libya, in which women stand in a circle around a group of male drummers. Each woman advances alone from the circle and invites one of the drummers to dance with her. She then retreats, falls stiffly backward, and is caught by the other dancers before she touches the ground. They then toss her in the air and she lands upright on her feet. A choreographer would have trouble sustaining this repetitious proceeding for a modern audience without adding stagecraft. In contrast, the courtesans' dances of Sokna and Mourzouk are *danse du ventre* and far too intimate to succeed in a theatrical setting—nor would they advance the Islamic ideal of womanhood.

While many traditional dances are not displayed, some are arbitrarily included. Because the nomadic Tuareg have romantic appeal for the rest of upper North Africa, Libyan and almost all other North African folk troupes include a Tuareg dance—even if it is performed by dancers who are not Tuareg.

Unlike most other North African countries, Morocco has not created a national dance company. Instead, the ministries of culture and tourism rely on dancers and musicians from tribal strongholds, where music and dance are still vital. The dances at the annual folk festival at Marrakesh, for example, are performed by the local population. Whereas some performances, such as the traditional Moroccan wedding ceremony, are obviously staged, most dances are untouched, although they may be somewhat shortened for a foreign audience. The relatively simple movement patterns of some of the dances are compensated for by the authenticity, vitality, and sheer numbers of the performers. Most remarkable, perhaps, are the choreographic sophistication and outstanding performing skills of such groups as the Kelaa M'gouna.

[*For general discussion, see* Aesthetics, *article on* Islamic Dance Aesthetics; Islam and Dance; *and* Music for Dance, *article on* Arab Music. *See also* Algeria; Danse du Ventre; Egypt; Morocco; Ouled Naïl, Dances of the; *and* Tunisia.]

BIBLIOGRAPHY

Ibn Muhammad el-Waziz al-Fasi. *The History and Description of Africa* (1600). Translated by John Pory. London, 1896.

Henricy, Casimir. *Les moeurs et costumes de tous les peuples*. 2 vols. Paris, 1847.

Lane, Edward W. *An Account of the Manners and Customs of the Modern Egyptians*. 5th ed. London, 1860.

Martial. *Epigrams*. Book 5, epigram 79.

Murdock, George Peter. *Africa: Its Peoples and Their Culture History*. New York, 1959.

Wood, Leona. "Danse du Ventre: A Fresh Appraisal." *Arabesque* (January–February 1979); (March–April 1980).

Aisha Ali, Mardi Rollow, and Leona Wood

NORTHCOTE, ANNA (also known as Anna Severskaya; born 1907 in Southbourne, died 6 July 1988 in London), English dancer and teacher. Northcote, who danced under the name Anna Severskaya, is a notable example of a dancer who developed her own successful methods of teaching from study with a wide range of teachers and ballet masters and years of stage experience in worldwide touring. Her early training was with Euphan Maclaren, Margaret Craske, and Nikolai Legat before she went to Olga Preobrajenska in Paris. She made her debut at the age of twelve as the First Fairy in *A Midsummer Night's Dream* with the Ben Greet Players, later appearing in the leading role of the children's play *Bluebell in Fairyland* at the Scala Theatre in London. With the Henriette Fuller Dancers she danced in revues, music halls, and cinemas in the United Kingdom and at London's Lyceum Theatre. She toured with the Oumansky Ballet, principally in Italy (where she took classes with Cia Fornaroli), and filmed with the company at Elstree Studios. At this time she also worked with Léonide Massine in England on a film project that proved abortive.

In Brussels in 1934, with a small group led by Molly Lake, Northcote was recruited for the Levitoff-Dandré Russian Ballet for a world tour. With this company she learned a repertory of Fokine ballets from Michel Fokine himself and classics such as *Swan Lake* from Aleksandra Fedorova. In 1936 she danced with the Ballets Russes de Paris and later that year joined Colonel W. de Basil's Ballets Russes (Second Company) to tour Australia, New Zealand, and Europe.

After the outbreak of World War II, Northcote found her vocation as a teacher. She opened a studio on West Street in London in 1941, where she built an international reputation as a teacher of professional dancers. In 1969 the West Street studio was closed and she transferred to the Dance Centre on Floral Street in Covent Garden until her retirement ten years later. During these years she was also a guest teacher in Finland, Sweden (Malmö and Gothenburg), the Netherlands (Dutch National Ballet), and Paris (for the Studio Paul Goubé).

BIBLIOGRAPHY

Cowper, Anthony. "School for Theatre." *Dance and Dancers* (April 1953): 19.

Mason, Edward C. "Schools and Teachers." *Dance and Dancers* (June 1958): 30.

Wilson, George. "Off Stage." *The Dancing Times* (October 1980): 40.

ARCHIVE. Dance Collection, New York Public Library for the Performing Arts.

KATHRINE SORLEY WALKER

NORTHERN BALLET THEATRE. Britain's first regionally based, medium-scale dance company was formed as a result of the Arts Council of Great Britain's Opera and Ballet Enquiry, 1966–1969, which recommended the formation of dance companies based in certain regions of the nation. Laverne Meyer, a Canadian dancer and choreographer formerly with Western Theatre Ballet, made a feasibility study of the Northwest region, resulting in his becoming founder-director of Northern Dance Theatre, based in Manchester.

At the start, the company consisted of seven female and four male dancers, with musicians from the Royal Northern College of Music. Meyer's policy placed emphasis on new work, and the company's opening program at Manchester's University Theatre, on 28 November 1969, included premiere performances of no fewer than four works by company members, along with a revival of Andrée Howard's *Death and the Maiden.* The new works were Meyer's *Meeting Places* and *Brahms Sonata,* Clover Roope's *Predators,* and David Toguri's *Preludes.*

By the time the company moved to a larger theater at the Royal Northern College of Music in 1973, it had been enlarged to sixteen members, its technical proficiency had reached a new level, and it boasted a repertory of about thirty ballets. Some of these were revivals of works by such well-known choreographers as Frank Staff, Peter Darrell, and Walter Gore, but the majority had been created by members of the company. Among the emerging choreographers, Jonathan Thorpe showed remarkable promise. His *Quartet* (1971), set to Beethoven's String Quartet in B-flat, op. 130, was the first of several distinguished creations to music by Beethoven, Brahms, Bach, and other classical composers. The first full-length ballets were made by Meyer—*Cinderella* (1973), set to music by Robert Stewart, and *Aladdin* (1974), set to music by Ernest Tomlinson, a Manchester native. By this time, too, the company was capable of giving polished performances of classic works from the international repertory, such as Michel Fokine's *Le Carnaval* and Kurt Jooss's *The Green Table.* When Meyer resigned as director in 1975, Northern Dance Theatre was firmly established in the Manchester area.

After a period when the company was run by a committee, Robert de Warren, formerly a dancer with the Royal Ballet and director of ballet and folk dance companies in Iran, was appointed artistic director. When he took over, Northern Dance Theatre consisted of twenty-five well-trained dancers. Although de Warren realized the importance of new work, he felt there was a need for greater emphasis on the classical repertory, and, accordingly, the company was renamed Northern Ballet Theatre in 1976. The first move toward establishing a classical repertory was a production of *Coppélia,* for which Peter Clegg adapted the traditional choreography to a Lancashire setting. Alicia Markova coached the dancers in *Giselle,* as well as mounting Fokine's *Les Sylphides,* and André Prokovsky staged a version of *The Nutcracker.* Other full-

NORTHERN BALLET THEATRE. Christopher Gable as L. S. Lowry with members of the ensemble in Gillian Lynne's *A Simple Man* (1987), one of the company's most acclaimed works. (Photograph courtesy of Northern Ballet Theatre.)

length works included de Warren's *Cinderella,* to music of Johann Strauss, and Rosemary Helliwell's *Alice in Wonderland,* to music by Joseph Horovitz. Although full-length works became the mainstay of the repertory, new works for well-balanced triple bills were also sought. One of the most interesting was Geoffrey Cauley's *Miss Carter Wore Pink.* Also set to music by Horovitz, it was based on the writing and paintings of a local celebrity, Helen Bradley.

In 1987, Christopher Gable succeeded de Warren as artistic director. Northern Ballet Theatre increased to twenty-nine dancers, and Gable initiated a policy of developing talent from within the company. As a former actor and Royal Ballet principal, he introduced a more theatrical emphasis. The repertory began to focus on narrative ballets such as Gable's production of *The Amazing Adventures of Don Quixote* (1989), choreographed by Massimo Moricone to the traditional score by Léon Minkus but following a new and original scenario. The company continued to reflect its northern roots, however, in such works as Gillian Lynne's *A Simple Man* (1987), set to music by Carl Davis. One of the company's most popular productions, Lynne's ballet brought to life many of the characters depicted in paintings by L. S. Lowry. With a cast featuring Gable and Moira Shearer as Lowry and his mother, this ballet enjoyed great success and, some claim, helped to save the company from extinction.

In 1989, a funding crisis threatened Northern Ballet Theatre's future. A successful survival campaign resulted in the restoration of Arts Council support and in a newfound awareness of the company's important contribution on both a regional and a national scale. The positive aftermath of the campaign led to the company's relocation to Halifax, some twenty miles northeast of Manchester, in 1991. With an increased local authority grant (from five West Yorkshire councils), private sponsorship from firms with the region, and better working conditions, Northern Ballet Theatre acquired a greater degree of stability and support than ever before.

Thanks to the artistic policies introduced by Gable, emphasizing drama and narrative, the company continued to win the approval of local audiences and sponsorship from local firms. The repertory included new productions of *Giselle* (1990), staged by Gable; *Romeo and Juliet* (1991), choreographed by Moricone; and *Swan Lake* (1992), mounted by Gable. For the 1993/94 season, Gable added two new, full-length works: *A Christmas Carol,* choreographed by Moricone to a commissioned score by Carl Davis, and Gable's own *Cinderella,* also set to a specially commissioned score, by Philip Freeny. The former, which features singing as well as dancing, is in effect a kind of Dickensian musical. In addition to these works, one-act, plotless ballets such as Graham Lustig's *D'Ensemble* and Derek Williams's *Extenzion* were acquired to make up a triple bill with a revival of Lynne's *A Simple Man.*

By 1995, Northern Ballet Theatre had grown to a company of thirty-five dancers. Among the principals were Graciella Kaplan, Jeremy Kerridge, Peter Parker, Jayne Regan, Lorena Vidal, William Walker, and Victoria West. A notable addition to the repertory in 1995 was Gable's full-length production of *Dracula,* designed to capitalize on the enduring popular appeal of Gothic romances about vampires and their victims. With this and other story ballets, the company gives regular performances to enthusiastic audiences in Manchester and the surrounding region.

BIBLIOGRAPHY

Parry, Jann. "United Kingdom: Subsidized Companies." In *World Ballet and Dance, 1993–1994,* edited by Bent Schønberg, pp. 137–144. Oxford and New York, 1994.

Percival, John. "Rehabilitating Don Quixote." *Dance and Dancers* (July 1989).

"The Road to Manchester." *Dance and Dancers* (September 1987).

Southern, R., comp. *Northern Ballet Theatre, 1969–1979.* Manchester, 1979. Includes lists of works in the repertory and members of the company to 1979.

PETER WILLIAMS and ANGELA KANE

NORWAY. [*To survey the dance traditions of Norway, this entry comprises six articles:*

Folk, Traditional, and Social Dance
Theatrical Dance before 1919
Theatrical Dance, 1920–1958

Theatrical Dance since 1958
Classical Dance Education
Dance Research and Publication

The first article presents traditional and social dances; the next three articles trace the history of theatrical dance; and the concluding articles explore education, scholarship, and research.]

Folk, Traditional, and Social Dance

In contemporary Norway there is no consensus on the definition of the term *folk dance.* Depending on a speaker's background, experience, attitude, and identity the term is used to cover a narrow or wide range of types, genres, local traditions, and styles. Because the term *folk,* ever since the Romantic movement, has given legitimacy and prestige to certain expressive forms and their performers, the application of the term also tends to provoke considerable debate and rivalry. Scholars and students of Norwegians culture therefore avoid the term by substituting more specific generic categories, such as *bygdedanser* (ancient, traditional rural dances), *folkevisedans* (choreographed revival chain and song dances), and *gammeldans* (nineteenth-century popular dances).

The Romantic nationalist movement of the early nineteenth century—with its emphasis on ancient items of folk culture serving as symbolic vehicles for the history and unity of the nation—clearly reinforced cultural self-assurance and pride. It also inspired the growth of regionalism and of national preservationist movements of the rural grass-roots type, to oppose the cultural hegemony of the modern cosmopolitan elite. These are some of the most important reasons for why ancient dance forms and a multitude of local stylistic variants still constitute a living tradition, to exist side by side with so-called popular folk dances.

Solo and Couple Dances. In Norway, couple dances have predominated since the late 1800s in a great variety of forms and genres. Traditional solo dancing, however, is now fairly uncommon and only exists as a living tradition in a few areas.

Bygdedanser. The *bygdedans* genre consists of three subcategories. The first comprises men's solo dances known as *halling* or *laus* (*laus* means "unbounded", "without a partner"). Sachs (1937) describes these as "bravura and skill dances on the borderline between dance and sport." Performed with deep bends, jumps, leaps, and revolutions in a variety of local and individual styles, they are danced to fiddle music in triple (3/8 or 6/8) or duple (2/8 or 2/4) meter in a relatively fast tempo and certain characteristic patterns of bowing.

The second subcategory, couple dances called *gangar* and *rull,* have a fairly moderate tempo and are danced to music that, apart from its tempo, is similar to that of the *halling.* The third, couple dances called *springar, springdans, rundom,* or *pols,* vary among localities but are usually danced to music in 3/4 or 9/16 meter. Two regional varieties can be identified: the style of the west and southwest, danced with light, rapid steps in uneven (3/16) beats; and the style of the central region, the east, and the northeast, danced with assymmetric (approximately 5:7:6) three-beat steps modified by a recurrent and stable rubato.

The *gangar* and *springar* share a number of characteristic features. The essence of both types is the integration of patterns of locomotion and patterns of cooperative interchange between partners. Movement and postures are adapted to the natural floating gait. Expressive gestures are mostly extensions or exaggerations of the dance movement. Rotations of the hip, knee, and ankle joints are emphasized, and the flow of stretching and bending efforts shows significant variations in local and regional styles.

Couples in these dances invariably form rings moving counterclockwise, and their movements are symbolic of

NORWAY: Folk, Traditional, and Social Dance. A man performing the *halling,* or *laus,* an athletic solo dance for men, involving deep knee bends, jumps, and turns. (Photograph by Rolf Karlberg © 1970 by the Rådet for Folkemusikk og Folkedans, Dragvoll, Norway; used by permission.)

NORWAY: Folk, Traditional, and Social Dance. Targeir Heistad and Torbjørg Åmlid Paüs performing a *gangar* from Setesdal, a region of southern Norway. The *gangar* is a couple dance of the *bygdedansar* genre, the traditional dances of small rural communities. (Photograph by Egil Bakka © 1963 by the Rådet for Folkemusikk og Folkedans, Dragvoll, Norway; used by permission.)

the relationship between the sexes. The contrast between male exhibitionism and female modesty underscores the metaphor of courtship. The men, who lead, control the inner circle, and the counterclockwise direction reflects the symbolic significance of initially leading the woman by the right hand. Nowadays the coordination between the different couples is limited to the maintenance of the ring. A patterned exchange of partners, however, used to be fairly common, and old ceremonial dances for two female partners still survive.

Couples alternate between two kinds of holds: open hand and arm holds allow partners to move somewhat independently of each other; and locked holds require them to move as one body. The idealized expression of the contrast and complementarity between the sexes is most striking. Within the limits of the structure, couples can improvise by selecting dance phrases and motifs from a shared repertory of alternatives. Similarly, male dancers can select among alternative step figures.

The preferred musical instrument for accompaniment is the *hardingfele,* the Italian-style violin. The musical form and playing style parallel the formal construction of the dance: small themes are linked by repetition, variation, and transition.

The essential features of these national dances date back to the late Middle Ages. The *gangar* and the western and southwestern variations of the *springar* demonstrate features of couple dancing that predate the well-documented dual patterns of early sixteenth-century north and central European folk dance (open figure dancing followed by a close embrace during spiral turns). While the traditional *gangar* and the *springar* of the west and southwest feature only side-by-side body contact, most variations of *springar* today reflect the influence of these "modern" features, which are particularly identified with the *pols* ("Polish") dance.

Since the nineteenth century the traditions of *bygdedanser* have been restricted to the mountain valleys and the inner fjord districts—the poorest but also the most independent and geographically mobile sectors of the rural population. Generally speaking, the *bygdedanser* are no longer integral to household or community festivities; their community functions have in fact been declining since the turn of the century. This decline is probably related to social changes and the spread of the German-Austrian folk and social dances of the eighteenth century.

Gammeldans. The waltz–polka genre, collectively known as *gammeldans* ("old dance"), consists of the fast waltz (3/4 meter); polkas (2/4) such as *hamborgar, pariser-polka, hoppvals,* and *skotsk* ("Scottish") or *polka;* the *reinlender* (6/16) from *Rheinländer* ("German") (3/16 × 2), which is next to the *vals* in popularity; and mazurkas (3/4 or 9/16) such as *polka-masurka, springpolka* or *hambo,* and *masurka* or *springdans*.

Some of the variations in these Norwegian dance terms refer to differences in kind, while others arise from local usage. Apart from the *vals,* all the dances have a two-part symmetrical structure consisting of open holds and parallel face-to-face or side-by-side movement in the line of direction, followed by locked holds and the spiral turn. Group formations and line of direction are similar to those of *bygdedanser*.

Differences between the kinds of dances lie mainly in

NORWAY: Folk, Traditional, and Social Dance. Couples in a dance hall performing *vals,* a popular type of *gammeldans* ("old dance"). *Gammeldans* is a Norwegian genre of dance similar to the waltz or polka. (Photograph by Egil Bakka © 1983 by the Rådet for Folkemusikk og Folkedans, Dragvoll, Norway; used by permission.)

steps, rhythm, and tempo. Thus the *reinlender,* with its characteristic step-dip or step-hop, has a triple meter, whereas the polka has a duple meter. There are, however, also significant rhythmic differences within categories.

The *gammeldans* genre, probably of Polish and south Germanic origin, reached Norway during the early nineteenth century as fashionable dances. During the second half of the century the dance spread from the cities and coastal towns to the rural districts, where it replaced and mingled with older dances. The genre differs from the *bygdedanser* in several ways. It is simpler in rhythm and formal structure, following the dual pattern; it requires synchronized coordination of couples within the group; and it emphasizes similarity and unison of the sexes rather than dichotomy and complementarity.

In the nineteenth and twentieth centuries, when immigration to cities and new industrial centers caused rapid mingling of people from different regions, a need arose for a common and fairly standardized dance language. The dialect-specific national dances did not suffice. These social factors, together with increasing social mobility and international exchange, help to explain the rapid diffusion of the waltz–polka genre and of later imported forms such as tango, fox trot, slow fox, and swing–rock. These latter forms are sometimes quite logically classified as *gammeldans*.

Change and Continuity. Despite the changes, important continuities persist. First, dances within the old genres have been gradually modified over the centuries. In particular, the *pols* and *springdans* of the east and northeast are now similar in terms of their simplicity, standardization, and formal dualism. Second, a definite continuity of tradition is evident in the style of body usage. Finally, old and new forms have no doubt been blended; for example, the *masurka* or *springdans* of the eastern lowlands seems to be a blend of the *polka-masurka* and the older *springdans* of the area. Thus the fast clockwise spiral turns of the *masurka* are similar to those of the *springarpols.* Even more striking is the so-called *rull* of western Norway, which appears to be a fusion between the formal structure of the polka and the rhythm of the *gangar.*

The *bygdedans* and *gammeldans* genres, however, remain distinct. Apart from their differing symbolic implications, this distinction is based on musical contrasts. According to the principles of functional harmony (the tonic-dominant cycle), the music associated with the waltz–polka genre is, in comparison to the modal tonalities of the *springar* and *gangar* tunes, generally easy on modern ears. It is therefore well adapted to harmonic arrangements for ensembles, typically accordion, fiddle, guitar, and bass.

Figure Dances. Collectively named *turdanser* (from the French *tour,* "turn"), figure dances are less common than couple dances. A group of contradances, mostly English,

NORWAY: Folk, Traditional, and Social Dance. Children performing the triple-meter *reinlender,* a type of *gammeldans.* (Photograph by Egil Bakka © 1982 by the Rådet for Folkemusikk og Folkedans, Dragvoll, Norway; used by permission.)

was introduced to Norway during the second half of the nineteenth century by wealthy city dwellers and subsequently spread into the community of prosperous farmers in the lowlands. The *feier* (2/4), with fast step-hop movements, and the *engelskdans* (3/4), with waltz steps and rhythm, represent two distinct genres within the category. The repertory also includes dances known as *figaro* and *fandango.* French *contredanses* such as the *francese* and the quadrille or Lancers arrived much later but were common in the cities around 1850. Apart from the *feier,* the *contredanses,* with their emphasis on the courtly manners associated with the private parties of wealthy society, never became very popular among the general population.

In contrast, the *ril* ("reel") seems to represent a widespread folk genre, especially in the coastal southeast. Circle reels are most common, but rows and figure-eights are also known. The genre is probably of Scottish origin, but it appears to have blended with traditional Norwegian couple dances, especially those for two female partners.

Song Dances. Norway has no indigenous tradition of song dancing, but there exists a repertory of choreographed revival dances based on Norwegian folk songs and Faeroese chain dancing. The genre is nevertheless categorized by most people as Norwegian folk dance under the label *folkevisedans* (referring to remnants of medieval epic song, analogous to Faeroese ballads). The existence of these remnants, together with the close historical connections between Norway and the Faeroe Islands, gives legitimacy to the song-dance movement particularly identified with the names of Hulda Gorborg and Klara Semb. The origins of this movement are rooted in the desire of the puritan and nationalist liberal youth movement of Norway for a symbolic and coherent tradition. [*See* Denmark, *article on* Dance in the Faeroe Islands.]

Mimic Play and Song. The Sword Dance, the Bear Dance, and various courtship games are examples of a type of dancing that is almost extinct. Other relicts of this once rich tradition are children's street-corner and schoolyard pantomimic songs and certain forms of dancing and singing around the Christmas tree *(ringmoro, joleleik)*. Generally speaking, dances of this category emphasize play and rhyming rather than movement and therefore feature very simple steps and rhythms.

Folk Dance in Modern Context. Norwegian folk dancing of the twentieth century has been under the growing influence of voluntary organizations. The liberal youth movement adopted the *folkevisedans* both as a means to organizational ends and as a central symbol of their ideology and unity. Of special value to the organization is a large repertory of *turdanser;* some few standardized versions of *bygdedanser* also became part of the repertory. These organizations teach folk dancing, generally without much concern for authenticity or the problems of distorting tradition through formal training. Because of their large membership and organizational strength, the various associations connected with Noregs Ungdomslag (NU) until recently exercised a dominating influence on the codification, teaching, and public presentation of national traditions, including dance and costume.

In contrast, *bygdedans* has gradually come to be identified with the National Association of Fiddlers (LfS) whose members today perform at various local and national festivals. Unlike the NU, the LfS has no specific political or social ideology or purpose.

Unlike *folkevisedans* and *bygdedans,* the *gammeldans* genre represents a neutral meeting ground. Together with some popular imported social dances, it is seen at ordinary dance gatherings, including those arranged by the LfS and NU. These dances constitute the genuine popular dance repertory of Norway today. Independent of organizational efforts to preserve them, they are still common in many parts of Norway and are not identified with any particular social class or region.

NORWAY: Folk, Traditional, and Social Dance. Men and women forming concentric circles in *songdans* ("song dance"), performed as part of a Leikfest (dance celebration) at the 1977 annual national festival of the Norwegian Youth League in Gol. (Photograph by Egil Bakka © 1977 by the Rådet for Folkemusikk og Folkedans, Dragvoll, Norway; used by permission.)

BIBLIOGRAPHY

Bakka, Egil. *Danse, danse, lett ut på foten: Folkedansar og songdanser.* Oslo, 1970.

Bakka, Egil. *Norske dansetradisjonar.* Oslo, 1978.

Bakka, Egil. "Folk Dance Research in Norway." *Dance Studies* 5 (1981): 22–47.

Bakka, Egil. *Danstraditisjonar frå Vest-Agder.* Flekkefjord, Norway, 1990.

Bakka, Egil, et al. *Springar and Pols: Variation, Dialect, and Age.* Trondheim, Norway, 1995.

Beal, Daniel Sundstedt. "Two Springar Dance Traditions from Western Norway." *Ethnomusicology* 28 (1984).

Beal, Daniel Sundstedt. *Dances from Norway.* 2d ed. Minneapolis, 1988.

Blom, Jan-Petter. "Diffusjonsproblematikken og studiet av danseformer." In *Kultur og diffusjon,* edited by A. M. Klausen. Oslo, 1961.

Blom, Jan-Petter. "The Dancing Fiddle: On the Expression of Rhythm in Hardingfele Slåtter." In *Norske folkemusikk,* ser. 1, vol. 7, edited by Jan-Petter Blom et al. Oslo, 1981.

Blom, Jan-Petter. "Structure and Meaning in a Norwegian Couple Dance." *Studia Musicologica Academiae Scientiarum Hungaricae* (1991): 33.

Blom, J. P., and T. Kvifte. "On the Problem of Interferential Ambivalence in Musical Meter." Ethnomusicology (1986): 30–33.

Lange, Roderyk. *The Nature of Dance: An Anthropological Perspective.* London, 1975.

Nielsen, H. Grüner. "Dans i Norge." In *Idrott och lek, utgiven av Johan Götlind,* edited by H. Grüner Nielsen. Nordisk Kultur, vol. 24. Oslo, 1933.

Sachs, Curt. *World History of the Dance.* Translated by Bessie Schönberg. New York, 1937.

Semb, Klara. *Norske folkedansar.* 2 vols. Oslo, 1934.

Sevåg, Reidar. "Geie und Geigenmusik in Norwegen." In *Die Geige in der europäischen Volksmusik,* edited by Walter Deutsch and Gerlinde Haid. Vienna, 1975.

Urup, Henning, et al. *Gammaldans i Norden.* Trondheim, Norway, 1988.

Wolfram, Richard. *Die Volkstäntze in Österreich und verwandte Tänze in Europa.* Salzburg, 1951.

JAN-PETTER BLOM

Theatrical Dance before 1919

For reasons primarily historical and geographical, professional theater did not develop in Norway until the first part of the nineteenth century. Norway's union with Denmark, which lasted from 1388 until 1814, and the personal union with Sweden, which lasted from 1814 until 1905, suppressed the development of an indigenous theatrical tradition. The Norwegian nobility was almost nonexistent; the Danish royal family lived in Copenhagen (Denmark), and the Swedish royal family lived in Stockholm (Sweden), while a viceroy or his representative was stationed in Christiania (today's Oslo, Norway). The upper classes spoke either Danish or a Dano-Norwegian dialect. With its small population, harsh climate, and rugged mountainous terrain, Norway was regarded as a poor country on the fringe of Europe. Its cities and towns were small and far apart, and transportation was difficult. Not until the eighteenth century, when the economy improved, did Norwegians demand greater autonomy and a national university (the only one in Denmark-Norway was then in Copenhagen). At the same time, the educated classes started to establish dramatic societies and, in the late 1700s to the mid-1800s, small theaters were built in the larger towns.

NORWAY: Theatrical Dance before 1919. Gyda Christensen in *The Naughty Little Princess,* a musical play written by Gabrielle Kjelland and performed at the National Theater in 1905. (Photograph courtesy of the Senter for Dansekunst, Oslo.)

In connection with local dramatic societies, small orchestras were formed, mainly with amateur musicians, since in addition to plays, the groups performed opera, operetta, and vaudeville. Dance intermezzi were sometimes included, usually performed by members of the amateur society.

It was a Swede, Johan Peter Strømberg (1772–1834), however, who in 1827 tried to establish the first professional theater in Oslo. The theater's first program included dance solos and pas de deux. In addition to his duties as theater manager, Strømberg was also a dance teacher, and his wife had been a professional dancer. When the theater burned down in 1835, the well-to-do citizens built another theater, named for their city, Christiania. (Named Christiania [also spelled Kristiania] by King Christian IV in 1624, the city was so called until

NORWAY: Theatrical Dance before 1919. Lillebil Ibsen, Gyda Christensen's daughter, in *Die Shäferin* (The Shepherdess), a children's play written by Hugo von Hoffmannsthal and performed in Berlin in 1915. Max Reinhardt helped cast Ibsen in this role and coached her during rehearsals, although he was not, it seems, otherwise involved in the production. (Photograph courtesy of the Senter for Dansekunst, Oslo.)

1925.) The main performers during the next decades were Danish-speaking actors. A small orchestra was attached, and, usually in summer, troupes from the opera houses in Stockholm and Copenhagen performed at the theater. These performances and those of the theatrical season included dance spectacles.

In 1850, the first professional theater with Norwegian actors was established in Bergen; it had been backed by the internationally known violin virtuoso and composer, Ole Bull (1810–1880), who had been born in Bergen. The opening night included dances by young peasants from the neighboring districts. During its fairly short existence, this theater counted Henrik Ibsen among its directors and dramatists. It is today regarded as the forerunner of Bergen's National Theater.

In the late nineteenth century, despite pressure for Norway's independence from Sweden and for Norway's cultural independence from the Danish influence on language and culture, both Swedish and Danish troupes continued to perform in Norway. Many featured well-known dancers, including the Danish Alexander Genée and his niece Adeline. Norwegian lyric theater was therefore only established in 1899, when the National Theater opened in Oslo. Until its orchestra dissolved in 1919, the National Theater presented regular performances of opera, operetta, and ballet.

At first, ballet was included either as *divertissements* during an opera or as separate events. A more professional corps de ballet was attached to the theater under the direction of Gyda Christensen, an actress and later a prominent Norwegian director and manager; she had been known for her dance recitals in the style of Isadora Duncan. She persuaded professional ballet teachers such as the Royal Danish Ballet's Emilie Walbom to visit Norway, and for a few years during World War I she employed the Russian Nikolai Tarasov of Diaghilev's company as a teacher to the company.

Gyda Christensen was principal choreographer and producer as well as principal dancer from 1899 to 1919. The first ballet to be performed was Ernő Dohnányi's ballet-pantomime *The Bridal Veil*, in 1910. During Tarasov's stay, *Coppélia* was staged in a two-act version titled *Dukken* (The Doll), with Tarasov as Doctor Coppélius. Swanilda was played by Norway's first *prima ballerina*, Christensen's daughter Lillebil, who later married a grandson of Henrik Ibsen.

Lillebil Ibsen and Christensen visited Berlin during World War I, when Norway was a neutral country. They worked there with Max Reinhardt for some seasons, Christensen as choreographer and Ibsen as principal dancer. Just before the war, they had become acquainted with Michel Fokine. With other members of the small ballet ensemble at the National Theater, Ibsen later studied with Fokine in Denmark.

Because of economic difficulties and a growing opposition to the idea of opera and ballet sharing the theater repertory, the National Theater musicians left in 1919 and formed the nucleus of what became the Oslo Philharmonic. No new theater orchestra was established, so Norway did not get another professional, permanent ballet company until after World War II. Norway's first ballet ensemble played a vital role, however, by providing a number of well-qualified teachers for the generation of dancers that later founded the forerunner of the Norwegian National Ballet.

BIBLIOGRAPHY

Aabel, Per. *Den stundesløse Per Aabel.* Oslo, 1980.
Hansteen, Valdemar. *Historien om norsk ballett.* Oslo, 1989.
Ibsen, Lillebil. *Det begyndte med dansen.* Oslo, 1961.
Jennson, Liv. *Teaterliv i Trondhejm, 1800–1835.* Oslo, 1965.
Jensson, Liv. *Teater i drammen inntil 1840.* Oslo, 1974.
Jensson, Liv. *Biografisk skuespillerleksikon: Norske kanske og svenske skuespillere på norske scener sqolig på 1800–tallet.* Oslo, 1981.
Mjøen, Reidar. *Lillebil.* Kristiania, 1919.
The Norwegian National Ballet (in English). Oslo, 1990.
Sinding, Leif. *Gyda Christensen.* Kristiania, 1919.
Sjögren, Margareta. *Skandinavisk balett.* Stockholm, 1988.

Sørensen, Hans Christian. "Gyda Christensen og hennes betydning for norsk ballett." *Ergo*, no. 4 (1978).

Store Norske Leksikon (The National Encyclopedia of Norway). 2d ed. Oslo, 1987.

Theatre and Dance in the Nordic Countries. Copenhagen, 1995.

HANS-CHRISTIAN ARENT

Theatrical Dance, 1920–1958

Although the ballet company at the National Theater in Oslo was dissolved in 1919, the Opera Comique had been established there in 1918. It was an ambitious enterprise with talented singers and gave many fine performances. The Opera's ballet company included about twenty dancers, with Gunvor Ullring as *prima ballerina* and Christiani Aamodt as *premier danseur*. The Swedish-born Augusta Johannesen was the ballet mistress and main choreographer. She was also a well-known teacher. The German Ernst Matray worked with her as dancer and choreographer. The ballet presented few programs of its own and appeared mainly in operas and operettas. After three seasons, the Opera had to close despite the acclaim of both critics and audiences, victim to crippling costs.

Between 1921 and 1924 there existed a small but charming theater, the Mayol, where ballet performances alternated with plays. On this stage Lillebil Ibsen and Per Aabel both appeared as soloists. They were dancers of a high professional standard, both educated abroad and extremely popular; both later became actors and performed into their eighties. Per Aabel was also a talented choreographer and designer. An English dancer, Ernest Marini, held a leading position at the Mayol and also did some choreography. Unfortunately, this theater also had to close.

The succeeding years were difficult for Norwegian dancers. The only dance work available was in revue or cabaret theaters. Some serious dancers tried to make careers abroad. Among those who succeeded were Gerd Larsen, who achieved fame in England, and the talented twin brothers Paal and Lief Roschberg, who went to Paris and became partners of the great music-hall star Mistinguett. Nonetheless, quite a few dancers remained in the Norwegian theater. Lillebil Ibsen and Per Aabel both gave concert performances, and several other dancers also performed to a high professional standard. On the whole, however, classical ballet in Norway lacked vitality during these years. Even guest performances were rare. One explanation may be the lack of a strong ballet tradition.

In contrast, interest in modern dance was growing. The choreographer and teacher Inga Jacobi came to Norway from Germany around 1918, educated at the Dalcroze school in Geneva and strongly influenced by Isadora Duncan's dancing. She ran a school in Oslo for more than twenty years. Jacobi had close contact with the dance community in Germany, but she also had ideas of her own and developed into a choreographer for the dramatic theater, using her own group of dancers.

One of Jacobi's pupils was the dancer and choreographer Signe Hofgaard, also adept at dramatic works. Gerd Kjølaas continued more or less in this tradition. She also started a school for professional dancers that became vitally important for the future of theatrical dance in Nor-

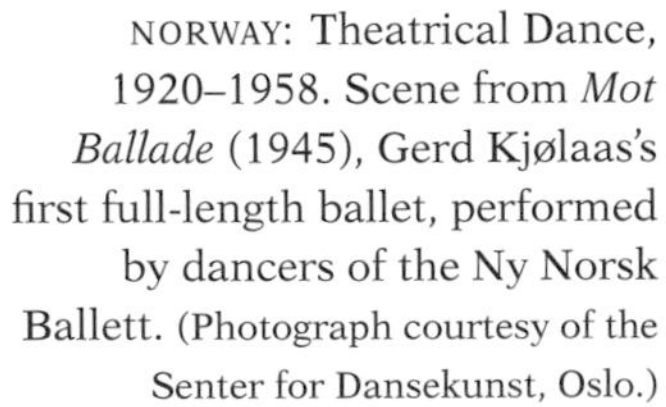

NORWAY: Theatrical Dance, 1920–1958. Scene from *Mot Ballade* (1945), Gerd Kjølaas's first full-length ballet, performed by dancers of the Ny Norsk Ballett. (Photograph courtesy of the Senter for Dansekunst, Oslo.)

way. During World War II, Norwegian artists refrained from public performances but kept working; thus, after the war Kjølaas was able to mount her first full-length ballet, *Mot Ballade,* based on a Norwegian novel and featuring music by a Norwegian composer. In 1948 Kjølaas and the British dancer Louise Browne established the first Norwegian professional ballet company, Ny Norsk Ballett. Their aim was to present ballets based on works by Norwegian writers and composers or on Norwegian folklore. Their performances were generally a great success.

An important result of this collaboration was that classical and modern technique and training were combined for the first time in Norway. Even more importantly, the Ny Norsk Ballett created a kernel of well-trained dancers who could maintain its standards and traditions even after it succumbed to financial troubles. They had to face some lean years but managed to survive by working in musicals. When Louise Browne left Norway, Rita Tori joined Gerd Kjølaas as leader of the group, which was then called Den Norske Ballett. Tori ran the leading school of classical ballet in Oslo. They staged several ballets from both the classical and the modern repertories, giving their last performance in 1958. In the fall of that year they were engaged by the Norwegian Opera.

Bibliography

Hansteen, Valdemar. *Historien om norsk ballett.* Oslo, 1989.
Ibsen, Lillebil. *Det begyndte med dansen.* Oslo, 1961.
Jensson, Liv. *Biografisk skuespillerlesikon: Norske kanske og svenske skuespillere på norske scener sqolig på 1800–tallet.* Oslo, 1981.
Kjølass, Gerd. *Fri dans.* Oslo, 1946.
Parmer, Vidar. *Teatr på Fredrikshald.* Halden, 1965.

Eva Krøvel

Theatrical Dance since 1958

When Den Norske Ballett, the successor to the Ny Norsk Ballett (New Norwegian Ballet), joined with the former Opera Society in establishing a National Opera House in Oslo, there were nine dancers—five women and four men—plus the ballet master Harcourt Algeranoff. There was no separate corps de ballet, and the dancers gave ballet performances and also took part in operas and operettas.

To set ballet on an equal footing with opera, however, the new company, called Operaballetten, started its first season with a ballet performance on 2 November 1958 in the town of Hamar. The site was chosen to emphasize that this ballet company would be truly national, not one limited to performances in the capital, and that it would maintain the tradition of touring Norway, as the old ballet company had done under the name of Ny Norsk Ballett from 1948.

On the program that first night was *Coppélia.* Other ballets presented during the 1958/59 season were Birgit Cullberg's *Medea* and Algeranoff's *Pilemønsteret (*Willow Pattern*),* as well as several *divertissements,* including a pas de deux from *Giselle,* the pas de trois from *Swan Lake,* and a dance from *The Nutcracker.*

The following year, Nicholas Orloff took over as ballet master. During his one season as artistic leader, he commissioned two ballets from the Swedish choreographer Ivo Cramér. One, *Blåskjeggs Mareritt (*Bluebeard's Nightmare*),* was set to original music by the Norwegian composer Harald Saeverud. The second ballet, based on a theme from medieval Norway, *Bendik og Årolilja (*Bendik and Arolilja*),* was set to music composed by the Norwegian Gunnar Sønstervold.

The person who actually had the decisive influence on the development of Norwegian ballet was Joan Harris, a British dancer and former ballet mistress of the Munich State Opera. Harris arrived in 1961 and stayed until 1965. During her term as ballet mistress she added a corps de ballet of ten. She added to the repertory the complete three-act version of *Coppélia; Giselle;* a two-act version of *Swan Lake;* and *Aurora's Wedding.* She also introduced

NORWAY: Theatrical Dance since 1958. *Coppélia* was presented by the Operaballetten during its 1958 inaugural season and has been restaged for the Norwegian Ballet several times. Brenda Last staged a version in 1979, during her three-year tenure as artistic director. Seen here are Sissel Westnes as Swanilda and Ketil Gudim as Franz in a 1983 performance of Last's production. (Photograph by Erik Berg © Den Norske Opera; used by permission.)

works of contemporary choreographers such as Antony Tudor's *Jardin aux Lilas* and *The Judgment of Paris,* Walter Gore's *Street Games,* and Alan Carter's *The Miraculous Mandarin.* Cullberg contributed two of her own ballets, *Månerenen (*Moon Reindeer*)* and *Eden.* Norwegian composer Arne Nordheim was commissioned to write the music for Ivo Cramér's ballet *Katharsis,* which the company performed at the International Bergen Festival in 1962.

The principal dancers of the Norwegian Ballet during these formative years included Henny Mürer, Grete and Mette Møller, Edith Roger (who created an unforgettable Medea), and Anne Borg, a fine technician and a dancer who played an important part in the development of Norwegian ballet. Among the first male principals were Rolf Daleng, the Dane Palle Damm, and the character dancer Egil Åsmann.

During the 1965/66 season, Brian Macdonald served as part-time artistic leader, while also working as the ballet director of the Royal Swedish Ballet. Henny Mürer was the day-to-day leader of the company in Oslo.

From the fall of 1966 until 1971, the Bulgarian-born Sonia Arova was artistic director of the company, the first person to hold this title. More dancers were added to the company, and their dance technique was improved. Arova brought international contacts with her, and famous dancers such as Rudolf Nureyev and Erik Bruhn appeared with the company. She also introduced several of George Balanchine's ballets to Norwegian audiences, among them *Apollo* (1966), *Symphony in C* (1968), *The Four Temperaments* (1968), and *Serenade* (1970). The first complete performance of *Swan Lake* came in 1967 and *La Sylphide* in 1969. These ballets were well received by the relatively small ballet audiences, although several more modern ballets did not stay long in the repertory.

The next ballet director, Anne Borg, took over in 1971, after being assistant ballet director during the previous season. She was the company's artistic director until 1977; in 1979 she left to become principal classical teacher at the newly founded National State College of Ballet. She returned as artistic director from 1983 to 1988 and was headmistress (rector) from 1991 to 1995. Borg had danced with the company from its first years and was a fine dancer, remembered for the title part in Cullberg's *Miss Julie,* among other dance roles. She was also the first official Norwegian ballet director with a sound knowledge of the Norwegian dance milieu and Norwegian dancers.

Borg commissioned a number of new ballets, and several Norwegian choreographers now made their debut with the Norwegian Ballet. Kari Blakstad, a former dancer with the company, created her first ballet, *In All Evighet* (In All Eternity), for the company's workshop. Later came *Vi Har Ikke Tid* (We Haven't Time) and her full-length ballet *Johannes og Anima* (1975). Other Norwegian choreographers include Edith Roger, whose work *Haugtussa* (1972) was inspired by the lyric poems of Arne Garborg (1851–1924), a major Norwegian dramatist, author, and poet. This ballet, with its folkloric theme, became very popular with audiences. The music was composed by Finn Ludt, with additional music by Edvard Grieg. Another former dancer, Henny Mürer, created the full-length ballet *Pinocchio,* set to music by the Norwegian-Italian composer Antonio Bibalo.

NORWAY: Theatrical Dance since 1958. Scene from the original production of Kari Blakstad's *Hedda* (1978), with Marte Sæther (center) in the title role. (Photograph © Den Norske Opera; used by permission.)

In the regular ballet workshops initiated by Anne Borg, many other choreographers have made their debuts, among them dancers attached to the company. Not all have been Norwegians, and not all have met with great success; but the workshops created new opportunities for choreographers, giving them access to the technical resources of the Opera House and to a company of professional dancers.

In 1971, Anne Borg invited the American Glen Tetley to stage his *Mythical Hunters* for the Norwegian Ballet. Two years later, Tetley created *Strender (*Beaches*)* for the company, to the music of Arne Norheim. Their collaboration also produced the popular ballet *Stormen* (The Tempest), which Tetley mounted in 1980.

Anne Borg persuaded the Hungarian dancer Viktor Róna to stay on for several years, as both the company's leading male principal and its ballet master. He produced Vasily Vainonen's *The Nutcracker* in 1975 and, as in many other countries, this ballet has become a Christmas favorite. Also in 1975, Doris Laine from the Finnish Opera Ballet created a new production of *Giselle.* Other works introduced during these years were Nicolas Beriozoff's *Tornerose* (The Sleeping Beauty), John Cranko's *Spill med Kort* (Game of Cards), Michel Fokine's *Petrouchka,* Frederick Ashton's *Les Patineurs,* and Charles Czarney's *Concerto Grosso* and *Haffner Symphony.*

In 1972 Peter Brinson's lecture-demonstration troupe, Ballet for All, was brought to Norway by Anne Borg, to tour many parts of the country. As an educational effort by the Norwegian Ballet, it presented *The Two Coppélias* and provided many schoolchildren with an introduction to ballet.

NORWAY: Theatrical Dance since 1958. *(left)* The Norwegian Ballet's production of *Swan Lake* was staged by John Field in 1978, with Ellen Kjelberg as Odette-Odile and Viktor Róna as Siegfried. *(right)* Glen Tetley's *Stormen* (The Tempest), created for Ballet Rambert in 1979, was added to the repertory of the Norwegian Ballet in 1980 and immediately became a popular hit. This photograph was taken during a 1982 performance at the Brooklyn Academy of Music, New York. (Left photograph by Karsten Bundgård © Den Norske Opera; used by permission. Right photograph from the Dance Collection, New York Public Library for the Performing Arts.)

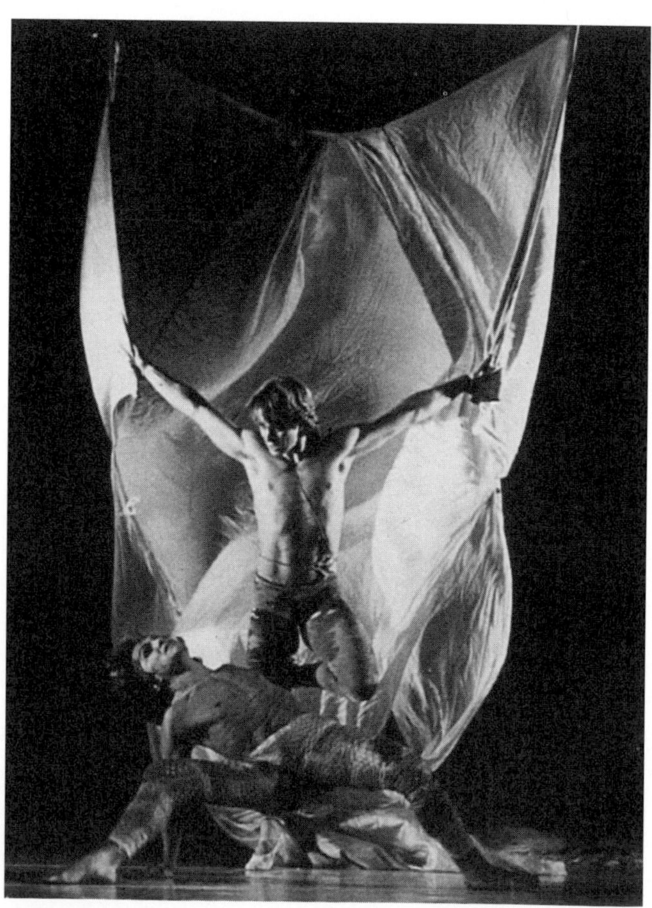

The successor to Anne Borg was another dancer from England's Royal Ballet, Brenda Last. During her directorship, which lasted from 1977 until 1980, the technical standard of the dancers rose again. She started by giving the company a new production of *Swan Lake,* choreographed by John Field, and her own production of *Coppélia.* During the centenary celebration for Henrik Ibsen in 1978, the new ballet *Hedda* was commissioned from Kari Blakstad. The full-length Bournonville ballet *Napoli,* as restaged by Poul Gnatt, was presented in 1980.

Glen Tetley's *Stormen,* set to Arne Norheim's music, was to become one of the most popular and important ballets during Last's tenure. Originally performed in 1980, it is still probably the most popular ballet in Norway; it also drew the attention of American critics and audiences when the Norwegian company toured to New York in 1982.

From 1980 to 1983, Jens Graff, a Norwegian and a principal with the Royal Swedish Ballet, took over as artistic director. He added Nureyev's production of *Don Quixote* (1981), László Seregi's charming and amusing *Sylvia* (1982), and a new work on a Norwegian theme by Flemming Flindt. He ended his directorship with another production of *Swan Lake,* adding some of his own choreography. Graff had also pursued a project initiated by his predecessor—a club for ballet enthusiasts, which started in 1980.

In the early fall of 1983, the twenty-fifth anniversary of the Opera House and the Norwegian Ballet, Anne Borg resumed the directorship. It was a year notable mostly for increasing economic hardships for the Norwegian arts, but it was also the year when the state took over full responsibility for the Norwegian Opera, including the Norwegian Ballet.

The future of dance in Norway has become more promising, since it has been generally accepted, both as a pastime and as an art form. Ballroom dancing and competitive dancing are popular. Ballet schools, both private and public as part of municipal schools of music, which include classical as well as modern dance technique, exist all over Norway, with competent teachers. There are also some three to four times the number of theaters that there were just after World War II. Many of these, particularly those in the bigger cities and towns, stage regular productions of musicals and operettas, which include dancers. The second national theater in Oslo, Det Norske Theater (The Norwegian Theater) has attached a small regular ensemble of dancers, actors, and singers; it has become the leading producer of well-known international musicals under the well-known choreographer-director Runar Borge.

Foreign ballet and other dance companies visit Norway regularly since the 1980s and tour the capital and other major cities. The spring International Festival, in Bergen, often includes major international dance companies as well as smaller Norwegian companies.

Despite the problems, a new generation of talented dancers with strong technical preparation is gradually gaining prominence in the Opera House and in other theaters. As yet there has been no Norwegian choreographer who has made a lasting impact on the public and whose works have survived to become part of the ballet repertory. The greatest obstacle to the development of ballet is financial, but interest in it and other different forms is not lacking among the general public.

The Swede Viveka Ljung took over in 1988 as artistic director of the Norwegian Ballet after Anne Borg, a difficult task since Borg was director of the company for about fifteen years. Ljung resigned after two seasons and is best known for the success of her production of *Volven,* choreographed by Norway's Kjersti Alveberg, who has also won European acclaim for her ballets for television. The Danish dancer and Bournonville expert Dinna Bjørn became ballet director in 1990.

In the years after World War II many small companies had to survive great hardships. Among the modern dance companies, most based in the Oslo region, that have received some financial support from the state are the

NORWAY: Theatrical Dance since 1958. Richard Suttie and Beatrix Balazs in the Norwegian Ballet's production of *The Nutcracker,* staged by artistic director Dinna Bjørn in 1994. (Photograph by Erik Berg © Den Norske Opera; used by permission.)

Høvik Ballet, established in 1969 with Merete Bergesen as principal choreographer, but dormant since 1988; Collage Dansekompani, Norway's leading modern company, founded in 1974, with Sølvi Edvardsen, Lise Nordal, and Inger Buresund as principal choreographers; until it folded in 1995 because of lack of financial support, Imago Danseteater, founded and run by one of Norway's most original choreographers, Lise Eger, who rarely offer more than one production annually. A postmodern dance group, Dance Design, was founded by the couple Anne Grete Eriksen and Leif Hernes; it has enjoyed success both in Norway and abroad for its multimedia works. In the zone between theater and dance is Kjetil Skøien and his Passage Nord Theater. Other modern choreographers and dancers are Ina Chriostel Johannesen (who in 1996 became company choreographer at New Carte Blanche) and Un-Margit Nordseth, with their Scirocco Dance Group; they were Norway's winners in the Nordic Choreographer Competition that was held at the Norwegian Opera in 1987. Other promising newcomers are Ingunn Bjørnsgaard and Jo Strømgren, who have also been favorably received in the other Scandinavian countries.

The Carte Blanche Dance Company, founded in 1985 by Norwegian-British Jennifer Day, has enjoyed great popular success with its mix of jazz dance and conventional modern dance forms. In 1989 it moved to Bergen to become the second state-supported dance theater. Through mismanagement, the company was declared bankrupt, but it was soon revived as the New Carte Blanche Dance

Company, with Anne Borg as its new director in 1990, followed by Jessica Iwanson, and from 1992 to 1995 by Fredrik Rütter.

The companies that emphasize modern dance are made up almost exclusively of women, with male dancers brought in only occasionally as guests. This is usually because male dancers are in short supply and because male dancers in Norway are under great pressure to provide security and a regular income for their families. Since the 1980s, more men have taken up dance as a profession, as Norway's interest in dance has increased and the state has provided more opportunities (by providing grants and inexpensive loans) for them to attend professional schools.

Norwegian dance in the latter 1980s and early 1990s has been marked by transition. Many of the leading dancers and choreographers have retired, but a new generation of well-schooled and ambitious dancers exists. Worth mentioning here are Kristina Gjems McGill and Arne Fagerholt in addition to Øyvind Jorgensen and Anderz Døving and his Andanse company. Government and local authorities are less generous with their financial support as the welfare state becomes more costly, but the interest in all dance forms has increased among the theatergoing public. However, the final decade of the twentieth century seems to form a kind of culmination of Norwegian dance after half a century of progress. First, there is a larger audience than ever before, but no less important, a larger diversity in the Norwegian dance scene. This was well proven during the Year of Dance in 1993, when the Norwegian dance scene was encouraged throughout the country, with extra financial support from the government, from local authorities, and by royal patronage. Nonetheless, the main obstacle remains one of finances as the companies become increasingly dependent on public support. The government promised in their 1992 official report on the arts that the field of dance would be of primary interest since it had been neglected in the past compared with other arts. Extra money has been provided for the National Touring Theater, to organize and send on tour various private dance groups as well as to increase the interest in dance among younger people through a youth program directed at primary and secondary schools. Outside the larger cities, the Norwegian public seems less receptive to dance performance, especially to modern dance.

As the higher institutions of dance graduate more dancers, teachers, and choreographers, the lack of jobs and the increasing competition from dancers from other countries has become a subject for concern and discussion. Norway's three national colleges of ballet, opera, and theater will be joined into a national school of the arts in 1997, which may also include other fine arts colleges.

Artistically, Norwegian dancers and choreographers are part of the Nordic and European dance scene, with a strong dramatic component that impresses many interested visitors. This has been enhanced by the renewal of ballet director Dinna Bjørn's contract at the opera in Oslo and the position of Jens Graff as the new artistic director of the New Carte Blanche in Bergen, both in 1995. Probably typical of the general attitude toward dance among Norwegians was the fact that the two classical works,

NORWAY: Theatrical Dance. Scene from the Imago Dance Company's production of *Tunnellen* (The Tunnel; 1992), choreographed by Lise Eger. The dancers are (left to right) Therese Skauge, Henriette Slorer, Jens Stueng, and Marit Schade Ødegaard. (Photograph by Mona Gundersen; courtesy of Imago Dance Company.)

NORWAY: Theatrical Dance. Niklas Gundersen and Yoshifumi Inao float side by side in Jo Strømgren's *Benpibernes Bøn* (Murmur of the Bonepipes; 1996), a production of the New Carte Blanche Dance Company. The costumes were designed by Ingvild Hovind. (Photograph by Øystein Klakegg; courtesy of Carte Blanche Dance Company.)

Romeo and Juliet in 1994 and *A Midsummer Night's Dream* in 1996, were the most popular; also, not until 1995 was the main classical ballet company at the Norwegian Opera officially designated the Norwegian National Ballet, for many years now its internationally recognized name. Dance in its many forms has, however, become a part of Norway's national cultural heritage, and with many new talents among its dancers and choreographers, the future looks both promising and exciting.

BIBLIOGRAPHY

Cruickshank, Judith. "Talent Isn't Measured in Inches." *Dance and Dancers* (June 1979): 28–31.

Frich, Elisabeth. "Dance in Norway." *Ballett International* 10 (April 1987): 12–16.

Garske, Rolf. "The Norwegian Ballet Today." *Ballett International* 12 (October 1989): 17–25.

Hansteen, Valdemar. "On scenedansens utvikling og vikår i Norge." Ph.D. diss., University of Oslo, 1987.

Hansteen, Valdemar. *Historien om norsk ballett.* Oslo, 1989.

Jensson, Liv. *Biografisk skuespillerleksikon: Norske kanske og svenske skuespillere på norske scener sqolig på 1800–tallet.* Oslo, 1981.

Livas, Haris. "Modern Dance in Norway." *Ballett International* 11 (October 1988): 40–43.

Loney, Glenn. "Towards the Sun." *Dance Magazine* (November 1970): 62–65.

Lumsden, Malvern. "Norskt dansliv 1981: En saga om Askungen och styvmodern." *Dans* (May 1981):20–23.

Lyngholm, Karene. "Looking Out and Looking Back." *Ballett International* 16 (February 1993): 36–37.

Maynard, Olga. "Sonia Arova: An Interview with the Director of Den Norske Ballet." *Dance Magazine* (May 1969): 41–43, 70–73.

Näslund, Erik. "Norska operaballetten 15 år." *Dans* (March 1974): 4–17.

Norwegian Ballet Union. *Arbeids-og inntektforhold for norske dansekunstnere.* Oslo, 1986.

Parmer, Vidar. *Teatr på Fredrikshald.* Halden, 1965.

HANS-CHRISTIAN ARENT

Classical Dance Education

Professional dance education is relatively new in Norway. The first dance day school, started during World War II, taught the free dance or expressionist techniques of central Europe. Little or no systematic training was available, except at the National Theater, between 1910 and 1919. Children attended private ballet schools, and those who could afford it went abroad for further education and employment.

The day school was short-lived, and twenty years elapsed before a new school, Ballettinstituttet, was started in 1966, headed by Jorunn Kirkenær. This school was privately run but received funds from the state for some years until the State School of Ballet was founded in 1968. A few years later a day school, with Joan Harris as principal, was opened in connection with the Norwegian National Opera and the National Ballet Company. It not only trained dancers but also prepared future teachers of ballet, using the system devised by London's Royal Academy of Dancing. The course lasted two years, with an optional third year.

Two schools now offered professional dance education in Oslo. Since both were recognized by the Department of Education, pupils could apply for grants and loans from the state. This system was intended to advance the knowledge of dance throughout the country, but in reality it has led to an oversupply of dancers, most of whom live in Oslo.

Under pressure from the Dancers and Dance Teachers Union, the problem of education was included in the Arts Report that was passed into law by Parliament in fall 1976. Parliament decided to establish an advanced ballet school run by the state. As a result, the two existing private schools lost their state financial support in 1980. The State School of Advanced Ballet Education enrolled its first students in fall 1979. A maximum of fifteen students are admitted each year, divided among three courses of study, dance, choreography, and teaching. The pedagogical course qualifies graduates to teach in Norwegian schools.

All applicants to the school must take a juried examination in dance technique. Dance students are required to have completed nine years of schooling, as is compulsory in Norway; choreography and pedagogy students must have an advanced secondary education (equivalent to the university entrance level) and thorough preparation in dance. Choreography applicants must present a choreographed work. The principal of the school in 1990 was Henry Miller.

The three years of education at the school are free, and students are awarded scholarships and loans on the same terms as other students in higher education. The school also plans to offer further education and retraining, which will be of great importance in addressing the problems of unemployment and early retirement among dancers.

The school at the Opera House now continues with a somewhat reduced teaching schedule, but its syllabus is being linked to that of the State School. The teachers' course has come to an end, but children between the ages of ten and fifteen are still taught on five levels. Those between fifteen and eighteen are taught at an additional three levels. Secondary-school students can combine academic education with advanced dance studies at one of Oslo's high schools.

BIBLIOGRAPHY

Aabel, Per. *Den stundesløse Per Aabel.* Oslo, 1980.
Hansteen, Valdemar. *Historien om norsk ballett.* Oslo, 1989.
Ibsen, Lillebil. *Det begyndte med dansen.* Oslo, 1961.

EMTE STAG

Dance Research and Publication

Dance scholarship in Norway is not an established and well-defined discipline, but it does exist in various contexts. The oldest and strongest tradition is in folk dance research. During the period of Romantic nationalism in the eighteenth century, cultivated townspeople took an interest in Norwegian folk culture, first concentrating on poetry, crafts, architecture, and music. Because of church disapproval, dance had a very low status, especially in the small communities of Norway, and in many locales dancing had not been practiced since the sixteenth or seventeenth century. [*See* Christianity and Dance.]

Around 1900, however, systematic recording and publication of Norwegian folk dances began. Klara Semb and Hulda Gorborg were leading figures. This interest in folk dance was part of a wider movement with the goal of reestablishing Norwegian cultural identity, which was weak after the Industrial Revolution. Several folk organizations included dancing and dance teaching as an important part of their activities. Thus a base was established for the study, reconstruction, and protection of Norway's cultural heritage.

At the University of Trondheim, Rådet for Folkemusik og Folkedans (The Council for Folk Music and Folk Dance) is the most important institution overseeing scholarly research in this field. Egil Bakka has recorded folk dances and has written several books and articles, among them the survey *Norske dansetradisjonar* (Norwegian Dance Traditions; Oslo, 1978).

The only dance bibliography in Norway is that included in *Folkedanslitteratur i Norden* (Folk Dance Literature in the Nordic Countries), published in 1983 by Nordisk Forening for Folkedansforskning (Nordic Society for Research in Folk Dance). Egil Bakka was the editor for Norway. Dance as a theatrical art is also represented in Bakka's bibliography. In Norway, dance was established very late as an independent art, even though it became an important element in the Norwegian theater early in the nineteenth century. Very little documentation of theatrical dance exists; material in archives has not been systematized and research is as yet minimal.

Drama critics deal with dance both as part of a theatrical performance and as an art in its own right. Occasionally the small theaters are reviewed; there dance is more common than in the larger, more established theaters. Until 1945 newspaper criticism gave an incomplete picture of the dance world. Reidar Mjøen wrote some informative articles in the 1920s and 1930s, as well as a short book, *Lillebil,* on the ballerina Lillebil Ibsen. Lisi Carén focused on the rising modern dance movement from the 1930s onward. Norway's influential and knowledgeable ballet critics, such as Eva Krøvel of *Aftenposten* and Erik Pierstorff of *Morgenbladet og Dagbladet,* became established after World War II.

A sense of the development of theatrical dance can often be found in artists' autobiographies. For example, in *Detbegynte med dansen* (It Started with the Dance, 1961), Lillebil Ibsen wrote about her own international career as well as the development of ballet at the National Theater under the guidance of her mother Gyda Christensen from 1910 to 1919. In *Den stundesløse Per Aabel* (The Fussy Per Aabel; 1980), Per Aabel described the ballet world around the turn of the twentieth century. *Fri Dans* (Modern Dance; 1946) by Gerd Kjølaas is a general introduction to modern dance and its position in Norway.

Dance is also described in nineteenth-century literature about theater history. In later books, dance and music are often regarded as relatively unimportant factors in theater, even when they play a featured part in the repertory. The theater historian Liv Jensson has collected materials to document all types of scenic performances, including dance. Her books *Teater i Drammen inntil 1840* (Theater in Drammen until 1840; Oslo, 1974) and *Teaterliv i Trondheim, 1800–1835* (Theater Life in Trondheim; 1800–1835, Oslo, 1965), are important for dance historians, covering more than their titles indicate. Jensson's *Biografisk skuespillerleksikon* (Dictionary of Actors) includes articles about dancers.

Vidar Parmer has written *Teatr på Fredrikshald* (Theater at Fredrikshald; Halden, 1965), which gives a description of all types of entertainment presented at the Frederikshald Theater. Nevertheless, much basic research still has to be done in the archives holding materials on theater history. Only in this way will information about the history of dance become synthesized and useful. Det Norske Teatret (The Norwegian Theater) has a modern archive with a computer database; the archives of Den Norske Opera (The Norwegian Opera), dating only from 1958, are insufficient to such a degree that important documentation from its early years cannot be found.

The Theater Archive and the Theater Museum in Bergen (connected to the Institute for Theater Research in Bergen) have important collections concerning theater in that city. The Theater Collection at the university library in Oslo and the Theater Museum there contain mostly documentation on Oslo's theaters. A good deal of material is also in private collections.

Research on theatrical dance also takes place at organizations such as the Institute for Theater Research at the University of Oslo. Since 1986, Live Hove has taught international ballet history there. Some theses have been written on theatrical dance in connection with specific performances from the 1980s. Valdemar Hansteen's 1987 thesis "On Scenedansens utvikling og vikår i Norge" ("Stage Dance in Norway: Development and Premises") is the first survey of this topic.

At the Institute for Drama, Film and Theater at the University of Trondheim, several papers on modern choreography have been written. At the School for Physical Education in Norway, some students have written papers dealing with dance as a theater art (and some about its physiological aspects).

In addition to these institutions where dance history and aesthetics are taught, some individuals should be mentioned. Gerd Bugge teaches ballet and theater history at the State School for Ballet; she has worked especially with modern and contemporary dance in Europe, the United States, and Norway. Hans-Christian Arent, critic at *Arbeiderbladet,* wrote an article in 1987 on Gyda Christensen and her importance for Norwegian ballet; he also writes on dance for *Store Norske Leksikon* (Great Norwegian Encyclopedia).

The Norwegian Ballet Union has sponsored research on the working conditions and salaries of Norwegian dancers, published as *Arbeids-og inntektforhold for norske dansekunstnere* (1986), and ongoing work on the recording of choreography. In 1987 the Riss Dance Company did research with deaf children in connection with the Federation for Deaf People in Norway. Tina Hessel, physiotherapist at the Norwegian Opera, has published *Tøyninger for dansere* (Oslo, 1987), about preventing injuries among dancers.

VALDEMAR HANSTEEN

NOTATION. Dance notation, the written recording of movement through signs, has, over the centuries, taken many forms. Pictorial representation (figure drawings) provides a record of a kind; certainly much about contemporary dances can be gleaned from tomb paintings and Greek vases, but by themselves, figural illustrations convey positions and omit much of the information necessary to serious movement research and reconstruction. However, even in this scientific age, visual representation is still used for quick jottings. Verbal description is another familiar method of recording information on movement, but one that is far from satisfactory even among people working in the same dance form and employing a common terminology. In movement, as in law, words must be chosen with care and sentences carefully constructed to avoid ambiguity. Words change meaning over the years, and in English particularly, one word may have more than one meaning. Thus, neither pictures nor words can be considered a "system" of movement notation.

Organized systems vary in three important respects: in the choice of movement analysis—that is, how movement is viewed and described; in the choice of graphic representation; and in the level of description. The last may range from an abbreviated memory aid to a high degree of specificity in how the body uses space (and/or other basic forms of movement), time, and energy. Also to be considered are the interests and expertise of the inventor(s), as well as the degree to which a system was—or is—used by others and the degree of the users' expertise. In Europe the development of dance (movement) notation followed closely the development of dance.

Renaissance. The earliest known manuscript of dance notation, found in the municipal archives of Cervera, Spain, dates from the second half of the fifteenth century. This notation method, based on a letter code for the five steps of Renaissance *bassesdanses* ("low dances"), is also found in *L'art et instruction de bien dancer* (anonymous, late fifteenth century), which may be the first printed book on the subject of dance. [*See* Bassedanse.]

In *L'art et instruction,* the names of the steps are abbreviated to their initial letters: R for *révérence, s* for *simple, d* for *double, b* for *branle* (swaying step), and *r* for *reprise* (backward step). A dance was recorded by placing the particular sequence of letters—*r ss ddd b ss rrr*—under the appropriate notes of the music score. The Dance Book of Margaret of Austria, also known as the Burgundian Manuscript, now in the Royal Library in Brussels, employs this letter system. The music and dance are written in gold and silver on a black background. The Cervera score, though older, goes further: simple signs are used to replace the letters—the first such abstraction.

Information about how these steps were performed and on the general decorum required at stately balls is provided by the many dance books and manuscripts from the Renaissance, particularly in those by the renowned Italian dance masters Domenico da Piacenza, Antonio Cornazano, and Guglielmo Ebreo. The best-known book—that of Thoinot Arbeau (pseudonym for Jehan Tabourot, canon of Langres), first published in 1588 and subsequently translated and republished several times—describes in some detail the manner of performing the steps (Arbeau, 1948). Arbeau's method of notation was to place

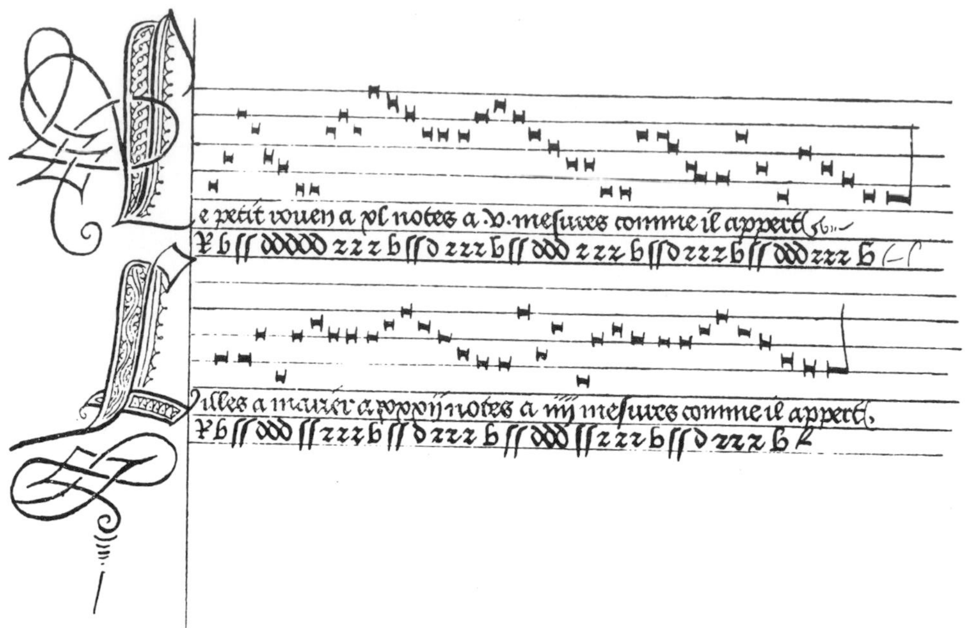

NOTATION. This example of Burgundian *bassedanse* notation is from a manuscript now in the Bibliothèque Royale in Brussels. The letters *R, s, d,* and *b,* used to abbreviate the step names, can be seen below the words of the song "Filles a Marier." Here, *z* is used as an abbreviation for a step called *reprise,* found in other sources as *r.* Represented by the breves of the tenor melody, each step is the equivalent of one musical note, except for the single steps (notated as *s*), which require two notes. As the *bassedanse* is a processional dance, floor patterns are not necessary. (Photograph from the Dance Collection, New York Public Library for the Performing Arts.)

the music vertically on the page and to write the name of each step next to the note on which it should occur. As has happened with all such descriptions of dance steps through the ages, Arbeau took for granted much knowledge on the part of the reader. As a result, there are inevitable gaps in what is understood of just how certain steps should be performed. [*See the entry on Arbeau.*]

The importance of where performers stood and the design of their progression across the dance floor resulted in the development of floor plans. The rose pattern, published in 1600 in Fabritio Caroso's *Nobiltà di dame,* appears to indicate the progression of the dancers in what later was called a hey. John Playford's *The English Dancing Master,* published in many editions between 1651 and 1728, describes steps through words, adding a few symbols for abbreviations and signs to indicate placement for men and women.

Though relying mainly on words, these books provide a wealth of country dances of the period. Graphic indication of the paths taken in these *contredanses* (as they were called in France) came later. The first examples of elaborate floor plans appear in the diagrams of horse ballets published in 1661 by Alessandro Carducci.

Baroque Dance. The notation system Raoul-Auger Feuillet published in Paris in 1700 flourished as a result of the social status dancing had achieved through the influence of Louis XIV in the French court. Being able to "read" dances became an expected skill for the educated class, creating a market for the regular publication of *recueils,* collections of new dances by the leading dancing masters. Translations of Feuillet's book soon appeared in English by John Weaver and Paul Siris in 1706 and John Essex in 1710; German and Spanish translations followed.

The so-called Feuillet system, which appears to have been originated by Pierre Beauchamps and perhaps even by André Lorin, was well suited to the dances of the Baroque period. The majority of dances were couple dances with an occasional solo either for a man or a woman. Floor design was important, and footwork was quite intricate, despite the heeled shoes of the time. In contrast, except for bowing, the torso was kept upright, and arm and hand movements followed a few simple patterns.

The notation was based on the track drawings that trace the path of dancers across the floor. Each page of notation represents the room, the path traversed being shown by a line. On this line strokes mark off the bar lines to coordinate with the accompanying music written at the top of the page. Signs for the steps are written on the right or left side of the track line. On the basic sign for a step is placed a variety of minor signs, to indicate rising, sinking, turning, beating, and springing, for example. As use of the system spread, improvements were made and details added. Kellom Tomlinson's *The Art of Dancing,* published in 1735, provided plates as well as valuable detailed explanations of dances. The wealth of publications using the Feuillet system provides a rich heritage from that era.

The Feuillet system fell into disuse because of the gradual separation of social and theatrical dance and the general effect of the French Revolution in removing the center of social dance from the court and the educated class. By the turn of the century, social dances had become much simpler; the popular *contredanses* required mainly floor patterns; words sufficed to describe the simple steps used in the polkas and waltzes that soon became fashionable and required much less skill and training. In contrast, theater dance developed beyond the complex footwork of the Baroque dance, incorporating greater use of the torso and leg and arm gestures. As the stage was the realm of the less-educated working class, dance literacy did not survive, nor did the system that had served so splendidly the style of dance for which it had been designed. [*See* Ballet Technique, History of, *article on* French Court Dance; *and* Feuillet Notation.]

Romantic Period. The mid-nineteenth century saw the publication of four notation systems, none of which gained a foothold, but each of which provides much information on contemporary dance and how it was taught. In 1831, E. A. Théleur, an English dance teacher who had studied in Paris, published *Letters on Dancing,* which included a system of notation based on abstract symbols. Using comparatively few symbols, he spelled out basic leg positions and movements, concluding with the complete "Gavotte de Vestris." For speedier writing, he introduced shorthand signs for familiar composite steps.

A Frenchman, Arthur Saint-Léon—unlike Théleur a much traveled and well-known dancer, teacher, and choreographer—published his system in *La sténochorégraphie* (1852). Based on the use of stick figures, it would seem to have had a chance of success, but then, as now, physically oriented dancers were reluctant to take the time to learn to read and write dance. [*See* Saint-Léon Notation.]

The system of the German Friedrich Albert Zorn gained support from dance teacher organizations, but their official resolutions to adopt it seem to have come to naught. Zorn's book, *Grammatik der Tanzkunst* (1887), the result

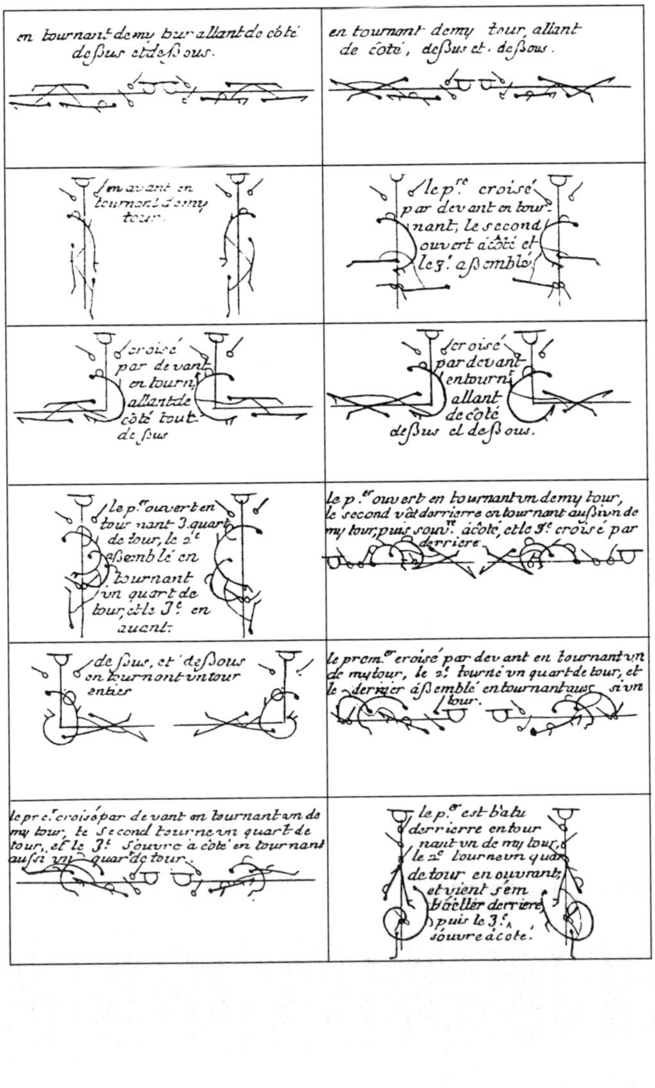

NOTATION. *(left)* The system published by Raoul-Auger Feuillet in 1700 was well suited for the elaborate social and theatrical solos and duets of the early eighteenth century, represented here by a page of Feuillet's table for notating the *pas de bourée.* When the steps were organized into dances, each dance phrase would fit a phrase of music that would be printed across the top of the page. *(right)* The larger group dances of the late eighteenth and early nineteenth centuries emphasized spatial patterns and placed less importance on footwork, as seen in this early nineteenth-century German notation for a quadrille. Each of the four couples is indicated by a number. Although the floor patterns are clear in this type of notation, steps, the number of measures, and coordination with music are not illustrated. (Left photograph from the Dance Collection, New York Public Library for the Performing Arts. Right photograph courtesy of Elizabeth Aldrich.)

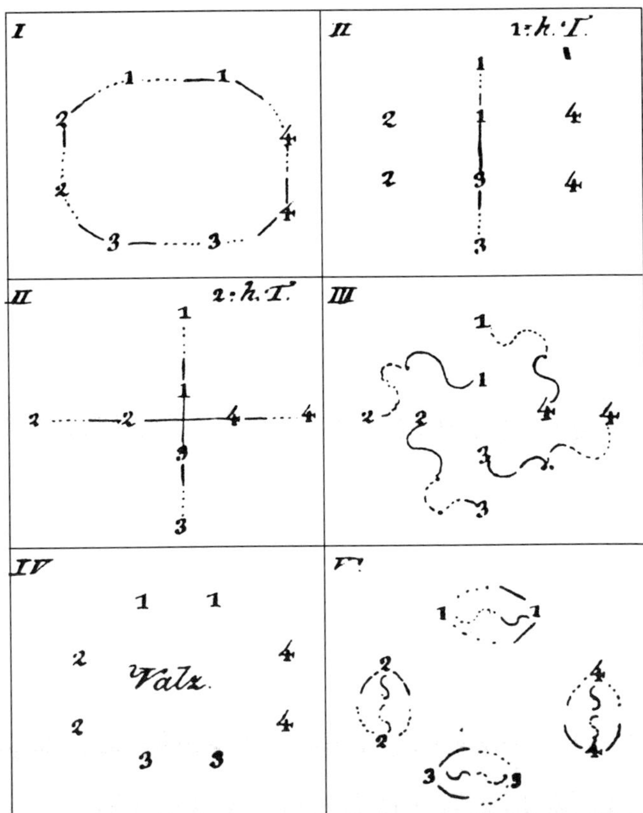

of years of work, contained careful instructions on how dance positions and movements should be performed. Each was carefully illustrated and spelled out in his stick-figure notation. [*See* Zorn Notation.]

A much simpler system, combining a few abstract signs with music notes to indicate timing, was introduced by Bernard Klemm in *Handbuch der Tanzkunst* (Leipzig, 1855). This book was so successful that it went into several editions through 1910. Klemm explained the correct performance of ballet steps and included details on the social dances of the time.

The first full system of movement notation based on music notes was that of Vladimir Stepanov, a Russian dancer at the Maryinsky Theater, whose study of anatomy led him to Paris. He published *Alphabet des mouvements du corps humain* there in 1892. Stepanov's system, taught for a period at the Imperial Ballet schools in Saint Petersburg and Moscow, was used for a while to record Marius Petipa's repertory. Both Léonide Massine and Vaslav Nijinsky were influenced by this system. [*See* Stepanov Notation.]

Twentieth Century. A great advance in understanding the human body, and hence in teaching movement, has taken place in the twentieth century. Scientific developments are gradually being applied to improve dance training. The numerous systems of notation that have been developed—on average a new one every four years since 1928—in some cases show a universal scientific approach and in others a limited view in which only the needs of a particular dance form are considered. This is particularly true of folk dance notations. (Ballroom notations, which predominantly use verbal descriptions combined with footprints, are not considered here.) The devices used hark back to those already met: stick figures (visual representation), music notes, and abstract signs, with the greatest variety being the choice of abstract signs.

Nijinsky's notation system has aroused much interest but was never published. The most tangible evidence of it is in the score he wrote in about 1915 of his ballet *L'Après-midi d'un Faune*. The score reveals the degree to which he used Stepanov's ideas—but there are differences that affected decipherment. In 1987 his system was deciphered, and his ballet *L'Après-midi d'un Faune* was revived from his score. Nijinsky's 1918 and 1919 notes on his notation ideas suggest that he had in mind more than one line of development. Nijinsky's notations of ballet exercises reveal the same lack of care in movement analysis found in the Stepanov scores (e.g., writing an *assemblé* as a spring off the ground from two feet rather than from one). Some of his other jottings have been found and perhaps one day the alleged score of *Le Sacre du Printemps* will come to light.

Rudolf Laban's *Choregraphie* (1926) included a shorthand memory aid for the space-harmony developments described. His 1928 book *Schrifttanz* (Written Dance) introduced his universally applicable abstract-symbol system Kinetography Laban, now more generally known as Labanotation. Laban's concern for movement of all kinds and his lack of schooling in any one dance style led to universally based principles that provided an impersonal analysis of movement. The broad view he established was subsequently combined with contributions made to the system by people using it in a variety of different movement fields. The result is a highly developed, flexible system capable of being used in a simple form to provide a general statement or at a high level of specificity to capture fine details of movement.

NOTATION. In 1831, E. A. Théleur described a type of notation that aligned step symbols with music. Here, in this two-phrase, sixteen-bar example from Théleur's notation for the "Gavotte de Vestris", the gentleman's part is notated above the music, the lady's below. Directional arrows within the score supplement the two boxes that provide the dancers' floor pattern for each of the two phrases. (Photograph from the Dance Collection, New York Public Library for the Performing Arts.)

N° 3. — **Jambe d'appui : *Pas sautés et mouvements tournants***

NOTATION. Many creators of dance notations have been accomplished musicians, as was Pierre Conté, who used a five-line staff and music notes for his system published in 1931. (Photograph from the Dance Collection, New York Public Library for the Performing Arts.)

Laban took his initial idea of a center line representing the center line in the body, dividing right and left, from the Feuillet system. From it he also borrowed the idea of marking off the music measures on this center line. The vertical staff representing the body reflects the symmetricality in the build of the body; symmetrical positions and movements appear as symmetrical designs on the page. A surprising number of systems do not provide symmetrical images for symmetrical movements. The vertical staff, a new idea, allows for representation of the body as it is usually imagined in the vertical standing situation, together with the possibility of writing continuous, unbroken movement through continuous indications up the page.

Because the basic beat of the music is established on the center line by a regular length, and the length of each movement indication gives its duration, there is no need to place the music alongside the movement notation to indicate timing. When music and dance are combined, the music is placed vertically to the left of the dance score, a separate music-only score being used by the pianist or orchestra. This feature—timing integrated in the movement symbol in a nonmusic note system—is unique to Laban.

Spread of the Laban system resulted in the establishment of notation centers in England, France, Germany, and the United States. Texts and teaching materials have been published in Dutch, English, Finnish, French, German, Hungarian, Polish, Serbo-Croatian, and Spanish. Many publications now include notated examples of dance exercises or steps. In Hungary, Kinetography Laban is the official system for preserving and publishing the traditional dance heritage. Because of its basic movement analysis, its use is spreading in the fields of movement education and choreographic composition. Libraries of notated choreographic scores have made possible comparative research and choreographic study. The Dance Notation Bureau in New York City was the first center to establish levels of qualification in training professional teachers, notators, and reconstructors. [*See* Labanotation; Laban Principles of Movement Analysis; *and the entry on Laban*.]

In 1928, Margaret Morris's *Movement Notation* was published in London. Morris, who also based her system on abstract symbols, had much in common with Laban. She also had a universal view of movement. As a dancer, she was largely self-taught, and thus not influenced by any one school. She set aside her teaching and performing career for a time to concentrate on the medical field, on prenatal care and the application of dance to remedial work. As a result of this, she based her system on an anatomical analysis of movement, on forms of flexion, extension, and rotation. Unlike any previous system, her system included breathing, pronation and supination of the feet, and other less commonly recorded actions.

The horizontal staff in Morris's notation provides a lower section for the legs and an upper section for the arms, the body and head notations written in between. Indications written on a line show movements for the right limbs; under a line are movements for the left. Dots between bar lines indicate timing with spaces between the dots being beats. Phrasing bows indicate legato movements.

Morris's inventiveness reflected her use of a different symbol for each possible movement for each body joint; other systems simplify description by combining signs for each part of the body with signs for the appropriate actions. In only a few instances are Morris's symbols pictorial—for example, in showing levels for arm and leg gestures by placement of the direction signs higher or lower on the staff.

Whereas Laban soon handed responsibility for further development of his system to others, Morris lacked an enthusiastic notation-oriented younger generation to carry on her work. Her many movement-centered activities left no time for the further development and application of her notation system. A renewed interest in her work in the early 1980s included the use of the system.

La danse classique, a system based on word abbreviations, was published by Antonine Meunier, a dancer and teacher at the Paris Opera, in 1931. Meunier presents a generous survey of previous systems, a description of each ballet step with its abbreviation, and several extracts from ballets.

Music notes were again the device used by Pierre Conté, a musician and ex-soldier who became involved with dance through the application of rhythm to gymnastics. He evolved his system of notation when he discovered that none was in general use. His *Écriture de la danse théâtrale,* published in 1931, places music notes on a modified music staff that represents the body. Directions are indicated by the numbers: *0* (for down), *1* (forward), *2* (side), *3* (backward), and *5* (up). The number *4* was used for twists in the body. The number *5* was chosen for "up" because arms overhead is the fifth position in ballet. Other balletic influences were evident: *CP,* for example, is the *cou-de-pied* position of the free foot. Various signs, some pictorial, indicated additional movements. From 1933 to 1936, Conté contributed many notated dance materials in his *Le guide chorégraphique,* which appeared in the publication *Arts et mouvement.*

A film about Conté's system, made in 1946 by Jean Painlevé, created much interest, but the system has never been used by professional dancers. For his amateur group, Conté composed a great number of ballets, all meticulously recorded in his notation. Work with his system is being carried on by the Arts et Mouvement center in Paris.

Lieutenant Antoinio Chiesa's system, based on music notes, was first presented in 1932 as *Ritmografia: L'arte di scrivere la danza.* In 1934 a series of articles on the system, then called *Motographia,* appeared in the Milan magazine *Perseo.* These articles discuss much about the value of notation and the need for it but provide comparatively little about the system itself.

Chiesa used a round note for forward and a diamond-headed note for backward. He showed right and left by placing the stem of the note on the right or left side of the note head. Level was demonstrated by a sharp for up, a flat for down, and the natural sign for normal level. Chiesa, who began work on his system in 1922, seems to have been interested in music, mathematics, and dance. No further materials have come to light and there is no evidence that others used his system.

The inclusion of modern dance in several colleges in the United States led to a concern with recording movement. Several academic theses have featured the invention of a movement-notation system. The first of these was a master's thesis by Gertrude Cross in 1934 at Claremont College in California. None of these systems has evolved further.

In the mid-1930s the Reverend Remy Zadra, an Italian priest working in Boston, published his system in a series of books, each undated, designed to provide music appreciation and graded daily exercises for children. Zadra used large wall charts so that the children could read and move at the same time. His abstract signs were drawn as pictorially as possible, with angular lines for gymnastic exercises and curved lines for artistic, dancelike movements.

The system devised in 1939 by Sol Babitz, a musician and the brother of Thelma Babitz, a dancer in Martha Graham's company, is of interest because he combined a visual representation of movement with indications of timing, adding the note value to the movement symbol. Babitz used a matrix of six squares on graph paper to represent the body and placed the movement lines in relation to the matrix. Although his system never developed, its basis was a forerunner of the Benesh system (see below), created independently several years later.

Srbui Lissitzian used her stick-figure system mainly to record Armenian folk dances. In her 1940 book on the notation of movement, *Zapis dvizhenija,* published in Moscow and Leningrad, she provided a substantial introduction to notation in general, describing and illustrating many other systems.

Jia Ruskaja created an abstract-symbol system in the 1940s that was published in Italian magazines during the 1950s. Based on a directional analysis of movement, her system used angular-shaped signs placed on a five-line music staff that represents the body. She recorded positions and the arrival points in space or points to be passed through, with the movement between them being assumed.

The first mathematician as such to concentrate on devising a movement notation was Joseph Schillinger (1895–1943), a New York musician who, in his 1946 book *The Schillinger System of Musical Composition,* taught rhythm by representing time values as lengths on graph paper—comparable to Laban's indication of duration. Schillinger's method, unfinished at his death, plotted movement on two coordinates, *V* for *vertical* and *H* for *horizontal,* with a third coordinate, *T* for *time,* lying between the two. The range of movement anatomically possible for each part of the body was analyzed. Such analysis, used also in some other systems, has the disadvantage of not allowing for the increased range of movement resulting from training or from hyperflexible bodies.

A strong music background led Alwin Nikolais to modify the Laban system he had studied when he encountered Laban's work at the Hanya Holm studio in the early 1940s. Nikolais converted the block Laban symbols into music notes, showing direction visually by appropriate placement of the tail of the note. A small diagonal tick was added above or below the direction sign to indicate level. Nikolais also divided the vertical staff representing the body into two sections, comparable to the treble and bass

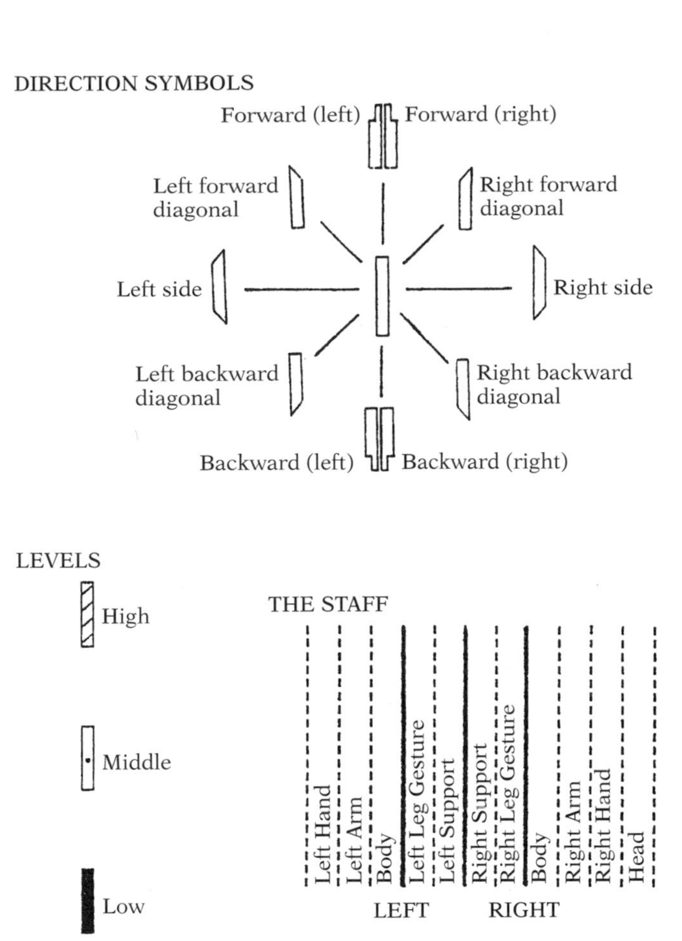

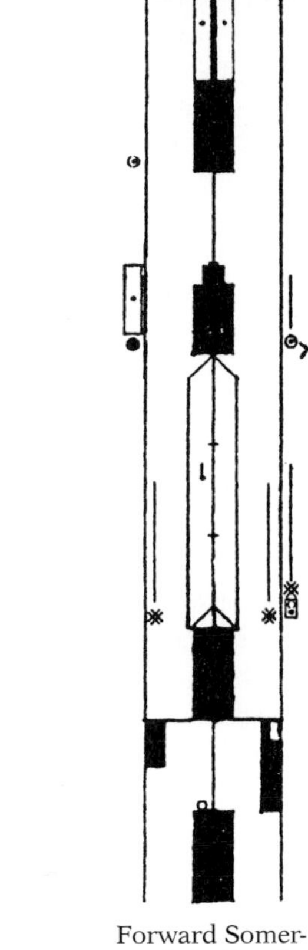

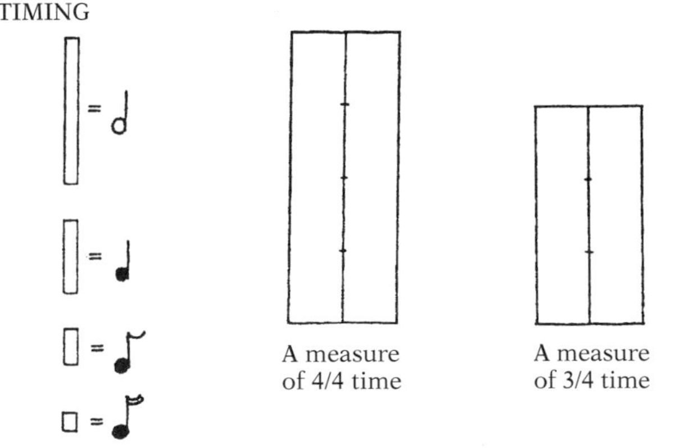

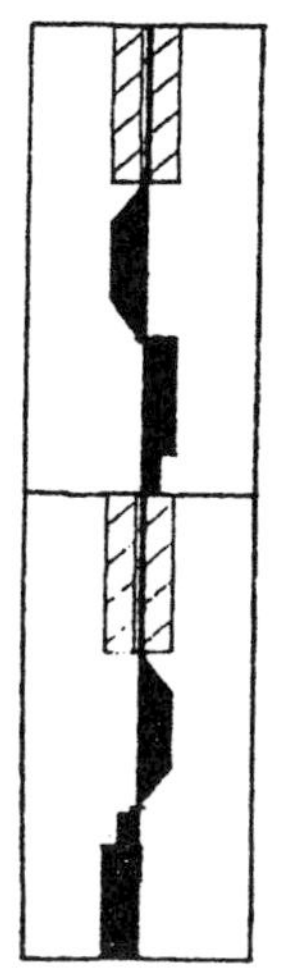

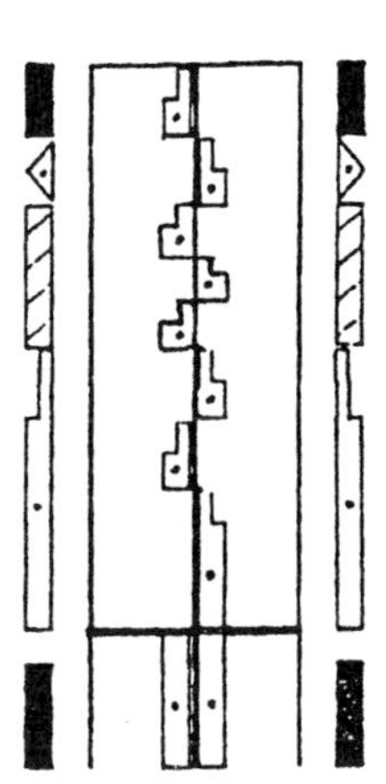

NOTATION. (*above*) In Labanotation, symbols are placed on a staff that indicates which body part is in action. The symbol's shape indicates the direction of the movement, while its shading indicates the level of the movement. The staff is read from bottom to top, with the duration of a movement indicated by the staff's height. (*right*) Several simple movements transcribed in Labanotation. (Courtesy of the Dance Notation Bureau, New York.)

music clefs—legs and arms were written on the left and head and parts of the torso on the right. Timing followed the standard music note values. Although the system was used for a time in his dance school and some notations were made of his choreography, none of Nikolais's students carried on his work. Articles on the system appeared in the *Dance Observer* and *Theatre Arts Magazine* in 1946.

Reluctance on the part of dancers to learn a system of notation led Richard Drake Saunders to make practical use of word descriptions. In 1946 he published his idea as *Danscore,* a series of sheets with lists of appropriate words to be circled to state the desired movement: for example, "right leg forward left arm up." Special sheets were supplied for each dance form—ballet, modern, ballroom, and interpretive. Each sheet also included blank floor plans for location and traveling, as well as a music staff on which to write the music (rhythm).

Stanley Kahn, who had studied Labanotation, wanted a tap-dance shorthand and made use of pictorially based abstract signs in his 1951 publication *Kahnotation: The K Symbols for Writing Tap Dancing* (rev. ed., 1977). Tap dance, with its comparatively small basic vocabulary, calls out for a shorthand system.

Walter Paul Misslitz used colors—red and black—to indicate right or left limbs in his stick-figure system, pub-

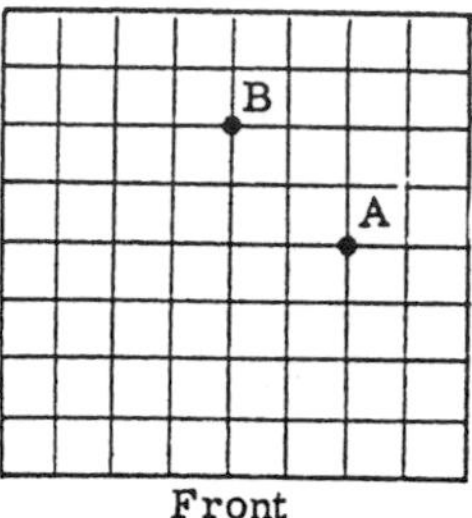

NOTATION. Noa Eshkol and Abraham Wachman developed a system, known as Eshkol-Wachman notation, and used numbers to indicate positions and movements, as seen in this example from the work *Island Birds.* (Photograph from the Dance Collection, New York Public Library for the Performing Arts.)

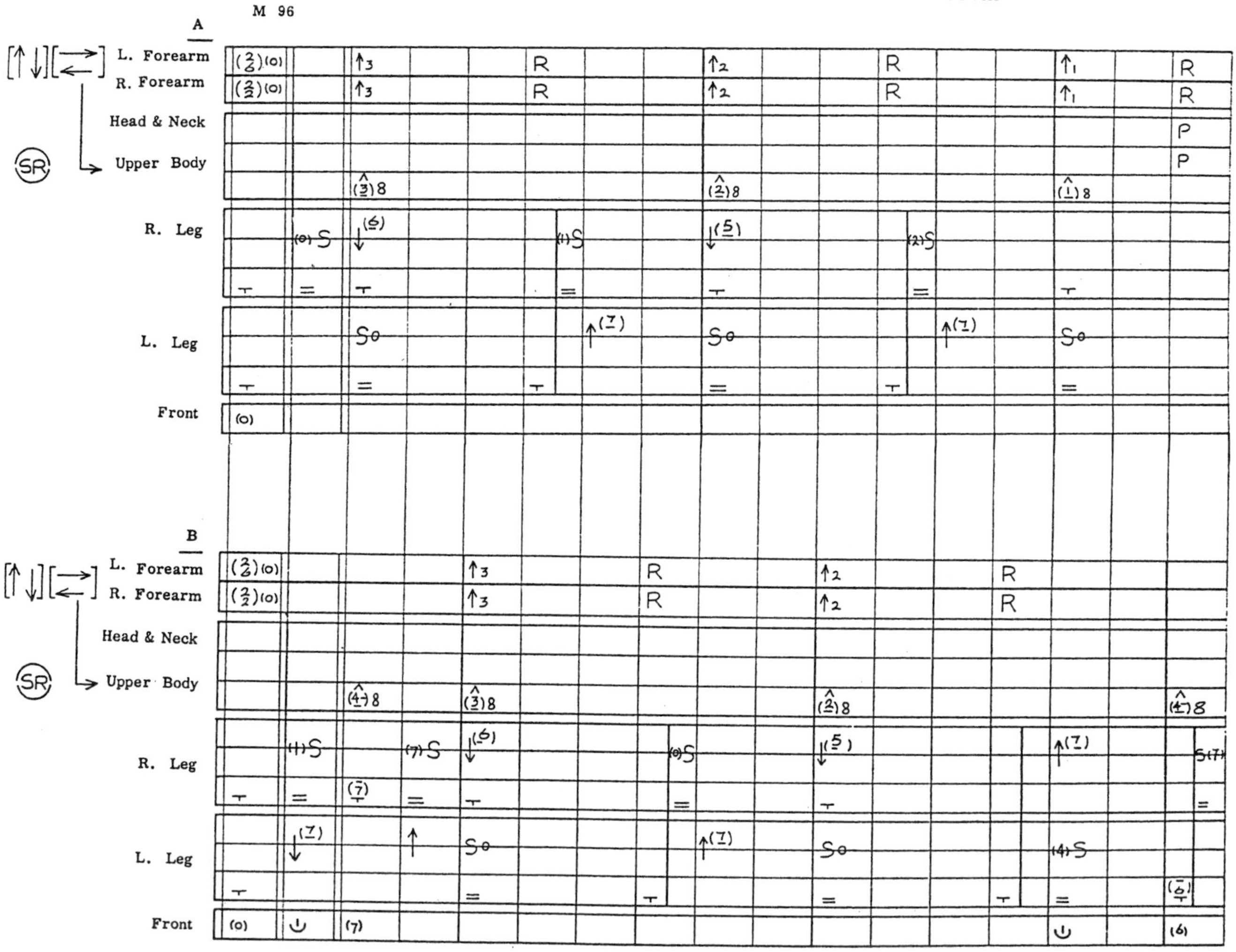

lished as *Tanzfigurenschrift* in 1954. Additional signs are used with the full figure to establish the third dimension and provide details that could not be shown on the figure. He published *Balletlehre* and *Gymnastiklehre,* on ballet technique and gymnastics, in 1960 and 1977, respectively. Misslitz considered the Laban system too analytical. For him, as with many others, the simplified drawn figure gave an immediate idea of body placement.

Eugene Loring and his associate D. J. Canna revealed a unique way of looking at movement in *Kinesiography,* published in 1955. Loring, an American ballet-trained dancer, teacher, and choreographer, analyzed movement as comprising four categories: direction, degree, emotion, and "special." The first two are self-evident—the degree category refers to the level of a directional movement or the degree of flexion. The category of emotion is a complete departure from any existing analysis of movement. It consists of intravert [*sic*] movements, such as raising the shoulders, making the chest concave, and rotating the legs inward; and extravert [*sic*] actions, which include lowering the shoulders, expanding the chest (to make it convex), and rotating the legs outward.

Loring's system was the first to use a staff that provided columns for each section of the body (such as upper arm, lower arm, hand), so that signs for the individual parts were not needed. The resulting eighteen-column staff is placed vertically on the page and is read from the top down. Regular units marked off on the staff indicate the regular beats of the music. The duration of a movement is the amount of space (beats) available after the movement indication—unless a hold sign is written. Loring based his symbols on the sign for *1,* the symbol of unity. A horizontal stroke on this vertical line (usually a slanted line when handwritten) indicates—by its placement at the upper right, upper left, lower right, or lower left—which of the four categories of movement is being described. Also unique to this system is use of a verbal "language"—numbers and letters (upper and lower case) used to call out the desired movement in the dance class. The system was taught for many years in Loring's American School of Dance in Los Angeles. Loring notated his *Billy the Kid,* in his system, but never published the promised second volume on the method. [*See the entry on Loring.*]

Two visual stick-figure systems came to light in 1956. Letitia Jay, an ethnic dancer in New York, used figure drawings much as Zorn had done, but with many additional signs to meet the needs of different dance forms. The figure could be written from different points of view: audience reader or upstage reader. Arrows showed the path of movement, and bubbles showed height in jumping. Letters such as *PU* ("palm up") were added to give details not easily drawn. Jay's system was registered for copyright but never formally published. Despite articles and advertisements in dance periodicals, it drew little support.

In contrast to Jay's attempts, the Benesh system, first published in 1956 as *An Introduction to Benesh Dance Notation,* had the advantage of being designed by an artist-accountant, Rudolf Benesh, who combined a flair for visual representation and practical presentation to publicize the system. Benesh had the added advantage of being closely connected to the British Royal Ballet: his wife Joan was a member of the then Sadler's Wells Ballet. Benesh's involvement in dance notation grew from his wife's desire to write down ballet choreography. With no knowledge of the existence of other systems, he based his on the belief that because dance is a visual art, its notation must be based on a visual representation of movement. The figure is not actually drawn; instead, a section of the five-line music staff forms a matrix representing the body. Locations of the extremities and of the midjoints are plotted on the matrix. The body is viewed from behind, which places right and left on their correct sides on the paper. Three main directional signs indicate whether placement is in the lateral plane, forward of this plane, or behind it, thus overcoming the problem of indicating the third dimension. Movement factors that cannot be indicated on the staff itself are indicated through additional signs placed above and below the staff. Timing is indicated by stating the number of beats in the measure (bar); individual beats and their subdivisions are indicated when needed through special signs placed above the dance staff.

Benesh believed in "redundancy avoidance" and so pared the movement description to the essentials. For each style of dance the notator learns which details can be taken for granted and omitted. Through practical shorthand devices he provided the means for stating several pieces of information in a few strokes.

The system, originally devised to record classical ballets, was adopted by the Royal Ballet for its needs. It established a staff notator, setting an example followed by other ballet companies. The Benesh Institute of Choreology, founded in 1962, has provided training for notators and reconstructors. Benesh adopted the word *choreology* for his system, apparently without being aware that the term had been used by others and was established as a generic term. [*See* Benesh Movement Notation.]

Marguerite Causley applied the system to physical education in 1967 in *An Introduction to Benesh Movement Notation.* In Benesh's 1977 book *Reading Dance: The Birth of Choreology,* additional symbols were presented as well as details of Benesh's philosophy and theories. The system has been applied to various forms of movement, to anthropology, and to remedial work in recording a patient's progress.

Vera Proca-Ciortea led in the development of a notation for Romanian folk dance. Known as Romanotation (or

NOTATION. Another musican-dancer, Charles B. McCraw, developed a system called Scoreography that used pitch to indicate direction. In this example, the triangle on the note C, found on the second half of the third beat, indicates that the left foot is in *relevé* and turning to the right and the right foot is in *passé.* (Photograph from the Dance Collection, New York Public Library for the Performing Arts.)

sometimes Procanotation), it was first published in 1956 in *Revista de Folclor* in Bucharest. This system, to which others contributed, was based on the letters *S* and *D* for left and right foot; the size of the letter—a large capital, upper case, lower case, or with a stroke through the letter—indicated the note value (half note, quarter note, and so on). Various minor signs were added to indicate the part of the foot being used (rising in the air, turning) and—important in Romanian dances—the various arm positions. Floor plans indicate the dancers' arrangement and progression. The limited vocabulary of Balkan folk dances allowed for such a simple notation system.

A complete departure from systems inspired by or tailored to particular dance forms was developed by Noa Eshkol and Abraham Wachman (*Movement Notation;* London, 1958). Eshkol, an Israeli modern dancer who had briefly studied the Laban system with Sigurd Leeder, was concerned with the body as a moving instrument and wanted a way to record her choreographic ideas. These involved progressions in degrees of motion of a particular kind, comparable to compositions based on intervals in music. Movement in this system is analyzed as being circular in nature, so that actions are rotary, planal, or conical in a plus or minus direction. Motion occurs horizontally (clockwise being plus) and vertically—rising or sinking (rising being plus). Positions and location in space are indicated through numbers based on two coordinates, horizontal and vertical. The system allows for choice in the basic unit of measurement. Eshkol-Wachman is the only system other than Laban's to provide both a choice in systems of reference for direction and description in terms of motion as well as destination.

The horizontal staff representing the body contains twenty columns, a space being provided for each body segment as well as for indication of weight placement and front. Designated sections of the staff can be used separately, e.g., the right arm only. Timing is indicated by marking off the staff at regular intervals with lines for the beats and bars. The duration of a movement is the time available after the indication before a new movement occurs or a thick vertical line shows cessation of the movement and the start of a pause.

Choreographing ahead on paper, Eshkol has also produced unusual movement sequences. She views movement objectively and is not concerned with subjective descriptions—that is, with the performer as an expressive human being. Many publications on movement techniques and dances have been published by the Movement Notation Society in Israel, which Eshkol directs. These include *Lessons* by Dr. M. Feldenkrais, *Physical Training, Classical Ballet, The Golden Jackal* (animal movement), *Shapes of Movement,* and two publications comparing Labanotation and Eshkol-Wachman notation. Because numbers are the chief means of describing positions and movements, the system has appealed to computer users. A special project using the system was undertaken in 1970 at the University of Illinois, in connection with the Department of Electrical Engineering.

Mary Fee of the University of Wisconsin dance department developed a system she published in 1959 in a thesis entitled *The Anatomical Notation.* The system grew out of her classroom work, in which rhythm and use of the body, angles of limbs, contact with the floor, and weight bearing, for example, were experienced and represented on paper—a rare example of a system growing out of practical application.

Music notes again made their appearance when Charles McCraw, a musician-dancer, published his system, *Scoreography,* in 1964. Having accompanied classes in which Labanotation was taught, he felt that a musical basis would be more suitable. His system was unusual in that, more than any other, he tried to link dance and music by giving directional meaning to the standard location of pitch on the staff: *A, B, C,* and so on. Thus, *A* became *A droit* (to the right), *B* was backward, *C* was center, *D* was down, and so on. The shape of the note head (round, triangular, square) indicated level (horizontal, high, low). The bass clef was used for the legs; the treble clef for the arms, head, and neck; and, between the staves, torso and hip were indicated. As has often been the case, the system suffered from lack of practical application before being published.

A second system called Romanotation appeared in 1967, the invention of Theodor Vasilescu, a Romanian who published many folk-dance books featuring the system. In it, flat-based music notes point right or left to indicate right and left feet. Timing is shown by modifying the basic sign, adding tails to the stem or making the base a white oblong. Additional signs placed above or below the note indicate the part of the foot being used, the size of a step (a detail omitted in several systems), turning, and so on. Also indicated are variations for arm positions, head and torso movements such as shifting and twisting, and orientation both in the room as well as in relation to a partner. The many folk dances published in this system have made it more widely known than the Proca-Ciortea system.

The undulating motion typical of certain Norwegian folk dance steps led Egil Bakka to publish his own system in 1970 in which that feature predominates. Rising and sinking lines are combined with word abbreviations to indicate step direction and the foot to be used.

Language of Dance, a method of viewing, reading, and writing movement, with particular focus on dance, was conceived by Ann Hutchinson Guest. It is based on an understanding and implementation of the basic elements of movement (the "alphabet") of which all movement is composed, together with application of the visual aid of the Motif symbols, derived from Labanotation. In 1967, the Language of Dance Centre was established in London.

The M S Method was developed by Marillyn Schwalbe-Brame and published in *Folk Dancing Is for Everyone* in 1973. Her system combines pictorial indications for the arms with different arrows for step direction and direction faced and a number of abstract symbols for leaps, taps, kicks, and the like. Some of its features are reflected in the stick-figure system published by Valerie Sutton as *Sutton Movement Shorthand* in 1973, a system then geared mainly to ballet movement. In a 1975 supplement to this book, Sutton introduced many modifications. The Sutton stick figure, placed on a music staff, is drawn as visually representative as possible. Abstract signs are added under the staff or between the figures to clarify the drawing or to provide additional information. Application to other forms of dance, sports, and physical therapy followed, and the system has been further developed to record sign language for the deaf. Publication of the periodical *The Sign Writer*, using her system, fills a significant need.

Since the mid-1970s developments in notation in Europe and the United States have appeared mainly for ballroom and folk dances. No doubt new systems will continue to appear because people do not know that other systems exist or believe it is easier to invent a new system than to learn an existing one. In fact, serious work on any system of notation that is to meet the needs of others at different levels and for different types of movement is a lifetime's work.

There is also a tradition in the Far East for recording movement. Ancient Chinese and Japanese documents reveal the use of word descriptions for dance steps, of figural illustrations, of footprints, and of stage plans. In 1987 *The Coordination Method of Dance Notation* by Wu Ji Mei and Gao Chun Lin was published in English in Shanghai. In 1988 the English edition of the North Korean *Chamo System of Dance Notation*, evolved by U Chang Sop, was published in Pyongyang. A stick-figure-based system for East Indian dance was devised by Luise Scripps in 1965 for *bharata nāṭyam* and another by G. Venu for *mohiniattam*. A simple music-note-based system by Subrahmanyana was included in the book *Bharata Nāṭyam*, published in 1979.

Conclusion. In five centuries, notation systems have progressed from the need to preserve the sequence of a limited number of conventional dance steps to the sophisticated and highly demanding requirements of contemporary life. No longer is dance alone to be served: a versatile present-day system must be able to record all forms of movement, including those of animals and objects and of movement in the weightless state. Industry, gymnastics, sports, and other arenas of movement that require specific indications for how to handle tools, apparatus, and assorted equipment need to be studied. Movement description must now range from the most general indications to the most precise.

When the creative use of movement—the basis of choreographic study—requires a description such as a "turning action followed by forward traveling and concluding with the body curled up," leeway is given for the kind of turn, the manner of traveling, how the body achieves its final shape, and exactly what that shape is. A specific description may, however, require, in some degree of detail, precise spatial placement; exact timing, particularly for how one part of the overall movement relates to another; a refined description of the energy pattern; and precise indications of how parts of the body are involved in the movement, where the movement is initiated, and how it flows through the body. Between the extremes of very general and very precise lie many gradations.

Movement notation has an important role to play in education, and a system must function at all levels from kindergarten, where movement is first discovered, to the university, where the tool of notation can be a valuable adjunct to classroom investigation into the nature of movement, the study of dance as an art form, dance history, contemporary techniques, or choreographic style and content.

NOTATION. Sutton Movement Shorthand, Valerie Sutton's stick-figure system of notation, has been further refined to record sign language for the deaf. (Courtesy of the Center for Sutton Movement Writing, Boston.)

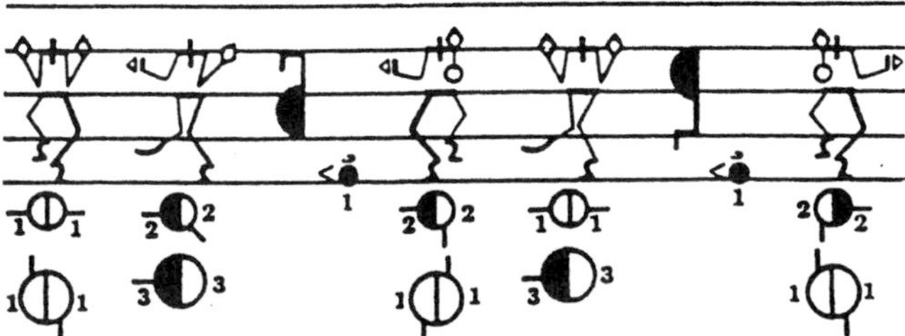

To meet these needs, a library of notated materials needs to be available. Whether a notated system succeeds or fails may rest as much on the salesmanship of the inventor—and on supportive colleagues who contribute to the system and prove its worth through practical application—as on how well the system is constructed and meets the requirements of being visual, logical, and flexible. Technological advances and the growing availability of film, videotape, and computer imaging are presenting new challenges to dance-notation systems. Systems that are widely used in the future will likely be compatible with the new technology but will not be supplanted by it.

[*See also* Reconstruction *and the entries on the principal figures mentioned herein.*]

BIBLIOGRAPHY

Arbeau, Thoinot. *Orchésographie* (1589). Translated as *Orchesography* by Mary Stewart Evans. London, 1948. Reprinted with introduction, corrections, and notes by Julia Sutton with Labanotation by Mireille Backer, New York, 1967.

Babitz, Sol. *Dance Writing.* Los Angeles, 1939.

Benesh, Rudolf, and Joan Benesh. *An Introduction to Benesh Dance Notation.* London, 1956.

Benesh, Rudolf, and Joan Rothwell Benesh. *Reading Dance: The Birth of Choreology.* London, 1977.

Caroso, Fabritio. *Il ballarino.* Venice, 1581.

Caroso, Fabritio. *Nobiltà di dame.* Venice, 1600. Translated and edited by Julia Sutton. Oxford, 1986.

Conté, Pierre. "Le Guide Chorégraphique." *L'Art et mouvement* (1933–1936).

Conté, Pierre. *Ecriture.* Paris, 1955.

Derra de Moroda, Friderica. "Chorégraphie, the Dance Notation of the Eighteenth Century: Beauchamp or Feuillet?" *Book Collector* 16 (Winter 1967): 450–476.

Eshkol, Noa, and Wachman, Abraham. *Movement Notation.* London, 1958.

Eshkol, Noa. *Moving, Writing, Reading.* Tel Aviv, 1973.

Eshkol, Noa, and Nul, Rachel. *Classical Ballet.* Tel Aviv, 1968.

Feuillet, Raoul Auger. *Chorégraphie, ou L'art de décrire la danse.* Paris, 1700. Translated by John Weaver as *Orchesography or The Art of Dancing* (London, 1706).

Guest, Ann Hutchinson. *Dance Notation: The Process of Recording Movement on Paper.* London, 1984.

Guest, Ann Hutchinson. *Choreo-Graphics: A Comparison of Dance Notation Systems from the Fifteenth Century to the Present.* New York, 1989.

Guest, Ann Hutchinson, with Claudia Jeschke. *Nijinsky's "Faune" Restored: A Study of Vaslav Nijinsky's 1915 Dance Score "L'Après-midi d'un Faune" and His Dance Notation System.* Philadelphia, 1991.

Guilcher, John-Michel. "André Lorin et l'invention de l'écriture chorégraphique." *Revue d'histoire du théâtre* 21 (1969): 256–264.

Hutchinson, Ann. *Labanotation.* New York, 1977.

Klemm, Bernard. *Katechismus (Handbuch) der Tanzkunst.* Leipzig, 1910.

Laban, Rudolf. *Schrifftanz: Kinetographie Methodik.* Vienna, 1928.

Laban, Rudolf. *Principles of Dance and Movement Notation.* London, 1956.

Loring, Eugene, and D. J. Canna. *Kinesiography: The Loring System of Dance Notation.* Hollywood, 1955.

Meunier, Antonine. *La danse classique (école française).* Paris, 1931.

Morris, Margaret. *The Notation of Movement.* London, 1928.

Preston-Dunlop, Valerie. *An Introduction to Kinetography Laban.* London, 1966.

Preston-Dunlop, Valerie. *Practical Kinetography Laban.* London, 1969.

Reynolds, William C. "Film versus Notation for Dance: Basic Perceptual and Epistemological Differences." In *The Second International Congress on Movement Notation at the Fifth International Dance Conference.* Hong Kong, 1990.

Saint-Léon, Arthur. *La sténochorégraphie.* Paris, 1852.

Stepanov, Vladimir. *L'alphabet des mouvements du corps humain.* Paris, 1892. Translated by Raymond Lister as *Alphabet of Movements of the Human Body* (New York, 1969).

Sutton, Valerie. *Sutton Movement Shorthand Book I, The Classical Ballet Key.* Irvine, Calif., 1973.

Théleur, E.A. *Letters on Dancing.* London, 1831. Reprinted with introduction by Sandra Hammond. Studies in Dance History, 2.1. (Pennington, N.J., 1990).

Thomlinson, Kellom. *The French Art of Dancing.* London, 1744.

Vasilescu, Theodor. *Rumanian Choreographic Folklore.* Bucharest, 1969.

Zorn, Frederich Albert. *Grammatik der Tanzkunst.* Leipzig, 1887. Translated by Benjamin P. Coates as *Grammar of the Art of Dancing* (Boston, 1905).

Ann Hutchinson Guest

NOVERRE, JEAN-GEORGES (born 29 April 1727 in Paris, died 19 October 1810 in Saint-Germain-en-Laye), French dancer and choreographer. Noverre was the son of Swiss soldier Jean Louys Noverre and a Frenchwoman from Lausanne, born Marie Anne de la Grange. At an early age, Noverre rejected a military career for the dance. He first became a pupil of Marcel, a Parisian dancing master, and then of Louis Dupré, *premier danseur* of the Paris Opera. As part of a newly formed troupe directed by Dupré and Jean-Barthélémy Lany, Noverre probably made his debut in Monnet's Opéra-Comique, Paris, at the Foire Saint Laurent on 8 June 1743 in Favart's *vaudeville Le Coque du Village.* His name first appeared on the program on 31 August in *L'Ambigu de la Folie, ou Le Ballet des Dindons* (a parody of Jean-Philippe Rameau's *Les Indes Galantes*), and in October he danced before the French court at Fontainebleau. His early contacts with Marie Sallé at the Opéra-Comique and with the music of Jean-Philippe Rameau proved to be extremely influential on his development. When the company broke up in 1744, Noverre traveled to Berlin to join Lany, who had become Frederick the Great's ballet master. There he danced in the entr'acte ballets for Johann Hasse's *Arminio* (1745) and probably also in works by Karl Graun.

About the end of 1747, Noverre returned to France, becoming ballet master at Marseille (or at Strasbourg; Tugal, 1959) and choreographing his first work, *Les Fêtes Chinoises* (1748). He probably met his future wife the dancer and actress Marie-Louise Sauveur, in Strasbourg. In 1750, he became principal dancer and partner of Marie Camargo in Lyon, and there, as explained in his *Lettres sur la danse,* he "undertook in the year 1751 to put onstage the magnificent subject of *Le Jugement de Pâris*" (Letter XV; vol. 2, 1803 ed.), his first serious pantomime ballet. It preceded by at least eight years not only his own next similar venture but also Christophe Willibald Gluck's *Don Juan* (1761), which his later rival, Gaspero Angiolini, claimed was the first of its kind.

Noverre seems to have been restricted to more conventional entertainments during his subsequent 1753/54 engagement at Strasbourg and his 1754/55 season at the Paris Opéra-Comique, but by introducing changing asymmetrical patterns, carefully coordinated costumes, scenery, lighting, and occasional mimed episodes, he considerably altered the effect of traditional *entrées*. The Paris revival of his *Les Fêtes Chinoises* (1 July 1754) occasioned a prophetic comment in Collé's *Journal:*

> It is not by the *pas* and the *entrées* that he pleased; it is by the variegated and novel tableaux that he achieved this prodigious success. If there is anyone who can drag us out of the childhood in which we are still in the matter of ballets, it must be a man such as this Noverre. The Opéra should secure and pay well for such a talent.

Having tried without success to gain a post at the Paris Opera, Noverre accepted the invitation of the actor and theater director David Garrick to prepare a group of dancers for the Theatre Royal, Drury Lane, London, for the 1755/56 season. When Noverre arrived in England with his company in October 1755, however, anti-French sentiment ran high; his elaborate staging of *Les Fêtes Chinoises* on 8 November 1755 provoked riots and was withdrawn. Although he remained in charge of dance at Drury Lane until March 1756, and returned there on 1 December for another engagement, aborted this time on account of illness, his name never reappeared on the playbills. His close work with the celebrated actor Garrick had its advantages, however. Not only had Noverre been so powerfully affected by Garrick's histrionic talents that he took him for his own model but also, during his convalescence at Garrick's home where he had access to a vast library of modern French literature and ancient Latin treatises on pantomime, Noverre wrote his book on dancing and the theater, entitled *Lettres sur la danse et sur les ballets*.

Noverre soon began putting his ideals, espoused in the as-yet-unpublished treatise, into practice at the new Lyon Opera. There, between autumn 1757 and February 1760, he collaborated with the composer François Granier on thirteen new works, three on serious themes: *La Descente d'Orphée aux Enfers, La Mort d'Ajax,* and *Renaud et Armide.* A greater success attended his lighter, very colorful pantomime ballets, however, such as *Les Caprices de Galathée, La Toilette de Vénus,* and *Les Jalousies du Sérail.* Soon, his works were reproduced by former colleagues, like Vincent Saunier, who staged *Le Jugement de Pâris* at Turin from 1755 to 1756 and *La Fontaine de Jouvence* at Milan from 1759 to 1760; yet Noverre's enthusiastic Lyon reviews were but a prelude to the renown he gained with the publication in autumn 1759 of his *Lettres.* Published with the date "1760" simultaneously at Lyon and Stuttgart, where Noverre had agreed to serve at the court of Duke Karl Eugen of Württemberg, his treatise caused a sensation throughout Europe. Although generally esteemed by the literary elite, it was bitterly criticized by Noverre's colleagues, particularly those in Paris.

During Noverre's tenure at Stuttgart from 1760 to 1767, he worked with the scenographer Servandoni, the costumer Louis René Boquet, and the composers Niccolò Jommelli, Florian Deller, and Johann Joseph Rudolph; the large company of dancers included, as guests from Paris, Gaëtan and Angiolo Vestris. Among the twenty new ballets he staged there, *Médée et Jason* (1763) proved his most popular. Like others of his Stuttgart ballets (especially *Psyché et l'Amour, La Mort d'Hercule, Admète et Alceste, Orpheus und Eurydice, Diane et Endimion,* and *Der Raub der Proserpina*), *Médée et Jason* was produced all over Europe during the next four decades by other choreographers, especially by Noverre's own pupils. He later complained that, when the Stuttgart company dispersed in 1767,

> thirty dancers all at once became as many *maîtres de ballet;* rich with my musical scores, my scenarios and my costume designs, they spread out into Italy, Germany, England, Spain and Portugal . . . and rendered only very imperfectly the products of my imagination. (Letter XII, vol. 2, 1803 ed.)

In November 1766, shortly before the expiration of his Stuttgart contract, Noverre attempted to secure a post as ballet master to the Polish court. He sent a written tender of services to Stanisław II Augustus and offered to sell eleven manuscript volumes entitled *Théorie et pratique de la danse simple et composée, de l'art des ballets, de la musique, du costume et des décorations.* The volumes contained a shortened version of his treatise, scenarios to eighteen ballets, and his correspondence with Voltaire; also twelve ballet scores (with music by Granier, Deller, Rudolph, and Renaud), 445 costume sketches in color by Boquet, and technical remarks for scene designers. The king purchased all but the last section on stage design—the volumes exist in the Warsaw University library—but he did not engage Noverre. Nevertheless, in Warsaw as elsewhere in Europe, revised versions of Noverre's ballets were staged both at the court and in public theaters by former colleagues and pupils, at first using Italian dancers and then, after 1785, the Polish company called His Majesty's National Dancers.

Despite Noverre's failure to gain an appointment in Warsaw, he delayed for nearly a year accepting an offer from Vienna for the position of ballet master to the imperial family and the two principal theaters. A letter of Garrick (5 April 1767) reveals that Noverre preferred to return to London. By the end of November, Noverre's unsuccessful negotiations with Drury Lane finally persuaded him to accept the post at Vienna, where public enthusiasm had already been excited by the Vestris staging of *Médée et Jason* at the Burgtheater.

The engagement in Vienna was to prove the high point of Noverre's career. Having applauded the choreographic experiments of Franz Hilverding in the 1740s and 1750s and then in the early 1760s the collaborations of his pupil Angiolini with Gluck and Raniero Calzabigi, the Viennese were receptive to Noverre's pantomimic approach to ballet. Between December 1767 and spring 1774, Noverre staged about thirty-eight new ballets and revived many earlier ones; he also choreographed several operas, most notably Gluck's *Alceste* and *Paride ed Elena.* Under his supervision, the two resident composers, Joseph Starzer at the Burgtheater and Franz Asplmayr at the Kärntnertor Theater, wrote ballets that proved to be their best music. They offered, as was to be expected, conventional closed forms for the set-piece dances, but their rhapsodic and overtly programmatic sections to accompany mimed episodes anticipated developments in purely instrumental music. Best received were *Agamemnon Vengé* (1771) and *Apelles et Campaspe* (1773), with music by Asplmayr, and the Starzer scores to *Les Cinq Soltanes* (1771, a revival of *Les Jalousies du Sérail*), *Adèle de Ponthieu* (1773), and *Les Horaces et les Curiaces* (1774). Noverre's long nineteen-page introduction to the program notes for *Les Horaces,* "Petite Réponse aux grandes lettres du Sr. Angiolini," answered Angiolini's critical "Lettere a Monsieur Noverre sopra i balli pantomimi (Milan, 1773), which initiated a series of polemics that continued for three years, raging hottest in Milan.

Despite his successes in Vienna, Noverre had evidently never been satisfied with his post. Nearly from the start of his seven-year employment there, he was looking about for a situation that would allow him more artistic freedom. Having failed to renegotiate contracts with Stuttgart or London, in early 1774 Noverre accepted an invitation from Milan's Teatro Regio Ducal. Angiolini replaced Noverre in Vienna, and the rivalry between them still raged. The Milanese had already seen more than twelve Noverre ballets in productions by his colleagues and pupils, such as Jean Favier, Giuseppe Salamoni *fils,* Vincenzo Galeotti, and Charles Le Picq. Not one of these revivals, however—even those of Noverre's most faithful disciple, Le Picq—was an exact reproduction; all were modified to suit both the performers and prevailing Italian tastes. Thus, Milanese audiences actually experienced the full effect of Noverre's style only when he himself took charge of productions. His own uncompromising efforts were poorly received, however, and his complaints in printed programs showed his growing despondency. "The more I work the more I sense my insufficiency," he wrote in the preface to *Euthyme et Eucharis,* and the program notes "express clearly what the Dance only says confusedly." Especially bitter toward the end of his stay, he addressed the Milanese in the preface to *La nuova sposa persiana:*

> That which characterizes delicacy of good taste is not bitter criticism at all, but rather reasoned indulgence. . . . Applause is a most delicious nourishment, but distaste is capable of burying forever a plant that might have produced the most beautiful fruit if it had not been the object of others' disdain. . . . In vain have the poisoned arrows of jealousy and calumny recently traversed two hundred leagues [i.e., from Angiolini in Vienna] in order to wound me.

Angiolini's publications and the barrage of anonymous pamphlets denigrating Noverre reflect an Italian aesthetic viewpoint put most clearly by the Milanese count Pietro Verri in his letters of 1775:

> Even the [choreographic] periods of the Noverre pantomimes seem greater from a distance than from close to. Here he has failed and has done everything in order to succeed. His backbiting, brutalizing the dancers, the spectators, the nation . . . is the cause of the failure. . . . There remains nothing but his supreme taste in costumes, the art of grouping the figures gracefully and the excellent technical aspects of the dance; he has prostituted the whole poetic part of it.
>
> Angiolini brings greater correspondence between the music and the gesture . . . he condenses his art on the single protagonist; he has a more logical development in the story, greater judgment in selecting expressible and intelligible subjects and in not entrusting pantomime with situations that cannot be discerned. . . . Consequently here Angiolini will come to triumph over his rival, who makes a regal show of pitying our Italian coarseness. I should like to see him put on his blunders at the theater of Paris, and I imagine that he would be booed.
>
> (Count Pietro Verri, 1775)

Verri's prediction that Noverre would fail in Paris soon proved right. Leaving Milan to spend the spring and summer of 1776 managing a company at Vienna's Kärntnertor Theater, Noverre abandoned plans for an engagement in London to take up the position he had long sought at the Paris Opera, a post secured for him through the intervention of a former pupil, Queen Marie Antoinette. The engagement was not a success. Although Noverre blamed the intrigues instigated by his rivals Maximilien Gardel and Jean Dauberval for his failures and eventual resignation, comments by dispassionate Parisian observers were quite similar to those voiced at Milan.

Some of the criticism was unique to Paris, for example, his "manner of making the principal subject of the spectacle what ought only to be the accessory" (Bachaumont, 13 October 1776)—that is, his insistence on producing whole and independent ballets in preference to dances that complemented an opera. Most of the criticism, however, focused on the works themselves. The themes he selected were thought unsuited for dance, while his extended productions, which were often considered enigmatic, were faulted for preferring pantomime over pure dance. Hostility was also sparked by his pretentious program notes decrying opposition to his aesthetic ideas.

Paris audiences applauded chiefly his lighter works: the revivals of his early French ballets *(Les Caprices de Galathée, La Toilette de Vénus,* and *Les Fêtes Chinoises),* as well as *Les Petits Riens* and *Annette et Lubin* (both 1778). Others, like the "arch-tragedy" *Les Horaces et les Curiaces,* failed utterly. In November 1779, his resignation had already been accepted and, although his employment continued to July 1781, he was given little to do; he was not even assigned ballets for operas, although these had been among his Paris successes.

As soon as his Paris contract was finished, Noverre signed once again with the King's Theatre in London, where he began a brilliant season's engagement in November 1781. Bringing dancers from Paris, he mainly concentrated on staging revivals of his Stuttgart and Vienna successes, creating few new dances. His London triumphs were soon reported in Parisian journals: "It is not without reason that Garrick called this artist the Shakespeare of the dance" (Bachaumont, 4 June 1782).

Then Noverre retired for nearly five years, from June 1782 until March 1787, when he revived three ballets at

NOVERRE. *Médée et Jason,* originally performed in 1763 at the Grand Ducal Theater, Stuttgart, was one of Noverre's most popular works; it was frequently produced in theaters throughout Europe. This satirical print showing Giovanna Baccelli as Creusa, Gaëtan Vestris as Jason, and Adélaïde Simonet as Medea in the 1781 London production was made by Francesco Bartolozzi, after an engraving by Nathaniel Dance. (Courtesy of Madison U. Sowell and Debra H. Sowell, Brigham Young University, Provo, Utah.)

Lyon. Returning to London for the 1787/88 and the 1788/89 seasons, he again fell back on his earlier successes, while the few new works—*Les Offrandes à l'Amour, Les Fêtes de Tempe* and *Les Fêtes Provençales*—were spectacular *divertissements,* of the kind he had long fought against as of lesser importance.

During the French Revolution (1789), Noverre retired to the French countryside at Triel, but he soon resumed his career because of financial necessity. Seeking a court appointment that would offer advantages like those he had enjoyed at Stuttgart, Noverre made a gift in 1791 to King Gustav III of Sweden: two large, handsomely copied and bound volumes (now at the Royal Library, Stockholm). The first had a selection of his ballet scenarios, and the second had an essay on dancers' dress, with four hundred costume designs in color by Boquet. Although similar to, if less extravagant than, the prospectus Noverre had offered the king of Poland a quarter-century earlier, its opening petition to the Swedish king no longer rings with the same confidence; he offers the "last efforts of my talent, which is burning low" and hopes that "at your court I would regain my youth and my talents."

His application once again unsuccessful, he spent his final two seasons as an active choreographer in London, where his only important new creation was the successful *Iphigenia in Aulide* (1793). For one whose fortunes had collapsed with the French monarchy, it is interesting that his final work was an allegorical ballet to the conclusion of Giovanni Paisiello's cantata *La Vittoria* (1794), which celebrated an English victory over the French. Retiring to Saint-Germain-en-Laye, he revised and amplified his earlier writings, particularly complaining about the rise and decline of pantomime ballet since the publication of his *Lettres.* The prevailing French taste for virtuosity and spectacle he saw as a relapse into the immature state against which he had fought in both words and practice.

Of the two main traditions dominating European dance around 1750, the Italian tradition had provided the most favorable conditions for the significant choreographic developments of the next seventy-five years, whereas the French tradition had lost ground. At the chief French theaters, ballets of the *divertissement* sort, those intimately linked and subordinated to a larger spectacle—opera, *vaudeville,* or theater—continued to predominate. By contrast, in Italy, ballets performed during the entr'actes of operas tended increasingly to be pantomime actions or character dances completely independent of the vocal works. The French serious style with its discreet motions, *terre-à-terre* dancing, and restrictive costumes was presented in Italy too, but the preference there was decidedly for the so-called grotesque type, a more acrobatic style that stressed rhythmic precision and encouraged freer dress. At midcentury, the Italian manner had held sway over much of Europe—in London, Vienna, and many German court theaters—while the French tradition had persisted chiefly in Russia. Even in France, fairground theaters and lesser houses inclined to put on ballets approaching in spirit the varied Italian repertory. Thus Noverre's career and aesthetic ideas flowered chiefly outside the confines of the tradition-bound French opera, especially in foreign environments—this despite the central position that the Paris Opera commanded in his reformist efforts and his lifelong defense of the fundamental principles of French dance.

In his writing and ballets, Noverre attempted the application of ideas about the dance that had come to the fore by the 1750s, after a century of speculative literature. He was most immediately influenced by the theories of Louis de Cahusac (*La danse ancienne et moderne,* 1754) and Denis Diderot (*Troisième entretien sur le fils naturel,* 1757). He was also influenced by Rameau's dance music, combining programmatic and strongly individual elements, by the expressive dancing of Sallé, the realistic acting of Garrick, and by the powerful accompanied recitatives in Johann Hasse's and Niccolò Jommelli's operas. Although others, notably Hilverding and Angiolini, had worked toward the *ballet d'action,* Noverre's *Lettres sur la danse* had raised the most important questions about the function of theatrical dance. For him, dramatic pantomime ballets brought together dance, ballet, and pantomime. As he pointed out:

> Dance is the Art of steps, of graceful movements and of lovely positions. Ballet, which borrows a part of its charms from Dance, is the Art of Design, of forms and of figures. Pantomime is purely that of feeling and of the emotions of the Soul expressed through gestures.
>
> (Noverre, Preface to *Euthyme et Eucharis,* 1775)

Noverre believed, like the French encyclopedists, in the "imitation of nature," but a nature selected and embellished:

> Nature does not always afford us models of perfection, hence one must possess the art of correcting them, of presenting them in a pleasing light, at an appropriate moment, in agreeable situations which, while veiling their defects, still confer on them the graces and charms that they ought to have to be really beautiful. . . . A fine picture is but the image of nature; a finished ballet is nature herself embellished with every ornament of the art. (Noverre, Letter IV, *Lettres sur la danse*)

That this concept actually held sway over any other goes far in illuminating Noverre's successes and failures as a choreographer and a critic. During his lifetime, despite his professed scorn for the marvelous and what he called the mere "mechanics of the dance," Noverre's ballets succeeded precisely because of his genius for both scenic and technical display. By contrast, his tragedies were criticized because the complexity of their plot made them difficult to comprehend, even with detailed program notes; they required too much attention and necessitated a virtual abandonment of dancing:

> In the ballets of Noverre . . . one dance only in the great movements of passion, in the decisive moments; in the scenes one walks in time, to be sure, but without dancing. . . . Dancing for the sake of dancing can only take place when the play-in-dance is finished. (Grimm, 1771)

Angiolini's success with heroic pantomimes, using streamlined plots with the action concentrated on a few protagonists, brought forth from Noverre during the height of their rivalry a spiteful but revealing statement of his fundamental aesthetic position:

> In the matter of Pantomime, multifarious incidents, tableaux, varied theatrical effects and unexpected events are preferable to those abbreviated plans which reason coldly measures.
> (Noverre, Preface to *Les incidents,* 1775)

The two choreographers' opposing views on the position of music and the utility of choreographic notation illustrate their radically differing approaches to dance composition. While Noverre inspired composers to create forward-looking descriptive music, he spoke of music last in his writings and believed that the musician should not begin work until the choreographer's plans were well advanced. He objected strongly to fitting choreography to existing music. Nevertheless, contemporary criticisms complained of a lack of correspondence between gestures and music. Angiolini, however, was both a composer and a choreographer, so for him music came before the dance and his appreciation of the significance of notation for music led him to plead for the development of adequate choreographic notation:

> Let us say, that every forward step in the dance will perish with its inventor until we have found the method for writing it down. (Angiolini, 1773)

Since Noverre prized spontaneity and intuition above all, he believed choreographic notation superfluous and restrictive, doubting that it could be made both comprehensive and practical.

The same qualities that evoked widespread appreciation for Noverre's genius in integrating the visual aspects of his ballets generated an immediate and far more lasting estimation for his *Lettres sur la dance,* which was reprinted many times. More than his ballets, it has contributed to a distorted view of his importance: he continues to receive credit for reforms put into practice by other choreographers at the same time. Nevertheless, the elegance and urgency of his prose and his practical, far-sighted approach make his treatise an undisputed landmark. Not only did he demand an end to repressive traditions peculiar to the Paris Opera—the masks, the elaborate headdresses, the often irrelevant, stereotyped, cumbersome costumes—and to the prevalence of old-fashioned musical styles, choreographic routines, and the "marvelous" but he also made cogent remarks of a universal pertinence. To become a good ballet master, he felt it necessary to gain a knowledge of great paintings, from which could be learned the laws of perspective, lighting, and color gradation; to read literature and history, for the selection of interesting subjects and correct costuming; to study contemporary drama, for the establishment of a realistic acting style; to listen to contemporary music, for a knowledge of the kinds of music composers were writing; and to know something about stage machinery and geometry. For him, the important thing in a ballet was not the parts, although he wanted diversity, with rapidly changing tableaux and dancing styles suited to characters and themes, in place of the old static, symmetrical arrangements. Virtuosic displays were admissible only if they did not interfere with dramatic truth.

Equally valuable are Noverre's detailed discussions of methods for training dancers. He encouraged the student to capitalize on his or her own talents rather than to imitate a teacher or the style of a dancer in vogue. The teacher's duty was to have a command of anatomy that would permit him to develop a student's natural potential and correct faults associated with particular body types. Noverre deplored the grimaces and contortions that betrayed many a dancer's poor training, which often led to permanent physical disabilities. Anatomical questions, which he believed were generally disregarded, occupy considerable space in the *Lettres;* there, he emphasized the need for careful training to make the inherently unnatural physical movements and positions required in dancing appear easy and beautiful.

Noverre's desire, to have ballet link the parts of an opera as pantomimes recalling the operatic situation, pertained only to French opera—not, as often stated, to productions at Stuttgart and Vienna. In France, dance sequences had been a part of the opera; at theaters following Italian custom, ballets between the opera's acts had been entirely independent spectacles. Not until Noverre worked at German and Italian theaters did he gain the freedom to develop ambitious, self-contained dramatic pantomime ballets, which often lasted as long or longer than the opera acts they followed. His declared bias later in life for German music and German audiences was no doubt due to a retrospective fondness for a nation that supported him. In reality, he placed little importance on ballet themes complementary to opera, programming heroic ballets with comic operas and vice versa. He used his ballets with different operas and even with dramas. His productions were so strongly unified that revivals often included not just the original choreography but also costume designs and musical scores. Largely because this self-contained species was viewed at the Paris Opera as a threat to the native genus did its transplantation not succeed, so Noverre's Paris engagement was aborted. Nevertheless, he directed many of his new observations toward the Paris Opera, as he had in the original version of his treatise of 1760 and in the revised version and additional texts for the collected editions of 1803 (Saint Petersburg) and 1807 (Paris).

Noverre began the summary of his life's work in the preface to the 1803 edition of *Lettres sur la danse,* by declaring his unswerving devotion to the Paris Opera, that theater "which was, is, and will continue for a long time to be the first and most magnificent of the temples of Terpsichore." He united it unhesitatingly with his principal accomplishments: "If one reflects on what *opera* [italics added] was in 1760 and on what it is today, it will be difficult not to recognize the effect produced by my *Lettres.*" Yet one of the most striking aspects of the Saint Petersburg edition is his pessimistic outlook on the future of pantomime ballet:

> After fifty years of study, research and work I have perceived that I made only a few forward steps in my career, and that I was stopped at that point where the obstacles appeared insurmountable to me. The ballet-masters who have adopted my genre have not been able to pass the barrier where I have been forced to suspend my course. (Letter VII, vol. 2, 1803 ed.)

Earlier, he had believed that ballet could become an imitative art on a par with contemporary poetry and drama, achieving the effects attributed to ancient pantomimes. Later, his failures in dealing with complex plots had forced him to review the Roman treatises. To remove his own efforts from unfavorable comparisons with the authoritative sources he had once used in justifying his ambitions, Noverre reinterpreted the Roman treatises. Contrary to his earlier views, he now understood that Roman mimes had not danced at all but rather performed a complex sign language like that used by the deaf. In restricting himself to the language of dance, Noverre had advanced as far as it was possible to go, and as proof, he pointed to the decline suffered at the Paris Opera after his resignation. The best dancers (his pupils) were gone; the themes were ridiculous and once again revolved around acrobatic displays by soloists "who run, who jump, who lunge and who no longer dance"; the corps de ballet languished in consequence as before; the overcomplicated new music (derided scornfully as "concertos for dancers") was only serving to hasten the demise of a once graceful art.

Since developments of the sort Noverre had introduced were no longer feasible, he believed his image, as the "one true reformer of the dance," to be untarnished. He believed his work had accomplished "a revolution in dance as striking and as lasting as that achieved by Gluck in music."

[*See also* Médée et Jason *and* Psyché et L'Amour.]

BIBLIOGRAPHY

Abert, Hermann. "J. G. Noverre und sein Einfluss auf die dramatische Ballettkomposition." *Jahrbuch der Musikbibliothek Peters* 15 (1908): 29–45.

Angiolini, Gaspero. *Lettere di Gasparo Angiolini à Monsieur Noverre sopra i balli pantomimi.* Milan, 1773.

Angiolini, Gaspero. *Riflessioni sopra l'uso dei programmi ne'balli pantomimi.* Milan, 1775.

Bachaumont, Louis Petit de. *Mémoires secrets pour servir à l'histoire de la République des Lettres en France.* 36 vols. Paris, 1777–1789.

Campardon, Émile. *L'Académie Royale de Musique au XVIIIe siècle.* 2 vols. Paris, 1884.

Greppi, Emanuele, and Alessandro Giulini, eds. *Carteggio di Pietro e di Alessandro Verri,* vol 1.1, *Ottobre 1766–Luglio 1767.* Milan, 1923.

Grimm, Friedrich Melchior von, et al. *Corréspondence littéraire, philosophique et critique.* Paris, 1879.

Haas, Robert. "Die Wiener Ballett-Pantomime im 18. Jahrhundert und Glucks Don Juan." *Studien zur Musikwissenschaft* 10 (1923): 6–36.

Hansell, Kathleen Kuzmick. "Noverre, Jean-Georges." In *The New Grove Dictionary of Music and Musicians.* London, 1980.

Hansell, Kathleen Kuzmick. "Opera and Ballet at the Regio Ducal Teatro of Milan, 1771–1776: A Musical and Social History." Ph.D. diss., University of California, Berkeley, 1980.

Lynham, Deryck. *The Chevalier Noverre: Father of Modern Ballet.* London, 1950.

Noverre, Jean-Georges. *Letters on Dancing and Ballets* (1803). Translated by Cyril W. Beaumont. Reprint, Brooklyn, N.Y., 1975.

Sasportes, José. "Noverre in Italia." *La danza italiana* 2 (Spring 1985): 39–66.

Sittard, Josef. *Zur Geschichte der Musik und des Theaters am württembergischen Hofe, 1458–1793, nach Original-Quellen.* 2 vols. in 1. Stuttgart, 1890–1891.

Sonnenfels, Joseph von. *Briefe über die wienerische Schaubühne.* Vienna, 1768.

Tugal, Pierre. *Jean-Georges Noverre der grosse Reformator des Tanzes.* Berlin, 1959.

Winter, Marian Hannah. *The Pre-Romantic Ballet.* London, 1974.

KATHLEEN KUZMICK HANSELL